Knocking On Heaven's Door

ISBN: 1-84609-091-1
ISBN 13: 978-1-84609-091-2
Order No: OP 51161

Exclusive Distributors
Music Sales Limited,
8/9 Frith Street,
London W1D 3JB, UK.

Music Sales Corporation,
257 Park Avenue South,
New York, NY 10010, USA.

Macmillan Distribution Services,
53 Park West Drive,
Derrimut, Vic 3030,
Australia.

To the Music Trade only:
Music Sales Limited,
8/9 Frith Street,
London W1D 3JB, UK.

Edited by Chris Charlesworth,
Johnny Rogan and Andy Neill

Cover and book designed by
Pearce Marchbank, Studio Twenty,
London.

Typeset by Galleon Typesetting,
Ipswich.
Printed by William Clowes Ltd,
Beccles, Suffolk.

A catalogue record for this book is available from the British Library.

Visit Omnibus Press on the web at
www.omnibuspress.com

Rock Obituaries

Knocking On Heaven's Door

Nick Talevski

OMNIBUS PRESS
London/New York/Paris/Sydney/Copenhagen/Madrid/Tokyo

Acknowledgements

A number of dedicated and knowledgeable individuals have aided in the development of this work. Their input is sincerely appreciated.

In the US, a number of friends and music historians have proofread the text for factual errors: John M. Riley, Professor Robert West, Peter Wilgus and Gary Felsinger (whose 40-year record collection was often employed to contradict "the facts" offered by many rock reference books).

Also helpful were library assistant Stuart Move and the interlibrary loan department at Kent State University; Karla Steward and Mary Lyons of the Fine Arts Department at the Akron Public Library; Megan Taylor; Bill Murphy; and curator William L. Schurk and the staff of the music library at Bowling Green State University.

For the original 1999 edition of this book, editor Chris Charlesworth called upon an experienced team in the editing and revision of the text, most notably co-editor Johnny Rogan. Thanks are also due to Keith Badman, Andrew King, Dave Lewis, Mick Middles, Mark Paytress, and Chris Welch. For this new edition, my thanks go to Andy Neill who edited the new additions as well as updating and revising certain entries.

Lastly, my gratitude goes out to the late Anne J Glasby who assisted in the early preparation of the manuscript.

Nick Talevski

Introduction

Over the years several attempts have been made to chronicle the many deaths in the world of rock'n'roll. Without exception, these works have primarily documented rock's major players alongside those minor sidemen whose deaths were either controversial or particularly sensational. Far from being a finale, death has repeatedly reignited the careers and record sales of faded, once proud musical artists.

An entire cottage industry has sprouted up around the departed Elvis Presley whose late-in-life excesses have been overlooked in favour of his post-mortem role of surreal icon. Performing for throngs of adoring fans has always had its occupational hazards. And with the unhealthy trappings that accompany rock stardom, old age is seldom the cause of death.

The human fascination with tragedy and the subsequent theatre of voyeurism makes us slow down to gape at the tangled metal offered by a traffic accident. Following the demise of Kurt Cobain, there was a morbid expectation among Nirvana fans that his widow Courtney Love would soon follow in his path. While this book does not gloss over the unpleasant details of the deaths of Presley, Cobain and all too many others, it does seek to avoid the "Babylon" method of cataloguing rock's more sensational tragedies.

When planning this book, the central concerns were who to include and what criteria to employ. Initially, only major artists were targeted, with the secondary and backing musicians relegated to a brief glossary. Eventually the two sections were merged and the secondary entries substantially lengthened. While the scope of this book is limited to hit acts within the fields of pop, rock, R&B, and to a limited extent, blues, prominent crossover artists from other genres (jazz, reggae, gospel, country and folk) who have impacted rock and pop music are also included.

It later became apparent that rock'n'roll would have never flourished without the talents of peripheral figures such as Alan Freed, Brian Epstein and Bill Graham. It was therefore necessary to include noteworthy deejays, managers, promoters, songwriters, record company founders, A&R men and critics. A final issue was resolved when recording artists popular only in Britain were granted the same treatment as their American counterparts.

The methodology of researching this book was fairly straightforward. Hundreds of rock reference books and biographies were scoured for information. With a host of impressive tomes published in the last few years, most notably Colin Larkin's extraordinary eight volume *Encyclopedia Of Popular Music*, it has become increasingly effortless to locate accurate source material.

While scores of newspapers and periodicals were also used, the following were especially useful: *Billboard*, *Discoveries*, *Goldmine*, *Guitar Player*, *Juke Blues*, *Living Blues*, *Musician*, *The New York Times*, *Record Collector*, *Variety*, and *The Washington Post.* It is worth noting that many reported deaths could not he verified, and in some cases, proved not to be true. And, sadly, many musical entertainers have doubtlessly passed away without receiving their deserved fanfare, their deaths eluding the press and this book. And, in an undertaking of this kind, it is inevitable that errors will occur.

The author and editors encourage any additions or amendments which, when verified, will be included in future editions. Please send any correspondence to: PO Box 2364, Akron, Ohio 44309, USA.

Nick Talevski, July 1999

A

June Abbit

(Joe Abbit, Sr.)
Born June 3, 1932
Died November 22, 1995
Short-term member of the Fifties doo-wop vocal group, The "5" Royales, June Abbit did not record with the group. One of the most popular groups of the early Fifties, the North Carolina-based "5" Royales evolved out of a gospel act, The Royal Sons.
Cause: Unknown.

Ewart Abner

(Ewart G. Abner, Jr.)
Born May 11, 1923
Died December 27, 1997
A veteran record company executive, Ewart Abner enjoyed considerable success at Chance, Vee-Jay, and Motown Records. After graduating from Howard University, Abner worked in a Chicago record pressing plant, before starting Chance Records in 1950 with his former boss Art Sheridan. Recording the finest examples of early Chicago doo-wop, Abner oversaw the sessions of The Moonglows and The Flamingos. With the shuttering of Chance in 1954, Abner landed at the nearby Vee-Jay Records, becoming a part owner by 1961. Here, he was instrumental in the development of the Chicago "Soul Sound" with acts such as Jerry Butler, Dee Clark, and Gene Chandler. Abner also had the foresight to issue The Beatles' first American releases, after Capitol Records had initially passed on the group. After gambling away record company funds, Abner was fired in 1963. Launching his own label, Constellation Records, Abner had success with former Vee-Jay act Gene Chandler. Abner briefly returned to Vee-Jay in 1965 in an unsuccessful attempt to revive the collapsing label. After giving an impassioned speech at a record industry convention in 1967, Abner was subsequently hired by Berry Gordy Jr. as an A&R director for Motown, and promoted to the position of company president in 1973. After retiring in 1975, for the next decade Abner managed the career of Stevie Wonder. With Berry Gordy Jr. selling Motown in 1988, Abner was later hired by Gordy in his new corporation.
Cause: Complications related to pneumonia. He died at Cedars-Sinai Medical Center in Los Angeles.

Herb Abramson

(Herbert C. Abramson)
Born November 16, 1916
Died November 9, 1999
As co-founder of the pioneering R&B and jazz label Atlantic Records, Herb Abramson was a major catalyst in the genesis of rock'n'roll. While studying dentistry in his native New York, Abramson moonlighted as a part-time A&R man at National Records, where he oversaw recording sessions with Billy Eckstine, Big Joe Turner, and the pioneering doo-wop group, The Ravens. Teaming with fellow jazz aficionado Ahmet Ertegun, the son of a Turkish ambassador, Abramson secured financial backing and launched a pair of labels, Quality and Jubilee, quickly selling the latter to Jerry Blaine. Learning from their failures, Abramson and Ertegun launched Atlantic Records in 1947. With $2,500 of their own seed money and another $10,000 from a Turkish dentist, the New York City-based label opened up as an outlet for jazz, its first two signings coming with Tiny Grimes and Joe Morris. Struggling in its early days, Atlantic veered towards R&B out of financial necessity, scoring its first national hit with Stick McGhee's raunchy 'Drinkin' Wine, Spo-Dee-O-Dee' (1949). Atlantic became a powerhouse in the R&B field during Abramson's six-years

as president, dominating popular black music with a diverse pool of talent which included Clyde McPhatter & The Drifters, LaVern Baker, The Clovers, Big Joe Turner, and the label's early warhorse, Ruth Brown. Also crucial to the label's success was the bookkeeping and administrative skills of Abramson's wife, Miriam. Recalled by the Army Dental Corps in 1953, Abramson was replaced by former *Billboard* writer Jerry Wexler. On his return to Atlantic in 1955, Abramson was given his own subsidiary Atco Records, soon home to Bobby Darin, King Curtis, and The Coasters. Unable to reintegrate into Atlantic and divorcing Miriam, he sold his share of the label in 1958 to his ex-wife and Ahmet Ertegun's brother Nesuhi. Abramson subsequently launched a string of labels with varying success, beginning with Triumph, whose roster included Varetta Dillard, The Majors, and Gene Pitney. Remaining active in the industry throughout the Sixties, he produced a host of R&B acts including Esquirita, a latter version of the former Atlantic group The Clovers, and Tommy Tucker.

CAUSE: Natural causes. He died at St. Rose Dominican Hospital in Henderson, Nevada.

Buddy Ace

(JAMES LEE LAND)
Born November 11, 1936
Died December 24, 1994

Nicknamed the Root Doctor (after one of his hits), Texas-born R&B guitarist and vocalist Buddy Ace recorded his best work on Duke Records in the Sixties. Excelling in soul ballads, his biggest hit came in 1966 with 'Nothing In This World Can Hurt Me (Like You)'. Ace belatedly released his first album in 1991, *Don't Hurt Me No More*.

CAUSE: He suffered a heart attack while performing in Waco, Texas, and died soon after.

Johnny Ace

(JOHN MARSHALL ALEXANDER, JR.)
Born June 9, 1929
Died December 25, 1954

Early Fifties R&B balladeer and prototype rock'n'roll star, Johnny Ace was reared in a strict home by his Baptist minister father. After dropping out of high school near the end of World War II, Ace was drafted into the US Navy. Dishonourably discharged, he spent six months in jail on trumped up trespassing charges in the Jim Crow South. Musically a late bloomer, he taught himself guitar, before switching to piano. Aggressive, he earned a spot with the "Teen Town Singers" at WEIA in Memphis, the country's first all-black formatted radio station. There he met deejay and blues guitarist, B.B. King, leader of a local, loose-knit R&B group, The Beale Streeters, which also included future R&B stars, Bobby "Blue" Bland and Junior Parker. Fronting the band after King's departure in late 1952, the former John Alexander changed his name to Johnny Ace. Recording for Duke Records (the label newly acquired by Don Robey), Ace scored a string of moody, romantic ballad hits with his fluid voice, beginning with 'My Song'(1952), the song a reworked rendition of Russ Morgan's 'So Long'. Backed in the studio by the Johnny Otis Orchestra, beginning in 1953, Ace's hit run continued with 'Cross My Heart' and 'The Clock'. A huge star in the black community, Ace broke the colour barrier with the posthumous hit, 'Pledging My Love' (1955).

CAUSE: Backstage after a performance at Houston's City Auditorium, Ace was playing solitary Russian roulette on Christmas Day. There were seven acts on the bill, including blues shouter, Big Mama Thorton. While another act was performing on stage, Ace was drinking with Thorton, several fans, and his girlfriend who was sitting on his lap. A show-off who was obsessed with firearms, Ace first pointed and pulled

the trigger of the inexpensive .22 calibre Saturday night special at two other people, before putting the gun to his head. With only one bullet in the chamber, he shot himself. He died instantly. Although Ace's death is usually attributed to a game of solitary Russian roulette, he believed that the gun's chamber was empty. Alphabetically and chronologically, Ace was rock music's true first death, and various fictionalised stories were invented by the rock press and by his record company to sensationalise his death and increase interest. Paul Simon recorded a song entitled 'The Late Great Johnny Ace' on his *Hearts and Bones* album (1983) which was written as a tribute to both Ace and John Lennon.
FURTHER READING: Salem, James M. (1999). *The Late, Great Johnny Ace and The Transition From R&B To Rock'n'Roll.* Urbana: University of Illinois Press.

Barbara Acklin

Born February 28, 1943
Died November 27, 1998
A popular Chicago-style R&B singer, Barbara Acklin first sang gospel music at her Baptist church in her native California. Moving to Chicago in 1957, as a teenager Acklin divided her time between studying classical music and singing R&B in the city's plentiful nightclubs. Then while working as a secretary at St. Lawrence Records in 1964, Acklin also provided backing vocals for a number of the label's acts. After recording at a competing label under the name of Barbara Allen, she then took a position as a secretary at Brunswick Records in 1966. Though initially rebuffed as a singer by label head Carl Davis, Acklin found success co-writing the Jackie Wilson hit 'Whispers (Gettin' Louder)'. Teaming with labelmate Gene Chandler, Acklin managed her first R&B chart hit in 1968 with 'Show Me The Way To Go'. She then scored a pop-crossover hit with her signature piece, 'Love Makes A Woman', the title track of her début album. Another Acklin/Chandler duet hit, 'From The Teacher To The Preacher', was followed by several solo R&B hits including, 'Just Ain't No Love' (1968) and 'I Did It' (1970). During this period, Acklin also enjoyed songwriting success, co-penning several Chi-Lites hits beginning with the ballad smash, 'Have You Seen Her'. Switching to Capitol Records, Acklin scored her final major hit with 'Raindrops' (1974). After flirting with reggae in the early Eighties, Acklin retired from music.
CAUSE: Pneumonia. She died in Omaha, Nebraska, while visiting a friend.

Chris Acland

(CHRISTOPHER JOHN DYKE ACLAND)
Born September 7, 1966
Died October 17, 1996
Founding drummer of the Nineties Britpop quartet, Lush, Chris Acland backed the Miki Berenyi-headed London-based group since their inception in 1988. Acland had previously been a member of several minor groups including Panik and Infection. After releasing their début album *Scar* in 1989, Lush scored several guitar-driven, alternative chart hits including 'Sweetness And Light' (1990) and 'For Love' (1992).
CAUSE: He committed suicide by hanging inside a barn while visiting his parents' home in Cumbria, England. He had been despondent over the break-up with his girlfriend and the shaky financial state of his eight-year-old band.

Johnny Adams

(LATHEAN JOHN ADAMS)
Born January 5, 1932
Died September 14, 1998
New Orleans-born R&B/blues artist, Johnny Adams began as a religious singer in a pair of professional gospel

groups, The Soul Revelers and Bessie Griffin & The Soul Consolators. But with his searing, versatile voice, Adams was drawn into secular R&B in the late Fifties after an odd episode. Overheard singing 'Precious Lord, Take My Hand' by his songwriter neighbour Dorothy LaBostrie while in his bathtub, Johnny Adams was convinced to record her composition, 'Oh Why'. With LaBostrie getting Adams signed with Ric Records, the retitled 'I Won't Cry', became a regional hit. Adams scored his first national hit the following year when he recorded 'A Losing Battle', the song written by his producer, Mac "Dr. John" Rebennack. Nicknamed "The Tan Canary" by a New Orleans deejay, Adams recorded for a pair of local labels before landing at SSS International Records in 1968, where he enjoyed several hits including a cover version of the much-recorded standard, 'Release Me' (1968) and his only Top 40 entry, the stunning falsetto-laden 'Reconsider Me' (1969). Not a major star until signing with Rounder Records in 1983, Adams jumped across several genres including jazz and blues as he recorded nine albums for the label, his finest being *One Foot In The Blues* and a pair of tribute albums to Doc Pomus and Percy Mayfield. Still wearing his trademark brightly coloured suits, Adams was performing until several months before his death.
CAUSE: Prostate cancer. He died in Baton Rouge, Louisiana.

Justin Adams

Born June 1, 1923
Died July 2, 1991
Popular New Orleans session guitarist at the J&M studio, Justin Adams backed Little Richard, Fats Domino and dozens of other hit acts. The talented group was headed by bandleader and producer Dave Bartholomew.
CAUSE: Heart attack. He died in New Orleans.

Don Addrisi

(DONALD JAMES ADDRISI)
Born December 14, 1938
Died November 11, 1984
The co-leader of the veteran pop duo, The Addrisi Brothers, Don Addrisi scored a pair of pop hits with 'We've Got To Get It On Again' (1972) and 'Slow Dancin' Don't Turn Me On'(1977). Also a successful songwriter, Don teamed with brother Michael Addrisi in penning The Association's Top 10 ballad, 'Never My Love'.
CAUSE: Cancer. He died in Los Angeles.

Eden Ahbez

(ROBERT BOOTSIN)
Born April 15, 1908
Died March 4, 1995
Brooklyn-born beatnik songwriter and poet who penned Nat "King" Cole's melancholy 1948 million-selling hit 'Nature Boy', Eden Ahbez was a spoken-word performing artist and itinerant troubadour. Nicknamed both "The Yogi" and "The Hermit", he dressed in white sheets and preferred to live on the streets even after earning thousands of dollars in royalties. Trained as a pianist, Ahbez also composed 'Nature's Symphony', 'Sacramento' and 'Hey, Jacques'.
CAUSE: He was hit by a car in Sky Valley, California.

Jim Alaimo

Born 1934
Died June 30, 1992
A member of the San Francisco rock band The Mojo Men, Jim Alaimo enjoyed a Top 40 hit in 1967 with 'Sit Down, I Think I Love You' written by Stephen Stills. The group was originally led by Sylvester Stewart (Sly Stone).
CAUSE: He died after heart surgery.

Bill Albaugh

(William E. Albaugh)
Born January 9, 1946
Died January 20, 1999
As the drummer of the Oxford, Ohio-based pop-psychedelic band The Lemon Pipers, Bill Albaugh landed in the Top 40 with the bubblegum-styled 'Green Tambourine'. The group disbanded in1969 after releasing its second album *Jungle Marmalade*. Lead guitarist Bill Bartlett later surfaced inthe hard rock group Ram Jam.
Cause: Undisclosed causes. He died in Batesville, Indiana.

Arthur Alexander

(Arthur Bernard Alexander, Jr.)
Born May 10, 1940
Died June 9, 1993
Noteworthy Sixties R&B singer-songwriter, Arthur Alexander was the son of a semi-professional blues player-turned-full-time-farmer, who had discouraged his son from playing the blues. After first joining a gospel group called The Heartstrings, in 1955 the younger Alexander met his soon-to-be manager, music publisher Tom Stafford, who encouraged the teenager to compose music. With Stafford's help, Alexander first recorded in a rudimentary, make-shift, two-track studio above an Alabama drug store. Released on the Judd Phillips-owned Judd Records, 'Sally Sue Brown' was a local hit. Recording his own composition, the soulful 'You Better Move On', Alexander landed his first pop hit. Much of his material was made more famous by The Beatles, including 'Anna', a song he wrote about his first wife, and The Rolling Stones, who covered 'You Better Move On'. After suffering through bouts of alcohol and drug abuse, Alexander quit music in 1975, his last hit coming with 'Every Day I Have to Cry Some'. He was also angry at record companies who had refused to pay him royalties. Moving to Cleveland in 1977, he worked as a bus driver. Drawn back into music by his colleagues in 1991, Alexander was in the midst of a comeback at the time of his death.
Cause: Suffering a massive heart attack on Monday, June 9, he died two days later at the Memphis Baptist Hospital. Earlier in the week, he had performed at the city's Summer Lights Music Festival. It was the third show of a much-anticipated comeback tour.

Dave Alexander

Born June 3, 1947
Died February 10, 1975
The bassist for the Detroit-based, Iggy Pop-led, proto punk-rock group The Stooges, Dave Alexander performed on the group's first two albums. The Stooges were formed by Pop in 1967 after he caught a Chicago performance of The Doors and was motivated to launch his own similarly styled group. Two weeks after The Stooges débuted at a Halloween dance at the University of Michigan as The Psychedelic Stooges, Alexander was added to the group. Renamed The Stooges, the group churned out a raw pounding fury, a backdrop to the self-mutilating antics of Iggy Pop; after smearing peanut butter on his shirtless torso, Pop would cut himself with glass and dive into the audience. When Elektra Records talent scout Danny Fields arrived in Detroit intending to sign MC5, he also signed The Stooges. Influential though selling poorly at the time, The Stooges' self-titled début album was produced by John Cale, and was highlighted by the tracks 'No Fun' and the often-recorded 'I Wanna Be Your Dog'. A subsequent release *Fun House* (1970) also fared poorly. Alexander was fired by Pop in mid-1970 for taking a debilitating quantity of drugs before a performance at the Goose Lake Festival in Saginaw, Michigan; he was replaced by James Williamson. While the entire group was abusing drugs, Alexander was an especially heavy user. The group

disbanded the following year, and the renamed Iggy & The Stooges emerged in 1972. Iggy Pop was later canonised as "The Godfather of Punk".
CAUSE: After years of alcohol and chemical abuse, he succumbed to pneumonia. He died in Detroit.

Ernestine Allen

(ERNESTINE ALLEN)
Born November 11, 1920
Died August 10, 1992
Discovered by Louis Jordan, Ernestine Allen was the featured singer in Lucky Millinder's proto-R&B orchestra from 1945 to 1954, appearing on hits such as 'I'll Never Be Free' (1951) and 'I'm Waiting Just For You' (1951). Allen's best known solo hit came with 'Let It Roll' (1947) and the Top 10 R&B entry, 'Baby I'm Doin' It' (1953). Backed by talented saxophonist King Curtis, in 1961 Allen recorded the fine album, *Let It Roll.* She retired from the music industry soon after.
CAUSE: Heart attack. She died at her apartment in Harlem.

Bill "Hoss" Allen

(WILLIAM ALLEN III)
Born December 3, 1922
Died February 25, 1997
Pioneering white deejay who garnered fame in the Fifties at WLAC in Nashville, Bill "Hoss" Allen helped usher in R&B music. A native of Gallatin, Tennessee, he attended Vanderbilt University, and was inspired to play R&B music after his childhood exposure to the blues and gospel music of his black neighbours.
CAUSE: Suffering a thoratic aneurysm in December, he died three months later at St. Thomas Hospital in Nashville.

Charles Allen

Born 1942
Died May 7, 1990
Vocalist for the West Coast rock group Pacific Gas & Electric, Charles Allen enjoyed his biggest hit with the gospel-styled 'Are You Ready?', the single culled from their third album of the same name. Formed in 1968, the group mixed gospel, soul and rock. With the group experiencing frequent line-up changes, Charles Allen was the last remaining original member in 1973. After switching from CBS to Dunhill Records for their final album, *Pacific Gas and Electric, Featuring Charlie Allen,* the group added a horn section.
CAUSE: Unknown. He died in Los Angeles.

Janna Allen

Born May 12, 1957
Died August 25, 1993
Songwriter who composed several Hall & Oates hits including 'Kiss On My List', 'Private Eyes' and 'Did It In A Minute', Janna Allen also provided material for Cheap Trick, Peter Wolf, and Louise Goffin.
CAUSE: Leukaemia. She died in Millbrook, New York.

Lee Allen

Born July 2, 1925
Died October 18, 1994
A classically trained musician, Lee Allen was a talented, much in-demand session saxophonist at the famed J&M Studios in New Orleans. There he backed R&B greats such as Little Richard and Lloyd Price. As a solo act, Allen's biggest hit came with 'Walking With Mr. Lee' (1956). Also a member of Fats Domino's band beginning in 1954, he frequently recorded and toured with the performer until 1965. Relocating to Los Angeles, he joined the Eighties neo-rockabilly band, The Blasters, appearing on their first three albums.
CAUSE: Lung cancer. He died in Los Angeles.

Leonard Allen

Born March 11, 1900
Died July 16, 1985
The owner of Chicago-based R&B

label, United Records, and its subsidiary States, Alabama-born Leonard Allen spent two decades on the streets of Chicago as a police officer. After leaving the force to work as a tailor, a frequent customer, Lew Simpkins, suggested they launch a record label. A former record man himself, Simpkins bankrolled Allen. With Simpkins' sudden death in 1953, Allen assumed control of the label and landed national hits with 'Because Of You' (Tab Smith), 'Mary Jo' (The Four Blazes), and the R&B standard, 'Night Train' (Jimmy Forest) before closing the label in 1957. Though he returned to tailoring, Allen would occasionally make forays into the record business. Allen later joined the Cook County Sheriff's Department and in 1975 sold the rights to the United and States catalogue to Delmark Records.
CAUSE: He died of natural causes in Chicago. Having lost much of his wealth, he continued to take in tailoring work to supplement his monthly Social Security cheque.

Papa Dee Allen

(THOMAS SYLVESTER ALLEN)
Born July 18, 1931
Died August 30, 1988
The percussionist of seminal Seventies soul-rock band War, Papa Dee Allen emerged from a jazz background. A native of Wilmington, Delaware, Allen in his teens joined a band led by jazz trumpeter Clifford Brown, and during the Sixties Allen collaborated with a number of major jazz acts including Herbie Mann and Dizzy Gillespie. Moving to California in 1967 at the age of 36, Allen joined The Creators, a Long Beach, California, group which evolved into War. Originally joining as the keyboard player, Allen switched to congas. Signing with MGM Records in 1970, War was hired initially as the backing group for former Animals' lead singer Eric Burdon. With his African and Caribbean polyrhythmic style, Allen predated the World Music movement of the Nineties. After releasing two albums and a Top 10 single, 'Spill The Wine' (1970), Burdon left the group to pursue a solo career. Now signed with United Artists Records, War began a fruitful string of gold and platinum albums, beginning with their second release, *All Day Music* (1971). Allen wrote or co-wrote most of the group's hits including, 'Cisco Kid' (1973), 'Why Can't We Be Friends?' (1975), and 'Low Rider' (1976). One of the most popular groups of the Seventies, War enjoyed fanbases in both the rock and soul communities. The group's final pop hit came in 1978 with 'Galaxy', from the album of the same name.
CAUSE: Suffering an aneurysm during a concert at the Talk Of The Town nightclub in Vallejo, California, he collapsed on stage while performing the song 'Gypsy'. He died a short time later.

Peter Allen

Born February 10, 1944
Died June 18, 1992
Australian-born cabaret singer-songwriter and pianist, Peter Allen penned a number of pop hits including 'Arthur's Theme', 'Don't Cry Out Loud', 'I Honestly Love You', and his signature piece, 'I Go To Rio'. Discovered by Judy Garland, he later married her daughter Liza Minnelli.
CAUSE: AIDS-related ailment. He died in San Diego.

G.G. Allin

(KEITH MICHAEL ALLIN)
Born August 29, 1956
Died June 28, 1993
A notorious underground new York City punk-rock performer, G.G. Allin shocked audiences with his lewd behaviour. Born and raised in a backwoods cabin in Littletown, New Hampshire, Allin left his wife of five years in 1980 to pursue music. Moving to Boston and then New York City, he

joined a series of counterculture bands including Drug Whores, Sewer Sluts and Murder Junkies. Often performing in the nude, Allin would cover himself in his own faeces, urine, and blood, sometimes throwing the mixture at audiences. Living up to his motto, 'My mind is a machine gun, my body is the bullets and the audience is the target', Allin frequently brawled with concert goers. Arrested over 50 times throughout the US on various charges, Allin spent 18 months in a Michigan prison for aggravated assault, convicted of slashing a female groupie and pouring hot wax into the wounds. He spent another year in prison in 1992. A media star late in life, Allin appeared on the *Geraldo* and *Jerry Springer* shows. He recorded 20 albums, the first in 1978, the last the posthumously released *Bloodshed And Brutality For All.*
CAUSE: Taking drugs with friends, he accidentally overdosed on heroin in his New York City apartment following a performance at the Gas Station nightclub. The concert ended early when he began to fight with several audience members and had to flee to avoid police. Allin had promised to one day commit suicide onstage, and to take others with him.

Luther Allison

Born August 17, 1939
Died August 12, 1997
Arkansas-born blues guitarist Luther Allison was exposed to blues as a child at the home of Muddy Waters. An unmatched live performer, Allison toiled away in Chicago blues clubs for much of the Fifties and Sixties, with his mix of traditional and modern blues. The first blues artist to sign with Motown Records, Allison went unnoticed outside of Chicago. Spending much of his latter years in Europe, Allison became a huge overseas star, during which time he did not record in his native US for nearly two decades. Signing with the US-based blues label Alligator Records in 1994, he released three sizzling albums, with 1995's *Blue Streak* and 1998's *Reckless* dominating the W.C. Handy Awards.
CAUSE: Inoperable lung and brain cancer. He was diagnosed just weeks before his death. He died in Madison, Wisconsin.

Duane Allman

(HOWARD DUANE ALLMAN)
Born November 20, 1946
Died October 29, 1971
Guitarist and co-leader of the pioneering Southern-rock band The Allman Brothers, Duane Allman was a much-copied blues-rock virtuoso. Born in Nashville but raised in Daytona, Allman was taught to play guitar by his younger brother, Gregg. His father an Army sergeant who was killed during the Korean War, Duane Allman dropped out of school at 15 to work full-time in bar bands, often gigging with his brother. In 1965, the brothers formed a rock foursome, The Allman Joys, releasing an obscure single. Joining Hour Glass two years later, the brothers recorded a pair of commercially disastrous albums. But with Duane Allman earning a reputation as a masterful slide- guitarist, he was in great demand as a session player, backing the likes of King Curtis and Aretha Franklin, often recording at the Fame Studios in Muscle Shoals, Alabama. While performing at a party, Duane Allman was discovered by Atlantic Records vice-president Jerry Wexler who bought out his contract with the hopes of shaping the guitarist into a solo act. Teamed in 1969 with producer Phil Walden of Otis Redding fame, Duane Allman resurrected Hour Glass and the group evolved into The Allman Brothers Band. While Duane was originally the lead singer, the better-suited Gregg now took over on vocals and keyboards. The group's début

album garnered little airplay, but it was followed by the classics, *Idlewild South* (1970) and *At Fillmore East* (1972). With blues-flavoured hits like 'Whipping Post' and 'Midnight Rider', the group spawned scores of imitators and became the pioneer band in the Southern rock movement of the early Seventies. Eric Clapton invited Allman to play on his *Layla And Other Assorted Love Songs* album which he recorded under the guise of Derek and The Dominoes, and it is Duane's slide guitar that can be heard on the well-known title track.
CAUSE: Motorcycle accident. Swerving to avoid colliding with a long-bed truck at an intersection in Macon, Georgia, Allman fell under his bike and suffered multiple injuries. He was taken by ambulance to the Macon Medical Center where he died three hours later. The remaining members of the Allman Brothers performed at his funeral. A year later, bandmate Berry Oakely died less than one mile away from the site of Allman's demise – also in a motorcycle accident.
FURTHER READING: Freeman, Scott. (1995). *Midnight Riders: The Story Of The Allman Brothers Band.* Boston: Little, Brown.

Roland Alphonso

Born January 12, 1931
Died November 20, 1998
Jazz-trained ska pioneer, saxophonist Roland Alphonso began as a professional musician in the late Forties. Emerging as a respected session player in Jamaica, he was frequently employed by producer Coxsone Dodd at his recording complex, Studio One. Joining the Don Drummond-led ska group The Skatalites in 1963, Alphonso popularised the genre. Gaining fame in their native land and in Britain, The Skatalites scored their biggest hit in 1967 with 'Guns Of Navarone'. The Skatalites were also employed as session players behind acts such as The Maytals and a young Bob Marley. Tragedy struck the group when the mentally imbalanced Drummond murdered his girlfriend. With Drummond imprisoned, the group disintegrated shortly thereafter. Receiving numerous job offers, The Skatalites reformed during the Eighties ska revival.
CAUSE: After collapsing on stage during a Skatalites concert at the West Hollywood venue the Key Club on November 2, he fell into a coma on November 17, succumbing three days later. He died at Cedars-Sinai Medical Center in Los Angeles.

Barbara Alston

(BARBARA LEE ALSTON)
Born 1944
Died May 15, 1992
A member of the Brooklyn-based early Sixties girl group The Crystals, Barbara Alston hailed from the Bedford-Styvescent section of Brooklyn. The group was assembled by Alston's uncle Benny Wells. While rehearsing at a publishing company, the teenage girls were overheard by a young producer named Phil Spector who signed them to his new label, Phillies Records. Although Alston was the group's original leader, Pat Wright usually assumed the lead vocal duties. Phillies Records' first release came with The Crystals' 'Oh Yeah, Maybe Baby'. While the A-side landed little airplay, the B-side, 'There's No Other (Like My Baby)' (1961) – which featured Alston's straightforward lead vocals – became the group's first hit. However, while The Crystals were on an East Coast tour, Spector employed a substitute 'Crystals' group, led by Darlene Love, to record 'He's A Rebel' (1964). Spector had rushed the single in an effort to fend off a competing version. Ironically, the real Crystals were forced to learn 'their' new hit while on the road. Returning to the studio, the Crystals' hit run continued with 'Da Doo Ron Ron' (1963) and

'Then He Kissed Me' (1963), both singles featuring Lala Brooks on lead vocals. After splitting with Spector the group struggled to survive, and were forced to disband in 1967. Alston and Thomas joined the Teri Nelson Group, releasing an obscure record in 1969. Marrying and raising a family, Alston moved to North Carolina. She joined several revival versions of The Crystals during the early Seventies, and by the late Seventies was leading her own Crystals group.
CAUSE: Heart Attack. She died in Brooklyn.

Stig Andersson

(STIKKAN ANDERSSON)
Born January 25, 1931
Died September 12, 1997
As the producer and manager of Seventies Swedish pop quartet Abba, Stig Andersson was responsible for the group's crisp sound on all of their international hits, from their 1974 breakthrough 'Waterloo' onwards. The group's chart run encompassed 19 UK Top 10 entries, including nine number 1s, and 10 US Top 20 hits. Involved in the music industry since 1950 when he published his first song, he worked exclusively in English. Andersson later launched the annual Polar Music Prize. At one time he was famously quoted as saying that Abba was Sweden's biggest export commodity after Volvo cars.
CAUSE: Heart attack. He died in Stockholm.

Mike Anthony

(MICHAEL JOSEPH LOGIUDICE)
Born October 19, 1930
Died March 9, 1999
A pop/rock songwriter who frequently collaborated with Barry Mann, Mike Anthony co-wrote 'Poetry In Motion' (Johnny Tillotson), 'The Grass Is Greener' (Brenda Lee), 'I'll Never Dance Again' (Bobby Rydell), and 'She Say (Oom Dooby Doom)' (The Diamonds). Turning his attention to country music, the New York-born Anthony co-wrote 'You Can't Buy Your Way Out Of The Blues' (George Strait) and 'I Miss You A Little' (John Michael Montgomery). (Not to be confused with Michael Anthony of Van Halen.)
CAUSE: Suffering a stroke and heart attack in early February, he never recovered. He died at Columbia Centennial Medical Center in Nashville.

Mel Appleby

(MELANIE SUSAN APPLEBY)
Born July 11, 1966
Died January 18, 1990
Teaming with older sister Kim, Mel Appleby formed the British dance-pop singing duo Mel and Kim. A school dropout who had worked as a nude model, Mel Appleby landed a record contract by singing and dancing outside a London record company. Enjoying a brief but strong hit run, Mel and Kim dominated the British charts beginning in 1986 with the club hits, 'Showing Out', 'Respectable', and 'That's The Way It Is'. Falling ill, Mel Appleby was forced to end her music career.
CAUSE: Diagnosed with spinal cancer in late 1986, she had to be wheeled out of the 1988 Montreux Festival in a wheelchair. While her press agent attributed the incident to a slipped disc, word of her illness was leaked to her fans. She succumbed to the disease four years later in a London hospital, after being stricken with pneumonia.

Floyd Arceneaux

Born 1934
Died May 13, 1992
Duke/Peacock Records session trumpet player, Floyd Arceneaux recorded with Bobby "Blue" Bland and Little Junior Parker, and toured with Chuck Willis and Ray Charles.
CAUSE: Unknown.

Archibald

(LEON T. GROSS)
Born September 14, 1912
Died January 8, 1973
New Orleans singer and pianist, Archibald scored his only nationally charting R&B hit in 1950 with the Top 10 entry, 'Stack-A-Lee (Parts I & II)', the precursor of 'Stagger Lee'. Previously known as "Archie Boy", he was a popular draw in New Orleans, influencing Fats Domino in the Forties.
CAUSE: Heart attack. He died in New Orleans.

West Arkeen

(AARON WEST ARKEEN)
Born June 18, 1960
Died May 30, 1997
Paris-born songwriter, West Arkeen collaborated with Sly Stone, Johnny Winter, Jeff Buckley, and Brother Cane. Arkeen was also an unofficial member of Guns N' Roses, and in the mid Nineties, led his own band hard-rock band, Outpatience.
CAUSE: He overdosed on the prescription drugs which he was taking for severe burns suffered in a barbecuing accident. He died at his home in Los Angeles.

Louis Armstrong

Born August 4, 1901
Died July 6, 1971
A major figure in the development of jazz, Louis Armstrong was among the century's greatest entertainers. Changing the face of popular music, the gravelly voiced trumpet player would also influence blues and rock. Orphaned at an early age, Armstrong was sentenced to the Colored Waifs' Home for firing a gun in public; here he would learn to play the cornet. Released in 1914, Armstrong sold his first composition, reworked by the buyer as 'I Wish I Could Shimmy Like My Sister Kate'. After replacing Joe "King" Oliver's in Kid Ory's band in 1919, Armstrong left New Orleans for lucrative work as a riverboat musician. Relocating to Chicago in 1922, Armstrong landed a spot as second cornet player with King Oliver, and married the group's pianist Lil Hardin, his second wife. Making his recording début the following year, he would back Oliver on 41 historic tracks. The dual cornet style they favoured was in evidence on many classic tracks, including 'Working Man's Blues', 'Chimes Blues' and 'Riverside Blues'. Armstrong next joined Fletcher Henderson's New York-based orchestra in 1924. While there, he recorded his first vocal outing, 'Everybody Loves My Baby'. In 1925, Armstrong returned to Chicago to form his own group, although he also guested in various bands during this period, working with Erskine Tate, Lil Armstrong and others. Recording for OKeh Records, alternately with The Hot Fives and The Hot Sevens, Armstrong turned the jazz world on its ear with a series of revolutionary improvisational recordings such as End Blues', 'Hotter Than That' and 'Heebie Jeebies'. During this period he switched from cornet to trumpet. Updating his sound in 1929, Armstrong replaced his combo with a larger jazz orchestra. During the Thirties, Armstrong appeared in Broadway revues and recorded several key ballads, including 'You're Driving Me Crazy', 'I'm Confessin'' and his signature 'When It's Sleepy Time Down South'. After severely damaging his lips in 1934, Armstrong would spend more time singing than playing his trumpet. His popularity among white audiences during this time was assisted by various collaborations with other big name artists, including the Mills Brothers, Louis Jordan and Ella Fitzgerald. A promising career in the movies also increased his profile. Reprising his small-combo in the Forties to the delight of his early fans, Armstrong embraced bebop jazz. Returning to his roots in 1947,

Armstrong formed a New Orleans-styled sextet, The All-Stars, with founding members Jack Teagarden and Earl Hines. Emerging as a superstar and crowned "The King of Zulus" at the 1949 Mardi Gras, Armstrong was one of the first entertainers to break long-standing colour barriers. Astutely recording for a number of labels during the Fifties, Armstrong continued to enjoy acclaimed collaborations with Ella Fitzgerald and Duke Ellington. His success continuing into the rock era, Armstrong landed on the charts with 'A Theme From The Threepenny Opera (Mack The Knife)' (1956), a reissue of 'Blueberry Hill' (1956), and his first million-seller, 'Hello, Dolly!' (1964). While 'What A Wonderful World' initially bombed in the US, it topped the British charts in 1968; the song was later popularised in the US by its inclusion in the 1988 film, *Good Morning, Vietnam.*
CAUSE: In poor health in the last few years of his life, he suffered a massive heart attack. He died in New York City.
FURTHER READING: Bergreen, Laurence. (1997). *Louis Armstrong: An Extravagant Life.* New York: Broadway.

Kokomo Arnold

(JAMES ARNOLD)
Born February 15, 1901
Died November 8, 1968
A trailblazing, left-handed, blues artist who played Hawaiian-styled blues guitar, Kokomo Arnold earned his nickname from his Thirties hit 'Kokomo Blues'. A whiskey bootlegger from Georgia, Arnold recorded three dozen 78s for Decca Records in the Thirties. When Elvis Presley recorded Arnold's first Decca release, 'Milk Cow Blues' (1934), as 'Milkcow Blues Boogie', the ageing bluesman was rediscovered. In poor health, Arnold skipped the blues revival of the Sixties.
CAUSE: Natural causes. He died in Chicago.

Matthew Ashman

Born 1962
Died November 21, 1995
A member of a pair of various pioneering British new wave groups, London-born guitarist Matthew Ashman was raised on jazz music. Switching to rock during his teens, he first joined the pop-rock group, The Kameras. In 1978, Ashman joined the second line-up of Adam & The Ants, a group led by the frilly-clothed, make-up wearing Adam Ant. Ashman played piano and guitar on the group's début album, *Dirk Wears White Sox,* with most of the album's tracks written by Ashman and Mark Gaumont. A Top 20 entry in England, the album was highlighted by the single 'Young Parisians'. The group's success was due in part to the outrageous antics of their manager Malcolm McLaren. But in 1980, McLaren stole Adam Ant's backing group and placed them behind another of his discoveries, 14-year-old Burmese singer Annabella Lwin, in the group Bow Wow Wow. The group's début release and a British Top 20 hit, 'C30, C60, C90, Go', encouraged home-taping. A controversial group, Bow Wow Wow was dropped by EMI Records after issuing their second single 'W.O.R.K.' Though ignored by American radio, the group landed MTV hits with a cover of the Strangeloves' 'I Want Candy' (1982)and 'Do Ya Wanna Hold Me'(1983). The group disbanded in 1983 after the start of a US tour in New York City when Ashman fell off the stage, breaking his wrist, while yelling at the soundman. Although his eyesight was failing as a result of his worsening diabetes, Ashman was wearing dark sunglasses at the time. In 1988, Ashman joined former Sex Pistols drummer Paul Cook in the group Chiefs Of Relief. At the time of his death, Ashman was working on an album for Epic Records as a member of Agent Provocateur. Bow Wow Wow reformed in 1998.

CAUSE: Diabetes-related complications. He had lapsed into a coma before his death.

Winifred Atwell

Born February 27, 1914
Died January 31, 1983
A Trinidadian-born honky-tonk pianist, Winifred Atwell was a major British star in the Fifties. Fascinated by the piano as a child, she became a local sensation after performing Chopin in public at age six. After entertaining troops during the Second World War, she arrived in New York, studying piano under Alexander Borovski. Relocating to London in 1946 with the goal of becoming a classical pianist, she furthered her education at the Royal Academy of Music. Redirected by her tutor Professor Harold Craxton, she took his advice and embraced a rollicking honky-tonk style, complete with vestiges of vaudeville. Discovered by future BBC producer Michael Gilliam, Atwell was an immediate sensation across Britain. A fixture on television, the pleasant natured Atwell landed her own ATV programme in 1956, *The Winifred Atwell Show*. But with the rise of skiffle, and then rock'n'roll, Atwell soon fell out of favour with British audiences. Always popular in Australia, she would emigrate there in 1971 and host her own television series. Occasionally returning to Britain, her last appearance was in the Seventies performing the theme tune for the BBC snooker show, *Pot Black*. After suffering a stroke in 1979, she retired from the stage.
CAUSE: Heart attack. She died in Sydney, Australia. (Two months before her death, she lost nearly all of her possessions in an apartment fire.)

Joseph August

(JOSEPH AUGUSTUS)
Born September 13, 1931
Died October 9, 1992
Nicknamed "Mr. Google Eyes", pioneering New Orleans R&B shouter Joseph August scored a number of regional hits including 'Poppa Stopa's Be-Bop Blues'. He later recorded for Columbia Records and penned the Johnny Ace hit 'Please Forgive Me'.
CAUSE: Heart attack. He died at his home in New Orleans.

Hoyt Axton

(HOYT WAYNE AXTON)
Born March 25, 1938
Died October 26, 1999
A talented country and pop singer-songwriter and actor, Hoyt Axton is best known for writing Three Dog Night's smash hit 'Joy To The World'. Born in Oklahoma, Axton was classically trained on piano but instead wanted to write literary prose. After his mother, Mae Boren Axton, co-authored Elvis Presley's smash 'Heartbreak Hotel', he followed her lead into music. Hitting the folk clubs of San Francisco in 1960, the likable, large-framed former college football player landed his first success as co-writer of The Kingston Trio's hit 'Greenback Dollar' (1963). Leaving his folk roots in the late Sixties, Axton recorded an orchestral-pop album in 1969, *My Griffin Is Gone*. While opening up for Three Dog Night in 1969–70, Axton offered the group what would become their career-defining hit, the novelty-styled, singalong 'Joy To The World', as well as penning another of their hits, 'Never Been To Spain'. Axton's other hit compositions included a pair of anti-drug themed numbers, 'The Pusher' (Steppenwolf) and 'No No Song' (Ringo Starr). As a solo act Axton was ignored by the pop market, his success coming on the country charts with hits such as 'Boney Fingers' (1974), 'Flash Of Fire' (1976), and 'A Rusty Old Halo' (1979). Making his acting début in 1959 on an episode of *Bonanza*, Axton appeared in nearly three dozen films including *The Black Stallion* (1979), *Gremlins* (1984), and *We're No Angels* (1989).
CAUSE: He suffered a heart attack at

his ranch in Helena, Montana. In poor health since suffering a debilitating stroke three years earlier, he was also in the advanced stages of diabetes.

Mae Boren Axton

(MAE BOREN)
Born September 14, 1914
Died April 8, 1997
Country deejay, publicist for Hank Snow, Mae Boren Axton was also a songwriter, co-composing Elvis Presley's hit, 'Heartbreak Hotel'. Axton is the mother of singer-songwriter Hoyt Axton.
CAUSE: She accidentally drowned in a hot tub at her home in Henderson, Tennessee. She had been ill for some time.

Packy Axton

(CHARLES AXTON)
Born February 17, 1941
Died January 1974
Leader and saxophonist of the Memphis-based teenage group, The Mar-Keys, Packy Axton scored an instrumental hit in 1961 with the quirky, 'Last Night'. The Mar-Keys, minus Axton, would later evolve into Booker T. & The MG's. In the mid Sixties, Axton would lead The Packers, landing an R&B hit in 1965 with 'Hole In The Wall'.
CAUSE: Heart attack.

Tom Ayres

Born 1933
Died May 30, 2000
A veteran producer who worked with artists ranging from Gene Vincent to David Bowie, Tom Ayres' first major success was with 'Hot Pastrami' for The Dartells. As a staff producer, Ayres worked at Hanna-Barbera Production and a number of labels including United Artists, ABC, Columbia, RCA, and Kama Sutra.
CAUSE: Unknown. He died at his home in Shreveport, Louisiana.

B

Buddy Bailey

(John H. Bailey)
Born December 29, 1931
Died February 3, 1994
A member of pioneering R&B/doo-wop group The Clovers, tenor vocalist Buddy Bailey provided the lead vocals on most of their hits. Founded by Harold "Hal" Lucas in Washington DC in 1946, Bailey was added later that year. Discovered by record store owner "Maxie Waxie" Silverman, The Clovers recorded an obscure single for Rainbow Records in 1950 before signing with Atlantic. Breaking through with a doo-wop styled B-side hit, the group first appeared on the R&B charts in 1951 with 'Don't You Know I Love You?', a track penned by Atlantic chief Ahmet Ertegun. Helping to define doo-wop, The Clovers were crucial in the transition of R&B from its old-styled blues tradition to smooth, group harmony, spawning a host of imitators in the process. They continued their hit run with 'Fool, Fool, Fool' (1951), 'One Mint Julep'/ 'Middle Of The Night' (1952), 'Hey, Miss Fannie'/'I Played The Fool' (1952) and 'Crawlin'' (1953). Drafted in 1952, Bailey was replaced by Charlie White and then Billy Mitchell. Upon Bailey's return in 1954, The Clovers' final hits at Atlantic were 'Nip Sip' (1955), 'Devil Or Angel' (1956) and 'Love, Love, Love' (1956). Dropped by Atlantic, The Clovers achieved their last chart hit in 1959 with the Leiber & Stoller composition, 'Love Potion No. 9'. By 1960, The Clovers split into two camps, one led by Bailey and the other by Lucas; neither fared well.
Cause: Unknown. He died in Las Vegas.

J.R. Bailey

(James R. Bailey)
Born 1937
Died 1985
Tenor vocalist of The Cadillacs beginning in mid 1956, J.R. Bailey had replaced LaVern Drake, appearing on the group's hit singles, 'Reindeer' (1957) and 'Peek-a-Boo' (1959). Bailey later shared lead vocal duties after the departure of original lead vocalist Earl Carroll. Bailey had previously been a member of the second line-up of The Crickets (not Buddy Holly's group) in 1953 and The Velvetones. He briefly joined a new line-up of The Cadillacs in 1970.
Cause: Unknown.

Bill Baker

Born 1936
Died August 10, 1994
Replacement lead singer for The Five Satins from 1957 to 1959, Bill Baker had filled for founding member Fred Parris, who was serving an army stint in Japan. With Baker on vocals, the Connecticut-based doo-wop vocal group scored a hit with the ballad, 'To The Aisle'. Baker later led a revival version of the group.
Cause: He suffered a stroke while under treatment for lung cancer. He had been diagnosed with the disease earlier in the year. He died in New Haven, Connecticut.

Jo Baker

Born 1948
Died November 11, 1996
Vocalist with the blues-rock band, The Elvin Bishop Group from 1968–1973, Jo Baker left before the release of the album, *Juke Joint Jump*. Joining Stoneground in 1974, she recorded one album for Warners. Also a popular session vocalist, she later collaborated with Eddie Money, The Doobie Brothers, and John Lee Hooker.
Cause: Suffering with liver disease for two years, she died in Oakland, California.

LaVern Baker

(DELORES LAVERN BAKER)
Born November 11, 1929
Died March 10, 1997
A pioneering queen of R&B, LaVern Baker was raised in a comfortable home on Chicago's south side. The niece of blues songstress Memphis Minnie, Baker earned her musical education as a soloist in her Baptist church choir. Drawn to the city's bustling blues scene, at 17 Brown landed a residency at Chicago's Club DeLisa under the stage name of "Little Miss Sharecropper", a bare-footed country bumpkin. After attracting the attention of Nat "King" Cole, Baker joined a band led by Fletcher Henderson. Developing a wide repertoire of blues and pop, Brown was especially drawn to jazz balladry. After brief stints at OKeh, National and King Records, Baker landed at Atlantic Records where she scored her first major crossover hit with the novelty-styled, 'Tweedlee Dee', featuring the blistering saxophone of Sam "The Man" Taylor. Possessing a fluid, husky voice, Baker continued her hit run with 'Jim Dandy' (1956) and her biggest pop hit, 'I Cried A Tear'. Baker's final major chart entry came in 1962 with 'See See Rider'. Leaving Atlantic for Brunswick Records at her manager's insistence, Baker experienced a career slump. She scored her final chart entry in 1966 with 'Think Twice', in a duet with labelmate Jackie Wilson. Divorcing comedian Slappy White, and then joining a USO tour in 1969, Baker nearly died from bronchial pneumonia which she contracted while performing just miles from the battle line in Vietnam. Miraculously recovering, she relocated to the Philippines, landing a position as the entertainment manager at the US military base nightclub in Subic Bay. With the closing of the base in 1988, Baker returned to the US for the first time in nearly two decades. Rediscovered, Baker landed the leading role in the Broadway musical *Black And Blue*, and recorded a new album, *Woke Up This Mornin'*. Diagnosed with diabetes in 1992, Baker had both of her legs amputated. She would occasionally return to the stage with the aid of a motorised wheelchair.
CAUSE: In the midst of a comeback, Baker died from complications from heart disease, a stroke, and diabetes. She died at St. Luke's-Roosevelt Hospital in Manhattan.

Lefty Baker

(EUSTACE BRITCHFORTH)
Born January 7, 1942
Died August 11, 1971
Guitarist and banjo player for the late Sixties folk-pop outfit Spanky And Our Gang, Lefty Baker formed a precursor of the group in Miami as a music and comedy trio. Relocating to Chicago and adding new lead vocalist Elaine "Spanky" McFarlane, Spanky And Our Gang followed in the wake of vocal harmony group The Mamas & The Papas on hits such as 'Sunday Will Never Be The Same' (1967) and 'I'd Like To Get To Know You' (1968). With their hit run ending, the group disbanded in 1970. Baker later joined The Folkers and The Bitter End Singers, and operated a recording studio.
CAUSE: Cirrhosis of the liver. He died in Burbank, California.

Florence Ballard

Born June 30, 1943
Died February 21, 1976
A member of the hugely popular Motown girl group, The Supremes, Florence Ballard was the group's initial leader. Possessing a powerful voice, she had been encouraged to pursue a singing career by her high school music teacher. After her manager Milton Jenkins formed an all-male singing group, The Primes in 1959, he decided that The Primes needed a female back-up group.

Although Jenkins had originally hired Ballard as a solo act, he asked her to form The Primettes. After a few personnel changes, The Primettes consisted of Ballard, Diana Ross, Mary Wilson, and a short-lived fourth member, all residents of the Brewster housing projects near the small Berry Gordy, Jr.-founded Hitsville USA Studio. Soon The Primes evolved into The Temptations and were signed by Gordy for his Motown label. After an initial failed audition, The Primettes were also signed by the label in 1961. Renamed The Supremes, the group toured extensively in "Caravan of Stars" tours for both Motown and Dick Clark. Nicknamed "Blondie", "Flo" Ballard had also moonlighted in the touring version of The Marvelettes. By late 1963, The Supremes' exposure began paying off, their first Top 40 hit coming with 'When The Lovelight Starts Shining Through His Eyes'. But aided by the brilliant songwriting skills of Holland-Dozier-Holland, The Supremes became Motown's most successful female singing group, unleashing a string of number 1 hits including 'Where Did Our Love Go', 'Baby Love', 'You Can't Hurry Love', and 'You Keep Me Hangin' On'. But with Diana Ross slowly moving to the forefront of the trio, an angry Ballard gained weight and began abusing alcohol and pills. Trying to distinguish herself from the group's two other members, Ballard abandoned her classic Supremes' bouffant hairstyle and cut her hair. As a result of the turmoil within the group, Ballard was fired in April of 1967 before a major concert at the Hollywood Bowl. Replaced by Cindy Birdsong, formerly of Patty LaBelle's Blue Bells, Ballard was given a brief reprieve, but was then officially fired in July of 1967. For decades, the media would blame Ross for Ballard's firing. 'The Happening' would be Ballard's final Supremes hit. Marrying Motown employee Tom Chapman (who became her manager), Ballard had a disastrous, brief solo stint at ABC Records. After leaving Motown, she led a desperate life. Claiming that Motown Records and her lawyer had cheated her of millions of dollars, Ballard ran out of money and was unable to fund her litigation. Losing her confidence to perform, she put on weight, reaching 200 pounds in the mid Seventies. With pride keeping her from asking friends for help, Ballard was forced to go on welfare to feed her three daughters in the mid Eighties. While Ballard's husband had stopped paying support, he reconciled with her when she received a $50,000 settlement from Motown.

CAUSE: Ballard died at Detroit's Mt. Carmel hospital of cardiac arrest. Suffering from chronic stress, high blood pressure and obesity, she had been prescribed various medications. But as a consequence of consuming alcohol while taking prescription drugs, she developed a blood clot that moved to her heart, causing it to stop. In her autobiography *Supreme Faith*, fellow Supremes member Mary Wilson blamed Ballard's longtime drinking habit on a rape at age seventeen. Guilty or not, Diana Ross has been blamed for Ballard's downfall, and was heckled at her funeral.

FURTHER READING: Wilson, Mary; & Romanowski, Patricia. (1986). *Dreamgirl: My Life As A Supreme*. New York: St. Martin's Press.

Phillip Ballou

(PHILLIP DEMITRIUS BALLOU)
Born February 22, 1950
Died March 19, 2005

A session vocalist, Phillip Ballou worked with James Taylor, Aretha Franklin, Todd Rundgren and Billy Joel among others, and also toured as a backing singer behind Luther Vandross. From Pittsburgh, Ballou followed the path of his father and sang in church settings during his youth.

After studying art at Carnegie Mellon University, Ballou settled in New York City where he co-founded the pop-gospel and RSO Records act Revelation, who occasionally opened up for labelmates The Bee Gees. Ballou also appeared in the Alan Freed film biography *American Hot Wax*.
CAUSE: Stroke.

Baltimora

(JAMES "JIMMY" MCSHANE)
Born May 27, 1957
Died March 28, 1995
A one-hit wonder in both the US and UK, Baltimora was a superstar in his adopted land of Italy. Born in Londonderry, Northern Ireland, Baltimora relocated to London in the late Seventies to study music and dance. Hired as a stage dancer and back-up singer by British artist Dee D. Jackson (of 'Automatic Lover' fame), Baltimora toured Europe and, during a swing through Italy, was attracted to the country's underground dance scene, which led to him settling in Milan. His stage persona shaped by songwriters Naimy Hackett and Maurizio Bassi, Baltimora recorded their composition, 'Tarzan Boy', which topped the charts in Italy for nearly four months. Although he failed to chart with his subsequent releases, Baltimora enjoyed a minor resurgence in 1993 when 'Tarzan Boy' was featured in both a television commercial and the film *Teenage Mutant Ninja Turtles III*.
CAUSE: Diagnosed with AIDS in 1994, he returned to Ireland and died the following year in his hometown.

Joe Banashak

Born February 15, 1923
Died October 1985
A native of Baltimore, Joe Banashak joined partner Larry McKinley in founding a pair of New Orleans-based R&B labels, Minit and Instant Records. With house producer Allen Toussaint, the labels had successes with Chris Kenner, Ernie K-Doe, and Jessie Hill. Selling Minit to Imperial Records in 1963, Banashak kept Instant Records active with its sole star, Chris Kenner.
CAUSE: Unknown. He died in Deer Park, Texas.

Lester Bangs

Born December 13, 1948
Died April 30, 1982
A legendary rock-music critic, Lester Bangs was originally a jazz aficionado who was raised on the music of Charlie Mingus and John Coltrane. With rock becoming Bangs' passion, he was first published by the fledgling *Rolling Stone* magazine in 1969. Leaving college and moving to Detroit in 1971, he became editor of *Creem*, a new monthly magazine started on a shoestring budget by Barry Kramer. Bangs, along with fellow *Creem* writer Dave Marsh, came to define the cutting edge of rock journalism with their stinging, insightful, and very opinionated pieces. Championing rock performers from The Troggs to Iggy Pop, Bangs also popularised the term "heavy metal". Leaving *Creem* in 1976, Bangs assumed the role of a rock personality, all the while attacking the very nature of rock stardom. The antithesis of the rock'n'roll idol/musician, Bangs was himself a musician, in 1980 joining the Austin punk-rock band, The Delinquents. Bangs' book credits include biographies of Rod Stewart and Blondie. Bangs finest essays were posthumously collected in the tome, *Psychotic Reactions and Carburetor Dung*.
CAUSE: An accidental death, Bangs died of a heart attack in his Manhattan apartment, resulting from a combination of the flu, long-term respiratory problems and the prescription drug, Darvon. His wake was held at New York City's famed punk nightclub, CBGBs.
FURTHER READING: Bangs, Lester. (1987). *Psychotic Reactions and*

Carburetor Dung. New York: Knopf.
DeRogatis, Jim. (2000). *Let It Blurt: The Life And Times Of Lester Bangs, America's Greatest Rock Critic*. New York: Broadway.

Al Banks

(Andrew Banks)
Born July 26, 1937
Died July 1977
As the lead singer of the 1950s doo-wop group The Turbans, Al Banks enjoyed a brief hit run with the Philadelphia-based quartet. Discovered by entrepreneur Herman Gillespie, the teenage group was Philadelphia's first nationally charting R&B group. Although The Turbans experienced a series of early line-up changes, Banks remained at the helm during their entire run. After a brief stint at Money Records, The Turbans were signed by Herald Records where they scored their only major hit with the early rock classic, 'When You Dance' (1955). Written by bass singer Andrew "Chet" Jones, and featuring Banks' soaring falsetto tenor, the song combined doo-wop vocals with Latin-tinged percussion. Banks and The Turbans managed several more regional hits including 'Congratulations' (1958), their last at Herald. After recording at a succession of labels, the group disbanded in the early 1960s. Maintaining a career in music, Banks worked as a solo act in Philadelphia and along the East Coast. In 1972, Banks joined the Charlie Thomas version of The Drifters and appeared on the album, *Live At Harvard*, before leaving the group in 1974.
Cause: Unknown.

Darrell Banks

(Darrel Eubanks)
Born July 25, 1937
Died February 24, 1970
A Sixties Northern soul singer, Buffalo-born Darrell Banks first found fame in the nightclubs of Detroit. After working with hard-soul singer Donnie Ebert in the mid Sixties, Banks joined the Daddy B. Combo. Pursuing a solo career in 1966, Banks recorded for Soultown and then Revilot Records. At the latter, he released the self-penned soul chestnut, 'Open The Door To Your Heart'. Spotting a rising star, Atlantic Records signed Banks in 1968, releasing the album *Darrell Banks Is Here*. After moving to the Stax Records subsidiary, Volt, Banks faded from the charts.
Cause: He was mortally wounded in the neck by a gun shot. Banks got into an altercation with a Detroit policeman who was dating Banks' former girlfriend. When police officer Aaron Bullock dropped off Marjorie Bozeman after a date, Banks sprang from his waiting car, grabbed Bozeman, and demanded to speak with her. When Bullock ordered Banks to release Bozeman, the singer aimed a gun at Bullock, who identified himself as a policeman. Bullock responded with a single gunshot. No arrests were made.

John Banks

Born September 23, 1943
Died April 20, 1988
The drummer for The Merseybeats, John Banks joined the Liverpool-based beat group in 1962 replacing original sticksman Frank Sloane. Though joining Brian Epstein's stable of acts, they soon parted ways over musical conflicts. The group also turned down a Decca Records contract offer on the grounds of exploitation. In the wake of Beatlemania, The Merseybeats were eventually signed by Fontana Records in 1963 and had several UK chart single successes, beginning with a cover of The Shirelles' ballad 'It's Love That Really Counts', continuing with their biggest hit 'I Think Of Love', 'Don't Turn Around', and the often recorded 'Wishin' And Hopin''. A self-titled album (1964) and further singles followed but The Merseybeats' fortunes had dwindled by the time Who managers, Kit Lambert and Chris

Stamp took over their management in mid 1965. After The Merseybeats disbanded in early 1966, Banks formed a duo, Johnny & John with bandmate Johnny Gustafson and was under consideration for the drummer's job backing Jimi Hendrix later that year. He eventually quit the music business.
CAUSE: Throat cancer.

George Barajas

Born June 17, 1949
Died August 17, 1982
Bassist of the Rochester, New York-based, hard-rock group, Duke Jupiter, George Barajas enjoyed a hit in 1982 with 'I'll Drink To You'. He was replaced in the group by Rickey Ellis.
CAUSE: Unknown. He died in Wisconsin.

Grover "Dean" Barlow

Born c. 1935
Died 1982
Lead vocalist of the Fifties doo-wop group, The Crickets (not Buddy Holly's group), Grover Barlow had joined the group in 1952. With the aid of manager and producer Joe Davis, the Bronx-anchored group scored a national hit with their début release, the velvety ballad, 'You're Mine'. With their follow-up single bombing, The Crickets were placed with Davis' new label, Jay-Dee Records. Though remaining a popular concert draw, the Crickets managed no more chart hits. Renamed by his manager, "Dean" Barlow later pursued a solo career, scoring airplay in 1961 with 'Third Window From The Right'. Leaving music, he later took a position with Western Union.
CAUSE: Unknown.

Roosevelt "Booba" Barnes

Born September 25, 1936
Died April 3, 1996
Mississippi-born, Chicago-based blues singer and guitarist, Roosevelt "Booba" Barnes began as a harmonica player during his teens. Arriving in Chicago in 1946, he became a fixture in the city's blues scene. After returning to Mississippi in 1971, he formed a blues group, The Playboys, and opened a blues nightclub in 1985, the Playboy Club. Barnes' belated first album, the raw *The Heartbroken Man,* was released in 1990.
CAUSE: Lung cancer. He died in Chicago.

Carlie Barrett

(CARLTON LLOYD BARRETT)
Born December 17, 1950
Died April 17, 1987
The drummer for the Bob Marley-led reggae group The Wailers, Jamaican-born Carlie Barrett had formed his first group in 1967, The Hippy Boys, with his older brother, Aston "Family Man" Barrett. Graduating to session work, the brothers formed The Upsetters, working at Lee "Scratch" Perry's small but influential, backroom studio in Kingston, Jamaica. With his muscular hands, Carlie Barrett employed a "one-drop" drumming style, emphasizing every fourth beat. Under Perry's direction, The Upsetters backed Bob Marley on a full-time basis, beginning with his 1969 groundbreaking works, *Soul Rebels* and *Soul Revolution.* But soon after, Marley disbanded the group to live with his mother in Delaware. With Marley returning to Jamaica, The Wailers regrouped as reggae became an international sensation. When Marley converted to Rastafarianism, the faith was injected into The Wailers' lyrics. Other themes of The Wailers' music included unemployment, tyrannical government and human rights. While Marley and The Wailers received scant airplay in the US during the Seventies, they garnered a loyal following and sold plenty of records. The Wailers' popularity was furthered by Eric Clapton's recording of the Marley-penned 'I Shot The Sheriff'

(1974). Barrett co-wrote a number of Wailers' classics including 'Them Belly Full (But We Hungry)' and 'Talkin' Blues'. When Marley died in 1981, the group's status went into limbo. Barrett later joined a reformed version of The Wailers. "Carlie Barrett was a genius at the one-drop style of drumming," wrote Timothy White in *Catch A Fire*, the definitive biography of Bob Marley, "the bass drum finding the basement on two and four, and he had a rapid sticking hi-hat accent that sounded like the first savage rattle in a snake pit."
CAUSE: Barrett was shot twice in the head outside his home in Kingston, Jamaica, en route to a grocery store. Charged with Barrett's murder were his wife, Albertine and her lover, 34-year-old taxicab driver, Glenroy Carter. Barrett was the third member of The Wailers to die an untimely death after Bob Marley and Peter Tosh. At the time of his death, Barrett was entangled in a messy legal dispute with Marley's widow, Rita, over the ownership of The Wailers' name.
FURTHER READING: White, Timothy. (1983). *Catch A Fire: The Life Of Bob Marley*. New York: Holt, Rinehart and Winston.

Keith Barrow

Born September 27, 1954
Died October 23, 1983
Falsetto-voiced Chicago-born singer/songwriter, Keith Barrow moved to New York City in 1974 to pursue a music career. He landed on the disco charts in 1978 with his sole hit, 'You Know You Wanna Be Loved'.
CAUSE: AIDS. The cause of death was not publicised for several years.

Lionel Bart

(LIONEL BEGLEITER)
Born August 1, 1930
Died April 3, 1999
Songwriter best known for *Oliver!*, his musical adaptation of Charles' Dicken' novel *Oliver Twist*, Lionel Bart also wrote 'Livin' Doll', Cliff Richard's first number 1 hit, and 'Do You Mind', a number 1 hit for Anthony Newley. Born in the East End of London, the youngest of seven children, Bart was a child prodigy on the violin but he gave up formal lessons in favour of making up his own songs. Two early musicals, *Fings Ain't What They Used To Be* and *Lock Up Your Daughters* were modest successes but *Oliver!* was a smash which brought Bart enormous wealth. His riches enabled him to become a key social figure of the 'swinging Sixties' in London, the host of legendary parties at his opulent Fulham home. Unfortunately he was to lose his fortune in an ill-advised rescue attempt of a subsequent musical called *Twang!!* In so doing he lost the rights to past and future works, including the *Oliver!* goldmine. Thereafter Bart became a tragic figure, an amiable alcoholic who never again tasted serious success. At one point in his life Bart was consuming three bottles of vodka a day, but he conquered his alcoholism in the Eighties through joining Alcoholics Anonymous. In the Nineties *Oliver!* enjoyed a revival under the aegis of producer Cameron Mackintosh who owned half the rights, and he gave Bart a share of the production royalties.
CAUSE: Cancer. He died at Hammersmith Hospital in West London.
FURTHER READING: Roper, David (1994). *Bart!* London, Pavilion Books.

Alan Barton

(ALAN LESLEY BARTON)
Born September 16, 1953
Died March 23, 1995
The lead vocalist of the British pop group Black Lace, Alan Barton enjoyed a brief hit run in the early Eighties. Founded by Barton and Colin Gibb, Black Lace had garnered publicity as Britain's entry in the Eurovision Song Contest in 1979. Considered somewhat of a novelty group, Black Lace scored several British hits

including 'Superman' (1983) and the overplayed singalong 'Agadoo' (1984). But Black Lace was blackballed after a public indiscretion by Gibb, who was subsequently fired from the group. But when Barton quit Black Lace, he asked Gibb to replace him. Joining a latter line-up of the rock group Smokie in 1986, Barton replaced Chris Norman as lead singer. Smokie was enjoying renewed popularity at the time of Barton's death.
CAUSE: En route to the Dusseldorf Airport following a concert, Smokie's minibus plunged into a ravine, flipping over several times during a hail storm near Gummersbach, Germany. Barton suffered head injuries. Entering a coma, he died six days later in a Cologne hospital without ever regaining consciousness. Bandmates Alan Silson and Terry Uttley suffered minor injuries.

Ralph Bass

(RALPH BASSO)
Born May 1, 1911
Died March 5, 1997
Pioneering R&B producer at the Cincinnati-based King-Federal, Ralph Bass aided the rise of rock music with the Dominoes, Etta James, and an act he signed over the label owner's strong objections, James Brown. The Bronx, New York native had previously worked in the Los Angeles-based, pioneering R&B and jazz label, Black and White Records, as a talent scout and record producer, where he oversaw two of the most important records in rock's early evolution, T-Bone Walker's 'Stormy Monday' (1946), and a rare, early crossover pop hit, Jack McVea's 'Open The Door Richard'. In 1948, Bass launched Bop Records, and then joined Herman Lubinsky's embryonic R&B label, Savoy Records, as West Coast A&R chief. Leaving Savoy in 1951, Bass landed at Cincinnati's King Records, with label founder Syd Nathan giving Bass his own Federal subsidiary. Leaving King-Federal in 1958, Bass headed the A&R department at Chess Records, where he worked with Muddy Waters and Howlin' Wolf. By 1976, Bass had landed at T.K. Records, a Miami-based disco label.
CAUSE: He suffered a heart attack aboard an aeroplane en route to Nassau, Bahamas, to visit his wife.

Stiv Bators

(STEVEN JOHN BATORS, JR.)
Born October 22, 1949
Died June 3, 1990
Early punk-rock personality, Youngstown, Ohio-native Stiv Bators joined the Cleveland-based group The Rockets in 1975. The Rockets had evolved from the legendary group Rocket From The Tombs, which had included Peter Laughner and future Pere Ubu-leader, David Thomas. As The Rockets' lead singer, Bators went under the name of Steve Machine, but was soon fired due to his peculiar, strained vocal delivery. Co-founding the early punk-rock group The Dead Boys in 1977, Bators was aided by The Ramones in landing gigs at New York City's famed punk nightclub, CBGBs. During the height of the disco era, The Dead Boys wore leather and safety pins, and mutilated themselves on stage. After signing The Dead Boys to a recording contract, CBGBs' owner Hilly Crystal sold the group's contract to Sire Records. Releasing a pair of albums, *Young, Loud, And Snotty*, and the Felix Pappalardi-produced *We Have Come For Your Children*, the projects yielded only a minor hit with 'Sonic Reducer' (1977). Though not a mass appeal group, The Dead Boys developed a cult following in the punk community. Drifting to London in the Eighties, Bators joined up with former Damned member Brian James and two others to form the first punk supergroup, Lords Of The New Church, which in the MTV era were more commercially viable than The Dead Boys. Lords Of The New

Church garnered a hit with the guitar-driven single, 'Open Your Eyes' (1982). Disbanding the group in 1986, Bators moved to Paris and appeared in a pair of films, including Michael Nesmith's *Tapeheads* in which he portrayed Dick Slammer, the leader of a heavy metal band called Blender Children. Before his death, Bators had formed a new version of Lords Of The New Church and was working on a new album. Guns N' Roses reprised The Dead Boys' 'Ain't it Fun' in 1991.
CAUSE: Internal injuries. Riding his motorcycle on the streets of Paris, he collided with a car. Bators was accustomed to hurting himself on stage and considered the injuries minor. Instead of seeking medical attention, he walked home, where he died in his sleep from a blood clot. His body was cremated and the ashes were spread over Jim Morrison's Paris grave.

Joe Bauer

Born September 26, 1941
Died November 1983
The drummer for the Sixties folk-rock group The Youngbloods, Joe Bauer came out of the jazz tradition. When singer-guitarist Jesse Colin Young formed The Youngbloods in 1965, Bauer, who hated rock music, reluctantly joined the group. Landing a long-term gig as the house band at New York City's Cafe A-Go-Go, The Youngbloods adopted a psychedelic persona with their pre-hippy hair and clothing. After Young fulfilled his recording obligations for Mercury Records, The Youngbloods signed with RCA in 1966. Their début album, *The Youngbloods* (1966), produced a pair of minor chart hits in 1967, 'Grizzly Bear' and the folk-rock, peace ballad, 'Get Together'. But after 'Get Together' was featured in radio and TV spots in 1969 for the National Conference of Christians and Jews, the Dino Valenti composition was re-released, landing in the Top 40. A popular live draw, The Youngbloods were booted off *The Tonight Show* in a well-publicised affair for their boisterous behaviour. After the group disbanded in 1972, Bauer joined Youngblood member Banana (Lowell Levinger) in Noggins, and then, Banana and The Bunch.
CAUSE: Unknown.

"Little" David Baughan

Born 1938
Died 1970
A solo R&B artist and member of The Drifters, "Little" David Baughan was initially a member of a Dominoes copy group called the Checkers. Then after recording a handful of obscure solo singles, in 1952 Baughan joined Clyde McPhatter's brief, first line-up of The Drifters at Atlantic Records. From the sessions, only one track, 'Lucille', was ever released, later appearing as a B-side. Disappointed with the sessions, McPhatter fired the entire group and hired a new version of The Drifters. Baughan then joined another King-Federal act, The Checkers, on lead vocals as the replacement for Perry Heyward. Baughan appeared on several of the group's singles including a 'Sixty Minute Man' rip-off called 'Don't Stop Dan'. Meanwhile, when McPhatter was drafted in 1954, Baughan was hired as his replacement for the group's road dates. Unable to deal with the stress of success, Baughan began to abuse alcohol and missed a number of the group's rehearsals. Tricked by their road manager Bill Pinkney into leaving the group after a show in Cleveland, Baughan was replaced by Johnny Moore. Signed as a solo act by Herman Lubinsky at Savoy Records as Little David And The Harps, Baughan found little success with his McPhatter-like vocal leads. Baughan joined a revival version of The Drifters in the late Sixties.
CAUSE: Unknown.
FURTHER READING: Allan, Tony. (1993). *Save The Last Dance For Me:*

The Musical Legacy Of The Drifters, 1953–1992. Ann Arbor, MI: Popular Culture Ink.

Bernie Baum

Born October 13, 1929
Died August 28, 1993
A pop songwriter, Bernie Baum penned 'Music, Music, Music (Put Another Nickel In)', 'That's Old Fashioned' and the Elvis Presley hit, '(You're The) Devil In Disguise'. He also provided the musical scores for several Presley films and penned material for Ray Charles, Bobby Darin, Eartha Kitt, and Peggy Lee.
CAUSE: Complications from diabetes. He died in Yonkers, New York.

Mel Bay

Born February 25, 1913
Died May 14, 1997
The author of a series of music instruction books, Mel Bay sold over 20 million copies of various editions of *Modern Guitar Method.* Born in Missouri, he taught himself to play the guitar on a Sears Roebuck model he received as a Christmas present in 1926. After passing through a series of bands in the Ozarks, and then St. Louis, Bay emerged as a much sought-after session player, and as a music teacher at his Kirkwood, Missouri, music shop. Releasing the first of his many instruction books in 1947, Mel Bay later published guides on the violin, piano, hammered dulcimer and a host of other instruments.
CAUSE: Long-term heart ailment. He died at Missouri Baptist Hospital in St. Louis.
FURTHER READING: Dankenbring, Ray. (1997). *The Mel Bay Story.* Pacific, MO: Mel Bay Publications.

Bobby Baylor

(ALVIN BAYLOR)
Born 1938
Died c. 1980
Baritone singer of the early Fifties, Harlem-based teenage doo-wop group, The Mello-Tones, Bobby Baylor sang back-up in the Ray "Buddy" Wooten-led outfit. Recording for Robin Records, the group landed its sole R&B chart entry with a cover of the 1936 standard, 'Where Are You (Now That I Need You)' (1952). Baylor later joined some of his bandmates to form The Solitaires.
CAUSE: Unknown.

Daniel Beard

Born November 4, 1949
Died July 27, 1982
A member of the 5th Dimension from 1976–1981, Daniel Beard had replaced Billy Davis Jr., who had left to form a duo with bandmate Marilyn McCoo. Signing with ABC Records, the retooled 5th Dimension managed only a few minor hits including 'Love Hangover' (1976). After a brief stint at Motown in the late Seventies, the group became popular on the dinner club circuit. Beard was also a budding Broadway actor.
CAUSE: When a fire broke out in his six-storey Manhattan apartment building, Beard fled down the stairs, succumbing to the smoke and flames on the fourth floor. His roommate headed to the roof and survived. The fire was set by an arsonist.

Beatmaster V

(VICTOR RAY WILSON)
Born February 20, 1959
Died May 1996
As the drummer for Ice-T's backing rap/heavy metal band Body Count, Beatmaster V was continually dogged by controversy. Formed by classmates from Crenshaw High School in the south central section of Los Angeles, Body Count initially backed Ice-T on his 1991 album *OG Original Gangster.* Later that year, Ice-T and Body Count drew positive reviews for their performances on the Lollapalooza tour. Body Count's self-titled 1992 début album was initially ignored until a

Texas police force threatened a boycott of Time-Warner because of the track 'Cop Killer'. Although the track was eventually deleted from the disc, the surrounding controversy propelled the group's rise in popularity. Leaving Time-Warner, Body Count issued their second album, *Born Dead*, on Ice-T's fledgling label, Priority Records. Although the group failed to sustain their popularity, Ice-T and Body Count followed up with the critically acclaimed 1997 album, *Violent Demise*, which was issued around the time that Beatmaster V fell ill. Following the deaths of three members of Body Count, Ice-T formed a new line-up of the group in 2004.
CAUSE: Leukaemia.

Paul Beaver

Born 1925
Died January 16, 1975
A jazz-trained session player who worked with The Beach Boys and The Beatles, Paul Beaver formed the pioneering electronic-rock duo, Beaver and Krause, with former Weavers member, Bernard Krause. Merging spoken-word lyrics with Moog synthesizers and complex studio technique, the duo released four influential, but commercially disappointing albums, beginning with 1969's *Ragnarock: Electronic Funk*. Beaver and Krause were aided in the studio by top musicians including Dave Grusin, Mike Bloomfield, and Ronnie Montrose. Beaver and Krause disbanded in 1972. Beaver completed a solo album, *Perchance To Dream*, shortly before his death in 1975.
CAUSE: Heart attack.

Lou Bedell

(LEWIS J. BEDELL)
Born March 21, 1919
Died July 6, 2000
Bedell was the co-founder, with Herb Newman, of Era Records and its subsidiary Dore. Formed in 1955, Era issued pop, country and jazz, while Dore was launched three years later and specialised in rock and R&B. (Dore's A&R department was headed by Herb Albert and Lou Adler.) After breaking onto the charts in 1955 with Gogi Grant's 'Suddenly There's A Valley', Bedell and Newman would enjoy success with Jan & Dean, The Teddy Bears, and Billy Joe & The Checkmates. Bedell sold his share of the labels to Newman in 1959, and later worked with a number of soul artists including The Whispers.
CAUSE: Cancer. He died in Los Angeles.

Jimmy Bee

(JAMES O'FARRELL)
Born September 20, 1934
Died April 22, 1993
Member of the Los Angeles-based doo-wop group, The Flairs, Jimmy Bee later joined the Billy Williams revue in 1959, staying for four years. Also a solo artist, Bee recorded for several labels beginning Hilton Records in 1959. Turning to artist promotions in the mid Sixties, Bee aided the careers of The Bee Gees, Gladys Knight & The Pips, Quincy Jones, and Johnny "Guitar" Watson. In 1973, Bee recorded his only solo album, *Live*. In the Eighties, Bee and partner Maury Alexander founded Bee/Alexander Productions.
CAUSE: Heart attack. He died while driving in New York City en route to the airport to catch a flight to Atlantic City where he was scheduled to receive the coveted Living Legend Award.

Carl Belew

Born April 21, 1931
Died October 31, 1990
Oklahoma-based singer-songwriter, Carl Belew penned 'Stop The World' (Johnnie & Jack; Waylon Jennings), 'Lonely Street' (Andy Williams) and 'What's He Doing In My World?' (Eddy Arnold). Also a performer who straddled the rockabilly and country fields, Belew scored several hits

including 'Crystal Chandelier' and 'Hello Out There'.
CAUSE: Cancer. He died in Selina, Oklahoma.

Chris Bell

Born January 12, 1951
Died December 27, 1978
Guitarist, vocalist and co-founder of the influential Memphis-based rock group, Big Star, Chris Bell had previously formed a local, British rock, cover-band in 1971 group called Ice Water. Inviting former Box Tops singer Alex Chilton to join, the group was renamed Big Star. Emerging as a potent songwriting team, Bell and Chilton penned a series of matched British Invasion meets Memphis R&B classics including 'In The Street' and 'Feel'. Releasing the stunning melody-driven, début album, *#1 Record*, Big Star earned far more accolades than record sales, becoming a musicians' favourite. Arguing with Chilton over the musical direction of the group, Bell left Big Star in 1973 to pursue solo projects. Bandmate Alex Chilton later emerged a solo star, his 1976 album, *I Am The Cosmos*, remaining unreleased until 1992.
CAUSE: Driving home from a Memphis recording studio following a rehearsal with his new group, Bell struck a telephone pole and died instantly.

Fred Below

Born September 6, 1926
Died August 13, 1988
A popular Chicago-based blues drummer, Fred Below backed Memphis Slim, Muddy Waters, Howlin' Wolf, and Chuck Berry on his pioneering early releases at Chess Records. As a member of the Aces, a popular studio blues band formed in 1950, Below spent several years backing a pair of harmonica players, Junior Wells (1950–52), and Little Walter (1952–55). Citing internal squabbles, Below left the group in 1955.
CAUSE: Heart attack. He died in Chicago.

John Belushi

(JOHN ADAM BELUSHI)
Born January 24, 1949
Died March 5, 1982
A comedian who stumbled upon musical success via a *Saturday Night Live* skit as half of white R&B duo The Blues Brothers, John Belushi had always wanted to be a singing star, forming a rock group during his teens. At his suburban high school, the popular Belushi was the homecoming king and the captain of the football team. After four years of occasional college coursework and stage acting, in 1971 Belushi became the Chicago's Second City comedy troupe's youngest ever cast member at the age of 22. Then hired as an original member of *Saturday Night Live*'s Not Ready For Prime Time Players in 1975, Belushi was almost passed up by the programme's producer Lorne Michaels over personality differences. A groundbreaking comedy programme, *SNL* made stars out of Belushi and several fellow cast members including Chevy Chase and Steve Martin. Starring in the 1978 low-budget smash National Lampoon's *Animal House*, Belushi also gave a vocal performance, singing Barrett Strong's R&B classic, 'Money'. After a series of impromptu, off-camera *Saturday Night Live* warm-up skits, on April 22, 1978 Belushi and cast member Dan Aykroyd débuted the singing duo called The Blues Brothers. Under the personas of "Joliet" Jake Blues and "Elwood" Blues, the campy duo wore black suits, hats, and sunglasses, while singing old R&B and blues songs. The Blues Brothers soon took their act on the road opening for Steve Martin. Originally considered a novelty act, The Blues Brothers reached the top of the charts with the Grammy-winning, three million selling album, *Briefcase Full Of Blues*. But while the ensuing feature film, the John Landis-directed *The Blues Brothers* was panned by critics, it became a surprise box-office

smash. The film also reinvigorated the careers of cast members James Brown, Aretha Franklin and Cab Calloway. Enjoying Top 40 airplay, The Blues Brothers scored a series of R&B cover hits including 'Soul Man' and 'Rubber Biscuit'. By the spring of 1979, Belushi had left the cast of *SNL*. Tired of his typecasting in comedy roles, Belushi in 1981 starred in a romantic feature, *The Continental Divide*. But although his acting was believable and sincere, box-office receipts indicated that fans wanted no part of Belushi as a serious actor. A long-planned sequel, *Blues Brothers 2000*, hit theatres in 1998.
CAUSE: During the Seventies Belushi was abusing large amounts of cocaine, and in the last few months of his life, heroin. After a drug and drinking binge at a $200-a-day suite at the Chateau Marmont Hotel in West Hollywood, Belushi overdosed on a mixture of cocaine and heroin and died in his sleep. The fatal cocktail was administered by his female friend, professional back-up singer Cathy Evelyn Smith. His hometown of Chicago was devastated by the news of his drug death. Attempting to elude prosecution, Smith fled to Canada but later turned herself in to authorities in Toronto. She was charged with murder and 13 counts of supplying and administering drugs. Pleading no contest in a Los Angeles courtroom, she was convicted of involuntary manslaughter and was sentenced to a three-year prison term, serving 18 months. In 1991, Smith was arrested on drug charges in Canada.
FURTHER READING: Woodward, Bob. (1984). *Wired: The Short Life & Fast Times Of John Belushi*. New York: Simon & Schuster. Belushi, Judith Jacklin. (1990). *Samurai Widow*. New York: Carroll & Graff.

Jesse Belvin

(JESSIE LORENZO BELVIN)
Born December 15, 1933
Died February 6, 1960

A popular Fifties R&B balladeer and composer who recorded under a variety of names, San Antonio-born Jesse Belvin was raised in California after his father's death. Settling in Los Angeles, five-year-old Belvin sang in a Baptist church choir at his mother's urging. In church, he also learned to play the piano. But against his mother's wishes, in 1948 15-year-old Belvin entered and won Johnny Otis' famed talent contest as an R&B balladeer. A year later, he joined Three Dots & A Dash, an R&B styled vocal group in Big Jay McNeely's Orchestra. With Belvin on lead vocals, McNeely scored a hit with 'All That Wine Is Gone' (1950). Leaving McNeely to pursue a solo career, Belvin recorded 'Dream Girl' at John Dolphin's Hollywood Records. Recording a new version of the song at Specialty Records with Marvin Phillips as Jesse & Marvin in 1952, it became an R&B hit. After a stint in the Special Services division of the army during the Korean War, Belvin returned to Los Angeles where he continued his high profile in the local music community. Recording under dozens of names on a series of labels, Belvin initially earned co-writing credits for 'Earth Angel', a hit for The Penguins. A smooth baritone singer, Belvin landed his biggest hit in 1956 with the romantic ballad, 'Goodnight My Love', the song popularised by New York deejay Alan Freed as his closing theme. Recording at Modern Records, Belvin joined Eugene Church in a duo called The Cliques, and also provided the falsetto backing vocals on The Shields' 1958 hit, 'You Cheated'. Signing with RCA Records, Belvin originally formed The Challengers, before scoring a pop hit as a solo act with 'Guess Who' (1959). But with the label steering Belvin toward a pop-standard direction in the tradition of Nat "King" Cole, Belvin lost much of his black fanbase. Wanting to reclaim his past glory, Belvin joined an R&B caravan tour in 1960.

CAUSE: He died in an auto accident near Little Rock in Hope, Arkansas, after a performance. Travelling from Little Rock to the tour's next stop in Dallas in a three-car caravan, Belvin and his wife JoAnn were passengers in a Cadillac whose driver, Charles Shackleford, nodded off and swerved into oncoming traffic, hitting an approaching car head-on. Shackleford had been fired several weeks earlier by another musical act for dozing at the wheel. Both Belvin and the driver died at the scene, and the crash claimed five lives in all including that of Belvin's wife's a week later. Some sources incorrectly claim that Belvin's car was drag racing, or that the car's tires had been slashed. The car's only survivor was a member of The Moonglows, who was sitting in the back seat. (One of the other two cars in the caravan was driven by former Midnighters member Al Frazier, who was chauffeuring Jackie Wilson.) Belvin had gone on tour to resuscitate his floundering career.

Chris Bender

(CHRISTOPHER LAMONT BENDER)
Born August 2, 1972
Died November 3, 1991
A rising R&B/rap singer, Chris Bender had brief success in the early Nineties. Frequently in trouble with the law in his youth, he was expelled from high school for fighting. Though receiving no formal musical training, Bender discovered his singing talent aged 10. Although initially signing with Epic Records at 17, he later signed a $500,000, seven-album deal with the Atlantic Records subsidiary, East/West. At the time of his death, he had just released his second album, *Draped.*
CAUSE: He was shot four times in the back while trying to shield his cousin, a passenger in his automobile. Shortly after arriving at the Crescent Court public housing project where he was raised, his Mercedes was riddled with at least 16 bullets. While police assumed that he was involved in an illicit activity at the time of the shooting, his family attributed the gunfire to a crosstown feud between two teenage gangs.

Louis Benjamin

(ISAAC LOUIS BENJAMIN)
Born October 17, 1922
Died June 20, 1994
Although best known as the chief of the British label Pye Records, mogul Louis Benjamin spent his lifetime in various facets of the entertainment industry. The son of a shoemaker, he began his career at age 14 as an office boy for Moss Empire, the British theatre chain. Emerging as its managing director by the Sixties, along the way Benjamin had displayed a knack for spotting talent. When Moss purchased Pye Records in 1959, Benjamin took the reins of the company in spite of his scant musical background. An unorthodox executive who destroyed the domination of the UK record industry by Decca and EMI Records, Benjamin introduced a lower-priced record line (Golden Guinea), was quick to embrace rock and R&B, and signed and nurtured a host of young, emerging recording artists, including The Searchers, The Kinks and Sandie Shaw. The label also secured the rights to US Mercury, thereby releasing in the UK records by Chuck Berry, Bo Diddley and Muddy Waters. In the mid Sixties their principal act was Donovan, but the company was slow to pick up on the changes in the rock climate brought about by the 'underground' market, and relied too heavily on marketing its back catalogue as budget lines. Heading both Pye Records and the Stroll Moss theatre chain by 1970, Benjamin wielded great power in the entertainment industry. Benjamin also founded The Children's Royal Variety Show, and was the presenter of The Royal Variety Performance from 1979 to 1985. Benjamin was forced into retirement in 1989.

CAUSE: Suffering from longterm lung and kidney maladies, he died in a London hospital.

William "Benny" Benjamin

Born July 15, 1925
Died April, 1969
The house drummer for Motown Records, William "Benny" Benjamin appeared on scores of soul/pop hits. An employee at Motown since the label's inception, Benjamin was a vital member of "The Funk Brothers", backing acts such as The Four Tops, Marvin Gaye, The Supremes, and his close friend, Stevie Wonder. Instantly recognisable, Benjamin's drumming was characterised by its strong, danceable, heart beat-like beat. But like most of his bandmates, Benjamin remained virtually unknown to the public during the label's heyday in the Sixties. Abusing alcohol by the late Sixties, Benjamin's duties were gradually assumed by his understudies, drummers Richard Allen and Uriel Jones. With his health worsening, Benjamin retired shortly before his death.
CAUSE: Stroke.

Duster Bennett

(ANTHONY BENNETT)
Born September 23, 1946
Died March 26, 1976
British blues singer, guitarist and harmonica player who was a member of John Mayall's Bluesbreakers in the late Sixties, Duster Bennett had previously worked as half of a duo with Yardbirds' guitarist Tony "Top" Topham. Signing with Blue Horizon Records in 1967, Bennett's début album, *Smiling Like I'm Happy* (1968), featured members of Fleetwood Mac. Recording for RAK Records beginning in 1974, Bennett scored a minor hit with 'Coming Home.'
CAUSE: He died in a car crash in Warwickshire, England. He was returning home after sharing a bill with bluesman Memphis Slim.

Wayne Bennett

Born December 13, 1933
Died November 18, 1992
A prolific R&B/blues guitarist and vocalist, Wayne Bennett hit the professional circuit at age 15 when he landed a stint with R&B shouter Amos Milburn. Drawn to the blues scene of Chicago, Bennett recorded behind Otis Spann and Elmore James at Chess Records, and Magic Sam and Buddy Guy at Cobra Records. Frequently backing Bobby "Blue" Bland, Bennett appeared on the standard 'Farther Up The Road' and provided the guitar solo on Bland's reading of 'Stormy Monday'. After recording a solo single in 1968, Bennett joined Operation Push's politically charged Operation Breadbasket band, recording two albums at Chess Records. Though he would occasionally rejoin Bland's touring band, Bennett moved to New Orleans and became a local fixture as a session player.
CAUSE: Scheduled to receive a donor heart, he died at a Veteran's Administration hospital in New Orleans.

Les Bennetts

Born 1940
Died 1995
A popular skiffle bandleader, Les Bennetts was one of the genre's most talented guitarists. After forming the group Les Hobeaux in 1957, he subsequently joined the bands of Chas McDevitt and Lonnie Donegan. Moving to the US in 1959, Bennetts operated a series of nightclubs but returned to England several years later, working outside of the music industry.
CAUSE: Lung cancer.

Wes Berggren

(WESLEY JOSEPH BERGGREN)
Born April 3, 1971
Died October 28, 1999
The guitarist of Nineties alternative-rock group Tripping Daisy, Wes Berggren joined the Dallas-based

group shortly after its inception in 1991. Formed by vocalist Tim DeLaughter, drummer Mitch Marine, and a college classmate from the University of North Texas, bassist Mark Pirro, the psychedelic/alternative flavoured group garnered a strong following on US college campuses. After releasing an indie album in 1992, the group signed with Island Records the following year. With a new drummer, Tripping Daisy landed their first hit with 'I Got A Girl' (1995), the track culled from their second studio album, *I Am An Elastic Firecracker.* Dropped by Island after the poor sales of *Jesus Hits Like An Atomic Bomb* (1998), Tripping Daisy turned to the internet as a vehicle for issuing material. Disbanding two months after Berggren's death, the group's final tracks were compiled on the album, *Tripping Daisy* (2000).
CAUSE: Overdosing on a combination of cocaine, propoxyphene, and benzodiazepine, he was found dead in his Dallas apartment by his wife.

Brook Benton

(BENJAMIN FRANKLIN PEAY)
Born September 1, 1931
Died April 16, 1988
A glossy-voiced soul singer and prolific songwriter, Brook Benton began as a gospel singer in his father's Methodist church in Camden, South Carolina. Joining a series of notable East Coast gospel groups, Benton passed through The Golden Gate Quartet, The Camden Jubilee Singers and The Jerusalem Stars. Moving to New York in 1948, he supported himself as a dishwasher and truck driver. Leaving gospel for R&B, Benton joined a group called The Sandmen, recording at OKeh Records in 1955. Also that year, he formed a songwriting partnership with Clyde Otis, who had joined Mercury Records as the head of their A&R department. With Otis signing Benton to Mercury, Benton first found success as a songwriter as three Benton/Otis collaborations hit the Top 10 in 1958: 'Looking Back' by Nat "King" Cole, 'A Lover's Question' by Clyde McPhatter, and 'The Stroll', a huge seller for The Diamonds. But with his sweet, mellow, baritone voice, Benton soon reeled off his own string of hits, including 'It's Just A Matter Of Time' (1959), 'Endlessly' (1959), and 'Thank You Pretty Baby' (1959). Otis and Benton parted in 1961 after the release of Benton's million-selling R&B version of the folk standard, 'The Boll Weevil Song'. In the early Sixties Benton scored a series of duet hits with Dinah Washington, with whom he constantly clashed. After a career lull, in 1970 Benton scored his last major chart entry with an elegant cover of the Tony Joe White classic, 'Rainy Night In Georgia'. In the Seventies Benton continued to record for a series of labels including Stax and MGM. Benton reunited with Otis in 1978 to score an R&B hit with the title track of his album, *Makin' Love Is Good For You.* Finding religion, Benton preached at a Bronx church in the early Eighties. He later sued Mercury Records for $750,000 over unpaid royalties, the case settled in 1988.
CAUSE: Although Benton's family refused to disclose the exact cause of death, initial reports claimed pneumonia and related diabetes. Later it was revealed that he succumbed to bacterial meningitis. He died at Mary Immaculate Hospital in Queens, New York.

Bert Berns

(BERTRAND BERNS)
Born November 8, 1929
Died December 30, 1967
Bronx-born R&B producer who once worked as a nightclub pianist in pre-Castro Cuba, Bert Berns pursued a solo career in the early Sixties, releasing several obscure singles under the stage name of Russell Byrd. But Berns first garnered fame for his production work with The Drifters

after the departure of Leiber & Stoller from Atlantic Records in 1963. Continuing The Drifters' chart run, Berns oversaw the sessions for the group's final hits including the rock standard, 'Under The Boardwalk' and 'Saturday Night At The Movies'. During 1964, Berns visited England, producing 'Here Comes The Night' for both Them and Lulu. Berns later launched a pair of labels, Shout and Bang Records, whose rosters featured Neil Diamond, The McCoys, The Strangeloves and Van Morrison, for whom he produced his breakthrough solo hit, 'Brown Eyed Girl'. Also a prolific songwriter – often in collaboration with Jerry Ragavoy – Berns employed the pseudonym of Bert Russell on hits such as 'Piece Of My Heart', 'Time Is On My Side', 'Twist And Shout', 'Cry To Me', 'A Little Bit Of Soap' and 'My Girl Sloopy', the latter an early version of 'Hang On Sloopy'. Three decades after Berns' death, his widow Illene Berns launched Bang II Records, having sold the original label's name and masters to CBS in 1969. Berns' finest work is compiled on the two CD set, *Sloopy II Music Presents The Songs Of Bert Russell Berns (1997)*.
CAUSE: Heart attack. He died suddenly in a New York City hotel room.

Richard Berry

Born April 11, 1935
Died January 23, 1997
A central figure in the Fifties Los Angeles doo-wop and R&B scene, Richard Berry is best known for his frat-rock classic 'Louie Louie'. A Louisiana native, Berry was raised in Los Angeles, stricken with polio as a toddler. Attending Jefferson High School, Berry was surrounded by a host of future R&B stars including Jesse Belvin and Curtis Williams. Working with a series of vocal groups, he collaborated on recordings with The Crowns, The Flairs, and The Robins. Berry first appeared on a hit record in 1954 as a guest lead vocalist on The Robins' 'Riot In Cell Block #9'. Also that year, he traded vocals with Etta James on her smash hit 'The Wallflower (Roll With Me Henry)'. Recording 'Louie Louie' in 1957 as by Richard Berry and The Pharaohs, the record was a minor hit at the time, the song detailing the exploits of a bartender and a love-starved customer in a Jamaican bar. Needing money to get married, in 1957 Berry sold the copyrights of seven of his songs, including 'Louie Louie', for $750. Over the years, the three-chord song was covered by several Pacific Northwest rock groups; after The Wailers scored a regional hit in 1960, both Paul Revere & The Raiders and The Kingsmen recorded the song, with the latter's version becoming a rock classic. Although Berry remained a fixture on the Los Angeles music scene throughout the Sixties, he was unable to garner national success. When Rhino Records was compiling an all 'Louie Louie' compilation album in 1986, the label asked Berry to submit a newly recorded version after the song's copyright owners demanded an exorbitant fee for Berry's original rendition. By the mid Eighties, Berry reclaimed partial ownership rights to the song, winning about $2 million of its $10 million accrued royalties.
CAUSE: He died in his sleep at his Los Angeles home after suffering an aneurysm. He had previously experienced heart problems.
FURTHER READING: Marsh, Dave. (1993). *Louie Louie: The History and Mythology Of The World's Most Famous Rock'n'Roll Song.* New York: Hyperion.

Claude Bessy

Born June 20, 1945
Died October 2, 1999
Best known as the editor of Los Angeles based punk magazine/record label Slash, French-born, Sorbonne-educated Claude Bessy had

relocated to Los Angeles in 1973. Launching a reggae magazine, *Amgeleno Dread*, he took the pen name Kickboy Face. Teaming with graphic artist Steve Samiof and others, Bessy launched *Slash*, one of the country's first punk rock periodicals, in the mid Seventies. A passionate writer, Bessy championed emerging local punk bands such as X and The Germs. Retaining his Kickboy Face moniker as the frontman for his own hardcore punk group, Catholic Discipline, the articulate and hard-drinking Bessy also appeared in the punk film documentary, *The Decline Of Western Civilization*. Catholic Discipline spawned the careers of two solo acts, El Vez, a Mexican Elvis impersonator, and Phranc, the self-styled "Jewish American lesbian folk singer". Having studied film, Bessy took the role of Frenchy in *The Hardy Boys* television series. Meanwhile, *Slash* magazine had evolved into a punk record label. Angered by the presidential election of Ronald Reagan in 1980, Bessy fled the US for England, where he worked as the press officer for Rough Trade Records and, later, a nightclub deejay and music video producer. As a back-up singer, he appeared on projects with Howard Devoto, Sonic Youth and Graham Lewis (of Wire). Bessy settled in Spain in 1987.
CAUSE: A heavy smoker, he died from lung cancer at his home in Barcelona.

Alan Betrock

Born 1950
Died April 9, 2000
A noteworthy publisher, producer, and label owner, Alan Betrock became fascinated with rock music during the rise of the British Invasion. Reared in the Queens borough of New York City, he frequently travelled to England in his youth to hunt for rare records. In the early Seventies, he founded the music magazine, *Jamz*, and a pioneering record collecting publication, *The Rock Marketplace*. During this period he also freelanced for a number of music magazines including *Rock Scene* and *Hit Parader*. Founding the influential *New York Rocker* magazine in 1975, Betrock chronicled the rising punk rock scene and other musical trends, during which time he moonlighted as the East Coast editor for *Bomp* magazine. Passing the reins of *New York Rocker* in 1978 to Andy Schwartz, Betrock launched Shake Books as a vehicle to explore pop culture, publishing tomes such as *Pin-up Mania*, *Illustrated Price Guide To Cult Magazines*, and the critically acclaimed *Girl Groups: The Story Of A Sound*. Adding a music division, Shake Records, in 1979, he produced demos for the then-unknown Blondie, including a track that would later re-emerge as 'Heart Of Glass'. Betrock also issued singles by such artists as The Smithereens, Richard Hell, Marshall Crenshaw, and The dB's.
CAUSE: Cancer. He had been diagnosed two months before his death. He died in New York City.

Big Bopper

(JILES PERRY RICHARDSON, JR.)
Born October 10, 1932
Died February 3, 1959
A Texas disc jockey turned rock'n'roll singer who had the misfortune of being immortalised by his death in the same plane crash that killed Buddy Holly, "J.P." Richardson was the son of a Texas oil worker. Given a guitar by his father, the musically inclined youth taught himself by playing along with country and gospel songs on the radio. After attending technical school and earning a degree in radio and television, he landed a deejay position at KTRM in Beaumont, Texas in 1953. Adopting the radio persona of The Big Bopper, and calling his programme Club 990, he spoke in a black dialect with his deep bass voice. Drafted a year later, he began to compose music while in the service. Returning to KTRM in 1957, his

popularity soared. Entering a recording studio in 1958, The Big Bopper recorded a mediocre parody song, 'The Purple People Eater Meets The Witch Doctor' for "D" Records, in an effort to capitalise on a pair of recent novelty hits. With the song a flop, deejays instead played the B-side, 'Chantilly Lace'. Picked up by Mercury Records, the single went on to sell over six million copies and catapulted the Texas deejay to stardom. The Big Bopper landed one more hit, 'Big Bopper's Wedding' (1958) and wrote Johnny Preston's hit 'Running Bear' on which he can be heard making Indian calls in the background.
CAUSE: In January, 1959, The Big Bopper joined the "Winter Dance Party" tour during which he would sing 'Chantilly Lace' into a prop telephone. Also featuring Holly and Ritchie Valens, the tour began on January 23, 1959, at George Devine's Ballroom in Milwaukee, Wisconsin, and was scheduled to end at the Illinois State Armory in Springfield on February 15, 1960. The admission to the sold-out show at Surf Ballroom in Clear Lake, Iowa, was $1.25. With a blistering winter freeze outside, a sell-out was not expected. In spite of night-time temperatures which plummeted to well below-zero, the entire caravan, including Dion & The Belmonts, were forced to tour in a dilapidated former school bus with a broken heater. Refusing to freeze on the trip to the next concert, a frustrated Buddy Holly decided instead to charter a plane, and was joined by Ritchie Valens. Shortly before the plane's departure, The Big Bopper convinced Waylon Jennings, Holly's then-unknown bass player, to give up his seat on the chartered craft. Taking off in a blinding snowstorm, the private plane departed from an airfield in Mason City, Iowa, and was destined for Fargo, North Dakota. With newlywed, local resident Roger Peterson at the controls, the craft went down minutes after takeoff, at 1:50 a.m. An investigative team ruled that pilot error caused the crash. After a successful take-off, Peterson experienced vertigo and flew directly into the ground. Instead of being a footnote in rock music history as the artist who scored one major rock hit, The Big Bopper was thus immortalised as a rock'n'roll casualty.

Big L

(LAMONT COLEMAN)
Born May 30, 1974
Died February 15, 1999
A member of New York City-based rap outfit Diggin' In Tha Crates (a.k.a. DITC), Big L was murdered shortly before the release of the group's Tommy Boy Records début. Big L had previously released a solo album at Columbia Records, *Lifestylz ov da Poor and Dangerous* (1995).
CAUSE: He was shot to death in front of his home in Harlem.

Big Maybelle

(MABEL LOUIS SMITH)
Born May 1, 1924
Died January 23, 1972
A pioneering R&B shouter, Big Maybelle earned her musical training in a sanctified church in Jackson, Tennessee. Leaving her gospel choir at the age of 12 in 1936, she joined a black, all-girl musical revue, The Sweethearts Of Rhythm. Touring extensively through the deep South until her twentieth birthday, she then joined The Christine Chatman Orchestra as lead vocalist, before leaving to front Tiny Bradshaw's R&B orchestra. Recording for the first time under her own name, Maybelle Smith, in 1948, she released several singles at King Records. Discovered by Fred Mendelsohn at a Detroit nightclub and signed to the CBS-owned OKeh Records as Big Maybelle, she scored a series of R&B hits with 'Gabbin' Blues' (1952), 'Way Back Home' (1953), and 'My Country Man' (1953). A

swaggering, rotund woman, Big Maybelle did not have the finesse of Ruth Brown or the class of Dinah Washington, nor was she able to cross over into the pop market. A gritty, full-voiced, growling and gyrating R&B shouter, Big Maybelle was a superstar in the black community during the early Fifties. But after developing a severe drug habit, her recording success waned. With OKeh Records refusing to renew her contract in 1956, she switched to Savoy Records. Her career slumping, she landed her final hit of the decade with 'Candy' (1956). Making a comeback in the late Sixties, she scored a pair of soul-flavoured hits with 'Don't Pass Me By' (1966) and a cover of ? and The Mysterians' '96 Tears' (1967). Enjoying a new wave of popularity during the blues revival of the late Sixties, Big Maybelle performed occasionally until 1971. Late in life, she moved to Cleveland to live with her mother.
CAUSE: She died while in a diabetic coma in a Cleveland hospital.

Big Punisher

(CHRISTOPHER CARLOS RIOS)
Born November 9, 1971
Died February 7, 2000
A rotund rapper, Big Punisher was a major figure in the rap community in the late Nineties. Of Puerto Rican-descent, the Bronx-born singer was a former teenage athlete who was forced to leave sports after ballooning in his late teens. Dropping out of high school at 15 to raise a family, he remained faithful to Catholicism in spite of the fact that he sold crack cocaine to earn a living. Originally known as Big Moon Dog, he met frequent singing partner Fat Joe (Joseph Cartagena) on a street corner, and was invited to join The Terror Squad. Signed to RCA subsidiary Loud Records, Big Punisher first came to prominence with the track 'You Ain't A Killer' from the soundtrack, *Soul In The Hole*. Infusing Latin rhythms into straightforward raps on his Grammy nominated, double-platinum, début album *Capital Punishment* (1998), he landed a crossover hit with 'I'm Not A Player'. Often photographed with a Puerto Rican flag and infusing Spanish snippets into his raps, he was embraced by the US Puerto Rican community. At the time of his death, "Pun" was enjoying chart success with an appearance on the Jennifer Lopez single, 'Feelin' So Good', and had completed his posthumously released second album, *Yeeeah Baby*. With his weight approaching 700 pounds, he was unable to perform. Rapper Cuban Link recorded the tribute single 'Flowers For The Dead' in 2000.
CAUSE: With his weight nearly quadrupling in ten years, he suffered a heart attack at the Crowne Plaza Hotel near White Plains, New York. Emergency workers had a difficult time performing CPR due to his large girth. Using a construction trolley to wheel him into an ambulance, he died en route to a nearby hospital. An autopsy revealed an acutely enlarged heart.

Jules Bihari

Born September 8, 1913
Died November 17, 1984
The founder of the pioneering West Coast R&B label, Modern Records, Jules Bihari operated the company with his younger siblings. Moving from Oklahoma with his Hungarian-Jewish family to the Watts section of Los Angeles in 1941, Bihari launched a jukebox company, relegated by his established competitors to the ignored black sections of the city. Unable to fully stock his jukeboxes with jazz and blues records, Bihari was forced to start his own label. Aided by a pair of brothers – Joe (who was still in high school) and Saul who was attending business college) – Jules was the driving force behind Modern Records, the label's name taken from Modern Music Jukebox, the former employer of yet

another brother, Lester Bihari. Eventually, three Bihari sisters – Roz, Maxene, and Florette – were brought on board. Modern's first release, 'Swingin' The Boogie' by pianist/singer Hadda Brooks, cost $800 and was a strong West Coast seller. Although initially targeting bebop jazz, the Bihari Brothers signed artists like Russel Jacquet and Gene Phillips. Expanding their empire in 1948, the Biharis established the first of several subsidiaries beginning with RPM, and later including Kent, Flair, and a budget label, Crown. And in 1952, Lester Bihari settled in Memphis to launch the affiliated, Meteor label. Embracing blues, jazz, doo-wop, and R&B, the Biharis were regularly scoring paydirt with artists such as B.B. King, John Lee Hooker, Elmore James, Jimmy Witherspoon, Jesse Belvin, and Etta James. After the death of Saul Bihari and retirement of Joe Bihari in 1975, the label subsisted chiefly as a reissue company. The Biharis sold Modern and its subsidiaries in 1984.
CAUSE: He died in Los Angeles after being hospitalised for an undisclosed, long-term illness.

Bill Black

(WILLIAM PATTON BLACK, JR.)
Born September 17, 1926
Died October 21, 1965
The stand-up bass player and the "Bill" of Elvis Presley's famous backing duo "Scotty & Bill", Bill Black played a key role in Presley's meteoric ascent to fame in the mid Fifties. Moving to urban Memphis in his teens, Black quit high school at the age of 16 to work for a rail shipping company. After a stint in the army, he returned to Memphis in 1947, eventually finding work at a Firestone tyre plant. Playing a huge, rockabilly-style, stand-up bass, he formed a fiddle-based, honky-tonk country group with several co-workers, Doug Poindexter and The Starlight Wranglers. A popular local draw, the group members were acquainted with Sam Phillips of Sun Records, where Black and bandmate Scotty Moore did occasional session work. In 1954, Black and Moore were hired by Phillips to back a young, raw Presley at his first sessions. Unimpressed by their initial recordings, Phillips was instead mesmerised by an impromptu performance of 'That's Alright Mama' during a break in the sessions. Signed to Sun, the trio was billed on the record label as Elvis Presley with "Scotty and Bill". But with Presley coming under the grip of new manager Col. Tom Parker, who signed the emerging singer to RCA Records in 1956, Scotty and Bill were relegated to mere backing musicians. While Elvis earned millions, Scotty and Bill received basic union scale. As well as the now legendary Sun recordings, the pair also appeared on most of Elvis' early RCA records including 'All Shook Up', 'Heartbreak Hotel' and 'Jailhouse Rock'. Parting with Presley in 1958, the pair were fired for asking for an increase in their $100 per week salary ($200 if they were on the road). Scotty and Bill returned for a handful of concert dates, but then left for good. In late 1958, Black formed a successful instrumental group, The Bill Black Combo, scoring hits with 'Smokie – Part 2' (1959), the million-selling, 'White Silver Sands' (1960), and a cover of Presley's 'Don't Be Cruel' (1960). Black launched his own record and production company in 1962, Lyn-Lou, and appeared with his combo in the film, *Teenage Millionaire*.
CAUSE: Diagnosed with a brain tumour in early 1965, Black died several months later. After the onset of his illness, Black signed over the reins of The Bill Black Combo to guitarist Bob Tucker, who led the group into the Eighties. Black died in Memphis.
FURTHER READING: Guralnick, Peter. (1994). *Last Train To Memphis: The Rise Of Elvis Presley*. New York: Little, Brown.

Robert "Bumps" Blackwell

(ROBERT A. BLACKWELL)
Born May 23, 1918
Died March 9, 1985
A prolific songwriter and producer, the classically trained, Seattle-born Robert "Bumps" Blackwell had formed an R&B band in the late Forties with a pair of then-unknowns, Ray Charles and Quincy Jones. A successful entrepreneur, Blackwell soon operated a nightclub, butcher shop, jewellery store, and even a fleet of taxicabs. Working at Specialty Records in the Fifties, Blackwell managed and co-wrote most of the hits of Little Richard including 'Good Golly, Miss Molly', 'Long Tall Sally', 'Rip It Up' and 'Ready Teddy'. And although he prodded Sam Cooke to switch from gospel to R&B, he was unable to convince labelmates The Blind Boys of Alabama to do the same. After leaving his position as bandleader and arranger at Specialty Records, Blackwell helped launch Keen Records, where Sam Cooke scored his early pop hits beginning with 'You Send Me'. Blackwell later worked with Herb Alpert, Ike & Tina Turner, and Sonny Bono.
CAUSE: He died from a heart attack and pneumonia at Whittier Hospital in Los Angeles. Suffering from glaucoma, he was nearly blind in the last years of his life.

Matty Blag

(MATTHEW ROBERTS)
Born 1964
Died February 22, 2000
The frontman of British worldbeat style, rap/punk band Blaggers I.T.A., Matty Blag is best known for attacking a *Melody Maker* interviewer for suggesting that assaulting a Fascist was as bad as being a Fascist. In the aftermath, the group was snubbed by the media, and dropped from the Reading Festival. A politically charged group that was often compared to The Clash, Blaggers I.T.A's biggest hit came with 'Abandon Ship' (1994). With Blag a better lyricist than singer, he would spout leftist ideologies and anti-fascist/capitalistic slogans at the group's often violent concerts and anti-Fascist rallies. Shortly after Blag was found not guilty of assault due to technicalities in 1995, he was booted from the group.
CAUSE: Drug overdose. He died in London.

Jerry Blaine

Born December 10, 1910
Died March 1973
A former jazz bandleader turned music mogul, Jerry Blaine broke into the industry in the Forties as he moved through the ranks of National Records. After a promotion to sales manager, he teamed with the label's A&R chief Herb Abramson in forming the tiny Jubilee Records. With Abramson struggling with another venture, the fledgling Atlantic Records, Blaine assumed control of Jubilee. Initially recording a former National Records act The Orioles, Blaine managed a string of pioneering doo-wop hits at Jubilee. Wanting to launch an R&B/rock label, Blaine débuted the Josie imprint in 1954 and enjoyed success with The Cadillacs, Bobby Freeman and J. Frank Wilson. In the early Sixties, Blaine organised his many labels – including Port, Dana, and Chex – under The Jay-Gee Record Company umbrella.
CAUSE: Unknown.

Alan Blakely

Born April 1, 1942
Died June 10, 1996
Rhythm guitarist and keyboard player of The Tremeloes, Alan Blakely formed the group in 1959 with schoolfriends in Dagenham, England. Blakely was originally the group's drummer in the Brian Poole-fronted group. Originally a cover band billed as Brian Poole & The Tremeloes, they enjoyed British success in 1963 with

the singles 'Twist And Shout' and 'Do You Love Me'. The group was signed by Decca in preference to The Beatles, largely because they were based closer to Decca's London headquarters. In 1964 the group again topped the UK charts with the ballad 'Someone Someone', which featured Buddy Holly's manager Norman Petty on piano. With Brian Poole leaving the group for a solo career in 1966, new lead singer/bassist Len "Chip" Hawkes led The Tremeloes on a series of hits including the Cat Stevens-penned 'Here Comes My Baby', the chart topping 'Silence Is Golden' and 'Even The Bad Times Are Good'. In an attempt to keep up with changing tastes The Tremeloes took a progressive rock turn in 1970 with the album *Master* but they were unable to adapt to the underground music of the era and soon found themselves on the cabaret and "oldies" circuit. With Hawkes quitting the group after suffering an injury in a car crash in 1974, Blakely left soon after in January 1975. Switching to production work in the late Seventies, Blakely oversaw The Rubettes and Bilbo. Rejoining The Tremeloes later in the Seventies (as did Len Hawkes), Blakely fronted the group until he was forced to retire in 1984 due to worsening health.
CAUSE: Cancer.

Edgar V. Blanchard

(EDGAR V. BLANCHARD, SR.)
Born 1924
Died October 17, 1972
Pioneering New Orleans R&B guitarist and bandleader who worked with Little Richard, B.B. King, Roy Brown, Paul Gayten and others, Edgar Blanchard also provided the backing guitar on Sam Cooke's breakthrough pop hit 'You Send Me'. Leading bands such as The Gondoliers, Blanchard occasionally recorded under his own name.
CAUSE: Heart attack. He died in New Orleans.

Richard Blandon

Born August 16, 1934
Died December 30, 1991
The lead singer of the 1950s R&B group The Dubs, Richard Blandon was raised in the deep south city of Montgomery, Alabama. While stationed in New York City during an Air Force stint in the mid Fifties, he formed a vocal group called The 5 Wings, supplying lead tenor vocals. Blandon then joined his cousin Bill Carlisle on second tenor to form The Marvels. Renamed The Dubs in 1957, the group recorded a Blandon composition, 'Don't Ask Me (To Be Lonely)' for the tiny Johnson label. With the song garnering national attention, The Dubs landed at the larger, George Goldner-owned Gone label, where the re-released single would become their first hit. Also written by Blandon, The Dubs' follow-up release, 'Could This Be Magic' (1957), featured Blandon's impassioned vocals. A romantic, doo-wop ballad, it would be the group's biggest hit. The Dubs' final hit came in 1958 with a non-Blandon composition, 'Be Sure My Love' (1958). Blandon would form various incarnations of The Dubs into the 1990s, releasing a series of singles on a variety of labels.
CAUSE: Unknown. He died in New York City.

Howard Blauvelt

(HOWARD ARTHUR BLAUVELT)
Born 1949
Died October 25, 1993
Bass player for the Seventies hard-rock group, Ram Jam, Howard Blauvelt had once played alongside Billy Joel. In the late Sixties, Blauvelt had been a member of the Long Island, New York-based surf rock group, The Echoes, when he asked schoolmate Billy Joel to join on piano. A popular bar band, the Echoes evolved into a British Invasion cover band called the Lost Souls. But when the Lost Souls

shared a bill with the Hassles in 1967, Joel and Blauvelt left to join the more skilful band. Signing with United Artist Records, the Hassles released a pair of obscure albums, with Joel leaving the group in 1969. By 1974 Blauvelt had joined Ram Jam, a hard-rock group that scored a hit with a reworked cover of Leadbelly's 'Black Betty' (1977). Calling the song offensive, the NAACP launched a boycott against the group. Wounded by the negative publicity, Ram Jam released just two albums before disbanding. In 1991, Blauvelt joined a local New York City group called Spitball.
CAUSE: Heart attack. He died on arrival at the Downtown Hospital in New York City.

Archie Bleyer

Born June 12, 1909
Died March 20, 1989
A popular bandleader who found fame on the radio and television programmes *The Arthur Godfrey Show*, Archie Bleyer formed Cadence Records in the early Fifties with another Godfrey-alumni, singer Julius LaRosa. When Bleyer left Godfrey, he took along The Chordettes with him. Cadence's first star act, The Chordettes included Bleyer's soon-to-be wife, Janet Ertel. Other Cadence successes came with Andy Williams, The McGuire Sisters, and The Everly Brothers. Retiring from music in the mid Sixties, Bleyer mothballed Cadence.
CAUSE: Parkinson's disease. He died in Sheboygan, Wisconsin.

Janet Bleyer

(JANET ERTEL)
Born September 21, 1913
Died November 22, 1988
The bass vocalist for the all-girl, barbershop group, The Chordettes, Janet Ertel was asked to join them by her college friend, Jinny Osborn. Formed in Sheboygan, Wisconsin, in 1946, the group blossomed under the musical guidance and financial assistance of Osborn's father (a former barbershop singer). An immediate success, The Chordettes toured heavily in the late Forties. While taking college classes, Ertel was replaced on road dates by Nancy Overton. The Chordettes garnered national exposure as regulars on Arthur Godrey's popular radio and television programmes. In 1950, Godrey aided the group in landing a recording contract with Columbia. But fired by Godrey in 1953, The Chordettes were replaced on the programme by The McGuire Sisters. Signing with Cadence Records in 1954 (the label launched by Godrey's former bandleader and Ertel's fiancee, Archie Bleyer), The Chordettes moved away from their traditional sound, scoring several pop hits including 'Mr. Sandman' and 'Lollipop'. In 1955, Ertel married Bleyer. The Chordettes appeared on the first episode of the national version of Dick Clark's *American Bandstand* in 1957. After the Chordettes disbanded in the early Sixties, Ertel and her husband moved to Freeport, and then back to Sheboygan in 1986. Ertel last sang with The Chordettes at a barbershop music convention in 1984.
CAUSE: Cancer. She died in Black River, Wisconsin. Archie Bleyer died shortly after on March 20, 1989, of Parkinson's disease at the age of 80.

Bobby Bloom

Born 1946
Died February 28, 1974
A multifaceted pop and soul singer-songwriter, Bobby Bloom broke into music during the early Sixties as a member of a small R&B combo, The Imaginations. A skilled musician, Bloom soon found success as a popular session player. Also a songwriter, Bloom in the late Sixties wrote or co-wrote a number of hits including 'Mony, Mony' for Tommy James And The Shondells, and 'Indian Giver' and 'Special Delivery' for the

bubblegum-pop group 1910 Fruitgum Company. Bloom also performed as a session man for Don Kirshner fictitious, cartoon group, The Archies, on their hits, 'Sunshine' and 'Shang-A-Lang'. Recording as a solo artist in 1966 at Kama Sutra Records, he first used the moniker, Bobby Mann. Finally recording under his real name in 1970, he turned out a number of singles on several labels. A solo effort *The Bobby Bloom Album*, spawned his only Top 40 hit, 'Montego Bay' (1970). He released a second solo album the following year.
CAUSE: He accidentally shot and killed himself in Hollywood, California.

Michael Bloomfield

Born July 28, 1944
Died February 15, 1981
A talented, white, Jewish, blues guitarist and singer, Bloomfield taught himself to play on borrowed instruments from his uncle's pawnshop. A natural leftie, Bloomfield forced himself to play the guitar right-handed. Reared in an affluent Chicago family, he switched from the rockabilly of his idol, Elvis' guitarist Scotty Moore, to the blues he heard on local black radio. Riding the bus to Chicago's south side nightclubs, he was tolerated by the city's blues players and before long blues legends like B.B. King, Big Joe Williams and Muddy Waters accepted the "little rich white kid", teaching him proper techniques. After graduating from high school, Bloomfield joined the newly electric folkie Bob Dylan at the Newport Folk Festival, and on the album *Highway 61 Revisited* (1965), which featured the hit 'Like A Rolling Stone'. By age 20, Bloomfield was also managing a blues club. Then along with longtime collaborator Nick Gravesnites, Bloomfield joined the Paul Butterfield Blues Band in 1965 to record the classic début album *The Paul Butterfield Blues Band*. A rocking, bluesy record featuring tracks such as 'Born In Chicago', it made blues stars out of both Bloomfield and Butterfield. Bloomfield and Gravenites left Butterfield's group in 1967 and along with drummer Buddy Miles formed the experimental group, Electric Flag. The horn and guitar-based blues-rock band débuted at the Monterey Pop Festival. Leaving Electric Flag after releasing one disjointed studio album, *A Long Time Comin'* (1968), Bloomfield teamed with Al Kooper and Steven Stills on the pioneering, guitar-rock album, *Super Session* (1968). Shunning the studio tricks of his contemporaries, Bloomfield preferred unadorned, straightforward electric blues. Bloomfield rejoined Butterfield in 1969 to assist their mentor Muddy Waters on the appropriately titled album, *Fathers And Sons*. Pursuing a solo career in the Seventies, Bloomfield released several fine albums including the heralded *Triumvirate*. Though not a particularly heavy drug user, Bloomfield's output was negatively affected by his substance abuse in the Seventies. His final album, *Living In The Fast Lane*, was released in 1980. In the last years of his life, he taught college-level blues courses.
CAUSE: Drug overdose. While the press attributed his death to cocaine, he had actually ingested both cocaine and a form of heroin. He was found dead in his Mercedes with no identification, the keys still in the ignition and all four doors locked, near his home in San Francisco. Some of his friends suspected foul play, claiming that Bloomfield was in great spirits during this period.
FURTHER READING: Ward, Ed. (1983). *Michael Bloomfield: The Rise And Fall Of An American Hero*. Port Chester, NY: Cherry Lane.

Cheese Blotto

(KEITH A. STEPHENSON)
Born July 31, 1956
Died October 3, 1999
The bassist for novelty-styled rock

group Blotto, the former Keith A. Stephenson shaved his head and assumed the role of Cheese Blotto (*à la* The Ramones). A native of Florida, he was educated at the Berklee School of Music in Boston. In the late Seventies, while employed as a bartender in Albany, New York, he formed Blotto out of the remnants of a local folk-rock group called The Star Spangled Washboard Band. Releasing a four-track EP in 1980, Blotto landed a college hit with the track 'I Wanna Be A Lifeguard', and with MTV desperate for material in its first year, Blotto received massive exposure from the song's video, shot by two college students for a class assignment. The band's first full-length album contained another MTV favourite, a heavy-metal spoof 'Metal Head'. Produced by and featuring Buck Dharma, the lead guitarist of Blue Oyster Cult, the comedic video cost $3,000 to produce, and would later rank in the Top 100 of *The Rolling Stone Book Of Video*. As a promotional stunt, the group hired TV actor Burt Ward (Batman's sidekick, Robin) as their manager. Unable to sign with a major label and struggling to distribute their independently produced discs, Blotto remained on the verge of stardom in the early Eighties. After the group disbanded in 1984, Cheese Blotto returned to Albany, New York, and joined a local rockabilly band. He later ran a restaurant.
CAUSE: He suffered heart failure as the result of a diseased liver, while sitting in his pickup truck in the car park of Saratoga Springs State Park in New York. He was found by a park ranger.

David Blue

(STUART DAVID COHEN)
Born February 18, 1941
Died December 2, 1982
Born in Providence, Rhode Island, folk-rock singer and songwriter, Stuart Cohen gravitated to the Greenwich Village folk scene in the early Sixties, garnering a strong following with his politically charged performances. Enthralled with the compositions of fellow folk singer Bob Dylan, Blue became a prolific folk-style songwriter. But upon hearing The Beatles in 1964, Blue took a turn toward rock music. Moving from guitar to organ in 1965, he joined Country Joe & The Fish, now as David Cohen. Formed by McDonald and Barry Melton at Berkeley University, the group was leading large-scale, on-campus student demonstrations. The ultimate, anti-Vietnam War, anti-establishment, hippy protest band, The Fish had a loyal underground following that lasted into the early Seventies. After recording three EPs, it was the title track of their second album, *I Feel Like I'm Fixin' To Die* (1967), that captured the sentiment of the war protesters. Cohen left the group after their third album, *Together* (1968). Returning to a solo career as David Blue, he released a series of poorly received EPs and albums before moving to stage acting in the Seventies. In 1976, he backed Dylan on his Rolling Thunder Revue. Also a film actor, he appeared in *American Friend* (1978).
CAUSE: He died from a heart attack while jogging through Washington Park in New York City.

Curt Boettcher

Born 1944
Died June 1987
Producer of many Sixties surf and psychedelic rock hits, Curt Boettcher worked on recordings by Tommy Roe and The Association (including the hits 'Along Comes Mary' and 'Cherish'). Along with Gary Usher, he was involved in the studio groups Sagittarius and The Millenium. Boettcher also recorded a solo album *There's An Innocent Face* in 1973. As Curt Becher he produced many artists, and co-produced The Beach Boys' 'Here Comes The Night'.
CAUSE: Liver complications.

Neil Bogart

(Neil Bogatz)
Born February 3, 1941
Died May 8, 1982
Singer-turned-record executive, Neil Bogart launched his musical career in 1961 as Neil Scott, scoring a pop hit with 'Bobby'. Then after briefly pursuing an acting career under the name Wayne Roberts, he returned to music, landing a position with the industry trade publication *Cashbox*. After heading Cameo-Parkway Records in the mid Sixties, Bogart founded Buddah Records along with Jeff Katz and Jerry Kasenetz. Assuming production duties at the label, Bogart oversaw dozens of bubblegum style pop hits beginning with The Lemon Pipers ('Green Tambourine') and continuing with Ohio Express and 1910 Fruitgum Company. Leaving Buddah in 1974, Bogart launched Casablanca Records, the label dominated by Kiss and a number of disco artists, including Donna Summer and the outrageous five-man band, The Village People. During its short life Casablanca became known for gratuitous excess and the extravagance of parties thrown to herald new signings and successful records. Vast quantities of cocaine were allegedly consumed on company premises, drug orders being taken daily by a girl who dashed from office to office on roller skates. Establishing the Casablanca film division with Peter Gruber in 1976, Bogart scored a box-office hit with *Midnight Express*. But with Casablanca haemorrhaging millions of dollars after repeatedly pressing millions more records than it could sell, PolyGram bought out the half of the label it didn't already own, with Bogart receiving $15 million. Following the demise of disco, Bogart and partners Peter Gruber and Jon Peters launched Boardwalk Records in 1980, their early success coming with the chart-topping 'I Love Rock And Roll' by Joan Jett.

Cause: Cancer. He had been diagnosed a year earlier. He died at the Cedars-Sinai Medical Center in Los Angeles.

Marc Bolan

(Mark Feld)
Born September 30, 1947
Died September 16, 1977
The leader of the popular British rock group T. Rex, Marc Bolan launched his show business career as a child actor on the BBC television series *Orlando*. As a teenage model, he took the stage name of Toby Tyler. Receiving his first guitar at age nine, Bolan formed a skiffle group a year later. Headstrong, he was expelled from school at the age of 14. During an extended stay in Paris in 1964, Bolan became enthralled by black magic, a subject which he would later explore in his lyrics. Pursuing a musical career, initially as Marc Bowland, he recorded the poorly received single 'The Wizard' (1965). Joining the rock group John's Children in 1967, he quickly left to form his own band, Tyrannosaurus Rex. Evolving into a quirky folk duo with drummer Steve Peregrine-Took, Tyrannosaurus Rex found a huge following among the new British underground and were championed by the influential DJ John Peel. Then, in 1969, Bolan fired his partner and shocked longtime fans by going electric and adopting a glam-rock image. Leading the renamed T. Rex, Bolan became an unlikely teen-idol and found international fame with the breakthrough album, *Electric Warrior* (1971), highlighted by the group's only US hit 'Bang A Gong (Get It On)' (1972). Donning an androgynous look with long corkscrew curls, feather boas and spangled outfits, Bolan was in the forefront of the British glitter-rock movement alongside David Bowie and Elton John. T. Rex's only rival on the UK singles charts during the early Seventies was the more downmarket but marginally more successful Slade.

Nevertheless T. Rex enjoyed 11 Top 10 singles, including four number 1s, between 1970 and 1973. Not surprisingly in view of the disparity in taste between UK and US rock fans, Bolan was unable to translate his UK success into American success, and he alienated the US press with boastful comments and was subsequently ignored there. Bolan remained a star in Britain and T. Rex released a series of critically acclaimed albums including *The Slider* (1972) and *Tanx* (1973). Bolan had plenty of high profile friends with whom he was often photographed, including David Bowie, Elton John and Ringo Starr. The former Beatles' drummer even directed a movie about the success of T. Rex, entitled *Born To Boogie*, in which Elton was featured. With his popularity waning by 1973, Bolan hired a female back-up trio, which included his future girlfriend, American soul singer Gloria Jones (who would give birth to his son Rolan). Jones, who became the group's keyboard player a year later, attempted to infuse soul into the group's sound. Bolan became a British tax exile in 1974, fleeing to Monte Carlo where he suffered a heart attack later in the year. By this time he had developed a cocaine habit and had alienated many of his allies. By the mid Seventies his popularity was waning in England. After disbanding T. Rex in 1975, Bolan formed a new line-up in 1976, landing his final British hit with 'I Love To Boogie' (1976). At the time of his death, Bolan was hosting a British children's television programme.
CAUSE: Car crash. Leaving a London nightclub shortly before 5 a.m., the inebriated Bolan was a passenger in his own purple sub-compact, Mini GT. Since Bolan did not drive, at the wheel was his common-law wife and back-up vocalist since 1973, American soul singer Gloria Jones. After driving across a bridge, she rammed into a tree in Barnes Common, south London at 45 mph. Trailing in another car was Jones' brother, Richard, who arrived at the crash scene within seconds. Bolan was crushed by the impact and died instantly. Jones was subsequently charged with drink driving. Neither passenger was wearing a seat belt. Jones recovered from her wounds and eventually continued her recording career. It was the third accident involving the tree that year alone; the damaged horse-chestnut tree became a tourist attraction, and was saved from removal in 1993 by the local council.
FURTHER READING: Paytress, Mark. (1992). *Twentieth Century Boy: The Marc Bolan Story*. London: Sidgwick & Jackson.

Jesse Bolian

Born June 8, 1941
Died August 24, 1994
Second tenor of the Sixties Chicago R&B group The Artistics, Jesse Bolian appeared on the hit, 'I'm Gonna Miss You' (1966). Formed in 1958, The Artistics signed with OKeh Records in 1963, before moving to Brunswick three years later. The group disbanded in 1974.
CAUSE: Unknown.

Tommy Bolin

Born December 4, 1950
Died December 4, 1976
Solo artist as well as a member of Deep Purple, Zephyr and The James Gang, the legendary Tommy Bolin was raised on electric blues and Fifties rock. Although his mother was a music teacher, Bolin never learned to read music. After mastering the drums, he switched to guitar at age 15. Relocating to Boulder, Colorado, in 1968, Bolin formed a blues-rock band called Ethereal Zephyr. After adding David and Candy Givens to the renamed Zephyr, the group recorded two albums, including the Warner Brothers release *Going Back To Colorado*. Leaving Zephyr along with bandmate Bobby Berge in early 1971, Bolin formed a jazz-metal group called Energy, the

outfit serving as a vehicle for Bolin's compositions and intricate guitar work. After a brief stint with former Zephyr bandmates Candy and David Givens in an oldies band called The 4-Nikators, Bolin was out of work for a year, during which time he composed nearly a hundred songs. Returning to music, Bolin played session guitar on Billy Cobham's jazz-rock fusion album, *Spectrum* and went on tour backing bluesman Albert King. In August 1973, Bolin joined The James Gang, as a replacement for Joe Walsh. Leaving The James Gang after recording just one album, *Miami*, Bolin formed his own group, The Tommy Bolin Band, and launched his own label. After recording a solo album and scoring a minor album-rock hit with 'Teaser', Bolin subsequently joined the perennial British hard-rock Deep Purple as Ritchie Blackmore's replacement, appearing on the album *Come Taste The Band* (1975). Purple organist Jon Lord has stated that Bolin was even more fluent than Blackmore when it came to blues playing, although Blackmore was a better all round technical guitarist. With Bolin's drug use intensifying, his onstage playing suffered to the extent where towards the end of his Purple career Bolin was reduced to playing straightforward chords. When Deep Purple disbanded, Bolin returned briefly to his solo career but died before re-establishing himself. His guitar wizardry would not be fully appreciated until years after his death.

CAUSE: He overdosed on morphine, cocaine, Lidocaine and alcohol. Bolin was barely breathing when he was discovered unconscious by his bandmates in his room at the Newport Hotel in Miami. He was pronounced dead on arrival at a local hospital. He had performed the night before at the Jai-A Lai Fronton club in Miami.

FURTHER READING: Charlesworth, Chris. (1983). *Deep Purple: The Illustrated Biography*. London: Omnibus.

Graham Bond

(JOHN CLIFTON BOND)

Born October 28, 1937

Died May 8, 1974

A British blues-rock legend, Graham Bond launched his professional career in the jazz field in the late Fifties as a saxophone player for The Don Rendell Quintet. In 1962 Bond joined the pioneering, British blues band, Alexis Korner's Blues Incorporated, as a replacement for organist Cyril Davies. Davies was largely responsible for the introduction of American blues music into Britain. In 1963 Bond left Korner, and with Ginger Baker and Jack Bruce formed a jazz-R&B group, The Graham Bond Trio. With the addition of John McLaughlin, the group evolved into The Graham Bond Organisation, an R&B-flavoured outfit. Switching from the saxophone to the electric organ, by 1964 Bond also experimented with a mellotron, an early synthesizer. Though critically acclaimed, the group had little commercial success, scoring infrequent hits with 'Long Tall Shorty' (1964) and 'Tammy' (1965). Disbanding the group in 1965, Bond left for the US where he recorded a pair of solo albums, *Love Is The Law* and *The Mighty Graham Bond.* Returning to London in late 1966, Bond formed the group, Initiation, before joining Ginger Baker's underrated group, Airforce. Selling moderately well in Britain in 1970, the Bond compilation album *Solid Bond* was an uneven collection of Sixties tracks. In 1971 Bond formed a mystical-styled group, Magick with his future wife Diane Stewart. After divorcing Stewart, Bond formed Magus, the group's name taken from the title of a high level sorcerer. Bond's later collaborative releases with folk artists Pete Brown and then Carolanne Pegg were met with little interest. At the time of his death he

was becoming increasingly obsessed by his interest in black magic and the occult, to the extent that he was telling friends he was the son of noted mystic Aleister Crowley. Along with John Mayall and Alexis Korner, Graham Bond was a pivotal figure in the birth of the British blues movement of the mid Sixties.
CAUSE: In the last year of his life, Bond had become financially destitute. Frustrated by his lack of success, his drug use intensified and he suffered a nervous breakdown. He was found dead beneath a London subway train at Finsbury Park Station. The body was so badly mangled that it took two days for positive identification, which was achieved by a fingerprint match. Authorities were uncertain whether he fell or committed suicide. With Bond often dabbling in the occult, it has been rumoured that he had performed an exorcism ceremony on the day of his death, which resulted in a demon taking over his body, and forcing him onto the train tracks.
FURTHER READING: Shapiro, Harry. (1992). *Graham Bond: The Mighty Shadow*. London: Guinness.

Johnny Bond

(CYRUS WHITFIELD BOND)
Born June 1, 1915
Died June 29, 1978
A popular country and western singer and cowboy actor, Johnny Bond began as a backing musician with Roy Rogers in the film *Saga Of Death Valley*, one of his dozens of film roles. After a stint in the Jimmy Wakely Trio on Gene Autry's *Melody Ranch* programme, Bond later formed his own band, the Red River Roys. By the Fifties, Bond emerged as a solo act on Gene Autry's Republic Records, enjoying several novelty hits about drinking including 'Sick, Sober And Sorry' (1951) and '10 Little Bottles' (1965). Bond's only crossover pop entry came in 1960 with 'Hot Rod Lincoln', a song revived in the Seventies by Commander Cody and his Lost Planet Airmen.
CAUSE: Heart attack.

Ronnie Bond

Born May 4, 1942
Died November 13, 1992
A member of the British Sixties group, The Troggs, Ronnie Bond provided the drums on their hits, including the garage group classic 'Wild Thing', the UK chart topping 'With A Girl Like You', the frantic 'I Can't Control Myself' and the ballad 'Love Is All Around'. A former construction worker, he joined the band in 1964. The group garnered greater success in their native England than in the US. With the group disbanding in 1969, Bond pursued a solo career, releasing several singles. But by 1972, Bond reteamed with former Troggs singer Reg Presley in a new line-up. Following a series of unpleasant incidents, Presley fired Bond from the group in the mid Eighties. A few months before his death, Bond had collaborated on the R.E.M. project *Athens Forever*.
CAUSE: He died after a brief, undisclosed illness at Winchester General Hospital in Hampshire, England.

John "Bonzo" Bonham

(JOHN HENRY BONHAM)
Born May 31, 1948
Died September 25, 1980
The drummer with the legendary blues-metal band Led Zeppelin, John "Bonzo" Bonham worked as a bricklayer before launching his musical career in a series of Birmingham, England-based bands, beginning with Terry and The Spiders in 1964. With the group The Band Of Joy, Bonham backed his future bandmate Robert Plant. Bonham subsequently worked on the British touring circuit backing Tim Rose and had been invited to join Joe Cocker's touring band when the offer to join Led Zeppelin came up. Meanwhile, in 1968 guitarist Jimmy

Page of The Yardbirds was left without a group when the other members quit. Transforming The Yardbirds into Led Zeppelin, he added singer Plant, bassist John Paul Jones and finally Bonham, though Page's first choice for drummer had been B.J. Wilson of Procol Harum. Led Zeppelin was signed by Atlantic Records, allegedly receiving a then-unheard of advance of $200,000, thanks to negotiations settled by their astute manager, Peter Grant. Releasing a self-titled début album in 1969, Zeppelin saluted their blues roots with the inclusion of a pair of Willie Dixon songs, 'I Can't Quit You Baby' and 'You Shook Me', alongside genre-defining tracks such as 'Dazed And Confused' and 'Communication Breakdown'. Despite lukewarm press reviews the group ultimately set attendance records on its US tours, but took longer to ignite similar interest in England. The album *Led Zeppelin II* (1969), was an international smash, containing the group's only US Top 10 pop hit, 'Whole Lotta Love'. Another track, 'Moby Dick', featured a 15-minute drum solo by Bonham. An active songwriter within the group, Bonham wrote or co-wrote 'Communication Breakdown', 'D'Yer Maker', 'Good Times, Bad Times' and 'Heartbreaker'. Mischievous and a heavy drinker, Bonham set the standard for hard rock drummers with his uncanny ability to play lightly one moment then come crashing down on his kit with fearsome intensity the next. The group's untitled fourth album in 1971 featured the AOR classic 'Stairway To Heaven', the most-played song in US radio during the Seventies. Dominating album-rock radio during the decade, Led Zeppelin would spawn hundreds of imitators. Arrested for assaulting an employee of promoter Bill Graham at an Oakland concert in 1977, Bonham was convicted of battery. Also that year, Bonham broke three ribs in an automobile accident. After a three-year respite from recording, Led Zeppelin released their final studio album, *In Through The Out Door*, in 1979. Led Zeppelin's final concerts were on a European tour in June, during which Bonham at one point collapsed through "exhaustion".

CAUSE: Drug and alcohol overdose. He choked to death on his own vomit at bandmate Jimmy Page's English home in Mill Lane, Windsor, after a night of heavy drinking and drugs. Bonham reportedly consumed a lethal amount of vodka, dying in bed. His friends claim that Bonham's demise was inevitable. The band's North American tour, which was to have kicked off at the Montreal Forum on October 17, was cancelled and the group promptly disbanded. In 2000, Jimmy Page was successful in a libel suit against *Ministry Magazine*, which had accused him of contributing to Bonham's death. The magazine alleged that upon discovering his unconscious bandmate, Page was more concerned about the vomit soiling his bed than aiding his dying friend. It was actually Zep bassist John Paul Jones and a roadie who first attempted to resuscitate the drummer.

FURTHER READING: Davis, Stephen. (1985). *Hammer Of The Gods*. New York: William Morrow. Lewis Dave. (1991). *Led Zeppelin: A Celebration*. London: Omnibus.

Sonny Bono

(SALVATORE PHILLIP BONO)
Born February 16, 1935
Died January 5, 1998

The son of Sicilian immigrants, singer-turned-politician "Sonny" Bono spent years trying to succeed in music. Working for producer Phil Spector as a backing vocalist in the early Sixties, Bono performed on dozens of records. At one of the sessions Bono was attracted to a fellow back-up singer named Cherilyn Sarkisian LaPiere, whom he nicknamed Cher. Divorcing his first wife of nine years, and marrying Cher in 1964, Bono and his new singing partner initially recorded as Caesar and Cleo, before settling on a new moniker, Sonny and Cher. Their first chart single, the million-selling 'I Got You Babe' (1965), introduced the beatnik couple to America, and was followed by a string of hits including 'Baby Don't Go' (1965) and 'The Beat Goes On' (1968). Bono also scored a solo hit in 1965 with 'Laugh At Me'. Bono wrote his own material and also co-wrote The Searchers' 1964 smash 'Needles And Pins'. Considered out of fashion by 1970, Sonny and Cher went from performing in large auditoria to becoming a lounge act. Spotted at one of their nightclub shows by a CBS producer, Sonny and Cher were offered their own television show. In the loosely scripted variety programme, *The Sonny And Cher Comedy Hour*, Bono appeared as the self-demeaning, punch-bag recipient of Cher's wisecracks. The show was cancelled in 1974 with the couple divorcing soon after. While Cher became a popular actress and solo singer, Bono dropped out of music and operated a series of restaurants. Frustrated by the strict regulations which impeded local businesses, Bono successfully ran for mayor of Palm Springs in 1988. Setting his sights on the national level, in 1994 Bono won a landslide victory in the first of two Congressional wins as a conservative Republican.

CAUSE: Skiing accident. After leaving the main slope at the Upper Orion trail at the Heavenly Ski Resort near Lake Tahoe along the Nevada and California line, he struck a tree and died instantly of massive blunt trauma. An experienced skier who had frequented the resort for 20 years, Bono was dead for four-and-a-half hours before his partially obscured body was found by searchers. Earlier in the day he had discussed the purchase of a skiing helmet in the wake of a similar accident which had recently taken the life of Michael Kennedy. Although the coroner later ruled out drugs and alcohol as factors in Bono's death, Bono's widow blamed the accident on her husband's battle with prescription pain killers.

FURTHER READING: Bono, Sonny. (1991). *And the Beat Goes On*. New York: Pocket.

James Booker

(JAMES CARROLL BOOKER III)

Born December 17, 1939

Died November 8, 1983

A New Orleans boogie-woogie style pianist whose mentor was Dave Bartholomew, James Booker was given a saxophone as a Christmas gift by his mother at age nine. Receiving classical music training until age 12, Booker soon favoured the piano. Nicknamed "The Piano Prince of New Orleans" by age 11, he played the organ on a gospel radio programme on WMRY. A flamboyant figure, the teenage Booker was soon pounding out R&B in New Orleans nightclubs, becoming the city's first electric organ player. Joining Joe Tex's group in the mid Fifties, Booker also worked as a session player for Fats Domino, appearing on a number of recordings in place of the touring Domino. Enrolled at Southern University, Booker dropped out shortly before graduation in 1960 to join Dee Clark's group. About this time, Booker lost an eye during an altercation. After Clark disbanded his backing group, Booker pursued a solo career and scored a hit with the instrumental 'Gonzo' (1960), a song that was first rejected by Clark. After serving two years in prison for heroin possession in the Seventies, Booker worked as a session player for Ringo Starr, Labelle, The Doobie Brothers and others. In the same league as Dr. John and Professor Longhair, Booker inspired scores of imitators.

CAUSE: He died of a heart attack at his New Orleans' apartment, after years of alcohol and drug use. Booker claimed his drug addiction began at age 10 when paramedics gave him drugs after their ambulance struck and critically injured him.

Dennis Boon

Born April 1, 1958
Died December 22, 1985
The guitarist of legendary, underground alternative-rock band, The Minutemen, Dennis Boon also employed the stage name D. Boon. Formed in 1980, the California-based Minutemen released a series of politically charged punk-flavoured recordings including the angry 'Double Nickles On The Dime'. After Boon's death, members Mike Watt and George Hurley disbanded The Minutemen and formed Firehose.
CAUSE: Car crash. Driving the group's van through Arizona, Boon's girlfriend nodded off at the wheel. Boon, who had been sleeping in the back, died instantly. The vehicle was previously owned by the Meat Puppets.

Henry Booth

Born 1935
Died 1967
Tenor for the Fifties R&B vocal group, Hank Ballard and The Midnighters, Henry Booth had first joined the group's earlier precursor, The Thrillers, in 1949. Formed at Dunbar High School in Detroit, the group then evolved into The Royals in 1950. Spotted by Los Angeles-based bandleader and talent scout Johnny Otis, The Royals signed with King-Federal in 1952, releasing several poor-selling singles beginning with 'Every Beat Of My Heart' (which was later a hit for Gladys Knight & The Pips). With the departure of Lawson Smith in May 1953, Alabama-native Hank Ballard joined the group, pushing aside Booth as lead tenor. At first, Booth resented Ballard and cared little for his singing. But with Ballard at the helm, the group scored their first hit with the Ballard co-composition, the racy, 'Get It'. But their bawdy 'Work With Me Annie' (1954) catapulted the renamed Midnighters to stardom, and spawned several follow-up answer hits. As Hank Ballard and The Midnighters, the group remained popular into the early Sixties. After leaving the group, Booth released solo material on Deluxe Records in 1961. A 1967 court judgement gave Ballard legal ownership of The Midnighters name.
CAUSE: Unknown.

Adrian Borland

Born December 6, 1957
Died April 26, 1999
A pioneer of Britain's punk rock movement, singer-songwriter and guitarist Adrian Borland released the first indie punk album in 1977 as a member of The Outsiders (not the US group of the same name). He subsequently formed a similar group, Second Layer, and for a time collaborated with the Dead Kennedy's outspoken frontman Jello Biafra. Forming his best-known outfit, the critically acclaimed punk/psychedelic The Sound, in 1980 Borland and his group were eventually dropped by Korova Records. Also pursuing a solo career, he was in the midst of recording his sixth album at the time of his death.
CAUSE: Suicide. He jumped under a moving train in London. Chronically depressed, he had stopped taking his prescribed medication.

Earl Bostic

Born April 25, 1913
Died October 28, 1965
Alto saxophone player and arranger who worked with Hot Lips Page, Lionel Hampton, and Cab Calloway, the talented Earl Bostic formed his own band in 1944. Signing with King Records, Bostic landed several R&B hits including 'Temptation' (1948) and 'Flamingo' (1951).
CAUSE: Heart attack. He had suffered his first heart attack in 1956, which had sidelined him for three years.

Mike Botts

Born December 8, 1944
Died December 9, 2005
As a member of Seventies soft-rock band Bread, drummer Mike Botts appeared on most of their albums. Born in Oakland but raised in Sacramento, Botts honed his skills while performing with a number of local jazz greats including Jimmy Smith and Wes Montgomery. Quitting college, Botts moved to Los Angeles and joined a folk-rock group, The Travelers Three, who recorded several unreleased demos for Capitol Records, some of the tracks being produced by budding singer-songwriter David Gates. After passing through a group called Joshua Fox, Botts turned to studio work and spent two years working with Righteous Brothers member Bill Medley. By late 1969, Botts was asked to join David Gates' new studio group Bread as replacement for original drummer Jim Gordon, shortly after the release of their début album. Joining in time for the group's second album *On The Waters*, Botts provided the backbeat on a string of often melancholy ballads such as 'Make It With You', 'It Don't Matter To Me', 'If', 'Baby I'm-A Want You', 'Everything I Own', 'The Guitar Man', 'Aubrey' and 'Lost Without Your Love'. With the group taking a break in 1973, Botts spent two years touring and recording with Linda Ronstadt. After Bread disbanded in 1977, Botts worked as a session player and producer, before joining Dan Fogelberg's touring band. In 2001, Botts issued a solo album, *Adults Only*, and after completing a two-year tour with Bread in the mid Nineties, Botts rejoined Fogelberg.
CAUSE: Colon cancer. He died at Providence St. Joseph Medical Center in Burbank, California.

Donald James Bowden

Died 1963
Born November 18, 1993
Also known as Donald Dee, songwriter and producer Donald James Bowden worked with Chaka Khan, Rob Base, and SWV.
CAUSE: Long-term, undisclosed illness.

Thomas "Beans" Bowles

Born May 7, 1926
Died January 29, 2000
A Motown session player and executive, Thomas "Beans" Bowles was an essential cog in the Motown hit machine. Born in South Bend, Indiana, he relocated to Detroit in 1944 to enrol at Wayne State University. Dropping out to enlist in the services, he toured internationally as a member of a US Navy band. Returning to Detroit, he was a fixture of the city's jazz clubs, including The Flame Showbar, where he backed touring acts such as Billie Holiday and Billy Eckstine. Drawing the attention of one-time jazz record store owner Berry Gordy Jr., he was hired at Motown as both a session player and an A&R man. Trained in jazz – as were most members of Motown's house band – Bowles played the flute and baritone saxophone, appearing on several hits, including 'Stubborn Kind Of Fellow' (Marvin Gaye), 'Heat Wave' (Martha and The Vandellas), and 'Baby Love' (The Supremes). He also composed the harmonica solo in Stevie Wonder's breakthrough, chart-topping hit 'Fingertips Part II'. Nicknamed "Bean" due to his thin 6′ 5″ frame, he continued to lead a local jazz group called The Swinging Dashikis even after he joined Motown.
CAUSE: Suffering from prostate cancer, his health deteriorated after a blood clot passed through his heart. He was diagnosed with cancer at a Veteran's Administration hospital in 1990. He died in Detroit.

Priscilla Bowman

Born 1928
Died July 24, 1988
Kansas City-based R&B singer best known for her hit, 'Hands Off' (1955), Priscilla Bowman had previously been

a member of Jay McShann's band, where she shared vocal duties with Jimmy Witherspoon.
CAUSE: Lung cancer. She died in Kansas City.

Tommy Boyce

(SIDNEY THOMAS BOYCE)
Born September 29, 1944
Died November 24, 1994
A prolific Sixties songwriter and performer, Tommy Boyce was best known for his involvement with the television supergroup, The Monkees. A Virginia native, Boyce moved to Los Angeles as a child, where his minister father taught him to play the guitar. As a songwriter, his first success came in 1959 with the Fats Domino recording of 'Be My Guest'. Boyce and singer-songwriter Curtis Lee hooked up with producer Phil Spector in 1961, resulting in a pair of doo-wop styled hits for Lee, 'Pretty Little Angel Eyes' and 'Under The Moon Of Love'. Moving to New York City and settling into the famed Brill Building, Boyce teamed with new partner Bobby Hart to write hundreds of songs including 'Come A Little Bit Closer' for Jay and The Americans, and 'She' By Tommy James & The Shondells. Many of the compositions were commissioned by promoter/manager Don Kirshner. Collaborating with Kirshner, Boyce and Hart led the studio band of the manufactured TV group, The Monkees. Boyce and Hart wrote The Monkees' theme song as well as their hits 'I'm Not Your Stepping Stone', and – based on the last notes of The Beatles' 'Paperback Writer' – the similar 'Last Train To Clarksville'. Pursuing their own singing career, Boyce and Hart scored hits with 'I Wonder What She's Doing Tonight' (1967) and 'Alice Long (You're Still My Favorite Girlfriend' (1968). In 1975, Boyce and Hart toured with Monkees members Davy Jones and Mickey Dolenz as a quartet. Parting with Hart in 1976, Boyce continued working in music, collaborating with Meat Loaf and Iggy Pop among others. Boyce suffered a serious brain aneurysm in 1983, and experienced steadily worsening health. At the time of his death, he was about to start a job as a deejay in Cincinnati.
CAUSE: Suicide. He shot himself in the head at his Nashville home. Leaving a suicide note, his body was discovered by his wife the next morning.

Eddie Boyd

Born November 25, 1914
Died July 13, 1994
Mississippi-born, Chicago-style blues pianist and vocalist whose biggest hits came with 'Five Long Years' (1952) and 'Third Degree' (1953), Eddie Boyd was a self-taught player. Learning his trade in the blues clubs of Memphis with his band the Dixie Rhythm Boys, Boyd moved to Chicago in 1941. Finding regular club work, he was also a frequent session player for Sonny Boy Williamson (#1). By 1951, Boyd signed his first recording contract, joining J.O.B. Records. Tired of battling his record companies over underpaid royalties and wanting to escape the racial tensions in the US, Boyd spent three decades living in Europe.
CAUSE: Natural causes. He died in Helsinki, Finland, having made the country his home in 1971.

David Box

(HAROLD DAVID BOX)
Born August 11, 1943
Died October 23, 1964
Lubbuck, Texas-based rockabilly singer, David Box was a Buddy Holly soundalike who briefly recorded with Buddy Holly's Crickets after Holly's death, providing the lead vocals on a re-recording of the single, 'Peggy Sue Got Married'. Also heading his own group, Box recorded for Candix and Coed Records in the early Sixties.
CAUSE: Box and the rest of his group perished in a plane crash while returning home after a gig.

Jimmy Bracken

Born May 23, 1908
Died February 20, 1972
The "Jay" in Vee-Jay Records, Kansas City-born Jimmy Bracken launched the successful Chicago-based record R&B/soul label in 1953 with his deejay wife, Vivian Carter. The label had evolved from their Gary, Indiana record store, Vivian's Record Shop. Competing with Chess Records, Vee-Jay had a strong roster with acts such as the doo-wop group The Spaniels, bluesman Jimmy Reed, and several Chicago soul acts, Dee Clark, The Impressions, and Gene Chandler, who gave the label its first million-seller with 'Duke Of Earl'. Entering the pop fray in the early Sixties, Vee-Jay signed The Four Seasons and issued The Beatles' early material. The label folded in 1966 due to financial misappropriations. Carter and Bracken later operated smaller labels such as J.V. and Ra-Bra.
CAUSE: Unknown. He died in Chicago.

Tommy Braden

Born c. 1920
Died 1957
Bass player and lead tenor vocalist of the Chicago-based R&B combo The (Four) Blazes, Tommy Braden joined the 11-year-old outfit in 1951. Playing a stand-up bass, Braden quit J.T. Brown's group to replace Prentice Butler in The Blazes. Signed to United Records, the group had a trio of Top 10 R&B hits: the Braden composition 'Mary Jo' (1952), 'Please Send Her Back To Me' (1952) and 'Perfect Woman' (1953). After leaving The Blazes to form his own group in 1954, Braden briefly returned for some recording sessions the following year.
CAUSE: Unknown.

Louis Bradley

Born 1937
Died June 1991
Second tenor of the Fifties doo-wop group, the El Dorados, best known for their hit 'At My Front Door' (1955), Louis Bradley joined the group at Chicago's Englewood High School in 1952. After winning a talent contest, the El Dorados were signed by Vee-Jay Records in 1954.
CAUSE: Heart attack.

Tiny Bradshaw

(MYRON BRADSHAW)
Born September 23, 1905
Died November 26, 1958
Popular R&B and jazz bandleader who backed many famous R&B acts, Tiny Bradshaw studied psychology at Wilberforce University before turning to a career in music in the late Twenties. After passing through several groups, his last being Luis Russell's band, Bradshaw launched his own orchestra in 1934, recording for Decca Records later in the year. Landing several long-term nightclub residencies and touring prolifically, the raspy-voiced Bradshaw also scored several hits at King Records in the early Fifties including 'Well, Oh Well' (1950) and the instrumental 'Heavy Juice' (1953). One of Bradshaw's compositions, 'The Train Kept a-Rollin'' was later popularised by The Yardbirds, Led Zeppelin, Aerosmith and Johnny Burnette & The Rock and Roll Trio. Suffering with poor health, Bradshaw retired from music in the early Fifties. Bradshaw's band subsequently recorded without him until 1958.
CAUSE: He passed away after suffering two strokes.

Junior Braithwaite

(FRANKLIN DELANO ALEXANDER BRAITHWAITE)
Born April 4, 1949
Died June 2, 1999
An original member of ground-breaking reggae group The Wailers, Junior Braithwaite joined Bob Marley and others in the Trenchtown ghetto of Kingstown, Jamaica in the early Sixties. Initially called The Teenagers,

Braithwaite was the group's original leader, providing the vocals on lesser known works including 'It Hurts To Be Alone' and 'Habits'. With Marley emerging as the chief songwriter and group's leader, Braithwaite left The Wailers in late 1964, although he would frequently provide backing vocals for both Marley and another Wailer, Peter Tosh. Joining his family in Chicago, Braithwaite hoped for a career in the medical field, which never materialised. Following Marley's untimely death in 1981, Braithwaite reunited with Bunny Wailer and Peter Tosh for an album project in 1984, *Never Ending Wailers*; belatedly released in 1991, the album contained new instrumental backings over unreleased Marley demos. At the time of his death, Braithwaite was working with the all-female group, Fourth Street Sister.
CAUSE: He was murdered at the home of fellow musician, Laurence "Chakka" Scott, in Kingston, Jamaica, by two intruders. Braithwaite was shot in the head; Scott was also killed. Braithwaite had recently returned to Jamaica after living in Chicago for three decades. Authorities attributed the break-in to an earlier murder at the residence when thieves were looking for firearms.

Jacques Brel

Born April 8, 1929
Died October 9, 1978
Brussels-born singer and songwriter who is considered the French Elvis, Jacques Brel emigrated to Paris after releasing a pair of singles in 1953. A sensitive artist whose charismatic nature enthralled French audiences, Brel became a superstar, beginning in 1955 after scoring a hit with 'Quand On N'a Que L'Amour'. Enjoying a long string of successes, Brel was a media sensation whose outrageous behaviour and public statements added to his mystique. But in 1966, Brel announced that he would never again perform in public. Brel is best known overseas through the stage production, *Jacques Brel Is Alive And Well And Living In Paris*; the show premiered in New York City in 1968, featuring 26 Brel songs translated into English by Mort Shuman and Eric Blau. Brel's compositions have also been recorded by noted acts such as Scott Walker, David Bowie and Gene Vincent. One of his compositions, 'Le Moribond', was reworked into English by Rod McKuen as 'Seasons In The Sun', and was later a hit for Terry Jacks.
CAUSE: Lung cancer. After he was diagnosed with the disease in 1974, he refused all treatment.

Jackie Brenston

Born August 14, 1927
Died December 15, 1979
A pioneering artist, Jackie Brenston was the unlikely singer of one of rock's first hits. Born and raised in Clarksdale, Mississippi, Brenston was taught to play the saxophone in the Forties by friend Jesse Flowers. Joining a band led by Ike Turner, Brenston switched to lead vocals as a replacement for O'Neal Johnson (who had just signed as a solo artist with King Records). Travelling to the Memphis Recording Studio (operated by Sam Phillips), the group recorded four tracks, two with lead vocals by Turner, and two by Brenston. Released by Chess Records in 1951, 'Rocket 88' was credited to Jackie Brenston and His Delta Cats. Topping the R&B chart, 'Rocket 88' (about an Oldsmobile 88 car) is often considered the first rock'n'roll song with its classic 2/4 time, an electric guitar in the forefront, and standard rhythm section. Angry at the undue attention that Brenston was receiving, his backing band soon abandoned him. Forming his own group with Sam Phillips' help, Brenston was unable to maintain his popularity. Returning to Clarksdale, Brenston later joined Lowell Fulson's group on saxophone. Finding limited success in the Sixties, Brenston drifted through a number of bands, at one time joining Ike & Tina Turner's revue.

Fading from the music scene in the Seventies, Brenston later drove a truck for a living.
CAUSE: He died from a heart attack in a Veterans Administration hospital in Memphis.

Ty Brian

CHARLES O'BRIAN
Born 1941
Died 1967
The guitarist with the early Liverpool rock group Rory Storm and The Hurricanes from 1960 to 1967, Ty Brian enjoyed little fame in spite of the fact that Ringo Starr played with The Hurricanes until invited to replace Pete Best in The Beatles.
CAUSE: He collapsed on stage days after undergoing appendectomy surgery, having contracted a massive infection.

Gene J. Bricker

Born August 3, 1938
Died December 1983
Second tenor for the Pittsburgh-based, Cornelius Harp led doo-wop group, The Marcels, Gene J. Bricker had previously sang with a series of local groups. Bricker left The Marcels several months after the release of the group's chart-topping reworking of the Rodgers & Hart standard, 'Blue Moon' (1961).
CAUSE: Unknown.

Shirley Brickley

Born December 9, 1944
Died October 13, 1977
The lead singer of Sixties Philadelphia girl-group The Orlons, Shirley Brickley formed the group as a quintet with her junior high school classmates, disbanding after several months. When Len Barry of The Dovells discovered Brickley, he insisted she reform the group. Now attending Overbrook High School in Philadelphia, Brickley, an alto vocalist, was joined by two other former Orlons, Rosetta Hightower and Marlena Davis. Signed to Cameo/Parkway Records, the trio added a male member, baritone/bass vocalist Steve Caldwell. With their classic, danceable girl-group sound, The Orlons biggest hits included 'The Wah Wahtusi' (1962) and 'South Street' (1963). Brickley also sang back-up for labelmates, Dee Dee Sharp and Bobby Rydell. The Orlons disbanded in 1966 at the height of the British Invasion. Brickley later worked as a bartender.
CAUSE: She was shot to death at her Philadelphia home. No arrests were made.

David Briggs

Born February 29, 1944
Died November 26, 1995
A prolific record producer, Briggs is best known for his 26-year association with Neil Young. The Wyoming-born Briggs moved to California in the Sixties, first working as a staff producer at Bill Cosby's Tetragrammaton record label, where he worked with comedian Murray Roman. Settling in Topanga, he became a focal point for local musicians, including members of Spirit, with whom he worked on the critically acclaimed *Twelve Dreams Of Dr Sardonicus*. An inveterate maverick, Briggs proved the perfect foil for Neil Young. Like the Canadian, he maintained a guarded mystique, and was seldom interviewed or photographed. He appears on the back cover of Young's *Everybody Knows This Is Nowhere* clutching a rifle. His most successful work with Young was on the guitar-laden albums with Crazy Horse, most notably *Everybody Knows...*, *Tonight's The Night*, *Zuma* and *Ragged Glory*. He also worked with a number of other late Sixties/Seventies' acts including Tom Rush, Alice Cooper, Grin/Nils Lofgren, Nicky Hopkins, Jerry Williams, Simon Stokes and Kathy McDonald. In his later years, he produced Willie Nelson and was involved with a younger generation of performers, including Nick Cave and Royal Trux.
CAUSE: Lung cancer. He died at his home in San Francisco.

Lillian Briggs

(LILLIAN BIGGS)
Born 1934
Died April 11, 1998
One-hit wonder who scored a pop hit in 1955 with 'I Want You To Be My Baby', Lillian Briggs had been discovered by deejay/promoter Alan Freed when she was a member of the New York City-based Joy Cayler's All-Girl Orchestra.
CAUSE: Lung cancer.

Lee Brilleaux

(LEE GREEN)
Born May 10, 1952
Died April 7, 1994
The lead singer, and harmonica player for Seventies British R&B-styled band Dr. Feelgood, Lee Brilleaux formed the outfit in 1971 with guitarist Wilko Johnson. Born in South Africa, Brilleaux emerged out of the jug/skiffle tradition. Though a popular pub-rock group in England, Dr. Feelgood (named after the pseudonym of American bluesman Willie Perryman) experienced little US success. The group's highest-charting British album, *Stupidity* (1976), was a live project culled from a pair of concerts at Southend and Sheffield, England. Brilleaux co-wrote most of the group's material with Johnson, and, following Johnson's departure in 1977, with his replacement, John Mayo. With their outrageous stage antics and sharp suits, Dr. Feelgood were at the heart of the London pub rock/new wave movement which, in turn, gave rise to punk-rock. After scoring its only Top 10 British hit with 'Milk And Alcohol' (1979), Dr. Feelgood fell out of fashion by the Eighties. Releasing a poorly selling solo album, *Brilleaux*, in 1983, Lee Brilleaux continued forming various incarnations of Dr. Feelgood. Falling ill in 1993, Brilleaux temporarily disbanded the group. Touring with a new version of the band at the time of his death, he was the last remaining original member.
CAUSE: He died of throat cancer in Canvey Island, England.
FURTHER READING: Moon, Tony. (1997). *Down By The Jetty: The Dr. Feelgood Story*. Bordon, England: Northdown.

Bruce "Damian" Broadus

(BRUCE EDWARD BROADUS)
Born September 13, 1966
Died June 27, 1996
Half of R&B duo Damian Dame, Bruce "Damian" Broadus joined Debra "Deah Dame" Hurd to form the first act signed to the Arista subsidiary Laface Records. Raised in Battle Creek, Michigan, Broadus was a self-taught musician, beginning with piano and moving to guitar and drums. Playing keyboards, he joined an Eighties group called Shy Boy before meeting Debra Hurd at a Los Angeles studio in 1990. Composing their own material, Hurd provided the lyrics to Damian's melodies. An immediate sensation on R&B radio, Damian Dame scored a trio of hits in the early Nineties with 'Exclusivity', 'Right Down To It' and 'Gotta Learn My Rhythm'. After Hurd was killed in a traffic accident in 1994, Broadus pursued a solo career, but died only days after his début solo album, *199Sex*, was released.
CAUSE: Colon cancer. Deah Dame (Debra Hurd) died exactly two years earlier.

Dennis Brooks

(JAMES MEALEY)
Born April 1, 1942
Died 1978
Bass vocalist of the early Sixties vocal group The Dovells, Dennis Brooks appeared on the hits 'Bristol Stomp' (1961), 'Bristol Twistin' Annie' (1962), and a cover of Phil Upchurch's instrumental hit, 'You Can't Sit Down' (1963). Brooks had replaced original member Mark Stevens.
CAUSE: Unknown.

Marv Brooks

Born 1946
Died February 23, 1998
A radio pioneer, Marv Brooks was instrumental in the conception of the oldies radio format. He introduced an all-oldies playlist at WMOD in Washington DC, in September 1968. The format grew slowly before exploding in popularity during the mid Eighties.
CAUSE: Heart attack. He died at his home in Silver Spring, Maryland.

Big Bill Broonzy

(WILLIAM LEE CONLEY BROONZY)
Born June 26, 1893
Died August 15, 1958
Prolific and influential jazz/blues singer and guitarist who inspired many R&B musicians, the Mississippi-born Big Bill Broonzy was taught to play the fiddle by an uncle at age 10. Leaving his family of 17, Broonzy worked as an itinerant preacher and then joined the service, before moving to Chicago in the late Twenties. Abandoning his fiddle for a guitar, Broonzy helped to usher in modern blues, his first recordings coming at Paramount Records in 1927. Forming a series of combos, he recorded prolifically throughout his life, appearing on hundreds of sessions with fellow blues pioneers such as Sonny Boy Williamson (#1), Washboard Sam, and Tampa Red. Simultaneously pursuing a solo career, Broonzy composed over 200 blues including 'Key To The Highway'. Although immensely popular in the Thirties with his acoustic, country-blues, Broonzy still had to maintain a day job. Broonzy gained added notoriety in 1938 when he appeared at the Spirituals to Swing concert at Carnegie Hall. His career waning in the US with the rise of electric blues in the Fifties, Broonzy later emerged as a star throughout Europe, and especially Britain, alongside folk-blues artists Sonny Terry and Brownie McGhee.
CAUSE: Throat cancer.

Bill Brown

Born 1936
Died 1958
An original member of the early R&B group The Dominoes, Bill Brown joined the Billy Ward-managed group in 1950. A deep bass singer, Brown was teamed with Charlie White, Willie Lamont and former gospel singer Clyde McPhatter. Signed to the new King Records subsidiary, Federal, The Dominoes worked under the guidance of producer Ralph Bass. With McPhatter on lead, the group landed on the R&B charts with their début release, the ballad 'Do Something For Me' (1950). Two singles later, the group would score the biggest R&B hit of the decade with 'Sixty Minute Man'. With Brown's deep, booming, older-style voice, the song was banned by many radio stations and considered a novelty by others. It was especially explicit for its time, even with its euphemistic lyrics. After recording 'When The Swallows Come Back To Capistrano' (1952), Brown and White were fired by Ward. The pair then joined The Checkers, a Dominoes' copy band. The group disbanded in 1953. Brown wanted to sign with another label, but was contractually obligated to stay with King Records where he formed a new Checkers group which lasted until 1955.
CAUSE: Unknown.

Buster Brown

(WAYMAN GLASCO)
Born August 14, 1911
Died January 31, 1976
Blues singer and harmonica player whose biggest hits came with 'Fannie Mae' (1960) and 'Sugar Babe' (1962), Buster Brown was unknown outside Florida and Georgia until the Sixties. Moving to New York City in the late Fifties, the Georgia native was discovered by Bobby Robinson of Fury/Fire Records. Brown later recorded for a series of labels including Chess.

CAUSE: Unknown. He died in Brooklyn, New York.

Charles Brown

Born September 13, 1922
Died January 21, 1999

Born in Texas City, Texas, Charles Brown was raised by his grandmother following the death of his mother. Brown took music lessons beginning at age ten at the urging of his grandmother, a church pianist. Graduating high school at age 15 and earning a degree in chemistry at Prairie View College by age 20, Brown also played music as a sideline during this period. After teaching high school chemistry, Brown took a government position as a chemist in Arkansas. Then, after transferring to Berkeley, he found the position filled. Quickly finding a stint as a pianist in the San Francisco servicemen's club, Brown discovered his musical niche. Settling in Los Angeles, Brown soon emerged as a major figure in the rise of West Coast R&B. Teaming with guitarist Johnny Moore and bassist Eddie Williams in a trio called Johnny Moore's Three Blazers, Brown and the group quickly built a local fanbase. After recording several singles at the tiny Atlas label, the group found fame at Eddie Messner's Philo Records. Composed by Brown and characterised by his melancholy, blues piano strains and brooding, sad vocals, 'Drifting Blues' was a very influential hit. Refusing to be tied down to a single label, The Blazers enjoyed hits with several record companies. Featuring Brown's jazz-blues, elegant, ballady voice, The Blazers dominated jukeboxes with hits such as 'Sunny Road', 'So Long', 'New Orleans Blues', and his signature piece and perennial favourite, 'Merry Christmas, Baby'. Leaving in 1948 to pursue a solo career, Brown was unhappy about the addition of Johnny Moore's brother, Oscar. Signing with Eddie Messner's new label, Aladdin Records, Brown scored a remarkable run of hits in 1949 including 'Get Yourself Another Fool', 'Long Time', and 'Trouble Blues'. His hit run continued into the Fifties with 'Black Night' and 'Seven Long Days'. Brown suffered a career blow after suing his label for back royalties. Leaving Aladdin, he spent several years working at a Cincinnati nightclub. After decades of relative obscurity, Brown was rediscovered after a 1991 tour with Bonnie Raitt. His album *All My Life* was nominated for a Grammy.

CAUSE: Congestive heart failure. He died in his sleep at Summit Medical Center in Oakland.

Dennis Brown

(DENNIS EMANUEL BROWN)
Born February 1, 1957
Died July 1, 1999

Nicknamed "The Crown Prince of Reggae", the velvet-voiced Dennis Brown earned much acclaim when Bob Marley dubbed him his favourite singer. A perennial favourite in Jamaica, Brown recorded prolifically for three decades, teaming with a who's who of reggae artists and producers. Performing on stage since age nine, he was discovered by reggae producer Byron Lee at age 12, landing a local hit with 'No Man Is An Island' (1969). Releasing his finest material in the mid Seventies under the guidance of producer Niney The Observer, Brown forsook his Afro for dreadlocks and followed Marley's lead into Rastafarianism, recording politically charged material such as 'Whip Them Jah Jah', 'Tribulation', and his signature piece, 'Here I Come (With Love Not Hatred)'. Teaming with producer Joe Gibbs in the late Seventies, Brown scored his biggest British hit with 'Money In My Pocket' (1979). Moving to London and signing with A&M Records, he started his own label, DEB Records, overseeing a number of female artists including former Soul II Soul leader Caron

Wheeler. Brown continued to chart in Britain with 'Halfway Up, Halfway Down' (1982) and 'Love Has Found Its Way' (1982) and after a brief flirtation with electronic music in the late Eighties, Brown returned to his reggae roots, earning a Grammy nomination in 1994 for his album, *Light My Fire*. Brown's 'Ghetto Girl' was reprised in 1998 by former Simply Red frontman Mick Hucknall. Struggling with cocaine and then crack addiction since the Seventies, Brown frequently sabotaged his own career.
CAUSE: Becoming ill during a tour of Brazil, he suffered a heart attack while battling respiratory failure and pneumonia. He died at University Hospital in Kingston, Jamaica.

Eddie Brown

Born 1941
Died August 9, 1966
Half of the California-based black vocal duo, Joe and Eddie, Eddie Brown had joined partner Joe Gilbert in the early Sixties. Recording for Capitol and GNP/Crescendo, the duo managed little airplay with their pop-flavoured sound.
CAUSE: Gilbert drove off the road, killing both himself and Brown.

J.T. Brown

(JAMES THOMAS BROWN)
Born April 2, 1910
Died November 24, 1969
A tenor saxophonist, J.T. Brown gained fame backing Chicago bluesman Elmore James, Eddie Boyd, and Roosevelt Sykes. Brown was also a member of a popular stage and studio group, the Boogie Band. Brown later collaborated with Muddy Waters, and in 1969, Fleetwood Mac.
CAUSE: Unknown.

Romaine Brown

Born c. 1915
Died 1987
Baritone singer and pianist of the pioneering, Forties/Fifties Los-Angeles-based doo-wop vocal group, the Red Caps, the classically trained Philadelphia-born Romaine Brown had joined the group in 1943 as the replacement for Beryl Booker. Signing with Beacon Records, the (Five) Red Caps scored hits with the Mills brothers-styled, 'I've Learned A Lesson I'll Never Forget' (1943) and 'No One Else Will Do'. Moving to Mercury Records in 1946, the renamed Steve Gibson and the Red Caps landed a hit with 'Wedding Bells Are Breaking Up That Old Gang of Mine' (1948). Moving to RCA, the group scored their final hit in a duet with Damita Jo, 'I Went To Your Wedding' (1952). In 1953, Brown led a side project called The Romaines, issuing some material at Decca Records. By 1960, Brown had disbanded The Romaines and quit The Red Caps.
CAUSE: Unknown.

Roy Brown

(ROY JAMES BROWN)
Born September 10, 1925
Died May 25, 1981
A pioneering New Orleans R&B blues shouter, Brown is best known for his composition, 'Good Rockin' Tonight', later a hit for Elvis Presley. Reared on old-time spirituals, Brown had despised blues music during his youth. Moving to Los Angeles and changing his name to Billy Hale, he entered the boxing ring. Soon quitting over his aversion to the sight of blood, he returned to Louisiana. Pursuing a career in music, Brown found clubwork as a novelty act, a black Bing Crosby imitator. Relocating to Galveston, Texas, Brown gravitated toward blues in the late Forties, honing his soulful, gospel-based high-pitched voice. Also a songwriter, he offered 'Good Rockin' Tonight' to Wynonie Harris who initially turned it down, changing his mind when he heard Brown's version on the radio. But

unfortunately for Brown, Harris' remake fared better on the charts. With his sax and piano-heavy sound, Brown's R&B hits continued with 'Boogie At Midnight' (1948), 'Hard Luck Blues' (1950), and 'Bar Room Blues' (1951). Blackballed by the music industry after demanding unpaid royalties from King Records, Brown saw his career slump. Signing with Imperial Records in 1957, Brown scored his only pop hit with 'Let The Four Winds Blow'. In the Sixties, Brown issued a series of self-produced records on several different labels. Touring with the Roomful Of Blues in 1981, Brown saw his career reinvigorated.
CAUSE: Suffering a heart attack near his home in the San Fernando Valley, he died at nearby Pacoima Lutheran Memorial Hospital. He checked into the hospital after suffering an insulin rejection on May 23, two days before his death.

Walter Brown

Born 1916
Died 1956
A blues-ballad styled vocalist and pianist, Walter Brown got his start in 1941 as the featured vocalist in a band led by Jay McShann (which also included a young Charlie Parker on sax). Brown provided the lead vocals on the McShann hits, 'Hootie Blues', 'Lonely Boy Blues', and the million-selling 'Confessin' The Blues'. His career hampered by a drug habit, Brown left McShann's band in 1944. Pursuing a solo career, he recorded unsuccessfully for several top labels including King and Capitol, and was frequently backed on sessions by his former associates in McShann's group.
CAUSE: Long-term drug abuse.

Jimmy Bruno

Born c. 1925
Died c. 1980
As the jazz-trained guitarist of one-hit wonders The Virtues, Jimmy Bruno scored a Top 10 instrumental rock'n'roll hit in 1959 with 'Guitar Boogie Shuffle'. The Philadelphia-based group was formed in 1946 by Frank Virtue.
CAUSE: Unknown.

Boudleaux Bryant

(DIADORIUS BOUDLEAUX BRYANT)
Born February 13, 1920
Died June 25, 1987
Classically trained violinist turned songwriter who penned dozens of hits in the Fifties and Sixties, Boudleaux Bryant is mostly associated with The Everly Brothers. Marrying the former Felice Scaduto, Bryant and his new wife teamed up as songwriters in 1945, their first success coming with 'Country Boy', a hit in 1948 for Jimmy Dickens. Hired as staff writers at Acuff-Rose Publishing in Nashville, the Bryants penned hits in the Fifties for Tony Bennett, Frankie Laine, and Eddy Arnold. But their biggest success came with a long and fruitful collaboration with the youthful Everly Brothers. Starting with 'Bye Bye Love', the Bryants provided a string of hit compositions for the country-tinged Everlys including 'Wake Up Little Susie', 'All I Have To Do Is Dream', 'Bird Dog' and 'Devoted To You'. Returning to their country roots in the late Sixties, the Bryants provided a hit for the Osborne Brothers with the folk gem, 'Rocky Top'. Bryant, who had previously recorded several obscure singles, joined his wife on their lone album in 1979, the British-only release, *Surfin' On A New Wave*; the project featured eight new songs and four of their classics including 'Bye Bye Love'. Boudleaux Bryant's composition 'Love Hurts' was later a hit for heavy metal group, Nazareth. In all, Bryant composed over 1,500 songs.
CAUSE: Cancer. He died at the Baptist Memorial Hospital in Knoxville, Tennessee.

Beryl Bryden

(BERYL AUDREY BRYDEN)
Born May 11, 1920
Died July 14, 1998
Nicknamed the "British Queen of the Blues", Beryl Bryden enjoyed a 50-year career in music, having performed with Ella Fitzgerald and Billie Holiday. A former typist, the flamboyant singer started out in the vaudeville tradition, accompanying herself with a washboard in the Forties. After stints with George Webb and Chris Barber, Bryden secured her own radio show in 1948, joined by her new backing band, Beryl's Backroom Boys. She scored her début British hit in 1954 with 'Rock Island Line', duetting with skiffle king Lonnie Donegan. Her other UK hits included a cover of Bessie Smith's 'Gimme A Pigfoot' (1961) and 'Million Dollar Secret' (1965). Bryden's first US tour came in the Seventies.
CAUSE: Lymphatic cancer. She died at St. Mary's Hospital in London.

Bill Buchanan

Born April 30, 1930
Died August 1, 1996
Half of the late Fifties novelty duo, Buchanan and Goodman, which scored a hit with the break-in record, 'The Flying Saucer', Bill Buchanan met his partner Dickie Goodman while working in the music department of 20th Century Fox. Using an unusual interview style, the pair scored follow-up hits with 'Flying Saucer The 2nd' (1957) and 'Santa And The Satellite (Parts I & II)' (1957). Buchanan left in 1959 to pursue songwriting, and later, production work, penning Bobby Vee's hit, 'Please Don't Ask About Barbara'. Buchanan also teamed with a new partner Mickey Shorr, as Spencer and Spencer, releasing a pair of singles in 1959.
CAUSE: Cancer. He died in Los Angeles.

Roy Buchanan

Born September 23, 1939
Died August 14, 1988
Overlooked blues-rock guitar virtuoso and much in-demand session musician, Roy Buchanan was the son of a conservative Pentecostal preacher and farmer. Born in Arkansas but raised in Pixley, California, at a young age Buchanan was inspired by the fervent black gospel music of tent revivals. Receiving his first guitar at age five and taking guitar lessons at age seven, he soon switched his allegiance from gospel to R&B music. After playing in Las Vegas show bands in 1954, Buchanan's big break came the following year when he joined the Los Angeles-based Johnny Otis Revue. Buchanan had idolised Otis' R&B group, and was particularly impressed by guitar player Jimmy Nolan. A popular Los Angeles session player, Buchanan was soon working for Leiber & Stoller and others. After a brief stint as the leader of his own group The Heartbeats, Buchanan moved to Oklahoma and backed rockabilly singer Dale Hawkins on the hits, 'My Babe' (1958) and 'Lifeguard Man' (1958). In 1960 Buchanan joined Ronnie Hawkins' Hawks, a precursor of The Band (he was later replaced by Robbie Robertson). Returning to session work, Buchanan backed artists such as Freddie Cannon, Al Jones, and Cody Brennan. Disenchanted by the music industry, in 1962 Buchanan moved to the Washington DC area to raise a family. Content with occasional club work behind local country and blues acts, Buchanan would sell his own self-pressed releases at these shows. Garnering national exposure in 1971 on the PBS programme, *The Best Unknown Guitarist In The World*, Buchanan had also turned down an offer to join Eric Clapton's group Derek and The Dominos. Finally discovered by major labels, Buchanan later recorded for Polydor, Atlantic, and lastly, Alligator Records. At the

peak of his career at the time of his death, Buchanan seemed poised for stardom.
CAUSE: Suicide. Buchanan had been arrested for public drunkenness after a verbal altercation with his wife. His wife had called the police who picked him up a few blocks from his home in Reston, Virginia. He had been in a jail cell at the Fairfax County (Virginia) Adult Detention Center for 30 minutes before deputies checked on him. He had hung himself by tying his shirt to a window grate.

Jeff Buckley

(JEFFREY SCOTT BUCKLEY)
Born August 1, 1966
Died May 29, 1997
The son of folk-rocker Tim Buckley, the mystical and charismatic Jeff Buckley followed his father into music. The younger Buckley met his father only once at age eight, two months before the elder Buckley's tragic death from a heroin overdose at aged 28, and was instead raised by his mother, a classically trained pianist, and his stepfather. A sensitive singer-songwriter who cut across various musical styles from folk and rock to jazz and R&B, the California-born and raised Jeff Buckley was classically trained at the Los Angeles Musicians' Institute. Moving to Manhattan, he first made waves after performing his father's composition, 'One I Was', in 1991 at a star-studded Tim Buckley tribute. After a brief stint in an avant-garde band called Gods & Monsters, Buckley went solo, becoming a regular on the New York City folk club circuit with his dramatic, heartfelt performances. Rejecting several major label record deals before signing with Columbia, Buckley débuted in 1993 with an eclectic jazz, rock and R&B-styled four-song, limited edition mini-album, *Live At Sine*, taken from a performance at his favourite venue, the Sine folk club in New York City. Following up with *Grace* in 1994, the critically acclaimed album was met with little sales, but spawned the minor hit, 'Last Goodbye'. Hailed as a musical genius, Buckley came under intense, self-doubting pressure, and the constant comparisons with his famous father. At the time of his death, Buckley was recording tracks for his follow-up album, belatedly released in 1998 as the 2-CD set, *Sketches For My Sweetheart*. The project included both demo recordings and ten new, Tom Verlaine-produced studio tracks. Buckley enjoyed greater fame in the UK than in his native country.
CAUSE: Fully clothed, Buckley waded in the Wolf River, doing the backstroke and singing the Led Zeppelin song, 'Whole Lotta Love'. First a tugboat passed and then a barge, and as he was swimming in the path of the wake, Buckley was swept under and drowned. His body was washed ashore several days later at the base of the city's famed Beale Street. Despite rumours, no drugs were found in his body.

Tim Buckley

(TIMOTHY CHARLES BUCKLEY III)
Born February 14, 1947
Died June 29, 1975
An influential Sixties folk-rock singer and guitarist, Tim Buckley formed his first band while in high school. The folk/country group also featured bassist Jim Fielder (later with Blood, Sweat & Tears) and drummer Larry Beckett, who became an integral part of Buckley's success. Revered for writing ethereal, mystical lyrics, Buckley was discovered by Frank Zappa's manager Herb Cohen, and signed to Elektra Records in 1966. Buckley's second album *Morning Glory* (1967), utilised classical instrumentation and was highlighted by the title track and the utopian, 'Goodbye And Hello'. Buckley's subdued articulation and lyrical idealism differed from Dylan's often angry, blunt delivery. In 1970, Buckley joined Zappa's label Straight

Records, beginning with the album *Blue Afternoon*. Moving away from folk music in the Seventies with the poor-selling but critically acclaimed album *Greetings From L.A.*, Buckley began experimenting with vocal overdubbing, poetry, jazz fusion, and funk rhythms. Taking ethnomusicology courses at UCLA, he was also attracted to African and Southeast Asian music. Losing his fan base with his new sound, he became despondent. Buckley's last years were marked by inconsistent and poor-selling rock-oriented albums such as *Sefronia* (1973) and *Look At The Fool* (1974). Buckley was experiencing much personal strife during this period including a divorce and management problems. He was planning to record a live anthology of his hits at the time of his death.
CAUSE: Drug overdose. He had taken heroin, morphine, and alcohol at a friend's house in Santa Monica, California. Friends had brought him home, still alive, to his wife Judy Buckley. He died shortly thereafter. Allegedly, Buckley believed he was taking cocaine. The man who supplied the drugs, doctoral music student Richard Keeling, was indicted on charges of second degree murder, and convicted of involuntary manslaughter.

Allen Bunn

(ALDEN BUNN)
Born September 24, 1924
Died August 21, 1977
Gospel, doo-wop, and then blues star, Allen Bunn was born in Bailey, North Carolina. Learning to play the guitar in his teens, he joined a local gospel choir at age 20, before moving to a series of leading gospel groups including The Gospel Four and The Selah Jubilee Singers. By the late Forties, Allen and fellow Selah member Thurman Ruth left the group to form The Jubilators. Joined by former bandmate Eugene Mumford and three others in 1950, the group released both gospel and pop music under a variety of names. As The (Five) Larks, the quintet scored several doo-wop hits on Apollo Records including the gorgeous 'My Reverie', 'Eyesight To The Blind' and 'Little Side Car'. With the Larks disbanding in 1952, Bunn joined another doo-wop group, The Wheels, scoring a hit with 'My Heart's Desire' (1956). Simultaneously pursuing a solo career, he recorded soul music as TBunn for Red Robin Records. Metamorphosing, Bunn later emerged as a Chicago-styled, electric blues singer under the name of Tarheel Slim, initially recording with his future wife Little Ann as The Lovers, the duo landing a hit in 1962 with 'Darling It's Wonderful'. Leaving music for much of the Sixties, Bunn returned to the blues scene in the Seventies and recorded for Trix Records.
CAUSE: Suffering from throat cancer, he succumbed to pneumonia and died at Montefiore Medical Center in New York City.

Dorsey Burnette

(DORSEY BURNETTE, JR.)
Born December 28, 1932
Died August 19, 1979
The bass player in the pioneering rockabilly group, The Rock and Roll Trio, Dorsey Burnette was initially attracted to the sound of Forties pop vocalists. A tough street fighter, he won a Golden Gloves championship in his youth. Working as an electrician, in 1952 Dorsey joined his younger brother (by 15 months) Johnny, and a neighbour, ex-boxer Paul Burlison, for jam sessions. First joining a local group called The Daydreamers, the Dorsey brothers soon teamed with Burlison as Johnny Burnette and The Rock and Roll Trio. Dorsey played slap-style stand-up bass behind Johnny on lead vocals and Burlison on guitar. After backing a white R&B artist, Doc McQueen, the trio failed their audition for Sam Phillips at Sun Records. Moving to New York City in 1956,

expecting to make it big, the group earned first place honours on the Ted Mack Amateur Hour. Signing with Coral Records, the group recorded a series of stinging, underrated rockabilly classics such as 'Train Kept A-Rollin'' (1956). Struggling financially, Dorsey worked as an electrician while in New York City to pay bills. After disbanding the group, the Burnette brothers moved to Los Angeles where they composed a pair of hits for Ricky Nelson, 'Waiting In School' and 'It's Late'. Rejected by Nelson, 'Tall Oak Tree' was instead a solo hit for Dorsey Burnette. Later making a transition into country, Burnette signed with Capitol Records in 1972, landing several hits beginning with 'In The Spring' and 'Darlin' (Don't Come Back)'. Dorsey Burnette's son, Billy Burnette, was a member of Fleetwood Mac in the 1980s.
CAUSE: Heart attack. He died at his Canoga Park, California home. He had just signed with Elektra/Asylum Records.

Johnny Burnette

Born March 25, 1934
Died August 1, 1964
The lead singer in the Memphis-based rockabilly group, Johnny Burnette and The Rock and Roll Trio, Burnette showed an interest in music after his mother bought him an inexpensive acoustic guitar at age five. While his older brother, Dorsey, was fighting in the ring, Johnny was a star athlete in high school. After a disastrous cross-country job search after graduating from high school, Johnny set aside his musical dreams, and followed Dorsey into the boxing ring. Returning to music, Johnny was joined by Dorsey, and neighbour, Paul Burlison in 1952 to form a rockabilly group, Johnny Burnette and the Rock and Roll Trio. Also working as a solo act, Johnny performed on a local radio show on KWEM. Rejected by Sun Records, the trio moved to New York where at Coral Records, they recorded a series of rockabilly classics including 'Train Kept a Rollin'' (1956). With a fill-in member, the trio appeared in Alan Freed's low budget film, *Rock Rock Rock* (1956) in which they performed 'Lonesome Train'. After disbanding the group, the Burnette brothers moved to Los Angeles, working as songwriters for Ricky Nelson. Johnny Burnette signed with Liberty/Freedom Records as a solo artist, breaking through with the rockabilly-styled hits, 'Dreamin'' (1960) and 'You're Sixteen' (1960). While his chart run quickly ended in the US, Burnette managed a few more British hits in the early Sixties. Shortly before his death, he formed his own label, Magic Lamp Records. Burnette's son, Rocky Burnette scored a Top 10 hit in 1980 with a rockabilly-flavoured single, 'Tired Of Toein' The Line'.
CAUSE: He drowned in a boating accident near Clear Lake, California. He was fishing in a small, unlit boat at dusk and was rammed by a larger craft. It took several days for divers to recover the body.

August Burns

Born 1940
Died 1982
A member of the first act to perform at the original Woodstock Music Festival, cellist August Burns co-founded the seven-member interracial group Sweetwater in 1967. Burns was studying classical music at UCLA when he joined forces with Alan Malarowitz. Attracting attention around Los Angeles with their Latin-styled percussion, Sweetwater recorded three albums for Reprise and opened up for many of the top acts of the day, but achieved only limited success in their own right. After lead singer Nancy Nevins was seriously injured in a car crash in December 1969, the group drifted before disbanding two years later. Burns later continued his musical education, with the goal of becoming

an orchestra conductor. The group's biopic, *Sweetwater: A True Rock Story*, aired on the VH-1 network in 1999.
CAUSE: He fell from an open-air construction lift while in Germany. Though surviving the fall, he contracted pneumonia while in hospital.

Harold Burrage

Born March 30, 1931
Died November 25, 1966
A northern US soul singer, Chicago-based pianist Harold Burrage scored his solitary hit in 1965 with 'Got To Find A Way', and penned the blues standard 'Crying For My Baby'. Burrage later discovered and mentored R&B singer Tyrone Davis.
CAUSE: Heart attack.

Cliff Burton

(CLIFFORD LEE BURTON)
Born February 10, 1962
Died July 27, 1986
The bass player for the thrash-metal band, Metallica, Cliff Burton was trained in classical music, dividing his time in junior college between classical piano and heavy metal guitar. Around 1980, Burton joined a hard-rock group called Vicious Hatred with future Faith No More guitarist Jim Martin. By the early Eighties, Burton joined San Francisco heavy metal band, Trauma. But when Metallica's first bassist, Ron McGovney, quit the band in 1982, the group's drummer Lars Ulrich (a transplanted Dane), pleaded with Burton to quit Trauma and join his group. After discovering that Burton would not join because he was unwilling to move to Los Angeles, the entire group relocated to San Francisco. Burton then reluctantly joined Metallica in late 1982. With his formal training, Burton applied his knowledge of chords and harmony structure to the group's music. Somewhat of a character, Burton's retro, bell-bottom jeans, Deadhead-like style of clothing were in striking contrast to the rest of the group. With James Hetfield on vocals and guitar, and Kirk Hammett on guitar, Metallica's début LP, *Kill 'Em All*, was released in 1983 on a small independent label, Megaforce, whose owner had discovered the group from a bootleg copy of their demo tape. Highlighted by tracks such as 'Seek And Destroy' and 'Whiplash', the album would define the emerging speed-metal genre. Garnering a large underground following, Metallica would move further away from speed-metal with each successive release. Their second album, *Ride The Lightning*, was highlighted by their first commercially oriented song, 'Fade To Black'. But even with the strong sales of their third album, *Master Of Puppets* (1986), and an opening slot on an Ozzy Osbourne tour, the group was still unable to land radio or MTV airplay.
CAUSE: In September of 1986, Metallica began their first headlining European tour. The group had finished a concert in Stockholm and was headed for a date in Copenhagen, Denmark. Burton was killed instantly when the group's bus spun around and landed on its side on icy roads near the town of Ljumgbye in southern Sweden. Burton had been sleeping in an upper bunk by a window. When the window buckled, he fell out and the bus landed on top of him. Burton had won a bet earlier in the day and swapped bunks with Kirk Hammett, who normally slept in that spot. The 48-year-old British driver suffered a minor foot injury and the eight other passengers were also hurt. Most severely injured were Ulrich and the group's manager, Bob Schneider. The second half of the tour was postponed. The band, which continues to tour heavily, now travels in its own private aeroplane.
FURTHER READING: Crocker, Chris. (1993). *Metallica: The Frayed Ends of Metal*. New York: St. Martin's Press.

Billy Butler

Born 1925
Died March 20, 1991
Jazz and R&B guitarist who provided the classic solo on Bill Doggett's hit 'Honky Tonk', Bill Butler had first improvised the opening chords of the song while performing on stage in western Ohio. Forming his own group in the late Sixties, Butler released five albums on Prestige Records. Later a much in-demand session player in New York City, he worked with Dinah Washington and Dizzie Gillespie.
CAUSE: Heart attack. He died at his home in Teaneck, New Jersey.

Floyd Butler

Born June 5, 1941
Died April 29, 1990
The co-leader of the pop-soul band, Friends Of Distinction, Floyd Butler formed the quartet with Harry Elston, the pair first meeting in a San Diego public housing project at age five. Lifelong friends, Butler and Elston attended the same high school and college, before they both entered the service. After their discharges, both Butler and Elston settled in Los Angeles, where they continued their college education and part-time music pursuits. They first formed The Hi-Fi's, an R&B group that also included Marilyn McCoo and Lamonte McLemore. The group was befriended by Ray Charles who hired the band as an opening act, and then produced their only single (released as by The Vocals). After the group disbanded, McCoo and McLore formed The Fifth Dimension. But while Butler first took a job at the Urban League, he soon rejoined Elston in a group called The Friends Of Distinction. Financially supported by former football star Jim Brown, the group landed a recording contract with RCA Records. Their début hit came in 1969 with a million-selling remake of the Hugh Masekela instrumental, 'Grazing In The Grass', featuring newly written lyrics by Harry Elston. With RCA taking the group in an R&B direction, their follow-up single 'Going In Circles' was their second million-seller. Another smash hit came in 1970 with, 'Love Or Let Me Be Lonely'. After experiencing several personnel changes, the group fell out of popularity and disbanded in 1975.
CAUSE: Heart attack.

Paul Butterfield

Born December 17, 1942
Died May 4, 1987
A white, Jewish, blues singer-songwriter, Paul Butterfield was raised in Chicago's south side in a predominately black neighbourhood, where in the late Fifties he discovered the city's bustling blues scene. Befriended by Muddy Waters in 1958, Butterfield was occasionally permitted to share the stage with his musical mentor. While studying the classical flute at the University of Chicago, Butterfield was instead drawn to the blues harmonica, with "harp" master Little Walter soon becoming his tutor. Forming The Paul Butterfield Blues Band in 1963, he was joined by college friend Elvin Bishop (later of 'Fooled Around And Fell In Love' fame) and guitarist Mike Bloomfield. Butterfield garnered national exposure when members of his group were heckled by folk purists as they backed Bob Dylan at the début of his controversial electric concert at the Newport Folk Festival. Signing with Elektra Records in 1965, Butterfield's group combined Chicago-style blues with hard rock on their classic début release, *The Paul Butterfield Blues Band*, the album highlighted by 'Born In Chicago'. Introducing blues music and its black originators to white America, Butterfield recorded seven albums for Elektra, and appeared at Woodstock in 1969. Though a master harmonica player, Butterfield was only an average singer. In 1969 Butterfield and former bandmate Mike Bloomfield joined their

mentor, Muddy Waters, on the album, *Fathers And Sons*. Moving to Woodstock, New York, in the early Seventies, Butterfield formed a folkier-styled group, The Better Days, releasing several moderately successful albums for Bearsville Records. In the late Seventies, Butterfield teamed up with Levon Helm in The All Stars, and then with Rick Danko in The Danko-Butterfield Band. After coming down with peritonitis (a digestive disorder) in 1981, Butterfield was unable to record or publicly perform for several years. He was stricken while recording the album, *North South*. He subsequently underwent several operations. Returning to the stage in 1987, Butterfield toured with The Allman Brothers and Santana.

CAUSE: He died of intestinal maladies after years of alcohol and drug abuse. He was found dead in the kitchen of his North Hollywood apartment by his manager.

Glen Buxton

Born November 10, 1947
Died October 19, 1997

The original lead guitarist and keyboardist for theatrical rock outfit Alice Cooper in the early Seventies, Glen Buxton provided some of the most identifiable guitar licks in hard rock. Born in Akron, Ohio, but raised in Phoenix, Buxton formed The Spiders in 1965 with several of his high school classmates. The group, featuring singer Vincent Furnier on lead vocals, scored a local smash with 'Don't Blow Your Mind'. With Furnier taking on the Alice Cooper persona, the group, previously known as The Nazz, took the same name. Moving to Los Angeles, they auditioned for Frank Zappa who signed them to his Straight label but, heckled by California audiences, Alice Cooper returned to Detroit for a period before relocating to the New York area. Signing with Warner Brothers in 1971, the group unleashed a string of grinding, guitar-driven hard-rock anthems including 'Eighteen', 'School's Out', 'Elected' and 'No More Mr. Nice Guy'. Alice Cooper drew much media attention for their macabre stage act which incorporated live snakes, a guillotine and a full-size electric chair. With Buxton's hard drinking interfering with his duties, the group had to be augmented by a session guitarist for both stage and studio work, including much of their seventh album *Muscle Of Love* (1974). At one point Buxton's irrational behaviour extended to pulling a knife on the group's road manager. Experiencing problems with his record company, Cooper fired the entire band in 1975 (several members, minus Buxton, formed the offshoot group Billion Dollar Babies). Instead of recording a planned solo album, Buxton began collecting antiques, and when he neglected to pay taxes on an investment, he lost his home to the IRS in 1979. Settling in New York City for a time, Buxton was drawn to the burgeoning punk scene; after frequenting the genre's epicentre, CBGB's, he formed his own outfit, Shrapnel. Broke and now living with his parents in Phoenix, Buxton was relegated to performing Top 40 cover hits in a local bar band called Virgin, and working at a Goodyear plant during the day. Invited to live on a farm in Iowa in 1990 by a rock memorabilia collector, Buxton jumped at the opportunity. Living a quiet life, Buxton performed in local bands and gave music lessons.

CAUSE: Although viral pneumonia was the ultimate cause of death, Buxton had ignored years of doctors warnings against drug and alcohol abuse. On his return home from performances in Texas, Buxton was taken to hospital. Insisting that he needed to take a nap, he died shortly thereafter. Buxton had begun his love of alcohol while at high school and his body was wracked by years of substance abuse.

FURTHER READING: Cooper, Alice. (1996). *The Last Temptation Of Alice Cooper*. New York: Marvel Entertainment.

David Byron

Born January 29, 1947
Died February 28, 1985

The vocalist and founding member of the perennial hard-rock group, Uriah Heep, David Byron began his professional career in 1965 as the singer for the popular British pub band, Spice. In 1970, Byron and guitarist Mick Box left Spice to form Uriah Heep. Singing in a lusty, hard-rock fashion, Byron hit the stage in bare-chested flashy costumes. Signing with Mercury Records, Uriah Heep's breakthrough album, *Salisbury* (1971), was highlighted by its orchestral, 16-minute title track. Though garnering little airplay, the group proved that success could be gained by marathon touring, initially as an opening act for Deep Purple, Vanilla Fudge and T. Rex. Uriah Heep landed its first million-seller in 1972 with *Demons And Wizards* which featured their only Top 40 hit, 'Easy Livin''. Leaving Mercury in 1973, the group signed with Warner Brothers, their label début album *Sweet Freedom* highlighted by the track, 'Stealin''. After much internal squabbling, Byron left the group (most sources claim he was fired) in July, 1976, his last Uriah Heep album coming with *High And Mighty*. Releasing his first solo album, *Take No Prisoners*, on Mercury, Byron was backed by Box and other Uriah Heep alumni. After joining the heavy metal group Rough Diamond in 1977, Byron returned to a solo career, releasing the albums *This Day And Age* (1980) and *On The Rocks* (1982).
CAUSE: A heart attack brought on by long-term, excessive drug and alcohol abuse.

C

Tommy Caldwell

(THOMAS MICHAEL CALDWELL)
Born November 9, 1949
Died April 28, 1980
The bass player for the Southern-rock group, The Marshall Tucker Band, Tommy Caldwell picked up the guitar at age 10, taught to play by his country musician father, and older brother, Toy Caldwell. Two years later, Tommy switched to the electric bass. After a stint in the US Marines in the late Sixties, Tommy Caldwell joined his brother's group, Toy Factory. But since that group already had a bass player, Toy and Tommy alternated on lead guitar. When Toy Factory evolved into The Marshall Tucker Band in 1972, Tommy switched to bass. Signing with Capricorn Records, the group released a self-titled album, highlighted by acoustic guitar hit, 'Can't You See', the song featuring the flute playing of Jerry Eubanks. With little fanfare, the group hit the road for a long series of one-nighters, initially opening up for labelmates and fellow Southern-rockers, The Allman Brothers Band. A strict technique bass player, Caldwell later experimented with jazz stylings. Throughout the decade, The Marshall Tucker Band churned out a series of gold and platinum certified albums, including *Searchin' For A Rainbow* (1975), which was highlighted by 'Fire On The Mountain', and *Carolina Dreams* (1977), which included their biggest hit, 'Heard It In A Lovesong'. Their final Capricorn album came in 1978 with *Together Forever.* Switching to Warner Brothers in 1979, the group recorded a pair of poorly received, jazz-flavoured albums, including *Tenth* (1980) which was released shortly before Caldwell's death. A scratch golfer, Caldwell was a member of the Professional Golfers' Association.
CAUSE: Tommy Caldwell died five days after sustaining injuries suffered in an auto accident in Spartanburg, South Carolina, on April 23. He hit a stalled car and his vehicle, a Toyota Landcruiser, rolled over. Caldwell's other brother, Tim, had died in a separate car crash a month earlier.
FURTHER READING: Smith, Michael B. (1997). *Carolina Dreams: The Musical Legacy Of Upstate South Carolina.* Beverly Hills, CA: Marshall Tucker Ent.

Toy Caldwell

(TOY TALMADGE CALDWELL, JR.)
Born November 13, 1947
Died February 25, 1993
Guitarist, principal songwriter and lead singer of the Southern-rock band, The Marshall Tucker Band, Toy Caldwell was born into a musical family in Spartansburg, South Carolina, his father a veteran of local country music groups. During his late teens, Toy Caldwell occasionally performed with his father at square dances. Forming his first rock group in 1965, The Rants were a British Invasion cover band. The group disbanded in 1967 when Caldwell and the rest of the group were drafted. Returning home in April 1969 after being injured in Vietnam, Toy Caldwell had to relearn how to play his Les Paul guitar. Forming Toy Factory, he was soon joined by his brother Tommy. The group was soon opening up for Wet Willie, who recommended them to Phil Walden of Capricorn Records. Evolving into The Marshall Tucker Band, the group débuted with *The Marshall Tucker Band* (1973), the album highlighted by the acoustic guitar hit, 'Can't You See'. A string of consistently selling albums followed including, *Searchin' For A Rainbow* (1975), which included the hit, 'Fire On The Mountain', and *Carolina Dreams* (1977), which featured 'Heard It In A Lovesong'. Also a session

player, Toy Caldwell worked with Elvin Bishop, Waylon Jennings, and Hank Williams, Jr. Playing with his thumb instead of a pick, Caldwell was a melodic guitar player who had absorbed some of his father's Southern influences. Toy Caldwell left the Marshall Tucker Band in 1985 after the death of his brother (see above) in an automobile accident. Pursuing a solo career, he was completing his second album at the time of his death.
CAUSE: Caldwell suffered from chronic bronchitis and was ill with the flu. He saw a doctor the day before his death, but succumbed to acute respiratory failure at his Spartanburg home. The Spartanburg County coroner later ruled that Caldwell's death was cocaine related. Caldwell had been scheduled to perform at a fund-raiser for a Ronnie Van Zant memorial park on the day of his death.
FURTHER READING: Smith, Michael B. (1997). *Carolina Dreams: The Musical Legacy Of Upstate South Carolina.* Beverly Hills, CA: Marshall Tucker Ent.

Roy Calhoun

(ROYALSTON CALHOUN)
Born c. 1936
Died 1970
First tenor and occasional songwriter of the Fifties doo-wop group, Lee Andrews and The Hearts, Roy Calhoun enjoyed several hits at Chess Records including 'Long Lonely Nights' (1957) and 'Teardrops' (1958). Managed by Philadelphia deejay Kae Williams, The Hearts initially recorded for a pair of local labels, Rainbow, and then, Gotham Records.
CAUSE: He died in an apartment fire.

Randy California

(RANDOLPH CRAIG WOLFE)
Born February 20, 1951
Died January 2, 1997
A talented guitarist, Los Angeles born and raised Randy California was exposed to rock music during his early teens at his uncle Ed Pearl's Ash Grove nightclub, where he was also permitted to jam with the likes of Mance Lipscomb, Sleepy John Estes and Lightnin' Hopkins. Forming a jazz-fusion group, the Red Roosters, California was joined by keyboardist John Locke and his soon-to-be stepfather, drummer Ed Cassidy. Moving to New York and joining Jimmy James And The Blue Flames, California received his stage name from the group's then-unknown bandleader, Jimi Hendrix. Returning to Los Angeles, Randy California reteamed with Locke, Cassidy, and two more ex-Red Roosters, to form Spirits Rebellious. Placing former bluegrass musician Jay Ferguson at the helm as lead singer, the group shortened its name to Spirit. Their first three albums *Spirit, The Family That Plays Together* and *Clear* were highly accomplished works that brought the group critical acclaim for their jazzy experimentation. Creative tensions would eventually sunder the unit but not before they issued their masterpiece – *Twelve Dreams Of Dr Sardonicus*. This album revealed California at the peak of his powers, composing the ecological anthem 'Nature's Way', among others. Ferguson and Andes subsequently formed Jo Jo Gunne, who enjoyed chart success with 'Run Run Run'. Meanwhile, California entered a dark period, first falling from a horse and sustaining serious injuries, after which he released the flawed *Kaptain Kopter And The Fabulous Twirlybirds* (1972), with Hendrix bassist Noel Redding and drummer Les Sampson. A move to London almost ended in premature death when Randy threw himself off London's Waterloo Bridge into the River Thames. He subsequently reactivated Spirit, entering another fascinating phase with the double album *Spirit Of '76*, followed by the sometimes enigmatic *Farther Along* and *Future Games*. A previously doomed

project *Journey Through Potatoland* was exhumed from the vaults and re-recorded in 1981. The following year, California released a solo album, *Euro American*. In 1984, the original Spirit regrouped for *The Thirteenth Dream*, but the old invention was lacking. Further releases, included *Rapture In Chamber* (1989), *Tent Of Miracles* (1990) and *Live At La Paloma*, which succeeded in keeping the band's name alive. Sony's remastering of the group's early catalogue elicited favourable reviews and indicated a renewed interest in the band's classic period, prompting hopes of a resurgence in popularity.
CAUSE: He drowned while swimming with his 12-year-old son, Quinn, near Molokai, Hawaii. Caught in a riptide, California was lost at sea. Authorities called off their search after one day due to bad weather. His body was never found.

Cab Calloway

(CABELL CALLOWAY III)
Born December 25, 1907
Died November 18, 1995
Legendary zoot-suited jazz performer whose career was re-ignited in the Eighties by his performance of 'Minnie The Moocher' in the film *The Blues Brothers*, the Rochester, New York-born Cab Calloway broke into showbusiness in his late teens via his older sister Blanch, who helped him get a part in a "The Plantation Days" touring revue. Gigging in Chicago with Louis Armstrong in the mid Twenties, Calloway built upon Armstrong's scat vocal delivery, forming his own band in 1929. An immediate sensation, Calloway won a residency at Harlem's famed Cotton Club in 1931 after the departure of Duke Ellington. Appearing in many films and touring extensively for the next few decades, Calloway enjoyed a long hit run in the Thirties and Forties that included 'The Scat Song', 'The Jumpin' Jive' and 'The Great Lie'. Also hitting the stage, he joined productions of *Porgy And Bess* and an all-black Broadway revue of *Hello, Dolly!*
CAUSE: Suffering a stroke on June 12, 1995, he did not recover. He died in a nursing home in Hockessin, Delaware.

Robert Calvert

Born March 9, 1945
Died August 14, 1988
South African-born poet, and sometimes vocalist, Robert Calvert was from 1970–73 a member of Hawkwind, the British psychedelic space-rock group, who became as famous for their alternative lifestyle as their music. The group's biggest hit came with the Calvert-penned single 'Silver Machine' (1972), a new version of the song in which Calvert's vocals had been overdubbed. Calvert rejoined Hawkwind in 1977, before launching a solo career in the Eighties with a pair of album releases.
CAUSE: Heart attack.

John Campbell

Born January 20, 1952
Died June 13, 1993
Southern blues guitarist and singer who employed voodoo imagery in his stage shows, John Campbell first recorded in 1988 before teaming with guitarist Alexander Kennedy. Signing with Elektra Records in 1991, Campbell released his first of two albums at the label, *One Believer*, the project recorded with Robert Cray's former backing band.
CAUSE: Heart disease. He died in his sleep at his home in New York City.

Stephen Canaday

(STEPHEN PAUL CANADAY)
Born September 12, 1944
Died September 25, 1999
A member of perennial country-rock group, The Ozark Mountain Daredevils, Stephen Canaday joined a stripped-down line-up of the group in 1977, providing both guitar and

drums. The group was formed in 1971 in Springfield, Missouri, comprising primarily classmates from Southwest Missouri State University. First appearing on the album *Don't Look Down*, Canaday joined the group at a time of declining fortunes. He also joined a new line-up of the group in the early Nineties. He later worked in photography, and as a tour manager for Lee Roy Parnell, Tammy Wynette, Marshall Chapman, and others.
CAUSE: Aeroplane crash. He was a passenger in a light plane that crashed in the Germantown section of Nashville. The vintage World War II craft piled through treetops, glided across a lawn before smashing into the side of an unoccupied triplex apartment. While pilot Rick Loudermilk perished immediately, Canaday died en route to the hospital. No one on the ground was injured. Ironically, Canaday was a helicopter pilot during the Vietnam War.

Jerry Capehart

(JERRY NEIL CAPEHART)
Born August 22, 1928
Died June 7, 1998
Based in Nashville, producer and songwriter Jerry Capehart is best known as the catalyst behind rockabilly singer Eddie Cochran. First meeting Cochran in a music store, Capehart became his manager from 1955–59. Helping Cochran sign with Liberty Records, Capehart co-wrote a number of his songs, including the rock standards 'Summertime Blues' and 'C'mon Everbody'. Capehart and Cochran split shortly before Cochran's untimely death in a road accident in England in 1960. Capehart later managed Glen Campbell and entertainer Frank Gorshen. He also composed 'Beautiful Brown Eyes', a hit for both Rosemary Clooney and Jimmy Wakely, and 'Turn Around, Look At Me', a hit for both Glen Campbell and The Vogues.
CAUSE: Brain cancer; he had been diagnosed a month before his death. He died in Nashville.

Leonard "Chick" Carbo

(LEONARD "CHICK" CARBO)
Born December 28, 1927
Died August 18, 1998
Leader of the Fifties, New Orleans-based doo-wop vocal group The Spiders, baritone-vocalist Leonard "Chick" Carbo formed the group in 1947 as a gospel quartet called The Zion Harmonizers. Adding brother Hayward "Chuck" Carbo, the renamed Delta Southernaires signed with Imperial Records in 1953. But with Imperial refusing to record the group as a gospel act, The Southernaires recorded as a secular doo-wop group under the pseudonym The Spiders. After being outed by a local deejay, the group was banned from singing in its home Baptist church. One of the few successful doo-wop vocal groups to emerge from the Crescent City, The Spiders enjoyed airplay with hits such as 'I Didn't Want To Do It' (1954), 'I'm Slippin'' (1954), and 'Witchcraft' (1955). Oddly, the group did not have a following in its hometown, but was popular on tours with artists such as Ray Charles and The Drifters. After The Spiders disbanded in 1957 from lack of success, Chick Carbo recorded for Revue Records in the Sixties. The Spiders remain a favourite among vocal group collectors.
CAUSE: Unknown.

Jake Carey

(JACOB A. CAREY)
Born September 9, 1926
Died December 10, 1997
The bass vocalist and eldest member of the early doo-wop group, The Flamingos, Virginia-native Jake Carey moved to Chicago in 1950 along with his cousin Zeke Carey. There the cousins joined the choir at a local Black Jewish synagogue. Forming The Swallows (not the more famous Baltimore group) in 1951 with Johnny

Carter and Paul Wilson, the group installed Earl Lewis as their lead singer. Renamed The (Five) Flamingos in 1952 after the addition of Sollie McElroy as their new lead singer, the group recorded a series of much sought after singles on the Chance, Parrot and Checker labels. Providing some of the most elegant harmonies in the doo-wop genre, The Flamingos scored a series of regional hits with 'If I Can't Have You' and the marvellous 'Golden Teardrops'. The Flamingos finally reached the national R&B charts in 1956 with the Nate Nelson-penned, 'I'll Be Home', the song also hitting the pop charts via a cover version by Pat Boone. Moving to New York and recording on Decca, and then End, the group entered the second phase of its career, landing a major smash in 1959 with the romantic standard, 'I Only Have Eyes For You'. Carey continued a version of The Flamingos into the Nineties.
CAUSE: Heart attack. He died at his home in Lanham, Maryland.
FURTHER READING: Pruter, Robert. (1996). *Doowop: The Chicago Scene.* Urbana, IL: University of Illinois Press.

Zeke Carey

(EZEKIEL J. CAREY)
Born January 24, 1933
Died December 24, 1999
The bass vocalist and eldest member of early doo-wop group, The Flamingos, West Virginia-native Zeke Carey moved to Chicago in 1950 along with his cousin Jake Carey, joining the choir at a local black Jewish synagogue. Forming The Swallows (not the more famous Baltimore group) in 1951 with Johnny Carter and Paul Wilson, the group installed Earl Lewis as their lead singer. Renamed The (Five) Flamingos in 1952 after the addition of Sollie McElroy as their new lead singer, the group recorded a series of much sought-after singles on the Chance, Parrot and Checker labels. Providing some of the most elegant harmonies in the doo-wop genre, The Flamingos scored a series of regional hits with 'If I Can't Have You' and 'Golden Teardrops'. The Flamingos finally reached the national R&B charts in 1956 with the Nate Nelson-penned, 'I'll Be Home', the song also hitting the pop charts via a cover version by Pat Boone. With both Jake Carey and Johnny Carter joining the military in July 1956, the group took a break but re-formed in 1957, signing with End Records. Reinvigorated, the group returned to the R&B charts with 'Lovers Never Say Goodbye' (1959). This was their most successful period during which The Flamingos charted with the timeless ballad 'I Only Have Eyes For You' (1959), the Sam Cooke-penned 'Nobody Loves Me' (1960), and 'Mio Amore' (1960). In 1969, the group managed its only British hit with a three-year-old track, 'The Boogaloo Party'. Zeke and Jake Carey maintained The Flamingos well into the Nineties.
CAUSE: Cancer. He died at Walter Reed Army Medical Center in Washington, DC.
FURTHER READING: Pruter, Robert. (1996). *Doowop: The Chicago Scene.* Urbana, IL: University of Illinois Press.

John Carnegie

Born 1934
Died 1979
Original tenor vocalist of the early Fifties Dominoes' copy group The Checkers, John Carnegie provided the lead on their single 'Night's Curtains'. Signed with King-Federal Records, the group released a series of non-charting singles. Carnegie was drafted in early 1953 and forced to leave the group.
CAUSE: Unknown.

Karen Carpenter

(KAREN ANNE CARPENTER)
Born March 2, 1950
Died February 4, 1983
Drummer and vocalist of the soft-rock duo, The Carpenters, Karen Carpenter was born and raised in suburban New

Haven, Connecticut. A boisterous tomboy in her teen years, Karen initially studied piano before switching to drums. Moving to Downey, California, in 1964, Karen played drums in her high school band. By 1967, she had joined her brother Richard, and Wes Jacobs, in a jazz combo called The Richard Carpenter Trio. The group soon evolved into a soft Top 40 covers group, Spectrum, playing Los Angeles nightclubs. During this period both Karen and Richard attended Cal State University. Pared down to a duo in 1969 following Jacobs' departure for The Detroit Symphony, the renamed Carpenters were discovered by trumpeter Herb Alpert and signed to his A&M Record label. Their début album, *Offering*, released later in the year, featured a cover of The Beatles' 'Ticket To Ride' and would be their only commercial failure. Utilising top-notch songwriters, The Carpenters scored a string of light-rock, soft-spoken hits beginning with 'Close To You' (1970), and continuing with 'We've Only Just Begun' (1970), 'Rainy Days And Mondays' (1971), 'Sing' (1973), and 'Top Of The World' (1973). With their blend of unpretentious harmonies and heartfelt lyrics, The Carpenters were considered very unhip. Constantly on the road from 1970 with their Vegas-style act, both Karen and Richard Carpenter were in ill health by late 1975. With Karen's weight down to 80 pounds, a tour had to be cancelled. Richard, meanwhile, had become addicted to a prescription drug, Quaalude. With disco on the rise in the late Seventies, The Carpenters saw their fame diminish. In 1979 Karen began working on a solo album with producer Phil Ramone. After abandoning the project, Karen married in 1989 but the relationship didn't last, and she rejoined Richard on their comeback album, *Made In America*, landing a final hit with 'Touch Me When We're Dancing' (1981). With her health in decline, Karen Carpenter spent little time in the studio during the early Eighties. Her solo album was finally released posthumously in 1996.
CAUSE: Anorexia nervosa. Following her divorce, Karen Carpenter had been living with her mother in Downey, California. There she was found unconscious and transported to the city's Community Hospital. Initially, the cause of death was listed as a heart attack. Karen's health had been declining since 1975 as a result of a heavy touring schedule. The excessive media coverage surrounding the circumstances of her death focused attention on the eating disorder, anorexia nervosa. A CBS television movie, *The Karen Carpenter Story* (1989), presented an accurate portrayal of her long-term illness.
FURTHER READING: Garcia, Ronald. (1994). *Close To You: The Story of Richard & Karen Carpenter*. Glendale, CA: Good Reading Co. Coleman, Ray. (1994). *The Carpenters: The Untold Story*. London: Boxtree.

Eric Carr

(PAUL CARAVELLO)
Born July 12, 1950
Died November 24, 1991
The drummer for perennial, fire-breathing hard-rock group, Kiss, Brooklyn-born and raised Eric Carr was a veteran of several New York City and East Coast bar bands from the late Sixties, passing through such groups as Flasher and Mother Nature Father Time. Carr joined Kiss in 1980 as a replacement for the group's original drummer, Peter Criss, who left to pursue a solo career. Teaming with Kiss founders Gene Simmons, Paul Stanley and Ace Frehley, Carr (in fox make-up) first appeared with the band at a New York City performance at the Palladium on July 25, 1980. Carr recorded eight albums with the group, beginning with an uncharacteristic concept album *Music From The Elder* (1981), written for a planned, but

unreleased film of the same name. Carr also helped to produce that album which contained the unlikely Kiss ballad, 'World Without Heroes'. Switching to Mercury Records, and finding a new audience with the inception of MTV, Kiss reprised the confident, rocking sound of their early years on their 1983 comeback album *Lick It Up*. A video for 'Lick It Up' featured the group's first-ever make-up free appearance. Riding a new crest in heavy metal popularity, Kiss enjoyed a string of album-rock hits in the 1980s with 'Heaven's On Fire' (1984), 'Tears Are Falling' (1985), and 'Reason To Live' (1987). Carr's last album with Kiss came in 1990 with *Hot In The Shade*. Also a session player, Carr worked with Gary Moore, Black Sabbath and Alice Cooper.
CAUSE: Complications from cancer of the heart and lungs. Ultimately, he died of a cerebral haemorrhage in New York City's Bellevue hospital while in a coma. He had undergone open-heart surgery in April, 1991.

Leroy Carr
Born March 27, 1905
Died April 29, 1935
An influential self-taught Nashville-born blues pianist, Leroy Carr teamed with Scapper Blackwell in Indianapolis to form the most popular blues duo of the late Twenties and early Thirties. Signing with Vocalion Records in 1928, Carr was joined by Blackwell on a string of melancholy blues standards including 'Blues Before Sunrise', 'Hurry Down Sunshine' and his signature piece, 'How Long, How Long Blues'.
CAUSE: An alcoholic, he drank himself to death.

Robert Carr
Born c. 1938
Died May 18, 1993
Member of the New York City-based R&B duo Robert & Johnny, with Johnny Mitchell. The pair scored a minor hit in 1958 with 'We Belong Together'.
CAUSE: Unknown.

Johnny Carroll
(JOHN LEWIS CARROLL)
Born October 23, 1937
Died February 18, 1995
A rockabilly artist, Johnny Carroll scored a pair of minor hits in the late Fifties with 'Crazy Lovin'' and 'Wild Women', and appeared in the film *Rock Baby, Rock It*. The Fort Worth, Texas-native's best work is compiled on the Bear Family Records release, *Rock Baby, Rock It: 1955–1960.*
CAUSE: He died from complications from a liver transplant in Godley, Texas.

Vivian Carter
Born March 25, 1921
Died June 12, 1989
The "Vee" of Vee-Jay Records, Mississippi-born Vivian Carter launched the successful Chicago-based record R&B/soul label in 1953 with husband, Jimmy Bracken. The label had evolved from their Gary, Indiana record store, Vivian's Record Shop. Staying on top of the city's blues and R&B scene, Carter was also employed as a deejay at the time. A quick success, Vee-Jay's roster included Jimmy Reed, The Spaniels, Gene Chandler, Dee Clark, and The Impressions. Taking a pop approach in the early Sixties, Vee-Jay signed the Four Seasons, and issued The Beatles' early material when Capitol had refused. The label folded in 1966 due to a series of financial misappropriations. Carter and Bracken subsequently operated a pair of smaller labels, J.V. and Ra-Bra. Carter later operated a radio station in Gary, Indiana.
CAUSE: Complications from diabetes. She died in Gary, Indiana.

John Cascella
Born April 29, 1947
Died November 14, 1992

Keyboard and accordion player for mainstream, midwest rocker, John (Cougar) Mellencamp, John Cascella won a New York City accordion playing contest at age 11. After mastering a series of instruments during his teen years, he studied jazz with Phil Woods. Switching to rock in the mid Seventies, he joined the Faith Band, appearing on two albums, *Rock'n'Romance* and *Face To Face*. The Faith Band's sole hit came in 1978 with 'Dancin' Shoes'. Leaving the group in 1979, Cascella worked as a session player and film scorer, before launching his own production company, Cascella Music Productions. Joining John Mellencamp's band in 1984, Cascella was slowly weaned away from the keyboard to the accordion. On Mellencamp's 1987 hit, 'Paper And Fire', Cascella's frenetic accordion was coupled in a fierce exchange with the fiddle of Lisa Germano. Cascella also appeared on the Mellencamp hits, 'Small Town', 'Rain On The Scarecrow', 'R.O.C.K. In The USA.', and 'Lonely Ol' Night'. As a session player, Cascella also worked with Sue Medley, Kim Carnes and Ronna Reeves.
CAUSE: Traffic accident. He died while driving home after watching the Evander Holyfield/Riddick Bowe heavyweight World Championship. His car veered off the road into a cornfield in central Indiana. The car was later discovered by a passing motorist.

Alvin Cash

(ALVIN DE FOREST WELCH)
Born February 15, 1939
Died November 21, 1999
A Sixties R&B singer, Alvin Cash launched a minor dance craze in 1963 with 'Twine Time'. A native of St. Louis, he first hit the stage as a tap dancer in a family group with his younger brothers named The Crawlers. Hoping to land a recording contract, Cash and his brothers relocated to Chicago in 1963. Signed by One-Der-Ful Records as a solo act, Cash was teamed with a Louisville, Kentucky, group called The Nightlighters (the group was renamed The Registers by the record label). Scoring a Top 20 hit with his début release 'Twine Time', Cash capitalised on a Chicago dance craze (the single was misattributed to Alvin Cash & The Crawlers). As Alvin Cash & The Registers, he followed up with 'The Barracuda' (1965), 'The Philly Freeze' (1966), and 'Alvin's Boogaloo' (1966). In 1967, Cash released a novelty record about boxer Mohammed Ali, 'Doin' The Ali Shuffle'. Although the single attracted only moderate interest, a follow-up 'The Ali Shuffle' (1976) was a European hit. With his career in deep decline, Cash was arrested in New York City for trying to pass himself off as James Brown. Cash later appeared in several films, including the portrayal of a member of The Five Satins in *The Buddy Holly Story*.
CAUSE: Suffering from stomach ulcers, he died in his sleep at his home in Chicago.

Johnny Cash

(J.R. CASH)
Born February 26, 1932
Died September 12, 2003
Spanning rock, folk and country, Johnny Cash emerged from poverty to become a musical superstar in both the country and rock fields. Raised in a backwoods shack in rural Arkansas, Cash grew up in a hard-working, dirt-poor environment. Lacking electricity during his early childhood, Cash listened to country music on a battery-powered radio. Devastated by the industrial accidental death of older brother Jack, the event forever moulded Cash as he adopted an impermeable, unsmiling exterior. During his youth, Cash took private singing lessons and his family somehow afforded a piano. Singing an original composition, Cash won first prize at an amateur contest at age 17. During an Air Force stint in the

early Fifties, Cash was stationed in West Germany where he worked as a radio operator. Practising on his newly acquired guitar, he wrote a number of songs during this period including 'Folsom City Blues', which was inspired by the film, *Inside The Walls Of Folsom Prison*. Experimenting with lyric writing, Cash's poetry was published in the military newspaper, *Stars And Stripes*. After his discharge in 1954, Cash moved to Memphis and took a job as a salesman to support his first wife. But drawn to music, he enrolled in an evening radio announcers' course. Forming a gospel-flavoured country group, The Tennessee Three, Cash was backed by electric guitarist Luther Perkins, bassist Marshall Grant and steel guitarist, Red Kernodle. After Kernodle's departure, Cash and The Tennessee Two adopted a more rockabilly-oriented approach and in the wake of Elvis Presley's success, the group approached Sun Records. Label owner Sam Phillips was intrigued by the group's sincerity and musical simplicity. Straddling the line between rock and country, Cash unleashed a string of hits beginning in 1955 with 'Hey Porter'/'Cry! Cry! Cry!', 'Folsom Prison Blues' and 'I Walk The Line'. A pair of pop-crossover hits, 'Ballad Of A Teenage Queen' and 'Things Happen That Way', were Sun's attempts to shape the "Man in Black" into a teen idol. Singing in a dry, restrained style, Cash's deep voice and limited vocal range was augmented by Phillip's innovative production technique of using the slapback style of tape echo. With the addition of drummer, W.S. Holland, the band expanded back into The Tennessee Three. Unhappy with Sun's excessive studio production and instrumentation on his later releases, Cash joined the larger Columbia label in 1958. Veering from rock and becoming a regular on *The Grand Ole Opry*, Cash continued his hit run starting with 'Don't Take Your Guns To Town'. After spending time in the burgeoning Greenwich Village music scene, Cash scored with folk-leaning hits such as the mariachi-flavoured 'Ring Of Fire' (1963) and a cover of Bob Dylan's 'It Ain't Me Babe'. In 1967, Cash tackled his decade-long amphetamine dependency, reaching rock-bottom after his divorce, an arrest and a series of car crashes. Soon after, Cash landed an ABC variety show and he returned to the charts in a big way with the old-time country song, 'Daddy Sang Bass' (1968). Written by Carl Perkins (then a member of Cash's band), it featured the co-vocals of his soon-to-be-wife, June Carter of the Carter country-music dynasty. He followed up with his best-selling single ever, the novelty tune, 'A Boy Named Sue' (1969), extracted from the live album, *At San Quentin*. Again flirting with folk music, in 1970 Cash recorded a hit cover of Tim Hardin's 'If I Were A Carpenter'. Cash retreated to his roots in the Seventies, recording a prolific string of country and gospel albums. In 1985, after sharing the bill at a televised Christmas special, Cash formed a country supergroup with Waylon Jennings, Willie Nelson and Kris Kristofferson, scoring a smash country hit with the Jimmy Webb-penned 'Highwayman'. Winning a Grammy Award, the foursome regrouped in 1989 for a second album project. After being let go by CBS Records in 1986, Cash signed with Mercury, which tried to limit his output strictly to country music. Though his health began to wane, Cash continued recording. Signing with the Rick Rubin label American Recordings, Cash issued a series of albums which featured interpretations of numerous modern rock hits. *American Recordings IV* contained a stunning reworking of the Nine Inch Nails song, 'Hurt'; the accompanying video was nominated for an MTV award. The 2005 hit biopic *Walk The Line* starred Joaquim Phoenix as Johnny Cash and Reece Witherspoon as June Carter.

CAUSE: He died from respiratory failure as the result of complications from diabetes, just three days after he was discharged from Baptist Hospital in Nashville, where he had been admitted following an attack of pancreatitis. Cash's wife, June Carter Cash, had died in May 2003.

Leonard "Baby Doo" Caston

(LEONARD CASTON, SR.)
Born June 2, 1917
Died August 22, 1987
A prolific Mississippi-born, Chicago-based blues pianist and guitarist, Leonard "Baby Doo" Caston was taught to play guitar by his cousin Alan Weathersby. After teaching himself to play piano, Caston headed north to Chicago in 1936, first gaining fame in 1939 after teaming with former boxer Willie Dixon. The two formed The Five Breezes, a popular club band around Chicago. But with Dixon imprisoned as a conscientious objector in 1941, Caston formed a new group, the Rhythm Rascals Trio. As part of the war effort, Caston and The Rhythm Rascals Trio joined a USO tour, teamed with Alberta Hunter. Returning to Chicago in 1945, Caston joined Willie Dixon and Bernardo Dennis (later replaced by Ollie Crawford) in the legendary, Big Three Trio. Recording for several labels including Bullet and Columbia, the group landed its sole hit with 'You Sure Look Good To Me' (1948). After the group disbanded, Caston was a much in-demand session player. Also pursuing a solo career, Caston released on album on Hot Shot Records.
CAUSE: Suffering from heart disease, he underwent a triple-bypass procedure in 1982. He died at the Hennepin County Medical Center in Minneapolis.

William Cathey

Born 1937
Died January 17, 1970
Member of Billy Stewart's band, William Cathey appeared on the singer's several Sixties R&B hits including, 'I Do Love You' and a frenetic cover of George Gershwin's 'Summertime'.
CAUSE: Car crash. Experiencing brake problems, the new car that Stewart and the group were riding struck a bridge abutment and plunged into a river.

Danny Cedrone

Born 1921
Died June 18, 1954
A session guitarist who provided the solo on Bill Haley and The Comets' groundbreaking hit 'Rock Around The Clock,' Danny Cedrone had previously performed on several Bill Haley and The Saddlemen releases. Cedrone was also a member of The Esquire Boys.
CAUSE: He fell down a flight of stairs while in Philadelphia.

Eddie Chamblee

(EDWIN L. CHAMBLEE)
Born February 21, 1920
Died May 1, 1999
A Chicago-based R&B saxophonist, Eddie Chamblee worked with The (Four) Blazes, Lionel Hampton, The Four Buddies and others. Born in Atlanta but raised in Chicago, Chamblee attended school with future singing star Dinah Washington. Working as a session player at Miracles Records, Chamblee backed Sonny Thompson on a pair of R&B hits and subsequently recorded his own Top 10 R&B hit – the instrumental 'Back Street' – for the label in 1949. Chamblee later worked with Dinah Washington and was briefly her fifth husband. Settling in New York City, Chamblee performed in a number of jazz acts.
CAUSE: Natural causes. He died in a nursing home in New York City.

Chas Chandler

(BRYAN JAMES CHANDLER)
Born December 18, 1938
Died July 17, 1996

A native of Tyneside in north-east England, Chas Chandler was the bass player in The Animals though he would find greater fame as the manager and producer of Jimi Hendrix. In the early Sixties, Chandler joined the Newcastle jazz-blues trio The Alan Price Combo, led by keyboard player Price. When the charismatic Eric Burdon was brought on board in 1963 as lead vocalist, the group evolved into The Animals. The group's début studio album, *The Animals*, spawned the international hit, 'House Of The Rising Sun'. Featuring Price's bluesy organ riffs and Burdon's soaring vocal lead, the song – reportedly recorded live in the studio in just 20 minutes – was initially considered far too long for a single by both the group's producer and record company, but it rapidly rose to number 1 in both the US and UK. A first wave British Invasion group, The Animals enjoyed a string of hits with 'We Gotta Get Out Of This Place' (1965), a cover of Sam Cooke's 'Bring It On Home To Me' (1965), 'It's My Life' (1965), and 'Don't Bring Me Down' (1966). But with members squabbling and abusing drugs, The Animals began disintegrating. Following Chandler's departure in 1967, the group was subsequently known as Eric Burdon and The Animals. Setting his sights on rock management, Chandler discovered Jimi Hendrix playing in a bar in New York's Greenwhich Village. Taking the unknown virtuoso guitarist to England, Chandler teamed Hendrix with two British musicians, Noel Redding and Mitch Mitchell, to form The Jimi Hendrix Experience. Chandler also produced the first two Hendrix albums, *Are You Experienced?* and *Axis: Bold As Love*. Following Hendrix's untimely death, Chandler then managed the Wolverhampton, England-based Slade, who enjoyed a string of UK hits in the early Seventies. Over the years, the original Animals attempted a number of ill-fated reconciliations. Brief reunions in 1968 and 1977 fared poorly due to battling egos. In 1982, a reconstituted group minus Burdon began touring as The Animals. Chandler, who hadn't played the bass in almost two decades, had to relearn the instrument. A 1983 reunion album and tour ended with onstage physical brawls. Chandler sold most of his musical interests in 1982 and returned to the north eastern coastal town of Cullercoats, semi-retired from music. Although outspoken, Chandler was a much respected and loved figure in the UK music industry. His last project was the building of a large rock venue in Newcastle.

CAUSE: Heart attack.

FURTHER READING: Burdon, Eric. (1986). *I Used To Be An Animal.* Boston: Faber and Faber. Blackford, Andy. (1986). *Wild Animals: The Story Of The Animals*. London: Sidgwick & Jackson.

Kermit Chandler

Born October 27, 1945
Died February 22, 1981

Guitarist of the early Sixties soul group, The Sheppards, Kermit Chandler later worked as a session player, playing guitar on recordings for The Dells and Gene Chandler.

CAUSE: Unknown. He had been ill for some time.

Herman "Sunny" Chaney

Born February 16, 1939
Died January 29, 1989

Lead singer of the Fifties doo-wop group The Jaguars, Herman "Sunny" Chaney was born and raised in Dallas, Texas. Moving to Los Angeles as a teenager, Chaney formed a vocal doo-wop quartet with classmates from the choir at Freemont High School. First calling themselves The Miracles, then The Shadows, the group settled on The Jaguars. A then-rare interracial group, they featured Chaney on lead vocals, and included tenor Val Poliuto, baritone Manuel Chavez and bass

vocalist Charlie Middleton. Signed to R-Dell Records, The Jaguars scored their only national hit in 1956 with an updated version of the Jerome Kern composition, 'The Way You Look Tonight', recorded in 1936 by Fred Astaire. After spending a year as The Velvetones, The Jaguars scored a double-sided regional hit with 'Look Into My Eyes'/'Thinking Of You' (1959), joined by new bass vocalist, Richard Berry. The group disbanded shortly thereafter and Chaney entered the military. Chaney worked with a number of other R&B vocal groups in the Fifties and Sixties including The Robins, The Coasters, and Don Julian's Larks. Drafted in 1966, Chaney left music for several years. Later reuniting The Jaguars of the oldies circuit, Chaney retired in the early Eighties, blind from diabetes. The group reunited for a time in 1987.
CAUSE: Complications from diabetes. He died in Culver City, California.

Andy Chapin

Born February 7, 1952
Died December 31, 1985
A member of a latter version of Steppenwolf in the mid Seventies, Andy Chapin was later a keyboard player in Ricky Nelson's back-up group, The Stone Canyon Band.
CAUSE: He died of burns and smoke inhalation resulting from an on-board fire in the passenger compartment of a DC-3 plane, near Dekalb, Texas. Also killed were Ricky Nelson and six others. The plane was en route from Guttersville, Alabama to Dallas for half-time festivities at the Cotton Bowl. His widow Lisa Jane Chapin, later sued two aviation companies for wrongful death.

Harry Chapin

(HARRY FORSTER CHAPIN)
Born December 7, 1942
Died July 16, 1981
A popular folk-rock singer, songwriter and charity worker, Harry Chapin was born and raised in Greenwich Village. Encouraged by his father Jim, a drummer for both Tommy Dorsey and Woody Herman, the younger Chapin began on the trumpet before switching to the guitar. In 1964 Chapin joined a group with his father and brothers Steve and Tom, called The Chapin Family, releasing one album, *Chapin Music*. But while training in the Air Force Academy, Chapin was drawn to folk music. After a stint as an architecture major at Cornell University, Chapin left to work in film, producing the Academy Award nominee, and New York Film Festival winner, *Legendary Champions* (1969). Signing with Elektra Records in 1972, the folk-rock styled Chapin scored a pair of Top 10 singles 'Taxi' (1972) and 'Cat's In The Cradle' (1974), both melancholy story songs. Embraced as a folk troubadour, Chapin enjoyed hit albums such as *Heads & Tails* (1972) and *Verities And Balderdash* (1974). Turning his attention to the stage, Chapin wrote and starred in the 1975 Broadway musical, *The Night That Made America Famous*, the production earning two Tony nominations. Remaining a popular concert draw but landing little airplay in the late Seventies, Chapin reaped a pair of gold-certified albums, *Greatest Story: Live* (1976) and *Dance Band On The Titanic*. Signing to Boardwalk Records in 1980, Chapin landed his final Top 40 hit with a sequel to his 1972 hit 'Taxi', which was appropriately titled 'Sequel'. A political activist, much of Chapin's energy and income went to causes such as human rights and arts funding. He was also an active member of President Jimmy Carter's commission on world hunger.
CAUSE: He died in an auto accident on a six-lane Long Island Expressway bridge near Jericho, New York, en route to New York City. Chapin's 1975 Volkswagon Rabbit was struck from the rear by a longbed truck. The truck's driver pulled Chapin out of

the blazing car. The coroner originally ruled that Chapin died of a heart attack but changed the cause to massive blood loss. It was not certain whether Chapin had a heart attack before or after the crash. Chapin was driving on a suspended driver's licence. Later that day, Chapin was scheduled to have given a free concert at Long Island's Eisenhower Park. Not knowing of the singer's fate, thousands of fans showed up expecting a performance.
FURTHER READING: Coan, Peter M. (1990). *Taxi: The Harry Chapin Story*. New York: Carol.

Charlie Charles

(HUGH GLENN MORTIMER CHARLES)
Born 1945
Died September 5, 1990
Drummer for the British rock group, Ian Dury & The Blockheads, the Guyana-born Charlie Charles emigrated to England in 1959. After serving in the British Army for six years, he formed a touring rock band in 1970 called No Sweat. Returning to London in 1972, he passed through a series of rock bands and worked as a session drummer behind acts such as Lulu, Elkie Brooks and Arthur Conley. Joining a group called Loving Awareness in 1975, Charles recorded the critically acclaimed album *Loving Awareness* the following year. In 1977, Charles was a founding member of Ian Dury & The Blockheads, the group achieved instant fame with their début album, *New Boots And Panties*. Garnering little airplay in the US except for 'Sex And Drugs And Rock And Roll' and 'Hit Me With Your Rhythm Stick', The Blockheads were major British stars with hits such as 'What A Waste', 'Reasons To Be Cheerful', and 'I Want To Be Straight'. Charles also pursued several side projects including his own group, Multi Pleasure Music, for which he also sang lead vocals.
CAUSE: Cancer. He died in London.

Don Charles

(WALTER STANLEY SCUFFHAM)
Born December 10, 1933
Died December 4, 2005
A British pop singer, Don Charles scored a minor UK hit in 1962 with the Joe Meek-produced remake of John Leyton's 'Walk With Me My Angel'. Signed by George Martin to EMI's Parlophone subsidiary, Charles had no further hits. He later operated a nightclub in Malta with Rolf Harris.
CAUSE: Unknown. He died in Herstmonceux, East Sussex.

Mark Charron

Born 1944
Died June 17, 1994
Songwriter who penned hits for the Partridge Family, Bill Anderson, and the Vogues, Mark Charron also wrote the B.J. Thomas hits 'Billy And Sue' and 'Mama'.
CAUSE: Unknown. He died in Nashville.

Bill Chase

(WILLIAM EDWARD CHIAIESE)
Born October 20, 1934
Died August 9, 1974
Leader and trumpeter of the jazz-rock group, Chase, Bill Chase studied trumpet at the Berklee College of Music in the mid Fifties. After a several-year stint in Woody Herman's group in the early Sixties, Chase joined The Thundering Herd. Forming a nine-man group in 1970 called Chase, he attracted the attention of Epic Records. A pioneering jazz-rock fusion band, Chase recorded three albums, *Chase* (1971), *Ennea* (1972), and *Pure Music* (1974). The group's only Top 40 single came in 1971 with 'Get It On'. Follow-up releases, 'So Many People' (1971), and a song recorded by Rod Stewart in 1969, 'Handbags And Gladrags' (1971), were only minor hits.
CAUSE: Bill Chase died in an aeroplane crash in a Minnesota soybean field en route from Chicago. The accident also

killed three backing members of his revamped band: drummer Walt Clark, guitarist John Emma, and organ player Wally Yohn. Both pilots of the twin-engine Comanche also perished. The five other members of Chase were not on board.

Brandon Chase

(Alan Gary Zekley)
Born January 4, 1943
Died June 26, 1996
Songwriter who penned The Grass Roots' hits, 'Sooner Or Later' and 'Wait A Million Years', Brandon Chase was also a member of the rock group, Yellow Balloon.
Cause: Heart attack. He died at his home in Marina del Rey, California.

Clifton Chenier

Born June 25, 1925
Died December 12, 1987
Self-taught, Grammy-winning, accordion player nicknamed the King of Zydeco, Clifton Chenier had been in the forefront of the genre since the early Fifties, releasing his début single in 1954, 'Clifton Blues'. Signing with Specialty Records the following year, he recorded his finest work, the tracks compiled on the album, *Bayou Boogie*. With his squeezebox accordion, the gritty-voiced Chenier, became a star in the Seventies in the US, and then across Europe. He retired from music in the early Eighties.
Cause: Kidney failure and complications from diabetes. He died at Lafayette General Hospital in Louisiana.

Leonard Chess

(Lazer Shmuel Chez)
Born March 12, 1917
Died October 16, 1969
A Soviet-Jewish immigrant, Leonard Chess had settled in Chicago's predominantly black South side in 1928. By the mid Forties, Leonard and his younger brother Phil operated several nightclubs including their flagship venue, The Macomba, which booked blues and jazz acts. Unable to fully stock their jukeboxes with jazz and blues records, the Chess brothers were forced to start their own label, Aristocrat Records, in 1947, landing their first major hit in 1948 with Muddy Waters' groundbreaking '(I Feel Like) Going Home'. In order to concentrate on the growing record company, Leonard Chess abdicated control of the nightclubs to his brother Phil. In 1950, the Chess brothers landed their first hit on their renamed Chess label with the Gene Ammons release, 'My Foolish Heart'. Largely ignorant about blues music, Leonard Chess hired blues bassist Willie Dixon as the house musical director, and within a few years, Chess had emerged as the country's leading blues label, its roster boasting stars such as Muddy Waters, Howlin' Wolf and Little Walter. By 1955, Chess expanded into rock'n'roll with a pair of trailblazing, electric guitar-rooted artists, Bo Diddley and Chuck Berry. With blues falling out of popularity in the black community, Chess Records experienced a downturn in the late Fifties. Hiring former King-Federal Records producer Ralph Bass and songwriter and A&R-man Billy Davis in the early Sixties, Chess emerged as a soul-based label with new signings, Etta James, Billy Stewart, and The Dells. With the rise of blues among white college students in the late Sixties, Chess experienced a boom with much of its early material repackaged on LPs, but with the sale of Chess to General Recorded Tape (GRT) in 1969, the label lost its focus. After Leonard Chess' death later that year, his son Marshall was named president. Chess was closed in 1975, with MCA Records acquiring the 25,000 title Chess catalogue ten years later.
Cause: Heart attack. He died in Chicago.

Bobby Chouinard

Born June 23, 1953
Died March 8, 1997
A prolific drummer, Massachusetts-born Bobby Chouinard launched his professional career in his mid teens, joining a series of groups before landing in a neo-rockabilly band led by Robert Gordon. Later joining Billy Squier's hard rock group in the late Seventies, Chouinard appeared on the hard-rock anthems 'Everybody Wants You', 'In The Dark', and 'The Stroke'. A popular session player, Chouinard also worked with Cher, Peter Wolf, Chuck Berry, Alice Cooper, and Ted Nugent. Chouinard was later a member of Duke and The Drivers, and in the second line-up of the rock group TKO.
CAUSE: Massive heart attack. He died in New York City.

Arlester "Dyke" Christian

Born June 13, 1943
Died March 1971
R&B performer who headed the late Sixties group Dyke & The Blazers, Arlester "Dyke" Christian was born in Brooklyn, but raised in Niagara Falls and Buffalo. After dropping out of high school, he began hanging around nightclub musicians. Although an inexperienced bassist, in 1960 Christian joined a local quartet called Carl LaRue and His Crew. At first, the musically inept Christian played only a small part in the LaRue's keyboard-heavy band. Becoming a big draw in northwestern New York state with their gritty soul and danceable R&B sound, the youthful group caught the attention of The O'Jays in 1964. Soon, Carl LaRue and His Crew toured with The O'Jays as both their backing group and as a separate, opening act. But after relocating to Phoenix in 1965, Carl LaRue and His Crew disintegrated. Then along with former bandmate Alvester Jacobs, Christian formed his own band, Dyke and The Blazers. A hard-edged soul outfit, the group scored its first hit with the self-penned, gritty but sensual, soul classic, 'Funky Broadway, Pt. 1 & 2'. Featuring Christian on bass and lead vocals, the single was first released by the tiny Artco Records. Reissued on the larger Art Laboe's Original Sound label in early 1967, it hit the national charts, though it was eclipsed by Wilson Pickett's gritty cover version. The first chart hit to include the word "funky" in its title, the song was banned by a number of radio stations. After losing most of his backing group over a financial dispute, Christian returned to Buffalo where he formed a new version of The Blazers. The group's chart-run continued with the Christian-penned, hard-R&B hits 'We Got More Soul' (1969), 'Let A Woman Be A Woman – Let A Man Be A Man' (1969), 'Uhh' (1970) and 'Runaway People' (1970). But with new money problems, Christian was abandoned by his new group. In early 1971, Christian was set to record again with Barry White as the producer.
CAUSE: He was shot to death outside a bar in Phoenix, in a dangerous part of town. The perpetrator was set free after a jury ruled that he had acted in self-defence.

Charlie Christian

Born July 29, 1916
Died March 2, 1942
Revolutionary jazz guitarist who popularised the electric guitar in that field, Texas-born Charlie Christian mastered several instruments in his teens including the trumpet, piano, bass, and guitar. Making Oklahoma City his home in the Thirties, Christian initially played a mixture of Texas blues and jazz. After stints in his brother's band, The Jolly Jugglers, and then The Anna Mae Winburn Band, Christian formed his own quartet in 1937. Discovered playing the guitar in a pool hall by Count Basie's guitarist, Eddie Durham, Christian received a series of lessons. Recommended by producer John Hammond, Christian

joined the Benny Goodman Orchestra in 1939, after outplaying the bandleader in an impromptu on-stage contest. Often joined in the studio by jazz masters such as Cootie Williams and Count Basie, Christian made only a limited number of recordings including his co-composition, 'Flying Home' and 'Solo Flight'. With his unmatched, improvised guitar solos, Christian would expand the role of the guitar in jazz music. Diagnosed with tuberculosis in 1941, he was confined to Bellevue Hospital in New York.
CAUSE: Succumbing to tuberculosis, he died at the Seaview Sanitorium in Staten Island. Benny Goodman paid all of his medical bills.

Miss Christine

(CHRISTINE FRKA)
Born 1950
Died November 5, 1972
Member of Frank Zappa protégé rock group and groupie quintet, The GTOs (short for, among other things, Girls Together Outrageously), "Miss Christine" was a native of San Pedro, California. The GTOs emerged out of a small circle of young women who cavorted with visiting rock stars in Los Angeles. The GTOs toured with Zappa and his Mothers Of Invention as stage dancers, and recorded a sole album, the Zappa produced *Permanent Damage*, before disbanding in late 1969. Miss Christine also appeared on the cover of Zappa's LP, *Hot Rats*, and frequently baby-sat Zappa's daughter Moon Unit. She also dated both Todd Rundgren and Albert Grossman and was name-checked in The Flying Burrito Brothers' 'Christine's Tune (Devil In Disguise)'. Fellow GTOs member "Miss Pamela" (Pamela Miller) later wrote the groupie autobiography, *I'm With The Band*, under her married name, Pamela Des Barres.
CAUSE: She overdosed in a Boston hotel room on prescription painkillers that she was taking following treatment to repair her curved spine.

Lew Chudd

(LEWIS R. CHUDD)
Born July 1, 1911
Died June 15, 1998
The founder of Imperial Records, Toronto-born Lew Chudd broke into the music industry as a promotions man in the Thirties, hyping the big bands of the day. Joining NBC radio by the mid Thirties, Chudd developed a popular radio programme starring Benny Goodman. Promoted to the head of NBC's Los Angeles Bureau, Chudd also worked for the Office of War Information where he produced Armed Forces Radio programmes. After launching and then selling Crown Records in the mid Forties, he established the pioneering Los Angeles-based R&B label Imperial Records, originally targeting folk and Mexican music. Soon embracing R&B and rock'n'roll, Imperial was responsible for the rise of Little Richard, Fats Domino, Smiley Lewis and Ricky Nelson. With intuitive producers and A&R men such as Henri Rene and Al Young, Imperial was a dominant player in the Fifties. Chudd also ran a satellite operation in New Orleans, with producer Dave Bartholomew overseeing sessions at the tiny J&M studio. Eventually crowded out by the major labels, Chudd sold Imperial to Liberty Records in 1963, and retired from music. Chudd later purchased several radio stations.
CAUSE: Heart failure. He died in Los Angeles.

Eugene Church

Born January 23, 1938
Died April 16, 1993
A talented singer who had successes in both the doo-wop and soul fields, Eugene Church was raised in St. Louis. Relocating to Los Angeles, Church became enthralled by vocal harmony groups such as The Clovers and The Drifters. Meeting his idol, singer and songwriter Jesse Belvin at a recording session for Church's cousin Mel

Williams, Church and Belvin immediately struck up a friendship. Forming the studio group The Cliques, Church and Belvin enjoyed a doo-wop hit with 'Girl Of My Dreams' (1956). Often in collaboration with Belvin, Church wrote or appeared on dozens of hits in the late Fifties, many of them at clandestine sessions for competing labels under a variety of names. Blessed with good looks and a smooth baritone voice, Church also pursued a solo career beginning in 1957. Backed by Jessie Bevin and Turks members Alex and Gaynell Hodge, Church scored his first solo hit with 'Open Up Your Heart' (1957) on Specialty Records. Aided by Bobby Day in signing with Class Records, Church scored his first crossover hit with 'Pretty Girls Everywhere' (1958) as Eugene Church & the Fellows. A follow-up release, the thematically similar 'Miami' (1959), hit the R&B charts. Signing with King Records in 1961, Church released several singles, most noteworthy was 'Mind Your Own Business' (1961). But unfortunately for Church, Syd Nathan's King label was experiencing a decline during this period. Church last recorded for the World Pacific label in 1967. Leaving music in 1970, he became wealthy operating a chain of hair salons. Inspired by Lou Rawls, he returned to music in 1981 and recorded gospel music on his own Church label. Church toured on the oldies circuit until shortly before his death.

CAUSE: AIDS-related cancer. He died in Los Angeles.

Savannah Churchill

(SAVANNAH VALENTINE)

Born August 21, 1920

Died April 19, 1974

Trained as a violinist, the Louisiana-born Savannah Churchill was forced into a singing career to support her children after the car-crash death of her husband in 1941. After recording with Benny Carter in 1942, she toured with Nat "King" Cole and Hoagy Carmichael. Pursuing a solo career, she adopted an early R&B vocal style with her deep voice, scoring several hits including 'Daddy Daddy' (1945), the smash, 'I Want To Be Loved By You' (1947), and 'Time Out For Tears' (1948). Severely injured in a bizarre theatre accident in 1956 when a drunken man fell on top of her from a balcony, Churchill suffered a broken pelvis. While hospitalised, she was diagnosed with cancer. By the time she returned to the stage in the late Fifties, her torch ballad style had fallen out of vogue.

CAUSE: Pneumonia.

John Cipollina

Born August 24, 1943

Died May 29, 1989

Prolific studio musician and founding member of early "San Francisco Sound" band Quicksilver Messenger Service, John Cipollina was a former child virtuoso, trained on the piano since age two. Moving to classical guitar in his teens, his allegiance switched to rock'n'roll guitar at age 16 after hearing Mickey & Sylvia's guitar-oriented hit, 'Love Is Strange'. Living on a houseboat in coastal Sausalito, California, Cipollina formed a pair of local Top 40 covers groups in 1960, Penetrator, and then, The Deacons. The Deacons took a psychedelic turn in 1964 when Cipollina hired a popular local singer Dino Valenti. Practising heavily with the then-unnamed group, Valenti was jailed on a drug charge before the group had made its stage début. Influenced by a pioneering San Francisco rock troupe The Charlatans, the renamed Quicksilver Messenger Service came to define the new sub-genre of "acid rock". Playing self-designed guitars, Cipollina employed complex, rhythm-heavy arrangements within a hard-rock framework. Hitting the stage in late 1965, QMS was an immediate sensation, soon playing alongside

Jefferson Airplane, Big Brother & The Holding Company, and an early version of The Grateful Dead. Rejecting offers from several major labels, the anti-establishment QMS was already making plenty of money and feared losing artistic freedom. Finally signing with Capitol Records, QMS remained an outlaw group. Although landing hit albums with *Quicksilver Messenger Service* (1968) and *Happy Trails* (1969), the group managed little radio airplay. Cipollina left QMS in 1970 during the sessions for *Just For Love* after a dispute with the returning Dino Valenti. From this album, the group would score its biggest hit with 'Fresh Air'. In all, Cipollina played on five QMS albums as well as on a mid Seventies reunion. Intending to produce an album for Jim Murray, Cipollina instead turned the sessions into his new band, Copperhead. But after signing a lucrative deal with Columbia Records in 1973, the group disbanded after one album. Cipollina later joined Terry & The Pirates, Raven, and the Welsh group Man who were heavily influenced by QMS. Plagued with health problems, Cipollina would often perform in a wheelchair. Cipollina's brother, Mario, is the bass player in Huey Lewis & the News.
CAUSE: Chronic Asthma. Diagnosed with emphysema in 1988, Cipollina was hospitalised for several months. His condition was aggravated by his heavy smoking and by his performances in cigarette-smoke filled venues. He often performed wheelchair bound or on crutches. He died in San Francisco's Marin General Hospital after being admitted for a severe asthma attack.

Dee Clark

(DELECTAS CLARK, JR.)
Born November 7, 1938
Died December 7, 1990
Chicago pop and R&B tenor vocalist Delectas "Dee" Clark was born in Blytheville, Arkansas, but moved to Chicago at age three. Teaming at age 13 with Sammy McGrier and Ronny Strong in 1951, Clark joined a juba trio called The Hambone Kids. Backed by The Red Saunders Orchestra, The Hambone Kids scored a novelty hit with 'Hambone', which was based on a rhyming children's game and consisted of slapping out a rhythm on their thighs, sides and mouths. The song inspired a dance, and a new "Hambone" beat later popularised as the "Bo Diddley beat". While attending Chicago's Marshall High, Clark joined a vocal group which evolved into The Kool Gents, the name taken from the nickname of local deejay Herb Kent who aided the group. Clark was the group's chief (uncredited) songwriter, and later on, shared lead vocal duties. The Kool Gents recorded for Vee-Jay Records, and scored a minor hit as The Delegates with a novelty number, 'The Convention'. Clark went solo in 1957, scoring his first hit in 1958 with the self-penned, 'Nobody But You'. He followed with 'Just Keep It Up' (1959), his first pop-crossover hit, 'Hey Little Girl' (1960), and a Doris Troy composition, 'How About That' (1960). Returning to Vee-Jay, he scored several hits including the gut wrenching smash 'Raindrops' (1961). Leaving Vee-Jay, Clark focused on songwriting, co-writing the Dovells' hit, 'You Can't Sit Down' (1963). He also recorded on Constellation Records (where Gene Chandler was a labelmate) scoring moderate R&B hits with 'Warm Summer Breezes' (1964) and 'TCB' (1965). With Constellation closing in 1966, Clark would drift from label to label. At the time of his death, he was planning to record an album with his brother.
CAUSE: He suffered a heart attack at a Knights Inn motel in Smyrna, Georgia. His death could not have come at a more tragic time since he had successfully fought back from a

debilitating heart attack in July of 1987. Although warned not to perform by his doctors, he did so anyway. At the time of his death, he was on his way to California to appear on the syndicated television programme, *Star Search.*

Gene Clark

(HAROLD EUGENE CLARK)
Born November 17, 1944
Died May 24, 1991
Composer, singer and co-founder of the pioneering Californian group, The Byrds, Clark was born in Bonner Springs, Kansas, and raised in Tipton, Missouri. After playing in several local groups, Clark was discovered by Randy Sparks and inducted into the hit folk group The New Christy Minstrels during early 1963. After brief contributions to the albums *Merry Christmas* and *Land Of Giants*, he moved to Los Angeles, where he met singer/songwriters Jim McGuinn and David Crosby at the Troubadour. Together, they formed a trio, the Jet Set, which evolved into The Byrds with the arrival of drummer Michael Clarke and Chris Hillman. After signing to CBS Records, the group hit number 1 in the summer of 1965 with 'Mr Tambourine Man'. Other hits followed that year: 'All I Really Want To Do' and another US number 1, 'Turn! Turn! Turn!' Clark was the most prominent writer in the group, composing the bulk of the songs on their first two albums, including many tales of fractured love such as 'Feel A Whole Lot Better', 'Here Without You', 'You Won't Have To Cry', 'The World Turns All Around Her' and 'Set You Free This Time'. A fear of flying, exacerbated by tensions within the group, prompted his shock departure in March 1966, just after the release of the groundbreaking 'Eight Miles High', one of the best singles of the decade. It is generally accepted that Clark wrote the lion's share of that song, which was completed by contributions from McGuinn and Crosby. Clark's solo career was erratic but fascinating and punctuated with moments of brilliance. His first solo album, *Gene Clark & The Gosdin Brothers*, included the superb single 'Echoes', an innovative work that failed to chart. In the late Sixties, he recorded two groundbreaking albums for A&M with Doug Dillard (as Dillard & Clark), which helped kickstart the country rock explosion. In 1971, he issued his second solo album, *White Light*, a highly accomplished work. A third solo album, produced by Terry Melcher, was abandoned, but a work-in-progress effort was subsequently issued on A&M Holland as *Roadmaster.* Meanwhile, the original Byrds reformed for a one-off album on Asylum Records, which was again dominated by Clark's vocal and songwriting contributions. Staying with Asylum, Clark recorded the startling *No Other* (1974), one of the most ambitious albums of its era and subsequently a cult classic. A continued reluctance to tour blighted Clark's progress as a soloist and his last major label recording alone appeared in 1976 on RSO as *Two Sides To Every Story.* He then rejoined his former colleagues in McGuinn, Clark & Hillman, who toured the world and issued two albums before foundering at the end of the Seventies. Thereafter, Clark was reduced to recording for small labels and issued only two more albums in his lifetime, *Firebyrd* and *So Rebellious A Lover*, a duet album with Carla Olson. A few months before his death, he rejoined the original Byrds onstage for their induction into the Rock 'n' Roll Hall of Fame.
CAUSE: Heart attack. Clark was found unconscious at his home in Sherman Oaks, California. He had been a drug user and extremely heavy drinker for many years and had previously undergone a stomach operation. It is thought he had also developed an aneurysm.
FURTHER READING: Rogan, Johnny. (1997). *The Byrds: Timeless Flight*

Revisited – The Sequel. London: Rogan House.

Steve Clark

(STEPHEN MAYNARD CLARK)
Born April 23, 1960
Died January 8, 1991
Guitarist and founding member of the successful, 1980s heavy-metal rock band Def Leppard, Steve Clark was born in suburban Sheffield, England. Receiving his first guitar at age 10, he took lessons in classical guitar beginning at age 14. Briefly attending Stannington College, Clark was asked by Pete Willis to join Def Leppard. With his good looks, long blond hair, and strong musical skills, Clark was a perfect addition to the Joe Elliot-headed group. Financed by the members' families, a 1979 3-track EP, *Getcha Rocks Off*, led to a contract with Phonogram's Vertigo label. From their début 1980 album, *On Through The Night*, Def Leppard landed British airplay with the singles 'Wasted' and 'Hello America'. But with AC/DC producer Robert "Mutt" Lange at the controls, Def Leppard's 1981 release, *High'n'Dry* began a string of US successes, the album highlighted by the AOR smash, 'Bringin' On The Heartache'. The follow-up album *Pyromania* (1983) was embraced by MTV, selling seven-million copies, and spawning the hits 'Photograph', 'Foolin'', and 'Rock Of Ages'. The group's massive success soon spawned a new wave of British heavy metal, "hair" groups. But tragedy struck the group on December 31, 1984, when their drummer Rick Allen lost an arm in an auto accident. After a three year hiatus, Def Leppard released their best-selling album to date with *Hysteria* (1987), dominating rock radio for the next two years with several hit tracks including, 'Animal', 'Pour Some Sugar on Me', 'Love Bites' and 'Rocket'. The group was working on a new album at the time of Clark's death.
CAUSE: Clark died in his sleep at his London apartment after attending a drinking party the night before. He died from a lethal mixture of alcohol, barbiturates, and anti-depressant drugs. He was found by his girlfriend. Clark was replaced in the group by Vivian Campbell, formerly of the groups Dio and Whitesnake.
FURTHER READING: Dickson, Dave. (1995). *Biographize: The Def Leppard Story*. London: Sidgwick & Jackson.

Michael Clarke

(MICHAEL JAMES DICK)
Born June 3, 1946
Died December 19, 1993
Drummer for Sixties rock group The Byrds during their heyday, Clarke was born in Spokane, Washington. At the age of 16, he journeyed to San Francisco, occasionally playing congas and bongos in coffee houses. After meeting both Jim McGuinn and David Crosby on his travels, he moved to Hollywood, teaming up with the duo and Gene Clark, who had recently formed The Jet Set. Michael changed his name from Dick to Clarke and joined the group as their drummer, initially playing on cardboard boxes until he could afford a drum kit. The group eventually found a fifth member, bassist Chris Hillman and evolved into The Byrds, finding instant success with the chart-topping 'Mr Tambourine Man' in the summer of 1965. Clarke proved an instant teen idol and sex symbol in the group. Nicknamed "the champion of 4/4" he played on all their big hits after 'Mr Tambourine Man', including 'All I Really Want To Do', 'Turn! Turn! Turn!', 'Eight Miles High', 'So You Want To Be A Rock 'n' Roll Star' and 'My Back Pages'. His chunky playing was evident on the excellent 'The Bells Of Rhymney' and the funky 'Captain Soul', which he largely wrote himself. By the time of their fourth album, *The Notorious Byrd Brothers*, Clarke was losing interest in the group, who were undergoing various internal problems. He

nevertheless named and co-wrote one of the best songs on that album, the anti-drug anthem 'Artificial Energy'. Leaving the Byrds in late 1967, Clarke subsequently teamed up with former colleague Gene Clark on Dillard & Clark's first album and later joined Chris Hillman in The Flying Burrito Brothers, appearing on their second and third albums. After they split, he briefly reconvened with The Byrds for their reunion album, released in 1973. A born hedonist and optimist, Clarke usually managed to fall on his feet and ended the Seventies as the most commercially successful member of the group and the only one with a major record contract to his name, courtesy of Firefall. The latter enjoyed six Top 40 hits, but fell apart in the Eighties. By this time, Clarke was heavily into drink and, to a lesser extent, drugs and squandered most of his money. For a time, he took up painting in earnest and several of his watercolours were later included in the book *Musicians As Artists*. He worked with Jerry Jeff Walker, then rejoined Gene Clark in a series of Byrds tribute gigs in the mid Eighties, before touring under the group name in his own right. In 1989, McGuinn, Crosby and Hillman took legal proceedings to try and copyright The Byrds name for themselves, but the judge ruled in favour of Clarke, who continued to use the name up until his death.
CAUSE: Liver failure, resulting from alcohol abuse. He died at his home in Treasure Island, Florida. Even his ashes were the subject of dispute and were distributed between his mother and estranged wife.
FURTHER READING: Rogan, Johnny. (1997). *The Byrds: Timeless Flight Revisited – The Sequel*. London: Rogan House.

Tony Clarke

Born c. 1944
Died 1970
New York City-born Sixties soul singer, Tony Clarke scored his biggest hit with the Chess Records release 'The Entertainer' (1965). Also a songwriter, he penned the Etta James hits 'Pushover' and 'Two Sides To Every Story'.
CAUSE: Unknown.

Tom Clay

(THOMAS CLAYQUE)
Born August 20, 1929
Died November 11, 1995
Buffalo, New York-native Tom Clay was a notable Los Angeles deejay when he scored an unlikely hit in 1971 with a musically overdubbed montage of speeches by Martin Luther King and John and Bobby Kennedy, titled 'What The World Needs Now Is Love'/ 'Abraham, Martin And John'. His previous radio nickname was Guy King.
CAUSE: Cancer. He died at St. Joseph's Hospital in Burbank, California.

Josh Clayton-Felt

Born May 18, 1967
Died January 19, 2000
The lead singer and backing guitarist of Nineties alternative-rock band School Of Fish, Josh Clayton-Felt was drawn into music by his stepfather, folk musician Henry Felt. Raised in Boston, he quit college and moved to Los Angeles in 1988. After a brief stint in Francis X and The Bushmen, Clayton-Felt and guitarist Michael Ward left the group to form a duo, employing a drum machine for percussion. Expanding in 1989 into a quartet called School Of Fish, the guitar-oriented outfit enjoyed a major alternative-rock hit with the psychedelic styled 'Three Strange Days', culled from their 1991 self-titled début album. Clayton-Felt disbanded the group in 1993 as he was unhappy with the confines of alternative rock. Embarking on a solo career in 1994, he recorded a self-released album and was subsequently signed by A&M who in 1996 released the folk-leaning *Inarticulate Nature Boy*, on which

Clayton-Felt played all of the instruments. Opening up for Tori Amos and Jewel, he also provided session guitar work on the Jewel album, *Spirit*. Recording a second studio album over a three-year period, Clayton-Felt was dropped by A&M when the label was sold, and was told that the project would be shelved. The album, *Invisible Tree*, was posthumously released.
CAUSE: Diagnosed with inoperable testicular cancer in December 1999, he died one month later at the UCLA Medical Center in Los Angeles.

Alfred W. Cleveland

Born March 11, 1930
Died August 14, 1996
Pittsburgh-born staff lyricist at Motown, Alfred W. Cleveland penned 'I Second That Emotion', 'Holy, Holy', and inspired by the Detroit riots, 'What's Going On' Cleveland was hired by Motown after a chance meeting with the label's vice-president and star act, Smokey Robinson. After leaving Motown in the mid Eighties, Cleveland turned to production work. Cleveland began in music as a member of the New York City doo-wop group, the Halos, which had scored a hit with the novelty-styled, 'Nag'. After the group sang back-up on the Curtis Lee hit, 'Pretty Little Angel Eyes', Cleveland later sang on hits behind Gene Pitney and Bobby Vinton.
CAUSE: Long-term heart disease. He died in Las Vegas.

Rev. James Cleveland

Born December 5, 1931
Died February 9, 1991
Popular gospel singer and choir leader who reinvigorated the genre in the Sixties, the Rev. James Cleveland was the founding pastor at the Cornerstone Institutional Baptist Church in Los Angeles. A native of Chicago, he had learned his craft under the tutelage of gospel pioneer Thomas A. Dorsey. Invited to Detroit by the charismatic Rev. C.L. Franklin in 1949, Cleveland directed the choir at Franklin's New Baptist Church and frequently tutored Franklin's young daughter, the future Queen of Soul, Aretha Franklin. A three-time Grammy winner, the Chicago-born baritone singer was responsible for the return in popularity of gospel choirs in the Sixties after a decade when only gospel quartets were in fashion. A prolific composer and recording act, Cleveland is best known for his powerful performances of 'Peace Be Still' and 'I Stood On The Banks Of The Jordan'. His stature in gospel music was solidified when in 1968 he established the annual Gospel Music Workshop of America.
CAUSE: Heart and respiratory problems. He died in Culver City, California.

Patsy Cline

(VIRGINIA PATTERSON HENSLEY)
Born September 8, 1932
Died March 5, 1963
A country and pop crossover singer who remained popular decades after her death, Virginia native Patsy Cline began in showbusiness as a child dancer in talent contests. A fan of The Grand Ole Opry, Cline received a piano for her eighth birthday and by her teen years she was singing in a Baptist church choir with her mother. With her father abandoning the family, Cline quit high school to support her mother, landing gigs at local dinner clubs. Soon working in honky-tonks and country bars, she gained much regional exposure. In 1953, she married for the first time to Gerald Cline. About this time, her manager Bill Peer suggested she change her first name to Patsy. Assertive and confident, Cline often appeared on radio, and by 1955, her appearance on The Grand Ole Opry led to a contract with Decca Records. With her simple, heartfelt and sentimental vocal style she scored her first major crossover hit in 1956 with 'Walkin' After Midnight', premiering the song on *Arthur Godrey's Talent Scouts* television show. On

January 9, 1960 Cline achieved her long desired wish to become a member of The Grand Ole Opry but tragedy struck Cline in June of 1961 when she almost died from injuries sustained in an auto accident. Recovering by the year's end, she enjoyed a strong hit run with 'I Fall To Pieces' (1961) and, most notably, with the Willie Nelson-penned, 'Crazy'. A moody song that she cared little for, 'Crazy' became Cline's biggest seller and signature tune. Cline scored with several more pop hits before her death including 'She's Got You' (1962) and 'When I Get Through To You' (1962). Cline had just finished recording the album *Faded Love* and had completed an engagement at the Mint in Las Vegas shortly before her death. In 1973, Cline became the first female solo artist inducted into the Country Music Hall of Fame. Cline landed an unlikely Top 10 country hit in 1981 with 'Have You Ever Been Lonely', in an eerie electronically generated duet with the late Jim Reeves.

CAUSE: Cline died in a plane crash three miles west of Camden, Tennessee, which also killed Cowboy Copas (44), Hawkshaw Hawkins (43), and Randy Hughs (35). Flying in turbulent weather, the single engine aeroplane disintegrated over two miles of tree tops. The trio were returning to Nashville from Kansas City after performing at a tribute for Kansas City disc jockey, Cactus Jack Call, who had died tragically in a car crash. Scheduled to fly with his friends, Grand Ole Opry member Billy Walker was unable to find room on the plane and instead took a commercial flight.

FURTHER READING: Nassour, Ellis. (1993). *Honky Tonk Angel: The Intimate Story Of Patsy Cline*. New York: St Martin's.

Bruce Cloud

Born 1941
Died 1971

Second tenor of Billy Ward & the Dominoes from 1959–62, Bruce Cloud joined a few years after the end of their hit period. By this time, the group had supplanted its doo-wop sound with a more big band, Vegas-style revue.

CAUSE: Suicide.

Odia Coates

Born 1942
Died May 19, 1991

Mississippi-born singer, Odia Coates was reared on the gospel music heard in her preacher father's church. By 1967 she joined the 42-member Edwin Hawkins Singers, meeting Paul Anka when he was producing the group's hit 'Oh Happy Day'. Switching to pop music, she found nightclub work in Los Angeles. After some session work behind Sly & The Family Stone, she joined Merry Clayton in the soul group Sisters Love. Offered a solo record deal, Coates asked Edwin Hawkins for advice. Hawkins suggested that she contact Paul Anka. Instead hired as Anka's singing partner in 1974, Coates scored several duet hits including 'One Man Woman/One Woman Man' and the million-selling chart-topper, '(You're) Having My Baby'. Also pursuing a solo career, Coates scored a minor hit in 1975 with a cover version of E.L.O.'s 'Showdown'.

CAUSE: Diagnosed with breast cancer in 1987, she succumbed to the disease four years later. She died at Kaiser Hospital in Oakland, California.

Kurt Cobain

(KURT DONALD COBAIN)
Born February 20, 1967
Died April 5, 1993

At the forefront of the early Nineties Seattle grunge rock movement, guitarist Kurt Cobain emerged as a much-copied anti-hero. Born in Abertdeen, Washington, but raised in Seattle, Cobain was a poor student who began writing rock songs at age 14. Devastated by the divorce of his parents, he would slip into a lifelong depression. A loud, crunching guitarist, Cobain formed a series of bands during

his teen years. Teaming with bassist Krist Novoselic to form Skid Row (not the heavy metal band), the group evolved into Nirvana. After recording an obscure single in 1988 on the Sub-Pop label, Nirvana followed with the album *Bleach* in 1989. The trio would soon fall into place with the addition of Ohio-born drummer Dave Grohl. Popularising the Seattle grunge movement, Nirvana's 1991 album *Nevermind* was highlighted by the blistering, hard-rocking, angst-filled anthem of the era's disenfranchised youth, 'Smells Like Teen Spirit'. Sporting plaid shirts, stringy long hair, and an irreverent attitude, Cobain spawned scores of imitators. Initially rejected by label executives as too uncommercial, Nirvana's follow-up album *In Utero* was a number 1 smash, and was highlighted by the alternative-radio 'All Apologies' and the moody 'Heart-Shaped Box'. A media star, Cobain graduated from his decade-long marijuana use to heroin. Marrying the lead singer of Hole, Courtney Love, Cobain fathered one child, Frances Bean Cobain. In December 1993, MTV aired Nirvana's *Unplugged* set, highlighted by the tracks 'About A Girl' and the David Bowie cover 'The Man Who Sold The World'. Although seemingly at the top of the world, Cobain was terribly depressed and unhappy with his role as a rock star. After eight years of legal wrangling between Courtney Love and the surviving members of Nirvana, an unreleased Cobain track, 'You Know You're Right', was included on a compilation album in 2002.
CAUSE: Suicide by gunshot. Exhibiting signs of depression, on March 4, 1993, Cobain had slipped into a drug-induced coma while in Rome after consuming a combination of champagne and 60 tablets of Rohypnol. Some media outlets described the episode as a suicide attempt. Then on March 18, wife Courtney Love called Seattle police claiming that Cobain was threatening suicide. Convinced by his wife, Cobain agreed to receive treatment for heroin addiction at the Exodus Recovery Center in Marina Del Ray, California. But Cobain would leave after two days on April 1. When Cobain's mother reported him missing on April 4, neither Seattle police nor a private investigator hired by Love were able to locate him. On April 5, Cobain killed himself with a Remington model-11 20-gauge shotgun in a greenhouse room above his garage at his home in Seattle, while sitting in a chair and staring through a window. Next to Cobain's body was a cigar box containing heroin paraphernalia. Cobain's body was discovered by electrician Gary Smith on April 8. Smith called police and then local radio station KXRX. A police photograph of the suicide scene was later released to newspapers. The coroner found heroin and Valium in Cobain's bloodstream. Leaving a suicide note, Cobain included a cryptic line from Neil Young's 1979 song 'Hey Hey, My My (Into The Black)'; the note was read by an angry and emotional Courtney Love to a crowd in Seattle, during which time she spewed many obscenities, calling Cobain an "asshole" for taking his own life. In a strange ceremony, many in the crowd of 7,000 burned their flannel shirts (a trademark piece of grunge clothing) in a bonfire. Cobain's mother Wendy O'Connor raged: "Now he's gone and joined that stupid club", referring to dead rockers like Janis Joplin, Jim Morrison and Jimi Hendrix, all of whom died at 27. Two of Cobain's great-uncles had committed suicide in the Seventies. Despite the threat of a lawsuit brought by Love, a 1998 documentary, *Kurt And Courtney*, suggests that Cobain's death was not a suicide, and that musician El Duce (now dead) claimed that Love offered him $50,000 to murder Cobain. The only mystery surrounding the case is

the fact that someone tried to use Cobain's credit card after his death. FURTHER READING: Sandford, Christopher. (1995). *Kurt Cobain*. London: Victor Gollancz. Wall, Mick & Dome, Malcolm. (1996). *Nirvana: The Legacy*. London: Omnibus Press.

Ed Cobb

(EDWARD C. COBB)
Born July 16, 1918
Died December 27, 1999
A singer-songwriter and member of The Four Preps, Ed Cobb is best known for composing a pair of rock classics, 'Dirty Water' and 'Tainted Love'. An original member of The Four Preps, Cobb joined three friends he had known since high school to form the group in the early Fifties. With their peppy harmonies, the quartet enjoyed pop hits with '26 Miles (Santa Catalina)' (1958), 'Big Man' (1958), 'Lazy Summer Night' (1958) and 'Down By The Station' (1960). Embraced by folk audiences on college campuses in the early Sixties, the group's apolitical material was soon out of vogue, and they were displaced by folk activists like Bob Dylan and Peter, Paul & Mary. The Four Preps' final hit came in 1964 with the mocking parody, 'A Letter To The Beatles'. During the mid Sixties, Cobb was also a member of The Piltdown Men, a seven-man studio group at Capitol Records. The group landed surprise instrumental hits in the UK with 'MacDonald's Cave' (based on the children's nursery rhyme, Old MacDonald), 'Piltdown Rides Again' and 'Goodnight Mrs. Flintstone'. Turning to management, Cobb assumed the reins of a Los Angeles band, The Standells, and penned their sole garage-rock hit, 'Dirty Water'. He unsuccessfully tried to repeat this success with fellow Californian garage band, The Chocolate Watch Band. Another of Cobb's compositions, 'Tainted Love', was rejected by The Standells but was instead recorded by soul singer Gloria Jones (later Marc Bolan's common-law wife). The track was given a new lease of life by techno-pop duo, Soft Cell who turned the song into a hit in 1982. Returning to his roots, Cobb founded The New Four Preps in 1988. During his long tenure in the music industry, Cobb had been nominated for three Grammys, and earned 32 gold and platinum awards for producing or engineering tracks for artists as diverse as Fleetwood Mac, Pink Floyd, Steely Dan, and The Lettermen.
CAUSE: Unknown. He died in Massachusetts.

Eddie Cochran

(EDWARD RAY COCHRANE)
Born October 3, 1938
Died April 17, 1960
A rockabilly legend, Eddie Cochran grew up in Minnesota, a fan of country and western music. Playing the trombone in high school, Cochran quit when the band director told him his musical skills were sub-par. Borrowing his brother's Kay model guitar, he became infatuated with the instrument. Moving with his family to suburban Los Angeles at age 15, Cochran made few friends in school and spent most of his time practising the guitar. He soon formed a duo with a bass-playing schoolmate Connie "Guybo" Smith, performing the popular country and western hits of the time. Cochran then teamed with Hank Cochran (no relation) as the Cochran Brothers. Starting out as a country and western outfit, the pair was quick to jump to rockabilly and, after hearing Elvis Presley, rock'n'roll. With help from Los Angeles songwriter Jerry Capehart, Cochran signed with Liberty Records where he scored a Top 20 hit with a cover version of John D. Loudermilk's 'Sittin' In The Balcony'. Cochran previously landed a small role in the Jayne Mansfield film, *The Girl Can't Help It* (1956) where he performed the song, 'Twenty Flight Rock'. In 1958, at

the age of 19, Cochran released his million-selling signature tune, and rock classic, 'Summertime Blues'. The following year he issued 'C'Mon Everybody', another memorable call-to-arms teen anthem which reached the UK Top 10. Cochran had planned to stop touring, preferring the producing and recording aspects of music. But with rockabilly out of fashion in the US by 1960, Cochran co-headlined a British tour with Gene Vincent. At the time of Cochran's death, his record company had just released the single 'Three Steps To Heaven' which – ironically in view of its title – topped the UK charts in June 1960. Cochran's rhythmic guitar style has influenced a number of top players, most notably The Who's Pete Townshend.

CAUSE: Cochran and fellow rockabilly artist Gene Vincent were in Britain for a concert tour. A surprise success, a second 10-week tour was quickly scheduled. Homesick and invited by his record company to finish recording an album, Cochran planned to return to the US for a two-week respite. His final performance, a last-minute addition to the tour, was at the Bristol Hippodrome. Shortly after midnight, en route from the Royal Hotel in Bristol to Heathrow Airport in London for a flight the next afternoon, tour manager Patrick Thompkins informed the driver, George Martin (not The Beatles producer), that he was going in the wrong direction. While attempting to stop and turn round just outside Chippenham, Martin lost control of the Ford Consul Saloon, blew a tyre and struck a solid lamp-post. The car had spun around, leaving a 50-yard skid mark. Cochran was thrown from the vehicle, striking his head on the ground. The accident seriously injured Gene Vincent; another passenger, Cochran's girlfriend, songwriter Sharon Sheeley, suffered a broken pelvis. Cochran was seated in the middle of the back seat, and had shielded Sheehan from the brunt of the force. Cochran was taken to Chippenham Cottage Hospital but transferred to St Martin's Hospital in Bath, where he died later that day from massive head injuries. Both men in the front seat, Martin and Thompkins, were uninjured. The driver was later fined £50 and his licence was suspended for 15 years. The car had been used for a wedding earlier in the day and was littered with confetti. Future UK pop singer, then policeman, Dave Dee (real name David Harman), was the first officer called to the scene. Singer Jimmy Bowen recalled in his autobiography *Rough Mix*: "Eddie had a brooding, fatalistic, destructive streak. He was always muttering how he wasn't going to live long. That seemed so weird to me, but he seemed to *know*. I asked him once why he drank so much and he snarled, 'Why not? It's all one big party. I'm not making it past 30 anyway.' "

Jackie Lee Cochran

Born February 5, 1934
Died February 1998

Louisiana-born rockabilly performer and songwriter, Jackie Lee Cochran primarily recorded with Ray Campi. Cochran's best known compositions are 'Georgia Lee Brown' and 'Hip Shakin' Mama'. His finest work is compiled on the 1997 album, Rockabilly Music.

CAUSE: Heart attack.

Cub Coda

(MICHAEL CODA)
Born October 1, 1948
Died July 1, 2000

A much respected and well-liked musician, writer and rock archivist, Detroit-native Cub Coda composed and provided the guitar work on the Seventies rock anthem, 'Smokin' In The Boys' Room' (1973) by Brownsville Station. Playing the drums at age five, before switching to guitar at 14, Michael "Cub" Coda had taken his nickname from Cubbie in *The Mickey Mouse Club*. After attending Northern

Michigan University for a year in 1968, he dropped out to pursue a career in music. Forming Brownsville Station in 1969 in Ann Arbor, Michigan, the group signed with Warner Brothers Records the following year. Culled from their third album *School Punks*, 'Smokin' In The Boys' Room' became a massive pop success but Brownsville Station managed only one further hit with 'Kings Of The Party' (1974). After the group disbanded in 1979, Coda joined the roots-rock bands, The Points and The Bone Gods, and released about a dozen solo albums. Coda was a knowledgeable rock aficionado and record collector who wrote the "Vinyl Junkie" column for the record collector magazine *Goldmine*, and later *Discoveries*. He also co-authored the book, *Blues For Dummies*. 'Smokin' In The Boys' Room' was reprised in the Eighties by hair metal band, Mötley Crüe.
CAUSE: Suffering from diabetes and kidney ailments, he died following complications of kidney dialysis.

Alma Cogan

Born May 19, 1932
Died October 26, 1966
Popularly known as "the girl with the laugh in her voice", London-born Cogan was the most successful UK singing star of the Fifties with 18 chart entries to her name, including 'Bell Bottom Blues', 'Little Things Mean A Lot', 'I Can't Tell A Waltz From A Tango' and the chart-topping 'Dreamboat'. As well as appearing in musicals and films, she was a regular on television, renowned for her lively sense of humour and ostentatious collection of dresses. A favourite of the showbusiness elite, she numbered among her close friends composer Lionel Bart and Beatles' manager Brian Epstein. Paul McCartney played tambourine on one of her B-sides and she responded by recording Lennon/McCartney's 'Eight Days A Week' as a single. During the height of pirate radio, she released a tribute record to television's *Man From UNCLE* star David McCallum, 'Love Ya Illya', under the pseudonym Angela And The Fans. She continued performing up until her death.
CAUSE: Stomach cancer. In the autumn of 1966, Cogan collapsed while working in Sweden. She flew back to England and died soon after at London's Middlesex Hospital.

Brian Cole

(BRIAN LESLIE COLE)
Born September 8, 1944
Died August 2, 1972
Founding member of popular Sixties vocal rock group, The Association, Washington-born Brian Cole was initially trained on the clarinet. Trading the instrument for a stand-up bass, he moved to Los Angeles and joined a jazz band. Flirting with acting, Cole then joined a comedy skit and folk-rock trio, The Gnufolk. A burly man with an intense expression, Cole in 1965 joined a 13-piece rock group called Men. Trimmed to six members within months, the group was renamed The Association. While Cole played both bass and occasional clarinet in the group, most of the bass duties were actually relegated to studio musicians. After switching from Jubilee to Valiant Records, The Association had its first success in 1966 with 'Along Comes Mary', featuring Cole's clarinet solo and characterised by the group's tight vocal harmony. A major hit, 'Along Comes Mary' came under attack for its alleged marijuana references. Taking a pop-rock approach, The Association followed up with a pair of ballad hits, 'Cherish' (1966) and 'Never My Love' (1967). The group charted its final hits in 1968 with 'Everything That Touches You', 'Time For Livin'', and 'Six Man Band'. The Association would release several moderately successful albums into the Seventies, including the soundtrack to the film, *Goodbye Columbus*.

CAUSE: Heroin overdose. He died at his Hollywood home.

David Cole

Born June 3, 1962
Died January 24, 1995
Keyboardist of the Top 40 duo C+C Music Factory, Tennessee-born David Cole was raised in New Jersey. A musical virtuoso, as a teenager Cole was the choir director at his Baptist church, training singers twice his age. While attending the Berklee School of Music, he also taught music courses at his former high school in Passaic, New Jersey. Entering the music industry as a deejay in 1985 at the Better Day's nightclub in New York City, by 1987 Cole had teamed with lifelong partner, club deejay Robert Clivilles. The duo initially found fame as the remixers of Natalie Cole's cover hit 'Pink Cadillac'. Hired as producers and remixers at the A&M subsidiary Vendetta Records, the pair continued their run with Seduction's 'Two To Make It Right', Mariah Carey's 'Make It Happy', and Whitney Houston's 'I'm Every Woman'. Forming their own group, Cole and Clivilles scored a minor club hit in 1987 with 'Do It Properly' as 2 Puerto Ricans, A Black Man and A Dominican. Forming C+C Music Factory in 1990, Cole and Clivilles enjoyed a trio of massive club/pop hits beginning with 'Gonna Make You Sweat (Everybody Dance Now)', the hook-filled track featuring the powerful intro by veteran studio singer Martha Wash and a rap by Freedom Williams. The single was culled from their début album *Gonna Make You Sweat,* which also yielded the hits 'Here We Go' and 'Things That Make You Go Hmmm'. In 1994, the duo won a Grammy for their production work on *The Bodyguard* soundtrack. Cole and Clivilles bought a building in Greenwich Village in 1994, converting it into a recording and entertainment complex. But a second *C+C Music Factory Anything Goes!* went virtually ignored on its release in 1994. Columbia Records dropped C+C Music Factory several days after Cole's death.
CAUSE: Spinal meningitis. He had been ill for several months. He died in a Manhattan hospital.

Nat "King" Cole

(NATHANIEL ADAMS COLES)
Born March 17, 1917
Died February 15, 1965
An elegant jazz musician turned pop crooner, Nat "King" Cole was born in the Deep South city of Montgomery, Alabama, but raised in Chicago. The son of a preacher, Cole formed his own jazz band, The Royal Dukes, at 17. He first recorded in 1936 as a backing pianist for his brother, Ikes. Emerging from the south side of Chicago, in 1939 Cole formed the King Cole Trio, an instrumental jazz combo featuring guitarist Oscar Moore and bassist Wesley Prince (later Johnny Miller). Winning many *Downbeat* magazine popularity polls, the combo enjoyed a series of crossover hits with 'All For You' (1943), 'Straighten Up And Fly Right' (1944), 'Gee, Baby, Ain't I Good To You' (1944), 'I'm A Shy Guy' (1945), and their signature piece, 'Get Your Kicks On Route 66'. By the late Forties, Cole adopted a more polished sound, choosing lush orchestral backing in place of his trio. Scoring his first hit in 1946 with the perennial holiday classic, 'The Christmas Song', he followed up with a series of smash ballad hits including 'Nature Boy' (1948), a song written by a homeless man, Eden Ahbez, 'Mona Lisa' (1950), 'Unforgettable' (1951) and 'If I May' (1955). Hosting his own musical television show in 1956, Cole usually sported a proper tuxedo while sitting at a grand piano, whispering elegant strains of romantic songs. But Cole had trouble landing national advertisers and his programme was dropped in mid-season. Suffering a string of vicious public attacks in the

press from both sides of the race controversy in the mid Fifties, Cole received numerous death threats when he moved to a suburban Los Angeles neighbourhood, and was severely beaten by six members of the White Citizens Council at a show in Birmingham, Alabama, because of his mixed-race backing band. Cole continued to record successfully until shortly before his untimely death in 1964. In 1991, Cole enjoyed a revival with a newly recorded version of 'Unforgettable', which featured an electronically spliced duet with his daughter Natalie.
CAUSE: Lung cancer. He died in Santa Monica, California.
FURTHER READING: Gourse, Leslie. (1991). *Unforgettable: The Life And Mystique Of Nat King Cole*. New York: St. Martin's.

Cornelius "Tenoo" Coleman

(CORNELIUS JESSIE COLEMAN)
Born 1929
Died February 20, 1973
Longtime drummer for Fats Domino's band, Cornelius "Tenoo" Coleman appeared on many of Domino's hits beginning in 1955, including 'Blue Monday' and 'Blueberry Hill'. A New Orleans-native, Coleman later joined Dave Bartholemew's talented studio band.
CAUSE: He died after a brief undisclosed illness at his home in New Orleans.

Ray Coleman

Born June 15, 1937
Died September 10, 1996
A pioneering British rock journalist and biographer, Ray Coleman is best remembered for editing *Melody Maker*. A native of Leicester, England, Coleman worked at a series of major British newspapers before landing a reporter's position at *Melody Maker* in 1960. He soon brought a hitherto unknown degree of professionalism to pop reporting, infusing politics and more thorough reporting into a field largely looked upon as trivial. Finding himself at the vanguard of the beat boom, Coleman frequently obtained exclusive interviews with The Beatles. He became a friend and confidant of the group, especially John Lennon. Leaving *Melody Maker* in 1967, Coleman took over the reins of a spin-off magazine, *Disc*. Returning to *Melody Maker* in 1969 as editor-in-chief, he held the post until 1979, during which time he strengthened the magazine's position in the crowded British music field. Coleman became a freelance writer in the early Eighties, writing columns for various magazines and eventually turning to books. After penning a biography of Gary Numan, Coleman became a serious musical writer, writing a definitive two-volume John Lennon biography, the first with the assistance of Cynthia Lennon, the second with Yoko Ono Lennon. He followed with an authorised biography of Eric Clapton and then of the late Beatles manager Brian Epstein, the latter with the aid of Epstein's invalid mother, Queenie. Coleman's subsequent works included a tome with Bill Wyman (*Stone Alone*), Gerry Marsden (*I'll Never Walk Alone*), The Carpenters and Frank Sinatra. At the time of his death, Coleman was completing an authorised biography of Phil Collins. Coleman was deeply upset by *Melody Maker*'s drop in stature and circulation after his departure.
CAUSE: Kidney cancer. He died at his home in Shepperton, England.

Albert Collins

Born October 1, 1932
Died November 24, 1993
A gritty Texas-style blues guitarist, Albert Collins was born on a farm in Leona, Texas, moving to Houston at age nine. Studying piano and listening to the jazzier big bands of the Forties, Collins had aspirations to be a professional keyboard player until his instrument was stolen when he was 15. Undaunted, he switched to guitar,

fronting a jazz combo called The Rhythm Rockers. By the mid Fifties, Collins was playing blues and upbeat R&B in a Southern touring group headed by Piney Brown. Returning to Houston, Collins honed his blues skills in the city's rougher bars during the late Fifties and early Sixties. Playing with a movable metal capo bar on the neck of his instrument, Collins emulated fellow-Texas bluesman Gatemouth Brown. Nicknamed "The Master of the Telecaster", Collins hated to sing, and as a result recorded mostly instrumentals. Collins scored a series of regional hits in the first half of the Sixties including 'The Freeze' and the million-selling, 'Frosty' (1962). After a few more one-shot recording deals, mostly on several Bill Hall-owned labels, Collins earned some national notoriety. Releasing a collection of his early singles, the album *The Cool Sound Of Albert Collins* (1965) also featured his rare vocal hit, 'Dyin' Flu'. Aided by Canned Heat vocalist Bob Hite in 1968, Collins signed with Imperial Records and was hired as the group's opening act. After releasing three uninspired albums at Imperial, and one on Tumbleweed Records in 1971, Collins experienced a career slump. But Collins was rediscovered after signing with Alligator Records in 1978. Backed by a group called Icebreaker, Collins recorded *Ice Pickin'* (1979). The album reintroduced Collins to a new audience of blues aficionados, and he returned to touring on a full-time basis. During the second phase of his career, Collins landed in the R&B charts with 'Frostbite' (1980), 'Frozen Alive' (1981), and 'Don't Lose Your Cool' (1983). Collins' 1985 album *Showdown!*, earned a Grammy in the Best Traditional Blues Recording category, and featured the talent of guest players Robert Cray and Johnny Copeland. A star in the blues community into the Nineties, Collins later recorded for the Charisma Records subsidiary, Pointblank.
CAUSE: Lung cancer. Although ill, he continued to perform up to his death. He died in Las Vegas.

Allen Collins

Born July 19, 1952
Died January 23, 1990
Guitarist and original member of the legendary southern-rock group, Lynyrd Skynyrd, Allen Collins was taught to play the guitar at age 12 by his mother, a fan of country music. Attending Robert E. Lee High School in Jacksonville, Florida, Collins formed a group called My Backyard with several classmates in 1965. They soon evolved into Lynyrd Skynyrd – named after an unpopular gym teacher, Leonard Skinner. Headed by vocalist Ronnie Van Zant, the group featured the dual guitar lead of Collins and Gary Rossington. After extensive clubwork, and a few local record releases in the late Sixties and early Seventies, Lynyrd Skynyrd signed with MCA Records in 1973. Produced by Al Kooper, their début album *Pronounced Leh-Nerd Skin-Nerd* (1973), was highlighted by the rock standard, 'Free Bird'. With their guitar-oriented, southern-rock hybrid sound, the group was in the forefront of the new genre. Their second album *Second Helping* (1974) featured their first Top 10 pop hit, 'Sweet Home Alabama', the song an angry answer to Neil Young's anti-Southern laments, 'Southern Man' and 'Alabama'. In the fall of 1977, Lynyrd Skynyrd launched a 50-city tour to promote its new album release *Street Survivors* but tragedy struck when their rented plane ran out of fuel and crashed, killing three members of the group, and their road manager. In 1979, Collins joined former bandmate Gary Rossington in forming The Rossington-Collins Band, their biggest hit coming with 'Don't Misunderstand Me' (1980), from their gold album, *Anytime, Anyplace, Anywhere*. Rossington-Collins lasted until 1982 when Collins quit to form

The Allen Collins Band. Tragedy again struck Collins in 1986 when he was paralysed in a car crash which also killed his girlfriend. Performing in a wheelchair, he later joined a Lynyrd Skynyrd reunion.
CAUSE: Pneumonia. After years of ill health, he was hospitalised for several months. He died at Memorial Hospital near Jacksonville, Florida.

Rob Collins

(ROBERT COLLINS)
Born February 23, 1963
Died July 22, 1996
Founding keyboardist and songwriter for the British alternative-rock group The Charlatans, Rob Collins began playing the piano as a child, switching to a second-hand Hammond organ in the mid Eighties. Fronted by singer Tim Burgess, The Charlatans emerged out of the Manchester music scene in 1989. (The group was known as Charlatans UK in the US to differentiate them from the Sixties San Francisco band). Topping the British charts in 1990 with their début album *Some Friendly*, The Charlatans enjoyed a pair of hits with 'The Only One I Know' and 'Then'. A British sensation, The Charlatans were voted "best new group" in a 1990 *New Musical Express* readers' poll. From their second album, *Between 10th & 11th*, the hit track 'Weirdo' (1992) featured Collins' frenetic, synth-rock organ stylings. Convicted of driving the getaway car in a bizarre armed robbery attempt in 1993, Collins served four months of an eight-month jail sentence. At the time of his death, Collins was working on The Charlatans' fifth album.
CAUSE: He died in an automobile accident while driving from a pub to a recording studio for a late-night session. He flipped his BMW 520 into a cornfield on a curve near Monmouth, South Wales. Thrown out of the sun-roof, Collins died from head injuries. His passenger, the group's sound engineer, Richard Peet, was unhurt. Collins' blood-alcohol level measured twice the legal limit.

Marc Conners

Born April 15, 1949
Died March 25, 1989
Original member of the Canadian a cappella group The Nylons, Ottawa-born Marc Conners began as an actor in college in 1967, earning a Bachelor's degree in Fine Arts. A busy stage actor who worked the stages of Edmonton's Citadel, Montreal's Centaur, Halifax's Stradford and Neptune Theaters, he also played the role of Jesus in a Toronto production of *Godspell*. Joining fellow actors Paul Cooper, Claude Morrison, and Dennis Simpson in singing doo-wop harmonies as a diversion during rehearsals, Conners soon found himself performing informally at private parties. While singing at a party in Toronto in early 1979, the group was overheard by a nightclub owner who suggested they enter his talent show. Winning first place, they earned a paying gig. Conners' strong tenor and good looks fitted well with the upbeat group of singers. Released by Attic Records, the group's début album *One Size Fits All* (1982) spawned their first Canadian hit, an a cappella version of 'The Lion Sleeps Tonight'. Singing mostly oldies, the group broke into the American market in 1985, scoring their first hit two years later with a cover of the 1969 Steam hit, retitled 'Kiss Them Goodbye', from the album *Happy Together*. Though initially looked upon as a novelty act, the group went on to fill venues throughout the country. Conners' final Nylons album came in 1989 with the Windham Hill album *Rockapella*.
CAUSE: AIDS. He died in Toronto.

Brian Connolly

(BRIAN FRANCIS CONNOLLY)
Born October 5, 1945
Died February 10, 1997
Flamboyant lead singer of Seventies

British glam rock group Sweet, Scottish-born Brian Connolly received his first guitar as a Christmas present at age 12. Leaving home at 18 after discovering that he was raised by foster parents, he jumped into a career in music. Forming The Wainwright Gentlemen in 1966, Connolly renamed the group The Sweet Shop in 1968. Featuring drummer Mick Tucker, guitarist Andy Scott and bassist Steve Priest, the group was signed by Fontana Records. Switching labels and desperate for a hit, the renamed Sweet agreed to the demands of songwriters Mike Chapman and Nicky Chinn (of Mud and Suzi Quatro fame) and had Connolly backed by a session band for the group's first five singles. Sweet hit the British charts between 1971 and 1973 with bubblegum/rock hits like 'Funny Funny', 'Co-Co', 'Little Willy' and 'Blockbuster'. Gradually evolving into a make-up wearing, glam-rock group, Sweet enjoyed greater US success in the mid Seventies with the hits 'Ballroom Blitz' (1974) and 'Fox On The Run' (1975). Tired of targeting a young audience, in 1974 Sweet recorded the less commercial efforts, *Desolation Boulevard* and *Sweet Fanny Adams*, and then parted from Chinn and Chapman. From the album *Level Headed*, Sweet scored its final hit in 1978 with the Top 10 entry, 'Love Is Like Oxygen'. Leaving Sweet over personality conflicts in 1979, Connolly pursued a rocky solo career. A hard drinker all of his life, his career was interrupted by a series of heart attacks, a divorce, and near-bankruptcy. Enjoying a revival in the mid Eighties, he formed Brian Connolly and Sweet in direct competition with a Sweet group led by Andy Scott.
CAUSE: Kidney and liver failure. He died in Slough, England. Although Connolly had quit drinking in the early Eighties, his health was in terminal decline during the last decade of his life.

Bert Convy

Born July 23, 1933
Died July 15, 1991
A successful stage and film actor and game show host, Bert Convy broke into the entertainment industry as a musician. Born in St. Louis, he moved to California with his family at age seven. While attending UCLA in the mid Fifties, Convy was drawn to acting but spent most of his free time in a vocal trio called The Cheers. Signing with Capitol Records, Convy and the group enjoyed two Top 10 hits with '(Bazoom) I Need Your Lovin'' (1954) and the gritty 'Black Denim Trousers' (1955). After starring in a Los Angeles stage production, Convy left music and moved to New York. Later hosting several television game shows including *Win, Lose Or Draw* and *Super Password*, he won an Emmy for *Tattletales*.
CAUSE: Brain cancer. He died at his home in Los Angeles 15 months after being diagnosed with the illness.

Sam Cooke

(SAMUEL COOK)
Born January 2, 1931
Died December 11, 1964
A legendary and highly influential American soul singer, Chicago-born Sam Cooke first hit the stage at age six as a member of The Singing Children Choir at his minister father's church. While in high school, he joined a popular local gospel group, The Highway QCs. Going professional at the age of 19, he joined the legendary Soul Stirrers in 1950, hand-picked by the group's departing founder R.H. Harris. With his emotion-laden vocal delivery, Cooke sprung from the background to the lead vocal spot in the group. Attracting younger women to the group's performances, the good-looking and charismatic Cooke had become a superstar in the gospel field by the mid Fifties, with his quivering lead vocals on hits such as 'Nearer To Me' (1955) and 'Touch The Hem Of His Garment' (1956).

Unhappy with his meagre salary, Cooke took the advice of producer Robert "Bumps" Blackwell and left gospel for secular music, though many of Cooke's fans would never forgive him for abandoning his gospel roots. Initially recording under the pseudonym Dale Cooke, he found no success with his Specialty releases. Buying Cooke's contract from Specialty owner Art Rupe, Blackwell took Cooke to Keen Records, where the singer unleashed a long string of pop hits beginning with the chart-topping, 'You Send Me', having performed the song on *The Ed Sullivan Show*. Meanwhile, in 1959 Cooke launched SAR Records on discovering that The Soul Stirrers had been dropped by Specialty Records. Named for Cooke, his managers, J.W. Alexander and Roy Crain, SAR signed both gospel acts and pop acts such as Johnnie Taylor, Mel Carter and The Valentinos, whose single 'It's All Over Now' was later a hit for The Rolling Stones. Moving to the larger RCA label where he was overseen by the production team of Hugo Peretti and Luigi Creatore, Cooke became a pop/soul superstar with a string of self-penned hits such as 'Chain Gang' (1960), 'Cupid' (1961), 'Twistin' The Night Away' (1962), 'Bring It On Home To Me' (1962) and 'Another Saturday Night' (1963). A savvy businessman, Cooke hired entertainment lawyer Allen Klein after finding discrepancies in his royalty statements at RCA. Wanting to hit the big screen, in 1964 Cooke had taken a successful screen test for a part in the film, *In The Heat Of The Night*. Moving away from his pop-styled material and returning to his soulful roots shortly before his death, Cooke recorded the socially aware, posthumous hit 'A Change Is Gonna Come'. After Cooke's death, SAR Records was closed.

CAUSE: Cooke died in a mysterious shooting incident at the Hacienda Motel in Los Angeles. Home during a Christmas break, Cooke had picked up a young Eurasion woman, Linda Boyer, at a party earlier in the evening. (Some reports claim that the two had known each other for a few years.) The two first went to a bar before going to a cheap hotel, where Cooke signed in as "Mr. & Mrs. Cook". But minutes later, Boyer ran out of the hotel room carrying Cooke's clothing. He ran after her and broke into the manager's office, where he mistakenly accused the manager's wife, Bertha Franklin, of hiding Boyer. Franklin shot Cooke three times with a .22 calibre gun. She then poked Cooke with a stick to make sure he was dead. There were no witnesses to the killing. Boyer was at a nearby phone booth. Later, she was found to possess a black book with the names and numbers of powerful Hollywood moguls. A court later ruled that Franklin shot Cooke in self-defence and that the killing was justifiable homicide. There were no charges of racism since Franklin was herself black. Whether Cooke was being robbed or, as Boyer charged, Cooke was attempting to rape her, will never be known. The circumstances of Cooke's death remained a mystery for years in order to shield his wife and two children. Cooke's life had been marred with tragedy: in 1958, Cooke almost died in a car crash that also nearly killed the then-unknown Lou Rawls; in 1959 his first wife died in another car crash; in 1963 his one-year-old son (by his second wife) drowned in a swimming pool.

FURTHER READING: Wolff, Daniel; Crain, S.R.; White, Clifton; & Tenenbaum, G. David. (1995). *You Send Me: The Life And Times Of Sam Cooke*. New York: Morrow.

Johnny "Clyde" Copeland

Born March 27, 1937
Died July 5, 1997

Born in Louisiana but raised in Arkansas and Texas, guitarist Johnny

"Clyde" Copeland apprenticed on stage under several local Houston blues artists including Big Mama Thorton and Sonny Boy Williamson. By 1954, Copeland had formed his first band, the Dukes of Rhythm. After touring in the Sixties with Otis Redding and then O.V. Wright, Copeland settled in New York City in 1975. Signing his first recording contract in 1981, he enjoyed fame with début album, *Copeland Special*. Riding the blues revival, he scored several hits including 'Make My Home Where I Hang My Hat' and his signature piece, 'Houston'. Recording five albums for Rounder Records and three for Verve, Copeland won a Grammy in 1996 for *Showdown!*, a collaborative album with Albert Collins and Robert Cray.
CAUSE: He died from complications from heart surgery to repair the valve of a transplanted organ which he had received in January. It was his eighth heart operation. He died at Columbia-Presbyterian Hospital in Manhattan.

Warren Corbin

Born September 12, 1938
Died June 1978
Bass vocalist of the Fifties doo-wop vocal group, The Cleftones, Warren formed the group with a classmate at Jamaica High School in New York City, Herbie Cox. Signing with George Goldner's Gee Records, the group scored several hits including, 'Little Girl Of Mine' and covers of the standards, 'Heart And Soul', and 'For Sentimental Reasons'. Corbin left the group in 1965.
CAUSE: Cancer.

Denny Cordell

(DENNIS CORDELL-LAVERACK)
Born August 1, 1943
Died February 18, 1995
A legendary Argentinian-born producer, Denny Cordell got his start in the music industry as the manager of jazz trumpeter Chet Baker. Switching to rock music, Cordell landed his first success as producer for the first line-up of The Moody Blues. After hearing the original version of 'Go Now' by Bessie Banks, Cordell insisted The Moody Blues record the song, which gave the group a UK number 1 in 1965. After a succession of British hits for Georgie Fame ('Getaway') and The Move ('Night Of Fear'), Cordell formed his own production company and garnered an international smash with Procol Harum's 'Whiter Shade Of Pale'. Cordell reactivated the Regal Zonophone label and went on to work with Joe Cocker ('With A Little Help From My Friends'). Launching Shelter Records in 1970 with keyboard player/singer Leon Russell, who shared production duties, Cordell saw the label succeed with J.J. Cale and Tom Petty. Cordell later launched Mango Records with Chris Blackwell of Island Records. Leaving the music industry in 1980, Cordell worked as a horse breeder. Lured back into music by Island Records in 1990, he produced Melissa Ethridge and was an early supporter of the Irish group, The Cranberries.
CAUSE: Lymphoma. He died in Dublin, Ireland.

Ritchie Cordell

(RICHARD JOEL ROSENBLATT)
Born March 10, 1943
Died April 13, 2004
A prolific songwriter and producer, Ritchie Cordell was responsible for a number of pop and bubblegum rock hits during the late Sixties. Emulating Elvis Presley, the Brooklyn-born Cordell began playing the guitar and writing songs during his teens. At 18 years old, Cordell broke into the music industry with the aid of Sid Prosen, the manager of the pop duo Tom and Jerry (better known as Art Garfunkel and Paul Simon). With Prosen's help, Cordell teamed with Simon to compose and produce several singles issued under various names. Drawn to the

songwriting side of music, Cordell became friends with a number of Brill Building songwriters, and was hired in 1966 as a staff writer at Roulette Records. In the wake of 'Hanky Panky', Tommy James and The Shondells' début smash for the label, Cordell was assigned to the group, producing and co-writing (often with Bo Gentry) several of their hits including 'Mirage', 'Getting Together', 'She' and the rock standard, 'Mony Mony'. Leaving Roulette to join the production duo of Jerry Kasenetz and Jeff Katz – known for their bubblegum defining releases at Buddah Records – Cordell penned the hits 'Gimme Gimme Good Lovin'' (Crazy Elephant) and 'Indian Giver' (1910 Fruitgum Co.). After a long sabbatical from the music industry for most of the Seventies, Cordell joined Kenny Laguna, his former session player and then manager of Joan Jett & The Blackhearts, to co-produce the group's chart-topping hard-rock anthem 'I Love Rock 'N Roll'. Cordell subsequently produced The Ramones' 1983 album, *Subterranean Jungle*. In 1987, two of Cordell's Sixties hits returned to the charts via cover versions: 'Mony Mony' by Billy Idol and 'I Think We're Alone Now' by Tiffany.
CAUSE: Pancreatic cancer. He died in New York City.

Carter Cornelius

Born 1948
Died November 7, 1991
The leader of the early Seventies soul band, The Cornelius Brothers with Sister Rose, Carter Cornelius had formed the group in Dania, Florida, out of a musical family of 15 children. Discovered by producer Bob Archibald, who became their manager, he recorded the group on his own Platinum label. Their 1971 recording of 'Treat Her Like A Lady' became a local hit, and drew the attention of United Artists Records, which picked up national distribution rights. With Eddie Cornelius their chief songwriter, the group continued its hit run with 'Too Late To Turn Back Now' (1972) and 'I'm Never Gonna Be Alone' (1972). In 1973, another sibling, Billie Jo, was added to the group. After scoring a few more hits, the group disbanded in 1976 when Cornelius became a follower of the Miami-based Yahweh Ben Yahweh and changed his name to Prince Gideon Israel. The sect was founded by Hulon Mitchell Jr. with Mitchell and Cornelius as its leaders. The former Carter Cornelius recorded the group's music and videos.
CAUSE: Heart attack. He died at his Dania, Florida, home.

Denny Correll

(DENNIS P. CORRELL)
Born February 19, 1946
Died November 30, 2002
A one-time member of the hard rock band Blues Image, Denny Correll spent most of his career in the field of contemporary Christian rock. Correll joined Blues Image in the late Sixties and assumed lead vocal duties following the departure of original lead singer Michael Pinera to join Iron Butterfly. Correll appeared on Blues Image's last two albums and provided the backing vocals on their sole Top 40 hit, 'Ride Captain Ride'. After the group disbanded in 1970, Correll later joined some of his former bandmates in the pioneering contemporary Christian rock act, Manna, and launched a successful solo career in Christian rock.
CAUSE: Suffering from heart problems, Correll was treated at the Hoag Hospital in Newport, California. After he was released, he attempted to drive himself home but suffered a heart attack. He drove into a school car park where he later died.

Hank Cosby

(HENRY COSBY)
Born May 12, 1928
Died January 22, 2002
An early member of Motown's house

band, saxophonist Henry Cosby had previously been a member of The Joe Hunter Band, a Detroit-based jazz combo that the label often hired for session work. Promoted by the label, Cosby was soon employed as a songwriter, arranger and producer. At Motown, Cosby worked with a number of acts including Martha And The Vandellas, The Temptations, Smokey Robinson And The Miracles, Gladys Knight And The Pips and The Marvelettes, and co-wrote 'Tears Of A Clown' for Smokey Robinson And The Miracles as well as several hits for Stevie Wonder and Jr. Walker & The All Stars. Cosby left Motown in 1973 after the label relocated to Los Angeles.

CAUSE: Undergoing triple bypass surgery at the William Beaumont Hospital in Detroit in July 2001, he contracted a number of infections and was forced to undergo three additional surgeries. He never recovered.

Don Costa

Born June 10, 1925
Died January 19, 1983

A prolific conductor, arranger, and producer, Don Costa worked with hundreds of acts during his long career. Of Columbian ancestry, Costa was a self-taught guitarist, joining the CBS radio orchestra in his hometown of Boston at age 15. Moving to New York to find work as an arranger, he was a session player, providing the haunting guitar behind Vaughn Monroe on the smash hit 'Riders In The Sky' (1949), as well as being the musical arranger for Monroe's radio and television programmes. Hired as an arranger by the team of Eydie Gorme & Steve Lawrence, Costa oversaw their early releases at Coral Records, then followed the duo to ABC-Paramount, where he was soon hired as an arranger and chief A&R man, discovering Canadian teenage crooner Paul Anka. Costa also released a number of his own records, landing on the charts with 'Theme For The Unforgiven' and the million-selling 'Never On Sunday'. Establishing Don Costa Productions in the early Sixties, he nurtured a number of acts including Little Anthony & The Imperials and Trini Lopez. Lured away from Gorme & Lawrence by Frank Sinatra in the late Sixties, Costa worked as Sinatra's arranger and bandleader until the early Eighties. Costa also worked with Barbra Streisand, Dean Martin, and The Osmonds. A year before his death, Costa recorded the three-million selling duet single with his 10-year-old granddaughter Nikka, 'Out Here On My Own'.

CAUSE: Experiencing severe respiratory distress while in a New York City hotel room, he was rushed to Lenox Hill Hospital where he suffered a series of heart attacks and died soon after. He had a history of heart disease.

Robert Cotoia

(ROBERT N. COTOIA)
Born August 28, 1953
Died September 3, 2004

The keyboardist of the rock act John Cafferty and The Beaver Brown Band, Robert Cotoia attained unforeseen fame via the film *Eddie And The Cruisers*. Formed in 1972 as a cover band, the New Jersey-based group first garnered some exposure in 1980 with the regional hit, 'Wild Summer Nights'. Then in 1981 when Kenny Vance (formerly of Jay & The Americans) took film director Martin Davidson to one of their concerts, Davidson commissioned Cafferty to compose the music for the film, *Eddie And The Cruisers*. Although the film was initially ignored during its release in 1983, frequent airings the following year on the cable outlet, HBO, spawned renewed interest in both the film and its music. With the album reaching the Top 10, Jerry Cafferty And The Beaver Brown Band had a string of radio hits, including 'On The Dark Side',

'Tender Years', 'Tough All Over' and 'C-I-T-Y'.
CAUSE: Unknown. He died in Burlington, Massachusetts.

Cousin Joe

(PLEASANT JOSEPH)
Born December 20, 1907
Died October 2, 1989
New Orleans R&B and jazz pianist, Cousin Joe recorded for a number of labels including Aladdin, Savoy, DeLuxe, Decca, and the Mezz Mezzrow-owned King Jazz Records. A self-taught player, Cousin Joe remained popular on the jazz and blues circuit into the Seventies.
CAUSE: He died of natural causes in his sleep at his home in New Orleans.
FURTHER READING: Cousin Joe: *Blues From New Orleans.*

Robert Covington

Born December 13, 1941
Died January 17, 1996
Mississippi-born blues-based drummer, Robert Covington first worked professionally behind Big Joe Turner. By the early Sixties Covington and his band worked as session players behind Ted Taylor and Ernie K-Doe. Moving to Chicago, Covington worked with the city's finest bluesmen including Buddy Guy and Little Walter. Joining Sunnyland Slim's group beginning in 1983, Covington later recorded a solo album, *Blues In The Night*.
CAUSE: Kidney failure and complications from diabetes. He died in Chicago.

Peter Cowap

Born June 29, 1944
Died July 16, 1997
A veteran British guitarist and singer, Peter Cowap enjoyed minor success with the single 'Crickets' and was the lead singer of Herman's Hermits in the early Seventies after Peter Noone's departure from the group. Joining in 1971, Cowap led the group on a series of singles beginning with 'She's A Lady'. He left the group in 1975.
CAUSE: Pneumonia.

Cowboy

(ROBERT KEITH WIGGINS)
Born September 20, 1960
Died September 8, 1989
A member of the pioneering Melle Mel-led, rap group The Furious Five, Bronx-born Cowboy (Robert Keith Wiggins) was one of the first singers to perform in a then-unnamed vocal style later called rap. Cowboy had previously been an MC with trailblazing rap artist Grandmaster Flash and the 3MCs. Inspired by the success of the Sugarhill Gang's 'Rapper's Delight', the group recorded a pair of poorly received singles as the Young Generation. Attracting the attention of Sugarhill Records, the renamed Grandmaster Flash and The Furious Five recorded the politically charged, socially conscious rap anthem, 'The Message', a song that would set the stage for the rise of gangster rap in the late Eighties. But when Grandmaster Flash left the group in 1984, Cowboy remained with the renamed Grandmaster Melle Mel and The Furious Five. Their highest charted single, 'Beat Street Breakdown – Part I', featured in the breakdance film, *Beat Street.* When Grandmaster Flash reunited his original group in 1987, Cowboy was serving a prison term.
CAUSE: His career on a downslide, Cowboy began using crack cocaine. Frequently arrested on drug charges in the last years of his life, he died of an undisclosed illness at Elmhurst Hospital in New York City. Although he had been an important pioneer of rap music, he died in obscurity.

Patrick Cowley

(PATRICK JOSEPH COWLEY)
Born October 19, 1950
Died November 12, 1982
A synthesizer player, Patrick Cowley backed gender-bending singer Sylvester on his disco hits, 'Dance (Disco Heat)'

and 'You Make Me Feel (Mighty Real)'. A native of Buffalo, Cowley was working at San Francisco's City Disco when he first met Sylvester, who was performing at the time. Cowley had several solo disco hits including 'Mengery'/'I Wanna Take You Home' and wrote and produced Paul Parker's 'Right On Target'. In 1981, Cowley teamed with producer-keyboardist Marty Blecman to form the label, Megatone Records, where he joined Sylvester in producing the single, 'Do You Wanna Funk'.
CAUSE: AIDS. He died in San Francisco.

Barbara Cowsill

Born July 12, 1928
Died January 31, 1985
Nicknamed "The Singing Mom", Barbara Cowsill was a member of the late-Sixties family, bubble-gum rock group, The Cowsills, joining her five sons and one daughter on a string of pop hits. Evolving out of a rock duo formed by brothers Bill and Bob Cowsill in their hometown of Middletown, Rhode Island, The Cowsills were managed by Barbara's husband, retired naval officer William "Bud" Cowsill. The last to join the group, Barbara Cowsill provided backing vocals but did not play an instrument. After honing a nightclub singing act around the Rhode Island area, The Cowsills moved to New York City to be closer to the music industry. Signing with MGM Records in 1967, the group enjoyed a quick string of chart successes with the million-selling, 'The Rain, The Park & Other Things' (1967), 'We Can Fly' (1968), 'Indian Lake' (1968), and from the rock musical of the same name, 'Hair' (1969). In 1969 The Cowsills became involved with the ABC network, first singing the theme song for the television series, *Love American Style*. But when ABC offered the group its own television sitcom, The Cowsills turned down the offer when the network demanded that Shirley Jones play their mother. Instead, ABC launched *The Partridge Family*. After disbanding the group in 1972, the Cowsill family declared bankruptcy. Several of the group's members turned to drugs or alcohol during the next two decades.
CAUSE: She died in Tempe, Arizona, after a long bout of emphysema. Her death was kept a secret for years, and the cause was not publicised. She died while working the overnight shift at a nursing home. Bud Cowsill died on September 29, 1992, from leukemia.

Barry Cowsill

Born September 14, 1954
Died circa September 2, 2005
The bassist and backing vocalist of The Cowsills, Barry Cowsill joined his brothers, a sister and his mother in the family act. Evolving from a rock duo formed by brothers Bill and Bob Cowsill in their hometown of Middletown, Rhode Island, The Cowsills were managed by their father, retired naval officer William "Bud" Cowsill. Although Barry yearned for a career in a harder rock group, his fortunes came with light pop music. After earning a regular spot at a nightclub in Newport, Rhode Island, the group was discovered by a producer from NBC's *The Today Show* and was given the opportunity to perform for a national audience. Signed by MGM Records in 1967, the Cowsills enjoyed a quick string of quirky hits including the million-selling, 'The Rain, The Park & Other Things' (1967), 'We Can Fly' (1968), 'Indian Lake' (1968), and from the rock musical of the same name, 'Hair' (1969). Barry Cowsill sang lead vocals on several album tracks including 'Please Mr. Postman' and 'Painting The Day'. In 1969, The Cowsills began an association with the ABC network, performing the theme song for the television series, *Love, American Style*, but when ABC offered the group its own television sitcom, the family

rejected the offer after the network demanded Shirley Jones play their mother. After disbanding in 1972, the Cowsill family declared bankruptcy. Barry continued to perform, and while in Boston during the early Eighties, he was a member of the bands Blind Lemon Pledge and The Allston Brothers. By the Nineties, Barry pursued a solo career and occasionally teamed with three of his siblings for Cowsills reunion concerts; in 1998, the group released an album of new material, *Global*.
CAUSE: In the aftermath of Hurricane Katrina, Barry Cowsill took refuge in a warehouse and left his sister a chilling telephone message on September 2, asking for help in escaping the violence and looting. When he failed to make further contact, his family feared he was one of the 1,000 unidentified hurricane victims housed in a New Orleans morgue. On December 27, Barry's body was discovered by police near a pier in New Orleans, and was identified six days later through dental records. He had relocated to New Orleans the previous year.

Kevin Coyne

Born January 27, 1944
Died December 2, 2004
An eccentric British blues-rock singer-songwriter, Kevin Coyne nurtured a cult following during his four decades of work. Joining a number of amateur rock bands during his teens, he gave up music while attending art college. After leaving school in 1965, he worked in a mental hospital, which was the creative seed for much of his musical output. Joining forces with guitarist Dave Clague, the duo evolved into Siren, a London-based blues-folk group led by Nick Cudworth, featuring Coyne on lead vocal. Siren recorded a pair of fine but ignored albums which were released on David Peel's label, Dandelion Records. Pursuing a solo career, Coyne was aided by Clague on the 1972 album, *Case History*. Signing with the then-fledgling label Virgin Records in 1973, Coyne issued several solo albums, the last *Sanity Stop* (1980) employing the punk band The Ruts. A heavy drinker, Coyne remained in Germany after the completion of a tour in 1985. Sobering up and turning his attention to songwriting, he continued issuing albums, most of which were ignored outside Germany, and wrote several books. Both John Lydon and The Police have cited Coyne as an influence.
CAUSE: Lung fibrosis. He died at his home in Nuremberg, Germany.

Lee Crabtree

Born c. 1946
Died February 6, 1973
A member of the Sixties anti-establishment rock band The Fugs, Lee Crabtree joined in 1966 and appeared on two albums, *The Fugs* (which included liner notes by Allen Ginsberg) and *Virgin Fugs*. Formed in 1965 by poet/writers Ed Sanders, Ken Weaver and Tuli Kupferberg, The Fugs challenged conformity with their outrageous lyrics and found little in the way of radio airplay. Though a talented keyboard and flute player, Crabtree was forced from the band. He later joined the Holy Modal Rounders.
CAUSE: Undetermined, but some reports suggest suicide.

Carl Crack

(KARL BOHM)
Born May 6, 1971
Died September 6, 2001
A co-founder of the German hardcore-techno band Atari Teenage Riot, Swiss-born vocalist Carl Crack merged left-wing politics with experimental dance music. Formed in 1992 as a trio, the group initially garnered attention with their controversial début single, 'Hunting For Nazis'. Featuring Crack's often shouted lyrics, the group's music was accentuated by samples and occasional metal guitar riffs. After releasing a

number of singles on the British label Phonogram Records, the group broke their contract and in 1994 launched their own label, Digital Hardcore Recordings (DHR). Following their growing popularity in Europe, Atari Teenage Riot broke into the US market with their third album, *60 Second Wipe Out* (1999). The group took a break to permit Crack to treat his debilitating addictions. At the time of his death, he was working on the follow-up to his solo début album, *Black Ark*.
CAUSE: He was found dead in his Berlin apartment after accidentally overdosing.

Floyd Cramer

(FLOYD CRAMER, JR.)
Born October 27, 1933
Died December 31, 1997
A pop styled, country pianist with an instantly recognisable bent-note playing style, Floyd Cramer was born in Samti, Louisiana, but raised in Huttig, Arkansas. Self taught, Cramer received his first instrument at age five. Joining the house band for *The Louisiana Hayride* in Shreveport in 1951, Cramer performed behind a host of national performers including Hank Williams and a young Elvis Presley. First recording for Abbott Records, where he also worked as a session player, Cramer then took friend Chet Atkins' advice and moved to Nashville. A much in-demand session player, Cramer provided the piano on Elvis Presley's 'Heartbreak Hotel', Boots Randolph's 'Yakety Sax', Jimmy Dean's 'Big Bad John', Roy Orbison's 'Only The Lonely', and Patsy Cline's 'Crazy'. Pursuing a solo career, Cramer kicked off his chart run with his signature piece, the melancholy self-penned instrumental, 'Last Date'; with lyrics added by Boudleaux Bryant, the song was a hit later in the year for Skeeter Davis. Cramer scored several more instrumental hits including 'On The Rebound' (1961), which became a UK number 1, and 'San Antonio Rose' (1961). Touring in Elvis Presley's band and releasing dozens of albums at RCA, Cramer helped define the modern Nashville sound. Cramer scored his final hit in 1980 with the theme from television's *Dallas*.
CAUSE: Lung cancer. He had been diagnosed with the disease six months earlier. He died at his home in Madison, Tennessee.

Joe Crane

Born March 11, 1946
Died April 1980
Crane was the guitarist and keyboardist for the underrated Seventies West Coast-based, blues-rock band The Hoodoo Rhythm Devils, featuring vocalist Glenn Walters. Formed in the Sixties the group released a number of albums but were only able to garner regional attention with the track, 'Too Hot To Handle'.
CAUSE: Leukaemia.

Vincent Crane

Born May 21, 1943
Died February 4, 1989
Best known as the leader of Atomic Rooster, British-born Vincent Crane had previously joined Arthur Brown's London-based psychedelic rock group, The Crazy World Of Arthur Brown. Featuring Crane's eerie, frenetic, organ-work, the group landed its sole hit with the international smash, 'Fire'. Leaving Arthur Brown's group, Crane was joined by former bandmate, guitarist Carl Palmer, in 1969 to form Atomic Rooster. Featuring Crane on vocals and keyboards, Atomic Rooster experienced numerous line-up changes as it metamorphosed from a hard-rock to a blues-rock group, their best known singles coming in 1971 with 'Tomorrow Night' and 'The Devil's Answer'. After disbanding Atomic Rooster in 1974, Crane reteamed with Arthur Brown for the album, *Chisholm In My Bosom*. Crane formed a new version of Atomic Rooster in 1979. In 1983 Crane joined Dexy's Midnight

Runners, appearing on their album *Don't Stand Me Down*. He also penned material for Kim Wilde.
CAUSE: Suicide. He had suffered from long-term depression.

Darby Crash

(JAN PAUL BEAHM)
Born September 26, 1959
Died December 7, 1980
Lead singer of the influential Los Angeles-based punk rock band, The Germs, Darby Crash formed the outfit in 1977 after changing his stage name from Bobby Pyn. A spikey-haired anarchist, the charismatic and self-mutilating Crash led a band of inexperienced musicians, including for a brief period, future Go-Go's singer Belinda Carlisle. With the group's performances regularly marred by violence and food fights, The Germs had difficulty landing club gigs. After improving on their rudimentary musical skills, the group recorded a début independent single, 'Forming', followed by an album on Slash Records, *GI*. Leaving the group in early 1979, Crash travelled to England. Returning with a mohawk haircut, he formed the short-lived Darby Crash Band. With The Germs reuniting for one concert in December 1980, Crash spent his earnings on a lethal dose of heroin. Crash later emerged as a cult figure in punk rock, with two film makers planning biopics.
CAUSE: Heroin overdose. He killed himself at his home in Los Angeles as a tribute to his fallen idol Sid Vicious. Crash entered into a suicide pact with his girlfriend who survived; he had reportedly been planning his suicide for five years. Unfortunately for Crash, the press took little notice because John Lennon was killed the following day.

Pee Wee Crayton

(CONNIE CURTIS CRAYTON)
Born December 18, 1914
Died June 25, 1985
West Coast electric, blues guitarist, Pee Wee Crayton was tutored by T-Bone Walker in the mid Forties. After a stint with pianist Ivory Joe Hunter from 1945–49, the Texas-born Crayton was discovered in Los Angeles by Modern Records owner Jules Bihari. Scoring his first solo hit in 1949 with 'Yours Truly', Crayton continued with 'Blues After Hours', 'The Texas Hop' and 'I Love You So'. By the Sixties, Clayton was performing in a band behind Ray Charles. Leaving music for the most part in the Seventies, he worked as a truck driver. Rediscovered in 1982, he returned to the blues circuit.
CAUSE: Heart attack. He died during his sleep in a Los Angeles hospital.

"Papa" John Creach

Born May 28, 1917
Died February 22, 1994
Electric violinist who found fame as a member of Jefferson Airplane, Pennsylvania-born "Papa" John Creach was given his first violin at age 10 by his sailor uncle, who also played the instrument. Tiring of farming, Creach left his family farm in Michigan at the age of 20. Moving to Chicago in the late Thirties intending to work as a jazz musician, he briefly worked with the Illinois Symphony Orchestra. Later forming The Chocolate Music Bars, Creach performed in the city's many jazz clubs and mob-owned speakeasies. When the National Steel Company introduced the electric violin in 1943, Creach ordered a custom model and emerged as the country's first electric jazz violinist. Settling in Los Angeles in 1945, Creach secured a five-year residency on a cruise ship, the S.S. Catalina. Working as a session player during the next two decades, Creach at age 53 was discovered by Jefferson Airplane at the Parisian Room in San Francisco when Airplane drummer Joey Corington brought the band to hear the spirited player. Joining the Grace Slick fronted group in 1970, Creach was at first poorly received by audiences. Twice the age of the other

band members, the tall, skinny, and bony-fingered musician was soon embraced for his spirited, bluesy fiddle playing. First recording with Jefferson Airplane on their 1971 album *Bark*, Creach also launched a simultaneous solo career, releasing his first of seven solo albums with *Papa John And Friends*. Creach also joined a pair of Airplane members in the spin-off group, Hot Tuna. Joining the renamed Jefferson Starship in 1974, he appeared on the albums, *Dragonfly* and *Red Octopus*. Though stricken with arthritis, Creach remained an active performer in the Eighties, headlining a number of jazz and blues festivals. In 1992, Creach earned a W.C. Handy Award.
CAUSE: He died of natural causes at Midway Hospital in Los Angeles. He had been hospitalised for recurring heart and respiratory problems.

Linda Creed

Born December 6, 1948
Died April 10, 1986
A defining figure in the creation of the "Philadelphia Sound" of the Seventies, Linda Creed wrote hits for groups such as The Delfonics and The Stylistics. Born into a Jewish family in Philadelphia, Creed was drawn to black culture in her teens. Pursuing a career in music, she passed through a series of R&B bands including The Motivations, a group that featured 11 backing male singers. Introduced to producer Thomas Bell, Creed was initially hired as a secretary at a record company headed by the production team of Gamble & Huff. But with Bell encouraging Creed to try writing songs, her first attempt, 'Free Girl', was recorded by Dusty Springfield. Subsequently teaming with writing partner Bell, Creed enjoyed a string of mostly romantic ballad hits. With Bell usually composing the music and Creed the lyrics, the duo dominated the pop and R&B charts in the mid Seventies with 'I'm Stone In Love With You', 'You Are Everything', 'Break Up To Make Up', 'Betcha By Golly, Wow', 'You Make Me Feel Brand New' by The Stylistics; and 'Rubberband Man', 'I'm Coming Home' and 'Ghetto Child' by The Spinners. Creed co-wrote 'Greatest Love Of All' with Michael Masser for George Benson, featured in the 1977 Muhammad Ali film biography, *The Greatest*. Originally issued as a B-side, the song was a chart-topping hit for Whitney Houston at the time of Creed's death.
CAUSE: Cancer. Creed had been ill for a number of years and had refused to quit working. She died at her home in Ambler, Pennsylvania.

Arthur Crier

(ARTHUR GRIFFIN LEWIS CRIER JR.)
Born April 1, 1935
Died July 22, 2004
A gospel schooled singer-songwriter, Arthur Crier joined a series of doo-wop groups in the Fifties. Reared on the pop vocal music of The Ink Spots, Crier initially joined a local gospel group in his teens called The Heavenly Five. By the age of 18, he had formed his first doo-wop group, The Chimes. After issuing a pair of singles with little fanfare, Crier joined fellow band member Gary Morrison in The Mellows as the replacement for Harold Johnson but after recording several ignored singles, the group disbanded. Crier formed The Halos, finally hitting paydirt in 1961 with 'Nag', a novelty-styled R&B hit that prominently features Crier's deep bass vocals. The group had greater success as session vocalists, appearing on hit records for such artists as Dion, Johnny Nash, Bobby Vinton, Johnny Mathis, Little Eva, The Coasters, Connie Francis and Brian Hyland. Crier's recognisable bass voice can also be heard on Curtis Lee's 'Pretty Little Angel Eyes' and Barry Mann's 'Who Put The Bomp'. Relocating to Detroit in 1972, Crier worked at Motown Records in various roles including

songwriter and producer, but he left the label when it relocated to Los Angeles. By the mid Eighties, Crier returned to his doo-wop roots and re-formed The Mellows. Crier spent the last two decades of his life promoting the historical significance of doo-wop music and, in 1999, organised the "Another Great Day In Harlem" photograph, which featured hundreds of vocal group singers. He also produced a local television programme, *Doo-Wop Is Alive*. Crier's son, Keith, was a member of the R&B band GQ.
CAUSE: He died at his home in Warsaw, North Carolina, after suffering a heart attack.

Jim Croce

(JAMES JOSEPH CROCE)
Born January 10, 1943
Died September 20, 1973
A popular Seventies singer/songwriter who earned a dozen gold and platinum records during his brief career, Jim Croce was born and raised in suburban Philadelphia. He bought his first guitar at a toy store where he was working in the early Sixties. While attending college at Villanova, he joined a local rock group that played campus parties at weekends, and it was while hosting a folk music programme at the college's radio station that he met his future wife, Ingrid. By 1966, Jim and Ingrid Croce worked as counsellors at a summer camp in the woods of Pennsylvania. During this period Croce would compose the music for an Emmy Award winning documentary, *Miners' Story*. Moving to New York City in 1967, Jim Croce struggled financially as a coffee-house folk musician. Aided by musician friend, Tommy West, the Croces were soon signed as a duo by Capitol Records. Featuring self-composed material, their album *Jim And Ingrid Croce: Another Day, Another Time* (1969) was a commercial failure. Returning to a simple life in rural Lyndell, Pennsylvania, the Croces would recall this period away from city life as the happiest of their lives. Here, Jim Croce would write many of his future hits. During this time, he also worked as a construction worker and a remedial teacher. After sending several of his new compositions to West and his new partner, producer Terry Cashman, Croce was invited back to New York to record. Signed by ABC Records in 1972 as a solo artist, he scored a breakthrough with the title track of the album, *You Don't Mess Around With Jim*. His hit run continued with 'Operator' (1972), the million-selling 'Bad Bad Leroy Brown' (1973), and 'I Got A Name' (1973). Touring to the point of exhaustion from 1972–73, Croce died while flying to a performance. Croce scored several posthumous hits including 'I Got A Name' (1973), a song popularised by the television film *She Lives*, the lovely 'Time In A Bottle' (1973), and 'I'll Have To Say I Love You In A Song' (1974). Croce's widow Ingrid would spend millions of dollars in court during the next two decades fighting record companies and former business colleagues over her late husband's royalties and recording rights, before settling the case in 1985.
CAUSE: He died in a plane crash near Natchitoches, Louisiana, which also killed five others, including his manager Dominick Cortese, his guitarist Maury Muehleien, and comedian George Stevens who would open up for Croce. Hitting a tree, the charted plane went down shortly after its takeoff. Investigators would later rule that the craft had failed to gain sufficient altitude.
FURTHER READING: Jacobs, Linda. (1976). *Jim Croce: The Feeling Lives On*. St. Paul, MN: EMC.

G.L. Crockett

(GEORGE CROCKETT)
Born September 18, 1928
Died February 15, 1967
A Mississippi-born blues singer, G.L.

Crockett landed on the charts with his sole hit in 1965 with 'It's A Man Down There'.
CAUSE: Unknown.

Howard Crockett

(HOWARD HAUSEY)
Born December 25, 1925
Died December 27, 1994
A songwriter who provided Johnny Horton with his 1956 hit, 'Honky Tonk Man', Howard Crockett was a performer in the Fifties on *The Louisiana Hayride* programme. Previously a professional baseball player, he was a pitcher on the Brooklyn Dodgers' farm team, forced to retire after a shoulder injury. In 1986, Dwight Yoakam landed his début hit with a cover of Crockett's 'Honky Tonk Man'.
CAUSE: Lung cancer. He died at his home in Fort Worth, Texas.

Tony Crombie

(ANTHONY JOHN CROMBIE)
Born August 27, 1925
Died October 18, 1999
A self-taught British jazz drummer, Tony Crombie is best known for his associations with Ronnie Scott and John Dankworth. After backing Duke Ellington on a European tour in 1948, Crombie launched a bebop band in London, Club Eleven. Mastering the piano in the early Fifties, Crombie sometimes played both instruments on recordings. With the rise of rock in the mid Fifties, Crombie formed Tony Crombie's Rockets, his own rock outfit, with former jazz musicians whose reputation for unruly behaviour caused them to be banned at many venues. When former bandmate Ronnie Scott opened his legendary London jazz spot in 1959, Crombie was hired as the house drummer, and was a member of Scott's various jazz ensembles. Crombie later joined Georgie Fame's Blue Flames, and worked as a touring drummer for acts such as Tony Bennett and Jack Jones. Leaving music in the Nineties, he became an antiques dealer.
CAUSE: Natural causes.

Robbin Crosby

(ROBBINSON LANCE CROSBY)
Born August 4, 1959
Died June 6, 2002
The burly lead guitarist of the popular Eighties pop-metal band Ratt, Robbin Crosby provided a number of memorable riffs. Conceived in 1981 by Crosby and vocalist Stephen Pearcy, Ratt was at the forefront of the "hair band" genre, and Crosby (from La Jolla, California) was primarily influenced by Jimi Hendrix. After issuing a self-titled début release in 1983, Ratt earned a recording contract with Atlantic Records by means of its connections to Mötley Crüe. Issued in 1984, the three-million-selling *Out Of The Cellar* spawned a trio of radio and MTV hits, 'Round And Round', 'Back For More' and 'Wanted Man'. Frequently touring with another metal act Poison, Ratt released a series of hit albums including *Invasion Of Your Privacy*, *Reach For The Sky* and *Detonator*. Following the departure of Stephen Pearcy, Ratt disbanded in 1992, but later re-formed with Jizzy Pearl on vocals and John Corabi on guitar.
CAUSE: Heart attack due to AIDS. He died at his apartment in Hollywood, California. A heroin user, he was diagnosed with the disease in 1994 as a result of using dirty needles.

Jimmy Cross

Born April 27, 1939
Died October 8, 1978
A singer-songwriter, Jimmy Cross scored a minor hit in 1965 with the necro-rock, novelty classic 'I Want My Baby Back'. The single received additional exposure in the Eighties via regular airplay on *The Dr. Demento Show*. A false rumour later circulated

that Jimmy Cross was really Harry Nilsson.
CAUSE: Heart attack. He died in North Hollywood, California.

Arthur "Big Boy" Crudup

Born August 24, 1905
Died March 28, 1974
A popular Forties jump-blues artist best known for having written 'That's All Right', the first song recorded by Elvis Presley, Mississippi-born Arthur "Big Boy" Crudup was a musical late bloomer who did not pick up the guitar until in his twenties. A large man, Crudup earned his nickname "Big Boy" during his youth. Soon, like millions of American blacks, Crudup migrated to the North. Arriving in Chicago in 1941 as part of a loose knit gospel group, within days Crudup was homeless, forced to work as a street singer. Miraculously discovered during a sidewalk performance by talent scout Lester Melrose, Crudup was introduced to legendary bluesman Big Bill Broonzy. Switching to an electric guitar by 1942, Crudup recorded a series of straight-forward, Delta-styled blues records, accentuated by his high piercing voice. During this period, Crudup spent his days working in a Chicago tyre factory. Taking an R&B turn in the late Forties, Crudup signed with RCA/Bluebird Records. After scoring a regional hit with one of his compositions, 'That's All Right', he took his earnings and returned to Mississippi to work on a farm. Whenever he was in need of additional funds, he would sporadically visit Chicago over the next few years to record new material. But when RCA began issuing 45-rpm records in 1949, the label's first R&B single release was Crudup's 'That's All Right', heard on the radio by the young hillbilly Elvis Presley. Presley would record 'That's All Right' as the A-side of his début single at Sun Records in 1954. (Presley would later cover two more Crudup songs, 'So Glad You're Mine' and 'My Baby Left Me'.) Paid no royalties for Presley's hit, Crudup was for a time again homeless. Disillusioned, Crudup quit the music business and moved to Virginia where he bought a farm. Returning to the stage, he enjoyed a revival in the late Sixties, and teamed with a young Bonnie Raitt in the Seventies.
CAUSE: Stroke. He died at the North Hamthamton-Accomac Memorial Hospital in Nassawadox, Virginia. He had been hospitalised for a week, and never regained consciousness.

Joseph Cubert

Born 1947
Died 1991
The founding rhythm guitarist of the Detroit-based rock/blue-eyed soul act Mitch Ryder & The Detroit Wheels, Joseph Cubert shared guitar duties with James McCarty (later a member of The Electric Flag). Cubert had previously been a member of another local act The Tempest. Formed as Billy Lee & The Rivieras, the high energy Detroit Wheels were originally rejected by Berry Gordy of Motown Records but were signed by The Four Seasons' producer Bob Crewe to his Dyno-Voice label in 1965 after he saw them outperform headlining act, The Dave Clark Five. Beginning with 'Jenny Take A Ride!' The Detroit Wheels performed a string of urgent, upbeat hits in the mid Sixties with 'Little Latin Lupe Lu', 'Devil With A Blue Dress On'/'Good Golly Miss Molly' and 'Sock It To Me Baby!' but after Crewe attempted to foster Ryder as a solo act, the group fell apart.
CAUSE: Liver cancer.

Joe Cuoghi

Born May 15, 1922
Died July 1970
The long-time proprietor of Hi Records since shortly after its inception

in the mid Fifties, Joe Cuoghi operated the Memphis-based label along with partner John Novarese. Cuoghi and Novarese had combined the label with their 10-year-old record wholesale business, Poplar Tunes. A successful organisation, Hi Records was home to hit acts such as The Bill Black Combo and Ace Cannon. Hiring Willie Mitchell as the label's music director, Hi Records had success with soul acts Al Green and Syl Johnson.
CAUSE: Unknown.

Steve Currie

Born May 21, 1947
Died April 28, 1981
The bass player for Marc Bolan's group, T. Rex from 1970 to 1975, the British-born Steve Currie had previously been a member of a group called The Rumble. After switching from folk to electric rock in 1970, Bolan hired several musicians in 1970, including Mickey Finn, Bill "Legend" Fyfield, and Steve Currie. Currie had auditioned for Bolan after answering a newspaper advertisement. Sporting a glam-rock look, T. Rex would lead the popular movement in England alongside David Bowie and David Essex. In 1971, the quartet released its breakthrough, *Electric Warrior*, the album highlighted by the group's only US Top 10 single, 'Bang A Gong (Get It On)' (1972). T. Rex followed with a number of critically acclaimed albums, including *The Slider* (1972) and *Tanx* (1973). Bolan reworked his band in 1974, firing everyone but Currie. That year, the group released the poorly received album, *Zipgun Boogie*. Bolan disbanded T. Rex in 1975, but would form a new version of the group in 1976 minus Currie. Currie continued performing and recording with a number of acts including Wreckless Eric and Chris Spedding.
CAUSE: Car crash. Around midnight on April 28, 1981, Currie's car veered off the road near his home in Val Da Parra, Portugal.

Chris Curtis

(CHRISTOPHER CRUMMY)
Born August 26, 1941
Died February 28, 2005
The drummer and backing vocalist of the Merseybeat band The Searchers, Chris Curtis joined in 1962 as the replacement for Norman McGarry. Originally formed as a skiffle group, The Searchers often performed at the Star Club in Hamburg, Germany, the same venue in which The Beatles honed their stage act. In the wake of The Beatles' success, British labels swooped into Liverpool and signed a number of acts, with The Searchers landing at Pye Records under Tony Hatch. Beginning with their début single in 1963 – a cover of The Drifters' 'Sweets For My Sweet' – The Searchers followed up with a string of smash hits including 'Sugar And Spice' and the often covered Jackie DeShannon/Sonny Bono composition, 'Needles And Pins'. Curtis composed a number of tracks for the group, including 'No One Else Could Love Me', 'I Pretend I'm With You' and 'He's Got No Love'. Exhausted by the rigours of the pop business, Curtis left The Searchers in 1966 during a tour with P.J. Proby and subsequently teamed with his brother Dave, guitarist Ritchie Blackmore and keyboard player Jon Lord in the rock band, Roundabout; the group later evolved into Deep Purple. Leaving the group, Curtis produced Paul & Barry Ryan, and occasionally returned to the stage. He later took a civil service job.
CAUSE: Unknown. He was found dead at his home after a long illness.

Ian Curtis

(IAN KEVIN CURTIS)
Born July 15, 1956
Died May 18, 1980
Vocalist for the innovative Joy Division, Ian Curtis joined the group in 1977. From Manchester, and originally called Stiff Kittens and then Warsaw,

the group was launched by bassist Peter Hook and guitarist Bernard Sumner. Installing the moody Ian Curtis as lead singer, Joy Division was completed with the addition of drummer Steven Morris. Curtis played additional guitar. Renamed Joy Division (the SS term for the Nazi brothel corps), the group started out as a guitar-oriented band, before adopting a multi-layered, textured synthesiser sound. An introspective lyricist who was attracted to the dark rock of The Velvet Underground, Curtis found in the group his ideal musical vehicle. An engaging, charismatic figure, Curtis frequently shocked audiences with onstage manic movements, made more intense as he was prone to epileptic seizures. Joy Division recorded for their manager Tony Wilson's label, the under-funded Factory Records, and benefited from the support of prominent British deejay John Peel, twice performing on his radio show. By early 1979, any vestiges of their punk influences had faded from their sound and Joy Division was moving towards a bleaker, gothic rock style. After supplying a bevy of tracks to various compilation projects, Joy Division released its début LP, *Unknown Pleasures*, in 1979. Recorded on a shoestring budget, the much-copied album was produced by electronic whiz, Martin "Zero" Hannett. Often referred to as the group's fifth member, he played an important part in the group's sound as he constantly purchased and applied state of the art technologies to their record production. This energetic and strangely romantic record would find Curtis vamping through dark, chilling and disturbing images on hit tracks such as 'Transmission' and 'Atmosphere'. Released two months after Curtis' death in 1980, a second Joy Division studio album, *Closer*, confirmed their standing as one of the most important and influential groups of the era. Commercially, they achieved their greatest success with the posthumously released 'Love Will Tear Us Apart'.

CAUSE: Curtis committed suicide by hanging the night before the start of the group's first American tour. He hung himself on a clothes line in the kitchen of his flat in Macclesfield which he shared with his girlfriend and bandmates. An Iggy Pop record was playing on the stereo at the time. He had attempted suicide on a previous occasion. Curtis was despondent about his failed marriage. Joy Division had agreed to drop their name if any of its members ever "left" the group. Consequently, Joy Division evolved into the popular modern/dance group New Order, and Bernard Sumner took over the lead vocals.

FURTHER READING: Edge, Brian. (1985, revised 1988). *Joy Division & New Order: Pleasures And Wayward Distractions*. London: Omnibus.

Mann Curtis

(NORMAN KURTZ, SR.)
Born 1911
Died December 6, 1984

Lyricist who penned 'The Jones Boy', The Everly Brothers' 'Let It Be Me' and 'The Story Of A Starry Night', Mann Curtis also wrote many uncredited songs with Duke Ellington, for which he was paid little.

CAUSE: Unknown. He died in San Francisco.

Rick Curtis

Born c. 1956
Died January 31, 1996

A vocalist and guitarist with Neil Young's occasional backing band Crazy Horse from 1972–73, Rick Curtis and his brother Mike joined the group at the invitation of drummer Ralph Molina, with Rick writing or co-writing half of the *Crooked Lake* album. The Curtis brothers had previously been members of Sixties psychedelic rock band, These Vizitors.

In 1974, the brothers recorded some demos with the duo Lindsey Buckingham & Stevie Nicks; one of the songs, the Rick Curtis composition 'Blue Letter', was later recorded by Fleetwood Mac. Another track, 'Seven League Boots', was later reworked by Stephen Stills as 'Southern Cross', and became a hit in 1982 for Crosby, Stills & Nash.
CAUSE: Suffering a seizure, he died at his home.

John Curulewski

Born October 3, 1950
Died February 1988
The original guitarist of the Seventies heartland rock act Styx, John Curulewski left just before the group achieved massive fame. Formed from the nucleus of a rock band led by twins Chuck and John Panozzo and Dennis DeYoung, the trio hired Curulewski, their classmate at Chicago State University. Originally known as TW4, the group then expanded with the addition of James Young and Tommy Shaw. Discovered in 1971 by label owner Bill Traut, the renamed Styx was signed to Wooden Nickel Records; releasing their début album *Styx* in 1971, and building a solid Midwest fanbase with heavy touring. Finally, in 1975, the group belatedly landed its breakthrough pop hit with a three-year-old track, the Dennis DeYoung-penned power ballad, 'Lady'. Curulewski quit shortly after the release of the group's A&M Records début release, *Equinox*. Disillusioned by the record industry and wanting to spend more time with his family, Curulewski subsequently performed with a number of local Chicago bands and operated a music store and recording studio.
CAUSE: He died after suffering a brain aneurysm at his mother's home.

Johnny Cymbal

Born February 3, 1945
Died March 16, 1993
Pop and country singer-songwriter, Johnny Cymbal was born in Ochiltree, Scotland, but raised in Goderich, Ontario. A fan of country and western music in his youth, he began a singing career at age 13. Moving to Cleveland a year later, there he had formed his first rock band. Hiring Baltimore deejay Jack Gale as his manager, Cymbal was signed by MGM Records in 1960. Cymbal's MGM releases failed miserably, as did those at Kedlin Records. Signing with Kapp Records, Cymbal scored his first hit with the self-penned, doo-wop throwback, 'Mr. Bass Man' (1963). The song featured the booming bass vocals of former Coasters member, Ronnie Bright. Cymbal followed with a minor hit, the morbid 'Teenage Heaven'. By the late Sixties Cymbal had jumped into the bubblegum music craze. After recording unsuccessfully as Milk on the Buddah label, he signed with Bang Records where, under the name Derek, he returned to the charts with the hits, 'Cinnamon' (1968) and 'Back Door Man' (1969). Turning to production work, he collaborated with The Partridge Family and wrote David Cassidy's 1972 solo hit 'Rock Me Baby'. Attempting another comeback later in the decade, Cymbal teamed with Peggy Clinger as a rock duo, Cymbal and Clinger. Cymbal later moved to Nashville to work as a full-time producer in the country music field. Also continuing to record, he used yet another alias, George Tobin.
CAUSE: Heart attack. He died in Nashville.

D

D-Roc

(Dennis L. Miles)
Born March 28, 1959
Died August 17, 2004
As the rhythm guitarist for Ice-T's rap/heavy metal band Body Count, D-Roc was continually dogged by controversy. Wary of fame, he wore an ominous hockey mask and wool cap both on and off stage. Formed by Crenshaw High School classmates in the south central section of Los Angeles, Body Count initially backed Ice-T on his 1991 album *OG Original Gangster*, and drew positive reviews after their performances together on the Lollapalooza tour that same year. Body Count's self-titled 1992 début album was initially ignored until a Texas police force threatened a boycott of Time-Warner because of the track, 'Cop Killer'. Although the track was eventually deleted from the disc, the surrounding controversy elevated the group's rise in popularity. Leaving Time-Warner, Body Count issued their second album, *Born Dead*, on Ice-T's fledgling label, Priority. Although they failed to sustain their popularity, Ice-T and Body Count followed up with the critically acclaimed 1997 album, *Violent Demise*. Nicknamed "The Executioner", D-Roc later worked with Macy Gray and his own band Pitch Black.

Harry Dailey

Born December 22, 1951
Died April 18, 2003
A member of Jimmy Buffett's Coral Reefer Band, bassist Harry Dailey co-wrote the Buffett hit, 'Volcano'. Joining in 1975, Dailey performed on the hits, 'Changes In Latitudes, Changes In Attitudes', 'Coconut Telegraph', 'Son Of A Son Of A Sailor' and 'You Had To Be There', and his final performance with Buffett came in 2001 at a Coral Reefer reunion concert. A native of Bethesda, Maryland, Dailey had previously been a member of a folk-blues duo with Gove Scrivenor.
Cause: He suffered a heart attack and died at his home in Falls Church, Virginia. In poor health for several years, he was also stricken with the Epstein-Barr disease virus.

Dalida

(Yolande Gigliotti)
Born January 17, 1933
Died May 3, 1987
Born in Egypt to Italian parents, but living in France, Dalida enjoyed success as both a singer and actress. Best known for her international hit, 'Bambina' (1954), she sang primarily in French or Italian, selling in excess of 85 million records worldwide.
Cause: Suicide by barbiturate overdose. She was found dead in her Paris apartment. A nearby suicide note read: "Life is unbearable. Forgive Me."

Damita Jo

(Damita Jo DuBlanc)
Born August 5, 1930
Died December 25, 1998
Jazz and R&B songstress, Damita Jo was attracted to show business while living in California in the early Fifties. Joining her future husband's group as the featured singer, Steve Gibson & The Red Caps, she provided the vocals on their 1952 hit, 'I Went To Your Wedding'. Also a solo artist, she scored hits with 'I Don't Care' (1953); the million-selling 'I'll Save The Last Dance For You' (1960) (an answer record to The Drifters' 'Save The Last Dance For Me'); and 'I'll Be There' (1961) (an answer record to Ben E. King's 'Stand By Me'). She followed with an international hit a few years later in a duet with Billy Eckstine, 'Loves A Ball' (1964). Costumed in sequined gowns, she toured internationally into the mid Eighties. A

regular on Redd Foxx's late Seventies variety programme, Damita Jo also toured with the comedian. Retiring in Baltimore, she later turned to gospel music, releasing an album of religious material in 1985.
CAUSE: Respiratory illness. She died in Baltimore.

Denis "Piggy" D'Amour

Born 1959
Died August 26, 2005
The guitarist of the Canadian thrash-metal band Voivod, Denis "Piggy" D'Amour blended complex jazz chords with progressive rock. Raised in suburban Montreal, he earned his childhood nickname "Piggy" due to his weight. Fronted by vocalist Denis "Snake" Belanger, Voivod released their début album in 1984, *War And Pain*. Building a loyal following, the group was at its peak in 1989 with the release of *Nothingface*, which was highlighted by a cover of Pink Floyd's 'Astronomy Domine' and a US tour, featuring opening acts Faith No More and Soundgarden. After briefly disbanding in 2001, a new line-up included former Metallica bassist Jason Newsted. Voivod was working on its 14th album at the time of D'Amour's death.
CAUSE: Colon cancer. He died in a Montreal hospital. He had survived thyroid cancer in 1988.

Dennis Danell

Born June 24, 1961
Died February 29, 2000
The guitarist of California-based punk band, Social Distortion, Dennis Danell joined in 1979 at the invitation of singer Mike Ness, a heroin-using classmate from Fullerton High School. Danell's addition to the group caused a rift, with two of the members leaving to form The Adolescents. Initially a bassist, Danell switched to lead guitar as the group's line-up evolved. After releasing their first single '1945', they followed with a well-received album, the thrashing, self-abusing *Mommy's Little Monster* (1983). The group's low-budget tour that same year was captured in the documentary *Another State Of Mind*. Although Ness wrote most of the group's material, Danell co-wrote tracks on the 1988 album, *Prison Bound*. After surviving the rise and fall of punk's popularity, Social Distortion went on a sabbatical with the release of the 1998 album, *Live At The Roxy*. Danell subsequently took a day job in the property field and produced a number of acts at the group's recording studio in Fullerton, California. Pursuing a side project, Danell and Social Distortion bassist John Maurer formed Fuel, sharing lead vocals in the quartet. Danell had launched a second side venture, The Strung Gurus, nearly completing a début album which was to be released on Danell's own Masterpiece Records.
CAUSE: He suffered a brain aneurysm in the driveway of his new home, in Newport Beach, California, while moving furniture.

Rich Dangel

(RICHARD DANGEL)
Born December 1, 1942
Died December 3, 2002
A member of the Washington state surf-instrumental group The (Fabulous) Wailers, who had a hit with 'Tall Cool One' in 1959. A native of Texas, guitarist Rich Dangel joined the John Greek-led teenage group in 1958. 'Tall Cool One', composed by Dangel and Greek, unexpectedly recharted in 1964, a year after Dangel had left the band.
CAUSE: Suffering a brain aneurysm, he died at his home in Seattle.

Rick Danko

Born December 29, 1942
Died December 10, 1999
The bass guitarist and occasional singer in The Band, Rick Danko was born into a musical family in the small town of Simcoe, Ontario. He quit

school at 14 to pursue a career in music and at 17 landed his first professional gig as a member of the Ronnie Hawkins-led rockabilly band, The Hawks. Although hired as a rhythm guitarist, he soon switched to bass guitar and by late 1961 The Hawks had settled into the classic line-up of Danko, Richard Manuel, Garth Hudson, Robbie Robertson, and Levon Helm. When Danko was fired by Hawkins in 1964 for bringing a girlfriend to a club, the remaining Hawks quit, formed Levon & The Hawks and headed for North America. After a period of playing in bars up and down the east coast they settled in New York where they backed blues guitarist John Hammond, Jr. Danko and co. were hired as Bob Dylan's touring musicians, just as he was switching from acoustic to electric folk rock, but night after night, Dylan and the group (minus Helm), now referred to as The Band, were booed around the globe by folk purists. With Dylan settling into a rented pink house (nicknamed "The Big Pink") near Woodstock, New York, after suffering a near-fatal motorcycle crash, Danko and the others joined him. Here they spent their days playing music informally but the tracks were bootlegged on the widely issued *The Great White Wonder* album and officially released in 1975 as *The Basement Tapes*. Signing with Capitol Records, The Band enjoyed much critical praise for their début release *Music From Big Pink* (1968), which featured all of the members, apart from Hudson, contributing lead vocals. Embracing a rustic sound that combined country, folk and blues, The Band followed up with the self-titled *The Band* (1969), which was highlighted by the group's highest-charting US single 'Up On Cripple Creek', and the often recorded 'The Night They Drove Old Dixie Down' (later a Top 10 hit for Joan Baez). The Band continued to release albums including *Stage Fright* (1970), *Cahoots* (1971), *Rock Of Ages* (1972), and the Alan Freed tribute, *Moondog Matinee* (1973). They rejoined Dylan in 1973, backing him on *Planet Waves*, and on a 1974 tour which spawned the subsequent live release, *Before The Flood*. In 1976, at Robertson's behest, the group disbanded and to mark their exit, an all-star concert was organised on November 25, 1976 at the Winterland Ballroom in San Francisco. Billed as 'The Last Waltz', the Thanksgiving Day concert was captured on a three-album set, and an acclaimed Martin Scorsese documentary. After recording a contractually required studio album *Islands*, The Band formally disbanded. In 1978, Danko became the first member of The Band to release a self-titled solo album, featuring guest appearances from Eric Clapton, Ronnie Wood and Doug Sahm. Reunited in 1986, The Band (minus Robertson) launched a series of small venue tours, with Danko assuming more vocal duties. In 1989, Danko and Helm were touring members of Ringo Starr's All-Star Band. Switching gears, in 1991, Danko found European success in a trio with folk singer Eric Anderson and Norwegian singer-songwriter Jonas Fjeld, releasing the first of two highly regarded albums.

CAUSE: He died in his sleep at his home in Woodstock, New York. Standing at 350 pounds, he was not in good health for the last few years of his life. His weight gain was the result of his battle against heroin addiction.

FURTHER READING: Hoskyns, Barney. (1993). *Across The Great Divide: The Band And America*. New York: Hyperion.

Bobby Darin

(WALDEN ROBERT CASSOTTO)

Born May 14, 1936

Died December 20, 1973

A versatile rock, jazz and standards singer, Bobby Darin was a success across several genres. Born and raised in East Harlem, New York, Darin suffered rheumatic fever in his childhood which permanently damaged his heart. Often bedridden as a child, he was advised by doctors that he would not survive past age 18. Expecting to die young, Darin would be an aggressive risk-taker his entire life. After attending Hunter College for one semester, Darin quit school to fulfil his dream to become an entertainer. Aided by his friend, songwriter Don Kirshner, Darin signed with Decca Records where he bombed with a cover version of Lonnie Donegan's 'Rock Island Line' (1956). Switching to Atlantic Records at age 21 in 1957, Darin was the first white rock artist signed to the R&B label. After releasing a series of flop singles, Darin scored a million-selling début hit with 'Splish Splash', the song written by Darin but credited to his mother and New York disc jockey Murray The K. During the same period, Darin used a pseudonym at Brunswick Records where he scored a pop hit with 'Early In The Morning' as by The Ding Dongs (after legal action, the record was re-released at Atlantic as by The Rinky-Dinks). Darin's Atlantic hits continued with a pair of self-composed numbers, 'Queen Of The Hop' (1958) and 'Dream Lover' (1959). Unhappy as a pop singer, Darin was instead attracted to the sound of crooners like Tony Bennett and Frank Sinatra. Ignoring Dick Clark's advice that it would be a career-ending move, Darin recorded a jazzy, orchestrated rendition of 'Mack The Knife', a Kurt Weill composition from 1928's *The Threepenny Opera*. With the song a smash hit, Darin continued his hit run with covers of pop standards, 'Beyond The Sea' (1960), 'Clementine' (1960), 'Won't You Come Home Bill Bailey' (1960), and 'You Must Have Been A Beautiful Baby' (1961). Leading a story-book life, Darin married starlet Sandra Dee in December 1961 (they divorced in 1968). Switching to Capitol Records in 1962 as a replacement for Frank Sinatra, Darin enjoyed hits with 'You're The Reason I'm Living' (1963) and '18 Yellow Roses' (1963). Targeting an adult fanbase, Darin adopted the persona of a tuxedoed cabaret singer, playing to packed houses in Las Vegas. Also a popular actor, Darin appeared in several films including *Come September* (1959), *Pepe* (1960), *State Fair* (1961), *Pressure Point* (1962), and the movie in which he earned an Oscar nomination as Best Supporting Actor, *Captain Newman M.D.* Returning to Atlantic Records in 1965, Darin entered the acoustic, folk singer phase of his career. An unlikely protest singer who would turn his back on the excesses of stardom, Darin scored folk-styled hits with the John Sebastian-penned 'Lovin' You', and one of the seven Tim Hardin compositions he would record, 'If I Were a Carpenter'. Launching his own label, Direction Records in 1967, Darin recorded the much-ignored protest album *Born Walden Robert Cassotto*. Signing with Motown in the early Seventies, Darin released a pair of poorly selling albums. Hosting a summer replacement variety show on NBC beginning in 1972, Darin was signed to star in his own series the following year. The Bobby Darin film biography *Beyond The Sea* (2004) starred Kevin Spacey as Darin and Kate Bosworth as Sandra Dee. Dee passed away a few months after the film's release.

CAUSE: Suffering from a recurring heart condition caused by childhood rheumatic fever, Darin died after surgery to replace a heart valve. He had undergone an operation two years earlier to have two artificial valves implanted. According to Darin's son, Dodd Darin, in his biography of his father, a trip to the dentist was the precursor of Bobby Darin's death, as he forgot to take his usual antibiotics.

FURTHER READING: DiOrio, Al. (1981).

Borrowed Time: The 37 Years Of Bobby Darin. Philadelphia: Running Press.

Larry Darnell

(LEO EDWARD DONALD)
Born December 21, 1928
Died July 3, 1983
A popular balladeer who merged jump-blues with the passion of the gospel music of his youth, Larry Darnell left home at age 15 to join the backing band of a travelling burlesque troupe, The Brownskin Models. Relocating to New Orleans, he found work at the Dew Drop Inn and scored a series of R&B ballad hits including 'For You, My Love' (1949) and 'I Love You Baby' (1950). Retiring from music in the late Sixties, he returned to his hometown of Columbus, Ohio, where he sang in church choirs.
CAUSE: He died of lung cancer in Columbus, Ohio. He was diagnosed with the disease in 1979 during an operation for injuries sustained in a beating by three men in Akron, Ohio.

Eugene "Bird" Daughtry

Born 1939
Died December 25, 1994
Member of the Sixties soul vocal group The Intruders, whose biggest hit came in 1968 with the million-seller, orchestrated ballad, 'Cowboys To Girls', Eugene "Bird" Daughtry sang back-up behind the lead of Sam "Little Sonny" Brown. The first act to sign with the Philadephia-based production team of Gamble & Huff, The Intruders scored two dozen R&B hits at Gamble Records including 'Love Is Like A Baseball Game' and 'I'll Always Love Me Mama'. After disbanding in 1973, The Intruders reformed for occasional performances at oldies shows beginning in 1983.
CAUSE: Liver and kidney disease.

Billy Davenport

Born April 23, 1931
Died December 24, 1999
A blues drummer who worked with a host of legends, Billy Davenport is best known for his stunning performance on the ground-breaking blues-rock album *East West* by The Paul Butterfield Blues Band (1966). Learning to play the drums at age six after he found a pair of drumsticks on the pavement, Davenport played jazz while in high school. He later performed in Chicago's many jazz clubs before joining the military in 1951 and spending four years with the US Navy's Mechanical Drum and Bugle Corps. With the decline of jazz in Chicago, Davenport was forced to switch to blues, regularly performing with Muddy Waters, James Cotton, Junior Wells, and Howlin' Wolf. Davenport first met Butterfield in 1964, but joined his band the following year on the recommendation of Mike Bloomfield, as a replacement for Sam Lay who had accidentally shot himself. After illness in 1968 forced him to take a break, Davenport later joined the bands of Jimmy Dawkins, Willie Dixon and, later, The Pete Baron Jazztet.
CAUSE: Unknown. He died in Chicago.

Mack David

Born July 5, 1912
Died December 30, 1993
The older brother of prolific songwriter Hal David, Mack David scored his first collaborative hit composition in 1939 with 'Moon Love', a hit for Glenn Miller. A talented lyricist, he often teamed with Burt Bacharach beginning with The Shirelles' hit 'Baby It's You'. Frequently working on film scores in the Sixties, David's credits included *The Hanging Tree* and *It's A Mad, Mad, Mad, Mad World.* David's other pop hits included 'It Must Be Him' (Vikki Carr) and 'Cherry Pink And Apple Blossom White' (Perez Prado). He also penned the lyrics to several television themes including *Surfside 6*, *Caspar The Ghost* and *77 Sunset Strip*.
CAUSE: Natural causes. He died in Rancho Mirage, California.

Cyril Davies

Born 1932
Died January 7, 1964
A pioneer of British blues, Cyril Davies emerged as a popular bandleader and influence on future superstars in the early Sixties. Born in Denham, England, he began to hone his skills on the guitar and banjo while working as a carpenter in the early Forties. Drawn to American Dixieland jazz, he joined Chris Barber's jazz group in the early Fifties. By the mid Fifties, Davies teamed with bandmate Alexis Korner in forming a separate blues ensemble within Barber's group. Davies and Korner thus became crucial to the popularisation of the blues in Britain. Leaving Korner's group, Davies and Korner operated the Roadhouse Blues Club from 1957 to 1962. Besides showcasing American soul, blues and R&B artists, the small venue gave British artists such as Brian Jones, Mick Jagger and Eric Clapton their professional starts. Forming the legendary Blues Incorporated with Korner in 1961, Davies provided the vocals and harmonica. The group found a residency at the Marquee Club, a performance captured on the album *R&B From The Marquee*. Experiencing frequent personnel changes, a who's who of British blues-rockers passed through the group's ranks, including Charlie Watts, Long John Baldry, Jack Bruce and Ginger Baker, and Robert Plant was also a disciple. Leaving Blues Incorporated in 1962 to form his own group The All-Stars, Davies built the group from the remnants of Screaming Lord Sutch's backing band. With the addition of Long John Baldry in early 1963, The All-Stars enjoyed some airplay with 'Country Line Special' and 'Preachin' The Blues'. Achieving cult status in the UK, The All-Stars were renamed The Hoochie Coochie Men after Davies' death in 1964.
CAUSE: During an engagement at a nightclub on Eel Pie Island, Richmond, England, Davies collapsed from the combination of alcohol abuse and complications from leukemia. Some sources cite the cause of death as alcohol poisoning.

Roy Davies

Born c. 1950
Died 1986
A core member of the British R&B/disco ensemble Gonzalez, keyboardist Roy Davies played on their 1979 hit, 'Haven't Stopped Dancing Yet' – a Gloria Jones composition recorded two years previously and remixed for its release. In 1974, Davies had joined former Doors members Robby Krieger and John Densmore in a blues-rock quintet called The Butts Band but he was replaced after recording one album. Davies also recorded with Freddie King.
CAUSE: Cancer.

Billy Davis

(ROQUEL BILLY DAVIS)
Born July 11, 1932
Died September 2, 2004
A talented songwriter and producer, Billy Davis was at the forefront of Chicago soul in the Sixties. Breaking into music as a songwriter and member of a Fifties doo-wop group called The Thrillers, Davis later became their manager. Recording for a series of labels and experiencing a number of name changes – including The 5 Jets and The Voice Master – the group never managed a national hit. By 1957, a co-manager, Berry Gordy (who was also managing a young Jackie Wilson at the time), was added. Davis also became the manager for his cousin Lawrence Payton's group, The Four Aims, but when Davis sent a demo tape of original material to Chess Records, the label was more interested in the compositions than the group. The Four Aims were renamed The Four Tops and recorded two of Davis' compositions, while two other Davis songs, 'See Saw' and 'A Kiss From

Your Lips', became hits at Chess for The Moonglows. Encouraged by his success as a songwriter, Davis took the pseudonym Tyran Carlo and teamed with Berry Gordy in his pre-Motown days to write several hits for Jackie Wilson – including 'Lonely Teardrops', 'I'll Be Satisfied', 'Reet Petite' and 'To Be Loved' – as well as 'You Got What It Takes' for Marv Johnson. Unhappy with the meagre royalties he was earning, Davis joined Berry's sister, Gwen, to launch Anna Records but in 1961 the label was sold and incorporated into Motown. Subsequently, Davis was hired by Chess Records to oversee a Detroit-based satellite label called Check-Mate. Unable to score a national hit, Davis was brought to Chess' Chicago studio where he was hired as the head of the A&R department. Davis hired topnotch session players and songwriters and, taking the label in a different direction, he helped define Chicago soul with acts such as Jan Bradley, Fontella Bass, Billy Stewart, The Dells, Etta James and Little Milton. But with Chess undergoing management upheavals, Davis left in 1968 to work in advertising, co-writing jingles such as 'It's The Real Thing' for Coca-Cola and 'If You've Got The Time' for Miller Beer. He retired from the advertising business in 1987.
CAUSE: Suffering from a long-term, undisclosed illness, he died at his home in New Rochelle, New York.

Huey Davis

(HUEY MARVIN DAVIS)
Born August 17, 1938
Died February 23, 2002
A member of soul-vocal group The Contours, Mississippi-born guitarist Huey Davis joined an early incarnation of the group called The Blenders (not the Forties group of the same name) in 1959. Auditioning for Motown the following year, the group was initially rejected by label head Berry Gordy Jr., but were signed to the label in 1962 with the aid of Jackie Wilson. The Contours were responsible for Motown's first million-selling single with the raucous hit penned by Gordy, 'Do You Love Me?' The explosive dance record flopped in the UK, where an inferior cover version by Brian Poole & The Tremeloes topped the charts. Unable to return to the Top 40, The Contours continued their hit streak on the R&B charts with 'Shake Sherry', ' Can You Jerk Like Me?', a song written by Smokey Robinson and later covered by the J. Geils Band, 'First I Look At The Purse' and 'Just A Little Misunderstanding'. When the group disbanded in the late Sixties, Davis took positions in construction and private security. The 1987 hit film *Dirty Dancing* highlighted 'Do You Love Me?', with the reissued single returning to the charts. However, Davis did not join the re-formed touring version of the group.
CAUSE: Unknown. He died at his home in Detroit.

James "Jimmie" Davis

Born 1922
Died March, 1970
Bass player for Fats Domino from the mid Fifties until 1970.
CAUSE: He died in an automobile accident which injured Domino and several other band members.

James "Thunderbird" Davis

(JAMES HOUSTON)
Born November 10, 1938
Died January 23, 1992
Blues guitarist and singer, James "Thunderbird" Davis began as a gospel singer in his native Alabama. Switching to blues, he was a member of Guitar Slim's band, often used as a separate opening act. Following Guitar Slim's death in 1959, Davis joined the bands of Nappy Brown and Lloyd Lambert. Emerging as a solo act in the mid Sixties, Davis scored a pair of hits with 'Blue Monday' and 'Your Turn

To Cry'. Having abandoned music and been presumed dead by the Eighties, Davis was sought out by Black Top Records in 1988. Experiencing a stunning comeback, he recorded his first album, *Checkout Time* (1989).
CAUSE: Collapsing on-stage at the Blues Saloon in St. Paul, Minnesota, he died from a heart attack.

Jesse "Ed" Davis

Born September 21, 1944
Died June 22, 1988
Popular session guitarist who worked for Bob Dylan, George Harrison, Eric Clapton, Willie Nelson, Gene Clark, Leon Russell, John Lennon, Rod Stewart and Joe Cocker, the Oklahoma-born Jesse "Ed" Davis got his first break with Taj Mahal, appearing on the bluesman's first three albums in the late Sixties, beginning with *Statesboro Blues*. He can be seen backing Taj on the film of The Rolling Stones' *Rock'n'Roll Circus*. Leaving Taj Mahal in 1969, Davis pursued a solo career, releasing three albums in the early Seventies. A native-American of the Kiowa tribe, Davis in 1985 teamed with native-American poet John Trudell to form the group, Graffiti Man. Davis is still regarded as one of the best bottleneck guitar exponents of his era.
CAUSE: Heroin overdose. He was found in the laundry room of an apartment building in Venice, California, with drug paraphernalia next to him.

Larry Davis

Born December 4, 1936
Died April 19, 1994
Kansas City blues guitarist who was best known for his much recorded 1958 hit, 'Texas Flood', Larry Davis released his final album, *Sooner Or Later* in 1992.
CAUSE: Cancer. He died in Los Angeles.

Miles Davis

(MILES DEWEY DAVIS, III)
Born May 25, 1926
Died September 18, 1991
A jazz giant, trumpeter Miles Davis led a series of noteworthy ensembles throughout a fruitful career that varied from bebop to funk. Hiring talented sidemen, the innovative Davis nurtured players such as John Coltrane, Wayne Shorter, Chick Corea and Herbie Hancock. Reared in a middle-class family, the son of a dentist and gentleman farmer, Davis acquired a trumpet at age 13 and was soon permitted by his parents to frequent the jazz clubs of his native St. Louis. Relocating to New York City to attend Juilliard, he searched out Charlie Parker; recording with his mentor at age 19, Davis also took Parker's lead in abusing heroin (Davis gave up heroin for cocaine in the early Fifties). After passing through the bands of Billy Eckstine and Benny Carter, Davis entered into a long-term collaborative relationship with arranger Gil Evans. Forming his own nine piece band in 1949, which featured Max Roach and Gerry Mulligan, Davis released the then ignored, groundbreaking "cool jazz" album *The Birth Of Cool* (1950). Usually performing with a quintet after 1955, Davis worked with a who's who of jazz, issuing a host of innovative albums at Columbia Records including *Kind Of Blue* (1959). His voice soft and raspy following throat surgery in 1956, Davis took another stylistic turn and in 1959 abandoned bop. Leading a tight quintet from 1964–1968 in the avant-garde school of jazz, Davis hired a pair of young sidemen, Tony Williams and Herbie Hancock. Electrifying his sound and veering toward jazz-rock fusion in the late Sixties, the unpredictable Davis shocked his longtime fans with albums such as the rocking *A Tribute To Jack Johnson* (1970), the R&B-flavoured *On The Corner*, and his best-selling release *Bitches Brew*. Wanting a hipper audience, he infused contemporary

musical strains into his music as he performed for young crowds at venues such as the Fillmore East. Retreating from the music scene in 1975, he re-emerged in 1981, the same year that he wed actress Cicely Tyson. Further antagonising the jazz world, Davis toyed with his role of cultural icon as he performed with Prince, and recorded songs by popsters Cyndi Lauper and Michael Jackson.
CAUSE: In delicate health for decades, he succumbed to a stroke, pneumonia, and respiratory failure at St. John's Hospital in Los Angeles.
FURTHER READING: Carr, Ian. (1998). *Miles Davis: The Definitive Biography*. London: HarperCollins.

Raymond Davis

Born March 29, 1940
Died July 5, 2005
A founding member of the bombastic soul-funk ensemble Parliament-Funkadelic, Ray Davis provided the deep bass vocals on their hits, such as 'Tear The Roof Off The Sucka (Give Up The Funk)', 'Flashlight', 'Aqua Boogie' and 'One Nation Under A Groove – Part I'. Wearing outrageous costumes and employing outlandish stage props – including a massive spaceship – the band was led by the dreadlocked George Clinton. Originally formed in the Sixties as a doo-wop soul act called The Parliaments, the band helped to create the funk genre of the Seventies. For much of the decade, the large conglomerate of singers, dancers and musicians operated in two overlapping camps, Funkadelic and Parliament, which eventually merged as "P-Funk". In the mid Nineties, following the death of Melvin Franklin, Davis joined a touring version of The Temptations, and also later toured with former members of The P-Funk All Stars.
CAUSE: He succumbed to respiratory complications at Robert Wood Johnson University Hospital in New Brunswick, New Jersey.

Skeeter Davis

(MARY FRANCES PENICK)
Born December 30, 1931
Died September 19, 2004
A country singer who had occasional pop crossover success, Skeeter Davis is best known for her romantic lament, 'The End Of The World'. Performing since the early Fifties, Davis (who was nicknamed "Skeeter" by her grandfather) signed with RCA, with a two-decade-long chart run, as well as a long-term stint on *The Grand Ole Opry*. Her other pop hits included a vocal version of Floyd Cramer's 'Last Date' which she retitled 'My Last Date' and 'I Can't Stay Mad At You'. Late in life, Davis adopted Christian music.
CAUSE: Breast cancer. She died at St. Thomas Hospital in Nashville.

Tyrone Davis

(TYRONE BRANCH)
Born May 4, 1938
Died February 9, 2005
A Chicago-based soul singer best known for his smooth ballads, Tyrone Davis experienced a two-decade reign on the R&B charts. A native of Greenville, Mississippi, he moved north to Chicago with his father. Spending a year working as a personal valet for bluesman Freddy King, befriended by soul-gospel singer Otis Clay and mentored by pianist Harold Burrage, Davis recorded two Burrage-produced singles in 1965 under the name Tyrone (The Wonder Boy). Eventually landing at Carl Davis' Dakar Records, Tyrone scored a Top 10 crossover, B-side hit in 1968 with 'Can I Change My Mind?'. Although 'Turn Back The Hands Of Time' (1970) would be Davis' final Top 10 entry on the pop charts, he was a staple on R&B radio with songs such as 'Is It Something You've Got?', 'I'll Be Right Here', 'I Had It All The Time', 'Without You In My Life', 'Turning Point', 'Give It Up (Turn It Loose)' and 'Are You Serious?'. He subsequently recorded for a series of

different labels. A flashy dresser, Davis would hit the stage in an elaborate costume.

CAUSE: Pneumonia. He had been in a coma since suffering a stroke on September 7, 2004. Placed in a convalescence home, he later died at Hinsdale Hospital in the Chicago suburb of Hinsdale, Illinois.

Ronnie Dawson

(RONALD M. DAWSON)
Born August 11, 1939
Died September 30, 2003

A celebrated rockabilly singer-guitarist who had limited success on the pop charts, Ronnie Dawson launched his professional musical career when still a teenager. Victorious for 10 weeks straight at a Dallas talent competition as Ronnie Dee And The D Men, Dawson drew the attention of Gene Vincent's manager and was soon scoring regional hits. Signing with and recording several singles for the Dick Clark-affiliated label Swan Records, Dawson made an appearance on Clark's *American Bandstand* show but was unhappy with his new teen idol status. Poised on the brink of stardom, Dawson watched his career dissolve as Clark became embroiled in the payola scandal of 1959. Unable to reignite his career in the Sixties, Dawson then worked as a session musician, playing drums on Paul & Paula's 'Hey Paula' and Bruce Channel's 'Hey! Baby'. After joining a series of regional bands, including Steelrail, Dawson was rediscovered in the mid Eighties by British audiences thanks to the rockabilly revival. He returned to the stage and recorded several albums of new material.

CAUSE: Throat cancer. He died at his home in East Dallas, Texas.

Bobby Day

(ROBERT JAMES BYRD, SR.)
Born July 1, 1930
Died July 27, 1990

A popular West Coast doo-wop singer, Texas-born Bobby Day moved to Los Angeles in the late Forties to attend college, where he majored in maths. Trained as a child in gospel, the music minded Day was drawn to Johnny Otis' famed Barrelhouse nightclub where he earned his education in R&B. Forming The Flames with Earl Nelson and others in 1949, Day had little aspirations of becoming a professional singer. Recording for a series of labels including Unique, Decca, and Money, The Flames were local stars in spite of their lack of a national hit. Signing with Class Records in 1957, the group was renamed Bobby Day And The Satellites. Recording the Day-composed 'Little Bitty Pretty One', the single was squashed on the charts by a competing version by Thurston Harris. Simultaneously recording at Hollywood Records, billed by the record company as the Hollywood Flames, the group scored its first national hit with another Day composition, 'Buzz-Buzz-Buzz'. Then backed by The Flames/Satellites, but promoted as a solo act, Bobby Day landed his first solo hit with the Leon Rene-penned 'Rockin' Robin' (1958). The record's B-side 'Over And Over' was also a hit, out-charting a competing cover version by Thurston Harris. When Class Records sold to RCA in 1960, Day was saddled with substandard material and was never able to match his prior successes. Recording prolifically during this period, Day appeared on dozens of labels under various names including The Jets, The Turks, Bob & Earl, Bobby Garrett, and even his real name, Bobby Byrd. Several of Day's compositions later became bigger hits for other artists, including 'Over And Over' by The Dave Clark Five and 'Rockin' Robin' by Michael Jackson. Day's widow unknowingly lost the rights to his song 'Little Bitty Pretty One' in the Seventies by not refiling the copyright. She later appeared before a congressional committee to

lobby for a change in the US music copyright laws.
CAUSE: Cancer and a related stomach haemorrhage. He had been diagnosed with cancer only two weeks earlier and died in a Los Angeles hospital.

Rusty Day

Born c. 1945
Died June 3, 1982
A short-term member, from 1969–71, of Ted Nugent's Sixties hard-rock group The Amboy Dukes, Rusty Day replaced John Drake on vocals but fell out with Nugent over drug use. Day then joined Cactus and later led Rusty Day and The Midnighters.
CAUSE: He was shot dead in Orlando, Florida, during a drug deal gone bad. Two others were also killed.

Dead

(PER YNGVE OHLIN)
Born January 16, 1969
Died April 8, 1991
The lead singer of the Norwegian black metal/satanic group Mayhem, "Dead" joined the group in 1988. A native of Sweden, he had previously been a member of a similarly dark group, Morbid. Communicating little with his bandmates, Dead was notorious for practising Satanic rituals along with Mayhem's leader Euronymous. The first black metal musician to employ "corpse" make-up, Dead brought realism to the stage by burying his stage clothes before every concert, and inhaling air from a plastic bag holding a decayed raven. The album *Live In Leipzig* (1982), with tracks such as 'Carnage' and 'Necrolust', was the only official Mayhem release to feature Dead.
CAUSE: Suicide by gunshot. Before contacting the police, bandmate Euronymous took photos of the scene (later used as an album cover) and collected pieces of Dead's skull and brain. Ironically, Dead had once stabbed Euronymous.

Bill Deal

(WILLIAM F. DEAL)
Born December 8, 1944
Died December 10, 2003
The lead singer of The Rhondels, Bill Deal helped to define the East Coast "beach music" sound. While studying business at college, Deal spent his evenings performing in local bars and, joining forces with drummer Ammon Tharp, formed a series of soul-flavoured rock bands. After first recording an obscure single as Bill Deal and The Big Deals on Mala Records in 1965, the group was eventually renamed The Rhondels. By 1968, Deal and the band pressed 3,000 copies of a remake of Maurice Williams and The Zodiac's 'May I'. A local hit, the song was picked up by Heritage Records for national distribution and became the group's first hit. Subsequent releases, 'I've Been Hurt' and 'What Kind Of Fool Do You Think I Am?' were also successful. Following the closure of Heritage in 1970, Deal switched labels but was unable to garner further hits. During the Seventies, Deal co-owned a Virginia Beach nightclub, The Rogue's Gallery, and led the house band but sold his stake in the club in 1977 to work in real estate. After selling The Rhondels' name to another act, Deal bought back the rights in the late Eighties and began performing regionally with his former bandmates.
CAUSE: He died after suffering a heart attack at his home in Virginia Beach, Virginia.

Louise Dean

Born 1971
Died July 8, 1995
An emerging British soul/dance singer in the trio Shiva, Louise Dean reached the Top 40 chart with 'Working Out' just a month before her death. The lead vocalist of Shiva, she scored a Top 20 posthumous hit with 'Freedom'.
CAUSE: Walking across the street near her apartment in Linthwaite, England, she was struck and killed by an

unlicensed and uninsured drunk driver. She died instantly from head injuries.

Bobby DeBarge

Born March 5, 1956
Died August 16, 1995
Member of the R&B groups Switch and DeBarge, Bobby DeBarge had first joined an Ohio funk band in the early Seventies called White Heart. After releasing a poorly selling, Barry White-produced album in 1975, the group disbanded with the core trio of members of DeBarge, Greg Williams and Jody Sims forming the Mansfield, Ohio-based funk group, Switch. After adding brother Tommy DeBarge and others, Switch was aided by Jermaine Jackson in signing with Motown Records. Jackson went on to produce their début album. Featuring Bobby DeBarge's high-tenor lead vocals, the popular disco-styled group enjoyed R&B airplay with the hits, 'There'll Never Be' (1977), 'I Call Your Name' (1979), and 'Love Over And Over Again' (1980). By 1983, brothers Bobby and Tommy DeBarge would leave Switch. Meanwhile, several other DeBarge siblings had formed a gospel, turned R&B family singing group called DeBarge. Hailing from Grand Rapids, Michigan, DeBarge was made up of four of the 10 DeBarge brothers and sisters, with Bobby producing their début album, *The DeBarges* (1981). Again, Jermaine Jackson had aided the group in landing a record contract with Motown. Following DeBarge's healthy hit run in the mid Eighties, a new, less successful line-up of the group featuring Bobby DeBarge emerged in 1987. Switching to Striped Horse Records, the new DeBarge bombed with their album, *Bad Boys*. In 1988, brothers Bobby and Chico DeBarge were convicted in Michigan of selling cocaine and sent to prison. Bobby DeBarge released a solo album, *It's Not Over*, shortly before his death.
CAUSE: AIDS.

Abel De Costa

(ABEL DICOSTA)
Born c. 1929
Died 1985
The first tenor of the doo-wop groups, The Blenders and The Cues, Abel De Costa joined The Blenders in 1949. The Blenders were formed in 1946 as a Ravens-like vocal group by former Ravens tenor Ollie Jones. Although a popular concert draw, The Blenders only managed one hit, 'Don't Play Around With Love', issued on Jay-Dee Records in 1953. De Costa later followed Ollie Jones to Atlantic Records to form The Cues. An invention of producer Jesse Stone, The Cues were primarily a backing session vocal group, appearing on hit records for Ruth Brown, LaVern Baker, Ray Charles, Ivory Joe Hunter, Roy Hamilton and others. With Atlantic unwilling to record The Cues as a separate act, the group released several singles for Capitol Records. De Costa later performed with a revivalist version of The Ink Spots for over three decades.
CAUSE: Unknown.

Mercy Dee

(MERCY DEE WALTON)
Born August 3, 1915
Died December 2, 1962
A blues singer and pianist, Mercy Dee scored a pair of hits with 'Lonesome Cabin Blues' (1949) and 'One Room Country Shack' (1953). Born in Texas, Mercy brought his rural blues to California in the Forties.
CAUSE: Cerebral haemorrhage.

Zenon De Fleur

Born September 9, 1951
Died February 17, 1979
Guitarist of the Seventies, British R&B/rockabilly, pub-rock turned punk-rock group, Count Bishops, Zenon De Fleur shared the lead guitar duties in the group with Johnny Guitar. Originally featuring American lead vocalist Mike Spenser, and then Dave

Tice, the group was known for raw and riveting tracks such as 'Route 66' and the self-penned 'Train Train'. The group was renamed The Counts in 1978 with the release of the single 'I Want Candy'.
CAUSE: Involved in a car crash in London, he died from a heart attack.

Pete DeFreitas

Born August 2, 1961
Died June 14, 1989
Drummer for the Eighties group Echo And The Bunnymen, Pete DeFreitas joined the group as the human replacement for the group's broken drum machine. Formed in Liverpool, England, in 1978 by a trio of musicians – Will Sergeant, Les Pattinson, and lead singer Ian McCulloch – the group initially utilised a drum machine nicknamed "Echo" for their percussion needs. They were signed to the local independent Zoo label but soon they switched to the WEA distributed Korova who demanded the group hire a drummer. A native of Port of Spain, Trinidad, DeFreitas was brought into the group right out of school. As important members of a Liverpool musical renaissance, the group was embraced by the British rock press beginning with their first single 'Rescue' and début album *Crocodiles*. Attracting US attention with their 1981 album *Heaven Up There*, the Bunnymen first targeted the dance market before jumping on the early Eighties British new-wave movement. More upbeat than contemporaries The Cure and New Order but less commercial than U2 and Big Country, Echo And The Bunnymen offered uplifting, classy British hits such as 'The Back Of Love' (1982), 'The Cutter' (1983), 'Never Stop' (1983), 'The Killing Moon' (1984), 'Seven Seas' (1984), and 'Bring On The Dancing Horses' (1985). Tired of playing the drums, DeFreitas temporarily left the group in early 1986, moved to New Orleans, changed his name to Mad Louie, and went on a partying spree with three new-found friends. He stayed in the city until he'd spent all of his savings, then rejoined The Bunnymen somewhat worse for wear. He returned in time to appear on the disappointing album *Echo & The Bunnymen* (1987), and although the group scored a pair of international hits with 'Lips Like Sugar' and 'Bedbugs And Ballyhoo', the writing was on the wall and DeFrietas left the group again. Lead singer Ian McCulloch also quit the group in 1988 to pursue a solo career. DeFreitas formed a group he called The Sex Gods but they never released anything.
CAUSE: He died in a motorcycle accident in Rugeley, Staffordshire, England. He crashed into a car.
FURTHER READING: Fletcher, Tony. (1990), *Never Stop: Echo And The Bunnymen*. London: Omnibus.

Bobby Del Din

Born May 18, 1942
Died April 15, 1992
The first tenor of the early Sixties vocal group, The Earls, whose biggest hit came in 1963 with 'Remember Then', Bobby Del Din had first joined a precursor of the group in 1957, the Larry Figueiredo-led High Hatters. Del Din left the Earls in 1964.
CAUSE: Unknown.

Randy Delay

Born November 30, 1952
Died May 12, 1993
The drummer with The Georgia Satellites for much of the Eighties, Randy Delay performed on the group's hits, the raucous, hard-rocking anthem 'Keep You Hands To Yourself' and 'Battleship Chains'. He later worked with The Kentucky Headhunters, Drivin' N' Cryin' and a number of lesser known metal acts.
CAUSE: Unknown.

Junior Delgado

(OSCAR HIBBERT)
Born August 25, 1958
Died April 10, 2005
A roots-style reggae singer-songwriter, Jamaican-born Junior Delgado spent his latter years in London. Under the name Junior Hibbert, he was originally a member of Time Unlimited but, despite patronage from legendary reggae producer Lee Perry in 1973, the group had limited success. Changing his name to Junior Delgado, he left the group in 1975 to pursue a solo career, signing with Dennis Brown's DEB label and producer Earl "Chinna" Smith. After a début hit with 'Tition', Delgado launched his own Incredible Jux label in 1979 and continued to thrive in the reggae field but a drug bust in the early Eighties resulted in an 18 month prison sentence. The social commentary of his 1985 release 'Broadwater Farm' predicted the violence at a housing project in north London. Following the so-called Tottenham riots and the brutal murder of police officer Keith Blakelock, the single was banned in the UK. After dabbling for a time with dance hall style, Delgado reunited with Augustus Pablo for a number of releases and on 1998's *Fearless*, he was joined by a number of guests including rapper Maxi Jazz and Jerry Dammers of The Specials. The following year, Delgado played both the Glastonbury and Roskilde festivals.
CAUSE: Unknown He died in his sleep at his home in London.

Denis D'Ell

(DENIS JAMES DALZIEL)
Born October 14, 1943
Died July 6, 2005
The lead singer of the Sixties pop-rock act The Honeycombs, London-born Denis D'Ell broke into music after his fellow railway workers encouraged him to enter a local talent contest, which he won. As a member of The Sherabons, D'Ell was discovered at the Mildmay Tavern in north London by songwriters Ken Howard and Alan Blaikley, who became their managers. Taking the act to the Holloway studio of independent producer Joe Meek, the renamed Honeycombs recorded the Howard/Blaikley composition, 'Have I The Right?' which became a worldwide hit in 1964. Follow-up singles, 'Is It Because?', 'Something Better Beginning' (written by Ray Davies of The Kinks) and 'That's The Way' (featuring the lead vocals of D'Ell with the group's female drummer, Annie "Honey" Lantree) were minor British chart entries. Following the demise of The Honeycombs, D'Ell recorded some solo singles.
CAUSE: Cancer.

Darryl DeLoach

(DARRYL JAMES DELOACH)
Born September 12, 1947
Died October 3, 2002
The original vocalist and guitarist of the Sixties psychedelic rock band Iron Butterfly, Darryl DeLoach co-founded the group in 1966 and played on their début album, *Heavy*. DeLoach left Iron Butterfly (with two other original members) before their 1968 smash breakthrough *In-A-Gadda-Da-Vida* and was replaced by Doug Ingle. DeLoach toiled in the music industry for a short period before returning to San Diego, where he worked as a restaurateur. In an odd twist, Ingle provided guest vocals on DeLoach's 1995 solo album, *Through The Hand Of Time.*
CAUSE: Liver cancer. He died at his mother's home in San Diego.

Martin Denny

Born April 10, 1911
Died March 2, 2005
The father of the "exotica" genre, Martin Denny combined light jazz, classical, Latin and Pacific Island styles with sound effects such as bird calls and croaking frogs. A native of New York City, Denny played big band style jazz in a combo from 1931 until just

after the Second World War. Following a stint in the US Army Air Corps, he attended college on the G.I. Bill, studying classical music and composition. Landing in Waikiki, Hawaii, he performed as a solo act before forming a trio in 1955 with bassist John Kramer and vibraphonist Arthur Lymon. With the addition of percussionist Augie Colon the following year, Denny's trademark exotica sound had gelled. Attracting large audiences in Hawaii, Denny signed with Liberty Records, resulting in a trio of Top 10 albums during the late Fifties and early Sixties: *Exotica,* featuring the Top 10 title track, *Quiet Village* and *A Taste Of Honey.* Following the departure of Arthur Lymon who started a similar ensemble, Denny hired another future bandleader, Julius Wechter. Denny's revival occurred during the lounge music movement of the Nineties and, although in poor health in his last years, he continued to perform.
CAUSE: Natural causes. He died at his home in Hawaii Kai, Hawaii.

Sandy Denny

(ALEXANDRA ELENE MACLEAN DENNY)
Born January 6, 1947
Died April 21, 1978
Solo folk singer and member of Fairport Convention, Wimbledon, England-born Sandy Denny had a delicate soprano voice and was skilled on guitar and piano. Inspired by her friend Paul Simon, then living in the UK, Denny quit her studies at Kensington Art College in London to become a folk singer. Briefly joining the bluegrass-tinged, British folk group The Strawbs in late 1967, Denny recorded an early version of her folk standard, 'Who Knows Where The Time Goes' (the song was also recorded by Judy Collins on an album of the same name). Leaving The Strawbs in the summer of 1968, Denny joined Fairport Convention after an invitation by guitarist Richard Thompson. Signing with Island Records in 1969, the group released *What We Did On Our Holidays* (issued by A&M in the US under the title *Fairport Convention*), the album was highlighted by the Denny-influenced tracks, 'Fotheringay' and 'She Moved Through The Fair'. The group's follow-up *Unhalfbricking* featured the definitive version of Denny's 'Who Knows Where The Time Goes', and the group's only pop hit, a French version of the Bob Dylan composition, 'If You Gotta Go, Go Now' retitled as 'Si Tu Dois Partir'. Angering their fans with their electric-folk set *Liege And Lief* (1969), Fairport Convention experienced much infighting. Leaving the group in early 1970, Denny formed the folk group Fotheringay, joined by her boyfriend (and soon, husband) guitarist Trevor Lucas, guitarist Jerry Donahue, and two others. After releasing a sole album, *Fotheringay* (1970), the group disbanded in January 1971. Pursuing a solo career, Denny was frequently backed by former Fairport Convention members on albums such as *Northstar Grass Man* and *The Ravens* (1971), *Sandy* (1972) and *Like An Old Fashioned Waltz* (1973). Sandy also worked as a session vocalist, her best known guest spot being her duet with Robert Plant on the Led Zeppelin ballad 'The Battle Of Evermore' (1971). Denny and Lucas rejoined Fairport Convention in 1974 for a pair of albums, *Fairport Live: A Moveable Beast* and the group's best US seller, *Rising For The Moon.* Denny would release her final solo effort in 1977, *Rendezvous,* the album highlighted by 'One Way Donkey Ride'.
CAUSE: After falling down a flight of stairs at a friend's home, she suffered severe head injuries. She went into a coma and died four days later at Atkinson Morley's Hospital in London.
FURTHER READING: Humphries, Patrick. (1982). *Meet On The Ledge: A*

History Of Fairport Convention. London: Eel Pie.

John Denver

(John Henry Deutschendorf, Jr.)
Born December 31, 1943
Died October 12, 1997
Popular folk-pop singer-songwriter, John Denver enjoyed massive success in the Seventies. The son of an Air Force pilot, Denver moved frequently while growing up. Given his first guitar by his grandmother, Denver played the instrument in high school. Dropping out of Texas Tech University in 1964 and moving to Los Angeles, he joined the folk and acting troupe, The Back Porch Majority. Replacing the leader of The Chad Mitchell Trio, the group soon evolved into Denver, Boise and Johnson. A prolific songwriter, Denver had his first success in 1967 when folksters Peter, Paul & Mary scored a hit with his composition 'Leaving On A Jet Plane' (1967). Subsequently signing with RCA Records in 1969, he released a pair of poorly received albums, with his début set *Rhymes And Reasons* containing a rendition of 'Leaving On A Jet Plane'. From his third album *Take Me To Tomorrow*, Denver landed his breakthrough hit with the country-tinged, chart-topping paean to the state of West Virginia, 'Take Me Home, Country Roads'. A major US pop star by the mid Seventies, he continued his string of hits with 'Sunshine On My Shoulder' (1974), 'Annie's Song' (1974) written for his wife, 'Thank God I'm a Country Boy' (1975), and 'I'm Sorry' (1975). Launching his own label, Windsong Records, he signed The Starland Vocal Band who landed in the Top 10 with the suggestive 'Afternoon Delight'. With his music out of fashion in the Eighties, Denver scored his final pop hit in 1982 with 'Shanghai Breezes'. Later in his career he embraced country music and appeared in celebrity golf tournaments. Also a successful actor, Denver co-starred with George Burns in *Oh, God!* Although suffering a pair of divorces and two drunk-driving convictions, Denver also kept up a public profile with his extensive charity work and interest in ecology.
Cause: Denver plunged his experimental, lightweight aeroplane into the Monterey Bay, just off the California coast near Monterey. His craft, a homemade model Long E-Z, had run out of fuel and it spiralled down into the ocean. It was later revealed that his pilot's licence had been suspended in March 1997 due to his multiple drunk-driving convictions. A coroner's report found no traces of drugs or alcohol were in Denver's system. A report by the National Transportation Safety Board suggested that the crash was caused by modifications to the aeroplane which made it difficult to grasp a handle to switch to a reserve fuel tank. The report also theorised that a collision with a large bird might have affected Denver's control of the craft.
Further Reading: Denver, John; & Tobier, Arthur. (1994). *Take Me Home: An Autobiography*. New York: Harmony.

Karl Denver

(Angus McKenzie)
Born December 16, 1931
Died December 21, 1998
As leader of the Karl Denver Trio, Karl Denver was a popular singer in the UK in the immediate pre-Beatles era. He was best known for his 1961 hit 'Wimoweh', which was based on a Zulu folk song, and featured Denver's characteristic yodelling voice. Born in Glasgow, Denver left school at 15 to join the Norwegian merchant navy and subsequently fought in the Korean war with the Argyll & Sutherland Highlanders. He learned to play the guitar while recovering from a war wound and, having

become interested in country music, went back to sea, jumped ship in the United States and headed for Nashville. Adopting the name Karl Denver in the country music capital, he appeared on radio and TV and even on the prestigious *Grand Old Opry* show, but he was discovered by the US immigration department and deported. Resettling in Manchester, England, he teamed up with Gerry Cottrell and Kevin Neill to form the Karl Denver Trio and played local clubs until he was discovered by TV producer Jack Good and appeared on his *Wham!* TV show. Good was also responsible for Denver signing to Decca Records for which he recorded four UK Top 10 hits during 1961 and 1962, including 'Marcheta' and 'Wimoweh'. Eclipsed by The Beatles and the beat-boom, Denver faded from popularity in the mid Sixties but his trio continued to perform in cabaret in the UK and elsewhere over the next 30 years. There was a brief return to the limelight in 1989 when The Happy Mondays invited Denver to guest on their single 'Lazyitis – One Armed Boxer', and an updated recording of 'Wimoweh' was released by Manchester based Factory Records.
CAUSE: Brain tumour. He died in a hospice in Manchester.

Delia Derbyshire

Born May 5, 1937
Died July 3, 2001
A composer, arranger and musician, Delia Derbyshire was a pioneer in electronic music and, in 1963, she was asked to create the theme to a new BBC serial, *Dr. Who*. Aided by recording engineer Dick Mills, Derbyshire created the unique space-age piece that was used to open each episode. A classically trained musician, she worked for the United Nations before landing a position in 1960 with the BBC, and as a member of the BBC's Radiophonic Workshop, she continued to explore electronic music, before leaving the corporation in 1973.
CAUSE: Kidney failure. She died in Northampton, England.

Tony Destra

Born September 20, 1954
Died February 8, 1987
The drummer for the Eighties glam-metal act Britny Fox, Tony "Stix" Destra passed away before the band achieved fame. Originally a founding member of the Tom Keifer-led blues-based, heavy metal band Cinderella, Destra and guitarist Michael Kelly Smith were fired in 1985 at the behest of their record company. The pair soon formed Britny Fox, and hired "Dizzy" Dean Davidson as their lead vocalist. Wanting to reside in the hair-metal capital, the group left Philadelphia for Los Angeles, and a 1987 cassette demo, *In America*, featured two tracks written by Destra. He died shortly before Britny Fox was signed to Columbia Records, and did not therefore appear on the band's self-titled major label début release in 1988, which included six re-recorded versions of songs from the cassette demo. Destra was replaced by former Waysted member Johnny Dee.
CAUSE: Following a concert performance in Pennsylvania, he was involved in an auto accident at 4 a.m. and died at the scene.

Tony De Vit

Born September 12, 1957
Died July 2, 1998
A noteworthy British deejay and remixer, Tony De Vit remixed a total of 16 British Top 40 hits during his career. Born in Kidderminster, he began deejaying at 17, gaining fame, aged 20, after spinning records at Birmingham's legendary Nightingale Club. A former computer programmer, De Vit then deejayed at London's after-hours club, Trade, and hosted his own weekly radio programme in

London. As a remixer, De Vit worked with a host of acts including Adam & The Ants, Louise, Taylor Dayne, The Shamen, and East 17. A recording artist himself, he scored a trio of British Top 40 hits in the mid Nineties with 'Burning Up', 'Hooked', and 'I'll Be There'. De Vit also ran his own record label, TDV.
CAUSE: He succumbed to AIDS-related bronchial pneumonia and bone marrow failure. His health worsened during a visit to Miami (for his first US tour) when he was stricken with food poisoning and diagnosed with exhaustion.

James Dewar

Born October 12, 1946
Died May 16, 2002
A talented Scottish musician and vocalist who joined a series of successful British rock acts, James Dewar remained out of the limelight for most of his career. A native of Glasgow, Dewar was playing bass in a local band, The Gleneagles, while in his teens but when a local singer, Marie Lawrie (a.k.a. Lulu), needed a backing band, Dewar, as a member of the renamed Luvvers, got into the UK Top 10 in 1964 with a cover of The Isley Brothers' 'Shout'. Dewar quit the Luvvers in 1965 and, two years later, joined Frankie Miller's R&B group, Sock 'Em JB, who disbanded after two members were killed when their tour van crashed. From the group, Dewar and John McGinnis teamed with singer Maggie Bell and guitarist Les Harvey to form Power, a popular Glasgow soul-rock pub band. Discovered by Led Zeppelin's manager Peter Grant, the group was renamed Stone The Crows, featuring Dewar and Bell sharing lead vocal duties. Although the group was greeted with critical acclaim, they sold few records and, by 1971, Dewar had reunited with Frankie Miller, adding former Procol Harum guitarist Robin Trower to form a band called Jude. The group was short-lived and by the following year Dewar had teamed with Trower and drummer Reg Isadore to form The Robin Trower Band, featuring Dewar on bass guitar and lead vocals. The progressive rock trio built a loyal following in the Seventies, recording eight guitar-driven albums including *Bridge Of Sighs* (1974), *For Earth Below* (1975) and *In City Dreams* (1977). Dewar parted with Trower in the early Eighties.
CAUSE: Pneumonia. He died in hospital after a long illness.

Keith Diamond

Born 1951
Died January 18, 1997
Trinidad-born producer and songwriter, Keith Diamond worked with Mick Jagger, Michael Bolton and Donna Summer, and earned a Grammy nomination for co-writing Billy Ocean's 'Caribbean Queen'. He first arrived in the US in 1969, and was hired as a staff songwriter at the Zomba Publishing Company in 1980.
CAUSE: Heart attack. He died at his home in New York City.

Norman "Dinky" Diamond

Born 1951
Died September 10, 2004
A member of quirky rock band Sparks, drummer Norman "Dinky" Diamond joined after answering an advertisement in *Melody Maker*. (Diamond was dubbed "Dinky" during his childhood due to his undersized physique.) Formed by the eccentric American-born brothers Russell and Ron Mael, Sparks had previously failed with a pair of US releases and had decided to start again in London. Recommended by John Hewlett (of the group John's Children) to Island Records producer Muff Winwood, Sparks signed with the label in 1974. Recording the critically acclaimed glam-influenced album *Kimono My House*, Sparks were

heralded by British record buyers and scored a pair of Top 10 UK hits with 'This Town Ain't Big Enough For The Both Of Us' and 'Amateur Hour'. Often compared to Roxy Music, the group continued its hit run with the albums *Propaganda* and the Tony Visconti-produced *Indiscreet*, which spawned the hits 'Never Turn Your Back On Mother Earth', 'Something For The Girl With Everything', 'Get In The Swing' and 'Looks, Looks, Looks'. Although Diamond was voted drummer of the year in 1975 in a poll conducted by Premier Drums, he was fired from Sparks the following year when the Mael brothers decided to employ session players. Diamond later joined a series of groups including Sparks spin-off outfit The Four Squares.
CAUSE: Suicide. After repeatedly complaining to local authorities about his chronically noisy neighbours for playing loud music, he got drunk and hung himself at his home in Berkshire. One of the accused neighbours told *The Mirror*: "I can't believe I'm being blamed."

Joe Dias

Born March 11, 1932
Died July, 1982
The original bass singer of The Chords, Joe Davis left in 1953 to join the Bronx-based doo-wop vocal group, The Crickets (not Buddy Holly's band), appearing on obscure singles such as, 'Changing Partners', and 'Just You'. But when The Crickets evolved into The Bachelors in 1956, Dias rejoined The Chords.
CAUSE: Unknown.

Lance Dickerson

Born October 15, 1948
Died November 11, 2003
As a longtime member of the rock act Commander Cody & His Lost Planet Airmen, drummer Lance Dickerson played an upbeat mix of rockabilly and Texas boogie. Born in Latovia, Michigan, the son of big-band drummer Robert Dickerson, he joined Cody's band around 1968, having been lured away from Charlie Musselwhite's band. From their début album *Lost In The Ozone*, Commander Cody & His Lost Planet Airmen scored a surprise Top 10 hit with a remake of the novelty song 'Hot Rod Lincoln' (1972). Dickerson remained with the band until 1976 when he and bandmate "Buffalo" Bruce Barlow joined Roger McGuinn's post-Byrds group Thunderbyrd. Dickerson also worked with Hoyt Axton, David Bromberg, Maria Muldaur and John Lee Hooker.
CAUSE: Suicide.

Renee Diggs

Born July 23, 1954
Died March 18, 2005
As the lead singer of R&B/dance group Starpoint, Renee Diggs provided the polished vocals on over two dozen R&B chart singles. Originally called Licyndiana, the previously all-male group gelled after adding Diggs. Signed in 1980 by Casablanca/Chocolate City Records, Starpoint scored club hits with 'I Just Wanna Dance With You' and 'Keep On It'. After passing through Boardwalk Records, Starpoint joined Elektra in 1984 and scored their only Top 40 hit with the club classic, 'Object Of My Desire'. Nonetheless, the group remained a staple of R&B radio for the rest of the decade with hits such as 'What You Been Missin'', 'Restless', 'He Wants My Body' and 'Say You Will'. After Diggs was diagnosed with multiple sclerosis in 1985, she was unable to continue touring, and after releasing their tenth studio album *Have You Got What It Takes?*, Starpoint disbanded in the early Nineties. Although Diggs recorded a solo album for Capitol Records in 1990, the project was shelved until its release 10 years later by Expansion Records. Also a session

vocalist, Diggs worked with James Ingram and Bob James.
CAUSE: Viral infection.

Varetta Dillard

Born February 3, 1933
Died October 4, 1993
Popular Fifties R&B singer, the Harlem-born Varetta Dillard had spent much of her youth in hospitals due to a debilitating bone condition. After winning a pair of Apollo Theater amateur contests, she was signed to Savoy Records in 1951. With her early singing partner H-Bomb Ferguson, Dillard landed on the R&B charts with 'Easy, Baby Easy' (1952), 'Mercy, Mr. Percy' (1953), and the Johnny Ace tribute, 'Johnny Has Gone' (1955). Leaving Savoy for a series of labels beginning with RCA/Groove, her hit run ebbed. In the late Sixties, she joined her husband's militant black musical group, The Tri-Odds.
CAUSE: Cancer. She died in Brooklyn, New York.

Peter "Dino" Dines

Born December 17, 1944
Died January 28, 2004
A talented keyboardist best known for his work with Marc Bolan's band T. Rex, Peter "Dino" Hines was previously a member of The Keef Hartley Band, performing on their only album that reached the charts, *The Time Is Near* (1970). A native of Hertford, England, Hines joined a later line-up of T. Rex at the end of 1974 and appeared on three albums: *Bolan's Zip Gun*, *Futuristic Dragon* and *Dandy In The Underworld.* The group disbanded after Bolan's death in 1977. In 1998, Dines joined the T. Rex tribute band, T. Rextasy.
CAUSE: Heart attack.

Mark Dinning

(MAX DINNING)
Born August 17, 1933
Died March 22, 1986
A one-hit wonder, Oklahoma-born Mark Dinning was raised in a musical family, the youngest brother of the popular Forties sibling trio, The Dinning Sisters. Dinning grew up on a farm near Nashville, his father a salesman and an evangelical singer. Picking up the guitar at age 13, Mark Dinning soon joined his older brother Ace for a number of nightclub performances. His career aided by his famous sisters and producer Mitch Miller, Dinning signed with MGM Records. Dinning's sister Jean, an employee of Capitol Records, gave him a song which she had written called 'Teen Angel'. Backed on the session by The Jordanaires and Dinning's sister Delois, 'Teen Angel' was a smash hit in 1960 selling three million copies. Banned in England, the morbid song was about a girl who was killed by a train while retrieving her boyfriend's ring. One of the first examples of the death-rock sub-genre, 'Teen Angel' spawned dozens of similar songs. Dinning followed up with a few minor hits, 'A Star Is Born (A Love Has Died)' (1960), 'The Lovin' Touch' (1960), and the novelty song, 'Top Forty, News, Weather And Sports' (1961). In 1963, Johnny Mathis scored a Top 10 hit with a cover of Dinning's 'What Will Mary Say'. Dinning returned to the stage in the early Seventies with the help of his brother Ace.
CAUSE: He suffered a heart attack while driving home from a club appearance at the Red Bird Inn in Jefferson City, Missouri. He died in his car.

Sacha Distel

Born January 29, 1933
Died July 22, 2004
Paris-born singer-actor, Sacha Distel made his sole appearance on the British pop charts in 1970 with a cover version of B.J. Thomas' 'Raindrops Keep Falling On My Head'. A jazz-trained guitarist, Distel recorded and worked prolifically with such acts as Dizzy Gillespie and Quincy Jones. Also a film and

television actor, he was a major star in his native France and found fame in the UK following his performance in the London production of the Bob Fosse musical, *Chicago*. Distel dated Brigitte Bardot for a time.
CAUSE: He died near Saint-Tropez, France, following a long-term, undisclosed illness.

Divine

(HARRIS GLENN MILSTEAD)
Born October 19, 1945
Died March 7, 1988
A former hair-stylist turned campy entertainer, Divine was an obese, transvestite actor and singer, his most famous role coming as the mother of Ricki Lake's character in the John Waters' film, *Hairspray*. At over 300 pounds, the rotund Baltimore-born drag queen was typecast in a series of female roles. Also a singer, Divine scored several disco-styled hit singles in England including 'You Think You're A Man' and 'Walk Like A Man'.
CAUSE: He suffered a heart attack during his sleep at the Regency Plaza Hotel in Hollywood, California. He was in town, scheduled to film an episode of the Fox sitcom *Married... With Children*.

Julius Dixon

(JULIUS EDWARD DIXSON)
Born May 20, 1912
Died January 30, 2004
A New York City-based songwriter, Julius Dixon penned the rock era hits 'Lollipop' (The Chordettes), 'Dim, Dim The Lights' (Bill Haley & The Comets), 'It Hurts To Be In Love' (Annie Laurie) and 'The Clouds' (The Spacemen).
CAUSE: Natural causes. He died in Manhattan, New York.

Willie Dixon

Born July 1, 1915
Died January 29, 1992
A prolific songwriter, producer, and occasional recording artist, Mississippi-born Willie Dixon made his mark on modern, urban blues in the Fifties during his reign at Chess Records. Reared on gospel music as a child, he joined The Union Jubilee Singers as the bass vocalist. But Dixon was also exposed to the blues via a local singer named "Little Brother" Montgomery. Following his sister to Chicago in his mid-teens, the already large-framed Dixon took a job delivering ice. After reluctantly returning to Mississippi to resume his schooling, he began to box at the local YWCA. Returning to Chicago in 1936, he entered the boxing ring as "James Dixon", winning the heavyweight championship in the amateur Golden Gloves tournament in 1937. But Dixon quit the sport after a year, banned from the ring after accusing his managers of stealing his earnings. Returning to music, Dixon began playing a one-string bass. Joined by Leonard "Baby Doo" Caston and Evan Spencer, Dixon and his group worked as street musicians in the early Forties. With the trio disbanding at the start of World War II, Dixon was jailed on charges of draft evasion. Released from prison in 1945, Dixon began playing an upright bass for a year with a new group, The Four Jumps of Jive. Reteaming with Caston in 1946 to form a jump blues outfit called The Big Three Trio (along with Bernard Dennis, and later, Ollie Crawford), Dixon and the group recorded for several labels before scoring their first national hit with '(Wee Wee Baby) You Sure Look Good To Me' (1948). Beginning a long-term relationship with Leonard and Phil Chess of Chess Records beginning in 1948, Dixon was initially hired as a session player. A central figure in the rise of modern blues, Dixon was also responsible for Chess Records' unparalleled success during the Fifties. Working chiefly as a producer and session bassist, Dixon also composed countless blues standards including 'I'm Your Hoochie

Coochie Man' (Muddy Waters), 'I Just Want To Make Love To You' (Muddy Waters), 'Backdoor Man' (Howlin' Wolf), 'The Red Rooster' (Howlin' Wolf), 'My Babe' (Little Walter), and 'The Seventh Son' (Willie Mabon). Often injecting voodoo imagery into his work, Dixon usually gave his finest compositions to Howlin' Wolf. Releasing his own single on the Chess subsidiary, Checker Records in 1955, Dixon scored the only solo chart hit of his career with 'Walking The Blues'. Then with the rise of rock in the mid Fifties, Dixon played bass on some of Chuck Berry's early classics including 'Maybellene' and 'Johnny B. Goode'. Leaving Chess for cross town rival Cobra Records in 1956, Dixon worked with Otis Rush and Buddy Guy. But with Cobra closing three years later, Dixon returned to Chess in 1960 where he worked as a producer and A&R man until 1970. With blues falling out of popularity in the US during the first half of the Sixties, Dixon teamed with bluesman Memphis Slim for several very popular tours through Europe. Returning to Chicago a musical legend, Dixon teamed with the city's best blues players in the late Sixties to form The Chicago Blues All-Stars. Returning to his roots and adopting a folkier blues style, Dixon recorded for a number of labels including Verve, Folkways and Bluesville. By the Seventies, Dixon formed the Soul Attraction talent agency, Soul Productions record production company, as well as a pair of labels, Yamboo and Spoonful. Although losing a leg to diabetes in 1977, Dixon remained a vibrant performer into the late Eighties. Late in life Dixon devoted much time to his non-profit, Blues Heaven Foundation, which awarded scholarships to needy, aspiring students of blues music. Dixon earned Grammys for the projects *Hidden Charms* and *The Chess Box*.
CAUSE: Heart failure. He died at St. Joseph's Medical Center in Burbank, California. Suffering from diabetes, he had been hospitalised for three weeks.
FURTHER READING: Dixon, Willie, & Snowden, Don. (1989). *I Am The Blues*. New York: Da Capo.

DJ Screw

(ROBERT EARL DAVIS, JR.)
Born July 20, 1971
Died November 16, 2000
A popular Houston-based producer, DJ Screw made a career out of issuing slowed-down cassette remixes of popular rap hits. Operating a retail store and record label, DJ Screw also discovered and mentored a number of Houston-based rap artists including Lil' Flip, Big Pokey, Lil' Keke and Z-Ro. Already a star in the Deep South, DJ Screw turned down a major label recording contract in the mid-Nineties.
CAUSE: Suffering a heart attack, he was found dead in his studio after ingesting a lethal combination of marijuana, alcohol, and a drug he often extolled in his songs, codeine-laced prescription cough syrup.

Sir Coxsone Dodd

(CLEMENT SEYMOUR DODD)
Born January 26, 1932
Died May 4, 2004
An important cog in the rise of modern Jamaican music, Sir Coxsone Dodd was responsible for discovering many of ska and reggae's most visible exponents. Dodd was reared on jazz before discovering American R&B music while travelling to the US to work on the sugar cane fields in the Deep South. Returning to Jamaica in the mid Fifties, he operated a mobile street deejay system which he dubbed Sir Coxsone's Downbeat Sound Systems, but with American music changing in the early Sixties, Cox lost a source of the R&B he played and was forced to produce his own material out of necessity. Launching Studio One Records in 1962 and opening a recording studio the following year, Dodd combined the sound of American R&B with the

emerging sounds of Ska and Rock Steady. Artists on his label included The Skatalites, Ken Boothe, Alton Ellis, The Maytals, and an early version of Bob Marley and The Wailers. In the Eighties, Dodd moved to Brooklyn, New York, and operated a record store, Coxsone's Music City.
CAUSE: He suffered a massive heart attack and died at his recording studio in Kingston, Jamaica just four days after the city had renamed a street in honour of his legendary studio.

Bill Doggett

(WILLIAM BALLARD DOGGETT)
Born February 16, 1916
Died November 13, 1996
Jazz-turned R&B organist and arranger, Philadelphia native Bill Doggett took piano lessons at age nine. After high school, he joined the house band at the Nixon Grand Theater in his native Philadelphia. After spending several years as a member of Jimmy Goreham's swing group, Doggett formed his first group in 1938. But by 1940, he was playing piano for Lucky Millinder's proto-jump blues band. The following year, he was hired by the soaring Ink Spots as a pianist and arranger, and in 1943, he accompanied songstress Ella Fitzgerald. Working as a musical arranger, Doggett worked for Lionel Hampton in 1946, and then Count Basie in 1947. Returning to the piano, Doggett was a member of Louis Jordan's Tympany Five in the late Forties. During this period, Doggett switched from piano to his more famous organ. Starting his own R&B band in 1952, Doggett was now playing a distinctive Hammond B-3 organ. Aided by former bandmate Henry Glover, an A&R man at King Records, Doggett was signed to the label. Doggett found crossover success with his début hit 'Honky Tonk' (1956), the groundbreaking instrumental featuring the grinding saxophone of Clifford Scott. The song had been written during a performance in Ohio after the group's guitarist Billy Butler launched into an unplanned blues solo. After 'Honky Tonk', Doggett scored a million-seller with a cover of Sil Austin's 'Slow Walk', and continued with 'Ram-Bunk-Shush' (1957), 'Hold It' (1958), and his final hit, 'Yocky Dock (Part 1)' (1959). Earning little at King Records, Doggett left the label in 1960 for Columbia, and then Warner Brothers Records. Doggett would tour heavily into the Eighties.
CAUSE: While battling cancer, he suffered a heart attack and died at Lennox Hill Hospital in Manhattan.

John Dolphin

Born c. 1915
Died February 2, 1958
The owner of several early rock'n'roll labels, former car salesman John Dolphin operated from his own Dolphins of Hollywood record store. Credited with helping to popularise R&B on the West Coast, the cigar-chomping Dolphin operated his store 24-hours a day. Buying late-night air time on Los Angeles radio station KRKD, Dolphin hired deejays such as Hunter Hancock and Dick "Huggie Boy" Hugg to spin records in the front window of his store. Dolphin was soon recording a number of pioneering Los Angeles jazz, blues and R&B acts including Errol Garner, The Robins, Damita Jo, Percy Mayfield and The Hollywood Flames. Launching the Recorded In Hollywood label in 1951, he would sell some of the master recordings to King-Federal Records of Cincinnati and, later, about 150 master recordings to Decca Records. Dolphin would start other labels including Lucky (1953), Money (1954) and Cash Records (1955). In 1955, Dolphin acquired masters from Swing Time Records including some by Lloyd Glenn and Lowell Fulson. Dolphin's widow, Ruth, continued to operate her husband's labels in the Sixties.

CAUSE: He was murdered by a young songwriter, Percy Ivey, who believed he had been cheated out of royalties. Dolphin had a habit of paying cash upfront rather than traditional royalties. While the two men were arguing inside Dolphin's record store, Dolphin pulled out a knife and was shot by Ivey at close range.

Patti Donahue

Born March 29, 1956
Died December 9, 1996
As the wry, lead singer of the early Eighties new wave group The Waitresses, Patty Donahue had joined the group on a lark. The Waitresses were the brainchild of songwriter Chris Butler, formerly of Tin Huey. Based in Kent, Ohio, they emerged out of a local music scene which had spawned the likes of Devo and The Rubber City Rebels. Recording a track for an Akron, Ohio, compilation album, *Bowling Balls From Hell*, The Waitresses created a buzz with the track, 'I Know What Boys Like'. Providing surly, spoken word-like vocals, Cleveland native Patty Donahue possessed no previous musical experience. Migrating to New York City in 1980, The Waitresses released the début album *Wasn't Tomorrow Wonderful?* (1981), which also included 'I Know What Boys Like'. Following up with an EP *I Could Rule The World*, the group scored a minor hit with the infectious 'Christmas Wrapping'. It was followed by the group's theme song for the CBS sitcom *Square Pegs*. After recording the Hugh Padgham-produced album *Bruiseology*, Donahue left the group in May of 1983 and was replaced by former Holly and The Italians singer, Holly Beth Vincent. Donahue briefly returned to the band in early 1984 before they disbanded. Donahue later landed a position at MCA publishing in New York City, her first signing coming with the alternative rock group, The Idle Wilds.
CAUSE: Cancer. She died in New York City.

Tom Donahue

(THOMAS COMAN)
Born May 21, 1928
Died April 28, 1975
West Coast deejay who invented the album-rock format, Tom Donahue began on East Coast Top 40 radio, leaving for California after being implicated in the payola scandal of 1960. After a brief stint as a talk-show host, in 1961 Donahue arrived in San Francisco, rejoining former fellow deejay Bobby Mitchell at Top 40 AM powerhouse, KYA. Entering concert promotion, Donahue and Mitchell booked acts such as The Beach Boys and The Beatles. The pair also started their own record label, Autumn Records, hiring the fledgling Sly Stone as producer, and landing on the charts with The Beau Brummels, Bobby Freeman, and The Mojo Men. Opening the city's first psychedelic nightclub, Donahue began experimenting with LSD. Quitting his position at KYA and closing Autumn Records, Donahue yearned to create an alternative to adolescent-targeted, Top 40 radio fare. Gradually taking over the near-bankrupt KMPX in April 1967, Tom "Big Daddy" Donahue (his nickname derived from his imposing 400-pound frame) introduced his free-form format, picking his own playlist across genre lines in which long, obscure album tracks were preferable to Top 40 hits. The genesis of the Album-Oriented Rock (AOR) format, KMPX also spouted anti-establishment political rhetoric and anti-war sentiment. But following a tense employee strike in 1968, the KMPX staff quit en masse, transplanting the station at cross-town rival KSFR, whose call letters were changed to KSAN. Spawning a series of local, then national imitators, Donahue's underground radio format was considered mainstream by the mid Seventies. Although KSAN was popular, the station made little money until 1972. In 1991, San Francisco

began a radio-awards gala called the Donahue Awards.
CAUSE: Heart attack. He was extremely overweight.

Lonnie Donegan

(ANTHONY JAMES DONEGAN)
Born April 29, 1931
Died November 4, 2002
A skiffle legend, Lonnie Donegan had great success in Great Britain during the late Fifties in the period before the rise of American rock'n'roll. A native of Scotland, he was reared on folk, blues and country, forming the Tony Donegan Jazz Band in 1952, before joining the similarly styled New Orleans dixieland "trad" band, The Ken Colyer Jazzmen. Following Colyer's departure in 1954, the renamed Chris Barber Jazz Band recorded for Decca Records, and also recorded a number of Donegan's skiffle songs, most notably a rousing version of Leadbelly's 'Rock Island Line' in 1956. Emerging at the forefront of the skiffle movement, Donegan soon spawned countless imitators across the UK, including John Lennon who formed his own skiffle group, The Quarry Men, in Liverpool. Donegan merged old-style jug band music with upbeat folk on hits such as 'My Old Man's A Dustman' (1959) and his best known US release, the novelty number 'Does Your Chewing Gum Lose Its Flavour (On The Bedpost Over Night)' (1960). In 1967, Tom Jones had a hit with the Donegan composition, 'I'll Never Fall In Love Again'. Three decades later, Van Morrison hired Donegan and Barber for a tour, issuing some of their performances as *Skiffle Session: Love In Belfast 1998.*
CAUSE: He complained of back pain and then suffered a heart attack in Peterborough, England. He had undergone heart surgery earlier in the year.

Francis A. Donia

Born August 25, 1945
Died November 16, 1984
Drummer for the disco group Tavares from 1973 to 1976, Francis Donia joined the New Bedford, Massachusetts-based band in 1973. Tavares was centred around a quintet of Tavares Brothers, Ralph, Arthur, Feliciano, Perry and Antone, the group having formed in 1964 as Chubby And The Turnpikes. The group's début album *Check It Out* spawned their breakthrough hit of the same name. Donia also appeared on the group's hits, 'It Only Takes A Minute' and 'Heaven Must Be Missing An Angel'.
CAUSE: Unknown. He died in Somerville, Massachusetts.

Ral Donner

(RALPH STUART DONNER)
Born February 10, 1943
Died April 6, 1984
Considered an Elvis Presley clone, Chicago-born Ral Donner enjoyed several pop hits in the early Sixties. First singing spirituals in his church, Donner picked up the guitar in his early teens. After earning exposure on a local television programme in 1958 as the leader of a rock group called Ral Donner and The Gents in 1958, Donner was hired as a backing musician by both Sammy Davis Jr. and Alan Freed. Though under age, Donner toured extensively on the East Coast and the Midwest. Then hiring his brother-in-law as his manager, Donner emerged as a solo act in 1959. After recording an obscure single on the small Scottie label in 1959, Donner landed at the larger Gone Records in 1961. Backed by a Miami-based group which was soon renamed The Starfires, Donner scored his first national hit with a cover version of an Elvis Presley album track, 'The Girl Of My Best Friend'. A novelty tune of sorts, Donner sang the song as an Elvis imitator. Donner was one of several successful Elvis clones during this period including Terry Stafford ('Suspicion') and Joe Dowell ('Wooden Heart'). But not wanting to be typecast

as an Elvis-clone, Donner followed an original composition which became his biggest hit, 'You Don't Know What You've Got (Until You Lose It)'. Donner's brief hit run continued with 'Please Don't Go' (1961), 'She's Everything (I Wanted You To Be)' (1962), and 'To Love Someone' (1962). Leaving Gone Records due to a royalty dispute, Donner never scored another hit as he passed through several labels including, Reprise, Red Bird, Fontana, and named after Donner's one-time backing group, Starfire. Donner re-emerged in the Seventies as the writer of the perennial musical, *Grease*, with a storyline based on his experiences in a Chicago high school. A Broadway smash, the production was later transferred to the big screen via a 1978 film starring Olivia Newton-John and John Travolta. Shortly after Presley's death in 1977, Donner released a tribute record, 'The Day The Beat Stopped'. In 1981, Donner was asked to impersonate Presley's voice for the documentary film, *This Is Elvis*. Donner met Presley only twice in his lifetime.
CAUSE: Lung cancer. He was diagnosed with the disease in the late Seventies. He died at his home in Chicago.

Freddy Donovan

Born June 26, 1939
Died May 1986
A later member of doo-wop act The Willows, bass vocalist Freddy Donovan joined the group in 1956 as the replacement for original member Thomas "Scooter" Steele, just after they scored their only hit with 'Church Bells May Ring'. Donovan was briefly a member of The Solitaires.
CAUSE: Unknown.

Harold Dorman

Born December 23, 1926
Died October 8, 1988
Country-pop singer who scored his sole hit in 1960 with 'Mountain Of Love', Harold Dorman enjoyed a revival version of the song in 1964 by Johnny Rivers. Charley Pride later scored a hit with Dorman's composition 'Mississippi Cotton Picking Delta Town'.
CAUSE: Heart attack. He had previously suffered two debilitating strokes.

Jane Dornacker

Born October 1, 1947
Died October 22, 1986
A member of the avant-garde rock act The Tubes, Jane Dornacker was initially hired in 1973 as a dancer. She was spotted by Tubes' member Michael Cotten, who was painting a mural at The Palms Café in San Francisco while Dornacker was performing as the leader of Leila T and The Los Frondos Fabulosos. All three women were brought into the band, and Dornacker is best known for co-writing and providing the co-lead vocal of the Tubes' bawdy melodramatic novelty hit, 'Don't Touch Me There'. Also a stand-up comedienne and an actress, she played Nurse Murch in the film *The Right Stuff*.
CAUSE: She was killed in a helicopter crash while doing a live traffic report for radio station WNBC in New York City. Stalling in mid-air, the craft plunged into the Hudson River. The pilot, Bill Pate, was seriously injured. Dornacker had survived a previous helicopter crash earlier in the year.

Lee Dorsey

(IRVING LEE DORSEY)
Born December 4, 1924
Died December 2, 1986
Although a prolific Fifties New Orleans R&B singer, Lee Dorsey never gave up his day job as a car mechanic. Born in New Orleans but moving with his family to Portland in 1935, Dorsey served in the US Navy during World War II, and was wounded in a Pacific battle. While serving in the navy,

Dorsey entered the ring and won a boxing championship in the lightweight division. After his discharge, Dorsey worked as a professional boxer in the Portland area under the moniker Kid Chocolate. After studying car repair, Dorsey returned to New Orleans in 1955, where he found a job at a garage owned by local deejay "Ernie The Whip". A hard-working family man and father of 11 children, Dorsey began his unlikely musical career in the late Fifties when overheard singing by an independent record producer, while working underneath a car. Beginning his long association with legendary New Orleans producer Allen Toussaint, Dorsey scored a pair of regional hits with 'Rock (Pretty Baby)' (1957) and 'Lottie-Mo' (1958). Signing with Bobby Robinson's Fury label, Dorsey landed on the national charts with 'Ya Ya' (1961) and 'Do-Re-Me' (1962). But following the collapse of Fury Records in 1963, Dorsey was free of contractual obligations. Reteaming with Toussaint and usually backed by The Meters, Dorsey recorded on a number of different labels in the Sixties, and landed on the charts with 'Ride Your Pony', 'Get Out Of My Life Woman', 'Working In A Coal Mine', and 'Holy Cow'. In the mid Sixties, Dorsey would tour with Chuck Berry, James Brown, and in 1966, The Beatles. Backed by The Meters in 1970, Dorsey released the critically acclaimed, but poor selling album, *Yes We Can*; two of the tracks were hits for others, 'Sneaking Sally Through The Alley' by Robert Palmer and 'Yes We Can' by The Pointer Sisters. Remaining active in the music industry, Dorsey appeared on Southside Johnny's début album in 1976, and after being cited as a major influence of the group, as the opening act for British punk-rock outfit The Clash on their 1980 US tour.
CAUSE: After a year-long battle with emphysema, he died in New Orleans.

Thomas A. Dorsey

(THOMAS ANDREW DORSEY)
Born July 1, 1899
Died January 23, 1993
The "Father of Gospel Music", Thomas A. Dorsey began his career in the blues field during the Twenties. A bawdy performer who used a variety of pseudonyms including "Barrelhouse Tom" and "Georgia Tom", he also penned a number of jazz and blues hits during this period, including 'Riverside Blues' (Joe "King" Oliver's Creole Jazz Band) and 'The Stormy Sea Blues' (Ma Rainey). But after falling seriously ill for the second time in the decade, Dorsey swore off blues in exchange for his health, and in 1926 penned his first gospel song, 'If You See My Saviour, Tell Him That You Saw Me'. Backsliding a year later, Dorsey returned to blues, lured by its financial rewards. Forming a duo with Hudson Whitaker (better known as Tampa Red) under the moniker The Famous Hokum Boys, their first hit came with the sexual innuendo-filled, 'It's Tight Like That'. Vacillating between gospel and blues in the late Twenties, Dorsey brought elements of each musical genre to the other. And instead of the traditional, solemn musical arrangements and bare-boned instrumentation of the old time sacred spirituals, Dorsey brought a hook-filled, melody-driven, percussion-heavy, pop-oriented approach to religious music. But Dorsey's world began to destruct. Believing that he was paying a price for his flirtation with the blues, Dorsey was beset by tragedy during this period. First he lost a large amount of money when his bank closed during the Depression; and in 1932, his wife, Nettie, and then their child, both died after brief illnesses. Returning to the gospel arena for good in 1932, Dorsey marked the conversion by composing 'Precious Lord, Take My Hand', a touching song that single-handedly ushered in the Gospel Age (the song

was further popularised in 1968 with Mahalia Jackson's rendition at the funeral of the Rev. Martin Luther King Jr.). Dorsey launched his own publishing company, and frequently teamed with gospel singer, Sallie Martin. But Dorsey's brand of religious music came under attack. Often challenged by old-line preachers who considered the music evil and worldly, modern gospel music was slow to earn respectability in the black church. Dorsey's other gospel compositions include 'When I've Done My Best', 'Search Me, Lord' and 'If I Could Hear My Mother Pray'.
CAUSE: Alzheimer's disease. He died in Chicago.

Steve Douglas

(STEVEN KREISMAN)
Born September 24, 1938
Died April 19, 1993
Popular session sax player who began in Duane Eddy's backing group, The Rebels, Steve Douglas was a self-taught player who picked up the instrument as a young child. While in high school in Los Angeles, Douglas had attracted the attention of classmate Phil Spector, who would later frequently employ him on tracks such as 'Be My Baby'. Besides a long-term stint with Duane Eddy, Douglas also worked with Chicano rocker Ritchie Valens and was a touring member of groups behind Elvis Presley, Eric Clapton and Bob Dylan. Douglas also appeared with Presley in the film, *Girls, Girls, Girls*. Based in Los Angeles since the Sixties, he moved to San Francisco in 1981 to pursue a solo career, releasing an instrumental album, *Hot Sax*, in 1982.
CAUSE: Heart disease. He died of heart failure in a Los Angeles recording studio while working with Ry Cooder.

Tom Dowd

(THOMAS JOHN DOWD JR.)
Born October 20, 1925
Died October 27, 2002
A prolific recording engineer at Atlantic Records, Tom Dowd was trained as a physicist, and worked on the secret Manhattan Project during World War II. Unable to find a job as a physicist after the war, he instead turned to his early love of music. While a junior recording engineer at Apex Studios in New York City in 1947, Dowd endeared himself to record company owners Ahmet Ertegun and Herb Abramson by breaking the established rules of recording. Hired by Atlantic Records as chief recording engineer, Dowd played a crucial role in the company's success. By convincing the label in the Fifties to record sessions in stereo as well as monophonic, Dowd gave Atlantic an edge over its competitors with the rise of stereo records. He also began recording onto tape rather than disc, and by 1959 he was using an eight track recording console. As both engineer and producer, Dowd worked with countless musical acts including Ray Charles, The Drifters, Otis Redding and Aretha Franklin. Leaving Atlantic in the late Sixties to work as an independent producer, he oversaw sessions by acts such as Dusty Springfield, Eric Clapton (a.k.a. Derek & The Dominoes), The Allman Brothers, and Lynyrd Skynyrd. Dowd's illustrious career was chronicled in Mark Moormann's 2003 documentary, *Tom Dowd & The Language Of Music*.
CAUSE: He succumbed to respiratory disease at his home in Aventura, Florida. He had suffered with the ailment for two years.

Big Al Downing

Born January 9, 1940
Died July 4, 2005
One of the few African-Americans to succeed in country music, pianist-vocalist Big Al Downing placed several hits on the country charts in the late Seventies and early Eighties, including 'Mr. Jones', 'Touch Me (I'll Be Your Fool Once More)' and 'Bring It On Home'. Joining Wanda Jackson's band

in the late Fifties, he performed on her biggest hit, the rockabilly standard, 'Let's Have A Party'. Downing is an inductee of the Rockabilly Hall of Fame.
CAUSE: He died at a hospital in Worcester, Massachusetts after losing his battle with leukaemia.

Peter Doyle

(PETER JOHN DOYLE)
Born July 28, 1949
Died October 13, 2001
Singer-songwriter Peter Doyle became a member of a new version of The Seekers (who had split in 1968) named The New Seekers. Assembled by original Seekers member Keith Potger, the Australian-British act had several MOR hits in the early Seventies beginning with a melancholy composition written by US folk singer Melanie Safka, 'Look What They've Done To My Song Ma', continuing with an adaptation of a Coca-Cola commercial, 'I'd Like To Teach The World To Sing' and a medley cover (from the Who's *Tommy*), 'Pinball Wizard'/'See Me, Feel Me'. Doyle shared lead vocals with Lyn Paul on 'Beg, Steal Or Borrow', the UK's Eurovision Song Contest entry in 1972. After leaving The New Seekers in 1973, Doyle pursued a solo career, and in 1982 joined former Wings drummer Steve Holly in the group Regis. A native of Melbourne, Australia, Doyle mastered the banjo and guitar as a child and, by the age of 16, had the first of several Australian hit singles with a cover version of Conway Twitty's 'Speechless'.
CAUSE: He died in Australia after battling throat and lung cancer for two years.

Willis Draffen

(WILLIS LEWIS DRAFFEN JR.)
Born March 18, 1945
Died February 8, 2002
Guitarist for the perennial pop/soul act Bloodstone, Willis Draffen co-founded the group in 1962 as The Sinceres. Originally an a cappella, doo-wop styled outfit, the group left its Kansas City base for Los Angeles in the late Sixties. Bloodstone earned accolades for their soulful performances on an English tour with singer Al Green in 1972, and had a Top 10 crossover hit in 1973 with 'Natural High' for Decca Records. The group followed up with a string of R&B hits, including 'Never Let You Go', 'Outside Woman', 'My Little Lady' and 'We Go Back A Long Way'. Bloodstone also appeared in the 1975 film, *Train Ride To Hollywood.*
CAUSE: Complications from diabetes. He died just as he was preparing for a US tour.

LaVerne Drake

Born October 8, 1938
Died c. 1979
Founding member of Fifties vocal doo-wop outfit, The Cadillacs, whose biggest hit came in 1955 with 'Speedo', LaVerne Drake was the only female in the group. Formed in 1953 as The Carnations, the group distinguished itself from its competitors with its choreographed stage moves. Signing with Josie Records and renamed The Cadillacs, the group was the first of many Fifties doo-wop outfits to be named after a car. Led by Earl Carroll, the group recorded a string of doo-wop gems including the often-recorded 'Gloria' and 'Wishing Well'. Drake was replaced in The Cadillacs in mid-1956 by J.R. Bailey.
CAUSE: Unknown.

Nick Drake

Born June 18, 1948
Died November 25, 1974
Earning a cult following in the years after his death, Nick Drake enjoyed little fame during his brief career. Born in Burma, the British-based folk singer-songwriter was reared on the saxophone and clarinet, switching to guitar in his late teens. Drawn to British and American folk music, he

joined a thriving local folk scene while attending Cambridge University on an academic scholarship in 1968. Discovered by Ashley Hutchings of Fairport Convention, Drake was signed to a management contract by the group's manager, Joe Boyd. A year in the making, Drake's début album *Five Leaves Left* (1969) featured several Fairport Convention members. Receiving little promotion, the album was a critical success but a commercial failure. After dropping out of college in 1969, Drake was joined on his follow-up album *Bryter Layter* (1970) by John Cale, Richard Thompson, and a host of session musicians. A favourite artist of the underground set, Drake was a mystical, reclusive figure who refused to grant press interviews. As a stage performer he would often ignore his audience altogether, by 1970 refusing to perform at all. After delivering the tapes for his third and final album, *Pink Moon* (featuring only Drake's vocals, and a piano and guitar), to Island Records in 1972, Drake disappeared. Suffering severe depression in early 1972, he voluntarily entered a clinic. Returning to recording in 1973, he had finished four tracks for a planned album and at the time of his death was preparing to move to Paris. Released posthumously in 1979, a boxed-set, *Fruit Tree*, spawned renewed interest in Drake, the material influencing dark, moody bands like Joy Division and The Dream Academy. Drake remained relatively unknown in the US until the Eighties. Drake gained a degree of further recognition in 2000 when his 'Pink Moon' was featured in a pair of car commercials.
CAUSE: Frustrated by his lack of commercial success, Drake overdosed on an anti-depressant, Tryptasol. He died in Birmingham, England. Though disputed by his family who reported an upswing in his mood, the coroner ruled the death a suicide.
FURTHER READING: Humphries, Patrick. (1997). *Nick Drake*. Bloomsbury: London.

Pete Drake

(RODDIS FRANKLIN DRAKE)
Born 1932
Died July 29, 1988
A popular pedal-steel guitar player, the Atlanta-born Pete Drake moved to Nashville in 1959 and landed a position as a sideman at the Grand Ole Opry. Briefly pursuing a solo career, he scored an instrumental hit in 1964 with 'Forever', billed as Pete Drake and His Talking Steel Guitar. Based in Nashville for the rest of his life, Drake was a popular session player, working with George Jones, Elvis Presley and Tammy Wynette. He played on Bob Dylan's albums *John Wesley Harding* and the country-styled album, *Nashville Skyline* (1969), and then Ringo Starr's *Beaucoups Of Blues* (1970). Pioneering the use of the voicebox, Drake was toying with a primitive version of the synthesizer between sessions for the 1971 George Harrison project, *All Things Must Pass*.
CAUSE: He died from complications of lung disease at his home in Brentwood, Tennessee.

Rusty Draper

(FARRELL H. DRAPER)
Born January 25, 1923
Died March 25, 2003
A pop-country singer, Rusty Draper broke into music, aged 12, via his uncle's Tulsa, Oklahoma, radio programme. Signing with Mercury Records in 1952, Draper had a country hit with 'Gambler's Guitar', and, when moved over to the label's pop division, a trio of Top 40 hits in 1955 with 'Are You Satisfied?', 'The Shifting, Whispering Sands' and a cover of Boyd Bennett's 'Seventeen'. During this period Draper recorded a number of rock-style songs including 'Rock 'n' Roll Baby'. Signing with Monument

Records in 1963, Draper returned to his country music roots.
CAUSE: In poor health, he died at a Seattle hospital. He suffered from throat cancer and heart disease, and had endured multiple strokes.

Jimmy Driftwood

(JAMES CORBETT MORRIS)
Born June 20, 1907
Died July 12, 1998
Schoolteacher turned folk singer-songwriter, Jimmy Driftwood penned the Johnny Horton hit 'The Battle Of New Orleans' (an updating of a square dance song called 'The Eight Of January') and the Eddie Arnold hit 'Tennessee Stud'. A member of the Grand Ole Opry, Driftwood later earned the nickname, "The Father of Arkansas Folk Music".
CAUSE: Suffering a stroke a few weeks before his death, he died of heart failure in Fayettesville, Arkansas.

Don Drummond

Born 1943
Died May 6, 1969
Leader of the Jamaican ska group, The Skatalites, Don Drummond had emerged as a popular session trombonist in the early Sixties. Forming the pioneering ska band the Skatalites in 1963, Drummond and the group landed a British hit in 1967 with 'Guns Of Navarone'. The Skatalites were also employed as session players behind acts such as The Maytalls and a young Bob Marley. A prolific songwriter, Drummond penned most of The Skatalites' material. Tragedy struck the group when the mentally unbalanced Drummond was intentionally given the wrong medication by his girlfriend Marguerite Mahfood so that she could go dancing on New Year's Eve, while he slept through a scheduled concert. When she arrived home the following morning on January 1, 1965, he stabbed her in the neck, killing her. With Drummond imprisoned, the group disintegrated shortly thereafter. Receiving job offers, The Skatalites reformed during the Eighties ska revival.
CAUSE: He committed suicide while imprisoned in a Jamaican insane asylum.

Spencer Dryden

Born April 7, 1938
Died January 11, 2005
A member of Jefferson Airplane, Spencer Dryden was the drummer during the group's glory years in the late Sixties. Born in New York City but raised in Los Angeles, Dryden was exposed to the entertainment industry as a child through his uncle, actor Charlie Chaplin. After graduating from the Army and Navy Academy, Dryden joined a series of rock and jazz groups including The Ashes, which in 1966 evolved into the psychedelic band The Peanut Butter Conspiracy. Leaving before the group recorded, on the recommendation of session drummer Earl Palmer, Jefferson Airplane hired Dryden as replacement for drummer Skip Spence, actually a guitar player, who left to form Moby Grape. Joining in time for Jefferson Airplane's second album, the psychedelic classic *Surrealistic Pillow* (1967), Dryden performed on a pair of Top 10 singles, 'White Rabbit' and 'Somebody To Love', which vocalist Grace Slick had first recorded with her previous group The Great Society. Dryden and Slick were briefly an item before Dryden married groupie Sally Mann. One of the most influential rock bands of the era, Jefferson Airplane performed at 1967's Monterey International Pop Festival, Woodstock Music and Arts Fair, as well as the ill-fated Altamont Festival in December 1969. In all, Dryden appeared on five of the group's albums up to and including 1970's *Volunteers*, which included the only Dryden composition recorded by the group, 'A Song For All Seasons'. After being fired that year, Dryden replaced Mickey Hart

in The Grateful Dead's offshoot country-rock band, New Riders Of The Purple Sage, eventually becoming their manager and appearing on several of their albums, including *The Adventures Of Panama Red.* After leaving the group in 1978, Dryden was beset by poor health and a series of personal tragedies. When Jefferson Airplane reunited for an album and tour in 1989, Dryden was not asked to participate.
CAUSE: Suffering from colon cancer, he died at his home near Petaluma, California. In poor health for a long time, he had previously undergone hip replacement surgery and suffered from advanced coronary disease. A benefit to raise money for Dryden's medical care was organised by Bob Weir of The Grateful Dead and Warren Haynes of Gov't Mule.

Steve Duboff

Born July 13, 1941
Died February 28, 2004
A singer-songwriter, Steve Duboff teamed with Art Kornfield to compose 'The Rain, The Park And Other Things' (The Cowsills), 'We Can Fly' (The Cowsills) 'The Pied Piper' (Crispian St. Peters) and garage-rock classic, 'How Is The Air Up There?' (The La De Da's, The Bangles). Duboff's other compositions have been recorded by acts such as The Turtles, Al Hirt, The Monkees and Ringo Starr. Duboff and Kornfield had previously been members of the rock group The Changin' Times, who toured as the opening act for Sonny and Cher. In the Seventies, Duboff was an A&R man for ABC Records. He later worked as a video game programmer.
CAUSE: Cancer. He died in Malibu, California.

Wendell Duconge

Born c. 1920
Died c. 1980
Alto saxophonist with Fats Domino in the Fifties, Wendell Duconge was also a popular session player at J&M Studio in New Orleans.
CAUSE: Unknown.

Dave Duddley

(DAVID DARWIN PEDRUSKA)
Born May 3, 1928
Died December 22, 2003
A popular country singer, Dave Duddley achieved a crossover pop hit in 1963 with the truck driving anthem, 'Six Days On The Road'. A former semi-professional baseball player, he broke into the music industry as a radio deejay.
CAUSE: Heart attack. He died in Danbury, Wisconsin.

Gus Dudgeon

Born September 30, 1942
Died July 22, 2002
A producer and engineer best known for his work with David Bowie and Elton John, Gus Dudgeon had a long and varied career. Breaking into music inadvertently in June 1964, Dudgeon was ordered to work the tape machine at Decca Studios in London because the technician was drunk; the session produced the hit, 'She's Not There' by The Zombies. Remaining at Decca he developed his skills as a recording engineer, working with Marianne Faithfull and John Mayall, among many other Decca acts. Promoted to producer, he first worked with Ten Years After on their self-titled début album but it was his imaginative work on David Bowie's 1969 hit, 'Space Oddity', where Dudgeon stepped in and completed the track after producer Tony Visconti refused the role, that brought him industry attention. Teaming with Elton John, Dudgeon produced most of Elton's classic Seventies albums including *Madman Across The Water* and *Goodbye Yellow Brick Road.* The pair launched the short-lived Rocket label, which fell apart in 1976, and after parting company with Elton, Dudgeon produced a number of acts

including The Beach Boys, Steeleye Span, Chris Rea, Lindisfarne, Joan Armatrading and XTC. Constructing Sol Studios in the early Eighties, Dudgeon later sold the operation to Chris Rea. In 1985, Dudgeon reunited with Elton John for three albums. In 2003, Dudgeon's estate sued David Bowie for £6m over unpaid royalties for 'Space Oddity'.
CAUSE: The Jaguar he was driving veered off the road in Berkshire, England, instantly killing both Dudgeon and his wife, Sheila. They were returning home from a 50th birthday party for Chris Hook, formerly of the Dudgeon-produced band Voyager.

Tony Duhig

Born 1942
Died January 1991
As the leader of the progressive-rock band Jade Warrior, guitarist/keyboardist Tony Duhig released three critically acclaimed but poor-selling albums at Vertigo Records. Also a prolific session player, Duhig would occasionally reform Jade Warrior.
CAUSE: Heart attack.

Al Duncan

(ALROOK CLIFFORD DUNCAN, JR.)
Born October 8, 1927
Died January 3, 1995
Chicago-based house drummer for Chess Records, Al Duncan performed on several of Chuck Berry's early hits at the label. Later hired by Vee-Jay, Duncan frequently worked with bluesman Jimmy Reed.
CAUSE: He died in his sleep from congestive heart failure; he had undergone heart surgery the previous year.

Johnny Duncan

(JOHN FRANKLIN DUNCAN)
Born September 7, 1931
Died July 15, 2000
Though unknown in his native country, American-born singer-guitarist Johnny Duncan scored a pioneering British skiffle hit in 1957 with 'Last Train To San Fernando'. Hailing from Tennessee, Duncan first sang in a gospel quartet in his teens. Teaching himself guitar, he joined a Texan hillbilly trio at 16. Drafted into the armed services in 1952, he was stationed in England where he married a local girl the following year. Though settling in the US after his discharge, he returned to Britain to appease his homesick wife. Performing on stage at the American Club in Bushey Park, Duncan was discovered by banjo player Dickie Bishop of The Chris Barber Jazz Band and was hired as a vocalist, spending a year on stage in the renamed Chris Barber Skiffle Group, before going solo. Working with producer Dennis Preston, Duncan formed The Blue Grass Boys, borrowing the moniker from Bill Monroe's backing group. Though initially straddling folk and country styles, Duncan jumped on the skiffle bandwagon, recording a cover version of a reworked calypso song, 'Last Train To San Fernando'. Duncan became a sensation in Britain and had two more hits, 'Blue Blue Heartache' and 'Footprints In The Snow', as well as landing his own BBC radio show, *Tennessee Songbag*. After a tour through Australia in the early Seventies, he remained in the country and remarried.
CAUSE: Diagnosed with inoperable bowel cancer, he died in Taree, New South Wales, Australia.

"Champion" Jack Dupree

(WILLIAM THOMAS DUPREE)
Born July 4, 1910
Died January 21, 1992
Legendary New Orleans jazz and barrelhouse piano player whose long recording career was kicked off at OKeh Records in 1940, "Champion" Jack Dupree was emotionally scarred in his childhood when both of his parents were killed in a Ku Klux Klan attack. Raised in a New Orleans orphanage, he

became a pounding barrelhouse player. Moving to Indianapolis in the Twenties, he came under the tutelage of pianist Leroy Carr. After a stint in professional boxing in the Thirties, Dupree signed with OKeh Records in 1940, recording the blues standards, 'All Alone Blues' and 'Gamblin' Man Blues'. Serving in World War II, he was captured and imprisoned in a Japanese camp. Settling in New York City in the late Forties, he recorded for a series of labels before signing with King Records where he recorded his only chart hit in 1955, 'Walking The Blues'. Taking a folk blues turn in the mid Fifties, Dupree frequently teamed with folk blues guitarist Brownie McGhee. Moving to Europe in 1959, he found plenty of club work, even playing alongside The Rolling Stones and Eric Clapton. Recording and touring heavily late in life, he rarely returned to the US.
CAUSE: Cancer. He died in Hanover, Germany.

Roger Durham

(ROGER LEE DURHAM)
Born February 14, 1946
Died July 27, 1973
Vocalist and percussionist for perennial pop/soul band Bloodstone, Roger Lee Durham was a founding member of the group when they were known as The Sinceres. Originally an a cappella, doo-wop styled outfit, the group left its Kansas City base for Los Angeles in the late Sixties. Though unsigned, Bloodstone toured England with singer Al Green in 1972. Earning accolades for their soulful performances, the group attracted media attention and were signed by Decca Records. Appearing on their first three albums including their best seller, *Natural High* (1973), Durham provided the vocals on several hits, including the million-selling 'Natural High' (1973), 'Never Let You Go' (1973), and 'Outside Woman' (1974). Durham was replaced in Bloodstone by Harry Wilkins.
CAUSE: He died from internal injuries after being thrown from a horse.

Ian Dury

Born May 12, 1942
Died March 27, 2000
The streetwise leader of the British funk band, Ian Dury & The Blockheads, the physically handicapped Dury had his greatest success in the late Seventies. A native of Harrow, North London, Dury promoted the widely held belief that he came from Upminster in the county of Essex, and many of his songs were based on fictional characters from this part of England. Dury contracted polio at age seven and after a two-year hospitalisation the disease had paralysed the left side of his body and withered his left leg and arm. After graduating from Walthamstow Art College and London's Royal College of Art, he taught painting at Canterbury Art College. In 1970 Dury was a leading figure in the formation of pub rockers Kilburn & The High Roads, and three years later he quit his teaching position for a full-time musical career. On the verge of success, the group came under the management of author/broadcaster Charlie Gillett, and landed an opening slot for a Who tour across Britain in November 1973. A single, 'Rough Kids', was released in November '74, while an album, *Handsome*, was released after the group disbanded. After disbanding in 1975, the group re-emerged briefly as Ian Dury and The High Roads. Teaming with bandmate Chaz Jankel, Dury signed to Stiff Records in 1977, and had his first hit with 'Sex & Drugs & Rock'n'Roll'. Essentially a solo album recorded with studio musicians, the critically acclaimed *New Boots And Panties* was a smash in Britain, including the tribute, 'Sweet Gene Vincent'. Assembling a backing band of experienced musicians calling themselves The Blockheads, the witty and lyrically inventive Dury enjoyed a series of pop smashes with 'What A Waste' (1978), 'Hit Me With

Your Rhythm Stick' (1978), 'Reasons To Be Cheerful (Part 3)' (1979), and 'I Want To Be Straight' (1980). After poor sales figures for the 1981 album *Lord Upminster*, Dury turned to acting, appearing in television, plays, and films such as *Pirates* and *The Cook, The Thief, The Wife And Her Lover*. On the musical front, he formed The Music Students, releasing the album *4000 Weeks Holiday* (1984) and subsequently released two further solo albums. An Ian Dury & The Blockheads reunion in 1998 spawned the acclaimed comeback album *Mr. Love Pants*, the group's first release in 17 years. Dury continued to perform until two weeks before his death.

CAUSE: He was diagnosed with colon cancer in 1996, the disease having spread to his liver. His first wife had died of cancer in 1994.

FURTHER READING: Balls, Richard. (2000) *Sex & Drugs & Rock'n'Roll: The Life Of Ian Dury*. London: Omnibus Press.

Willem Duyn

Born March 31, 1937
Died December 3, 2004

The "Mouth" of Seventies Dutch pop-rock duo Mouth & McNeal, Willem Duyn earned his nickname because he was a big talker. Formerly a construction worker who spent weekends playing the drums in a jazz band, Duyn graduated to working as a radio deejay and operating his own nightclub, followed by a stint in popular Dutch band Speedway. In 1971, Duyn quit Speedway to pursue a solo career, and after an unsuccessful single, he teamed with former classical singer Maggie MacNeal (real name: Sjouke Van't Spijker). Their second release, the million-selling 'How Do You Do?' featured Duyn's unusual, strained vocal delivery. A Top 10 US hit in 1972, their success continued mainly in their native Netherlands but an English-language version of Holland's Eurovision Song Contest entry, 'I See A Star', reached the British Top 10 in 1974, but by the end of the year, the duo disbanded and "Mouth" teamed up with wife Ingrid Kup to form the less successful duo, Big Mouth & Little Eve.

CAUSE: Heart attack. He died in the Netherlands.

Bernie Dwyer

Born September 11, 1940
Died December 4, 2002

A member of Sixties British Invasion act Freddie & The Dreamers, Bernie Dwyer played drums on all their hits. Formed in Manchester, England, the group was fronted by former skiffle player, ex-milkman Freddie Garrity. Honing their act at seaside resorts, the group found success by mixing rock'n'roll with slapstick-style humour. After passing a BBC audition in 1962, the group landed in the British charts with a Top 10 cover of James Ray's R&B based 'If You Gotta Make A Fool Of Somebody'. Hiring songwriter Mitch Murray, the group continued their hit run with 'I'm Telling You Now' and 'You Were Made For Me'. By early 1965, the group had its final British hits with 'Over You', 'Just For You' and a pair of remakes – Paul Anka's 'I Love You Baby' and The G. Clefs' 'I Understand'. But just as the group's fortunes were waning, in the wake of The Beatles success, American audiences craved all things British. Reaching the top of the US charts in 1965 with the two-year-old single 'I'm Telling You Now', Freddie & The Dreamers were soon appearing on all of the major music and variety programmes on US television. When asked to identify the dance which Garrity performed on stage, the group quickly dreamed up 'Do The Freddie' – another US Top 20 hit. In the UK, the group appeared in the film *Every Day's A Holiday* and recorded an album of Disney film music but changing musical trends left them high and dry. The group stayed the course, subsisting

mainly in cabaret, until 1970. Dwyer did not join a 1976 Freddie and The Dreamers reunion but did return to the group in his final years.
CAUSE: After learning he had terminal cancer six months earlier, Dwyer threw dozens of parties for friends. He died at St. Ann's Hospice near Heald Green, Cheadle, England, the day after one such party.

Ronnie Dyson

Born June 5, 1950
Died November 10, 1990
A popular Seventies R&B singer, Washington DC native Ronnie Dyson scored several Philadelphia Soul style hits including 'Why Can't I Touch You' (1970) and 'One Man Band' (1972). Also an actor, he starred in the Broadway production of *Hair*, singing the opening piece 'Aquarius', before graduating to films. Dyson scored a posthumous R&B duet hit in 1991 with Vicki Austin, 'Are We So Far Apart We Can't Talk Anymore'.
CAUSE: He died at a nursing home in Philadelphia following a short, undisclosed illness. He had been previously treated for heart problems.

E

Dave Early

Born 1957
Died October 1996
A percussionist who recorded and toured with Sade and Van Morrison, Dave Early joined Morrison's band in the late Eighties and performed on several albums including *Enlightenment*, *Avalon Sunset* and *Hymns To The Silence*. Drawn toward traditional Irish music, Early settled in Northern Ireland in 1992, and worked with Mary Black until his death.
CAUSE: He died in a car accident in Ireland.

Marlena Easley

(MARLENA DAVIS)
Born October 4, 1944
Died February 27, 1993
Member of the early Sixties girl-group, The Orlons, singer Marlena Easley had initially joined a precursor of the group, Audrey and The Teenetts, a decade earlier at a Philadelphia junior high school. After losing its female lead singer and adding male vocalist Stephen Caldwell, the renamed Orlons were aided by Len Barry in signing with Cameo Records. After backing labelmate Dee Dee Sharpe on her Top 10 hit 'Mashed Potato Time', The Orlons enjoyed their own hit run of innocent pop-flavoured ditties with 'South Street', 'Don't Hang Up', and spawning a dance craze, 'The Wah Wahtusi'. Easley left the group in 1964, and retired from music in the Seventies. Easley and original member Stephen Caldwell toured as The Orlons beginning in the late Eighties.
CAUSE: Lung cancer. She died in Philadelphia.

Eazy-E

(ERIC WRIGHT)
Born September 7, 1973
Died March 26, 1995
A controversial gangster rapper, Eazy-E was born and raised in the crime-ridden Los Angeles suburb of Compton. Though barely in his teens, in 1985 he launched his own label Ruthless Records (allegedly from drug profits). Co-founding militant rap group N.W.A. (Niggers With Attitude) in 1988 along with Dr. Dre, MC Ren, and Ice Cube, the group was at the forefront of the gangster rap genre, beginning with their début album, *Straight Outta Compton*. An angry, politically charged project, the album included several controversial tracks including one which attacked the police. Released in 1990, a follow-up album, *Efil4zaggin* (which backwards spells Niggaz4life), was thematically similar to its predecessor with its exploration of social taboos such as paedophilia, prostitution, and gang rape. N.W.A. member Ice Cube left the group for a solo outing in 1990. Pursuing his own solo career, Eazy-E released his début album in 1989, *Eazy-Duz-It* (1989). Much of Easy-E's solo output was centred on his rivalry with former bandmate Dr. Dre. Eazy-E made news in 1991 when he attended a Republican senatorial fundraiser attended by President George Bush; the rapper explained his $2,500 donation by praising the candidate for his pre-free speech stance. After leaving N.W.A. in 1990, Eazy-E concentrated on the Ruthless Records stable of acts including, Above The Law, Michel'le, Bone Thugs-N-Harmony, and before losing them to rival Suge Knight at Death Row Records, rappers Dr. Dre and Snoop Doggy Dogg. Eazy-E guested on Bone Thugs-N-Harmony's hit single, 'Foe Tha Love Of'. Eazy-E sired at least seven children by six different women, including Tomika Wood, whom he wed while he was hospitalised.

CAUSE: AIDS. Admitted to Cedars-Sinai Medical Center in Los Angeles in late February, he died seven months later. He went public with his condition only a few weeks before his death.

Billy Eckstine

(WILLIAM CLARENCE ECKSTEIN)
Born July 8, 1914
Died March 8, 1993
Velvety jazz vocalist, trumpeter and trombonist who was inspired by Cab Calloway, Bill Eckstine emerged out of the Pittsburgh music scene. After a stint in a band led by Earl "Fatha" Hines beginning in 1939 (during which time he brought Sarah Vaughan to his boss' attention), Eckstine formed his own band in 1943. Nicknamed "Mr. B", the always fashionably dressed Eckstine was the first black singer to make the cover of *Life* magazine. Possessing a stunning baritone voice, he enjoyed a long string of hits including 'I Stay In The Mood For You' (1944), 'A Cottage For Sale' (1945), 'Prisoner Of Love' (1946), 'Fools Rush In' (1949), and 'I Apologise' (1951). One of Eckstine's compositions, 'I Want To Talk About It', was recorded by John Coltrane. Eckstine's career nose-dived with the arrival of rock music in the mid Fifties, his final hit coming in a duet with Sarah Vaughan, 'Passing Strangers'.
CAUSE: Stroke. Although a resident of Las Vegas, he travelled to his native Pittsburgh in 1992 for treatment. He died at Montifiore Hospital.

Damon Edge

(THOMAS WISE)
Born 1950
Died September 1995
Vocalist and synthesizer player of the San Francisco psychedelic-styled hard-rock band Chrome, Damon Edge led the group on several albums between 1977 to 1983. After disbanding the group, Edge emerged as a solo act.
CAUSE: Heart attack.

Jerry Edmonton

(JERRY MCCROCHAN)
Born October 24, 1946
Died November 28, 1994
Drummer for the early hard-rock group Steppenwolf, Canadian native Jerry Edmonton had previously been a member of The Sparrows. Meeting John Kaye in New York City, Edmonton invited him to join the group as their new lead singer. After recording an early version of the future Steppenwolf hit, the Hoyt Axton-penned 'The Pusher', The Sparrows disbanded. But when ABC-Dunhill Records convinced Kay to reform the group, Edmonton was included in the new line-up, now called Steppenwolf. From their début album *Steppenwolf*, the group landed a massive hit with the hippy anthem 'Born To Be Wild', a song written by Jerry Edmonton's brother, Dennis. With its politically tinged lyrics, Steppenwolf became an AOR stalwart, scoring hits with 'Rock Me', 'Magic Carpet Ride', an updated version of 'The Pusher', the often banned, 'Sookie Sookie', and from the album of the same name, 'Monster'. After Steppenwolf disbanded in 1973, Edmonton reformed a new version of the group the following year, 1974, calling it quits after two years. Edmonton and his brother, Dennis, later moved to Los Angeles where they joined a series of rock groups. In the Eighties, Edmonton married the widow of the latter Steppenwolf keyboardist, Andy Chapin.
CAUSE: He died in an auto accident near Santa Barbara, California.
FURTHER READING: Kay, John, & Einarson, John. (1994). *Magic Carpet Ride: The Autobiography Of John Kay And Steppenwolf.* Kingston, Ontario: Quarry Press.

Bernard Edwards

Born October 31, 1952
Died April 18, 1996
Talented producer and co-founder of the disco/funk group Chic, North

Carolina-born Bernard Edwards moved to New York City at age 10. Trained on the saxophone, he switched to the electric bass in his mid-teens. Teaming with Nile Rodgers, a former member of the Apollo Theater's house band, Edwards entered into a lifelong musical partnership. Soon joined by drummer Tony Thompson, Edwards and Rodgers formed a jazz-rock outfit, The Big Apple Band. But following the success of another group called Walter Murphy and The Big Apple Band, Edwards' group changed its musical direction and was renamed Chic. With the addition of a pair of female singers, Chic enjoyed international fame in the late Seventies beginning with 'Dance, Dance, Dance' (1977), a four-million selling single. Featuring Edwards' funky, prominent bass line, the group's hits continued with 'Le Freak' and 'Good Times'. Besides penning Chic's material, Edwards and Rodgers wrote and produced Sister Sledge's massive hit, 'We Are Family'. Many of Chic's hits would later be sampled by rap acts, beginning with 'Rapper's Delight' by The Sugarhill Gang which was based on 'Good Times'. With Chic disbanding in 1982, Edwards released his first solo album that year with *Glad To Be Here*. He then rejoined Tony Thompson in the short-lived group, The Distance. Turning to production work, sometimes in collaboration with Rodgers, Edwards worked with Diana Ross ('Upside Down' and 'I'm Coming Out'), Robert Palmer ('Addicted To Love' and 'I Didn't Mean To Turn You On'), Rod Stewart/Ronald Isley ('This Old Heart Of Mine'); he also produced the self-titled début of Power Station, a group fronted by singer Robert Palmer and formed around members of Duran Duran. Reunited in 1992, Chic found scant airplay with the poorly received album *Chicism*. While producing the Power Station's second album in 1996, *Living In Fear*, Edwards was forced to join the group after the departure of bassist John Taylor.

CAUSE: He died from pneumonia in a hotel room in Tokyo after a Japanese tour.

Bob "Chico" Edwards

Born June 12, 1937
Died March 11, 2001

The guitarist of Fifties R&B/doo-wop group The Diablos, Bob "Chico" Edwards was the only member who played a musical instrument at their recording sessions. Fronted by the brothers Nolan and Jimmy Strong, the Detroit-based group's only hit was 'The Way You Dog Me Around' (1956). Another of their releases, a ballad 'The Wind', became a doo-wop standard. Leaving the group in the late Fifties, Edwards settled in New York City where he worked in a number of jazz combos. Returning to Detroit, Edwards joined Nolan Strong for some recording sessions in 1972.

CAUSE: Unknown. He died in Detroit.

Jackie Edwards

(WILFRED GERALD EDWARDS)
Born 1939
Died August 15, 1992

Jamaican-born singer-songwriter, Jackie Edwards penned the Spencer Davis Group UK number 1 hits 'Keep On Running' (1965) and 'Somebody Help Me' (1966). A prolific composer, his other compositions include 'Your Eyes Are Dreaming' and 'Tell Me Darling'. Edwards was also instrumental in the rise of Chris Blackwell's Island Records, penning many ska and reggae songs. Edwards emigrated to England in the mid Sixties, where his début album sold poorly. He returned to Jamaica in 1987.

CAUSE: Heart attack. He died in Jamaica.

James "Ricky" Edwards

Born c. 1933
Died c. 1965

The bass singer of Fifties, New York-based doo-wop group, The

Chords, James "Ricky" Nelson had been an original member of the group in the early Fifties, joining the new better-known line-up in 1954. Signing with Atlantic Records, The Chords scored a rare crossover pop entry with the million-selling smash, 'Sh-Boom'.
CAUSE: Unknown.

Pearl Edwards

Born June 6, 1934
Died November 30, 2001
A member of the New Orleans-based R&B band Huey "Piano" Smith & The Clowns, Pearl Edwards was hired by Smith after he heard her singing along with the juke box in a bar. In addition to appearing on a number of Smith's releases, Edwards was also a member of The Pitter Pats, The Soul Shakers, The Hueys and John Williams & The Tick Tocks. She recorded just one solo single for Ace Records, 'It Do Me Good' (1964).
CAUSE: Kidney failure.

Raymond Edwards

Born September 13, 1924
Died March 4, 1997
The bass singer of the Fifties Philadelphia-based doo-wop group The Silhouettes, the group scored one of the era's finest examples of the genre with the hit 'Get A Job' (1958). The Silhouettes had evolved from a religious group called The Gospel Tornadoes. Edwards left the group in 1962.
CAUSE: Prostate cancer. He died in Philadelphia.

Tommy Edwards

Born February 17, 1922
Died October 22, 1969
Popular Fifties pop/R&B crooner, Richmond, Virginia-born Tommy Edwards had worked in show business since his childhood. Landing his own radio show in Richmond as a singer and piano player in the Forties, Edwards garnered his first national success when Louis Jordan scored a million-selling hit with an Edwards co-composition, 'That Chick's Too Young To Fry' (1946). After briefly recording several obscure singles in the late Forties at Top, and then National Records, Edwards moved to New York City in 1950 to pursue a career as a songwriter. But he was instead signed as a solo act by MGM Records. Backed by The Leroy Holmes Orchestra, he enjoyed a decade-long string of pop hits beginning in 1951 with 'The Morning Side Of The Mountain'. But with the rise of rock'n'roll in the mid Fifties, Edwards updated his earlier hits with the aid of Leroy Holmes' new arrangements, and recharted with new versions of his previous hits, 'Please Mr. Sun', 'The Morning Side Of The Mountain', and his best-selling single, a chart-topping ballad written in 1912 by future Vice-President Charles Dawes (under Calvin Coolidge, 1925–29), 'It's All In The Game'. Edwards' final hits came with a pair of remakes, 'My Melancholy Baby' and 'I Don't Want To Know'. After enjoying several hit albums, Edwards left MGM Records in 1965. Cliff Richard reprised 'It's All In The Game' for a British hit in 1964, as did The Four Tops in 1970.
CAUSE: Brain aneurysm. He died in Henrico County, Virginia.

Donnie Elbert

Born May 25, 1936
Died January 26, 1989
A solo R&B singer, Donnie Elbert was born in New Orleans but raised in Buffalo. Joining The Vibraharps in 1954, he recorded a few obscure singles in 1955, hitting the R&B charts with 'What Can I Do?'. Leaving the group to pursue a solo career, Elbert scored his début hit with 'What Can I Do?' (1957). After serving a two-year army stint, Elbert had only limited success in the next decade. After

recording a fine, but obscure album on King Records, *The Sensational Donnie Elbert Sings* (1959), Elbert recorded for several labels, once turning down a contract with Motown Records. Launching his own Gateway/Upstate label in 1964, he scored regional hits with the soulful, falsetto-heavy, 'Run Little Girl' (1964) and the danceable, 'A Little Piece Of Leather' (1964). Experimenting with Jamaican ska music and moving to Britain, Elbert found a new fanbase as well as a bride. Returning to the US in 1970, he entered the R&B charts with 'Can't Get Over Losing You'. The following year Elbert scored his first of two pop crossover hits with a pair of remakes, The Supremes' 'Where Did Our Love Go' and The Four Tops' 'I Can't Help Myself (Sugar Pie, Honey Bunch)'. By the late Seventies, Elbert had fallen into obscurity. In 1984, he joined Polygram Records, Canada, as an A&R man.
CAUSE: Stroke. He died in Philadelphia.

Tommy Eldridge

(THOMAS A. ELDRIDGE)
Born October 23, 1940
Died June 19, 2000
As a member of the one-hit-wonder R&B group The Jarmels, bass vocalist Tommy Eldridge had a hit in 1961 with the Bert Berns composition, 'A Little Bit Of Soap'. Formed in Richmond, Virginia, by five teens who attended the same high school and church, the group was one of the few African-American acts signed by Laurie Records. Eldridge joined a revival version of The Jarmels in the Nineties.
CAUSE: Unknown.

Ivan Elias

Born March 23, 1950
Died June 4, 1996
The bass player of the Eighties pop-rock group Scandal, Ivan Elias was the beneficiary of MTV airplay. Scandal was founded in 1981 by New York City-based guitarist Zack Smith. Wanting to add a female vocalist, he auditioned nearly 100 women before settling on the energetic Patty Smyth, the daughter of a nightclub manager. Signed by Columbia Records, Scandal were an early MTV favourite, with the video for 'Goodbye To You' receiving heavy play. After scoring three more AOR hits, 'The Warrior', 'Beat Of A Heart' and 'Hands Tied', the group was struck by infighting, and eventually founder Zack Smith was forced out of his own group. The surviving members of Scandal re-formed for a documentary on the VH1 network in 2004.
CAUSE: Lung cancer. After complaining of back pain, he sought medical treatment and discovered that he had lung cancer that had spread to his backbone. He was not a smoker.

(Mama) Cass Elliot

(ELLEN NAOMI COHEN)
Born September 19, 1941
Died July 29, 1974
The visual focus of the Sixties folk-rock group, The Mamas & The Papas, Baltimore born and raised (Mama) Cass Elliot was trained on the piano and guitar. After moving to Virginia and briefly attending American University, she moved to Greenwich Village in 1960. Working as an actress, she landed several off-Broadway roles. Also singing in local coffee houses as a solo folk singer, she then joined her first husband, James Hendricks (whom she divorced in 1969), in a folk group called The Big Three. Elliot subsequently formed another shortlived trio, The Mugwumps, which included future Lovin' Spoonful members John Sebastian and Zalman Yanovsky. Then, while on vacation in the Virgin Islands in 1964, Elliot ran into a trio of friends from New York City who performed as The New Journeymen. After spending weeks on the beach singing with Denny Doherty,

John Phillips and his wife, Michelle (nee Gilliam), Elliot left for California. The New Journeymen would soon relocate to Los Angeles, and reunite with Elliot. Now expanded to a quartet, they were hired to sing back-up on Barry McGuire's album, *Precious Time*. But after impressing Dunhill Records owner Lou Adler with their tight, melodic four-part harmony, The New Journeymen were signed to the label. Renaming themselves The Mamas & The Papas, the group débuted in 1966 with their version of a song from the McGuire sessions, 'California Dreamin'', composed by John and Michelle Phillips. Overnight stars, The Mamas & The Papas enjoyed a two-year string of folk-flavoured rock hits with the million selling, 'Monday, Monday' (1966), 'I Saw Her Again' (1966), 'Dedicated To The One I Love' (1967); and the autobiographical, 'Creeque Alley' (1967). Nicknamed Mama Cass, the overweight Elliot was the only group member who did not compose material. Elliot scored a solo hit with a cover of 'Dream A Little Dream', taken from the group's abum *The Mama's & The Papas*. Going on a crash diet in late 1968 and losing 110 pounds in three months, Elliot collapsed onstage on the first night of a Las Vegas solo engagement. After recuperating, she recorded a pair of albums, hitting the pop charts with the hits 'It's Getting Better' (1969) and 'Make Your Own Kind of Music' (1969). Introduced by Gram Parsons, Elliot teamed with former Traffic guitarist Dave Mason for an album, *Dave Mason And Mama Cass* (1971). Drawing an unusual fan mix of young teenage girls and older progressive rockers, a successful tour followed. After a brief reuniting with The Mamas & The Papas for the disappointing *People Like Us*, Elliot resumed her solo career. Returning to Las Vegas in 1973 this time healthy and successful, she continued a series of nightclub performances which would find her in England by 1974.

CAUSE: Elliot died in the London apartment of her friend Harry Nilsson. While initial reports claimed that she had choked on a ham sandwich, it was later determined that she had suffered a massive heart attack. Her heart was in poor shape as a result of severe weight loss (a one meal a week diet) and alternating weight gain. Elliot was in London for a two-week stint at the Palladium. In 1978, Who drummer Keith Moon would die in the same apartment.

FURTHER READING: Phillips, John. (1986). *Papa John*. New York: Doubleday.

Jim Ellison

Born April 18, 1964
Found dead June 20, 1996

Lead singer and guitarist of the Chicago alternative rock group, Material Issue, Jim Ellison had formed the band while a student at Columbia College. Headstrong, Ellison would boast that his group was destined for fame. Signing with Mercury Records in 1991, the group enjoyed success with their début album, *International Pop Overthrow*, which was highlighted by a pair of modern rock chart hits, 'Valerie Loves Me' and 'Diane'. The group's success continued with 'What Girls Want', culled from their follow-up album, *Destination Universe*. But although the Chicago rock scene was raging with alternative acts such as The Smashing Pumpkins and Urge Overkill, Mercury dropped Material Issue in 1994. Ellison launched a side project group with bandmate Mike Zelenko called AMX. Ellison's final work appeared on the AMX album, *Telecommando Americano* (1997).

CAUSE: Suicide. He died from carbon monoxide poisoning in the garage of his Chicago home. He left a suicide note. His body was discovered several days after his death.

Lorraine Ellison

Born 1935
Died August 17, 1985
Philadelphia-based gospel-turned-soul singer, Lorraine Ellison was originally a member of The Ellison Singers and then The Golden Chords. Pursuing a solo career in 1964, she scored a pair of soulful, emotion-laden R&B hits with 'I Dig You Baby' (1965) and the Jerry Ragavoy produced and co-written chestnut, 'Stay With Me' (1966). Her best works were compiled on the album, *Stay With Me: The Best Of Lorraine Ellison* (1995). Janis Joplin later recorded a cover of Ellison's 'Try Just A Little Bit Harder'.
CAUSE: Unknown.

Sims Ellison

(SIMS EDGAR ELLISON)
Born March 10, 1967
Died June 6, 1995
Bassist of the Austin, Texas-based hard-rock band Pariah, Sims Ellison had formed the group while attending a San Antonio high school with his brother Kyle on guitar and Shandon Sahm on drums. Expanding the group with vocalist Dave Derrick, Pariah relocated to Austin in 1990. Signing with Geffen Records in 1990, the group waited three years for the release of their début album, the poor-selling, *To Kill A Mockingbird.* The band was dropped by Geffen in 1995.
CAUSE: Suicide by gunshot. Killing himself in his Austin apartment, Ellison had been suffering from depression. Alarmed by the rise of deaths in the music industry, the former manager of Pariah, Wayne Nagle, launched the SIMS foundation, offering musicians mental health and drug counselling.

Jack Emerson

(JOHN WILLIAM EMERSON III)
Born April 29, 1960
Died November 22, 2003
Breaking into music as an original member of the alt-country band Jason & The Scorchers, Jack Emerson emerged as the group's manager. He launched the A&M affiliated label and management company, Praxis International, where he worked with The Georgia Satellites, Steve Forbert, John Hiatt and others. In 1995, Emerson launched E-Squared Records and, shortly before his death, had formed another label, Jack Of Hearts.
CAUSE: Suffering from respiratory problems for some time, he succumbed to a heart attack at home.

John Entwistle

(JOHN ALEC ENTWISTLE)
Born October 9, 1944
Died June 27, 2002
As bass player for The Who, John Entwistle provided the solid foundation for some of the most memorable performances in rock music. Nicknamed "The Ox", as well as "Thunderfingers" thanks to his digits becoming a blur across the four-string fretboard, Entwistle appeared to be the most reserved and stable member of this most combustible of groups. Born into a musical family in Chiswick, west London, Entwistle was a classically trained musician who played the French horn in the Middlesex Youth Orchestra. Drawn to rock'n'roll in his early teens, Entwistle abandoned the trumpet for a home-made bass guitar, thanks to his idol Duane Eddy, and played in school groups The Confederates and The Scorpions with his friend Peter Townshend. In 1961, he was approached to join fellow Acton County Grammar School pupil Roger Daltrey's group, The Detours. Six months later, John persuaded Roger to let Townshend join. Initially lead guitarist, Daltrey eventually assumed the role of vocalist and The Detours became The Who in February 1964. The last piece of The Who's unique chemistry fell into place when original drummer Doug Sandom was replaced by the irrepressible Keith Moon in April '64. Entwistle contributed to The

Who's distinctive sound by cultivating a lead style of bass, underpinning Townshend's more rhythmic style of guitar playing with inventive runs in a higher register than most bass players while at the same time keeping the group's timing rigid during Moon's volatile thrashings. That summer, the neophyte group were convinced by publicist Peter Meaden to jump on the contemporary "mod" scene by cutting their hair, wearing mod-style clothing and adopting a new name, The High Numbers. After an obscure single, 'Zoot Suit'/'I'm The Face' was issued on Fontana Records, the group were taken over by new managers Kit Lambert and Chris Stamp, both assistant film directors. Reassuming the name The Who, the group's January 1965 début single, 'I Can't Explain', was influenced by The Kinks' early releases, and was produced by that group's recording boss Shel Talmy. Although it became a British Top 10 hit, it fared poorly in the US, as did the follow-up British hits, 'Anyway Anyhow Anywhere', 'My Generation', featuring a prominent bass solo by Entwistle – the first of its kind on a rock record – and 'Substitute'. While Townshend emerged as The Who's songwriter-in-chief, Entwistle also began writing; his distinctive macabre contributions to The Who's oeuvre started with 'Whisky Man' and the imperishable 'Boris The Spider' on the *A Quick One* album (1966), continuing with 'Doctor, Doctor' and 'Someone's Coming' (1967), 'Silas Stingy' (from 1967's *The Who Sell Out*), 'Dr. Jekyll & Mr. Hyde' (1968), 'Heaven And Hell' (with which The Who opened their formidable live shows between 1968 and 1970), 'Cousin Kevin' and 'Fiddle About' (both written for The Who's 1969 magnum opus *Tommy* – Townshend specifically requested Entwistle to write these "nasty songs" as he felt uncomfortable with the subject matter) and 'My Wife', from 1971's *Who's Next*, another popular stage number. An integral part of the second wave of the British Invasion, The Who eventually made inroads into America with their first US Top 40 hit, the unrepresentative 'Happy Jack', in spring 1967. Having earned valuable exposure at the Monterey Pop Festival and as the unlikely opening act for Herman's Hermits on a gruelling cross-country American tour, The Who achieved their only US Top 10 hit with 'I Can See For Miles' (1967). With the release of 'Pinball Wizard' and *Tommy* in 1969, The Who's status as the most exciting live act treading the boards was established and for the next two years they consolidated that accolade by touring relentlessly, particularly in America where a whole new rock audience opened up for them. They returned to England as millionaires, at last able to clear an astounding level of debt that had accrued thanks to their destructive and spendthrift habits over the previous five years. While the other members moved out of London, Entwistle remained true to his west London roots. Having married his childhood sweetheart Alison Wise in 1967 he bought a large semi-detached home in Acton, and filled it with all sorts of extraordinary artefacts, ranging from a full suit of armour to a tarantula. His eccentricity and taste for the bizarre was to remain with him throughout his life, and when he finally moved out of the city to Stowe-on-the-Wold in Gloucestershire in 1975, his 17-bedroomed mansion Quarwood resembled a major museum. It also housed one of the largest guitar collections belonging to any rock musician. John and Alison separated in the late Seventies and he was subsequently married to an American girl, Maxine, but this relationship also ended. The Who's stature continued throughout the Seventies and beyond with *Who's Next* (1971) and *Quadrophenia* (1973) being major artistic and commercial successes. John's impressive musicianship continued apace and his work on 'The Real Me' (from *Quadrophenia*) and 'Dreaming From The Waist' (from 1975's *The Who By Numbers*) was particularly memorable. However, The Who being a volatile proposition, dissent was never far from the surface and Entwistle privately threatened to quit on more than one occasion. While accepting that the group conformed more to Pete Townshend's style of songwriting, John sought an outlet for a backlog of songs. In 1971, he became the first band member to release a solo album, *Smash Your Head Against The Wall*, which earned him a cult following in the US for fans of his brand of black humour. Other solo studio albums followed: *Whistle Rymes* (1972), *Rigor Mortis Sets In* (1973), *Mad Dog* (1975), *Too Late The Hero* (1981) and *The Rock* (1996). He also compiled a Who leftovers collection, *Odds And Sods*, in 1974 and with The Who out of action because of business problems and filming commitments on Ken Russell's bombastic vision of *Tommy* (1975), Entwistle went out on the road with his own band, Ox – a venture that cost him in the region of $70,000. The Who snapped out of their inactivity with a new album, *Who Are You* (1978) and the films, *The Kids Are Alright* (a biopic of The Who's history) and *Quadrophenia* (both released in 1979). However, tragedy struck in September 1978 with the death of 32-year-old Keith Moon from an accidental drug overdose in the same London apartment in which "Mama" Cass Elliot had suffered a fatal heart attack in 1974. The Who resolved to continue with ex-Small Faces, Faces drummer Kenney Jones but suffered another blow on December 3, 1979, when 11 fans were crushed to death as a result of a flawed festival seating policy at Cincinnati's Riverfront Stadium. The Who staggered on into the early Eighties, releasing a pair of forgettable albums, *Face Dances* (1981) and *It's Hard* (1982), before Pete Townshend announced he was leaving in 1983. For Entwistle, it was a body blow as he considered that a group's *raison d'être* was to play live. Regrouping for Live Aid in 1985 and a 25th-anniversary tour in 1989 (featuring Simon Phillips on drums), The Who added a horn section and three back-up vocalists. In 1996, The Who took a stage production of *Quadrophenia* on the road, featuring a cast of Gary Glitter, Billy Idol, Zak Starkey and Townshend's brother, Simon. By the end of the millennium, a stripped-down version of The Who – consisting of Entwistle, Daltrey, Townshend, keyboard player John "Rabbit" Bundrick, and Ringo Starr's son, Zak Starkey (who had drummed in Entwistle's studio band) – were touring again, amply demonstrating to diehard fans and a new generation of musicians just how they had established their diehard credentials. In 2002, The Who was scheduled to begin yet another US tour.

CAUSE: On the eve of an American tour, Entwistle was in Las Vegas to open a show of his artwork – a sideline he had developed to music. He was found dead in bed at the Hard Rock Hotel and Casino in Las Vegas, having suffered a heart attack after ingesting four coffee brandies and an undetermined quantity of cocaine. A 27-year-old Las Vegas showgirl had been his last companion. The coroner's report listed the official cause of death as cocaine intoxication and hypertensive cardiovascular disease. Entwistle had been taking prescription medication for his heart problems. After cancelling two concerts, the surviving members of The Who completed their scheduled US tour with Pino Palladino substituting on bass.

Rust Epique

(CHARLES ANTHONY LOPEZ)
Born February 29, 1968
Died March 8, 2004
One of two guitarists in the rock-rap

group Crazy Town, Rust Epique played guitar alongside Anthony "Trouble" Valli. A native of Stockton, California, Epique was an eccentric who left junior college and, after passing through a series of local bands, moved to Hollywood in 1989, where he formed a group that later evolved into Rust & The Superheroes. In 1999, Epique joined Crazy Town, a group founded by Shifty Shellshock and Epic Mazur. Issued in 2000, their début album, *Gift Of Game*, was initially a slow seller until the third single, 'Butterfly', topped the US charts; the song sampled The Red Hot Chili Peppers' track 'Pretty Little Ditty'. After scoring a follow-up hit with 'Revolving Door', the group was added to the Ozzfest tour, but following the relative failure of their second album *Darkhorse*, the group disbanded. In 2002, Epique formed a hard rock band, Pre)thing, and at the time of his death, the group's début single, 'Faded Love', was an emerging hit on alternative rock radio. The track was included on the posthumously released album, *22nd Century Lifestyle*.
CAUSE: Suffering a heart attack, he died at his home in Las Vegas.

"Sweet" James Epps

Born March 30, 1947
Died September 8, 2000
A member of the Detroit-based vocal R&B band The Fantastic Four, "Sweet" James Epps co-founded the quartet in 1965. Signing with Ric-Tic Records, the group had several R&B chart hits in the late Sixties, beginning with their début single, 'The Whole World Is A Stage' (1967). But after Ric-Tic was acquired by Motown in 1968, the group managed just one more hit over the next several years, with the reissued single, 'I Love You Madly'. Unhappy with their status at the label, the members of the group eventually stopped recording until the expiration of their contract in 1974. Signing with Westbound Records, The Fantastic Four recorded four albums during the Seventies but reaped limited rewards during the disco era with their soul-rooted sound.
CAUSE: Heart attack.

Brian Epstein

(BRIAN SAMUEL EPSTEIN)
Born September 19, 1934
Died August 27, 1967
Brian Epstein, manager of The Beatles, was one of the most famous and successful impresarios of all time. Born and raised in a privileged middle-class family in Liverpool, he attended private schools, then worked in his father's furniture business. He was conscripted for national service, but found army life oppressive. Off duty, he became involved in homosexual liaisons and was placed before an army psychiatrist, then honourably discharged. He next enrolled in the Royal Academy Of Dramatic Arts, but his hopes of becoming an actor were dashed after three terms and he elected to take over the record department of his parents' NEMS stores in Liverpool. His life changed forever after witnessing a lunch-time performance by The Beatles at the city's Cavern Club on December 3, 1961. He was instrumental in changing their visual image and encouraging a more professional approach. Initially, he was unable to sign them to any British label, suffering rejections from Decca, Philips, Pye and Columbia. Eventually, George Martin of Parlophone, a predominantly comedy label and part of EMI, took on the group. In the meantime, Epstein oversaw the sacking of Pete Best and installation of Ringo Starr as The Beatles' new drummer. Epstein did not officially sign The Beatles until as late as October 1962. As with his later signings, he took 25 per cent of their earnings. Following the release of their first single, 'Love Me Do', Epstein arranged for their publishing to be handled by Dick James and helped set up Northern

Songs. Once The Beatles broke big Epstein moved his operation to London. Expanding his stable of acts, he oversaw the careers of Gerry And The Pacemakers, Billy J. Kramer, Cilla Black, The Fourmost, and a host of others. His strike rate by 1964 was extraordinary, with Gerry notching up three consecutive number one hits, while Billy J. and Cilla Black registered two chart toppers each. Inevitably, the onslaught of Beatlemania took up much of his time, especially when the group exploded across America in early 1964. Epstein was later criticised for failing to take fiscal advantage of the group's merchandising potential, although this was largely the fault of his solicitor David Jacobs. At a time when pop music was regarded as ephemeral, the concept of merchandising was largely unknown territory. With The Beatles' appearance at the Hollywood Bowl, Epstein can take credit for ushering in the era of stadium rock, a full decade before most of his rivals. In that alone, he altered rock economics forever. When The Beatles decided to cease touring in 1966, Epstein became gradually less involved in their daily lives. By 1967, the entrepreneur was losing control. He sold off a majority holding in his NEMS empire to rival Robert Stigwood and became increasingly addicted to prescription drugs and doomed homosexual affairs. His contract with The Beatles was due to expire in October 1967 and his increasing isolation caused concern to his other artists, most notably Cilla Black. What might have been a second stage of his career was cut short in the summer of 1967.

CAUSE: He overdosed on a combination of brandy and barbiturates at his London home. At the time of his death, The Beatles were in Wales, receiving guidance from the Maharishi Mahesh Yogi. A coroner later ruled that Epstein's death was the result of an accidental overdose.

FURTHER READING: Rogan, Johnny. (1988). *Starmakers & Svengalis: The History Of British Pop Management*. London: Queen Anne Press. Coleman, Ray. (1989). *Brian Epstein: The Man Who Made The Beatles*. London: Viking.

Howie Epstein

(HOWARD NORMAN EPSTEIN)
Born July 21, 1955
Died February 23, 2003

The bassist of heartland rockers Tom Petty & The Heartbreakers, Howie Epstein replaced original member Ron Blair. Born in Milwaukee, Wisconsin, Epstein had previously played in a series of local bands including The MHG Experience, Winks and The Craze. Relocating to Los Angeles, Epstein joined John Hiatt's band and appeared on the Tom Petty-produced Del Shannon comeback album, *Drop Down And Get Me*. Then when original bassist Ron Blair quit the Heartbreakers to spend more time with his family, Epstein was the only musician who was auditioned. Joining the group, beginning with the 1985 album *Southern Accents* he played on *Pack Up The Plantation*, *Let Me Up (I've Had Enough)*, *Into The Great Wild Open*, *Wildflowers* and his final Heartbreakers album, 1999's *Echo*. Epstein also contributed to Petty's successful solo album, *Full Moon Fever* (1989). Possessing a similar voice to that of Petty's, Epstein occasionally sang lead vocal in concert and also recorded with Bob Dylan, Stevie Nicks, Warren Zevon, as well as working on three albums with his longtime girlfriend, Carlene Carter. He also produced John Prine's Grammy-winning 1991 album, *The Missing Years*. In 2001, Epstein and Carter were arrested near Albuquerque, New Mexico, when police discovered heroin in the stolen car they were driving. Although the drug charges were later dropped, Epstein struggled with his addiction and parted with Petty in 2002, at which time Ron Blair returned to the band.

CAUSE: He collapsed in a friend's

bathroom after taking heroin and prescription antibiotics, and was driven to St. Vincent's Hospital in Santa Fe, New Mexico. He never regained consciousness.

Coke Escovedo

(THOMAS ESCOVEDO)
Born April 30, 1941
Died July 13, 1986
The co-leader of the Seventies, Latin-based jazz-rock group Azteca, Los Angeles-born percussionist Thomas "Coke" Escovedo first made a name for himself as a backing musician for Santana in the early Seventies, touring with the group in 1971 as a replacement for ailing tambales player Jose Chepito. Also working with Carlos Santana's brother Jorge in the group Malo, Escovedo performed on the Top 20 hit, 'Suavecito'. Launching his own group in 1972, Escovedo teamed with his brother, vocalist Pete Escovedo; the salsa-influenced jazz-rock ensemble enjoyed its best-selling release with the album, *Azteca* (1974). With the group disbanding later in 1974, Coke Escovedo launched a solo career in the mid Seventies, recording a trio of Latin-tinged albums for Mercury Records. As a session player, Escovedo also performed with Jefferson Starship, Gabor Szabo, and Jean-Luc Ponty. Escovedo's niece is R&B singer Sheila E.
CAUSE: Unknown. He died in Montebellow, California.

Esquerita

(ESKER REEDER, JR.)
Born 1932
Died April 23, 1986
An extravagant pianist who greatly influenced Little Richard, the outrageous Esquerita sported black sunglasses, an exaggerated pompadour, and a pencil-thin moustache. The South Carolina-born, gospel-trained performer had first appeared as a duo with singer Sister Rosa. Moving to New York City, he backed a gospel trio called The Three Stars, before joining another gospel group, The Heavenly Echos. A wild, frenetic piano player and falsetto-voiced singer, Esquerita left gospel and fully embraced the excesses of rock'n'roll. Pursuing a solo career, he was discovered by a member of Gene Vincent's backing band The Blue Caps. Signing with Capitol Records, Esquerita was backed on many of his sessions by members of The Blue Caps. Recording several singles, he failed to crack the charts except for an instrumental version of 'Green Door', a song he claimed to have written. Ahead of his time, he was not appreciated until after his death. Esquerita was jailed at Rikers Island for a few years in the Eighties.
CAUSE: AIDS. He died at Harlem Hospital in New York.

Esquivel

(JUAN GARCIA ESQUIVEL)
Born November 26, 1931
Died January 3, 2002
A quirky lounge-music pianist and bandleader, Esquivel concocted unique light-hearted, Latin-tinged arrangements of popular songs, as he became the king of "space-age bachelor music". Esquivel was already a massive star in his native Mexico when he began touring through the US in the Fifties. Recording for RCA Records, he became a featured entertainer in Las Vegas. A womanizer who married six times, Esquivel was an extravagant and demanding showman. Losing popularity during the late Seventies disco era, Esquivel returned to Mexico but found new popularity during the lounge music revival of the Nineties.
CAUSE: Suffering a stroke, he died at his home in Morelos, Mexico.

Euronymous

(OYSTEIN AARSETH)
Born April 15, 1968
Died August 10, 1993
The leader of the Norwegian black metal/satanic heavy-metal group

Mayhem, Euronymous launched the outfit in 1984, inspired by the British metal band, Venom. Taking heavy metal to its extremes, Mayhem employed meandering power chords over angry and blatantly anti-Christian lyrics. After Mayhem's lead singer committed suicide in 1991, Euronymous claimed to have consumed a portion of his brain. After receiving a government arts grant in 1991, the group relocated to Oslo, where Euronymous would open a combination record label (Deathlike Silence), occult book store, and record shop called Helvete (Norwegian for "hell"). Influencing a new generation of black metal fans, Mayhem reinvigorated the genre with images of Satanic worship, cold hatred and the celebration of death. Euronymous' final sessions, the posthumously released *De Mysteris Dom Sathanas*, featured his murderer on bass.
CAUSE: He was stabbed to death by Varg Vikernes (a.k.a. Count Grishnacky), the lead singer of a competing black metal band Burzam, after arguing about which of their groups were the true kings of black metal, and over money Euronymous allegedly owed. Euronymous was stabbed 23 times in the head and back. Vikernes was sentenced to 21 years in prison, the maximum permitted under Norwegian law. Vikernes was also convicted of torching dozens of historical churches; police discovered 150 kilos of explosives in his apartment. An accomplice, musician Snorre Rush (a.k.a. Blackthore), drove the getaway car and was sentenced to nine years in prison. Vikernes' mother was arrested in 1997 for hiring a neo-Nazi organisation to break her son out of prison.

Mark Evans

Born May 12, 1956
Died January 26, 2005
The drummer of the Nineties politically charged heavy metal band Warrior Soul, Mark Evans performed on the albums *Drugs, God & The New Republic* (1991), *Salutations From The Ghetto Nation* (1992) and *Chill Pill* (1993). Headed by Kory Clarke, the group recorded with little success for Geffen Records.
CAUSE: He was strangled and then his body torched. The corpse was found in a rubbish bin in a London car park. Two men and a woman from Essex were charged with the murder.

Samie "Sticks" Evans

Born February 5, 1923
Died April 11, 1994
Popular R&B session player who toured with Ray Charles and James Brown, Samie "Sticks" Evans also recorded behind dozens of acts, including Ornette Coleman and Tony Bennett. Performing professionally since 1942, he also authored a pair of drumming instruction manuals.
CAUSE: Stroke. He died in New York City.

Tom Evans

Born June 21, 1947
Died November 23, 1983
Bass player for The Beatles' protégés Badfinger, Liverpool, England-born Tom Evans initially pursued a career in engineering. After a stint in a hometown rock group called The Calderstones, Evans in 1968 joined The Iveys as the replacement for David Jenkins on rhythm guitar and vocals. With the addition of Joey Molland later in the year, Evans switched to bass. Signed to The Beatles' Apple label by Paul McCartney, The Iveys recorded the Evans penned single, 'Maybe Tomorrow'. Renamed Badfinger in late 1969, the group landed in the Top 10 with the Paul McCartney produced and composed 'Come And Get It', the track written for the Ringo Starr film *The Magic Christian*. Collaborating with George Harrison, Badfinger played on his album *All Things Must Pass*, and appeared at the

Harrison-promoted charity event, Concert for Bangladesh, at New York's Madison Square Garden. Released in 1970, Badfinger's début album *No Dice* (1970) contained their second Top 10 hit 'No Matter What', and 'Without You' which was covered by Harry Nilsson and became a massive international hit. Produced by Todd Rundgren, the group's follow-up album *Straight Up* spawned the hits 'Baby Blue' (1971) and guitar-oriented 'Day After Day' (1972). Leaving Apple for Warner Brothers in 1973, Badfinger's career began to slide. Then in 1974, Warner Brothers pulled the group's album, *Wish You Were Here*, off the market when $100,000 owed to the band came up missing. In the ensuing legal morass which was centered around the group's manager, Badfinger disbanded and singer/guitarist Pete Ham committed suicide. Evans and bandmate Bob Jackson subsequently joined The Dodgers, releasing a sole album, *Love On The Rebound*. For a time Evans left the music industry and worked in mechanical drawing. Evans and Molland later reformed Badfinger, recording two disappointing albums, *Airwaves* (1978) and *Say No More* (1981), the latter spawning a minor chart hit with 'Hold On'. Badfinger disbanded in 1983 over a royalty dispute.
CAUSE: Suicide. Evans killed himself in a similar fashion to bandmate Pete Ham. He was despondent over a royalties dispute as well as a series of personal problems. Some reports claim that Evans had been diagnosed with a tumour in his throat.
FURTHER READING: Matovina, Dan. (1997). *Without You: The Tragic Story Of Badfinger*. San Mateo, CA: Francis Glover.

Tommy Evans

Born c. 1934
Died c. 1981
A member of The Drifters, Tommy Evans was one of three dozen vocalists who would pass through the perennial R&B doo-wop group. Previously forming his own group in Detroit in the early 1950s, he recorded several obscure singles. Evans then replaced the talented bass singer of The Ravens, Jimmy Ricks, for their road appearances, on and off from 1954 to 1956. But in late 1956, Evans was asked by Jimmy Oliver to replace The Drifters' bass vocalist Bill Pinkney who left to form The Flyers. Evans appeared on the 1957 Johnny Moore-led Drifters hits, 'It Was A Tear', 'Hypnotized', and 'I Know', as well as the 1958 Bobby Hendricks-led 'Drip Drip'. But Evans was fired along with the rest of The Drifters in 1958 by their manager George Treadwell, who would hire The Crown as the new Drifters. Thin, with dashing good looks, Evans then briefly sang with Charlie Fuqua's Inkspots, before returning to The Ravens. But when Drifters' member Elsbeary Hobbs was drafted in 1961, Evans returned to the group. During this period, Evans appeared on The Drifters hits, 'Some Kind Of Wonderful' (1961), 'Sweets For My Sweet' (1961), 'When My Little Girl Is Smiling' (1962), 'Up On The Roof' (1962), and 'On Broadway' (1963). Evans and bandmate Doc Green left The Drifters in late 1962 to form an unsuccessful Drifters copy group, The Drapers. Then in 1964, Evans and Green toured in a shortlived, unauthorised, competing Drifters group that was assembled by Lover Patterson. Disbanding after legal threats in 1966, Evans and Green formed a quartet called The Floaters (not the group of 'Float On' fame), recording briefly for B&B Records. Then in the early Seventies, Evans and Green joined the R&B group, The Exciting Changes. By the mid Seventies, Evans formed another group, The Masters, before joining a revival version of The Ravens.
CAUSE: Unknown.

Betty Everett

Born November 23, 1939
Died August 19, 2001

A Sixties soul singer-pianist, Betty Everett is best remembered for her upbeat chestnut, 'The Shoop Shoop Song (It's In His Kiss)'. After singing gospel music in her hometown of Greenwood, Mississippi, she moved to Chicago and switched to blues, aided early in her career by bluesman Magic Sam. Recording for Cobra Records in 1959, before moving to Vee-Jay, Betty fared poorly with her original version of 'You're No Good' (the song was taken to the UK Top 10 in 1964 by The Swinging Blue Jeans and to the number one position on the US charts in 1975 by Linda Ronstadt) but the follow-up, the oldies standard 'The Shoop Shoop Song (It's In His Kiss)' gave her a US Top 10 hit in 1964. The song belatedly reached the British Top 10 in 1975 via a disco cover version by Linda Lewis, and topped the charts on both sides of the Atlantic in 1990 when recorded by Cher (from the movie *Mermaids*). Everett reached the British Top 30 in early 1965 with another soul classic, 'Getting Mighty Crowded' (later covered by Elvis Costello). Teaming with soul singer Jerry Butler for an album in 1966, Everett charted with the lovely ballad, 'Let It Be Me'. After Vee-Jay Records closed in 1967, Everett signed with Uni, scoring R&B hits with 'There'll Come A Day' and 'It's Been A Long Time', but her hit run slowed when switching to Fantasy Records in 1970. Her final performance came on a PBS television programme in 2000.
CAUSE: Unknown. She died at her home in Beloit, Wisconsin.

Tommy Eyre

Born June 5, 1949
Died May 23, 2001

A talented keyboard player, Tommy Eyre played with a remarkable assortment of pop, rock and jazz artists during his long and varied career. A native of Sheffield, England, Eyre came to the attention of Joe Cocker in 1968, joining Cocker's backing outfit The Grease Band. The 19-year-old Eyre provided the bluesy organ on Cocker's pair of hit remakes 'Feeling Alright' and 'With A Little Help From My Friends', as well as the 1969 album, *With A Little Help From My Friends*. Leaving the group that same year, Eyre joined an all-star blues-rock group, Aynsley Dunbar Retaliation. Recording just one album (which was produced by John Mayall), the group disbanded when Eyre and drummer Aynsley Dunbar were asked to join Frank Zappa's Mothers Of Invention, but when Zappa's keyboard player decided to stay with the band, Eyre was not needed. Eyre reunited with Dunbar in late-1969 to form Blue Whale featuring vocalist Paul Williams, whom Eyre recommended to Dunbar, but after recording a self-titled progressive rock album in 1970, the group disbanded. Subsequently, Eyre passed through a number of Seventies rock acts, Janklin, Juicy Lucy, Strabisnus, the duo Mark-Almond, Riff-Raff, the jazz-rock group Zzebra and Dan McCafferty (lead singer of Nazareth). Joining The Sensational Alex Harvey Band in 1977 as the replacement for Hugh McKenna, Eyre appeared on the album *Rock Drill*, and when Harvey quit his own band for a solo career, he was joined by Eyre for the album, *The Mafia Stole My Guitar*. In the Eighties, Eyre recorded an album as a member of John Martyn's band, before joining The Greg Lake Band and, in 1982, The Gary Moore Band. Taking a major turn towards mainstream pop, Eyre spent almost four years as the musical director and keyboardist for the George Michael-led group, Wham! Joining in time for their second album, Eyre appeared on a string of international hits, including 'Wake Me Up Before You Go Go', 'Everything She Wants', 'Freedom' and 'I'm Your Man', as well as George Michael's solo hit, 'Careless Whisper'. Following the break-up of Wham! in 1986, Eyre turned to production work, but still found time to join a series of bands: the jazz-rock act Mr. Gone, The Ray Russell Band, Ian Gillan and a second stint with Gary Moore. Relocating to New York City, Eyre joined a number of rock and jazz acts. A popular session player, he worked with numerous artists including Mick Jagger, Barry Melton, Daryl Hall, The Strawbs, The Pez Band, and appeared on Gerry Rafferty's major hit single 'Baker Street'. Eyre was married to violinist Scarlet Rivera.

CAUSE: He battled esophageal cancer for two years.

F

Yvonne Fair

Born 1942
Died March 6, 1994
After breaking into music as a later member of The Chantels, Virginia-born Yvonne Fair joined the James Brown Revue in the early Sixties. Recording with Chuck Jackson, Fair drew the attention of Motown and was signed to the label in the early Seventies, teamed with talented producer Norman Whitfield. Following 'Love Ain't No Toy', she had an R&B hit with the often-recorded composition 'Funky Music Sho Nuff Turns Me On' (1974) and, in 1976, reached the UK Top 10 with a remake of Kim Weston's 'It Should Have Been Me'. Also that year, Fair released her only album, *The Bitch Is Black*. Fair had a minor role in the Berry Gordy-produced film, *Lady Sings The Blues*, and was married to Sammy Strain, a member of The O'Jays and Little Anthony & The Imperials.
CAUSE: Unknown. She died in Las Vegas.

Bruce Fairbairn

Born December 30, 1949
Died May 17, 1999
Bruce Fairbairn had more than earned his reputation as "the best producer of hard rock records in the world". A native Canadian, Fairbairn began his musical career in the early Sixties as a trumpet player in various R&B acts, before settling into the role of musician/producer with Vancouver-based pop group Sunshyne. By the Eighties, he had largely abandoned trumpet duties in favour of record production, earning his first major credit in 1986 with Bon Jovi's breakthrough LP, Slippery When Wet. Fairbairn next turned his attentions to resurrecting the career of previously washed up Seventies rock act Aerosmith. His association with the band saw them return to the top of the US charts with three multi-platinum LPs – 1987's Permanent Vacation, 1989's Pump and 1993's Get A Grip. The producer also scored platinum discs for his work in the Nineties with Van Halen, AC/DC and The Cranberries. Bruce Fairbairn's last high profile project was overseeing the return of original shock-rockers Kiss, whose 1998 LP, Psycho Circus, broke into the US Top Five.
CAUSE: Heart attack. He was found dead in his apartment in Vancouver by studio manager Shel Preston and Jon Anderson, the singer with Yes.

Steve Fairnie

(STEPHEN ANGUS FAIRNIE)
Born February 21, 1951
Died February 22, 1993
A member of several British post-punk/new wave acts, Steve Fairnie was involved with The Fish Co., Famous Names, Writz and The Techno Twins (later renamed The Technos). Earning little from his music, he branched out into production work, acting, painting, creating board games and teaching at college level, and late in his career he turned to contemporary Christian music.
CAUSE: He suffered a heart attack and died in Brixham, England, while on a field trip with students from Weston-super-Mare College, where he taught.

Adam Faith

(TERENCE NELHAMS)
Born June 23, 1940
Died March 8, 2003
A pioneering pop artist in pre-Beatles Britain, singer-actor Adam Faith was one of the most successful British acts during this period. Hailing from Acton, west London, Faith quit school, aged 15, and took a position at Rank Screen

Services as a messenger boy and apprentice film editor. During the skiffle boom of 1956, he joined several of his fellow employees in forming an amateur group called The Worried Men, and was nurtured as a solo act when discovered at a Soho club by producer Jack Good of the BBC TV's *6.5 Special.* Signing with Parlophone, Faith's hit run began with the Buddy Holly-influenced string laden ditty 'What Do You Want?', a UK number one in 1959, and continued with a series of innocent but endearing songs such as 'Poor Me', 'Someone Else's Baby', 'Johnny Comes Marching Home', 'How About That!', 'Lonely Pup (In A Christmas Shop)', and 'Who Am I?' Turning to acting in the early Sixties, he starred in films such as *Beat Girl, Never Let Go, What A Whopper!* and *Mix Me A Person.* Following the example set by the emerging British Beat groups, in 1963, Faith had his own backing band, The Roulettes, but by 1965, Faith had his final British Top 40 hit. (In the US, Faith managed just one minor hit with 'It's Alright'.) With his musical career fading, in the early Seventies, he focused on acting, garnering renewed fame as the star of the British television series *Budgie*, playing an upbeat ex-convict. He also managed then-unknown Leo Sayer and produced Roger Daltrey's first solo album, *Daltrey*, which generated the Top 10 UK hit single 'Giving It All Away' in 1973. After a serious car crash that same year, Faith was sidelined for a year and almost lost a leg. In 1974, he attempted a comeback; being aided by Paul McCartney on the album *Survive* and co-starring with David Essex in the film *Stardust.* Turning his attention to financial investments in the Eighties, Faith lost tens of millions of pounds and eventually declared bankruptcy. By the Nineties, Faith returned to the small screen, starring in the BBC sitcoms, *Love Hurts* and *The House That Jack Built.* In 1996, Faith published his autobiography, *Acts Of Faith.*

CAUSE: He suffered a heart attack in Stoke-on-Trent, Staffordshire, England, after performing in a stage production of *Love And Marriage* at the Regent Theatre. Later the following morning, his condition worsened and he died shortly after arriving at a local hospital. He had undergone open heart surgery in 1986.

Peter Falcaglia

Born 1948

Died May 3, 1995

Touring member of Dion's band in the early Sixties after Dion's departure from The Belmonts, Peter Falcaglia did not record with Dion.

CAUSE: He was shot in the neck during a robbery attempt, while working in a friend's music store in the Bronx. The store's owner, Michael Polomba, was also shot. The robbers escaped with a briefcase containing unknown items.

Falco

(JOHANN HOLZEL)

Born February 19, 1957

Died February 6, 1998

Austrian-born techno-pop singer Falco enjoyed a brief hit run in the Eighties. Discouraged by his parents to pursue a career in music, Falco nonetheless attended the Vienna Music Conservatory. Relocating to West Germany he joined a jazz-rock group, and changed his name to Falco Sturmer (the last name taken from that of a popular skier). Returning to Austria in 1978, he scored a regional hit came in 1980 with a banned-by-radio, club anthem whose lyrics chronicled the heroin scene in Vienna. Falco scored a German-language hit in 1983 with 'Der Kommissar', the novelty-styled rap song recorded two years earlier. But soon after, 'Der Kommissar' was covered by the English rock band After The Fire, becoming an international smash hit. Trying to win back airplay

for his version, an angry Falco shot a very amateurish, low-budget video. Falco finally landed a US hit in 1986 with 'Rock Me Amadeus' from his third US album, *Falco 3*, the track co-written with his producers; the synthesizer-heavy song was about fellow Austrian, 19th century composer Wolfgang Amadeus Mozart. A follow-up single 'Vienna Calling', hit the Top 20. Shortly before his death Falco had completed a new album, *Out Of The Dark*.
CAUSE: He died in a traffic accident in the Dominican Republic, where he had established a residence for tax purposes. His sports utility vehicle collided with a bus as he was driving onto a highway. Taken to a hospital near the resort town of Puerta Plata, he died of head injuries.

Leroy Fann

Born November 9, 1936
Died November, 1973
Bass vocalist of the Sixties R&B group, Ruby & The Romantics, the Akron, Ohio-born Leroy Fann had launched the group as an all-male group called The Supremes while in high school. Discovering singer Ruby Nash who was leading a local all-girl band, Fann added her to The Supremes line-up. Relocating to New York City in 1962, the group was aided by music promoter Leroy Kirkland in signing with Kapp Records. But with the rise of Diana Ross and The Supremes, Fann's group was forced to adopt a new name. With Kapp insisting that Nash front the group, the renamed Ruby and The Romantics enjoyed a string of soul-pop classics including, 'Our Day Will Come' (1963), 'My Summer Love' (1963) and 'Hey There Lonely Boy' (1963). Switching to ABC-Paramount Records in 1967, the group faded from the charts. Fann left the group soon after. Many of the group's songs became bigger hits for other artists, including 'When You're Young And In Love' by The Marvelettes (1967) and 'Hurting Each Other' by The Carpenters (1972).
CAUSE: Heart attack.

Mimi Farina

(MARGARITA MIMI BAEZ)
Born April 30, 1945
Died July 18, 2001
A folk-rock singer and social activist, Mimi Farina is best known for her collaborations with husband, Richard Farina, who died in a 1966 motorcycle accident. The daughter of a scientist/professor and the younger sister of Joan Baez, Farina studied dance, piano and violin during her childhood and was drawn to folk music after watching a performance by The Charles River Valley Boys. In 1963, aged 17, she married singer Richard Farina in secret. The couple moved to a small cabin in Carmel, California, and began performing as Richard & Mimi Farina, featuring Mimi on guitar and Richard on dulcimer. The duo occasionally performed on stage with Joan Baez and, signing with Vanguard Records in 1965, the duo issued the classic folk album, *Richard & Mimi Farina*, which was highlighted by the Richard Farina-co-composition , 'Pack Up Your Troubles', later a hit for Mimi's sister. A favourite at the 1965 Newport Folk Festival, the duo recorded a second album, *Reflections In A Crystal Wind*, which was issued shortly after Richard's death. Moving to San Francisco later in 1967, Mimi Farina joined the comedy troupe, The Committee and, continuing to work in folk music, Farina had a relationship with singer-songwriter Tom Jans, who would also meet an untimely death. In 1974, Farina founded the benevolent organisation Bread & Roses, which brought musical performances to non-traditional audiences in places such as prisons and psychiatric institutions. She belatedly issued her first solo album in 1986, *Mimi Farina Solo*.
CAUSE: She died at her home in Mill

Valley, California, after battling neuro-endocrine cancer for two years.

Richard Farina

Born March 8, 1937
Died April 30, 1966
Leftist folksinger and songwriter, Richard Farina found fame in the mid Sixties with wife Mimi Farina in the duo Richard & Mimi. Raised by a Cuban father and Irish mother in Brooklyn, Farina was a revolutionary who affiliated himself with the Irish Republican Army in the mid Fifties. While attending Cornell University off and on in the late Fifties, he ventured to Cuba, leaving when Castro seized power. Returning to New York City as a protest singer, he performed in Greenwich Village coffee houses alongside his first wife, Carolyn Hester, and Bob Dylan. In 1963, Farina secretly married 17-year-old dance student Mimi Baez, the younger sister of Joan Baez whom he had met earlier that year in London. Moving to a small cabin in Carmel, California, the couple began performing as Richard & Mimi. Featuring Richard on dulcimer and Mimi on guitar, the duo occasionally performed on stage with Joan Baez. Signing with Vanguard Records, Richard & Mimi débuted with *Richard & Mimi Farina* in 1965, the album highlighted by the Richard Farina co-composition, and Joan Baez hit, 'Pack Up Your Troubles'. The duo was embraced by the folk community after their appearance at the 1965 Newport Folk Festival. Richard & Mimi's second album, *Reflections In A Crystal Wind* (1966), was released shortly before Richard's death. Also a poet, author, and playwright, Farina penned prose and poetry for a variety of magazines including *Atlantic* and *Mademoiselle*, had his plays staged at a number of venues including Cornell University, and had published the book *Been Down So Long It Looks Like Up*.
CAUSE: He died in a motorcycle accident in Carmel, California, on his way home from a party celebrating both the publication of his first novel and his wife's 21st birthday. During the middle of the party he had decided to take a ride. He was a passenger on a speeding motorcycle which skidded out of control and flew over a five-foot embankment and crashed through two fences. Farina died instantly. After her husband's death, Mimi Farina continued working as a folk singer and social activist. In the early Seventies she had a relationship with singer/songwriter Tom Jans who also met an untimely death.
FURTHER READING: Farina, Richard. (1983). *Been Down So Long It Looks Like Up*. New York: Random House.

Pete Farndon

Born June 12, 1952
Died April 14, 1983
The bass player for the rock group The Pretenders, Pete Farndon was born and raised in Hereford, England, a musically isolated town near the Welsh border. Expelled from school at age 15, he worked as a manual labourer before joining a series of local "pub-rock" bands. A rough, loud bass player, in the mid Seventies Farndon joined a touring version of the popular Sydney, Australia-based folk-rock band The Bushwackers. Then, after wasting a year drinking in the bars in Hong Kong, Farndon returned to Hereford to recuperate. In the spring of 1978, Farndon joined The Pretenders, a London-based band led by transplanted Ohio singer Chrissie Hynde. Adding guitarist James Honeyman-Scott and drummer Jerry Mackleduff, The Pretenders were instant critical and commercial favourites with their post-punk, hard guitar oriented sound. Recording on their manager's Real Records label, the group enjoyed a hit with their début single, a cover of The Kinks' 'Stop Your Sobbing'. With drummer Martin Chambers replacing Mackleduff and Sire buying Real

Records, The Pretenders teamed with Sex Pistols/Roxy Music producer Chris Thomas for their début album *The Pretenders*. Featuring Farndon's untamed playing, and Hynde's sexual growls, the album spawned the hit 'Brass In Pocket' (1979). Soon, Farndon and Hynde began a two-year affair, which ended in 1981, after which Hynde dated Kinks' leader Ray Davies. On a roll, The Pretenders returned to the charts with *Pretenders II* (1981), the album highlighted by 'Message Of Love' and 'Talk Of The Town'. Farndon's playing suffered due to heavy alcohol and drug use, and he was fired by Hynde after the completion of a world tour on June 14, 1982. Two days later, bandmate James Honeyman-Scott died of a drug overdose. Hynde considered allowing Farndon to return but drummer Martin Chambers and the group's manager were against it. In 1983, Farndon was attempting to form a new group with Rob Stoner and former Clash member Topper Headon.
CAUSE: Farndon drowned in the bathtub of his London apartment as the result of a heroin-induced sleep. He was found with a needle still in his arm.
FURTHER READING: Wrenn, Mike. (1990). *The Pretenders: With Hyndesight*. London: Omnibus.

Edward Farran

(EDWARD JOHN ELIAS)
Born June 17, 1937
Died January 2, 2003
Formed at the University of Michigan by two sets of brothers, Edward and Fred Farran and Scott and Thomas Herrick, The Arbors had just one Top 20 hit, a psychedelic-tinged remake of The Box Tops' 'The Letter'. Formed in 1965, the group moved to Chicago to work as session singers in advertising. Edward Farran later worked as a professional vocal coach.
CAUSE: Kidney failure. He died in Chicago.

Wes Farrell

(WES FOGEL)
Born December 21, 1939
Died February 29, 1996
A legendary Brill Building songwriter, Wes Farrell co-wrote 'Boys' (The Shirelles/The Beatles), 'My Girl Sloopy' (later retitled as 'Hang On Sloopy'), 'Come On Down To My Boat' and 'Come A Little Bit Closer'. Establishing the Wes Farrell Organisation in the mid Sixties, he turned to music publishing, production work, and record promotion. Farrell worked with a variety of pop-rock acts including The Everly Brothers, The Cowsills, and, writing most of their music including their television theme song, The Partridge Family.
CAUSE: Cancer. He died while vacationing in Fisher Island, Florida.

Fat Pat

(PATRICK HAWKINS)
Born 1971
Died February 3, 1998
A Houston-based rapper, Fat Pat died shortly before the release of his début album, *Fat Pat & Wreckshop*, which went on to sell 100,000 copies, and spawned the hit 'Tops Drop'. He also supplied the co-vocals on Li'l Troy's rap hit, 'Wanna Be A Baller' (1999). Fat Pat's life was chronicled in the documentary, *Ghetto Dreams*.
CAUSE: He died after being shot. While three of his friends waited in a car, the rapper was shot at the Meadow Southwest Apartments in Houston while collecting money from a concert promoter.

Jimmy Lee Fautheree

(JAMES WALTON FAUTHEREE)
Born April 11, 1934
Died June 29, 2004
A rockabilly pioneer, Jimmy Lee Fautheree was rooted in honky-tonk style country music when he performed at the Big D Jamboree in Dallas and the Louisiana Hayride during the early Fifties. Passing

through several labels under the name "Jimmy Lee", he recorded a number of Fifties' country and rockabilly singles. Forming the duo Jimmy & Johnny with Country Johnny Mathis (not the pop ballad singer), Fautheree had a Top 10 country hit in 1954 with 'If You Don't Somebody Else Will', and during this period, a young Elvis Presley was his occasional opening act. With Fautheree's brother, Lenny, replacing Mathis, Jimmy & Johnny joined Faron Young's backing band, The Deputies, and in the late Seventies, Fautheree produced several gospel albums.
CAUSE: Cancer. He died at his home in Dallas.

Carl Feaster

Born September 24, 1930
Died January 23, 1981
Member of the Fifties New York-based doo-wop group, The Chords, Carl Feaster was born and raised in the Bronx. Around 1950, Carl Feaster, and his brother Claude, formed a vocal group called The Tunetoppers. Carl sang lead tenor, while Claude sang baritone. In 1951, The Tunetoppers met up with a Jimmy Keys-led group called The Four Notes. Impressing each other, the two groups merged into The Tunetoppers in 1952. After winning the amateur contest at the Apollo Theater, the youthful and good-looking doo-wop sextet were introduced to the Associated Booking Agency. Fronted by lead tenor Carl Feaster, they were discovered by Atlantic Records which placed them on their subsidiary, Cat Records. Recording 'Cross The Bridge' as the A-side of their début single, The Chords instead landed a hit with the B-side, their self-penned 'Sh-Boom'. Victims of the cover version phenomenon, The Chords lost sales and airplay to The Crew-Cuts' rendition of the song. The Chords followed up with the moderately selling single, 'Zippity-Zum', which would be their last hit. With only the Feaster brothers remaining in the group, the renamed Sh-Booms switched to Vic Records in 1957. Briefly returning to Atlantic in 1960, they quickly faded after recording a cover of The Marcels' hit, 'Blue Moon'. Beginning in the late Fifties, Carl Feaster also recorded at Roulette Records under the pseudonyms, Lionel Thorpe and Carl "Lionel" Thorpe. In the Sixties, Carl Feaster went into songwriting. By the late Seventies, Carl Feaster and Jimmy Keys reformed The Chords, performing at oldie shows.
CAUSE: Cancer.

Claude Feaster

Born September 23, 1933
Died November 1975
Member of the Fifties New York-based doo-wop group, The Chords, Claude Feaster was born and raised in the Bronx. Around 1950, Claude Feaster, along with his brother Carl, formed a vocal group called The Tunetoppers. Claude sang baritone, while Carl sang lead tenor. In 1951, the Tunetoppers met up with a Jimmy Keys-led group called The Four Notes. Impressing each other, the two groups merged into The Tunetoppers in 1952. After winning the amateur contest at the Apollo Theater, the youthful and good-looking doo-wop sextet were introduced to the Associated Booking Agency. Fronted by lead tenor Carl Feaster, they were discovered by Atlantic Records which placed them on their subsidiary, Cat Records. Recording a cover of Patti Page's pop hit 'Cross The Bridge' as the A-side of their début single, The Chords instead landed a hit with the B-side, their self-penned 'Sh-Boom'. The song also set off a series of nonsense lyric songs such as 'Be-Bop-A-Lula' and 'Tutti Frutti'. Victims of the cover version phenomenon, The Chords lost sales and airplay to The Crew-Cuts' rendition of the song. But The Chords were especially angry at Stan Freeberg

who had recorded a demeaning, novelty hit of the song. The Chords followed up with the moderately selling single, 'Zippity-Zum', which would be their last hit. With only the Feaster Brothers remaining in the group, the renamed Sh-Booms switched to Vic Records in 1957. Briefly returning to Atlantic in 1960, The Chords quickly faded after recording a cover of The Marcels' hit, 'Blue Moon'.
CAUSE: Unknown.

Charlie Feathers

(CHARLES ARTHUR FEATHERS)
Born June 12, 1932
Died August 29, 1998
Rockabilly singer and songwriter, Mississippi-born Charlie Feathers was taught to play guitar by bluesman Junior Kimbrough. After leaving school at age 10 to work with his father in the oil fields of Oklahama, Feathers relocated to Memphis in 1950 where he worked as a truck driver at Crown Electric and became friendly with co-worker Elvis Presley. Frequently hanging around the Sun Records studio, Feathers was hired as a demo singer. Adding a smart part to the song, Feathers was given a portion of the songwriting credit of Elvis Presley's final Sun single, 'I Forgot To Remember To Forget'. Although Feathers frequently claimed in interviews to have played a large role in Presley's early sessions, historical evidence has refuted that claim. Recording sporadically in the Fifties at Sun, Meteor and King Records, Feathers garnered little success with singles such as 'Defrost Your Heart' (1955) and the novelty-styled, 'Tongue-Tied Jill' (1956). Enjoying the British rockabilly revival of the late Seventies, Feathers experienced a career boost with the aid of Nick Lowe. A compilation of Feathers' finest output entitled *Get With It* was released a month before his death. Although remaining a respected figure in music, Feathers sold few records in his career.
CAUSE: Stroke. He died at St. Francis Hospital in Memphis after lapsing into a coma two weeks earlier.

John Felton

Born 1934
Died May 18, 1982
Latter member of the Fifties doo-wop pop group The Diamonds, California-born John Felton joined the group in late 1958 as a replacement for original tenor vocalist Ted Kowalski. Formed in Toronto, Canada, in the mid Fifties, The Diamonds had just scored a major hit with 'The Stroll'. Although primarily a cover band, the hugely popular group would switch to recording mostly original material in the late Fifties with 'Kathy-O' (1958) and the novelty-styled 'She Say (Oom Dooby Doom)' (1958). They also scored a pair of cover hits 'Walking Along' (1958) and their final Top 40 entry, 'One Summer Night' (1961). With the departure of David Somerville for a solo career in the early Sixties, Felton would take over the lead vocal duties. The Diamonds finally disbanded in 1967, but when Felton attempted to launch a new version of the group in 1973, he had to secure the permission of the group's longtime manager, Nathan Goodman. Felton led one of two touring Diamonds group into the Eighties, and was working on a new album at the time of his death.
CAUSE: Plane crash. A private aeroplane en route from Reno, Nevada, to Grants Pass, Oregon where Felton lived, crashed into Mount Shasta in California killing Felton and his wife, and the pilot and his wife. Felton had last performed two days earlier at a casino in Sparks, Nevada.

Leo Fender

(CLARENCE LEO FENDER)
Born August 10, 1909
Died March 21, 1991
Inventor and tinkerer who revolutionised the electric guitar, Leo Fender studied piano and saxophone

in his early teens, but never the guitar. After attending Fullerton College, he took an accounting position with the California Highway Department. But with the Depression taking his job, Fender opened a radio repair business in the mid Thirties. Then in a fateful meeting, Doc Kaufman brought a broken amplifier into Fender's shop in 1941. Intrigued by its inferior design, Fender proposed building his own model. Teaming with Kaufman, Fender formed the K&F Company. After buying out Kaufman in 1947, the organisation was renamed Fender Electrical Instruments. Hiring chief assistant and engineer George Fullerton, Fender launched a guitar line in the late Forties, the first Fender instrument played by country guitarist Jimmy Bryant while backing Little Jimmy Dickens. The single-cutaway Fender "Broadcaster", renamed "The Telecaster" in 1950, was the first mass market solid bodied electric guitar and a great improvement over existing electric guitars. But it was "The Stratocaster", introduced in 1954, which revolutionised the modern electric guitar. Nicknamed "The Strat", the instrument eliminated problems such as feedback and access to the upper frets, and sold for under $100. Constructed of modern components in a sleek, sexy shape, the Strat was embraced by a number of emerging rockers, most notably Buddy Holly. Fender employed 600 workers by the mid Sixties and was an unpretentious, hands-on employer who demanded perfection. He sold his company to CBS for $13 million in January 1965, and thereafter pre-1965 instruments have continued to command high prices in the collectors' market. In the early Seventies, Fender opened the G&L Guitar company and the CLF laboratories to further improve the guitar. Continuing to work on inventions up to his death, Fender held over 100 patents. Guitarists who have used Fender guitars include Jimi Hendrix, Eric Clapton, Stevie Ray Vaughan and Mark Knopfler.
CAUSE: Suffering from Parkinson's disease, he was found unconscious by his wife at their home in Fullerton, California.

Shane Fenton

(JOHNNY THEAKSTON)
Born 1944
Died 1961
The original lead singer and namesake of the early Sixties British rock outfit Shane Fenton and The Fentones, he died before the group was signed to Parlophone Records. A replacement Shane Fenton was found in the group's roadie, Bernard Jewry, who later emerged as Alvin Stardust.
CAUSE: His heart damaged by a childhood bout of rheumatic fever, he died of heart failure.

Keith Ferguson

Born July 23, 1947
Died April 29, 1997
Left-handed bassist and backing vocalist for the blues-rock band The Fabulous Thunderbirds, Houston-born Keith Ferguson joined the Austin, Texas-based group shortly after its inception in 1974. Estranged from his father, a classical pianist with the Chicago Symphony, Ferguson belatedly picked up the bass guitar at age 20, first touring throughout the West Coast as a member of Sunnyland Special during the late Sixties. Relocating to Austin in 1970, he joined Jimmy Vaughan in the group Storm, before backing Vaughan's brother, a then-unknown guitarist named Stevie Ray Vaughan in a blues-rock band called The Nitecrawlers. By 1974, Ferguson had turned down an offer to join an emerging Texas blues-rock band, ZZ Top to join The Fabulous Thunderbirds. Formed by guitarist Jimmie Vaughan, The Fabulous Thunderbirds were hired as the house band at Antone's nightclub in Austin. Befriended by bluesman Muddy

Waters, the group signed with Takoma Records. Beginning with the 1979 release *The Fabulous Thunderbirds*, Ferguson appeared on the group's first four albums. In 1980 the group toured with the Nick Lowe/Dave Edmunds band Rockpile, and both Lowe and Edmunds would later produce albums for The Fabulous Thunderbirds. By the early Eighties, The Fabulous Thunderbirds began garnering AOR airplay with tracks such as 'Tip On In' and 'One's Too Many'. Ferguson was booted from The Fabulous Thunderbirds in 1985 shortly before their pop breakthrough, and was replaced by Preston Hubbard. Years of bitter litigation between Ferguson and the band followed. Joining The Tailgators in 1995, Ferguson co-wrote the group's signature piece, 'Mumbo Jumbo'. But with a heroin habit intensifying, Ferguson would be fired from The Tailgators in 1990. He performed in a series of local Austin bands until shortly before his death.
CAUSE: He succumbed to liver failure caused by long-term heroin use. He died at Brackenridge Hospital in Austin.

Michael Ferguson

(BYRON MICHAEL FERGUSON)
Born c. 1942
Died 1979
Pianist for the San Francisco-based, proto-psychedelic group The Charlatans, San Diego-born Michael Ferguson suffered from childhood diabetes and was in poor health all his life. Thin and balding, Ferguson formed an artists community in the early Sixties in the San Francisco head shop he operated. It was here that vocalist George Hunter formed the group, originally as George And The Mainliners. Dressing in Western and turn-of-the-century garb, and decorating the stage with old theatre props from Ferguson's personal collection, the renamed Charlatans combined folk, jug, and rock influences. Ferguson also designed the group's psychedelic posters, inspiring a new artform. The first local rock group to sport long hair, The Charlatans garnered a large following during an extended engagement at the Red Dog Saloon in Virginia City, Nevada. Returning to the Haight-Ashbury district of San Francisco in the autumn of 1965, Hunter and several employees from the Red Dog Saloon formed a concert production company called the Family Dog, predating Bill Graham's more commercial venture. After recording some unreleased sessions for the Tom Donahue-operated Autumn Records, The Charlatans were signed by Kama Sutra in late 1965. But Ferguson would quit in September 1967, two years before the group recorded its sole album. Landing a post office job, Ferguson later teamed with singer Lynn Hughes to form a group called Tongue and Groove. An entirely different British rock group, The Charlatans, emerged in the Nineties.
CAUSE: Complications from diabetes.

Jimmy Fernandez

Born September 30, 1965
Died May 23, 1994
Bassist of the heavy metal group God Machine, Jimmy Fernandez was an original member of the San Diego-based band. Relocating to London in 1989, the group signed with Friction Records, releasing three EPs and two albums, one posthumously. The group disbanded after his death.
CAUSE: Brain tumour. He died in London.

Bobby Fields

Born September 11, 1928
Died January 6, 1981
A tenor saxophonist, Bobby Fields played in bands behind Buddy Clark and Ike Turner.
CAUSE: Cancer. He died at the V.A. Hospital in Chicago.

Richard "Dimples" Fields

Born March 21, 1941
Died January 12, 2000

A popular Eighties R&B vocalist, Richard "Dimples" Fields was nicknamed by a female fan because of his pleasant demeanour. From Louisiana, he moved to Oakland aged nine and, after performing in Bay Area clubs, he partnered Kenneth Taylor in launching his own nightclub in San Francisco, The Cold Duck Music Lounge. Installing himself as the entertainment, Fields performed on a weekly basis and released a series of moderately selling albums on his own DRK label. During the Seventies he provided backing vocals for soul heavyweights such as Millie Jackson, Betty Wright, The Dramatics, and Wilson Pickett, and also produced The Ohio Players' album, *Ouch*. Although Fields managed local hits beginning in the Sixties with 'Tears As Big As Cantaloupes', he failed to attract notice until signing with Boardwalk Records in 1981. After garnering some attention with his cover of the doo-wop standard 'Earth Angel', he became an R&B favourite with hits such as 'If It Ain't One Thing, It's Another' (1982), 'Taking Applications' (1982), and 'Tell It Like It Is' (1987).

CAUSE: Stroke. He died at Novato Community Hospital in Los Angeles.

Clayton Fillyau

Born August 16, 1934
Died July 18, 2001

A talented R&B drummer, Clayton Fillyau was a member of James Brown's Famous Flames, providing spirited performances on hits such as 'I Got You (I Feel Good)' and 'Papa's Got A Brand New Bag' as well as on the ground-breaking album *Live At The Apollo*. An influential musician, he popularised what later became known as the "break beat". Fillyau also worked with Ike & Tina Turner, Etta James and Sam & Dave.

CAUSE: Unknown. He died in Florida.

Mickey Finn

(MICHAEL NORMAN FINN)
Born June 3, 1947
Died January 11, 2003

As a member of T. Rex, Mickey Finn was at the forefront of the Glam movement. Drawn to the hippie scene during the late Sixties, Finn joined an artist collective that also played music named Hapshash & The Coloured Coat. In 1969, Tyrannosaurus Rex leader Marc Bolan fired bongo player Steve Peregrine-Took citing personal differences after a US tour, and hired good-looking Finn as his replacement, shortening the name to T. Rex. Bolan shocked his underground following by abandoning folky acoustic music for electric glam-rock, and with the addition of bassist Steve Currie and (later) drummer Bill Legend, the group's first Top 10 single came with 'Ride A White Swan' in 1970. Expanded into a quartet, T. Rex was incredibly successful in the UK with a long string of hit singles and albums between 1970 and 1973. In the US, the group managed just one Top 40 hit, 'Get It On'. Due to constant infighting, Finn quit the group in late 1974 after completing sessions for the album, *Bolan's Zip Gun*. The final version of T. Rex disbanded following Bolan's tragic death in 1977. After leading his own group for a time, Finn teamed with former members of T. Rex for a reunion concert in 1997. Encouraged by fan response, he formed Mickey Finn's T. Rex with Paul Fenton and Jack Green.

CAUSE: Unknown. Suffering from both kidney and liver ailments, he died at Mayday Hospital in London.

Larry Finnegan

(JOHN LAWRENCE FINNEGAN)
Born August 10, 1938
Died July 22, 1973

A country-pop performer, Larry Finnegan is best known for his 1962 hit, 'Dear One'. Moving to Switzerland in the late Sixties, he

launched his own record company.
CAUSE: Brain tumour. He died shortly after returning to the US.

Adrian Fisher

Born c. 1950
Died April 2000
A member of quirky rock band Sparks, guitarist Adrian Fisher joined the band after answering an advertisement in *Melody Maker*. Formed by the eccentric American-born brothers Russell and Ron Mael, the duo had released a pair of commercially unsuccessful albums in the US and had decided to start anew in London. Recommended by ex-John's Children bassist John Hewlett to Island Records producer Muff Winwood, the group signed with the label and recorded the glam album *Kimono My House* (1974), which yielded two UK Top 10 hits – 'This Town Ain't Big Enough For The Both Of Us' and 'Amateur Hour'. Fisher was fired from the band in late 1974 and replaced by Trevor White. In 1977, Fisher joined Mike Patto and Tim Bogert in the group Boxer, co-writing two tracks on their poor-selling album *Absolutely*. After playing in a band with former Free bassist Andy Fraser, Fisher moved to Thailand around 1990.
CAUSE: A heavy beer drinker who engaged in an unhealthy lifestyle, he collapsed after a performance and suffered a heart attack. He died on the resort island of Koh Samui in Thailand, where he had been performing in rock and blues bands for nine years.

Miss Toni Fisher

Born 1931
Died February 12, 1999
A pop singer who scored a Top 10 hit in 1959 with 'The Big Hurt', Los Angeles-born Miss Toni Fisher followed with the Top 40 lament about the Berlin Wall, 'West Of The Wall' (1962).
CAUSE: Heart attack. She died in Hyrum, Utah.

Rob Fisher

Born November 5, 1959
Died August 25, 1999
A member of two Eighties pop/new-wave groups, Naked Eyes and Climie Fisher, keyboardist Rob Fisher was also a talented songwriter. The Cheltenham-born Fisher formed Naked Eyes in 1979 with vocalist Pete Byrne. The group released three albums and scored a pair of hit singles with the Burt Bacharach/Hal David-penned 'Always Something There To Remind Me' and 'Promises, Promises'. After parting with Byrne, Fisher was hired as a session player by U2 producer Steve Lillywhite. While working at Abbey Road Studios, Fisher teamed with session musician Simon Climie to form a songwriting partnership. After penning songs for the likes of George Michael, Jeff Beck and Aretha Franklin, the duo formed their own musical outfit, Climie Fisher. After releasing a pair of albums, the duo enjoyed hits in 1988 with the ballads, 'Rise To The Occasion' and a re-released earlier single, 'Love Changes (Everything)'. Before falling ill, Fisher had planned to resurrect Naked Eyes.
CAUSE: Stricken with acute pancreitis, he underwent emergency surgery shortly before his death.

Ella Fitzgerald

(ELLA JANE FITZGERALD)
Born April 25, 1917
Died June 15, 1996
One of the century's greatest jazz singers, Ella Fitzgerald emerged as "The First Lady Of Song". A native of Newport News, Virginia, she had yearned to be a dancer in the tradition of Snake Hips Tucker, but after winning an Apollo Theater amateur contest at age 15 with a rendition of The Boswell Sisters' 'The Object Of My Affection', Fitzgerald was discovered by trumpeter Benny Carter who was in the audience. Introduced to drummer and bandleader Chick Webb, she was hired in 1935 and

became synonymous with his small orchestra, scoring a massive hit with the swinging, 'A-Tisket, A-Tasket'. Following Webb's sudden death aged 30 in 1939, Bill Beason assumed the drummer duties and the group continued under Ella Fitzgerald's moniker. Going solo in 1942, Fitzgerald was embraced by both pop and jazz audiences on hits such as 'It's Only A Paper Moon', and teamed with The Ink Spots, 'I'm Making Believe'/'Into Each Life Some Rain Must Fall'. A talented improvising bebop and scat vocalist, Fitzgerald's talent was evident on her 1947 recording, 'How High The Moon'. By 1948, she joined a band led by her then-husband, Ray Brown. Dropped by Decca in 1956, Fitzgerald signed with her manager/producer's new label, Verve Records. Reigniting her career with her label début, Fitzgerald tackled an album's worth of Cole Porter standards. She would follow with similar projects, redefining the works of great American composers such as Irving Berlin, Duke Ellington and George and Ira Gershwin. Her career remained strong into the rock era, and Fitzgerald landed on the pop charts with 'Mack The Knife' (1960) from the Grammy-winning live album *Mack The Knife: Ella In Berlin*. Suffering ill health by the late Sixties, her masterful voice began to wane. Last recording in 1989, she won a total of 13 Grammy Awards and appeared in several films including *St. Louis Blues*.
CAUSE: Stricken with numerous illnesses including heart problems and severe diabetes, she suffered a stroke two weeks before her death. She died at her home in Beverly Hills, California.
FURTHER READING: Nicholson, Stuart. (1996). *Ella Fitzgerald: A Biography Of The First Lady Of Jazz*. London: Indigo.

Charles Fizer

Born June 3, 1940
Died August 1965
Second tenor/baritone singer for the Fifties doo-wop group, The Olympics, Charles Fizer joined the group while attending high school in Compton, California. Aided by Jesse Belvin, The Olympics signed with Demon Records in 1958. Taking a comic approach on much of their material, The Olympics scored their biggest hit with their Demon début, 'Western Movies' (1958). Fizer left The Olympics before the release of their next single, but returned to the group in 1959. Switching to Arvee Records, the Olympics scored a series of moderate R&B hits including 'Big Boy Pete', 'Shimmy Like My Sister Kate' and 'Dance To The Light Of The Moon'.
CAUSE: He was killed in the Watts race riots in Los Angeles.

Gabe Fleming

Born c. 1930
Died December 1989
Trumpet player who worked with Ike & Tina Turner, Gabe Fleming later headed the horn section behind Albert Collins. Fleming had also been a member of Charles Wright and the Watts 103rd Street Rhythm Band, from 1969–71, appearing on several hits including 'Do Your Thing' and 'Express Yourself'.
CAUSE: Heart attack. He died in Los Angeles.

Wade Flemons

Born September 25, 1940
Died October 13, 1993
Raised in Kansas but moving to Battle Creek, Michigan, Wade Flemons formed an R&B group at age 15 called The Newcomers. Recording for Vee-Jay Records as a solo artist beginning in the late Fifties, he scored several hits including 'Here I Stand' (1958), 'Easy Lovin'' (1960), and his final chart entry, a cover of Percy Mayfield's 'Please Send Me Someone To Love' (1961). By the mid Sixties he joined Vee-Jay session vocalist Maurice White in the soul group The Salty Peppers, which by 1970 had evolved into Earth,

Wind & Fire. After releasing two albums at Warner Brothers – *Earth, Wind & Fire* and *The Need Of Love* – White fired most of the group in 1972, including Flemons. Also a songwriter, Flemons co-wrote the 1968 Dells hit, 'Stay In My Corner'.
CAUSE: Unknown.

Matthew Fletcher

Born November 5, 1970
Died June 12, 1996
Member of the British independent label, pop-rock group Heavenly, Matthew Fletcher played drums behind his vocalist sister, Amelia Fletcher. He died shortly before the release of the group's fourth album, *Operation Heavenly*, for which he wrote most of the tracks.
CAUSE: He committed suicide by hanging at his home in London.

Tom Fogerty

(THOMAS RICHARD FOGERTY)
Born November 9, 1941
Died September 6, 1990
Rhythm guitarist of the bayou-rock band Creedence Clearwater Revival, Tom Fogerty was born and raised in southern California. Fogerty passed through a series of rock bands in his teen years beginning with The Playboys, for which he provided lead guitar and vocals. Meanwhile, his younger brother John Fogerty had formed The Blue Velvets in 1959 at Potola Junior High in El Cerrito, California, along with bass player Stu Cook and drummer Doug Clifford. With Tom joining The Blue Velvets on rhythm guitar and co-lead vocals, the renamed Tommy Fogerty and The Blue Velvets performed at frat parties and school dances in the San Francisco Bay area. When Tom Fogerty landed a shipping clerk position at Fantasy Records, he convinced the label to sign his band. Forced to change their name to The Golliwogs, the quartet scored a local hit with 'Brown Eyed Girl' (1965). But after Saul Zauntz purchased Fantasy Records in late 1967, The Golliwogs were renamed Creedence Clearwater Revival (CCR). The group soon landed a slow-rising national hit with a bluesy cover of Dale Hawkins' rockabilly standard 'Suzie Q', a track that would be included on their début album, *Creedence Clearwater Revival*. With John Fogerty emerging as the group's leader and chief songwriter, CCR would unleash a string of politically and socially tinged, Top 10, million-selling hits including, 'Proud Mary' (1969), 'Bad Moon Rising' (1969), 'Down On The Corner'/'Fortunate Son' (1969), 'Travelin' Band'/'Who'll Stop The Rain' (1970), 'Up Around The Bend' (1970) and 'Looking' Out My Back Door' (1970). But resenting John's increasing control of the group, in January of 1971 Tom Fogerty left CCR shortly after the release of their sixth album *Pendulum*. From it, the hit single 'Have You Ever Seen The Rain' (1971) foretold the group's impending demise. CCR would limp along for another 18 months before disbanding. Tom Fogerty initially performed with a looseknit group of musicians which included Jerry Garcia before pursuing a solo career. Fogerty would record several rock and country albums for Fantasy Records including two with his group Ruby, with only *Goodbye Media Men* (1972) hitting the best sellers charts. Fogerty's last album came in 1985 with *Precious Gems*. He later relocated to Hawaii where he worked as a real estate agent. Except for performances at Tom Fogerty's 1980 wedding and a high-school reunion, CCR members would remain estranged.
CAUSE: He succumbed to respiratory failure as a result of tuberculosis. He died in Scottsdale, Arizona. He had been ill for several months.
FURTHER READING: Hallowell, John. (1971). *Inside Creedence*. New York: Bantam.

Zak Foley

(ZACHARY FOLEY)
Born December 9, 1970
Died December 31, 2001
The bassist for dance/alternative rock act EMF, Zak Foley enjoyed success just months after the group was launched. Formed in 1989 in the Forest of Dean, England, EMF (short for Epsom Mad Funkers) was fronted by lead vocalist James Atkin, and their début single 'Unbelievable', released in 1990, was a hit on both sides of the Atlantic. The catchy, upbeat song prominently sampled politically incorrect comedian Andrew "Dice" Clay. Releasing the million-selling *Schubert Dip* album the following year, the group drew unwanted attention after Yoko Ono objected to a vocal sample of John Lennon's murderer Mark David Chapman reading a Lennon lyric. Although EMF's US fortunes waned after the single 'Lies', they continued their British hit run with 'I Believe', 'Children', 'It's You', and in a collaborative effort with the comedy team of Reeves & Mortimer, a cover of The Monkees' 'I'm A Believer'. After being dropped by Parlophone Records, EMF disbanded. Foley subsequently joined a retro-rock band, Carrie.
CAUSE: His body was found in his Camden, New Jersey, apartment. Next to him were pieces of crack cocaine, a crack pipe, burned tin foil, beer cans and a vodka bottle.

Clarence Ford

Born December 16, 1929
Died August 8, 1994
New Orleans session saxophonist and member of Fats Domino's band (1954–1970), Clarence Ford left Domino after a serious car crash in 1970. He returned to New Orleans where he worked as a session player. Ford had first broken into the music business in 1945 in a jazz combo called The Eureka Brass Band.
CAUSE: Unknown. He died in New Orleans.

Mary Ford

(IRIS COLLEEN SUMMER)
Born July 7, 1928
Died September 30, 1977
Musical partner and one-time wife of Les Paul, the former Iris Colleen Summer became a major star in the early Fifties. A country singer on Gene Autry's radio programme, the 27-year-old teamed with Les Paul in 1945, having been recommended by Eddie Dean (brother of Jimmy Dean). First naming his musical partner Mary Lou, and then Mary Ford, Paul married her four years later. Combining Paul's love of jazz and Ford's affinity for country music, the duo of "Les Paul and Mary Ford" scored a string of massive pop hits beginning with a cover of 'Tennessee Waltz' (1950); the song was characterised by Les Paul's groundbreaking use of double-tracked vocals which allowed Ford to harmonise with herself. Promoting their releases on their own radio show, the frequently touring duo continued their hit run with 'Mockin' Bird Hill' (1951), 'How High The Moon' (1951), and their best-seller, taken from the 1940 Broadway play *Two For The Show*, 'Vaya Con Dios' (1952). By 1952, Paul and Ford had transferred their daily radio show to television. But with the rise of rock in the mid Fifties, Paul and Ford faded from the charts. Switching to Columbia Records in 1956, Paul and Ford released their final album, *Time To Dream*, and had their television programme cancelled four years later. With Les Paul spending most of his time working, Mary Ford divorced him in 1964 and retired soon after marrying her high school sweetheart. Most of their recorded output is included on the boxed set, *Les Paul: The Legend And The Legacy*.
CAUSE: Cancer. She had been in a diabetic coma for 54 days before passing away in a Los Angeles hospital.

Earl Forest

(EARL LACY FOREST)
Born December 1, 1926
Died February 26, 2003
A singer-songwriter and drummer, Earl Forest was a member of the loose-knit Fifties Memphis-based R&B ensemble The Beale Streeters, which at times included Johnny Ace, Bobby Bland, Junior Parker, B.B. King and Rosco Gordon. Forest's only hit (in 1953) was 'Whoopin' And Hollerin'', which featured Johnny Ace on piano.
CAUSE: Cancer. He died at the Memphis Veterans Administration Medical Center.

Joey Forgione

(JOSEPH P. FORGIONE)
Born November 22, 1943
Died October 20, 2003
The original drummer for blue-eyed soul band The Soul Survivors, Joey Forgione had previously been in Steeplechase, a band led by Dean Parrish. The Soul Survivors were formed in 1966, and the Gamble & Huff produced 'Expressway To Your Heart' became their only hit the following year. The group disbanded after releasing an album for Atlantic, with most of the tracks being produced by Rick Hall at Fame Studios in Muscle Shoals, Alabama. Rejoining Dean Parrish in a revived version of The Vagrants, Forgione drummed on sessions for a new album.
CAUSE: He suffered a heart attack after a performance at Downtime nightclub in New York City.

Gene Forrest

(EUGENE FORREST III)
Born September 3, 1931
Died July 24, 2003
One half of the R&B duo, Gene & Eunice. Born in San Antonio, Texas, but raised in Harlem and Los Angeles, Forrest took piano lessons in his teens before learning to play Hawaiian style guitar. Forming a doo-wop group Gene Forrest & The Four Feathers, he performed in Los Angeles nightclubs and recorded two singles. After competing in a talent contest, Forrest asked another contestant, Eunice Levy, to join his group but after Forrest's backing band left him, he formed the duo Gene & Eunice; the couple also became romantically involved. Writing their own material, they scored two R&B hits in 1955, 'Ko Ko Mo' and, backed by Johnny Otis' group, 'This Is My Story'. (Perry Como's remake of 'Ko Ko Mo' hit the pop charts.) Although Gene & Eunice remained popular in Southern California, they had no further hits. Forrest later worked at Hughes Aircraft and Levy died in 2002.
CAUSE: Kidney failure. He died in Las Vegas.

Jimmy Forrest

Born June 24, 1920
Died August 26, 1980
A popular jazz and R&B artist, Jimmy Forrest had earned his dues in the Forties in bands led by Jay McShann, Andy Kirk and Duke Ellington. Emerging from the St. Louis jazz scene, Forrest gravitated towards R&B in the early Fifties. He is best known for his self-composed hit, 'Night Train', a song based on Ellington's composition, 'Happy-Go-Lucky Local'. Released by United Records during his stint at the label from 1951–53, the R&B standard was reprised by James Brown in 1962. Forrest later joined bands led by Harry Edison and then Count Basie. In the mid Seventies, he toured the US and England with jazz trombonist Al Grey.
CAUSE: Unknown. He died at Butterworth Hospital in Grand Rapids, Michigan.

Rhett Forrester

Born September 22, 1956
Died January 22, 1994
The lead vocalist and harmonica player of the New York City-based, Eighties hard-rock group Riot, Rhett Forrester

launched his musical career in a series of bar bands in Atlanta. After a two-year navy stint and a one-year jail term for robbing a gas station, Forrester joined Riot in 1982 as a replacement for founding vocalist Guy Speranza. After releasing their major label début on Elektra Records, *Restless Breed*, Riot landed the opening slot on a tour with Rainbow. After Riot disbanded, Forrester returned to his hometown of Atlanta and joined a local rock band called Mr. Dirty.
CAUSE: He was murdered in Atlanta, shot in his car at an intersection during an argument with two men. After flagging down a police cruiser, he died soon after. His killers were never found.

Albert "Sonny" Forriest

(ELBERT MCKINLEY FORRIEST)
Born May 21, 1934
Died January 10, 1999
Session guitarist for legendary R&B act The Coasters, Albert "Sonny" Forriest (sometimes known as Albert Forrest and Sonny Clarke) recorded with the group from 1959 to 1961. In the Fifties, Forriest also worked with Jackie Wilson, Dee Clark and Big Jay McNeely and, in 1962, joined Ray Charles' touring group. Later veering toward jazz and blues, Forriest released the blues album, *Tuff Pickin'*, and played vibes on the Hank Crawford album, *After Hours*.
CAUSE: Unknown. He died in Capital Heights, Maryland.

Thomas "Quorthon" Forsberg

Born 1965
Died June 7, 2004
The leader of Swedish black-metal band Bathory, Thomas "Quorthon" Forsberg formed the outfit in the early Eighties with Jonas Åkerlund. The group first made waves with its 1989 album, *Hammerheart*. Forsberg recorded a pair of solo albums in the Nineties.
CAUSE: Heart attack. He was found dead in his apartment in Stockholm, Sweden.

Ken Forssi

Born 1943
Died January 5, 1998
The bassist of the psychedelic, folk-rock flavoured group Love, Cleveland-born Ken Forssi replaced short-term, original member Johnny Fleckenstein. Formerly with the surf group The Surfaris (of 'Wipe Out' fame), Forssi joined that group in time for their fifth and final album. Forssi then joined Arthur Lee and Bryan MacLean in a new psychedelic-flavoured folk-rock group called The Grass Roots. Forced to change their name after the discovery of another group with the same moniker, the renamed Love was the first rock signing to the folk music label, Elektra Records. Love enjoyed critical-acclaim with their masterful début album *Love*, which spawned the singles 'My Little Red Book' and 'Seven And Seven Is'. After releasing the impressive *Da Capo* in 1967, Love followed up with the masterpiece, *Forever Changes*, the album highlighted by the touching Bryan MacLean-composition, 'All Alone Or'. Forssi also deputised for Bruce Palmer when The Buffalo Springfield bassist faced voluntary deportation for drugs offences. Abusing drugs and in trouble with the law in 1968, Forssi was imprisoned, and subsequently fired by Arthur Lee.
CAUSE: Brain cancer. He died in Florida.

Steve Foth

Born October 4, 1963
Died September 29, 1999
A rock singer/songwriter, Steve Foth is best known as the boyfriend of pop singer Jewel, co-writing her hit, 'You Were Meant For Me' (he also appeared in the song's video). As a member of alternative rock group The

Rugburns, he landed a college radio hit with the oddball single, 'Hitchhiker Joe' (1998), a song Foth co-wrote with Steve Poltz. Leaving The Rugburns in 1998, Foth joined the acoustic folk trio, Carnivorous Lunar Activity (C.L.A.), and simultaneously pursued a solo career. During this time, Foth also operated a financially struggling record shop in San Francisco, Rocket Records.
CAUSE: He was stabbed to death in San Diego, California. He borrowed a friend's car to meet friends at a restaurant but never arrived. Instead, his unclothed body was discovered the following day in a field in northern San Diego County. He had been repeatedly stabbed. The burnt wreckage of his car, a 1996 Audi, was discovered on October 3. In what was later judged to be a drug-related slaying, two men and a woman were charged with his murder.

Charlie Fox

Born September 23, 1939
Died September 18, 1998
Songwriter best known for 'Mockingbird', Charlie Fox also penned the pop hits 'I Got A Name' (Jim Croce), 'My Fair Share' (Seals & Croft), 'Ready To Take A Chance Again' (Barry Manilow) and the chart-topping 'Killing Me Softly With His Song' (Roberta Flack). Charlie Fox wrote his first hit, the nursery rhyme-based 'Mockingbird' for his former gospel-singer sister Inez Foxx (the extra "x" added by her record company), also providing backing vocals and guitar on the Top 10 hit. Charlie and Inez released several more singles at Sue Records and were equally billed on their latter releases. For a time, Charlie Fox pursued a solo career, and produced Gene Pitney's 'She's a Heartbreaker'. Fox also penned the themes for the television programmes, *Angie, Love Boat, Laverne And Shirley* and *Happy Days*. Fox had left North Carolina for New York City in the late Fifties to become a full-time songwriter. James Taylor and Carly Simon reprised 'Mockingbird' in 1974.
CAUSE: Leukaemia. He died in Mobile, Alabama.

David "Panama" Francis

Born December 21, 1918
Died November 13, 2001
The longtime leader of The Savoy Sultans, jazz-rooted drummer David "Panama" Francis was a prolific session player who performed on scores of rock hits including Bill Haley & The Comets ('Shake, Rattle And Roll' and 'ABC Boogie'), Buddy Holly ('Peggy Sue Got Married'), Bobby Darin ('Splish Splash'), Ray Charles ('Hallelujah I Love Her So'), Screamin' Jay Hawkins ('I Put A Spell On You'), Neil Sedaka ('Calendar Girl') and Connie Francis ('Lipstick On Your Collar'). A professional performer since age 13 when his mother would collect him from the clubs where he performed, Francis worked with the finest bandleaders in jazz, including lengthy stints in the orchestras of Cab Calloway and Lucky Millinder. Francis continued to perform even after he turned 80 and appeared in the Madonna video for 'Secrets'.
CAUSE: Unknown.

Claude Françoise

Born February 4, 1942
Died March 11, 1978
An Egyptian-born, jazz-trained French pop singer, Claude Françoise crossed over into the British market in 1976 with 'Tears On The Telephone'. Since the early Sixties, Françoise had made a career out of covering Anglo hits for the French market. Nicknamed "Clo-Clo", he switched to ballad material to target older audiences and one of his co-compositions, 'Comme d'Habitude', was translated into English by Paul Anka as 'My Way', becoming a standard and being

covered by artists as diverse as Frank Sinatra and Elvis Presley.
CAUSE: He was electrocuted while changing a light bulb in his bathroom, at his home in Paris.

Carolyn Franklin

(CAROLYN ANN FRANKLIN)
Born May 13, 1944
Died April 25, 1988
Songwriter and R&B singer who is chiefly identified as a backing vocalist for her legendary sister Aretha Franklin, Carolyn Franklin simultaneously pursued her own solo career. Born in Memphis, but raised in Buffalo and then Detroit by her famous preacher father, the Rev. C.L. Franklin, Carolyn Franklin played the piano and began writing songs in her teen years. Beginning with Aretha Franklin's 'Do Right Woman, Do Right Man' (1967), Carolyn was joined by another sister, Erma, in providing exquisite gospel-rooted vocal harmony. Never attaining any level of solo success comparable to Erma or Aretha, Carolyn Franklin released a total of four studio albums beginning with her 1969 début, the Jimmy Radcliffe-produced *Baby Dynamite*. Also a songwriter, Carolyn Franklin penned several hits for sister Aretha including, 'Baby Baby Baby' and 'Angel'. In 1979, Franklin appeared as a backing singer behind Aretha in *The Blues Brothers*, for a rousing performance of 'Think'. Franklin also provided vocals on the Dan Hartman-produced, Paul King album, *Joy*. Although in the advanced stage of cancer, Franklin earned a law degree shortly before her death.
CAUSE: Cancer. She died in Bloomfield Hills, Michigan.

Erma Franklin

(ERMA VERNICE FRANKLIN)
Born March 13, 1938
Died September 7, 2002
A Sixties soul singer, Erma Franklin honed her musical talent alongside her sisters, Carolyn and future superstar Aretha, at the New Bethel Baptist Church where their celebrated father, the Rev. C.L. Franklin, officiated. After Erma formed a teenage singing group, The Cleo-Patrettes, she was asked by budding songwriters Berry Gordy and Billy Davis (in their pre-Motown period) to record three of their compositions, but her father convinced her to continue her formal education, attending the tiny Clark College in Atlanta, majoring in business administration. Erma Franklin eventually recorded for Epic (part of the same company that had signed her sister, Aretha) and released a poor-selling jazz-pop album in 1962, *Her Name Is Erma*. She would not record again until her contract expired in 1967 by which time, with her sister's career on the ascent, Erma signed with songwriter Bert Berns' Shout label. She recorded the Bert Berns/Jerry Ragovoy soul classic 'Piece Of My Heart' which became her only hit; a reworked version of the song by Janis Joplin would become a blues-rock standard. Erma and Carolyn provided backing vocals on some of Aretha's biggest hits including 'Respect' and 'Chain Of Fools'. After working with Aretha for much of the Seventies and Eighties, Erma took a position as a fundraiser for a social organisation which aided high-risk youth. 'Piece Of My Heart' was reissued and reached the British Top 10 in 1992 after the song was featured in a Levi's 501 jeans commercial.
CAUSE: Throat cancer. She died at her home in Detroit.

Melvin Franklin

(DAVID ENGLISH)
Born October 12, 1942
Died February 23, 1995
The bass singer for the Sixties vocal harmony group The Temptations, Melvin Franklin played an essential

role on the group's many Motown hits. A native of Montgomery, Alabama, Franklin was raised in Detroit. First singing backing vocals with The Voicemasters on a session at Gwen Gordy's Anna Records, Franklin then joined The Distants, a group led by Otis Williams. After releasing a single at Northern Records, The Distants merged with another Detroit group in 1961 to become The Temptations. Having attended Wayne State University in Detroit, Franklin had planned to return to earn a degree in theology. Signing with Motown Records, The Temptations scored a series of pop-soul classics including 'My Girl' (1965), 'Ain't Too Proud To Beg' (1966), '(I Know) I'm Losing You' (1966) and 'I Wish It Would Rain' (1968). Franklin's deep bass vocals became prominent in The Temptations' sound during its psychedelic phase on the hits 'Cloud Nine' (1968), 'Psychedelic Shack' (1970), and 'Ball Of Confusion' (1970). With the group experiencing frequent personnel changes, Franklin and bandmate Otis Williams were the only original members by the early Seventies, when the group scored its final Top 10 entries with 'Papa Was A Rolling Stone' (1972) and 'Masterpiece' (1973). Though landing little airplay with their newer material in a group built around the nucleus of Franklin and Williams, The Temptations remained a mainstay on the concert circuit. Becoming ill, Franklin stopped performing with The Temptations in July 1994.
CAUSE: Admitted into Cedars-Sinai Medical Center in Los Angeles after experiencing seizures, he died a week later from heart failure. In poor health for several years, he suffered from diabetes and severe rheumatoid arthritis.
FURTHER READING: Williams, Otis; & Romanowski, Patricia. (1989). *Temptations*. New York: Firesign.

Al Frazier

Born 1930
Died November 13, 2005
A member of the R&B group The Rivingtons, Al Frazier had passed through a series of acts before achieving fame. While attending high school in Los Angeles, Frazier formed his first vocal group, The Mello-Moods (which included future Platters member Paul Robi). Drafted before the group was able to record, Frazier served in Korea. Upon his discharge in 1952, Frazier formed The Emanons, a group whose only accomplishment was an appearance on a local television programme. Then at a 1953 amateur contest promoted by notable disc jockey Hunter Hancock, Frazier joined forces with some of the other contestants – including the talented Thurston Harris – to form The Lamplighters. Signing with King-Federal Records, the group enjoyed regional success throughout the West Coast. After Harris left the group to return to Indiana, the remaining members re-emerged as The Tenderfoots. With Harris briefly returning to the fold, the group surfaced as The Jacks, providing backing vocals for Paul Anka; with Harris again leaving, the group recorded as The Sharps on Jamie Records, before coming full circle and backing Harris on his solo hits including 'Little Bitty Pretty One'. Frazier's group then recorded under a bewildering series of names including The Rebels (behind Duane Eddy), The Four After Fives, The Crenshaws, and their final incarnation, The Rivingtons. Signing with Liberty Records in 1962, The Rivingtons scored a pair of raucous, novelty-styled R&B hits with 'Papa-Oom-Mow-Mow' and 'The Bird Is The Word'. The garage-rock band The Trashmen later revived the two songs as a hit medley. By 1965, Frazier had moved to the role of the group's manager and was replaced by

Darryl White. Frazier occasionally joined revival versions of The Rivingtons, and performed right up to his death.
CAUSE: Suffering a heart attack, he died at his home in Las Vegas.

Freaky Tah

(RAYMOND RODGERS)
Born May 14, 1971
Died March 28, 1999
A member of the socially conscious, anti-drug, rap quartet The Lost Boyz, Freaky Tah joined three childhood friends from Queens, New York, to form the dreadlocked group in 1995. From their gold-certified début album *Legal Drug Money* (1996), The Lost Boyz landed on the charts with 'Music Makes Me High' and 'Get Up'. Shortly after the release of their follow-up *Love, Peace & Nappines* [sic], the group earned a slot on the Lollapolooza tour.
CAUSE: He was shot in the back of the head by a masked gunman at 4 a.m. in the morning as he was leaving a party at the Four Points Sheraton Hotel in New York City. He was declared dead on arrival on reaching Jamaica Hospital Medical Center.

Eddie Freche Jr.

Born October 10, 1947
Died April 6, 1995
A member of the veteran New Orleans based R&B outfit The Neville Brothers, guitarist Eddie Freche was hired in 1994. Freche was also a member of The Nobles and The Boogie Kings.
CAUSE: Unknown.

John Fred

(JOHN FRED GOURRIER)
Born May 8, 1941
Died April 15, 2005
A native of Baton Rouge, Louisiana, pop-rock singer John Fred was the son of professional baseball player, Fred Gourrier. Forming an R&B outfit, John Fred & The Playboys, while in high school, Fred had a minor hit with 'Shirley' (1959) and because he was a member of his school's basketball team, he declined an offer to perform on *American Bandstand* as he was competing in the state playoffs. After disbanding The Playboys, Fred attended Southeastern Louisiana University and, in the early Sixties, formed what evolved into John Fred & His Playboy Band. After releasing several singles, the group finally hit chart paydirt in 1967 with 'Judy In Disguise (With Glasses)', a tongue-in-cheek parody of The Beatles' 'Lucy In The Sky With Diamonds', composed by Fred and bandmate Andrew Bernard. Following up with a series of cover versions of R&B songs, the group never returned to the Top 40 and disbanded in 1968. The following year, Fred assembled another pop-rock group, and was later a producer and vice-president at RCS Studios in Baton Rouge, Louisiana. He last performed in 2002.
CAUSE: After undergoing a kidney transplant in late 2004, he never recovered. He died at Tulane Hospital.

Alan Freed

(ALDON JAMES FREED)
Born December 15, 1921
Died January 20, 1965
Legendary disc jockey often credited with popularising the term "rock'n'roll", Pennsylvania-born Alan Freed was raised in Salem, Ohio. Playing the trombone in a local New Orleans-style jazz band called The Sultans Of Swing during his teen years, Freed was also a fan of classical music. After briefly attending Ohio State University in 1940, he joined the army the following year. Receiving a medical discharge in 1942, he returned to Salem and enrolled in broadcasting school. After working at a series of radio stations, he landed at WAKR in nearby Akron. It was here that in 1946 Freed first used the term "rock'n'roll", more as an expression than as a

musical term. His popularity soaring, Freed became a local star with his salary tripling. Fired for demanding a raise, Freed was barred from talking a job within a 75-mile radius for two years. Returning to radio in June 1951 at WJW in Cleveland, Freed initially played classical music in the graveyard shift. But when Cleveland record store owner Leo Mintz informed Freed of a new trend of white teenagers listening to black popular music, Freed began to play R&B records. His popularity skyrocketing overnight, Freed called himself The Moondog, and his programme, *The Moondog Rock'n'Roll House Party*. Also promoting local music concerts, Freed created a firestorm when on March 23, 1952, he staged what is considered the first modern rock'n'roll concert, the Moondog Coronation Ball. The oversold 10,000 seat Cleveland Arena erupted into a riot after just one song. Soon promoting R&B caravan tours, Freed became a national figure. Lured to New York City in 1954, Freed took the microphone at WINS and created a sensation by giving listeners the original versions of rock and R&B songs instead of watered-down pop cover versions by white artists. Freed was soon forced to drop his "Moondog" moniker after being sued by a local musician, Louis Hardin, who had used the name since 1947. Continuing to promote concerts, Freed rented out the Paramount Theater in Brooklyn for a long residency of all-star revues. Moving to film, Freed oversaw several quickie rock'n'roll flicks including *Rock Rock Rock* and *Mister Rock'n'Roll*. Under a constant barrage of attacks, Freed was set up in a career-damaging riot at a concert in Boston. Fired by WINS, he briefly landed at WABC. Then as the chief target of congressional payola hearings, Freed was hauled before investigators in 1962. Punished for what everyone else in the industry was doing, Freed was abandoned by the music industry after he pleaded guilty to charges of bribery, and was fined and given a suspended sentence. Drifting from station to station, Freed died a broken and forgotten man. A week in Freed's life formed the basis of the 1978 film, *American Hot Wax*. Because of Freed's pioneering use of the term "rock'n'roll", Cleveland was picked as the site for The Rock'n'Roll Hall of Fame and Museum.

CAUSE: After the payola scandal of the late Fifties, Freed was made a scapegoat and his career came to an end. He became despondent and his health failed. He entered the Desert Hospital in Palm Springs, California, in early January 1965, suffering from a kidney disease, uremia. He died at the hospital shortly thereafter. In 2002, a brass urn containing Freed's ashes was relocated from a mausoleum in New York to the Rock and Roll Hall of Fame in Cleveland and installed inside a wall.

FURTHER READING: Jackson, John A. (1991). *Big Beat Heat: Alan Freed And The Early Years Of Rock & Roll.* New York: Schirmer.

Ernie Freeman

Born September 16, 1922
Died May 16, 1981

Arranger, producer, and pianist, the Cleveland-born Ernie Freeman was classically trained at the Cleveland Institute of Music. After a military stint in the early Fifties, Freeman relocated to Los Angeles. Rooted in jazz, Freeman became a much in-demand session player, working with artists such as Frank Sinatra, Dean Martin and Sammy Davis, Jr. Also pursuing a solo career, he hit the charts with 'Jivin' Around' (1956), 'Lost Dreams' (1956), and his Top 10, signature instrumental hit, 'Raunchy' (1957). Freeman often recorded as the leader of a studio-only group, B. Bumble, scoring a pair of instrumental hits in the early Sixties with 'Bumble Boogie' and 'Nut Rocker'. Freeman also

co-wrote, 'Percolator (Twist)', a hit for Billy Joe & The Checkmates (1962). In the Seventies, Freeman was the musical director at Reprise Records. In 1988 Rhino released the Freeman compilation disc, *Greatest Hits*.
CAUSE: Heart attack. He died in Hollywood, California.

Derek J. Frigo

Born July 26, 1966
Died May 28, 2004
The lead guitarist of the Eighties metal band Enuff Z'Nuff, Derek J. Frigo was the son of actress Brittney Browne and violinist Johnny Frigo. Intending to go to medical school, Frigo instead pursued a career in music. After recording a 1985 solo album *LeMans*, he joined the Chicago-based glam rock band Enuff Z'Nuff in 1988, headed by Donnie Vie and Chip Znuff, and their 1989 self-titled début album included the AOR radio hits, 'New Thing' and 'Fly High Michelle'. After leaving the group in 1992, Frigo relocated to Los Angeles, working with a series of local bands. Several months before his death, he reunited with Enuff Z'Nuff and began recording an album.
CAUSE: Overdose. He was found dead outside his girlfriend's home in Beverly Hills.

Joe Fritz

Born November 3, 1924
Died June 1983
Nicknamed "Papoose", Texas-based singer/saxophonist Joe Fritz landed a Top 10 R&B hit in 1950 with 'I Love You My Darlin''.
CAUSE: Unknown. He died in Houston.

Yafeu Fula

Born October 9, 1977
Died November 10, 1996
Nicknamed Kadafi, rapper Yafeu Fula is best known for his association with Tupac Shakur. As a member of Shakur's back-up group Outlaw Immortalz, he appeared on the massive-selling gangsta-rap albums, *Me Against The World* and *All Eyez On Me*. In 1994, Outlaw Immortalz evolved into Dramacydal.
CAUSE: He was shot in the head during a drug altercation while visiting a friend at a housing project in Orange, New Jersey. Discovered by police at 3 a.m., he died the following afternoon at University Hospital in Newark. He was murdered by two juveniles, a crime that investigators insist was not related to Shakur's murder two months earlier. Fula had been sitting in a car behind Shakur who was shot on the Las Vegas strip. Although the thoroughfare was packed with cars and pedestrians, Fula was the only individual who claimed that he saw the gunmen. After hiring a lawyer, Fula became uncooperative and refused to meet with investigators.

Bobby Fuller

(ROBERT GASTON FULLER)
Born October 22, 1943
Died July 18, 1966
Leader of the Sixties garage rock band The Bobby Fuller Four, Texas-born Bobby Fuller built a rudimentary recording studio in the basement of his parents' house while in his teens. After studying music at North Texas University in 1960, Fuller returned to his home in El Paso where he joined a series of rock groups. Releasing a number of singles, including several on his own Eastwood and Exeter labels, Fuller emerged as a local star, landing airplay with singles such as 'King Of The Beach'. Joined by his brother Randy Fuller, Jim Reese, and Dewayne Bryant (Querico), Bobby Fuller relocated his new group to Los Angeles. After performing under several names including Bobby Fuller and The Cavemen and Bobby Fuller and The Fanatics, the group settled on The Bobby Fuller Four. In 1965, the group performed a pair of songs in the surf film *Ghost In The Invisible Bikini*; on the set, Phil Spector unsuccessfully

tried to sign the group to his Philles label. The Bobby Fuller Four would instead sign with Bob Keene, owner of Donna and Del-Phi Records (of Ritchie Valens fame). Keene first recorded Fuller's group on the Donna imprint, before placing them on his new Mustang subsidiary for which they recorded their seminal version of 'I Fought The Law', written by Sonny Curtis of Buddy Holly's Crickets. It reached number nine in the US singles charts in 1966 and became a garage rock classic, subsequently recorded by hundreds of acts including The Clash, Johnny Rodriguez and The Stray Cats. The Bobby Fuller Four returned to the Top 10 with a Buddy Holly composition, 'Love's Made A Fool Of You'. Following a disagreement with Keene over the selection of future singles, Fuller quit the group in June 1966. Fuller intended to pursue a solo career but died a month later.
CAUSE: He died from asphyxiation under mysterious circumstances. According to witnesses, Fuller's body was found in his car in the parking garage of his Hollywood apartment, beaten, bruised, and smelling of gasoline. But a coroner's report disputed the eye witnesses, and claimed that there were no bruises on the body. Though Keene pushed for an investigation, no arrests were ever made. Rumours that Fuller was having an affair with the wife of a Mafia gangster support the murder theory. It was later revealed that murder attempts were made on two members of Fuller's backing group.

Jesse "Lone Cat" Fuller

Born March 12, 1896
Died January 29, 1976
Folk-blues singer and multi-instrumentalist, Georgia-born Jesse "Lone Cat" Fuller is best known for his 1954 composition 'San Francisco Bay Blues'. Playing a 12-string guitar, he incorporated various folk, jug and gospel influences into his music. A jack of all trades, Fuller considered music a sideline as he shined shoes, operated a hot dog stand, and even landed film roles alongside Douglas Fairbanks. At age 55, Fuller became a full-time musician, benefiting from the blues revival of the late Sixties.
CAUSE: Natural causes. He died in Oakland, California.

Lowell Fulson

Born March 31, 1921
Died March 6, 1999
A polished West-Coast bluesman, Lowell Fulson enjoyed a string of hits beginning in the Forties. Born on a Choctaw Indian reservation in Oklahoma (his grandfather was a member of the tribe), Fulson was reared on gospel and country & western music. After passing through a white, western swing outfit, The Dan Wright String Band, Fulson veered toward the blues, in 1939 replacing Chester Burnette (a.k.a. Howlin' Wolf) in harmonica-player Texas Alexander's Gainesville, Texas-based blues band. Leaving the group on his draft into the US Navy in 1943, Fulson formed a band while serving in Guam; relocated to a base in Oakland, California, he decided to remain in the warm climes of California. Recording for a series of labels under the tutelage of producer/label owner Bob Geddins, Fulson was backed by brother Martin Fulson on guitar on his début hit in 1948, 'Three O'Clock Blues' (the song later reprised by B.B. King). Joined by Lloyd Glenn and switching to Swingtime Records, Fulson scored a major hit with a reworking of Memphis Slim's 'Nobody Loves Me' as 'Everyday I Have The Blues' (1950); a follow-up single 'Blue Shadow' topped the R&B charts. During this time, Fulson had hired a young Ray Charles as both an opening act and member of his group. Landing at Chess-Checker Records in 1954,

Fulson recorded 'Reconsider Baby', a song later immortalised by Elvis Presley. Leaving Checker in 1962, he landed at the Modern/RPM subsidiary Kent Records as Lowell "Fulsom"; here he enjoyed a comeback with the soulful 'Black Night' (1965) and 'Tramp' (1966). Written by Fulson and Jimmy McCracken, 'Tramp' would be surpassed on the charts in a duet by Otis Redding and Carla Thomas. Primarily touring through Europe later in his career, Fulson recorded sporadically. His 1995 album *Them Update Blues* was nominated for a Grammy.
CAUSE: Suffering from kidney disease and diabetes, he succumbed to congestive heart failure. Also displaying early signs of Alzheimer's disease, he had been hospitalised for six weeks. A resident of Los Angeles, he died at Pacific Hospital in Long Beach, California.

Johnny Funches

Born July 13, 1935
Died January 23, 1998
The original lead singer of the perennial vocal group The Dells, Johnny Funches was raised by foster parents in suburban Chicago. Forming a vocal group at Thorton Township High School in 1953 called The El Rays, Funches and the group recorded a sole single at Checker Records. Evolving into The Dells by 1955, they signed with Vee-Jay Records. With Funches providing the lead vocals, the group scored regional doo-wop styled hits with 'Dreams Of Contentment' (1956), 'Pain In My Heart' (1957), and 'Dry Your Eyes' (1959). But their biggest hit during this period came with the Funches co-written, romantic ballad, 'Oh What A Nite' (1956). Involved in a serious car crash in 1958, The Dells disbanded for a time. Leaving the group in 1959, Funches found work in a steel mill. When The Dells regrouped in 1961, former Flamingos member Marvin Junior assumed lead vocal duties. The Dells returned to the charts with a newly recorded version of 'Oh, What A Night' in 1969. The film *The Five Heartbeats*, was loosely based on The Dells.
CAUSE: Emphysema.

Billy Fury

(RONALD WYCHERLY)
Born April 17, 1941
Died January 28, 1983
British pop and rock star once considered a contender for the title the "British Elvis", Billy Fury was born in the Dingle section of Liverpool, England. Sickly as a child, he worked as a ferry boat hand in the mid Fifties. A songwriter by hobby, Fury boldly confronted singer Marty Wilde in 1958, hoping to sell him a pair of compositions. By impressing Wilde's manager, Larry Parnes, Fury instead earned an audition as Wilde's opening act. Signed by Decca Records and renamed Billy Fury, the former Ronald Wycherly possessed a slight, vulnerable voice and a rocker's sneer. Touring heavily, Fury first landed on the British charts with his début single 'Maybe Tomorrow' (1959). In early 1960, Fury shared the bill on the 10-week tour that ended in tragedy for the headlining US rockabilly star Eddie Cochran. After Decca released an album of Fury singing original rockabilly tracks, *The Sound Of Fury* (1960), the label decided to take him in a ballad and pop cover direction. In 1961, Fury began to suffer heart problems which resulted in a number of cancelled performances (he would suffer three heart attacks). Though unknown in the US, Fury enjoyed a long string of British hits including 'Colette' (1960), a Tony Orlando cover (and Goffin-King composition), 'Halfway To Paradise' (1961), 'Jealousy' (1961), 'Like I've Never Been Gone' (1963), 'When Will You Say I Love You' (1963), 'In Summer' (1963), a cover Conway Twitty's 'It's

Only Make Believe' (1964), and 'In Thoughts Of You' (1965). Landing his own television show in 1964, Fury also starred in a pair of films, *Play It Cool* (1962) and *I Gotta Horse* (1965). After scoring his final hit in 1966 with a cover of Tennessee Ernie Ford's 'Give Me Your Word', Fury was dropped by Decca Records. Though continuing to record a string of unsuccessful singles for Parlophone Records, Fury was forced to retire from touring due to declining health. In 1973 he landed a small role in the David Essex film *That'll Be The Day* as a cameo of his younger self, an aspiring, fictional rock singer named Stormy Tempest, and sang a composition written by Pete Townshend, 'Long Live Rock', which was later a minor hit for The Who. After declaring bankruptcy in the mid Seventies, Fury retired to a farm in Wales where he followed his favourite hobby, ornithology. The album *The Only One* was posthumously released. CAUSE: Heart failure. He was found at his home by his housekeeper; he died at St. Mary's Hospital in London.

G

Milt Gabler

(MILTON GABLER)
Born May 20, 1911
Died July 20, 2001
Best known as the producer who oversaw musical pioneers Louis Jordan and Bill Haley, Milt Gabler's six-decade-long career in the recording industry played a significant role in the rise of bebop jazz, R&B and rock'n'roll. Remarkably, Gabler could neither read music nor play an instrument. Working at his father's radio shop in the late Twenties, he began stocking jazz records after pedestrians began requesting the songs heard over the store's pavement speaker. Promoted to store manager in 1931, Gabler built the renamed Commodore Record Shop into the city's top jazz outlet. Unable to fill requests for out-of-print jazz records, Gabler began leasing the masters from record companies and started the first reissue record label, Commodore Records. However, when the labels began reissuing their own material, Gabler was forced to cut his own records, including Billie Holiday's stunning protest song, 'Strange Fruit'. Gabler kept Commodore active until 1954, recording Ben Webster, Roy Eldridge, Eddie Condon and Sidney Bechet. Hired by Decca Records in 1941, he worked with the label's top crooners including Guy Lombardo and Bing Crosby, jazz acts Ella Fitzgerald, Woody Herman and Lionel Hampton, and vocal harmony groups The Mills Brothers and The Ink Spots but his most enduring Decca assignment was with ground-breaking proto-R&B bandleader Louis Jordan. Beginning in 1942 with 'I'm Gonna Leave You At The Outskirts Of Town', Gabler produced Jordan's revolutionary crossover hits, including 'Five Guys Named Moe', 'Caladonia', and the Gabler co-composed, 'Choo Choo Ch'Boogie' (1946). Appointed the head of Decca's A&R department, Gabler also oversaw Decca's newly created Coral division and a second subsidiary, Brunswick. Soon after Decca announced in 1953 that it was dropping Jordan, Gabler signed Jordan's stylistic successors, Bill Haley & The Comets. Updating the formula used in dozens of Jordan's hits, Gabler produced Haley's cover version of Big Joe Turner's R&B stomper, 'Shake, Rattle And Roll', and shaped Haley's revolutionary single, 'Rock Around The Clock'. Recorded in just two takes at the cavernous Pythian Temple Studio in Manhattan, Gabler overdubbed one take directly over the other. Released in 1954, the single was only a moderate hit; but the following year, Gabler sold the rights to the song for one-dollar to MGM, which featured the guitar-and-sax anthem over the opening credits of the controversial film, *The Blackboard Jungle*. A smash hit, the reissued single became the first number one single of the rock era. Meanwhile, the Commodore Record Shop continued apace, selling a remarkable 100,000 jazz records in 1950 alone, before closing eight years later. As Decca's vice-president in the Sixties, Gabler produced artists such as Brenda Lee, but was let go in 1971 when the company's new owners, MCA, wanted to employ a more youthful approach. Gabler was inducted into the Rock and Roll Hall of Fame in 1993, in the non-performers category.
CAUSE: Natural causes. He died in New York City.

Cassie Gaines

Born January 9, 1948
Died October 20, 1977
Backing vocalist of the legendary southern-rock group, Lynyrd Skynyrd, Oklahoma-born Cassie Gaines was

hired as part of a female vocal trio that also featured Leslie Hawkins and Jo Jo Billingsley. Gaines appeared on three of the group's albums, beginning with *Gimme Back My Bullets* in 1976. With the departure of guitarist Ed King, Cassie's brother Steve Gaines, who also died in the plane crash (see below), was added to the group. Cassie and Steve Gaines both appeared on the 1977 album *Street Survivors*, which was released just days before their tragic deaths.
CAUSE: The group was en route from Greenville, South Carolina, to Baton Rouge, Louisiana, when their private aeroplane ran out of gas and was forced to crash land near McComb, Mississippi. Cassie Gaines bled to death as rescuers were unable to drive or fly into the marshy, wooded site. As well as her brother Steve, the crash also claimed the lives of Lynyrd Skynyrd singer Ronnie Van Zandt, the group's roadie, Dean Kilpatrick, and both pilots.

Steve Gaines

Born September 14, 1949
Died October 20, 1977
Born in Seneca, Missouri, Steve Gaines joined Southern-rock band Lynyrd Skynyrd as their third guitarist after the departure of Ed King in 1976. Gaines' sister, Cassie Gaines, had joined the group earlier in the year as part of a female backing trio. Influenced by Sixties soul music, Gaines became a songwriting partner in group, teamed with Ronnie Van Zant and Allen Collins. He first appeared on the double-live album, *One More For The Road* (1976), which was recorded in Atlanta. He also appeared on the Lynyrd Skynyrd studio album *Street Survivors*, which was released just days before the plane crash that claimed his life.
CAUSE: Steve Gaines died in the plane crash (see above) which also killed his sister Cassie, Ronnie Van Zant, Dean Kilpatrick and two pilots. The craft had run out of gas and crashed into a wooded marsh. The group's album *Street Survivor* was recalled because of its cover art which featured Steve Gaines' eyes closed and his hair on fire.

Serge Gainsbourg

(LUCIEN GINSBURG)
Born April 2, 1928
Died March 2, 1991
French painter turned pop-singer whose outrageous behaviour made him a sensation, Serge Gainsbourg was trained in classical piano by his Jewish-Russian father. Identified by his characteristically scruffy beard and dishevelled clothing, Gainsbourg was infamous for heavy womanising, drinking and smoking. Often controversial, Gainsbourg enjoyed a hit single with the erotic, 'Je T'aime (Moi Non Plus)', which he recorded with his then wife, the British actress Jane Birkin. (The original, equally erotic, version of the song was recorded with Brigette Bardot but this was withdrawn at the last minute at Bardot's request.) Also an actor, Gainsbourg appeared in 22 films, and directed four others.
CAUSE: Heart attack. He died at his apartment in Paris.

Tommy Gaither

Born 1930
Died November 5, 1950
Backing vocalist and guitarist in the pioneering R&B group The Orioles, Tommy Gaither joined the group in 1947. Meeting at a Baltimore talent show, Gaither and three other contestants teamed with the night's winner, Sonny Til, to form a group called The Vibranairs. Playing a slightly oversized guitar, Gaither sported a thin moustache, and cheery demeanour. The group was discovered at a tiny nightclub by songwriter Deborah Chessler who became their manager. After months of rehearsals, Chessler got the group a spot on Arthur Godrey's Talent Scout programme in 1948. Losing to George

Shearer but impressing Godrey, the group was asked to perform on his more popular daytime show. Here they met record distributor Jerry Blain, who renamed the group after the Maryland state bird, The Orioles. A harmony based group, The Orioles landed a rare crossover hit with the Chessler composition, 'It's Too Soon To Know', the single released on Blain's New York-based It's A Natural label. Featuring the stunning, elegant lead of tenor Sonny Til, The Orioles were instrumental in the launch of a new doo-wop genre. Gaither's hits with The Orioles continued on Blaine's renamed Jubilee label which include '(It's Gonna Be A) Lonely Christmas' (1948), 'Forgive And Forget' (1949), and 'What Are You Doing New Year's Eve'.
CAUSE: Returning from a concert in Massachusetts, one of the group's two cars crashed just outside Baltimore. The car was struck when Gaither had fallen asleep at the wheel. Riding in the same car as Gaither, Johnny Reed and George Nelson were both hurt. Sonny Til and Alexander Sharp were riding in a second car. As a result of the crash, the group lost its enthusiasm for touring outside of their home region. As a result, their popularity was curtailed from lack of exposure. For about two months, neither Nelson nor Reed appeared at the group's concerts. Eventually Ralph Williams joined as the group's guitarist. The group's next release 'I Miss You So', was dedicated to Gaither, with the royalties going to his family.

Eric Gale

Born September 20, 1939
Died May 25, 1994
Self-taught guitar player, Brooklyn-born Eric Gale began his career in a pair of Sixties R&B groups, King Curtis and Little Anthony & The Imperials. Having pursued a degree in chemistry at Niagara University, Gale quit school for a career in music. As a session player, he worked with Jimi Hendrix, Marvin Gaye and Grover Washington, Jr. Later based in Los Angeles, Gale formed the influential R&B group, Stuff, in 1976. Eric Gale and Stuff appeared in Paul Simon's 1982 film *One Trick Pony.*
CAUSE: Lung cancer. He died in a Mexican hospital.

Danny Galindo

(DANIEL RAYMOND GALINDO)
Born June 29, 1949
Died May 17, 2001
The bass player for the 13th Floor Elevators, Danny Galindo was born in San Antonio, Texas, joining his brother, Robert, in a series of local bands in Austin. In 1967, he joined the Elevators, headed by the crazed Roky Erickson, as replacement for Ronnie Leatherman, and appeared on the psychedelic outfit's second album, *Easter Everywhere.* Although the ground-breaking group was a critical favourite, few radio stations dared play their records due to the overt drug connotations; the band being proselytisers for LSD. The band drifted after Erickson tried to get round a drug charge in 1968 by pleading insanity and subsequently spending nearly four years in a mental institution. After their record label issued two piecemeal albums in the late Sixties, the group disbanded. Galindo later joined a series of Texas based bands, including Storm which featured guitarist Jimmie Vaughan.
CAUSE: Suffering from Hepatitis C, he succumbed to liver failure. He died in San Antonio, Texas.

Rory Gallagher

Born March 2, 1948
Died June 14, 1995
The respected Irish-born blues guitarist and singer, Rory Gallagher was raised on American blues and the folk-pop of Lonnie Donegan. First picking up a guitar at age six, he joined a popular Irish showband, The

Fontana, at age 15. Bored by playing cover material in a band uniform, Gallagher formed the blues-rock trio Taste, which made waves after moving to London in 1968. Recording for Polydor Records, Gallagher disbanded the group after its 1970 chart album, *On The Boards*. Playing a battered Fender Stratocaster, Gallagher earned a reputation as a top-notch blues guitarist, his prowess showcased on several solo albums in the Seventies, including his biggest seller, *Live In Europe* (1972). Also a popular session man, he joined Muddy Waters in 1972 on the album, *London Sessions*. A quiet, rather shy man, Gallagher suffered from stagefright for most of his life. Almost always dressed in check shirts and faded denims, Gallagher eschewed the star factory, preferring to live modestly and work in small clubs. Although he faded from the music scene in the Eighties, he attempted a comeback in 1990 with the album *Fresh Evidence*. At the time he was reported to be drinking heavily.
CAUSE: Receiving a liver transplant in April 1995, he died from a chest infection six weeks later at King's College Hospital in London.

Cliff Gallup

(CLIFTON ELWOOD GALLUP)
Born June 17, 1930
Died October 9, 1988
Guitarist for Gene Vincent and The Blue Caps in 1956, Cliff Gallup provided the stark, haunting performances on the hits 'Race With The Devil', 'Be-Bop-A-Lula' and 'Bluejean Bop'. A much revered player, he influenced an entire generation of rock-styled guitarists. In all Gallup recorded 31 tracks with Vincent during a seven month period. Disliking the rigours of touring, Gallup left the band and was replaced by Johnny Meeks. Returning home to Norfolk, Virginia, Gallup performed locally for the next three decades, and also frequently worked as a session player for local gospel acts. In 1993, Jeff Beck and The Big Town Playboys recorded a tribute album to Gallup, *Crazy Legs*.
CAUSE: He died of a heart attack in Norfolk, Virginia. He had suffered chest pains while playing at a private party at the Norfolk Yacht & Country Club in nearby Virginia Beach. After returning home, he went into cardiac arrest and was rushed to the hospital.

Margie Ganser

(MARGUERITE GANSER DORSTE)
Born February 4, 1948
Died July 28, 1996
A member of the Sixties girl-group The Shangri-Las along with her twin sister Mary Ann, Margie Ganser was born in Oceanside, Long Island, but raised in Queens, New York. Attending Andrew Jackson High School in Queens, New York, the Ganser twins formed the group with another pair of sisters, Betty (Liz) and Mary Weiss. Margie was the most mature and confident of the group. With all four members growing up in the tough Queens neighbourhood of Cambra Heights, their streetwise attitude would be manifested in their musical output. Discovered by songwriter/producer George "Shadow" Morton, the group passed through several labels before signing with Leiber and Stoller's Red Bird label; the label sported several other girl groups on their roster, including The Dixie Cups and The Jelly Beans. A much shortened version of a lengthy Morton composition, 'Remember (Walkin' In The Sand)' (1965) with eerie, ethereal vocals and ocean sounds, became The Shangri-Las' first hit. They followed up with the definitive teen death classic, 'Leader Of The Pack', a song about an innocent teenage girl's romance with a motorcycle-riding hoodlum, and his subsequent death in a bike crash. Other Shangri-Las hits included 'Give Him A Great Big Kiss' (1965), another death-rock themed song, 'Give Us Your Blessings' (1965), 'I Can Never

Go Home Anymore' (1965), and 'Long Live Our Love' (1966). Projecting both innocence and sensuality, the group members dressed in leather or other skin-tight clothing, wore high boots, and were photographed in provocative poses. While there were four women in the group, most often only three (the Ganser twins and Mary Weiss) would tour at a time. (Recruited by Morton, drummer Joseph Alexander would briefly join the group.) Leaving Red Bird for Mercury Records in 1966, the group faded from the charts. With lawsuits raging between their past record companies, The Shangri-Las disbanded in 1968. Marguerite Ganser then returned to her schooling, earning a high school diploma. She married Bill Dorste in 1972, becoming Margie Ganser Dorste. There were false reports of Ganser's death in 1972. The surviving members of The Shangri-Las regrouped in 1977 and recorded a number of unreleased tracks for Sire Records. The trio would perform in public only twice more – at CBGB's in 1977 and at a Palisades Park tribute concert at the Meadowlands Arena in 1989. Ganser later worked for the Nynex corporation.
CAUSE: Breast cancer. She died at Calvary Hospital in New York City.

Mary Ann Ganser

Born February 4, 1948
Died March 14, 1970
A member of the Sixties girl-group The Shangri-Las along with her twin sister Margie (see above), Mary Ann Ganser was born in Oceanside, Long Island, but raised in Queens, New York. Attending Andrew Jackson High School in Queens, New York, the Ganser twins formed the group with another pair of sisters, Betty (Liz) and Mary Weiss. With all four members growing up in the tough Queens neighbourhood of Cambra Heights, their streetwise attitude would be manifested in their musical output. Discovered by songwriter/producer George "Shadow" Morton, the group passed through several labels before signing with Leiber and Stoller's Red Bird label. (Still legally bound to Kama Sutra Records, the group would later be targeted in a lawsuit.) Recording a much shortened version of a lengthy Morton composition, 'Remember (Walkin' In The Sand)' (1965), they followed up with the definitive teen-death classic, 'Leader Of The Pack'. (A group called The Detergents would later score a hit with a spoof of 'Leader Of The Pack' called 'Leader Of The Laundromat'.) Other Shangri-Las hits include 'Give Him A Great Big Kiss' (1965), another necra-rock themed song, 'Give Us Your Blessings' (1965), 'I Can Never Go Home Anymore' (1965), and 'Long Live Our Love' (1966). Projecting both innocence and sensuality, the group members dressed in leather or other skin-tight clothing, wore high boots, and were photographed in provocative poses. While there were four women in the group, most often, only three (the Ganser twins and Mary Weiss) would tour at a time. Leaving Red Bird for Mercury Records in 1966, the group faded from the charts. With lawsuits raging between their past record companies, The Shangri-Las disbanded in 1968.
CAUSE: Encephalitis. Many sources incorrectly cite a drug overdose as the cause of death.

Cecil Gant

Born April 4, 1913
Died February 4, 1951
Nashville-born boogie-woogie pianist and singer, Cecil Gant was nicknamed the G.I. Singsation. Gant made musical history when in 1945 his single 'I Wonder' became one of the first R&B hits to cross over to the pop charts. Later recording for a series of labels including King and Decca, Gant was unable to match his early success.

CAUSE: He died in an automobile crash in Memphis.

Rick Garberson

Born November 15, 1950
Died July 15, 1979
Drummer with the early new-wave group, The Bizarros, Rick Garberson emerged from a musical scene in the Akron-Kent, Ohio-area that produced Tin Huey, The Waitresses and Devo. The Bizarros released a self-titled album on Mercury Records in 1979.
CAUSE: Suicide by carbon-monoxide poisoning.

Frankie "Cannibal" Garcia

(FRANCISCO M. GARCIA)
Born April 22, 1946
Died January 21, 1996
Founder and leader of the Sixties Los Angeles-based rock group Cannibal and The Headhunters, Frankie "Cannibal" Garcia formed the group in 1965. The Mexican-American group scored its only hit with the frat-rock standard, 'Land Of A 1,000 Dances' (1965). Wilson Pickett landed a bigger hit with his rendition of the song in 1966. With the group disbanding in early 1967, Garcia attended college for a year. Returning to music, he ventured out as a solo act before fronting a local trio. In 1979, Garcia recorded an obscure disco remake of 'Land Of A 1,000 Dances'.
CAUSE: Suffering from an undisclosed long-term illness, he died in Los Angeles.

Jerry Garcia

(JEROME JOHN GARCIA)
Born August 1, 1942
Died August 9, 1995
As the central figure of the pioneering hippie band The Grateful Dead, guitarist and songwriter Jerry Garcia became a much loved American cultural icon. Born in the San Francisco Bay area, Garcia was the son of a Spanish immigrant father who was a former big band musician turned bar owner. Raised by his maternal grandparents (who exposed him to the Grand Ole Opry), he later lived with his mother. Given an accordion for his 15th birthday, Garcia exchanged it for an electric guitar. Enlisting in the army at 17, Garcia was court-martialled a year later for going AWOL. Switching his attention from rock to folk music and buying a banjo, he settled in Palo Alto, California, where he would become friends with future Grateful Dead lyricist Robert Hunter. There Garcia would briefly form a folk group with Ron "Pigpen" McKernan called The Zodiacs. Teaming in 1964 with McKernan, Bob Weir and others, Garcia formed a jug band, Mother McCree's Uptown Jug Champions. After finding their acoustic folk material attracted little interest, the group went electric in early 1965. Renamed The Warlocks and adding new members, they settled into a commune in a large house in the Haight-Ashbury section of San Francisco. Renamed The Grateful Dead by Garcia in late 1965, the group performed on the same bill as Jefferson Airplane and The Mothers Of Invention at the opening night of Bill Graham's Fillmore Auditorium. At the forefront of the emerging Sixties drug culture, The Grateful Dead also served as the house band for Ken Kesey and his Merry Pranksters public "acid test" parties, with Garcia nicknamed Captain Trips. As San Francisco became the epicentre of youth culture, The Dead created a following with a series of free concerts in local public parks. Signing with Warner Brothers Records and releasing a self-titled début album in early 1967, the group garnered national attention after performing at the Monterey Pop Festival later in the year. Expanded with several new members, The Grateful Dead enjoyed chart success during this period with albums such as *Anthem Of The Sun*, *Aoxomoxoa* and, featuring their first radio hit,

'Truckin'', *American Beauty*. With the group's fame in decline in the mid Seventies, Garcia and other members pursued various independent ventures. Often employing several Grateful Dead members, Garcia dabbled in several side projects, beginning with a collaborative album with Howard Wales, *Hooteroll*, and continuing with solo albums such as *Garcia (The Wheel)* (1972), *Garcia (Compliments of Garcia)* (1974), and *Reflections* (1976). Regrouping in 1977, The Dead signed with Arista Records. Their popularity rekindled, they enjoyed a rare radio hit in 1980 with 'Alabama Getaway', culled from the album *Go To Heaven*. After decades of constant touring, The Dead had achieved cult status by the Eighties, spawning an entire subculture of loyal followers called Deadheads who followed the band from city to city in their tie-dyed tent communities. Usually outfitted in a black T-shirt, the bespectacled, grey-haired, slightly tubby and bushy-bearded Jerry Garcia remained as the group's focal leader but while touring with Tom Petty & The Heartbreakers and Bob Dylan in 1986, Garcia collapsed, his body wracked by years of drug abuse. In 1987, The Dead finally scored their first bona fide pop Top 10 hit with 'Touch Of Grey'. The accompanying video served to enforce Garcia's image as a benign father figure to the Dead and the hippie movement in general. Now an American institution, Garcia and The Dead toured regularly until Garcia's death, whereupon the group promptly disbanded. Always more popular as a live attraction than on (official) record, they encouraged fans to tape their shows, even going as far as to provide outlets to tapers from their own soundboard. As a result, scores of live tapes of the Dead's shows continue to circulate amongst fans. Garcia also launched a pair of commercial projects, a line of neckties and the Ben & Jerry's ice cream flavour, Cherry Garcia. After his death a star in the distant solar system was named in Garcia's honour.
CAUSE: A diabetic and long-term drug user who was in poor health for the last years of his life, Garcia was trying to kick a heroin habit. In and out of drug treatment centres in his last decade, he checked himself into the Marin County rehab centre and died two days later. The cause of death was attributed to a heart attack.
FURTHER READING: Greenfield, Robert. (1997). *Dark Star: An Oral Biography Of Jerry Garcia*. New York: Broadway.

Paul Gardiner

Born c. 1955
Died February 4, 1984
The founding bassist of Gary Numan's synthesizer-based band The Tubeway Army, Paul "Scarlett" Gardiner appeared on a number of hits including Numan's only US Top 40 effort, 'Cars'. With Numan disbanding his backing group in 1981, Gardiner attempted a solo career. Scoring a minor British hit with 'Storm Trooper In Drag', the single featured Numan as a guest musician. Shortly before his death, Gardiner recorded 'Venus In Furs', the first single on Numan's new label, Numa Records. Gardiner also worked with Robert Palmer.
CAUSE: Overdosing on heroin, he was found dead on a park bench.
FURTHER READING: Coleman, Ray. (1982). *Gary Numan: The Authorized Biography*. London: Sidgewick & Jackson.

Kim Gardner

Born January 27, 1948
Died October 24, 2001
A talented bassist who played with several British rock acts, Kim Gardner formed his first band, The Thunderbirds, eventually shortened to The Birds, in 1964 while attending art college. The group had a minor UK hit in 1965 with 'Leaving Here' but were most visible when their manager

arranged a publicity coup by serving the touring Byrds with a writ at London Airport over the name in August 1965. The Birds disbanded in 1967 and Gardner then joined another cult Sixties British group, The Creation, who were popular on the Continent. His old Birds' bandmate and neighbour from their Middlesex childhood, Ronnie Wood, joined briefly in 1968 but the group disbanded not long after. Gardner then joined with Wood, Rod Stewart (both fresh from the recently disbanded Jeff Beck Group), ex-Small Faces' Ian McLagan and Kenny Jones, as well as Ronnie's brother, Art Wood, in the pre-Faces group, Quiet Melon. Gardner then teamed with drummer Ron Dyke and pianist Tony Ashton to form Ashton, Gardner & Dyke; infusing jazz and blues into much of their material, the trio reached the UK Top 5 in 1971 with the blues-rock single 'The Resurrection Shuffle'. After recording three albums, the group disbanded in 1972. Subsequently, Gardner joined drummer Roy Dyke's progressive-rock band Badger, but shortly after recording the album *White Lady*, at the New Orleans studio of producer Allen Toussaint, the group disbanded. Gardner later operated an English pub restaurant in Hollywood called The Cat & Fiddle.
CAUSE: Cancer. He died in Los Angeles.

Ron Gardner

Born 1945
Died 1992
As a member of the Washington state surf-instrumental group The (Fabulous) Wailers, sax player and songwriter Ron Gardner joined the group as replacement for Mark Marush, a few years after their sole hit 'Tall Cool One'. Previously a member of a Tacoma-based group called The Bootmen, Gardner joined The Wailers in 1963 and left in 1969. Gardner later led a pair of Seattle rock bands, Sweet Rolle and The Ron Gardner Group, and in the early Seventies, he recorded a solo album for Blue Thumb Records.
CAUSE: He died in a fire.

Hank "Sugarfoot" Garland

(WALTER LOUIS GARLAND)
Born November 11, 1930
Died December 27, 2004
A legendary Fifties Memphis-based guitarist, Hank "Sugarfoot" Garland had a brief but prolific career. After performing on radio shows beginning at age 12, he was discovered aged 14 by bandleader Paul Howard of The Arkansas Cotton Pickers, and first worked as a session player and solo act at Decca Records in 1949. One of his releases, the self-composed 'Sugarfoot Rag', became a hit through a cover version by Red Foley; the song also gave Garland his nickname. By 1954, Garland and musician Billy Byrd had invented the short scale neck guitar named the Byrdland and manufactured by Gibson. Though unsuccessful as a recording artist, Garland quickly emerged as a leading Nashville session player and was part of a select group of top players nicknamed the A-Team. Garland performed on numerous rock and country hits, including 'Oh, Lonesome Me', 'Sea Of Heartbreak' (both Don Gibson), 'Gone' (Ferlin Husky), 'In The Jailhouse Now' (Webb Pierce), the Christmas standards 'Rockin' Around The Christmas Tree' (Brenda Lee) and 'Jingle Bell Rock' (Bobby Helms), as well as on tracks for The Everly Brothers, Roy Orbison, Marty Robbins, Conway Twitty, Hank Williams and Patsy Cline. Garland also worked with Elvis Presley beginning in 1956, appearing on hits such as 'Hound Dog', 'A Big Hunk O' Love', 'A Fool Such As I', 'Are You Lonesome Tonight?' and 'It's Now Or Never'. After appearing on 'Little Sister', Garland suffered serious injuries during a suspicious car crash in 1961 near Springfield, Tennessee. In a coma for months, he never recovered

from his injuries, and he spent much of his later years battling record companies over royalties. Garland was portrayed by actor Waylon Payne (godson of country star Waylon Jennings) in the much delayed 2006 biographical film, *Crazy*.
CAUSE: Staphylococcal infection. He died at Orange Park Medical Center in Orange Park, Florida.

Sherman Garnes

Born June 8, 1940
Died February 26, 1977
Bass vocalist of the Fifties New York City doo-wop group, Frankie Lymon & The Teenagers, Sherman Garnes met future bandmate Jimmy Merchant while in the 9th grade at Edward W. Stitt Junior High School. Merchant was interested in getting to know the tall basketball player because of his very low, bass voice. The pair formed a group called The Earth Angels, named after the hit by their favourite group, The Penguins. In 1954 Garnes convinced Merchant to join two nearby Puerto Ricans, Herman Santiago and Joe Negronie, to form a vocal harmony group. Initially reluctant, Merchant agreed to the group and The Coupe De Villes were born. After adding the young Frankie Lymon as a backing vocalist, the renamed Premiers/Ermines were discovered by former Valentines' lead singer turned producer Richard Barrett. Signed to George Goldner's Gee Records in late 1955, the group recorded their self-penned composition called 'Why Do Birds Sing So Gay?' At Barrett's suggestion, Frankie Lymon replaced Herman Santiago as lead singer. The group was renamed The Teenagers and their song title was changed to 'Why Do Fools Fall In Love?' A multi-million selling smash, the song catapulted the five teens to massive fame. Dropping out of school, Garnes and the rest of the group hit the road for a succession of tours. The Teenagers enjoyed a brief hit run with 'I Want You To Be My Girl' (1956), 'I Promise To Remember' (1956) and from the Alan Freed film *Rock Rock Rock*, 'I'm Not A Juvenile Delinquent' (1956). Though promised a trust fund by their record company, each member would receive only $1,000 each at age 21. With Lymon convinced to leave the group for a solo career, The Teenagers struggled along. Signing away all future rights to their music in exchange for the use of The Teenagers name, the group replaced Lymon with Bill Lobrano, recording their final single in 1960.
CAUSE: He died during heart surgery.

Ralph Garone

Born February 27, 1940
Died May 5, 1986
Baritone and second tenor of the vocal group, The Bob Knight Four, Ralph Garone had previously been a member of the Bobby Dells. Signing with Laurie Records, The Bob Knight Four frequently performed as session backing vocalists, before scoring their sole hit with the ballad, 'Good Goodbye' (1961). After the group disbanded in 1964, Garone worked in New York radio as an advertising representative.
CAUSE: Cancer. He died in New York City.

Danny Gatton

Born September 4, 1945
Died October 4, 1994
A popular Washington DC-born and based guitarist who was nicknamed "The World's Greatest Unknown Guitarist", Danny Gatton combined blues, rock and country to create a distinctive sound. Picking up the guitar at age nine after hearing a Les Paul record, Gatton joined his first band at 15 while in junior high. Forming his first serious group in 1975, Danny and The Fat Boys, Gatton recorded an obscure album for Aladdin Records. But after injuring his hands, he was forced to abandon his music career for a time. A prolific session player, he

turned down many offers to join high profile artists. Usually playing a Fender Telecaster, Gatton garnered much respect among fellow guitarists with the solo album *Unfinished Business* (1987), the project a combination of various styles. Signed by Elektra in 1991, Gatton recorded an all-instrumental, Grammy-nominated album *88 Elmira Street*, and– featuring the vocals of his saxophonist-keyboardist Bill Holloman – a Fifties-styled project, *Cruisin' Dueces*. Gatton also guested on Chris Isaak's 1993 album, *San Francisco Days* (1993).
CAUSE: Suicide by gunshot. He killed himself in a garage on his farm in Newburg, Maryland. His life was in turmoil at the time of his death; he had been dropped by Elektra Records and was suffering financial problems.

Marvin Gaye

(MARVIN PENTZ GAY, JR.)
Born April 2, 1939
Died April 1, 1984
An immensely popular soul singer, Marvin Gaye enjoyed a two decade long string of successes despite a lifetime of personal troubles. Born in Washington DC where he sang in the choir of an Apostolic church, Gaye was emotionally scarred by his overly strict, sometimes preacher father. A self-taught pianist, the introverted Gaye joined his high school friends in forming The DC Tones, and after quitting school in the mid Fifties he was enlisted in the US Airforce and honourably discharged. Returning to Washington, Gaye joined a doo-wop group, The Marquees, and recorded an obscure Bo Diddley-produced single. Then, in a fateful meeting following a shared bill at Washington's Howard Theater, Harvey Fuqua fired his backing Moonglows and hired Gaye and The Marquees as his replacement group. Relocating to Chicago, the newly billed Harvey and The Moonglows recorded for Chess, where Gaye provided his first lead vocal on a song he co-wrote with Fuqua, 'Mama Loocie'. With The Moonglows disbanding, Fuqua took Gaye to Detroit where he launched a pair of record labels on which Gaye was hired as a session man. When Fuqua sold his companies to Motown boss Berry Gordy Jr., Gaye was retained by Motown, initially as a session drummer. A quick learner, Gaye provided the drum parts on recordings for The Miracles and The Marvelettes, and was hired as touring drummer for The Miracles. With singer-songwriter Smokey Robinson encouraging Gaye to try writing songs, Gaye scored his first co-credit at the label with The Marvelettes' hit 'Beechwood 4-5789'. Pursuing a solo career, Gaye bombed with his débût album, *The Soulful Moods Of Marvin Gaye*, and thereafter abandoned his goal to become a "black Sinatra" and turned to soul for his first hit, 'Hitch Hike' (1963). By the end of 1963, Gaye had married Berry Gordy's sister Anna, who was 17 years his elder. Meanwhile, Gaye's hit run continued with 'Pride And Joy' (1963), 'I'll Be Doggone' and 'Ain't That Peculiar'. Gaye also enjoyed success with several duet hits, teaming with Mary Wells, Kim Weston, Diana Ross, and his confidante, Tammi Terrell. Gaye scored his biggest hit of the decade in 1968 with 'I Heard It Through The Grapevine', previously recorded by labelmates Gladys Knight & The Pips. Following the death of Tammi Terrell in 1970, Gaye became severely depressed and withdrew from his career. When he eventually returned to the studio he broke away from Motown's assembly-line tradition, releasing the self-produced, ideological album, *What's Going On*, an all-time classic release which features mature tracks such as 'What's Going On', 'Save The Children' and 'Mercy Mercy Me'. Recorded over a two-year period, Gaye's follow-up album *Let's Get It On* (1973) propagated Gaye's virile image with the sensuous title cut.

But after signing a new and lucrative contract with Motown, Gaye had limited success in the Seventies. Divorced from Anna Gordy, Gaye remarried in 1977 and titled his 1979 album *Here My Dear* because all profits went to his first wife. His personal life in chaos, Gaye was abusing cocaine, in trouble with the IRS, and constantly hounded by Motown for new material. Fleeing to Hawaii before settling in London in 1980, Gaye again entered the recording studio but when Motown prematurely issued Gaye's unfinished tracks on the album *In Our Lifetime*, an angry Gaye left the label. Signing with CBS Records in 1982, Gaye enjoyed a major comeback hit with the US chart-topping, Grammy-winning 'Sexual Healing', the track culled from the album of the same name produced by his old friend Harvey Fuqua. On the run from the IRS, Gaye subsequently spent time living in Belgium and his behaviour remained erratic for the rest of his life.
CAUSE: His father shot him to death after a verbal and physical altercation. After years of pent-up frustration, Marvin Gaye finally worked up the nerve to confront his father, Marvin Gay, Sr. (no "e"). Gaye was struck in the chest and died at California Hospital in Los Angeles. Gaye was murdered during an argument which began over a lost insurance form. His father shot Gaye twice in the chest with a handgun, once while he was standing and then again after he had collapsed on the floor. Gaye's mother, who was standing nearby, pleaded with her husband not to shoot her. Originally charged with murder, Gay was sentenced to five years probation on the reduced charges of voluntary manslaughter and was also prohibited from residing on the street where the shooting occurred. The elder Gay died in 1998 at the age of 84.
FURTHER READING: Ritz, David. (1995). *Divided Soul: The Life of Marvin Gaye*. London: Omnibus.

Billy Gayles

(WILLIE JAMES GAYLES)
Born October 19, 1931
Died April 8, 1993
St. Louis-based drummer, Billy Gayles was an on-and-off member of Ike Turner's backing band, The Kings Of Rhythm, from 1953–1963. He was usually utilised for his vocal rather than drumming skills. Providing some blistering, soulful lead vocals on several of Turner's singles, Gayles was credited as a solo act on his self-penned 'I'm Tore Up'. Leaving Turner to form his own band, Gayles remained a fixture on the St. Louis music scene. He also played drums behind several blues acts including Richard "Groove" Holmes and Albert King.
CAUSE: Inoperable cancer. Hospitalised for three months, he died in St. Louis.

Paul Gayten

Born January 20, 1920
Died March 27, 1991
New Orleans-based R&B pianist, Paul Gayten first recorded on DeLuxe Records in 1947. He enjoyed a brief string of hits beginning that year with 'Since I Fell For You' (1947), 'True' (1947), 'I'll Never Be Free' (1950), and backed by The Coleman Brothers, 'Goodnight Irene' (1950). Beginning in 1954, Gayten worked as a talent scout for the New Orleans branch of Chess Records, producing and supplying musical accompaniment for acts such as Bobby Charles and Clarence "Frogman" Henry. Assigned to the new Los Angeles branch of Chess in 1960, he remained with the label until its sale in 1969. Gayten then launched his own short-lived label, Pzazz Records. Also a songwriter, Gayten's best known song is 'For You, My Love', a hit for both Larry Darnell and The Nat King Cole Trio. Gayten's uncle is pianist Little Brother Montgomery.

CAUSE: Bleeding ulcer. He died in Los Angeles.

Pete Geddes

(PETER W. GEDDES)
Born April 28, 1956
Died June 29, 2004
The bassist of popular touring ensemble The Southern Rock All-stars, Pete Geddes backed a core of Southern rock veterans including Dave Hlubek of Molly Hatchet, Jakson Spires of Blackfoot, Jay Johnson of The Rossington Band and Charles Hart of Radio Tokyo. Performing material by their respective bands and cover versions by other acts in the genre including Lynyrd Skynyrd and The Allman Brothers, The Southern Rock All-stars were unable to garner airplay with their original material.
CAUSE: Suicide.

Bob Geddins

Born February 6, 1913
Died February 16, 1991
A pioneering black entrepreneur, Bob Geddins launched a series of record labels beginning in the mid Forties including Big Town, Cava-Tone, Downtown, and Irma. A native of Texas, Geddins was a crucial figure in the development of West Coast blues and R&B. Setting up a recording studio in his living room in Oakland, he often leased his bigger hits to major labels (which frequently resulted in his losing the acts). Geddins worked with pioneering acts such as Lowell Fulson, Jimmy McCracklin, Sugar Pie Desanto, Johnny Fuller, and 17-year-old Etta James. Also a songwriter, Geddins penned 'Hello San Francisco', 'Haunted House', 'My Time After A While', 'Last Letter' (Johnny Ace) and 'Mercury Boogie'. Disillusioned by the economics of the record industry, he left to operate a radio and television repair business from his home.
CAUSE: Liver cancer. He died in Oakland.

Lowell George

(LOWELL GEORGE JR.)
Born April 13, 1945
Died June 29, 1979
A widely admired slide guitar player and founding member of the rock group Little Feat, Lowell George was also an alumni of several other groups. Born in Hollywood, California, the son of a furrier, George was raised in a privileged environment (his next-door neighbour was actor Errol Flynn). Studying the flute, at the age of six George performed on The Ted Mack Amateur Hour. Attracted to the guitar at age 11, George borrowed his brother's instrument. Emerging as a talented guitarist while attending college, in 1965 George formed a Byrds' cover group called Factory (Of Man), joined by future Little Feat member Fred Martin and future CSN&Y drummer Dallas Taylor. Though aided by the production skills of Frank Zappa, the group floundered. After briefly returning to college, George passed through a pair of one-hit wonder garage-rock bands, The Standells and The Seeds, both of whom were in their waning days. George subsequently joined Frank Zappa's Mothers Of Invention as the replacement for singer Ray Collins. A better guitarist than vocalist, George displayed his talent on the Zappa albums *Hot Rats* (1969) and *Weasels Ripped My Flesh* (1970). During this time George honed his songwriting skills, composing 'Willin'', which was recorded by Linda Ronstadt, and 'Truck Stop Girl' which was included on The Byrds' *Untitled* album. Leaving The Mothers in late 1969, George joined Fraternity Of Man, appearing on the group's second album, *Get It On* (1969). Then, at the urging of Zappa, George formed his own group in early 1970. From the Mothers, George recruited bassist Roy Estrada, and from The Fraternity of Man, Bill Payne and Richie Hayward, to form the first line-up of Little Feat. Signing with Warner Brothers Records, the group

was a huge critical success, often considered a country-rock or folk-rock extension of Zappa. Beginning with *Little Feat* (1971), Lowell George supplied the rhythm guitar on eight of the group's albums. Uncomfortable as the group's leader, George preferred to take a democratic approach to decisions. After Little Feat briefly disbanded in late 1973, George worked as a session player. Reforming in 1974, Little Feat enjoyed a radio hit with the funky George co-penned 'Rock And Roll Doctor' from the album *Feats Don't Fail Me Now*. In late 1975, during the recording of the album *The Last Record Album*, George was stricken with hepatitis. After recording three more albums, none of them big sellers despite the rave reviews they earned, and touring extensively in America and Europe, the group disbanded in 1979. By this time their reputation as a hot and funky stage act was without peer but they were unable to translate their prowess and popularity on the concert circuit into record sales. Pursuing a solo career after Little's Feat dissolution, George was unhappy by Warner Brothers' decision to release his horn-heavy, mostly cover-version album *Thanks, I'll Eat It Here*. Besides producing most of his group's albums, George was also a prolific session player, working with Jackson Browne, John Cale, The Grateful Dead, Robert Palmer, Bonnie Raitt and others.
CAUSE: Overweight and unable to conquer various drug problems, he died from a heroin-induced heart attack in an Arlington, Virginia, motel room during the middle of his first solo tour. The night before, he performed at nearby George Washington University. A few years later, John Belushi expressed interest in playing the part of George in a planned film biography.

Samuel George

Born October 1, 1942
Died March 17, 1982
Lead singer and drummer of the Detroit-based R&B trio The Capitols, Samuel George signed with the Ollie McLaughlin-operated Karen label in 1963. Bombing with their début release, 'Dog And Cat' (1963), the group almost faded into obscurity. But with an expanded line-up, The Capitols belatedly returned for a second Karen single in 1966, scoring an upbeat, funky, danceable hit with 'Cool Jerk' (1966). After following with a trio of minor, follow-up R&B chart hits with 'I've Got To Handle It' (1966), 'We Got A Thing That's In The Groove' (1966), and 'Soul Brother, Soul Sister' (1969), the group disbanded in 1969.
CAUSE: He was stabbed to death during a domestic argument in Detroit.

Andy Gibb

(ANDREW ROY GIBB)
Born March 5, 1958
Died March 10, 1988
A popular teen idol in the late Seventies, Andy Gibb was the youngest brother of Bee Gee brothers Maurice, Robin and Barry Gibb. Born in Lancashire, England, but moving to Australia with his family at the age of six months and thereafter to Ibiza in 1973 and the Isle Of Man the following year, Gibb was reared on his parents' big band and vocal-group record collection. In Ibiza at the age of 13, Gibb began performing in a number of local Spanish rock groups before starting his own band. When he started to compose his own material, the younger Gibb was encouraged by brother Barry to return to Australia to try to break into the music business. Performing in nightclubs and releasing a single in 1975, Andy Gibb initially met with little interest. But with Barry convincing Bee Gees' manager Robert Stigwood to listen to his brother's demos, 19-year-old Andy Gibb was signed to RSO Records. Released in 1977, Andy Gibb's début album *Flowing Rivers* featured tracks that were composed by his brothers, as well as

the vocal backing of brother Barry. An immediate sensation, Gibb released a string of radio-friendly, teen-flavoured, soft pop-rock hit singles, beginning with a pair of chart-topping Barry Gibb-penned smashes, 'I Just Want To Be Your Everything' (1977), and '(Love Is) Thicker Than Water' (1978). Often employing falsetto vocals, Andy Gibb patterned his technique after his successful brothers. From the album of the same name, Gibb scored the best-selling single of his career with a track he co-wrote with The Bee Gees, 'Shadow Dancing'. He followed up with the Top 10 hits, 'An Everlasting Love' (1978), and a track originally planned as a Bee Gees song, '(Our Love) Don't Throw It All Away On Love' (1978). In 1980 Gibb teamed up with Olivia Newton-John for the hit, 'I Can't Help'. The following year he recorded The Everly Brothers' 'All I Have To Do Is Dream' in a duet with his then-girlfriend, the *Dallas* actress Victoria Principal. Tied to the disco era, Gibb's career suffered in the early Eighties, and he never returned to the charts after 1981. Turning to stage work, Gibb starred in a 1981 Los Angeles production of *The Pirates Of Penzance*, before hitting the small screen as the host of television's *Solid Gold*. Fired from the programme in 1982 after missing shoots, he was similarly dismissed in 1983 from the Broadway play, *Joseph And The Amazing Technicolour Dreamcoat*. Devastated by the break-up of his relationship with Victoria Principal, the despondent Gibb was abusing cocaine. Saddled with debts of $1 million, he was forced to file for bankruptcy. In 1985, Gibb checked into the Betty Ford Clinic for his drug addiction. At the time of his death, he had left RSO Records and was working on his first album for Island Records. His older brothers later established the Andy Gibb Foundation to support his favourite charities.
CAUSE: Complaining of stomach pains, Gibb checked himself into the John Radcliffe Hospital in Oxford, England, where he soon died. Although the tabloids blamed his death on cocaine use, the ultimate cause of death was viral infection of his damaged, enlarged heart.
FURTHER READING: Berman, Connie. (1979). *Andy Gibb*. Middletown, CT: Xeros Education Pub.

Maurice Gibb

(MAURICE ERNEST GIBB)
Born December 22, 1949
Died January 12, 2003
The most quiet and reserved member of The Bee Gees, Maurice Gibb was an integral part of their success. Though recognised for their disco run in the late Seventies, The Bee Gees first dominated the pop charts in the late Sixties with their tight, Beatle-influenced vocal harmonies. Born on the Isle of Man, England, the Gibb twins returned with their family to Manchester, England, in 1955. Their first public performances came when nine-year-old Barry Gibb and his seven-year-old brothers, fraternal twins Robin and Maurice, mimed to records during intermissions at a Manchester movie theatre. When the record player malfunctioned in mid-song, the group was forced into spontaneous harmonising and a singing trio was born. After brother Andy's birth in 1958, the Gibb family emigrated to Australia because of Barry and Robin's juvenile delinquency. Initially managed by their parents, the Gibb brothers signed with Australia's Festival Records in 1962. Originally called The Rattlesnakes, and then Wee Johnny Hays & The Bluecats, the trio finally settled on the B.G.'s (after Brothers Gibb), which was later spelled Bee Gees. With Maurice on bass and keyboards and Barry playing guitar, the group managed a few Australian hits over a four year period, finally topping the charts there in 1966 with 'Spicks And Specks'. Encouraged, the boys'

father hawked the Bee Gees' demos to several British labels, attracting the attention of Cream manager (and expatriate Australian) Robert Stigwood. Returning to England in early 1967, the group was signed to a five-year contract by Stigwood, who took over managerial duties. Adopting mop-top haircuts and velvet, Victorian clothing, The Bee Gees were promoted by Stigwood as "the new Beatles". Expanding the trio to a quintet with the addition of Australian friends, drummer Colin Peterson and guitarist Vince Melouney, The Bee Gees landed their first UK/US hit with 'New York Mining Disaster 1941'. With the departure of Melouney in late 1968, the group began to splinter. Robin, who had provided lead vocals on most of their hits, left after a dispute with Barry for a solo career, and Gibb sister, Lesley, briefly joined the group. In 1969, Maurice Gibb married UK pop singer Lulu, but they divorced five years later. Also during this period, he starred in the short-lived London musical, *Sing A Rude Song*, and collaborated with Steve Kipner, an Australian artist from the group Tin Tin, including a single, 'Have You Heard The Word?' as The Fut which fooled some into thinking it was The Beatles under a pseudonym. Welcomed back in the early Seventies by US (but not UK) fans, the reunited original Bee Gees trio returned to the charts with 'Lonely Days', 'Run To Me', and 'How Can You Mend A Broken Heart', featuring their soon to be trademark falsetto vocals. With Atlantic refusing to release an all-ballad album in 1973, The Bee Gees left the label for Stigwood's new RSO label and hired R&B producer Arif Mardin for the poor-selling album, *Mr. Natural*. Retaining Mardin and hiring a studio band, The Bee Gees returned with a vengeance in 1975 with the dance-flavoured album *Main Course*, which spawned a trio of hits, 'Jive Talkin'', 'Nights On Broadway' and the ballad 'Fanny (Be Tender With My Love)'. Dropping Mardin, and adopting a harder-edged disco sound built around Maurice's Moog synthesiser, The Bee Gees received heavy airplay with the 1976 album, *Children Of The World*, which featured the hits, 'You Should Be Dancing', 'Love So Right' and the funky 'Boogie Child'. Retreating to Paris in 1977 to mix a live album, and start work on their next studio album, The Bee Gees were asked by Stigwood to supply songs for a movie he was producing, *Saturday Night Fever*. From that blockbuster film, The Bee Gees saturated the airwaves in 1977/78 with their disco-defining hits, 'Night Fever', 'Stayin' Alive' and the ballad 'How Deep Is Your Love'. A massive hit, the two-disc soundtrack sold over 40 million copies worldwide. Stigwood followed with the film musical, *Sgt. Pepper's Lonely Hearts Club Band*, which starred The Bee Gees and Peter Frampton in the role of Billy Shears. A major artistic turkey, the film flopped and was promptly disowned by all. Recorded over a 10-month period, and released with little hype, The Bee Gees' 1979 album *Spirits Having Flown* spawned a trio of chart-topping singles in the US but while the group never identified itself with disco music, it could never escape the label, which in the US was a pejorative term. The band's private life was subject to drama, not least the death of brother Andy in 1988. Maurice's alcoholism became a concern to his family and friends, although he eventually dried out by dint of his own will. When the group's US hit run ended, The Bee Gees continued to achieve European success well into the Nineties with 'You Win Again', 'Secret Love', 'Alone' and 'Immortality'. The group's final album, *This Is Where I Came In*, was issued in 2001. In all, the group won seven Grammy Awards. Maurice Gibb occasionally pursued a solo career, releasing just a few singles.

CAUSE: After collapsing at his home in Miami Beach, he was taken to Mount Sinai Medical Center. He suffered a heart attack before undergoing emergency surgery for an intestinal blockage; it took doctors 10 minutes to restart his heart, by which time he had suffered brain damage. He died three days after his surgery. The coroner attributed the cause of death to ischaemic enteropathy, which restricted the blood flow to the intestines. Maurice's family later sued the hospital for negligence.

Mike Gibbins

Born March 12, 1949
Died October 4, 2005
The drummer for Beatles' protégés Badfinger, Mike Gibbins encountered success and tragedy within the group. Hailing from Swansea, Wales, Gibbins joined the group, then called The Iveys, in 1965, led by guitarist Pete Ham. Discovered by British bandleader Bill Collins who became their manager, The Iveys attracted the interest of several companies but signed with The Beatles' Apple label in 1968. After scoring a minor pop hit with 'Maybe Tomorrow', the renamed Badfinger reached the Top 10 in early 1970 with the Paul McCartney produced and composed 'Come And Get It' (appearing on the group's Apple début LP, *Magic Christian Music*), which was written for the film *The Magic Christian*, starring Peter Sellers and Ringo Starr. The Beatles connection was furthered by the group's road manager, Mal Evans, producing Badfinger's second album *No Dice* which contained a second Top 10 hit in 'No Matter What', and a track later recorded by both Harry Nilsson and Mariah Carey, 'Without You'. Badfinger backed George Harrison on parts of his solo album *All Things Must Pass*, and appeared at the Harrison-promoted charity event, The Concert for Bangladesh in 1971. That same year, several members played on John Lennon's *Imagine* album. Initially produced by Harrison but completed by Todd Rundgren, the third Badfinger album *Straight Up* (1972) spawned hits in the haunting 'Day After Day', and 'Baby Blue' (in the US). Leaving Apple for Warner Brothers in 1973, the group fared poorly with their label début *Badfinger*. Warner Brothers pulled their next album off the market when $100,000 owed to the band was discovered missing. Ensnared in a legal morass with its label and manager, the group disbanded. Overwhelmed by frustration and rage, Badfinger member Pete Ham committed suicide in 1975, as did Tommy Evans in 1983. Surviving members Gibbins and guitarist Joey Molland later formed a new short-lived version of Badfinger. Gibbins then pursued a solo career, often with the aid of former UFO guitarist Paul Chapman.
CAUSE: Natural causes. He died in his sleep at his home in Oviedo, Florida.

Bob Gibson

Born November 16, 1931
Died September 28, 1996
A Greenwich Village folk singer of the Sixties, Bob Gibson was best known as the co-writer of the standard 'Abilene', a country chart-topper for George Hamilton IV in 1964. His other compositions included 'Well, Well, Well', 'You Can Tell The World About This' and 'There'a A Meeting Here Tonight'. Gibson had first achieved fame in 1959 when he invited Joan Baez to make her début at the Newport Folk Festival. Later settling in Chicago, he helped popularise the use of the 12-string guitar in folk music.
CAUSE: He died of a degenerative brain disease, supranuclear palsy, at his home in Portland, Oregon. He had been diagnosed in 1994.

"Master" Henry Gibson

Born August 9, 1942
Died December 18, 2002

A popular session percussionist at Chess Records in the Sixties, "Master" Henry Gibson also spent several years in Curtis Mayfield's touring band, and worked with Aretha Franklin, Minnie Riperton, Natalie Cole, The Rotary Connection, The Staple Singers and others.
CAUSE: He suffered a heart attack in Stockholm, Sweden.

David Lee Gilbert

Born December 4, 1951
Died August 1, 2001
As lead singer of the Detroit-based hard rock band The Rockets, David Lee Gilbert had a sole Top 40 hit in 1979 with a cover of Fleetwood Mac's 'Oh Well'. Gilbert had previously been a member of a number of Detroit groups including The Shades Of Light, The Free (not the British band of the same name), Richard & The Young Lions, and in 1971, Ted Nugent's backing band. The Rockets, which included two former members of Mitch Ryder & The Detroit Wheels, formed in 1972 and disbanded 11 years later.
CAUSE: Contracting liver cancer caused by chronic cirrhosis, he died in Waterford, Michigan.

Joe Gilbert

Born November 7, 1940
Died August 9, 1966
Half of the California-based black vocal duo, Joe and Eddie, Joe Gilbert had joined partner Eddie Brown in the early Sixties. Recording for Capitol and GNP/Crescendo, the duo managed little airplay with their pop-flavoured sound.
CAUSE: Gilbert drove off the road, killing both himself and Brown.

Kevin Gilbert

(KEVIN MATHEW GILBERT)
Born November 20, 1966
Died May 19, 1996
Songwriter and musician, Kevin Gilbert is best known for co-writing seven songs on one-time girlfriend Sheryl Crow's breakthrough album, *Tuesday Night Music Club*, including 'All I Want To Do' and 'Leaving Las Vegas'. Also the leader and vocalist of his own groups, N.R.G, Giraffe, Kaviar, and Toy Matinee, Gilbert later released a solo album. In the Nineties, he toured with Eddie Money.
CAUSE: He died of accidental asphyxiation at his home in Eagle Rock, California.

Terry Gilkyson

(HAMILTON H. GILKYSON III)
Born June 17, 1916
Died October 15, 1999
A prolific songwriter, Terry Gilkyson also led his own folk group, The Easy Riders. The wealthy Pennsylvanian honed his musical trade during a stint in the US Army Corps, appearing weekly on Armed Forces Radio as a folk singer. After his discharge in 1948, he relocated to Los Angeles to work as a songwriter, scoring his first hit in 1950 with 'Cry Of The Wild Goose' (Frankie Laine) and continuing his hit run with 'Memories Are Made Of This' (Dean Martin) and 'Fast Freight' (Richard Hayes; The Kingston Trio). Gilkyson also sang back-up on The Weavers' hit renditions of 'On Top Of Old Smoky' and 'Across The Wide Missouri'. Joining a folk trio, The Easy Riders, Gilkyson had chart success with a number of self-penned compositions including 'Everybody Loves Saturday Night', 'The Sea Of Green', 'Marianne' (based on a gypsy melody) and 'Greenfield', a song that was covered by The Brothers Four. Hired in the Sixties as a songwriter by Disney Films, Gilkyson provided hundreds of songs for both their weekly television programme and films such as *Swiss Family Robinson*. 'The Bare Necessities', from the animated *Jungle Book*, earned an Academy Award nomination. Gilkyson's compositions were recorded by a host of country and pop artists including Johnny Cash, Tony Bennett, Doris Day, and Louis Armstrong.

CAUSE: Suffering an aneurysm while visiting his daughters, he died in Austin, Texas.

Ray Gillen

Born May 12, 1959
Died December 1, 1993
A good-looking, high-voiced singer who worked with Black Sabbath and his own group Badlands, Ray Gillen was raised on the music of Led Zeppelin and Bad Company in his native New Jersey. Though he excelled in sports during his teen years, music remained his untapped passion. After training with a vocal coach, Gillen passed through a series of local hard-rock groups. Then in 1985 Gillen spent three years with Rondinelli, a heavy-metal outfit led by former Rainbow drummer Bobby Rondinelli (sessions would be released in 1996 on *Wardance*). But in a strange twist of fate, shortly after auditioning for a role in the Broadway show *Cats*, Gillen received an invitation to join Black Sabbath. With Gillen leaving Rondinelli, the group disbanded. Four dates into his first tour with Black Sabbath, Gillen was forced to take over the lead vocal duties when Glenn Hughes bowed out of the band. Ray quit Sabbath when the group imploded during the recording sessions for the album, *Eternal Idol*. After passing through a pair of groups, including Blue Murder, Gillen in 1988 co-founded the blues-based, hard-rock band Badlands, along with former Sabbath drummer Eric Singer and Jake E. Lee, a blazing guitarist formerly with Dio and Ozzy Osbourne. Signing with Atlantic Records, the group released a self-titled début disc in 1989, and landed an MTV hit with 'Dreams In The Dark'. Following the release of a second album, Gillen left the group in 1992. He had briefly formed another group, Sun Red Sun, before falling ill.
CAUSE: He died from AIDS-related complications.

Steve Gilpin

Born April 28, 1950
Died November 25, 1991
Lead singer of the New Zealand synthesiser band Mi-Sex, Steve Gilpin was at the forefront of the techno movement. Trained as a jewellery maker, he worked as a nightclub singer during the mid Seventies. Joining forces with former Father Time bassist Don Martin, Gilpin formed a hard-rock group, Fragments Of Time. Cutting their long hair, the group evolved into a new wave outfit called Mi-Sex. Signed with CBS Records, the group made waves with its label début *Graffiti Crimes* (1979). Landing an international hit with the title track of their 1980 album *Computer Games*, Mi-Sex spawned a number of copy-cat bands.
CAUSE: Driving home after a concert, he was involved in an accident near his home in Mullunbimby, New South Wales, Australia. In a coma, he died several weeks later at the Gold Coast Hospital in Queensland.

James Gilreath

Born November 14, 1938
Died September 7, 2003
A singer-songwriter who was taught to play guitar by country artist Bill Anderson, Mississippi-native James Gilreath had his only Top 40 hit in 1963 with 'Little Band Of Gold'. Another of his compositions, 'Why Not Tonight', was recorded by Jimmy Hughes.
CAUSE: He was killed during a farming accident in Saltillo, Mississippi.

Bobby Gimby

Born October 15, 1918
Died June 20, 1998
Nicknamed "The Pied Piper of Canada", the Saskatchewan-born radio and television actor scored a massive hit in Canada in 1967 with the anthemic 'Ca-na-da: A Centennial Song'. All of the song's royalties were donated to the Boy Scouts of Canada.

Also a trumpet player, Bobby Gimby was a member of the big band, Mart Kenney and His Western Gentlemen.
CAUSE: After briefly being hospitalised for pneumonia, he died at the Leisure World Retirement Home in North Bay, Ontario.

J.C. Ginyard

(JULIUS CALEB GINYARD)
Born January 15, 1910
Died August 11, 1978
The lead vocalist of the doo-wop group The Du Droppers, J.C. Ginyard had a long history in vocal harmony singing. Rooted in gospel music, Ginyard first joined a Florida-based gospel group The Royal Harmony Singers in 1936; two years later, the group evolved into The Jubilaires; then in 1948 he joined The Dixieaires. Comprised chiefly of seasoned former gospel singers, The Du Droppers were formed in Harlem in 1952. Originally signed with the tiny Red Robins label, the group released an amusing answer record to The Dominoes' 'Sixty Minute Man', called 'Can't Do Sixty No More' (the single bombed, as did The Dominoes' cover version of the single two years later). Moving to RCA Records, the group scored a pair of Top 10 R&B hits in 1953, 'I Wanna Know' and the similarly themed 'I Found Out'. Leaving the group in 1955 to return to his gospel roots, Ginyard joined the legendary Golden Gate Quartet. After a 16-year stint, he left the group to pursue a solo career.
CAUSE: Unknown. He died in his adopted country of Switzerland.

Candy Givens

Born 1947
Died January 27, 1984
Member of the Seventies Tommy Bolin-led, Colorado-based hard rock group, Zephyr, Candy Givens frequently shared the vocal duties with Bolin. Singing in a bluesy, Janis Joplin-like style, Givens appeared on the group's three albums. Bolin left Zephyr in late 1971, later joining The James Gang and Deep Purple. Candy Givens returned for a revival of Zephyr in 1980.
CAUSE: Drug and alcohol overdose. She was found dead in a hot tub at her home in Boulder, Colorado.

John Glascock

Born May 2, 1951
Died November 17, 1979
London-born studio bass player for Jethro Tull from 1975 to 1979, John Glascock joined the group for the recording of the album *Too Old To Rock And Roll, Too Young To Die*. He was previously a member of the British blues-rock band, Chicken Shack from 1971 to 1973, appearing on their 1972 album, *Imagination Lady*.
CAUSE: He died after open heart surgery.

Dick Glasser

(RICHARD EUGENE GLASSER)
Born December 8, 1933
Died July 10, 2000
Though a talented singer and songwriter, Ohio-born, Virginia-raised Dick Glasser is best known for his work as a producer. After breaking into music in the mid Fifties as a pop/rockabilly singer, he composed material for a number of artists including P.J. Proby and Gene Vincent. Taking the stage name of Dick Lory, Glasser scored an Australian Top 10 hit with a Proby composition, 'Handsome Guy'. Turning to production, Glasser worked with a host of artists including Freddie Cannon, Johnny Cash, The Ventures, The Everly Brothers, The Vogues, and Dean Martin. By the mid Sixties, Glasser headed the A&R department at Warner Brothers Records.
CAUSE: Lung cancer. He died in Thousand Oaks, California.

Pat Glasser

(PATRICK J. GLASSER)
Born March 17, 1941
Died June 29, 2005
A music producer, Pat Glasser oversaw

the demos for an unknown hard rock band, Night Ranger, in 1981. Securing a recording contract with Boardwalk Records, he produced the group's first three albums and the radio hits with 'Don't Tell You Love Me', '(You Can Still) Rock In America', 'Sister Christian', 'When You Close Your Eyes' and 'Sentimental Street'. Glasser also worked with Rail, Refugee and Giuffria.
CAUSE: Unknown. He died in California.

Ralph Gleason

Born 1917
Died June 3, 1975
Co-founder of *Rolling Stone* magazine, jazz critic Ralph Gleason was the first American music journalist to treat rock'n'roll as a respectable art form. Reared on jazz music, he embraced the counterculture before it became fashionable. After being kicked out of New York's Columbia University in the Thirties for pulling a prank, Gleason launched his own independent jazz publication. Working for CBS and ABC in the Forties, he relocated to San Francisco where he initially worked as an insurance salesman. He was a columnist for *Downbeat* from 1950–58, and in 1950 landed the coveted position as music columnist for *The San Francisco Chronicle*, his articles nationally syndicated. Championing bebop and modern jazz artists, Gleason made his mark in that genre when in 1958 he joined Jimmy Lyons in launching the annual Monterey Jazz Festival. But Gleason also made the occasional misstep, panning both Charlie Parker and Bob Dylan. Sensing a musical change in the air, in 1966 Gleason advised promoter Bill Graham to rent out the Fillmore auditorium to showcase the many innovative local rock acts. Soon, Gleason was proclaiming that San Francisco had become "the new Liverpool", as seemingly dozens of local acts were being signed by national record labels. He later chronicled the movement in the book, *San Francisco Scene*. In a fateful meeting in 1965, Gleason was approached by Berkeley dropout Jann Wenner at a psychedelic music concert also attended by poet Allen Ginsberg. Leaving the editorial board of *Ramparts* magazine in 1967, Gleason aided Wenner in launching a new, serious rock music magazine. He rejected Wenner's suggestion of calling it *The Electric Newspaper*, and came up with *Rolling Stone*, borrowed from the Muddy Waters song of the same name. Bringing his reputation to the magazine, Gleason was consulting editor and a columnist. After years of sparring with Wenner, Gleason resigned from *Rolling Stone* in 1973. In the Seventies, Gleason was also named the vice-president of Fantasy/Prestige/ Milestone Records. In 1990, BMI launched the annual Ralph Gleason Music Book Awards, celebrating the finest literary achievements in popular music journalism. As a mark of respect, Gleason's name still appears beneath the masthead in every issue of *Rolling Stone*.
CAUSE: Heart attack. He died in San Francisco.

Lloyd Glenn

Born November 21, 1909
Died May 23, 1985
Pioneering West Coast jazz and R&B pianist whose hits included 'Old Time Shuffle Blues' and 'Chica Boom', Texas-born Lloyd Glenn also produced T-Bone Walker's 'Stormy Monday Blues'. Glenn recorded for several labels during his career including Aladdin, Imperial and Swing Time. In the Seventies he toured with Big Joe Turner, and later recorded with Clarence "Gatemouth" Brown.
CAUSE: Heart attack. He died in San Antonio, Texas.

Henry Glover

Born May 21, 1921
Died April 7, 1991
Pioneering black producer and

songwriter at King Records, Arkansas-native Henry Glover quit graduate school in the late Thirties to join the jump-blues bands of Buddy Johnson and Tiny Bradshaw. While working as an arranger and trumpet player for Lucky Millinder's R&B orchestra in the mid Forties, Glover wrote and co-penned the R&B hit 'I Love You Yes I Do', for Millinder's vocalist Bull Moose Jackson at King/Queen Records. Retained at King by label head, Syd Nathan, Glover was named vice-president, overseeing many of the King's early R&B acts including Wynonie Harris and Little Willie John. Glover also travelled to Nashville to record country acts such as Moon Mullican and The Delmore Brothers. Leaving King Records in 1956, Glover produced hit records for Bobby "Blue" Bland, Arthur Prysock, and The Fiestas. After briefly operating his own label in the early Sixties, Glover landed at Roulette Records as the head of the A&R department, where he produced The Essex, Sonny Stitt, Dinah Washington, and co-wrote 'Peppermint Twist', for a group he discovered, Joey Dee & The Starliters.
CAUSE: Heart attack. He died in New York City.

Keith Godchaux

Born July 19, 1948
Died July 22, 1980
The keyboard player in the Seventies for the perennial tie-dyed, hippie group The Grateful Dead, San Francisco-born Keith Godchaux was the son of a professional pianist. Following the departure of The Grateful Dead's founding keyboardist, Ron "Pig Pen" McKernan, Godchaux was hired as his replacement in 1972. Godchaux had originally performed with the group in the fall of 1971 when McKernan began to miss shows during the middle of a tour which would be chronicled on the triple album, *Europe '72*. Godchaux's wife, Donna Jean, would also join the group, hired as a back-up soprano vocalist. The Godchauxs joined a group that was now led by guitarist Jerry Garcia, and included rhythm guitarist Bob Weir, bassist Phil Lesh, keyboardist Tom Constanten and percussionists Bill Kreutzmann and Mickey Hart. While Godchaux did not display the stage presence nor the showmanship of his predecessor, he was a much more proficient and nimble keyboard player. Freed from contractual obligations with Warner Brothers Records, the group formed its own record label, Grateful Dead Records. The first Grateful Dead studio album to include the Godchauxs was *Wake Of The Flood* (1973), with Keith Godchaux's lead vocal on the first single 'Let Me Sing Your Blues Away'. With Godchaux, Grateful Dead albums include *From The Mars Hotel* (1974), *Blues For Allah* (1975), *Steal Your Face* (1976), and after signing with Arista Records, the overproduced, *Terrapin Station* (1977) and *Shakedown Street* (1978). The Godchauxs also recorded their own album in 1975 on the Grateful Dead Records' subsidiary label, Round Records; panned by critics, *Keith And Donna Godchaux* sold few copies. The Godchauxs then teamed with bandmate Mickey Hart to form The Heart Of Gold Band. Then in early 1978 the Godchauxs toured in the Dead side project The Jerry Garcia Band, after appearing on the Garcia album *Cats Under The Stars* (Keith's brother, violinist Brian Godchaux, guested on the album). But following many personal and musical disputes with other band members, the Godchauxs were forced out of The Grateful Dead in April, 1979. Keith Godchaux was replaced by Brent Midland. Shortly before Keith Godchaux's death, the Godchauxs had just formed their own group, Ghost, along with John Cipollina, and had performed on stage with Dave Mason.
CAUSE: He died in a car crash in Marin County, California.

FURTHER READING: Jackson, Blair. (1983). *Grateful Dead: The Music Never Stopped*. New York: Delilah.

Geoff Goddard

Born 1938
Died May 15, 2000
A British songwriter best known for his association with producer Joe Meek, Geoff Goddard had a brief hit run in the Sixties. A pianist by trade, Goddard was an unknown music scribe when he penned the haunting 'Johnny Remember Me', a hit for independent producer Joe Meek's discovery, John Leyton. For Leyton's follow-ups, Goddard wrote 'Wild Wind' and 'Son This Is She', also produced by Meek. Goddard and Meek co-wrote 'Don't You Think It's Time', a hit for Mike Berry. As a trained musician and talented singer, Goddard (along with Dave Adams) frequently provided uncredited vocals on a series of Meek productions. After briefly performing as Anton Hollywood, Goddard reverted to his birth name and released four obscure singles. Goddard and Meek parted on poor terms after Goddard claimed that The Honeycombs' hit 'Have I The Right' was a rewrite of his composition 'Give Me The Chance'. Leaving the music industry, Goddard took a position in the food service department at Reading University.
CAUSE: Heart attack.

Dwayne Goettel

(DWAYNE RUDOLPH GOETTEL)
Born February 1, 1964
Died August 30, 1995
Classically trained keyboard player and inventive electronics wizard of the Canadian industrial-rock band Skinny Puppy, Dwayne Goettel had first appeared in a duo with vocalist Sandy Weir called Water. A native of Edmonton, Goettel then released an EP as part of a techno-rock band, Voice. Skinny Puppy had formed in Vancouver in 1983, with Goettel leaving another industrial band, Psych, to join the Dave Oglivie-fronted group as a replacement for Wilhelm Shroeder. With Skinny Puppy signing with Capitol Records, Goettel added his sampling wizardry to the group's album, *Cleanse Fold And Maunipulate* (1987). With their macabre theatrics of simulated self-mutilation on stage, Goettel and the group were primarily an underground sensation. The group first made waves in 1989 with the critically acclaimed *Rabies*, the album featuring the guitar and vocals of Ministry's Al Jourgenson. Drawn toward techno music in the early Nineties, Goettel pursued a side career under the name Duck. Although Goettel was a prolific songwriter, few of his compositions were recorded by Skinny Puppy. Goettel was working on Skinny Puppy's ninth album at the time of his death. The band was experiencing internal problems at the time and disbanded soon after.
CAUSE: Accidental heroin overdose. He was found in the bathroom of his parent's home in Edmonton, Canada. He had started taking heroin the previous year, and had entered a detox programme two months earlier.

Glenn Goins

Born January 2, 1954
Died July 30, 1978
Guitarist and vocalist for George Clinton, Glenn Goins was one of dozens of musicians employed as part of the Parliament/Funkadelic funk and R&B congregation. Joining Clinton in 1975, Goins appeared on the hits, 'Bop Gun', 'Handcuffs' and 'Do That Stuff'. Leaving the group in mid-1977, Goins produced his brother Kevin's group, Quazar, and led his own group, Mutiny, which had just signed with Arista Records shortly before his death.
CAUSE: Complications related to Hodgkin's disease. He died at a Plainfield, New Jersey, hospital two days after collapsing at his home.

Wally Gold

Born May 28, 1928
Died June 7, 1998

A songwriter who frequently teamed with Aaron Schroeder, Wally Gold composed several rock hits including 'It's My Party' (Lesley Gore), 'Because They're Young' (Duane Eddy), and the Elvis Presley hits 'It's Now Or Never' (words only – the music came from an Italian ballad) and 'Good Luck Charm'. Gold had broken into music as a member of the Four Esquires, who in 1957 landed a pop hit with 'Love Me Forever'. By the early Sixties, Gold was a staff producer at CBS Records, working with artists such as Barbra Streisand and Tony Bennett. He was later appointed vice-president of Don Kirshner Entertainments.
CAUSE: Colitis. He died in Teaneck, New Jersey.

Albert Goldman

Born April 15, 1927
Died March 29, 1994

Albert Goldman can lay claim to having been rock music's most loathed biographer, having written scathing, mean-spirited, high-profile biographies of Elvis Presley and John Lennon, and also comedian Lenny Bruce. Georgia-born Goldman earned a PhD in English from Columbia University. Attracted to popular music in the Sixties, Goldman earned a reputation for firing volleys at cultural icons. A reckless journalist, in a 1968 *Life* magazine article he compared a Rolling Stones concert to a Nazi rally. Receiving a $1 million advance, Goldman viciously attacked Presley in the 1981 tome *Elvis*, offering exaggerated accounts of gluttony, drug abuse and peculiar sexual habits. Although promoted as the definitive Presley biography, *Elvis* was subsequently discredited by Presley scholars, notably the American writers Greil Marcus and Peter Guralnick, not least for its many factual inaccuracies. Similarly, in *The Lives Of John Lennon*, Goldman portrayed the former Beatle as arrogant and self-absorbed, and suggested that Lennon might even have committed murder while in Germany. Much of his evidence relied on dubious speculation, and it was said that if Goldman were ever to show his face in Liverpool he might face a lynch mob. A key premise of Goldman's books on both Presley and Lennon was that the subjects lacked serious talent and that their fans had somehow been deceived into believing otherwise; that their celebrity was a sham and their fans were foolish dupes. This was hardly likely to win Goldman any friends among devotees, and hardback copies of both *Elvis* and *The Lives Of John Lennon* wound up on the shelves of cut-price bookshops, which suggests that the public were unimpressed by Goldman's hatchet jobs despite the controversy they aroused. In 1999 both books were out of print. At the time of his death, Goldman was preparing a biography on Doors' leader Jim Morrison. Many of Goldman's essays from *Life* magazine were compiled in the book, *Freakshow*.
CAUSE: Heart attack. He died aboard an aeroplane en route from Miami to London.

George Goldner

Born 1918
Died April 15, 1970

Legendary music industry mogul, Manhattan-born George Goldner got his start in 1951 at a Latin music label, Tico Records. Starting Rama Records as a subsidiary of Tico in 1953, Goldner was quick to jump on the doo-wop bandwagon with the label's roster boasting The Harptones, Heartbeats, Wrens, Valentines and Crows, who delivered a million-selling smash with 'Gee'. Launching, buying, and selling a series of labels during the next decade, Goldner was instrumental in the rise of R&B and rock via record

companies such as Gone, End and Roulette, where he kick started the careers of acts such as Frankie Lymon & The Teenagers, The Chantels, and Little Anthony & The Imperials. But with his underworld connections and serious gambling habit, Goldner was forced to sell off his companies. Returning to the record business in 1964, he teamed with songwriters/producers Jerry Leiber and Mike Stoller to launch the primarily girl-group label, Red Bird Records, working with The Dixie Cups and The Shangri-Las. After Goldner acquired the label from his partners for $1, Red Bird went out of business in 1966. Goldner launched his final label, Firebird, in 1970. Along with many of his associates, Goldner has been frequently attacked for the poor financial treatment of early musical acts.
CAUSE: Heart attack. He died in New York City.

Cliff Goldsmith

Born May 10, 1925
Died June 14, 1991
Los Angeles-born producer and songwriter, Cliff Goldsmith joined Fred Smith in composing a pair of hits for The Olympics, 'Western Movies' (1958) and 'Hully Gully' (1960). As a producer, Goldsmith later worked with Little Johnny Taylor and Leon Haywood.
CAUSE: Heart failure. He died in Burbank, California.

Dickie Goodman

(RICHARD DORIAN GOODMAN)
Born April 19, 1934
Died November 6, 1989
Perennial novelty songwriter and performer who pioneered "the break-in record", Dickie Goodman was the son of a lawyer. Dropping out of New York University, Goodman formed a songwriting partnership with novice music publisher Bill Buchanan. The pair took a unique approach, writing comedy dialogue pieced together by vocal snippets of rock and R&B hits. Released in 1956, 'The Flying Saucer (Parts 1 & 2)' employed an Orson Welles *War Of The Worlds* framework, featuring Goodman as a reporter named John Cameron Cameron (after John Cameron Swayze). After leading New York deejay Alan Freed played the song on WINS, Buchanan & Goodman were signed by Roulette Records and given their own label imprint. A Top 10 hit, 'The Flying Saucer' inadvertently helped bring attention to the snippeted songs, bringing them additional sales. Employing a similar interview style, the duo scored follow-up hits with 'Flying Saucer The 2nd' (1957) and 'Santa And The Satellite (Parts I & II)' (1957). With Buchanan leaving Goodman in 1959, the latter continued his hit run with a series of topical releases, including: a pair of parody hits based on the television show *The Untouchables*, 'The Touchables' and 'The Touchables In Brooklyn' (1961); a parody of the *Ben Casey* theme called 'Ben Crazy' (1962); 'Batman And His Grandmother' (1966); 'On Campus' (1969); 'Watergate' (1973); 'Energy Crisis' (1974); 'Mr. Jaws' (1975); and 'Kong' (1977). Goodman last charted in 1982 with the minor hit, 'Hey E.T.' (1982). Goodman recorded on a remarkable 30-plus labels during his long career, under both his own name and under several psuedonyms including Jeckyl and Hyde. Goodman also worked as a jingle writer for 20th Century Fox, and as a comedy writer for *The Ed Sullivan Show* and for a number of stand-up comics, including Jackie Mason.
CAUSE: Self-inflicted gunshot. He died at his son's home in Fayetteville, North Carolina. His wife had left him and he had a serious gambling addiction.

Shirley Goodman

Born June 19, 1936
Died July 5, 2005

The female half of the teenage R&B duo Shirley & Lee, Shirley Goodman teamed with Leonard Lee on a series of gritty releases. Honing her singing while a member of a Baptist church in New Orleans, Goodman later recorded a Cosimo Matassa-produced demo with a group of teens. When Aladdin Records chief Eddie Messner heard the disc, he was impressed by Goodman's unique vocal delivery and paired her with the mature sounding 15-year-old Leonard Lee. After notching their début hit in 1952 with the Dave Bartholomew-produced 'I'm Gone', the duo was billed as "The Sweethearts of the Blues", in an attempt to promote a non-existent romance between the couple on songs such as 'Shirley Come Back To Me', 'The Proposal' and 'Two Happy People'. Backed by New Orleans' finest session players on mostly Lee-composed material, Shirley & Lee hits included the million-selling 'Let The Good Times Roll' (1956) and the similar-sounding 'I Feel Good' (1957). Leaving Aladdin, Shirley & Lee then recorded for Warwick Records in 1961–62, before parting in 1963. Moving to Los Angeles, Goodman was teamed with Jessie Hill by producer Huey Meaux; their unsuccessful singles were compiled on the album, *You'll Lose A Good Thing*, in 1970. Briefly reuniting with Lee in 1972, Goodman performed at a series of revival concerts. After providing session vocals for The Rolling Stones and Dr. John, she retired from music and took a clerical position at the offices of *Playboy* magazine. While answering the phones, Goodman spoke with former R&B singer Sylvia Robinson, the co-founder of All Platinum Records, and Robinson offered her the opportunity to provide lead vocal on the early disco hit single 'Shame, Shame, Shame', with the song credited to Shirley & Company. After returning to the stage for two years, Goodman retired.

CAUSE: Suffering a stroke, she died at Cedars-Sinai Hospital in Los Angeles.

Steve Goodman

Born July 25, 1948
Died September 20, 1984

Born and raised in Chicago, folk-rock singer and songwriter Steve Goodman began playing the guitar at age 13. After joining several local, rock bar-bands, Goodman soon discovered and fell in love with folk music. Graduating from high school, he travelled to New York City where he played his original compositions on street corners. Returning to Chicago and enrolling at Lake Forest University, Goodman spent his evenings performing in folk clubs. Finding success as a commercial jingle writer, he composed a ditty for a Maybelline cosmetic product, Blushing Eye Shadow. Then with the help of Kris Kristofferson and Paul Anka, Goodman signed to Buddah Records in 1970 as an acoustic folk-rocker. His first album, *Steve Goodman* (1971), contained his standard 'City Of New Orleans', 'Would You Like To Learn to Dance', and the first version of 'You Never Even Called Me By My Name'. With his short stature, full beard, and warm persona, Goodman sang in a sincere, unpretentious manner, crossing the boundaries of pop, folk, country, and blues. But Goodman had greater fortune as a songwriter with his 'City Of New Orleans', a huge hit for Arlo Guthrie in 1972. After releasing a second, more mainstream album *Someone Else's Trouble* (1973), Goodman switched to Asylum Records in 1975. That year, an updated version of a Steve Goodman-John Prine composition 'You Never Even Called Me By My Name', became a hit for country music outlaw, David Allen Coe. Though Coe's version would become a bar-room classic, many radio stations banned the song. Joined by Jethro Burns of the comedy duo Homer and Jethro, Goodman then

released the self-produced folkish album, *Jessie's Jig And Other Favourites* (1975). Though remaining popular in the Chicago area, Goodman continued to record a series of poorly selling albums including *Say It In Private* (1977), which contained the Goodman/John Prine composition 'The Twentieth Century Is Almost Over', a song that Prine would also record. Reciprocating, Goodman produced an album for Prine in 1978, *Bruised Orange*. Collapsing on stage in New York City in 1982, Goodman had been suffering a decade-long bout with leukaemia; he had hidden his illness from the public. In 1983, Goodman began recording on his own label, Red Pajamas; his first release, *Artistic Hair*, contained new recordings of his earlier hits. Goodman's last hit came with a local favourite, a novelty song about the Cubs baseball team winning the World Series called 'A Dying Cub Fan's Last Request'. Goodman released his final album *Santa Ana Winds*, just days before his death.
CAUSE: Complications from leukaemia. He died at the University of Washington Medical Center in Seattle after undergoing a bone marrow transplant.

Ronnie Goodson

(RONALD GOODSON)
Born February 2, 1945
Died November 4, 1980
Lead singer of the R&B vocal group, Ronnie and The Hi-Lites, New Jersey born and raised Ronnie Goodson began singing in his Baptist church choir. At the age of 12 in 1957, Goodson was asked to join a local group called The Cascades as a Frankie Lymon-like lead singer; fronting the quintet, Goodson was backed by four older high-schoolers. Aided by music industry veterans Hal and Mariam Weiss, the renamed Ronnie and The Hi-Lites landed their only national hit with the Mariam Weiss composition, 'I Wish That We Were Married'. Signed to the new Joy label, the group would manage only regional interest with several follow-up releases. Attempting a solo career in the mid Sixties, Goodson was hampered by his deepening, maturing voice. But with his professional career seemingly over, he returned to high school. Though enrolled in a community college, Goodson yearned for a career in music. In the late Sixties, Goodson joined John Fred & His Playboy Band as a trumpeter, appearing on the group's horn-heavy garage hit 'Judy In Disguise'.
CAUSE: Brain tumour. Goodson had been diagnosed in the Sixties and had been ill off and on into the Seventies. He died at his home in Jersey City, New Jersey.

Sam Goody

(SAMUEL GUTOWITZ)
Born February 25, 1904
Died August 7, 1991
Pioneering record store entrepreneur who founded the US record chain called Sam Goodys, he opened his flagship store in Manhattan in 1945. In 1978 Goody sold the chain for a reported $5.5 million to the Primeric Corporation, which merged the company with Musicland.
CAUSE: Heart failure. He died at St. John's Hospital in Far Rockaway, New York.

Irving Gordon

Born January 28, 1915
Died December 1, 1996
Prolific jazz songwriter whose biggest rock-era hit came with Nat "King" Cole's 'Unforgettable', Irving Gordon also wrote Abbott and Costello's timeless comedy skit 'Who's On First?', which premiered in the 1941 film, *Buck Privates*. Trained as a classical violinist, the Brooklyn songwriter was first signed by Mills Music in the Thirties, where he penned hundreds of songs, including material for Duke Ellington.

CAUSE: Cancer. He died at his home in Los Angeles.

Rosco Gordon

Born April 10, 1928
Died July 11, 2002

A Fifties R&B artist, Rosco Gordon was a member of the loose-knit Memphis-based R&B ensemble The Beale Streeters, which at times included Johnny Ace, Bobby Bland, Junior Parker, B.B. King and Earle Forest. Breaking into music after winning an amateur contest, Gordon parlayed the victory in a popular weekly radio programme on powerhouse WDIA, where he sang and played piano. Recording his sessions at the studios of Sun Records, Gordon had several shuffle-beat R&B hits at Modern-RPM and Vee-Jay, including 'Saddled By The Cow', 'Booted' and 'No More Doggin''. Gordon's most enduring hit, the self-composed 'Just A Little Bit' (1960), would be his final chart entry before leaving the music industry in the early Sixties to devote time to his second marriage. Gordon was also disillusioned over a lack of royalty payments. Operating a dry cleaning business in New York City, he later launched his own small label out of his home, and after his wife died from cancer in 1984, Gordon returned to writing and performing. In 2000, he teamed up with blues guitarist Duke Robillard to record *Memphis, Tennessee*, an album that recaptured his early sound.

CAUSE: He died at his home in Queens, New York, following a heart attack.

Gwen Gordy

Born November 26, 1927
Died November 8, 1999

The co-founder of a pair of labels which evolved into Motown, Gwen Gordy was an older sister of Berry Gordy. Gwen had initially launched Anna Records in 1959, and then with her future husband, former Moonglows leader Harvey Fuqua, Tri-Phi Records. Anna Records had some success with David Ruffin, Barrett Strong, Joe Tex and The Falcons but with brother Berry starting Motown, Anna and its artist roster were absorbed, and Gwen Gordy remained a crucial part of the label's infrastructure. During Motown's rise in the Sixties, she took roles as a songwriter, producer and artist manager, working with Junior Walker, David Ruffin, Marvin Gaye, Tammi Terrell and others. She co-penned 'You've Got What It Takes' (Marv Johnson), 'All I Could Do Was Cry' (Etta James) and several early Jackie Wilson hits including 'Lonely Teardrops' and 'To Be Loved'. Gwen Gordy was also instrumental in the formation of Motown's all-important Artist Development department, and brought in Maxine Powell, hitherto the proprietor of a finishing and modelling school, to run the department and be responsible for the artists' stage costumes. When Motown relocated to Los Angeles in the early Seventies, she was one of the few executives to make the move. Gordy also headed a trio of music publishing companies, Gwen Glen, Der-Glenn, and Old Brompton Road. After leaving the music industry, she purchased a farm to breed and train thoroughbred horses.

CAUSE: Cancer. She died at her home in San Diego.

Carole Joyner Gourley

Born August 14, 1938
Died December 7, 1997

Co-writer of the hit, 'Young Love', a Top 10 chart entry for both Tab Hunter and Sonny James, Carole Joyner Gourley had collaborated on the song with her boyfriend, Ric Cartey.

CAUSE: Cancer. She was diagnosed with the disease one month before her death. She died in Atlanta.

Bill Graham

(WOLFGANG GRAJONCA)
Born January 8, 1931
Died October 26, 1991

Bill Graham was a legendary concert promoter and music industry entrepreneur, a crucial pioneer in the development of the San Francisco sound and rock in general as a multi-million dollar industry. A Russian-Jew reared in Nazi Berlin, after the death of his father Graham's mother placed him in a German orphanage to shield him against the anti-Jewish purges. Moving to a Paris orphanage for much of the War, Graham lost a sister during a long overland trek to reach a freighter to flee the country. While the emaciated Graham landed in the US, his mother and another sister perished in a German concentration camp. Raised in a foster home in the Bronx, Graham became a US citizen and earned a Bronze Star and Purple Heart while fighting in the Korean War. After gaining a business degree, Graham observed the inner workings of the entertainment industry while working as a waiter in the Catskill Mountains resort area from 1958 to 1963. Moving to the San Francisco bay, Graham left a safe, white-collar position to work as the business manager for a struggling mime troupe. With the troupe arrested on obscenity charges, Graham promoted his first concert on November 6, 1965, as a benefit to raise money for a legal defence fund. The bill featured Allen Ginsberg and the then-unknown Jefferson Airplane. With the concert a rousing success, Graham turned to promotion as a full-time job, transforming the former Winterland ice-skating rink into a music venue. Booking psychedelic rock, jazz and blues groups, Graham outgrew this location in 1968, and moved into the 4,000-capacity Carousel Ballroom, which was rechristened the Fillmore (West). He would later launch a Fillmore East in New York City's lower east side, and both became vitally important venues for artists and fans alike. Instrumental in the discovery or success of many local acts, Graham booked The Grateful Dead, Santana, Janis Joplin and Steve Miller into the Fillmore West, as well as those visiting British bands – The Who, Jimi Hendrix and Led Zeppelin – who were then at the cutting edge of rock. Graham was quick to spot the potential of serious rock music to become a thriving industry and he made a point of befriending and creating the right on-stage environment for the top bands, thus ensuring that they would continue to work with him for years to come. With both Fillmores closing by 1971, a film documenting the Fillmore West's last days *Fillmore*, was released in 1972. Turning concert promotion into big business in the Seventies, Graham filled large arenas and stadiums with acts such as Led Zeppelin, The Who, Bob Dylan, The Grateful Dead and The Rolling Stones, for whom he acted as tour manager in the early Eighties. He also branched into management, managing Santana and Van Morrison, and launched his own record label. A tough, brash negotiator, Graham earned both respect and disdain from performers and venue operators alike, but by 1990 he was grossing over $100 million annually. But Graham still made time to promote charity concerts such as the US Live Aid concert in Philadelphia. He also had a passion for acting, and co-produced and landed a small role in the Jim Morrison film biography, *The Doors*. Additionally, he portrayed a show promoter in *Apocalypse Now*, and mobster Charles "Lucky" Luciano in *Bugsy*.

Cause: He was killed when his helicopter hit a utility tower in Sonoma County, about 25 miles north of San Francisco. The crash also took the lives of his longtime companion Melisa Gold (42), and the pilot Steve Kahn. At the time Graham was flying home from a Huey Lewis & The News concert in Concord.

FURTHER READING: Greenfield, Robert (1992). *Bill Graham Presents: My Life Inside Rock And Out*. New York: Doubleday.

Ernie Graham

Born June 14, 1946
Died April 27, 2001
A British singer-guitarist, Belfast-born Ernie Graham broke into music in 1965 as a member of a local beat band, Tony & The Tellstars. Graham and future Wings' guitarist Henry McCulloch subsequently formed The People (not the American band of the same name) who were managed by ex-Jimi Hendrix roadie and future Stiff Records' co-founder Dave Robinson, and renamed Eire Apparent. Sharing the same management as Jimi Hendrix, the group toured with him, as well as Pink Floyd and Soft Machine. Eire Apparent recorded only one album, the Hendrix-produced *Sunrise* (1969), but it sold poorly resulting in their disbanding in 1969. While working on an album with the Welsh group Help Yourself, Graham enlisted his bandmates (as well as members of Brinsley Schwarz) to back him on a folk-rock solo project issued in 1971, but it sold poorly. Meanwhile, Help Yourself's folk-meets-hard rock self-titled début album was also a commercial disappointment and Graham left during the sessions of their psychedelic second album, *Strange Affair*. Teaming with Martin Belmont and other musicians, Graham then formed Clancy, who issued a pair of soul-flavoured rock albums on Warner Brothers. Graham's final recording, a cover of Phil Lynott's 'Romeo And The Lonely Girl', was released in 1978 on Stiff Records.
CAUSE: Unknown.

Eudell Graham

Born May 24, 1933
Died January 1995
The lead singer of a later version of The "5" Royales, North Carolina-native Eudell Graham replaced John Tanner in late 1963. The group did not have any hits after leaving King-Federal Records in 1960 and disbanded after Graham and bandmate Larry Robinson were arrested for armed robbery in 1968. Graham was previously a member of The 4 Dukes.
CAUSE: Unknown.

Earl Grant

Born January 20, 1933
Died June 10, 1970
Classically trained former music teacher, Earl Grant is best known for his soothing pop organ hit, 'The End' (1958). Primarily an album artist in the Sixties, he managed only one more chart entry, 'Sweet Sixteen Bars' (1962).
CAUSE: He died in a car crash near Lordsburg, New Mexico.

Jim Grant

Born July 29, 1943
Died November 29, 2004
The bassist of pop-rock group The Five Americans, Jim Grant had formed the quintet with classmates at Southeastern Oklahoma State University in 1962. Adopting a pirate motif and calling themselves The Mutineers, the group spent the summer of 1964 in Dallas with the goal of earning enough money for the following term's tuition. Discovered by John Abdnor, the owner of Abnak Records, the renamed Five Americans were swept up in the current British Invasion sound, reaching the charts in 1966 with their self-penned single, 'I See The Light'. Featuring Mike Rabon on lead vocal, the group continued their hit run in 1967 with the million-selling (in the US) 'Western Union', 'Sound Of Love', and 'Zip Code'. After the group disbanded in 1969, Grant went to work in advertising design. The Five Americans reunited in 2002.
CAUSE: He died at his home in Dallas after suffering a heart attack.

Peter Grant

Born April 5, 1935
Died November 21, 1995

Defiant wrestler turned legendary rock manager, the gruff Peter Grant made his name as the manager of Led Zeppelin, helping to turn them into rock's biggest attraction by the mid Seventies. Grant came from a very poor background and was hardened as a child during the Nazi bombings of London. Receiving little schooling, by 13 he was working as a stagehand at the Croydon Empire Theatre, and he later took a job as a messenger boy in Fleet Street. Through his connections, Grant also appeared as an extra in the film *The Guns Of Navarone*, and as a body double for actor Robert Morley. Bulking up to 250 pounds, Grant worked as a bouncer and doorman at London's earliest rock'n'roll venue, the 2Is coffee bar in Soho's Old Compton Street, and as a wrestler under the name of Prince Mario Alassio. Drawn to the music industry, the intimidating Grant then became a tour manager for visiting American rock acts such as Chuck Berry, The Everly Brothers and Gene Vincent. Grant first visited the US as the tour manager for British Invasion act, The Animals, in whose employ he allegedly displayed extraordinary personal bravery by facing down a gunman in Arizona. By 1967 Grant had acquired a thorough grounding in the way the music industry worked and an instinctive feeling for the way cash flowed, and that year he joined forces with pop producer Mickie Most to buy out the contract of the rock group The Yardbirds from their manager Simon Napier-Bell. While Most was content to work with the group in the studio, Grant joined The Yardbirds on the road as their tour manager. With Grant threatening and bullying unscrupulous nightclub owners and promoters alike, The Yardbirds were finally earning good wages, a fact not lost on guitarist Jimmy Page. When The Yardbirds disbanded in July of 1968, Page recruited three others to fulfil contracted tour dates, and Grant became the manager of the new group. Originally calling themselves The New Yardbirds, Page, John Paul Jones, Robert Plant and John Bonham soon evolved into the all conquering blues rock supergroup Led Zeppelin. After the group recorded tracks for what would be their first album, Grant flew to the US and negotiated a lucrative contract with Atlantic Records. With the fearless, intimidating and massively built Grant at the helm, Led Zeppelin were *always* paid in full, in cash, and stories about their legendary manager became common currency in rock circles. Once, in New Orleans, Grant spotted two US Marines making fun of Page and Plant for their long hair. "What's your problem Popeye?" Grant allegedly growled, picking up both Marines by the collars of their uniforms and repeatedly knocking their heads together. Making both himself and the group rich through hit albums and constant tours, Grant alienated rock promoters in 1972 when he demanded 90 per cent of the gate receipts at all of the group's concerts. Thereafter he maintained Led Zeppelin's legendary and somewhat mystical status by shrewdly distancing them from their fans, and touring selectively as the Seventies progressed. Grant's policy of never allowing Atlantic to release a Led Zeppelin single in the UK and refusing all requests to appear on television further enhanced his and the group's uncompromising status. With Led Zeppelin given its own Swan Song subsidiary by Atlantic in 1974, Grant headed the label, signing Bad Company, whom he also managed, The Pretty Things, and former Stone The Crows vocalist, Maggie Bell. Now weighing in at 300 pounds, Grant was joined by others in attacking an employee of promoter Bill Graham at the Oakland Coliseum in 1977. Grant

and the others had beaten Jim Matzorkis to a pulp. Though arrested and later found guilty, Grant received a suspended sentence. Following the sudden death of Led Zeppelin drummer John Bonham in 1980, the group disbanded and a devastated Grant, rumoured to be addicted to heroin, left the music industry. A subsequent dispute over royalties between Led Zeppelin and Grant was quietly settled. Retiring to the South Coast resort of Eastbourne, Grant became something of a recluse but he remained a legendary figure from an era when the music industry was run by trailblazing pioneers as opposed to lawyers and accountants. Towards the end of his life Grant re-emerged into the public eye, much slimmed down, and appeared at music industry functions as a benign father figure, much respected by younger managers.
CAUSE: He suffered a heart attack in the back of a car on the way to his home in Eastbourne.
FURTHER READING: Davis, Stephen. (1985). *Hammer Of The Gods*. New York: William Morrow.

James Graves

Born 1941
Died 1967
Drummer for the R&B group, Junior Walker & the All Stars, James Graves joined the Battle Creek/Detroit-based group in the early Sixties. Discovered by former Moonglows singer Harvey Fuqua, the saxophonist-centred instrumental group first recorded on the Fuqua-owned Harvey Records in 1962. With Harvey Records purchased by Motown, Walker and the band recorded on the Motown subsidiary, Soul Records, landing a Top 10 entry with its first song with vocals, 'Shotgun'. The group's hit run continued into the early Seventies with the Holland-Dozier-Holland number, '(I'm A) Road Runner' (1966) and a live cover version of Marvin Gaye's 'How Sweet It Is To Be Loved By You' (1966).
CAUSE: Car crash.

Rob Graves

(ROBERT RITTER)
Born c. 1960
Died June 28, 1990
A veteran of the Los Angeles punk scene, Rob Graves passed through a number of groups, especially thriving in the noted goth-metal outfit, 45 Grave. Graves subsequently joined The Bags, Thelonius Monster, and his final group, Zelig of Hollywood.
CAUSE: He died of a heroin overdose in New York City.

Les Gray

(THOMAS LESLIE GRAY)
Born April 9, 1946
Died February 21, 2004
The animated lead singer of glam-rock group Mud, Les Gray was a popular entertainer in the UK during the mid Seventies. A native of Carshalton, Surrey, Gray formed Mud in 1966. Having released records on both CBS and Philips but with no success, the group were rediscovered in 1973 by legendary pop producer Mickie Most, and signed to his label, RAK. An immediate success, Mud achieved a trio of chart-topping singles in the UK, 'Tiger Feet', 'Lonely This Christmas' and 'Oh Boy'. After the group disbanded in 1977, Gray pursued a solo career, including a British hit with a cover of The Mindbenders' 1966 hit, 'A Groovy Kind Of Love'. Continuing to tour as Les Gray's Mud, he performed until throat cancer forced him from his career in December 2002.
CAUSE: He suffered a heart attack while battling throat cancer. He blamed his malady on heavy smoking. Choosing chemotherapy over surgery which would have required the removal of his vocal cords, he had hoped to save his voice. He died at his home in the Algarve, Portugal, where he had lived for 12 years.

Milt Grayson

(Milton B. Grayson, Jr.)
Born August 22, 1931
Died September 3, 2005
A member of the R&B group Billy Ward & The Dominoes during their pop-oriented period in the late Fifties, Milt Grayson left his job as a waiter in 1955 to replace Prentice Moreland (who would occasionally return to the fold). A Juilliard-trained vocalist, Grayson often shared lead vocal duties with the group's tenor, Jackie Wilson (who would leave The Dominoes in 1957 for a solo career). With their King-Federal Records contract expiring, the group landed at Decca Records in 1955. Abandoning their signature blues-rooted R&B sound for mainstream pop, the group scored a trio of Top 40 hits (none of which landed on the R&B charts) with 'St. Therese Of The Roses', 'Star Dust' and 'Deep Purple'. Grayson left the group in 1958 and, after a stint as a solo artist at Keen Records, began a three-year term in 1960 as a vocalist with Duke Ellington. Grayson subsequently worked as a Las Vegas entertainer, a member of Harry Belafonte's backing band The Belafonte Folk Singers, and then performed in a number of Broadway musicals including *Porgy & Bess* and *Trumpets Of The Lord.* Late in his career, he joined Wynton Marsalis & The Lincoln Center Jazz Orchestra.
Cause: Unknown. He died in New York City.

Ric Grech

Born November 1, 1946
Died March 17, 1990
Noteworthy bass player and a member of a series of progressive British rock bands, Ric Grech was born in Bordeaux, France, but reared in Britain. Joining a local soul-rock band The Farinas in Leicester, England, in the mid Sixties as the bass player, the group also included guitarist John Whitney and saxophonist Jim King. The Farinas evolved into Family in 1966 with the addition of singer Roger Chapman and drummer Rob Townsend. After a successful residency at the UFO Club in London, the group was discovered by pop producer John Gilbert who became their manager. An eclectic, progressive group marked by Chapman's unorthodox vocals and Grech's bass and violin, Family was a British cult favourite with their début album, the Dave Mason-produced *Music In A Doll's House* (1968). A follow-up album, *Family Entertainment* (1969), was highlighted by the tracks, 'Hung Up Down' and 'The Weaver's Answer'; Grech had composed several of the album's tracks, including 'How Hi The Li'. Shortly after the start of their first US tour, Grech quit Family to join Blind Faith with Eric Clapton on vocals and guitar, Steve Winwood on vocals and keyboard, and Ginger Baker on drums. Blind Faith was arguably rock's first supergroup, but they released only one album, *Blind Faith.* With Blind Faith dissolving, Grech, Winwood and others joined Baker in his new group, Airforce. After recording two albums with the group in 1970, *Airforce* and *Airforce 2*, Grech left in late 1970 to join Traffic, first appearing on the live album *Welcome To The Canteen* (1971). Leaving Traffic in late 1971 after the sessions for *The Low Spark Of High Heeled Boys*, Grech would later emerge in the short-lived Mike Bloomfield-headed supergroup KGB. A popular session player, Grech would work with a slew of musical acts in the Seventies including The Bee Gees, Graham Bond, Jim Capaldi, Eric Clapton, Gram Parsons, Rod Stewart, Muddy Waters, and the duo of Ron Wood and Ronnie Lane. Grech's finest work is collected on the anthology album *The Last Five Years.*
Cause: Kidney and liver failure. He died in Leicester, England. At the time of his death he was reported to be destitute.

Cal Green

(CALVIN HENRY GREEN)
Born June 22, 1935
Died July 6, 2004
The guitarist of pioneering R&B/doo-wop group The Midnighters, Cal Green performed on most of the group's output in the Fifties, and co-wrote their 1957 hit 'Is Your Love For Real?' Reared on the blues, guitarist Green was hired during a 1954 tour stop in Texas, as the replacement for Arthur Porter who had been drafted. Joining in time for the group's massive hit, the bawdy 'Work With Me, Annie', Green also appeared on the follow-ups, 'Annie Had A Baby' and 'Annie's Aunt Fanny'. As a session musician, Green worked with Bill Doggett, providing guitar on Little Willie John's 'Fever'. Imprisoned for possession of marijuana in 1959, Green spent three years behind bars and, upon his release, he briefly rejoined The Midnighters. He later issued solo material and worked with the jazz acts, Charles Kynard and Brother Jack McDuff.
CAUSE: He died in Lake View Terrace, California, after suffering an aneurysm.

Doc Green

Born October 8, 1934
Died March 10, 1989
Baritone singer for The Drifters from 1959–1962, Doc Green was born and raised in Harlem where he would sing on street corners. An upbeat, big-boned man, Green formed a group called The Harmonaires in 1952. From that group, Green and childhood friend, Wilbur "Yonkie" Paul, joined three brothers – James, John and Claude Clark – in forming The Five Crowns. Recording for Rainbow Records, the group would score a regional hit with 'You're My Inspiration' (1952). After numerous personnel changes including the addition of Ben E. King, the group shortened its name to The Crowns. (Beginning in 1955, Green and Crown member Paul would simultaneously record with The Duvals.) Meanwhile, after The Crowns completed a one-week engagement at the Apollo Theater in 1958, The Drifters manager George Treadwell fired his group and hired The Crowns as the new Drifters. Headed by vocalist Ben E. King and adding a string section, The Drifters scored their first hit with a King composition, 'There Goes My Baby' (1959), and continued with 'This Magic Moment' (1960) and 'Save The Last Dance For Me' (1960). With Rudy Lewis taking over lead vocal duties, The Drifters hits continued with 'Some Kind Of Wonderful' (1961), 'Sweets For My Sweet' (1961), and 'Up On The Roof' (1962). Having never provided lead vocals on any Drifter's song, Green left the group in late 1962 along with bass singer Tommy Evans, and formed an unsuccessful Drifters copy group called The Drapers. In 1964 Green joined a new touring version of The Moonglows which was formed by lead singer, Alexander Graves, recording at Lana Records. Also in 1964, Green and Evans toured in an alternate, short-lived Drifters outfit which had been formed by The Crowns' manager Lover Peterson. By 1966, Green and Evans led a quartet called The Floaters (not the same group of 'Float On' fame), before joining a group called The Exciting Changes. Then in 1971, Green joined Charlie Thomas' version of The Drifters, recording three albums and performing mostly outside the US. In 1978, Green attempted to form his own Drifters group but was legally challenged by Thomas who had a copyright on the group's name. Later that year a court assigned the group's name to three members: Doc Green, Charlie Thomas and Elsbearry Hobbs. In the Eighties, Green also performed with a touring version of Vito & The Salutations.
CAUSE: Cancer. He died at home in Fresh Meadows, New York.

FURTHER READING: Allan, Tony (1993). *Save The Last Dance For Me: The Musical Legacy Of The Drifters, 1953–1993*. Ann Arbor, MI: Popular Culture.

Tyrone "Crusher" Green

Born October 30, 1944
Died January 8, 2002
The drummer in Wilson Pickett's backing band The Midnight Movers, Tyrone "Crusher" Green joined the soul outfit in 1965. Eventually becoming Pickett's musical director, Green worked on his many hits including 'Land Of A Thousand Dances', 'Mustang Sally' and 'Funky Broadway'. Green stayed with Pickett for four decades, until falling ill. Green also worked with The Shirelles, Maxine Brown and Lucky Peterson.
CAUSE: Pancreatic cancer. He died in Long Island, New York.

Vernon Green

Born May 1, 1937
Died December 24, 2000
As the lead singer and founder of the doo-wop act The Medallions, Vernon Green had a pair of West Coast hits in the mid Fifties with 'The Letter' and its flip side, 'Buick '59'. Green also sang lead for The Cameos and The Phantoms but after being involved in a serious car accident in the mid Sixties, Green left music for nearly a decade.
CAUSE: Suffering a debilitating stroke, he never recovered. He died at his home in Los Angeles.

Florence Greenberg

Born September 16, 1913
Died November 2, 1995
A housewife turned record company founder, Florence Greenberg had no musical or business training when she entered the music industry. A former Republican campaign worker who was married to an accountant, she managed to do the impossible, heading one of the biggest independent labels of the Sixties. Initially launching the tiny Tiara label, she recorded The Shirelles, leasing some of the masters to Decca Records in 1958. Joined by songwriter and producer Luther Dixon (of '16 Candles' fame), Greenberg formed Scepter Records. With Decca losing interest in The Shirelles group, Greenberg re-signed the group the following year. With Greenberg also acting as their manager, the bouffant-wig wearing Shirelles scored a string of girl-group hits including a cover of The 5 Royals' 'Dedicated To The One I Love', the seminal 'Will You Love Me Tomorrow' (No. 1), 'Mama Said', 'Baby It's You' (covered by The Beatles) and 'Soldier Boy' (also No. 1). When Scepter expanded to include the Wand Records subsidiary, Greenberg enjoyed a series of hits with The Kingsmen ('Louie, Louie'), The Isley Brothers ('Twist And Shout'), Dionne Warwick ('Walk On By'), Chuck Jackson ('Any Day Now'), and B.J. Thomas ('Raindrops Keep Falling On My Head'). After refusing an offer to sell the label for $6 million to Gulf & Western in 1965, Greenberg watched as the major record companies reclaimed their turf. She was forced to shutter Scepter in 1977.
CAUSE: Stroke, she died at the Hackensack University Medical Center in New Jersey.

Chuck Greenberg

Born March 25, 1950
Died September 4, 1995
Co-founder of the eclectic folk/rock/jazz fusion sextet Shadowfax, saxophonist and keyboardist Chuck Greenberg launched the group in an Illinois farmhouse in 1972. Recording 10 albums in all, the group broke through with the jazz-influenced album *Shadowfax* in 1982; their 1988 release *Folk Songs For A Nuclear Village* earned a Grammy. The group's chief songwriter, Greenfield played the flute, piccolo, saxophone, and an instrument he popularised, the lyricon.
CAUSE: He suffered a heart attack

while holidaying with his family on Santa Cruz Island in southern California.

Lorne Greene

(LORNE HYMAN GREENE)
Born February 12, 1915
Died September 11, 1987
Silver-haired star of TV's *Bonanza* who scored a number one hit single with the spoken word song 'Ringo' (1964), the Canadian-born Lorne Green began in show business as an announcer for CBC in 1940.
CAUSE: He died of complications following abdominal surgery for a bleeding ulcer at a Santa Monica, California hospital.

Howard Greenfield

Born March 15, 1936
Died March 4, 1986
A prolific lyricist who partnered Neil Sedaka, Howard Greenfield co-penned most of Sedaka's hits. As classmates at Lincoln High School in Brooklyn, Greenfield and Sedaka formed a neighbourhood teenage rock group before launching their fruitful songwriting partnership. After Sedaka spent a brief stint as a member of The Tokens, he teamed with Greenfield on their first success – the Connie Francis hit 'Stupid Cupid'. Selling a number of compositions to Atlantic Records, the pair's songs were recorded by LaVern Baker and Clyde McPhatter. Recommended by songwriter Doc Pomus, Greenfield and Sedaka were hired as house writers at the Don Kirshner/Al Nevins operated Aldon Music. Recognising the vocal talents of the Juilliard-trained Sedaka, Nevins and Kirshner helped him land a recording contract with RCA. Providing the melodies to Greenfield's lyrics, Sedaka churned out a series of hits including 'Happy Birthday, Sweet Sixteen', 'Breaking Up Is Hard To Do', 'Calendar Girl' and 'Next Door To An Angel'. Apart from Sedaka, Greenfield collaborated with Quincy Jones, Phil Everly, Carole King, and Paul Anka. Maintaining his songwriting partnership with Sedaka, Greenfield won a Grammy for the chart-topping hit 'Love Will Keep Us Together' (The Captain & Tennille).
CAUSE: AIDS-related heart failure. He died at Cedars-Sinai Hospital in Los Angeles.

"Big" John Greer

(JOHN MARSHALL GREER)
Born November 21, 1923
Died May 12, 1972
Singer and saxophonist who was a member of Lucky Millinder's band in the late Forties, "Big" John Greer was the featured vocalist on Millinder's R&B hit 'Little Girl Don't Cry' (1949). Leaving to pursue a solo career at RCA-Victor and its Groove subsidiary, he scored a Top 5 R&B hit in 1952 as by John Greer & His Rhythm Rockers with 'Got You On My Mind', featuring the piano talents of Bill Doggett. Recording at King Records, he scored no further hits, but did play saxophone on labelmate Annisteen Allen's hit, 'Baby I'm Doin' It' (1953).
CAUSE: Unknown.

Bryan Gregory

(GREGORY BECKER)
Born 1955
Died January 10, 2001
The co-founder of Midwest punk-psychobilly band The Cramps, Bryan Gregory formed the group in 1975 with his sister Pam Beckerleg, Lux Interior and Poison Ivy Rorschach. A native of Detroit, Gregory had met the band's leader, Lux Interior, while working in a record store. Making their début at CBGB's in New York City, the group cultivated a loyal legion of fans. Unable to attract record company interest, The Cramps released material on their Vengeance label but were signed by Miles Copeland's IRS Records, and recorded the Alex Chilton-produced *Songs The Lord Taught Us* album. In May 1980,

for reasons never fully explained, Gregory absconded with the group's van, which contained all their equipment, and never returned. He later joined a series of lesser known bands such as The Dials, Beast and Shiver.
CAUSE: Suffering a heart attack, he died several weeks later after contracting pneumonia. He died at Anaheim Memorial Hospital.

Gerald "Bounce" Gregory

Born 1934
Died February 12, 1999
The bass singer of The Spaniels, Gerald "Bounce" Gregory formed the doo-wop group with classmates at Roosevelt High School in Gary, Indiana, originally as Pookie Hudson and The Hudsonaires. Recording the Hudson/Gregory composition, The Spaniels landed in the R&B Top 10 with 'Baby, It's You'. Featuring Gregory's extremely low bass voice, The Spaniels would follow up with the doo-wop classic, 'Goodnight Sweetheart, Goodnight' (the song was supplanted on the pop charts by The McGuire Sisters' white-bread cover version). Following several personnel changes, The Spaniels landed their final hit in 1960 with 'I Know'. Gregory left the group in 1961. An imposing man who often wore a patch over his glass eye, Gregory later abused alcohol.
CAUSE: Unknown. He died in Gary, Indiana.
FURTHER READING: Carter, Richard G. (1994). *Goodnight Sweetheart, Goodnight: The Story Of The Spaniels.* Sicklerville, NJ: August.

Winston Grennan

Born September 16, 1944
Died October 27, 2000
A pioneering Jamaican drummer, Winston Grennan is credited with inventing and popularising the "one drop" style reggae rhythm. Ignoring his mother's pleas to become a doctor, he instead followed the lead of his many relatives who were professional musicians. Emerging during the ska/rock-steady period of Jamaican music, Grennan worked with The Paragons, Phyllis Dillon and the emerging Bob Marley & The Wailers. Encouraged to move to the US by jazzman Dizzy Gillespie, Grennan settled in Woodstock, New York, and began working with a number of rock and R&B artists including Paul Simon ('Mother And Child Reunion'), The Rolling Stones (*Goat's Head Soup*), The O'Jays, Marvin Gaye, Aretha Franklin and Kid Creole & The Coconuts. Returning to Jamaica for a period, he recorded under the name of Winston Richards. In the Nineties, Grennan led The Ska Rocks, recording five albums.
CAUSE: He died at his home in Nantucket, Massachusetts, as a result of lung and bone cancer.

Rob Gretton

(ROBERT LEE GRETTON)
Born January 15, 1953
Died May 15, 1999
Manchester born Rob Gretton was the manager of Joy Division and New Order and an important force in the rise of the post-punk Manchester music scene. He began his music career as a DJ at Rafters Club where he first saw Joy Division, then called Warsaw, in 1977. Taking over their management, he signed them to Tony Wilson's locally based Factory Records, originally to record a track on the *A Factory Sampler* EP. Instead of taking the much touted group to a major label, Gretton remained loyal to Factory in which he would later become a substantial shareholder. With the death of singer Ian Curtis, Gretton encouraged the other three members of Joy Division to regroup as New Order, a name he chose, and thereafter steered the group to international fame. More recently Greeton had launched his own label, Rob's Records. Prematurely

grey, Gretton was known for his love of gambling, especially on the chart potential of New Order records.
CAUSE: Heart attack.

Herman Lewis Griffin

Born November 25, 1936
Died November 11, 1989
Leader of the 11-piece soul group The Boys In The Band, Herman Lewis Griffin scored a minor R&B hit in 1970 with 'Money Music'. Griffin was once married to Motown singer Mary Wells.
CAUSE: Heart attack.

James "Sonny" Griffin

Born December 18, 1930
Died December 16, 2003
As the tenor of the New Haven, Connecticut-based doo-wop group The Nutmegs, James "Sonny" Griffin had a pair of hits in 1955 with 'Story Untold' and 'Ship Of Love'. Led by his brother Leroy Griffin, the group had formed two years earlier as The Lyres.
CAUSE: Unknown. He died in New Haven, Connecticut.

Jimmy Griffin

(JAMES ARTHUR GRIFFIN)
Born August 10, 1943
Died January 11, 2005
A singer-songwriter, Jimmy Griffin was a member of both Bread and The Remingtons. Born in Cincinnati but raised in Memphis, he took accordion lessons from the age of seven at the Central Academy of Music and performed locally during his teen years. Moving to California, he was befriended by his former neighbours, rockabilly musicians Dorsey and Johnny Burnette, who aided Griffin in securing a recording contract with Reprise Records. Working with legendary producer Jimmy Bowen, Griffin's début album, *Summer Holiday* (1963), was a collection of cover songs but he matured as a songwriter, with his material recorded by Lesley Gore, Bobby Vee, and Ed Ames among others. Expanding into other avenues, Griffin secured minor roles in a number of films including *Those Who Think Brave*. In 1969, Griffin joined fellow LA singer-songwriter David Gates and session man Larry Knechtal in forming the soft-rock group Bread. One of the most dependable acts on the US pop charts during the early Seventies, the group had a healthy hit run with a series of ballads including 'Make It With You', 'It Don't Matter To Me', 'If', 'Baby I'm-A Want You', 'Everything I Own', 'The Guitar Man', 'Aubrey' and 'Lost Without Your Love'. During this period, Griffin co-wrote 'For All We Know', the Academy Award-winning theme for the film *Lovers And Other Strangers*, which was a hit for The Carpenters. With Bread disbanding in 1977, Griffin returned to solo work, issuing a series of albums. By the late Eighties, Griffin joined Billy Swan and former Eagles member Randy Meisner in the group Black Tie; not a successful venture, the trio's only minor country hit came with a cover of the Buddy Holly composition, 'Learning The Game'. In 1991, Griffin teamed with former Cymarron members Richard Mainegra and Rick Yancey to form another country band, The Remingtons; the group had a trio of hits beginning with 'A Long Time Ago' (1991).
CAUSE: Complications from cancer. He died at his home in the Nashville suburb of Franklin, Tennessee.

Leroy Griffin

Born April 5, 1934
Died September 1966
Leader of the doo-wop group The Nutmegs, Leroy Griffin had previously formed a series of vocal outfits in his native New Haven, Connecticut. After recording an obscure single for the tiny J&G label with The Four Haven Knights, Griffin organized The Lyres; renamed The Nutmegs, the group signed with Herald Records where they would score a pair of Griffin-penned

hits in 1955 with 'Story Untold' and 'Ship Of Love'. Following Griffin's untimely death in 1966, the group continued with his nephew Harold James at the helm.
CAUSE: While working at a steel mill, he either fell or was pushed into a blast furnace.

Johnny Griffith

(JOHN ELLIS GRIFFITH JR.)
Born July 10, 1936
Died November 12, 2002
A member of the legendary Motown session band The Funk Brothers, Johnny Griffith provided the keyboards on countless hits for the label including Marvin Gaye's 'I Heard It Through The Grapevine', The Temptations' 'Ain't Too Proud To Beg' and The Supremes' 'Stop! In The Name Of Love'. A classically trained musician who earned two college degrees, Griffith had originally arrived at Motown to work at their short-lived jazz subsidiary, Workshop Jazz.
CAUSE: He suffered a heart attack after watching the Detroit premiere of the documentary film about The Funk Brothers, *Standing In The Shadows Of Motown*. He had performed at the Apollo Theater the night before his death.

Paul Griffith

Born 1938
Died June 14, 2000
A prolific session player, Paul Griffin provided piano and organ for myriad artists including Aretha Franklin, Bob Dylan, The Isley Brothers, Don McLean, and Steely Dan. Griffith honed his craft as a child by watching the organists at his Baptist church in Harlem, before studying classical music. Griffith also worked with Dionne Warwick on all of her Burt Bacharach/Hal David sessions. His most identifiable performance came on the intro to B.J. Thomas' smash hit, 'Raindrops Keep Fallin' On My Head'.
CAUSE: Stricken with diabetes and awaiting a liver transplant, he suffered a heart attack at his home in New York City.

Eric Griffiths

(ERIC RONALD GRIFFITHS)
Born October 31, 1940
Died January 29, 2005
A founding member of The Quarry Men, a group which evolved into The Beatles, Eric Griffiths was replaced in 1958 by a young George Harrison. A guitarist and backing vocalist, Griffiths would play alongside John Lennon and Paul McCartney. Minus their more famous Beatles progeny, members of The Quarry Men reunited for a tour and album in 1997.
CAUSE: Pancreatic cancer. He died at his home in Edinburgh, Scotland.

Tiny Grimes

(LLOYD GRIMES)
Born July 7, 1916
Died March 4, 1989
R&B and jazz guitarist and bandleader who worked with Screamin' Jay Hawkins and Red Prysock, Tiny Grimes also led his own popular jump-blues group, The Rocking Highlanders, in the Forties and Fifties. Grimes emerged from the field of jazz as a drummer in bands led by Charlie Parker and Art Tatum. In later years he worked in small combos in the New York City area.
CAUSE: Meningitis. He died at a New York City hospital.

Don Grolnick

Born September 23, 1947
Died June 1, 1996
Songwriter, producer, and session player, Don Grolnick was a member of Seventies jazz-rock group, Dreams. As a session pianist, he worked with Michael Brecker, Bonnie Raitt, Steely Dan, James Brown and Carly Simon. As a musical director, he worked with James Taylor on several albums including *New Moon Shine*. Grolnick completed a solo album, *Medianoche*,

shortly before his death.
CAUSE: Non-Hodgkins lymphoma. He died at Mount Sinai Hospital in New York City.

Albert Grossman

(ALBERT B. GROSSMAN)
Born May 21, 1926
Died January 25, 1986
Folk and rock music impresario, Albert Grossman is best known for managing Bob Dylan during the Sixties. Born in Chicago to Russian-Jewish immigrants, Grossman was fired from a position in the Chicago Housing Authority in the early Fifties (he would later falsely claim to have earned a business degree). Joining a friend in opening The Gate Of Horn, a pioneering Chicago folk and blues venue, Grossman booked acts such as Big Bill Broonzy. Turning his attention to management, Grossman oversaw the career of a frequent performer at his club, folk-blues singer Odetta. After co-directing the inaugural Newport Folk Festival, Grossman moved to New York City where he frequented the folk clubs of Greenwich Village. Assembling Peter, Paul & Mary, Grossman also brought them their biggest hit, the Bob Dylan composition 'Blowin' In The Wind'. Signing Dylan to a 10-year contract in 1962, Grossman gave himself a healthy percentage of the performer's earnings. Legendary for his evasiveness with the press and for his negotiating skills, Grossman was captured at his best in the Dylan documentary *Don't Look Back*, particularly during his bartering with London agent Tito Burns. Tutoring and inviting Dylan into his home for two years, Grossman was crucial in the marketing of the brilliant folk singer. Accused of orchestrating Dylan's switch from acoustic to electric music, Grossman got into a backstage brawl with researcher Alan Lomax over the issue at the 1965 Newport Folk Festival. Also that year, Grossman and Dylan launched their own music publishing company. With the signing of Janis Joplin, Grossman increased his stable of acts, which also included John Lee Hooker, Ian & Sylvia, Gordon Lightfoot, and Dylan's perennial backing group, The Band. By the late Sixties, Goldman was losing many of his star acts. Dylan left Grossman in 1969, the relationship dissolved by a court two years later; in 1970 Peter, Paul & Mary disbanded; and in 1971 Joplin died of an overdose. Moving away from the music industry, Grossman settled in rural Woodstock, in upstate New York. There he launched his own record label, Bearsville Records, signing Todd Rundgren, Foghat and Jesse Winchester.
CAUSE: Heart attack. He died while asleep on a flight to London.
FURTHER READING: Goodman, Fred. (1997). *Mansion On The Hill.* Scaduto, Anthony (1971, reprinted 1996). *Bob Dylan.* London: Helter Skelter/Rogan House. Shelton, Robert (1986). *No Direction Home: The Life And Music Of Bob Dylan.* London: New English Library.

Dave Guard

Born November 19, 1934
Died March 22, 1991
A member of the popular folk outfit The Kingston Trio, Honolulu-born Dave Guard was initially a fan of the island's jazz scene but after the bombing of nearby Pearl Harbor, Guard and his family moved to Washington DC. Discovering R&B and rock only after attending Stanford University in California, Guard subsequently jumped on the calypso craze. Playing banjo, Guard was joined by guitarist Nick Reynolds in a San Francisco-based quartet called The Calypsonians. With the addition of Bob Shane, Guard's singing partner from his teenage days in Honolulu, the group evolved into The Kingston Trio. After filling in for comedienne Phyllis Diller, the trio earned an extended

engagement at a San Francisco nightclub, where they caught the attention of Capitol Records. Signing with the label, The Kingston Trio emerged at a time when left-wing folkies like Pete Seeger were blacklisted for their political activities. Donning striped-shirts and short-hair, the clean-cut Kingston Trio made folk music a respectable, family genre, opening the doors for more political folk artists such as Joan Baez and Bob Dylan. Called the originators of the folk music craze, The Kingston Trio topped the pop charts with their second single 'Tom Dooley' (1958), a song which Guard had based on a 19th century folk song, 'Tom Dula'. With two of the three members hailing from Hawaii, Guard and others had little previous exposure to folk music and were forced to search many sources for material to record. Their hit run continuing with 'The Tijuana Jail' (1959), 'M.T.A.' (1959), 'A Worried Man' (1959), 'El Matador' (1960), and 'Bad Man Blunder' (1960), The Kingston Trio landed on the cover of *Life* and appeared at both the Newport folk and jazz festivals. Quitting the group shortly after getting married, Guard was angry over the disappearance of his songwriting royalties, and his record label's demand of three albums a year. Guard was replaced in the group by John Stewart (later of 'Gold' fame). Forming The Whiskeyhill Singers with lead vocalist Judy Henske, Guard released a sole album in 1962, and provided the music for the film *How The West Was Won*. With Capitol Records losing interest in his group, Guard moved to Australia to raise a family. There he wrote a pair of books and hosted his own television programme. Guard joined John Stewart for some sessions in 1979.
CAUSE: Diagnosed with skin cancer in 1978, he later died of lymphoma at his home in Rollinsford, New Hampshire.

John Guerin

(JOHN PAYNE GUERIN)
Born October 31, 1939
Died January 5, 2004
A prolific self-taught session drummer, John Guerin recorded with hundreds of jazz and rock acts. Born in Hawaii but raised in San Diego, he began his professional music career in the field of jazz, as a member of Buddy DeFranco's quartet, and then, The George Shearing Quintet. Relocating to Los Angeles later in the Sixties, he worked with the likes of Peggy Lee, Ella Fitzgerald, Frank Sinatra, The Byrds, Frank Zappa, Joni Mitchell, Thelonious Monk and Lou Rawls. Guerin also co-led his own group, LA Express, with sax player Tom Scott, recording four albums. During the Seventies Guerin composed and performed a series of film scores and advertising jingles. In the Nineties, he worked with Oscar Peterson, Ray Charles, John Faddis, Sonny Rollins, Jimmy Heath and others. He also wrote the instructional drumming book, *Jazz + Rock = John Guerin*.
CAUSE: Pneumonia.

Stacy Guess

Born November 21, 1964
Died March 11, 1998
A founding member of the jazz/neo-swing band The Squirrel Nut Zippers, trumpet player Stacy Guess died before the group achieved fame. Joining the group in 1993, he performed on their début album *The Inevitable Squirrel Nut Zippers*. Leaving the group in 1995 to seek treatment for his drug addiction, he did not appear on their breakthrough million-selling disc, *Hot*. The tribute album, *Legacy*, features Guess' work with The Squirrel Nut Zippers as well as tracks from his previous groups, The Pressure Boys and The Sex Police.
CAUSE: Heroin overdose. He had been in a coma for four days.

Eleanor O. Guest

Born 1940
Died August 23, 1997
Original member of Gladys Knight & The Pips, Eleanor O. Guest appeared on the group's first single, 'Whistle My Love' (1958). The group formed in 1952 when several extended family members had sung together after a record player broke at her brother Bubba's 10th birthday party. Married and pregnant with her first child, Guest left the struggling group in 1959. In the Seventies, Guest promoted gospel music as part of James Cleveland's Gospel Music Workshop of America.
CAUSE: Heart failure. She died at Southwest Hospital in Atlanta.

Greg Guidry

(GREGORY M. GUIDRY)
Born January 23, 1950
Died July 31, 2003
A singer-songwriter and pianist, Greg Guidry scored his only hit in 1982 with 'Goin' Down', a track from his début album *Over The Line*. Reared in his family's gospel group, Guidry got his first break in 1981 when he provided backing vocals on The Allman Brothers' album *Brothers Of The Road*. Guidry's compositions have been recorded by Rex Smith, Robbie Dupree, The Climax Blues Band and England Dan & John Ford Coley.
CAUSE: His charred body was found in a parked car inside the garage of his home in Fairview, Tennessee, five days after his death.

Isaac Guillory

Born February 27, 1947
Died December 31, 2000
A folk-rock singer-songwriter, Isaac Guillory is best known as a member of the pop-rock group The Cryan' Shames. Born on the US naval base at Guantanamo in pre-Castro Cuba, Guillory began studying classical piano at the Conservatory of Music in Havana beginning at age six; his mother later taught him to play guitar. While enrolled at St. John's River Junior College, Guillory joined a popular local band called The Illusions. Continuing his musical education at a pair of Chicago area colleges, he formed The Ravelles, who sometimes played on the same bill as rising local bands The Flock and The Cryan' Shames. But with The Cryan' Shames in need of a bass player, Guillory switched from guitar and joined the group for two albums, *A Scratch In The Sky* (1967), featuring four of Guillory's compositions, and *Synthesis* (1968). With the group disbanding in 1970, Guillory moved to Europe. Meeting Al Stewart in Holland, he was exposed to the emerging British folk scene, and on occasion, joined Stewart on stage. Joined by former Cryan' Shames member James Fairs, Guillory recorded his first solo album, *Isaac Guillory Side One* (1973). Subsequently joining Elkie Brooks' group, Guillory was then hired by Donovan and replaced guitarist Big Jim Sullivan in the jazz group, Pacific Eardrum. As a session player Guillory played guitar on Buggles' 1979 new wave hit, 'Video Killed The Radio Star'. In the Eighties, Guillory joined Barbara Dickson, first as her opening act, and then as her guitarist and musical director. Returning to his roots, Guillory reunited in 1982 with The Cryan' Shames for a massive concert in Chicago. He continued to record and tour until weeks before his death.
CAUSE: Cancer.

Johnny Guitar

(JOHN BYRNE)
Born December 4, 1939
Died August 18, 1999
The guitarist and vocalist for Rory Storm & The Hurricanes, Johnny Guitar was drawn into music during the mid Fifties British skiffle craze. He teamed up with Alan Caldwell (the future Rory Storm) to form, among other monikers, The (Raving) Texan Skiffle Group. Switching to rock in

1959, the renamed Rory Storm & The Hurricanes emerged as one of Liverpool's leading bands, and was the first such group to perform at the renowned Cavern Club. During this period John Byrne became Johnny Guitar (after the title of a 1953 film Western) and drummer Richard Starkey became Ringo Starr; it was Guitar who had convinced Starr to leave his factory job to join the band on a full-time basis. Sharing equal billing with The Beatles at the Kaiserkeller in Hamburg, The Hurricanes eventually lost their drummer to the group in 1962. Unable to recover from the loss of Starr, and only mediocre musicians, Rory Storm & The Hurricanes trudged along with a series of drummers but soon fell from popularity. With the group disbanding in 1966, Johnny Guitar took a position with an ambulance service, retiring in 1998. In 1980, he launched The New Hurricanes.
CAUSE: Suffering from undisclosed motor neurone disease, he collapsed and died at his home in Liverpool.

Guitar Slim

(EDDIE JONES)
Born December 10, 1926
Died February 7, 1959
Mississippi-born electric blues guitarist who made his base in New Orleans in the Fifties, Guitar Slim initially joined a group led by Huey "Piano" Smith. An exquisite showman who employed a 300-foot guitar chord, Guitar Slim combined gospel-rooted vocals with blasting, swampy, single-note solo guitar riffs. Signing with Specialty Records, he scored his million-selling signature piece in 1954 with 'The Things That I Used To Do'. Dropped by his label, he wound up at the Atlantic subsidiary, Atco, from 1956–58, where his heavy drinking had diluted the quality of his recorded output. In his band in the late Fifties was James "Thunderbird" Davis.
CAUSE: Pneumonia. He died in New York City.

Mark Guktowski

Born 1948
Died 1998
Guitarist of the Sixties bubblegum group, 1910 Fruitgum Company, Mark Guktowski was essentially a session player in the manufactured group overseen by producers Jerry Kasenetz and Jeff Katz. Giving the new Neil Bogart-headed Buddah Records its first hit in 1968 with the million-selling 'Simon Says', The 1910 Fruitgum Company invented a new subgenre of pop music aimed at the pre-adolescent. With bubblegum experiencing its last hurrah, the group's final hit came in 1969 with 'Special Delivery'.
CAUSE: Unknown.

Arthur Gunter

Born May 23, 1926
Died May 16, 1976
Nicknamed "Hardrock", Arthur Gunter gained fame for his original R&B/blues version of his self-composed hit, 'Baby, Let's Play House' (1954), a song later reprised at Sun Records by Elvis Presley. With none of Gunter's other Excello Records releases charting, he was dropped by the label in 1961.
CAUSE: Unknown. He died in Port Huron, Michigan.

Cornell Gunter

(CORNELIUS E. GUNTER)
Born November 14, 1938
Died February 26, 1990
Member of several R&B and doo-wop groups including The Coasters and The Flairs, Cornell Gunter was born in Coffeyville, Kansas, but raised in Las Vegas. Singing and playing the piano at his church, Gunter was encouraged to explore music by his mother, a professional R&B singer. Moving to Los Angeles in the early Fifties and attending Fremont High School,

Gunter was the original lead singer of The Platters. After performing with the group in several talent shows, an impatient Gunter quit (The Platters would soon find fame thanks to their mentor and manager, Buck Ram). A tall, muscular teen with good looks and a sharp smile, Gunter then joined The Hollywood Blue Jays, the group evolving into The Flairs. Featuring Richard Berry and Young Jessie, The Flairs recorded a series of doo-wop classics including 'You Should Care For Me', 'Love Me Girl', and their only real hit, the controversial 'She Wants To Rock'. But after Gunter brought his sister Shirley Gunter into the group in 1955, its members began to quarrel. Gunter left The Flairs and briefly rejoined The Platters for their live performances. Then, after a short stint with Charlie Fuqua's Ink Spots, in 1955 Gunter formed another vocal group, The Ermines, releasing several singles at Loma Records. The Ermines would evolve into a new Flairs group, and under Buck Ram's management, would record and tour with some of Ram's other groups. Leaving The Ermines in 1958, Gunter joined the Leiber & Stoller created group The Coasters as second tenor. With his exaggerated pompadour, Gunter fit right in with the comical R&B group. Featuring Gunter, The Coasters enjoyed crossover hits with 'Yakety Yak' (1958), the million selling 'Charlie Brown' (1959), 'Along Came Jones' (1959), and 'Poison Ivy' (1959). The group's final pop hit came in 1961 with a song about a stripper, 'Little Egypt'. Leaving The Coasters soon after, Gunter was replaced by ex-Cadillacs lead singer, Earl Carroll. Gunter then briefly joined Dinah Washington's revue before teaming with his sister Shirley to form his own version of The Coasters. Touring on the oldies circuit, Gunter was sued in 1971 by The Coasters' manager H.B. Barnum, and forced to drop any claims to the group. Gunter then joined a legitimate version of The Drifters in the late Seventies. But beginning in 1980, Gunter was leading the only authorised version of The Coasters.
CAUSE: Gunter was gunned down sitting at the wheel of his 1978 Camaro while stopped at an intersection in Las Vegas. Witnesses reported a loud argument between Gunter and a man who was standing at the driver's side of the car. After his windshield was showered by bullets, Gunter attempted to speed away. But due to his severe injuries, he drove into a brick wall. The motive for the shooting was never known. Gunter had been performing that week at the city's Lady Luck Hotel. His funeral expenses were paid by Bill Cosby and Sammy Davis, Jr. Gunter would not be the only Coasters member murdered in Las Vegas: Nate Wilson was killed in 1980. A suspect in Gunter's death, Kinnie Deon Poole, 19, was acquitted of the murder in a Las Vegas district court.
FURTHER READING: Millar, Bill. (1974). *The Coasters*. London: W.H. Allen & Co.

Billy Gussak

Born c. 1925
Died c. 1995

A session player and informal member of Bill Haley & The Comets, Billy Gussak played drums on the group's ground-breaking single, 'Rock Around The Clock'. Haley had first met Gussak at Essex Records, where he worked as a session drummer. Gussak performed on some of Haley's recordings at the label in the early Fifties, including the hit 'Crazy, Man, Crazy'. After Haley left the label to join Decca, producers wanted to replicate his early rock sound and hired Gussak for some sessions in place of Haley's regular drummer, Dick Boccelli. Recorded in just two takes at the cavernous Pythian Temple Studio in Manhattan, 'Rock Around The Clock' was a rushed affair because Sammy Davis Jr. was waiting in the

wings for his scheduled session. Released in 1954, the single was only a moderate hit, but the following year when the song was played over the opening credits of the controversial film *The Blackboard Jungle*, it returned to the charts and became the first number one single of the rock era. In 1955, Gussak joined a Comets' splinter group, The Jodimars.
CAUSE: Unknown.

Gwen Guthrie

Born July 14, 1950
Died February 4, 1999
A silky-voiced R&B singer who is best known for her solo hit 'Ain't Nothin' Goin' On But The Rent', Newark, New Jersey-native Gwen Guthrie had a long and fruitful career as a session vocalist. After backing Billy Preston on the album *Music Is My Life* (1972), singing on jingles for national ads such as Chevrolet and Avon, and passing through a pair of local groups, The Ebonettes and The Matchmakers (the latter group featuring future Cameo singer Larry Blackmon), Guthrie tried to settle into a position as a school teacher. In 1974, Guthrie joined Aretha Franklin on the road and in the studio, and appeared on the album *I'm In Love*. Also a songwriter, Guthrie teamed with Patrick Grant to pen seven songs on Sister Sledge's début album, Ben E. King's Top 10 British hit 'Supernatural Thing', and Angela Bofill's 'This Time I'll Be Sweeter'. In the late Seventies, Guthrie backed Roberta Flack, and penned her 1978 track 'God Don't Like Ugly'. Then, after backing former Wailer Peter Tosh, Guthrie was befriended by Island Records sessionmen Sly Dunbar and Robbie Shakespeare, the pair backing her on a pair of soulful albums, *Gwen Guthrie* and *Padlock*. Leaving Island Records, and still backed by Dunbar and Shakespeare, Guthrie wrote and produced her most successful, 'Ain't Nothin' Goin' On But The Rent' (1986). She followed up with a pair of British hits, a cover of '(They Long To Be) Close To You' and the title track of her album *Good To Go Lover*. Leaving Polydor for Warner-Reprise Records, her career floundered.
CAUSE: She had been diagnosed with uterine cancer a year before her death. She died in Orange, New Jersey.

Billy "Bip" Guy

(FRANK WILLIAM PHILLIPS)
Born June 20, 1936
Died November 5, 2002
A member of popular R&B group The Coasters, baritone vocalist Billy "Bip" Guy was a former child actor, earning his nickname from a stint in an R&B duo called, Bip & Bop, formed with Emmanuel Perez. When a popular Los Angeles doo-wop group, The Robins, splintered into two camps, members Carl Gardner and Bobby Nunn formed The Coasters. Gardner (who was Guy's former neighbour) added Guy, Leon Hughes and Adolph Jones to the group. Coming under the tutelage of hit producers and songwriters Leiber & Stoller, the group developed a comic routine, with Guy often playing a country rube. Recording for Atlantic Records subsidiary Atco, The Coasters' string of infectious, upbeat hits – most of which featured Guy on lead vocals – included the double-sided single 'Searchin''/'Young Blood', 'Yakety Yak', 'Charlie Brown', 'Along Came Jones' and 'Poison Ivy'. In the early Sixties, Guy occasionally hired substitute vocalists for The Coasters' live performances while he simultaneously pursued a solo career. Leaving the group in 1973, Guy worked as a session singer in Los Angeles. Beginning in the late Seventies, Guy began touring with a number of Coasters revues.
CAUSE: Suffering from cardiovascular disease, he passed away at his Las Vegas apartment. With Guy having

died penniless, former Coaster member Carl Gardner and fans held fund-raisers for a proper burial.

Eddie Guzman

Born March 10, 1944
Died July 29, 1993
Percussionist for white, Motown soul-rock band, Rare Earth, Eddie Guzman joined in 1971, first appearing on the album, *One World.* His hits with the group included 'Hey Big Brother' (1972) and 'Warm Ride' (1978). Guzman also appeared on the 1974 Doobie Brothers album, *What Were Once Vices*. He joined a revival version of Rare Earth in the Eighties.
CAUSE: Unknown.

H

Paul Hackman

Born 1953
Died July 5, 1992

Guitarist for the Canadian heavy metal group Helix, Paul Hackman joined the three-year-old Kitchener/London, Ontario-based outfit in 1978. Featuring the lead vocal duties of Brian Vollmer, Helix enjoyed hits with 'Rock You' and 'Runnin' Wild In The 21st Century'.

CAUSE: He was mortally wounded in a tour bus accident after the driver fell asleep at the wheel. Thrown from the vehicle, he later died at Royal Inland Hospital in Kamloops, British Columbia.

Robert "Buddy" Hagans

Born December 18, 1922
Died June 1980

Tenor saxophonist with Fats Domino's touring band in the Fifties, Robert "Buddy" Hagans toured internationally to packed houses.

CAUSE: Unknown.

Malcolm Hale

Born May 17, 1941
Died October 31, 1968

Lead guitarist for the Sixties folk-rock group Spanky And Our Gang, Malcolm Hale was born and raised in Butte, Montana. By the early Sixties, Hale was a member of a musical performance troupe called The New Wine Singers, along with budding vocalist Elaine "Spanky" McFarlane. Relocating to Chicago in 1966, Hale rejoined McFarlane in Spanky & Our Gang. With Hale on guitar and trombone, the harmony-based quintet employed four-part backing harmony behind McFarlane's lead vocals. Initially incorporating stage theatrics and comedy into their act, Spanky And Our Gang enjoyed success in the shadow of the similar sounding The Mamas and The Papas. Infusing rock into their folk-based melodies, Spanky And Our Gang landed on the charts with 'Sunday Will Never Be The Same' (1967), 'Making Every Minute Count' (1967), 'Lazy Day' (1967), 'Sunday Mornin'' (1968) and 'Like To Get To Know You' (1968).

CAUSE: Alternately cited as cirrhosis of the liver or walking pneumonia. He was found dead in his Chicago apartment.

Bill Haley

(WILLIAM JOHN CLIFTON HALEY, JR.)
Born July 6, 1925
Died February 9, 1981

The undisputed father of rock'n'roll, Bill Haley emerged from the hillbilly country tradition and was an unlikely candidate for a pioneer of rock. Born in Highland Park, Michigan, Haley received piano lessons from his British-born mother. Blinded in one eye after a botched operation in his childhood, Haley became a social outcast in his teens. Searching for work during the Depression, Haley's mechanic father moved his family to Chester, Pennsylvania. Drawn to the music of singing cowboys, Haley was given a guitar at age 13 and taught to play by his father. Dropping out of school at 15, Haley was hired as a singer in a local band. Costumed in a cowboy outfit much like his idol Gene Autry, Haley assumed the stage name Silver Yodeling Bill. Getting a break in 1943, Haley was hired as a replacement yodeller in The Downhomers, a popular hillbilly group with its own national radio show. Haley briefly rejoined the group in 1945, appearing on a pair of their records. Then forming his own hillbilly group The Range Drifters, Haley secured a position on the WLS National Barn Dance tour. First exposed to jazz and blues while at a stop in Kansas City, Haley would contemplate infusing the music into his repertoire. Disbanding the group, Haley found work as a radio deejay, eventually landing the position of programme director at WPWA in Chester, Pennsylvania. Programming an eclectic mix of pop, country and even R&B radio programmes, Haley also performed on air with his new group, The Four Aces of Western Swing. Leaving WPWA and forming The Saddlemen in 1950, Haley landed a long-term stint at a New Jersey nightclub. Combining elements of R&B with the group's country-based sound, Haley hired a saxophonist and drummer to produce a self-described "cowboy jive" sound. The group first scored a regional hit with a cover of Jackie Brenston's 'Rocket 88'. Renamed Bill Haley & His Comets, the group dropped its hillbilly/cowboy image and signed with Essex Records, scoring national hits with 'Crazy, Man, Crazy' (1953), 'Fractured' (1953), and 'Live It Up' (1953). Aided by songwriter Jim Meyers, Haley and The Comets then signed with Decca Records and recorded the Meyers-penned 'Rock Around The Clock'. Produced by Milt Gabler, 'Rock Around The Clock' was initially a moderate hit, and was followed by a bowdlerised version of Big Joe Turner's, 'Shake, Rattle And Roll' (1954), and the double-sided 'Mambo Rock'/'Birth Of The Boogie' (1955). But when Decca sold the rights to 'Rock Around The Clock' for inclusion in the opening scene of the juvenile delinquent film *The Blackboard Jungle*, the single was re-released. Topping the pop charts and launching the rock era, the song catapulted Haley to stardom on both sides of the Atlantic. Following the success of *The Blackboard Jungle*, Haley and The Comets starred in their own film, *Rock Around The Clock* (1956), and continued their string of rockabilly-flavoured hits with 'Razzle-Dazzle' (1955), 'Burn That Candle' (1955), 'See You Later Alligator' (1956), 'R-O-C-K' (1956), a cover of Little Richard's 'Rip It Up' (1956), and the sax-driven Haley/Pompilli composition, 'Rudy's Rock' (1956). Slightly overweight and sporting a cow-lick curl over his forehead, Haley scored a final hit in 1958 with 'Skinny Minny', by which time he had been supplanted on the charts by the younger and much sexier Elvis Presley. Like many pioneering American rock acts, Haley extended his fame to England where he attracted negative publicity after overzealous 'Teddy Boy' fans rioted at one of his British concerts. With much of his wealth squandered by his manager, the desperate Haley signed with Warner Brothers in 1959. Unable to pay his back taxes, he was forced to flee the US in the Sixties. Regularly recording in Mexico, Germany and Sweden, little of Haley's material would be available in the US. Settling his IRS bill in 1971, Haley joined the oldies circuit and was always assured of a generous welcome in the UK. With Haley's 'Rock Around The Clock' used as an early theme song in 1973 for the Fifties sitcom *Happy Days*, the song recharted the following year. Returning to the US in 1973, Haley settled in Harlington, Texas. Haley was devastated by the death of his long-term sax player Rudy Pompilli in 1976, and never recovered. Touring only intermittently, Haley's final performance came in South America in 1979.

CAUSE: There are several versions of Haley's death. Some reports attributed his demise to a heart attack, while others cite a brain tumour or other cerebral malady such as Alzheimer's disease. He died at his home in Harlington, Texas, with a bottle in his hand.

FURTHER READING: Swenson John. (1982). *Bill Haley*. London: W. H. Allen. von Hoelle, John; & Haley, John W. (1990). *Sound And Glory: The Incredible Story Of Bill Haley*. Wilmington, DE: Dyne-American.

Joey Hall

Born 1939
Died 1972
Lead singer of the Philadelphia-based R&B quartet Little Joey & The Flips whose only hit came in 1962 with 'Bongo Stomp', Joey Hall also released several solo singles under a one-name moniker, Joey.
CAUSE: Unknown.

Rene Hall

Born September 26, 1912
Died February 11, 1988
A jazz-trained New Orleans session guitarist and composer, Rene Hall worked with The Clara Ward Singers, The Soul Stirrers and The Dominoes, for whom he provided the prominent guitar backing on their massive hit, 'Sixty Minute Man'. After moving to Los Angeles, he backed the finest in rock and R&B including Ray Charles, Eddie Cochran, Little Richard, The Platters, and Brook Benton. In B. Bumble and The Stingers, Hall joined several session men in the Ernie Freeman-led group, scoring a pair of instrumental hits in the early Sixties with 'Bumble Boogie' and the Kim Fowley-produced 'Nut Rocker'. Hall also recorded under his own name on several labels in the Fifties and Sixties.
CAUSE: Heart disease.

Roy Hall

(JAMES FAYE HALL)
Born May 7, 1922
Died March 2, 1984
Early rockabilly/country pianist and songwriter, Roy Hall scored a minor hit with the self-penned 'Dig That Boogie' during a brief stint at Decca Records in the mid Fifties. The song was later recorded by Bruce Hornsby for inclusion in the *Backdraft* soundtrack. Co-written with Dave Williams, Hall's best known composition was 'Whole Lotta Shakin' Goin' On', which was a career-making début hit for Jerry Lee Lewis; the song was written while Hall and Williams were drinking wine on a fishing boat. Moving to Nashville in 1950, Hall joined Webb Pierces' band. Quitting to open his own bar in 1953, he later worked as a session player for the likes of Marty Robbins, Hawkshaw Hawkins and Red Foley.
CAUSE: Heart attack. He died in Nashville.

Ollie Halsall

(PETER JOHN HALSALL)
Born March 14, 1949
Died May 29, 1992
Innovative guitarist/vibraphonist with early Seventies British jazz-rock group Patto, Ollie Halsall demonstrated his talent on the group's album, *Hold Your Fire*. Leaving Patto, Halsall joined Tempest in 1973 for one album, a band that included guitarist Allan Holdsworth. He left in mid-1974 to join Kevin Ayers and The Soporifics. Reuniting in 1975 with Mike Patto in the group Boxer, Halsall created controversy for the nude image on the cover of their first of two albums, *Below The Belt*. With Boxer disbanding in 1978, Halsall worked as a session player, subbing in the studio for non-musician Dirk McQuickly in The Beatles' spoof group The Rutles. Sometimes referred to as "the Fifth Rutle", he earned the nickname Leppo. Halsall experienced drug problems late in his life.
CAUSE: Heart attack. He died in Madrid, Spain.

Bianca Halstead

Born May 5, 1965
Died December 15, 2001
The lead singer and bassist of Hollywood-based, all-female, hard rock/punk band Betty Blowtorch, Bianca Halstead (a.k.a. Bianca Butthole) formed the outrageous, glam-influenced outfit in 1998. Born in the Bronx, New York, the heavily tattooed Halstead had previously been a member of the acts Sin, Butt

Trumpet and Humble Gods. After releasing a Duff McKagen produced EP, Betty Blowtorch issued their début album in 2001, *Are You Man Enough,* which featured a guest appearance by rapper Vanilla Ice. A month before Halstead's death, two of the four members quit the band and threatened legal action if Halstead continued to tour as Betty Blowtorch.

CAUSE: Several hours after a performance at The Howlin' Wolf nightclub in New Orleans, Halstead was being driven to the band's hotel by 33-year-old music journalist Brian McAllister. She was riding in his 1986 Corvette with two other passengers when the speeding driver sideswiped another car while changing lanes, lost control of the vehicle, jumped the central reservation and struck an oncoming car. Halstead was killed instantly and the two other passengers were hospitalised. Legally inebriated, McAllister's blood-alcohol content was measured at 0.12 per cent; Halstead had quit drinking years earlier. McAllister later pleaded guilty to vehicular homicide, charges and was sentenced to five years in prison.

Pete Ham

(PETER WILLIAM HAM)
Born April 26, 1947
Died April 23, 1975

Leader, chief songwriter, and guitarist of The Beatles' protégé rock group Badfinger, Welsh-born Pete Ham had previously passed through a number of local covers bands. In 1966, Ham joined the backing group of British vocalist David Garrick who struck out on their own as The Iveys and were discovered by British bandleader Bill Collins who became their manager. At this time, the quartet consisted of Ham, rhythm guitarist Tommy Evans, drummer Mike Gibbons and bassist Ron Griffiths. Following Griffiths departure, guitarist Joey Molland was added to the group, forcing Evans to switch to bass. Signed to The Beatles' Apple label, The Iveys scored a minor pop hit with 'Maybe Tomorrow' and would thereafter always be associated with The Beatles – and compared to them by critics, at least as far as their melodic harmonies were concerned. Renamed Badfinger in late 1969, the group reached the Top 10 with the Paul McCartney produced and composed 'Come And Get It', written for the film *The Magic Christian* which featured Ringo Starr. The soundtrack album also included several Iveys tracks. Collaborating with George Harrison, Badfinger backed him on his album *All Things Must Pass,* and appeared at the Harrison-promoted charity event, The Concert for Bangladesh, at New York's Madison Square Garden. Badfinger members would also work on solo projects by Ringo Starr and John Lennon. Released in 1970, Badfinger's début album *No Dice* contained their second Top 10 hit 'No Matter What', and a track soon covered for a number 1 hit by Nilsson, the Ham co-composed 'Without You'. Produced by Todd Rundgren, the group's follow-up album *Straight Up* spawned the hits 'Baby Blue' (1971) and guitar-oriented 'Day After Day' (1972). Leaving Apple for Warner Brothers in 1973, Badfinger fared poorly with their label début *Badfinger*. Ham briefly left the group in 1974, and was replaced by Bob Jackson. Warner Brothers pulled the group's album *Wish You Were Here* (1974) off the market when $100,000 owed to the band was found to be missing. Molland left Badfinger in early 1975, and the remaining members recorded an album's worth of material. But with Warner Brothers refusing to release the project, the group disbanded. Embroiled in a legal morass, Badfinger was unable to work during this period.

CAUSE: Suicide. He hung himself in the garage/recording studio of his London home. Ham had been drinking earlier in the day and was despondent over the disputed royalties for his co-composition 'Without You', and the band's general long-term misfortunes with their managers and record label. Ham had quit the group just a few days earlier.

FURTHER READING: Matovina, Dan. (1997). *Without You: The Tragic Story Of Badfinger*. San Mateo, CA: Francis Glover.

Dan Hamilton

(DANIEL ROBERT HAMILTON)

Born June 1, 1946

Died December 23, 1994

Born in Spokane, Washington, vocalist and guitarist Dan Hamilton entered the music business at age 16 as a session player and songwriter, composing several songs for The Ventures including 'Diamond Head'. Teaming with Tommy Reynolds in the mid Sixties, Hamilton then formed a studio-only group The T-Bones, registering a Top 10 novelty instrumental hit with, 'No Matter What Shape (Your Stomach's In)', the song adapted from an Alka Seltzer commercial. In 1970 Hamilton and Reynolds were joined by Joe Frank Carollo in a pop vocal trio, Hamilton, Joe Frank & Reynolds. Hamilton was the group's guitarist and chief songwriter. Signing with Dunhill Records, the trio landed a million-selling hit with 'Don't Pull Your Love' (1971). Although Reynolds would be replaced by Alan Dennison in 1972, the group retained its Hamilton, Joe Frank & Reynolds moniker, and enjoyed a pair of hits in 1975 with 'Fallin' In Love' and 'Winners And Losers'. After releasing an album in 1976 as by Hamilton, Joe Frank and Dennison, the group disbanded. The original trio later reformed, hitting the Las Vegas circuit.

CAUSE: Suffering from an undisclosed, long-term illness, and undergoing abdominal surgery, he died in Sherman Oaks, California.

Gerald Hamilton

Born c. 1934

Died c. 1967

Bass vocalist of The Crows, Gerald Hamilton had formed the early Fifties doo-wop group with neighbourhood friends in Harlem. Discovered at Apollo's Amateur Night, the group signed with George Goldner's Rama Records where they landed an early pop-crossover hit with the million-selling, 'Gee'. Enjoying only a brief stab at fame, the group disbanded in 1955. 'Gee' is sometimes considered the first rock'n'roll song.

CAUSE: Unknown.

Roy Hamilton

Born April 16, 1929

Died July, 20, 1969

Popular Fifties baritone balladeer, Roy Hamilton was born in Leesburg Georgia but moved with his family at the age of 14 to Jersey City, New Jersey. His vocal talent nurtured in his church choir, Hamilton won an Apollo Theater talent contest in 1947. A man of several talents he then joined The Searchlight Gospel Singers, was a semi-pro boxer and worked as a professional painter. But after fighting in the Golden Gloves heavyweight division, he gave up the sport, disturbed by the violence. Possessing good looks and a powerful voice, Hamilton began performing secular music in the mid Fifties. With the aid of influential black deejay Bill Cook, Hamilton was signed to the Columbia subsidiary, Epic Records. Heavily promoted on Cook's radio programme, Hamilton's gospel-based début single, the Rodgers & Hammerstein composition from *Carousel*, 'You'll Never Walk Alone' was a smash hit. Though not overtly sexual, the charismatic Hamilton drew legions of screaming young women to his performances. Applying some of the exaggerated emotional aspects of gospel music to his pop material, he enjoyed a hit run with another song

from *Carousel*, 'If I Loved You' (1954); 'Ebb Tide' (1954); a song later reprised by Timi Yuro, 'Hurt' (1954); 'Everybody's Got A Home'; and one of four Top 10 versions of 'Unchained Melody' that would chart in 1955. Forced to abandon his musical career in June 1956 due to a bout of tuberculosis-related pneumonia, Hamilton re-emerged in 1958, co-starring in the film *Let's Rock*. Returning to the charts, Hamilton scored crossover hits with 'Don't Let Go' (1958), a cover of Johnny Ace's 'Pledging My Love' (1958), and 'You Can Have Her' (1961). Switching to MGM, and then RCA Records, Hamilton would be unable to match his previous success. With soul music displacing Hamilton's style of pop balladry, he later returned to his gospel music roots.
CAUSE: Hospitalised for hypertension, pneumonia, and a stroke, he died a few weeks later in New Rochelle, New York.

Nicky Hammerhead

(JOHN SCOTT PALLOTTA)
Born August 30, 1960
Died November 20, 1992
Drummer in Julian Lennon's group, Nicky Hammerhead also backed the touring Fifties rocker Bo Diddley. Also a struggling actor, he later appeared in a few stage plays.
CAUSE: He died from internal injuries suffered in a motorcycle accident.

John Hammond

(JOHN HENRY HAMMOND)
Born December 15, 1910
Died July 10, 1987
Music journalist, promoter, producer and CBS Records talent scout, John Hammond was a member of the massively affluent American Vanderbilt family and raised in a wealthy home. Receiving piano lessons at age four, he later switched to the viola. More fascinated with the gritty jazz he heard played on the phonographs of his black servants, Hammond frequented black nightclubs in his teens. Donning his trademark crew-cut at age 18, Hammond worked as a music journalist at *The Gramophone* and *Downbeat*, later becoming the US jazz correspondent for *Melody Maker*. Settling in Greenwich Village after dropping out of Yale, Hammond became an independent producer, discovering a number of jazz greats including Billie Holiday and Teddy Wilson. Hammond garnered national notoriety in 1938 when he produced his first of two "From Spirituals To Swing" concerts. Staged at Carnegie Hall, it marked the first instance of an integrated audience at the prestigious 57th Street venue. Showcasing jazz, blues and spirituals, the concerts introduced black acts such as Big Bill Broonzy, Sonny Terry, Big Joe Turner, Pete Johnson and Sister Rosetta Tharpe to white audiences. Hired by Columbia Records to head their pop division, in 1939 Hammond recorded both Lionel Hampton and Benny Goodman. A social outcast for supporting unpopular causes of Jews and blacks, Hammond joined the NAACP board of Directors in 1935 at age 25, and helped raise money for the legal defence of the Scottsboro Boys. After working for a series of labels in the late Forties – Keynote, Majestic, and Mercury Records – Hammond returned to Columbia in 1959. Here he signed blacklisted singer Pete Seeger, and discovered Aretha Franklin and Bob Dylan. Hammond was initially ridiculed by his colleagues for signing the skinny folk singer, who was initially referred to inside the company as "Hammond's folly". With Dylan emerging as a superstar, Hammond was vindicated and his status as one of the world's leading talent scouts confirmed for all time. After the loss of Aretha Franklin to Atlantic Records in 1965, Hammond signed jazz singer George Benson, and in 1972, rocker Bruce Springsteen. Retiring from CBS

in 1975, Hammond turned to independent production work.
CAUSE: He died of natural causes while listening to a Billie Holiday record.
FURTHER READING: Hammond, John, with Townsend, Irving. (1977). *John Hammond On Record: An Autobiography*. New York: Ridge Press.

Paul Hammond

Born 1952
Died 1992
A British drummer, Paul Hammond is best remembered for his work with Atomic Rooster, a British progressive rock band formed in 1969 by former Crazy World Of Arthur Brown members Vincent Crane and Carl Palmer. A native of Marlow, Buckinghamshire, Hammond began drumming at age 12. After winning a *Melody Maker* competition, Hammond joined a group called Farm, which shared a bill with Atomic Rooster. Following Palmer's departure in 1970 to form Emerson, Lake & Palmer, Atomic Rooster hired Hammond, who appeared on two albums, *Death Walks Behind You* and *In Hearing Of Atomic Rooster*, and the UK hit singles, 'Tomorrow Night' and 'Devil's Answer'. While recuperating from a broken leg suffered in a car crash during a German tour, Hammond learned that bandmate John DuCann was leaving Atomic Rooster. Hammond joined DuCann, bassist John Gustafson and vocalist Al Shaw to form the group Daemon, and recorded one album, *Entrance To Hell*. Following Shaw's departure from the band, it evolved into Bullet, and then Hard Stuff, which released two critically acclaimed albums, *Bullet Proof* and *Bolex Dementia*, on Deep Purple's Purple label, but disbanded in 1973. Involved in another crash, this time in Belgium, Hammond hurt his arm and re-injured his leg and spent two years convalescing. In 1977, Hammond joined The Intellektuals, a London-based art/punk group led by Jack Hues and Nick Feldman. The group disbanded in 1978, with Hues and Feldman later forming Wang Chung. In 1980, Hammond rejoined Atomic Rooster who recorded the poor-selling *Atomic Rooster* album. He left the group again in 1984.
CAUSE: Accidental barbiturate overdose.

Smokey Hampton

(VANDY HAMPTON)
Born November 15, 1949
Died February 22, 2005
A soul vocalist, Smokey Hampton sang in a series of Chicago-based acts. After a stint with The Soul Majestics, Hampton joined The Chi-Lites for a brief stint in the late Seventies, during which time the group failed to chart. In 1982, Hampton joined the perennial R&B band The Impressions as replacement for Reggie Torian. Touring with The Impressions over the next 21 years, Hampton also recorded several albums with the group.
CAUSE: Unknown. He had been ill for some time and passed away in the Chicago suburb of East Chicago, Indiana.

Hunter Hancock

Born April 21, 1916
Died August 4, 2004
The first West Coast deejay to play R&B, Texas-native Hunter Hancock worked at KFVD in Los Angeles. Originally playing jazz on the radio show *Harlem Holiday*, Hancock began to take notice of the blossoming R&B and doo-wop scene in Los Angeles in the late Forties. As was the case with deejay Alan Freed, radio listeners were shocked to discover that Hancock was white. In 1955, Hancock débuted an R&B television programme in Los Angeles, *Rhythm & Bluesville*, and the following year, he was playing rock'n'roll on KGFJ. A partner in the label Swingin' Records, Hancock oversaw several hits including 'There Is Something On Your Mind' by Big Jay

McNeely and 'Once Upon A Time' by Rochell & The Candles. Hancock left radio for a position in public relations in 1968.
CAUSE: Suffering from a heart ailment, he died at a retirement village in Claremont, California.

W.C. Handy

(WILLIAM CHRISTOPHER HANDY)
Born November 16, 1873
Died March 29, 1938
Called "The Father Of The Blues", W.C. Handy was instrumental in the popularisation of blues music. A native of Florence, Alabama, Handy secretly purchased a cornet in his teens over the objections of his strict, religious father. Running away from home at age 15, Handy joined a quartet in a minstrel show. Abandoned far from home after the show went bust, Handy returned to Alabama and earned a teaching degree from Huntsville Teachers Agricultural and Mechanical College in 1892. Unhappy with a low paying teaching job, Handy worked in a steel mill. Leaving the mill to form a musical quartet, Handy travelled to St. Louis. Now playing trumpet, by 1896 Handy joined the famous W.A. Mahara's Minstrels, touring with the group as the bandleader on-and-off until 1903. After forming his own small orchestra in Clarksdale, Mississippi, Handy experienced an awakening at a Mississippi train station in 1903 where he overheard the wailings of a solitary blues singer and guitarist. Handy had never before heard such music but he was fixated. Calling the music blues, Handy reworked the genre into a more commercially accessible form, bringing blues into the jumping nightclubs of Memphis' Beale Street. While in Memphis, Handy wrote 'Boss Crump's Blues' in 1909 as the campaign song for Memphis mayoral candidate, Edward H. "Boss" Crump. Becoming a popular hit, the song was purchased by a music publisher for $50 and renamed 'Memphis Blues'. Angry that he was cheated out of his song, Handy formed the Pace & Handy Publishing Company with friend, Harry A. Pace. Becoming America's blues ambassador, Handy penned a series of much-recorded classics including his haunting signature piece, 'St. Louis Blues', 'Jogo Blues' (1913), 'Joe Turner Blues' (1915) and 'Beale Street Blues' (1917). By the Twenties, Handy was performing in the country's finest venues. Handy was left blind and wheelchair-bound after fracturing his skill in a subway accident in 1943. Inaugurated in 1980, the American Blues Awards are named after Handy.
CAUSE: In very poor health for the rest of his life after the subway accident, he died in 1958 of bronchial pneumonia.

Terry Hanley

Born July 25, 1958
Died October 7, 1999
The drummer of Eighties new wave group The Neats, Terry Hanley joined the Boston-based outfit in 1979. Hanley had met guitarist Phil Caruso while attending Kent State University and the pair arrived in Boston in 1978 to study at the Boston Architecture Center. Dropping out of school to form The Neats, Hanley and Caruso were joined by singer-guitarist Eric Martin and bassist David Lee, recording four artsy, retro psychedelic-styled, low-key albums, which failed to find a wide audience. Having evolved into a blues rock band by the late Eighties, The Neats disbanded in 1991. Relocating to Denver, Hanley took a position at an airline food service company.
CAUSE: He fell from the balcony of his fourth floor apartment in suburban Denver. Battling alcoholism for years, his blood-alcohol level stood at 0.24 per cent at the time of his death.

Jerome Hanna

Born c. 1944
Died 1965
The first tenor of New York City-based

doo-wop group The Jive Five, Jerome Hanna joined the Eugene Pitt-led outfit in 1959. After scoring a sizable crossover hit with 'My True Story' (1961), the group charted with the R&B entries 'Never Never' (1961) and 'Hully Gully Calling Time' (1962).
CAUSE: He contracted pneumonia while walking in Toronto.

Martin Hannett

Born May 31, 1948
Died April 9, 1991
Prominent Manchester, England-based producer, Martin "Zero" Hannett got his start in the music industry as a guitarist in a band with future Mike & The Mechanics singer Paul Young, 'Mike' being Mike Rutherford of Genesis. After a stint as a club soundman, Hannett produced The Buzzcocks' *Spiral Scratch*. Essential in the development of Joy Division's textured sound, Hannett produced the group's dark, moody Factory Records albums, *Unknown Pleasures* and *Closer*. Following the suicide of Joy Division singer Ian Curtis, Hannett carried on with the group's remaining members as New Order, beginning on the album *Movement*. A prolific producer, Hannett also worked with U2, OMD, The Psychedelic Furs and The Only Ones. With the rise of the Manchester sound in the mid Eighties, Hannett produced local bands such as The Stone Roses and The Happy Mondays.
CAUSE: He succumbed to a heart attack, brought about by years of unhealthy living.

Terome "T-Bone" Hannon

Born August 15, 1964
Died September 4, 2003
A bass player, Terome "T-Bone" Hannon joined several leading acts beginning in the Nineties. A native of Detroit, Hannon performed around the city for a decade before getting his big break. Befriended by contemporary Christian singer Michael W. Smith, Hannon was recommended to pop/Christian artist Amy Grant. After a stint with Grant, Hannon subsequently worked with The Boy Choir Of Harlem, Shania Twain and SheDaisey. In 2000, he was hired by folk-rocker Jewel as a member of her touring band.
CAUSE: He suffered a brain aneurysm and died at Beaumont Hospital in Royal Oak, Michigan.

Mary Hansen

Born November 1, 1966
Died December 9, 2002
Guitarist, keyboardist and occasional vocalist with the influential, alternative rock outfit Stereolab, Mary Hansen joined the band in mid-1992 shortly before they were signed by Elektra Records. Born near Brisbane, Australia, Hansen relocated to London in the late Eighties and joined the group, The Wolfhounds. Hansen was asked to join Stereolab by its founder Tim Gane, who had first met her when he was a member of the group McCarthy. Far more popular in their native UK than in the US, Stereolab was revered in the indie scene for their avant-garde approach and the ethereal vocals of Laetitia Sadier. The group's recordings include *Mars Audiac Quintet*, *Refried Ectoplasm*, *Emperor Tomato Ketchup* and *Dots And Loops*. Hansen's final album with the group, *Sound-Dust*, was issued in 2001. An album of Hansen's work, *Hybrid*, was posthumously released in 2004.
CAUSE: While riding a bicycle in central London, she was struck by a truck, which backed into her.

Tim Hardin

(EUGENE HARDIN)
Born December 23, 1941
Died December 29, 1980
An autobiographical folk-rock tunesmith, Tim Hardin was born in New Jersey, but raised in Eugene, Oregon. Hardin would claim (though not always seriously) to be a descendant of western outlaw, John

Wesley Hardin. After dropping out of high school, he spent two hard years in the US Marines. Discharged in 1961, he moved around the country before arriving in Greenwich Village in 1963. After briefly attending the American Academy of Dramatic Art, Hardin began playing folk guitar in the area coffee houses. Leaving for Boston, Hardin was beckoned back to New York City by manager Erik Jacobsen to record some demos (to Hardin's horror, these tracks would later emerge on the 1969 album *Tim Hardin IV*). Signed to the new Verve-Forecast label, Hardin in 1966 released the groundbreaking jazz-infused, folk album *Tim Hardin 1*. Moving to Woodstock, New York, in 1967, Hardin settled near the home of Bob Dylan. A contemporary of Dylan, Hardin considered the singer-songwriter his rival. Dylan himself enjoyed antagonising Hardin, releasing an album in 1968 called, *John Wesley Harding*, although whether this had anything to do with Tim seems doubtful. A talented songwriter, many of Hardin's compositions were bigger hits for other artists. His best-known work, 'If I Were A Carpenter', was a smash for both Bobby Darin and The Four Tops. Angry that Darin had copied his vocal arrangement of the song, Hardin turned the tables, and scored his only pop hit with a cover of the Bobby Darin composition 'Simple Song Of Freedom'. Another Hardin song 'Reason To Believe', was a hit for Rod Stewart in 1971. It is generally accepted that Hardin peaked as a songwriter on his first two albums. Addicted to heroin and living in London, Hardin released his final album, *Nine*, in 1974. Returning to the US in 1975, Hardin spent a year recuperating at his parents' home after ingesting "bad" drugs. At the time of his death, Hardin had planned to record an album with Herbie Hancock.
CAUSE: He died from an overdose of heroin and morphine in his Hollywood apartment. For years, he spent most of his recording income on drugs.

Leon Hardy

Born May 12, 1932
Died June 1985
Nicknamed "Tee Top", Leon Hardy was the tenor vocalist of the pioneering doo-wop vocal group, The Cardinals. Formed in 1946 as a pop-ballad group in the tradition of The Mills Brothers, the group was originally named The Mellotones. Signing with Atlantic Records, The Cardinals scored the hits, 'Shouldn't I Know' (1951), 'The Wheel of Fortune' (1952) and 'The Door Is Still Open' (1955).
CAUSE: Unknown.

Auburn "Pat" Hare

Born December 20, 1930
Died September 26, 1980
Talented guitarist, Auburn "Pat" Hare performed in bands led by Howlin' Wolf and Muddy Waters, and was a member of Little Junior Parker's Blue Flames. As a session player, Hare also worked for Sam Phillips at his studio in his pre-Sun period. Murdering his girlfriend and a police officer in 1964, Hare spent the rest of his life behind bars.
CAUSE: He died of cancer while serving a life prison term.

Slim Harpo

(JAMES ISAAC MOORE)
Born January 11, 1924
Died January 31, 1970
Smoky-voiced Delta-styled blues virtuoso, Slim Harpo found mainstream success in the Sixties after scoring a pair of crossover pop entries with 'Rainin' In My Heart' (1961) and 'Baby, Scratch My Back' (1966). A native of Baton Rouge, Louisiana, the former James Isaac Moore was nicknamed Slim Harpo by producer Jay D. Miller, the moniker taken from a harmonica the bluesman was playing. The influential Harpo was frequently covered by British Invasion acts

including The Rolling Stones who recorded his 'I'm A King Bee'. With fame eluding him, Slim Harpo spent most of the Sixties away from the stage heading his own trucking company. His finest work is collected on the Rhino album, *The Best of Slim Harpo* (1989).
CAUSE: Heart attack. He was in London where he had just finished recording an album and was about to begin a European tour.

Don "Sugarcane" Harris

(DONALD BOWMAN)
Born June 18, 1938
Died November 30, 1999
A doo-wop singer turned blues-rock violinist, classically trained Don "Sugarcane" Harris began his musical career with The Squires, a doo-wop vocal group formed at John Muir High School in Pasadena, California. The Squires, featuring Harris' sixth part harmony and occasional piano work, landed a local hit with 'Sindy'. Harris then teamed with childhood friend Dewey Terry from the group to form the R&B duo, Don & Dewey. Although the pair had only limited success, their self-composed recordings were bigger cover hits for other acts: 'Justine' (The Righteous Brothers), 'Big Boy Pete' (The Olympics), 'I'm Leaving It All Up To You' (Dale & Grace), and 'Farmer John' (The Premiers, The Searchers, Neil Young). While touring with R&B bandleader Johnny Otis, Harris was given his "Sugarcane" nickname, a reference to his finesse with women. After disbanding the duo in the early Sixties, Harris toured in Little Richard's band (which at the time included Jimi Hendrix), before becoming an unlikely session player as an electric violinist for acts such as Frank Zappa and John Mayall. Flirting with experimental, improvisational jazz, Harris recorded a number of solo albums in the Seventies. Re-teaming with Terry in 1975, Harris occasionally played the oldies circuit.
CAUSE: He had been abusing drugs for many years and suffering from heart disease when he was found dead in a boarding house in south central Los Angeles.

Eddie Harris

Born October 20, 1934
Died November 5, 1996
Chicago-born tenor saxophonist and songwriter, Eddie Harris began his musical career in his teens, backing Gene Ammons on piano. A solo artist in the Fifties, Harris scored his biggest chart hit with a jazz- pop version of the theme from *Exodus* (1961). On the album *Eddie Harris In The U.K*, Harris was joined by guest musicians Steve Winwood and Jeff Beck. As a songwriter, Harris penned *The Bill Cosby Show* theme. Also an author, he penned several books on music instruction.
CAUSE: Bone cancer and kidney disease. He died in Los Angeles.

Lester Harris

(HARRY LESTER)
Born 1920
Died February 25, 1953
As lead vocalist and drummer of the early R&B combo The Ray-O-Vacs, Lester Harris landed on the R&B charts with 'I'll Always Be In Love With You' (1949) and the double-sided entry 'Besame Mucho'/'You Gotta Love Me Baby Too' (1950). Formed in New York City, the outfit was named after a battery brand. In 1952, Harris left the group and was replaced by Herb Milliner.
CAUSE: Pneumonia.

Norman Harris

Born February 10, 1958
Died March 21, 1987
A record company owner, producer, songwriter and prolific session musician, New York-born guitarist

Norman Harris was a fixture in the Philadelphia music scene. Harris broke into music in the late Fifties in a Philadelphia-based R&B duo featuring bassist Ron Baker. Adding drummer Earl Young, the production and session trio of Baker-Harris-Young were in much demand within the city's thriving soul scene. The trio eventually morphed into M.F.S.B., the large studio band at Kenny Gamble and Leon Huff's label Philadelphia International Records. Recording at Philadelphia Sigma Sound Studios, M.F.S.B. backed hundreds of acts including Loleatta Holloway, Harold Melvin, The Delfonics, The Intruders, Archie Bell, The O'Jays and Barbara Mason. Apart from their duties as session players, M.F.S.B. landed their own hits, including the chart-topping instrumental 'TSOP', which was the theme song of the syndicated music programme, *Soul Train*. In 1973, Harris signed the female trio First Choice to his Philly Groove label, scoring several R&B hits including, 'Armed And Extremely Dangerous', 'The Player – Part 1' and 'Doctor Love'. By 1976, Baker-Harris-Young established their own production and music-publishing company, Golden Fleece, and Harris launched another label, Gold Mind Records; Harris retained First Choice, and signed Bunny Sigler and Loleatta Holloway. As a recording artist, he released a disco album under the moniker, The Harris Machine. Meanwhile, M.F.S.B. disbanded after scoring a Top 10 UK hit with the title track of their album, *Mysteries Of The World* (1981).
CAUSE: Heart attack.

Peppermint Harris

(HARRISON D. NELSON, JR.)
Born July 17, 1925
Died April 12, 1999
An early, Texas-based R&B artist, Peppermint Harris first picked up the guitar while serving in the navy during World War II. Settling in Houston in 1947, he studied speech and drama at a local university. Befriended by Lightnin' Hopkins 1948, Harris recorded at Houston's Gold Star Records, the tracks released under the name Peppermint Nelson. Following Gold Star producer Bob Shad to Sittin' In With Records, Harris landed an R&B hit with 'Raining In My Heart' (1950). Signed the following year by Aladdin Records, Harris topped the R&B charts with 'I Got Loaded' (1951), his first of several booze-themed singles at the label. After a stint as a lyricist, Harris performed and recorded intermittently for the rest of his life, releasing a final album in 1995, *Texas On My Mind.*
CAUSE: Unknown. He died in New Jersey.

Ray Harris

(HOMER RAY HARRIS)
Born September 7, 1927
Died November 13, 2003
Although a Rockabilly Hall Of Fame Inductee, Ray Harris had far greater success as a label owner than a recording artist. Born into a poor Southern farm family near Tupelo, Mississippi, Harris enlisted with the Air Force at age 17. Starting a family and working at a Firestone factory in Memphis, he played country music as an avocation but fellow Firestone employee Bill Black, who would soon be backing a young Elvis Presley, got Harris interested in the professional side of music. A pair of upbeat, rockabilly singles for Sun Records – 'Hey Little Mama' and 'Greenback Dollar, Watch And Chain' – were only regional hits for the label so instead, owner Sam Phillips hired Harris as an assistant producer. Later deciding to form his own label, Harris and three others, including record wholesaler Joe Cuoghi, launched Hi Records. While Presley was in the military, Harris helped Presley's sideman Bill Black to form his own successful project, The Bill Black Combo, which, in 1959, had

the first of several Top 40 hits, 'Smokie – Part 2'. Other artists that Harris produced at the label included Ace Cannon, Gene Simmons, Jerry Jaye and Charlie Rich. Leaving Hi in 1970, Harris sold his share to producer/musician Willie Mitchell. In the mid Seventies, Harris tried to return to the music industry but was hampered by a series of lawsuits. He later recorded a pair of solo albums.
CAUSE: Unknown. He died at his home in Tupelo, Mississippi.

Richard Harris

(RICHARD SAINT JOHN HARRIS)
Born October 1, 1930
Died October 25, 2002
A stage and film actor, Richard Harris had an unexpected major pop hit in 1968 with the Jimmy Webb composition that was originally offered to The Association, 'MacArthur Park'. Although he would chart with three more singles, he never returned to the Top 40. His best known acting role was as King Arthur in both the stage and big screen versions of *Camelot*. The soundtrack, featuring Harris' vocals, was a longtime best seller.
CAUSE: Lymphoma. He died in London.

Thurston Harris

(THURSTON THEODORE HARRIS)
Born July 11, 1931
Died April 14, 1990
A popular R&B singer, Indianapolis-born Thurston Harris launched his musical career during his childhood in the gospel group, The Canaan Crusaders. After returning from the service in 1952, Harris switched from gospel to secular R&B. Discovered by jump blues guitarist Jimmy Liggins, Harris was introduced to his more successful brother, R&B band leader Joe Liggins, who asked him to join his touring band as a vocalist. Harris left Liggins in an argument over wages at a stop in Los Angeles. After winning a talent contest at the city's Johnny Otis' Barrelhouse Club, Harris joined one of the competing acts on the bill, The Lamplighters. Signing with Federal Records, The Limelighters recorded a series of obscure singles from 1953 to 1956, beginning with 'Part Of Me'. Scoring a regional hit with 'Be Bop Wino', Harris and The Lamplighters were sabotaged by their own reckless hard drinking and skirt chasing. Signing with Aladdin Records in 1957 and backed by The Lamplighters who were now known as The Sharps (soon to be The Rivingtons), Harris scored the biggest hit of his career with an upbeat, crossover smash with a cover of Bobby Day's 'Little Bitty Pretty One' (1957). Harris followed up with the R&B hit 'Do What You Did' (1958) and another Bobby Day cover, 'Over And Over'. His musical career waning by the early Sixties, Harris jumped from label to label while working a day job in construction. Harris was arrested several times in the Seventies on drug possession charges. Bitter and nearly destitute by the Eighties, Harris was unsuccessful in his fight to secure the rights to his early recordings.
CAUSE: Heart attack. He died in a rest home in Pomona, California.

Willie Harris

(WILLIAM HARRIS)
Born April 14, 1925
Died December 6, 1988
Guitarist for the pioneering doo-wop group The Clovers, North Carolina-born Willie Harris learned to play the organ in church. Moving to the Baltimore/ Washington DC area after serving in World War II, Harris studied classical guitar, receiving instruction from the great Django Reinhardt. After earning a music degree from Howard University, Harris became the first black to enrol at the Columbia School of Music. Beginning his professional career as the guitarist in the backing band for an

all-female dancing troupe, The Brown Skin Models, Harris left the troupe in 1950. Joining the four-year-old Buddy Bailey-led Clovers later in 1950, Harris was employed as a guitarist and arranger. Discovered by record store owner "Waxie Maxie" Silverman, The Clovers were originally rejected by Atlantic Records. With new manager Lou Krefetz, The Clovers recorded for Rainbow Records in 1950, scoring a minor hit with a cover of the standard, 'Yes Sir, That's My Baby'. But with Atlantic Records now interested in the group, The Clovers scored a B-side hit with 'Don't You Know I Love You' (1951), the song penned by Atlantic chief, Ahmet Ertegun. Though landing on the national charts, the group was initially unhappy with its new, glossy sound. The Clovers' R&B hits continued with: 'Don't You Know I Love You' (1951), 'Fool, Fool, Fool' (1951), 'One Mint Julip' (1952), 'Ting-A-Ling' (1952), 'Lovey Dovey' (1954), 'Your Cash Ain't Nothing But Trash' (1954), 'Nip Sip' (1955), 'Devil Or Angel' (1956) (which was a bigger pop hit for Bobby Vee in 1960), and 'Love, Love, Love' (1956). In 1956, Harris had recorded a solo album of jazz and classical guitar on the Mercury subsidiary, EmArcy Records, his first of three releases at the label. Dropped by Atlantic in 1958, The Clovers would sign with their manager's Poplar label. But wanting to return to his family, Harris left the group in late 1958. Harris later taught jazz at both college level and in his own studio in Washington DC. He also opened a pair of jazz venues, the Hog Meat Club, which operated out of his house, and The Pigfoot. Falling behind on his taxes, Harris lost his businesses in 1980, and then his home in 1987. Inexperienced in business matters, Harris also lost his writer's credit for his many Clovers compositions. The Rhythm and Blues Foundation held a benefit for the ailing Harris in 1988.

CAUSE: Pancreatic cancer. He died at Howard University Hospital in Washington DC.

Wynonie Harris

Born August 24, 1915
Died June 14, 1969

A prolific, upbeat blues and early R&B shouter, Wynonie Harris attended Creighton University in his native Omaha, Nebraska, during the mid Thirties. Dropping out of school to take a position as a tap dancer and drummer in a travelling revue, by 1940 Harris had relocated to Los Angeles. Performing and emceeing in the nightclubs of Central Avenue, Harris began honing his skills as a blues shouter in the Big Joe Turner tradition. After a stop in Chicago in 1944, Harris was hired as the featured vocalist in Lucky Millinder's orchestra. Billed as Wynonie "Mr. Blues" Harris, he enjoyed a series of hits with Millinder's band on Decca Records, beginning with 'Who Threw The Whiskey In The Well?' (1965). Although he would soon leave Millinder, Harris would frequently borrow his former boss' orchestra for recording sessions. A consummate performer whose comedy antics made him a nightclub favourite, Harris would tour with the leading orchestras of the day including Johnny Otis, Jack McVea, Cab Calloway and Lionel Hampton. Recording for a series of record labels in the late Forties, including Hamp-Tone, Bullet, Aladdin, Philo and Apollo, Harris scored R&B hits with 'Playful Baby' and 'Wynonie's Blues'. After joining the Cincinnati-based King label in late 1947, Harris sold a tremendous amount of records, beginning with a cover version of Roy Brown's 'Good Rockin' Tonight' (1948). Harris followed with another cover hit, Stick McGee's smash, 'Drinkin' Wine Spo-Dee-O-Dee', and continued his chart trailblazing with 'All She Wants To Do Is Rock' (1949), the double-sided sexual innuendo-filled,

'Sitting On It All The Time'/'I Like My Baby's Pudding' (1950) and 'Oh Babe' (1950). But by the early Fifties, Harris' career had begun to slip as R&B was changing, being taken over by vocal groups. He would manage only two more hits, a cover of Hank Penny's 'Bloodshot Eyes' (1951) and 'Loving Machine' (1952). Leaving King Records in 1954, Harris would record only sporadically. To capitalise on the calypso craze in 1955, he released an updated version of 'Good Rockin' Tonight' reworked as 'Good Mambo Tonight'. Harris left music in the late Fifties, and settled in Brooklyn where he operated a tavern. Though occasionally recording into the Sixties, he was unable to secure airplay.
CAUSE: Throat cancer. He died in Oakland.
FURTHER READING: Collins, Tony. (1995). *Rock Mr. Blues: The Life And Music Of Wynonie Harris*. Milford, NH: Big Nickel.

George Harrison

Born February 25, 1943
Died November 29, 2002
George Harrison was always known as the 'quiet' Beatle, which he came to detest, not least because of his droll sense of humour and ability to foster and maintain warm friendships within the rock community in which he was always held in the highest respect. A more appropriate nickname would have been "Dark Horse", which he chose for his own record label in the Seventies. Harrison found enormous fame as The Beatles' lead guitarist and occasional songwriter, but this fame weighed heavily on his fragile psyche and he spent much of his life trying to shake it off, largely unsuccessfully, through a devotion to Indian spiritual beliefs. This commitment caused Harrison to demonstrate a curious humility for one so celebrated, and to this end he would describe himself as a gardener, as opposed to a musician, a reflection of his deep love of all matters botanical and the care he devoted to tending the magnificent grounds at his palatial home, Friar Park, in Henley-on-Thames, Oxfordshire.
George Harrison was born into a large working-class family in Liverpool, his father a Liverpool bus driver, and both parents were former professional ballroom dancers, so the household was filled with music. His mother Louise gave him a guitar which he practised assiduously to master. Attending the Liverpool Institute in 1954, Harrison was in the year behind Paul McCartney. (He'd also attended Dovedale Primary School which counted John Lennon as a former pupil.) With the rise of skiffle, Harrison formed his own band in 1956, The Rebels. Becoming friends with McCartney, Harrison was eventually asked to join McCartney's group with John Lennon, The Quarry Men. His ability to play a note perfect version of Bill Justis' instrumental hit 'Raunchy' got him the gig with Lennon, who was initially put off by Harrison's young age. Briefly leaving The Quarry Men in January 1959 because of a lack of work, Harrison joined The Les Stewart Quartet. But by August, Harrison had reunited with Lennon and McCartney. Playing a selection of American R&B and rockabilly hits at a series of poorly paid gigs, the group adopted a new moniker, Johnny & The Moondogs and in 1960, Lennon's art school friend Stuart Sutcliffe joined on bass to form (among various names) The Silver Beatles. Later in the year, with Pete Best on drums, the group began a four month stint in Hamburg, Germany, shortening their name to The Beatles. Playing exhausting several-hour-a night schedules in red-light district clubs, their showmanship and musical skills were sharpened, providing the platform for what was to follow. An early fan, art student Astrid Kirchherr changed the group's image with new outfits and page-boy haircuts. She got engaged to

Sutcliffe, who remained behind in Germany, furthering his art career (which was tragically terminated at his death as the result of a cerebral haemorrhage in April 1962). Having been deported from Hamburg on various charges including the fact that Harrison was underage at 17, The Beatles returned to Liverpool and, in December 1960, caused a local sensation with their new sound and look with a gig at the city's Litherland Town Hall, where they were billed as being "Direct from Germany". The Beatles also débuted at a dingy Liverpool cellar, the Cavern Club, formerly a jazz haunt where their reputation was built up over the next two years with almost 300 performances. During a subsequent visit to Hamburg in the summer of 1961, the group backed Tony Sheridan on his updated cover of the standard 'My Bonnie', released as by Tony Sheridan & The Beat Brothers. That October, after a customer requested a Beatles record from NEMS, his well-stocked Liverpool record store, Brian Epstein saw a lunchtime Cavern performance, and became their manager. After failing an audition with Decca Records, The Beatles signed with EMI's Parlophone subsidiary in 1962, impressing 36-year-old producer George Martin (a classically trained oboe player) with their charm rather than their music. In August, drummer Best was ignominiously fired and replaced by Ringo Starr, who they knew from playing the same Hamburg clubs with Rory Storm & The Hurricanes. The first Beatles single, 'Love Me Do', was issued in October 1962 (reaching the UK Top 20) and marked the first Lennon-McCartney composition to grace an unprecedented run of chart singles. After refusing Martin's orders to record 'How Do You Do It?' (instead a hit for Gerry & The Pacemakers), The Beatles followed up with 'Please Please Me', their first number one in Britain (despite some UK chart books stating that it only reached number two). On a roll, The Beatles toured Britain on bills with Helen Shapiro, Chris Montez, Tommy Roe and Roy Orbison, released another number one in 'From Me To You', a best-selling LP, their début *Please Please Me*, and EP *Twist And Shout*, topped off by appearances on the British television institution *Sunday Night At The London Palladium* and a Royal Command Performance – both events signifying the birth of Beatlemania in Britain. With fourth single 'She Loves You' breaking British sales records, Brian Epstein travelled across the Atlantic to investigate the group's inability to break through into the American market. While EMI's American counterpart, Capitol refused to issue The Beatles early records, labels such as Vee-Jay, Tollie and Swan took chances with the group. Capitol eventually relented and launched an expensive promotional campaign as Beatlemania was imported to the States. In January 1964, 'I Want To Hold Your Hand' (the group's fifth single in the UK, released November '63) débuted on the US singles charts, and was soon at the number one position – a feat that only two prior English acts had managed to attain. On February 7, 1964, The Beatles made their triumphal arrival at New York's Kennedy Airport, greeted by 3,000 screaming girls. Two days later, 73 million American viewers were introduced to the mop-topped "Fab Four" on *The Ed Sullivan Show*. In their banner year of 1964, when Beatlemania spread worldwide, The Beatles were responsible for dozens of chart entries, on several labels, setting sales and chart records, rivalling only Elvis Presley. The group also made a successful venture into celluloid with *A Hard Day's Night*, a black and white, day in the life quasi documentary that provided the antidote to all the anodyne pop musicals that had preceded it. Harrison had contributed his first composition, 'Don't Bother Me' to the group's second album *With The Beatles*, following through with 'I Need You' and 'You Like Me Too Much' for the 1965 *Help!* LP. While The Beatles' early albums largely consisted of innocuous, upbeat material, by 1965, their experiences had resulted in a more worldly wise group adopting a more mature sound. On *Rubber Soul* Harrison experimented with the sitar on the track 'Norwegian Wood', after being introduced to the instrument by sitar maestro Ravi Shankar (he would use the instrument on his Beatles tracks, 'Love You Too', 'Within You, Without You' and 'The Inner Night'). *Rubber Soul* also contained the jangly 'If I Needed Someone' influenced by US contemporaries The Byrds. *Revolver* was also another major leap forward in terms of studio experimentation and featured an unprecedented three Harrison songs, 'Taxman', 'Love You Too' and 'I Want To Tell You'. Citing difficulties in recreating their new sound outside a studio environment and the pressures of simply being Beatles, the group gave their last concert at San Francisco's Candlestick Park on August 29, 1966. Earlier in the year, George had married model, Patti Boyd, whom he had met on the set of *A Hard Day's Night.* Continuing to explore and expand the boundaries of pop music, the group issued the double-sided single, 'Penny Lane' / 'Strawberry Fields Forever' (1967), the latter track signalling their increasing technological experimentation in the studio. After five months of inspired session work, The Beatles released their critically acclaimed masterpiece, *Sgt. Pepper's Lonely Hearts Club Band* in June 1967; the album, featuring the world-weary Harrison composition 'Within You, Without You', becoming the soundtrack for 1967's psychedelic Summer of Love. In August, The Beatles travelled to Bangor to meet Indian mystic, the Maharishi Mahesh Yogi – a visit that was curtailed by the news of manager Brian Epstein's death from an accidental overdose. A poorly received made-for-TV film venture *Magical Mystery Tour* (December '67) featured George's ethereal 'Blue Jay Way'. In the early part of '68 the group went to India to study transcendental meditation properly with their newfound guru but Harrison was the only member of the group to continue to follow Indian religion seriously. Without the firm guidance of Epstein, the group launched Apple Corps in 1968, and eventually lost millions in a series of imprudent business ventures. However, their début release on Apple, the double-sided hit – 'Hey Jude'/ 'Revolution' – successfully launched their own Apple record label with yet another worldwide number one. In November 1968, Harrison released the all-instrumental film soundtrack, *Wonderwall Music*, some of which was recorded in his beloved India. During this period, Harrison also began producing material for other artists including Badfinger, Jackie Lomax and Billy Preston. After following up with the two-disc set *The Beatles (The White Album)* – which included four Harrison compositions, the most successful of which was 'While My Guitar Gently Weeps', featuring George's friend Eric Clapton on lead guitar – internal disputes began to broil, and during the sessions, Ringo briefly quit the band. During the January 1969 'Get Back' sessions, Harrison did the same but was coaxed back. Performing an unannounced lunchtime show on the roof of their Apple offices, in Savile Row, London on January 30, 1969, joined by keyboardist Billy Preston, The Beatles performed together one last time in public, to climax the documentary film, *Let It Be* (1970). With the break-up imminent, the group asked George Martin to produce one last album, *Abbey Road*, which contained a pair of Harrison classics, the romantic 'Something' (which none other than Frank Sinatra called the greatest love song of the past 50 years) and the optimistic 'Here Comes The Sun'. With Apple in near financial ruin, new manager Allen Klein reorganised the company, beginning with the release of *Let It Be*, which featured Harrison's 'I Me Mine' and 'For You Blue'. Citing internal differences, The Beatles officially disbanded in April 1970 with McCartney's announcement that he had quit. That year, all four Beatle members would release solo albums. Retaining Spector, Harrison issued the commercially and artistically successful three-disc set *All Things Must Pass*; a collection of songs that George had written over the latter Beatle years. From the album, the worldwide chart-topping single 'My Sweet Lord' was found by a court to have plagiarised The Chiffons hit 'He's So Fine' and a judge later awarded damages against Harrison; the situation was later alluded to in his 1976 composition, 'This Song'. At the urging of Ravi Shankar, Harrison staged the charity all-star Concert For Bangladesh; a triple-album and film raising $15 million for UNICEF and a studio single, 'Bangla-Desh', giving Harrison another Top 40 hit. Throughout the Seventies and into the Eighties, Harrison continued to release a periodic sequence of albums – *Living In the Material World* (1973), *Dark Horse* (1974), *Extra Texture (Read All About It)* (1975), *Thirty Three And A Third* (1976), *George Harrison* (1979), *Somewhere In England* (1981) and *Gone Troppo* (1982) – that met with diminishing critical and sales returns. Forming Dark Horse Records in 1974, Harrison produced records for artists he admired like Splinter, Stairsteps, Attitudes and Ravi Shankar, though none was particularly successful. By this time Harrison had separated from his wife Patti, who went on to become the partner of Eric Clapton, and met Olivia Arias, a secretary from Dark Horse Records in Los Angeles, whom he would eventually marry. Their only child, a son they named Dhani, was born in 1978. In 1979, being a major fan of their anarchic humour, Harrison helped to finance *Monty Python's Life Of Brian* – a venture which established him as an unlikely saviour of the British film industry in the Eighties with his Handmade Films company. Unfortunately, the venture ended in rancour when it was discovered that Harrison's business adviser, Denis O'Brien had misappropriated considerable funds. When John Lennon was murdered in December 1980, McCartney and Starr reunited informally in a tribute to Lennon on the Harrison single, 'All Those Years Ago' (1981). In 1988 Harrison became part of an ad-hoc quintet of well-known musicians who called themselves The Traveling Wilburys, the others being Bob Dylan, Roy Orbison, Tom Petty and Jeff Lynn. Although convened in an atmosphere that suggested an element of droll humour, the Wilburys released two first rate albums which brought out the best qualities in each musician and proved a fine epitaph for Orbison who died soon after the release of the first. Then in 1994, The Beatles (or 'The Threetles' as Harrison dubbed them) released new material by building upon unfinished Lennon demos, 'Free As A Bird' and 'Real Love', released in conjunction with a much-hyped television documentary, *The Beatles Anthology*, and three double-album sets of previously unreleased demos, works-in-progress and live material which sold a combined 10 million copies. In 1996, the remaining Beatles turned down a quarter-billion dollar offer to perform in concert, matching a pair of earlier overtures. Harrison's final years were characterised by his evident distaste of the current state of popular music and many of those who performed it, a deliberate shunning of the limelight and his quixotic support

of the Natural Law Party, a Bedfordshire based organisation which promoted transcendental meditation and a spiritual lifestyle. He lived variously in Henley, Los Angeles and Hawaii, was often seen in the pits at Formula One motor racing meetings and devoted his energies to maintaining the superb gardens at Friar Park which included a grotto and a substantial lake which was fitted with a submerged walkway that enabled him to appear to 'walk on water', much to the amusement of his guests. He also became a world-class ukulele player, a keen fan of George Formby and an environmentalist with strong views about the ways in which mankind was eroding the planet's natural resources. In December 1999, Harrison and his second wife Olivia barely survived a knife attack by an intruder at his Henley home; the attacker, Michael Abram, was acquitted of attempted murder by reason of insanity and sent to a psychiatric hospital. After his long recuperation, Harrison worked on sessions for an album that would be posthumously released, *Brainwashed*.
CAUSE: Harrison had surgery and radiation treatment in 1997 for throat cancer, which condition he blamed on smoking. In May 2002, Harrison entered the Mayo Clinic to undergo surgery for lung cancer. In July, he went through a course of radiotherapy for a brain tumour at a hospital in Switzerland. Securely away from paparazzi, Harrison died at a friend's home in the Hollywood Hills, California.

Wilbert Harrison

Born January 5, 1929
Died October 26, 1994
Best known for his reinterpretation of the Jerry Leiber/Mike Stoller song 'Kansas City', Charlotte, North Carolina-born Wilbert Harrison had originally jumped on the calypso bandwagon following his discharge from the navy in the early Fifties. Recording for several labels in the Fifties including Savoy, Harrison was approached by Fire/Fury owner Bobby Robinson in 1959. Featuring Harrison's breezy vocal delivery, the million-selling 'Kansas City' (1959) was recorded for just $40. But while Harrison insisted that he wrote the song, Leiber & Stoller prevailed in a subsequent lawsuit. And with Savoy Records owner Herman Lubinsky insisting that he still owned Harrison's contract, legal proceedings kept Harrison from recording. Falling into obscurity, Harrison landed a minor comeback hit in 1970 with the Sue Records release, 'Let's Work Together (Part 1)', the song reprised by blues-rock band, Canned Heat and later reworked by Bryan Ferry. Financially destitute for the remainder of his life, Harrison performed as an unaccompanied solo act in the Seventies.
CAUSE: Stroke. He died in a nursing home in Spencer, North Carolina.

Dan Hartman

Born November 4, 1951
Died March 22, 1994
A native of Harrisburg, Pennsylvania, Dan Hartman became proficient on a number of instruments as a teenager. Joining The Edgar Winter Group in 1972 on bass guitar, Hartman appeared on the hits, 'Frankenstein' (1973) and the Hartman-penned 'Free Ride' (1973). In 1976 both Hartman and Rick Derringer left the band. Pursuing a solo career, Hartman signed with Blue Sky Records, where he scored a million-selling disco hit with 'Instant Replay' (1978). Recording and producing several film scores, Hartman scored a Top 10 rock dance hit in 1984 with 'I Can Dream About You', from the film *Streets Of Fire*. He followed up with the Top 40 entries, 'We Are The Young' (1984) and 'Second Nature' (1985). Constructing the Schoolhouse recording studio in Westport, Connecticut, Hartman recorded

albums by Foghat, Muddy Waters, and Johnny and Edgar Winter. Hartman also produced sessions for James Brown, Paul Young and Tina Turner. CAUSE: Suffering from AIDS, he died from a brain tumour in Westport, Connecticut.

Alex Harvey

Born February 5, 1935
Died February 4, 1982
Leader of the avant-garde rock group The Sensational Alex Harvey Band, Alex Harvey was raised in a poor section of Glasgow, Scotland. Dropping out of school at age 15, he took a series of menial jobs. Passing through several jazz groups in the early Fifties, he played trumpet, and after that instrument was stolen, the banjo. Jumping on the skiffle craze, he switched to guitar and joined a number of skiffle groups. Emerging as a solo artist, Harvey won a talent competition, and was dubbed "Scotland's Tommy Steele". Forming The Alex Harvey Big Soul Band in 1959, Harvey would back visiting acts such as Gene Vincent and Eddie Cochran. Touring heavily throughout Scotland, Harvey's band occasionally played in Hamburg, Germany, where they performed behind singer Tony Sheridan. Releasing their début album in 1964, The Alex Harvey Soul Band disbanded two years later. In 1965, Harvey teamed with his 17-year-old younger brother, Les, to record an album, *The Blues*. After a couple of major career shifts (one as a British folk ballad singer), in 1967 Harvey was hired to play rhythm guitar in the orchestra pit for the London production of *Hair*. Staying for five years, this extended theatrical gig would expose Harvey to the stage techniques he would later incorporate into his own act. During this time, Harvey recorded a pair of solo albums with other musicians in the pit, including *Roman Wall Blues* (1969). After forming his own short-lived group with a young Mike Oldfield in 1972, Harvey then joined forces with a two-year-old Scottish band, Tear Gas, then on the verge of disbanding. Renamed The Sensational Alex Harvey Band, the pioneering theatrical-rock ensemble incorporated costumes, props, and acting into their concerts. Musically, the group blended British pop, light avante-garde jazz, and R&B. With his large-frame, long black hair, grimacing smile, and weathered face, Harvey came over as a rebel and seasoned performer. Produced by the group's former lead singer David Batchelor, SAHB enjoyed success in the UK with albums such as *Tomorrow Belongs To Me* (1975), *Live* (1975), and *SAHB Stories* (1976). Emerging as a cult favourite, the group had hits with 'Vambo' (1973), 'Faith Healer' (1974), 'Delilah' (1975), 'Gamblin' Bar Room Blues' (1975) and 'Boston Tea Party' (1976). After releasing seven albums, the group disbanded in 1977. Joined by various backing bands, Harvey continued his heavy touring schedule, but after suffering a back injury in the late Seventies he was forced to scale back his stage antics. His only post-SAHB album, *The Mafia Stole My Guitar*, came in 1980.
CAUSE: He suffered a heart attack brought on by an unhealthy lifestyle and years of hard touring and hard drinking. He was stricken on a ferry boat from Calais, France, on his way home to London after a tour of West Germany. He died in Zeebrugen, Belgium.

Bryan Harvey

Born 1957
Died January 1, 2006
A member of indie blues-rock duo House Of Freaks, Bryan Harvey recorded several critically acclaimed albums with drummer Johnny Hott, garnering airplay with 'Sun Gone Down' and 'Rocking Chair'. Harvey and Hott later worked with former Dream Syndicate leader Steve Wynn in the group Gutterball.

CAUSE: Harvey, his wife and their two children were murdered in the basement of their home in Richmond, Virginia, by a pair of 28-year-old burglars. The killers, Ray J. Dandridge and Ricky Gray, were also charged with the murders of a second family.

Les Harvey

(LESLIE HARVEY)
Born 1947
Died May 3, 1972
The guitarist for the British rock group, Stone The Crows, Les Harvey was born and raised in Glasgow, Scotland. At 16, he joined his first rock band, The Kinning Park Ramblers. Reared in the shadow of his older musician brother Alex Harvey, Les teamed with Alex for an album, *The Blues*, in 1965. In the late Sixties, Alex Harvey introduced Les to a white soul singer named Maggie Bell. An impressed Les Harvey joined forces with Bell in 1969 to form a group called Power. Discovered by Led Zeppelin's manager, Peter Grant, the renamed Stone The Crows were signed to Atlantic Records. Combining soul with hard rock, the group released two albums in 1970, *Stone The Crows* and *Ode To John Law*, which featured the shared vocals of Bell and Jim Dewar. While neither album sold well, the group retained a strong draw through Britain with their powerful stage shows which featured Harvey's intricate guitar solos and Bell's Janis Joplin-like full-tilt vocals. By this time, Harvey and Bell had become romantically involved. After two members of Stone The Crows quit and were replaced in 1971, the group's next album, *Teenage Licks* (1971) was their breakthrough release. Also in 1971, Harvey joined Aretha Franklin on a European tour, filling in for her ailing guitarist. Harvey died after partially completing the group's final studio album, *Ontinuous Performance* (1972). He was replaced by Jimmy McCulloch of Thunderclap Newman.

CAUSE: He died as a result of an electrical shock from a poorly grounded microphone at the start of a performance in the Top Rank Ballroom at Swansea University in Wales before an audience of 1,200.

Rick Harvey

Born 1950
Died April 5, 1993
A popular Memphis-based blues session guitarist, Rick Harvey was influenced by Albert King before playing with B.B. King, Stevie Ray Vaughan and Billy Joel. In 1985, Harvey played on Bobby "Blue" Bland's Grammy-winning album, *Members Only*. He later pursued a solo career, forming The Rick Harvey Band.
CAUSE: Kidney failure. He died in Memphis.

Tony Harvey

Born c. 1940
Died February 1993
A pioneering British rock guitarist, Tony Harvey was a member of the influential but short-lived outfit Vince Taylor & The Playboys, a group that also featured Tony Sheridan. Frequent guests on the BBC television show, *Oh Boy!*, the group scored a brilliant rock hit with the Taylor-penned 'Brand New Cadillac'. With the group disbanding in 1959, Harvey and Taylor assembled a new version of The Playboys, and backed shock-rocker Screaming Lord Sutch in 1960. Parting from Taylor when he emigrated to France, Harvey joined an instrumental group, Nero & The Gladiators, best known for the hit 'Entry Of The Gladiators' (1961). The group was headed by guitarist Mike O'Neal who wore a toga on stage.
CAUSE: Cancer.

Bobby Hatfield

(ROBERT LEE HATFIELD)
Born August 10, 1940
Died November 5, 2003

As half of the popular blue-eyed soul duo The Righteous Brothers, Bobby Hatfield performed on a series of stirring classics. Born in Michigan but raised in California, he abandoned his budding baseball career for music. Forming The Variations, he performed throughout Southern California, and joined a white R&B band called The Paramours, which at the time was headed by lead singer Bill Medley. After the group recorded an obscure single on Moonglow Records in 1962, Hatfield and Medley left to form The Righteous Brothers. After scoring a regional hit with a Medley composition, 'Little Latin Lupe Lu' (1963), the duo recorded with Phil Spector, who had purchased their contract from Moonglow. Released on Spector's Philles label, the soulful lament, 'You've Lost That Lovin' Feelin'', was a deserved smash in late 1964 and was followed by a cover of the pop standard, 'Ebb Tide'. Tiring of Spector's unpredictable behaviour, The Righteous Brothers left Philles to record for Verve. Borrowing from Spector's patented sound, Hatfield and Medley reached the Top 10 with the lush, self-produced '(You're My) Soul And Inspiration'. Quitting the duo in 1968, Hatfield then teamed up with Jimmy Walker, but reunited with Medley in 1973, for a Top 10 comeback about departed singers, 'Rock And Roll Heaven'. Relegated to the oldies circuit for the remainder of their career, The Righteous Brothers enjoyed a lucrative comeback in the Nineties, thanks to the inclusion of 'Unchained Melody' in the film, *Ghost*.

CAUSE: He passed away in his sleep at the Radisson Plaza Hotel in Kalamazoo, Michigan. His body was discovered in his bed, an hour before a scheduled performance at nearby Western Michigan University. An autopsy attributed the death to cocaine-induced heart failure. His singing partner, Bill Medley, claimed never to have witnessed Hatfield using the drug.

Donny Hathaway

Born October 1, 1945
Died January 13, 1979

Soul singer/songwriter and frequent duet partner of Roberta Flack, Donny Hathaway was born into a poor family in Chicago. Raised in a St. Louis, Missouri, housing project by his grandmother Martha Cromwell, a professional gospel singer, Hathaway joined her on the gospel road as "Donny Pitts, the Nation's Youngest Gospel Singer". A skilled classical pianist in his high school years, Hathaway earned a full academic scholarship, majoring in music theory at Washington DC's Howard University in the mid Sixties. During this period, Hathaway considered joining the church. But while performing the keyboards in a student jazz group, The Ric Powell Trio, Hathaway was spotted for the first time by fellow music student Roberta Flack; impressed, she would run into him again. Moving back to Chicago in the late Sixties, Hathaway produced a number of sessions for Jerry Butler, The Impressions, Pop Staples, and recorded a duet at the Curtis Mayfield-operated Curtom Records, 'I Thank You Baby'. But with the aid of King Curtis, Hathaway was signed to Atlantic/Atco Records as a songwriter, producer and solo recording artist. A sensitive, soulful singer and talented pianist, Hathaway combined strains of gospel, soul, and classical music on his début album *Everything Is Beautiful* (1970). But with the album spawning only a minor R&B single, Hathaway was personally aided by Atlantic producer Jerry Wexler for his second album, *Donny Hathaway* (1971); from the project, Hathaway landed a Top 30 pop hit with a cover version of James Taylor's 'You've Got A Friend' (1971) in a duet with Roberta Flack. The following year, Hathaway scored a pair

of hit albums, *Donny Hathaway Live*, and *Roberta Flack And Donny Hathaway*; from the latter project, the jazzy, million-selling duet ballad 'Where Is The Love' hit the Top 10. Also that year, Hathaway supplied the music for the film, *Come Back Charleston Blue* and provided the vocals for the theme to the CBS television show *Maude*. By the mid Seventies, Hathaway concentrated on production duties, working with artists such as Roberta Flack, Aretha Franklin, Jerry Butler, and Carla Thomas. In 1978 Hathaway scored his final pop hit with another Roberta Flack duet, 'The Closer I Get To You'. Daughter, Lalah Hathaway, became a successful urban-contemporary singer who released her début album in 1990.
CAUSE: He either fell or jumped from a 15th floor waist-high window of the Essex House Hotel in New York City. He landed on a second floor ledge. If he had jumped, he would have been projected further away from the building. Though prone to depression, earlier that day he was upbeat during a recording session with his singing partner Roberta Flack. His hotel room was found intact with no suicide note. But while the coroner ruled the death a suicide, the Reverend Jesse Jackson, who gave the eulogy, maintained that Hathaway's death was neither suicide nor murder; Jackson cited Hathaway's attire at the time of his death – a hat, coat and scarf – suggesting that no one would get dressed up "just to jump out of a window". But the coroner asserted that adults don't fall out of windows. At his 17th floor apartment in Chicago, Hathaway would frequently preach and sing, while leaning out of a window; he had previously been evicted from several hotels for doing the same thing.

Felix Haug

Born March 27, 1952
Died May 1, 2004
As half of the Swiss duo Double, Felix Haug was behind an international hit in the mid Eighties with 'The Captain Of Her Heart'. A drummer and keyboardist, he was previously a member of jazz-rock trio Ping Pong. In 1983, Haug and fellow bandmate, singer and guitarist Kurt Maloo, formed the pop-rock duo Double. After the outfit disbanded, Haug worked as a journalist in Zurich.
CAUSE: Suffering a heart attack, he died in Uster, Switzerland.

Nick Hawkins

Born February 3, 1965
Died October 10, 2005
The guitarist with the Clash spin-off group Big Audio Dynamite II, Nick Hawkins joined the Mick Jones-led project in 1990. Originally from Luton, Hawkins was an immense Clash fan during his youth and had previously worked in a series of local bands including Lutitia Network and Romeo Street Gang. After releasing the much ignored album *Kool-Aid* (1990), Big Audio Dynamite II made waves with *The Globe*, which spawned a pair of hits, 'Rush' (which samples The Who's 'Baba O'Riley') and 'The Globe' (which samples The Clash's 'Should I Stay Or Should I Go'). Despite opening for U2 in 1992/93 and appearing at a number of major music festivals, Big Audio Dynamite II failed to establish itself as a major act. Renamed Big Audio and then reverting to its original moniker Big Audio Dynamite, the group continued to struggle on the charts. Hawkins left the group in 1997 and relocated to Las Vegas. He was working on a posthumously released solo album, *Dusk To Dawn*, at the time of his death.
CAUSE: He suffered a heart attack and died at his home in Las Vegas. Suffering from severe diabetes, he was told as a teenager that he would not survive past his thirties.

Screamin' Jay Hawkins

(JELACY J. HAWKINS)
Born July 18, 1928
Died February 12, 2000
An early R&B artist who combined jungle rhythms with ghoulish imagery, Screamin' Jay Hawkins made a career out of his standard, 'I Put A Spell On You'. Hawkins' birth was unusual in that his pregnant mother disembarked from a Greyhound bus to give birth at the bus station in Cleveland. Having done her biological duty, she boarded the bus leaving her child behind. Hawkins was raised in a series of orphanages and would offer fictionalised accounts of his childhood, one of which had him being raised by Indians. Though self-taught on the piano and saxophone, he honed his skills at the Ohio Conservatory of Music. Also a boxer, Hawkins won a series of titles during his youth including a Golden Gloves championship. Entering the US Air Force in 1944, he was placed into the special services as an entertainer in Europe and Asia. Discharged in 1950, he hit the road as a solo act. Although fond of opera, he was more suited to gritty R&B and as a pianist and sax player he joined Tiny Grimes & The Rocking Highlanders in 1951, providing the vocals on 'Why Don't You Waste My Time'. Leaving Grimes, Hawkins came under the wing of R&B shouter Wynonie Harris and as a session musician he played the saxophone on tours behind The Turbans and Fats Domino. Settling in New York City, Hawkins passed through a trio of labels before recording his breakthrough single, 'I Put A Spell On You', in 1956. It became a legendary rock'n'roll track, with the drunken Hawkins slobbering and grunting his way through the voodoo-laden lyrics. Though written as a ballad, Hawkins had other ideas, perhaps because recording took place after an evening of drinking with session players Mickey Baker and Sam "The Man" Taylor. Banned by radio, but a strong seller, 'Spell' became a rock standard recorded by countless acts including Creedence Clearwater Revival, Alan Price, Arthur Brown and Nina Simone. Convinced by deejay/promoter Alan Freed to take the stage in a coffin, Hawkins expanded his ghoulish repertoire of props to include a skull head-on-a-stick named Henry; for a time, he adopted a Zulu warrior costume of white face paint, a bone through his nose, and a jungle loincloth. A regular of Freed's Fifties rock'n'roll revues, Hawkins also appeared in Freed's cheapie rock flick *Mister Rock And Roll* and in the 1978 Freed biopic *American Hot Wax*. For a while, Hawkins retired from music and ran a bar in Hawaii, but returned to the stage and in 1969 signed with Philips Records where he would record the outrageous 'Constipation Blues'. Remaining a cult figure late in life, Hawkins turned to acting, appearing in the 1989 Jim Jarmusch film, *Mystery Train* and *A Rage In Harlem* (1991). Hawkins spent many of his latter years in Europe.
CAUSE: After undergoing surgery for an obstructed bowel at a hospital near his Paris home, he died from a related haemorrhage. A month after his death, a website was launched to locate his reported 57 children.

Ted Hawkins

(EDWARD THEODORE HAWKINS, JR.)
Born October 28, 1936
Died January 1, 1995
Acoustic guitarist and songwriter who blended country, blues and folk influences, the fluid-voiced Ted Hawkins spent three years in a Mississippi reform school from the age of 15 for stealing a leather jacket. On his release, he was inspired by the gospel-soul of Sam Cooke and he turned to a career in music. Relocating to Los Angeles in 1966, Hawkins recorded the single 'Baby'. Angry that

he was paid no royalties, Hawkins became a full-time street singer in the artsy Venice Beach section of the city. Sitting on his trademark milk crate, Hawkins would work for tips that were dropped into a Mason jar. Convinced by producer Bruce Bromberg in 1971 to re-enter a recording studio, Hawkins recorded a series of tracks, many of which were collected on the 1982 Rounder Records album, *Watch Your Step*. Rediscovered by deejay Bill Harris during one of his sidewalk performances, Hawkins began recording at a regular pace in the Eighties. Lured to England in 1986 by a British deejay, Hawkins was celebrated as a star during four years of touring. Returning to the US in 1990, Hawkins restarted his street corner performances. Finally earning acclaim with the release of his sixth album, *The Next Hundred Years* (1994), Hawkins passed away soon after.
CAUSE: Suffering a stroke on December 28, 1994, he died three days later. Hawkins had been afflicted with diabetes and high blood pressure.

Roger Hayes

Born 1942
Died December 11, 2003
The second tenor with Fifties youthful doo-wop/R&B group The Schoolboys (a Frankie Lymon & The Teenagers soundalike), who had an R&B hit with 'Please Say You Want Me' and the crossover-pop hit 'Shirley'. Formed at Cooper Junior High School in Harlem, The Schoolboys were discovered by disc jockey Tommy Smalls. After the group disbanded, Hayes joined another doo-wop act, The Collegians, landing a chart hit with 'Zoom Zoom Zoom'. The other members of The Schoolboys turned to heroin, and all of them suffered drug-related demises. While high on heroin, Hayes committed murder and served 30 years behind bars. While in jail, he converted to Islam and took the name Talib Muhammad.
CAUSE: Kidney failure. He died at Staten Island University Hospital in New York.

Ofra Haza

Born November 19, 1959
Died February 23, 2000
Israeli-born techno artist, Ofra Haza combined traditional Hebrew music with techno beats. Launching her solo career at the age of 19, she broke onto the European music scene with the 1985 album *Yemenite Songs*, and scored her biggest hit with the dance club single, 'Im Nin Alu' (1988). Produced by Don Was, her 1992 album *Kirya* was nominated for a Grammy in the World Beat category. Haza also worked with Thomas Dolby, Lou Reed, Paula Abdul, and Iggy Pop.
CAUSE: AIDS-related pneumonia. Her family attempted to keep the cause secret. She died in Tel Aviv. In 1987, Haza had survived an aeroplane crash.

Eddie Hazel

Born April 10, 1950
Died December 23, 1992
An intricate part of the pioneering funk-rock ensemble Parliament-Funkadelic, guitarist Eddie Hazel was much influenced by the psychedelic style of guitar virtuoso Jimi Hendrix. Born in Brooklyn, New York, but moving to Plainfield, New Jersey, in his early teens, Hazel would meet hairdresser-turned musician George Clinton. Hazel initially joined Clinton's soul group The Parliaments in 1967, shortly after the group scored its break-through hit with '(I Wanna) Testify'. But after losing the ownership of the group's name, Clinton would launch an extended family of up to 40 musicians under the Parliament/Funkadelic umbrella, and various incarnations such as The P. Funk All Stars and Parlet. With Hazel primarily a member of Funkadelic (a moniker used since 1969), the group recorded the perennial album-rock favourite 'Maggot Brain' (1971), the track

highlighted by Hazel's searing, 10 minute guitar solo. Clinton would later hire guitarist Phelps Collins to share the lead duties with Hazel. A member of George Clinton's groups off and on for much of the Seventies, Hazel co-wrote a number of the group's songs including, 'Red Hot Mama' and 'Free Your Mind And Your Ass Will Follow'. But in 1974, Hazel was convicted and jailed for taking drugs on an aeroplane. Released from prison, Hazel joined Motown, playing guitar on The Temptations hit, 'Shakey Ground'. Pursuing a solo career, Hazel signed with Warner Brothers in 1977, his début album coming with *Games, Dames, And Guitar Thangs*. Hazel toured as part of the Clinton's P-Funk All Stars in 1992 but was forced to leave due to declining health.
CAUSE: The cause is alternately given as stomach cancer and complications from liver failure. Refusing to listen to his doctor's advice, Hazel toured until a few months before his death. Hazel died in Plainfield, New York.
FURTHER READING: Mills, David. (1998). *George Clinton And P-Funk: An Oral History*. New York: Avon.

Dick Heard

(RICHARD MARTIN HEARD)
Born 1937
Died September 8, 1998
Songwriter and music industry executive, Dick Heard broke into the music industry in 1970 after co-penning with Eddie Rabbit the Elvis Presley hit, 'Kentucky Rain'. By 1978 he formed the Dick Heard Television Productions. Also a writer, he co-authored *Elvis Up Close*.
CAUSE: Cancer.

"Huby" Heard

(JAMES HUBERT HEARD)
Born May 31, 1951
Died July 29, 2004
A native of suburban Cincinnati, singer-songwriter "Huby" Heard formed his first group while in high school with future R&B star Roger Troutman. While singing at his local church, Heard was discovered by R&B singer Billy Preston. Relocating to Los Angeles at age 22, Heard joined Preston's backing band The God Squad, and appeared on a number of soul/rock hits including 'Outa-Space', 'Will It Go Round In Circles?', 'Space Race' and 'Nothing From Nothing'. In 1973, Heard was hired as a member of The Rolling Stones' band for a European tour and, in 1975, performed on Stones' bassist Bill Wyman's second solo album, *Stone Alone*. Parting with Preston in the early Eighties after a 13-year association, Heard also worked with The Gap Band, Ray Charles, Teddy Pendergrass, Stephanie Mills and The Brothers Johnson. Returning to Cincinnati in 2001, Heard became active in his church choir and recorded the gospel album, *Eternal Praise*.
CAUSE: Suffering from a heart ailment, he died at Good Samaritan Hospital in Cincinnati.

Mark Heard

Born 1951
Died August 16, 1992
A folk-pop and Christian rock songwriter and artist best known for his composition 'Satellite Sky', Georgia native Mark Heard had his songs recorded by Joan Baez, Phil Keaggy and Olivia Newton-John. Also a producer, Heard joined R.E.M.'s Peter Buck on the album *Killing Floor*, by Athens, Georgia duo Vigilantes Of Love. On the brink of major success with the release of his 15th album, *Mark Heard*, he was being courted by a pair of major labels just before he died. Heard was the subject of two tribute albums, *Orphans Of God* and the Grammy-nominated *Strong Hand Of Love*.
CAUSE: Heart attack. He had suffered a previous heart attack while performing on July 4, at the Cornerstone Festival near Chicago.

John Heartsman

Born February 9, 1937
Died December 25, 1996
A singer, guitarist and organist, electric bluesman John Heartsman was a fixture on the West Coast, managing his only national hit in 1957 with 'Johnny's House Party (Parts 1 & 2)'. A versatile performer, the shaven-headed Heartsman worked as a session player behind Kimmy Wilson, Al King, and Tiny Powell.
CAUSE: Unknown. He died in Sacramento, California.

Rob Heaton

(ROBERT CHARLES HEATON)
Born July 6, 1961
Died November 4, 2004
As a key member of the politically charged UK modern rock act New Model Army, Rob Heaton garnered a loyal following. The group was conceived in 1980 by Justin Sullivan (a.k.a. Slade The Leveller) and writer Joolz Denby as an anti-establishment, post-punk venture. Initially reared on his father's trad jazz records, Heaton later immersed himself in an eclectic mix of classical, country music and classic rock. After working with a series of drummers, Sullivan hired Heaton in time for the sessions for New Model Army's débút single 'Bittersweet'. Signed to the independent Abstract label, the group quickly attracted attention with tracks such as 'Great Expectations', 'Spirit Of The Falklands' and 'The Price'. While touring throughout the UK for a series of miners' benefit shows as the opening act for Billy Bragg, the group garnered a great deal of press coverage. Signing with a major label, EMI Records, and alienating many of their fans in the process, New Model Army's prolific string of UK chart entries began with 1983's 'No Rest'. Heaton and Sullivan would co-write most of the group's hits including 'Better Than Them', 'Brave New World', 'Poison Street', 'White Coats', 'Space', 'Here Comes The War', and a controversial song that resulted in a ban by the American Musician's Union, 'The 51st State'. Following a respite during the mid Nineties, NMA re-formed in 1998. Adding a string section, they issued *Strange Brotherhood* and a double live album . . . *& Nobody Else*. Following surgery in 1998 to remove a brain tumour, Heaton left the group and opened a recording studio in Bradford. Heaton would later issue solo material under the moniker Gardeners Of Eden.
CAUSE: Pancreatic cancer. He died after collapsing at his recording studio.

Dick Heckstall-Smith

(RICHARD MALDEN HECKSTALL-SMITH)
Born September 26, 1934
Died December 17, 2004
An influential British bluesman, Dick Heckstall-Smith was a member of a series of ground-breaking blues-rock acts. Influenced by sax player Sidney Bechet, Heckstall-Smith mastered the alto saxophone at a young age. While studying agriculture at college, the tall and lanky Heckstall-Smith was drawn to the trad jazz movement and led his college's jazz band. After winning a second-place prize in a collegiate jazz competition, he was asked to join the group of one of the judges, clarinettist Sandy Brown. After recording with Brown, Heckstall-Smith issued solo material before joining a band led by banjoist Hugh Rainey that also included Acker Bilk and drummer Ginger Baker. Veering towards blues, Heckstall-Smith was an original member of Alexis Korner's Blues Incorporated which changed the course of British rock by influencing a generation of pioneering British bluesmen, among them the embryonic Rolling Stones, during residencies at the Ealing Jazz Club and the Marquee Club in London. Joining the Graham Bond Organisation in 1963, featuring

organist Bond, bassist Jack Bruce and drummer Ginger Baker, Heckstall-Smith merged jazz and blues with rock. The group was popular on the club circuit but their records failed to sell in great quantities and are consequently now collectors' items. In 1967, Heckstall-Smith and Bond bandmate Jon Hiseman joined John Mayall's Bluesbreakers. The following year, Heckstall-Smith and Hiseman teamed up with vocalist Chris Farlowe to form Colosseum, a pioneering jazz-rock outfit who recorded a trio of albums featuring Heckstall-Smith's free-form jazz solos. Following Colosseum's break-up in 1971, Heckstall-Smith formed his own group, Manchild, releasing the album *A Story Ended.* While recuperating from back injuries during the Seventies, Heckstall-Smith completed a Doctorate in Sociology. Though out of the spotlight for much of the next two decades, he continued to record with various groups including his longtime outfit Big Chief. After suffering a severe stroke during a heart bypass operation in 1992, he briefly left music before re-forming Colosseum in 1994. His final album, *Blues And Beyond*, was issued in 2001 and featured guests Jack Bruce, John Mayall and Mick Taylor. Heckstall-Smith wrote a pair of autobiographies, including *Blowing The Blues*, which chronicled the rise of the British blues scene.
CAUSE: Cancer. He had been in poor health for many years.

Michael Hedges

Born December 31, 1953
Died November 28, 1997
Classically trained jazz-fusion, acoustic guitar virtuoso, Michael Hedges helped establish Windham Hill Records. Known for his unique guitar style of using both hands to play notes, Hedges signed with the fledgling label in 1981. Born in Enid, Oklahoma, he was trained on piano and cello, before taking guitar lessons at age 11. Joining his first rock band at 13, he later switched to classical music, attending the Peabody Conservatory in Baltimore. A varied player, he meshed electronic music with jazz and even hard rock. Recording a total of seven albums, including his defining *Aerial Boundaries* (1984), Hedges earned a Grammy nomination in 1990 for Tarpot. His final sessions were released on the 1999 album *Torched.*
CAUSE: His 1986 BMW went over an embankment near Boonville, California, on his way home from a San Francisco airport. The wreckage was discovered four days later by a road repair crew.

Heinz

(HEINZ BURT)
Born July 24, 1942
Died April 7, 2000
A legendary figure in early Sixties British pop music, German-born Heinz Burt was the bassist of the British instrumental group, The Tornados. Leaving Germany at age seven, he was raised in Hampshire, England. After failing an audition for bassist in the Joe Meek-managed Outlaws, Heinz so impressed Meek with his charisma and good looks, he was placed in a new group, The Tornados. Assembled initially as a session band, the quintet provided musical backing for Meek's stable of acts which included John Leyton, Don Charles, Glenda Collins, and Andy Cavell. Aside from their session duties, The Tornados recorded hit records of their own, including the chart-topping 'Telstar' (1962), named after an early communications satellite, which was an amalgamation of synthesised sounds and surreal, space-age effects. Predating The Beatles and The Rolling Stones, The Tornados were the first British group to land a number one single in the US with the record. Subsequent releases such as 'Ride The Wind' and the Meek composition 'Globetrotter' failed to repeat its success. Subsequently

groomed by Meek as a solo artist and dropping his last name, Heinz left The Tornados in January 1963. With Meek landing Heinz a role in the film *Farewell Performance*, the youthful teen idol garnered solo chart success with 'Just Like Eddie' (a tribute to the fallen rockabilly star Eddie Cochran) which featured a young Ritchie Blackmore on guitar, 'Country Boy' (1963), 'You Were There' (1963), and 'Questions I Can't Answer' (1964). Heinz became distanced from homosexual Meek after announcing that he was in love with a woman. Leaving the music industry with little money, Heinz hit the oldies circuit in the Seventies.
CAUSE: Suffering Lou Gehrig's disease (amyotrophic lateral sclerosis), he died at Southampton General Hospital. Diagnosed with the condition in 1990, he had been confined to a wheelchair for the last years of his life.

Bobby Helms

(ROBERT LEE HELMS)
Born August 15, 1936
Died June 19, 1997
An early pop-rock artist, Bloomington, Indiana-born Bobby Helms was reared in a musical family. A child performer, he landed on a local radio programme at age nine, later joined by his brother. Regularly appearing on his father's local television show beginning at age 13, Helms was a guest performer on the Grand Ole Opry by 1950. Helms was discovered by country star Ernest Tubbs who spotted Helms on television as he was passing through the city. Signing with Decca Records in 1957, Helms hit the pop charts that year with a trio of hits beginning with 'Frauline' and his signature piece, 'Special Angel'. A perennial classic, Helm's 'Jingle Bell Rock' (1957) was the first pop hit to tie a Christmas theme with rock music. Returning to his country roots, Helms was relegated to the country charts with the hits, 'Just A Little Lonesome' (1958), from the film *The Case Against Brooklyn*, 'Jacqueline' (1958), 'New River Train' (1959), and 'Lonely River Rhine' (1960). Recording occasionally, Helms managed a few minor hits in the late Sixties. Signing with MCA, Helms recorded his final album in 1983, *Pop-A-Billy*.
CAUSE: Suffering from emphysema and asthma for the last few years of his life, he died from general ill health in Martinsville, Indiana. Performing for the last time six months before his death, he brought his oxygen tank onstage.

Chet Helms

(CHESTER LEO HELMS)
Born August 2, 1942
Died June 25, 2005
The architect of San Francisco's psychedelic sound, Chet Helms was a key figure behind the movement which culminated in 1967's "Summer of Love". Though born in Santa Maria, California, Helms was raised in Texas and after dropping out of the University of Texas, he grew his trademark bushy beard and long hair. A stepchild of a mixed-race marriage, Helms began staging fund-raising benefits for civil rights groups, skills which he would later apply to concert promotion. Relocating to San Francisco at age 20, he settled in the city's Haight-Ashbury district where his home soon became a popular venue for jam sessions by various local groups including Big Brother & The Holding Company, a budding blues-based outfit which he managed. By 1966, Helms had convinced his former college friend, singer Janis Joplin, to front the group. Launching Family Dog Productions, Helms began organising free concerts and open-air counter-culture parties at Golden Gate Park that were dubbed "Human Be-Ins". By early 1966, Helms was staging concerts at the Fillmore Auditorium with new partner Bill Graham but, after Graham formed his own production company and took over the Fillmore, Helms opened the

competing Avalon Ballroom where Janis Joplin and Big Brother & The Holding Company would make their début in June 1966. The venue introduced psychedelic-style light-shows to rock music and hosted a who's who of West Coast rock royalty including The Doors, Country Joe & The Fish and, most frequently, The Grateful Dead. But in the growing world of professional concert promotion, Helms left the field in 1970. By 1978, Helms returned to concert promotion and, in 1980, operated the art gallery, Atelier Dore.
CAUSE: While battling hepatitis C, he succumbed to complications from a stroke. He died at California Pacific Medical Center in San Francisco. (Following erroneous media reports of his death in 2001, Helms staged a mock funeral and invited 200 friends. Driven to San Francisco's Gold Coast restaurant in a hearse, he sprang from a coffin to answer a cell phone positioned on his chest.)

Guy Bonson Hemric

Born June 30, 1931
Died January 10, 1993
Teaming with composer Richard Loring, Guy Bonson Hemric penned the lyrics for several early Sixties beach genre films including the Frankie Avalon/Annette Funicello feature *Beach Blanket Bingo*. Hemric's first success came with Petula Clark's 'What Good Does It Do Me?' Hemric worked in Hollywood into the Seventies.
CAUSE: Cancer. Diagnosed in 1981, he died in Maitland, Florida.

Dorris Henderson

Born February 2, 1933
Died March 3, 2005
A US born singer-songwriter who found fame after relocating to the UK, Dorris Henderson is best known for her stint with Eclection. Her father was a clergyman and her mother was a full-blooded Indian. Inspired to become a musician after attending a concert by folk legend Odetta, Henderson became a fixture on the Los Angeles folk scene, playing autoharp. After quitting her civil service job, she discovered the booming folk scene in Greenwich Village, where she was befriended by Bob Dylan. Within weeks of relocating to England in 1965, she became a sensation with the folk community at the Troubadour café in London, and earned a six-month residency on the BBC music programme *Gadzooks, It's All Happening*. Teaming with folkie John Renbourn (later with Pentangle), Henderson released a pair of albums, *There You Go* and *Watch The Stars*. In 1968, Henderson was hired by Trevor Lucas to replace lead vocalist Kerrilee Male in the electric folk-rock group Eclection; a year later, the group disbanded. Henderson joined another line-up of Eclection before turning to jazz and continued to perform throughout Europe until shortly before her death.
CAUSE: Cancer. She died in London.

Joe Henderson

Born April 24, 1937
Died October 24, 1964
A gospel-trained vocalist, Joe Henderson scored a Top 10 soul hit in 1962 with 'Snap Your Fingers'. At the time of his death, Henderson had just finished recording several tracks for RIC Records. Ronnie Milsap topped the country charts in 1987 with an updated version of Henderson's 'Snap You Fingers'. (Not to be confused with the saxophonist of the same name.)
CAUSE: Heart attack. He died at his apartment in Nashville.

Jimi Hendrix

(JOHNNY ALLEN HENDRIX)
Born November 27, 1942
Died September 18, 1970
A ground-breaking blues rock guitarist of almost supernatural fluency who greatly expanded the boundaries of

rock music and the vocabulary of the electric guitar, Jimi Hendrix was born in Seattle, and raised by his working-class father following the departure of his part-Cherokee Indian mother. After mastering the ukulele and harmonica, Hendrix taught himself to play a cheap, five-dollar acoustic guitar. Though left-handed, Hendrix re-stringed the right-handed guitar, playing it upside-down, a strategy he would always employ. Playing an electric guitar in 1959 in a Top 40 band called The Rocking Kings, he quit school the following year and, although underage, enlisted in the army. A member of the 101st Airborne Division, stationed at Fort Campbell, Kentucky, Hendrix was discharged after injuring his ankle and back in a parachuting accident. Hendrix then formed a blues group, The King Kasuals, with a fellow soldier, bassist Billy Cox, performing around Memphis. Hendrix spent the next few years as a backing guitarist for various acts including The Isleys, and he provided the guitar-work on their single 'Testify' (1964). Returning to Memphis and taking the stage name Maurice James, Hendrix joined Little Richard's band but was fired for his attention-stealing guitar work. Settling in New York City in late 1965, Hendrix joined an R&B group led by Curtis Knight. Eventually, although under contract to Knight's manager, Hendrix formed his own group, Jimmy James & The Blue Flames. Creating a buzz in the music community and drawing rock's royalty to his performances, Hendrix was signed to a management contract by former Animals' bassist, Chas Chandler. Taken to London by Chandler, Hendrix was teamed with guitarist-turned-bassist Noel Redding and former child actor, drummer Mitch Mitchell. Dubbed The Jimi Hendrix Experience, the group enjoyed a British hit, a blues-rock cover of the folk standard, 'Hey Joe', which was followed by the British-only chart hits, 'Purple Haze' and 'The Wind Cries Mary'. A rare, black rocker, Hendrix dressed in exotic, psychedelic clothing, accented by his long, noncomformist hair. With Hendrix still unknown in his home country, Paul McCartney insisted that he be added to the line-up at the Monterey Pop Festival in June of 1967. Receiving his first notable US exposure, Hendrix wowed the audience with his stage antics; maximising reverb, and employing deafening feedback, the outrageous Hendrix played his guitar with his teeth, before setting the instrument on fire. Releasing a pair of critically acclaimed Top 10 albums in 1967, *Are You Experienced?* and *Axis Bold As Love*, Hendrix set the standard for rock guitar with tracks such as 'Are You Experienced?', 'Foxy Lady', and 'Fire'. From the 1968 double-album, *Electric Ladyland*, Hendrix would score his US pop breakthrough with a reworked, electrified rendition of Bob Dylan's 'All Along The Watchtower'. With Chandler leaving Hendrix, Michael Jeffries, the former manager of The Animals, assumed managerial duties. Shortly after Hendrix's much-publicised arrest for heroin possession in Canada in May 1969, The Experience disbanded. The highest paid act at Woodstock, Hendrix was backed by a group called The Electric Sky Church, which included Mitchell and Cox, but not Redding. The highlight of Hendrix's performance was a distorted, solo electric guitar version of 'The Star Spangled Banner'. Buckling to pressure from his black critics, Hendrix then formed an all-black backing group, The Band Of Gypsys, which featured drummer Buddy Miles and Billy Cox on bass, but the group disbanded after their second concert. Reforming The Experience with Mitchell and Cox, Hendrix performed at the Isle of Wight Festival in the summer of 1970. Completing the

construction of his new, state-of-the-art Electric Lady studio in July 1970, Hendrix would be dead two months later. His assets at the time of his death were reportedly worth only $21,000. Although the album *Cry Of Love* (1971) would mark Hendrix's final completed project, producer Alan Douglas would regularly issue new Hendrix albums, beginning with *War Heroes*, by overdubbing unfinished or raw tracks. Decades after his death, Hendrix is still revered as the most innovative instrumentalist in the history of rock, his entire music catalogue remaining a strong seller. Since his death, the Hendrix catalogue and legacy has been the subject of endless litigation but Hendrix's father Al finally regained control of his son's musical output in 1995.
CAUSE: Drug overdose. He was found unconscious in a basement bedroom at the Samarkand Hotel in Notting Hill Gate which had been let to Monika Danneman who subsequently claimed that she and Hendrix were to be married. Hendrix came home at 3 a.m. from a party held by ex-Monkee Mike Nesmith where he had imbibed a large quantity of red wine. After eating a tuna sandwich, he chatted with Danneman for approximately the next four hours. Hendrix, who did not have a high tolerance to drugs, had consumed about nine pills of a German barbiturate, quinalbarbitone – 18 times the normal dose. Awakening at 10:30 in the morning, the panicky Danneman delayed calling authorities and instead telephoned a friend for advice on what to do. There was no truth to Danneman's claim that Hendrix was still alive when help arrived, and that the paramedics had inadvertently rushed his demise by their faulty actions. While Hendrix was dead on the scene, he was pronounced DOA at St. Mary's Abbots Hospital in London. The coroner's report ruled the death an "open verdict" with the cause of death attributed to "inhalation of vomit due to barbiturate intoxication". His final public performance was two nights before his death at a London nightclub where he sat in with the group, Eric Burdon & War. Following his death, Hendrix's New York apartment was looted. In December 1993, Scotland Yard reopened the investigation of Hendrix's death; a new inquest was requested by former girlfriend Kathy Etchingham, who had commissioned her own investigation and discovered discrepancies in how and when an ambulance was summoned. Monika Danneman was later discredited and attacked in the press for a series of "fantasies" and untruths she would repeat about Hendrix. She sued, though never successfully, the publishers of several books that suggested her delay in calling an ambulance made her culpable in Hendrix's death, and in 1996 committed suicide shortly after losing a well reported libel case brought by Kathy Etchingham. In late 1999, Hendrix's family announced controversial plans to disinter and re-bury the late singer in a new 27-foot-high, stone and bronze dome-shaped mausoleum, financed in part by corporate "ad" space around the memorial and future admission fees.
FURTHER READING: Henderson, David. (1996). *The Life Of Jimi Hendrix: 'Scuse Me While I Kiss The Sky*. New York: Bantam. Brown, Tony (1997). *Jimi Hendrix: The Final Days*. London: Omnibus Press.

Margie Hendrix

Born March 13, 1939
Died July 1973

A member of The Cookies and The Raelettes, Margie Hendrix appeared on dozens of hit records. The Cookies were formed in New York City in 1953 by Hendrix, Ethel McCrea and Pat Lyles. Signing with Atlantic Records, the trio scored the Top 10 R&B hit 'In Paradise' (1956) and provided the backing harmony for a variety of the label's acts including Joe Turner,

LaVern Baker and Chuck Willis. In 1957, Ray Charles hired The Cookies as his new backing vocal group, whom he renamed The Raelettes. Provocatively attired, the group was a hit with audiences and appeared on many of Charles' hits, including '(Night Time Is) The Right Time' and 'What'd I Say'. In the early Sixties, Hendrix had an out-of-wedlock child fathered by Charles which was the inspiration for the song 'Hit The Road Jack'. Hendrix later recorded solo material on Charles' record label, Tangerine, and was portrayed by Regina King in the Charles biopic *Ray*.
CAUSE: Drug overdose.

Jim Henson

Born September 24, 1936
Died May 16, 1990
The creator of the children's programmes *Sesame Street/Muppets Show*, Jim Henson also scored a pair of pop hits with his "Muppet" characters, 'Rubber Duckie' as by Ernie, and the Grammy-winning, Jim Brickman-penned 'Rainbow Connection' as by Kermit the Frog, the latter taken from a full-length Muppets feature film. Born in the US, but a resident of London for 15 years, Henson created several other characters such as Big Bird and Miss Piggy. Jim Henson's estate sold the rights to his Muppet characters for $680 million in 2000.
CAUSE: Pneumonia. He died shortly after his diagnosis from an especially bad strain of the disease. He died in New York City.

Bob Herbert

Born February 4, 1942
Died August 9, 1999
Manager and mastermind of the prefabricated pop supergroup, The Spice Girls, former accountant Bob Herbert assembled the vocal quintet by advertising in the entertainment trade journal, *The Stage*. He was helped in the selection process by his son Chris, selecting the girls (initially called Touch) from 600 applicants. After they'd honed a stage act, Herbert signed them to Virgin Records but The Spice Girls fired Herbert in 1997, just as they were breaking through with their début hit 'Wannabe', and hired new manager Simon Fuller. Herbert subsequently managed another British teenage-targeted group, Five, and was poised to launch another girl group at the time of his death. Herbert's first exposure to the music industry came in 1985 when he nurtured and financed a teenage pop group called Gloss. Later renamed Bros, the successful outfit was taken over by manager Tom Watkins.
CAUSE: Car crash. He was killed instantly when he lost control of his MGF sports car during a heavy rainstorm and collided with another car in Windsor, Berkshire.

Gregory Herbert

Born May 19, 1947
Died January 31, 1978
A tenor saxophonist, Gregory Herbert was a latter member of Blood, Sweat & Tears. A professional musician at 16, he first performed with The Miles Davis Group. Joining the Thad Jones/Mel Lewis Orchestra, he appeared on their 1978 release of an earlier concert, *Live in Munich*. Joining Blood, Sweat & Tears in early 1977, he recorded only one album with the group, *Brand New Day*.
CAUSE: Accidental heroin overdose in his hotel room. He was staying in Amsterdam with Blood, Sweat & Tears on the eve of a European tour.

Bobby Herne

(ROBERT HERNE, JR.)
Born January 18, 1938
Died May 27, 1998
Guitarist and producer, Bobby Herne is best known for producing the album, *The Philosophy Of The World* by The Shaggs.
CAUSE: Heart attack. He died in York, Maine.

Rene Herrera

Born October 2, 1935
Died December 20, 2005
A member of the Laredo, Texas-based Mexican-American pop-rock duo Rene & Rene, Rene Herrera reached the US Top 20 in 1968 with 'Lo Mucho Que Te Quiero (The More I Love You)'. Herrera had formed the duo with Rene Ornelas after a decade-long stint in a popular regional rock group, The Quarter Notes.
CAUSE: Cancer. He died at a Houston hospital.

Paul Hester

(PAUL NEWELL HESTER)
Born January 8, 1959
Died March 26, 2005
The drummer in Antipodean bands Split Enz and Crowded House, who achieved international success. Previously a member of the Sydney-based funk group Deckchairs Overboard, Hester was hired by Split Enz in 1983 on the recommendation of Midnight Oil's Rob Hirst. His recruitment occurred at a time when elder Finn brother Tim was ceding his role in the band to younger brother Neil, and Hester only played on Enz's final studio album, *See Ya 'Round.* In late 1985, Hester and Neil Finn (with bassist Nick Seymour) launched a new band, The Mullanes, which quickly evolved into Crowded House. Relocating to Los Angeles and signing with Capitol Records in 1985, the group enjoyed stateside success with their self-titled début album which spawned the hits 'Don't Dream It's Over' and 'Something So Strong'. Unable to capitalise on this promising start, the group was later reinvigorated with the temporary addition in 1990 of Neil's brother Tim, who had pursued a solo career after leaving Split Enz. From the 1991 album *Woodface*, Crowded House made the UK pop charts with 'Fall At Your Feet', 'Weather With You', 'Four Seasons In One Day' and 'It's Only Natural'. The subsequent release *Together Alone* (1993) contained further hit singles in 'Distant Sun', 'Nails In My Feet' and 'Locked Out'. Unhappy with the hardships of constant touring, Hester left Crowded House in 1994. Returning to his hometown of Melbourne, Australia, he pursued several business ventures, including operating a recording studio. Hester also hosted an Australian cable television programme, *The Music Max Sessions.*
CAUSE: Suicide by hanging. He was found dead, dangling from a tree in Elsternwick Park near his home in Melbourne.

Ersel Hickey

Born June 27, 1934
Died July 9, 2004
A budding rockabilly idol who was dubbed the next Elvis, Ersel Hickey failed to live up to expectations. Alone after the death of his father and the institutionalisation of his mother, Hickey was drawn to music by teen idols Johnnie Ray and Elvis Presley. Initially recording in 1955 under the name Mickey Evans, Hickey is best known for self-composed rockabilly standard, 'Bluebirds Over The Mountain' (1958).
CAUSE: Suffering complications from bladder cancer, he contracted a fatal infection. He died at New York University Medical Center in New York City.

Ulysses "Ronnie" Hicks

Born 1929
Died February 1, 1955
A member of the Five Keys from 1953–54, Ulysses Hicks sang on their hits 'Ling, Ting, Tong' (1954) and 'Deep In My Heart' (1954). Hicks had been hired as a temporary replacement for Rudy West who had been drafted.
CAUSE: While on tour through Massachusetts, Hicks was staying in Boston after a performance in

Springfield. Fainting in a hotel lobby, he was pronounced dead on arrival at a local hospital. He died from a rheumatic heart condition.

Monk Higgins

(Milton Bland)
Born October 3, 1930
Died July 3, 1986
Classically trained R&B/soul performer, session pianist and saxophone player, Arkansas-born Monk Higgins recorded on several labels including MCA, Chess, and his own label, Almon, scoring a pair of hits with 'Who-Dun-It?' (1966) and 'Gotta Be Funky' (1972). Hired as a music director at Onderful Records in the early Sixties, he later took a similar position at Chess Records. In the Eighties, Higgins led the West Coast-based outfit, The Whodunit Blues Band. For a time, Higgins worked as a social worker and a music teacher in Chicago.
Cause: Respiratory disease. He died at Centinela Hospital in Englewood, California.

Joe Higgs

Born June 4, 1940
Died December 18, 1999
Nicknamed "The Father of Reggae", Joe Higgs remains a footnote in musical history despite the fact that he mentored a host of Jamaican performers including Jimmy Cliff, Bob Marley, Bunny Livingston, and Peter Tosh. From Kingston, Jamaica, Higgs worked as a high school music teacher, initially garnering popularity as a songwriter. Managed by the future prime minister of Jamaica, Edward Seaga, Higgs scored his first hit in 1960 with 'Oh Manny Oh' in a duet with Delroy Wilson and by the early Sixties, Higgs was tutoring a host of budding reggae musicians. When Bunny Wailer quit The Wailers in 1973 during a US tour as opening act for Sly & The Family Stone, Higgs was called in as his replacement. Higgs later toured and recorded a number of duets with Jimmy Cliff and penned Peter Tosh's signature hit 'Steppin' Razor'. Higgs' first solo album, *Life Of Contraction*, was issued in the mid Seventies and featured guest guitarist Eric Gale. When his politically charged single 'So It Go' (1983) was banned in Jamaica, Higgs was unable to work and consequently emigrated to the US where he made Los Angeles his home. In 1990, members of The Wailers backed Higgs on the album, *Blackman Know Yourself*.
Cause: Cancer. He died at Kaiser-Permanente Hospital in Los Angeles.

Rico Hightower

Born 1947
Died January 17, 1970
A member of Billy Stewart's band, Rico Hightower appeared on the singer's Sixties R&B hits including, 'I Do Love You' and a frenetic cover of George Gershwin's 'Summertime'.
Cause: Car crash. Experiencing brake problems, the new car that Stewart and the group were riding in struck a bridge abutment and plunged into a river.

Z.Z. Hill

(Arzel Hill)
Born September 30, 1935
Died April 27, 1984
Veteran, Texas-styled blues and soul singer, Z.Z. Hill enjoyed a hit run which spanned the Sixties until his death in 1984. With his hard soul sound, Hill landed on the R&B charts with 'You Were Wrong' (1964), 'Don't Make Me Pay For His Mistakes' (1971), and 'Love Is So Good When You're Stealing It' (1977). Signing with Malico Records in 1981, Hill saw his career was in the ascent with the album, *Down Home*. The album was highlighted by his signature piece, the gritty, George Jackson-penned, 'Downhill Blues' (1982). With the album a strong seller for two years, Hill enjoyed a major revival in the Eighties,

especially among Southern audiences. Hill frequently toured with Millie Jackson.
CAUSE: Two months after a traffic accident, he died in a Dallas hospital from a related blood clot.

Kenny Hillary

Born c. 1960
Died June 5, 1996
The bassist with heavy metal band Quiet Riot, Kenny Hillary was a member from 1993 to 1995. Hillary had initially joined Heat, a group that featured two former Quiet Riot members, vocalist Kevin DuBrow and guitarist Carlos Cavazo. Reverting to their Quiet Riot moniker, the group issued the album *Terrified* (1993). Hillary left shortly before their 1995 follow-up studio release, *Down To The Bone.*
CAUSE: Suicide.

Eddie Hinton

(EDWARD CRAIG HINTON)
Born June 15, 1944
Died July 28, 1995
A popular session guitarist, Eddie Hinton worked primarily at the Fame Studio in Shoals Alabama, backing the likes of Aretha Franklin, Joe Tex, and Wilson Pickett. Also a songwriter, he penned The Box Tops' hit, 'Choo Choo Train'. As a solo act, Hinton was unable to find an audience for his blue-eyed soul. Painfully shy, Hinton had turned down the lead singer spot in a band that became The Allman Brothers.
CAUSE: He died of a heart attack at his parents' home in Birmingham, Alabama.

Joe Hinton

Born November 15, 1929
Died August 15, 1968
Originally a gospel singer with the Spirit of Memphis Quartet, Indiana-born Joe Hinton signed with Duke/Peacock Records in 1953. Following the lead of former gospel singer, Sam Cooke, Hinton reluctantly entered the pop fray in 1958 at the insistence of label owner, Don Robey. After a series of poor-selling releases, in 1963 Hinton broke through with the soul-charged, Joe Scott production, 'You Know That Ain't Right'. A falsetto singer, Hinton followed with a guitar-driven rendition of Willie Nelson's 'Funny (How Time Slips Away)' (1964), and 'I Want a Little Girl' (1965).
CAUSE: Skin cancer. He died in Boston.

Bob Hite

Born February 26, 1945
Died April 5, 1981
A talented harmonica player and singer, Torrance, California-born Bob Hite was the co-founder of pioneering blues-rock band Canned Heat. Nicknamed "Big Bear" because of his 300-pound girth, Hite was a blues scholar, amassing a wealth of rare 78s during his stint as the manager of Rancho Music, a Los Angeles record shop. Hite co-founded Canned Heat in 1966 from the remnants of an acoustic California jug band, along with guitarist, harmonica player and singer Al Wilson. Electrifying its sound, the unsigned group delivered a solid set at the Monterey Pop Festival in June 1967, and as a result of this exposure, the group was signed by Liberty Records. Their début album Canned Heat (1967) was a critical success and a moderate seller, containing blues standards such as Elmore James' 'Dust My Broom'. Breaking through with the follow-up release, *Boogie With Canned Heat* (1968), the band enjoyed their début hit single with a reworking of an old Floyd James song, 'On The Road Again', a jug-flavoured, hippy anthem. Combining psychedelic textures over a folk and blues foundation, the group became a favourite of the late Sixties flower power crowd. Their next album, *Living The Blues*, featured their

hit single 'Going Up The Country', which borrowed the melody of Henry Thomas' blues standard, 'Bulldoze Blues'. In August of 1969, a revamped Canned Heat nearly stole the show at the Woodstock festival. During this time, Hite befriended blues guitarist Albert Collins, and was instrumental in Collins' signing to Imperial Records. Tragedy struck Canned Heat in September 1970 when Al Wilson died from a drug overdose a week before the start of a European tour, a loss from which the group would never fully recuperate. Shortly thereafter, Canned Heat scored its last pop hit with a cover of Wilbert Harrison's 'Let's Work Together' from their album *Future Blues* (1970). The following year Canned Heat teamed with blues legend John Lee Hooker for the album, *Hooker 'N' Heat*. After releasing a final album at Liberty, the dispirited group switched to Atlantic Records where their fortunes continued to fade. Considered out of vogue, Canned Heat toured primarily as a nostalgia act in the Seventies. But with blues music on an upswing in the early Eighties, Canned Heat was experiencing a revival when Hite died.
CAUSE: He died shortly after suffering a drug-related (heroin) heart attack while performing at the Hollywood nightclub, the Palamino. He was severely overweight. His bandmates took him to his home in Mar Vista, California where he later died. A serious blues collector and archivist, Hite left his collection of over 60,000 blues records to United Artists for their work on the *Legendary Masters* blues compilations.

Richard Hite

(RICHARD JAMES HITE)
Born May 18, 1951
Died September 21, 2001
A latter member of the blues-rock band Canned Heat, bassist Richard Hite joined in 1972. The group was launched in 1966 by Alan Wilson and Hite's brother, singer-harmonica player Bob Hite. Although Canned Heat continued to record throughout the Seventies, the group was past its heyday and was considered a nostalgia act. After the group disbanded in 1978, Richard Hite did not join later reincarnations. A serious blues historian, he was the curator of the Memphis Blues Museum, hosted the radio programme *The Beale Street Caravan* and co-published the magazines *R&B Collector* and *R&B Magazine*. Also operating a record company, Memphis Archives, he reissued early blues tracks and recorded such artists as Clarence "Gatemouth" Moore, Hammie Nixon and John Lee Hooker.
CAUSE: Lung cancer. He died at the Regional Medical Center in Memphis.

Elsbearry Hobbs

Born July 27, 1936
Died May 31, 1996
Bass singer of The Drifters in the early Sixties, Elsbearry Hobbs had previously joined the second line-up of The (Five) Crowns in 1956, which at the time included lead singer Benjamin Earl Nelson (later known as Ben E. King). Meanwhile after The Crowns completed a one-week engagement at the Apollo Theater in 1958, The Drifters' manager George Treadwell fired his group and hired The Crowns as the new, replacement Drifters. Headed by vocalist Ben E. King, the new Drifters belatedly scored their first hit with a King composition 'There Goes My Baby' (1959), the song featuring a string section and Hobb's prominent bass vocals in the introduction. Hobbs appeared on several more Drifters hits including 'This Magic Moment' (1960) and 'Save The Last Dance For Me' (1960). Drafted, Hobbs would leave The Drifters shortly after the departure of King. Hobbs was replaced in the group by Tommy Evans. After his army duty, Hobbs returned to New York City and

worked as a therapist at Knickerbocker Hospital. He joined a revival version of The Drifters in 1969.
CAUSE: Throat and lung cancer. He died in New York City.
FURTHER READING: Allan, Tony (1993). *Save The Last Dance For Me: The Musical Legacy Of The Drifters, 1953–1993*. Ann Arbor, MI: Popular Culture.

Randy Hobbs

(RANDALL JOSEPH HOBBS)
Born August 5, 1945
Died August 5, 1993
Bass player for The McCoys, Indiana-born Randy Hobbs joined the group in 1965 as the replacement for Dennis Kelly. Formed in 1962 by brothers Randy and Rick Zehringer (later changed to Derringer), the group was befriended by members of The Strangeloves (of 'I Want Candy' fame), and signed to the Bert Berns-operated Bang Records. Berns insisted the group record a cover version of The Vibrations' recent pop hit, 'My Girl Sloopy', reworked as 'Hang On Sloopy'. With its gritty, guitar-oriented rock arrangement, 'Sloopy' became a US chart-topping garage-rock classic in 1965. The group followed with two more cover version hits, Little Willie John's 'Fever' (1965), and Ritchie Valens' 'Come On, Let's Go' (1966). With several of their follow-up releases charting but missing the Top 40, The McCoys left Bang Records following Bert Bern's sudden death in late 1967. Moving to Mercury Records, The McCoys recorded a pair of poor selling albums. Falling out of the public spotlight, the group in 1970 was forced to take the position as house band at the New York City nightclub, Steve Paul's Scene. The club's owner, Steve Paul, who doubled as Johnny Winter's manager, would also sign The McCoys to a management deal. With Winter looking for a more pop-oriented backing band to make his music more commercially accessible, he hired the former McCoys. With drummer Bobby Caldwell and others, the group joined the blues guitar virtuoso on the road and on his album, *Johnny Winter And . . .* (1970). Hobbs and the others met the challenge and adapted to Winter's demanding blues set. A follow-up release, *Live: Johnny Winter and . . .* (CBS/1971) was a much better seller, and like the previous album, was produced by Rick Derringer. But the group was forced to disband in 1972 due to Johnny Winter's debilitating heroin habit. Hobbs subsequently worked with Johnny Winter's brother, Edgar, in his band White Trash, appearing on the albums, *Road Work* (1972) and *They Only Come Out At Night* (1973). In 1976, Hobbs guested on the Montrose album *Jump On It*.
CAUSE: Unknown. He died in Dayton, Ohio.

Jimmy Hodder

Born December 17, 1947
Died June 5, 1990
The drummer for Steely Dan during their early years, Boston-born Jimmy Hodder had previously been a member of a group called Bead Game. Primarily a studio group formed by the partnership of songwriters Donald Fagan and Walter Becker, Steely Dan signed with Dunhill Records in 1972. Named after a dildo in the William Burroughs book *Naked Lunch*, Steely Dan enjoyed immediate fame with their complex, jazz-based rock sound, beginning in 1972 with the certified gold Can't Buy A Thrill, which was highlighted by the hits 'Do It Again' and 'Reeling In The Years'. *Countdown To Ecstacy* (1973) was equally impressive with 'The Boston Rad' proving one of several highlights. *Pretzel Logic* (1974) was highlighted by the group's highest-charting single, 'Rikki, Don't Lose That Number' (on which drummer Jim Gordon, and not Hodder, appears). After a brief tour, Steely Dan would not perform live for another three years. Hodder left the

group in July of 1974 and was replaced by future Toto drummer Jeff Porcaro and, as time went on, every top rated session drummer from New York to Los Angeles. Hodder continued to record as a session musician, appearing on albums behind The Rowan Brothers and Sammy Hagar.
CAUSE: Found at the bottom of a swimming pool in Point Arena, California, he died at a nearby hospital. His blood-alcohol content was measured at 0.28 per cent, nearly triple the legal driving limit in much of the US.
FURTHER READING: Sweet, Brian. (1994). *Steely Dan: Reelin' In The Years*. London: Omnibus.

Carl Hogan

Born 1938
Died December 23, 1997
The second tenor of The Valentines, Carl Hogan joined several friends in Harlem in 1952 to form the doo-wop group. Originally called The Dreamers, the quartet was expanded with the addition of lead tenor Richard Barrett. Hogan would leave the group in late 1954 before a session at Old Town Records. After a stint in the Fury Records group The Miracles (not the Motown outfit), Hogan returned to The Valentines just in time to appear on their final release, a Hogan-Barrett composition, 'Don't Say Goodnight'. With the group disbanding in 1958, Hogan turned to songwriting, frequently teaming with Richard Barrett on compositions such as 'Be Sure My Love' (The Dubs) and 'So Much' (The Imperials). Hogan's grandfather, Broadus Hogan, wrote the gospel standard, 'Amen'.
CAUSE: Unknown.

Silas Hogan

Born September 15, 1911
Died January 8, 1994
Louisiana blues guitarist, harmonica player, and vocalist, Silas Hogan worked with Lightnin' Slim and Slim Harpo in the early Forties. Forming his own group in 1958, Hogan signed with Excello Records in the Sixties, the tracks compiled on the 1972 album, *Trouble*. Touring through Europe in the Eighties, Hogan was greeted by appreciative audiences. Returning to his native Baton Rouge, Louisiana, he retired from music in the Nineties.
CAUSE: Heart disease. He died in Baton Rouge.

Smokey Hogg

(WILLIE ANDERSON HOGG)
Born January 27, 1914
Died May 1, 1960
A rural blues singer and guitarist, Smokey Hogg had a pair of major hits at Modern Records with 'Long Tall Mama' (1948) and 'Little School Girl' (1950). First recording for Decca Records in 1937, he returned to the studio after a 10-year absence, recording for a series of Los Angeles labels including Fidelity, Federal, Hollywood, Showtime and, lastly, Lee Rupe's Ebb Records. The Texas-born bluesman is the cousin of Lightnin' Hopkins.
CAUSE: Unknown. He died in McKinney, Texas.

Ron Holden

(ROLAN HOLDEN)
Born August 7, 1939
Died January 20, 1997
A one-hit R&B wonder, Ron Holden landed a Top 10 entry in 1960 with the million-selling, 'Love You So'. He had written the song with fellow inmates during a brief jail stint at King County Jail in Seattle. He later operated a nightclub. His father was jazz great Oscar Holden.
CAUSE: Heart attack. He died in a jail cell in Roarito Beach, Mexico. He had been in town for a performance.

Jimmy Holiday

Born July 24, 1934
Died February 15, 1987
A soulful R&B singer-songwriter,

Mississippi-born Jimmy Holiday's début, the self-composed 'How Can I Forget?', competed on the R&B charts with a cover by Ben E. King in 1963. Leaving Everest Records for Minit, Holiday scored a few more hits including 'Baby I Love You', which was a bigger success for Little Milton in 1970. Holiday later collaborated with songwriters Randy Myers and Jackie DeShannon to compose several hits including 'Put A Little Love In Your Heart'.
CAUSE: Heart failure.

Michael Holliday

(NORMAN MILNE)
Born November 26, 1928
Died October 29, 1963
A diminutive, Liverpool-born pop crooner who was nicknamed "The British Bing Crosby", Michael Holliday scored a string of ballad hits in the last half of the Fifties. After dropping out of school at 14, Holliday joined the Merchant Marine and the Royal Navy, during which time he would entertain his shipmates. After winning a talent contest in New York City, he returned to Liverpool and launched a professional singing career. After a stint in The Eric Winstone Band, Holliday turned solo. Signed by Columbia in 1955, Holliday enjoyed a strong hit run on the British charts with 'Nothin' To Do' (1956), 'Gal With The Yaller Shoes' (1956), 'Hot Diggity' (1956), 'The Story Of My Life' (1958), 'Stairway Of Love' (1958), and 'Starry Eyed' (1960). A baritone vocalist with impeccable phrasing but a feeble memory, he would frequently garble song lyrics on stage. Appearing on his own television programme *Relax With Mike*, he later turned to film acting. Appearing in the comedy film *Life Is A Circus* (1962), he was unable to transfer his success to the big screen. Refusing to update his sound, Holliday failed to reach the charts after 1960.
CAUSE: Insecure about his career in the face of the rise of rock music, he committed suicide by overdosing on drugs.

Buddy Holly

(CHARLES HARDIN HOLLEY)
Born September 7, 1936
Died February 3, 1959
Legendary Fifties guitarist, singer, songwriter and musical innovator, Buddy Holly was an important rock pioneer. In an era when almost all pop stars were manufactured by the music industry, he wrote his own material, led his own group, and recorded a catalogue of classic songs that influenced and inspired everyone from The Beatles and Bob Dylan to Bruce Springsteen and Elvis Costello. He was also the first major rock star to play a Fender Stratocaster guitar. Though Holly's career was brief, sales of his records run into the many millions, and each year the anniversary of his birth is celebrated across two continents. Born in Lubbock, Texas, Holly took piano lessons at age 11 before switching to the guitar, and was greatly influenced by *The Grand Ole Opry* radio programme. Teaming with guitarist Bob Montgomery as Buddy & Bob, the country and bluegrass duo became regulars on local radio station KDAV. Adding bassist Larry Welbourn, and hiring deejay "Hi Pockets" Duncan as their manager, the trio took a rockabilly turn as they performed throughout western Texas. The group got its break in 1955 when they were hired as a last-minute replacement for Bill Haley's absent Comets and were spotted by Nashville music agent Eddie Crandall. With Jerry Allison now on drums, the group was aided by Crandall and talent scout Jim Denny in signing with Decca Records, which at the time was envious of RCA's signing of Elvis Presley. Joined by sidemen guitarist Sonny Curtis and bassist Don Guess, and later, Jerry Allison, Holly recorded a few unsuccessful singles, including a first

version of 'That'll Be The Day'. Decca quickly lost interest in the group. Forming his more famous backing band The Crickets with his former drummer Jerry Allison and new members Niki Sullivan on rhythm guitar, and Joe B. Maudlin on bass, Holly travelled to Clovis, New Mexico, to work at independent producer Norman Petty's small studio. Recording an improved version of 'That'll Be The Day', the song was released as by The Crickets on the Decca subsidiary, Brunswick Records; topping the charts, the single propelled Holly and his group to national fame. With Norman Petty becoming their new manager, Holly and The Crickets were granted unprecedented artistic control in the studio. In many ways Buddy Holly and The Crickets were the first bona fide *rock group*, with Holly singing and playing lead guitar popularising the Fender Stratocaster in the process – with a rhythm guitarist, bassist and drummer, some of whom provided backing vocals. In a brilliant marketing move, Decca would release Holly solo work (often backed by The Crickets) on another Decca subsidiary, Coral Records. A follow-up "solo" hit single on Coral, 'Peggy Sue', was originally titled 'Cindy Lou' after Jerry Allison's future wife. Performing on *The Ed Sullivan Show* on December 1, 1957, Buddy Holly and The Crickets would sing their first two hits. Other Holly/Crickets hits included 'Oh Boy!', 'Maybe Baby', 'Think It Over' and 'Rave On'. Also, a number of Holly's minor songs such as 'Not Fade Away', 'Everyday' and 'It's So Easy (To Fall In Love)' would become hits years later. After marrying Puerto Rico-born Maria Elena Santiago in August 1958, Holly split from The Crickets for a solo career, abandoning all legal claims to The Crickets name; but neither The Crickets nor Holly would be as successful apart, although Holly did manage hits with 'Heartbeat' and the posthumous UK chart topping 'It Doesn't Matter Anymore'. Desperately short of cash, Holly signed up for the ill-fated Winter Dance Party tour, forming a new backing band with Tommy Allsup on guitar, Charlie Bunch on drums, and the then-unknown Waylon Jennings on bass. The tour was to span the Northern plains and the Midwest but would be scarred by the death of Holly and others. Although his professional career lasted just two years, Holly would greatly influence future rockers, most notably The Beatles, who recorded 'Words Of Love', and The Rolling Stones, who enjoyed an early career success with 'Not Fade Away'. While his hit run in the US would end following his death, in England Holly continued with a remarkable string of a dozen Top 40 hits. Meanwhile, Holly's former producer Norman Petty released reworked early Holly home tapes, the tracks overdubbed with backing by The Fireballs. Holly's life and career were celebrated in the film, *The Buddy Holly Story* (1978), with Gary Busey in the title role, and a statue of Holly was erected in his hometown of Lubbock, Texas, in 1980. Buddy, a musical based on the life of Holly, has been one of the London stage's most popular attractions in recent years. In the late Seventies Paul McCartney bought the rights to Holly's song catalogue from his widow and each year the former Beatle organises a Buddy Holly week to celebrate Holly's musical legacy. Holly's family took legal action against MCA Records in 1999 over the issue of underpaid royalties.

CAUSE: A much chronicled event, Buddy Holly, The Big Bopper, Ritchie Valens, and the pilot died in an aeroplane crash. Frustrated with the broken heater in their dilapidated tour bus, Holly and the others had wanted to avoid the region's sub-zero temperatures and had instead chartered a small aeroplane, paying a combined $108 in cash. Holly had also

wanted time to do his laundry. Instead of an uncomfortable 10-hour bus ride, the trip by air was scheduled to take slightly more than three hours. With weather conditions worsening further, the tour's road manager telephoned the promoter in an unsuccessful attempt to cancel the next day's performance. With Holly and the pilot seated up front and Valens and The Big Bopper in the back, the plane departed from nearby Mason City, Iowa, in a blinding snowstorm en route to their next show in Moorhead, North Dakota. After a routine take-off at 1:50 a.m., the craft went down minutes later. Pilot error was cited as the cause of the crash; suffering a case of vertigo, 21-year-old newly-wed Roger Peterson flew the plane directly into the ground. The mangled wreckage of the plane was discovered the following morning perched against a fence at the edge of a cornfield in Clear Lake, Iowa. It is unknown whether the four men aboard perished from the crash or the inclement elements. Tragedy or not, the Winter Dance Party Tour continued with a revised line-up, including Frankie Avalon, Jimmy Clanton and, at one stop, 15-year-old Robert Velline (a.k.a. Bobby Vee) and his band The Shadows. The tour had begun on January 23, 1959 at George Devine's Ballroom in Milwaukee, Wisconsin, and ended on schedule at the Illinois State Armory in Springfield on February 15.
FURTHER READING: Goldrosen, John; & Beecher, John. (1996). *Remembering Buddy: The Definitive Biography Of Buddy Holly*. London: Omnibus.
Norman, Philip. (1996). *Buddy: The Biography*. London: Macmillan.
Amburn, Ellis. (1995). *Buddy Holly: A Biography*. New York: St Martin's.

Hollywood Fats

(MICHAEL MANN)
Born December 1953
Died December 8, 1986
A guitarist with The James Harmon Band and The Blasters, Los Angeles-born Hollywood Fats had dropped out of junior high school to work in a series of blues-rock bands. Nicknamed by Buddy Guy, the rotund Hollywood Fats performed with a number of blues greats in the Seventies and Eighties including Muddy Waters, John Lee Hooker, Canned Heat, and Albert King. In 1978, Hollywood Fats formed his own group, the on-and-off-again, Hollywood Fats Blues Band. But his notoriety came in 1981 when he joined the Orange County, California-based John Harmon Band, a popular regional outfit which released a number of EPs and albums. In the Chicago-style blues outfit, Fats would unleash scorching guitar solos alongside fellow guitarist David "Kid" Ramos. Hollywood Fats later garnered much press when he replaced Dave Alvin (who left to join the punk-rock group, X) in the 1986 reorganised roster of The Blasters. But Hollywood Fats was under appreciated, and worse, misplaced in the neo-rockabilly outfit. The Blasters were planning to record a new album in early 1987 and were scheduled to tour Louisiana and Texas at the time of Hollywood Fats' death. Dave Alvin temporarily returned to the group to help out.
CAUSE: Suffering a drug-induced heart attack, he died in a Santa Monica hospital.

Richard "Groove" Holmes

(RICHARD ARNOLD HOLMES)
Born May 2, 1931
Died June 29, 1991
Self-taught jazz/blues organist, New Jersey-born Richard "Groove" Holmes originally began as a bass guitarist. Discovered in 1955 by Les McCann at a Pittsburgh performance, Holmes signed with the Pacific Jazz label. Aided on his early albums by sax players Gene Ammons and Ben Webster, in 1966 Holmes scored an enduring cover version hit of Erroll

Garner's 'Misty'. Establishing a long residency at Los Angeles's Black Orchid Club, Holmes later recorded a live album there. Holmes recorded regularly into the Eighties, usually with his group, The Richard Holmes Trio, his final release coming in 1989 with *Blues All Day Long*.
CAUSE: Prostate cancer. He died in St. Louis.

Gary Holton

(WAYNE WINSTON NORRIS)
Born 1952
Died October 25, 1985
Lead singer of the London-based hard-rock group The Heavy Metal Kids, the unpredictable Gary Holton led the over-amplified, guitar-crunching band in the mid Seventies. Signing with Atlantic Records in 1974, the group recorded a pair of albums including *Anvil Chorus*, which was highlighted by the bizarre track, 'Call The Cops'. Dropped by Atlantic Records, The Heavy Metal Kids recorded a final album for RAK Records in 1977, *Kitsch*, before disbanding soon after. After a brief stint in the punk rock group The Damned, Holton released a solo album, scoring a minor hit with 'Catch A Falling Star' (1984). Holton later turned to acting, appearing in the London production of *Guys And Dolls*. At the time of his death, he was starring in the critically acclaimed British TV series, *Auf Wiedersehen, Pet*, about a gang of displaced construction workers, which also featured Jimmy Nail.
CAUSE: Accidental drug overdose.

James Honeyman-Scott

Born November 4, 1957
Died June 16, 1982
Lead guitarist for British/American rock group, The Pretenders, James Honeyman-Scott was born in Hereford, England. Growing up listening to his mother play church hymns on the family piano, he took piano lesson for two years beginning at age seven, and was given a guitar at 10. A fan of California beach music, he was attracted by its intricate guitar work, preferring fast-fingered playing. Dropping out of school and leaving home at age 15, he joined a series of blues and rock groups, and worked as a session player on albums by Robert John Godfrey and Tommy Morrison. By 1974, Honeyman-Scott and drummer Martin Chambers joined a group called Cheeks, which was led by ex-Mott The Hoople keyboard player, Verden Allen. After the group disbanded in 1977 without ever recording, Honeyman-Scott worked as a guitar salesman at a music store where he received a call from a transplanted American singer, songwriter and guitar player, Chrissie Hynde. Hynde had decided to form her own rock band, first hiring Pete Farndon who had recommended Honeyman-Scott; drummer, Jerry Mackleduff, was lastly added to the group. The Pretenders were instant critical and commercial favourites with their post-punk, hard guitar oriented sound. Recording on their manager's Real Records label, the group enjoyed a hit with their début single, a cover of The Kinks' 'Stop Your Sobbing'. With drummer Martin Chambers (Honeyman-Scott's former bandmate) replacing Mackleduff and Sire buying Real Records, The Pretenders teamed with Sex Pistols/Roxy Music producer Chris Thomas for their début album *The Pretenders*. With Hynde's sexual growls, the album spawned the Honeyman-Scott/Hynde-penned UK number 1 hit 'Brass In Pocket'. Besides being a powerful guitarist, Honeyman-Scott was also the best singer of the three players behind Hynde. But instead, he preferred to play his hard-rock-meets-rockabilly guitar licks, and would occasionally play the keyboards. Addicted to amphetamines and experiencing problems with his liver from excessive

drinking and cocaine use, "Jimmy" Honeyman-Scott was receiving treatment for his addictions. In April 1981, Honeyman-Scott married American model, Peggy Sue Fender in London. Meanwhile, on a roll, The Pretenders returned to the charts with *Pretenders II* (1981), the album highlighted by 'Message Of Love' and 'Talk Of The Town'. During a Pretenders' tour of the US, Honeyman-Scott discovered The Violent Femmes, and invited the group to open for them. Pete Farndon's playing suffered due to heavy alcohol and drug use, and he was fired by Hynde at the completion of a world tour on June 14, 1982. Two days later, Honeyman-Scott would die. Replaced by Robbie McIntosh, a former member of the groups Manfred Mann's Earth Band and Night, Honeyman-Scott had himself recommended the guitarist as a possible backing player earlier in the year.
CAUSE: He died of a cocaine and heroin overdose at a friend's London apartment.
FURTHER READING: Wrenn, Mike. (1990). *The Pretenders With Hyndesight.* London: Omnibus.

Earl Hooker

Born January 15, 1930
Died April 21, 1970
Popular Chicago-based blues slide-guitarist, Earl Hooker was tutored as a child by Robert Nighthawk. By the Fifties he was touring with Ike Turner and Sonny Boy Williamson. First recording as a solo act in 1952 at Sun and Rockin' King Records, he soon emerged as a session guitarist on tracks for Junior Wells, A.C. Reed and Muddy Waters, backing the latter bluesman on the standard, 'You Shook Me'. Enjoying a revival in the late Sixties, Hooker collaborated with Steve Miller on the album *Hooker & Steve.*
CAUSE: Tuberculosis. He died in Chicago.

John Lee Hooker

Born August 21, 1917
Died June 21, 2001
One of the last classic, 20th century Delta blues guitarists, John Lee Hooker was reared in the poverty of the Deep South, hailing from the blues breeding ground of Clarksdale, Mississippi. Born into a sharecropper's large family of 11 children, Hooker was taught to play the guitar by his stepfather. Leaving home by age 14, Hooker drifted north and enlisted in the army by lying about his age. Stationed in Detroit, he was discharged after three months. Landing in Memphis in 1931, Hooker spent two years playing with Robert Nighthawk and other bluesmen, before moving to Cincinnati in 1933, where he worked as a theatre usher, as well as joining several gospel groups including The Fairfield Four. Returning to Detroit in 1943, Hooker worked as a janitor at a car factory, and with the help of a record shop owner, he spent months working on a marketable demo disc. Stomping on a board for percussion in a rudimentary studio, Hooker recorded an improvised track, 'Boogie Chillen'; one of the most influential modern blues songs of all time, the song was a link between the pre-war country blues style and modern electrified R&B. Hooker's nimble, fast-paced playing style contrasted with his drowsy and distant persona. Forming his own band, Hooker unleashed such distinctively identifiable blues classics as 'Hobo Blues' (1949), 'Crawling King Snake Blues' (1949) and an unlikely pop-crossover hit with 'I'm In The Mood' (1950). Unhappy with the terms of his recording contract at Modern Records, Hooker subsequently recorded for various labels under numerous pseudonyms including Texas Slim, Johnny Williams and John Lee Booker. Landing at Vee Jay Records in 1955, Hooker performed with a full band, featuring guitarist Eddie Taylor, but with the waning

popularity of the blues in America during the late Fifties, Hooker retreated to Europe. Adopting a pared-down sound on his return, Hooker scored his second crossover hit with the retro-styled 'Boom Boom' (1962); performing at the Newport Folk Festival that same year, Hooker solidified his stature in the blues world. Hooker recorded his last album for Vee Jay in 1964, the same year that The Animals and other white British R&B groups introduced his material to a wider audience. Moving to San Francisco, Hooker collaborated with the blues-rock band Canned Heat, releasing the album *Hooker 'N' Heat.* Remaining on the road for the next two decades, Hooker was revered as a living legend. Hooker's 1989 album *The Healer* featured guests George Thorogood, Robert Cray and Bonnie Raitt, and won a Grammy for the track 'I'm In The Mood'.

CAUSE: He died in his sleep of natural causes at his home in Los Altos, California.

FURTHER READING: Murray, Charles Shaar (1999). *Boogie Man: The Adventures Of John Lee Hooker In The American Twentieth Century.* London: St. Martin's Press.

Shannon Hoon

(RICHARD SHANNON HOON)
Born September 26, 1967
Died October 21, 1995

As the charismatic leader of the Nineties alternative rock group Blind Melon, Shannon Hoon was influenced by Seventies hard rock. Born in Lafayette, Indiana, the rebellious Hoon moved to Los Angeles in 1990 to pursue a musical career. Joining guitarist Rogers Stevens and bassist Brad Smith to form Blind Melon, Hoon and the group recorded their first demos within a week. Expanded to a quintet and unhappy with the competitive Los Angeles music scene, the group set up base in Durham, North Carolina. But when their demo tape wound up on the desk of an entertainment lawyer, the group landed a lucrative contract with Capitol Records the following year. Hyped heavily by the label, Blind Melon received heavy exposure, with Hoon making a cameo appearance in labelmate's Guns N' Roses video for 'Don't Cry' and on their albums, *Use Your Illusion, Vols. 1 & 2.* A critics' favourite with their jazzy, Grateful Dead-like stylings, *Blind Melon* landed a surprise hit with their début album Blind Melon, and a Top 10 multi-format hit with the melancholy 'No Rain', the song's video featuring the group's "bee girl" mascot. Playing Woodstock 2 in 1994, Blind Melon was nominated for both a Grammy and American Music Award. A heavy drug user, Hoon soon earned a reputation for his unpredictable, idiosyncratic behaviour. Released eight weeks before Hoon's death, the group's second album *Soup* fared poorly; Hoon had been arrested for disorderly conduct during the recording sessions in New Orleans. Named after Hoon's daughter Nico Blue, the posthumously released Blind Melon album *Nico* assembled various Hoon sessions.

CAUSE: He died from an accidental cocaine overdose. He was found dead in his tour bus by the group's soundman. Blind Melon was scheduled to perform that night in New Orleans. The group had twice forced Hoon into a detox programme due to his propensity for psychedelic drugs. Fearing for Hoon's health and safety, the group hired a drug counsellor to join the group on their final tour. But Hoon resented the intrusiveness and fired the counsellor shortly before his death.

Douglas Hopkins

Born April 11, 1961
Died December 4, 1993

Songwriter and original guitarist for the rock group, The Gin Blossoms, Douglas Hopkins was raised in Tempe,

Arizona. Co-founding The Gin Blossoms in 1986, Hopkins and the group garnered a large fanbase around Phoenix. After issuing an independent label album *Dusted*, the group signed a major label contract with A&M Records. Finding success at modern rock radio stations with their début album, *New Miserable Experience* (1993), the group was also embraced by MTV. But the erratic, binge-drinking Hopkins was quickly fired from the group, and replaced by Scott Johnson. Hopkins became increasingly angry at the success of his former band, as his compositions – 'Hey Jealousy' and 'Found Out About You' – were receiving heavy airplay. Subsequently forming the short-lived group, Chimeras, Hopkins later performed in Tempe as a solo act, and occasionally joined other local acts on stage.
CAUSE: Suicide. He shot himself at his home in Tempe, Arizona. Two weeks earlier, he had been admitted into the detox centre of Phoenix's St. Luke Hospital after a suicide attempt.

James Hopkins-Harrison

Born 1949
Died May 16, 1991
The Scottish-born lead singer of the German progressive-rock band Lake, James Hopkins-Harrison provided the soaring vocals on their sole US hit, 'Time Bomb' (1975), taken from the group's self-titled album. The group recorded four studio albums for CBS Records, before signing with the German Polydor label. Lake disbanded in 1987.
CAUSE: Heroin overdose.

Lightnin' Hopkins

(SAM HOPKINS)
Born March 15, 1912
Died January 30, 1982
Blues vocalist and guitarist extraordinaire who influenced countless white "serious" rockers, Sam "Lightnin" ' Hopkins was born and raised in Centerville, Texas, near Houston. Building his own guitar, and taught the basics by his older brother, he left home at a young age to perform as an itinerant musician, rarely crossing the state line. During his treks, he performed with other blues musicians such as Blind Lemon Jefferson. Teaming in 1929 with his cousin, noted blues singer Texas Alexander, Hopkins would join him for tours off and on for the next two decades. Settling in Houston in the early Forties, Hopkins performed in the city's more dangerous bars. But although Hopkins' professional career began in the Twenties, his recording career didn't occur until much later when in 1946, he was invited to Los Angeles by Aladdin Records where he cut some sides with pianist "Thunder" Smith. Hopkins then returned to his adopted hometown of Houston and recorded for the Gold Star label. He would subsequently record prolifically for a number of labels, demanding a cash settlement after each recording session instead of depending on a less than profitable royalty arrangement. A prolific songwriter who would employ unorthodox musical metres, he would compose material on the spot. With his downhome, autobiographical verses, Hopkins projected a very distinguishable, high, dry, pained, and sometimes cracking or wailing voice. Often performing unaccompanied, he would augment his guitar playing with the heavy tapping sounds of his shoes. As the leader of country blues alongside John Lee Hooker, Lightnin' Hopkins enjoyed a number of chart hits including 'Tim Moore's Farm' (1949), '"T" Model Blues' (1949), 'Shotgun Blues' (1950), 'Give Me Central 209' (1952), and 'Coffee Blues' (1952). Hopkins created some controversy when in 1952 he recorded a then rare anti-war, protest song, 'Sad News From Korea'. But by the mid Fifties, Hopkins' earthy, Delta-based style of blues had fallen out of favour. He then returned to

Houston, playing in the city's many nightclubs. After music historian Sam Charters cut an album with Hopkins, the brilliant *Texas Bluesman*, Hopkins was again in demand, soon performing at Carnegie Hall. Hopkins recorded heavily in the Sixties, appearing on dozens of labels with his best work coming on Barnaby and Imperial Records. Hopkins life was chronicled in the 1967 film biography, *The Blues According To Lightnin' Hopkins*. His last public appearance came in 1981.
CAUSE: Untreatable cancer of the esophagus. He died in a Houston hospital after a bout of pneumonia.

Nicky Hopkins

Born February 24, 1944
Died September 6, 1994
A prolific session player, Nicky Hopkins performed on dozens of hit singles and albums in a long career blighted by ill health. Born in London, Hopkins learned to play the piano at age three, taking lessons by age ten. His first group was The Savages, the backing band of British shock-rocker Screaming Lord Sutch, followed by pop-rock group Cliff Bennett and The Rebel Rousers and the blues outfit, Cyril Davies & The All-Stars. Life on the road left Hopkins debilitated and he quit music for a time, returning in 1965 for session work with The Who and The Kinks, amongst others. Attempting a solo career in 1966, he released the poor-selling album *The Revolutionary Piano Of Nicky Hopkins*. After working as a session player for The Rolling Stones, he joined The Jeff Beck Group in the late Sixties, appearing on the hit blues-rock albums, *Truth* (1968) and *Beck-Ola* (1969). Hopkins then settled in San Francisco after discovering its music scene during a US tour. There he worked with local acts Steve Miller, Quicksilver Messenger Service, and The Jefferson Airplane, appearing with the latter act at Woodstock. During the Seventies, Hopkins played on albums by George Harrison, Ringo Starr, John Lennon and The Who, among others. In the Eighties, he worked with Bob Seger and Paul McCartney, and provided the arrangement for the Julio Iglesias/Willie Nelson hit, 'To All The Girls I Loved Before'. Settling in Nashville in the Nineties, Hopkins worked with Guns N' Roses' guitarist Izzy Stradlin.
CAUSE: Abdominal and heart problems. Suffering stomach problems and sickly since childhood, he died in Nashville after undergoing stomach surgery.

Bob Horn

(DONALD LLOYD HORN)
Born February 20, 1916
Died July 31, 1966
Original MC of the television dance programme *Bandstand*, Bob Horn was later replaced by Dick Clark. Born in West Virginia, but raised in eastern Pennsylvania, Horn landed his first deejay stint at WIP in Camden, New Jersey. Débuting a pop-music show called *Bandstand* in 1952 on WFIL in Philadelphia, Horn had transferred the programme from radio. Playing records and showing music video-like kinescopes, Horn became a celebrity in Philadelphia. The hugely popular *Bandstand* drew thousands of local teenagers who lined outside of the studio door each afternoon, and the programme was even name-checked in Chuck Berry's hit 'Sweet Little Sixteen'. But Horn's career was shattered in June 1956 when he was fired after being charged with drunk driving and relations with a minor. After some initial picketing by *Bandstand* regulars, the squeaky-clean Dick Clark was accepted as the new host. But a year later, the renamed *American Bandstand* would be broadcast to a nationwide audience on the ABC network. Horn later moved to Houston and changed his name to Bob Adams. With the IRS targeting Horn for unreported payola payments, he

was forced to declare bankruptcy.
CAUSE: Heart attack brought on by heat stroke. He died in Houston.

Cleveland Horne

(WESLEY CLEVELAND HORNE)
Born April 14, 1942
Died April 12, 2000
A latter member of the Detroit-based vocal R&B group The Fantastic Four, Cleveland Horne appeared on four albums, scoring R&B hits with 'Alvin Stone' (1975) and 'I Got To Have Your Love' (1977). A native of Detroit, Horne was previously a member of The Carstairs, and worked as a session vocalist with a variety of acts including Aretha Franklin and Bette Midler.
CAUSE: He died two weeks after suffering a stroke at Grace Hospital in Detroit.

Bill Horton

Born December 25, 1929
Died January 24, 1995
The lead singer of the Fifties doo-wop group The Silhouettes, Bill Horton led the Philadelphia-based quartet on one of the era's finest examples of the genre with the hit 'Get A Job' (1958), the song written by the group's tenor Rick Lewis. Originally called The Gospel Tornadoes, the group had previously sang only religious material. Discovered by deejay Kae Williams, The Silhouettes were signed to his label, Junior Records. Horton left the Silhouettes in 1962, and in the late Sixties formed a group called Dawn. He later worked in construction, occasionally reprising his group for oldies concerts.
CAUSE: He died from a heart attack at his home in Philadelphia. He had a long history of heart disease.

Johnny Horton

(JOHN GALE HORTON)
Born April 3, 1929
Died November 5, 1960
Pop and country singer, Los Angeles-born Johnny Horton was raised in Texas and Louisiana by his farm-worker parents. Excelling in athletics, he briefly attended Baylor University in 1951 on a basketball scholarship. Eventually moving north to Alaska to work as a fisherman, he then trekked south to California. Taught to play the guitar in his teens by his mother, Horton pursued a singing career after winning a talent contest. Nicknamed "The Singing Fisherman", he performed mostly self-composed numbers. Discovered by Fabor Robinson, who became his manager, Horton earned a prized spot on the *Louisiana Hayride* radio show in 1951. Singing an upbeat brand of country and western and becoming a national star via his radio exposure, Horton initially released some obscure singles for Cormac Records in 1951. Signing to Mercury Records in 1952 with little success, Horton kept up a heavy touring schedule, garnering exposure and increased popularity. Signing with Columbia Records, Horton was convinced by his new manager Tillman Franks to adopt a guitar-oriented, pop sound. Featuring Bill Black on bass, Horton's first hit 'Honky Tonk Man' was followed by a series of unsuccessful rockabilly-tinged releases. Settling back into a folk and country vein by 1958, Horton had a strong hit run beginning with 'I'm Just A One Woman Man' (1957) and 'All Grown Up' (1958). But it was the number 1 smash, 'The Battle of New Orleans' (1959) which solidified Horton's career. He followed up with a similar sounding, folkish 'North To Alaska' (1960).
CAUSE: He died in an auto accident in Milano, Texas, when his luxury car was struck head-on by a drunk driver. Injured were Horton's manager Tillman Franks and musician Gerald Tumlinson. The Skyline nightclub in nearby Austin is the last place where both Johnny Horton and Hank Williams, Sr. played before their

deaths. Also coincidentally, Horton's wife Billy Jean Eshlimar was previously married to Hank Williams.
FURTHER READING: Levine, Michael. (1982). *Johnny Horton: Your Singing Fisherman*. New York: Vantage.

Yogi Horton

(LAWRENCE HORTON)
Born October 1, 1953
Died June 8, 1987
A funk-style drummer, Yogi Horton spent several years behind R&B balladeer Luther Vandross in a band that also included Doc Powell, Skip Anderson and Nat Adderley Jr. Horton joined in 1982, first appearing on *Forever, For Always, For Love,* Vandross' second solo album. A popular session drummer, Horton also worked with David Byrne, Aretha Franklin, Kenny G, Peter Wolf, Diana Ross, Martha & The Muffins, Debbie Harry, The B-52's and others. As an educator, Horton issued an instructional video, *A History Of R&B Funk Drumming*.
CAUSE: Following a tense concert in New York City behind Luther Vandross, Horton was angry about the state of his career and jumped from a 17th floor window.

Tomaz Hostnik

Born 1961
Died December 21, 1982
A co-founder of the politically active Slovenian heavy metal band Laibach, gravelly-voiced lead singer Tomaz Hostnik drew international acclaim after re-recording The Beatles' *Let It Be* album. Formed in the post-Tito era, the group frequently clashed with the country's totalitarian government.
CAUSE: Suicide by hanging near his home.

Son House

(EDDIE JAMES HOUSE, JR.)
Born March 21, 1902
Died October 19, 1988
A former Baptist preacher turned Delta blues legend, the Mississippi-born Son House influenced Robert Johnson, Muddy Waters, and many other pioneering blues performers. After serving a year in jail for manslaughter, House picked up his first guitar at age 25 and earned his musical education in 1930 alongside guitarist Charlie Patton. House followed Patton in the early Thirties to a recording session in Wisconsin and recorded several brilliant, but obscure singles for Paramount Records. A phenomenal stage performer, Son House soon teamed with Willie Brown for much of the Thirties. Always displaying a sombre disposition on stage, House felt guilty for leaving the church for gin joint blues. After making a series of Library of Congress Recordings for Alan Lomax in 1941–42, Son House moved to Rochester, New York, and retired from music in 1948. Rediscovered in 1964, Son House was coaxed back to the stage. A living legend who inspired a new generation of college-aged blues fans, Son House recorded a fine album for Columbia Records in 1965 *Father Of Folk Blues*. The ailing performer retired from music for good in 1976.
CAUSE: He was stricken with both Parkinson's and Alzheimer's disease. He died in Detroit.

Mikey Houser

(MICHAEL HOUSER)
Born January 6, 1962
Died August 10, 2002
The guitarist of the alternative-rock band Widespread Panic, Mikey Houser met the group's leader singer John Bell in 1982 while attending the University of Georgia. By 1985, the pair was joined by three others to form Widespread Panic. Their sound rooted in the blues, the Athens, Georgia-based act drew fans along the same lines as such 'jamming' bands as Phish and The Grateful Dead. Signing with Capricorn Records, the group was a hit with audiences at the 1992 and 1993

HORDE musical festivals. Often the focus during the group's performances, Houser infused jazz and blues into his extended guitar solos. Houser also joined some of his bandmates to work with wheelchair-bound singer/songwriter Vic Chestnutt in the band Brute. Several months before his death, Houser became too ill to perform and was replaced in Widespread Panic by George McConnell. Houser's only solo album, *Door Harp*, was posthumously released in 2002.
CAUSE: Pancreatic cancer. He died at his home.

David Houston

Born 1936
Died November 30, 1993
A popular country singer, David Houston landed a pop crossover hit in 1966 with the honky-tonk styled, Grammy-winning single, 'Almost Persuaded'. Joining the Grand Ole Opry in 1972, he was an active member of the Opry until shortly before his death.
CAUSE: Brain aneurysm. He died in Bossier City, Louisiana.

Tim Hovey

Born June 19, 1945
Died September 9, 1989
A child actor turned rocker, Tim Hovey was a screen star during the Fifties and appeared in feature films such as *The Private War Of Major Benson*, *Slim Carter* and *Toy Tiger*. Drawn to music, Hovey mastered the slide guitar and became a member of the extended Grateful Dead camp, co-writing 'Importin' Exportin' Man' for The New Riders Of The Purple Sage – a spin-off country rock group created by Jerry Garcia – engineering two albums for Bob Weir's Kingfish and serving as the Dead's road manager for several years beginning in the late Seventies.
CAUSE: Drug overdose. He died in Watsonville, California.

Andy Howard

(ANDREW JAMES HOWARD)
Born June 9, 1982
Died September 16, 2005
A member of the emerging nu-metal band Twisted Method, guitarist Andy Howard co-wrote many of their early songs. Based in Cape Coral, Florida, the group was signed by MCA Records solely on the strength of its powerful live performances. Releasing début disc *Escape From Cape Coma* in 2003, the group was added to the Ozzfest line-up that year. Howard quit Twisted Method a few months before his death to spend more time with his twin daughters.
CAUSE: He died suddenly in his sleep at his home in Florida, possibly from heart disease.

George Howard

Born September 15, 1957
Died March 22, 1998
Saxophonist George Howard was a member of Harold Melvin and The Blue Notes before launching a solo career. The Philadelphia-born musician first joined Harold Melvin's group in 1972 as a touring session player. After a residency in Grover Washington Jr.'s band in 1979, Howard emerged as a successful jazz artist, scoring hit albums throughout the Eighties and Nineties. He earned two Grammy nominations, for the 1988 album *Reflections*, and for the 1992 track 'Just The Way I Feel'.
CAUSE: Lymphoma. He died in an Atlanta hospital.

William "Wee Gee" Howard

(WILLIAM FRANKLIN HOWARD II)
Born July 13, 1950
Died February 22, 2000
The raspy-voiced co-lead vocalist of perennial soul group, The Dramatics, Detroit-born William "Wee Gee" Howard began singing at age 12, mimicking his older brother who had formed a local soul group. After providing the lead on The Dramatics' début Volt Records release 'Your Love

Was Strange' (1969), Howard was relegated to providing backing vocals behind Ron Banks beginning with the group's hit 'Whatcha See Is Whatcha You Get' (1971). Howard returned to the helm on the Tony Hester-produced hits 'In The Rain' (1972), 'Toast To The Fool' (1972), and 'Hey You! Get Off My Mountain' (1973). In 1973, Howard and bandmate Elbert Wilkins left the group to form a competing version of The Dramatics; signed by Mainstream Records, the Howard/Wilkins lineup managed just one R&B hit with 'No Rebate On Love' (1975). Emerging as a solo artist in the late Seventies under the moniker "Wee Gee", Howard barely dented the R&B charts. He rejoined The Dramatics in the mid Eighties.
CAUSE: Unknown. He died at Lawrence Hospital in Bronxville, New York.

Alphonso Howell

Born 1937
Died May 7, 1998
Bass singer of a latter version of the vocal R&B group, The Sensations, Alphonso Howell appeared on their hits 'Music, Music, Music' (1961) and the Top 10 entry, 'Let Me In'. Howell was also the replacement bass singer of The Silhouettes (of 'Get A Job' fame) when original member Ray Edwards was drafted.
CAUSE: Unknown.

Hammy Howell

(WILLIAM HOWELL)
Born October 24, 1954
Died January 13, 1999
As a member of the British rock revivalist band Darts, blues-trained keyboardist Hammy Howell played on several hits in the late Seventies. A nine-man outfit conceived by bass vocalist Den Hegarty, Darts combined doo-wop styled harmonies with energetic stage routines. Befriended by BBC radio host Charlie Gillett, the group signed with Magnet Records during the height of the punk explosion in 1977, and gained a series of cover hits on the British charts including a medley of The Rays' 'Daddy Cool' and Little Richard's 'The Girl Can't Help It', The Wrens' 'Come Back My Love', The Ad-Libs' 'The Boy From New York City', Gene Chandler's 'Duke Of Earl', and an original composition 'It's Raining'. After quitting the group in 1978, Howell briefly returned the following year. Suffering a nervous breakdown after the death of his mother in 1979, he later taught music and occasionally worked as a session player, as well as joining a number of groups including Hoodoo Moon and The Beacon Band.
CAUSE: Heart Failure.

Howlin' Wolf

(CHESTER ARTHUR BURNETT)
Born June 10, 1910
Died January 10, 1976
Legendary Delta-born, Chicago bluesman whose powerful performances endeared him to audiences, Howlin' Wolf was one of the century's most talented entertainers. Born on a plantation near West Point, Mississippi, and named after the 21st President of the United States, Chester Arthur, Burnette later moved to another plantation near Ruleville, Arkansas, where a meeting with blues great Charley Patton would shape the 18-year-old labourer's future. After long sweaty days in the fields, Howlin' Wolf would blow his harmonica and strum his guitar on street corners. Settling in Parkin, Arkansas, in 1933, Howlin' Wolf would be tutored on harmonica by his soon to be brother-in-law, Sonny Boy (Rice Miller) Williamson. By the late Thirties, Howlin' Wolf would occasionally play a borrowed electric guitar. Still playing the guitar as a sideline, he remained a full-time farmer until World War II when he was drafted into the US Army; stationed in Seattle, he never saw action. Leaving farming in 1948, Howlin' Wolf moved to West

Memphis in search of better wages. Purchasing an electric guitar and forming a band which featured talented guitarist Willie Johnson, the hulking, 300-pound Howlin' Wolf perfected his explosive stage show. By 1949, Howlin' Wolf had his own popular 15-minute show on a local radio station, KWEM. Diverging from his contemporaries by veering toward uptempo blues, Howlin' Wolf recorded for independent producer Sam Phillips at his Memphis Recording Studio (later, renamed Sun Records). Sometimes recording slightly different versions of the same song, Howlin' Wolf would have his tracks leased to Modern/RPM and Chess Records – while Chess would get 'Moanin' At Midnight', RPM would receive 'Morning At Midnight'. But with both labels threatening to sue Phillips, Chess Records would sign the bluesman to an exclusive contract. Moving to Chicago in 1952, he quickly became a major force in the blues field. At Chess, Willie Dixon would produce and write most of Howlin' Wolf's hits, which included 'Who Will Be Next', 'Smokestack Lightning', 'I Asked For Water', 'I Ain't Superstitious', 'Back Door Man', 'Spoonful', 'Wang Dang Doodle' and 'Red Red Rooster', the latter reprised in 1964 by The Rolling Stones as 'Little Red Rooster' for a chart-topping hit in Britain. Breaking with Dixon in 1964, Howlin' Wolf began to record his own material, including 'Killing Floor'. Churning out a number of fine albums in the Sixties, he collaborated with Muddy Waters and Bo Diddley, and landed his final chart hit in 1969 with an updated psychedelic, electric version of 'Evil'. After severely damaging his kidneys in an auto accident, he slowed his touring pace. Howlin' Wolf later sued his record and publishing companies over disputed royalty payments. The Blues Heaven Foundation of Chicago awards an annual "The Howlin' Wolf – Keepin' The Blues Alive" prize.
CAUSE: He succumbed to complications from kidney disease and a heart condition. He died in Chicago.

Tippie Hubbard

(ROOSEVELT HUBBARD)
Born c. 1935
Died c. 1982
The lead vocalist in a latter line-up of the R&B/doo-wop act The Clovers, tenor Tippie Hubbard joined an outfit headed by founding member Hal Winley. The outfit unsuccessfully recorded for several labels under various names – The Clovers, Tippie & The Covers, and Tippie & The Clovermen – before disbanding around 1964. Hubbard later joined a revival version of The Clovers.
CAUSE: Unknown.

R.B. Hudman

Born August 6, 1954
Died August 25, 1995
An R&B artist and songwriter, Georgia-born R.B. Hudman charted with several minor hits in the late Seventies, his biggest in 1977 being 'Whatever Makes You Happy'.
CAUSE: Cancer.

Keith Hudson

Born March 18, 1946
Died November 14, 1984
A Jamaican-born reggae star, Keith Hudson pioneered the dub style of singing over instrumental tracks, his finest work coming at Atra Records on the album, *Pick A Dub* (1974). As a producer, he worked with U Roy, Ken Booth and Big Youth. He signed with Arista Records in 1976.
CAUSE: Diagnosed with lung cancer in 1984, he collapsed and died later in the year.

Billie Hughes

(WILLIAM KEITH JONES)
Born 1948
Died July 3, 1998
The songwriter and leader of Seventies group Lazarus, Texan Bill Hughes studied the violin as a child. Befriended

by Peter Yarrow (of Peter, Paul & Mary), Lazarus relocated to Woodstock, New York and signed with Albert Grossman's Bearsville Records, recording a pair of albums, produced by Yarrow and Phil Ramone. Pursuing a solo career in 1978, Hughes signed with Epic Records, scoring a European hit with 'Martin Eden'. Entering into a partnership with Roxanne Seeman in 1983, Hughes composed, produced, and recorded music for television and film. Reprising his solo career, Hughes earned an Emmy nomination for the title track of his album, *Welcome To The Edge* (1991), after the song was featured on the television soap opera *Santa Barbara*.
CAUSE: Heart attack. He died in Los Angeles.

Gene Hughes

(EUGENE V. HUGHES)
Born July 11, 1936
Died February 3, 2004
As a member of Cincinnati-based vocal group The Casinos, Gene Hughes provided the impassioned lead vocals on their only Top 40 hit, a cover of an obscure track by Johnny Nash, 'Then You Can Tell Me Goodbye'; issued in 1967, the doo-wop styled single was an anomaly during the psychedelic rock of the period. Exhausted by constant touring, Hughes quit The Casinos in 1968, but occasionally hit the oldies circuit with a re-formed version of the group. Settling in Nashville, Hughes headed his own record promotion firm in 1977, and later worked at MCA Records as vice-president of promotions before being hired as A&M's national director of promotion.
CAUSE: He belatedly succumbed to injuries sustained in an October 2003 car accident. He died at Saint Thomas Hospital in Nashville.

Glenn Hughes

(GLENN R. HUGHES)
Born July 18, 1950
Died March 4, 2001
The leather-clad, mustachioed biker in the campy Seventies disco group Village People, Glenn Hughes was a biker in real life. While working as a toll bridge attendant in Brooklyn, he answered an advertisement placed by record producer Jacques Morali seeking "macho" singers with moustaches. Aside from Hughes' biker character, the group would also include an Indian chief, cowboy, soldier and construction worker and was fronted by lead vocalist Victor Willis who dressed as a motorcycle cop. Initially intended as a studio-only group, Village People became media darlings in the late Seventies with hits such as 'San Francisco', 'Macho Man', 'Y.M.C.A.' and 'Go West'. Another of their hits, 'In The Navy', was used in a recruitment campaign by the US Navy until the Pentagon officials ordered the ads to be axed because of the group's gay persona. Following the People's appearance in the box office bomb *Can't Stop The Music* and with the waning popularity of disco in the early Eighties, Village People disbanded. Hughes re-formed the group in 1987, leaving in 1995 due to declining health; he was replaced by Eric Anzalone. The following year, Hughes staged a popular cabaret act in New York City.
CAUSE: Lung cancer. He died at his home in New York City. In accordance with his instructions, Hughes was buried in his leather biker costume.

Jimmy Hughes

Born 1935
Died April 1, 1997
Alabama-born R&B singer-songwriter, Jimmy Hughes registered his biggest hit in 1964 with the ballad, 'Steal Away', one of the first tracks recorded at the legendary Muscle Shoals, Alabama-based Fame Studio. Hughes is the cousin of Percy Sledge.
CAUSE: Cancer.

Richard Hughes

Born March 31, 1950
Died 1983

A drummer for blues rocker Johnny Winter from 1973–76 and 1981, Richard Hughes appeared on several albums including *Still Alive And Well*, *Saints & Sinners*, *Captured Live* and *Together*. Previously a member of New Jersey-based rock outfit Cobalt, Hughes and bandmate Doug Brockie (who stayed only briefly) were hired by Winter following a recommendation by Winter's producer Rick Derringer. Performing since his mid-teens, Hughes had previously recorded a number of singles while a member of the groups Calliope and The Millburnaires.

CAUSE: He committed suicide as the result of personal problems and the rigours of touring.

Alan Hull

Born February 20, 1945
Died November 18, 1995

Singer, songwriter and guitarist best known for leading the British folk-rock group Lindisfarne, Alan Hull began his career with future Ian Dury & The Blockheads' pianist Mickey Gallagher in The Chosen Few. Greatly influenced by American protest singers, notably Woody Guthrie, Hull formed Downtown Faction in 1967; evolving into Lindisfarne the following year. Though he was not their sole songwriter, the group's best known hits came with the Hull-composed folk standards, 'Lady Eleanor' and 'Meet Me On The Corner'. Lindisfarne became synonymous with their hometown of Newcastle in north east England, and their singalong style made them favourites on the UK festival circuit in the early Seventies. After a disastrous US tour in 1972, the group splintered, with three of the members quitting to form Jack The Lad. While maintaining a version of Lindisfarne, Hull issued the first of five solo albums beginning with the fine *Pipedream* (1973), influenced by his work as a nurse in a psychiatric ward and featuring several members of Lindisfarne. With the original line-up reuniting in 1977, Lindisfarne returned to top form the following year with the hit single 'Run From Home', their first US chart success. Experiencing frequent personnel changes in the Eighties, Lindisfarne landed a surprise hit with a novelty rap version of 'Fog On The Tyne' recorded with then-Newcastle United FC football hero Paul Gascoigne. Hull was rejoined by the original members of the group for an annual Christmas performance at Newcastle City Hall. Hull continued to perform solo at folk clubs in the latter part of his career, and took an active role in local Labour politics in the Newcastle area.

CAUSE: Heart attack.

Helen Humes

Born June 23, 1913
Died September 13, 1981

Jazz and R&B songstress who first gained notoriety in bands behind Count Basie and Harry James, Helen Humes began her career in her teen years writing blues songs. Recording several tracks at age 14 at OKeh Records, she was accompanied by guitarist Lonnie Johnson. Discovered by Basie at the Cotton Club in 1937, she was hired as the replacement for Billie Holiday. Humes gained further fame in 1938 at the John Hammond-produced Spirituals To Swing concert at Carnegie Hall. Later pursuing a solo career her hits included the million-selling, scat-styled crossover entry recorded with Bill Doggett's group, 'Be Baba Leba' and the double-entendre 'Million Dollar Secret' (1950). Joining Red Norvo's group in the mid Fifties, she took a jazz turn, her work captured on several albums for Contemporary Records. Retired from music in 1967 to take care of her ailing father after the death of her mother, Humes performed only sporadically.

CAUSE: Cancer. She died at the Beverly Manor Convalescent Hospital in Santa Monica, California.

Alberta Hunter

Born April 1, 1895
Died October 17, 1984
A pioneering classic blues singer, Memphis-born Alberta Hunter was responsible for standards such as 'My Castle's Rocking', 'I Got A Mind To Ramble' and 'Rough And Ready Men'. Running away from home at age 11 to Chicago, she took a job as a cook before finding club work a year later. Spending her teen years belting out mostly blues songs in the city's seedier clubs, she was primarily influenced by Sophie Tucker. After a brief stint at Black Swan Records in 1921, Hunter signed to Paramount Records in 1922 where she was accompanied by top players such as Fletcher Henderson, Eubie Blake, and Louis Armstrong. Meanwhile in 1922, Bessie Smith had scored a million-selling dèbut hit with the Hunter-penned 'Downhearted Blues'; conversely in 1923, Hunter replaced Smith in the all-black musical *How Come*. Alternating her time between Chicago and New York for the next decade, Hunter arrived in London in 1929 where she teamed with Paul Robeson in the musical *Showboat*. During World War II and continuing into the Korean War, Hunter regularly performed for US troops in USO tours. Abandoning music for humanitarian activities following her mother's death in 1954, Hunter spent the next two decades working at a hospital on Roosevelt Island. But Hunter enjoyed an unlikely revival in 1977 after an impromptu performance at a birthday party for Mabel Mercer; after a stunning performance the following year at the Newport Jazz Festival, she was subsequently asked to record the soundtrack for the 1978 film, *Remember My Name*. She spent subsequent years performing to packed houses at The Cookery nightclub in Greenwich Village.
CAUSE: Natural causes. She died at her home in Roosevelt Island, New York.
FURTHER READING: Taylor, Frank C. (1988). *Alberta Hunter: A Celebration In Blues*. New York: McGraw-Hill.

Ivory Joe Hunter

Born December 10, 1914
Died November 8, 1974
Smooth proto-R&B piano playing balladeer, Ivory Joe Hunter was born into a musical family in Kirbyville, Texas. Playing the piano since his childhood, he joined his school band. Forming his own group at 19, Hunter toured throughout Texas, making Houston his base. By the early Forties, he had also secured his own radio programme in nearby Beaumont. Relocating to California in 1942, Hunter first worked with Slim Jenkins. With his combination of elegant vocals atop a Texas blues base, Hunter was a popular draw in West Coast jazz and blues clubs. Forming Ivory Records, Hunter scored a national hit when he leased one of his tracks to Leon Rene's Exclusive Records: 'Blues At Sunrise' (backed by Johnny Moore and The Three Blazers). Launching another label, the San Francisco-based Pacific Records, Hunter enjoyed a chart hit with 'Seventh Street Boogie' (1946). The 4-Star label purchased Hunter's Pacific masters in 1947, including the future Top 10 R&B chart hit, 'Blues At Midnight'. Signing with the then-fledgling label King Records, Hunter became a hot commodity with hits such as 'Pretty Mama Blues' (1949), 'Don't Fall In Love With Me' and 'I Quit My Pretty Mama'. But Hunter was soon lured to MGM Records. Toning down his blues persona, he switched to ballad-oriented material. His dèbut release, 'I Almost Lost My Mind' (1949), became his first million-seller (and was later a pop hit for Pat Boone). Hunter's hits at MGM continued with 'S.P. Blues'

(1949) and 'I Need You So' (1950). Signing with Atlantic Records in 1954, Hunter continued his hit run with 'A Tear Fell' (1955) and the charming, pop crossover hit, 'Since I Met You Baby' (1956). Hunter's last hit, a minor R&B entry, 'Yes I Want You', came in late 1958. Unable to adapt to the demands of rock'n'roll, he left Atlantic Records in 1958. His career on the skids, Hunter would drift from label to label, including Dot, Capitol, VeeJay and Epic. Backed by session men in Nashville and Memphis, Hunter switched gears in the Seventies, pursuing a career in country music; Hunter was drawn to country after Sonny James scored a million-selling hit with a cover of 'Since I Met You Baby' in 1969.
CAUSE: Lung cancer. He died in a Memphis nursing home, after being admitted to a Memphis hospital the previous December.

John Hunter

(JOHN WILLIAM HUNTER)
Born November 23, 1941
Died February 1976
Drummer for the one-hit Sixties psychedelic Memphis-based band The Hombres, John Hunter was born and raised in Memphis. In 1964, Hunter was asked to joined the touring version of Ronny & The Daytonas; a studio-only congregate comprised of session players. The group had a pair of hits with 'G.T.O.' and 'Sandy'. Unhappy with the arrangement after a few years, Hunter and the road group were only occasionally permitted to appear on the group's records. Hunter and his bandmates formed The Hombres in 1966, and signed with Verve/Forecast Records. Recorded in 1966, the folk/psychedelic, novelty-styled, hippy anthem, 'Let It Out (Let It All Hang Out)' took a year to chart. It was followed with other novelty-styled singles including 'Mau, Mau, Mau', 'Take My Overwhelming Love' and 'Cram It Up Your Heart'. The group released an album on Verve, *Let It Out*; a second album was recorded but never released. Hunter returned to Memphis, passing through a number of local bands.
CAUSE: Suicide by gunshot.

Ty Hunter

(TYRONE HUNTER)
Born July 14, 1940
Died February 24, 1981
Originally the lead vocalist of The Voicemasters, Ty Hunter left the group to pursue a solo career. In 1960 he joined the Detroit-based R&B group, Glass House, enjoying a series of minor R&B hits beginning with 'Crumbs Off The Table' (1969). With the departure of member Scherrie Payne who turned solo, the group disbanded. In 1971, Hunter replaced C.P. Spencer in the R&B group, The Originals.
CAUSE: Lung cancer.

Willie Hunter

Born March 24, 1936
Died April 1978
The baritone vocalist of the Fifties R&B/doo-wop act The Diablos, Willie Hunter formed the group with friends while in high school. Fronted by brothers Nolan and Jimmy Strong, the Detroit-based group scored its only hit with 'The Way You Dog Me Around' (1956). Another of their releases, the fine ballad 'The Wind', became a doo-wop standard. Hunter remained with the group until the mid Sixties.
CAUSE: Unknown. He died in Detroit.

Debra "Deah Dame" Hurd

(DEBRA JEAN HURD)
Born September 20, 1958
Died June 27, 1994
Half of the R&B duo Damian Dame, Debra "Deah Dame" Hurd was teamed with Damian (Bruce Edward Broadus), the first act signed to the Arista subsidiary Laface Records. Born in Houston but raised in San Jose, Hurd sang in her gospel choir and, at 18, she toured with her sister and

brother-in-law in an R&B band. Signed by Geffen Records as a solo act, Hurd recorded a much ignored album in 1983. Turning to session vocals in the Eighties, she backed The Deele and Karyn White, as well as recording a duet with Babyface. After meeting Damian at a Los Angeles studio in 1990, Hurd agreed to form the duo, Damian Dame. Composing their own material, Hurd provided the lyrics to Damian's melodies. An immediate sensation on R&B radio, Damian Dame scored a trio of hits in the early Nineties with 'Exclusivity', 'Right Down To It' and 'Gotta Learn My Rhythm'. Hurd was working on a second Damian Dame album at the time of her death.
CAUSE: Car crash. Her singing partner, Damian, died exactly two years later.

Willie Hutch

(WILLIAM MCKINLEY HUTCHINSON)
Born December 6, 1944
Died September 19, 2005
A Motown producer and soul singer, Willie Hutch broke into music as a solo act and songwriter for The 5th Dimension. After Hutch co-wrote The Jackson 5 hit, 'I'll Be There', he was hired by Motown chief Berry Gordy as a producer and songwriter. Hutch oversaw sessions by Marvin Gaye, Diana Ross and the first post-Smokey Robinson release by The Miracles. Turning his attention to film soundtracks, Hutch composed the music for the 1973 Richard Pryor blaxploitation classic *The Mack*, which gave Hutch two R&B hit singles, 'Brother's Gonna Work It Out' and 'Slick'. Hutch also composed the music for the film *Foxy Brown* and scored a series of R&B hits including 'Get Ready For The Get Down', 'Love Power' and 'Party Down'. Hutch continued to work in music until shortly before his death.
CAUSE: Unknown. He died at his home in the Dallas suburb of Duncanville, Texas.

Michael Hutchence

(MICHAEL KELLAND FRANK HUTCHENCE)
Born January 20, 1960
Died November 22, 1997
Born in Sydney but spending much of his youth in Hong Kong where his father worked as an international trader, Michael Hutchence lived briefly in Los Angeles with his mother following his parents' divorce. He met Andrew Farriss in a Sydney high school in 1975, and quit school in 1977 to join Farriss' band which also featured two more Farriss brothers, Jon and Tim. Originally called The Farriss Brothers, the group retained a stable line-up for the next 20 years. On the nightclub circuit in Perth, and then Sydney, the group was discovered by Midnight Oil's manager Garry Morris. Signing with the Australian RCA-distributed Deluxe label in 1979, the renamed INXS released its self-titled début album the following year. Clad in leather, the handsome, cocky, charismatic Hutchence would frequently be compared to Mick Jagger and Jim Morrison. Signing with Atlantic/Atco Records (Mercury in the UK), INXS was introduced to international audiences in 1982 with their third album, *Shabooh Shoobah*, and their dance-rock style was welcomed by MTV which aired their video for 'The One Thing'. The group followed with the Nile Rodgers-produced hit single 'Original Sin' from the album, *The Swing*. One of the most successful groups of the Eighties, INXS unleashed a string of multi-format hits with 'The One Thing', 'What You Need', 'Devil Inside', and 'Need You Tonight'/'Meditate', the latter winning five MTV video awards in 1988. Hutchence flirted with acting, starring in a couple of films including *Dogs In Space* (1986). Also a savvy businessman, Hutchence had helped finance the 1986 hit film, *Crocodile Dundee*. Nearly leaving the group in 1989 over the strains of constant

touring, Hutchence formed a side band project, Max Q, with friend Ollie Olsen. Released in 1992, INXS's fine album *Welcome To Wherever You Are* topped the charts in the UK, but signalled the group's decline in US popularity as its dance-rock sound did not fit in with radio's then fascination with grunge-rock. After a three-year recording hiatus, INXS returned to the charts in 1997 with the uneven *Elegantly Wasted*. The group was planning to launch a new album and begin a 20th anniversary tour in late 1997. Hutchence's good looks and wayward lifestyle made him an unwilling target for the tabloid press, a situation exacerbated after he was linked with high-profile girlfriends like Kylie Minogue, the model Helena Christensen and, finally, Paula Yates, the former wife of Bob Geldof. Recorded over a two-year period, a posthumously released self-titled solo album was poorly received. The remaining members of INXS went through a series of replacement lead singers including Terence Trent D'Arby and Jimmy Barnes, before settling on the Hutchence-lookalike, former Noiseworks vocalist Jon Stevens, who quit the band after three years. INXS selected J.D. Fortune as their next lead vocalist through a competition on the CBS television programme *Rock Star*.

CAUSE: Meeting his end in a soap opera-like, scandal-ridden incident, Hutchence was found dead in a hotel room at the Ritz-Carlton in Sydney, having apparently hung himself. Earlier the same evening Hutchence had been visited (for six hours) by British television star Kym Wilson and her lawyer-boyfriend Andrew Rayment; the couple left the hotel at 4:45 a.m. Then, shortly before 9 a.m., Hutchence received a call from Paula Yates, informing him that her children would not be accompanying them for the upcoming Australian leg of INXS' 20th anniversary tour. Already involved in a messy custody case between Yates and the father of three of her daughters, Bob Geldof, Hutchence then telephoned Geldof. Hutchence had been on the phone for a great deal of time in the last hours of his life, but instead of reaching most of the people, he was forced to leave answering machine messages. One of the calls was to an old friend, Michelle Bennett, who, when realising the poor state he was in, rushed to the hotel but there was no answer at his door at 10:30 a.m., at which time he was probably dead. Some time later Hutchence's unclothed body was found by a maid on the floor of his hotel suite. He had hung himself from a door hinge with a leather belt, the belt buckle subsequently breaking off and dropping Hutchence to the floor. Hutchence had been drinking vodka, beer and champagne, with an autopsy also finding Prozac and traces of a number of other drugs including cocaine in his system. Hutchence had met with his therapist a week before his death. While the coroner ruled the death as suicide by asphyxiation, in a 1999 BBC TV documentary, Yates insisted he died accidentally as the result of autoerotic asphyxiation. At the funeral, Yates was shoved and verbally attacked by Hutchence's mother, Patricia Glassop. The grief-stricken Yates attempted suicide several months later, and died from an accidental overdose on September 17, 2000.

FURTHER READING: Gee, Mike. (1998). *The Life And Death Of Michael Hutchence.* London: Omnibus.

Joseph Hutchinson

Born February 28, 1931
Died September 1, 1985

Tennessee-born founder of the gospel group, The Hutchinson Sunbeams, Joseph Hutchinson assembled the quartet with his three daughters, Jeanette, Wanda, and Sheila. The group soon evolved into the R&B/disco group The Emotions, who in 1969 scored a million-selling hit with 'So I Can Love You' (1969), a song written by Hutchinson and his daughters. Easing himself out of the group by the mid Seventies, the elder Hutchinson assumed a managerial position. The Emotions won a Grammy in 1978 for the single, 'Best Of My Love'. In 1995 Hutchinson's daughters staged the autobiographical play, *Bigger Than Bubblegum*.

CAUSE: Unknown. He died at Northwestern Memorial Hospital in Chicago.

J.B. Hutto

(JOSEPH BENJAMIN HUTTO)

Born April 29, 1926

Died June 12, 1983

A blues composer and bandleader, J.B. Hutto was born in South Carolina but raised in Georgia, moving to join his family in Chicago in 1947. Reared on gospel music, he was the leader of a family group, The Golden Crown, with his three brothers and a sister. Embracing the music of Chicago and inspired by Muddy Waters, Hutto abandoned gospel for secular blues. Initially a drummer and pianist, Hutto emerged as a masterful slide guitarist and after spending time in a local bar band, Johnny Ferguson & His Twisters, Hutto left to form his own band, The Hawks. Recording for Chance Records, they released gritty tracks such as 'Things Are Slow', 'Dim Lights', and 'Now She's Gone'. Quitting music in the late Fifties, he returned to the industry the following decade during the genre's rebirth in popularity.

CAUSE: Diagnosed with lung cancer, he was unable to undergo surgery due to his diabetic condition. The cancer spread, and he died at his home in Harvey, Illinois.

Phyllis Hyman

Born July 6, 1949

Died June 30, 1995

Jazz, R&B singer and Broadway actress, Pittsburgh-born Phyllis Hyman worked in the Seventies as a legal secretary by day and a club singer by night. Discovered by Norman Conners, Hyman was hired as the vocalist of his jazz group, Starship. Emerging as a solo act, Hyman signed with Buddah, and then Arista Records, scoring a pair of hits with the Barry Manilow written and produced, 'Somewhere In My Lifetime' and 'You Know How To Love Me'. As an actress, Hyman garnered much fame for her Tony-winning role in the Broadway production of *Sophisticated Ladies*. Veering toward jazz, she scored a hit album in 1977 with *Living All Alone*. Remaining a popular draw into the Nineties as a torch jazz singer, Hyman performed in the country's most elegant venues. Her final album *I Refuse To Be Lonely*, was posthumously released.

CAUSE: Taking an overdose of pills, she had left a suicide note. She was found unconscious lying in bed in her New York apartment, dying two hours later at Roosevelt Hospital. She had been depressed over the death of her mother.

I

Ripley Ingram

Born January 21, 1930
Died March 23, 1995
Tenor vocalist of the early doo-wop group The Five Keys, Ripley Ingram was a student in Newport News, Virginia when he and his brother Raphael joined The Sentimental Four in 1949. Following an amateur night win at the Apollo Theater, the Rudy West-led group signed with Aladdin Records in 1951. Recording on several labels, and experiencing numerous line-up changes, the group scored several hits including the doo-wop standard, 'The Glory Of Love' and 'Ling Ting Tong'. Ingram left the group in the early Sixties.
CAUSE: Unknown. He died in Newport News, Virginia.

Rick Intveld

Born 1962
Died December 31, 1985
A member of Rick Nelson's back-up group, The Stone Canyon Band, Rick Intveld appeared on Nelson's 1972 comeback hit, 'Garden Party'.
CAUSE: On-board fire in a DC-3 aeroplane, near Dekalb, Texas, en route from Guttersville, Alabama, to Dallas for half-time festivities at the Cotton Bowl. Killed were Ricky Nelson and six others. The pilots survived.

I-Roy

(ROY SAMUEL REID)
Born June 28, 1944
Died November 27, 1999
A popular "toaster" (the Jamaican precursor of rap), Jamaican-born vocalist I-Roy borrowed his moniker in 1969 from the genre's inventor, Ewart "U-Roy" Beckford. After making his first recordings in 1972, I-Roy left his civil service accounting position. Sticking out from his contemporary Rastafarians, I-Roy preferred flashy white suits and rum over loose-fitting multi-coloured garments and ganja. Travelling to England in 1973, he helped usher in reggae with a long residency at London's Roaring Twenties Club. Returning to Jamaica in 1975, he worked as a producer at Jo Jo Hookim's Channel One studio, and landed a local hit with 'Welding'. Signing with Virgin Records in 1977, he released five albums.
CAUSE: Financially destitute, homeless, and in very poor health in the last years of his life, he succumbed to heart failure. He died at the Spanish Town Hospital. One of his sons had been violently murdered a month earlier.

Weldon Irvine

(WELDON JONATHAN IRVINE, JR.)
Born October 27, 1943
Died April 9, 2002
A songwriter and pianist, Weldon Irvine is best known for co-writing Nina Simone's often recorded African-American anthem, 'To Be Young, Gifted And Black'. A jazz-trained musician, Irvine first arrived in New York City in 1965 and joined a 17-piece jazz orchestra. His compositions have been recorded by Donny Hathaway, Aretha Franklin, Dionne Warwick, The Fat Back Band and numerous jazz artists. As a solo act, Irvine recorded at least nine albums for Hubbab, RCA, Saucerman, Luv N' Haight, Tuff City, Nodlew and Strata East labels. He also recorded with Freddie Hubbard, Lenny White and various hip-hop artists.
CAUSE: Suicide. He shot himself in the head with a rifle while on the lawn of the Uniondale office complex near Nassau Coliseum in Long Island, New York.

Big Dee Irwin

(DIFOSCO ERVIN)
Born July 8, 1939
Died August 27, 1995

Lead singer of the Fifties doo-wop group The Pastels, Big Dee Irwin formed the vocal group in 1955 when he was an air force sergeant stationed at a base in Greenland. Originally called The Rocketeers, all of the group members were soon transferred to a base in Washington DC. After performing in local USO clubs, the group came second in a national military talent contest behind Pittsburgh's Del-Vikings. Renamed The Pastels, the group was quickly signed by New York-based Hull Records in 1956. Recording the Irwin co-composition 'Been So Long' in 1956, the ballad was a belated hit in 1958. With Irwin discharged from the service that year, he led The Pastels on a series of tours until the early Sixties. As a solo act, Irwin enjoyed a hit in 1963 with a cover of Bing Crosby's 'Swinging On A Star', with uncredited backing vocals by Little Eva. In the Seventies, he recorded under the name DiFosco, and wrote material for Ray Charles and The Dells.
CAUSE: Heart failure. He died in Las Vegas.

Kelly Isley

(O'KELLY ISLEY, JR.)
Born December 25, 1937
Died March 31, 1986
A member of the perennial R&B vocal group The Isley Brothers, Kelly Isley earned his musical education at a Baptist church choir in Cincinnati. The eldest of six brothers, Kelly formed a gospel quartet with three of his siblings in the early Fifties. But when his brother Vernon was killed in a bicycle accident, the group disbanded for one year. Urged by their parents to reform the group, the three eldest Isley brothers assembled a six-man group. Now performing secular R&B, The Isley Brothers trekked to New York City. After recording several flops on a series of labels, the group signed to RCA Records. Teamed with the production duo of Hugo & Luigi, The Isley Brothers released a rollicking, million-selling smash with the frat-rock classic, 'Shout – Pts. 1&2'; angering the congregation at their church, the song employed a gospel-style, call-and-response vocal pattern, and a frenetic church-like organ. Unable to repeat their success, The Isley Brothers were dropped by RCA and signed by Atlantic Records. But after a mismatched, unfruitful pairing with Leiber & Stoller, the Isleys moved to Wand Records, where in 1962 they would record another much-covered rock standard, 'Twist And Shout', which The Beatles would record on their UK début album and release as a hit single in the US. Signing with United Artists, the Isleys hired the unknown Jimi Hendrix as their guitarist. Then switching to Motown, the Isleys would manage only one pop hit at the label with the Holland-Dozier-Holland composition 'This Old Heart of Mine (Is Weak For You)' (1966). Having earlier attempted to launch their own label, The Isley Brothers formed T-Neck Records, with Kelly in charge of the finances. At T-Neck, they recorded a million-selling hit album with *It's Our Thing*, highlighted by the funky, 'It's Your Thing'. Expanding the group to include two more siblings and a cousin, The Isley Brothers moved to a harder, rockier sound in the early Seventies. On the cutting edge of funk and soul, the group enjoyed crossover airplay with hits such as '(Who's) That Lady' and 'Fight The Power', and sold millions of albums with gold and platinum releases such as 3 + 3, *Go For Your Guns* (1977), *Showdown* (1978), Go All The Way (1980), and Grand Slam (1981). The Isley's rock standard 'Shout', having already proved a success for Sixties singer Lulu, received renewed attention via Otis Day & The Nights' remake from the John Belushi, college frat-film, *National Lampoon's Animal House*. The Isleys would splinter into two separate groups in

1984, with the eldest three members moving to Warner Brothers Records and retaining The Isley Brothers moniker. Kelly Isley would last appear on the album *Masterpiece* (1985), an elegant set of ballads and standards.
CAUSE: Cerebral haemorrhage. Kelly suffered a heart attack on March 29. He died two days later at Englewood Hospital in Englewood, New Jersey.

J

Steve Jablecki

(STEPHEN H. JABLECKI)
Born February 15, 1946
Died April 14, 2005
The guitarist and lead singer of the Providence, Rhode Island-based one-hit wonders Wadsworth Mansion, Steve Jablecki wrote their Top 10 hit 'Sweet Mary' (1971). In 1973, Jablecki and bandmate Howie "Forrest" McDonald moved to Los Angeles where they formed a group called Slingshot.
CAUSE: Unknown.

Adam Jackson

Born March 10, 1938
Died February 1995
Lead singer and songwriter of the Fifties doo-wop group, The Jesters, Adam Jackson joined the New York-based year-old outfit in 1957. After winning three Apollo Theater talent contests, the group signed with Winley Records. The Jesters landed East Coast airplay with the single, 'So Strange' (1957) and a cover of The Chatels' hit, 'The Plea' (1958). The Jesters are better known for their strong selling album, *The Paragons Meet The Jesters*, in which the group was teamed with its labelmate. The Jesters regrouped in the Nineties.
CAUSE: Unknown.

Al Jackson, Jr.

Born November 27, 1935
Died October 1, 1975
The drummer for the prolific Sixties soul band Booker T. & The MGs, Memphis-born Al Jackson was known primarily as an immaculate time-keeper. He first hit the stage in his childhood, and after performing professionally in his father's 11-piece orchestra in his teen years, he backed R&B singer Roy Milton in the late Fifties. During this period Jackson also attended AM&N College in Pine Bluff, Arkansas. A talented drummer, Jackson then joined the Willie Mitchell-led house band at Hi Records. Soon lured to Stax Records by organist Booker T. Jones, Jackson was joined by a bandmate from his days with Roy Milton, bassist Lewis Steinberg, and guitarist Steve Cropper. Intended as a B-side, Booker T. & The MGs scored their first hit with the hook-laden instrumental, 'Green Onions'. Then, with Steinberg replaced on bass by former Mar-Key Donald "Duck" Dunn, the group settled into its classic line-up, with Jackson the eldest member. Content with their role as studio musicians, The MGs became Stax's premier house band, backing most of the label's artists including Otis Redding, Carla Thomas and Sam & Dave. Employing very danceable rhythms on hundreds of tracks, Jackson drove his powerful, perfect-time percussion behind the group's organ-heavy sound. Working with the production and songwriting team of Isaac Hayes and David Porter, Booker T. & The MGs also continued to release their own material and enjoyed hits with: 'Hip Hug-Her' (1967), 'Soul Limbo' (1968) which is best known in the UK as the signature tune for BBC TV's cricket coverage, 'Hang 'Em High' (1968) from the Clint Eastwood film of the same name, 'Time Is Tight' (1969) and a cover of Simon & Garfunkel's 'Mrs. Robinson' (1969). As a songwriter, Jackson joined Al Green and Willie Mitchell in the late Sixties to compose the hit songs, 'Let's Stay Together' and 'I'm Still In Love With You'. But after the departure of Jones and Cropper from the group, Jackson and Dunn teamed in 1973 to record the poor-selling album *The MGs*. In the Seventies, Jackson was a popular and much respected session player, working with artists such as Al Green, Leon Russell,

Rod Stewart and Eric Clapton. Also a producer, Jackson oversaw albums for Major Lance and Shirley Brown. After Jackson's untimely death in 1975, Booker T. & The MGs would regroup for special projects and occasional recording sessions.

CAUSE: He was shot to death by two burglars at his Memphis home after returning from a telecast of the third Mohammad Ali/Joe Frazier fight. Jackson's wife was tied up and unable to warn her husband. She watched as he was robbed of the money in his wallet and then shot five times. The police had first suspected his wife because she had shot Jackson the previous July. But with no one in the Memphis police department willing to discuss the still unsolved murder, unsubstantiated rumours have persisted about the killer's identity.

Bull Moose Jackson

(BENJAMIN CLARENCE JACKSON)
Born April 22, 1919
Died July 31, 1989

A pioneering R&B recording artist, Cleveland-born Bull Moose Jackson was a soloist in the junior choir at his AME church at the age of three. Taking violin lessons from the age of five, he joined the orchestra at Cleveland Central on tenor saxophone. Given the nickname "Bull Moose" due to his disproportionately large head, Jackson was the target of much teasing in his youth. Turning professional right after high school, Jackson moved to New York City and formed The Harlem Hotshots with Freddie Webster. Then after passing through a few bands in Buffalo in the early Forties, Jackson returned to Cleveland. Discovered on a local stage by popular bandleader Lucky Millinder, Jackson was hired as a saxophonist but was placed in the featured vocalist position following the departure of Wynonie Harris. But when King/Queen Records owner Syd Nathan tried to sign Millinder who was still under contract, the bandleader instead suggested Jackson. Backed by Millinder's orchestra until 1947, Jackson barrelled onto the R&B charts with the Top 10 entry, 'I Know Who Threw The Whiskey In The Well'. Stealing away several members of Millinder's orchestra including sax great Sam "The Man" Taylor, Jackson formed his own backing band, The Buffalo Bearcats (which for a brief time would include John Coltrane). With his schoolboy glasses, rugged appearance, and football player body, Jackson became an unlikely R&B star. The gravely voiced Jackson enjoyed a strong string of hits with: the chart-topping, crossover entry, 'I Love You, Yes I Do' (1947), 'All My Love Belongs To You'/'I Want A Bowlegged Woman' (1948), 'I Can't Go On Without You' (1948), 'Little Girl, Don't Cry' (1949), 'Why Don't You Haul Off And Love Me?' (1949). The latter part of Jackson's career would be marked by a number of racy and novelty records such as 'Nosey Joe' (1952) and 'Big Ten Inch Record' (1952), the latter reprised by Aerosmith in 1975. With his career ebbing, Jackson left King Records in 1956, scoring his final hit in 1961 with a newly recorded version of his early hit, 'I Love You, Yes I Do'. Essentially retiring from music for the next two decades, James worked for a catering company. But in a strange twist of fate, when a Pittsburgh rock band, The Flashcats, scored a local hit with Bull Moose Jackson's 'Nosey Joe' in 1983, the ageing Jackson was lured back on stage. Recording a cassette-only album, *Moosemania*, in 1984, James scored a minor hit with the novelty number, 'Get Off The Table, Mable (The Two Dollars Is For The Beer)'. Rediscovered by audiences, Jackson toured through Europe in 1985, backed by the Johnny Otis Show. But with his health worsening, Jackson moved back to Cleveland.

CAUSE: Diagnosed with untreatable

cancer, he died after a long-term confinement at Mount Sinai Hospital in Cleveland.

Harold Jackson

Born 1930
Died c. 1980
Tenor and guitarist of the doo-wop group, The Crickets (not the Buddy Holly group of the same name), Harold Jackson was an original member of the Bronx-based quartet. The Crickets scored their sole national chart hit with their début release, 'You're Mine' (1953). Lead singer Barlow "Dean" Barlow fired the entire group in late 1953.
CAUSE: Unknown.

J.J. Jackson

(JOHN JULIAN JACKSON III)
Born April 8, 1941
Died March 17, 2004
As one of the original five MTV veejays, J.J. Jackson was at the forefront of the music video revolution. A radio veteran, Jackson had perfected his on-air banter at rock outlets WBCN in Boston and KLOS in Los Angeles, and also provided the deejay voice-overs in the 1976 film *Car Wash*. Jackson gained television experience when he was hired in 1979 by Los Angeles television station KABC for a rock news segment. When MTV débuted in 1981, Jackson was joined by veejays Nina Blackwood, Martha Quinn, Mark Goodman and Alan Hunter. The eldest MTV host, Jackson was also the most knowledgeable when it came to rock history. With his friendly demeanour and smooth, deep voice, Jackson interviewed the cream of rock royalty from Kiss to Robert Plant. After leaving MTV in 1986, Jackson worked at a series of Los Angeles radio stations – as a deejay at KROQ, the music director at KEDG and, lastly, a deejay on KTWV – and as the host of a pair of Westwood One syndicated radio series, *The Beatle Years* and *Super Star Concert Series*. The original MTV veejays were hired in 2005 to host an all-Eighties channel on Sirius satellite radio.
CAUSE: Heart attack. He had undergone open-heart surgery a few years earlier. He died in Los Angeles while driving home from dinner with a friend. Stopping his vehicle at the side of the road, he passed away and could not be revived by paramedics.

Ray Jackson

(RAYMOND JACKSON)
Born 1943
Died 1972
Stax Records pianist and producer, Ray Jackson was also a songwriter, co-penning 'Who's Making Love' (Johnnie Taylor), 'If You're Ready' (The Staple Singers), 'Take Care Of Your Homework' (Johnnie Taylor), and '(If Loving You is Wrong) I Don't Want To Be Right' (Luther Ingram).
CAUSE: He died in a house fire.

Rodney Jackson

Born c. 1933
Died 1978
The original bass singer of the Bronx-based, Fifties doo-wop group The Crickets (not Buddy Holly's band), Rodney Jackson was hospitalised shortly after the group's inception in 1951. After convalescing, Jackson appeared on their début single, and only national chart hit, 'You're Mine' (1953). Lead singer Barlow "Dean" Barlow fired the entire group later in 1953.
CAUSE: Unknown.

Tony Jackson

(ANTHONY PAUL JACKSON)
Born July 16, 1940
Died August 18, 2003
The lead vocalist and bass player for The Searchers, Tony Jackson was at the forefront of the Merseybeat movement in the early Sixties. A Liverpudlian, Jackson was caught up in the skiffle craze of the mid Fifties and formed a group called The Martinis.

Abandoning his career goal of becoming an electrician, in 1960 Jackson formed Johnny Sandon & The Searchers with Mike Pender, John McNally and Chris Curtis, with vocalist Billy Beck (as Johnny Sandon), taking their name from the John Wayne Western. When Beck quit in 1962 to join The Remo Four, Jackson assumed the role of lead vocalist. In common with most of Liverpool's beat combos, The Searchers honed their sound in the seedy nightclubs of Hamburg, Germany, where a live recording was made at the city's famed Star Club. After Pye Records had rejected The Beatles, an A&R man from the label, Tony Hatch, scoured Liverpool for similar talent and signed The Searchers, who by then were playing a residency at the Iron Door Club. An instant hit in the UK, The Searchers chart run began with a cover of The Drifters' 'Sweets For My Sweet', a Tony Hatch composition, 'Sugar And Spice', 'Needles And Pins' (written by Phil Spector associates, Sonny Bono and Jack Nitzsche), and 'Don't Throw Your Love Away' (originally recorded by US girl group The Orlons). Unhappy with his diminishing role in the band, Jackson left The Searchers in mid-64 and formed his own, poorly received group, Tony Jackson & The Vibrations, scoring a minor hit that same year with a cover of Mary Wells' 'Bye Bye Baby'. Jackson later ran a nightclub in Spain and worked in management at a golf club. Later attempts to form his own Searchers group fared poorly. In 1994, Jackson returned to the British charts with a minor hit in collaboration with the band Q, covering Bryan Adams' major hit '(Everything I Do) I Do It For You'. Two years later, Jackson was sentenced to 18 months in prison for threatening a woman with an air gun during a confrontation at a telephone box.
CAUSE: He suffered from a number of ailments including cirrhosis of the liver.

Walter Jackson

Born March 19, 1938
Died June 19, 1983
Chicago-based soul artist, Walter Jackson sang mostly love ballads. First recording on OKeh Records, he enjoyed a long hit run into the Seventies including 'Suddenly I'm All Alone' (1965), 'It's An Uphill Climb To The Bottom' (1966) and his biggest, a cover of Morris Albert's 'Feelings' (1976). Forming a band in the late Seventies called Chills And Fuel, Jackson was active until his death. Stricken with polio in his teens, he performed on crutches.
CAUSE: Cerebral haemorrhage. He died at his home in Chicago.

Willis "Gator Tail" Jackson

Born April 25, 1932
Died October 25, 1987
R&B artist; saxophonist, and one-time musical partner and husband of Ruth Brown, Miami-born Willis "Gator Tail" Jackson had first joined a band in his teens led by jazzman Fats Navarro. After earning a degree at Florida A&M University, Jackson joined the Cootie Williams Orchestra. After providing the blistering saxophone on the Cootie Williams' 1950 hit 'Gator Tail', Jackson left for a solo career. In the Fifties Jackson recorded several albums, usually with blues organist Jack McDuff, his best work coming on the Prestige label. He was also a popular session player, often working behind acts such as Dinah Washington, Jackie Wilson, and his future wife, Ruth Brown. Jackson later settled in Manhattan, and performed in various local nightclubs.
CAUSE: A diabetic, he died a week after heart surgery at Columbia-Presbyterian Medical Center in New York City.

Jam Master Jay

(JASON MIZELL)
Born January 21, 1965
Died October 30, 2002
A member of influential rap group

Run-DMC, deejay Jam Master Jay helped to introduce the genre to mainstream audiences. Run-DMC was formed by a trio of longtime friends from a middle-class neighbourhood in Queens, New York: Joseph Mizell (Jam Master Jay), Joseph Simmons (Run) and Darryl McDaniels (DMC). As Jam Master Jay worked a pair of turntables, Simmons and McDaniels rapped and paced back and forth across the stage. While their contemporaries rapped over soul or funk records, Run-DMC stood out by rapping over samples by rock artists. Signed to Profile Records, the trio released their début in 1984, *Run-DMC*. The first rap album to be certified gold, it was highlighted by the tracks 'It's Like That' and 'Rock Box', and was followed by another fine effort in 1985, *King Of Rock*. It was Run-DMC's third album, the multi-platinum *Raising Hell* (1986), that featured a ground-breaking rap-rock cover version of Aerosmith's 'Walk This Way', featuring the song's original vocalist Steven Tyler sharing the lead; at the time, Aerosmith was in a career slump, and the track not only reinvigorated the veteran rock band's fortunes but also legitimised and introduced rap music to middle America. The album spawned further hits with 'It's Tricky' and 'My Adidas' (members of Run-DMC wore uniforms of black fedoras, thick gold chains and their trademark, white, shell-toe Adidas footwear, and as a result, Adidas shoes entered a sponsorship deal with the trio). Turning to the big screen, Run-DMC starred in the motion pictures *Krush Groove* and *Tougher Than Leather* but with the changing direction of rap in the late Eighties, Run-DMC's fortunes waned. The group reunited in 2001 for *Crown Royal*, their first studio album in eight years, and in a reverse of fortunes, Aerosmith hired Run-DMC to open up for the superstar rock band during a stadium tour that year. Jam Master Jay later launched a deejay school and produced various rap artists, including the first two albums for Onyx.

CAUSE: What is known for certain is that two men were allowed into the second-floor loft studio located in the Jamaica neighbourhood of Queens, New York, after being buzzed in at the entrance. While one man remained at the door, the other man (who was masked) ran directly toward Jam Master Jay and shot him in the head while he was sitting on a couch with a friend playing a video game. He died instantly. The other man in the studio, Uriel Rincon, was shot in the leg. Although the motive of the shooting was originally a mystery, there are multiple conspiracy theories. A reward of over $300,000 was collected by the Hip-Hop Summit Youth Council.

James "Jamie" Jamerson

(JAMES LEE JAMERSON, SR.)
Born January 29, 1936
Died August 2, 1983

Outstanding session bassist at Motown Records, James "Jamie" Jamerson played on most of the label's hits during the Sixties. A native of South Carolina, Jamerson was educated at Detroit's Wayne State University in the mid Fifties. After landing session work behind John Lee Hooker, Jamerson teamed up with future Motown drummer Benny Benjamin backing Dizzy Gillespie and other jazz greats. Arriving at Motown in the early Sixties, he assembled a superb jazz-trained house band that became known as The Funk Brothers and, aside from Jamerson, included Benjamin, guitarist Robert White and keyboard player Earl Van Dyke. Although his contributions to their records went uncredited, Jamerson appeared on hits by The Temptations, Four Tops, Jackson 5, Supremes, Marvin Gaye and others. Many of Motown's musical arrangements were written around Jamerson's memorable bass lines, and

it is no exaggeration to suggest that his expertise was largely responsible for their success. In 1972, Jamerson joined his boss Berry Gordy Jr. at Motown's relocated headquarters in Los Angeles, the only member of Motown's house band to make the move. After refusing to adapt his playing to the demands of new producers, Jamerson left the label in 1973. Despite his key role in defining the Motown sound, Jamerson died with little fanfare in near poverty. A previously unreleased instrumental track credited to Jamerson, 'Fever In The Funk House', was included in the 1995 Motown boxed set, Year-by-Year.
CAUSE: After years of hard drinking, he died of cirrhosis of the liver at USC Medical Center in Los Angeles.
FURTHER READING: Slutsky, Alan. (1989). *Standing In The Shadows Of Motown: The Life And Times Of Legendary Bassist James Jamerson.* Hal Leonard: New York. George, Nelson. (1985). *Where Did Our Love Go?: The Rise & Fall Of The Motown Sound.* Omnibus Press: London.

Dick James

(RICHARD LEON ISAAC VAPNICK)
Born 1919
Died February 1, 1986
A London-born music publisher who launched Northern Songs to publish the work of John Lennon and Paul McCartney, and subsequently discovered and published Elton John's catalogue, Dick James earned millions. The son of Polish-Jewish immigrants, he began as a pop crooner in Henry Hall's dance orchestra. Given the stage name of Dick James by bandleader Geraldo, he then gained fame with The Cyril Stapleton Orchestra, and landed a few hits in the mid Fifties as a member of The Stargazers. Signed by George Martin at Parlophone Records in 1956 as a solo act, James landed a hit with a Martin-produced single, the theme from television's *The Adventures Of Robin Hood.* Somewhere along the line James discovered the high profit potential of music publishing and went into business for himself. It was George Martin who recommended that Beatles manager Brian Epstein should contact James regarding song publishing, and James impressed the young manager by promptly fixing up for The Beatles to appear on a television show. In 1963 it was traditional for song publishers to pay 10 per cent to writers but James then proposed a unique deal for Epstein, the formation of a separate company to be called Northern Songs in which James and his partners would have a 50 per cent stake, with 20 each going to Lennon and McCartney and 10 per cent for Epstein. James also published Brian Epstein's other acts, Gerry and The Pacemakers, Cilla Black and Billy J. Kramer and The Dakotas, as well as non-Epstein artists such as The Hollies and The Spencer Davis Group. James would later place Northern Songs on the stock market, selling his shares in 1969 to Lew Grade's Associated Television (ATV), and concentrate his energies on a record label, DJM Records. In 1967 James discovered the former Reginald Dwight, who as Elton John was teamed with lyricist Bernie Taupin, and he signed them to both a songwriting and recording contract. Although Elton John was initially unsuccessful, his eventual superstar status further filled James' coffers. Elton John would later take James to court in an unsuccessful attempt to regain the rights to his songs and obtain a more favourable royalty rate.
CAUSE: James suffered a heart attack while playing cards with friends and died at his London penthouse. James had just finished two gruelling months of court testimony in the case brought by Bernie Taupin and Elton John, a catalyst in James' death. While James was forced to pay John a minor settlement, he did retain ownership of the lucrative Taupin/John library.

Elmore James

(ELMORE BROOKS)
Born January 27, 1918
Died May 24, 1963
An influential bottleneck-style, blues guitarist, Elmore James was born in the Deep South community of Richland, Mississippi. Born out of wedlock, James took his surname from his sharecropper mother's common-law husband, Joe Willie James. After working long, hard days in the fields, James would play primitive, home-made, stringed instruments. No longer willing to do back-breaking farm work, James moved to Belzoni, Mississippi, in the mid Thirties, and pursued a career as a juke and sidewalk musician. Borrowing much from his contemporary, Robert Johnson, James adopted the Johnson song '(I Believe I'll) Dust My Broom' as his trademark tune. Following Johnson's death, James frequently teamed with Sonny Boy Williamson, and in 1942 performed on his radio programme on KFFA in Helena, Arkansas. Serving in the US Navy until the war's end in 1945, James fought in Guam. Returning to Mississippi, James married and had seemingly retired from music but, in 1947, Williamson recruited James as a sidekick for his radio performances. Gaining fame as a loud, brash slide guitarist, James also found club work with Willie Love and Arthur "Big Boy" Crudup. Pursuing a solo career, James recorded the first of many versions of 'Dust My Broom' in 1951, credited to Elmo James, followed by 'I Believe' (1953), 'Dust My Blues' (1955), and 'It Hurts Me Too' (1957). After a career lull, James emerged with a more mature sound in the early Sixties. Rediscovered by Fire/Fury Records chief Bobby Robinson, James recorded the hastily written 'The Sky Is Crying', and with his impassioned vocals and raging slide guitar, he continued with 'Look On Yonder Wall'/'Shake Your Moneymaker' (1961), and an updated version of 'It Hurts Me Too'. After employing non-union players, the ailing James was forced by the Chicago musician's union to retreat to Mississippi. Returning to Chicago, James performed in the city's blues clubs until his death. James' standard 'The Sky Is Crying' was reprised by Stevie Ray Vaughn in 1992.
CAUSE: Heart attack. He died before a performance in Chicago, while showering at the home of his cousin, bluesman Homesick James. Elmore James had a history of heart disease dating back to the Forties.

Ethan James

(RALPH BURNS KELLOGG)
Born August 2, 1946
Died June 20, 2003
A latter member of the pioneering San Francisco-based heavy metal band Blue Cheer, Ethan James (a.k.a. Ralph Kellogg) appeared on two albums, *B.C. #5 The Original Human Beings* (1970) and *Oh! Pleasant Hope* (1971) before the group disbanded in late 1971. In the Eighties, James operated Radio Tokyo Studio in Venice, California, where he recorded artists such as The Rain Parade, Black Flag, The Descendents, fIREHOSE and The Minutemen. After changing his name from Ralph Kellogg to Ethan James, he began issuing a series of compilation albums, *Radio Tokyo Tapes*, featuring music by acts such as Henry Rollins, The Last, The Bangles and Phranc. Selling Radio Tokyo Studio in 1990, James teamed with Erin Kenney and recorded a pair of albums featuring medieval and other rudimentary musical instruments. After parting with Kenney, James continued to record and perform around Los Angeles.
CAUSE: Liver cancer. He died in San Francisco.

Rick James

(JAMES AMBROSE JOHNSON, JR.)
Born February 1, 1948
Died August 6, 2004
A flamboyant singer-songwriter and

multi-instrumentalist, Rick James dominated the R&B charts for nearly a decade beginning in the late Seventies. Raised in Buffalo by his mother after his father deserted the family, James had a chaotic childhood. Joining the US Naval Reserves while in his teens, he went AWOL and fled to Toronto, and under the stage name Ricky Matthews, he formed The Mynah Birds, which for a time included future Buffalo Springfield members Neil Young and Bruce Palmer. Although he recorded an album's worth of material for Motown Records, none of the tracks were released once the label discovered James' AWOL military status. After passing through a series of bands over the next decade, James signed with Motown in 1978 as a songwriter and producer but was far more successful as a performer, selling a million copies of his débút album *Come Get It!* which spawned the hit 'You And I'. Labelling his music "punk funk", James continued his hit run of rock-flavoured dance songs with 'Mary Jane', 'Bustin' Out', 'Give It To Me Baby' and the enduring 'Super Freak (Part 1)'. As a producer, James worked with Teena Marie on her débút album *Wild And Peaceful*; oversaw the R&B trio Mary Jane Girls, who scored a Top 10 hit in 1985 with the James composition, 'In My House'; and produced Eddie Murphy's first musical album *How Could It Be*, which spawned the unlikely dance hit 'Party All The Time'. Meanwhile, James' solo hit run continued with a duet with The Temptations on 'Standing On The Top – Part 1', 'Dance With Me – Part 1', a Smokey Robinson duet on 'Ebony Eyes', '17', 'Glow', 'Sweet And Sexy Thing' and R&B chart topper 'Loosey's Rap', featuring rapper Roxanne Shante. James topped the pop charts in 1990 via M.C. Hammer's 'U Can't Touch This', a reworked version of 'Super Freak'. However, amid mounting personal problems – a protracted lawsuit against Motown over unpaid royalties, heavy drug use and an assault conviction which led to jail time – James quickly hit rock bottom. After his release from prison in 1996, he suffered a severe stroke and underwent hip replacement surgery. At the time of his death, James had just finished recording an album and was in negotiations regarding a movie about his life.

CAUSE: He was found dead at his home in Los Angeles by his personal assistant. Although an autopsy revealed nine drugs in his system, including prescriptions for a host of ailments including diabetes and heart disease, the coroner's report insisted that "none of the drugs or drug combinations were found to be at levels that were life-threatening in and of themselves". James had suffered a severe stroke in 1998 and had a pacemaker implanted in his heart. The official cause of death was listed as a heart attack and the death was ruled accidental.

Skip James

(NEHEMIAH CURTIS JAMES)
Born June 2, 1902
Died October 3, 1969

An influential blues guitarist and pianist, Skip James was raised on a Mississippi plantation. Abandoned by his bootlegging Baptist minister father, the young James turned to music and was tutored by his frequent partner Henry Stuckey. Discovered by record store owner and talent scout H.C. Spears, James recorded 26 songs for Paramount Records over two days in 1931, including the blues chestnuts 'I'm So Glad' and 'Killing Floor Blues'. James employed an unorthodox tuning on his guitar and with his eerie, falsetto-styled voice, he was able to conjure shadowy images of the devil. Although his records sold poorly during the Depression era and James abandoned the blues, his influence was felt by other blues guitarists, most notably Robert Johnson who would rework James' 'Devil Got My Woman' as 'Hell Hound On My Trail'. Moving

to Dallas in 1932 and teamed with his preacher father, James formed a jubilee musical group. Ordained a Baptist minister, James would leave music altogether in the Forties but after being 'discovered' by a trio of folk aficionados in 1964, James enjoyed a triumphant return following a performance at the Newport Folk Festival. During the Sixties, James recorded a pair of albums for Vanguard Records, and toured the blues circuit with Mississippi John Hurt and others. James' early work has been recorded by countless British Invasion groups including Cream ('I'm So Glad').
CAUSE: Cancer. He died at the University of Pennsylvania Hospital in Philadelphia.
FURTHER READING: Calt, Stephen. (1994). *I'd Rather Be The Devil: Skip James And The Blues*. New York: Da Capo.

Horst Jankowski

Born January 30, 1936
Died June 29, 1998
German jazz pianist, Horst Jankowski is best known for the international 1965 instrumental hit, 'A Walk In The Black Forest'. A classically trained pianist, he switched to jazz in his twenties, and later worked with the German subsidiary of Muzak.
CAUSE: Cancer. He died in Bonn, Germany.

Tom Jans

Born February 9, 1949
Died March 25, 1984
A folk singer-songwriter, Tom Jans first garnered press for his musical association with his paramour Mimi Farina (the sister of Joan Baez) in the early Seventies. Parting with Farina, he later recorded four solo albums at A&M and CBS Records including the classic *Dark Blonde*. As a staff writer at Irving Almo Music, Jans penned 'Loving Arms' (Kris Kristofferson; Dobie Gray), 'Out Of Hand' (Gary Stewart), and 'Old Time Feeling' (Johnny Cash). Jans also collaborated with Jeff Porcaro, Jerry Swallow, Lowell George, and Bill Payne.
CAUSE: He died at his home in Santa Monica, California, probably from a drug overdose. Jans had damaged his kidneys the previous year in a motorcycle accident.

Joe "Yo Yo" Jaramillo

Born October 15, 1946
Died May 24, 2000
A founding member of Sixties rock band Cannibal & The Headhunters, Joe "Yo Yo" Jaramillo had initially teamed with his brother and two others in a doo-wop group called Bobby & The Classics. Based in east Los Angeles, the Chicano group replaced their lead singer with Frankie "Cannibal" Garcia, and, at the insistence of producer Eddie Davis, were renamed Cannibal & The Headhunters. Recording a cover of the Chris Kenner-composed and recorded New Orleans classic 'Land Of 1000 Dances', Cannibal & The Headhunters scored their only Top 40 hit in 1965. A college frat-rock classic, the song would be recorded by countless acts, most notably Wilson Pickett.
CAUSE: Natural causes.

Felton Jarvis

(CHARLES FELTON JARVIS)
Born November 16, 1934
Died January 3, 1981
Best known as Elvis Presley's latter Nashville-based producer, Charles Jarvis initially worked in the promotions department of ABC-Paramount in the early Sixties. Joining RCA Records in 1965 as a producer, Jarvis first worked with Presley on the Grammy-winning album *How Great Thou Art* (1966). As Presley's producer, in the late Sixties, Jarvis oversaw hits such as 'Suspicious Minds' and 'Kentucky Rain'. Wanting to devote more time to Presley, Jarvisleft RCA in 1970. Jarvis' final Presley production came with the

posthumously released album, *Guitar Man*. Jarvis also worked with Willie Nelson and others.
CAUSE: Stroke. He died at Baptist Hospital in Nashville.

Mike "Yas" Jastremski

(MICHAEL WAYNE JASTREMSKI)
Born March 16, 1963
Died May 23, 2005
The bassist of the San Francisco-based heavy metal band Heathen, Mike "Yaz" Jastremski performed on their 1987 début *Breaking The Silence*, but left shortly thereafter to form the group Pigs. Jastremski reunited with Heathen in 2001 for the "Thrash of the Titans" benefit show for Chuck Billy of Testament. Quitting Heathen for good in 2004, Jastremski was replaced by Jon Torres.
CAUSE: He suffered a heart attack while in a detox programme.

Matthew Jay

Born October 10, 1978
Died September 24, 2003
A rising star who was often compared to Nick Drake and Badly Drawn Boy, British-born, electric, folk-rock singer-songwriter Matthew Jay earned a recording contract on the strength of his compositions before he ever performed in public. After releasing a pair of well-received EPs on the independent Food label, Jay landed at Capitol Records from where his full-length début album, *Draw*, was released in 2001. Jay quickly found residency on American college radio and was tipped for greater success.
CAUSE: He plunged to his death from a window in his seventh floor apartment in Nottingham, England.

Blind Lemon Jefferson

Born July 11, 1897
Died December 1929
A pioneering rural blues guitarist, Texas-born Blind Lemon Jefferson was partially blind since childhood. Unable to join his large family working in the fields, Jefferson became a travelling blues singer. After releasing a pair of obscure religious 78s in his adopted home-town of Dallas in the mid Twenties, Jefferson recorded a string of influential records at Paramount from 1926 to 1929. A national star, Jefferson sang of sinful pleasures and the black experience on blues standards such as 'Long Lonesome Blues', 'Corrina Blues', 'Black Snake Blues', 'Pneumonia Blues', and his best known work, 'See That My Grave Is Kept Clean'. For a brief time, Jefferson toured with folk-blues musician Leadbelly. Jefferson was honoured with a commemorative US postage stamp in 1994, and the San Francisco group Jefferson Airplane took their name in his honour.
CAUSE: Acclimated to warm Southern weather, Jefferson left a rent party in Chicago and froze to death on a sidewalk while waiting either for his personal driver or a streetcar. Alternatively, it has been claimed that when Jefferson's chauffeur-driven car got stuck in a snowstorm, he froze to death after being abandoned by his driver.

Paul Jeffreys

(PAUL AVRON JEFFREYS)
Born February 13, 1952
Died December 21, 1988
Guitarist for British pop band Cockney Rebel, Paul Jeffrey joined the chart-topping Steve Harley-led group on a number of releases including 'Come Up And See Me (Make Me Smile)' (1975). With the group disbanding in 1977, Jeffreys joined Chartreuse. He later worked for a record company in London.
CAUSE: He died in the infamous Pan Am Flight 103 over Lockerbie, Scotland, along with his newlywed wife, 23-year-old Rachel. They were flying to the US to honeymoon and spend time with friends. The chief suspects, Libyan terrorists Abdel

Basset al-Megrahi and Lamen Khalifa Fhimah, were indicted in 1991 by both the US and Scotland but at the time of writing have yet to stand trial. All 259 passengers and crew aboard the plane perished, with an additional 11 people killed on the ground.

Otto Jeffries

Born c. 1928
Died c. 1980
Early bass singer-turned-manager of the Fifties vocal doo-wop group, The "5" Royales, Otto Jeffries was reared in Winston-Salem, North Carolina. The "5" Royales had evolved from a religious group led by brothers Lowman and Clarence Pauling, The Royal Sons Gospel Group. Landing at Apollo Records, the renamed Royal Sons Quintet recorded some gospel material before being convinced by label head Carl LeBow to tackle secular R&B. With the group renamed The "5" Royales by LeBow in 1952, Jeffries soon left his role as a performer and assumed managerial duties. The "5" Royales disbanded in 1965.
CAUSE: Unknown.

Tony Jenkins

(JAMES JENKINS)
Born March 26, 1934
Died September 21, 2001
An original member of Philadelphia-based doo-wop group The Silhouettes, Tony Jenkins was drafted into the military shortly before the recording session for the group's only hit, 'Get A Job'. The group had previously sung gospel music as The Gospel Tornadoes. After his discharge from the military, Jenkins joined a latter version of the hit Philly doo-wop act, The Turbans.
CAUSE: Lung cancer.

Ken Jensen

Born 1966
Died January 29, 1995
Drummer in the Nineties line-up of the pioneering, Vancouver hardcore punk band D.O.A., Ken Jensen joined the Joey Keithley-fronted band in 1992 beginning with the group's self-released album *13 Flavors Of Doom*. Jensen was the group's fifth drummer.
CAUSE: He was killed in a house fire which also destroyed much of the band's gear. According to a fireman on the scene, the blaze was probably started when a smouldering cigarette was dropped on a couch. Four of Jensen's friends escaped unharmed.

Stevo Jensen

(STEVEN RONALD JENSEN)
Born April 29, 1959
Died August 20, 2005
The original vocalist of seminal California-based punk rock outfit The Vandals, Stevo Jensen co-founded the group in 1980. After appearing on the group's first two albums, *Peace Through Vandalism* and *When In Rome Do As The Vandals Do*, he left in 1984 and was replaced by Dave Quackenbush. Jensen spent years battling a former bandmate over the ownership of the group's early material.
CAUSE: He accidentally overdosed on prescription medication which he was taking to treat arm and back injuries suffered in an accident. He died at his home in Kehei, Hawaii.

Antonio Carlos Jobim

(ANTONIO CARLOS BRASILEIRO DE ALMEIDA JOBIM)
Born January 25, 1927
Died December 8, 1994
Brazilian-born "father" of the bossa nova craze, Antonio Carlos Jobim was also a prolific composer. His initial success came with the score of 1958's *Black Orpheus*. At the end of the Fifties, Jobim pioneered the bossa nova – a highly commercial fusion of samba dance and jazz influences, characterised by staccato rhythms and the sultry vocals of singers like Astrud Gilberto. In late 1962, Stan Getz and Charlie Byrd registered a US Top 20 hit with Jobim's 'Desafinado' and, two

years later, Getz and Astrud Gilberto charted internationally with the standard 'The Girl From Ipanema'. At one point, Jobim's bossa nova style dominated the album charts and even inspired such pop novelty hits as Elvis Presley's 'Bossa Nova Baby' and Eydie Gorme's 'Blame It On The Bossa Nova'. A skilled guitarist and pianist, Jobim released 32 albums during his career, with his 1967 release *Frank Sinatra & Antonio Carlos Jobim* earning a Grammy nomination.
CAUSE: Heart failure. He died in New York City.

Jobriath

(BRUCE WAYNE CAMPBELL)
Born December 14, 1946
Died September 3, 1983
Eccentric, gender-bending, American glam-rocker, Jobriath recorded a pair of poor selling albums in the early Seventies. Heavily influenced by David Bowie's early Seventies incarnations, Jobriath was much hyped by his record label, Elektra. Ordered not to grant interviews by his manager Jerry Brandt, the gay, Pennsylvania-born Jobriath quickly alienated the rock press. Dropped by Elektra, he later worked as a cabaret and lounge singer. Also an actor, Jobriath had earlier appeared in the original Los Angeles production of *Hair*. British singer Morrissey has frequently cited Jobriath as one of his influences.
CAUSE: AIDS. He died in New York City.

Little Willie John

(WILLIAM EDGAR JOHN)
Born November 15, 1937
Died May 26, 1968
Popular R&B balladeer, Little Willie John was born in Ouachita County, Louisiana, and raised in Detroit after his factory-worker father moved the family in the mid Forties. There, John and his siblings formed a gospel group, The United Five, headed by his eldest sister, Mabel. Working for tips, John began singing R&B on street corners and in a neighbourhood bar. At 14, John made an impression at the Detroit stop of Johnny Otis's travelling amateur show. Though recommended by Otis, John was initially rejected by King Records. John then landed stints with Paul Williams (of 'The Hucklebuck' fame) and The Count Basie Orchestra. With the aid of Williams, John re-auditioned at King Records, and was signed by producer Henry Glover in 1955. Earning the nickname "Little" Willie John due to his short stature, the five-foot-four singer was short-tempered and quick to jump into a fight. An immediate sensation, John landed a strong run of hits beginning with 'All Around The World' (1955) and the double-sided, emotion-laden, 'Need Your Love So Bad'/'Home At Last' (1956). Combining jazz strains with elements of R&B and gospel, the elegantly attired John scored his first crossover hit in 1956 with his hauntingly beautiful signature piece, 'Fever'; unfortunately, John's version of 'Fever' was surpassed on the pop charts by Peggy Lee's cover version. During this period, John befriended labelmate James Brown, hiring him as opening act. John's hits continued with the Joe Seneca-penned 'Talk To Me, Talk To Me' (1958), 'Tell It Like It Is' (1958), 'Leave My Kitten Alone' (1959), 'Heartbreak' (1960), a cover of Fred Waring's 1924 recording, 'Sleep' (1960), and his final chart entry, 'Take My Love (I Want To Give It All To You)' (1961). A heavy drinker who squandered his money, John was dropped by King Records in 1963. The Beatles recorded a reworked version of John's 'Leave My Kitten Alone' (which finally saw release on their *Anthology* albums in the Nineties) and Madonna scored an international hit with 'Fever' in 1993. John's sister, Mabel John, recorded for Motown/Tamla and Stax, and sang back-up for Ray Charles in the Raelletes.

CAUSE: Charged with assault by authorities in Miami in 1964, John jumped bail and fled to the West Coast. There he was involved in a bar fight, killing Kendall Roundtree. When John had returned to his table after a trip to the restroom, he found Roundtree in his seat. When Roundtree refused to move, the pair engaged in a brief scuffle. Unconscious after falling and hitting his head, the dying Roundtree was ignored by bar patrons for over an hour. Charged with Roundtree's death, John again jumped bail. Recaptured, John was convicted of manslaughter in a lengthy trial, and given a sentence of eight to twenty years. Jailed at the Washington State Penitentiary in the city of Walla Walla, John died two years later. Although his death is almost always attributed to pneumonia, he actually died of a heart attack. In tribute, James Brown recorded 'Thinking About Little Willie John' in 1968.

Allen Johnson

Born 1940
Died September 28, 1995
The baritone singer of the Pittsburgh-based doo-wop group The Marcels, Allen Johnson replaced original member Richard Knauss. Johnson joined the group immediately after completing an army stint in 1961, a few months after the release of their smash hit, 'Blue Moon'. The group was led by Allen's brother, Fred Johnson. But within a couple of years, Allen Johnson left the group and rejoined the army, retiring from the service in 1982.
CAUSE: Cancer. He died in Pittsburgh.

Billy Johnson

Born 1929
Died May 6, 1987
The guitarist for the early R&B vocal group The Moonglows, Billy Johnson was born and raised in Hartford, Connecticut. A graduate of the Hartford Conservatory of Music, Johnson was a very nimble guitarist. Entering popular music as a session player for artists such as Charles Brown and Sonny Thompson, Johnson eventually settled in Chicago where in 1954 he joined the Harvey Fuqua-led doo-wop outfit The Moonglows, shortly after Chess Records bought the group's contract from the financially doomed Chance label. At Chess, The Moonglows scored their breakthrough hit with 'Sincerely', an emotion-laden ballad. Unfortunately for the group, The McGuire Sisters recorded a competing, 'whitebread' cover version which outpaced the original on the charts. But The Moonglows' hit run continued with 'Most Of All' (1955), 'We Go Together' (1956), another crossover entry 'See Saw' (1956), 'Please Send Me Someone To Love' (1957) and 'Ten Commandments Of Love' (1958), which featured Johnson's vocals prominently. Appearing in the 1957 Alan Freed film *Mr. Rock And Roll*, The Moonglows performed 'Barcelona Rock' and 'Rock Rock Rock'. Leaving The Moonglows, Johnson worked as a guitarist in bands behind Jackie Wilson and Brook Benton. But Johnson would soon follow Fuqua to Motown Records in the early Sixties, and worked with several of the label's hit acts including The Four Tops. Johnson was not part of The Moonglows' 1972 reunion, but continued to work in the music industry as a performer and producer.
CAUSE: Heart failure. He died in Los Angeles.

Buddy Johnson

(WOODROW WILSON JOHNSON)
Born January 10, 1915
Died February 9, 1977
A pioneering jump-blues/R&B bandleader, Buddy Johnson had first toured Europe as a part of The Cotton Club Revue. Returning to the US in 1939, he formed his own swing/jump blues group. After landing a long-term residency at the Savoy Club with his

big band in 1943, he scored a series of hits in the Forties including 'Let's Beat Out Some Love' (1943) and 'That's The Stuff You Gotta Watch'. Recording for Decca, Johnson usually worked with his sister, vocalist Ella Johnson, and with Arthur Prysock. Switching to Mercury Records in 1953 and surviving into the rock era, Johnson scored his final hit in 1956 with 'I Don't Want Nobody (To Have My Love But You)'. Also a songwriter, Johnson's composition 'Since I Fell For You' was a hit for several artists including Paul Gayten and Lenny Welch. Heading a small jazz group late in life, Johnson was also heavily involved in religious activities.
CAUSE: Sickle cell anaemia and brain tumour. He died in New York City.

Claude "Juan" Johnson

Born November 24, 1934
Died October 31, 2002
The "Juan" in the R&B duo Don & Juan, Claude Johnson was previously a member of The Genies. As the lead vocalist of The Genies, Johnson recorded the upbeat doo-wop classic, 'Who's That Knocking?'; although the song was a hit in early 1959, the group had disbanded by year's end. While working as the superintendent of an apartment complex in 1960, Johnson met Roland "Don" Trone, who was painting the exterior of the building. Joining forces as a doo-wop styled duo, Don & Juan landed a recording contract with Big Top Records with the aid of a customer who had heard them harmonising. Originally issued as a B-side, the ballad 'What's Your Name?' reached the Top 10 in 1962, but with management shuffling them from label to label, the duo managed only one more hit, 'Magic Wand', before disbanding in 1967. Johnson later joined the soul group New York City and scored a crossover hit with 'I'm Doin' Fine Now' (the song topped the British charts in 1982 via a cover version by The Pasadenas). Don & Juan returned to the stage in 1981, and following Trone's death in 1982, Johnson formed a new version of the act with former Genies bandmate Alexander "Buddy" Faison.
CAUSE: Unknown.

Ella Johnson

Born June 22, 1923
Died February 16, 2004
A pioneering sultry-voiced jazz-blues singer, Ella Johnson spent nearly two decades in her brother's jump blues-style big band, The Buddy Johnson Orchestra, where she provided lead vocals on a pair of crossover hits – 'When My Man Comes Home' (1944) and 'That's The Stuff You Gotta Watch' (1945) – as well as the R&B hits 'Because' (1950), 'Hittin' On Me' (1953), 'I'm Just A Fool' (1954), '(Gotta Go) Upside Your Head' (1955) and 'Bring It Home To Me' (1956). A native of Darlington, South Carolina, Ella followed her brother to New York City after he formed his own group, but with the rise of rock'n'roll in the mid Fifties, Buddy disbanded his orchestra. Following her brother's death in 1977, Ella retired from music.
CAUSE: Natural causes. She died in New York City.

Ernie "Sweetwater" Johnson

(ERNEST L. JOHNSON, JR.)
Born October 22, 1945
Died August 20, 2005
As a member of soul duo Eddie & Ernie, Ernie "Sweetwater" Johnson scored a minor R&B hit in 1965 with 'Time Waits For No One'. A native of Phoenix, Johnson teamed with singing/songwriting partner Eddie Campbell in the early Sixties, and some of their compositions were recorded by Dee Clark, Jackie Wilson and James Carr.
CAUSE: He was struck by a car in a hit-and-run accident in Phoenix.

Harold Johnson

Born July 4, 1931
Died May 8, 1985
Backing tenor vocalist of the Fifties, Bronx-based doo-wop group, The Crickets (not Buddy Holly's group), Harold Johnson was a member of its first line-up in 1951. Originally a quartet, the group was completed with the addition of lead singer Grover Barlow. Johnson and the group recorded for MGM, and then their manager's label, Jay-Dee, landing their only national hit with 'You're Mine' (1953). Barlow disbanded the original Crickets in mid-1953 and quickly assembled a new backing band.
CAUSE: Unknown.

Howie Johnson

Born 1938
Died January 1988
The original drummer of the pioneering, instrumental surf-rock group The Ventures, Howie Johnson joined the group in 1959. Formed as The Versatones in Seattle, the quartet recorded on its own Blue Horizon label. Within months, the renamed Ventures scored a genre defining hit with their second single, a cover of Johnny Smith's 'Walk Don't Run', the first of a long string of guitar-driven instrumentals. Signed to the larger Dolton Records, the group spawned a host of imitators. After sustaining severe injuries in an automobile accident in 1961, Johnson left the band. In all, he appeared on The Ventures' first three albums.
CAUSE: Unknown.

Hubert Johnson

Born January 14, 1941
Died July 11, 1981
A member of soul-vocal group The Contours, Detroit born and raised Hubert Johnson joined a predecessor of the group in 1960 called The Blenders (not the Forties group of the same name). Auditioning for Motown in 1960, the group was initially rejected by label head Berry Gordy Jr. But with the aid of Johnson's cousin Jackie Wilson, The Contours signed with Motown in 1962. The group scored its first hit with 'Do You Love Me?' (1962), a song that had originally been offered to The Temptations. Penned by Gordy, the explosive dance record catapulted the group into the charts, and gave Motown its first million-seller. Although the song failed to chart in England, a cover version by Brian Poole & The Tremeloes topped the charts. The Contours followed with several more hits, beginning with 'Shake Sherry' (1963), before Johnson left the group in 1964. The 1987 smash film Dirty Dancing highlighted The Contours hit 'Do You Love Me?', with the reissued single returning to the pop charts.
CAUSE: Suicide by gunshot.

Johnnie Johnson

(JOHNNIE CLYDE JOHNSON)
Born July 8, 1924
Died April 13, 2005
A talented pianist and songwriter who was pivotal in the success of Chuck Berry, Johnnie Johnson remained an obscure figure in rock'n'roll until a few years before his death. Following a stint in the Marines during World War II, Johnson settled in Chicago where he honed his piano skills in the city's blues clubs. Landing in St. Louis in the early Fifties, he formed The Sir John Trio. On New Year's Eve, 1952, Chuck Berry was hired as a replacement for an ailing member of the group. A natural showman, Berry was retained and quickly assumed the group's leadership. With Berry signing as a solo act to Chess Records in 1955, Johnson continued to back Berry for the next two decades. Never receiving credit for the songs he helped Berry compose, Johnson would instead be paid small lump sums, less than $1,000. After parting with Berry, Johnson rarely performed until the Nineties, when he returned to the stage

on a more regular basis. Alleging that he co-wrote many of Berry's hit songs, Johnson sued Berry in 2000 but lost because the statute of limitations had long expired. Despite the lawsuit, Johnson and Berry continued to perform together on occasion. At Johnson's 2001 induction into the Rock and Roll Hall of Fame, Keith Richards referred to him as "the foundation for Chuck's sound".
CAUSE: Natural causes. He died at his home in St. Louis.

Ken Johnson

(KENNARD JOHNSON)
Born July 3, 1951
Died March 19, 2005
A member of The Steve Miller Band in the mid Seventies, blues-trained drummer Ken Johnson appeared on Miller's hit albums *Fly Like An Eagle* (1976) and *Book Of Dreams* (1977). A native of St. Louis, Johnson was still in his teens when he worked with Ike & Tina Turner, and in the early Seventies, Johnson began a long stint with bluesman James Cotton. After working with The Chi-Lites and Steve Miller, Johnson moved to New Orleans where he worked with Louisiana Red before joining The Kenny Neal Band for a 13-year run.
CAUSE: Suffering from diabetes complications, he died at his home in Jonesboro, Georgia.

Kripp Johnson

(CORINTHIAN JOHNSON)
Born May 16, 1933
Died June 22, 1990
Lead singer for the doo-wop vocal group The Del Vikings, Kripp Johnson honed his vocal skills alongside his brothers in a series of church groups. Serving in the US Airforce in the mid Fifties, Johnson was stationed in Pittsburgh. There he formed an off-hours vocal group in 1956 with several other servicemen. After winning a number of Armed Forces talent contests, the group caught the attention of Pittsburgh DJ Barry Kaye. Recording in Kaye's small basement studio, the group was helped by local record distributor Joe Averbach. One of the first racially integrated rock groups, The Del Vikings enjoyed a genre-defining hit with 'Come Go With Me'; initially released by the small Fee Bee label, the record was picked up by the larger Dot label. Johnson sang behind the lead vocals of Norman Wright and Gus Baker; but because the group members were still serving in the Airforce, not every member appeared on every record. After following up with another upbeat hit, 'Whispering Bells', The Del Vikings splintered into two different groups. While Fee Bee retained the group led by Johnson and Don Jackson, Mercury controlled the group led by bassist Clarence Quick. While Quick's group scored a Top 40 hit with 'Cool Shake' (1957), the Mercury version was less successful. Fans, distributors and record stores soon backed off from both groups. Johnson eventually moved to the Mercury version of the group and by 1959 sang on tracks such as 'Flat Tire' and 'When I Come Home'. The group recorded with a number of labels including ABC-Paramount before disbanding in 1965. Johnson joined a revival version of the Del Vikings in 1981.
CAUSE: Prostate cancer. He died at his home in Pontiac, Michigan.

Lonnie Johnson

(ALONZO JOHNSON)
Born February 8, 1889
Died June 16, 1970
Prolific and influential New Orleans-born blues, R&B and jazz singer and guitarist, Lonnie Johnson began as a violinist in his father's group. After touring Britain in 1917–19, he returned home to find all but one brother dead from the flu epidemic. Devastated, John fled to St. Louis with his sole surviving brother

and joined a series of jazz bands. Then winning a talent contest in 1925, Johnson was signed by OKeh Records. Usually playing a 12-string guitar, Johnson often teamed with guitarist Eddie Lang, and recorded with Duke Ellington's orchestra and Louis Armstrong and his Hot Five. Moving to Chicago, Johnson recorded for Bluebird Records during the war years, his output highlighted by the hit, 'He's A Jelly Roll Baker'. Landing at King Records in 1947, Johnson often substituted an electric guitar for an acoustic model, landing on the R&B charts with hits such as 'Tomorrow Night', 'Pleasing You (As Long as I Live)' and 'So Tired'. Experiencing lean times in the late Fifties, Johnson took a job as a janitor. Rediscovered in the Sixties, Johnson switched to a more sleek jazz-styled blues.
CAUSE: Struck by a car in Toronto in 1969, he died the following year.

Marv Johnson

Born October 15, 1938
Died May 16, 1993
A popular gospel-trained Sixties soul artist, Detroit-born Marv Johnson originally toured in Southern carnivals as the featured vocalist in The (Junior) Serenaders. Quitting after a serious car crash, he returned to Detroit for a long recuperation. Meeting Berry Gordy Jr., who was operating a jazz record store, Johnson recorded a Gordy-produced single in 1958 on the Flick Records subsidiary, Kudo. Then, with Gordy parting with Jackie Wilson, Johnson became the recipient of Gordy's compositions, beginning with 'Come To Me' which became the first single issued on Gordy's new Tamla label. The song received national airplay and was then leased to United Artists in order to raise money for Gordy's record company. A smooth baritone, Johnson followed with a song he co-wrote with Gordy and others, 'You Got What It Takes' (1959), the track originally intended for Aretha Franklin's sister, Erma Franklin, but first recorded by Bobby Parker. Johnson's follow-up hits included the Gordy-penned 'I Love The Way You Love' (1960) and '(You've Got To) Move Mountains' (1960). Johnson managed two more hits with 'I Miss You, Baby' (1966) and the British Top 10 entry, 'I'll Pick A Rose For My Rose' (1969). With his career ebbing, Johnson worked as a Motown executive in the Seventies, overseeing promotions. Leaving Motown, Johnson remained a popular draw on the oldies circuit in the US and Europe. Johnson, Smokey Robinson and Martha Reeves later conceived the idea for a Motown Museum at the former Hitsville Studio in Detroit.
CAUSE: After performing at a tribute concert on May 14 for Bill Pinckney of The Drifters in Columbia, South Carolina, Johnson suffered a stroke backstage. He died two days later at Richmond Memorial Hospital.

Norman Johnson

Born 1935
Died February 1970
Bass singer of the early Sixties doo-wop group The Jive Five, Norman Johnson had teamed with several friends on a basketball court in the Bedford-Styvesant section of New York City. Featuring the lead vocals of Eugene Pitt, the group enjoyed several ballad and novelty-styled hits beginning with the Top 5 entry, 'My True Story'.
CAUSE: He contracted pneumonia while walking in Toronto.

Raymond Johnson

Born c. 1930
Died c. 1980
Best known as the bass singer of the early doo-wop group The Blenders, Raymond Johnson had previously been a member of The Beavers, a NewYork City-based Coral Records group formed in 1949 by music teacher/manager Joe Thomas. Johnson

left The Beavers in 1950 to join The Blenders, a Ravens-like vocal group formed two years previously by short-lived Ravens tenor Ollie Jones. Johnson left The Blenders in 1951 before they switched from MGM to their more successful stint at Jay-Dee Records. Johnson later joined the Savoy Records group, The Marshall Brothers.
CAUSE: Unknown.

Robert Johnson

(ROBERT LEROY JOHNSON)
Born May 8, 1911
Died August 16, 1938
Innovative and legendary blues guitarist, Robert Johnson gained massive fame and respect decades after his death. Born fatherless in Hazelhurst, Mississippi, Robert Johnson was dragged from farm to farm by his field labourer mother. Settling with her in Robinsonville, Mississippi, Johnson first learned how to play the harmonica. Sneaking into blues joints, he would pester guitar masters such as Son House and Charlie Patton into showing him how to play guitar. A proficient guitarist by his late teens, Johnson left his bleak sharecropping past for the blues road and toured heavily throughout the South (and even north into Canada). Characterized by an intricate, bottle-neck, slide guitar-style, Johnson's compositions were as revolutionary as they were intriguing. Johnson claimed that his musical skills were the result of a compact with the devil, the deed consummated at midnight on a Mississippi crossroads. With his high and shrill vocals, Johnson conjured up images of the underworld in songs such as 'Hell Hound On My Trail' and 'Me And The Devil Blues'. Managing only two recording sessions, the first in 1936 when he was 25, Johnson completed such standards as 'I Believe I'll Dust My Broom', 'Cross Road Blues', 'Sweet Home Chicago', 'Love In Vain', 'Traveling Riverside Blues', and his best selling 78, 'Terraplane Blues'. Playing a variety of musical styles, Johnson toured the country in 1938 with blues guitarist Johnny Shines, and he also gained a reputation as a notorious womaniser. Then with news of his death slow to emerge, Johnson was searched out by Vocalion Records, a pair of Library of Congress musicologists, and New York City promoter John Hammond who had planned to hire Johnson for the Spirituals To Swing concert at Carnegie Hall. Johnson was rediscovered when Columbia Records reissued an album of his material in 1961. His songs were covered mostly by British acts including Cream ('Crossroads'), The Rolling Stones ('Love In Vain' and 'Stop Breaking Down'), and Led Zeppelin ('Travelling Riverside Blues'). Always a shadowy figure, Johnson was heavily researched in the Seventies when the first of two known photographs of him finally emerged. A lost Johnson song is a sub-plot in the 1986 film *Crossroads* and Cleveland-based Robert Junior Lockwood, Johnson's step-son, is a blues star in his own right. Performances from every last living musical connection to Johnson were compiled on the 1992, Grammy-nominated album, *Root Of Rhythm And Blues: A Tribute To The Robert Johnson Era*. In 2004, Eric Clapton released an album of Johnson covers, *Me And Mr. Johnson*, selling about 500,000 copies. Clapton had unsuccessfully attempted to purchase the rights to some of Johnson's music before issuing the album. The Mississippi Supreme Court ruled in 2000 that 68-year-old Claude Johnson was Robert Johnson's illegitimate son, and therefore a legal heir, entitled to over a million dollars in royalties.
CAUSE: There are three competing explanations of how Johnson perished. Most likely, he died from ingesting rat poison. The victim of a jealous husband, the womanising Johnson

drank from a bottle of poison-laced moonshine whiskey unknowingly brought to him by his paramour. Johnson died after four excruciating days, allegedly swearing off the blues and accepting Christianity shortly before his death. CBS Records later donated $10,000 to a fund to mark a gravesite next to Mt. Zion Missionary Baptist Church near Morgan City, Mississippi. The 2,000-pound monument was dedicated on April 20, 1991. Some dispute also exists over his exact burial spot: Johnson might have been buried two miles away in the yard of the Payne Chapel Missionary Church in Quito, and a smaller marker was placed there.
FURTHER READING: Guralnick, Peter. (1998). *Searching For Robert Johnson*. New York: Plume.

Ruby Johnson

Born April 19, 1936
Died April 5, 1999
A one-hit artist, Memphis-based soul singer Ruby Johnson landed on the charts in 1966 with a Stax/Volt single, the emotionally charged 'I'll Run Your Hurt Away'. Trained in music at her Jewish temple, she first released some obscure discs at V-Tone and Nebs Records. Leaving the industry in 1974, she took a civil service job.
CAUSE: Unknown. She died in Lanham, Maryland.

Tommy Johnson

Born 1896
Died November 1, 1956
Delta blues pioneer who was a contemporary of Charlie Patton and Son House, Tommy Johnson recorded a number of groundbreaking discs in his brief recording career from 1928 to 1930. Recording for RCA-Victor and Paramount Records, his best known numbers included 'Maggie Campbell', 'Big Road Blues' and 'I Asked For Water'. His composition 'Canned Heat Blues' inspired the name of the Sixties blues-rock group Canned Heat. A hard drinker and womaniser who, like Robert Johnson (no relation), claimed to have sold his soul to the devil in exchange for musical prowess, Tommy Johnson was a consummate performer, who could play the guitar behind his back. A full-voice singer who would play for hours upon end, he toured with a medicine show in the Thirties. Although a major influence in the blues community, Johnson spent the last decades of his life working in Mississippi juke joints. Johnson's composition 'Cool Water Blues' was later reworked by Howlin' Wolf as 'I Asked For Water'.
CAUSE: He suffered a heart attack while performing at a house party in Crystal Springs, Mississippi.

Andrew "Chet" Jones

Born November 17, 1934
Died June 25, 1998
The bass vocalist of The Turbans, Andrew "Chet" Jones performed on the doo-wop standard, 'When You Dance' (1955). Written by Jones and featuring lead singer Al Banks' soaring falsetto, the song was highlighted by Latin tinged percussion. Following several more regional hits, including 'Congratulations', Jones quit The Turbans but rejoined in 1960 for some sessions on Roulette, before leaving again the following year.
CAUSE: Unknown.

Billy Jones

(WILLIAM HARRY JONES)
Born November 20, 1949
Died September 7, 1995
Original guitarist and backing vocalist of the Southern-rock outfit The Outlaws, Billy Jones co-founded the group in 1972. Jones shared lead guitar duties in the band with Hughie Thomasson and Henry Paul. Formed in Tampa, the group enjoyed hits with 'Green Grass And High Tide', 'There Goes Another Love Song', and a cover of the standard, '(Ghost) Riders In The Sky'. Jones left the group in 1981.

CAUSE: Suicide. He died in Spring Hill, Florida.

Brian Jones

(LEWIS BRIAN HOPKIN-JONES)
Born February 28, 1942
Died July 3, 1969
Founder and original lead guitarist of The Rolling Stones, Brian Jones craved fame like a junkie craves heroin, but when he found it he was unable to cope and his early death – like those of Jimi Hendrix, Janis Joplin and Jim Morrison – became a metaphor for the end of the Sixties' dream. "Brian died a little every day," was one comment from a fellow Sixties rock star, an indication that few who knew him were terribly surprised when his body was fished out of the swimming pool at his country home. Brian Jones was born in Cheltenham, England, to middle-class parents. His mother was a piano teacher and Jones inherited natural musical talent, although his tastes ran more to American jazz and blues than popular songs, and as a teenager he taught himself to play both the saxophone and guitar. He dropped out of school after impregnating a local girl, a scandal that embarrassed his family, and played briefly with a local group called The Ramrods while working in labouring jobs and as a bus conductor. Moving to London, he took a day job in a department store, and eventually worked his way up to an occasional gig in Alexis Korner's Blues Incorporated. By age 20, Jones had sired another illegitimate child; by the time of his death he would have fathered five children and possibly six. In 1962 Jones placed an advertisement in *Jazz News* seeking fellow R&B enthusiasts to form a blues group, hiring first pianist Ian Stewart; eventually, singer Mick Jagger, guitarist Keith Richard, saxophonist Dick Taylor, and future Kinks' drummer Mick Avory would also join his band. Taking their name from a Muddy Waters' song, The Rolling Stones, with Charlie Watts now on drums and Bill Wyman on bass, were performing regularly around the Richmond (West London) area in 1963 and drawing big crowds at London's Marquee. A blues fanatic, Jones was musically more skilled than the rest of the group and in these early days he, at least, considered himself their leader. Making a splash in the British press with their long hair, scruffy clothes and all-round contemptuous behaviour, Jones and the group signed with Decca Records and quickly gained a huge following in Britain, second only to The Beatles. Meanwhile, to Jones' chagrin, Jagger was slowly emerging as the group's leader, a situation that was compounded when he and Keith Richards began writing the group's material after their initial success with Chuck Berry's 'Come On' (1963) and the Lennon-McCartney composition, 'I Wanna Be Your Man'. In the summer of 1964, the Stones scored their first US Top 40 hit with 'Tell Me (You're Coming Back)' and later in the year they created a stir with their *Ed Sullivan Show* début. By the end of 1964, The Rolling Stones were at the forefront of the British Invasion alongside The Beatles, but fame sat uneasily within Jones' fragile psyche and it wasn't long before he experienced the first of several drug overdoses. At first it all helped to nurture their bad boy image while the group enjoyed a dazzling string of hits, including 'It's All Over Now', 'The Last Time', the polemic '(I Can't Get No) Satisfaction', 'Get Off Of My Cloud', 'Paint It Black', 'Let's Spend The Night Together' and more. By this time Jones was contributing a variety of unusual stylistic influences to the Stones' music, sitars, harpsichords and flutes amongst them, and there is no doubt this helped to keep the group fresh and interesting in an era when the competition – from both sides of the Atlantic – was at its zenith. By 1966 Jones had entered into a stormy

relationship with Anita Pallenberg, a beautiful but tempestuous German actress. For a while they were among pop's golden couples, their blond fringes and dandified clothes making them look so similar as to appear almost interchangeable, but there was a dark undercurrent to their relationship which manifested itself in violent fights. Behind the facade Jones was struggling to cope with fame and his diminishing role in the Stones, and turning increasingly to drugs of all kinds. In May, 1967, he was busted for marijuana possession, an incident that received much press coverage, not least because Jagger and Richards were remanded in court for drug offences on the same day. There were calls from the establishment for jail sentences to be handed down – to teach them all a sharp lesson – but Jones was fortunate to find himself up before a lenient judge who concurred with psychiatrists' evaluations, and he got off with a fine and three years probation. Within a week, however, Jones would require hospitalisation for his condition, euphemistically described in the press as "exhaustion", though "acute paranoia" would be a more accurate description. When the group recorded the drug-oriented, psychedelic-themed album Their *Satanic Majesties Request* (1967), Jones was disappointed by its relative failure and from this point on his actions served only to alienate him further and further from the rest of the band. Busted for drugs a second time in May 1968, Jones was again found guilty, but he eluded jail by promising to rehabilitate himself. By this time Pallenberg had left him for Keith Richards after a dramatic episode in Morocco, and her desertion in favour of a fellow Stone further upset inter-band relations. His new girlfriend was the high-profile model Suki Poitier, but thereafter Jones' behaviour became more and more erratic as he found himself pushed to the sidelines by Jagger and Richards. *Beggar's Banquet* (1968) was a return to form for the Stones, though it is generally believed that Jones' contribution to the album was minimal. Indeed, there was a telling dialogue in the studio when Jones asked Jagger, "What can I play?" "Good question. What *can* you play, Brian?" retorted Mick. The announcement – on June 9, 1969 – that Jones had left the group came as no surprise to insiders. He was replaced by Mick Taylor, a fine young blues guitarist who had cut his teeth with John Mayall. When he left, the now seriously unstable Jones claimed he was unhappy with the Stones' pop turn, but it is more likely that Jagger had forced him out since Jones' drug convictions, mental problems and inability to perform prevented the group from touring the US. Obviously, he'd become a liability. Announcing his intention to form a new band, Jones first asked to join Alexis Korner's band, New Church, but was turned down. He then approached John Lennon, The Beatles having all but called it a day, but Lennon was in no mood to humour Jones either. During the last few months of his life, Jones visited Morocco and his recordings of local pipe music were posthumously released.

CAUSE: What is known for certain is that Jones drowned after a midnight dip in the pool of his 16th century home, Cotchford Farm, in Hartford, Sussex, once the residence of Winnie The Pooh creator, A.A. Milne. After inviting friends over for the evening, Jones had decided to take a swim. Jones suffered from asthma and had placed his inhaler by the side of the pool. Joining Jones for a swim were his 21-year-old live-in girlfriend Anna Wohlin and building contractor Frank Thorogood, who was living in the garage while working on various projects throughout the estate, and Thorogood's friend Janet Lawson. Jones was later discovered in the deep end of the pool by Wohlin and pulled from the water. Both Wohlin and Lawson, who was a nurse, began performing CPR but were unable to revive him. Jones had consumed both drugs and alcohol that day, and the coroner's ruling was "death by misadventure". By all accounts, Jones was an excellent swimmer. Two days after Jones' death, a quarter of a million spectators assembled for a free Rolling Stones concert at London's Hyde Park (the show had already been planned and acted as a tribute). In remembrance of Jones, Mick Jagger recited poetry by Shelley and released 3,500 white butterflies. Alexis Korner's band, New Church, also performed. Less than a week after Jones' death, Jagger's girlfriend, Marianne Faithfull, was clinging to life in an Australian hospital after a drug overdose. The mystery of Jones' death intensified after the alleged deathbed confession of Frank Thorogood that he had murdered Jones, presumably by holding his head underwater, only hours after Jones had reprimanded him for poor workmanship. Thorogood resented the rich young musician and frequently insulted him. The alleged murder was explored in British director Stephen Woolley's 2005 documentary, *Stoned*. In the unreleased Rolling Stones film *Charlie Is My Darling* (1965), Jones said that he didn't expect to live past the age of 27. Tiles from the swimming pool were offered for sale to the public by a Brian Jones Appreciation Society in 2000.

Burnetta "Bunny" Jones

Born April 6, 1917
Died May 10, 1998
A former beauty salon owner turned music entrepreneur, Burnetta "Bunny" Jones emerged as a music socialite in the New York black community. With one of her nine salons located just a block from the Apollo Theater, she developed close ties with entertainers such as Jackie Robinson, Eddie O'Jay and Jimi Hendrix. She later operated the New York-based Astral Studios and collaborated with Stevie Wonder on his hit, 'Isn't She Lovely'.
CAUSE: Natural causes.

Busta Jones

(MICHAEL JONES)
Born 1951
Died December 6, 1995
Memphis-based session bassist Busta Jones toured with Albert King, Talking Heads, King and Stevie Wonder, and recorded behind David Byrne and Brian Eno. A self-taught musician, he was also a member of The Bombers, The Sharks, and had toured with Gang Of Four in 1981–82 as a replacement for Dave Allen.
CAUSE: Heart failure. He died at his home in Memphis.

Carl Jones

Born June 9, 1913
Died September 24, 1985
As an operator of a trio of Chicago-based labels – C.J., Colt, and Firms Records – Carl Jones issued gospel, Spanish, and doo-wop recordings, but had the most success with his R&B and blues acts, Hound Dog Taylor, Earl Hooker, Lee Jackson, and Betty Everett. A former musician, the Texas-born Jones had been a member of a succession of territorial bands in the Thirties. Landing in Chicago in 1937, he earned a music degree at the Chicago Conservatory of Music, and recorded sporadically as a solo act. He launched his first label, C.J. Records, in 1955.
CAUSE: Unknown. He died in Chicago.

David Jones

Born 1931
Died 1995
As a member of the Brooklyn-based doo-wop group The Four Fellows, David "Sugar Lump" Jones scored an R&B chart hit in 1955 with 'Soldier Boy'. Jones had co-written the song with bandmate Larry Banks while they

were stationed in Korea. Jones quit The Four Fellows in 1956 to join another doo-wop group, The Rays, and as the second tenor behind lead vocalist Walter Ford, he appeared on their double-sided hit, 'Silhouettes'/'Daddy Cool' (1957), while 'Soldier Boy' topped the charts in 1962 via a cover version by The Shirelles.
CAUSE: Unknown.

Jimmy Jones

Born January 31, 1944
Died November 7, 1995
A session bassist, Jimmy Jones performed with Eddie Floyd, T-Bone Walker, Wilson Pickett, and Peggy Scott.
CAUSE: He died of liver disease in Texas City, Texas.

Joe Jones

Born August 12, 1926
Died November 27, 2005
A New Orleans-style R&B pianist and singer, one-hit wonder Joe Jones reached the US Top 10 in 1960 with the comedic 'You Talk Too Much'. Following a stint in the Navy during World War II, he attended New York's Juilliard Conservatory and formed his own musical group, The Atomic Bebops. When Roy Brown recorded his 1948 breakthrough R&B hit 'Good Rockin' Tonight', he hired most of Jones' band for the sessions. After spending time in B.B. King's band in the early Fifties, Jones went solo in 1954. Aided in his career by Sylvia Vanderpool of Mickey & Sylvia, Jones was signed to Roulette Records, but when the label shelved Jones' recording of 'You Talk Too Much', it was issued by Ric Records instead. When the single began garnering airplay, Ric was forced by Roulette to withdraw the record. A follow-up single, 'California Sun', was a minor hit for Jones but reached the Top 10 in 1964 via a surf rock version by The Rivieras. Turning to production work at Red Bird Records, Jones oversaw The Dixie Cups and Alvin Robinson. Relocating to Los Angeles in 1973, Jones launched a music publishing firm.
CAUSE: He died in a Los Angeles hospital of complications following quadruple bypass surgery. He had previously battled colon and prostate cancer.

Linda Jones

Born January 14, 1944
Died March 14, 1972
A talented Sixties soul artist, Linda Jones gained experience in her family's gospel group, The Jones Singers. After unfruitful stints at Atco and Cub Records (at the latter as Linda Lane), she scored her biggest hit in 1967 with 'Hypnotized'. She later recorded for a series of labels including Gamble & Huff's Neptune Records.
CAUSE: After collapsing from a diabetic shock backstage at the Apollo Theater in Harlem, she was rushed to a hospital where she died several hours later.

Michael M. Jones

Born 1942
Died August 18, 1984
A pianist, Michael M. Jones worked with Ike & Tina Turner, B.B. King and others.
CAUSE: He died of cirrhosis of the liver in St. Louis.

Ollie Jones

(HENRY OLIVER JONES)
Born December 9, 1923
Died October 4, 1990
A tenor vocalist, Ollie Jones joined a series of pioneering doo-wop groups in the Forties and Fifties. A founding member of the Baltimore-based Ravens, Jones appeared on their first three singles but left in 1946 just as the group was poised for stardom. After touring throughout the East Coast as a member of The 4 Notes, Jones co-founded The Blenders in 1949. Mentored by Ravens co-founder Jimmy Ricks, The Blenders recorded a string of excellent singles, but only

'Don't Play Around With Love' received any airplay. With the group disbanding in 1954, Jones and bandmate Abel DeCosta formed session vocal group The Cues, with the aid of Atlantic Records arranger Jesse Stone, providing the backing harmonies on hits by Ruth Brown, LaVern Baker, Joe Turner, Ivory Joe Hunter, Ray Charles and Bobby Darin. Although they appeared on scores of records, The Cues' contributions were uncredited. Securing a recording contract, not with Atlantic but with Capitol, The Cues issued a series of singles, two of which scraped the bottom of the pop charts. After the group disbanded around 1960, Jones joined The Billy Williams Quartet and had success as a songwriter with 'Step By Step' (The Crests) and 'Tiger' (Fabian).
CAUSE: Unknown.

Ralph Jones

Born March 25, 1921
Died June 1, 2000
A member of Bill Haley & The Comets, drummer Ralph Jones left his job as a milkman to join the group in late 1955. He was brought in by Haley's sax player Rudy Pompilli, Jones and Pompilli having previously been members of Little Ernie's Four Horsemen, a group from Chester, Pennsylvania. Initially hired only as a touring member, Jones demanded to appear on the group's records and made his début on the 1956 million-selling hit 'See You Later, Alligator'. With the group's fortunes waning after leaving Decca for Warner Brothers Records, Jones quit at the end of a Mexican tour in 1960.
CAUSE: Heart failure. He died at a nursing home in Chester, Pennsylvania.

Randy Jones

(RANDALL JONES, JR.)
Born May 20, 1936
Died June 24, 2002
A baritone/bass vocalist, Randy Jones was a member of several West Coast doo-wop groups. Originally a member of The Meadowlarks – a group of high school students led by Don Julian – Jones was the eldest member but, after recording two singles, Jones left the group and replaced Bruce Tate in The Penguins (a devastated Tate had quit after killing a pedestrian with his car). Recording several singles with The Penguins, Jones provided the lead vocal on just one track, 'Kiss A Fool Goodbye'. Jones also filled in for Richard Berry in The Flairs, appearing on two singles, 'Hold Me, Thrill Me, Chill Me' and 'Love Me, Love Me, Love Me', which the record label credited to The Chimes. Jones subsequently passed through various doo-wop vocal groups including The Jac-O-Lacs, The Peppers, The Cadets and The Flares, and later did some film acting.
CAUSE: During rehearsals as a member of The Jacks (a.k.a. The Cadets) for the 2001 Southern California Doo-Wop Society concert, he suffered a stroke. He passed away 13 months later at a Los Angeles nursing home.

Ray Jones

Born October 2, 1939
Died January 20, 2000
The bassist of Sixties pop-rock group The Dakotas – the backing group for Billy J. Kramer – Ray Jones enjoyed transcontinental success in the shadow of The Beatles. Manchester born Jones had formed the group with original lead singer Pete Maclaine in 1959. Three years later, The Dakotas signed with manager Brian Epstein and were teamed with Liverpool singer Billy J. Kramer, who had previously been backed by a local group called The Coasters. A successful outing at Hamburg's Star Club then led to a contract with Parlophone Records and George Martin who became their producer. Billy J. Kramer & The Dakotas topped the British charts with

a pair of Lennon-McCartney compositions, 'Do You Want To Know A Secret?' and 'Bad To Me'. As a solo act, The Dakotas landed on the charts with the surf-styled instrumental, 'The Cruel Sea', their only hit, in 1963. Behind Kramer, the group continued their hit run with 'I'll Keep You Satisfied', 'Little Children', and 'From A Window'. Earning a pittance with The Dakotas, Jones quit the group in July 1964 and, after passing through a series of rock bands, Jones abandoned music in 1967. He later worked as a psychiatric nurse, and then as a computer instructor for the handicapped.
CAUSE: Unknown. He died in Morecambe, Lancashire.

Rob Jones

Born 1964
Died July 30, 1993
Bassist for the British rock group The Wonder Stuff, Rob Jones replaced founding member Chris Fradgley. Mixing folk with distorted guitar-heavy, garage rock, the group was launched in 1986 as a quartet. A popular club band, The Wonder Stuff recorded a pair of singles in 1987 on their own Far Out label, attracting the attention of Polydor/PolyGram Records. Though remaining relatively unknown in the US, The Wonder Stuff enjoyed British fame with its smart, indie-orientated material. Beginning with the début album, *The Eight Legged Groove Machine*, and continuing with the more successful Hup, The Wonder Stuff enjoyed and scored a string of British hits in the late Eighties with 'It's Yer Money I'm After Baby', 'Who Wants To Be The Disco King', and 'Don't Let Me Down Gently'. But following a series of much publicized internal squabbles, Jones left the group in 1989 and moved to New York City, where he wed Jessie Ronson. There, Jones and his wife formed The Bridge & Tunnel Crew, the eight-piece group signed to PolyGram Records.
CAUSE: Accidental heroin overdose. He died in New York City.

Will "Dub" Jones

(WILLIAM J. JONES)
Born May 14, 1928
Died January 16, 2000
A member of popular R&B/rock band The Coasters, Will "Dub" Jones provided the group with their prominent deep bass vocals. Louisiana-born Jones was reared on gospel music and, after a stint in the US army, he settled in Los Angeles. There he teamed with Ted Taylor and Lloyd McCraw in 1954 to form The (Santa Monica) Soul Seekers. Convinced by A&R man Maxwell Davis of Modern Records to record some non-religious numbers, the group evolved into The Cadets/Jacks. Expanding into a quintet, the group simultaneously recorded as The Cadets on Modern Records and as The Jacks on a subsidiary label, RPM. Jones assumed the nickname "Dub" in order to distinguish him from bandmate Willie Davis. Usually recording cover songs, The Cadets were the more popular of the two monikers, landing a national hit with a remake of The Jayhawks' raucous 'Stranded In The Jungle' (1956). With Bobby Nunn's departure from The Coasters in 1958, Jones replaced him in one of the country's top musical groups. Featuring Jones' prominent deep bass vocals, The Coasters continued their hit run with the chart-topping, 'Yakety Yak' (1958), the million-selling, 'Charlie Brown' (1959), 'Along Came Jones' (1959), and the amusing jab at women, 'Poison Ivy' (1959), a song much covered by beat-boom era British bands including The Rolling Stones. During this period, Jones briefly recorded with Cora Washington as Cora & Dub. With The Coasters leaving Atco Records in 1966, Jones departed from the group and was replaced by Ronnie Bright. Returning to his gospel roots in the Seventies,

Jones re-teamed with former Cadet bandmate Lloyd McCraw and joined several gospel groups including The Mighty Travelers. Jones formed a new version of The Coasters in the Eighties.
CAUSE: Diabetes. He died in Long Beach, California.

Janis Joplin

(JANIS LYN JOPLIN)
Born January 19, 1943
Died October 4, 1970
A blockbuster blues-rock singer in the tradition of Bessie Smith, Janis Joplin was an emotionally scarred woman notorious for her sexual exploits and bouts of drug and alcohol abuse. Born into a middle-class family in Port Arthur, Texas, Joplin was a social outcast who was taunted by her classmates. Schooled in the arts and drawn to poetry, she was taught to play piano by her mother. Also an accomplished painter, Joplin yearned to gain an art degree. Quitting college after one semester, Joplin returned home and took a course in key-punch operation. Unhappy in Port Arthur, she moved to Los Angeles and was drawn to the Venice Beach arts community. She soon found her way to San Francisco's fledgling folk scene and was embraced by like-minded artists and musicians. Returning to Texas in 1962, she enrolled in college and joined an Austin-based country/folk group, The Waller Creek Boys. Acutely embarrassed to have been nominated the "ugliest man on campus", Joplin left school and briefly performed in the folk clubs of New York City's Greenwich Village. She then joined former college classmate Chet Helms and returned to San Francisco in 1964. But with her drug use intensifying, Joplin was near death; emaciated at 88-pound, she returned to Port Arthur in mid-1965. After yet another attempt at college, she left school and became an immediate sensation in the nightclubs of Austin. Turning down an offer to join The 13th Floor Elevators, Joplin instead accepted Helms' offer to front a six-month-old San Francisco group that he was managing called Big Brother & The Holding Company. Financially strapped after being stuck in Chicago, the group reluctantly signed with the small Mainstream Records. Emerging as a star after a captivating, blues-wrenched performance at the Monterey Pop Festival in 1967, Joplin adopted a psychedelic costume of beads and feathers. Rush-released by Mainstream Records, the inconsistent album *Big Brother & The Holding Company* was highlighted by a blues-rock cover of Big Mama Thorton's 'Ball And Chain'. In 1968 manager Albert Grossman negotiated a lucrative contract with Columbia Records, and Joplin topped the album charts for two months with *Cheap Thrills*, the project highlighted by 'Down On Me', a cover of Erma Franklin's 'Piece Of My Heart', and a radical reworking of George Gershwin's 'Summertime'. Instructed by Grossman to hire a new backing band, Joplin assembled The Kozmic Blues Band. But despite this success Joplin was racked with insecurities, and she began abusing heroin. With her new group, Joplin recorded *I Got Dem Ol' Kozmic Blues Again Mama!*, which spawned the hits 'Kozmic Blues' (1969) and 'Try (Just A Little Bit Harder)' (1970). After briefly reuniting with Big Brother & The Holding Company for a pair of live appearances in April 1970, Joplin expanded The Kozmic Blues Band into the Full Tilt Boogie Band, Joplin's most proficient backing group. Though engaged to be married, and her career on an upswing, Joplin was unable to break her heroin habit. During the middle of recording sessions, Joplin was found dead, the victim of an accidental heroin overdose. Her final tracks were released on *Pearl*, a highly accomplished album which spawned the posthumous

number 1 single 'Me And Bobby McGee'.
CAUSE: Heroin overdose. She was found dead in her room at the Landmark hotel in Hollywood, California, with a needle sticking out of her left arm. She had been drinking at a club the previous night.
FURTHER READING: Friedman, Myra. (1973). *Buried Alive*. New York: William Morrow.

John Jordan

Born November 7, 1913
Died June 16, 1988
Lead singer of the black vocal harmony outfit The Four Vagabonds, John Jordan and his group were regulars on the radio programme *The Breakfast Club*.
CAUSE: Unknown. He died in Chicago.

Louis Jordan

(LOUIS THOMAS JORDAN)
Born July 8, 1908
Died February 4, 1975
The "Father of Rhythm & Blues", Brinkley, Arkansas-born Louis Jordan was taught to play clarinet and saxophone by his father, a former dance band leader turned music teacher. Spending his summers in his teen years in a travelling minstrel show, Jordan sang, danced and played his saxophone. While enrolled in the Arkansas Bible College in the late Twenties, he spent his evenings performing in local juke joints with artists such as Charlie Gaines. Restless, Jordan headed for the East Coast in the early Thirties. After passing through a series of groups in Philadelphia and New York, Jordan landed in Chick Webb's band, an all-star ensemble that recorded on Decca. Playing his sax and providing the occasional vocal, Jordan left the Harlem-based group after Webb's death in 1938. But while he was with Webb, Jordan organized his own smaller combo within the group, The Elks Rendezvous Band. Renaming the group Louis Jordan & his Tympany Five in 1939, Jordan originated the shuffle-boogie beat, a close precursor of rock'n'roll. A danceable outgrowth of blues music, Jordan's sound was later labelled "jump blues". Leading the top-selling black group of the Forties, Jordan charted with a remarkable string of hits including 'I'm Gonna Leave You At The Outskirts Of Town' (1942), 'G.I. Jive'/'Is You Is Or Is You Ain't (Ma' Baby)' (1944), the Little Richard-like 'Caledonia' (1945), 'Beware' (1946), a rare million-seller, 'Choo Choo Ch'Boogie', a cover of 'Open The Door, Richard' (1947) and 'Saturday Night Fish Fry' (1949). A pioneering crossover artist, Jordan had wide acceptance among whites, with his records issued on Decca's coveted "personality" imprint. With his often exaggerated comic stage antics, Jordan was occasionally attacked by black critics who viewed his behaviour to be racially demeaning. Jordan also appeared in a number of films including *Follow The Boys, Meet Miss Bobbysox*, and his self-financed, all-black musical, *Beware*. Unable to survive into the rock era, Jordan's final release at Decca came with the appropriately titled 'Nobody Knows You When You Are Down And Out'. After flirting with big band music in the early Fifties, he retired from music. Sporadically returning to the studio beginning in 1956, Jordan formed a new version of The Tympany Five in 1964. Jordan's final appearance came at the 1973 Newport Jazz Festival.
CAUSE: He died of a heart attack at his Los Angeles home. He had suffered his first heart attack the previous year.
FURTHER READING: Clifton, John. (1997). *Let The Good Times Roll: The Story Of Louis Jordan and His Music.* Ann Arbor: University of Michigan Press.

Tim Jordan

Born 1981
Died December 13, 2005
A touring member of punk band The

All-American Rejects, keyboardist Tim Jordan joined in mid-2005. He was previously a guitarist for the group Welton and keyboardist for Number One Fan.
CAUSE: He committed suicide in his hometown of Camden, Arkansas.

Nat Joseph

(NATHAN JOSEPH)
Born July 23, 1939
Died August 30, 2005
The founder of the pioneering independent British record label Transatlantic Records, Nat Joseph built his company by distributing American releases that the major UK labels had rejected. A native of Birmingham, he entered the record business after quitting his Columbia University teaching post in 1960, and was drawn to music after discovering the American folk and blues genres while traversing the country. Eventually recording his own artists, Joseph issued material by Alexis Korner, Mike Oldfield, Bert Jansch, Pentangle and The Humblebums (which included members Billy Connolly and Gerry Rafferty). Connolly later turned to comedy and recorded the label's biggest seller, *Solo Concert*. Selling a controlling stake in Transatlantic Records to the Granada television network in 1975, Joseph left the label two years later and turned to theatre production and management.
CAUSE: Stricken with Parkinson's disease, he died of pneumonia.

Judge Dread

(ALEX HUGHES)
Born May 2, 1945
Died March 13, 1998
Kent, England-born, Seventies ska/reggae-flavoured singer, Judge Dread enjoyed a series of hits including 'Big Six' (1972), 'Big Seven' (1972), and 'Je T'aime (Moi Non Plus)' (1975). A former bar bouncer and wrestler, Dread had based his first two hits on Prince Buster's bawdy club hit, 'Big 5'. But with their overtly sexual lyrics, many of Dread's songs appeared on the charts but received no radio airplay on the BBC. He continued to record and perform regularly into the Nineties.
CAUSE: He suffered a heart attack and collapsed onstage near the completion of a concert at Canterbury while performing one of his hits, 'The Winkle Man'. His final words were "Let's hear it for the band." With Dread a consummate prankster, the audience assumed that it was part of the stage act. He died soon after at a nearby hospital.

Don Julian

Born April 7, 1937
Died November 6, 1998
Lead singer and guitarist of the Fifties, Los Angeles-based, doo-wop group The Meadowlarks, Don Julian recorded at Dootone Records beginning in 1955. A much revered harmony outfit, The Meadowlarks landed their biggest hit with the ballad, 'Heaven And Paradise' (1955). Emerging as The Larks in 1961 (not be confused with the group of the same name that recorded for Apollo and Lloyds), Julian scored a hit in 1964 with 'The Jerk'. After flirting with soul and funk in the Seventies, he performed as Don Julian And The Larks until shortly before his death.
CAUSE: Complications of pneumonia. He died in Los Angeles.

Bill Justis

(WILLIAM E. JUSTIS, JR.)
Born October 14, 1926
Died July 16, 1982
A prolific session player and producer who crossed over from jazz into rock, R&B, jazz, and even country, Bill Justis was encouraged into music by his mother. Born in Birmingham, Alabama, and moving as a young child to Memphis, he first picked up the saxophone. After completing a Navy stint, Justis formed a swing jazz combo

in 1950. During this time he also worked as a musical director at Tulane and the University of Arizona. Embracing rock music, Justis was hired by Sam Phillips in 1954 as the musical director for Sun Records. There he worked with greats such as Elvis Presley, Johnny Cash, Jerry Lee Lewis, Roy Orbison, and others. But Justis was fired from Sun in 1959 after fighting with Phillips over the label's musical direction, preferring an R&B sound over Phillips' pop-orientated leanings. As a recording artist, Justis scored his own Top 10 hit with a saxophone-rooted song he co-wrote, which featured guitarist Sid Manker, 'Raunchy' (1957). After joining Mercury Records in 1961 as an A&R man, Justis became an independent arranger, working with a number of artists including Ray Charles, Willie Nelson, Brenda Lee, Bobby Vinton, and Brook Benton. In 1972, Justis moved to Memphis to be closer to the music industry. Justis also provided the music for several films including *Smokey And The Bandit* (1977) and *Hooper* (1978). In his career, Justis worked on hundreds of albums and singles with countless acts including, Fats Domino, Frank Sinatra, Ray Charles and Tom Jones.

CAUSE: Possibly cancer.

K

Ernie K-Doe

(Ernest Kador)
Born February 22, 1936
Died July 5, 2002
A New Orleans-based R&B singer, nicknamed "The Emperor", Ernie K-Doe scored his biggest hit with the rollicking Allen Toussaint novelty composition 'Mother-In-Law' (1961). A veteran performer, K-Doe recorded several regional hits including 'Popeye Joe' and 'Certain Girl' (covered by UK R&B group The Yardbirds for their first single) for a series of labels beginning with the Chicago-based United Records. In 1994, he opened a nightclub in New Orleans, the Mother-In-Law Lounge.
Cause: Suffering liver failure, he died at University Hospital in New Orleans.

John Kahn

Born June 13, 1947
Died May 30, 1996
Best-known as the bassist in the Grateful Dead side-project, The Jerry Garcia Band, John Kahn joined the group in 1972, appearing on several albums beginning with *Hooterall.* Kahn had met Garcia at a weekly, free-form jam session at the Keystone Korner nightclub in San Francisco's North Beach. Playing both the electric and stand-up bass, Kahn also worked with Maria Muldaur, Al Kooper, Nick Gravesnites, and another Grateful Dead alumni, Merle Saunders. Following Garcia in the bluegrass group, Old & In The Way, Kahn employed an acoustic bass on the group's self-titled album. Also an artist, Kahn provided the cover art for two of Garcia's albums.
Cause: He died at his home in Mill Valley, California, from a drug overdose.

Harold Kalin

Born February 16, 1934
Died August 23, 2005
A member of The Kalin Twins, Harold Kalin had sung with identical twin brother Herbert from a young age. Their career interrupted by Harold's stint in the Army, The Kalin Twins moved to Washington DC in 1957, where they were befriended by songwriter Clint Ballard who helped them land a contract with Decca. Recording a composition their manager hated, The Kalin Twins scored a surprise million-selling, B-side hit in 1958 with 'When', which topped the UK charts for over a month. Often compared to The Everly Brothers, Harold and Herbert Kalin continued their brief hit run with 'Forget Me Not' (1958) and 'It's Only The Beginning' (1959). 'When' returned to the UK charts in 1977 via a cover version by Showaddywaddy.
Cause: Auto accident. He died in Waldorf, Maryland.

Michael Kamen

Born April 15, 1948
Died November 18, 2003
A Grammy and Oscar winning composer who was prolific in both the classical and pop music fields, Michael Kamen was the son of liberal activists. Mastering a series of musical instruments as a child, he studied the oboe at Juilliard and, combining rock with classical music, formed The New York Rock And Roll Ensemble, recording a total of five albums. As a composer, he wrote film scores – including *Lethal Weapon* and *Die Hard* – and co-wrote the Bryan Adams hit '(Everything I Do) I Do It For You'. Kamen worked with an incredibly wide assortment of musical artists including the London Philharmonic, Pink Floyd, Sting, Rod Stewart, Aerosmith, Metallica, Eric Clapton, George Harrison, and David Sanborn. Inspired by the Richard Dreyfuss film *Mr. Holland's Opus,*

Kamen established the Mr. Holland's Opus Foundation in 1997 to raise money to make musical instruments available to children.
CAUSE: Suffering from multiple sclerosis, he suffered a heart attack and died at his home in London.

Arthur "Killer" Kane

(ARTHUR HAROLD KANE, JR.)
Born February 3, 1949
Died July 13, 2004
As a member of The New York Dolls, bassist Arthur "Killer" Kane was at the forefront of the glam-rock movement in the mid Seventies. A native of New York City, Kane was trained on the clarinet but switched to bass guitar at age 16. Influenced by the second generation of British Invasion bands, he joined high school friend Rick Rivets to form a covers group called London Fogg, which evolved into The Poor Boys, and then a roots rock band, The Berrys (in a nod to Chuck Berry). Kane studied hotel management at Pratt Institute but quit school in 1969 and, along with Rivets, left the US for the Netherlands and Britain. Deported on the expiration of his visa, Kane returned to New York City where, in 1971, he teamed up with David Johansen, Johnny Thunders, Sylvain Sylvain and Billy Murcia to form a pioneering gender-bending, glam-rock outfit, The New York Dolls. After emerging as the house band at the proto-punk nightclub Max's Kansas City, the group signed with Mercury Records, and recorded a pair of critically acclaimed albums, the Todd Rundgren-produced *New York Dolls* (1973) and the George Shadow Morton-produced *Too Much Too Soon* (1974). Earning patchy airplay with 'Personality Crisis' and 'Trash', the Dolls managed only one real hit, a cover of The Cadets' novelty number, 'Stranded In The Jungle'. Dropped by Mercury for their profligate behaviour, the struggling band hired visiting British impresario Malcolm McLaren as their manager. With McLaren unwisely forcing the group members to trade their make-up and glam clothing for Red Chinese Communist outfits, the Dolls were greeted with public outrage. After the group disbanded amid drug and alcohol problems, Kane formed a new group in Florida, Killer Kane and, relocating to Los Angeles, he joined a number of lesser-known outfits including The Corpse Killers and The Idols, but none of these post-Dolls projects achieved any level of success. After converting to the Mormon faith in 1989, Kane worked at a Mormon temple in LA and, shortly before Kane's death in the summer of 2004, British singer Morrissey convinced the surviving members of The New York Dolls to perform together for the first time in nearly three decades for two appearances at the Meltdown Festival in London. Falling ill almost immediately afterwards, Kane bowed out of the re-formed Dolls before a scheduled tour.
CAUSE: Believing he was suffering from influenza, Kane was unaware that he had contracted leukaemia, and died in Los Angeles shortly after the diagnosis. Kane was the fourth member of The New York Dolls to die an early death, following Billy Murcia (1972), Johnny Thunders (1991) and Jerry Nolan (1992).

Carlo Karges

Born July 31, 1951
Died January 30, 2002
A member of German new wave band Nena, guitarist Carlo Karges wrote their hit '99 Luftballons'. Nena was formed by singer Nena Kerner and her drummer boyfriend Rolf Brendel. Before joining, Karges passed through the bands Tomorrow's Gift, Novalis and Extrabreit. After scoring a hit in Germany with their début single 'Nur Geträumt', Nena followed up with '99 Luftballons', an English language

version of which ('99 Red Balloons') became a worldwide hit, propelled on to the US charts by a popular MTV video. Nena released a total of six albums before disbanding in 1987. Karges continued to collaborate with Nena Kerner during her solo career, writing much of her material. He later operated Cafe Carlo, a bar in Berlin.
CAUSE: A heavy drinker, he developed liver disease. He died at his mother's home in Hamburg, Germany.

Michael Karoli

Born April 29, 1948
Died November 17, 2001
As a member of German rock band Can, guitarist Michael Karoli scored a 1976 UK hit with the David Gilmour-composed 'I Want More'. An avant-garde, free-form psychedelic group, Can originally formed in 1968 as Inner Space and, with the departure of lead vocalist Kenji "Damo" Suzuki in 1974, Karoli began sharing lead vocal duties with Irmin Schmidt. After Can split in 1978, Karoli pursued a solo career in the mid Eighties. Can reunited in 1989 for the album, *Rite Time*.
CAUSE: Cancer. He died in Essen, Germany.

Terry Kath

(TERRY ALAN KATH)
Born January 31, 1946
Died January 23, 1978
Guitarist, singer and founder member of the jazz-rock group Chicago, Chicago-native Terry Kath first taught himself to play his older brother's drum kit. Moving to the banjo and, at 15, guitar, he learned riffs by playing along to surf tunes. He took guitar lessons from a jazz instructor at age 18 but yearned to play rock music. Joining a friend's band which had just completed a Dick Clark caravan tour, Kath was forced to switch to the bass guitar. Then teaming with future Chicago drummer Danny Seraphine, Kath formed The Missing Links. After hiring a manager, who changed the group's name to The Big Thing, Kath switched back to the rhythm guitar. The group's lead singer and songwriter, Kath was soon joined by several friends from the University of Chicago. The group's manager, record industry insider James Guercio, then renamed the band Chicago Transit Authority. Playing an eclectic brand of Latin, jazz, classical and rock, the group briefly relocated to Los Angeles in 1967, finding only sporadic club work. But with Guercio pulling strings at CBS Records, the group was signed to the label in early 1969. Produced by Guercio, the group's jazz-rock fusion packed double-album *Chicago Transit Authority* was a hit, highlighted by 'Questions 67 and 68' and a cover of The Spencer Davis Group's 'I'm A Man'. Threatened with legal action by the real Chicago Transit Authority (the city's bus line), the group shortened its name to Chicago. Containing their first US pop hits of 'Make Me Smile' (1970) and '25 Or 6 To 4' (1970), the group's next album *Chicago II*, reached the Top 10. Then in April of 1971, Chicago became the first rock group to play Carnegie Hall. The group was originally centred around Bobby Lamm's lead vocals and Kath's extended, fuzz-tone guitar solos, and they became almost as famous for their italicised logo (and the fact that each successive album was simply titled *Chicago III, IV, V* etc) as they did for their increasingly stylised music. Although ignored in Britain, Chicago remained one of the top bands in the US during the Seventies with hits such as 'Saturday In The Park' (1972), 'Feelin' Stronger Everyday' (1973), 'Just You'N'Me' (1973), 'Old Days' (1975), and 'If You Leave Me Now' (1976). *Chicago XI* was the group's final album produced by Guercio and the last one with Kath. From it came the Top 10 single, 'Baby, What A Big Surprise' (1977), as well as two

posthumous chart entries. Kath was planning a solo album at the time of his death. Shocked by Kath's death, the group considered disbanding. Eventually, Kath was replaced by Donnie Dacus, formerly with Boz Scaggs and Stephen Stills.
CAUSE: After three days on a booze and drugs binge without any sleep, he had arrived at a friend's home in Woodland Hills, California, having just returned from a session at a shooting range. While cleaning a gun with a bullet lodged in the chamber, he accidentally shot himself.
FURTHER READING: O'Shea, Mary. (1975). *Chicago*. Creative Education: Mankato, MN.

John "Speedy" Keen

(JOHN DAVID PERCY KEEN)
Born March 29, 1945
Died March 29, 2002
The drummer and lead singer of rock act Thunderclap Newman, London-born John "Speedy" Keen was previously a member of several minor British beat groups including The Tomcats and The Cat. As Pete Townshend's personal assistant and chauffeur, one of his earliest compositions, 'Armenia City In The Sky', was recorded by The Who, appearing on the 1967 album *The Who Sell Out*. The song sounded remarkably like something Townshend might have written himself. A year later, Townshend assembled a band around Keen, adding jazz pianist Andy "Thunderclap" Newman, a post office engineer, and 15-year-old Scottish guitarist Jimmy McCulloch. Written by Keen, Thunderclap Newman scored a psychedelic-tinged, UK number one over the summer of '69 with 'Something In The Air', which Townshend produced, arranged the string section and contributed bass under the pseudonym Bijou Drains. Never comfortable as a live act, the group released their only album, *Hollywood Dream*, in 1970. Keen later released two solo albums, *Previous Convictions* (1973) and *Y'Know Wot I Mean* (1975), which spawned the minor hit 'Someone To Love', and toured France with The Who. Turning to production work, Keen oversaw Johnny Thunders & The Heartbreakers' 1977 punk album *L.A.M.F.* (the poor mixing and mastering of which drew strong criticism) and Motörhead's 1977 début *Motörhead.* A perennial favourite on rock radio, 'Something In The Air' has appeared in numerous films and commercials and was a minor hit in 1993 for Tom Petty & The Heartbreakers.
CAUSE: Heart attack.

Brian Keenan

Born January 28, 1945
Died c. 1985
Drummer of the psychedelic-soul group The Chamber Brothers, New York City-native Brian Keenan was the last to join the previously all-sibling group. Relocating to London at 18, he played briefly with Manfred Mann but returned to New York in 1966 at age 21 and joined The Chamber Brothers, a group consisting of four Mississippi-rooted, gospel-trained brothers. Keenan was hired after Bob Dylan invited him to join the group for an impromptu performance at Ondine's nightclub in New York City. Swerving toward a psychedelic sound, the previously all-black group drew praise at the Newport Folk Festival in 1965, and at the Avalon and Fillmore Auditorium in San Francisco. Signing with Columbia Records in 1967, The Chamber Brothers landed a psychedelic-soul hit with 'Time Has Come Today' (1968); the five-minute single had been edited from the album's original 11-minute version. Labeled a "black hippie band", the Chamber Brothers were popular on college campuses until 1970. But following run-ins with record company brass and internal squabbling, Keenan left the

group in 1972. While Keenan joined Genya Revan's band, the rest of them returned to gospel music, backing Maria Muldaur and others. Keenan owned and operated his own recording studio in Connecticut during the Eighties.
CAUSE: Heart attack.

Tommy Keifer

Born August 21, 1957
Died December 24, 1986
The guitarist for Krokus, Tommy Keifer co-founded the Swiss-based heavy metal band in 1974. Originally a progressive rock outfit, Krokus made rapid strides in the US with the expertise of former Black Oak Arkansas manager Butch Stone. After recording several Europe-only releases, the group achieved its breakthrough in 1981 with *Hardware*, featuring the track 'Winning Man'. Keifer left the group soon after and was replaced by Randy Meier.
CAUSE: Suicide by hanging. He had been ill for some time.

Marion Keisker

Born September 23, 1917
Died December 29, 1989
Sam Phillips' secretary and assistant at Sun Records in Memphis, Marion Keisker played an instrumental role in the discovery of Elvis Presley. A native of Memphis, she knew Phillips from radio station WERC where they both worked. Keisker made history when on July 18, 1953, Elvis Presley came to the Memphis Recording Studio and recorded a vanity record. Impressed by his voice and appearance, she took notice of the shy young man. In early 1954, Keisker would suggest to Phillips that he record Presley. Keisker left Sun Records in 1957 and joined the US Air Force, working in Armed Forces television in West Germany (where at one point she ran into Presley). After returning to the US, she worked in the Office of Information. Retiring from the service in 1969, she returned to Memphis and worked in local theatre.
CAUSE: Cancer.

Jack Keller

Born November 11, 1936
Died April 1, 2005
A Brill Building songwriter in the Sixties, Jack Keller was hired by Don Kirschner of Aldon Music. In collaboration with lyricist Howard Greenfield, Keller co-wrote Frank Sinatra's 'When Somebody Loves You', Jimmy Clanton's 'Venus In Blue Jeans' and a trio of hits for Connie Francis, 'Breakin' In A Brand New Broken Heart', 'Everybody's Somebody's Fool' and 'My Heart Has A Mind Of Its Own'. After Aldon was absorbed by the television production firm Screen Gems in 1963, Keller and Greenfield composed a number of television themes including *Bewitched* (which originally featured a vocal) and *Gidget*, as well as writing and producing for The Monkees. Greenfield later teamed with Ernie Sheldon to write 'Seattle', the theme of the Bobby Sherman Western comedy, *Here Come The Brides*.
CAUSE: Leukaemia. He died at a Nashville hospital.

Kevin Kelley

(KEVIN DANIEL KELLEY)
Born March 25, 1943
Died April 6, 2002
Briefly a member of The Byrds, drummer Kevin Kelley appeared on only one album – the commercially unsuccessful but highly influential, country-oriented *Sweetheart Of The Rodeo*. Kelley was previously a member of The Rising Sons, a Los Angeles group which included Taj Mahal and slide guitarist Ry Cooder. After recording an unreleased (at the time) album, the group disbanded in 1966. After passing through a group called Fusion, in 1968, Kelley joined his cousin Chris Hillman in The Byrds, but by the end of that year, Kelley had been replaced by Gene Parsons. Kelley then joined Fever Tree, who had previously recorded the psychedelic classic 'San Francisco Girls'. After

recording just one album, *For Sale*, Kelley quit in 1970. He would later work with John Fahey, Phil Ochs (on the album *Gunfight At Carnegie Hall*) and then the Jesse Barish-led group, Jesse, Wolf & Whings.
CAUSE: Natural causes. He died in North Hollywood, California.

Alfonzo "Country" Kellum

(ALFONZO RAMANO KELLUM)
Born September 25, 1943
Died March 24, 2000
A pioneering funk-based guitarist in James Brown's backing band, Alphonso "Country" Kellum was a crucial part of Brown's rhythm section for a seven-year stint beginning in 1963. Though hired as a bassist, he soon switched to rhythm guitar behind Jimmy Nolan. Pioneering the "chicken scratch" style of rhythm, Kellum co-wrote a number of Brown hits including 'Lowdown Popcorn', 'Mother Popcorn', and 'I Love You'. Leaving Brown during a shake-up of the group in 1970, Kellum joined Maceo & All The King's Men. Settling in Rochester, New York, in 1972, Kellum made an occasional foray back on stage.
CAUSE: Heart disease. He died in Rochester, New York.

Jo-Ann Kelly

Born January 5, 1944
Died October 30, 1990
Early British R&B and blues artist who was inspired by Memphis Minnie, Jo-Ann Kelly often performed with her brother Dave. Recording for several labels including CBS, her best known hit came with 'Same Thing On Their Minds'. Late in her career, she incorporated jazz into her repertoire.
CAUSE: She died during surgery for a brain tumour. She had been diagnosed two years earlier.

Tim Kelly

Born January 13, 1963
Died February 5, 1998
Guitarist for heavy-metal band Slaughter, Tim Kelly was born and raised near Philadelphia, and was inspired to play guitar at 13 after buying a Kiss album. Meanwhile, in 1989 Mark Slaughter and Dana Strum had quit the Vinnie Vincent Invasion to launch their own group. Meeting Slaughter at a backyard barbecue, Kelly was asked to join the band. Based in Las Vegas, Slaughter arrived at the tail-end of the Eighties heavy-metal revival, their first live gig coming in 1990 as the opening act for Kiss. Produced by the entire group, Slaughter's début album Stick It To Ya sold three million copies, and was highlighted by hits such as the anthemic 'Up All Night' (1990), the power-ballad 'Fly To The Angels' (1990), 'Spend My Life' (1991) and 'Real Love' (1992). But the group was shaken in 1993 when Dana Drum was injured in a motorcycle accident and Kelly was arrested for possessing drugs, and charged with transporting cocaine in a nationwide smuggling ring. Pleading guilty, Kelly was fined $15,000, sentenced to three years probation and six months in a half-way house. Leaving EMI Records, members of Slaughter were unhappy with the label's inattention to their albums. But Slaughter was forced to compete with itself when EMI issued a greatest hits package at the same time as the group released its CMC International label début Fear No Evil. At the time of his death, Kelly had just finished recording tracks for a new Slaughter album.
CAUSE: He died in a car crash, six miles south of the mining town of Bagdad, Arizona. The car he was driving was struck head-on by a jack-knifing 18-wheel truck which had gone left of centre. Kelly's 1996 Hyundai struck a third vehicle and rolled over, leaving the road. Kelly died at the scene. His passenger Alice Montana, 25, of Las Vegas, was the owner of the Hyundai; she was treated

for minor injuries and released. The driver of the third vehicle, Pedrego Joscelynn, 30, was also injured.

Wells Kelly

Born 1949

Died October 29, 1984

The drummer for several Seventies rock groups, Wells Kelly first joined a band called Thunderfrog; led by future Orleans leader John Hall, the group disbanded in 1972 when Kelly left to form King Harvest. After appearing on one album and scoring a Top 20 hit with 'Dancing In The Moonlight' (1973), Kelly left soon after to join Boffalongo. But Wells and bandmate Larry Hoppen were lured by John Hall in 1975 into a Woodstock/Ithaca-based band called Orleans. Expanded into a quartet with the addition of Larry Hoppen's brother Lance, Orleans was a sensation on the East Coast, and quickly signed by ABC-Dunhill. Recording at the Muscle Shoals Studio, Orleans enjoyed hits with the pop-rock flavoured, 'Dance With Me' (1975), 'Still The One' (1976) and 'Love Takes Time' (1979). Leaving Orleans in 1980, Kelly then worked with rocker Meatloaf.

CAUSE: He choked to death on his own vomit after returning home from a party in London. According to the coroner, Kelly had been snorting heroin and cocaine. He was dropped off by a taxi and never made it inside.

Eddie Kendricks

(EDWARD JAMES KENDRICKS)

Born December 17, 1939

Died October 5, 1992

An original member of the legendary Motown vocal group The Temptations, Eddie Kendricks was born in Union Springs, Alabama, but raised in Birmingham. While attending high school, Kendricks met future Temptation Paul Williams, with both youths singing in local R&B doo-wop groups. Moving to Cleveland, Kendricks washed dishes during the day, and at night sang blues in a local group called The Majestics. After attempting a solo career in Detroit, Kendricks reunited with Williams in a group called The Primes. Managed by Milton Jenkins, The Primes were signed by Motown Records in 1960. Jenkins also managed a group called The Distants led by Otis Williams (no relation to Paul), and in 1961 he combined members of the two groups to form The Temptations. Featuring Elbridge Bryant on lead vocals, the group's first single was 'Oh, Mother Of Mine'. Though quiet and reserved, the bespectacled Kendricks fitted in well into the group's elegant look. After collaborating with Motown songwriter Smokey Robinson, The Temptations landed their first hit in 1964 with 'The Way You Do The Things You Do'; featuring Kendricks' tenor and mild-falsetto vocals, the song catapulted the group to stardom. Featuring the lead of David Ruffin, The Temptations enjoyed a remarkable string of hits including the pop standard 'My Girl' (1965), 'Get Ready' (1966), 'Ain't Too Proud to Beg' (1966), 'Beauty Is Only Skin Deep' (1966), '(I Know) I'm Losing You' (1966), 'All I Need' (1967), 'You're My Everything' (1967) and 'I Wish It Would Rain' (1968). A highlight of their stage show was the group's stunning choreography, with spins, twists and twirls all executed with a panache that would make today's 'boy bands' green with envy. Kendricks shared the lead vocals with Diana Ross on the Temptations/ Supremes duet, 'I'm Gonna Make You Love Me'. Following David Ruffin's departure in 1968, the group adopted a harder, rock-oriented sound on hits such as 'Cloud Nine' (1968) and 'Ball Of Confusion' (1970). After years of internal squabbling, Kendricks left the group in 1971, his final hit with The Temptations coming with 'Just My Imagination' which was later covered by The Rolling Stones. Kendricks' solo career was quick to take off, and he landed on the R&B chart with 'If You Let Me' (1972), the funk-based 'Keep On Truckin' (Part 1)' (1973), 'Boogie Down' (1973), 'Shoeshine Boy' (1975) and 'He's A Friend' (1976). Kendricks' solo output was more funk-flavoured and less pop-oriented than his Temptations output. After recording nine solo albums for Motown's Tamla subsidiary, Kendricks left Motown in 1977. Although his career faded at Arista Records, he managed an R&B hit in 1978 with 'Ain't No Smoke Without A Fire'. After a brief stint at Atlantic Records, Kendricks launched his own label, Dixie. He returned to The Temptations in 1982 for the group's *Reunion* album and tour, and they enjoyed renewed popularity during this period thanks to the film *The Big Chill.* In 1984 Kendricks dropped the "s" from his name, reportedly because Motown actually owned the trademark to his name. A year later, Kendrick and former bandmate David Ruffin scored a hit single, 'A Nite At The Apollo Live! The Way You Do The Things You Do/My Girl', in collaboration with Daryl Hall and John Oates. A subsequent album, *Ruffin And Kendrick*, spawned a pair of minor R&B hits, 'I Couldn't Believe' and 'One More For The Road'. In 1991, Kendrick sued Motown Records over royalties as both a solo artist and a member of The Temptations. Stricken with cancer and struggling to pay his medical bills, Kendrick's final tour was with former Temptation Dennis Edwards.

CAUSE: Cancer. He attributed his illness to years of smoking cigarettes. He had one of his lungs removed in 1989.

FURTHER READING: Turner, Tony; & Aria, Barbara. (1992). *Deliver Us From Temptation: The Tragic And Shocking Story Of The Temptations And Motown.* Emeryville, CA: Thundermouth. Williams, Otis, with Patricia Romanowski. (1988). *Temptations.* New York, Putnam.

Doris Kenner-Jackson

(DORIS COLEY)
Born August 2, 1941
Died February 4, 2000

A member of Sixties girl group The Shirelles, Doris Kenner-Jackson formed the outfit with her junior high classmates in Passaic, New Jersey. From Goldsboro, North Carolina, she moved to Passaic in her early teens. Originally called The Poquellas (Spanish for birds), the group of Kenner-Jackson (née Coley), Beverly Lee, Mickey "Addie" Harris and Shirley Owens sang an original composition at a school assembly, where an impressed schoolmate convinced the sceptical group to audition for her mother, Florence Greenberg, the owner of the small Tiara Records. With Greenberg also becoming their manager, the renamed Shirelles recorded several tracks which were leased to Decca Records. Issued a year later, 'Dedicated To The One I Love', The Shirelles reworked début cover of The "5" Royales doo-wop tune featuring Kenner-Jackson on lead vocals, was ignored. With Decca losing interest in the group, The Shirelles joined Scepter Records, a new label formed by Greenberg and songwriter Luther Dixon. The group found fame with songs about teenage romance, landing on the charts with the seminal 'Will You Love Me Tomorrow' (1960), a re-released 'Dedicated To The One I Love' (1961), 'Mama Said' (1961), 'Baby It's You' (1962), 'Soldier Boy' (1962), and 'Foolish Little Girl' (1963). Married to her first husband in 1963, she was frequently replaced on tour by Dionne Warwick. The Shirelles' final hit came in 1963 with 'Don't Say Goodnight When You Mean Goodbye'. Promised a trust fund at age 21 but paid nothing, Kenner-Jackson and The Shirelles left Sceptor Records. Unable to record due

to contractual obligations, The Shirelles eventually released a pair of albums at RCA Records. Remarried, Kenner-Jackson left the group in 1968 to become a housewife. Working for a shipping company in the Seventies, Kenner-Jackson rejoined The Shirelles in 1975 and assumed the role of lead singer.
CAUSE: Breast cancer. She died at Kaiser Permanente Medical Center in Sacramento, California.

Chris Kenner

Born September 30, 1929
Died January 25, 1976
An R&B singer and songwriter, Chris Kenner was born in suburban New Orleans. After a stint in the choir at his father's church, Kenner joined a gospel group The Harmonising Four. During this period, Kenner worked as a longshoreman. After discovering blues, he left gospel for secular music, and recorded briefly at the New York-based label, Baton Records. Signing with Imperial Records, he scored an R&B hit with 'Sick And Tired' (1957), the song hitting the pop charts the following year via a cover version by Fats Domino. After releasing two singles, Kenner was dropped by Imperial because label owner Lew Chudd saw no potential in the alcohol-abusing singer. Signing to the fledgling Instant label, Kenner scored his signature hit with a song he wrote two years earlier, 'I Like It Like That' (1961). Earning a Grammy nomination, the Allen Toussaint-produced single was inspired by the popular "Popeye" dance craze. Kenner's follow-up, 'Land Of A Thousand Dances', a reworked spiritual song, fared poorly. The song was later reprised by both Cannibal and The Headhunters and Wilson Pickett. Other Kenner cover hits included 'Something You Got' by Alvin Robinson (1964) and the duo of Chuck Jackson and Maxine Brown (1965), and 'I Like It Like That' by The Dave Clark Five (1965). Squandering his earnings, Kenner was destitute by the late Sixties. Convicted of statutory rape in 1968, Kenner was imprisoned; released in 1972, he spent the remainder of his life trying to jumpstart his career.
CAUSE: He died of a heart attack in a New Orleans' rooming house.

Richard Kermode

Born October 5, 1946
Died January 16, 1996
Noted San Francisco-based jazz-rock keyboardist, Richard Kermode worked with Janis Joplin, Santana, and others. Born in Wyoming but raised in Buffalo, he emerged as a jazz wizard on the Hammond-B3 organ. Recruited by Joplin, he joined her latter group The Kosmic Blues Band, backing the blues-rock singer for her stunning Woodstock performance. After her death, he joined Santana for three albums. He also worked with Carlos Santana's brother, Jorge Santana. Kermode later returned to his jazz roots.
CAUSE: Cancer. He died in Denver.

Ron Kersey

(TYRONE GARFIELD KERSEY)
Born April 7, 1949
Died January 25, 2005
A talented producer, keyboardist and songwriter at Philadelphia International Records, Ron Kersey played an essential role in the success of the label in the Seventies. A Philadelphia native, after completing a stint in the US Air Force, Kersey joined the record company in 1973 as a session player. As a member of the disco/soul group The Trammps, Kersey co-wrote their smash hit 'Disco Inferno', which greatly benefited from its inclusion on the *Saturday Night Fever* soundtrack. Quickly tiring of life on the road, Kersey left the group and returned to the session and production side, working with The O'Jays, Patti LaBelle, Lou Rawls, Robert Palmer,

Teddy Pendergrass and others. Kersey was also the lead keyboardist of the session group MFSB, which topped the charts in 1974 with the single 'TSOP', and played a key role in the disco/swing band Salsoul Orchestra.
CAUSE: Complications from pneumonia. He had been seriously ill after suffering a stroke in the mid Nineties. He died in Philadelphia.

Barney Kessell

Born October 17, 1923
Died May 6, 2004
A guitarist, producer, songwriter and session player, Barney Kessell was reared in the Big Band jazz tradition, joining orchestras led by Benny Goodman, Charlie Barnet, Charlie "Bird" Parker, and Artie Shaw. Drawn to bebop jazz in the Fifties, Kessell was hired as the guitarist in The Oscar Peterson Trio. As the A&R chief at Verve Records in the late Fifties, Kessell oversaw the career of teen sensation Ricky Nelson. Turning to session work during the rock era, Kessell performed on several Elvis Presley albums, numerous Lieber & Stoller productions and a number of Beach Boys hits including 'I Get Around' and 'California Girls'. Relocating to London in the late Sixties, Kessell was a popular draw at Ronnie Scott's nightclub in Soho, and in his later years he became a music educator, writing a monthly column for *Guitar Player* magazine.
CAUSE: Suffering from brain cancer, he died in San Diego. He was diagnosed in 2001. He survived a stroke in 1992.

Bert Keyes

Born 1934
Died July 21, 1980
A pop-rock songwriter and arranger, Brooklyn-born Bert Keyes was trained at the Brooklyn Conservatory of Music. A proficient arranger and conductor, he worked with hit acts such as Bobby Darin, The Marcels, Etta James, and Ike & Tina Turner. Also a songwriter, he penned The Moments' hit 'Love On A Two Way Street'.
CAUSE: He died from undisclosed causes at his home in Central Islip, New York.

Jimmy Keyes

Born May 22, 1930
Died July 22, 1995
As first tenor of the doo-wop group The Chords, Jimmy Keyes provided the lead vocals on one of rock's first breakthrough crossover hits, 'Sh-Boom'. Born in Kentucky, he moved to the Bronx in 1947, where by 1950 he formed a vocal group called The Four Notes. In 1953, Keyes and other group members joined The Tunetoppers. Signing with the Atlantic Records subsidiary Cat, the group became The Chords and gave Atlantic its first pop major crossover hit with 'Sh-Boom', the song penned by Keyes and Carl Feaster. Unfortunately, the song was a bigger hit via a cover version by an all-white group, The Crew Cuts. The Chords followed up with the moderately selling single, 'Zippity-Zum', their last hit. Forced to drop their name after legal threats from an obscure group also called The Chords, the renamed Chordcats (and then Sh-Booms) fared poorly. With the change in identity, the group faded from public view and soon disbanded. Joining a soul band, The Popular Five, Keyes re-recorded 'Sh-Boom'. Keyes and Carl Feaster reformed The Chords in the late Seventies. Feaster died in 1981 and Keyes maintained a touring group into the Eighties. Keyes backed Willie Mays on the novelty single 'Say Hey, Willie'.
CAUSE: He suffered an aneurysm during surgery in a Bronx, New York, hospital.

Johnny Kidd

(FREDERICK HEATH)
Born November 23, 1939
Died October 7, 1966

British singer, songwriter and leader of Johnny Kidd And The Pirates, Johnny Kidd left a lasting mark on popular music by composing the rock standard, 'Shakin' All Over'. One of a tiny handful of pre-Beatle British rockers to win lasting respect, Kidd earned his nickname from the eyepatch he wore over his right eye. Self-taught on the guitar and banjo, he boasted a strong tenor voice and was a natural showman. Trained from school as an interior decorator, Kidd turned to music in the late Fifties and formed a skiffle group The Five Nutters, which he renamed Johnny Kidd And The Pirates in 1958. Signing with EMI's subsidiary label HMV, the group reached the British Top 30 in 1959 with the Kidd co-penned, 'Please Don't Touch'. Adopting a pirate-style presentation, Kidd and group (guitarist Alan Caddy, bassist Brian Gregg and drummer Clem Cattini) donned pirate costumes and seafaring stage props, and Kidd was rarely seen without an antique naval cutlass. A sensation across Britain, the group enjoyed a trio of hits in 1960: a cover version of Marv Johnson's 'You Got What It Takes', 'Shakin' All Over' and 'Restless'. 'Shakin' All Over', a 12-bar blues variation in E minor with a repeated descending guitar riff echoed with a secondary riff on bass, really did send "shivers down the backbone" and is widely regarded as the greatest pre-Beatles British rock song. When the hits dried up in the summer of 1961 Kidd's group quit to back Tony Hicks, Tommy Steele's brother (Caddy and Cattini would later become members of The Tornados of 'Telstar' fame), but Kidd hired a new crew, amongst them the much underrated guitarist Mick Green whose ability to combine rhythm and lead influenced many fledgling players on the London scene. After waiting two years to return to the Top 40, Kidd scored a pair of British hits with the Merseyside-influenced 'I'll Never Get Over You' and 'Hungry For Love' (both 1963). A minor British hit, 'Always And Forever' (1964) would be Kidd's final chart entry. After a series of subsequent failures, Kidd disbanded the rapidly disintegrating Pirates. Shortly after, in 1965, Kidd hired The Regents (not the US group) as The New Pirates, but having lost its musical focus, the new outfit found little success with its mix of rock, R&B and country. The group toured heavily until Kidd's death. Meanwhile, two of Kidd's early hits would be revived, 'Shakin' All Over' by The Guess Who (1965) and 'You Got What It Takes' by The Dave Clark Five (1967). Kidd and his group The Pirates are important because they were among the earliest in England to feature a solo singer backed by bass guitar, drums and a *single* guitarist, alternating between rhythm and lead. The Pirates often supported The Who (then The Detours) on the West London gig circuit and proved influential in persuading Roger Daltrey to switch from guitar to sole lead vocalist. The Who later paid tribute to Kidd by releasing a stirring version of 'Shakin' All Over' on their million selling *Live At Leeds* album (1970).

CAUSE: He died in a car crash on the M1 motorway near Bury in Lancashire, England. The group's van was struck by a skidding truck. The recently married Kidd was killed instantly. One of the survivors of the crash in Kidd's car was The Pirates' last bass player Nick Simper, who later joined Deep Purple.

Theola Kilgore

Born December 6, 1926
Died May 15, 2005

A gospel rooted singer, Louisiana-native Theola Kilgore enjoyed a brief career in R&B, originally as Theola Kilgord. While singing gospel music, she was discovered by Sam Cooke's manager, J.W. Alexander, who introduced her to

singer-songwriter Ed Townsend. Townsend wrote and produced her 1963 singles, 'The Love Of My Man' and 'This Is My Love', while 'Sounds Of My Man' was written as an answer to Cooke's hit 'Chain Gang'.
CAUSE: Natural causes. She died in a Los Angeles convalescence home.

Tommy Killebrew

Born c. 1936
Died c. 1980
Later member of Fifties doo-wop group The Five Satins, Tommy Killebrew joined in 1957, appearing on the group's second and final hit, the melodious 'To The Aisle' (1957).
CAUSE: Unknown.

Walter Kimble

Born October 6, 1938
Died February 28, 1988
Saxophone player in Fats Domino's band, Walter Kimble also worked in bands behind Ray Charles, Professor Longhair, Huey Smith, and Bobby "Blue" Bland.
CAUSE: Pneumonia.

Junior Kimbrough

(DAVID KIMBROUGH)
Born July 28, 1930
Died January 17, 1998
Mississippi-born country blues singer and guitarist, Junior Kimbrough enjoyed fame only in the latter part of his career. Considered a regional act until late in life, his career took off after being profiled in the 1991 Robert Palmer film *Deep Blues*. Signed by Fat Possum Records in 1992, Kimbrough released three critically acclaimed albums. Kimbrough's finest output was compiled on the 1998 album, *God Knows I Tried*. In his lifetime, Kimbrough sired 36 children.
CAUSE: Heart failure.

King Biscuit Boy

(RICHARD ALFRED NEWELL)
Born March 9, 1944
Died January 5, 2003
The first Canadian blues artist to place an album on the US charts, King Biscuit Boy was a master of both the harmonica and slide guitar. A native of Hamilton, Ontario, he was originally a member of the blues-rock band The Barons from 1961 to 1965. In 1967, he joined Ronnie Hawkins' band and was dubbed King Biscuit Boy because of his ability to play the guitar like bluesman Sonny Boy Williamson, the host of the pioneering *King Biscuit Flour Hour* radio programme at KFFA in Helena, Arkansas. After Hawkins fired his backup band in 1969, King Biscuit Boy recorded a pair of albums with his former Hawkins bandmates under the name Crowbar. Signed as a solo artist by Epic in 1974, he teamed with producer Alan Toussaint and backing band The Meters on a self-titled album. King Biscuit Boy would record for a variety of labels over the next two decades, issuing fine albums such as *Mouth Of Steel*, *King Biscuit Boy AKA Richard Newell* and *Urban Blues Re: Newell*.
CAUSE: Unknown. He died in his sleep at his home in Hamilton, Ontario, Canada.

King Curtis

(CURTIS OUSLEY)
Born February 7, 1934
Died August 13, 1971
Legendary R&B saxophonist who worked with dozens of big name artists on hundreds of records, Texas-born King Curtis was a child prodigy and musical virtuoso. Initially playing alto sax, he switched to the more popular R&B-style, tenor sax in the tradition of Louis Jordan. Shortly out of high school, Curtis landed a coveted spot behind jazz great Lionel Hampton; here he was forced to adapt to Hampton's improvised playing style. After recording some obscure singles at the RPM and Monarch labels in 1953, Curtis was

hired as a session player at Atlantic Records, working behind a plethora of hit artists such as Bobby Darin, Wilson Pickett and Aretha Franklin. For a time he was considered an unofficial member of The Coasters, with his rasping sax prominent on raucous hits such as 'Yakety Yak'. In the Fifties, he was a central figure in promoter/deejay Alan Freed's house band at New York's Paramount Theater. Forming his own band in 1958 (The Noble Knights and later, The Kingpins), King Curtis was a regular in New York City clubs. Recording for several labels including Capitol and Atco, he scored a number of hits including 'Soul Twist' (1962), 'Soul Serenade' (1964), 'Memphis Soul Stew' (1967), and 'Ode To Billie Joe' (1967). In the late Sixties, King Curtis produced blues guitarist Freddie King and operated a thriving publishing company. King Curtis' album, *King Curtis Live At The Fillmore West* (1971), featured Billy Preston on organ, and later albums included *Mr Soul* (1972), *Everybody's Talking* (1973) and *Jazz Groove* (1974). At the time of his death, Curtis was working with John Lennon and Sam & Dave. Curtis' influence was a key element in the musical constituents of Bruce Springsteen's E Street Band whose saxophonist, Clarence Clemons, was clearly a respectful disciple. It was an influence that gave Springsteen and his band a style that, at its best, often seemed to encapsulate the entire history of rock'n'roll and R&B, turning them into what many critics in the Seventies and Eighties considered to be the best "bar band" in the world.
CAUSE: He was returning to an apartment building he owned with an air condition unit in his arms when he asked two junkies, who were shooting up on the front stoop, to move. One of the junkies stabbed him through the heart. King Curtis died the next morning at Roosevelt Hospital. The attacker, convicted felon Juan Montanez (aged 26), whom King Curtis had managed to stab after taking away his knife, was charged with murder.

King Tubby

(OSBOURNE RUDDOCK)
Born January 28, 1941
Died February 6, 1989
A former Jamaican electronics repairman, King Tubby invented the art of the instrumental dub, a process by which the non-vocal portions of a record are spiced together. Originally used by rock-steady and reggae deejays, the idea was later employed by rap artists. He also refined the mixing board used by deejays, and was employed by dozens of artists as a remix engineer.
CAUSE: He was murdered outside his home in Kingston, Jamaica, by an armed robber.

Albert King

(ALBERT NELSON)
Born April 25, 1923
Died December 21, 1992
A legendary blues guitarist who performed right up to his death, Albert King was born into a large, migrant farm-worker family in Indianola, Mississippi. Following the death of his lay preacher father, King and his family moved to Osceola, Arkansas, to escape farming. After a brief stint in a gospel quartet, King veered toward blues, building his own primitive guitar. After serving in World War II, and settling in St. Louis, he found plenty of work in the city's bustling music scene. Moving to Gary, Indiana, he joined a band led by guitarists Jimmy Reed and John Brim, and was forced to play drums. Emerging as a solo artist at Parrot Records in 1953, King had limited success with his sole release at the label, 'Walking From Door To Door'. A formidable figure at six-foot-four, King employed a unique style. Utilizing few chords, King played a

right-handed guitar upside-down, left handed, and tuned in an unorthodox fashion; instead of using a pick to play his Gibson Flying V guitar, he would often push the strings downwards with his thumb. Distrustful, King demanded immediate payment in cash after every show he performed, and preferred to sell the rights to his music for a flat fee instead of waiting for royalties. Recording at Bobbin Records, Albert King enjoyed his first national hit with a single that was leased to King Records, 'Don't Throw Your Love On Me So Strong' (1961). King then entered into the most successful phase of his career after signing with Stax Records. Befriended by promoter Bill Graham, King gained notoriety after a series of gigs at Bill Graham's Fillmore West Auditorium, where he shared bills with Jimi Hendrix and Janis Joplin. King's most successful album *Born Under A Bad Sign* was highlighted by the hits 'Laundromat Blues', a cover of Tommy McClennan's 'Crosscut Saw', and the scorching title cut, a song covered in a note for note version by Eric Clapton and Cream. King enjoyed further success with the crossover album, *Live Wire: Blues Power* (1968). After a career slump, King rode the early Eighties blues revival, enjoying healthy sales with his Fantasy Records releases, *San Francisco '83* (1983) and *I'm In A Phone Booth, Baby* (1984); he also appeared on Gary Moore's breakthrough album, *Still Got The Blues* (1990). With his stature in the blues community soaring, King was planning to tour Europe with B.B. King and Bobby "Blue" Bland in the spring of 1993.
CAUSE: Massive heart attack. Suffering from diabetes and looking very ill, at his last show King reportedly gave his guitar away to a younger musician in the band, claiming he would not need it anymore. He flew back to Memphis and died the next day at the Eastwood Medical Center.

Anna King
(ANNA DELORES WILLIAMS)
Born December 9, 1937
Died October 21, 2002
An R&B singer, Anna King pursued a solo career while a member of the James Brown Revue. With Brown producing her sessions at Smash Records, King landed on the R&B charts with the ballad 'If Somebody Told You' and a duet with Bobby Byrd 'Baby Baby Baby'. Under the name Delores King, she later recorded with a number of gospel acts.
CAUSE: Unknown. She died in her hometown of Philadelphia.

Earl King
(EARL SILAS JOHNSON IV)
Born March 17, 1934
Died April 17, 2003
A New Orleans based singer-songwriter and guitarist, Earl King composed hundreds of songs during his lengthy career. After a stint with Huey "Piano" Smith, King took over bluesman Guitar Slim's band. As a solo artist, King had two R&B chart entries, 'Those Lonely, Lonely Nights' (1955) and 'Always A First Time' (1962). King's most enduring compositions include 'Come On', 'Street Parade', 'Big Chief', and a song inspired by the death of his father, 'Trick Bag'. King remained an active performer well into the Nineties.
CAUSE: Suffering from diabetes-related complications, he died in New Orleans.

Freddie King
(BILLY MYLES)
Born September 3, 1934
Died December 28, 1976
Popular blues singer and guitarist, Texas-born Freddie King played with greats such as Muddy Waters and Willie Dixon. Taught to play guitar by his mother and uncle, King began as a country blues performer until discovering the electric guitar. After graduating from high school, King settled down in Chicago in 1954.

Working during the days in a paper mill, he spent his evenings performing in the city's many blues clubs behind Earl Payton and Little Sonny Cooper. Forming his own band The Every Hour Blues Boys, King would also work as a session player at Chess and Parrot behind acts such as Muddy Waters, B.B. King, Otis Rush, and Magic Sam. Playing in a somewhat twangy, Chicago-style blues fashion, King made his recording début with an obscure solo single in 1957, 'Country Boy'. Finally able to quit his day job in 1958, King was aided by friend Syl Johnson in signing with King-Federal Records as "Freddy" King. Recording what would become his signature piece 'Hideaway' (1960), King had written the song along with Magic Sam, the tune inspired by a Hound Dog Taylor instrumental. Primarily known for his instrumentals, King enjoyed hits with 'You've Got to Love Her With A Feeling', 'Lonesome Whistle Blues', 'San-Ho-Zay', 'The Stumble', and the often-recorded 'I'm Tore Down'. Unhappy by a lack of promotion and choice of material, King would leave King-Federal. Moving to Dallas and signing with Atlantic Records, he recorded two albums on their Cotillion subsidiary, with King Curtis producing and performing both projects. During this time, King was recording more standards such as 'Ain't Nobody's Business If I Do'. Also unhappy at Atlantic, King then signed with Shelter Records in 1971, releasing three albums. Adopting a more R&B approach, King began emphasizing his vocal prowess over his guitar playing. Joining RSO Records in 1974, King worked on his label début *Burglar* with Eric Clapton with whom he toured in the early Seventies.
CAUSE: He suffered from a serious heart condition, internal bleeding, and ulcers. He was hospitalised immediately after a Christmas day engagement. He died at Presbyterian Hospital in Dallas.

Jimmy King

Born 1949
Died December 9, 1967
A guitarist for The Bar-Kays, Jimmy King backed Sixties soul star Otis Redding on the road. Signed to Stax-Volt Records, The Bar-Kays had scored a riveting instrumental hit with the horn-heavy 'Soul Finger'.
CAUSE: On tour with Redding, King and the rest of The Bar-Kays were flying from Ohio to a performance in Wisconsin. Redding's new Beechcraft plane lost power, and went into a spin, dropping into the icy waters of Lake Monoma at 3:28 p.m., half a mile offshore. Besides Redding, four of the five members of The Bar-Kays perished – only Ben Cauley survived.

Pete King

Born 1961
Died August 1987
The drummer for the British new wave/dance group After The Fire, Pete King had joined in time for the group's hit, 'Der Kommissar'. Originally a member of the Coventry-based new wave band, The Flys (who recorded for EMI), he had replaced After The Fire drummer Ivor Twindell who had suffered a heart attack while performing on stage. Appearing on two albums, *80F* (1980) and *Batteries Not Included* (1982), King had success when the group recorded an English language version of German solo artist Falco's 'Der Kommissar', a huge MTV and dance-club hit in the US in 1983. While touring in the US as the opening act for ELO, King filled in, with only several hours notice, for ELO's ailing drummer Bev Bevan. After The Fire disbanded later in the year and King was working on a project called Zipcodes at the time of his death.
CAUSE: Stomach cancer.

Solomon King

(ALLEN V. LEVY)
Born August 13, 1931
Died January 20, 2005

An American-born ballad singer, Solomon King enjoyed success in the UK during the late Sixties. A native of Lexington, Kentucky, King served in the US Air Force during the Korean War. Originally recording under the name Randy Leeds, he fared poorly with his jazz-pop material and, hoping to jumpstart his career, he moved to London, taking the name Solomon King. Managed by Gordon Mills – whose charges included Tom Jones and Engelbert Humperdinck – the brawny King reached the UK charts in 1968 with a cover of a romantic ballad originally recorded by Roy Orbison, 'She Wears My Ring'. Although the song was a major hit, King would manage just one more chart entry, 'When We Were Young' (1968). As a popular cabaret singer, King performed throughout Britain during the Seventies before returning to the US in 1980.
CAUSE: Cancer. He died in Norman, Oklahoma.

Teddi King

(THEODORA KING)
Born September 18, 1929
Died November 18, 1977
Boston-based jazz-pop vocalist best known for her hit 'Mr. Wonderful' (1956), the diminutive Teddi King began her career in the early Forties after beating 500 other contestants in a local Dinah Shore sing-alike contest. She was subsequently approached by the agents of George Graham who was starting his own band. Pursuing a solo career on the jazz dinner-club circuit beginning in 1946, King would also record with George Shearing, Nat Pierce, and Dave McManus. King spent years working on the New England jazz circuit, frequently accompanied by pianist Dave McKenna. Suffering with Lupus since 1970, King hid her illness from the public, and performed until shortly before her death. Singer Carmen McRea has cited King as one of her greatest influences.
CAUSE: Lupus.

Sam Kinison

Born December 8, 1953
Died April 10, 1992
A shock-comic who would scream at his audiences, Sam Kinison also pursued a singing career, landing an AOR hit with a raucous, politically incorrect cover of The Troggs' garage-rock classic, 'Wild Thing' (1988), the track culled from his second of three albums, *Have You Seen Me Lately?* The song's video featured Billy Idol and Kinison's then girlfriend Jessica Hahn.
CAUSE: Car accident. He was driving his Pontiac Trans-Am near the California-Nevada state line to a sold-out performance in Laughlin, Nevada, when the car was struck head-on by a Chevrolet pick-up truck driven by a 17-year-old. The back of the pick-up was littered with empty beer cans. Kinison's third wife, whom he had married a week earlier, was with him. Driving behind, friends, family, and business associates witnessed the accident and saw Kinison emerge, seemingly unhurt, from the vehicle. But when they arrived at the scene to provide aid, Kinison began arguing with an unseen entity; then after uttering "I don't want to die . . . OK, OK, OK", he died.
FURTHER READING: Kinison, Bill. (1994). *Brother Sam: The Short, Spectacular Life of Sam Kinison.* New York: William Morrow.

Frank Kirkland

Born June 29, 1927
Died March 1973
Drummer in Bo Diddley's band at Chicago's Chess Records in the Fifties, Frank Kirkland was responsible for providing what became known as the "Bo Diddley beat" on hits such as 'I'm A Man', 'Bo Diddley', and 'Who Do You Love?' After his mother bought

him a drum kit, Kirkland joined Diddley's previous group The Langely Street Jive Cats in 1954.
CAUSE: Unknown.

Kenny Kirkland

(KENNETH DAVID KIRKLAND)
Born September 28, 1955
Died November 10, 1998
A jazz pianist who gained pop acclaim as part of Sting's recording and touring band from 1985, Kenny Kirkland was a much in-demand session instrumentalist. The Brooklyn-born Kirkland studied at the Manhattan School of Music, and first gained fame in trumpeter Wynton Marsalis' quartet, with whom he played from 1981 to 1985. Swerving into rock and joining Sting's group as a synthesizer player in 1985, Kirkland also worked with Crosby, Stills & Nash. Kirkland later joined saxophonist Branford Marsalis in the house band for television's *Jay Leno Show* from 1991–95. Although Kirkland appeared on dozens of albums, he released just one solo project.
CAUSE: He suffered hypertensive heart disease and a cerebral haemorrhage brought on by a cocaine overdose. His body was discovered on November 13, 1998, at his home in Queens, New York.

Lord Kitchener

(ALDWYN ROBERTS)
Born April 18, 1922
Died February 11, 2000
Nicknamed "The Grand Master of Calypso", Lord Kitchener popularised the native musical styles of Trinidad. Though he suffered with a lifelong speech impediment, his singing was unaffected. Trained originally as a blacksmith, he was taught to play guitar by his father and began making waves locally beginning in 1938, before his fame increased upon moving to Trinidad's capital, Port of Spain, in 1942, where he joined a group called The Roving Brigade. Taking the stage name Lord Kitchener (after British field marshal and war secretary, Lord Horatio Kitchener), he had his first hit in 1944 with 'Green Fig'. With trademark suit and fedora, he gained international prominence after touring England in 1947; garnering a large British following, he often booked several nightclub gigs in London on a single night. While in England, he recorded a number of singles with Cyril Blake's Calypso Serenaders, including the standard, 'Nora' (1950). After opening his own Manchester nightclub in 1958, he toured the US for the first time. Returning to Trinidad in 1963, Kitchener reinvigorated the calypso scene by infusing modern soul into the music to create the soca genre. In 1978, Kitchener landed a British hit with 'Sugar Bum Bum'. Diagnosed with cancer a year before his death, he retired from the industry.
CAUSE: Suffering from bone marrow cancer, he succumbed to a general infection and kidney failure. He died at The Medical Science Center at Port of Spain, Trinidad.

Baker Knight

(THOMAS BAKER KNIGHT, JR.)
Born July 4, 1933
Died October 12, 2005
A prolific songwriter, Baker Knight is best known for his association with Ricky Nelson. Teaching himself to play guitar while in the Air Force, Knight was drawn to rock'n'roll after his discharge. Forming Baker Knight & The Knightmares in the mid Fifties, he opened for acts such as Carl Perkins and Conway Twitty. Relocating to Los Angeles in 1958 after faring poorly as a solo act with Decca Records, Knight abandoned his goal of landing film roles and was instead drawn back into the music community. Writing 'Lonesome Town', Knight had hoped to submit the song to The Everly Brothers. Instead, Knight offered the song to teen idol Ricky Nelson, who

took it into the Top 10. In all, Nelson would record 21 of Knight's compositions. Although he continued to record throughout the Sixties, Knight had far more success as a songwriter, including 'Somewhere There's A Someone' (Dean Martin) and 'The Wonder Of You' (Elvis Presley). Suffering from agoraphobia, Knight returned to his hometown of Birmingham, Alabama, in the mid Eighties.
CAUSE: He died of natural causes at his home in Birmingham, Alabama.

Billy Knight

(DAVID LEON KNIGHT)
Born August 22, 1947
Died December 4, 2002
A percussionist and the youngest brother of R&B singer Gladys Knight, Billy Knight was an unofficial member of her backing band The Pips, and performed with the group for a number of years.
CAUSE: Complications of diabetes. He died in Las Vegas.

Curtis Knight

Born 1945
Died November 29, 1999
Kansas-born soul singer and guitarist, Curtis Knight is best known for the role he played in the early career of guitar virtuoso Jimi Hendrix who signed an early contract with Knight's manager Ed Chaplin. After serving in the military, Knight settled in California, and broke into show business with a role in the low-budget flick, *Pop Girl*. Relocating to New York City, he launched his own rock band, Curtis Knight & The Squires, recording several singles. Meeting Jimi Hendrix, Knight paid to have his guitar taken out of pawn. After aiding Knight on several recording sessions, Hendrix officially joined The Knights in 1966. Unhappy with the financial terms of his contract, Hendrix quit The Knights to form his own group, Jimmy James & The Blue Flames. Once Hendrix became a star, Capitol Records issued an album of impromptu studio jam sessions entitled *Get That Feeling* (1967), credited as by Jimi Hendrix & Curtis Knight. The project forever alienated Hendrix from Curtis. Following Hendrix's death, more Knight-era material was released. Relocating to Europe in the Seventies, Knight formed a new group and authored a pair of Hendrix biographies, *Jimi: An Intimate Biography* (1974) and *Starchild* (1992).
CAUSE: Unknown. He died at Lelystad, The Netherlands.

Gene Knight

Born c. 1942
Died August 1992
Lead tenor of the Norman Johnson-led, R&B vocal group The Showmen, Gene Knight appeared on the group's sole hit, 'It Will Stand' (1961).
CAUSE: Unknown. He died in Norfolk, Virginia.

Sonny Knight

(JOSEPH COLEMAN SMITH)
Born May 17, 1934
Died September 5, 1998
Illinois-born R&B vocalist, pianist, and songwriter, Sonny Knight is best known for the hits, 'Confidential' (1956) and 'If You Want This Love' (1964). Trained in blues and jazz, he composed the Amos Milburn hit, 'Vicious, Vicious Vodka'. Also an author, Knight penned *The Day The Music Died* (1981), an angry, insightful tome about blacks in the music industry. He spent his last two decades as a lounge singer in Hawaii, never quite completing a book on Jimi Hendrix.
CAUSE: He died in Maui, Hawaii. He had suffered a stroke two years earlier.

Terry Knight

(RICHARD TERRANCE KNAPP)
Born April 1, 1943
Died November 1, 2004

Although he was the leader of Terry Knight & The Pack, Michigan-native Terry Knight had far greater success as the manager and producer of Grand Funk Railroad. Breaking into music as a deejay on a small radio station, WTAC in Flint, Michigan, he quickly moved up to WJBK in Detroit and then Top 40 powerhouse CKLW in nearby Windsor, Ontario. A self-taught guitar player, Knight joined a Flint, Michigan-based group called The Jazz Masters. Renamed The Pack, and later, Terry Knight & The Pack, the group was popular in Southern Michigan and recorded a pair of albums and scored a hit cover version of Ben E. King's 'I (Who Have Nothing)'. Leaving the group before his 24th birthday in 1967, Knight wrote the score for the film, *The Incident*. In 1968, Knight was flown to England by Paul McCartney with the intention of signing him to Apple Records and, while staying at Ringo Starr's home, Knight turned down an offer to join The Hollies as replacement for the departing Graham Nash. In 1969, Knight reunited with Pack members Mark Farner and Don Brewer; switching to a management and production role, Knight renamed the group Grand Funk Railroad. Following a blistering performance at the Atlanta Pop Festival, Knight, aided by McCartney, negotiated a unique arrangement with Capitol to issue the group's independently produced records. Massively successful, Grand Funk Railroad filled stadiums and got their music on both AM and FM rock radio. But following numerous altercations, Knight was sued by the band in 1972 just three months before the scheduled termination of their contract. Subsequent lawsuits resulted in Knight receiving a large financial settlement and the publishing rights to the group's material. After parting with Grand Funk Railroad, Knight had limited success in the music field in subsequent years; he produced the hit 'D.O.A.' for Bloodrock and the self-titled album for the rock act Mom's Apple Pie, and launched the short-lived Brown Bag Records, a division of United Artists. In later years, Knight invested in professional auto racing.

CAUSE: He was murdered at his apartment in Temple, Texas. Knight was stabbed 17 times while trying to intervene in a quarrel between his daughter Danielle, aged 16, and her 26-year-old live-in boyfriend, Donald Alan Fair. Fair was later convicted of murder and blamed his actions on methamphetamine use.

Buddy Knox

(BUDDY WAYNE KNOX)
Born April 14, 1933
Died February 14, 1999

A rockabilly singer and songwriter, Buddy Knox enjoyed fame during the late Fifties. The son of a dirt-poor Texan farmer, Knox entertained himself with a guitar or harmonica in lieu of a radio which his family could not afford. After winning an athletic scholarship to West Texas State College in 1955, Knox formed a group with two classmates, bassist Jimmy Bowen and guitarist Don Lanier, the trio emerging as The Serenaders, soon renamed The Rhythm Orchids. Urged by Roy Orbison to seek out Norman Petty's tiny studio in Clovis, New Mexico, Knox sang lead vocal on 'Party Doll', a song he wrote in 1948. With Bowen providing the lead vocals on the Knox co-composition 'I'm Stickin' To You' as the B-side, the Triple-D single enjoyed regional airplay. When Roulette Records leased the disc, both sides were re-released as separate singles, with both artists landing pop hits. Drafted the same week that 'Party Doll' was topping the US charts in early 1957, Knox had to cancel a British tour. (Meanwhile, Knox would soon urge Buddy Holly to visit Norman Petty's studio.) His career stunted by a stint in the military,

Knox managed only a few more hits, 'Rock Your Little Baby To Sleep' (1957), a song he performed in the film *Jamboree*, 'Hula Love' (1957), and a remake of Ruth Brown's 'Somebody Touched Me' (1958). Faring poorly at Liberty Records in the early Sixties, Knox managed a final hit with a cover of The Clovers' often-recorded, 'Lovey Dovey' (1961). Settling in Canada in the Seventies, Knox was a favourite on the British oldies circuit.
CAUSE: He was diagnosed with cancer while hospitalised with a broken hip. He died at Harrison Memorial Hospital in Bremerton, Washington.

Keith Knudsen

Born February 18, 1948
Died February 8, 2005
As the drummer for the seminal rock act, The Doobie Brothers, Keith Knudsen provided the backbeat on a host of radio hits. Born in Iowa, but raised in Princeton, Illinois, Knudsen broke into music accompanying singer-keyboardist Lee Michael of 'Do You Know What I Mean' fame. Replacing Michael Hossack in 1974 as a second drummer in The Doobie Brothers, Knudsen shared the percussion with John Hartman. Knudsen performed on most of the group's major hits including 'Take Me In Your Arms', 'Takin' It To The Streets', 'What A Fool Believes' and 'Real Love' and co-wrote a number of album tracks such as 'Rocking Horse' and 'Time Is Here And Gone'. With The Doobie Brothers disbanding in 1982, Knudsen and bandmate John McFree joined forces in 1983 to form an all-star country-rock outfit, Southern Pacific, featuring Stu Cook of Creedence Clearwater Revival and David Jenkins of Pablo Cruise, whose country chart hits included 'Reno Bound', 'New Shades Of Blue' and 'Any Way The Wind Blows', before disbanding in 1991. Joining a revived version of The Doobie Brothers (without Michael McDonald) in 1993, Knudsen hit the road for a tour and subsequent live album, *Rockin' Down The Highway: The Wildlife Concert*. The "new" Doobies also recorded a studio album in 2000, *Sibling Rivalry*.
CAUSE: Hospitalised for a month, he succumbed to pneumonia and died at Kentfield Rehabilitation Hospital in Kentfield, California. He had been diagnosed with cancer in 1995.

Michael Knust

Born March 11, 1949
Died September 15, 2003
The founding member of Texas-based psychedelic band Fever Tree, guitarist Michael Knust wrote much of the group's material. Formed in 1967 as a garage band called Bostwick Vine, the renamed Fever Tree recorded a pair of obscure singles for Mainstream Records. Signing with Uni Records, the group recorded four late Sixties albums and are best remembered for the 1968 psychedelic classic, 'San Francisco Girls (Return Of The Native)', featuring Knust's frenetic fuzz guitar riffs. The group disbanded in 1970, but was later revived by Knust.
CAUSE: Unknown. He died in his sleep at his home in Spring Branch, Texas.

Ronald Koal

(ROBERT GOOSLIN, JR.)
Born 1959
Died May 8, 1993
Leader of the Eighties, Ohio-based, new-wave group Ronald Koal And The Trillionaires, who released a self-titled album in 1982. He would later form The Ronald Koal Band, and in 1992, The Messiah Factory.
CAUSE: He died of a self-inflicted gunshot wound to the head at his home in Columbus. He had just returned from a bar.

Helmut Koellen

Born 1950
Died May 3, 1977
Bassist and guitarist of the Seventies,

Jurgen Fritz-headed German progressive-rock group Triumvirat, Helmut Koellen appeared on the group's first four albums, including the symphonic *Mediterranean Tales* (1972), *Illusions On A Double Dimple* (1974), and the group's most successful, *Sparticus* (1975), the latter highlighted by the track, 'Dimplicity'. He left the group in 1976 and was replaced by Barry Palmer.
CAUSE: Suicide. He died in Cologne, Germany.

Leslie Kong

Born 1933
Died 1971
Reggae producer best known for overseeing the Desmond Dekker hit 'Isrealites', Leslie Kong first worked at the controls of a mixing board in 1961 on Jimmy Cliff's 'Dearest Beverly'. Then in 1962 Kong produced and released Bob Marley's first singles including 'Judge Not'. Recording the finest in local Jamaican talent including The Maytals and Joe Higgs, Kong released his output on either his own Beverly label or through a licensing arrangement with the larger Island Records. Kong reteamed with Marley in 1969, who was then with The Wailers, and assembled tracks for the album, *The Best Of The Wailers*. Kong also ran a combination record store and ice cream parlour in Kingston, Jamaica.
CAUSE: Heart failure.

Alexis Korner

Born April 19, 1928
Died January 1, 1984
Justly accorded the title "the father of British blues", Alexis Korner was born in Paris to a Greek mother and an Austrian father. Studying piano from the age of five, as a child he lived with various relatives, shuttling around Europe and North Africa. Emigrating to Britain in 1939 due to the start of World War II, the young and impressionable Korner was drawn to the blues in 1940 after hearing Jimmy Yancey's 'Five O'Clock Blues'. In the early Forties in England, he played boogie-woogie piano with London musician Chris Barber in nightclubs, a style of music that was completely foreign at the time. Drafted in 1946, Korner worked at a military radio station. Returning to England in 1947, he passed through several record companies and radio stations, including a stint at the BBC. Korner joined his first professional band in 1949 when he rejoined his former partner in the Chris Barber Jazz Group. Unhappy with Barber's traditional jazz, Korner and bandmate Cyril Davies formed a blues quartet within Barber's group. In 1952, Korner joined a pioneering skiffle group that was led by Ken Colyer and included vocalist Lonnie Donegan. Then, after passing through a series of jazz outfits, Korner joined Davies in 1957 to launch The London Blues and Barrelhouse Club on the second floor of the Roadhouse pub in Soho. The first club of its kind in the UK, it showcased American soul, blues and R&B artists. In 1961, Korner and Davies formed Blues Incorporated – Britain's first white, electric blues group. Within a year, they opened their own venue, the Ealing Rhythm & Blues Club which attracted many budding British musicians, including Brian Jones, Mick Jagger, Keith Richards and Eric Clapton. Blues Incorporated then landed a residency at the Marquee Club in Soho, a period captured on the album *R&B From The Marquee.* Although Davies soon left to form his own group, Blues Incorporated recruited many future British stars, including Charlie Watts, Long John Baldry, Jack Bruce and Ginger Baker. In 1964, Korner released the albums, *Red Hot From Alex and At The Cavern.* Retreating from a full-time music career in the mid Sixties to spend more time with his family, Korner turned to radio and television production.

Korner was the butt of purist criticism when in 1964 he led the house band on the children's television show, *Five O'Clock Club*, and later, *Gadzooks!*. Returning to touring in 1968, Korner teamed with the Danish blues band The Beefeaters. Forming New Church along with vocalist Peter Thorup, Korner combined gospel with jazz and blues, and encouraged a young singer called Robert Plant. By the early Seventies New Church evolved into CCS (Collective Consciousness Society), and the group landed a hit with an instrumental rendition of Led Zeppelin's 'Whole Lotta Love' which became the theme tune for BBC television's weekly chart show, *Top Of The Pops*. After releasing the album, *Bootleg Him!* (1972), a project comprised of tracks from various Korner-led groups, Korner went on his first and only tour of the US. In 1975, Korner teamed with Keith Richards, Steve Marriott and Peter Frampton for the album *Get Off My Cloud*. In 1981, he joined Ian Stewart's all-star outfit, Rocket 88. Korner possessed a wonderfully resonant speaking voice which came over particularly well on radio, and in the Eighties he did many commercial voice-overs in Britain. CAUSE: Hospitalized in London, he died soon after from lung cancer.

Paul Kossoff

Born September 14, 1950
Died March 19, 1976
Guitarist of the Seventies blues rock group Free, Paul Kossoff took classical guitar lessons for six years beginning at the age of nine. Reared in a show business family, his father was professional actor David Kossoff. Drawn into blues and rock, Paul bought an electric guitar at 16. After playing together in a British R&B group called Black Cat Bones, Kossoff and drummer Simon Kirke left to form Free in 1968. The London-based group was soon completed with the addition of vocalist Paul Rodgers and bass player Andy Fraser. Touring heavily in Britain, they garnered a sizable following, and in the autumn of 1969 were hired as the opening act for Blind Faith on their sold out US tour. Signing with Chris Blackwell's Island Records in 1968, Free released *Tons Of Sobs*, an album that spotlighted Kossoff's blues rock guitar prowess. The group's breakthrough came in 1970 with the hit single 'All Right Now', culled from the album, *Fire And Water*, but after the failure of their follow-up album *Highway* and much internal strife, the group disbanded on the completion of a West Coast tour in 1971. Ironically, later that year, their album *Free Live!* would land in the British Top 5. Kossoff and Kirke then formed a short-lived avant-garde quartet with Tetsu Yamauchi and John "Rabbit" Bundrick, releasing a self-titled album, *Kossoff, Kirke, Tetsu & Rabbit*. Reforming Free without Fraser, Kossoff and the group found further success with the album *Free At Last* (1972) but they never really gelled as before. By this time Kossoff was abusing drugs and missing concerts, and Tetsu and Rabbit were brought in as replacements. Free finally disbanded after the release of the album *Heartbreaker* in early 1973. During his time with Free, Kossoff had formed a side-project, Back Street Crawler; the group would find only limited success with their three album releases. CAUSE: He died of drug-induced heart failure while on an aeroplane en route from Los Angeles to New York City. In poor health in the last years of his life, he had suffered a heart attack seven months earlier.

Barry Kramer

Born February 25, 1943
Died January 1981
Founder of *Creem* magazine, Barry Kramer launched the monthly periodical in Detroit in 1969 with $1,200 in capital. Calling itself "America's Only Rock 'n' Roll

Magazine", *Creem* boasted the talents of writers such as Lester Bangs, Dave Marsh, and Cameron Crowe.
CAUSE: He was found dead alone in a hotel room. The coroner ruled the death an accidental overdose of nitrous oxide and other drugs.

Phil Kramer

(PHILIP TAYLOR KRAMER)
Born 1953
Died February 12, 1995
The vocalist and bassist of psychedelic/metal group Iron Butterfly in the mid Seventies, the 6′ 5″, Ohio-born Phil Kramer joined after the group's late Sixties era of popularity. A self-taught musician, Kramer was previously a member of Cleveland-based proto-punk band Max, which featured future punkster Stiv Bator. Forming a pop act with his sister Kathie, Kramer opened up for John Denver in the early Seventies and teaming with former Iron Butterfly drummer Ron Bushy, they formed a heavy metal group called Gold, recording one unreleased album. After Bushy ran into former bandmate Erik Braunn, a new line-up of Iron Butterfly was launched, with Kramer as bassist. During his three-year stint with the revived Iron Butterfly, Kramer appeared on two poor-selling albums, and opened up for acts such as Queen, Kansas, and Rush. Leaving music, Kramer earned a degree in physics, landing a position at Northrop Aerospace, where he worked on the guidance system of the MX missile. In 1987 he and Randy Jackson (of The Jackson 5) launched Midi City, a media production firm. Selling his share of the firm, he turned to the production of a specialty 70 mm camera. Kramer later launched a second media firm, TMM.
CAUSE: Missing for four years, Kramer was the subject of many conspiracy theories. Kramer's body was discovered by hikers, still buckled in the driver's seat of his Ford Aerostar van at the bottom of a 400-foot ravine. Shortly before he vanished in 1995, Kramer had telephoned 911 operators and announced his intention to commit suicide. His disappearance was the subject of a number of television programmes, and was attributed by some conspiracy theorists as related to his job. His family claimed that he had made a vital scientific discovery shortly before his death. What is known for certain is that Kramer had gone to the Los Angeles International Airport the day of his death to meet an arriving business associate; but for some reason he left the airport without picking up anyone, and then signed an IOU when leaving the airport car park. While driving along Highway 101 in southern California, he made numerous cellular calls, including a 911 emergency call that he was about to commit suicide. Driving off the road, he died from multiple blunt trauma injuries.

Kid Krupa

(JON KRUPA)
Born 1962
Died March 11, 2005
A latter member of the quirky, glam-influenced Scottish punk group The Revillos (previously known as The Rezillos, the group was forced to change its name after leaving Sire Records), guitarist Kid Krupa joined in 1979. After appearing on the albums *Rev-Up!* and *Attack*, Krupa quit to work as a session player and producer, collaborating with Tim Finn, Del Amitri, Shakin' Stevens, Roger Daltrey and Bonnie Tyler. Krupa returned to The Revillos for a number of reunion shows in the early Nineties.
CAUSE: Diabetes.

John C. Kuehne

Born February 6, 1942
Died February 12, 2000
A session bass player, John C. Kuehne worked with The Monkees, James Taylor, The Nitty Gritty Dirt Band, and Linda Ronstadt. While attending

San Antonio College, he frequently performed in clubs with classmate and future Monkee, Michael Nesmith. When Nesmith was chosen for The Monkees, he brought Kuehne on-board as a backstage player for the television programme. Taking the stage name of John London, he also appeared in several episodes. Leaving music in the Seventies, Kuehne left California for his native San Antonio, Texas, to work in newspaper advertising.
CAUSE: Unknown. He died in Rockport, Texas.

Andy Kulberg

(ANDREW M. KULBERG)
Born April 30, 1944
Died January 28, 2002
A bassist and flautist, Andy Kulberg was a member of The Blues Project and its successor Sea Train. A native of Buffalo, New York, Kulberg earned a music degree at New York University, and was hired as bassist for The Danny Kalb Quartet; changing musical directions, the renamed Blues Project was one of the country's first blues-rock groups. Adding Al Kooper, the group recorded a fine début in 1965 with the free-form style album *Live At The Café Au-Go-Go* – Kulberg's 'Flute Thing' later providing fruit for hip-hop samplers. After the departure of a number of original members – including Kooper who formed Blood, Sweat & Tears – Kulberg took the Blues Project in a more non-commercial, eclectic direction for their fourth album, *Planned Obsolescence*. Renamed Seatrain, the group moved to California and issued their self-titled début in 1969 but despite hiring George Martin to produce their next two albums in London, Seatrain found limited success. Experiencing a series of line-up changes, Seatrain disbanded after recording their fourth album. Kulberg subsequently composed music for television shows and worked as a producer for a number of New Age acts including Daniel Kobialka.
CAUSE: Lymphoma. He died at his home.

Les Kummel

(LESLIE KUMMEL)
Born February 23, 1945
Died December 18, 1978
Bassist with the Sixties Chicago-based folk-rock group, The New Colony Six, Les Kummel joined the group in 1967 as the replacement for Wally Kemp. Joining in time for their second album *Colonization*, Kummel appeared on their hits which he co-wrote with bandmate Ronald Rice, 'I Will Always Think About You' (1968) and 'Things I'd Like To Say' (1969). Suffering from drug problems, Kummel left the group in 1970 after the release of the single, 'People and Me'.
CAUSE: He died in a car crash.

Eddie Kurdziel

(EDWARD J. KURDZIEL II)
Born September 25, 1960
Died June 6, 1999
The guitarist for the modern glam-rock band Redd Kross, Eddie Kurdziel joined the 15-year-old band in 1993. Redd Kross was formed in Los Angeles by teenage brothers Steve and Jeff McDonald, originally as The Tourists, and then Red Cross. Previously a member of an eclectic hard-rock band, Shadowland, Kurdziel joined in time for Redd Kross' breakthrough album *Phaseshifter* (1993). Also a session player, he worked with Belinda Carlisle and Junior Braithwaite.
CAUSE: He overdosed on drugs at his apartment in Los Angeles.

L

Ed Labunski

Born May 14, 1937
Died October 1980

A jingle writer who composed commercial spots for Chevrolet and McDonalds, Ed Labunski was also a backing vocalist for Lonnie Mack. Labunski and Mack opened a studio in Pennsylvania in the late Seventies and were preparing to record a then-unknown guitarist named Stevie Ray Vaughan. Labunski had worked at Fraternity Records in the Sixties.
CAUSE: Car crash. He died in New Jersey.

Bobby LaKind

Born 1945
Died December 24, 1992

The percussionist for Seventies rock band The Doobie Brothers, Bobby LaKind joined as a member of the group's lighting crew. Usually seen pounding on conga drums alongside drummer Keith Knudsen, the boyish-looking LaKind became an official member in 1976, beginning with the album *Taking It To The Streets*. One of the decade's most successful rock acts, The Doobie Brothers enjoyed heavy radio airplay with hits such as 'What A Fool Believes', 'Minute By Minute', and 'Real Love'. LaKind remained with The Doobies until they disbanded in 1982, appearing on the album, *Farewell Tour*. After a reunion concert organised by drummer Keith Knudsen at a Vietnam veterans' fund-raiser, The Doobie Brothers hit the road for another tour in 1987. A subsequent album featured a LaKind/McDonald composition, 'Tonight I'm Coming Through (The Border)'. LaKind left the group in 1990 and was not part of a 1992 tour. LaKind rejoined his former bandmates just months before his death for a pair of benefit concerts to raise money for his two sons.
CAUSE: Colon cancer. He died in Los Angeles.
FURTHER READING: Bego, Mark. (1980). *The Doobie Brothers*. New York: Fawcett.

Kit Lambert

(CHRISTOPHER SEBASTIAN LAMBERT)
Born May 11, 1935
Died April 6, 1981

A charismatic character on the British rock scene in the Sixties, the unashamedly homosexual Kit Lambert was an entrepreneur of manic energy and an imaginative promoter, first as co-manager of The Who, and then as the co-founder of Track Records, one of the earliest and most successful British independent record labels. The son of classical composer Constant Lambert and grandson of George Lambert, a noted Australian painter, Kit was educated at Oxford and he acquired much of his organisational acumen while serving as an officer in the British army. He left the army to become a jungle explorer, joining an ill-fated expedition to trace the source of an undescended Brazilian river, on which a close friend was killed by a tribe of Indians. Shaken by the experience, he entered the entertainment business via film, becoming an assistant director and working on *The Guns Of Navarone* and *From Russia With Love*. Collaborating with another assistant director, Chris Stamp, at Shepperton Studios, Lambert hit on the idea of making a movie about fashion and music which would feature an unknown pop group. To this end he went out to look for one and discovered The Who (then called The High Numbers) at the Railway Hotel in Harrow, in north west London. Impressed by their energy, he and Stamp abandoned their movie plans and convinced the group's then management team to give up control. Under Lambert's energetic guidance,

The Who progressed rapidly, infusing elements of pop art into their image, with Pete Townshend dressed in a Union Jack coat, and incorporating Townshend's guitar smashing into a ritualistic act which he justified as 'situationism'. Lambert also encouraged Townshend to write songs, presenting him with two tape recorders, a gesture that secured the songwriter's loyalty through turbulent times ahead. Lambert was at the helm during 1965, The Who's breakthrough year, always dreaming up schemes to publicise and promote his charges. Early in 1966 Lambert fired The Who's record producer, Shel Talmy, with catastrophic long term financial consequences for the band, and assumed production duties himself. He was no technician in the studio, but his flair for imaginative ideas kept The Who at the cutting edge of pop for the rest of the decade. Flushed by The Who's success, Lambert and Stamp launched Track Records in 1966 and they were quick to sign The Jimi Hendrix Experience. Bankrolled by Polydor Records, Track achieved success early the following year when Hendrix landed in the British Top 10 with 'Hey Joe'. Other hit acts at the label included Thunderclap Newman (produced by Townshend) and The Crazy World Of Arthur Brown. In the studio Lambert oversaw all The Who's post-1965 hit singles and albums including *A Quick One*, which included Townshend's first extended work, the highly original *The Who Sell Out* and the group's first full-length rock opera, *Tommy*. As the creative foil for Townshend, Lambert was a key element in *Tommy*, giving the guitarist an early rough draft for the project and encouraging him all the way. He revelled in its success and took pride in presenting The Who at opera houses in Europe and America, but as the group became more and more successful, so Lambert seemed to lose interest. Although in earlier days he'd ingeniously managed to keep The Who afloat when the operation was in serious debt, he was a reckless business manager and overseeing a successful rock band did not appeal to his restless creative psyche. To Lambert, the challenge was making them successful in the first place. By 1970, his grandiose plans had become largely unnecessary as far as promoting The Who was concerned. In 1971, after a series of disastrous recording sessions with Lambert in New York, The Who opted to use Glyn Johns as their producer for what became *Who's Next*. The relationship never really recovered. In the early Seventies Lambert produced soul singer LaBelle. Lambert and Stamp's relationship with The Who had soured by 1974 and they gave up control the following year, handing over the reins to their subordinate, the far more business-minded Bill Curbishley. While Stamp returned to film, Lambert produced several early punk bands but by this time he was a victim of serious substance abuse, a chronic alcoholic and heroin addict, and his creative powers were seriously waning. By the time of his death he had squandered most of his wealth, much of it on a crumbling Venetian palace where he spent many of his last years.

CAUSE: He died in hospital from a brain haemorrhage incurred after falling down a flight of stairs at his mother's London house. The previous night he had been involved in a brawl in a Kensington nightclub, allegedly over a drug debt, and this may have contributed to his demise.

FURTHER READING: Motion, Andrew. (1986). *The Lamberts: George, Constant & Kit*. London: Chatto & Windus. Marsh, Dave. (1983). *Before I Get Old: The Story Of The Who*. New York: St. Martin's.

Martin Lamble

Born August 1949
Died May 14, 1969

The drummer for the influential British folk-rock group Fairport Convention,

Martin Lamble joined under unusual circumstances: while sitting in the audience at their début gig in June 1967, Lamble heckled the group's drummer. Agreeing with Lamble's assessment and impressed by his nerve, the group fired their original drummer Shaun Frater, and hired Lamble on the spot. A seven-piece band, fronted by vocalists Judy Dyble and Ian Matthews and featuring talented guitarist Richard Thompson, the group would nurture some of Britain's finest musicians over the years. Initially flirting with progressive rock, the Fairports toured as the opening act for Procol Harem. Signing with Polydor Records, the group issued a bland début *Fairport Convention* (1968), an album not released in the US for several years; the only highlight would come with the Richard Thompson composition, 'It's Alright Ma, It's Only Witchcraft'. Switching to Island Records and replacing Judy Dyble with Sandy Denny in 1968, the group pioneered a more traditional style, blending Denny's folk roots with Thompson's electric guitar work. They recorded the fine album *What We Did On Our Holidays* (1969) (released in the US by A&M as *Fairport Convention*), the project highlighted by 'Fotheringay' and 'She Moved Through The Fair'. Also that year, Lamble and the rest of the group would work on the Al Stewart album, *Love Chronicles*.
CAUSE: He died in a car crash near Mill Hill, London, England, which also took the life of passenger Jeanie Franklin, an American clothing designer (Jack Bruce's album *Songs For A Tailor* was dedicated to her). Bandmate Richard Thompson was also injured. With a roadie at the wheel of the group's touring van, they were returning to London after a performance in Birmingham.
FURTHER READING: Humphries, Patrick. (1997). *Meet On The Ledge: Fairport Convention; The Classic Years*. London: Virgin.

Jackie Landry

Born May 22, 1941
December 23, 1997

The second alto of the early girl-group The Chantels, New York City-born and raised Jackie Landry teamed with several classmates at St. Anthony of Padua High School. Singing in her church choir, Landry had been reared on traditional Catholic hymns. Signing with George Goldner's End label in 1957, the group was initially produced by Richard Barrett (of The Valentines). Featuring Arlene Smith's yearning lead vocals, The Chantels enjoyed several hits beginning with the million-selling 'Maybe' (1957) and 'Every Night (I Pray)' (1958). Switching to Carlton Records where they rejoined their early producer Richard Barrett, The Chantels returned to the charts with 'Look In My Eyes' (1961) and 'Well, I Told You' (1961), the latter an answer record to Ray Charles' 'Hit The Road Jack'. Jumping from label to label, the group was unable to match its early success. Retiring from music in 1970, Landry later took a post as a court reporter, holding the position until 1996. Occasionally hitting the oldies circuit, Landry rejoined some of her bandmates as The Original Chantels.
CAUSE: Cancer.

Ronnie Lane

(RONALD FREDERICK LANE)
Born April 1, 1946
Died June 4, 1997

The bassist of the pioneering British mod group The Small Faces, London-born guitarist Ronnie Lane teamed up with drummer Kenny Jones, singer Steve Marriott and keyboard player Jimmy Winston (soon to be replaced by Ian McLagan) to form the quartet in 1965. A rhythm guitarist turned bassist, Lane was also a talented songwriter, sharing the duties in the group with Marriott. In the forefront of the mod movement, along with The Who, the smartly dressed Small Faces were named because none of them stood over 5 foot 6 inches tall. An immediate sensation, the group enjoyed British hits with 'Whatcha Gonna Do About It' (1965), 'Sha-La-La-La-Lee' (1966), 'Hey Girl' (1966), 'All Or Nothing' (1966) and 'My Mind's Eye' (1966). Switching to the Immediate label and taking a slight psychedelic turn on the album *Odgen's Nut Gone Flake*, the group enjoyed its first US hit with 'Itchycoo Park'. With the departure of Marriott in 1969, the group temporarily disbanded. A year later, with the addition of Rod Stewart on vocals and Ronnie Wood on guitar, they re-emerged as The Faces. Under their new name the group became a much-loved rock institution at home and abroad despite, or perhaps because of, their sloppy, happy-go-lucky attitude. It was no secret that The Faces spent as much time in the pub as they ever did rehearsing. This often translated to the stage where untogetherness was the order of the day, a situation that often seemed to rile various members of the band, Lane included. But Lane was a fine foil for Rod Stewart, his diminutive height and laid-back manner in sharp contrast to the tall, rooster-haired, extrovert singer. In the early Seventies The Faces toured the UK and US to increasing acclaim but Stewart's concurrent (and more successful) solo career was a sticking point within the band. Unable to reconcile the situation, and embittered that his own songs were often ignored, Lane left The Faces in the spring of 1973 after the release of the poor-selling album *Ooh La La*. Later in the year, Lane formed Slim Chance, a folk-rock group which toured the UK in a circus tent but experienced limited success. Unfortunately Slim Chance ate up most of the money that Lane had made from The Faces, not that Lane was ever remotely concerned with pecuniary matters, a trait that served to exacerbate his chaotic personal life. In 1977 he teamed up with The Who's Pete Townshend, like Lane a disciple of the mute Indian guru Meher Baba, to record the acclaimed album *Rough Mix*. Lane suffered the first symptoms of multiple sclerosis in 1976, and publicly disclosed his diagnosis in 1981 after treatment had forced him into bankruptcy. That same year Lane appeared in a wheelchair on stage at London's Wembley Stadium during the final 20 minutes of a Rod Stewart solo concert when The Faces reformed to climax the show. Bill Wyman took over on bass and emotions ran high as Lane, watching from the sidelines, gamely raised himself from his wheelchair to sing 'Goodnight Irene' to an audience numbering over 70,000. A much revered and popular figure, Lane's reduced circumstances became a *cause-celebre* as music stars, including Wyman and fellow Stone Charlie Watts and British guitar heroes Eric Clapton, Jimmy Page and Jeff Beck, offered their services at a series of UK and US charity concerts to raise money for MS research. Relocating to Texas, the wheelchair-bound Lane formed a series of bands in the mid Eighties, his last recording session coming in 1992 on a duet with Ron Wood, 'Ooh La La'.

CAUSE: He succumbed to the effects of multiple sclerosis. He died at a hospital near his home in Trinada, Colorado, having moved there three years earlier. Lane had also been despondent over the death of former bandmate Steve Marriott. Lane's mother had also suffered from MS, dying from the condition in 1990.

FURTHER READING: Hewitt, Paolo. (1995). *Small Faces: The Young Mods' Forgotten Story*. London: Acid Jazz. Twelker, Uli. (1997). *Happy Boys Happy: A Rock History Of The Small Faces And Humble Pie*. London: Sanctuary.

Don Lang

Born January 19, 1925
Died August 3, 1992

As leader of The Frantic Five, chubby faced trombonist/singer Don Lang was

a regular face on *6.5 Special*, the first ever televised British rock'n'roll show, in 1957. He scored several hits including 'Cloudburst' (1955), 'School Day' (1957), and a cover of David Seville's 'Witch Doctor' (1958). Lang had previously played the trombone in big band orchestras led by Vic Lewis and Teddy Foster. Forming his own band in the mid Fifties, he spent the next two decades as a popular dance hall attraction.
CAUSE: Cancer. He died at the Royal Marsden Hospital in London.

Roy Lanham

Born January 16, 1923
Died February 14, 1991
A Kentucky-born session guitarist, Roy Lanham provided the guitar on The Fleetwoods' hits, 'Come Softly To Me' and 'Mr. Blue'. He had previously been a guitarist and vocalist in Roy Rogers' group The Sons Of The Pioneers, backing the singing cowboy on hits like 'Happy Trails'. Lanham toured with the Sons Of The Pioneers into the Eighties.
CAUSE: Cancer. He died in Camarillo, California.

George Lanuis

Born September 4, 1939
Died April 21, 1996
Lead singer of the Fifties pop vocal group The Crescendos, George Lanuis provided the vocals on the group's best known hit 'Oh Julie' (1958).
CAUSE: Unknown.

Scott LaRock

(SCOTT STERLING)
Born March 2, 1962
Died August 27, 1987
A mid Eighties rap singer and deejay, Scott LaRock was a partner in KRS-One and Boogie Down Productions. Working with The Ultramagnetic MC's, KRS-One popularised the term "by any means necessary" on their début gangster-rap album *Criminal Minded.* Before entering music, LaRock had worked as a counsellor.
CAUSE: He was shot dead outside a housing project. He was seated in his parked pick-up truck, there to diffuse a feud between two parties.

Frankie LaRocka

(FRANK LAROCCA)
Born April 17, 1954
Died May 12, 2005
A distinctive personality in the rock world, drummer Frankie LaRocka was a self-taught musician. A native of Long Island, New York, LaRocka passed through a series of popular local groups before joining The David Johansen Band in the late Seventies. A premiere drummer, LaRocka toured with John Waite, Patty Smyth & Scandal and Bryan Adams, and also performed on the Bon Jovi début smash 'Runaway'. Wanting to spend more time with his family, LaRocka quit touring and took a position as an A&R executive at Epic Records where he discovered The Spin Doctors and produced their 1991 début *Pocketful Of Kryptonite*. After promotion to head of A&R at Atlantic, LaRocka quit to form his own production company, Straight Line. Continuing to perform, LaRocka appeared on a live Noel Redding album and joined a New York City blues band, Hot Monkey Love.
CAUSE: He contracted pneumonia following surgery to treat his enlarged heart at St. Vincent's Hospital in West Brighton, New York.

Nicolette Larson

Born July 17, 1952
Died December 16, 1997
A session vocalist and solo artist, Nicolette Larson was born in Helena, Montana, but raised in Kansas City. Moving to California in 1974 at the age of 21 to pursue a music career, she found work in a band led by Hoyt Axton, and soon married Emmylou Harris' guitarist Hank DeVito. Teaming with Neil Young in 1978, she

provided vocals on his musical opus *Comes A Time*. Also pursuing a solo career, Larson scored the first of her two Top 40 pop hits in 1978 with a ditty penned by Neil Young, 'Lotta Love'; Young had given her the song after she heard a demo of the tune on a tape she found on the floor of his car. Larson then scored another hit with 'Let Me Go, Love' (1980) in a duet with Doobie Brothers vocalist Michael McDonald. Her last chart appearance came in 1986 with a Top 10 country hit, 'That's How You Know When Love's Right', featuring guest vocals by Steve Wariner. After appearing on albums by Andrew Gold, she toured with the musical *Pump Boy And Dinettes*, pursued a career as a country singer in Nashville, and was named Best New Vocalist in 1994 by the Academy of Country Music. Rejoining Young in the Nineties, she provided vocal harmony on his album *Harvest Moon* and on his MTV *Unplugged* session. Larson's final release came in 1994 with *Sleep Baby Sleep*, her sixth album. Latterly married to California-based session guitarist Russ Kunkel, Larson was also an actress, appearing in the film comedy Twins.
CAUSE: She died from complications of cerebral oedema at the UCLA Medical Center in Los Angeles.

Wick Larsen

Born May 2, 1951
Died February 14, 1989
A member of Southern-rock band Wet Willie briefly during the early Seventies, Wick Larsen joined in time for their second album *Wet Willie II* containing the instrumental 'Red Hot Chicken', featuring Larson on guitar and Moog synthesiser.
CAUSE: Diabetic coma.

David Lastie

Born November 11, 1934
Died December 5, 1987
A popular New Orleans R&B tenor saxophonist, David Lastie was trained in the bebop jazz tradition. After recording with Snooks Eaglin, James Booker, and others, he formed a group called A Taste Of New Orleans.
CAUSE: He suffered a stroke at his home in New Orleans.

Peter Laughner

Born August 22, 1952
Died June 22, 1977
The original guitarist and songwriter of the pioneering Cleveland-based punk group Pere Ubu, Peter Laughner worked closely alongside singer frontman David Thomas. Laughner and Thomas were previously members of the another proto-punk group called Rocket Of The Tombs. Formed in 1975, Pere Ubu was best known for the crowd pleasers '30 Seconds Over Tokyo' and 'Final Solution'. Another song, the Laughner composition 'Ain't It Fun', was later recorded by both The Dead Boys (another Cleveland punk group) and Guns N' Roses. Leaving Pere Ubu, Laughner then formed The Friction Band. Also a music critic, Laughner wrote reviews for a local weekly magazine, *Scene*. A Laughner compilation, *Take The Guitar Player For A Ride*, was issued in 1993.
CAUSE: Following several years of drug and alcohol abuse, he died from acute pancreatitis at his parents' home in suburban Cleveland. Laughner took drugs to emulate his musical hero, Lou Reed. Laughner was frequently hospitalised with liver ailments, but despite medical warnings, continued to abuse drugs.

Sammy Lawhorne

Born July 12, 1935
Died April 29, 1990
Born in Little Rock, Arkansas, electric guitarist Sammy Lawhorne got his first taste of fame at age 15 backing Sonny Boy Williamson on *The King Biscuit Boy* radio programme. Then after a five-year stint in the Navy during the Fifties, Lawhorne moved to Chicago and recorded 'You Don't Love Me'

with harmonica player Willie Cobbs. Lawhorne then joined the backing band of Junior Wells, and in the mid Sixties, Muddy Waters' group. After leaving Waters in 1974, Lawhorne rarely performed. Lawhorne released his only solo album in 1986, *After Hours*.
CAUSE: Natural causes. His health had deteriorated from years of heavy drinking.

Jimmi Lawrence

(JAMES LAWRENCE)
Born January 25, 1977
Died January 15, 2004
The guitarist for British alternative rock band Hope Of The States, Jimmi Lawrence formed the politically charged act in 2000. The group garnered press for the video to their eight-minute track 'Black Dollar Bills' (2003), which was banned for its controversial political message. After a bidding war, the group – which now included a violinist – was signed by Sony Records and charted in the UK with 'Enemies/Friends'. They were putting the final touches to their début album, *The Lost Riots*, when Lawrence died.
CAUSE: He was found dead by his bandmates at Real World Studios in Bath, England. He had hung himself.

Leadbelly

(HUDDIE WILLIAM LEDBETTER)
Born January 29, 1889
Died December 6, 1949
Legendary folk-blues singer-songwriter, keyboard player and guitarist, Louisiana-born Leadbelly was taught Cajun-style accordion at age six by an uncle. Attracted to liquor and women during his teen years, he left his family's farm to work as a gin joint entertainer, playing the piano in Shreveport brothels by the age of 16. Prone to violence and jailed several times, Leadbelly murdered a man in 1918, and served seven years of a 30-year sentence. He was pardoned after composing an impassioned song for the governor of Texas. Back in prison in 1930 for slashing a man, Leadbelly was visited by musicologist John A. Lomax for whom he recorded his signature piece 'Irene' (later recorded by The Weavers as 'Goodnight Irene'). Again pardoned, Leadbelly came under Lomax's tutelage and worked as his chauffeur. Moving to New York City in 1935, Leadbelly was embraced by America's East Coast liberals for his leftist lyrical messages. During this period he worked with a number of important contemporaries including Sonny Terry and Browie McGhee, Woody Guthrie and Josh White. He was jailed again in 1939, on assault charges, and served a year at Rikers Island. Recording for the labels Stinson, Capitol, and most-often, Moses Asch's Folkway Records, Leadbelly found little commercial success with songs such as 'Mr. Tom Hughs', 'Rock Island Line', 'Midnight Special', though the latter two would be revived as skiffle hits in the UK in the late Fifties. Others, like 'Cotton Fields', 'Black Betty' and 'Boll Weevil' became blues standards. Moving to Hollywood in the late Forties, Leadbelly failed to interest film-makers, and instead performed for dwindling nightclub audiences in Los Angeles and San Francisco. After returning to New York, he performed at Carnegie Hall. A film biography of his life *Leadbelly* was released in 1976. Following his death, his influence on a generation of musicians, from Bob Dylan to Van Morrison, was profound.
CAUSE: Lou Gehrig's Disease.
FURTHER READING: Wolf, Charles K. (1994). *The Life And Legend Of Leadbelly*. New York: Harper Perennial.

Lafayette Leake

Born June 1, 1920
Died August 14, 1990
A Mississippi-born blues pianist, Lafayette Leake played on hundreds of sessions at Chess Records in the Fifties

for acts such as Chuck Berry, Bo Diddley, Otis Rush and Howlin' Wolf. Leake had joined the label after replacing Leonard "Baby Doo" Caston in Willie Dixon's studio group. Leake later followed Dixon to Cobra Records.
CAUSE: Suffering a diabetic coma, he succumbed soon after. He died in Chicago.

Mike Leander

(MICHAEL FARR)
Born June 30, 1941
Died April 18, 1996
A British songwriter and producer, Mike Leander was best known for his collaborative efforts with Gary Glitter. Born in London, Leander joined a skiffle group in his teen years. After briefly attending law school, he enrolled at the London's Trinity College of Music. As musical director at Decca Records, one of Britain's leading labels, Leander produced hits for Billy Fury, Lulu and Marianne Faithfull, and worked with Alan Price, Gene Pitney, Roy Orbison and The Rolling Stones. Leander also arranged the string section on The Beatles' 'She's Leaving Home' from *Sgt. Pepper's Lonely Hearts Club Band.* After co-writing the theme for the British music programme *Ready Steady Go!*, Leander met assistant-director Paul Raven. Impressed with Raven's obvious talent, Leander added him to The Mike Leander Orchestra, which at the time was touring with The Bachelors. During this period Leander enjoyed hits with the compositions, 'I've Been A Bad Bad Boy' (Paul Jones), 'Early In The Morning' (Vanity Fare) and 'Lady Godiva' (Peter & Gordon). In 1964 he worked with The Drifters in New York City on the session for their classic song 'Under The Boardwalk'. Moving to MCA Records in 1969, Leander oversaw the London cast recording of *Jesus Christ Superstar.* More significantly, he re-shaped his former discovery Paul Raven into the successful pantomime rocker Gary Glitter. Collaborating with Glitter, Leander co-penned a series of British hits including his début, 'Rock And Roll Part 2', the perennial favourite 'Do You Wanna Touch Me' and his signature tune 'I'm The Leader Of The Gang'. Leander later oversaw the musical *Matador*, which chronicled the life of bullfighter El Cordobes.
CAUSE: Cancer. He died in London.

Ernie Leaner

(ERNEST LEANER)
Born August 15, 1921
Died April 1990
A former railroad worker, Ernie Leaner co-founded the Chicago-based label, One-Derful Records, along with his brother George Leaner. Operating a record distributorship since 1950, the Leaner brothers launched One-Derful in 1962, and later, the subsidiaries Mar-V-Lus, M-Pac and Midas. The Leaners recorded a number of Chicago soul and blues acts including Alvin Cash, McKinley Mitchell, The Five Dutones, and Otis Clay. With One-Derful folding in 1968, Ernie Leaner and his nephew Tony Leaner formed Toddlin' Town Records, recording many of the same artists as on his previous labels. Toddlin' Town folded in 1971.
CAUSE: Unknown. He died in Michigan City, Indiana.

George Leaner

(GEORGE WILLIS LEANER)
Born June 1, 1917
Died September 18, 1983
Hailing from Mississippi, George Leaner entered the record business in 1945 when his sister was awarded her ex-husband's Chicago record shop in a divorce settlement. While his brother Ernie worked at the store in 1940, George Leaner first worked at Groove Record in 1946. Expanding into record distribution in 1947, Leaner was hired as assistant to Lester Melrose. Both George and Ernie joined MS Distributers later that same year, with

George working as a salesman. In 1949, the brothers joined the Cord Distributing company, during which time they produced several singles that were released on Parkway Records. In 1950, the Leaners launched their own firm, United Record Distributors, with George the junior partner. Starting their own label, One-Derful Records, the Leaners had their first national hit in 1961 with McKinley Mitchell's 'The Town I Live In'. Also operating M-Pac, Mar-V-Lus, and Halo, the Leaners recorded hard soul artists such as The Five Du-Tones, Otis Clay, Johnny Sayles, and Alvin Cash. After the closing of One-Derful Records in 1968, Leaner worked in the music publishing business.
CAUSE: He died after an undisclosed short-term illness.

S.P. Leary

Born June 6, 1930
Died January 26, 1998
A prolific session drummer at Chess Records, S.P. Leary recorded and performed with Muddy Waters and Howlin' Wolf. A native Texan, he began his professional career in Dallas with T-Bone Walker, before arriving in Chicago in 1949. In the Sixties, Leary was a member of James Cotton's band before rejoining Muddy Waters' group. He later formed S.P. Leary and The Chicago All-Stars.
CAUSE: Complications from cancer and a stroke. He died at Trinity Hospital in Chicago.

Timothy Leary

Born October 22, 1920
Died May 31, 1996
A former Harvard psychology professor and LSD guru, Timothy Leary influenced the Sixties generation with his philosophy of "Turn On, Tune In, Drop Out". After experimenting with hallucinogenic mushrooms in 1960, Leary moved on to the then-legal drug LSD in 1961. A counter-culture hero, Leary was called "the most dangerous man in America" by President Nixon. Challenging drug laws, Leary was frequently jailed in the Seventies. Leary was celebrated in The Moody Blues' 'Legend Of The Mind (Timothy Leary's Dead)'. The 1997 tribute album *Beyond Life With Timothy Leary*, featured a new version of The Moody Blues' hit with the refrain changed to "Timothy Leary Lives". It was later revealed that Leary was an FBI informant during the Seventies.
CAUSE: Inoperable prostate cancer. He died in his sleep at his home in Beverly Hills. He had initially planned to commit suicide, hoping to broadcast the images over the internet.
FURTHER READING: Leary, Timothy. (1997). *Design For Dying*. London: Thorsons.

Otis Leavill

(OTIS LEAVILL COBB)
Born February 8, 1937
Died July 17, 2002
A soul music singer and producer, Otis Leavill also operated a record company. Born in rural Georgia but raised in Chicago, he started his musical education as a member of his family's gospel group, The Cobb Quartet. While in his teens, Leavill and future R&B star Major Lance gave up boxing to form an R&B quartet, The Floats. After attending college, Leavill issued a number of solo singles, some of which received local airplay. Hired in the early Sixties as record producer Carl Davis' assistant at Okeh Records, Leavill learned the music trade and discovered a number of hit acts including The Chi-lites and Tyrone Davis. Leaving Okeh, Leavill scored his first national hit with the Major Lance-produced ballad 'Let Her Love Me' (1965), which featured Leavill's signature, velvety falsetto. When Davis launched Dakar Records, Leavill was hired as the vice president, continuing to record hits for the label with 'I Love You' (1969) and 'Love Uprising' (1970). Following the closure of Dakar, Davis was hired by

Brunswick Records; Leavill followed Davis to Brunswick and issued several poor-selling records and, in 1976, Leavill and Carl Davis launched Chi-Sounds Records. Leavill later pursued a number of business ventures and, for a time, was a police officer in suburban Chicago.
CAUSE: Heart attack.

Lek Leckenby

(DEREK LECKENBY)
Born May 14, 1943
Died June 4, 1994
The guitarist for Herman's Hermits, Lek Leckenby was born in Leeds, England, but raised in Manchester. The group's tallest and eldest member, Leckenby dropped out of Manchester University, where he was studying civil engineering, to pursue a career in music. After leading his own local group The Wailers, he was asked by Herman's Hermits' manager Harvey Lisberg to join a new group as the bass player. He instead joined on guitar and brought along Wailers drummer Barry Whitwam. Last to join was a diminutive, struggling actor named Peter Noone. At the forefront of the British Invasion, Herman's Hermits hit number 1 in 1964 with a Carole King/Gerry Goffin composition, 'I'm Into Something Good'. With Leckenby adopting a folk guitar sound, 'Mrs. Brown You've Got A Lovely Daughter' was a surprise US chart topper; the band included the song on their début album as a joke, reluctantly releasing it after American deejays started playing the song; considered a perfectionist, Leckenby provided the blistering guitar solo on the Hermits' recording of the old British music hall favourite 'I'm Henry The Eighth, I Am'. Rivalling The Beatles for a time, Herman's Hermits enjoyed a string of lightweight chart hits on both sides of the Atlantic, but with the rise of serious rock in the late Sixties, the group's fame ebbed. The final blow came in 1971 when Peter Noone left for a solo career. Adding new vocalist Peter Cowap, the Hermits experimented with a country-rock sound. Noone returned to the group in 1973 for a reunion tour and then in 1974 unsuccessfully tried to claim ownership of the group's name. In the mid Seventies, Leckenby joined a revival version of the Noone-less group, which released several singles. Leckenby was still fronting a Hermits group at the time of his death, the group then fronted by lead singer C. Rod Gerrard.
CAUSE: He suffered from non-Hodgkins lymphoma, diagnosed two years earlier. Refusing to take his doctor's advice, he toured until two weeks before his death. He died in his hometown of Manchester, England.

Craig Lee

Born 1954
Died 1991
A pioneer within the Los Angeles punk scene, guitarist Craig Lee initially gained notoriety as a member of The Bags. An art school graduate, Lee was previously a screenwriter, penning scripts for television shows such as *The Mod Squad* and *Room 222*. Formed in 1977 as an all-girl band by sisters Alice and Pat Bag, The Bags were a first generation punk rock group. Expanded with the addition of male members, The Bags released their first single in 1979, 'Survive', and appeared in the punk documentary *The Decline Of Western Civilization*. A creative and motivated musician, Lee emerged as the group's chief songwriter and business manager. After The Bags disbanded in 1981, Lee joined Catholic Discipline, a punk band launched by Claude Bessy, that spawned the careers of two solo acts, El Vez (a Mexican Elvis impersonator) and an artist Lee would later join on tours, Phranc. Also a music journalist, Lee contributed to *Flipside* magazine, was the music editor of *The L.A. Weekly* and co-authored the book

Hardcore California: A History Of Punk And New Wave.
CAUSE: AIDS.

George Lee

Born March 24, 1936
Died October 25, 1994
The second tenor of the pop-soul group Ruby And The Romantics, George Lee teamed with several friends in Akron, Ohio, originally as an all-male outfit called The Supremes. After failing to find success in New York City, the group returned to Akron and added female vocalist Ruby Nash. Signing with Kapp Records, which insisted that Nash assume lead vocal duties, the redubbed Ruby And The Romantics enjoyed several hits including 'Our Day Will Come' and 'Hey There Lonely Boy'. But after leaving Kapp for ABC Records, Lee and the other male members of the group soon quit the group. Lee later worked as a truck driver.
CAUSE: Cancer; he suffered from the disease for eight years. He died in the Bronx, New York.

Jon Lee

(JON HENRY LEE)
Born March 28, 1968
Died January 7, 2002
A founding member of Welsh grunge rock act Feeder, drummer Jon Lee died just as the group had reached its commercial peak. A native of Newport, Lee first teamed with band member Grant Nicholas in the group Temper Temper. Relocating to London and adding Japanese bassist Taka Hirose, the group was renamed Real. Signing with Echo Records in 1995, the renamed Feeder emerged as a second generation grunge act, breaking through with their second album, *Polythene* (1997). Feeder achieved several hit singles including 'High' and reached the UK Top 10 with the albums *Yesterday Went Too Soon* and *Echo Park* (featuring 'Buck Rogers'). The group relocated to Florida in 2001.
CAUSE: Suicide. He died at his home in Miami.

Leonard Lee

Born June 29, 1936
Died October 23, 1976
The male half of the teenage, R&B duo, Shirley & Lee, Leonard Lee teamed with Shirley Goodman on a series of gritty releases. The duo notched their début hit in 1952 on Aladdin Records with 'I'm Gone', the session produced by the legendary Dave Bartholomew. The pair had first cut the tune on a self-financed demo disc. But when Aladdin co-owner Eddie Menser heard the song, he signed the squeaky-voiced, 14-year-old Shirley Goodman and the mature sounding 15-year-old Leonard Lee. Aladdin Records billed the duo as "The Sweethearts of the Blues", in an effort to promote a non-existent romance between the couple on songs like 'Shirley Come Back To Me', 'The Proposal', and 'Two Happy People'. Backed by the finest New Orleans session players on mostly Lee-composed material, Shirley and Lee enjoyed hits such as the million-selling 'Let The Good Times Roll' (1956) and the similar-sounding 'I Feel Good' (1957). Leaving Aladdin, Shirley & Lee then recorded for Warwick Records in 1961–62, before disbanding in 1963. Adopting a bluesy approach, Lee later pursued a solo career, recording for Imperial and Broadmoor Records. He also returned to his school, earning a degree in social work. (Shirley moved to the West Coast and teamed with Jessie Hill to perform as "Shirley & Jessie".) Shirley & Lee reunited in 1972 for some rock revival concerts.
CAUSE: Heart attack.

Peggy Lee

(NORMA DELORIS EGSTROM)
Born May 26, 1920
Died January 21, 2002
An elegant pop/jazz singer whose

career spanned several decades, Peggy Lee emerged from the big band tradition, getting her first break in 1941 when she was hired by Benny Goodman. During her two-year stint with Goodman, Lee was the featured vocalist on several hits including 'Somebody Else Is Taking My Place' and 'Why Don't You Do Right?' Marrying Goodman's guitarist Dave Barbour in 1943, Lee briefly retired before signing with Capitol Records the following year and continued her string of hits, many of which were penned with Barbour. At Decca in 1952, Lee recorded middle-of-the-road material including 'Lover' and 'Mr. Wonder'. Returning to Capitol in 1958, she thrived during the rock era, landing a Top 10 hit with her jazzy cover of Little Willie John's 'Fever'. Lee scored her final hit in 1969 with a Leiber & Stoller composition, the melancholy, Grammy-winning 'Is That All There Is?'. Also an actress, Lee starred in *The Jazz Singer*, portrayed a boozy singer in *Peter Kelly's Blues* and provided the voice for Peg and the Siamese cats in Disney's *Lady & The Tramp*.
CAUSE: Suffering from a host of maladies, she died from a heart attack at her home in Bel Air, California.

Marshall Leib

(MARSHALL PHILIP LEIBOVITZ)
Born January 26, 1939
Died March 15, 2002
As a member of The Teddy Bears – a short-lived group formed by a young Phil Spector – Marshall Leib enjoyed brief fame in the late Fifties. While attending Fairfax High School in Los Angeles, the 17-year-old Spector assembled The Teddy Bears, writing, producing and singing backup on a wry ballad inspired by the epitaph on his father's tombstone, 'To Know Him, Is To Love Him'. Featuring Leib on backing vocals and Annette Kleinbard on lead vocals, the song, originally a B-side, was a surprise chart-topper for the small Dore label; intended as a demo, and in stark form, it featured Spector on piano and guest Sandy Nelson on drums. Switching to the larger Imperial label, The Teddy Bears struggled on the charts, scoring a pair of minor hits, until the group disbanded after Kleinbard was seriously injured in a car accident. Leib later launched his own labels, Marsh and Capco, toured as a member of The Hollywood Argyles and provided backing guitar on a number of Duane Eddy sessions. He also worked in Hollywood, overseeing the music for a number of feature films including *Ode To Billy Joe* and *Macon County Line*. In 1996, Leib and Kleinbard were unsuccessful in their lawsuit against Spector over the non-payment of royalties for 'To Know Him, Is To Love Him'.
CAUSE: He died from a heart attack in Northridge, California.

Carolyn Leigh

(CAROLYN PAULA ROSENTHAL)
Born August 21, 1926
Died November 19, 1983
A pop songwriter whose first success came in 1951 with Lucky Millinder's 'I'm Just Waiting For You', Carolyn Leigh had previously worked as an ad writer at WQXR in New York City. Penning hundreds of songs, Leigh enjoyed hits with 'Young At Heart' (Frank Sinatra), 'The Day The Circus Left Town' (Eartha Kitt), and 'Witchcraft' (Frank Sinatra). She also composed material for several Broadway productions including *Peter Pan*, and starring Lucille Ball, *Wildcat*.
CAUSE: She suffered a heart attack while working with Marvin Hamlisch on a musical adaptation of *Smiles*.

Tony LeMans

Born 1963
Died June 24, 1992
A funk-rooted R&B singer-songwriter, Tony LeMans recorded for the Prince-owned Paisley Park label in the

late Eighties. LeMan's godfather was singer Billy Preston, and at one time he lived at the mansion of Motown Records founder Berry Gordy, Jr. After studying music for two years in college, he was discovered by Prince at a nightclub performance in San Francisco. From his début album, LeMans landed a minor R&B hit with 'Higher Than High' (1989). The San Francisco-based artist was working on his second album at the time of his death.
CAUSE: He was involved in a car crash while returning from a recording session in Los Angeles.

John Lennon

(JOHN WINSTON LENNON)
Born October 9, 1940
Died December 8, 1980
No rock death has caused such worldwide grief as that of John Lennon, senselessly gunned down outside his New York home by a deranged Beatle fan. From that day forward, all around the world, the image, legend and devotion surrounding The Beatles was never quite the same. As the pivotal member and social conscience of The Beatles, Lennon was a towering figure in rock, universally respected for his achievements not just as a musician, singer and songwriter but as a spokesman for his generation, a peace campaigner and a romantic philosopher. At the time of his death he was re-emerging after a self-imposed four-year exile from music, feeling his way once again into the public consciousness. John Lennon was born in Liverpool, England, a year after the start of World War II. His parents, Fred and Julia Lennon, split up when he was two. Julia Lennon gave up custody of young John to her sister Mary (Mimi) who raised him in a middle-class area of Liverpool. His seafaring father all but abandoned him, and his wayward mother lived close by and visited her son on a regular basis until she was killed in a traffic accident when John was 18. Given an inexpensive guitar by Mimi, Lennon was an impressionable teenager, eager to be a part of the British skiffle craze. In 1957 he formed The Quarry Men with his friend Peter Shotten on washboard, and met Paul McCartney the same year at a church fete. Impressing Lennon with his ability to tune a guitar, McCartney was brought on board. With the addition of a young George Harrison, and then drummer Pete Best, the group evolved into Johnny And The Moondogs. Heavily influenced by black American artists, they swopped skiffle for R&B and rockabilly hits, but at the same time Lennon and McCartney began writing their own material together and occasionally performing these original songs between the cover versions. In 1959 Lennon attended Liverpool Art College where he befriended Stuart Sutcliffe, a talented painter, who the following year became the group's bass player, and as The Silver Beatles they toured Scotland behind pop star Johnny Gentle. During this period, Lennon was also mastering the harmonica and piano. In search of regular club work, in August of 1960 the group fled Liverpool for the red-light district of Hamburg, Germany. There, Lennon and the group would hone their musical skills in gruelling, several-hour-a-night performances. Returning to Liverpool a much improved group, The Beatles made the first of almost 300 appearances at the Cavern club. Soon after, the group would lose Sutcliffe, but gain Brian Epstein as manager. Meanwhile, Lennon would marry his pregnant girlfriend Cynthia Powell in 1962, the union producing Lennon's first son, Julian. After failing an audition with Decca Records in January 1962, The Beatles were signed by George Martin at EMI's Parlophone subsidiary. Shortly thereafter, drummer Pete Best was

fired and replaced by Ringo Starr. The Beatles landed their début British hit with the modest chart entry 'Love Me Do' (1962), but followed up with the chart-topping, 'Please Please Me'. Thereafter The Beatles could do no wrong in their home country, and the chaos that followed in their wake was dubbed Beatlemania. They enjoyed a string of hits in Britain, all of them penned by Lennon & McCartney, and in so doing changed the face of pop music forever, establishing the self-contained 'group' as its dominant force, and wresting power from the music publishers and investing it in the artists and writers themselves. In 1964 The Beatles conquered America, topping the US charts early in the year with 'I Want To Hold Your Hand'. On February 9, 1964, The Beatles captured the heart of America with their appearance on *The Ed Sullivan Show*. Rivalling only the early Elvis Presley in their domination of the charts, The Beatles revolutionised pop music during this period with hits like 'From Me To You', 'She Loves You', 'Can't Buy Me Love', the title track of their first film *A Hard Day's Night*, and 'I Feel Fine'. At one point in 1964, the group occupied the first five places in the *Billboard* Hot 100, a feat never repeated. Lennon was already acclaimed as a powerhouse vocalist, most notably on the group's cover of The Isley Brothers' 'Twist And Shout'. He was also known for his word-play and clever song titles like 'Eight Days A Week'. His engaging Liverpudlian wit and love of puns were evident in the two books of prose he published during this period, *In His Own Write* (1964) and *A Spaniard In The Works* (1965). The Beatles' success story continued throughout 1965, a year when all four members received MBE awards from the Queen and enjoyed chart-topping hits with 'Ticket To Ride' and the film theme 'Help!', one of the first songs to expose Lennon's insecurity at the height of his fame. In America, McCartney enjoyed additional success with the solo-billed 'Yesterday'. The year ended with a double-sided number 1 'We Can Work It Out'/'Day Tripper' and the highly influential album, *Rubber Soul*, which featured several Lennon classics, including the sarcastic, punning, Dylan-inspired 'Norwegian Wood', the titillating 'Girl' and the stark, autobiographical 'In My Life'. In March 1966, Lennon created a furore when he was quoted in a British newspaper proclaiming that The Beatles "are bigger than Jesus". The group's subsequent US tour was beset with problems, including public burnings of Beatle memorabilia and death threats. It proved sufficient to convince the group that they should retire from public performances. In the studio their work continued in groundbreaking fashion. 1966's *Revolver* featured some of Lennon's most adventurous work, most notably the world-weary 'I'm Only Sleeping' and two LSD-inspired compositions 'She Said She Said' and 'Tomorrow Never Knows'. After a long break in singles releases, the group returned in early 1967 with the brilliant double A-side 'Penny Lane'/'Strawberry Fields Forever'. The latter was one of Lennon's most striking and experimental works. It was followed by the summer release of one of rock music's most famous albums, *Sgt. Pepper's Lonely Hearts Club Band.* One of the great studio albums of the era, it revolutionised rock music with its complex array of electronic recording techniques and strong lyricism. Lennon's influence was notable on several of the tracks, including the psychedelic-tinged 'Lucy In The Sky With Diamonds' (inspired by a drawing by his son, Julian), 'Good Morning, Good Morning', 'Being For The Benefit Of Mr Kite' and the awe-inspiring 'Day In The Life'. With the group members slowly drifting apart, Lennon became the first Beatle to pursue a film role apart from the group, cutting his long hair for the role of Private Gripweed in *How I Won The War.* In August 1967, while The Beatles were studying transcendental meditation with the Maharishi Mahesh Yogi, their manager Brian Epstein died from a drugs overdose. Lennon was stunned by the news of his mentor's death and later admitted that it signalled the demise of The Beatles. McCartney took the helm for their next venture *Magical Mystery Tour*, which included Lennon's Edward Lear-influenced 'I Am The Walrus'. Lennon continued to provide startling compositions during this period, including 'Revolution', the B-side of the single, 'Hey Jude', the first single to appear on their record label Apple. Over the next couple of years, the group would record three more major albums, the double *The Beatles, Abbey Road* and *Let It Be.* During this period, Lennon became romantically and artistically involved with Japanese artist Yoko Ono, whom he had first met at a London art gallery in late 1966. By November 1968, he had divorced his wife Cynthia. Four months later, on March 20, he married Yoko Ono in Gibraltar. The nuptials were immortalised in The Beatles' autobiographical 'The Ballad Of John And Yoko', recorded without George and Ringo. By this point, Lennon had effectively begun the second stage of his career, working with Yoko Ono on the avante-garde *Unfinished Music No. 1 – Two Virgins,* distributed by Track Records after EMI objected to its full-frontal nude shot of the two performers. The *audio-verite* album consisted of 30 minutes of voices, distorted instruments and various sound effects. The work was rapidly followed by two more avante-garde experiments, *Unfinished Music No. 2 – Life With The Lions* and *The Wedding Album.* Both offered snapshots of the pair's eventful lives, including Yoko's miscarriage and John's protective pleading of guilty to a marijuana charge. Lennon and Ono created more headlines when they embarked upon a series of "bed-in" peace missions, inviting television crews to their room at the Amsterdam Hilton where they stayed in bed for a week "to register our protest against all the suffering and violence in the world." One month later, Lennon launched his next project, The Plastic Ono Band, whose single 'Give Peace A Chance', recorded at Montreal's Queen Elizabeth Hotel with the world's media present, became a summer hit and remains a worldwide peace anthem. It was followed by the harrowing 'Cold Turkey', Lennon's brittle account of his withdrawal from heroin. With an instant supergroup, including Eric Clapton, Klaus Voormann and Alan White, The Plastic Ono Band issued *Live Peace In Toronto 1969* at the end of the year. A third POB single 'Instant Karma' displayed Lennon's talents to the fore once more and its chart success coincided with the return of his MBE to the Queen as a protest for world peace. Following The Beatles' dissolution in April 1970, the Lennons settled in New York. In March 1970, they enrolled in Arthur Janov's primal therapy programme, which inspired Lennon's first solo album proper – *John Lennon/Plastic Ono Band* – one of the most lacerating and self-analytical albums ever issued by a popular performer. It remains the most accomplished work of Lennon's post-Beatles period. The follow-up *Imagine* was more successful commercially and its title track became one of Lennon's most well-known and loved songs. Lennon's involvement in politics was evident on the sloganeering 'Power To The People' while his quest for peace reached an unexpected apogee on the festive standard 'Happy Xmas (War Is Over)'. Embraced by New York radicals such as Jerry Rubin and Abbie Hoffmann, John & Yoko teamed up with bar band Elephant's

Memory in 1972 for the overtly politicised *Some Time In New York City*, which offered Lennon's views on women's liberation, the IRA and US prison riots. By this time, the Lennons had scaled down their public appearances, although they did top the bill at Madison Square Garden for the One To One concerts for mentally handicapped children. The following year, Lennon released the accessible *Mind Games*, whose stand-out title track proved a highlight. By 1974, Lennon was temporarily separated from Yoko Ono, in what he later called his "lost weekend". Living with May Pang and hanging out with drinking/drug buddies Jesse Ed Davis and Nilsson (whose album *Pussycats* he produced), Lennon's high jinx were well reported in the US press. Despite his recklessness, he managed to complete the melodic and accomplished *Walls And Bridges* in 1974. It included two major hits, a chart-topping duet with Elton John – 'Whatever Gets You Through The Night' – and '#9 Dream'. Lennon's final concert appearance also occurred during this period when he guested with Elton John at Madison Square Garden and reunited with Yoko Ono. A long-standing legal dispute with publisher Morris Levy was settled by the release of 1975's *Rock'N'Roll*, a back to roots album of covers, which proved a modest success and included a US hit courtesy of Ben E. King's 'Stand By Me'. That same year, Lennon co-wrote David Bowie's hit 'Fame' and on October 9 his son Sean Taro Ono Lennon was born. Lennon effectively retired from professional music-making for the next four years to become what he termed a "house husband". In 1980 Lennon re-emerged into the public eye with a series of interviews promoting the comeback album *Double Fantasy* (1980) on which he and Ono had recorded alternate tracks. Released just weeks before Lennon's death, the first single, a retro-sounding pop-rocker '(Just Like) Starting Over' was zooming up the charts. With Lennon's death mourned on a worldwide scale, Ono vowed to continue releasing Lennon material to keep his memory alive, and there have been several posthumous releases including boxed compilations, books and videos.

CAUSE: Lennon was shot to death outside his apartment building, the Dakota on Central Park West in New York City, shortly before 11 p.m. by Mark David Chapman, a deranged, 25-year-old with mental problems. After finishing a recording session at the Record Plant studio, Lennon and Ono headed for their Dakota apartment on West 72nd Street, instead of going out for dinner. After Lennon stepped out of his limousine, Chapman appeared from the apartment alcove, called out, "Mr. Lennon", dropped into a combat stance and fired. The gunman did not flee. Instead he stood calmly by and read from a copy of J.D. Salinger's *Catcher In The Rye*. Arrested by police, he shouted "I am Holden Caulfield, the catcher in the rye of the present generation". Shot seven times, Lennon bled to death in a police cruiser en route to Roosevelt Hospital. Earlier in the day, Lennon had signed Chapman's copy of *Double Fantasy*; and the record was left on a window ledge of the building. Pleading guilty to first-degree murder on June 22, 1981, the killer was sentenced to 20-years-to-life at the Attica Correctional Facility. A former heroin and LSD user, he shunned his lawyer's advice to claim insanity and although he has been eligible for parole since December 1990, his release is unlikely. Lennon's murderer gave his first media interview in 1987; and in a letter to *The New York Times*, he justified the killing in a passage from *Catcher In The Rye*. He also read the verse from the novel in court: "I keep picturing all these little kids playing some game in this big field of rye and all. Thousands of little kids, and nobody's around – nobody big, I mean– except me. And I'm standing on the edge of some crazy cliff. What I have to do, I have to catch everybody if they start to go over the cliff – I mean, if they're running and they don't look where they're going I have to come out from somewhere and catch them. That's all I'd do all day. I'd just be the catcher in the rye."

FURTHER READING: Norman, Phillip. (1981). *Shout!: The True Story Of The Beatles*. London: Elm Tree Books. Coleman, Ray. (1995). *Lennon: The Definitive Biography*. London: Pan. Robertson, John. (1991). *The Art & Music Of John Lennon*. London: Omnibus.

J.B. Lenoir

Born March 5, 1929
Died April 29, 1967

A Mississippi-born, Chicago-based electric blues guitarist and songwriter, J.B. Lenoir is best known for 'Mama Talk To Your Daughter', and the controversial singles, 'Korea Blues' and 'Eisenhower Blues'. Possessing a high-pitched voice, Lenoir was performing mostly acoustic blues by the Sixties.

CAUSE: Struck by an automobile on a Chicago street, he died three weeks later from untreated complications. He died in Champaign, Illinois.

David Lerchey

Born December 3, 1937
Died January 29, 2005

A member of pioneering interracial doo-wop group The Dell-Vikings, Indiana native David Lerchey sang tenor and baritone. Serving in the US Air Force in the mid Fifties, Lerchey was stationed in Pittsburgh where five black servicemen had formed an off-hours singing group, The Dell-Vikings. After winning a series of Armed Forces talent contests, the group caught the attention of Pittsburgh DJ Barry Kaye but before the group could record, Bernard Robertson was shipped out to Germany and replaced by David Lerchey, the group's first white member. Recording at Kaye's small basement studio and aided by local record distributor Joe Averbach, The Del Vikings scored a genre-defining hit in 1957 with the innovative, 'Come Go With Me'. Initially released by the small Fee Bee label, the record went national after it was leased to the larger Dot label. The group followed with the rockabilly-inflected 'Whispering Bells', another Top 10 crossover hit. Because some of the members – including Lerchey – were underage when they signed with Fee Bee, the group splintered into two camps for a time, with Lerchey's group moving to Mercury Records and lead vocalist Kripp Johnson remaining at Fee Bee. At Mercury, the group achieved their final hit with 'Cool Shake' (1957), which charted at the same time as 'Whispering Bells' but this confused fans and record stores who backed off from both groups. After disbanding in the mid Sixties, The Dell-Vikings reunited in 1970, working the oldies circuit into the 21st century.

CAUSE: He died from cancer and heart problems at a veteran's hospital in the Miami suburb of Hallandale, Florida.

Bobby Lester

(ROBERT LESTER)
Born January 13, 1932
Died October 15, 1980

The tenor vocalist of the pioneering doo-wop group The Moonglows, Louisville, Kentucky-native Bobby Lester had joined the group in late 1952. Formed in Cleveland in 1949 by Harvey Fuqua as The Crazy Sounds, the group searched out local deejay Alan Freed, mistakenly believing he was black. Becoming their benefactor and their manager, Freed renamed the group The Moonglows after his own Moondog radio show. Recording for Freed's new Champagne label, the

group landed a regional hit with 'I Just Can't Tell No Lie' (1952). Following up with five singles on Chance Records in Chicago over the next year, the group managed only a minor hit with the ballad, 'I Was Wrong'. During this time, the heavy-set, pompadour-wearing Lester worked days in a coal yard. With Chess buying out The Moonglows' contract from the financially doomed Chance records, the group scored their breakthrough hit with the crossover entry 'Sincerely' (1954), which was forced to compete on the charts with a whitebread cover version by The McGuire Sisters. Lester sang lead on most of the group's hits which included, 'Most Of All' (1955), 'See Saw' (1956), 'Please Send Me Someone To Love' (1957), and a song he wrote, 'The Beating Of My Heart' (1958). The Moonglows also recorded on the Chess subsidiary, Checker as The Moonlighters, scoring R&B hits with 'Shoo Doo Bee Doo' (1954) and 'We Go Together' (1956). Lester left The Moonglows in early 1958 over monetary issues. As the lead tenor, Lester was receiving more money than the rest of the group, but less than Fuqua, who doubled as the group's producer. Returning to Louisville in the Sixties, Lester worked as a nightclub manager. In 1970 he formed The Aristocrats, a year later renaming the group The New Moonglows. This group recorded new versions of the group's old hits, landing a minor R&B hit with 'Sincerely '72'. Lester's son later joined the touring version of the group.
CAUSE: Lung cancer. Contracting pneumonia, he died in Louisville, Kentucky, after a 50-day hospital stay.

Irwin Levine

Born 1939
Died January 22, 1997
A songwriter, Irwin Levine co-penned 'This Diamond Ring' (Gary Lewis & The Playboys), and several hits for Tony Orlando and Dawn including 'Tie A Yellow Ribbon' and 'Candida'. He began his songwriting career in the early Sixties in collaboration with future rocker Al Kooper.
CAUSE: Kidney failure. He died at a Livingston, New Jersey, hospital.

Eunice Levy

(EUNICE LEVY FROST)
Born May 10, 1931
Died May 26, 2002
After performing at a talent contest in Los Angeles, Eunice Levy was asked to join a doo-wop group, Gene Forrest & The Four Feathers. When the band split from Forrest, he formed the duo, Gene & Eunice. Romantically involved, Levy and Forrest were nicknamed "The Sweethearts of Rhythm & Blues". Composing much of their own material, the duo scored two R&B hits in 1955, 'Ko Ko Mo' and 'This Is My Story'. (Perry Como's remake of 'Ko Ko Mo' hit the pop charts.) Although the duo remained popular in Southern California, no further hits followed. Gene Forrest died in 2003.
CAUSE: Liver failure. She died in Las Vegas.

Morris Levy

(MOISHE LEVY)
Born August 27, 1927
Died May 21, 1990
A notorious music business mogul who was involved in the many facets of the industry, Morris Levy built an extremely lucrative business empire, principally in song publishing. Born in the Bronx, Levy received little formal education but quickly progressed through the ranks of the East Coast crime underworld. In his first major acquisition, Levy joined eight partners in 1949 in opening the legendary Birdland nightclub in Manhattan. When agents of BMI and ASCAP came in and demanded royalty fees for playing music in his venue, his first thought was that a rival mob was moving in on his operation. Realising

that their "collections" were legally enforceable, Levy expanded into different aspects of the music industry, including jukebox companies, record distribution, label ownership and publishing. With his ties to major underworld figures (the FBI cited connections between him and the Genovese family), Levy built a massive web of businesses that included Roulette and several other record labels. His first publishing success would come with the George Shearing composition 'Lullabye Of Birdland'. Levy also earned much press in the mid Fifties when he teamed up with the charismatic deejay and promoter Alan Freed. By the Seventies Levy's holdings included the 160-store Strawberries Records chain. In the mid Seventies Levy sued John Lennon for an extraordinary $42 million in a case stemming from Lennon's alleged plagiarism of Chuck Berry's song 'You Can't Catch Me' on The Beatles' 1969 recording 'Come Together', Levy being Berry's publisher. Lennon had offered to record some Levy songs on his *Rock'N'Roll* album as compensation but Levy wasn't satisfied. The case was eventually thrown out. Targeted for decades by authorities for his business practices, Levy was finally convicted of extortion in 1988, but he cheated fate by dying before he could serve any prison time.
CAUSE: Liver cancer. He died at his home in Ghent, New York.
ADDITIONAL READING: Dannen, Frederic. (1991). *Hit Men: Power Brokers And Fast Money Inside The Music Business*. New York: Vintage.

Sir Edward Lewis

Born 1901
Died January 29, 1980
A giant in the British music industry, Sir Edward Lewis took over the reins of (British) Decca Records in 1931, two years after his family's stockholding company placed the company on the British stock market. Educated at Cambridge University, Lewis immediately altered the focus of Decca away from a manufacturer of gramophones to a modern record company. As the longtime chairman of Decca, Lewis oversaw its dominance in Great Britain for the next several decades. Decca was at the forefront of rock'n'roll, releasing Bill Haley's groundbreaking 'Rock Around The Clock' and also Buddy Holly's records through their Coral subsidiary. They also signed Britain's first rock'n'roll star, Tommy Steele. Although in early 1962, Decca missed out on the chance to sign The Beatles, in 1963, they got exclusive licence to release The Rolling Stones records worldwide, while riding the crest of the British Beat Boom by signing such acts as Brian Poole & The Tremeloes, The Nashville Teens, The Mojos, Them, The Zombies, The Small Faces, Marianne Faithfull, Lulu, and MOR artists The Bachelors, Tom Jones and Englebert Humperdinck. A leading record company up until the end of the Sixties, Decca issued its product in the US through subsidiary labels London and Parrot. Sir Edward and the board of Decca were pawns in a game played by The Rolling Stones newly appointed business manager Allen Klein whose cut-throat negotiating tactics got the Stones a favourable deal. Despite this the company insisted on exercising its powers of veto over the Stones product – most notably the sleeve to the band's 1968 album *Beggars Banquet* which depicted a graffiti-strewn toilet wall. With the company's adversarial relationship with The Rolling Stones ending in 1970 (the Stones set up their own label with Atlantic Records) the label lost its cachet, and other promising signings, including Cat Stevens and Genesis, also left to enjoy far greater success elsewhere. Lewis died only days after he agreed to sell Decca to PolyGram.
CAUSE: He died in his sleep at his home in London.

Ephraim Lewis

Born 1968
Died March 18, 1994
A talented British soul singer, Ephraim Lewis died before he could reap mass success. The youngest son of a devout Jamaican immigrant, the gospel-trained Lewis headed a Jackson Five-styled childhood gospel group with his siblings. Leaving home at 16 after his mother's sudden death, Lewis was discovered at 22 by the operators of Axis Studio in Sheffield. Tutoring and shaping Lewis for four years, Axis producers Kevin Bacon and Jonathan Quarmby placed him with the British branch of Elektra Records in 1991. Managed by David Harper (of UB40 and Robert Palmer fame), the charismatic Lewis recorded just one, much-acclaimed album *Skin*. Heavily promoted by Elektra in a multi-million dollar campaign, the album sold below expectations. With tensions breaking out between Elektra and Axis, Lewis was sent to the US by Elektra to work on his second album and was teamed with top producer Glenn Ballard. Arriving in California, he died six weeks later.
CAUSE: Suicide. He jumped from a balcony of a Los Angeles apartment under mysterious circumstances. Lewis' family filed charges against Los Angeles police, claiming that Elektra Records and David Harper were responsible for the death. Police reported that they had chased the unclothed Lewis for an hour. After climbing up the side of an apartment building, he had eluded them by jumping from balcony to balcony. The family also claimed police shot Lewis three times with a 50,000-watt stun gun, causing his fall.

Furry Lewis

(WALTER LEWIS)
Born March 6, 1893
Died September 14, 1981
A Mississippi-born, Memphis-based folk-blues guitarist, Furry Lewis initially worked with W.C. Handy. Following a railroad accident in 1916, his right leg was amputated. Moving to Memphis, Lewis first recorded in 1927 for Vocalion Records, adopting a country-blues, slide-guitar style on such blues ballads as 'Kassie Jones' and 'John Henry'. Rediscovered in the Fifties, he recorded for several labels and later toured with Don Nix. He also appeared in the Burt Reynolds film, *W.W. And The Dixie Dance Kings*. Joni Mitchell paid tribute to him on 'Furry Sings The Blues' on her 1976 album *Hejira*.
CAUSE: He suffered second-degree burns at his Memphis home in a blaze started by a faulty air conditioner. He subsequently died of heart failure on September 14.

Jimmy Lewis

(JAMES E. LEWIS)
Born April 11, 1939
Died September 11, 2004
An R&B singer/songwriter, Jimmy Lewis' first success came in 1968 when Ray Charles recorded his composition 'Understanding'. Lewis wrote or co-wrote every track on Charles' 1969 album, *Doin' His Thing*, which included a Lewis/Charles duet, 'If It Wasn't For Bad Luck'. Lewis subsequently released five, poor-selling singles on the Charles-owned label, Tangerine Records. Recording sporadically during the next two decades, Lewis also operated Miss Butch Records, scoring a novelty R&B hit in 1997 with 'Bill' by Peggy Scott-Adams.
CAUSE: Initially diagnosed with cancer of the pancreas in the early Nineties, the disease had spread to his liver. He died at his home in Los Angeles.

Joe E. Lewis

Born c. 1942
Died 1975
Conway Twitty's bassist, Joe E. Lewis later worked as a producer. Lewis appeared on all of Twitty's rock and

country hits until 1975, including 'It's Only Make Believe'. Before joining Twitty's group in 1956, Lewis had been a member of the Sun Records rockabilly group, Sonny Burgess & The Pacers.
CAUSE: Car crash.

Rick Lewis

Born September 2, 1933
Died April 19, 2005
The tenor vocalist of Philadelphia-based doo-wop group The Silhouettes, Rick Lewis began his singing career during childhood as a member of the Philadelphia All Boys Choir. While serving in the US Army, Lewis performed with future R&B stars Jesse Belvin and Curtis Williams, and after his discharge he joined a popular group, The Parakeets, before being hired as the road manager for The Turbans. Subsequently joining The Gospel Tornadoes, Lewis convinced the group to abandon religious for secular music. After singing gospel music on Sundays, the renamed Thunderbirds would moonlight during the week as a doo-wop group. Discovered by deejay Kae Williams, the group signed with his label, Junior Records. Recording the Lewis composition 'Get A Job' as the intended B-side for their début single, the renamed Silhouettes scored a massive, million-selling hit. One of the most enduring doo-wop singles of the era, 'Get A Job' spawned a number of answer records and even a revival group, Sha Na Na. With no further hits, The Silhouettes disbanded in 1968, later reuniting to tour the oldies circuit.
CAUSE: He died from kidney failure at Einstein Hospital in Philadelphia.

Rudy Lewis

Born August 23, 1936
Died May 20, 1964
One of over three dozen musicians who have sung with The Drifters, Rudy Lewis provided the lead vocals on several of their hits in the early Sixties. Born in Philadelphia, Lewis began in the gospel field as a backing member of The Clara Ward Singers. Joining The Drifters in late 1960, Lewis replaced Ben E. King, who was fired by the group's manager George Treadwell for complaining about his meagre salary. (Treadwell employed Johnny Williams and Charlie Thomas as interim lead singers.) With Lewis at the helm, The Drifters managed seven US Top 40 pop hits including 'Some Kind Of Wonderful' (1961), 'Please Stay' (1961), a Pomus & Shuman composition 'Sweets For My Sweet' (1961), a Goffin & King composition 'When My Little Girl Is Smiling' (1962), 'Up On The Roof' (1962) and 'On Broadway' (1963). Lewis often alternated the lead vocals with Johnny Moore. In 1963, Lewis also recorded a poor-selling solo single, 'Baby I Dig You', at Atlantic Records. The group lost much of its spark after Lewis' death.
CAUSE: He suffered a drug overdose-related brain seizure on the morning of a session where he was scheduled to record 'Under The Boardwalk'. Lewis was found in a hotel room with a needle in his arm. According to Drifters biographers Tony Allan and Faye Treadwell, fellow Drifters member Johnny Moore claimed that Lewis died by drowning on his own vomit after a night of over-eating.
FURTHER READING: Allan, Tony; & Treadwell, Faye. (1993). *Save The Last Dance For Me: The Musical Legacy Of The Drifters, 1953–1993*. Ann Arbor, MI: Popular Culture Ink.

Smiley Lewis

(OVERTON AMOS LEMONS)
Born July 5, 1913
Died October 6, 1966
A gritty-voiced R&B singer who emerged in the mid Forties, Smiley Lewis had a distinctive, melodic, shouting delivery. Born in DeQuincy,

Louisiana, Lewis ran away from home in his teens to work as a musician in New Orleans. There he joined The Thomas Jefferson Dixieland Band, a talented outfit that featured pianist Tuts Washington. A member of the band off and on for a decade, Lewis then formed a trio in 1945 with Tuts Washington and Herman Seale. A great stage performer but only an average guitarist, Lewis blended blues and R&B balladry, his vocals reminiscent of a rougher version of Louis Armstrong. Recording briefly at DeLuxe Records in 1947 as "Smiling" Lewis, he released just one single. Then signed as a solo artist with Imperial Records in 1950, Lewis was teamed with talented producer Dave Bartholomew. Determined to land on the national charts, Lewis finally broke through in 1952 with 'The Bells Are Ringing'; his hit run continued with: featuring Huey Smith on piano, 'I Hear You Knockin'' (1955); 'One Night (Of Sin)' (1956); and 'Please Listen To Me' (1956). Lewis was often compared to Imperial-labelmate Fats Domino and was said to have filled in for the popular singer on several recordings. Although 'I Hear You Knockin'' was an R&B hit for Lewis, the cover version by Gale Storm (1955) fared well on the pop charts; then in 1958 Elvis Presley recorded a sanitised version of Lewis' 'One Night (Of Sin)'. Leaving Imperial in 1960, Lewis recorded for several different labels in the Sixties, but never had another hit; at Loma Records, Lewis was produced by Allen Toussaint. 'I Hear You Knockin'' was reprised as a UK chart topping hit for Dave Edmunds in 1970.
CAUSE: Stomach cancer. He died at his New Orleans home a few days after undergoing an operation.

Ned "Ebn" Liben

Born April 18, 1953
Died February 18, 1998
Synthesizer player, and half of the Eighties pop-rock synthesizer duo Ebn-Ozn, Ned "Ebn" Liben enjoyed a pair of minor, early MTV hits with 'Bag Lady' and 'AEIOU (Sometimes Y)', both tracks culled from the duo's 1984 Elektra album, *Feeling Cavalier.*
CAUSE: Heart attack. He died in New York City.

Liberace

(WLADZIU VALENTINO LIBERACE)
Born May 16, 1919
Died February 4, 1987
A flamboyant pianist who combined classical music with an eclectic blend of popular styles, Liberace came to fame in the early Fifties via several popular television programmes. Dressed in a tuxedo and sequined cape, Liberace would be seated at a candelabra-lit grand piano. Selling millions of records and filling large venues, he became a favourite of middle-aged ladies. His repertoire featured many popular classics, augmented by show tunes. He was a huge influence on the popular pianists of the Fifties and one of the most celebrated entertainers of his era. In the Eighties, Liberace was outed when he was the target of a palimony suit filed by his former, young, male lover.
CAUSE: AIDS. He died in Palm Springs, California.
FURTHER READING: Thomas, Bob. (1989). *Liberace: The True Story*. New York: St. Martin's.

Jimmy Liggins

Born October 14, 1922
Died July 18, 1983
A popular guitarist and R&B bandleader, Jimmy Liggins scored a string of rocking hits. A self-taught musician, he was previously a driver for his brother's band, Joe Liggins & The Honeydrippers. Launching his own band in 1946, Jimmy Liggins joined Specialty Records where he scored a trio of R&B smashes with 'Teardrop Blues', 'Don't Put Me Down', and 'Drunk'. But while touring with his

band, The Drops of Joy, he was shot in the face in 1949 at a stop in Jackson, Mississippi. With Joe Liggins signed with Specialty Records in 1950, Jimmy Liggins frequently teamed with his brother. Switching to Aladdin Records, Jimmy Liggins recorded the often-covered 'I Ain't Drunk'. With his career waning, in 1958 Liggins opened his own label and artist management company, Duplex Records. He retired from music in 1978 to operate a music school in North Carolina.
CAUSE: Unknown. He died in Durham, North Carolina.

Joe Liggins

Born July 9, 1916
Died August 1, 1987
Pioneering jump-blues artist and leader of The Honeydrippers, Joe Liggins scored a career-defining hit in 1945 at Exclusive Records with the self-penned proto-R&B smash 'The Honeydripper'. Born in Oklahoma, he was a pivotal figure in the rise of West Coast R&B. A multi-instrumentalist, Liggins had previously been a member of bands led by Cee Pee Johnson and Sammy Franklin. Forming his own group in 1945, he followed his million-selling dèbut hit 'The Honeydripper' with a strong run of R&B chart entries including 'I Got A Right To Cry' (1946), 'Blow Mr. Jackson' (1947), and 'The Darktown Strutters' Ball' (1948). With the closure of Exclusive Records, Joe Liggins followed his brother Jimmy Liggins to Imperial Records. There, Joe Liggins scored several more hits including the crossover smash, 'Pink Champagne' (1951). At the label, the Liggins brothers often teamed on recordings. Jumping from label to label, Joe Liggins failed to survive into the rock'n'roll era. Reprising his jump-blues sound, Liggins was enjoying newfound popularity in the Eighties.
CAUSE: Stroke. He died in Los Angeles.

Mance Lipscomb

(BODYGLIN LIPSCOMB)
Born April 9, 1895
Died January 30, 1976
The son of an emancipated slave, Texas-born blues guitarist Mance Lipscomb did not record until late in life at the age of 65. A sharecropper who performed at weekends much of his life, Lipscomb was discovered by a pair of folklorists at 1960. These field recordings were issued later that year on Arhoolie Records as *Texas Songster.* Infusing old style gospel and ragtime into his music, he garnered a strong following during the blues boom of the Sixties. With his deep repertoire of songs, Lipscomb was embraced by blues purists as a musical genius in the tradition of Leadbelly. Lipscomb left the stage in 1974.
CAUSE: Natural causes. He died in Navasota, Texas.
FURTHER READING: Lipscomb, Mance. (1993). *I Say For Me A Parable: The Oral Autobiography Of Mance Lipscomb.* New York: W.W. Norton.

Little Caesar

(HARRY CAESAR)
Born February 18, 1926
Died June 14, 1994
A Fifties R&B singer, Little Caeser enjoyed his biggest hit with 'Goodbye Baby' (1952). Better known for his acting credits, he appeared in the films *Lady Sings The Blues and The Longest Yard.*
CAUSE: Unknown. He died in California.

Little Eva

(EVA NARCISSUS BOYD)
Born June 29, 1943
Died April 9, 2003
A popular pop-soul singer of the early Sixties, Little Eva recorded one of the most enduring dance records of the rock era. Discovered by hit songwriters Carole King and Gerry Goffin who had hired her as the babysitter for their two-year-old daughter, the couple

asked Eva to sing a demo version of 'The Loco-Motion'. Intended for Dee Dee Sharp (of 'Mashed Potato Time' fame), the song was rejected by Sharp's producers, but on hearing the demo, the composition's publisher, Don Kirshner, decided to record Little Eva. The first single released on Kirshner's Dimension Records, Little Eva's fully orchestrated, re-recorded version of 'The Loco-Motion' reached the top of the charts and, in the process set off a dance craze. Her follow-up hits included 'Keep Your Hands Off My Baby' (1962), 'Let's Turkey Trot' (1963) and a duet with Big Dee Irwin, 'Swingin' On A Star' (1964). Little Eva later recorded for a series of labels in the Sixties, sometimes under the name Little Eva Harris. 'The Loco-Motion' would return to the Top 10 on two more occasions via cover versions: by Grand Funk in 1974 and by Kylie Minogue in 1988, while Little Eva's original version returned to the British charts in 1972. Following the death of her mother in 1971, Little Eva left the music industry and returned to North Carolina where she raised her children and worked in a series of low-paying jobs. Lured back to the stage during the oldies revival of the Nineties, she often toured with Bobby Vee and Brian Hyland.
CAUSE: She died at Lenoir Memorial Hospital in Kingston, North Carolina, after battling cervical cancer for a number of years.

Little Milton

(MILTON CAMPBELL)
Born September 7, 1934
Died August 6, 2005
Straddling urban blues and Southern soul, singer-guitarist Little Milton never achieved the success that was his due. Born into a sharecropping family in Mississippi, he was a self-taught player who emulated his guitarist father and other local bluesmen at informal venues such as house parties. First recording in 1951, Milton backed Willie Love as a member of The Three Aces and worked with Ike Turner, who would become his lifelong mentor. On the recommendation of Turner, Little Milton recorded for Sam Phillips at Sun Records in 1953, followed by stints for Meteor and Bobbin Records, where he began to cultivate a reputation as a talented guitarist who understood the tonal intricacies of the instrument. Landing at Chess subsidiary Checker, he finally entered the charts with 'So Mean To Me' (1962). His only crossover hit 'We're Gonna Make It' (1965) was followed by a string of R&B hits over the next decade, including 'Feel So Bad', 'Grits Ain't Groceries', 'If Walls Could Talk', 'Baby I Love' and, after switching to Stax Records in 1971, 'That's What Love Will Make You Do'. Milton found renewed fame after he appeared in the 1973 concert film, *Wattstax*. In 1999, he was joined by guests Dave Alvin, Gov't Mule and Susan Tedeschi for a duets album, *Welcome To Little Milton.*
CAUSE: He suffered a stroke and died a week later in Memphis.

Little Miss Cornshucks

(MILDRED CUMMINGS)
Born May 26, 1923
Died November 11, 1999
A pioneering R&B vocalist, Little Miss Cornshucks was a conduit between blues and rock'n'roll. A native of Dayton, Ohio, the former Mildred Cummings honed her stage act during the Forties at venues such as Chicago's Club DeLisa. Costumed in a country bumpkin dress and straw hat with a basket at her side, she wowed audiences with her humour and commanding stage presence. A victim of poor career choices and marital difficulties, she recorded on occasion but never became a bona fide star. Instead, Little Miss Cornshucks influenced a number of pioneering R&B singers: LaVern Baker first hit the stage as a copycat

as Little Miss Sharecropper and Ruth Brown scored her first breakthrough hit with a note-for-note rendition of Little Miss Cornshucks' signature song, a bluesy reworking of Russ Morgan's 1940 hit 'So Long'. Another of Little Miss Cornshucks' songs, a bluesy lamenting rendition of the Thirties pop standard 'Try A Little Tenderness', was widely copied and later popularised by Otis Redding. Her career fading by the mid Fifties, Little Miss Cornshucks would perform sporadically around Chicago. After recording her only album in the early Sixties, she faded into obscurity, making infrequent public appearances over the next decade.
CAUSE: After suffering a series of strokes in the Nineties, she died in Indianapolis. Her death went unnoticed in the press.

Little Walter

(MARION WALTER JACOBS, SR.)
Born May 1, 1930
Died February 15, 1968
Chicago's finest post-war blues harmonica player, Louisiana-born Little Walter arrived in the Windy City after a brief stint with Sonny Boy Williamson. Playing the harmonica since his childhood, Little Walter had left home at age 12 to perform on the street corners of New Orleans. Settling in Chicago in 1946, he first teamed with Muddy Waters in 1948. Becoming an anchor of the Chess Records studio band, he appeared on dozens of the label's early hits. Also a solo star, his prolific hits began with the blistering instrumental 'Juke' (1952), the song recorded at the end of a Muddy Waters session. Infusing his gritty vocals into his Harmonica-based music, and backed by The Jukes, Little Walter enjoyed several more hits including 'Sad Hours' (1952), 'Blues With A Feeling' (1953), 'You're So Fine' (1954), and the often-recorded, 'My Babe' (1955). With his fortunes plummeting, he abused alcohol in the Sixties. Touring with The Rolling Stones in 1964, Little Walter's musical abilities had been dulled by his drinking habit.
CAUSE: Quick tempered and easily offended, he was involved in a vicious Chicago street brawl, and died soon after.

Carlo Little

(CARL O'NEILL LITTLE)
Born December 17, 1938
Died August 5, 2005
A lauded British drummer who passed through several notable musical acts, Carlo Little co-founded Screaming Lord Sutch & The Savages in 1960, appearing on their UK hit 'My Big Black Coffin'. Hailing from north-west London, Carlo became a local legend thanks to his prowess as a drummer and uncharacteristically offered drum tutelage to a young Keith Moon. In 1962 Little joined Cyril Davies & The R&B All-Stars, and while with the group, he reportedly turned down an offer to join The Rolling Stones, instead suggesting Charlie Watts. During the Stones' early years, Little and All-Stars bassist Ricky Fensen occasionally deputised for Watts and Wyman when they were indisposed. Little then rejoined Sutch for a brief period before drumming with Long John Baldry's Hoochie Coochie Men – who, ironically, were formed out of the remains of Cyril Davies' All-Stars (after Davies died in January 1964). Little also played in Neil Christian's Crusaders and a touring version of The Flowerpot Men before quitting music in 1969 to focus on family life. Together with Nick Simper (of Deep Purple and Johnny Kidd & The Pirates) he owned a grocery shop, as well as operating a fast food stand outside Wembley Stadium, occasionally when, with bittersweet irony, his old bandmates The Rolling Stones were performing. Occasionally returning to music Little formed the

groups Flying Fox, Florida Sun and Bandana.
CAUSE: Lung cancer.

Johnny Littlejohn

(JOHN FUNCHES)
Born April 16, 1931
Died February 1, 1994
A Delta-born Chicago-based, slide-guitar blues master, Johnny Littlejohn enjoyed limited success outside of the Windy City. Recording for Arhoolie Records, his finest release came in 1968 with the classic, *Chicago Blues Stars*.
CAUSE: Renal failure. He had been ill for some time.

Sir Joseph Lockwood

(JOSEPH FLAWITH LOCKWOOD)
Born November 14, 1904
Died March 6, 1991
A shrewd businessman who in spite of a limited education emerged as the chairman of EMI Records, Sir Joseph Lockwood earned his business acumen in the flour business. Working in the family's grain mill beginning at age 16, he lost his job three years later. Relocating to a mill in Chile, he was soon heading the company of 200 employees. He also made a small fortune betting on horse races. Returning to England in 1928, he was hired by Henry Simon Ltd as the technical manager at milling plants in Brussels and Paris. An expert in the field, he penned a pair of books beginning with *Provender Milling* (1939). Active in European food distribution during and after World War II, Lockwood honed his brilliant organisational skills. Named the chairman and managing director of Simon Ltd. in 1950, he took a new assignment when in 1954 he was appointed the chairman of EMI. At the time, EMI was losing money with its focus on classical music and the manufacture of radios and televisions. Eliminating the manufacturing side of the business, Lockwood transformed EMI into one of the country's leading record companies, with Decca as their only rivals. Although Lockwood personally favoured classical music and ballet, he chided EMI managers for ignoring popular musical tastes. EMI quickly embraced rock'n'roll and issued the records of Elvis Presley on their HMV label until RCA made their own distribution deal in the UK, and a host of other American acts. They also signed Britain's leading rock'n'roll star, Cliff Richard. In a stroke of genius Lockwood bought Capitol Records as a gateway into the US market. More importantly, EMI signed The Beatles after a number of competitors had rejected the group, and the success of The Beatles brought untold prosperity, though much of their profits were squandered on ill-advised investments in medical electronics and other aspects of the leisure industry. Lockwood retired from his chairmanship in 1974, and left the company's board of directors in 1979. Lockwood was the Chairman of The Royal Ballet (1960–78), and The Royal Ballet School (1971–85).
CAUSE: Natural causes. He died in London.

Larrie Londin

Born 1944
Died August 24, 1992
A Motown session drummer, Larrie Londin appeared on hit records by The Supremes, The Temptations, The Four Tops, and many of the label's other hit acts. He later became a much in-demand session player, playing behind The Carpenters, Journey, Glenn Frey, Vince Gill and Reba McEntire.
CAUSE: He died of heart failure in a Nashville hospital.

Shorty Long

(FREDERICK EARL LONG)
Born May 20, 1940
Died June 29, 1969
Latter Ink Spots member and solo

R&B pianist, Shorty Long enjoyed his biggest hit with the novelty tune, 'Here Comes The Judge' (1968). An Alabama native, he was tutored by W.C. Handy and in 1960 joined the Harvey Fuqua-owned Tri-Phi Records. Retained by Berry Gordy when Tri-Phi was acquired by Motown, Long served as an M.C. at Motown revues and also recorded for the Motown subsidiary, Soul Records. One of his releases 'Devil With A Blue Dress On' was a hit for Mitch Rider.
CAUSE: He died in a boating accident on the Detroit River in Michigan.

Teddy Long

Born c. 1935
Died July 1991
The second tenor of the Chicago doo-wop groups The Kool Gents and The El Dorados, Teddy Long had initially joined several friends at the Windy City's Marshall High School in 1951 to form The Golden Tones. After adding Delecta Clark (later known as Dee Clark) to the group in 1953, the group was later renamed The Kool Gents after a popular local deejay, Herb "Kool Gent" Kent. Signing with Vee-Jay Records in 1955, The Kool Gents recorded several singles, never managing to gain airplay outside Chicago. For a time, Vee-Jay also recorded the group as The Delegates. When Dee Clark left The Kool Gents in 1957 for a solo career, Long and the rest of his group teamed with original El Dorados lead singer Pirkle Lee Moses as the new El Dorados. After recording a pair of unsuccessful singles for Vee-Jay Records in 1958, the group disbanded.
CAUSE: Unknown.

Ty Longley

Born September 4, 1971
Died February 20, 2003
The guitarist for Great White, Ty Longley was a latter member of the band. Born in Sharon, Pennsylvania, but raised in the nearby Youngstown, Ohio, suburb of Brookfield, Longley took guitar lessons, beginning at age 12. Drawn to rock'n'roll in 1984 after watching the video for Ratt's 'Round And Round', Longley finished high school and then joined a series of local rock bands. Moving to Los Angeles in 1998, he joined the pop-metal band Great White in 2000 as replacement for founding guitarist Mark Kendall. The band was past its late Eighties hit heyday of 'Rock Me', 'Save Your Love' and a cover of Ian Hunter's 'Once Bitten Twice Shy'. When lead singer Jack Russell pursued a brief solo career in 2001, he hired Longley for his touring band. Russell re-formed Great White the following year, including both Longley and returning original guitarist Mark Kendall.
CAUSE: During a Great White performance at the Station nightclub in West Warwick, Rhode Island, the band employed a pyrotechnics display which ignited the foam above and behind the stage; the highly flammable polyurethane material was used as soundproofing insulation. As the fire and choking smoke quickly spread, the power went out and the room became pitch black. While the other members of Great White had managed to escape through a back door, Longley headed towards the main entrance, apparently to direct the panicked crowd, and perished in the inferno. In all, over 100 people died and 200 were injured – many with severe burns.

Ramon Loper

(RAMON NAVARRO LOPER)
Born November 25, 1935
Died October 16, 2002
The baritone vocalist of pioneering doo-wop group The Five Keys, Ramon Loper joined midway through their career. When lead singer Rudy West and tenor Dickie Smith were drafted into the army in 1953, they were replaced by Ulysses Hicks and Ramon Loper. Smith had recommended Loper, then a member of a Newport

News, Virginia-based vocal group, The Bob-O-Links. Leaving Aladdin Records, the group briefly recorded for RCA before the comedic 'Ling, Ting, Tong', featuring Hicks on lead vocals, reached the R&B Top 10 on Capitol Records. With Rudy West returning, The Five Keys' hit run continued over the next two years with the Chuck Willis-penned 'Close Your Eyes', 'The Verdict', ''Cause You're My Lover', the million-selling 'Out Of Sight, Out Of Mind' and 'Wisdom Of A Fool'. Following West's retirement from the group in 1958, The Five Keys signed to King Records without success and after leaving the group in late 1958, Ramon settled in New York City where he joined a touring version of The Ink Spots. He later worked in retail.
CAUSE: Unknown. He died at St. Luke's Hospital in New York City.

Lisa "Left Eye" Lopes

(LISA NICOLE LOPES)
Born May 27, 1971
Died April 25, 2002
A member of the Grammy-winning R&B trio TLC, Lisa "Left Eye" Lopes enjoyed massive R&B and pop crossover success. A native of Philadelphia, Lopes co-founded the Atlanta-based trio in 1991 with Rozonda "Chilli" Thomas and Tionne "T-Boz" Watkins. Superstars in the R&B field, the three women released a string of multi-platinum albums beginning with their 1992 début, the four-million-selling *Ooooooo . . . On The TLC Tip*, which spawned the hits 'Ain't 2 Proud To Beg', 'Baby-Baby-Baby' and 'What About Your Friends?'. One of the most successful US female acts in R&B, TLC continued their hit run with the ten-million-selling, Grammy-nominated album *CrazySexyCool*, featuring the chart-topping hits 'Waterfalls' and 'Creep'. But even with massive sales, the trio was forced to declare bankruptcy in 1995 due to a poorly negotiated contract. After a five-year recess, the group returned in 1999 with *Fan Mail*, featuring the track 'No Scrubs'. A flamboyant celebrity, Lopes pleaded guilty in 1994 to setting fire to her boyfriend's home and was sentenced to five years probation. Following Lopes' death, the surviving members of TLC launched a television reality show, *R U The Girl With T-Boz & Chilli*, with the winner joining the group to record a single and for the subsequent concert tour.
CAUSE: With Lopes at the wheel of a large sports utility vehicle on a road near the town of Jutiapa, Guatamala, she swerved to avoid something in the road. The vehicle flipped over twice and Lopes was thrown from a window. She died instantly. Lopes was visiting Central America to film a segment for possible use in a future music video and on a humanitarian mission to aid a child development centre. She was the only fatality among the eight occupants. Two passengers, including T'Melle Rawlings who was seriously injured, sued Lopes' estate, blaming her actions for the accident. Lopes' mother later sued Mitsubishi, alleging the SUV was prone to roll-overs.

Gil Lopez

(GILBERT LOPEZ)
Born July 4, 1934
Died July 3, 1998
A member of The Tune Weavers, tenor vocalist Gil Lopez backed his sister, lead vocalist Margo J. Sylvia, in the pop/R&B group. Originally a duo, Gil and Margo had competed in talent shows around Boston. After the completion of a military stint in 1956, Lopez re-formed the duo, which was soon expanded to a quartet called The Tone Weavers, but after a deejay at a dance mispronounced their name as The Tune Weavers, the group adopted the new moniker. Rooted in the light jazz/torch standards tradition, the group was discovered by Frank Paul who became their manager. For their

début release, the group recorded a song Lopez had co-written with Margo, the lamenting 'Happy, Happy Birthday Baby'. Released on Paul's tiny Casa Grande label, the single became a smash hit when picked up by the larger Chess/Checker label in 1957. Unhappy with the rigours of touring in caravan packages, Lopez left the group in 1959 and was replaced by his cousin's husband, William "Bunky" Morris. Lopez rejoined the following year just as the group was becoming a fixture on Boston's dinner club circuit until their disbandment in 1962. In 1986, Ronnie Milsap topped the country charts with 'Happy, Happy Birthday Baby', and in 1988, Lopez teamed with Margo to record a yuletide version of their hit, reworked as 'Merry, Merry Christmas Baby'. Lopez last performed on stage with The Tune Weavers in 1990, at a Richard Nader-promoted doo-wop extravaganza at the Meadowlands stadium in New Jersey.
CAUSE: Unknown.

Jerry Lordan

(JEREMIAH PATRICK LORDAN)
Born April 30, 1934
Died July 24, 1995
British songwriter and solo act, Jerry Lordan scored hits with 'I'll Stay Single' (1960) and 'Who Could Be Bluer' (1960). Several of his compositions were instrumental hits for The Shadows including 'Apache' and 'Wonderful Land'.
CAUSE: While battling liver disease, he died from renal failure shortly after being admitted to a London hospital.

Joe Hill Louis

(LESTER HILL)
Born September 23, 1921
Died August 5, 1957
A former boxer, Tennessee-born harmonica player and electric guitarist Joe Hill Louis garnered fame as B.B. King's replacement in 1949 at WDIA in Memphis. Aided by producer and record label owner Sam Phillips, Hill scored a local hit with 'I Feel Like A Million', the track leased to Modern Records. Louis was also employed as a session player at Phillips' label, Sun Records, where he backed acts such as Rufus Thomas and The Prisonaires. Louis later recorded for Columbia and Checker Records.
CAUSE: Cutting his thumb, he died from tetanus. He died in Memphis.

Preston Love

Born April 26, 1921
Died February 12, 2004
An alto sax player whose career spanned the big band to modern soul, Preston Love is best known for his work at Motown. A native of Omaha, Nebraska, Love joined The Count Basie Orchestra at age 22, substituting for an ailing Earle Warren who was stricken with an ulcer. After the six-week stint, Love was later rehired, and spent two additional years behind Basic. By 1942, Love joined The Serenaders, a touring swing group which included future bandleader Johnny Otis. By the following year, Love and Otis teamed to form a jump-blues outfit called The Otis-Love Band. Eventually forming The Preston Love Orchestra, Love toured throughout the Midwest and Plains regions. Settling in California, Love emerged as a much in-demand session player and later formed a record company with his old friend, Johnny Otis; Love and Otis also performed together at the legendary Monterey Pop Festival in 1967. With Motown moving most of its operations from Detroit to Los Angeles, Love soon headed the new West Coast studio band, and worked with the cream of the label's acts including Marvin Gaye, The Supremes, The Temptations and Stevie Wonder. Eventually returning to Omaha, Love continued to perform in the city's nightclubs, and also worked in journalism and broadcasting. Love chronicled his life in the 1997 autobiography, *A Thousand Honey*

Creeks Later: My Life In Music From Basie To Motown — And Beyond.
CAUSE: Lung cancer. He died in Omaha.

Hal Lucas

(HAROLD LUCAS)
Born 1932
Died January 6, 1994
The original lead singer of the pioneering doo-wop vocal group The Clovers, Hal Lucas had formed the group with classmates at Washington DC's Armstrong High School in 1946 originally as the 4 Clovers. With the addition of new lead singer John "Buddy" Bailey in 1946, Lucas switched over to the baritone spot. The Clovers were discovered by record store owner "Waxie Maxie" Silverman, who took the group to an unimpressed Atlantic Records. But with new manager Lou Krefetz, The Clovers recorded for Rainbow Records in 1950, scoring a minor hit with a cover of the standard, 'Yes Sir, That's My Baby', the group still rooted in the tradition of The Mills Brothers. But with Atlantic Records now interested in the group, The Clovers scored a B-side hit with 'Don't You Know I Love You' (1951), the doo-wop styled song penned by Atlantic chief, Ahmet Ertegun. Though landing on the national charts, the group was initially unhappy with its new, glossy sound. But with their updated approach, The Clovers were a vital link in the transition of old-style harmony singing into R&B. Helping to define doo-wop harmony, The Clovers notched a string of hits including, 'Don't You Know I Love You' (1951), 'Fool, Fool, Fool' (1951), 'One Mint Julip' (1952), and 'Ting-A-Ling' (1952). Drafted, Bailey was replaced in The Clovers by Charlie White and then Billy Mitchell. Upon Bailey's return to the group in 1954, The Clovers landed their final hits at Atlantic with 'Nip Sip' (1955), 'Devil Or Angel' (1956) (which was reprised by Bobby Vee in 1960), and 'Love, Love, Love' (1956). Dropped by Atlantic in 1956, The Clovers scored their last hit in 1959 with the Leiber & Stoller composition, 'Love Potion No. 9'. In 1960, The Clovers split into two camps, one led by Lucas, and the other by Bailey. Lucas led a Clovers group until 1992.
CAUSE: Lung cancer. He died in his native Washington DC.

Trevor Lucas

Born December 25, 1943
Died February 4, 1989
A veteran folk-rock singer-songwriter, Trevor Lucas gave Australian rock music an identity in the Eighties. Starting out as a solo nightclub performer in Sydney, he left for Britain in 1964 for a planned, short overseas stint that lasted over a decade. In England, Lucas initially formed a folk duo with fellow Australian Kerilee Male. Pursuing a solo career in 1966, the red-haired Lucas made his recording début with the Elektra album *Overlander.* The following year, he headed the pioneering British electric folk-rock Eclection, which disbanded after releasing a sole, self-titled album. During the same period, Lucas also teamed up with Burt Lloyd for two classic folk albums, *Legend* and *Leviathan.* Lucas then joined Fotheringay, a group launched by his future wife Sandy Denny (of Fairport Convention fame). Joined by Fairport Convention guitarist Jerry Donahue and two others, the group issued the poor-selling, but critically acclaimed album *Fotheringay,* which was highlighted by a Lucas composition 'The Ballad Of Ned Kelly'. During this time, Lucas was also employed as a producer at Island Records. With Fotheringay disbanding, Lucas joined Denny on her solo releases, including *The North Star Grassman And The Ravens, Sandy,* and *Like An Old Fashioned Waltz,* these works spawning folk-rock classics such as 'John The Gun' and 'Gone Solo'. After marrying

in 1973, Lucas and Denny joined Fairport Convention, appearing on the albums, Rosie (1973), *Fairport Nine* (1973), and an album featuring Lucas' lead vocals on several tracks, the strong-selling *Rising For The Moon*. But tired of infighting, Lucas and Denny would leave the turbulent group. After an extended respite from recording, Lucas would aid Denny on her final solo album, *Rendezvous* (1977). Following Denny's sudden death in 1978, Lucas returned to Australia where he became a successful record producer.
CAUSE: Heart attack. He died in Sydney, Australia.
FURTHER READING: Humphries, Patrick. (1997). *Meet On The Ledge: Fairport Convention; The Classic Years*. London: Virgin.

Peter Lucia

(PETER PAUL LUCIA, JR.)
Born February 2, 1947
Died January 6, 1987
The drummer of popular Sixties pop-rock group Tommy James & The Shondells, Peter Lucia performed on a series of hook-filled hits. A native of Morristown, New Jersey, Peter Lucia joined The Shondells in 1965 as replacement for Vincent Pietropaoli, but did not appear on the group's début hit, a three-year-old single 'Hanky Panky' which topped the charts in 1966. Signed to Morris Levy's Roulette label, the group was teamed with songwriters Richie Cordell and Bo Gentry who penned many of their hits, including 'Mirage', 'Getting Together', 'She' and the pop standard 'Mony Mony', later a hit again in the Eighties for Billy Idol. Lucia and James teamed in 1969 to co-write the psychedelic-tinged hit 'Crimson And Clover'; as well as vocals, James played all the instruments on the track except the drums. Later that year, the group declined an offer to perform at Woodstock. With James suffering from health problems, he disbanded the group in 1970. Renaming the group Hog Heaven, Lucia and the other members of The Shondells carried on with little success. 'Crimson And Clover' returned to the charts in 1982 via a cover version by Joan Jett & The Blackhearts.
CAUSE: Following a round of golf at a Los Angeles course, he suffered a massive heart attack.

Bob Luman

(ROBERT GLYNN LUMAN)
Born April 15, 1937
Died December 27, 1978
Underrated Fifties country and rockabilly artist, Bob Luman was born in Nacogdoches, Texas, the son of a talented fiddle player and harmonica player. Awestruck by The Grand Ole Opry, Luman formed a country & western group at Kilgore High School. Also a talented athlete, Luman turned down a tryout with the Pittsburgh Pirates in 1957. Then after Luman's band won a talent competition and caught the ear of a regional record producer, Luman recorded some rockabilly tracks (the material released two decades later). Asked by Johnny Cash in 1957 to join The Louisiana Hayride on a full-time basis, Luman would soon replace the ascending Cash. His career aided when The Everly Brothers sent him to music publishing mogul Wesley Rose, Luman signed with Imperial Records. Enjoying a minor hit with the rockabilly classic 'A Red Cadillac And A Black Mustache' (1957), Luman also appeared in the film *Carnival Rock*. Signing with Capitol, and then Warner Brothers Records, Luman scored his first big hit with 'Let's Think About Living' (1960); at the label, Luman would be backed by future guitar virtuoso Roy Buchanan; but enlisted in the Army reserves, Luman was unable to tour in support of the song, and for a time, was sent to Germany during the Berlin Crisis. Taking a country turn, Luman signed with Hickory Records in

1963. Becoming a *bona fide* country star, Luman finally joined The Grand Old Opry in 1965. Enjoying much success at Epic Records, Luman frequently recorded country versions of pop and R&B songs, his biggest hits coming with 'When You Say Love' (1972), 'Lonely Women Make Good Lovers' (1972), and 'Neither One Of Us' (1973). After a several-month hospitalisation in 1976 for heart disease, Luman recorded the Johnny Cash-produced album *Alive And Well*. Continuing to tour until the last year of his life, Luman remained an active member of the Opry until December 15, 1978. Also a producer, Luman worked with Ray Price, Jimmy Dean, and Tex Ritter.
CAUSE: Suffering heart problems throughout the Seventies, he succumbed to pneumonia. He died in Nashville.

Jo Lustig

Born October 21, 1925
Died May 29, 1999
Best known in music industry circles for having managed a number of British based folk rock artists during the Sixties and Seventies, Jo Lustig also had a colourful career as a Broadway press agent and film and TV producer. Born in Brooklyn, Lustig learned his trade in the late Forties and Fifties, touring with Louis Armstrong, publicising the Newport Jazz Festival, befriending comedy actor Mel Brooks and coming into contact with the Beat poets Allen Ginsberg, Gregory Corso and Jack Kerouac. Following a traffic accident that left him in hospital for six months, Lustig's business went downhill and he relocated to the UK after visiting Europe on a tour with Nat "King" Cole. In London he encountered the burgeoning folk scene and became the manager of Julie Felix. He also managed Nico before she sang with The Velvet Underground. In 1967 he took over the management of Pentangle, featuring the guitarists Bert Jansch and John Renbourn, and went on to manage Ralph McTell, Steeleye Span, Richard Digence, Richard and Linda Thompson, The Chieftains and Mary O'Hara. Lustig had a knack for promoting his artists outside of their obvious niche, and thus became one of the earliest music entrepreneurs to realise the concept of the 'cross-over act' long before the term became common currency in pop and rock circles. He was also known for his temper tantrums, especially down the phone, but any such displays of irascibility were invariably forgotten moments later. During the Eighties Lustig left the music industry but remained in Britain, turning his attention to films and TV, notably arts documentaries for the BBC and Channel 4.
CAUSE: Pancreatic cancer. He died in Cambridge, England.

Billy Lyall

Born March 26, 1953
Died December 1989
Keyboard player for the rock group Pilot from 1974–76, Billy Lyall was also a late member of the British hit group, The Bay City Rollers. Lyall joined Pilot while working at the Craighall Recording Studio in Edinburgh. The Scottish trio scored its only US hit with the Alan Parsons-produced million-seller, 'Magic' (1975). While the other two members of Pilot went on to join the Alan Parsons Project, Lyall pursued a solo career and released one album *Solo Casting*, before joining Dollar. In the Eighties, he played keyboards in Sheena Easton's band.
CAUSE: AIDS.

Frankie Lymon

Born September 30, 1942
Died February 28, 1968
Leader and soprano vocalist of Fifties vocal R&B group The Teenagers, Frankie Lymon grew up in a poor, extended family that shared his

grandmother's New York City apartment. Streetwise with both women and drugs before he even entered junior high, Lymon took a job at a grocery store in 1954. Musically gifted, Lymon played the bongos with his brother at a school talent show, and sang gospel songs with his family. In 1954 Sherman Garnes convinced Jimmy Merchant to join two nearby Puerto Ricans, Joe Negronie and Herman Santiago to form a singing group. Bringing Lymon into the fold to add a contrast to the other members' deeper voices, the group, then calling itself both The Premiers and The Ermines, practised in hallways and street corners. Discovered by singer and producer Richard Barrett (formerly with The Valentines), Lymon and the group were signed by Gee Records. While Barrett took much interest in the group, he was especially impressed by the raw talent of 13-year-old Lymon, whom he tutored. Signed to George Goldner's Gee Records in late 1955, the group recorded their self-penned composition 'Why Do Birds Sing So Gay?' But at Barrett's insistence, Lymon replaced Herman Santiago as the group's lead singer. The group was renamed The Teenagers, and their song was retitled 'Why Do Fools Fall In Love?' A multi-million selling smash, the song catapulted the five teens to massive fame, with little Frankie Lymon briefly emerging as a superstar. Dropping out of school, Lymon and the rest of the group hit the road for a succession of tours, and followed up with the hits, 'I Want You To Be My Girl' (1956), 'I Promise To Remember' (1956), and from the Alan Freed film *Rock Rock Rock*, 'I'm Not A Juvenile Delinquent' (1956). In 1957, Gee Records was taken over by Levy's larger Roulette Records and The Teenagers followed. The record company's biggest fear was that Lymon's voice could change at any time, but the singer took matters in his own hands when he was convinced by his girlfriend and record label to break away from The Teenagers and attempt a solo career. Others claim that Lymon's career ended when middle-America spotted him dancing with a white girl on the nationally televised programme, *Alan Freed's Rock 'N Roll Dance Party.* Lymon's first solo release came with 'Goody Goody' (1957), a song that had originally been recorded by the entire group, but was scratched in favour of the new version. With Lymon's voice having matured, he scored a minor hit in 1960 with the release of a two-year-old track, 'Little Bitty Pretty One'. That year was the beginning of Lymon's downfall: he was arrested several times for narcotics possession and was placed in a drug treatment programme. Entering the service in 1966 to avoid jail time, Lymon was stationed at Fort Gordon, Georgia. Dishonourably discharged for repeated AWOL violations, he married Elmira Eagle. Signed to a new recording contract in 1967, the excited Lymon celebrated with a night of drugs. But having stayed away from chemicals in the service, Lymon's body was not able to handle his old dosage, and he died. The Teenagers' biggest hit, 'Why Do Fools Fall In Love?' was a successful remake for Diana Ross in 1981. But when the royalties started flowing so did his wives – all three of them! In January 1990, a New York appellate court ruled that Erma Eagle was Lymon's legal widow. Lymon's life hit the big screen in 1998 with the hit film *Why Do Fools Fall In Love.*
CAUSE: He was found dead of a heroin overdose, a syringe next to his body, in the bathroom of his grandmother's Harlem apartment. He had been an addict for years. He had returned to New York City after getting a club gig. What his record companies didn't take from him, he squandered. Lymon was penniless at the time of his death. He was buried in an unmarked grave at St. Raymond's cemetery in the Bronx,

New York, his family unable to afford a headstone. A fan in Clifton, New Jersey, raised money for a marker, but because of continuing lawsuits over Lymon's estate, no one was legally empowered to grant permission for its placement.

David Lynch

Born July 3, 1929
Died January 2, 1981
Founding member of the popular Fifties vocal group The Platters, David Lynch was born and raised in St. Louis. Moving to Los Angeles in the mid Forties, Lynch, a tenor, joined several high school friends in forming an all-male vocal quartet. After entering numerous local talent shows, in 1953 the Tony Williams-fronted group came under the guidance of manager Buck Ram. Tutored by Ram, The Platters fared poorly with their début recordings at King-Federal Records; at the label, the group would record a raw version of their future hit 'Only You'. Then with another Buck Ram-managed group, The Penguins, signing with Mercury Records, Ram arranged a deal with the label to also take on The Platters. But while The Penguins faded from the charts, The Platters hit the Top 10 with a re-recording of 'Only You' (1955). The most successful R&B group of the decade, The Platters notched a strong run of elegant ballad hits, including 'The Great Pretender', '(You've Got) The Magic Touch', 'My Prayer', and 'Smoke Gets In Your Eyes'. But The Platters were irrevocably harmed in a scandal when on August 10, 1959, the four male members were arrested in a Cincinnati motel for having sex with women who were under 21. Although Lynch and the others were acquitted of the charges, the group never recovered. The Platters would score their final Top 10 hit in 1960 with a cover of the standard, 'Harbor Lights'. Waiting several years for another hit, The Platters landed at Musicor Records, taking a pop turn with 'I Love You A Thousand Times' (1966) and 'With This Ring' (1967). Lynch would leave the group in 1976.
CAUSE: Cancer. Lynch had been fighting the illness for four years. He died in a Veteran's Administration hospital in Long Beach, California.

Bill Lynn

Born 1932
Died January 5, 2006
A drummer who worked on the sessions for the Elvis Presley hit 'It's Now Or Never', Bill Lynn also appeared as Presley's drummer in the films, *Easy Come, Easy Go* and *Speedway*. Born in Columbia, Lynn was raised in the US and in 1960 he was hired as a session drummer by ABC- Paramount Records where he worked with numerous artists including Tommy Roe, The Impressions, Bryan Hyland, Bobby Vee and The Nitty Gritty Dirt Band. By the late Sixties, Lynn had become Presley's close confidant. In 1980, Lynn moved to Memphis and worked as marketing director for the Elvis Presley Museum.
CAUSE: Suffering from flu, he died from respiratory problems at his home in Villa de Leyva, Columbia.

Philip Lynott

(PHILIP PARRIS LYNOTT)
Born August 20, 1949
Died January 4, 1986
Bass player and lead vocalist of the Irish hard-rock band Thin Lizzy, Philip Lynott was born out of wedlock to an Irish mother and a Brazilian father. Raised in Dublin by his grandmother, Lynott had the unusual distinction of being a dark-skinned Irishman. He joined his first rock band at age 16 as the lead vocalist of a local soul outfit called Black Eagles, and then joined Skid Row, teaming up with future Thin Lizzy guitarist Gary Moore. Leaving the group over musical differences, the Afro-haired Lynott

taught himself to play the bass guitar, and then joined a blues group called Sugar Shack, which included childhood friend Brian Downey on drums. Lynott and Downey then formed Orphanage, landing a local hit with a cover of Tim Rose's 'Morning Dew'. Adding guitarist Eric Bell in 1970, the group evolved into Thin Lizzy. During this period, Lynott studied architecture at technical college. Earning a strong following in Dublin, Thin Lizzy initially released an obscure single on Parlophone Records. Then signed by Decca Records in late 1970, the group merged blues and folk on its début album *Thin Lizzy* (1971). While the group's two new albums, *Shades Of A Blue Orphanage* (1972) and *Vagabonds Of The Western World* (1973), were also poor sellers, Thin Lizzy enjoyed a breakthrough hit single with a rendition of the folk standard 'Whiskey In The Jar' (1973). Signing to the Vertigo Records in 1974, and replacing Eric Bell with Gary Moore (his first of three stints with the group), Thin Lizzy enjoyed hit albums with *Fighting* (1975) and *Jailbreak*, the latter highlighted by 'Jailbreak' and the group's sole US pop hit, 'The Boys Are Back in Town'. Although their success in the US was limited, Thin Lizzy continued their hit run in Britain with 'Don't Believe A Word' (1977), 'Dancin' In The Moonlight' (1977), 'Waiting For An Alibi' (1979), 'Sarah' (1979) and 'Killer On The Loose' (1980). In 1980 Lynott married Caroline Crowther, the daughter of a well known British comedian and game-show host, and that same year he released his first solo project, *Solo In Soho*, which was three years in the making. The album included the British hits, 'Dear Miss Lonely Hearts' (1980) and a tribute to Elvis Presley 'King's Call' (1980). With Lynott releasing a second solo album in 1982, Thin Lizzy disbanded the following year. In 1984, Lynott formed Grand Slam but the group never had time to achieve success.

CAUSE: He succumbed to heart and liver failure while in a coma in hospital at Salisbury, England. Having abused drugs for years, he had gone into the coma a week earlier as a result of a drug overdose.

FURTHER READING: Lynott, Philomena. (1996). *My Boy: The Philip Lynott Story*. London: Virgin. Putterford, Marc. (1998). *Philip Lynott: The Rocker*. London: Omnibus Press.

M

Jackie "Moms" Mabley

(LORETTA MARY AIKEN)
Born March 19, 1894
Died May 23, 1975
A bawdy, rotund black comedienne who launched her career in the tent shows during the Twenties, Jackie "Moms" Mabley was a fixture on the Vaudeville stage for four decades. Remaining popular into the Seventies, she recorded a series of successful, low-down comedy albums. She also landed a radio hit with a dramatic reading of the Dion classic 'Abraham, Martin And John'.
CAUSE: She died from natural causes related to a massive heart attack suffered two years earlier.

Willie Mabon

Born October 24, 1925
Died April 19, 1985
Influential Fifties R&B artist, Tennessee-born Willie Mabon taught himself to play piano in the boogie-woogie tradition. Relocating with his family from Memphis to Chicago in 1942, Mabon improved his piano skills following some formal training. He returned to Chicago after a brief marine stint in the closing days of World War II. Becoming a fixture in the blues clubs of the city's south side, Mabon frequently teamed with guitarist Earl Dranes in The Blues Rockers beginning in 1947. As a solo artist, Mabon recorded at Apollo Records as Big Willie. Signing with Chess Records in 1951, Mabon enjoyed a trio of major R&B hits with 'I Don't Know' (1952), 'I'm Mad' (1953), and 'Poison Ivy' (1954); he also waxed the first version of the Willie Dixon-penned 'Seventh Son'. Recording for several labels, Mabon scored his final hit in 1962 with the Formal Records release, 'Got To Have Some'. With Chicago remaining his base, Mabon frequently toured throughout Europe beginning in the Seventies.
CAUSE: Longterm illness. He died in Paris.

Ewan MacColl

(JAMES MILLER)
Born January 25, 1915
Died October 22, 1989
A folk revivalist who popularised the genre in his native land, Scottish folk singer Ewan MacColl was convinced by American musicologist Alan Lomax to pursue a career in British roots music. Scarred by the poverty he saw as a child growing up in Western Scotland and later in Salford, near Manchester, MacColl was an avowed Communist, his politics emerging in his music. He became involved in street theatre and co-founded the Theatre Workshop in London with his first wife, the actress Joan Littlewood. With Alan Lomax, he pursued the folk revival and featured on the radio programme *Ballads And Blues* alongside many important figures including A.L.Lloyd and Big Bill Broonzy. Although the skiffle craze was in full swing, MacColl continued to stress the importance of traditional British folk songs in favour of imported cover versions. After forming the influential Critics' Group, he met his second wife Jean Newlove, whose children included Kirsty MacColl, later a singing star in her own right. After divorcing Newlove, he married his touring partner Peggy Seeger (sister of Pete Seeger). They recorded *The Long Harvest*, a 10-volume set of child ballads and found fame with their *Radio Ballads* series, which featured several of their better-known songs, including 'The Travelling People'. They also formed their own record label, Blackthorne Records. As a composer, MacColl found unexpected worldwide success via Roberta Flack's

1972 hit recording of 'The First Time Ever I Saw Your Face', composed about his initial meeting with Peggy. MacColl's other great standard is the folk classic 'Dirty Old Town', made famous by The Dubliners and subsequently recorded by The Pogues.
CAUSE: Heart attack. He died in London.

Kirsty MacColl

Born October 10, 1959
Died December 18, 2000
An outspoken singer-songwriter who didn't achieve the level of fame she deserved, Kirsty MacColl was the daughter of folk singer Ewan MacColl and, for a time, the wife of hit producer Steve Lillywhite. A London native, Kirsty MacColl signed with Stiff Records at age 19, recording the self-composed 'They Don't Know' (which became a hit for Tracey Ullman in 1983). A talented and sharp-witted lyricist, MacColl enjoyed a sporadic string of UK hits, including 'There's A Guy Works Down The Chip Shop Swears He's Elvis' (1981), a cover of Billy Bragg's 'A New England' (1985), the cherished Christmas duet with Pogues leader Shane MacGowan, 'Fairytale Of New York' (1987), a cover of The Kinks' 'Days' (1989) and 'Walking Down Madison' (1991). Following her divorce from Lillywhite, MacColl took an extended break from recording and immersed herself in Latin music. Her final album, *Tropical Brainstorm* (2000), combined rock with Latin rhythms, and she later hosted a BBC radio series on Cuban music. As an in-demand backing vocalist, MacColl worked with Talking Heads, Frida, The Rolling Stones, Van Morrison and Simple Minds.
CAUSE: While scuba diving with her two sons near the Yucatan Peninsula in Cozumel, Mexico, she was struck on the head by a speedboat. Seconds before the impact, she managed to push one of her sons out of the direct path of the oncoming vessel which had wandered into an area reserved for swimmers. While MacColl was killed instantly, both of her sons received minor injuries. Despite conflicting witness accounts over who was steering the boat, a 28-year-old deckhand received a 34-month prison term – which he never served. The craft was owned by Mexican supermarket mogul Guillermo Gonzalez Nova, who was on board along with four other family members.

Byron MacGregor

(GARY MACK)
Born March 3, 1948
Died January 3, 1995
A Canadian broadcaster at CKLW in Windsor, Ontario, Canada, Byron MacGregor landed an unlikely hit with the spoken-word speech 'Americans' in 1974.
CAUSE: Pneumonia. He died in Detroit.

Billy MacKenzie

Born March 27, 1957
Died January 22, 1997
The lead singer and lyricist of The Associates, Billy MacKenzie formed the theatrical Scottish new-wave duo with multi-instrumentalist Alan Rankine. Signing with the Polydor Records subsidiary Fiction, the duo released their critically acclaimed début album in 1980, The Affectionate Punch. Switching to Warner Brothers Records, The Associates enjoyed a trio of British, New Romantic-era hits in 1982 with 'Party Fears Two', 'Club Country', and '18 Carat Love Affair'; the tracks were culled from the exotic album, *Sulk*. After disbanding for two years, the reformed group recorded the album *Perhaps*. The falsetto-voiced MacKenzie then recorded the poorly received album *Outernational* (1992). By 1995, he was forced to declare bankruptcy. MacKenzie signed with Nude Records shortly before his death, the sessions captured on the posthumously released *Beyond The Sun*.

CAUSE: Suicide by drug overdose. He had been despondent over his mother's death. He was found dead at his parents' home in Dundee, Scotland. FURTHER READING: Doyle, Tom. (1998). *The Glamour Chase*. London: Bloomsbury.

Bryan MacLean

Born September 25, 1946
Died December 25, 1998
Co-founder of the underrated, late Sixties folk-flavoured, psychedelic-rock band Love, Bryan MacLean played a vital role in the group alongside leader Arthur Lee. Raised in a privileged Hollywood Hills, California, home, MacLean was attracted to folk music in his teens. Dropping out of school at 17 to assume the role of folk troubadour, MacLean crossed paths with another folkie on the local Los Angeles coffee-circuit scene, David Crosby. With Crosby soon launching The Byrds, MacLean was hired in 1965 as the emerging group's roadie. But by the year's end, MacLean had left that post to join Arthur Lee to form The Grass Roots; forced to change their name after the discovery of another group with the same moniker, the renamed *Love* was the first rock signing to the folk music label, Elektra Records. The group enjoyed critical acclaim with their masterful début album *Love*, which spawned the singles 'My Little Red Book' (composed by Bacharach & David) and 'Seven And Seven Is'. But with the sensitive MacLean bullied by aggressive, R&B-trained Lee, few of MacLean's compositions were recorded by Love, save for classics such as 'Orange Skies', 'Softly to Me', 'Old Man' and the remarkable ballad, 'All Alone Or'. The last two songs featured on the group's musical opus *Forever Changes*, a landmark release that still features prominently in all-time great albums listings. Following much infighting during the sessions of the group's their album, their musical opus *Forever Changes*, MacLean quit the group for a solo career. His life in flux during the late Sixties, MacLean abused drugs and was frequently in trouble with the law before giving up rock music in 1970 due to his newfound Christian beliefs. In the Seventies, MacLean opened a Christian nightclub called The Daisey, and on occasion, reunited with Lee. In the early Eighties, he led The Bryan MacLean Band which sometimes featured his half-sister, Maria McKee. McKee later formed the country-rock group, Lone Justice; a MacLean composition that Lone Justice recorded 'Don't Toss Us Away' was a country hit for Patty Loveless in 1989. MacLean's final album *Ifyoubelievein* (1997), featured demos from his period with Love, and four tracks from 1982.
CAUSE: Heart attack. He was dining at a Los Angeles restaurant with Love biographer Kevin Delaney at the time of his death.

Gene MacLellan

Born February 2, 1938
Died January 19, 1995
A talented Canadian songwriter, Gene MacLellan is best known for composing 'Put Your Hand In The Hand' (recorded by Ocean) and Anne Murray's 'Snowbird'. Stricken with childhood polio, and wearing an eyepatch and suffering a facial disfigurement from a traffic accident (which killed his father), MacLellan remained shy and reclusive for much of his life. A native of Val d'Or, Quebec, he moved to Toronto in the mid Sixties, where he joined the folk-rock group, Little Caesar & The Consuls. In the Sixties and Seventies, he was involved with the Canadian television programmes, *Singalong Jubilee* and *Don Messer's Jubilee*; he wrote 'Snowbird' for a fellow cast member, Anne Murray. Turning to Christianity in 1972, he gave away his

money and possessions and moved to Europe to perform missionary work. As a recording artist, MacLellan penned deeply personal ballads, his finest output compiled on the EMI album *Lonesome River* (1997).
CAUSE: He committed suicide by hanging at his home in Summerside, Prince Edward Island.

Brian Macleod

Born June 25, 1952
Died April 25, 1992
A multi-instrumentalist with the Canadian rock group Chilliwack, Brian Macleod was a latter member of the veteran outfit. Born in St. John, Newfoundland, Macleod mastered the guitar, drums, and keyboard, as he passed through a series of groups – Huskey, Garrison Hill, and Pepper Time – before joining the nine-year-old Chilliwack in 1978. First appearing on the album *Lights On The Valley*, he contributed two compositions. But soon after, Chilliwack became involved in a legal dispute with their label, Mushroom Records, and were unable to record for two years. During this time, Macleod and bandmate Ad Bryant formed an alter-ego group called The Headpins. In this hard-rock group, Macleod co-wrote, produced, and played guitar, behind female vocalists Darby Mills; intended as a bar band, The Headpins were a surprise success. But soon, Chilliwack returned to the studio as the trio of Macleod, Bryant, and leader Bill Henderson. Already a hit act in Canada, Chilliwack finally broke through in the US with the catchy 'My Girl (Gone Gone Gone)', the single culled from their ninth album, *Wanna Be A Star*. Like 'My Girl' and the follow-up hits, 'I Believe' (1982) and 'Watcha Gonna Do' (1982), Macleod had authored much of the group's material; he had also penned songs for Chicago and Loverboy. Leaving Chilliwack in 1983 to concentrate on The Headpins, Macleod and Bryant recorded four albums before disbanding that group in 1986.
CAUSE: He had been diagnosed with lung cancer after collapsing on stage. He died at a hospital in Vancouver, British Columbia.

Angus MacLise

Born March 14, 1938
Died June 21, 1979
The original drummer of the avant-garde rock group The Velvet Underground, Angus MacLise quit the group because he did not like the idea of being paid to perform. MacLise had met VU member John Cale at an artist collective.
CAUSE: He died from a combination of malnutrition and hypoglycaemia at Shanta Bawan Hospital in Kathmandu, Nepal.

Kevin MacMichael

(KEVIN SCOTT MACMICHAEL)
Born November 7, 1951
Died December 31, 2002
As a member of pop-rock group Cutting Crew, guitarist Kevin MacMichael scored a pair of international hits. Born in Nova Scotia, Canada, MacMichael passed through a series of East Coast Canadian rock groups, most notably Spice, before meeting English-born vocalist, Nick Van Eede. After recording demos in Toronto, MacMichael and Van Eede moved to London to form Cutting Crew. Signing with Virgin Records, the group scored a chart-topping hit with the new wave-tinged '(I Just) Died In Your Arms', and managed one more Top 40 hit, 'I've Been In Love Before', before disbanding in 1993. Working with Robert Plant, MacMichael played guitar and co-wrote several tracks on *Fate Of Nation* (1993), but when Plant reunited with Jimmy Page, MacMichael's services were no longer needed. After spending two years in Pete Best's Beatles tribute act, MacMichael returned to Canada, where he performed in clubs and

produced local artists.
CAUSE: Lung cancer. He died in Halifax, Nova Scotia, Canada.

Alex MacNicol

Born c. 1960
Died 2004
The drummer of American band Green On Red, Alex MacNicol joined as replacement for Van Christian in 1981. Infusing elements of rockabilly and what would later be called "alt-country", Green On Red recorded for a series of labels including Enigma and Mercury. Previously a member of Lydia Lunch's backing band, MacNicol appeared on the albums *Gravity Talks* and *Gas Food Lodging*. MacNicol left the group in 1985 and was replaced by Keith Mitchell.
CAUSE: Unknown.

Rose Maddox

(ROSELEA ARBANA BROGDEN)
Born August 15, 1925
Died April 15, 1998
A pioneering female performer who crossed the boundaries of country, bluegrass and rockabilly, Rose Maddox launched her professional career in the Forties. A member of The Maddox Brothers and Rose, a group billed as "The Most Colorful Hillbilly Band in America", Maddox was popular among Southern audiences. An extravagant woman, she once shocked a Grand Ole Opry audience by appearing on stage in a bare midriff costume. With the break-up of the Maddox Brothers in 1956, Rose Maddox pursued a solo career, placing several hits on the country charts including 'Gambler's Love' and 'Kissing My Pillow'. She earned a Grammy nomination late in her career for the album, *$35 And A Dream* (1986).
CAUSE: Kidney failure. She died in Ashland, Oregon.
FURTHER READING: Whiteside, Jonn. (1997). *Ramblin' Rose: The Life And Career Of Rose Maddox*. Nashville: Vanderbilt University.

Eddie Madison

(EDWIN LEE MORRISON, SR.)
Born 1928
Died February 28, 1987
A popular Baltimore deejay, Eddie Madison provided the spoken portion of The Ray Bryant Combo's dance instruction pop hit, 'The Madison Time – Part 1' (1960).
CAUSE: Unknown. He died in Chicago.

Joe Madison

Born 1937
Died April 2, 1995
A session blues organist, Joe Madison had frequently performed with King Curtis.
CAUSE: Kidney ailment. He died in Buffalo.

Magic Sam

(SAMUEL MAGHETT)
Born February 14, 1937
Died December 1, 1969
A Mississippi-born, Chicago electric blues guitarist, Magic Sam initially recorded at the fledgling Cobra label in 1957. But his career was interrupted by an army stint and a subsequent jail term for desertion. Returning to Chicago, he helped revitalise the city's blues scene with his début album *West Side Soul*, highlighted by a cover of the blues standard 'Sweet Home Chicago'. Releasing his second album *Black Magic* and having gained notoriety after a stunning performance at the Ann Arbor Blues Festival, he was on the verge of stardom at the time of his death.
CAUSE: After complaining of heartburn, he collapsed from a heart attack. He died in Chicago.

Major Lance

Born April 4, 1939 (or 1942)
Died September 3, 1994
Mississippi-born soul singer Major Lance was raised in the same rough Cabrini-Green housing project as soulster Curtis Mayfield. A pioneer of

Chicago soul, Lance had initially pursued a career in boxing before turning to music. After garnering exposure via a regular spot on a local television music programme, Lance was signed to OKeh Records in 1962. At the label, Mayfield wrote most of Lance's hits including 'Hey Little Girl', 'Um Um Um Um Um Um', and 'The Monkey Time', the latter song spawning a dance craze. Apart from Mayfield, Lance scored an R&B hit with the self-composed, 'The Matador' (1964). Lance's fame spread further when Wayne Fontata & The Mindbenders secured a UK hit with 'Um Um Um Um Um Um'. On a UK tour in 1965 Lance was backed by Bluesology, whose pianist was Reg Dwight, the future Elton John. Leaving OKeh Records in 1968, Lance had scant success except for the Mayfield-penned 'Stay Away From Me', the single issued on the Mayfield co-owned Curtom Records. His career slumping in the US, Lance relocated to England in the early Seventies, and garnered a strong following on the soul circuit. Returning to the US in 1974, he launched Osiris Records with Booker T. & The MGs' drummer Al Jackson. Arrested for cocaine possession in 1978, Lance served a three-year prison term. Never able to recharge his career, Lance was later relegated to oldies status.
CAUSE: He died in his sleep at home in Decatur, Georgia, of heart disease. He had previously suffered a heart attack in 1987, and was nearly blind from glaucoma.

Alan Malarowitz

Born March 20, 1950
Died August 1981
A member of the first act to perform at the original Woodstock Music Festival, drummer Alan Malarowitz co-founded the seven-member interracial group Sweetwater in 1967. Malarowitz was studying classical music at UCLA when he joined forces with August Burns. Attracting attention around Los Angeles clubs with their Latin-styled percussion, Sweetwater recorded three albums for Reprise and opened up for many of the top acts of the day, but achieved only limited success in their own right. After lead singer Nancy Nevins was seriously injured in a car crash in December 1969, the group drifted before disbanding two years later. By that time, Malarowitz had already left the group to get married and later worked as a session drummer.
CAUSE: He perished in a car crash en route from Los Angeles to Las Vegas, after falling asleep at the wheel and striking an embankment.

Tony Mammarella

(ANTHONY SEPTEMBRE MAMMARELLA)
Born September 2, 1924
Died November 27, 1977
The producer of *American Bandstand,* Tony Mammarella was briefly the show's host. Originally a pre-med student, he instead earned a degree in theatre arts in 1950. Hired as a telephone operator at WFIL in Philadelphia in 1950, he was promoted several times and eventually named producer of a local music programme called *Bandstand* in 1952. But following the firing of original M.C. Bob Horn in 1956, Mammarella briefly took over the position before abdicating the duties to the clean-cut Dick Clark. The show was renamed *American Bandstand* upon its national broadcast in 1957, becoming a massively popular cultural institution. Mammarella stayed with the programme until 1960. Forming the Philadelphia-based Swan Records with Dick Clark and Bernie Binnick, Mammarella headed the company from 1960–68. He later worked in public relations.
CAUSE: Brain cancer. He died in Philadelphia.
FURTHER READING: Jackson, John A. (1997). *American Bandstand: Dick Clark And The Making Of A Rock 'n'*

Roll Empire. New York: Oxford University.

Robert Manardo

Born May 11, 1936
Died March 6, 2004
An original member of the Detroit-based doo-wop act The Falcons, tenor Robert Manardo appeared on their early singles, none of which charted. Joining the US Army in 1957, he left before the group scored its 1959 breakthrough hit, 'So Fine'. He later worked for *The Detroit News* and as a finance director and lobbyist for the Michigan state Democratic Party.
CAUSE: Cancer. He died at his home in Warren, Michigan.

Henry Mancini

(ENRICO NICOLA MANCINI)
Born April 16, 1924
Died June 14, 1994
A prolific Grammy-winning composer, Cleveland native Henry Mancini became a legendary figure in the realm of 20th century music. Breaking into the music industry following a stint in the Army Air Corps during World War II, the Julliard-trained Mancini was hired as pianist and arranger for the reformed version of The Glenn Miller Orchestra. Scoring the music for the 1954 film biography, *The Glenn Miller Story*, Mancini would launch a long and fruitful relationship with Hollywood that would continue for decades. Teaming with lyricist Johnny Mercer, Mancini won Oscars for *Moon River* and *The Days Of Wine And Roses*. He also composed music for *The Pink Panther*, *Breakfast At Tiffany's*, *Charade*, *Mr. Lucky*, and *Peter Gunn*. In all, he scored over 80 films and released over 90 albums. Nominated 72 times, Mancini would win an amazing 20 Grammys. His daughter Monica Mancini released her début album in 1998.
CAUSE: Pancreatic and liver cancer. He died in Los Angeles.
FURTHER READING: Mancini, Henry. (1989). *Did They Mention The Music?* Chicago: Contemporary.

Sidney Manker

Born January 25, 1932
Died January 1974
A guitarist in Bill Justis' band, Sidney Manker co-wrote Justis' biggest hit, the instrumental, R&B classic 'Raunchy'.
CAUSE: Heart attack.

Colin Manley

Born April 16, 1942
Died April 9, 1999
A talented guitarist and classmate of Paul McCartney's at Liverpool Institute, Colin Manley and Don Andrew formed The Remo Four in the early Sixties. Adding vocalist Keith Stokes and drummer Harry Prytherch, the Merseyside group honed their skills by playing at European military bases with Bill Buck replacing Prytherch, who in turn was replaced by Roy Dyke. Returning to Liverpool, they backed singer Johnny Sandon (who had previously been backed by The Searchers) and, landing a recording contract with Pye Records in the wake of The Beatles success, they were signed to Brian Epstein's NEMS organisation. Sandon & The Remo Four recorded two unsuccessful singles for the label before parting company in 1963. The Remo Four then became the backing band for Brian Epstein protégés Cilla Black and Tommy Quickly, as well as releasing two singles on Pye's subsidiary, Piccadilly, in 1964. Discovering that they owed large sums of money to both the tax collector and to NEMS, the group relocated to Germany in 1965, where they began experimenting with a jazzier direction, featuring new recruit Tony Ashton on keyboards. Returning to the UK in 1967, the group played on some George Harrison-produced sessions for the film, *Wonderwall*. With the group splintering in the late Sixties, Manley joined Billy J. Kramer & The Dakotas,

and then Georgie Fame's Blue Flames. He later worked with Freddie Starr, and an oldies version of The Swinging Blue Jeans.
CAUSE: Cancer. He died in Liverpool.

Kal Mann

(KALMAN COHEN)
Born May 6, 1917
Died November 28, 2001
As a lyricist and label owner, Philadelphia-born Kal Mann created some of rock music's most enduring dance crazes. Breaking into the entertainment field during the Forties, Mann worked as a comedy writer for Red Buttons, Jack Leonard and Danny Thomas. Turning to music during the start of the rock era, Mann teamed with business partner Bernie Lowe to launch Cameo Records in 1956 and a subsidiary, Parkway, two years later. Issuing some of the finest examples of Sixties American pop music, Cameo-Parkway enjoyed success with Chubby Checker, Dee Dee Sharp, Bobby Rydell, The Tymes, The Dovells and The Orlons. With the label based in Philadelphia, many Cameo-Parkway artists performed regularly on *American Bandstand*. As a songwriter (often under the pseudonym Jon Sheldon), Mann teamed with either Bernie Lowe or Dave Appell to compose many of his label's hits, beginning with the chart-topping 'Butterfly' and continuing with 'Bristol Stomp', 'Don't Hang Up', 'The Fish', 'Let's Twist Again', 'South Street', 'Wah Watusi', 'Wild One' and 'You Can't Sit Down'. Mann and Lowe also co-wrote the Elvis Presley hit 'Teddy Bear'. With popular music taking a turn toward more serious rock'n'roll and Dick Clark relocating *American Bandstand* to Los Angeles, Cameo-Parkway began fading from the charts. Around this time, Mann retired from the music industry and by 1967 the company's former accountant Allen B. Klein had acquired a controlling interest in the label. Two years later, Klein renamed the company ABKCO Records. But with Kal Mann retaining Cameo-Parkway's master tapes, Klein was unable to reissue the label's catalogue on CD until 2005.
CAUSE: Alzheimer's disease. He died at his home in Pompano Beach, Florida.

Dean Manuel

Born 1934
Died July 31, 1964
Originally the pianist in Bob Luman's country/rockabilly band ('Let's Think About Living'), Dean Manuel left Luman in 1960 to join Jim Reeves as both his pianist and manager.
CAUSE: He was killed in a plane crash in Nashville, which also took the life of country star Jim Reeves. En route from Batesville, Arkansas, to Nashville, the plane was piloted by Reeves. Members from a team of 700 volunteers found the wreckage two days later.

Richard Manuel

Born April 3, 1945
Died March 4, 1986
Pianist, singer and occasional composer with The Band, the Canadian group who backed Bob Dylan as well as becoming recognised in their own right, Richard Manuel was born and raised in Stratford, Ontario, Canada. While singing in a gospel group with his siblings, Manuel briefly took piano lessons followed by guitar at age 15. After Manuel's group The Rockin' Revols shared a bill with Canadian rock legend Ronnie Hawkins, Manuel joined Hawkins' popular touring group The Hawks. Taking a blues turn by late 1961, The Hawks settled into its classic line-up of Hawkins, Manuel, Garth Hudson, Robbie Robertson, Rick Danko and Levon Helm. When Danko was fired by Hawkins for bringing a girlfriend to a club, the remaining Hawks quit the group in 1964 and formed Levon & The Hawks. Backing blues guitarist John Hammond, Jr., Manuel and the

rest of the band were hired as Bob Dylan's touring group just as he was switching from acoustic to electric folk-rock; night after night, Dylan and his new electric group (minus Helm), rechristened The Band, were booed around the globe by folk purists. With Dylan settling into a rented pink house (nicknamed "The Big Pink") near Woodstock, New York, after suffering a motorcycle crash, Manuel and the rest of The Band joined him in recording what became known as *The Basement Tapes*. Signing with Capitol Records, The Band enjoyed much critical praise for their début release *Music From Big Pink* (1968); their sound was highlighted by Manuel's wracked and high falsetto vocals. Embracing a rustic sound that combined country, folk, and blues, the follow-up, *The Band* (1969), included the group's highest-charting US single 'Up On Cripple Creek', and the often recorded 'The Night They Drove Old Dixie Down' (later a Top 10 hit for Joan Baez). Manuel contributed the atmospheric 'Whispering Pines' but after this second album, Manuel abdicated songwriting duties to Robertson. The Band continued its string of strong sellers including *Stage Fright*, *Rock Of Ages*, and the Alan Freed tribute, *Moondog Matinee*. Throughout the Seventies, Manuel suffered drug and alcohol problems. Rejoining Dylan in 1973, The Band backed him on *Planet Waves*, and a subsequent live release, *Before The Flood*. In 1976 Robertson, tired of touring, pressured the others into disbanding and, in a major event that marked their exit, the group led an all-star concert on Thanksgiving Day 1976 at the Winterland Ballroom in San Francisco, billed as "The Last Waltz", that was captured on a three-album set, and a Martin Scorsese documentary. After recording a contractually required studio album, the remaining members of The Band reluctantly disbanded. Throughout the Seventies, Manuel suffered drug and alcohol problems and little was heard from him, other than that he entered a detox programme in 1979. Reunited in 1986, The Band (minus Robertson) launched a number of small venue tours, with Manuel assuming lead vocal duties. In the Eighties, Manuel also worked behind Bonnie Raitt and Willie Nelson.

CAUSE: He committed suicide by hanging himself in a Winterpark, Florida, motel room the day after a concert. He had hung himself with his belt in the bathroom, while his wife lay sleeping in the adjacent room at the Quality Inn. Manuel was under the influence of cocaine and alcohol at the time.

FURTHER READING: Hoskyns, Barney. (1993). *Across The Great Divide: The Band And America*. New York: Hyperion. Helm, Levon, with Davis, Stephen. (1993). *This Wheel's On Fire*. New York: William Morrow.

Bobby Marchan

(OSCAR JAMES GIBSON)
Born April 30, 1930
Died December 5, 1999

A New Orleans-based Fifties R&B singer, Youngstown, Ohio-born Bobby Marchan first hit the stage as a female impersonator. Organising a touring troupe of female impersonators, The Powder Box Revue, he landed at the legendary Dew Drop Inn in New Orleans. Impressed with the city, he rented a room above the nightclub and remained there. Hired as a singer and emcee at Club Tijuana, he performed in drag. Impressing Johnny Vincent, the owner of Ace Records, Marchan was teamed with R&B pianist Huey Smith as Huey "Piano" Smith & The Clowns. With Marchan providing lead vocals, the group landed on the R&B charts with raucous upbeat numbers such as 'Don't You Just Know It', 'Don't You Know Yockomo' and 'Havin' A Good Time'. With Smith concentrating on his songwriting, he

was eventually replaced in the touring version of the Clowns by pianist James Booker. Leaving The Clowns, Marchan signed as a solo artist with Fire Records, topping the R&B charts in 1960 with a soulful cover of Big Jay McNeely's 'There Is Something On Your Mind'. His only other solo chart entry came in 1966 with the Cameo release, 'Shake Your Tambourine'. Another of his releases, 'Get Down With It', was reprised by Slade in the early Seventies. Remaining in the music business well into the Nineties, he launched a rap promotion business and aided in the formation of Cash Money Records.
CAUSE: He was in poor health for some time, fighting a battle against cancer and having a kidney removed.

Bob Marley

(ROBERT NESTA MARLEY)
Born April 6, 1945
Died May 11, 1981
Innovative leader of the rebellious, pioneering reggae supergroup The Wailers, Bob Marley brought the genre into the mainstream. In doing so he became a Carribean superstar, and in death he has become a spiritual figure, widely revered for his beliefs as much as his music. The Jamaican-born Marley was the son of a black maid and a white civil servant. Raised by his mother in the Trenchtown ghetto of Kingston after his father abandoned the family, Marley played a home-made banjo as a child. Influenced by the local strains of ska music, Marley was first recorded by producer Leslie Kong in 1961. Working days as a welder, Marley then teamed with friends Bunny Livingston and Peter Tosh to form a proto-reggae group, called among other names, The Wailin' Wailers. Recording dozens of strong-selling local singles on Leslie Kong's Kong label, the group earned little but their reputation soared. But this didn't pay the bills and Marley left for Wilmington, Delaware, in 1966 to live with his mother, Cedella, at which time The Wailers disbanded. While in the US, Marley worked the night shift at a Chrysler plant. Wishing to avoid the Vietnam War military draft, Marley returned to Jamaica in late 1968 and reformed The Wailers. Converting to Rastafarianism, Marley infused tenets of the religion into his music. Teaming with producer Lee "Scratch" Perry in 1969, The Wailers were expanded with Aston and Carlton Barrett. During this period, The Wailers also launched their own Tuff Gong label, but were sidelined by Livingston's imprisonment and Marley's new association with Johnny Nash (who would score hits with the Marley-written 'Stir It Up' and 'Guava Jelly'). Though continuing to release Jamaican singles on their own Tuff Gong label, The Wailers signed with Chris Blackwell's Island Records, a move that was largely responsible for their eventual worldwide breakthrough. Released in 1972, the albums *Catch A Fire* and *Burnin'* contained politically charged tracks such as 'I Shot The Sheriff' and 'Get Up, Stand Up'. Marley's increasing profile received a further boost in 1974 when Eric Clapton took 'I Shot The Sheriff' to the top of the US charts. Marley's increasing fame did not sit well with Tosh and Livingston, who would quit for solo careers in 1974. Now featuring a female backing trio called The I-Threes (which included Marley's wife Rita), The Wailers enjoyed their first major US success with the album *Natty Dread*, which was highlighted by the track 'No Woman, No Cry'. As his fame escalated, Marley became a political force in Jamaica, promoting marijuana use among other issues, but he narrowly avoided death in an assassination attempt in 1976. Temporarily moving to the US, he would record *Exodus* (1977), the album containing his signature song, 'Jammin''. Though essential to the popularisation of reggae music, Marley

enjoyed scant radio airplay in the US. Shot and wounded in another assassination attempt in 1978, Marley would release two albums that year, *Kaya* and the live *Babylon By Bus*. By the late Seventies, Marley's Tuff Gong label was licensing Wailers albums for distribution outside Jamaica. Tragedy struck Marley when he was diagnosed with cancer after a fluid build-up in one of his toes, the condition caused by a soccer injury. Eventually the cancer spread to his brain. Continuing to record and perform as much as his health allowed him, Marley collapsed in September 1980 during the middle of a tour with The Commodores. Marley sired eleven children by seven different women; son David "Ziggy" Marley was joined by three other siblings in the group Ziggy Marley & The Melody Makers. For years after Marley's death, various parties fought for control of his estate, which by 1989 was valued at $30 million.
CAUSE: Suffering with lung and brain cancer, he was admitted to Cedar Lees Hospital in Miami, Florida, three days before his death. He had been in Florida visiting his mother and his wife, flying in from a German cancer clinic. He was given a Jamaican state funeral and buried with a guitar in one hand and a Bible in the other.
FURTHER READING: White, Timothy. (1983, 1992 & 1998). *Catch A Fire: The Life Of Bob Marley*. New York: Henry Holt; London: Omnibus Press. Davis, Stephen. (1983). *Bob Marley: The Biography*. London: Arthur Barker.

Steve Marriott

Born January 30, 1947
Died April 20, 1991
Guitarist and vocalist for British pop outfits The Small Faces and Humble Pie, east London-born Steve Marriott worked in show business from an early age, having been expelled from school for suspected arson. At the age of 12, Marriott appeared in the stage production of Lionel Bart's *Oliver* and recorded his début single on Decca Records, 'Give Her My Regards', a blatant homage to Buddy Holly, in 1963. By the end of the year Marriott was leading his own group, going under such names as Steve Marriott & The Moonlights and Steve Marriott & The Frantiks. After a shelved solo session under the guidance of Rolling Stones' manager Andrew Oldham in 1964, Marriott formed Steve Marriott & The Moments, and recorded a US only cash-in version of The Kinks' 'You Really Got Me'. Also during this time Marriott appeared in a number of low-budget youth films such as *Live It Up* and *Be My Guest*. While working in the J60 Music Shop in East Ham, London, in early 1965, Marriott sold a bass to his future bandmate and songwriting partner Ronnie Lane. Lane invited him to play with his group The Outcasts featuring drummer Kenny Jones at their regular pub gig. When the band was fired after Marriott went overboard on his Jerry Lee Lewis impersonation, resulting in a piano being wrecked, the three resolved to form their own group which became The Small Faces, additionally featuring Jimmy Winston on organ and vocals. The diminutive group caused an instant sensation in London's clubs, and manager Don Arden signed them to Decca Records in mid-1965. Within weeks the sharply dressed quartet was in the charts with their first single, 'Whatcha Gonna Do About It', which established them at the forefront of the Mod movement along with The Who. However Winston's days were numbered (not least because he stood over 5 foot 6 inches) and he was replaced by Ian McLagan. The group continued to score British hits, becoming teenybop idols thanks to Marriott's pin-up status and such hits as 'Sha-La-La-La-Lee' (1966), 'Hey Girl' (1966), 'All Or Nothing' (1966), and 'My Mind's Eye' (1966). Switching to the Immediate label and a new manager in Rolling Stones

svengali Andrew Oldham, the group spent more time in the studio, resulting in further classic singles with 'Here Come The Nice', 'Itchycoo Park' (a US Top 20 hit) and 'Tin Soldier' (all 1967) culminating in their 1968 masterwork *Ogden's Nut Gone Flake*, featuring the group's last major hit 'Lazy Sunday'. Unhappy with The Small Faces' pop image, Marriott left in 1969 to form Humble Pie, a more progressive rock band featuring former Herd guitarist Peter Frampton, Greg Ridley, and Jerry Shirley. (The remaining members of The Small Faces soldiered on, recruiting Rod Stewart and Jeff Beck to form The Faces.) Humble Pie's initial style mixed acoustic and rock on their first two albums, *As Safe As Yesterday Is* and *Town And Country*, and they had a British Top 5 hit with 'Natural Born Bugie' in 1969. When Frampton was replaced by ex-Colosseum guitarist Dave "Clem" Clempson, the band pursued a harder rock direction; from the album *Rock On*, the group landed its first US hit with 'I Don't Need No Doctor' and '30 Days In The Hole', culled from the album *Smokin'* in 1972. Other hit albums included the R&B flavoured *Eat It* (1973) and *Thunderbox* (1974). Their success was largely due to heavy touring, and the group took a break from the road before disbanding in early 1975. After recording a poorly received solo album, Marriott teamed with two members of Humble Pie to form Steve Marriott's All-Stars. Disbanding that group, he joined a re-formed Small Faces, minus Lane, in 1976. The group recorded two artistically and commercially disastrous albums before calling it quits in 1978. In 1980, in America, Marriott re-formed Humble Pie, but a year later he was sidelined after suffering from a number of health problems, including an injured hand. Returning to the UK, Marriott performed in a number of low-profile blues-rock groups in the Eighties, including his own outfit, Packet Of Three. At the time of his death, Marriott had finished work in Los Angeles on tracks with Peter Frampton.

CAUSE: He died in a fire at his 16th century home in Arkesden, Essex. Having arrived home earlier that day from America, Marriott and his third wife Toni had gone to their local pub but he had returned home alone after they argued. A jetlagged Marriott fell asleep with a cigarette burning. According to the coroner, although Marriott had consumed large quantities of alcohol and Valium, he had attempted to escape. He was found in his bedroom, dead from smoke inhalation.

FURTHER READING: Hewitt, Paolo. (2005). *All Too Beautiful*. London: Helter Skelter. McLagan, Ian. (1998). *All The Rage: A Rock 'n' Roll Odyssey*. London: Sidgwick & Jackson. Hewitt, Paolo. (1995). *Small Faces: The Young Mods' Forgotten Story*. London: Acid Jazz. Twelker, Uli. (1997). *Happy Boys Happy: A Rock History Of The Small Faces And Humble Pie*. London: Sanctuary Publishing Ltd.

Maithe Marshall

Born August 31, 1924
Died November 1989

A member of pioneering doo-wop group The Ravens, tenor Maithe Marshall introduced the prominent use of a falsetto as the lead vocal in R&B. Joining the Baltimore-based group in 1946 as replacement for Ollie Jones, Marshall complemented the booming vocals of bass singer Jimmy Ricks. Signing with Herb Abramson's National Records, The Ravens dominated the R&B charts with hits such as 'Write Me A Letter', 'Send For Me If You Need Me' and 'I Don't Have To Ride No More'. Following the group's switch to Columbia in 1950, Marshall and two other members quit the following year to form the short-lived act The Hi-Hatters. Briefly returning to The

Ravens, Marshall again quit and was replaced by Joe Van Loan. After forming another short-lived group, The Marshall Brothers, Marshall returned to The Ravens in 1954 for a number of tours. By the Sixties, Marshall had joined an Ink Spots revival group.
CAUSE: Unknown. He died in Minnesota.

Bobbi Martin

(BARBARA ANNE MARTIN)
Born November 29, 1943
Died May 2, 2000
A pop and rock singer, Bobbi Martin placed two songs in the Top 40, 'Don't Forget I Still Love You' (1965) and 'For The Love Of Him' (1970). Born in Brooklyn but raised in Baltimore, she began recording in 1960. Martin also toured with Bob Hope on his popular USO military Christmas shows.
CAUSE: Lung cancer. She died at Brighton Wood Knoll medical facility in Baltimore.

David Martin

Born 1937
Died August 2, 1987
Bass player of Sam The Sham & The Pharaohs, Texas-native David Martin had co-founded the Domingo Samudio-led group in the early Sixties. After landing regional success with the independent release 'Haunted House', the group signed with MGM Records in 1965. There, Sam The Sham & The Pharaohs scored several garage-rock hits including, the three-million selling 'Wooly Bully' and 'Little Red Riding Hood'. Martin left the group in 1966 and worked as a television repairman.
CAUSE: Heart attack. He died at his home in Garland, Texas.

Dean Martin

(DINO PAUL CROCETTI)
Born June 7, 1917
Died December 25, 1995
Actor and pop crooner, Dean Martin was the son of a Sicilian-born barber in Steubenville, Ohio. Leaving school in the 10th grade for the boxing ring, he spent time as an employee of the local mob, delivering moonshine and running numbers. After working in local gin-joints as Dino Martini, the renamed Dean Martin got his first break as the featured vocalist for The Sammy Watkins Orchestra at a Cleveland nightclub. But his singing career was interrupted by a 14-month stint defending his country in World War II, discharged after suffering a hernia. Then after sharing a bill with comedian Jerry Lewis at Atlantic City's Club 500 in 1946, a partnership was born. Signing a multi-film deal with Paramount, Lewis & Martin made 16 pictures from 1949–56. In the 1953 Martin & Lewis film *The Caddy*, Martin performed the sentimental, Italian-flavoured love song 'That's Amore', the single garnering an Academy Award nomination. Playing the straight man in his classic pairing with the zany Lewis, Martin was usually portrayed as a suave lady's man; the duo also landed their own television programme (1950–55), *The Colgate Comedy Hour*. But tired of Lewis' emerging star, a bitter Martin quit after refusing to play a police officer in the Lewis screenplay *The Delicate Delinquent*. While the entertainment media decreed Martin's career over, he emerged with a masterful role opposite Marlon Brando in the 1958 film *The Young Lions*, and offered convincing performances in *Rio Bravo* and *Some Came Running*. Martin would emerge as a hard drinking, chain-smoking member of the Rat Pack, alongside Frank Sinatra, Peter Lawford, and Sammy Davis Jr, with whom he co-starred in the films, *Ocean's 11* and *Robin And The 7 Hoods*. Having made his first recordings in 1948, the suave, baritone-voiced Martin oozed a smooth confidence in his mostly pop ballad hits which included 'Memories Are Made Of

This' (1955), 'Return To Me' (1958), 'Volare' (1958), 'Everybody Loves Somebody' (1964), and 'Send Me The Pillow That You Dream On' (1965). Returning to television, he hosted a variety show which ran on NBC from 1965–74; an informal programme with an on-stage bar stocked with alcohol, Martin assumed the role of a tipsy reveller. When The Rolling Stones appeared on his show in the mid Sixties he was deliberately rude, commenting on their appearance in a condescending manner that subsequently alienated him from rock fans (and Keith Richards in particular). Martin made his final film appearances in *Cannonball Run II* (1984). Devastated by the death of his son Dino Martin in 1987, Martin became a near-recluse. In 1988, Martin reluctantly rejoined his Rat Pack compatriots, Frank Sinatra and Sammy Davis Jr, for a large-venue tour; quitting after a week, he feigned kidney problems and briefly checked into a hospital (he would be replaced by Liza Minnelli). He subsequently returned to the Casino circuit, having become a caricature of himself. And with its inclusion in the 1987 film *Moonstruck*, Martin enjoyed renewed popularity with his recording of 'That's Amore'. Although Martin and Lewis feuded for years, Lewis attended Martin's 72nd birthday party in 1989, while Martin had guested on Lewis' annual telethon for Muscular Dystrophy.
CAUSE: Acute respiratory failure. He died at his home in Beverly Hills.
FURTHER READING: Tosches, Nick. (1993). Dino, *Living High In The Dirty Business Of Dreams*. New York: Dell.

Dino Martin

(DEAN PAUL MARTIN)
Born November 17, 1951
Died March 21, 1987
Actor, athlete, and member of the Sixties pop group Dino, Desi & Billy, Dino Martin was the eldest son of singer Dean Martin. At age 14, Dino formed a rock group with Desi Arnaz, Jr. and neighbour Billy Hinsche. Signing with Frank Sinatra's Reprise label, the trio was not especially talented, and compensated with their youthful charm and good looks. Targeting the teen market, the trio enjoyed two Top 40 hits in 1965 with 'I'm A Fool' and 'Not The Lovin' Kind'; the group disbanded in 1968. Enrolled in the pre-med programme at UCLA, Martin left school in 1970 and married English actress Olivia Hussey (divorcing her, he would later wed Dorothy Hammil). A remarkably talented athlete, Martin was a race car driver, a professional tennis player who made it to Wimbledon in 1978, and was drafted as a wide receiver by a World Football League team, the Las Vegas Casinos. Also an actor, he starred in the television programme *Misfits Of Science* (1985–86), and appeared in the films *Players* (1979), *Heart Like A Wheel* (1983), and with David Carradine, *Back Fire* (1987). Also a pilot, in 1980 Martin joined the Air National Guard.
CAUSE: Martin and co-pilot, Captain Ramon Ortiz (39), died instantly when their F-4C Phantom jet dropped several thousand feet in turbulent weather and flew into the snow-covered, 11,000-foot Mount San Gorgonio, near March Air Force Base in California. The wreckage was found five days later. Martin had earned his pilot licence at age 16.

Joe Martin

Born February 12, 1935
Died February 19, 2005
The co-founder of Fifties doo-wop group The (Five) Willows, baritone vocalist Joe Martin formed the act, as The Dovers, with his twin brother Ralph Martin and four others. The Harlem-based quintet originally included future record label owner Bobby Robinson and, later, future Drifters member Doc Green. After

recording a self-financed début single in 1953, The (Five) Willows continued to record for a series of labels until a crossover hit in 1956 came with the upbeat 'Church Bells May Ring', featuring a young Neil Sedaka playing chimes. Although failing to achieve any further hits, the group continued recording until 1964. Martin headed a touring revival version of the group in the Eighties.
CAUSE: Suffering a stroke, he died a year later at Presbyterian Hospital in New York City.

Nick Massi

(NICHOLAS MACIOCI)
Born September 19, 1935
Died December 24, 2000
The bass guitarist and backing bass vocalist of The Four Seasons, Mick Massi passed through a series of local rock bands before joining fellow Italian-American Frankie Valli in The Four Lovers. Signing with producer Bob Crewe in 1960, the group was initially employed as uncredited session vocalists behind Bobby Darin and others. Renamed The Four Seasons (taken from a New Jersey bowling alley), the doo-wop based vocal harmony group issued its first single on Gone Records in 1961, but after nearly disbanding due to a lack of success, member Bob Gaudio wrote 'Sherry' (originally titled 'Jackie' after Jackie Kennedy) in 15 minutes, suggesting Valli sing the lead in his soon-to-be trademark falsetto voice. Smelling a hit, Crewe shopped the single around, with the bidding war won by Vee-Jay Records. A chart-topping smash, many listeners assumed the group was black. The Four Seasons hit run continued with novelty-styled chart topper 'Big Girls Don't Cry', 'Walk Like A Man', 'Candy Girl', 'Dawn', 'Ronnie', 'Rag Doll' and 'Save It For Me'. Exhausted from touring, Massi quit the group in late 1964 and later teamed with former Four Seasons member Tommy DeVito to form the New Jersey-based production company, Vitomass Productions.
CAUSE: Cancer. He died at his home in West Orange, New Jersey.

Neal Matthews, Jr.

Born October 26, 1929
Died April 21, 2000
A member of harmony group The Jordanaires, Neal Matthews, Jr. is best known for his work with Elvis Presley. Formed in 1948 as a gospel quartet in Springfield, Missouri, The Jordanaires relocated to Nashville in the early Fifties. After several line-up changes, Matthews joined in 1953. A native of Nashville, Matthews learned to play the guitar in his teens; joining his father in The Crook Brothers gospel group, he appeared at The Grand Ole Opry. After a stint in the Korean War, Matthews studied psychology at Belmont College. Invited to join The Jordanaires by lead tenor Gordon Stoker, Matthews sang second tenor. The group's first break came when they were hired by Eddy Arnold to back him in concert and on his television show. The Jordanaires were soon providing backing harmonies on pop and country hits including 'Oh Lonesome Me' (Don Gibson), 'Big Bad John' (Jimmy Dean), 'Crazy' (Patsy Cline), 'It's Only Make Believe' (Conway Twitty), and several Ricky Nelson singles including 'Poor Little Fool'. Their sound rooted in old-time spirituals, The Jordanaires were teamed with the like-minded Elvis Presley when he signed with RCA in 1956. A fruitful pairing, The Jordanaires provided backing harmonies on dozens of Presley standards beginning with the double-sided hit, 'Hound Dog'/'Don't Be Cruel'. During their 15-year association with Presley, The Jordanaires appeared on most of his soundtrack albums (and made occasional cameo appearances in his many films), recorded religious material such as *His Hand In Mine*

(1960), and joined Presley on stage during the Seventies. The Jordanaires also issued their own material, landing a minor hit with 'Sugaree' (1956). Matthews also moonlighted in another backing vocal group, The Merry Melody Singers, and worked with a number of Mercury Records artists including Clyde McPhatter, Brook Benton, Ray Stevens, and Faron Young. After Presley's death, The Jordanaires released a tribute album, *The Jordanaires Sing Elvis' Gospel Favorites*. Suffering a stroke in 1995, Matthews was forced to retire. In 1985, Matthews authored the book, *Elvis: A Golden Tribute*.
CAUSE: He suffered a heart attack and died at his home near Nashville.

Rudy Maugeri

Born January 27, 1931
Died May 7, 2004
As a member of one of the most notable white cover bands during the start of the rock era, baritone vocalist Rudy Maugeri was instrumental in the success of The Crew-Cuts during the mid Fifties. Formerly a seminary student, Maugeri had intended to become a priest. Formed in Toronto originally as The Canadaires, the quartet scored its début hit in 1954 with the Maugeri composition, 'Crazy 'Bout Ya Baby'. Signing with Mercury Records, The Crew-Cuts built a career by recording pop cover versions of rock'n'roll songs, beginning with their million-selling rendition of 'Sh-Boom' which competed on the charts with the original doo-wop release by The Chords. Following the same effective formula, The Crew-Cuts continued with 'Earth Angel', 'Ko Ko Mo (I Love You)', 'An Untold Story' and 'Gum Drop'. After the group disbanded in 1964, Maugeri later worked in the broadcasting field in New York and Los Angeles.
CAUSE: Suffering from pancreatic cancer, he died at his home in Las Vegas.

Bill Maybray

(WILLIAM R. MAYBRAY, SR.)
Born May 14, 1944
Died December 5, 2004
As co-lead singer, bass player and occasional drummer for one-hit wonders The Jaggerz, Bill Maybray backed the group's leader Dominic Ierace (better known as Donnie Iris). A native of New Brighten, Pennsylvania, Maybray began drumming in his father's swing orchestra, beginning at age 10. Formed during the mid Sixties by Maybray and five others as a bar band in suburban Pittsburgh, The Jaggerz were discovered by former Skyliners manager Joe Rock and after recording an obscure album in 1969 for Kenny Gamble and Leon Huff at Gamble Records, The Jaggerz issued the million-selling single 'The Rapper' for the Kama Sutra label. Featuring Maybray's backing harmony vocals, the song nearly topped the charts in 1970, but with no further hits The Jaggerz disbanded in 1972. Maybray joined a revival version of the group in the Nineties.
CAUSE: Complications related to cancer.

Arthur Lee Maye

Born December 11, 1934
Died July 17, 2002
A doo-wop vocalist who split his time between music and professional baseball, Arthur Lee Maye was a member of The Crowns, The Rams, The Carmels and The Five Hearts, and often recorded with his close friend Richard Berry of 'Louie Louie' fame. With his baseball career taking precedence, Arthur Maye left The Crowns to play outfield as "Lee Maye" for The Milwaukee Braves and subsequently played for several other teams – including the Houston Astros, Cleveland Indians, and Washington Senators – achieving a respectable, lifetime .274 batting average before retiring from the sport in 1971. Continuing to make occasional forays

into music, Maye took a turn towards soul music in the late Sixties and for a time joined a touring version of The Platters, and later worked for Amtrak.
CAUSE: Liver cancer. He died in Riverside Community Hospital in Riverside, California.

Lenny Mayes

(LEONARD CORNELL MAYES)
Born April 5, 1951
Died November 8, 2004
A latter member of American soul group The Dramatics, baritone vocalist Lenny Mayes appeared on several of their hits. Quitting his job at a Ford factory in Detroit to work in music, Mayes was originally a member of an R&B/doo-wop group called The Casanovas, and recorded with The Sunrise Movement in 1968. In 1973, Mayes joined The Dramatics as the replacement for Elbert "Al" Wilkins and appeared on *A Dramatics Experience*, their final album for Stax-Volt. Signing with ABC, the group had a string of R&B hits over the next decade, including a cover of 'Me And Mrs. Jones', 'You're Fooling You', 'Be My Girl', 'Shake It Well' and 'Welcome Back Home'. Following the departure of lead singer Rob Banks, the group disbanded in 1982 and after briefly pursuing a solo career, Mayes reunited with The Dramatics in 1986 for the album *Somewhere In Time*. Mayes later worked in the computer and real estate fields.
CAUSE: While recuperating from a heart attack, he succumbed to lung cancer. He died in Southfield, Michigan.

Curtis Mayfield

Born June 3, 1942
Died December 26, 1999
The creative force in The Impressions, Curtis Mayfield was an influential figure in the world of soul music. Reared by his mother in the rough Cabrini-Green housing project of Chicago, Mayfield worked at odd jobs to help support his struggling family. Prodded by his grandmother, the Rev. A.B. Mayfield, he began singing gospel music at her Traveling Souls Spiritualist storefront church, and in his early teens, Mayfield formed The Northern Jubilee gospel quintet with three cousins and friend Jerry Butler. Several years later Butler joined an R&B group called The Roosters, and hired Mayfield, originally as a guitarist. Signing with Vee-Jay Records, the renamed Jerry Butler & The Impressions landed a gospel-drenched hit with the romantic ballad, 'For Your Precious Love' (1958). When Butler left to pursue a solo career, Mayfield took over on lead vocals but, unable to repeat their success, the group disbanded after a year. After taking a job at a tobacco shop to pay a tax bill, Mayfield re-formed The Impressions in 1961 and, signing with ABC-Paramount, they returned to the charts with 'Gypsy Woman'. Meanwhile, Butler had become a major R&B star and was often aided by Mayfield's guitar work and songwriting on hits such as 'He Will Break Your Heart' (1960), 'Find Another Girl' (1961) and 'I'm Telling You' (1961). Mayfield also wrote and produced material for Gene Chandler and his high school classmate, Major Lance. With Mayfield at the helm with his high-tenor voice, The Impressions continued a strong hit run with 'It's All Right' (1963) and a total of five Top 40 hits in 1964, including 'Amen' and the civil-rights themed 'Keep On Pushing'. With Mayfield harking back to his Christian roots, The Impressions scored an impressive crossover hit with 'People Get Ready' (1965), the song later reprised by both Aretha Franklin and Jeff Beck/Rod Stewart. Teaming with Eddie Thomas in 1968 to form Curtom Records, Mayfield signed a distribution deal with Buddah Records; a prosperous label, Curtom signed The Five Stairsteps, Linda Clifford, Baby Huey, and the pop-gospel group, The

Staple Singers, for whom Mayfield composed 'Let's Do It Again'. Leaving The Impressions in 1970, Mayfield continued to direct the group as a writer and producer. Veering towards hard soul in the early Seventies, Mayfield scored further R&B hits with 'Move On Up' (1971) and million-selling singles 'Superfly' and the anti-drug themed 'Freddie's Dead', the tracks culled from the soundtrack of low-budget, blaxploitation film, *Superfly* (1972). Moving to Atlanta, Mayfield closed Curtom Records in 1980 but reactivated the label in 1987, releasing the poor-selling soundtrack to the 1990 sequel, *Return Of Superfly*. Tragedy struck Mayfield at a free outdoor concert at Brooklyn's Wingate Field in 1990, when he was struck by a lighting scaffold and paralysed from the neck down. Receiving the Grammy Legend Award in 1994, Mayfield released his long-awaited solo album two years later, *New World Order*.
CAUSE: His health had deteriorated since his stage accident. Lapsing into a coma, he died at North Fulton Regional Hospital in Roswell, Georgia.

Percy Mayfield

Born August 12, 1920
Died August 11, 1984
An R&B pianist and ballad singer, Louisiana-born Percy Mayfield wrote songs throughout his youth. Moving to Los Angeles in 1942, he formed his own band, The May Tones. A reluctant singer, Mayfield was an emotional, blues-grounded vocalist. Recording on a pair of Los Angeles labels, before landing at Specialty Records, Mayfield first hit the R&B charts in 1950 with the million-selling single 'Please Send Me Somebody To Love'. Most of Mayfield's hits came in the early Fifties and included 'Lost Love' (1951), 'What A Fool I Was' (1951), 'Pray-in' For Your Return' (1951), 'Cry Baby' (1952), and 'Big Question' (1952). Involved in a serious traffic accident in 1952 which left his face seriously disfigured, Mayfield saw his career curtailed. Devastated by the change in his appearance, he struggled along for the rest of his life. Hired as a staff songwriter for Ray Charles in the late Fifties, his biggest seller came with 'Hit The Road Jack'. Returning to the charts in 1963, Mayfield scored an R&B hit with an updated version of his earlier release, 'River's Invitation', the single released on Charles' new Tangerine label. After parting with Charles, Mayfield continued to record and tour as a solo act.
CAUSE: He suffered a heart attack at his home in Los Angeles. Mayfield had been scheduled to perform on his birthday at a benefit concert for Big Mama Thornton who had passed away two weeks earlier.

Bob Mayo

(ROBERT JOHN MAYO)
Born August 25, 1951
Died February 23, 2004
A talented pianist and guitarist, Bob Mayo performed with a number of leading rock acts beginning in the Seventies. A child prodigy, the native New Yorker studied classical piano from age five. While a member of a pair of regional rock acts, Doc Holliday and Rat Race Choir, Mayo earned a degree from Iona College. Joining rocker Peter Frampton for an 11 month tour in 1975, Mayo performed on the live tracks which would be issued as the multi-platinum AOR double album *Frampton Comes Alive*. Coming off the road in 1980, Mayo worked in the studio with Joe Walsh, Joe Vitale and Foreigner. The latter, impressed with his work on the tracks 'Waiting For A Girl Like You' and 'Break It Up', hired Mayo for a series of subsequent tours beginning in 1981. During the Eighties, Mayo also joined the touring bands of rock heavyweights Aerosmith and Robert Plant as well as singer-songwriter Dan Fogelberg. In 1988, Mayo backed Daryl Hall and

John Oates on their album *Ooh Yeah*, and later joined Hall & Oates for a number of tours and two Daryl Hall solo albums. In 1992, Mayo reunited with Frampton for what was intended as a brief two-month tour; instead, the pair renewed their musical association for a number of touring and recording ventures. As a side project, Mayo was a member of the New York City-based, R&B-tinged rock band The Renovators. At the time of his death, Mayo was on the road with Frampton, who had just launched the European leg of a tour.
CAUSE: He died suddenly from a heart attack while on a train platform in Basel, Switzerland, a day after a concert in Paris.

Stuart McAllister

Born 1947
Died September 15, 2000
A rocker-turned-retailer, Stuart McAllister headed the 302-outlet, British based record store chain, HMV. A fine musician in his own right, he was the lead singer of the mid Sixties, Joe Meek-produced, pop-rock act Lee Scott & The Roulettes. After joining Thorn-EMI in 1984, McAllister was appointed CEO of the newly reorganised HMV group in 1986, and eventually expanded the record chain from 100 outlets in Britain, into a worldwide retailer with locations in nine countries.
CAUSE: After suffering a blood clot in 1998, his health deteriorated. He died in London.

Bob McBride

Born 1947
Died February 20, 1998
The lead singer of the Canadian pop-rock group Lighthouse, Toronto-born Bob McBride had previously spent a few years behind rockabilly artist Ronnie Hawkins. Formed in 1968 as a 13-piece group in Toronto by drummer Skip Prokop and songwriter Paul Hoffert, Lighthouse was signed to MGM Records. Though invited to perform at Woodstock in 1969, the group declined. Enjoying a string of Canadian hits, the group landed on the US charts with 'One Fine Morning' (1971) and 'Hats Off To A Stranger' (1972). Then after recording a solo album in 1973 for Capitol Records *Butterfly Records*, McBride was fired from Lighthouse; the group disbanded a year later. A successful solo act in Canada, McBride recorded a solo album for MCA Records in 1978, and also worked as a jingle writer. Lighthouse reunited for several concerts in 1982. But battling heroin addiction and in poor health, McBride was unable to join the group for a reunion in 1993. McBride was imprisoned the following year for robbing a drugstore.
CAUSE: Suffering from diabetes and Hepatitis-B, and in poor health for years, he died from a seizure at North York General Hospital in Toronto.

Patti McCabe

Born July 6, 1939
Died January 17, 1989
Member of the innocent, all-girl singing trio The Poni-Tails, Patti McCabe had joined the group as a replacement for original member Karen Topinka. After passing through two labels, the group was signed by ABC-Paramount. The Poni-Tails scored their only Top 40 hit with the yearning, puppy-love themed 'Born Too Late' (1958). After scoring a pair of minor, follow-up hits, 'Seven Minutes In Heaven' (1958) and 'I'll Be Seeing You' (1959), the trio turned down a contract extension and retired from music.
CAUSE: Cancer. She died in suburban Cleveland.

Tony McCall

(LOUIS ANTHONY MCCALL)
Born December 28, 1951
Died June 25, 1997
A member of the prolific soul/funk group Con Funk Shun, drummer Tony McCall formed the seven-piece outfit

with his high school classmates in Vallejo, California. Originally called Project Soul, the group toured in the early Seventies as the backing players for Stax act The Soul Children. Relocating to Memphis, Project Soul was hired by fellow Stax artist, veteran R&B singer Rufus Thomas, appearing in the performance film *Wattstax: The Living World.* Renamed Con Funk Shun and signed to Fretone Records (a label started by former Stax co-founder Estelle Axton), the group recorded a pair of poor-selling singles before signing to Mercury Records in 1976, and achieving a decade-long hit run on the R&B charts. Fronted by lead vocalists Michael Cooper and Felton Pilate, Con Funk Shun had one crossover hit with 'Ffun'. Employing a horn section, electric guitar riffs, funky electric keyboards and a sizzling backbeat, the group dominated urban radio with upbeat releases such as 'Shake And Dance With Me', 'Chase Me', 'Got To Be Enough', 'Too Tight', 'Baby, I'm Hooked (Right Into Your Love)', 'Electric Lady' and 'Burnin' Star'. Though disbanding in 1987, the group occasionally reunited, beginning in 1993.
CAUSE: He was murdered at his apartment complex in the Atlanta suburb of Stone Mountain, Georgia.

Allan McCarthy

Born c. 1958
Died August 1995
The drummer of Eighties new wave act Men Without Hats, Allan McCarthy appeared on their infectious 1983 MTV-era hit, 'The Safety Dance'. Formed in 1980 by vocalist Ivan Doroschuk, the Canadian-based group initially made waves with an independently issued EP, *Folk Of The '80s*, and reached its commercial apex with the 1983 album, *Rhythm Of Youth.* McCarthy left the group in 1987 prior to the recording of the album *Pop Goes The World.*
CAUSE: AIDS.

Linda McCartney

(LINDA LOUISE EASTMAN)
Born September 24, 1941
Died April 17, 1998
The wife of Paul McCartney, Linda Eastman was an accomplished photographer when the two met. Raised in a wealthy household in Scarsdale, New York, her father Lee Eastman was a successful entertainment business attorney who also represented various painters, including the noted abstract artist Willem de Kooning, and she majored in art history at the University of Arizona. Initially a receptionist at *Town And Country* magazine, she was assigned to photograph a number of musical acts beginning with The Dave Clark Five. During a trip to London in May 1967, she met Paul McCartney at a London nightclub. Married first to geophysicist John Melvyn See, she had one daughter, Heather, by him before marrying McCartney, the last Beatle bachelor, in 1969. She produced three further children, Mary, Stella and James, by McCartney. Joining her husband's group Wings on keyboards and backing vocals in 1972, she was initially criticised by fans for her rudimentary musical skills. Appearing on Paul McCartney's solo work and as part of his group, Linda was featured on dozens of hits including 'My Love' (1973), 'Band On The Run' (1974) and 'With A Little Luck' (1978). Linda McCartney wrote a handful of songs including 'Seaside Woman' (1977), the single released under the moniker Suzy & The Red Stripes; her final composition, a collaboration with her husband, was included on the 1997 Paul McCartney album, *Flaming Pie.* She also published several books, both collections of photographs and vegetarian cookery books. Like her husband, Linda was an outspoken vegetarian and promoter of animal rights, and in the Eighties she launched a very successful line of meatless frozen foods. After her death, Paul McCartney

released a commemorative tribute album, *Wild Prairie*, in 2000, with all the proceeds donated to cancer research.
CAUSE: Breast cancer. Diagnosed two years earlier, the disease had spread to her liver. Seeking privacy for his grieving family, Paul McCartney instructed his spokesman Geoff Baker to mislead the media by announcing that she had died while on vacation in Santa Barbara, California. She actually passed away at the family's 150-acre ranch near Tucson, Arizona. Linda McCartney's first husband, Joseph Melville See, Jr., committed suicide by gunshot on March 19, 2000
FURTHER READING: Miles, Barry. (1998). *Paul McCartney: Many Years From Now.* New York: Henry Holt.

Bobby McClure

Born April 21, 1942
Died November 13, 1992
A Chicago-based R&B singer, Bobby McClure was born in Chicago but raised in St. Louis. Reared on gospel music, he was hired to lead The Spirit of Illinois, a previously all-female gospel group. Returning to Chicago and switching to R&B in the late Fifties, McClure formed a doo-wop group, Bobby & The Vocals. Then after passing through a series of R&B bands, McClure teamed with Fontella Bass in 1965 for the duet hit, 'Don't Mess Up A Good Thing'. He subsequently recorded for a series of labels including Vanessa and Hi Records, before taking a job as a prison guard in Illinois. Moving to Los Angeles, he recorded his final sessions at Edge Records.
CAUSE: Brain aneurysm. He died in Los Angeles.

David McComb

Born February 17, 1962
Died February 2, 1999
The lead vocalist of The Triffids, David McComb had formed the Australian group while in high school, originally as Dalsy. A talented lyricist, the well-read McComb earned a journalism degree in the early Eighties. After relocating to Melbourne, then Sydney, and finally, London, McComb and The Triffids recorded the critically acclaimed *Born Sandy Devotional*, an album highlighted by the track 'Wide Open Road'. Experiencing only limited commercial success, the group disbanded after the release of their best-selling album, *The Black Swan* (1989). McComb later formed The Blackeyed Susans, while simultaneously pursuing a solo career. Returning to Australia and re-enrolling in college, he also formed a new group.
CAUSE: Involved in a traffic accident, he was treated at a hospital and sent home the following day. He died two days later from a heart condition. He had been the recipient of a heart transplant in 1995.

Tommy McCook

Born March 4, 1927
Died May 5, 1998
A Cuban-born saxophonist, Tommy McCook was a vital member of the Jamaican ska group The Skatalites. At 16, the jazz-trained McCook had joined a big band orchestra led by Eric Dean. But upon hearing John Coltrane and Thelonius Monk while briefly living in the US, he returned to Jamaica to form a jazz trio. But with the group disbanding, McCook worked as a session player at Studio One, for a time backing a young Bob Marley & The Wailers. By 1964, McCook joined a ska group The Skatalites. Featuring the talents of trombonist Don Drummond and saxophonist Roland Alphonso, The Skatalites scored a British hit in 1967 with 'Guns Of Navarone'. McCook later formed a studio group called The Supersonics, which in part, helped create the rock-steady genre by slowing down the tempo of ska. In spite of having not earned any royalties for his work with The Skatalites, McCook led a revival

version of the group in 1983. Suffering a heart attack in the mid Nineties, he was able to record but not tour with the group.
CAUSE: Heart failure and pneumonia. He died in Atlanta, Georgia.

Van McCoy

Born January 6, 1944
Died July 6, 1979
Session musician who found success as a disco artist in the mid Seventies, Van McCoy was born in Washington DC. Taking piano lessons as a young child, McCoy performed classical music around the city with his violinist brother. While attending Dunbar High School, the McCoy brothers formed a doo-wop quartet, The Starlighters. Moving to Philadelphia to work at his uncle's record label Rock'N Records, McCoy scored a minor hit in 1961 with 'Mr. D.J.' Returning to Washington DC, McCoy studied psychology at Howard University. But continuing his foray into the music field, he worked as a songwriter for Columbia Records, and as a producer at Sceptor where he gained much of his experience working with The Shirelles. Remaining an active songwriter in the mid Sixties, McCoy composed, 'Baby, I'm Yours' (Barbara Lewis), 'Before And After' (Chad & Jeremy), 'I Don't Wanna Lose You Baby' (Chad & Jeremy), and 'Sweet Bitter Love' (Aretha Franklin). Returning to Columbia, McCoy was signed to the label by Mitch Miller; recording the album *Nighttime is a Lonely Time* in collaboration with Miller, the project was too sophisticated for the pop market. Operating several music production companies by the late Sixties, McCoy had also formed Whitehouse Productions in a partnership with Joe Cobb. During his long career, McCoy produced albums for acts such as Gladys Knight, Ruby & The Romantics, The Stylistics and Brenda & The Tabulations; McCoy also discovered the Washington DC duo, Peaches & Herb. Then with the help of legendary producers Hugo & Luigi, McCoy scored a huge hit during the dawn of the disco era with the Grammy-winning dance classic 'The Hustle' (1975); the song was based on a new line-dance that was breaking out of New York City discos. Then after a brief stint at Hugo & Luigi's H&L label, McCoy recorded for MCA Records beginning in 1977. By the mid Seventies, McCoy had teamed with new partner Charles Kipps to form McCoy-Kipps Productions. Active in other areas of entertainment, McCoy hit the stage in the film musical *Sextette* (1978). Howard University awards an annual Van McCoy Music Scholarship.
CAUSE: After suffering a heart attack in late June at his Englewood, New Jersey, home, he died a week later at Englewood Hospital.

Lloyd McCraw

Born c. 1924
Died 1987
The baritone vocalist and manager of The Cadets (who simultaneously recorded as The Jacks), Lloyd McGraw was reared in the gospel tradition. A native of Chicago, he was previously a member of The Dixie Hummingbirds and The Royal Four. Relocating to Los Angeles, he formed a new gospel group called The Soul Seekers, which included future Cadets/Jacks members Will "Dub" Jones, Ted Taylor and Aaron Collins. Hired in 1955 as a session group at Modern Records, The Jacks/Cadets usually recorded competing cover versions of emerging R&B songs which Modern Records' owner Joe Bihari believed had hit potential. As The Jacks, Collins and the group had hits with 'Why Don't You Write Me' (1955), and as The Cadets, 'Don't Be Angry' (1955). McGraw quit in 1956 shortly before The Cadets scored their biggest hit, a cover of The Jayhawks' rollicking 'Stranded In The Jungle',

later covered in the mid Seventies by The New York Dolls.
CAUSE: Unknown.

Jimmy McCulloch

Born August 13, 1953
Died September 27, 1979
Guitarist in Paul McCartney's band Wings, Glasgow, Scotland-born "Little" Jimmy McCulloch began his professional career at age 13 in a group called One In A Million. Discovered in a Scottish pub by The Who's Pete Townshend, 15-year-old McCulloch was placed in a new group, Thunderclap Newman. Headed by Townshend's art school friend Andy Newman, Thunderclap Newman enjoyed a sole hit with the ethereal, chart-topping 'Something In The Air' which was produced by Townshend. When the group fell apart, McCulloch joined Stone The Crows, replacing Les Harvey who had died on stage from electrocution. McCulloch provided lead guitar on the group's partially completed album *'Ontinuous Performance* (1972); a strong live act, the band showcased the guitar solos of McCulloch and the gutsy blues of lead singer Maggie Bell. But without Harvey's spark, the group disbanded in 1973. After a stint in the RSO Records group Blue, McCulloch was hired by Paul McCartney as Henry McCullough's replacement in Wings. During his stint with Wings, McCulloch provided the lead guitar on a series of million-selling hits including 'Band On The Run' (1974), 'Listen To What The Man Said' (1975), 'Silly Love Songs' (1976), and 'Let 'Em In' (1976). Quitting McCartney's band in late 1977, McCulloch's final hit with the group came with 'London Town' (1978). McCulloch then joined a reformed version of the Steve Marriott-led Small Faces during a tour to promote their *Playmates* album. Forming his own group in 1979, The Dukes, McCulloch released just one album for Warner Brothers Records.
CAUSE: Heart failure as a result of a morphine and alcohol mixture. He died in his London apartment.
FURTHER READING: Grove, Martin A. (1978). *Paul McCartney, Beatle With Wings*. New York: Manor.

Butch McDade

(DAVID HUGH MCDADE)
Born February 24, 1946
Died November 29, 1998
The drummer and backing vocalist of the country-rock outfit The Amazing Rhythm Aces, Missouri-native Butch McDade co-founded the group in the early Seventies along with singer Russell Smith; the pair had previously backed Jesse Winchester beginning in 1972. But with Winchester fleeing to Canada to dodge the draft, McDade and Smith returned to the US to form their own group. Releasing five albums in the Seventies, The Amazing Rhythm Aces managed a sole crossover pop hit in 1975 with 'Third Rate Romance' and won a Grammy for the country hit, 'The End Is Not In Sight (The Cowboy Tune)' (1977); both Smith-penned songs previously recorded by Winchester. After the group disbanded in 1980, McDade worked with the likes of Lonnie Mack, Leon Russell, and Roy Clark. Joining an Amazing Rhythm Aces reunion in 1994, McDade was forced to bow out of the group in 1996 due to deteriorating health. McDade had also operated a restaurant and worked as a sports writer.
CAUSE: Bladder cancer. He died at his home in Marysville, Tennessee.

Floyd McDaniel

Born July 21, 1915
Died July 22, 1995
A remarkable performer who in his lifetime tackled jazz, doo-wop, and blues, Alabama-native Floyd McDaniel began his career in 1933 in a jug band called The Rhythm Rascals, the act débuting at the Chicago World's Fair. Then in 1941,

McDaniel joined The Five Blazes on guitar; signing with Aristocrat Records in 1947, the group would land a trio of R&B hits in the early Fifties with 'Mary Jo', 'Please Send Her Back To Me', and 'Perfect Woman'. With the group disbanding in 1954, McDaniel settled in Chicago and bought a bar. Returning to music in the Sixties, McDaniel backed soul superstar Sam Cooke. Then in 1971, he joined a revival version of The Ink Spots as a guitarist, a position he held for 10 years. Returning to his blues roots, by 1986 McDaniel joined the first of several Chicago-based blues bands, including the Willie Dixon-headed Big Tree Trio, and The Blues Swingers. McDaniel's final album *Let Your Hair Down* was released by Delmark Records in 1994.
CAUSE: Heart attack. He died in Chicago.

Sean McDonnell

Born October 2, 1965
Died January 11, 1995
Lead singer and guitarist of the rising New York City-based hard-rock group Surgery, Sean McDonnell formed the group in his hometown of Hartford, Connecticut. Surgery released a sole album at Atlantic Records in 1994.
CAUSE: Suffering a severe asthma attack, he went into a coma and died four days later at Brooklyn Hospital in New York City.

Mississippi Fred McDowell

Born January 12, 1904
Died July 3, 1972
A classic country-blues, Delta-styled, bottle-neck guitarist who enjoyed fame during the blues revival of the Sixties, Mississippi Fred McDowell was born in Tennessee but spent most of his life in Mississippi. Working as an itinerant blues musician following the death of his parents, McDowell later settled down as a farmer, playing blues on street corners at weekends. Discovered by musicologist Alan Lomax in 1959, McDowell recorded an obscure album for Atlantic Records. But it would be a pair of recordings at Arhoolie Records in the mid Sixties that would make McDowell a living legend. Suddenly a star in the folk and blues communities, McDowell became a much in-demand performer. Refusing to update his primal sound, he released his finest work in 1971 on Capitol, *I Don't Play No Rock 'N' Roll.* McDowell also recorded with his wife, Annie Mae. His material has been covered by both Bonnie Raitt and The Rolling Stones.
CAUSE: Cancer. Diagnosed in 1971, he continued performing until shortly before his death the following year.

Mitch McDowell

Born June 29, 1954
Died January 21, 1992
As the lead singer and multi-instrumentalist of the mid Eighties Motown rap/R&B group General Kane, Mitch McDowell scored a hit with the anti-drug song 'Crack Killed Apple Jack' (1986), from the album, *In Full Chill.* McDowell had previously released two obscure albums on Tabu Records in the early Eighties under the name, General Caine. Dropped by Motown in 1988, McDowell later started his own bail bondsman company.
CAUSE: He was shot and killed at his bail bondsman business in Los Angeles. Implicated in the death was suspected drug lord Joseph "Eddie" Arvizu. McDowell was possibly working as a police informant.

Brother Jack McDuff

(EUGENE MCDUFFY)
Born September 17, 1926
Died January 23, 2001
A talented keyboardist who was identified with playing his trademark Hammond B-3 electric organ, Brother Jack McDuff was at the forefront of the jazz/soul movement. A native of

Champaign, Illinois, McDuff spent much of the late Forties as a bass player in a series of R&B acts, taking a break to study music at the New York Technical College in Cincinnati. After heading his first group in 1957, he soon switched to the Hammond organ and by the early Sixties, McDuff was working with a host of jazz greats – including Roland Kirk, Grant Green and the then-unknown George Benson – issuing a number of successful solo releases on Prestige Records. McDuff reached the R&B singles chart just twice with a pair of funk-flavoured instrumentals, 'Let My People Go' (1968) and 'Theme From Electric Surfboard' (1970).
CAUSE: Heart attack. He died in a nursing home in Minneapolis, Minnesota. He had resided at the nursing home since 1990 and retired from performing after suffering multiple strokes in 2000.

Sollie McElroy

Born July 16, 1934
Died Jan 16, 1995
The lead vocalist of the much-respected doo-wop group The Flamingos, Sollie McElroy had replaced Earl Lewis (later with The Five Echoes). The Flamingos had been formed in 1950 by four cousins from the choir of the Jewish-affiliated, Chicago's Church of God and Saints of Christ. McElroy was hired into the group after being spotted singing in a Chicago talent show. Signing with Chance Records in 1952, the group recorded several stunning, regional hit singles including the lovely 'Golden Teardrops'. Feeling out of place in the all-Jewish, family group, McElroy quit in late 1954 and was replaced by Nate Nelson. McElroy then joined The Moroccos, appearing on their hit 'Somewhere Over The Rainbow' (1955). After scoring several regional hits, The Moroccos disbanded in 1957. McElroy later joined The Chaunteurs.
CAUSE: Cancer. He died in Chicago.

Addie (Micki) McFadden

(MICHELLE HARRIS)
Born January 22, 1940
Died June 10, 1982
A member of the Sixties girl-group The Shirelles, Addie (Micki) McFadden formed the outfit with her junior-high classmates in Passaic, New Jersey. Originally called The Poquellas (Spanish for birds), the group of McFadden (nee Harris), Beverly Lee, Doris Jackson and Shirley Owens sang an original composition at a school assembly, where an impressed schoolmate convinced the skeptical group to audition for her mother, Florence Greenberg, the owner of the tiny Tiara Records. With Greenberg becoming their manager, the renamed Shirelles recorded several tracks which were leased to Decca Records. Issued a year later, The Shirelles début cover of The "5" Royales' 'Dedicated To The One I Love' was ignored. With Decca losing interest in the group, The Shirelles joined Scepter Records, a new label formed by Greenberg and songwriter Luther Dixon. The group found fame with songs about teenage romance, landing on the charts with the classic 'Will You Love Me Tomorrow' (1960), a re-released 'Dedicated To The One I Love' (1961), 'Mama Said' (1961), 'Baby It's You' (1962), 'Soldier Boy' (1962), and 'Foolish Little Girl' (1963). In order to tour, McFadden was forced to drop out of high school in her junior year. The Shirelles' final hit came in 1963 with 'Don't Say Goodnight When You Mean Goodbye'. Promised a trust fund at age 21 but paid nothing, McFadden and The Shirelles left Sceptor Records. Unable to record due to contractual obligations, The Shirelles eventually released two albums for RCA Records before disbanding in the late Sixties.
CAUSE: She suffered a heart attack at Atlanta's Hyatt Regency Hotel after two performances with The Shirelles.

Initially complaining of stomach pains, she died soon after at Grady Memorial Hospital.

Gene McFadden

Born 1948
Died January 27, 2006
As one half of Philadelphia-based R&B duo McFadden & Whitehead, Gene McFadden had a disco-era hit in 1979 with the self-composed 'Ain't No Stoppin' Us Now'. Teamed with longtime collaborator John Whitehead, McFadden placed several additional singles on the R&B charts, most notably 'I Heard It In A Love Song'. Friends since high school, McFadden and Whitehead broke into music in a doo-wop group The Epsilons. After spending a year opening up for Otis Redding, the group later sang back-up for Arthur Conley. Following Redding's death in 1967, The Epsilons were renamed Talk Of The Town, and recorded a few obscure singles for producers Kenny Gamble and Leon Huff on their North Bay label. Continuing to work with Gamble & Huff at Philadelphia International Records, McFadden and Whitehead instead emerged as a successful songwriting team beginning with 'Back Stabbers' (The O'Jays), continuing with 'I'll Always Love My Mama' (The Intruders) and a number of hits for Harold Melvin & The Blue Notes including 'Bad Luck', 'Wake Up Everybody' and 'Where Are All My Friends?'. As producers, McFadden also worked with Archie Bell & The Drells, Melba Moore, Gloria Gaynor and Freddie Jackson. Whitehead was shot to death in 2004.
CAUSE: Diagnosed with liver and lung cancer in 2004, he died at his home in Philadelphia.

Sam "Flash" McFadin

Born March 30, 1952
Died August 31, 2001
The lead vocalist and guitarist of rock'n'roll revival band Flash Cadillac & The Continental Kids, Sam "Flash" McFadin joined the two-year-old outfit in 1971. Having formed at the University of Colorado for a lark, the oldies style act were featured as the prom band, Herby & The Heartbeats, in the 1973 film *American Graffiti*. This landed a record deal for Flash Cadillac & The Continental Kids who toured throughout the Seventies, often in the inappropriate opening slot for rock acts such as Alice Cooper and Black Sabbath. With three singles on the pop charts, including the Top 30 entry, 'Did You Boogie (With Your Baby?)' which featured spoken dialogue by Wolfman Jack, McFadin appeared in a 1975 episode of *Happy Days* as the leader of a band called Fish & The Fins. After his death, McFadin was replaced in The Continental Kids by Timothy P. Irvin.
CAUSE: He suffered a heart attack and died at his home in Colorado Springs, Colorado.

John McGeoch

(JOHN ALEXANDER MCGEOCH)
Born August 25, 1955
Died March 5, 2004
As a member of several notable British punk and new wave acts, guitarist John McGeoch was responsible for a series of memorable riffs. A native of Greenock, Scotland, McGeoch relocated to Manchester while in his teens and by the mid Seventies had embraced the burgeoning punk rock scene. In 1977, McGeoch answered an advertisement placed on a record shop wall by former Buzzcocks member Howard Devoto; the resulting band, Magazine, attracted immediate attention from Virgin Records. Appearing on the group's first four albums beginning with *Real Life*, McGeoch's distinctive guitar featured on tracks such as 'Shot By Both Sides' and 'Sweet Heart Contract'. During this period, McGeoch moonlighted in The Skids and Generation X but unhappy with Magazine's limited commercial success, he quit to join the

techno pop act Visage, recording the electro anthem 'Fade To Grey'. In 1980, McGeoch joined Siouxsie & The Banshees in time for the album *Kaleidoscope*; appearing on three further albums and singles such as 'Happy House', 'Christine', 'Spellbound' and 'Fireworks'. McGeoch also toured with the group during its first American dates but, succumbing to the stresses of constant touring, McGeoch suffered a breakdown and required hospitalisation. Returning to music in 1984, he teamed with former Skids member Richard Jobson to form The Armoury Show, and then joined John Lydon's Public Image Ltd., in time for their 1987 album *Happy?*, remaining until the group disbanded in 1992. Relocating to London, McGeoch trained to become a nurse and recorded music for television.
CAUSE: He suffered a heart attack and died in his sleep at his home in London.

Brownie McGhee

(WALTER BROWN MCGHEE)
Born November 30, 1915
Died February 16, 1996
A perennial folk-blues guitarist and singer, Brownie McGhee is best known for his 40-year collaboration with blind, harmonica player Sonny Terry. A native of Knoxville, Tennessee, McGhee was stricken by polio at age four; an operation at age 12 restored his mobility. Taught to play guitar by his musician father, McGhee vacillated between gospel and blues music in his youth. After a stint in The Golden Voices Gospel Quartet, McGhee quit to play the blues. Moving to Durham, North Carolina, he came under the influence of mentor Blind Boy Fuller and was befriended by talent scout J.B. Long. Then after Fuller's sudden death, Long convinced McGhee to tour for a time as Blind Boy Fuller #2. Moving to New York City and teaming with Sonny Terry, the duo were aided by Leadbelly in landing gigs in the city's folk and jazz clubs. Combining folk with blues strains, McGhee and Brown toured and recorded together prolifically for a variety of record labels. Also tackling electric R&B apart from Brown, McGhee landed a blistering hit in 1948 with the Savoy Records release 'My Fault'. And for a time, McGhee hit the stage for a 1955 Broadway production of *Cat On A Hot Tin Roof*. Arriving in Britain in the late Fifties, McGhee and Brown captivated audiences with their authentic folk-blues repertoire. But tired of each other's company, McGhee and Brown went their own ways in the mid Seventies.
CAUSE: Stomach cancer. He died in an Oakland hospital.

Stick McGhee

(GRANVILLE MCGHEE)
Born March 23, 1917
Died August 15, 1961
An early R&B artist, Tennessee-born Stick McGhee gave Atlantic Records its first major hit with the pioneering rock-styled single, 'Drinkin' Wine, Spo-Dee-O-Dee' (1949). Atlantic Records' head Ahmet Ertegun had hired McGhee to record a new version of the song when a Southern wholesaler asked him to ship him 5,000 copies of the previously recorded single. Wanting to cash in on the record, the financially strapped Ertegun landed a surprise million-seller. Having written the song during a World War II-era army stint, McGhee had initially recorded the song at Harlem Records in 1947. Managing only one more hit at Atlantic with a cover of Patti Page's 'Tennessee Waltz Blues', McGhee then moved to King Records, where he scored his final chart entry with 'Women, Whiskey And Loaded Dice'. Dropped by King, McGhee landed at Ember Records shortly before his death. Becoming a rock classic, 'Drinkin' Wine, Spo-Dee-O-Dee' has been recorded by countless acts including Jerry Lee Lewis.

CAUSE: Lung cancer. He died at a Veteran's Administration hospital in New York City.

Harold "Whiz Kid" McGuire

Born October 21, 1961
Died March 15, 1996
An early New York City-based Tommy Boy Records rap artist, Harold "Whiz Kid" McGuire scored a hit with 'Play That Beat Mr. DJ' in a collaboration with Soulsonic Force vocalist, M.C. G.L.O.B.E.
CAUSE: Unknown. He died in New York City.

Pat McGuire

Born c. 1942
Died 1963
The bass singer of doo-wop group The Chimes, Pat McGuire formed the quintet on a Brooklyn street corner in 1957. Signed to the tiny Tag label, the Leonard Cocco-headed outfit scored a pair of hits, a million-selling cover of Tommy Dorsey's 'Once In A While' and a cover of the 1934 Eddy Duchin hit, 'Let's Fall In Love' (1960).
CAUSE: Car crash.

Bob McIntosh

Born October 6, 1951
Died November 1972
The early drummer of theatrical rock band The Tubes, Bob McIntosh quit before the group entered a recording studio. The Tubes were formed in 1971 from members of two Phoenix-based rock acts, including McIntosh's band The Beans. The track 'Golden Boy' from The Tubes third album was written in his memory.
CAUSE: Cancer of the lymph nodes. He died after receiving treatment in Germany.

Robbie McIntosh

Born September 23, 1950
Died September 23, 1974
Drummer of British funk/soul group The Average White Band, Scottish-born Robbie McIntosh had initially been a member of the RCA recording group Forever More. Then joining Brian Auger's group, Oblivion Express, McIntosh appeared on three albums, *Oblivion Express* (1971), *A Better Land* (1971), and *Sacred Wind* (1972). After a stint in The Roy Young Band, McIntosh joined the Scottish R&B-influenced group The Average White Band, as a replacement for Clive Thacker. (In 1972, McIntosh and AWB-member Onnie McIntyre also backed Chuck Berry on his number 1 novelty single, 'My Ding-A-Ling'.) Signing with CBS Records, The Average White Band fared poorly with their critically acclaimed début effort *Show Your Hand* (1973). Switching to Atlantic Records in 1973, the group scored its breakthrough with the Jerry Wexler-produced album *Average White Band*, which was highlighted by the million-selling US hit 'Pick Up The Pieces' (1974). The AWB replaced McIntosh with Steve Ferrone and went on to enjoy substantial success in the early Seventies.
CAUSE: Believing it to be cocaine, he inhaled a lethal mixture of morphine and heroin at a Los Angeles party that had been thrown in the band's honour. McIntosh was taken back to his motel room where he died. A bandmate might have suffered the same fate if it were not for the help of party-goer Cher. The band had just finished a one-week stint at the Troubadour club. Indicted in the death for supplying McIntosh with the drugs, Kenneth Moss pleaded guilty to involuntary manslaughter charges; Moss, who denied knowing that the drug was heroin, served less than three months in jail.

Scotty McKay

(MAX KARL LIPSCOMB)
Born 1937
Died March 17, 1991
A later member of Gene Vincent's

band, Dallas-born Scotty McKay joined the rockabilly group as back-up rhythm guitarist and vocalist in late 1957 at the age of 17, while Vincent's 'Dance To The Bop' was on the charts. Although leaving the group in early 1958, he returned in mid 1958 for several months. Later pursuing a solo career, McKay recorded for a number of labels beginning with Parkway but his finest output came at Ace Records where he was backed on sessions by Dr. John and Allen Toussaint. In the Sixties, McKay released two solo albums, *Here's Scotty McKay* and *An Evening With Scotty McKay*. Also an actor, he appeared in films such as *The Black Cat* and *Creature From The Black Lagoon*. McKay reunited with the ailing Gene Vincent in 1970 on the Kama Sutra album *Gene Vincent*, the project featuring the McKay composition, 'I Need A Woman's Love'. McKay later worked as an independent promoter and producer, working with American Blues, a group that evolved into ZZ Top. Switching his attention to Christian contemporary music in 1982, he released the country flavoured album, *God, Texas, Tennessee And Me*. In the Eighties, McKay launched the Y'Shua Ministries.
CAUSE: Heart attack. He died in Dallas, Texas.

Ron "Pig Pen" McKernan

(RONALD C. MCKERNAN)
Born August 8, 1946
Died March 8, 1973
Founding keyboardist and harmonica player for The Grateful Dead, Ron "Pig Pen" McKernan was the group's blues anchor. McKernan was born in San Bruno, California, but raised in Palo Alto, his father a white R&B musician and San Francisco deejay. Dropping out of school, McKernan taught himself to play harmonica. Then while working in a music store, McKernan teamed with drummer Bill Kreutzmann to form The Zodiacs. McKernan then joined Bob Weir, Jerry Garcia, and others to form an acoustic jug band called Mother McCree's Uptown Jug Champions; switching to electric blues at McKernan's insistence, the renamed Warlocks were expanded with the additions of Phil Lesh and McKernan's earlier bandmate Bill Kreutzmann; in the group, McKernan was now playing Vox Continental and Hammond B-3 organs. Settling into San Francisco's Haight-Ashbury district, the group was at the forefront of the psychedelic era. Soon garnering attention as the house-band for Ken Kesey and his Merry Pranksters' "acid tests" parties, The Warlocks embraced the then-legal hallucinogenic drug, LSD. Renamed The Grateful Dead, the group gained a sizable local fanbase via a series of free, outdoor concerts. Signed to Warner Brothers Records in 1967, Bob Weir would emerge as the chief vocalist, with McKernan providing an occasional lead. Very overweight, and sporting long black whiskers and dishevelled, tie-dyed garb, the raspy-voiced McKernan would pace and structure the group's songs, which were punctuated by his long, improvised keyboard or harmonica solos. After adding Mickey Hart, Tom Constanten, and lyricist Robert Hunter, the group performed at both Woodstock and Altamont, and had commercial success with psychedelic-styled albums such as *Aoxomoxoa* and *American Beauty*, the latter containing their first radio hit, 'Truckin''. But suffering from liver damage and close to death, McKernan left the group in 1972, and was replaced by Merle Saunders, and then, Keith Godchaux. Garcia would emerge as the group's clear-cut leader, with Weir assuming greater lead-vocal duties.
CAUSE: An exceptionally heavy drinker much of his adult life, he suffered with liver disease and had undergone a series of stomach operations. With his

health failing, he dropped out of the band and waited to die. He was found dead in a friend's backyard in Corte Madera, California. McKernan was the only Grateful Dead member who did not use drugs in the group's post Acid-Test period.
FURTHER READING: Jackson, Blair. (1983). *Grateful Dead: The Music Never Stopped.* New York: Delilah.

Jason "Q.T." McKnight

(MICHAEL CUCCIONE)
Born January 5, 1985
Died January 13, 2001
A member of MTV spoof boy band 2gether, the charismatic Jason "Q.T." McKnight starred in the film and television series of the same name. Touring for a time, 2gether opened up for acts such as Britney Spears, while McKnight began his acting career in an episode of *Baywatch*, portraying a cancer patient. He also co-authored a book about his condition with his grandmother, *There Are Survivors: The Michael Cuccione Story*.
CAUSE: Suffering from Hodgkin's disease, he succumbed to lung failure due to treatment for a previous bout of cancer at age nine. He died in Vancouver, Canada.

Ollie McLaughlin

Born March 24, 1925
Died February 1984
Mississippi-raised, Michigan-based R&B garage-rock producer and disc jockey, Ollie McLaughlin is best known for discovering Del Shannon for whom he set up an audition with Big Top Records. In the wake of Motown's success, McLaughlin set up several Detroit-area labels including Carla Records; his hit acts included Barbara Lewis, Deon Jackson, and The Capitols. McLaughlin's output was assembled in a two-volume series issued by Solid Smoke Records in 1984, *Detroit Gold.*
CAUSE: Heart failure. He died in Detroit.

Tommy McManus

Born 1966
Died November 16, 1994
A member of Northern Ireland act Mama's Boys, drummer Tommy McManus formed the folk-rock outfit with his brothers Pat and John. The group found some success in the mid Seventies with the albums, *Mama's Boys* and *Power And Passion*, and was later expanded to a quartet with the addition of singer Keith Murrell.
CAUSE: Suffering from leukaemia since the age of nine, he contracted a lung infection following a bone marrow transplant.

Julius McMichael

Born November 25, 1935
Died June 1981
Member of the doo-wop group The Paragons, Julius McMichael formed the group while attending Jefferson High School in the Bedford-Stuyvesant section of Brooklyn. Recording for Winley Records, The Paragons scored a local hit with their début release, the McMichael co-penned ballad 'Florence' (1957). Though recording a series of stunning doo-wop singles, the group found its greatest success in the battle-of-the-bands album, *The Paragons Meet The Jesters*. Leaving the group in 1959, McMichael would later form a revival version of The Olympics.
CAUSE: Motorcycle accident.

Lillian Shedd McMurray

Born 1922
Died March 18, 1999
The founder of the Mississippi-based label, Trumpet Records, Lillian Shedd McMurray recorded a host of R&B, country, and gospel acts from 1951–55 including Elmore James, B.B. King, Little Milton, and Sonny Boy Williamson (#2). The label was closed shortly after it was renamed Globe Records in 1955.
CAUSE: Heart attack. She died in Jackson, Mississippi.

Harold McNair

Born November 5, 1931
Died March 26, 1971
A talented flautist and saxophonist, jazz-trained Harold McNair first garnered fame as part of Donovan's backing band; joining in 1966 beginning with the album *Sunshine Superman*, McNair performed on hits such as 'Sunshine Superman', 'Mellow Yellow' and 'Hurdy Gurdy Man'. Leaving Donovan in 1969, McNair joined Ginger Baker's group, appearing on his strong-selling début, live album *Ginger Baker's Airforce* (1970).
CAUSE: Lung cancer.

David McNeil

Born June 11, 1932
Died January 7, 2005
A gospel and R&B artist, bass singer David McNeil is best known for his stints with The Larks and Billy Ward & The Dominoes. North Carolina born, McNeil joined several friends in the late Forties to form The Southern Harmonaires, who evolved into The Jubilators. Abandoning religious for secular music in 1951, the renamed (Five) Larks recorded for Apollo Records, having doo-wop hits with 'Hopefully Yours' and the elegant ballad 'My Reverie'. With The Larks disbanding, McNeil joined Billy Ward & The Dominoes, replacing bass vocalist Bill Brown. As one of the most influential R&B vocal acts of the Fifties, The Dominoes enjoyed a strong hit run with 'Have Mercy Baby', 'I'd Be Satisfied', featuring McNeil on lead vocals, 'Pedal Pushing Mama' and 'These Foolish Things Remind Me Of You'. In mid 1953, The Dominoes lost their star lead singer, Clyde McPhatter, over monetary issues and McNeil to the US Army. Upon his discharge in 1955, McNeil joined the Charlie Fuqua-led Ink Spots revival act. Following Fuqua's death in 1971, McNeil launched a new version of The Ink Spots, which remained active until 1989.
CAUSE: Cancer. He died in New Haven, Connecticut.

Leroy McNeil

Born c. 1935
Died 1977
Bass vocalist of the New Haven, Connecticut-based, doo-wop group The Nutmegs, Leroy McNeil joined in 1954, when the group was known as The Lyres. Renamed The Nutmegs and signing with Herald Records, the group would score a pair of intricate, ballad hits in 1955 with 'Story Untold' and 'Ship Of Love'. McNeil left the group in 1959.
CAUSE: He was murdered.

Clyde McPhatter

(CLYDE LENSEY MCPHATTER)
Born November 15, 1932
Died June 13, 1972
A handsome tenor vocalist who graced two of the biggest R&B vocal groups of the Fifties, Clyde McPhatter was unable to maintain that success during his solo career. A native of Durham, North Carolina, McPhatter gained his vocal prowess as the featured soprano soloist in the choir of his preacher father's Baptist church. Moving to Teaneck, New Jersey, 14-year-old McPhatter formed The Mount Lebanon Singers. A strong high-tenor, McPhatter was the gospel group's lead singer. But soon attracted to Harlem's R&B night spots, McPhatter was discovered during an Apollo Theater amateur night performance by manager/musician Billy Ward. Assembling a group around McPhatter called The Cues, Ward followed an *Arthur Godrey's Talent Scouts* win with a recording contract at King-Federal Records. After placing their début release on the charts, McPhatter and The Dominoes scored the biggest R&B hit of the decade with the racy 'Sixty Minute Man' (1951); a rare crossover, pop chart entry, it was banned by many radio stations for its explicit lyrics. Featuring McPhatter's velvety,

gospel-trained stylings, The Dominoes' R&B hits continued with 'That's What Your Love Is Doing To Me' (1952), the blues-based, 'Have Mercy, Baby' (1952), 'I'd Be Satisfied' (1952), and 'The Bells' (1953). But after recording a cover of Billie Holiday's 'These Foolish Things Remind Me Of You', McPhatter was fired for demanding an increase of his meagre $100 weekly salary. Upon learning of McPhatter's release from The Dominoes, Atlantic Records founder Ahmet Ertegun searched out the singer by telephoning every McPhatter in the New York City directory. Signed to Atlantic, McPhatter assembled and then fired his first group. Forming a second line-up of what would emerge as The Drifters, McPhatter enjoyed a stunning run of harmony-based doo-wop hits beginning with the group's million-selling début release, 'Money Honey' (1953). The Drifters' hits would continue with 'Such A Night'/'Lucille' (1954), the McPhatter-penned 'Honey Love' (1954), and the group's first crossover entry, 'White Christmas'. Drafted in late 1954, McPhatter continued to record with the group while on leave, but was replaced on stage by a 15-year-old sound-alike, David Baughan. After scoring his final Drifters' hit with the Ahmet Ertegun-penned, 'What'cha Gonna Do' (1955), McPhatter officially left the group upon his discharge in April 1956, and sold the rights to the group's name to George Treadwell. Now backed with the pop-flavoured Ray Ellis Orchestra, McPhatter charted with 'Treasure Of Love' (1956), 'Without Love (There is Nothing)' (1957), 'Long Lonely Nights' (1957), 'Come What May' (1957), and his highest pop entry, 'A Lover's Question'. Lured to MGM Records by a $40,000 advance, McPhatter managed a sole chart entry at the label. Switching to Mercury in 1960, McPhatter struggled along at a time that The Drifters were dominating the pop charts. McPhatter's final major hits came with 'Lover Please' (1962) and a cover of Thurston Harris's 'Little Bitty Pretty One' (1962). Recording eight poor selling albums at Mercury before being dropped in 1965, the dispirited McPhatter then released five obscure singles at Amy Records. Relocating to England in 1968 in an attempt to recharge his career, he performed for dwindling crowds; charged with "loitering with intent", McPhatter returned to the US in 1970. Broke and despondent, he was crushed by Atlantic's refusal to sign him to a recording contract. Aided by Clyde Otis, McPhatter recorded a final album at Decca Records in 1971, *Welcome Home*.

CAUSE: After a decade of alcohol and drug abuse, he died of a heart attack during his sleep in a cheap, Bronx, New York, hotel room. His female companion awoke to find him dead. Though once a major star, McPhatter's death generally went unnoticed.

FURTHER READING: Allan, Tony; & Treadwell, Faye. (1993). *Save The Last Dance For Me: The Musical Legacy Of The Drifters, 1953–1993*. Ann Arbor, MI: Popular Culture Ink.

Don McPherson

Born July 9, 1941
Died July 4, 1971

The original lead singer of soul trio The Main Ingredient, Indianapolis-native Don McPherson formed the group as a quartet in Harlem in 1964. Originally called The Poets, the group recorded their début single at Red Bird Records in 1965, 'Merry Christmas Baby'. Pared down to a trio by 1966, the renamed Insiders signed with RCA and continued to falter with their releases. Now known as The Main Ingredient, the group began a long, R&B chart run beginning in 1970 with 'You've Been My Inspiration' (1970) and 'I'm So Proud' (1970). But with 'Black Seeds Keep On Growing' (his

last album with the group was *Black Seeds*) moving up the charts, McPherson fell ill and original member Cuba Gooding returned to the group, initially as temporary substitute. The group's biggest pop hit 'Everybody Plays The Fool', came a year after McPherson's death.
CAUSE: Leukaemia.

Matthew McQuarter

Born c. 1928
Died December 19, 2000
A member of pioneering R&B/doo-wop group The Clovers, Matthew McQuarter appeared on all of their Fifties hit records. Born in Dallas, McQuarter attended Morehouse University before enrolling at Howard University, Washington DC. Drawn to the city's numerous talent shows he met The Clovers, joining the three-year-old group in 1949 just as they were poised for success. Replacing Thomas Woods as a second tenor behind John "Buddy" Bailey, McQuarter provided harmony vocals on hits such as 'Don't You Know I Love You', 'Fool, Fool, Fool', 'One Mint Julep'/'Middle Of The Night', 'Hey, Miss Fannie'/'I Played The Fool' and 'Crawlin''. After Bailey was drafted in 1952, new lead singers Charlie White, and then, Billy Mitchell continued the group's hit run with 'Lovey Dovey' and 'Your Cash Ain't Nothin' But Trash'. Upon Bailey's return to the group in 1954, The Clovers final hits at Atlantic were 'Nip Sip' (1955), 'Devil Or Angel' (1956) and 'Love, Love, Love' (1956). Dropped by Atlantic, The Clovers had their last chart hit in 1959 with the Leiber & Stoller composition, 'Love Potion No. 9'. With The Clovers splitting into two camps in 1960, McQuarter joined a group led by Buddy Bailey. Leaving music in 1962, McQuarter took a position with the Postal Service. Returning to Dallas in 1972 to be with his ailing mother, he later worked in the insurance business.
CAUSE: Unknown.

Flap McQueen

(JACKSON MCQUEEN, JR.)
Born July 21, 1916
Died December 11, 2005
As bass player of early R&B combo The Ray-O-Vacs, Flap McQueen had hits with 'I'll Always Be In Love With You' (1949) and the double-sided entry 'Besame Mucho'/'You Gotta Love Me Baby Too' (1950). After the group disbanded in the late Fifties, McQueen ran a bar in Newark, New Jersey.
CAUSE: Natural causes. He died at East Orange General Hospital in New Jersey.

Blind Willie McTell

(WILLIAM SAMUEL MCTIER)
Born May 5, 1901
Died August 19, 1959
A pioneering, near-blind blues guitarist, Georgia-born Blind Willie McTell is best known as the composer of 'Statesboro Blues', the song named after his hometown. Emerging out of a musical family (he was also related to "Georgia Tom" Dorsey), McTell initially mastered the harmonica and accordion. Though proficient on the six-string guitar, the nimble-fingered McTell almost exclusively employed a 12-string model in the studio. A stunning vocalist, McTell first recorded in 1927, initially incorporating religious songs into his repertoire; by the Thirties, he recorded under various pseudonyms and occasionally teamed with his wife Ruthy "Kate" Williams. Turning his back on blues by the early Fifties, he would only record gospel material. McTell left music shortly before his death and became an ordained minister. Bob Dylan later immortalised his memory in the song 'Blind Willie McTell'.
CAUSE: Brain haemorrhage. He died in Almon, Georgia.

Jack McVea

(JOHN VIVIAN MCVEA)
Born November 5, 1914
Died December 27, 2000
A proto-R&B vocalist and tenor saxophonist who scored a massive crossover hit in 1947 with the novelty, partially spoken-word single 'Open The Door Richard!', Jack McVea had previously reached the R&B charts earlier the same year as the leader of Jack McVea and His All Stars who backed T-Bone Walker on the single, 'Bobby Sox Blues'. A former radio announcer, McVea began his professional musical career in his father's Los Angeles-based jazz band before joining Lionel Hampton's orchestra in 1941. In 1966, McVea began a 26-year stint as a clarinettist in a Dixieland jazz trio at the Disneyland amusement park.
CAUSE: Natural causes. He died in Los Angeles.

Carl McVoy

Born January 3, 1931
Died January 3, 1992
The original pianist of The Bill Black Combo, Arkansas-reared Carl McVoy joined the former Elvis Presley bassist in 1959, appearing on a number of hits including 'Smokie – Part 2', 'White Silver Sands', and a cover of Presley's 'Don't Be Cruel'. A former Sun Records session player, McVoy also became a partner in Hi Records, the label originally launched as a rockabilly and instrumental label that featured Black, Ace Cannon, and Jumpin' Gene Simmons. Other Hi Records acts included Al Green, O.V. Wright, Ann Peebles, Syl Johnson, and Otis Clay. Also a solo performer, McVoy scored a minor hit with 'You Are My Sunshine'. Leaving music to work in construction, McVoy would occasionally hit the stage to perform with his cousin Jerry Lee Lewis.
CAUSE: Heart attack. He died in Jackson, Mississippi.

Phil Medley

Born April 9, 1916
Died December 3, 1997
A noteworthy songwriter, Phil Medley penned 'Twist And Shout' (The Isley Brothers; The Beatles), 'Peace of Mind' (B.B. King; Nancy Wilson), and 'A Million To One' (Jimmy Charles; Donnie Osmond).
CAUSE: Cancer. He died in New York City.

Joe Medwick

(JOSEPH MEDWICK VEASEY)
Born June 22, 1933
Died April 12, 1992
A singer and songwriter at Duke/Peacock, Texas-native Joe Medwick primarily worked with Bobby "Blue" Bland and Junior Parker. Formerly a member of the Houston gospel group The Chosen Gospel Singers, Medwick became a secular songwriter, his first success coming with Bland's 'Don't Want No Woman'. Frequently collaborating with pianist Teddy Reynolds, Medwick would often use the pseudonym Joe Masters, his biggest hit compositions coming with 'I Pity The Fool', 'Two Steps From The Blues', 'Yield Not To Temptation', 'Cry, Cry, Cry', and the R&B standard, 'Further Up The Road'. Also a performer, Medwick released a spattering of singles in the Sixties.
CAUSE: Complications of liver disease. While watching *The Ten Commandments* at his Houston home, he started coughing uncontrollably and was dead before help could arrive.

Tony Meehan

(DANIEL JOSEPH ANTHONY MEEHAN)
Born March 2, 1943
Died November 28, 2005
A founding member of Cliff Richard's backing group The Shadows, drummer Tony Meehan also appeared on a series of instrumental hits – both with The Shadows and bassist Jet Harris. Born in Hampstead, London, Meehan was a

self-taught musician, landing a position as drummer in a London dance hall at age 13 and, soon after, as a tympani player with the London Youth Orchestra. Although he intended to pursue a career as a lawyer, Meehan took a break from his education for a series of gigs and never resumed his formal schooling. Hired in early 1959 as the replacement for drummer Terry Smart in Cliff Richard's backing band The Drifters, Meehan completed the famous line-up of Hank Marvin, Bruce Welch, and Jet Harris. When the popular American R&B group of the same name threatened legal action the British Drifters were renamed The Shadows. With Cliff Richard attaining the mantle of "the British Elvis", Meehan provided the backbeat on such UK smash hits as 'Living Doll', 'Travellin' Light', 'Please Don't Tease', 'Nine Times Out Of Ten' and 'I Love You'. Without Richard, The Shadows scored an impressive string of hits and became the most successful rock instrumental group in UK history. Beginning with the spine-tingling chart topper 'Apache', the group reached the UK Top 10 with 'Man Of Mystery', 'F.B.I.', 'Frightened City' and 'Kon Tiki'. Meehan also appeared with The Shadows behind Cliff in *Expresso Bongo* (1960). Leaving the group in 1961, Meehan signed with Decca Records as an A&R man and an independent producer, and worked on several hit records including Louise Cordet's 'I'm Just A Baby'. Meehan then joined former bandmate Jet Harris in a duo, who had a trio of Top 10 UK hits in 1963 with 'Diamonds', 'Scarlet O'Hara' and 'Applejack'. As a solo artist, Meehan scored a minor UK hit in 1964 with 'Song Of Mexico', and as a session drummer, he worked with Billy Fury, John Leyton and Frank Ifield. Meehan reunited with Cliff Richard (and The Shadows) for a pair of anniversary concerts at Wembley Stadium in 1989.

CAUSE: He died at St. Mary's Hospital in Paddington after sustaining head injuries in a fall at his home.

Joe Meek

(ROBERT GEORGE MEEK)
Born April 5, 1929
Died February 3, 1967

A pioneering independent British record producer, Joe Meek is best remembered for the instrumental 'Telstar' by The Tornados. Born in Newent, close to England's border with Wales, Meek was mesmerised by electronics in his youth. After a stint as a radio technician in the Royal Air Force, he worked as a sound engineer at Britain's leading independent recording studio, IBC; here he worked on Frankie Vaughan's 1956 hit 'Green Door'. Experimenting with reverb and other innovative studio techniques, he quit the company in 1957 to launch Lansdowne Studios along with jazz producer Denis Preston. Here Meek worked as an independent producer (a then unheard of practice in Britain) with acts such as Lonnie Donegan, Acker Bilk and Chris Barber. Leaving the studio after an argument, Meek established Triumph Records and worked at various London studios recording a series of acts, landing his first Top 10 hit in 1960 with 'Angela Jones' by Michael Cox. Utilising the money he earned from the proceeds of a Tommy Steele hit, Meek built RGM Sound studios in his North London flat. Employing primitive, often home-made equipment in his makeshift studio, Meek worked alongside a young, prolific songwriter named Geoff Goddard and leased out master recordings to record companies. Through RGM, Meek produced two 1961 UK hits, 'Johnny Remember Me' and 'Wild Wind', for stage actor John Leyton, as well as 'Tribute To Buddy Holly' by Mike Berry & The Outlaws. Meek then transformed two of Johnny Kidd's former backing band The Pirates, and three others, into The Tornados. The group became Meek's studio band, working behind various acts including John Leyton, Don Charles, Glenda Collins and Andy Cavell. But Meek's greatest accomplishment came with 'Telstar' (1962), a chart topper in the UK and the first ever single by a British group to top the US charts. Named after an early communications satellite, 'Telstar' was the first successful incorporation of synthesized sound into a pop hit; its melody performed on an early electronic organ, its powerful sound effects remain striking to this day. The Tornados would score further British hits in 1963, including the Meek composition 'Globetrotter'. Meek's other great success came with Tornados' member Heinz (Burt), who scored a number of solo British hits, including the Eddie Cochran tribute 'Just Like Eddie' (1963) and 'You Were There' (1964). Among the musicians who played on various Meek-produced records were Ritchie Blackmore, later of Deep Purple, Steve Howe, later of Yes, and bass player Chas Hodges, later one half of Chas & Dave. Meek's final major success came with The Honeycombs, whose 'Have I The Right' was a hit around the world. Ironically, the beat boom would finish Meek who found himself unable to compete with the post-Beatle rush of British groups. Losing his key songwriter Geoff Goddard, the temperamental, homosexual Meek was beset with financial problems and he drifted into severe depression during the last two years of his life.

CAUSE: He was found shot dead in his London recording studio, with his landlady, 52-year-old Violet Shenton, found nearby (though still alive, she died after reaching hospital). He had summoned her to his room and killed her with a shotgun after an argument. After shooting her, he then shot himself. Police at first charged Meek's assistant, and then singer Heinz Burt, whose fingerprints were found all over the gun. It was later learned that the gun had belonged to Heinz who had left it at Meek's studio.

FURTHER READING: Repsch, John. (1989). *The Legendary Joe Meek*. London: Woodford House.

Terry Melcher

Born February 8, 1942
Died November 19, 2004

A singer-songwriter and producer, best known for his work with The Byrds, Terry Melcher was the son of Doris Day and jazz musician Al Jorden. Born in New York City, Melcher was reared by his grandmother in Ohio while his mother established a career as an entertainer. Breaking into music as a producer at Columbia Records during the surf-rock era, Melcher also recorded solo material under the name, Terry Day. Teaming with future Beach Boys member Bruce Johnston, the pair recorded an album as Bruce & Terry, and also formed The Rip Chords, scoring a pair of surf-rock hits with 'Hey Little Cobra' and a track co-written by Jan Berry of Jan & Dean, 'Three Window Coupe'. Assigned by Columbia to work with the pioneering folk-rock act The Byrds, Melcher produced their ground-breaking first two albums, *Mr. Tambourine Man* and *Turn! Turn! Turn!* (both 1965), which included the rock standards 'Mr. Tambourine Man', 'All I Really Want To Do', '(I'll) Feel A Whole Lot Better', and 'Turn! Turn! Turn!' Although Melcher was responsible for polishing The Byrds' sound, he was fired by the group. Melcher also produced Paul Revere & The Raiders, whose records he sang backing vocals on and an album's worth of material by The Rising Sons (featuring Taj Mahal and Ry Cooder) that was not officially released until 1993. In a bizarre chain of events, Melcher was living in Los Angeles with his then-girlfriend, actress Candice Bergen, when he auditioned but ultimately rejected cult leader/aspiring singer-songwriter

Charles Manson. Some months later, Melcher moved out of the home which was subsequently rented to Roman Polanski and wife Sharon Tate, and was the site of the savage Manson murders. According to one of Manson's followers, the murders were committed in an effort to intimidate Melcher. Teaming again with The Byrds during their country-rock period, Melcher produced the albums, *The Ballad Of Easy Rider* (1969), *Untitled* (1970) and *Byrdmaniax* (1971). He later worked with ex-Byrd Gram Parsons on a series of sessions which remain unreleased. Briefly pursuing a solo career, Melcher issued a pair of albums at RCA in the mid Seventies, featuring the usual crew of LA session musicians he had worked with over the years, and Doris Day on backing vocals on one track. Melcher was hired as a producer on the TV series, *The Doris Day Show* and *Doris Day's Best Friends*, worked with The Beach Boys in the Eighties, co-writing the hits 'Getcha Back' (1985) and the chart-topper 'Kokomo' (1988), as well as producing their hit cover of 'California Dreamin'' (1986) which featured a guitar solo from Roger McGuinn.
CAUSE: He died at his home in Beverly Hills, California after battling melanoma for a number of years.

Brenda Melson

(BRENDA LEE JONES)
Born February 18, 1938
Died August 4, 2001
Best known as a member of pop duo Dean & Jean, Brenda Melson had sung professionally since the age of 12. During her teens, Melson worked with Eubie Blake, Tommy Tucker and Roland Kirk. In 1958 as "Jean", Melson formed the duo Dean & Jean with Welton "Dean" Young, and scored a regional hit with 'We're Gonna Get Married'. Drawing the attention of Laurie Records, Melson and Young were initially signed as songwriters, with their material recorded by Dion, The Jewels and The Charmers. Signed to Laurie subsidiary, Rust Records, Dean & Jean scored their own novelty hits with the self-composed 'Tra La La La Suzy' (1963) and the Ernie Maresca composition 'Hey Jean, Hey Dean' (1964). The duo also backed fellow Ohio-native Tommy Tucker on his hit, 'Hi-Heel Sneekers'. As a solo artist, Melson recorded as Brenda Jones, Brenda Lee Jones and Brenda Lee Melson. After surviving breast cancer in 1979, Melson turned to the contemporary Christian field.
CAUSE: Diagnosed with stomach cancer, she died two months later.

Harold Melvin

Born June 25, 1939
Died March 24, 1997
As the leader of Harold Melvin and The Blue Notes, Philadelphia-born Harold Melvin helped define the Philadelphia soul sound. Formed in 1954 in Philadelphia The Blue Notes were rounded out two years later with the addition of 16-year-old vocalist Harold Melvin. Melvin had previously headed his own group, The Charmagnes. After winning several Apollo Theater talent contests, The Blue Notes first recorded for Josie Records in 1957. They scored a pair of minor R&B hits in the Sixties, but it wasn't until 1970, when former drummer Teddy Pendergrass, who also assumed lead vocals, returned to their ranks, that the group excelled. Signing with Kenny Gamble and Leon Huff's new Philadelphia International label, they enjoyed a series of soulful hits with 'I Miss You (Part 1)', a career-making smash, 'If You Don't Know Me By Now', and 'Wake Up Everybody (Part 1)'. When the group splintered into two camps in 1976, both versions quickly faltered before disbanding. After pursuing a solo career, Melvin formed a new version of The Blue Notes with new lead singer David Ebo, and later, Gilbert Samuels;

though a strong concert draw, the group would land only few hits. Melvin also aided the career of one-time Blue Notes member Billy Paul.
CAUSE: After suffering his second stroke, he died at his home in Mt. Airy, Pennsylvania. His first stroke had left him unable to speak.

Jonathan Melvoin

(JONATHAN DAVID MELVOIN)
Born December 6, 1961
Died July 12, 1997
As a shortlived member of the Smashing Pumpkins, Jonathan Melvoin was the son of jazz pianist Mike Melvoin, a former chairman of the National Academy of Recording Artists and Sciences (NARAS). Playing drums since age five, Melvoin briefly joined his sister Susannah Melvoin in the Prince protégé band The Family, which recorded the original version of 'Nothing Compares To You'; Jonathan Melvoin also played drums on Prince's album *Around The World In A Day.* Drawn to the alternative scene, Melvoin joined the Los Angeles-based punk-rock group The Dickies in the late Eighties as the drummer and road manager, leaving in 1994. Though marrying and working as a paramedic, Melvoin maintained a simultaneous career in music. In December 1996, Melvoin joined the Billy Corgan-led alternative-rock group The Smashing Pumpkins for a much anticipated world tour; hired as the second keyboardist, the group was touring in support of the smash, multi-platinum album, *Melon Collie And The Infinite Sadness* when Melvoin died.
CAUSE: Returning to his room at the Regency Hotel in Manhattan, he joined bandmate Jimmy Chamberlin in injecting high-grade heroin purchased from a street dealer; both men had also been drinking heavily. Shortly after 3:30 a.m., Chamberlin awoke and found Melvoin unconscious. Chamberlin first telephoned the band's security manager, who rushed to the room and placed Melvoin in a cold shower in an attempt to resuscitate him. Chamberlin then called for paramedics, who pronounced Melvoin dead at the scene. A drug-free band, The Smashing Pumpkins fired Chamberlin five days later. Ironically, Melvoin's father had been active in fighting drugs in the music industry. Jimmy Chamberlin was rehired by The Smashing Pumpkins in 1999.

Memphis Minnie

(LIZZIE DOUGLAS)
Born June 3, 1896
Died August 6, 1973
Louisiana-born female blues guitarist and singer, Memphis Minnie ran away from home at age 13. Initially hitting the nightclubs of Memphis as a solo act, she often teamed with blues guitarist Willie Brown. Her recording début came in 1929 in a collaboration with long-term partner Kansas City McCoy on the duet hit 'Bumblebee'; parting with McCoy in 1935, she settled in Chicago. A gritty voiced, percussive player, Memphis Minnie was a favourite on the Chicago club scene; during this period she employed a larger group, which sometimes included her third husband, guitarist Little Son Joe. Forming a popular, travelling musical revue in the Forties, she was forced to retire from music in the late Fifties due to ill health.
CAUSE: Ill for some time, she spent much of her last years in nursing homes. She died in Memphis.
FURTHER READING: Garon, Paul. (1992). *Woman With Guitar: Memphis Minnie's Blues.* New York: Da Capo.

Memphis Slim

(JOHN LEN "PETER" CHATMAN)
Born September 3, 1915
Died February 24, 1988
Nicknamed America's official Ambassador of the Blues, Memphis Slim was born into a musical home in Memphis. A self-taught pianist, he was influenced by his mentor,

boogie-woogie bluesman Roosevelt Sykes. First playing in the clubs of Memphis' Beale Street district in the late Twenties, Chatman teamed for a while with blues great Robert Johnson. Relocating to Chicago in 1937, he frequently performed with folk-blues guitarist Big Bill Broonzy. Forming his own group in 1944, The House Rockers Band, Memphis Slim recorded 'Beer Drinking Woman' at Bluebird Records. With his booming voice and his refined style of blues piano, the 6 foot 6 inch Memphis Slim enjoyed hits with 'Messin' Around' (1948), 'Blue And Lonesome' (1949), 'Angel Child' (1949), and 'The Come Back' (1953). Memphis Slim's 1930s recording of 'Nobody Loves Me' was the basis for his 1951 release, 'Everyday I Have The Blues' (a song claimed by both Memphis Slim and Lowell Fulson, and later adopted by B.B. King as his theme song); and 'Mother Earth'. After leaving music for four years beginning in 1955, he later teamed with Willie Dixon for a very successful world tour and subsequent recording session. Adopting France as his new home in 1961, Memphis Slim performed at major European festivals and blues venues, and also ran his own blues venue in Paris, the Memphis Melodies Club. His 1990 album *Memphis Blues: The Paris Session* was nominated for a Grammy.
CAUSE: Kidney Failure. He died at Necker Hospital in Paris.

Michael Menson

Born July 1966
Died February 13, 1997
As a member of the British dance/ska group Double Trouble, Michael Menson landed on the charts with 'Just Keep Rockin'' (1989), 'Street Tuff' (1989), and 'Love Don't Live Here Anymore' (1990). The son of a Ghanaian diplomat, Menson formed the group with Leigh Guest and lead vocalist Michael West. With West leaving the group in 1989 to pursue a solo career as Rebel MC, Double Trouble teamed with vocalists Janette Sewell and Carl Brown. Later diagnosed with schizophrenia, Menson was forced to abandon his music career.
CAUSE: He was found in north London on January 28, 1997, apparently ablaze by means of gasoline. He died 16 days later. Although the hospitalised Menson insisted that he had been set alight by a group of white men, authorities attributed his death to suicide. Police had never interviewed Menson. Diagnosed as a paranoid schizophrenic, Menson was lying on the ground in a catatonic state when he was discovered by his attackers. With the case later reopened in what the media would soon dub "the human torch murder", Scotland Yard investigators admitted mistakes were made, and his death was ruled a murder. Two men were later prosecuted for the crime; Mario Pereira, 26, was convicted of murder and Harry Charalambous Constantinou, 26, was convicted of manslaughter. A third suspect, Ozgay Cevat, 24, fled to his native (Turkish) Cyprus and, in an unusual arrangement, was prosecuted for the crime by the Cypriot judicial system.

Freddie Mercury

(FAROOKH BULSARA)
Born September 5, 1946
Died November 24, 1991
The flamboyant, often bare-chested lead singer of the perennial British art-rock group Queen, Freddie Mercury combined various strains of heavy metal, glam and classical opera to produce a style that fans loved and critics hated. Born on the African island nation of Zanzibar, the former Farookh Bulsara moved with his native-born Zoroastrian family to Bombay, India, where Mercury attended school. In 1959, the Bulsara family were obliged to resettle in England somewhat hastily after Zanzibar gained its independence and became Tanzania. Their undignified

exit and the sharp downturn in their social status in England was not lost on Freddie, as he was now known, and seemed to have instilled in him a deep and unquenchable desire to attain (and thereafter maintain) a luxurious lifestyle. After passing through a pair of local British bands, Sour Milk Sea and a blues outfit called Wreckage, in the late Sixties Mercury joined a group called Smile as the replacement for departing vocalist Tim Staffell. Earning a degree in graphic arts from Ealing College of Art, Mercury sold clothing at a Kensington Market stall alongside Queen drummer Roger Taylor until fame beckoned. Joined by John Deacon in 1971, the renamed Queen was signed to EMI a year later. (During this time, Mercury would release a solo record under the name of Larry Lurex.) Making a respectable chart appearance with their eponymous début album, Queen attracted attention with the single 'Keep Yourself Alive', but with *Queen II*, the group would garner the first of many British Top 10 hits with 'Seven Seas Of Rhye'. In late 1975, Queen released its musical opus, *A Night At The Opera*; highlighted by the complex, five-minute and 52-second rock classic, 'Bohemian Rhapsody' (1975). The song was initially considered too long by the group's record company, though it was later named the best single of the previous 25 years by the British Record Industry. One of the hottest bands of the Seventies, Queen struck gold with their albums *A Day At The Races* and *News Of The World* (1977), the latter highlighted by the anthemic 'We Will Rock You' and 'We Are The Champions'. The group's highest-charting US studio album, *The Game* (1979), was a musically pared-down work, highlighted by the rockabilly-flavoured 'Crazy Little Thing Called Love' and the funky, 'Another One Bites The Dust' (1980). In 1981, Queen teamed up with David Bowie for 'Under Pressure' (the song would be the basis for the Vanilla Ice rap hit 'Ice, Ice Baby'). Queen's final American Top 40 hit during Mercury's lifetime came in 1984 with 'Radio Ga-Ga'. The video for the follow-up single 'I Want To Break Free' featured the band members in drag, with a moustached Mercury in a frilly French maid's outfit pushing a vacuum cleaner. On stage Mercury was as flamboyant as his friend Elton John, delivering Queen's songs with sweeping gestures and wearing elaborate costumes including, on one famous occasion, a queenly ballgown topped off with a royal crown. Mercury's unashamed bisexuality would alienate many of Queen's American fans, especially when he adopted the archetype male gay uniform of cropped hair, bushy moustache, skin-tight jeans and white T-shirt. This was not the case in England, where his much publicised luxurious lifestyle and hedonistic attitude attracted rather than repelled fans. Indeed, after his and Queen's crowd-pleasing performance at Live Aid in 1985, Freddie Mercury became a British institution, whose foibles were excused so long as he remained witty and entertaining. Although Queen would struggle to land airplay on US radio for the remainder of the decade, their British fan base remained steady as the group continued their chart domination with the albums *A Kind Of Magic*, *Live Magic*, and the chart-topping *The Miracle*. Mercury also pursued solo projects, recording 'Love Kills' for the new soundtrack for the 1926 film *Metropolis*; 'Foolin' Around' for the film *Teachers* (1985); and three songs for Dave Clark's London production of the musical, *Time* (1986). Mercury also released the solo album *Mr. Bad Guy* (1985), and teamed up with Spanish opera singer Montserrat Caballe on the album *Barcelona* (1988). A strong arena-rock act, Queen's final performance was at a festival appearance at Knebworth in

1986, after which Mercury gradually retired from public life. Mercury's final album with Queen, *Innuendo*, was released in 1991. Following Mercury's death, the single 'Bohemian Rhapsody'/'These Are The Days Of Our Lives' topped the British pop charts for the second time. Then in 1992, Queen's classic 'Bohemian Rhapsody' enjoyed another chart run after its inclusion in the film *Wayne's World*. In 2005, former Queen members Brian May and Roger Taylor joined vocalist Paul Rodgers for a Queen tribute tour, billed as "Queen & Paul Rodgers".
CAUSE: AIDS. He died at his home in Kensington, west London. Although rumours persisted for over a year before his death, with the tabloid press keeping a keen eye on developments, Mercury's AIDS diagnosis was kept secret until the day before he died, when it was evident that he was sinking fast. In early 1991, bandmate Brian May had publicly denied Mercury's AIDS diagnosis. Though candid pictures of an emaciated-looking Mercury had been published, his death was nevertheless a great shock and the British public reacted with a vast wave of sympathy, buying up Queen albums by the million. According to Zoroastrian tradition, he was cremated the day after his death. A large portion of Mercury's substantial estate was bequeathed to "those fighting AIDS", and on April 20, 1992, the Freddie Mercury Tribute Concert at London's Wembley Stadium, featuring many of rock's biggest names, raised £12 million for AIDS research.
FURTHER READING: Jones, Lesley-Ann. (1997). *Freddie Mercury: The Definitive Biography*. London: Hodder & Stoughton.

Wandra Merrell

Born February 24, 1923
Died November 2, 1994
A successful singer-songwriter who later worked as a music publisher, Wandra Merrell launched her career as a featured vocalist in The Sammy Kaye Band. Turning to songwriting, her credits included the Lou Monti hits, 'Pepino The Italian Mouse' and 'Calypso Italiano' (Monti was managed by Merrell's husband, George Brown). Merrell also penned 'Baby Lover' (Petula Clark) and 'Spanish Nights And You' (Connie Francis). Signed by RCA Records as a solo act, she later worked the nightclub circuit with Sammy Davis, Jr.
CAUSE: Cancer. She died in Hackensack, New Jersey.

Jerry Merritt

(JERRY LEE MERRITT)
Born December 25, 1933
Died May 4, 2001
A talented rockabilly guitarist, Jerry Merritt is best known for his membership in Gene Vincent's legendary backing band The Blue Caps. Born in Arkansas, Merritt moved to the Pacific Northwest where he played in a number of local rock acts including The Pacers, before joining Vincent's band in 1958 as a replacement for Johnny Meeks. During a 1959 tour of Japan, Vincent became homesick and left Merritt to assume leadership of The Blue Caps. Masquerading as Vincent, Merritt performed for the unsuspecting audiences. Returning to the US, Merritt joined Vincent in the studio to record tracks for the album *Crazy Times* (1960). Vincent recorded a number of Merritt compositions, including 'Hurtin' For You Baby', 'Born To Be A Rollin' Stone' and the enduring 'She She Little Sheila'. Unable to pay his band members' salaries, Vincent disbanded The Blue Caps and headed to England where he had a loyal following. Although Merritt parted professionally from Vincent, they remained close friends until Vincent's death in 1971. Merritt later led the popular Northwest band The Crowns, and in the Nineties he toured

with a revival version of The Blue Caps.
CAUSE: Long-term heart problems. He died in Dayton, Washington.

"Big Maceo" Merriweather

(MAJOR MERRIWEATHER)
Born March 31, 1905
Died February 26, 1953
Pounding blues pianist and vocalist who frequently recorded with Tampa Red, Atlanta-born "Big Maceo" Merriweather settled in Detroit in 1924. A fixture on Detroit's blues scene, Merriweather relocated to Chicago in 1941 where he was befriended by guitarist Big Bill Broonzy. Recording for RCA/Bluebird Records, Merriweather reached the charts with 'Worried Life' and 'Chicago Breakdown'. But after suffering a stroke in 1946, he would record only intermittently, and with the exception of a single session, would abdicate the piano playing to session players. Merriweather's finest work is complied on the Arhoolie album *King of Chicago Blues Piano*.
CAUSE: He never recovered from his stroke. He died in Chicago.

Ralph "Pee Wee" Middlebrooks

Born August 20, 1939
Died October 13, 1996
A horn player for the percussion-heavy funk band The Ohio Players, Clarence "Satch" Satchell initially joined a precursor of the Dayton, Ohio-based group in the Sixties, The Untouchables. Headed by Robert Ward, the trio was expanded with saxophonist Clarence Satchell and trumpet player Ralph "Pee Wee" Middlebrooks. Finding little interest with their early releases, the group also backed The Falcons on their 1962 R&B hit, 'I Found A Love'. Ward left in 1964, and was replaced by Leroy Bonner. Merging with another group in 1967 and now featuring Joe Harris (later of Undisputed Truth) on lead vocals, the renamed Ohio Players worked as session players at a hometown label, Compass Records. There, the group would also score a minor hit with 'Trespassin''. Signing with the Detroit-based Westbound Records in 1971, The Ohio Players achieved their first major hit with the synthesizer-heavy, novelty-styled 'Funky Worm' (1973). Moving to Mercury Records, the group recorded a string of funk-based crossover hits with 'Skin Tight' (1974); from a controversial album of the same name, 'Fire' (1974); 'Love Rollercoaster' (1975); and 'Who'd She Coo?' (1976). After switching to Arista Records in 1978, the group splintered into two camps, with two members leaving to form a group called Shadow. Middlebrook and The Ohio Players moved to Boardwalk Records in 1981, releasing the Richard "Dimples" Fields-produced album, *Tenderness*.
CAUSE: Unknown. He died in Dayton, Ohio.

Amos Milburn

Born April 1, 1927
Died January 3, 1980
Pioneering artist Amos Milburn was crucial in the transformation of jump-blues into R&B. Born into a very large family in Houston, he taught himself to play the piano at age five. An underage enlistee during World War II, Milburn fought in the Philippines. The toughened Milburn then became his family's bread-earner after the death of his father. Thanks to an aggressive manager, Milburn signed with Aladdin Records in 1946. Featuring the screaming tenor sax of Maxwell Davis, Milburn's upbeat boogie-woogie piano-styled release 'Chicken Shack Boogie' hit the charts in 1947; writing little of his own material, Milburn followed with a string of similarly styled danceable numbers including 'Hold Me Baby' (1949), 'In The Middle Of The Night' (1949), 'Rooming House Boogie' (1949),

'Empty Arms Blues' (1949), 'Real Pretty Mama' (1949), and 'Walking Blues' (1950). He soon earned the nickname "The King Of The Whiskey Songs" after a string of booze-related releases in the early Fifties, including 'Bad, Bad Whiskey' (1950), 'Thinkin' And Drinkin'' (1952); 'Let Me Go Home, Whiskey' (1953), and 'One Scotch, One Bourbon, One Beer' (1953), the latter reprised in 1976 by George Thorogood. But with rock music having changed the face of R&B, Milburn's hits stopped well before he was released by Aladdin in 1957; Milburn's old-fashioned R&B music was not in favour with record buyers who demanded the smooth sounds of The Drifters or Clovers. After recording for King, and then, Imperial Records, Milburn released an obscure album at Motown in 1963. Retiring from music, he settled in Cincinnati. After suffering a stroke in 1970, he returned to his hometown of Houston. Returning to the studio in 1976, Milburn was produced by Johnny Otis.
CAUSE: Suffering a series of strokes and heart attacks, Milburn had been paralysed for ten years. He died in a Houston hospital.

Lenny Miles

Born 1934
Died 1962
A Texas-based R&B artist, Lenny Miles scored a minor hit in 1960 at Sceptor Records with 'Don't Believe Him, Donna'.
CAUSE: Cancer.

Charles Miller

Born June 2, 1939
Died June 1980
Saxophone and clarinet player and original member of the soul/rock band War, Kansas-born Charles Miller had previously been a member of a group called Senor Soul. Then in 1965 he joined a Long Beach, California-based instrumental group, The Creators. Evolving into Night Shift, and eventually War, the group signed with MGM Records, as the backing band for ex-Animals front-man Eric Burdon. From the album *Eric Burdon Declares War*, the aggregation would land a psychedelic, soul-flavoured hit with 'Drink The Wine' (1970). With Burdon leaving the group in the middle of a European tour due to exhaustion, the Burdon-less War would sign with United Artists Records. One of only a handful of acts to merge soul with rock music successfully, War landed in the Top 10 with a series of hits such as 'Slippin' Into Darkness' (1972); 'The World Is A Ghetto' (1972); 'Cisco Kid' (1973); and 'Why Can't We Be Friends' (1975). Switching to MCA Records in 1976, War continued their hit run with 'Low Rider' (1976) and 'Summer' (1976). The group's fortunes waned during the disco era.
CAUSE: He was murdered during a robbery in Los Angeles.

Jacob "Killer" Miller

Born May 4, 1956
Died February 21, 1980
The charismatic vocalist of the reggae group Inner Circle, Jacob "Killer" Miller had previously recorded a series of solo singles during his teens. Joining Inner Circle in 1976, the group scored European hits with 'Everything Is Great' and 'Stop Breaking My Heart'. Disbanding after Miller's death, the band reformed in 1987, scoring a Top 10 hit with 'Bad Boys' (1993) better known as 'The Theme From Cops'.
CAUSE: Car crash.

J.D. Miller

(JAY D. MILLER)
Born May 5, 1922
Died March 23, 1996
A songwriter and producer, J.D. Miller worked with Slim Harpo, Lazy Lester, Lightnin' Slim, and other Louisiana-style swamp blues and Cajun players at Excello Records. While an A&R man at Decca Records, Miller wrote Kitty Wells' chart-topping

hit (the first-ever for a female country singer), 'Honky Tonk Angels', an answer song to Hank Thompson's 'Wild Side Of Life'. Miller operated several labels including Feature, Zynn, and Rebal.
CAUSE: Complications from quadruple bypass surgery. He died in Lafayette, Louisiana.

Jimmy Miller

Born 1942
Died October 22, 1994
A veteran record producer, Jimmy Miller is best known for his work with The Rolling Stones. Born in Brooklyn, he took up the drums in his youth. Turning to studio work, he moved to London in 1965 and was apprenticed with Island Records boss Chris Blackwell. Miller's composition 'Incense' was recorded by an Island studio aggregation featuring Steve Winwood (as Steve Anglo) on vocals. Miller first gained renown for his work with The Spencer Davis Group, producing 'Gimme Some Lovin'' and co-writing 'I'm A Man'. He continued working with Steve Winwood in Traffic, and also produced keyboard player Gary Wright in Spooky Tooth. On a creative roll, Miller was hired by Mick Jagger in early 1968 to work with The Rolling Stones, producing *Beggar's Banquet* (1968), *Let It Bleed* (1969), *Sticky Fingers* (1971), *Exile On Main Street* (1972) and *Goat's Head Soup* (1973), a series of classic albums that are widely acclaimed as representing the group's most productive period. He also played drums on 'Happy' (from *Exile . . .*), 'You Can't Always Get What You Want', and the cow bell intro to 'Honky Tonk Women'. Leaving the Stones circle due to personal problems in 1974, Miller dropped from sight but later produced such groups as Motörhead, The Plasmatics and, in the early Nineties, tracks for Primal Scream that were overly influenced by the work he'd produced for The Rolling Stones.
CAUSE: Liver failure. He died in Denver.

Keith Miller

Born April 15, 1947
Died May 17, 2005
As the keyboardist/synthesiser player of British rock act Sniff 'n' The Tears, Keith Miller played on the worldwide hit 'Driver's Seat'. Born in Manchester, Miller broke into music in 1965 as a member of the beat group St. Louis Union, who gained a recording contract with Decca after winning a *Melody Maker* contest. After the group's break-up in 1967, Miller passed through a series of rock acts including The Steve Gibbons Band. Though hired as a session musician to play Moog synthesiser on 'Driver's Seat', Miller became a full-time member just as the single began charting. A pioneering synthesiser player, he also worked with Ultravox, Rick Wakeman, Robert Plant, Culture Club, Paul McCartney, and Pete Townshend. Opening his own recording studio in London, Miller worked on music for film and television and co-composed Divine's 1984 novelty hit, 'You Think You're A Man'.
CAUSE: He suffered a brain haemorrhage.

Mrs. Miller

(IVA RUBY CONNES, a.k.a. ELVA MILLER)
Born October 5, 1907
Died July 5, 1997
When middle-aged suburban housewife Mrs. Miller was encouraged by her friends to record an album, she became an unlikely singing sensation on US college campuses. Wealthy and able to finance her own recording sessions, she initially waxed a series of traditional spirituals but with her recordings attracting the attention of Capitol Records, she released the novelty album, *Mrs. Miller's Greatest Hits*. With her campy, pseudo-operatic,

high-pitched warblings, she ran through a number of cover songs including Petula's Clark's 'Downtown' and The Beatles' 'A Hard Day's Night'. She appeared on a number of television programmes, and also performed for overseas US troops. She retired from music in 1973.
CAUSE: Natural causes. She died at a retirement home in Vista, California.

Roger Miller

(ROGER DEAN MILLER)
Born January 2, 1936
Died October 25, 1992
A county music star who enjoyed much crossover success in the Sixties, Roger Miller was taught to play guitar by a cousin by marriage, country star Sheb Wooley. Raised by an uncle after the death of his father from spinal meningitis, Miller was reared on a Texas cotton farm. Forced to join the army at 17 in lieu of a prison term for stealing a guitar, Miller fought in the Korean War. Shipped back to the States, he was transferred to the Special Services and joined a band called The Circle-A Wranglers. Moving to Nashville after his discharge, Miller recorded unsuccessfully for a series of labels. Faring better as a songwriter, Miller teamed with George Jones in 1957 to pen the Jones' single, 'Tall, Tall Trees', the song later reprised by Alan Jackson. Settling in Amarillo, Texas, Miller joined the band of Ray Price, and then, Faron Young. Signed as a solo act by RCA Records in 1960 by Chet Atkins, Miller scored his début hit, 'You Don't Want My Love'. Dropped by RCA but signed by Smash Records, Miller enjoyed a series of folk-flavoured, self-composed novelty-styled crossover hits such as 'Dang Me' (1964), 'Chug-a-Lug' (1964), his million-selling signature piece 'King Of The Road' (1965), and 'England Swings' (1965). Miller's self-composed hit 'Husbands And Wives' (1966) was reprised several times, most notably by Brooks & Dunn in 1998. During a two-year period, 1964–65, Miller would amass eleven Grammy Awards. In 1966, he hosted his own short-lived television variety programme. But with Mercury Records closing its Smash subsidiary in 1970, Miller's career took a downturn. After spending the next few years recording for Mercury, Miller passed through several labels. Miller gained his first Top 20 hit in nearly a decade when in 1982 he teamed with Willie Nelson and Ray Price on 'Old Friends'. Miller later earned a Tony Award for composing the music for the Broadway production of *Big River* (1985).
CAUSE: Diagnosed with lung cancer in 1991, he succumbed to the illness the following year at Century City Hospital in Los Angeles.

Lucky Millinder

(LUCIOUS VANABLE MILLINDER)
Born August 8, 1900
Died September 28, 1966
A popular jump-blues and R&B bandleader who discovered dozens of R&B acts, Lucky Millinder could not play an instrument and rarely sang. Born in Alabama but raised in Chicago, he broke into show business as an M.C. at a Chicago speakeasy, The Grand Terrace Club. Leading a series of jazz groups in the Thirties in both Chicago and New York, he first gained fame in 1934 as the leader of The Miss Blue Rhythm Band which landed a residency at Harlem's Cotton Club. After briefly taking over Bill Doggett's band in 1938, Millinder formed his own jazz/jump R&B group in 1940. Signed with Decca Records, Millinder enjoyed several pop and R&B hits including 'When The Lights Go On Again (All Over The World)' (1942), 'Apollo Jump' (1943), 'Sweet Slumber' (1943), and featuring the vocals of Wynonie Harris, 'Who Threw The Whiskey In The Well' (1945). Millinder hired a who's who

of musical talent, including Sam "The Man" Taylor, Eddie "Lockjaw" Davis, Dizzy Gillespie, and even gospel singer, Rosetta Tharpe; and after discovering a young Ruth Brown, he fired her after only a few dates. Millinder's band backed another of his sidemen, Bull Moose Jackson, at his early King-Queen sessions; recording for King Records, Millinder landed his final hit with 'I'm Waiting Just For You'. A catalyst who transformed jump blues into rock'n'roll, Millinder disbanded his group in 1952. Then except for a deejay stint at WNEW in New York, he would later work outside the music industry.
CAUSE: Liver problems. He died at Harlem Hospital in New York City.

Gordon Mills

Born 1935
Died July 29, 1986
Best known for his association with Tom Jones, Gordon Mills was born in Madras, India, the son of a Welsh army sergeant. Raised in Ton-y-Pandy, Wales, he worked as a bus conductor before breaking into the music business as a harmonica player with the seven-piece Morton Fraser Gang. In 1959, he formed The Viscounts with Ronnie Wells and Don Paul and they went on to become one of the most durable package tour backing groups of the era. By 1963, Mills was finding success as a hit composer, writing both 'I'll Never Get Over You' and 'Hungry For Love' for Johnny Kidd & The Pirates and 'The Lonely One' for Cliff Richard. In 1964, while on a visit to Wales, he discovered singer Tommy Scott "the twisting vocalist from Pontypridd". Mills took over his management and renamed him Tom Jones. What followed was nothing less than one of the most successful manager/artist relationships in pop history. Mills co-wrote Jones' second single, 'It's Not Unusual', which topped the UK charts. Over the next two years, Jones enjoyed several more hits, including the film theme 'What's New Pussycat?' and the massive-selling 'Green Green Grass Of Home'. Jones' hit run continued through the Sixties with songs such as 'I'll Never Fall In Love Again', 'Delilah' and 'Help Yourself'. Meanwhile, Mills launched another singer, his former best-man Engelbert Humperdinck who reached extraordinary heights in 1967 with three of the biggest UK selling singles of the year: 'Release Me', 'There Goes My Everything' and 'The Last Waltz'. By the end of the decade both Jones and Humperdinck were enjoying major-rating television series and succeeding on the Las Vegas circuit. Meanwhile, Mills launched his own record company MAM, one of whose stars was a new signing, Gilbert O' Sullivan. As with Jones and Humperdinck, Mills carefully groomed the star who achieved worldwide success in the Seventies – one of his biggest hits 'Clair' was written about Mills' daughter. Mills' empire continued to grow in the late Seventies and at one time he boasted the largest private collection of orang-utans in the world. Eventually, Humperdinck left his management and in a much-publicised court case during 1982, Gilbert O'Sullivan sued him and successfully won back the copyrights on his songs. Throughout this, Tom Jones remained loyal to the man he always acknowledged as his mentor.
CAUSE: Mills was diagnosed with stomach cancer and hospitalised at the Cedars-Sinai Medical Center in Los Angeles, California. Visited by Tom Jones, he asked his star: "What are my chances?" Jones replied: "50:50." Ever the gambler, Mills acknowledged, "That's not bad odds!" The following day, he died.
FURTHER READING: Rogan, Johnny. (1987). *Starmakers & Svengalis: The History Of British Pop Management.* London: Queen Anne Press.

Mike Millward

Born June 27, 1942
Died March 1966

The rhythm guitarist and backing vocalist of Liverpool-based group The Fourmost, Mike Millward joined the group, then known as The Four Jays, in 1962, featuring Brian O'Hara (guitar/vocals), Billy Hatton (bass/vocals) and Brian Redman (drums), who was replaced by Dave Lovelady. Changing their moniker after a lawsuit threat from a similarly named Scottish group, The Four Mosts alternated between skiffle and rock, and were favourites in Liverpool clubs and on the Isle of Wight. With Millward and his bandmates viewing rock as a semi-professional vocation, they initially refused Brian Epstein's management overtures but, in the wake of The Beatles' success, the renamed Fourmost signed with NEMS in 1963. When O'Hara asked friend John Lennon for a song, he was given 'Hello Little Girl', followed by a Lennon & McCartney composition, 'I'm In Love'. During 1964, The Fourmost became part of a long-running revue at the London Palladium, and appeared with Cilla Black in the film, *Ferry Cross The Mersey*. Millward remained with the group until shortly before his death, being replaced by George Peckham, and then Ian Edwards.
CAUSE: After beating throat cancer, he was stricken with leukaemia.

Roy Milton

Born July 31, 1907
Died September 18, 1983

A proto-R&B jump-blues singer and drummer, Roy Milton was raised on an Indian reservation in Oklahoma, before settling in nearby Tulsa. Launching his career in the late Twenties in the dance band of Ernie Fields, Milton joined as vocalist, and then, drummer. Moving to Los Angeles in 1933, Milton formed The Solid Senders; a direct predecessor of rock'n'roll, the group featured Milton's confident vocals and strong danceable drum rhythms, the jumping piano playing of Camille Howard, and an upbeat, rocking horn section. One of the first acts to record on Art Rupe's Jukebox label (the forerunner of Specialty) in 1945, Milton scored a pioneering, rare million-selling, electric jump-blues hit in late 1945 with 'R.M. Blues'. Prolifically recording for Specialty, Milton unleashed a string of rocking R&B hits including 'Thrill Me' (1947), a cover of Paul Williams' dance craze number 'Hucklebuck' (1949), 'Information Blues' (1950), 'Best Wishes' (1951), and 'Night And Day (I Miss You So)' (1952). Becoming a casualty of the emerging rock era, Milton left Specialty in 1955, and recorded for Dootone, and then, King Records. Recording sporadically in the Sixties, Milton would intermittently team with Johnny Otis, including a performance at the 1970 Monterey Jazz festival. Then after touring through Europe in 1977, Milton recorded a final album *Instant Groove*.
CAUSE: Suffering a massive stroke a year before his death, he never recovered. He died in Los Angeles.

Billy Mitchell

(WILLIAM JOSEPH MITCHELL, JR.)
Born January 30, 1931
Died November 5, 2002

A tenor vocalist, Billy Mitchell joined the R&B/doo-wop group The Clovers during the peak of their success. A native of Washington DC, he quit school, aged 17, for a career in music and as a member of The Joe Morris Blues Cavalcade, recorded four singles for Atlantic in the early Fifties. Joining The Clovers in 1954 upon the departure of Charlie White, Mitchell provided the lead vocal on the rocking 'Your Cash Ain't Nothin' But Trash'. The group's hits continued with a cover of Tony Bennett's 'Blue Velvet', 'Nip Sip', the enduring ballad 'Devil Or Angel'/'Hey, Doll Baby' and 'Love, Love, Love'. Leaving Atlantic for

United Artists in 1957, The Clovers' final hit came with 'Love Potion No. 9'. After the group disbanded around 1958, two competing line-ups emerged, and Mitchell eventually joined the group led by Harold Lucas. Mitchell later recorded an occasional solo single, but never reached the charts. Leaving music in the mid Sixties, he took a position at St. Elizabeths Hospital and reunited with The Clovers only once, at a Rhythm and Blues Foundation fundraising concert in 1988.
CAUSE: While suffering from colon cancer, he experienced a series of strokes. He died at the Washington Hospital Center in Washington DC.

Bobby Mitchell

Born August 16, 1935
Died March 17, 1989
A solo New Orleans R&B artist who recorded for Imperial Records in the Fifties, Bobby Mitchell landed on the charts with 'Try Rock and Roll' (1956) and 'I'm Gonna Be A Wheel Someday' (1957), the latter song also recorded by Fats Domino. Mitchell had previously been a member of a vocal group The Toppers, who had also recorded at Imperial. He later worked as an X-ray pathologist.
CAUSE: He died of kidney failure in New Orleans.

Brandon Mitchell

Born 1971
Died August 9, 1990
Member of the rap group Wreckx-N-Effects, Brandon Mitchell co-founded the trio in Harlem in 1987. Produced by Mitchell's half-brother Teddy Riley, the group helped define a new, rap sub-genre with its 1989 hit 'New Jack Swing'. First signed with Atlantic Records, the group had switched to Motown, which resulted in a lawsuit between the labels.
CAUSE: He was shot and killed in New York City during an argument over a woman.

Guy Mitchell

(ALBERT CERNICK)
Born February 27, 1927
Died July 2, 1999
Under the guidance of Columbia producer Mitch Miller, pop singer Guy Mitchell scored a long string of hits in the Fifties. Although he was a star in his native US, he was a much bigger attraction in Britain. The son of Yugoslavian immigrants, Mitchell was reared in Detroit but relocated with his family to the West Coast where the 11-year-old was groomed as an actor by Warner Brothers studios. Rejecting a career in acting, Mitchell moved north to San Francisco and became a singing sensation on a local country radio programme. After a stint in the US Navy, Mitchell was hired in 1947 as the featured vocalist in Carmen Cavallero's orchestra but quit after contracting food poisoning and pursued a solo career as Al Grant, recording tracks for King Records. After winning an Arthur Godfrey's Talent Scouts competition, he recorded a number of demo discs. Signed to Columbia Records by A&R director Mitch Miller, he was also given his stage name of Guy Mitchell. After his first five singles flopped, Mitchell landed a major break thanks to Frank Sinatra. With an orchestra already assembled, Sinatra refused to record a pair of songs and Miller called Mitchell into the studio. Those two songs, the standards, 'My Heart Cries For You' and 'The Roving Kind', gave Mitchell a double-sided Top 10 hit. Usually recording light-hearted, cheerful material, Mitchell was one of the last great crooners. With the rise of rock'n'roll, Mitchell turned in a pop/rockabilly direction with 'Rock-a-Billy', a cover of Marty Robbins' 'Singing The Blues' (which became a major hit) and 'Heartaches By The Number'. Unable to survive into the rock era, Mitchell flirted with country music for a time. Also an actor, he enjoyed big screen success

with films such as *Those Redheads From Seattle*, but fared poorly with his forays into television, first in 1957 as a variety series host and in 1961 with the Western, *Whispering Smith*. With his star fading in the US, Mitchell performed to large audiences in England. Leaving Columbia Records in 1961, Mitchell failed to dent the music charts with his releases at both Reprise and Joy. His star fading fast, Mitchell drank heavily and passed through a series of failed marriages.
CAUSE: He died during surgery at Desert Springs Hospital in Las Vegas, following an undisclosed accident.

James Mitchell

Born May 15, 1931
Died December 18, 2000
An arranger and saxophonist, James Mitchell was a member of The Memphis Horns, the famed house band at Stax-Volt Records. Memphis-born Mitchell worked on hundreds of hit records by artists such as The Doobie Brothers, Willie Mitchell, Ann Peebles, Otis Redding, Rufus Thomas, Sam & Dave, Al Green, Otis Clay, B.B. King, Aretha Franklin, Robert Cray, Johnny Taylor and Elvis Presley.
CAUSE: Bone cancer.

McKinley Mitchell

Born December 25, 1934
Died January 18, 1986
Chicago-based soul and blues singer, McKinley Mitchell first garnered fame in 1962 with his self-penned hit, 'The Town I Live In'. Born in Mississippi, Mitchell was a former teenage gospel singer who once led The Hearts of Harmony, and the Philadelphia-based group, The Mitchellaires. But after moving to Chicago in 1958, he was drawn to the blues scene. Recording on a series of labels, he was often produced by Willie Dixon. Recording for Retta Records during the Eighties, his final album was *I Won't Be Back No More* (1984).
CAUSE: Heart attack. He died at St. James Medical Center in Chicago.

Jimmy Mobley

Born c. 1938
Died 1979
Songwriter and short-lived member of the Fifties doo-wop group, The Four Fellows, Jimmy Mobley joined the group in 1956 beginning with the single 'Please Play My Song'. The group's second tenor, Mobley had previously been a member of The Starlight Toppers.
CAUSE: Heart attack.

Pierre Moerlen

Born October 23, 1952
Died May 2, 2005
The French percussionist of psychedelic jazz-rock band Gong, Pierre Moerlen also worked with Mike Oldfield in the Seventies, appearing on Oldfield's albums *Ommadawn*, *Incantations* and the live version of *Tubular Bells*. Moerlen first joined Gong in 1973 and appeared in various incarnations of the group over the next decade. In 1985, he joined the Sweden-based band Tribute.
CAUSE: He died in his sleep at his home in Strasbourg, France.

Matt Monro

(TERRY PARSONS)
Born December 1, 1930
Died February 7, 1985
Smooth voiced ballad singer Matt Monro enjoyed five top 10 hits in the UK between 1960 and 1965, including the first ever cover of The Beatles' 'Yesterday', now the most covered song in popular music history. Originally a bus driver, Monro first sang with bands using the pseudonym Al Jordon, but he had switched to Monro by the time of his first hit, 'Portrait Of My Love' in 1960. His other UK top 10 records were 'My Kind Of Girl' (1961), 'Softly As I Leave You' (1962), 'Walk Away' (1964) and 'Yesterday' (1965). Monro

achieved limited success in the US with 'My Kind Of Girl' and 'Walk Away' which prompted his move there in the mid Sixties and sustained his career there as a cabaret singer. During his lengthy career he recorded for EMI (the Parlophone and Capitol labels), RCA and Columbia. Numerous compilation albums have been released since his death.
CAUSE: Cancer.

Country Dick Montana

(DANIEL MCLAIN)
Born 1955
Died November 8, 1995
The leader of the alternative-rock group The Beat Farmers, Country Dick Montana headed the San Diego-based group for 12 years. While operating a record store and running a Kinks fan club in the late Seventies, Montana had first formed The Crawdaddys, the group releasing a pair of albums. Montana passed through The Penetrators, before forming The Beat Farmers in 1983 on drums and lead vocals. A roots-rock band that merged country, punk, and rockabilly influences, The Beat Farmers received little radio airplay during their tenure. A true showman who enjoyed stage high jinks, the California-born Montana would encourage crowds to throw beer in his face, and jump on tables and kick drinks onto patrons' laps. Earning a cult following, the group had just released their eighth album *Manifold* at the time of Montana's death.
CAUSE: Suffering an aneurysm on stage during a performance in Whistler, British Columbia, Canada, he fell backward into his drum set, and died within minutes. He had also suffered from thyroid and throat cancer.

Hugo Montenegro

Born September 2, 1925
Died February 6, 1981
A classical composer and conductor, Hugo Montenegro was an arranger for many artists during the Fifties, including Harry Belafonte. After recording a number of orchestral albums, he achieved surprise success in 1968 with the chart-topping instrumental 'The Good, The Bad And The Ugly' from Ennio Morricone's film of the same name. His other film score credits included *Hang 'Em High*, Elvis Presley's *Charro!*, and the Dean Martin-starring *The Ambushers* and *The Wrecking Crew*.
CAUSE: Emphysema. He died in New York City.

Ken "Dimwit" Montgomery

Born 1958
Died September 28, 1994
The lanky drummer of the Vancouver hardcore punk band D.O.A., California born Ken "Dimwit" Montgomery spent two stints with the group before leaving for good in the early Nineties. D.O.A. temporarily disbanded in 1991 after its contract with Restless Records was not renewed. Montgomery later formed a hard-rock group, The Four Horsemen.
CAUSE: Heroin overdose. He died in Vancouver.

Roy Montrell

(RAYMOND MONTRELL)
Born February 27, 1928
Died May 17, 1979
A New Orleans-based guitarist, Roy Montrell was a member of Fats Domino's band beginning in the early Fifties. As a solo act, Montrell recorded several singles at Imperial and Minit Records including 'Oooh-Wow!' and 'That Mellow Saxophone'.
CAUSE: Drug overdose. He died in his room at the Sonesta Hotel in Amsterdam with a syringe full of heroin next to his body. He was touring with Domino at the time.

Robert Moog

Born May 23, 1934
Died August 21, 2005
The inventor of the Moog synthesiser,

Robert Moog helped usher in the modern electronic age in popular music. Inspired by a rudimentary electronic instrument called the theremin (used on The Beach Boys' hit 'Good Vibrations'), Moog constructed the first Moog "Modular Synthesiser" in 1963 while a doctoral student in engineering at Cornell University, New York. The following year, he launched the R.A. Moog Company and manufactured the first commercial Moog. A costly device, the Moog was used by a number of rock acts including The Beatles, The Monkees, The Who, Emerson, Lake & Palmer and Stereolab and was prominently featured on the million-selling Walter Carlos album *Switched-On Bach.* Moog earned a Grammy Trustees Award for lifetime achievement in 1970. The Hans Fjellestad-directed biopic, *Moog*, was completed in 2004.
CAUSE: Brain tumour. He died at his home in Asheville, North Carolina.

David Mook

Born April 15, 1936
Died June 1, 1996
A music publisher and songwriter, David Mook co-wrote the themes of the television programmes, *Scooby Doo* and *The Dating Games*, and was the musical director for *The Banana Splits*.
CAUSE: Cancer. He died in Los Angeles.

Keith Moon

Born August 23, 1946
Died September 7, 1978
Keith Moon has been widely acclaimed as the greatest drummer in the history of rock. Certainly he played his massive drum kit differently from any of his peers, turning it into a lead instrument, and his up-front drumming was crucial in establishing The Who's passionate style, but his wilful abandon – and vast celebrity – often sat uneasily with the other players. Detractors argued that Moon couldn't keep time but this didn't matter – his playing ushered in an era wherein the drums became far more than simply a means of keeping the beat, and much of his recorded legacy from 1965–71 has a timeless quality that has never been repeated. In this respect Keith Moon was to the drums what Jimi Hendrix was to the guitar – a complete original, and as such he was probably the most influential drummer in hard rock. At the same time Moon was rock's wildest character in the Sixties and Seventies, an unapologetic freewheeling hedonist whose lifestyle became synonymous with the mad, carefree image of the rock star at large. He courted the press and became notorious as 'Moon The Loon', the incorrigible, brandy-swilling practical joker who respected no authority whatsoever and never knew the meaning of the word embarrassment. His drug and alcohol consumption were titanic and, of course, led directly to his early death, and in this respect it seemed that somewhere along the line Moon had decided to live out the reality of Who composer Pete Townshend's most famous line: "Hope I die before I get old." Hopelessly delinquent as a schoolboy, Moon became a surf music fan, took early lessons on drums as a teenager and played with local bands, The Escorts, Mark Twain & The Strangers, and The Beachcombers, before joining The Who in the summer of 1964. Shortly after his arrival, the group's management was usurped by Kit Lambert and Chris Stamp whose energy and ambition focused the group and who hooked them up with hot producer Shel Talmy in late 1964. Moon announced his arrival in spectacular form on the group's first real single 'I Can't Explain' (1965) on which his rifle-shot snare pre-empted singer Roger Daltrey's leap into the chorus. Mostly, though, his foil was guitarist Townshend with whom he developed an uncanny musical relationship, the product of which became one of The Who's great

trademarks: the chiming, bell-like, open-stringed power chord, cross cut against pounding drums and bass and allowed to feedback on itself and drone into a wall of electronic discord. Moon's drumming is outstanding throughout the group's début album *My Generation* and on several Sixties singles, most notably 'Happy Jack' (1966) and 'I Can See For Miles' (1967), but it is on the double album *Tommy* (1969) that his talents are best utilised. On Townshend's celebrated rock opera he becomes an orchestra within himself, driving the band along with an intelligence and sureness of touch that defies analysis. On *Who's Next* (1971) Moon is reined in somewhat but his playing on the bridge on 'Behind Blue Eyes' and throughout both 'Bargain' and 'Won't Get Fooled Again' ranks with anything he ever did. The Who's greatest strength, though, was in concert and by the end of the Sixties they were justifiably billing themselves as "the most exciting rock band in the world". To this Moon contributed an almost superhuman energy, his hands and feet battering his kit into submission night after night, the relentless power of The Who in full flight spiralling out from his arms and legs. Moon's kit was the biggest in rock, at one stage boasting at least 10 tom-toms, twin bass drums, twin timpani, snare, half-a-dozen cymbals and a gong. He developed an on-stage personality as a wise-cracker and often ad-libbed comical asides between numbers, and like Townshend he took an almost manic delight in wrecking his equipment at the close of a concert, especially in the group's early days. As The Who became massively popular worldwide, so Keith Moon became a celebrity, not just as a drummer, but as the mad joker in the rock pack, whose exploits included cross-dressing and a much-publicised episode when he and his friend Vivian Stanshall visited a London beerkeller dressed in Nazi SS uniforms. In 1966 Moon secretly married teenage model Kim Kerrigan and shortly afterwards became a father, but it made little difference to his reckless lifestyle. In 1970 he was involved in a tragic accident in which his chauffeur was killed, an incident which weighed heavily on his psyche and seemed to presage a slow and painful downfall. Tired of his philandering and manic behaviour, Kim left him in 1973 and he moved to California, Swedish model girlfriend in tow, but as The Who slowed down and Townshend sought creative outlets elsewhere so Moon found himself drifting with little motivation other than to get drunk and act the fool. He took cameo roles in several movies, made a dreadful solo album and returned to London in 1977, having squandered most of his fortune. He was fat and unfit, and his health – both mental and physical – was in a precarious state. His death later that year seemed somehow inevitable, although it still took the rock world by surprise to discover that Keith Moon wasn't indestructible after all. The Who carried on with Kenny Jones and others in the drum seat but were never the same. Moon took with him much of the group's passion and power, and also its sense of humour, and in the Eighties Townshend's sense of loss almost led him to follow Moon to an early grave.

CAUSE: Moon died from an accidental overdose of the prescription drug Heminevrin, prescribed to combat alcoholism, though his long-term abuse of alcohol, cocaine and prescription pills must have been a contributory factor. He died in the same flat in Park Street in London's Mayfair (belonging to Harry Nilsson) that Mama Cass had died in during 1974. On the eve of his death, he had been at a screening of *The Buddy Holly Story* during the Paul McCartney-sponsored, annual Buddy Holly week, but had drank little. Going home with his fiancee Annette Walter-Lax, he woke up the next

morning and demanded she cook him a steak. After eating the steak and washing down a quantity of Heminevrin pills with champagne, he returned to bed and died. An autopsy revealed that Moon had consumed 32 tablets of Heminevrin.
FURTHER READING: Fletcher, Tony. (1998). *Dear Boy: The Life Of Keith Moon*. London: Omnibus Press.

Moondog

(LOUIS THOMAS HARDIN)
Born May 16, 1916
Died September 9, 1999
Donning a Nordic costume of robe, horned-helmet and spear, and playing home-made instruments, street musician Louis "Moondog" Hardin was a fixture on New York City sidewalks during the Fifties. The son of an Episcopal preacher in Kansas, Hardin was blinded by an exploding blasting cap in his mid-teens. After studying music at the Iowa School For The Blind, he moved to New York City in 1943 and adopted the nickname Moondog in 1947, recording a number of obscure, esoteric jazz 78s. One of these records, 'Moondog Symphony', became the on-air theme for pioneering rock'n'roll deejay Alan Freed; more importantly, Freed also borrowed Hardin's Moondog nickname but when Freed transferred his popular programme from Cleveland to New York, Hardin went to court and successfully blocked Freed's appropriation of his Moondog moniker. When Hardin finally abandoned his street corner in 1974, many believed that he had died. Invited to perform in Frankfurt, Germany, he decided to stay there. Performing on the street corners of Frankfurt, he found a companion and business manager in archaeology student Ilona Goebel. Although Moondog continued to compose music prolifically, he recorded at a moderate pace.
CAUSE: Heart failure. He died in Munster, Germany.

Albert Moore

Born 1940
Died February 1994
A member of the first act to perform at the original Woodstock Music Festival, flute player and backing vocalist Albert Moore co-founded the seven-member interracial ensemble Sweetwater in 1967. Born in Pittsburgh, Moore had joined the US Air Force and mastered the flute while stationed in Morocco. Attracting attention around Los Angeles with their Latin-styled sound, Sweetwater recorded three albums for Reprise and opened up for many of the top acts of the day, but achieved only limited success in their own right. The group's biopic, *Sweetwater: A True Rock Story* aired on the VH-1 network in 1999.
CAUSE: Lung cancer.

Curley Moore

(JUNE MOORE)
Born c. 1933
Died December 14, 1985
A fixture on the New Orleans R&B scene, singer Curley Moore is best known for his stint with Huey "Piano" Smith & The Clowns. Joining The Clowns in 1960 as replacement for the outgoing Bobby Marchan, Moore provided the lead vocals on most of their output including the dance craze single, 'Popeye'. During the same period, Moore recorded solo material and a duet with Huey Smith, 'Huey And Curley At The Mardis Gras'. Leaving The Clowns in the mid Sixties, Moore scored a series of regional hits including 'Soul Train' and 'Sophisticated Sissy' and appeared on Huey Smith's 1978 album, *Rockin' And Jivin'*.
CAUSE: Unknown.

Gatemouth Moore

(ARNOLD DWIGHT MOORE)
Born November 8, 1913
Died May 19, 2004
An often overlooked blues legend, Gatemouth Moore was a star in the

Thirties and Forties. Born in Topeka, Kansas, but raised in Memphis, Moore broke into music after moving to Kansas City in 1930 where he found work in the city's plentiful jazz clubs. Nicknamed "Gatemouth" because of his booming voice, he worked with a number of leading bandleaders including Bennie Moten. In April 1940, Moore was one of the few survivors of the "Natchez Rhythm Club Fire" in Mississippi in which 207 people perished. Returning to Kansas City, he wrote 'I Ain't Mad At You', 'Somebody's Got To Go' and the often recorded blues standard, 'Did You Ever Love A Woman?' Moore subsequently worked with a series of jump-blues acts, including Dallas Bartley, Budd Johnson Orchestra and The Tiny Grimes Swingtet. Signing with King Records in 1947 as a solo artist, he recorded several jump-blues singles. While performing on a Chicago stage, Moore experienced a religious conversion; he went silent, unable to sing and then launched into an old spiritual, 'Shine On Me'. Ordained as a minister in 1949, Moore recorded mostly gospel material and worked for a time as a gospel deejay at WDIA in Memphis and as a television reporter in Alabama. Settling in Yazoo City, he became pastor of the Lintonia A.M.E. Church. Refusing to abandon secular music entirely, Moore occasionally performed in blues festivals and recorded his final album in 1977, *Great R&B Oldies*.
CAUSE: He died in Yazoo City, Mississippi, after a long illness.

Johnny Moore

(JOHN DUDLEY MOORE)
Born October 20, 1906
Died January 6, 1969
The leader of the popular, pioneering R&B group The Blazers, Johnny Moore formed the group with bassist Eddie Williams and singer/pianist Charles Brown. A native of Austin, Texas, Moore first performed on the violin and guitar in his father's group, before moving to Los Angeles. There Moore formed The Blazers in 1942. After recording several singles at the tiny Atlas label, The Blazers found fame at Eddie Messner's Philo Records. Composed by Brown, 'Drifting Blues' was a very influential hit during the rise of R&B. Refusing to be tied down to a single label, The Blazers enjoyed hit releases at several record companies. Featuring Brown's jazz-blues, elegant, ballady voice, and Moore's jazzy guitar, The Blazers dominated jukeboxes with 'Sunny Road', 'So Long', 'New Orleans Blues', and the perennial favourite, 'Merry Christmas, Baby'. But with the addition of Johnny Moore's younger brother, jazz guitarist Oscar Moore, Brown left soon after. Hiring replacement vocalist Bill Valentine, the group landed on the charts in 1949 with 'Walkin' Blues'. Brown briefly returned to record with the Blazers in the mid Fifties.
CAUSE: Unknown.

Johnny Moore

(JOHN DARREL MOORE)
Born December 15, 1934
Died December 30, 1998
Long-term member of the perennial, doo-wop vocal group The Drifters, Johnny Moore had joined the group on two separate occasions. Born in Selma, Alabama, Moore had relocated to Cleveland in his teens; there he joined a group called The Hornets, the doo-wop outfit releasing an obscure single on States Records; Moore and The Hornets also moonlighted as a gospel group called The Cleveland Quartet. Moore left the Hornets to join The Drifters in late 1954 after an impromptu audition during a tour stop in Cleveland. Hired as the replacement for the undependable David Baughan, Moore provided the lead tenor vocal on the group's hits 'Adorable', 'Ruby Baby', 'Soldier Of Fortune' and 'Fools Fall In Love'. Drafted, Moore left the

group in late 1957. Then after completing his military stint, he rejoined a reformed version of The Drifters in 1961. Initially backing lead singer Rudy Lewis, Moore was forced to assume the lead vocal duties upon Lewis' sudden death. Beginning with the stunning 'Under The Boardwalk', Moore fronted the group on 'I've Got Sand In My Shoes', and 'Saturday Night At The Movies'. Tired of internal squabbling, Moore and the rest of The Drifters disbanded in 1970. With a dispute over the US rights of the group's name, Drifter manager Faye Treadwell secured the European rights. Relocating to London, Johnny Moore formed a new version of The Drifters along with former bandmate Bill Fredericks. Adopting a modern, soul sound and relying heavily on session singers, the group landed British hits such as 'Kissing In The Back Row Of The Movies' and 'You're More Than A Number In My Little Red Book', none of which charted in the US. Moore left the group in 1978 to pursue a solo career. But following another battle over control of the group's moniker, in 1982 Moore formed a group called Slightly Adrift. Then after briefly reuniting with former Drifter Ben E. King in 1984, Moore regained control of The Drifters' name, and performed until days before his death.
CAUSE: He died of respiratory failure en route to a London hospital. Suffering from breathing problems a few months earlier, he was temporarily replaced by Wade Elliott.
FURTHER READING: Allan, Tony; & Treadwell, Faye. (1993). *Save The Last Dance For Me: The Musical Legacy Of The Drifters, 1953–1993.* Ann Arbor, MI: Popular Culture Ink.

Kenny Moore

(KENNETH M. MOORE)
Born 1952
Died March 25, 1997
A member of Tina Turner's band since 1977, keyboardist Kenny Moore performed on several of her albums. The Boston-born Moore had been raised on gospel music, joining a family group called The Moore Singers. Classically trained on piano, Moore got his first break in 1973 when he performed behind Duke Ellington on a television programme, and then as a vocalist behind the Rev James Cleveland. Finding work as a session player, he backed Aretha Franklin, Billy Preston, Carly Simon, Elton John, and Ray Charles. As a solo artist he released an album on his own label in 1987 *Have You Got A Moment?*
CAUSE: Apoplexy. He died in Sydney, Australia during a tour with Tina Turner; the trek through Australia and New Zealand was marred by two bomb threats.

Oscar Moore

(OSCAR FREDERIC MOORE)
Born December 25, 1912
Died October 8, 1981
Latter guitarist of the Three Blazers, Oscar Moore had made his mark in The King Cole Trio. A native of Austin, Texas, Moore had formed his first group at age 16 with his older brother Johnny Moore. In 1939, Oscar Moore joined Nat "King" Cole in an instrumental jazz combo, a group that also included bassist Wesley Prince (and later Johnny Miller). Winning many *Downbeat* magazine popularity polls, the combo enjoyed a series of crossover hits with 'All For You' (1943), 'Straighten Up And Fly Right' (1944), 'Gee, Baby, Ain't I Good To You' (1944), 'I'm A Shy Guy' (1945), and their signature piece, 'Get Your Kicks On Route 66'. But by the late Forties, Cole adopted a more polished sound, choosing lush orchestral backing in place of his trio. Relocating to Los Angeles in 1947, Oscar Moore joined his brother's group The Three Blazers, and took the R&B-flavoured combo in a jazz direction. With vocalist

and pianist Charles Brown leaving the group for a solo career, The Blazers' hit run slowed with new lead singer Billy Valentine. Launching a solo career in the early Fifties, Oscar Moore released three albums before leaving music to work as a bricklayer; he returned to music in the Sixties. A bebop pioneer, Moore also worked with Lionel Hampton, Lester Young, and Art Tatum.
CAUSE: He died of a heart attack during a visit to Las Vegas.

Tommy Moore

Born 1935
Died 1981
Briefly a member of pre-Beatles incarnation The Silver Beetles, drummer Tommy Moore quit after several clashes with John Lennon during a tour through Scotland in spring 1960 as the opening act for Larry Parnes' protégé Johnny Gentle. Moore returned to his job as a forklift operator and was eventually replaced by Pete Best.
CAUSE: Unknown.

Mooseman

(LLOYD ROBERTS)
Born c. 1958
Died 2000
The bass player for Ice-T's backing rap/heavy metal band Body Count, Mooseman was continuously dogged by controversy throughout his career. Formed by classmates from Crenshaw High School in the south central section of Los Angeles, Body Count initially backed Ice-T on his 1991 album *OG Original Gangster*. That year, Ice-T and Body Count drew positive reviews for their performances on the Lollapalooza tour. Body Count's self-titled 1992 début album was initially ignored until a Texas police group threatened a boycott of Time-Warner because of one track, 'Cop Killer'. Although the song was eventually deleted from the disc, the surrounding controversy magnified the group's notoriety. Leaving Time-Warner, Body Count issued their second album, *Born Dead*, on Ice-T's fledgling label, Priority. Mooseman left the group shortly after its release and later worked with rocker Iggy Pop on his album *Beat 'Em Up*. Following the deaths of three members of Body Count, Ice-T was forced to form a new line-up of the group in 2004.
CAUSE: He was murdered in a drive-by shooting in the south central section of Los Angeles. Mooseman was not the intended target.

Jacques Morali

Born 1947
Died November 15, 1991
A prolific disco producer who worked with The Ritchie Family and The Village People, Morocco-native Jacques Morali was raised in a dysfunctional home, dressed by his mother as a girl. Moving to France in his late teens to escape a civil war, Morali was befriended by fellow Moroccan Henri Belolo who had just started a publishing company; the pair soon entered into a fruitful songwriting partnership. Turning to production work, Morali had his first major success with The Ritchie Family whose 'Brazil' and 'The Best Disco In Town' were disco smashes. But Morali had his greatest success when in 1975 he discovered Felipe Rose (who is part Sioux Indian) dancing in full Indian regalia at a New York City nightclub. Morali placed Rose in the lead role of a group called The Village People. Signed to Casablanca Records, The Village People were intended as a studio-only group but after their material began getting airplay, Morali was forced to audition full-time members. A campy, costumed group that included an Indian, cop, biker, soldier and construction worker, The Village People defined disco with their Morali co-penned hits, 'Y.M.C.A', 'In The Navy' and 'Macho Man'.

Returning to Paris in 1984, Morali landed European chart success with rap and breakdance group, The Break Machine.
CAUSE: He succumbed to an AIDS-related ailment. He died in Paris, with his mother barred from the funeral.

Marc Moreland

Born January 8, 1958
Died March 13, 2002
As lead guitarist of new-wave band Wall Of Voodoo, Marc Moreland co-wrote one of the most enduring MTV hits of the early Eighties with 'Mexican Radio'. The nucleus of the group, Moreland and vocalist Stan Ridgway, had initially teamed in 1977 to record background music for low budget films. After the success of 'Mexican Radio' in 1983, Ridgway quit the group to go solo. After releasing the albums *Seven Days In Sammystown* (1985), *Happy Planet* (1987) and the mostly live *The Ugly Americans In Australia* (1988), Wall Of Voodoo disbanded in 1989. Moreland later formed a series of bands – Pretty & Twisted, Department Of Crooks and Marc Moreland's Mess – and worked with Johnette Napolitano of Concrete Blonde.
CAUSE: Suffering complications following a liver transplant, his body rejected the organ just five weeks after the procedure. He died in France.

Prentice Moreland

Born March 4, 1925
Died September 1988
A talented vocalist, Missouri-born Prentice Moore passed through a series of R&B groups in the Fifties. Joining the veteran doo-wop act The Du Droppers in early 1954 as high tenor, Moreland appeared on their single, 'How Much Longer'. Leaving the group later that year, Moreland then joined Billy Ward's Dominoes, who at the time featured Jackie Wilson on lead vocals. Moreland recorded only four tracks with the group, quitting after just a few months, including 'Can't Do Sixty No More' and 'If I Never Get To Heaven', featuring Moreland on lead. Moving to the West Coast, he joined The Chanteclairs, and provided the impassioned lead vocal on the ballad, 'Believe Me, Beloved' (1955), but by the following year Moreland had landed in The Cadets (who also recorded as The Jacks) as Ted Taylor's replacement. During his brief tenure, Moreland appeared on their biggest hit, a cover of The Jayhawks' 'Stranded In The Jungle'. Leaving soon after for a solo career, Moreland recorded for several labels over the next decade, with little success.
CAUSE: Unknown.

John Rushton Moreve

(JOHN RUSSELL MORGAN)
Born 1946
Died July 1, 1981
Bass player of the early heavy-metal group Steppenwolf, John Rushton Moreve had previously worked as a session player in his native Los Angeles. In 1967 Moreve joined a relocated Canadian group led by John Kay called Sparrow; the group briefly recorded for Columbia Records. Renamed Steppenwolf and signed by ABC-Dunhill, Steppenwolf released an eponymous album in 1968, landing a trio of rock smashes with the hippy anthem 'Born To Be Wild'; the anti-drug, 'The Pusher'; and the bawdy 'Sookie Sookie'. A subsequent album *Steppenwolf The Second* (Dunhill), was highlighted by the Moreve co-penned, hard-rocking, psychedelic classic 'Magic Carpet Ride'. Moreve left the group in 1968 and was replaced by Nick St. Nicholas.
CAUSE: He died in a car crash in Sunny Valley, California.
FURTHER READING: Kay, John; & Einarson, John. (1994). *Magic Carpet Ride: The Autobiography Of John Kay And Steppenwolf.* Kingston, Ontario, Canada: Quarry.

Ron Morgan

(Ronald B. Morgan)
Born June 8, 1945
Died June 1989
A talented guitarist, Ron Morgan played with a number of notable bands but never attained any degree of fame. Born in Colby, Kansas, Morgan moved to Los Angeles in 1965 where he formed Peter & The Wolves with Peter Lewis, the son of actress Loretta Young. Joining the art-rock ensemble The West Coast Pop Art Experimental Band, he appeared on their first three albums, beginning with *Part One*. When visiting his family in Denver, Morgan occasionally sat in with Tommy Bolin's first band, Zephyr, and by 1967 Morgan had joined another Denver-based group, Super Band, which featured Jimmy Greenspoon. Returning to Los Angeles, Morgan and Greenspoon joined an up-and-coming band called Three Dog Night. While Greenspoon remained with the group, Morgan balked at having to sign a contract and quit before they recorded their first album. Then in 1968, Morgan joined a version of The Electric Prunes as replacement for John Herron, while the group was recording the album *Just Good Old Rock And Roll*. By the early Seventies, Morgan had settled in Denver and was working as a taxi driver. Involved in a serious motorcycle crash around 1979, he never recovered.
Cause: In poor health for much of his last years, he died in his sleep at his home.

Johnnie Morisette

Born July 1, 1935
Died August 1, 2000
A one-hit wonder, Johnny Morisette scored an R&B hit in 1962 with the Sam Cooke composition, 'Meet Me At The Twistin' Place'. The single was issued on a label co-owned by Cooke, SAR Records. Born in South America but raised in Mobile, Alabama, Morisette had previously recorded as Johnny Two-Voice, because of his ability to jump across octaves. Much of his recording output was assembled on the 25-track collection, *Meet Johnnie Morisette At The Twistin' Place*.
Cause: Unknown. He died in San Francisco.

Jim Morrison

(James Douglas Morrison)
Born December 8, 1943
Died July 3, 1971
The charismatic, rebellious singer with the Sixties rock group The Doors, Jim Morrison emerged as a cult figure immediately after his death and has remained one ever since. Born in Melbourne, Florida, the son of a Naval officer, Morrison moved frequently in his youth before graduating from a Virginia high school. After studying at Florida State University, Morrison transferred to the UCLA film school where among his classmates was keyboard player Ray Manzarek. Dabbling in poetry and metaphysical philosophies, Morrison was drawn to the arty Venice Beach district where the like-minded Manzarek suggested they form a musical group after Morrison impressed him with a poem that would ultimately form the basis of the song 'Moonlight Drive'. Adding drummer John Densmore and guitarist Robby Krieger, The Doors became regulars at the famed Whisky A-Go-Go in Hollywood; but the group was fired by the club after performing the oedipally themed 'The End'. Signing with a former folk label Elektra Records, and releasing a self-titled album, The Doors topped the charts with an edited version of the Krieger-composed 'Light My Fire' (1967); featuring Manzarek's intricate keyboard, the song became the group's signature piece and an album-rock staple. Constantly challenging authority figures, the well-read and hedonistic Morrison enjoyed shocking people with his outlandish behaviour. His drinking was legendary, he

experimented with just about every drug he came across and he lived life constantly on the edge. His dark curls framing a face of unusual handsomeness, Morrison soon found himself on the cover of magazines that exploited his sexuality but he was a willing subject, at least in the early years of the group's fame. Frequently involved in controversy, Morrison reneged on a promise to change the lyrics of 'Light My Fire' for a 1967 *Ed Sullivan Show* appearance; in New Haven, Connecticut, Morrison was arrested for taunting police after he was maced backstage. Flirting with many influences including blues and Spanish flamenco music, The Doors remained in the charts with the albums, *Strange Days*, which spawned the pop hits, 'People Are Strange' and 'Love Me Two Times'; and *Waiting For The Sun*, which was highlighted by 'Hello I Love You' and 'Touch Me'. The self-described Lizard King, Morrison irrevocably damaged his career on March 1, 1969, at a concert at Miami's Dinner Key Auditorium when, during a chaotic performance of 'Touch Me', he allegedly flashed his genitals. With Morrison arrested and charged with "lewd and lascivious behavior", Doors' concerts were cancelled around the country. Now heavily abusing alcohol and drugs, Morrison joined the group in recording the bluesy *Morrison Hotel*, the album highlighted by the rollicking 'Roadhouse Blues'. (Morrison would also publish a book of poetry in 1970, *The Lords, And The New Creatures*.) Found guilty of profanity and indecent exposure by a Miami court, Morrison was fined and sentenced to eight months of hard labour; appealing the verdict, he was freed on bail. Morrison then recorded tracks of his own introspective poetry, and worked on what would be his final Doors album, *L.A. Woman* (1971); while the pop-flavoured 'Love Her Madly' landed in the Top 10, the album's title track featured Morrison's off-key vocals and became a rock classic. Obsessed with the deaths of Janis Joplin and Jimi Hendrix – both at age 27 – Morrison would often utter phrases such as "you're drinking with number three". Disillusioned with the music industry and the image it had bequeathed him, Morrison and his common-law wife Pamela Courson moved to Paris together in March 1971 to escape his problems, rest and plan his future; he also hoped that the artistic and literary community in the city would accept him as a poet. By this time he had put on a great deal of weight and was down-playing his image by growing an unkempt beard. After his sudden and somewhat unusual death, Morrison became a cult figure almost instantly, not least because of the manner of his passing. The remaining Doors members attempted to carry on, but they disbanded after recording two dispirited albums. Their music never fading from radio, The Doors achieved renewed interest when Francis Coppola featured 'The End' during a chilling scene in the Vietnam War film *Apocalypse Now*. The best-selling biography *No One Here Gets Out Alive* helped seal Morrison's legend and, with The Doors selling more albums a decade after Morrison's death than in the group's heyday, *Rolling Stone* featured a young, virile Morrison on its cover and proclaimed: "He's Hot, He's Sexy and He's Dead." In 1983, a collection of live Doors tracks *Alive, She Cried* spawned an unlikely MTV hit with 'Gloria'. Morrison's life was chronicled on the big screen in the 1991 feature film *The Doors*, with Val Kilmer in the lead role. In 2005, Doors drummer John Densmore, joined by the estate of Jim Morrison, successfully sued former bandmates Ray Manzarek and Robby Krieger, who had teamed with singer Ian Astbury, for touring as "The Doors Of The 21st Century".

CAUSE: Morrison was found dead in the bath tub of their Paris apartment by his common-law wife Pamela Courson. Although there were rumours that Morrison died from a heroin overdose, the French authorities ruled the cause of death was heart failure due to acute respiratory distress. Doctors had been called twice to treat his asthma while in Paris, but he refused to allow a doctor to be called on his final evening. Arguments surrounding his demise were fuelled by erroneous suggestions that beside Courson and the doctor who signed the death certificate, few people actually saw the body. In reality the body was seen by French police, ambulancemen, undertakers and various emergency personnel. The delay in the news of Morrison's death being circulated caused further questions to be asked and the debate took on a whole new dimension when the book *No One Here Gets Out Alive* propagated the theory that Morrison might have falsified his death and taken on a new identity, with Courson as his accomplice and the impending prison term as his motive. Either way, a coffin that everyone of sane mind now assumes contained Morrison's body was buried at the famous Père Lachaise cemetery in Paris alongside many other notables, including Chopin, Edith Plath and Oscar Wilde. The site of Morrison's grave has become a tourist attraction, second only in Paris to the Eiffel Tower, and the scene of several disturbances over the years, usually on the anniversary of Morrison's death. Pamela Courson died from a heroin overdose, probably suicide, in 1974, also aged 27.

FURTHER READING: Sugerman, Danny; & Hopkins, Jerry. (1980). *No One Here Gets Out Alive*. New York: Warner. Butler, Patricia. (1998). *The Tragic Romance Of Pamela And Jim Morrison*. Omnibus: London.

Sterling Morrison

(HOLMES STERLING MORRISON, JR.)
Born August 29, 1942
Died August 30, 1995

A founding member of the pioneering art-rock group, The Velvet Underground, Sterling Morrison traded guitar licks with leader Lou Reed. In spite of their lack of commercial success, The Velvet Underground influenced future generations of rockers, providing the blueprint for the rise of punk-rock in the late Seventies and much of the minimalist new wave music that followed. Born in the Long Island community of East Meadow, Morrison was classically trained on the trumpet. Attending Syracuse University for two semesters, he became friends with a fellow fan of R&B, literature major and budding poet, Lou Reed. Leaving college and settling in New York City in 1965, Morrison formed a rock band with Reed, John Cale, and Angus MacLise (who was soon replaced by the androgynous Maureen "Moe" Tucker). A far better guitarist than Reed, Morrison also played the bass and provided backing vocals. Adopting a series of names, the group settled on Velvet Underground, the moniker taken from Michael Leigh's book about New York's S&M culture, *The Velvet Underground*. Though alienating their early audiences with their brash sound, VU did find a fan in artist Andy Warhol; becoming VU's manager, he financed the group, added German-born *femme fatale* Nico as the co-lead vocalist, and incorporated the group into many of his multi-media projects. Signed to Verve Records in 1966, the group sold few copies of their début effort *The Velvet Underground And Nico*, which featured a Warhol-designed peeling-banana cover. A controversial album that went against the grain of the prevailing hippy culture and was consequently ignored by radio, its tracks included 'All Tomorrow's Parties' and the blatantly drug-oriented songs, 'Waiting For The Man' and 'Heroin'. With Warhol sidelined and Nico fired in 1968, VU released their follow-up album, *White*

Light/White Heat. (Morrison and Reed would co-write Nico's solo hit 'Chelsea Girls'). Cale left in 1969, unable to get along with Reed, and VU took a pared-down direction on their third album, *The Velvet Underground*, which was highlighted by Reed's 'Pale Blue Eyes'. Dropped by their label and switching to Atlantic Records, VU issued its most commercial project, *Loaded* (1970), which featured the original versions of the future Lou Reed hits 'Sweet Jane' and 'Rock & Roll'. Leaving Velvet Underground in 1971, Morrison returned to his studies, earning a doctorate in medieval literature from the University of Texas at Austin. His other love was boats and Morrison earned his living piloting a tugboat on the Houston shipping channel, eventually earning his captain's licence. On one occasional foray into music, he teamed with John Cale to score the film *Antartida*, and in the late Eighties, recorded and toured with Moe Tucker's band. Then, after a 1990 reunion performance at a Andy Warhol tribute, VU reunited for a tour in 1993, a performance captured on the album *Live MCMXCIII.* But with Reed and Cale bickering over who would produce a reunion album of new material, the group quickly disbanded. Morrison died in 1995 and was eulogised by the surviving members at their Rock'n'Roll Hall of Fame induction.
CAUSE: Suffering non-Hodgkin's lymphoma, he died at his home in Poughkeepsie, New York.
FURTHER READING: Bockris, Victor. (1995). *Up-Tight: The Velvet Underground Story.* London: Omnibus.

Melvin Morrow

Born c. 1930
Died 1981
The original second-tenor vocalist of Chicago-based doo-wop outfit The Moroccos, Melvin Morrow formed the group with several friends in 1952. Signing with United Records in 1954, The Moroccos found success after the addition of former Flamingos tenor Sollie McElroy, scoring regional hits beginning with a cover of 'Somewhere Over The Rainbow'. The group also recorded several singles with Lillian Brooks at King Records. After recording as The Morrocans in 1957, the group disbanded.
CAUSE: Unknown.

Ella Mae Morse

Born September 12, 1924
Died October 16, 1999
A pioneering, white, R&B/boogie-woogie singer, Texas born Ella Mae Morse was often mistaken for a black vocalist as her records crossed over to the R&B charts. The daughter of professional musicians, Morse sang in her father's jazz combo. Claiming to be 19 at an audition in Dallas, 14-year-old Morse joined Jimmy Dorsey's orchestra. On discovering her underage status, he fired her. Hired by former Dorsey pianist Freddie Slack, Morse gave fledgling Capitol Records its first million-seller with 'Cow-Cow Boogie' (Ella Fitzgerald had sung the song a year earlier as 'Cow-Cow Blues' in the film, *Ride 'Em Cowboy*). Teamed with a host of musicians including T-Bone Walker, The Bill May Orchestra, and The Dick Walters Orchestra, Morse enjoyed a hit run with 'Shoo Shoo Baby' (1943), 'Tess' Torch Song (I Had A Man)' (1944) and, with Freddie Slack, the ground-breaking proto-rock'n'roll number, 'House Of Blue Lights' (1946). Retiring in 1947 to raise a family with her second of four husbands, she returned to the studio after her marriage ended. Back at Capitol, she recorded a trio of hits, including the Nelson Riddle-arranged, 'Blacksmith Blues' (1951) but with the rise of the rock era, Morse made a career error by recording pop schmaltz. Although she made her final Capitol recordings in 1957, she continued to perform on a very limited basis for the next three decades, usually

accompanied by Ray McKinley's band. She retired in 1987.
CAUSE: Respiratory failure. Ill for several years, she died at Western Regional Medical Center in Bullhead City, Arizona.

Ronald G. Moseley

Born January 10, 1935
Died June 24, 2000
A songwriter, producer and artist manager, Ronald G. Moseley was a record industry veteran of nearly four decades. Breaking into the music business as a songwriter, he penned material for The Fiestas, The Jewels and Arthur Prysock. During the mid Sixties he was installed as the head of the Quincy Jones-owned label, Earth Music, and during this period, Moseley produced Mary Wells' post-Motown sessions at MGM Records. Moseley later worked as an executive at a series of labels including Warner Brothers, Capitol, ABC, Polydor and RCA. Forming Sussex Records with partners Clarence Avant and Art Kass, Moseley had success on the pop and R&B charts with Bill Withers, Dennis Coffey, The Presidents and Wadsworth Mansion. Later turning to artist management, Moseley worked with Isaac Hayes and others.
CAUSE: Myasthenia gravis. He died in New York City.

Pirkle Lee Moses, Jr.

Born October 4, 1937
Died December 16, 2000
Lead singer of doo-wop group The El Dorados, Pirkle Lee Moses, Jr. sang on a pair of mid Fifties hits. Formed as The Five Stars by a group of high school students on the south side of Chicago, they initially performed both gospel and doo-wop material. Winning a talent contest at the famed Club DeLisa, the group caught the attention of local deejay Al Benson, who signed them to Vee Jay Records. The El Dorados topped the R&B charts in 1955 with the upbeat rocker, 'At My Front Door', but although the single crossed over to the pop charts, it was eclipsed by Pat Boone's sanitised version. The El Dorados had a final hit in 1956 with 'I'll Be Forever Loving You', and in 1957, following a squabble over management, they split into two camps. Moses occasionally formed new line-ups of the group.
CAUSE: Cancer. He died in Chicago.

Mickie Most

(MICHAEL PETER HAYES)
Born June 20, 1938
Died May 30, 2003
One of the most prolific British record producers of the Sixties, Mickie Most worked with The Animals, Donovan, Herman's Hermits and others. Dropping out of school at 15 Most formed a pop covers band called The Most Brothers. After marrying a woman from South Africa, he moved to that country in 1959, where he formed a group called The Playboys, who had numerous successes with cover versions of overseas rock hits. Returning to England in 1962, Most recorded for Decca but was stymied in his efforts to continue as a successful performer, managing only one minor hit, 'Mr. Porter'. Turning to production work, Most gained his first major UK/US number one in the summer of 1964 with The Animals' cover of the American folk standard, 'The House Of The Rising Sun', which was famously recorded in two takes in 14 minutes flat, leaving just over three-quarters of an hour in which to record the B-side. With Most producing and selecting much of their singles material, The Animals continued their hit run with 'I'm Crying', 'Bring It On Home To Me', 'Don't Let Me Be Misunderstood', 'We Gotta Get Out Of This Place' and 'It's My Life' before parting company in late '65. Most also produced major hits for the UK beat groups The Nashville Teens ('Tobacco Road'), and especially Herman's Hermits

(including 'I'm Into Something Good', 'I'm Henry VIII, I Am', 'Mrs. Brown You've Got A Lovely Daughter' and 'There's A Kind Of Hush'), whose records almost outsold The Beatles in America in the year 1965. Most's production work with psychedelic folk-rocker Donovan spawned such memorable hits as 'Sunshine Superman', 'Mellow Yellow', 'Hurdy Gurdy Man' and 'Atlantis'. Most also produced Lulu's enduring ballad 'To Sir With Love', a US number one in 1967. But during this period, against the wishes of a number of more serious rock artists, Most preferred to remain in the pop camp. Although The Yardbirds begged to record self-composed blues-rock material, Most insisted that the band tackle professionally written pop tracks such as 'Little Games' and 'Ha Ha Said The Clown', while ex-Yardbirds guitarist Jeff Beck recorded the perennial party track 'Hi Ho Silver Lining' and the MOR standard 'Love Is Blue'. As well as these artists, Most also recorded teenage blues singer, Terry Reid. By the early Seventies, Most had opened his own RAK studios in London and, in 1970, operated a label of the same name. Most hired the services of the songwriting/production team of Nicky Chinn and Mike Chapman and oversaw a succession of hit pop-rock artists – Smokie, Suzi Quatro, Racey, Julie Felix, Mary Hopkins, Mud and Hot Chocolate – as well as a few non-mainstream acts such as Alexis Korner's CCS and Chris Spedding. Also in the Seventies, Most surfaced as a panelist on the pre-*Pop Idol* television programme, *New Faces* and, in 1978, produced the ATV music programme *Revolver*. Most's final production success came with pop chanteuse Kim Wilde (the daughter of Marty Wilde), who later dated Most's son Calvin Hayes, a member of the pop-rock group Johnny Hates Jazz. Most sold RAK to EMI Records in 1983.
CAUSE: He succumbed to mesothelioma, a cancer commonly associated with asbestos. He died at his home in London after battling the disease for three years.

Patrick Moten

Born March 17, 1957
Died November 22, 1999
A Los Angeles session musician and producer who is best known for his work with Anita Baker, classically trained Patrick Moten left this genre for R&B after watching a performance by Billy Preston. Moten formed his own band, Manufactured Funk, at age 15, opening for such headliners as B.B. King and Natalie Cole. Moten was a much in-demand session player, and produced his friend Bobby Womack's album *Roads Of Life*, co-writing his Top 10 R&B hit, 'If You Think You're Lonely Now' (1981). Moten similarly aided the career of Womack's labelmate Johnnie Taylor and also oversaw the début album by songstress Anita Baker, penning many of the tracks. Moten also worked with Syl Johnson, Tina Turner, Mica Paris, and Loleatta Holloway. Following a protracted lawsuit against Beverly Glen Records, Moten formed The Patrick Moten Orchestra in the mid Nineties.
CAUSE: Cancer. He died in Los Angeles.

Mr. Cee

(HUBERT KYLE CHURCH III)
Born 1973
Died December 31, 1995
Lead rapper of the San Francisco-based gangster-rap outfit R.B.L. Posse, Mr. Cee (also known as Mr. C) appeared on the group's first two albums, *Ruthless By Law* (1992) and *A Lesson To Be Learned* (1994). With partner Black C (Chris Matthew), the duo had signed with Big Beat/Atlantic.
CAUSE: He was shot eight times at close range after a drug deal had gone bad on a street corner near his home in the Hunters Point section of San Francisco.

Muddy Waters

(McKinley Morganfield)
Born April 4, 1915
Died April 30, 1983
A legendary post-war blues legend, Muddy Waters changed the landscape of Chicago blues. Born on a Delta sharecropping farm in Rolling Fork, Mississippi, Waters was sent to live with his maternal grandmother near Clarksdale following the death of his mother in 1918. Building a home-made guitar before buying a Sears model at age 17, Waters idolised masters such as Son House and Robert Johnson. Recorded in 1941 and 1942 by Alan Lomax for the Library of Congress folk music series, the inspired Waters left Mississippi in 1943 to pursue a career in music. Landing in Chicago, Waters was befriended by Big Bill Broonzy who found him a job with Sonny Boy Williamson. After switching from acoustic to electric guitar in 1944, Waters became a fixture in the southside clubs of Chicago. Then in 1947, Waters was invited by his frequent stage partner Sunnyland Slim to a session at Aristocrat Records; after backing Sunnyland Slim on 'Johnson Machine Gun', Waters sang lead on a pair of tracks, 'Little Anna Mae' and 'Gypsy Woman', which were released as his first 78 at Leonard and Phil Chess' label. Although the Chess brothers were unimpressed with Waters' first tracks, he returned the following year to record updated versions of tracks from his Alan Lomax sessions, 'I Be's Troubled' which was revised as 'I Can't Be Satisfied', and a reworked version of the Son House classic 'Walking Blues' as '(I Feel Like) Going Home'. A career-defining hit that bridged old-style Delta blues with modern Chicago, 'I Can't Be Satisfied' was a huge smash. Meanwhile, Waters had formed his own powerhouse stage band that eventually included guitarist Jimmy Rogers, drummer Elgar Edmonds and harmonica player Little Walter; a monumental outfit that was informally known as The Headhunters, the group reshaped and came to define modern Chicago blues. With Aristocrat Records evolving into Chess Records, Waters was aided by producer/songwriter Willie Dixon on a string of groundbreaking hits including 'Rollin' Stone' (1950), 'Louisiana Blues' (1950), 'Long Distance Call' (1951), 'Honey Bee' (1951), 'She Moves Me' (1952), 'I'm Your Hoochie Coochie Man' (1954), 'Mannish Boy' (1955), and 'I Got My Mojo Workin'' (1956). But with blues acts falling from popularity in the US during the Fifties, Waters found fame in Britain. Influencing a host of emerging blues hopefuls, Waters shared the stage with The Yardbirds, Eric Burdon, Eric Clapton and Jimmy Page. He even made an unlikely foray into psychedelic rock on *Electric Mud* (1968). Young American players such as Mike Bloomfield and Paul Butterfield were also emulating Waters, and appeared with their idol on the album, *Fathers And Sons* (1969). Severely injured in a car crash in 1969, Waters was sidelined for three years. In 1971, Waters won his first of six Grammys with the album, *They Call Me Muddy Waters*. It was followed by *The London Muddy Waters* (1972) on which he was joined by a who's who of UK proteges, including Steve Winwood, Georgie Fame and Rory Gallagher. After performing 'Mannish Boy' at The Band's 1976 finale, *The Last Waltz*, Waters worked with Texan bluesman Johnny Winter on retrospective albums, *Hard Again* (1977) and *I'm Ready* (1978), and a subsequent live album, *Muddy Mississippi Waters Live* (1979). Winter also produced Waters' final album, *King Bee* (1981).
Cause: Heart attack. He died in Chicago's Good Samaritan Hospital.
Further Reading: Rooney, Jim. (1991). *Bossmen: Bill Monroe & Muddy Waters*. New York: Da Capo.

Maury Muehleisen

(MAURICE MUEHLEISEN)
Born January 14, 1949
Died September 20, 1973
New Jersey-born guitarist for pop singer-songwriter Jim Croce, Maury Meuhleisen also co-wrote several songs with Croce including 'Salon Saloon'. Also a solo artist, Meuhleisen released the album *Gingerbread* (1972), which featured a guest appearance by Croce.
CAUSE: He died in a plane crash near Natchitoches, Louisiana which killed five others including Jim Croce and Croce's opening act, comedian George Stevens. Hitting a tree, the charted plane went down shortly after take-off. Investigators would later rule that the craft had failed to gain sufficient altitude.
FURTHER READING: Jacobs, Linda. (1976). *Jim Croce: The Feeling Lives On*. St. Paul, MN: EMC.

Karl Mueller

Born July 27, 1962
Died June 25, 2005
Bassist for rock band Soul Asylum, Karl Mueller co-founded the Minneapolis-based group with his roommate, Dan Murphy. Born and raised in suburban Detroit, Mueller played a variety of instruments during his youth before switching to guitar at age 15. Formed in 1981 as a garage-rock outfit called Loud Fast Rules, the group also featured future vocalist, then drummer, Dave Pirner. After adding new drummer Grant Young, the renamed group signed with the small Twin Tone label and released their début album, *Say What You Will, Clarence . . . Karl Sold The Truck* in 1984, produced by Bob Mould of Hüsker Dü. Signing with a major label, Soul Asylum adopted a more polished sound on its two releases for A&M Records, but nearly disbanded due to a lack of commercial success. Following an acoustic tour, the group was signed by Columbia Records and *Grave Dancers Union*, issued in 1992, became a strong seller, yielding the hits 'Somebody To Shove' and the Grammy-winning track 'Runaway Train'. During this time, Mueller continued his formal education and, in 1993, earned a Bachelor's degree in music from Rutgers University. Remaining favourites on the indie scene, the group continued its success with follow-up album *Let Your Dim Light Shine* (1994), which spawned the radio hits 'Promises Broken' and the fatalistic 'Misery'. Although Soul Asylum continued to tour and record, their follow-up releases fared poorly. In 1996, Mueller released the solo album, *Tea Leaves*.
CAUSE: Diagnosed with throat cancer in May 2004, he succumbed to the disease following complications and died at his home in Minneapolis.

Rich Mullins

Born October 21, 1955
Died September 19, 1997
A popular contemporary-Christian gospel songwriter, Rich Mullins recorded nine albums at Reunion Records, his best known compositions coming with 'Awesome God', 'The Jordan Is Waiting', and a song also recorded by Amy Grant, 'Sing Your Praise To The Lord'. His final sessions were posthumously released on the album, *The Jesus Record*.
CAUSE: He died in an automobile crash in rural LaSalle County, Illinois. A passenger, singer-songwriter Mitch McVicker, was severely injured. Both men were thrown from the vehicle.

Gene Mumford

(EUGENE MUMFORD)
Born June 24, 1925
Died May 1977
A gospel and doo-wop based singer, Gene Mumford is best known for his role as the lead singer of Billy Ward & The Dominoes. A native of North Carolina, Mumford was the youngest member of his family's gospel group,

The Mumford Brothers. As he was preparing to join a professional gospel group in 1945, Mumford was jailed. Falsely charged with attempted rape, he was pardoned in 1949 after serving two years. Then after passing through a pair of gospel groups, Mumford landed in The Jubilators (alternatively known as The Selah Singers among other names). But by 1951 the group evolved into The (Five) Larks, a secular, doo-wop ballad group that recorded on Apollo Records from 1951–53; usually featuring Mumford on lead tenor, the group enjoyed hits with the Mumford-penned 'Hopefully Yours' (1951), the beautiful ballad 'My Reverie' (1951), 'Eyesight To The Bland', and 'Little Sidecar'. Returning to gospel music, Mumford joined one of the country's leading groups, The Golden Gate Quartet; but by 1954, he left to form a new version of The Larks, which recorded some much-ignored singles for the new Apollo Records subsidiary, Lloyds. Then following the departure of tenor Jackie Wilson from The Dominoes in 1957, Mumford assumed the lead vocal role in the renamed Billy Ward & The Dominoes. During Mumford's residency, the group veered away from doo-wop in favour of Forties-styled material in the tradition of The Mills Brothers; during this period, the group employed lush orchestral backing on standards such as the Hoagy Carmichael/Mitchell Parish-penned 'Star Dust' and the big-band classic 'Deep Purple'. Mumford would stay with the group until 1959, his last release a cover of Jan & Arnie's 'Jennie Lee'. The Platters' label, Liberty Records, also coaxed Mumford into recording solo material in 1959. Mumford spent the remainder of his career in various incarnations of The Ink Spots and The Jubilee Four.
CAUSE: Unknown. He died in Los Angeles.

Scott Muni

(DONALD ALLEN MUÑOZ)
Born May 10, 1930
Died September 28, 2004
A pioneering deep-voiced deejay who worked at New York City Top 40 powerhouses WMCA and WABC, Scott Muni helped define AOR (Album Oriented Rock) – or "free-form" radio – in the late Sixties. After joining free-form outlet WOR-FM in 1966, he jumped to WNEW-FM, where he was promoted in the Seventies to programme director. After leaving WNEW in 1998, Muni hosted a pair of syndicated radio shows, *Ticket To Ride* and *Scott Muni's World Of Rock*.
CAUSE: Plagued by a host of medical problems, he suffered a stroke in January 2004 and never recovered.

Billy Murcia

Born 1951
Died November 6, 1972
The drummer of the pioneering, New York-based glitter-rock band The New York Dolls, Billy Murcia relocated to the city from his home town of Bogota, Columbia. A high school drop-out, Murcia initially joined guitarists Johnny Thunders and Sylvain Sylvain in the Johnny Thunders-fronted rock group, Actress. With the group evolving into The New York Dolls in 1971, Murcia brought in David Johansen as the new lead vocalist. A simple and straightforward drummer, Murcia was the catalyst behind the group's move to adopt an outrageous persona of make-up and outlandish feminine clothing. With its proto-punk sound, the group became a fixture at the city's counter-culture clubs such as Max's Kansas City. Murcia died on a trip to London with the band before the group recorded. He was replaced in the group by Jerry Nolan.
CAUSE: Although accounts vary, Murcia's death is usually attributed to a fatal reaction between alcohol and various illicit drugs, or subsequent

drowning, while in London for The New York Dolls' first European tour. Murcia had gone to a party with a group of people he had met at London's trendy Speakeasy nightclub. Earlier in the evening, a stand-offish Murcia had stormed off while under the influence of Methaqualone (Quaaludes), leaving his bandmates at their hotel. Though he possessed a strong tolerance for drugs, Murcia passed out from drinking heavily and, according to the coroner's report, a large quantity of drugs. Murcia probably drowned when a female partygoer tried to revive him by pouring cups of coffee down his throat. One conspiracy theory suggests that Murcia was killed when he accidentally stumbled upon a prostitution ring.
FURTHER READING: Antonia, Nina. (1998). *The New York Dolls: Too Much Too Soon*. London: Omnibus.

Alan Murphy

Born November 18, 1953
Died October 19, 1989
Latter guitarist for British synthesizer-based, pop-rock group Level 42, from 1988 until his death, Alan Murphy had replaced Boon Guild. Murphy appeared on several of the group's British hits including 'Heaven In My Hands' and 'Tracie'; he remained with the group until three months before his death, performing at the Prince's Trust concert in Birmingham. Murphy had also worked as a session player for Go West, Mike & The Mechanics, and Kate Bush.
CAUSE: AIDS-related pneumonia. He died at the Westminster Hospital in London.
FURTHER READING: Cowton, Michael. (1989). *Level 42: The Definitive Biography*. London: Sidgwick & Jackson.

Murray The K

(MURRAY KAUFMAN)
Born February 14, 1922
Died February 21, 1982
A catalyst in the rise of rock'n'roll, New York deejay Murray The K is best known for his association with The Beatles. Born in Richmond, Virginia, but raised in The Bronx, New York, the former Murray Kaufman worked as a child dancer in musical films and Broadway shows. After serving in World War II, he worked as an entertainer in the Catskill Mountain resorts, and then played minor league baseball. After landing his first disc jockey position at New York City's WMCA in 1952, he was hired by radio powerhouse WINS in 1958. Starting out in the overnight shift shortly before the station switched to an all rock format, he was soon promoted to the coveted evening slot a year later. Calling his show *The Swinging Soiree*, and now using the on-air moniker Murray "The K", he became famous for his fast-paced, vocal inflections and hyperactive enthusiasm. Shaping US Top 40 radio, he received nationwide exposure in February 1964 when he attached himself to The Beatles at their first US press conference, with George Harrison laconically referring to him as the "fifth Beatle"; Murray The K subsequently stayed by their sides throughout the rest of the trip and can be seen in the Maysles Brother's film documentary of The Beatles visit, *What's Happening: The Beatles In The USA*. The Beatles association continued, including him introducing the group in London at the *NME* Pollwinners' Concert (April 1964) and being a guest announcer at their mammoth Shea Stadium concert in New York (August 1965). Hosting a local television show, *It's What's Happening, Baby*, and opening his own nightclub, he also ran daily Murray The K concert seasons in New York City during the holiday periods, and it was on one of these in March 1967 that English groups The Who and Cream played their first US concerts. Disgusted with the tight playlists of Top 40 radio, Murray clashed with the heads of WINS and quit to join WOR-FM, becoming one of the country's first

deejays to employ a free-form format. A year later, he transferred the format to Toronto's CHUM-FM. Involved in many oldies projects in the Seventies, he hosted the syndicated radio programme *Soundtrack Of The Sixties*.
CAUSE: Cancer. Diagnosed with lymphoma, he fought the disease for 10 years. He died in Los Angeles.
FURTHER READING: Kaufman, Murray. (1966). *Murray The K Tells It Like It Is*. New York: Holt, Rineholt and Winston.

Dee Murray

(DAVID MURRAY OATES)
Born April 3, 1946
Died January 15, 1992
The bassist in Elton John's band for many years, Dee Murray appeared on dozens of hits. Born in Gillingham, England, the blond, athletically built Murray took infrequent piano lessons as a teen but was mostly self-taught. He played the bass with the group Mirage from 1965–68, and went on to become a session player where he met drummer and future Elton John-bandmate Nigel Olsson backing British band Plastic Penny on the hit 'Everything I Am' (1968). Later in the year, Murray and Olsson joined the final, short-lived, incarnation of The Spencer Davis Group, with Murray playing bass and providing backing vocals. Murray and Olsson went their separate ways when Davis split the group in 1969 but were reunited the following year when they joined rising singer-songwriter Elton John on a tour to promote his second album *Elton John*. Murray first played the bass behind John on 1970's *Tumbleweed Connection*, and also provided backing vocals on his early albums. With Elton John enjoying a remarkable chart run, Murray appeared on 'Crocodile Rock', 'Goodbye Yellow Brick Road', 'Don't Let The Sun Go Down On Me', 'Philadelphia Freedom' and more but he and Olsson were fired unexpectedly in April 1975, shortly before the release of *Captain Fantastic And The Brown Dirt Cowboy*. While Olsson attempted a solo career, Murray returned to session work behind acts such as John Prine, Yvonne Elliman, and the duo of England Dan and John Ford Coley. Murray returned to Elton John's band in 1980 on the album *21 At 33*, a project that also marked John's reunion with long-time songwriting partner Bernie Taupin. During this period, Murray and Olsson appeared on hits such as 'Kiss The Bride' and 'Sad Songs (Say So Much)'. Dropped by John in 1984, Murray found session work behind country artists in Nashville.
CAUSE: Murray had been diagnosed with skin cancer eight years before his death. While under treatment, he suffered a massive stroke. He died at Vanderbilt University Medical Center in Memphis.
FURTHER READING: Norman, Philip. (1991). *Elton*. London: Hutchinson.

Don Murray

(DONALD RAYMOND MURRAY)
Born November 8, 1945
Died March 23, 1996
The original drummer for the Sixties folk-rock group The Turtles, Don Murray joined them shortly after graduating from high school. The Turtles evolved out of a surf group called The Nightriders, forming at Westchester High School in suburban Los Angeles. After evolving into The Crossfires, Murray joined as the group's drummer. After winning a battle of the bands at The Revelaire Club, the group was hired as the house band, backing visiting acts such as The Righteous Brothers and Sonny & Cher. After issuing an obscure single, and ready to disband, the group was instead signed by a new label, White Whale Records. Renamed The Turtles, the group garnered immediate fame with their electric version of the Bob Dylan folk song, 'It Ain't Me Babe' (1965). Murray appeared on two more

hits, 'Let Me Be' (1965) and 'You Baby' (1966). He left the group in 1966 and was replaced by John Barbata. Also an artist, Murray worked at Hanna-Barbera from 1979 to 1982. He then joined a revival version of the surf rock band The Surfaris.
CAUSE: He died after surgery, following a short, undisclosed illness.

Juggy Murray

(HENRY MURRAY JONES, JR.)
Born November 24, 1923
Died February 8, 2005
The co-founder of Sue Records, Juggy Murray recorded Ike & Tina Turner, Don Covay, Wilbert Harrison, Ernestine Anderson, Jimmy McGriff, The Ray Bryant Combo, Inez Foxx and Baby Washington. A native of Charleston, South Carolina, Murray left a career in real estate to work in music. Launching the label in 1957, Murray named the company after his mother and daughter. Buying out his partners in 1960, he later sold Sue's master recordings and publishing rights to United Artists, and occasionally issued new material.
CAUSE: Stricken with Parkinson's disease, he died at his home in New York City.

Ruby Murray

(RUBY FLORENCE CAMPBELL MURRAY)
Born March 29, 1935
Died December 17, 1996
A very popular British singer, Belfast native Ruby Murray was a major star in the Fifties. Inspired to be an entertainer after witnessing a minstrel show at age four, she first appeared on Irish television at 12. Leaving school at 14 and passing through a series of menial positions, she was aided by her mother in joining a touring variety show through Northern Ireland. After performing in London at age 16, Murray was hired by BBC producer Richard Afton for a singing role in the television series, *Quite Contrary*. Signed by Columbia Records, she nearly topped the British charts with her second release, 'Heartbeat' (1954). Voted Britain's top female vocalist in a 1955 *Melody Maker* poll, Murray dominated the charts that year with six Top 10 entries including 'Happy Days And Lonely Nights' and her signature piece 'Softly Softly'. With her vulnerable "girl next door" persona, the husky voiced Murray sang in a natural, unadorned manner. Marrying singer Bernie Burgess of The Jones Boys in 1957, Murray begin an extremely rocky 16-year marriage. After returning from her first US tour, she had her final hit in 1959 with 'Goodbye Jimmy, Goodbye'. Although she remained in demand with both television and stage audiences, Murray semi-retired from music to raise a family. Her marriage in tatters, and drinking heavily, Murray became romantically involved with married comedian Frank Carson. After a messy divorce in 1977, Murray battled alcoholism for the rest of her life, and was twice hospitalised after suffering nervous breakdowns. Sporadically performing late in life, she last hit the stage in 1993 at London's Brick Lane Music Hall, her final performance marred by insecurity.
CAUSE: She succumbed to bronchial pneumonia and liver cancer at Torbay Hospital, in Torquay, Devon. Her body had been ravaged by years of hard drinking, and she spent her last eight months in a nursing home. In the UK her name has since become immortalised as Cockney rhyming slang for curry.

Brent Mydland

Born October 21, 1952
Died July 26, 1990
Keyboardist for the perennial hippy band, The Grateful Dead, Brent Mydland was a member of the group in the Eighties. Born in Munich, West Germany, his father an American army

chaplain, Mydland studied piano at age seven. Returning to the US, Mydland was raised in Long Island, and then San Francisco, where he joined a series of high school rock bands. Relocating to Los Angeles in the mid Seventies, he joined the Arista Records group, Silver, and appeared on the group's first album, *Silver* (1976). Mydland's association with The Grateful Dead began when he was hired by group member Bob Weir for a series of solo projects including the album *Heaven Help The Fool.* Consequently, when keyboardist Keith Godchaux was asked to leave The Grateful Dead, Mydland was hired as his replacement. A skilled musician with a strong understanding of electronic equipment, Mydland joined the group at a time when their popularity was skyrocketing. Mydland's first Grateful Dead recording came with the album *Go To Heaven* (1980), which was highlighted by the radio hit 'Alabama Getaway', and the Mydland composition, 'Far From Me'. In the Eighties The Grateful Dead became an American institution as legions of Deadheads made pilgrimages from show to show. Enjoying rare, MTV airplay with *Built To Last* (1989), the album was highlighted by the hit 'Touch Of Grey', and included three Mydland compositions including a song for his two young daughters, 'I Will Take You Home'. The live Grateful Dead album, *Without A Net* (1990) was released a month after Mydland's death. While Bruce Hornsby filled in for several Grateful Dead dates, Mydland was eventually replaced by former Tubes' keyboard player, Vince Welnick.
CAUSE: He was found dead in his home in Lafayette, California (near Oakland), from an overdose of cocaine and morphine, better known as a speedball.
FURTHER READING: Jackson, Blair. (1983). *Grateful Dead: The Music Never Stopped.* New York: Delilah.

James Myers

Born October 26, 1919
Died May 9, 2001
Co-writer of the rock standard 'Rock Around The Clock', James Myers wrote hundreds of songs during his career, many under the pseudonym, Jimmy DeKnight. A former big band drummer, he composed 'Rock Around The Clock' with Max Freedman in 1953. Originally recorded by Sonny Dae & His Nights, the song was recorded by Bill Haley & His Comets in 1954 and re-released in 1955 after the song's inclusion in the film *Blackboard Jungle,* whereupon it became the first number one single of the rock era. Myers would earn an estimated $10 million in royalties from the song.
CAUSE: Leukaemia. He died at a hospice in Fort Myers, near his home in Bonita Springs, Florida.

Donald Myrick

Born 1940
Died July 30, 1993
Jazz-rock saxophonist who played with Bobby Bland, Diana Ross and others, Donald Myrick was a member of Earth Wind & Fire from 1975–82. Then joining The Phoenix Horns, he backed Phil Collins, providing the bluesy sax solo on his hit 'One More Night'.
CAUSE: He was shot and killed in his suburban Los Angeles apartment in Santa Monica by a police officer. Searching for drugs, the police officer had first knocked on the door with a warrant in his hand. Upon entering, police mistook a seven-inch pencil-style butane lighter that Myrick was holding for a gun, and shot him dead. Crack pipes and other drug paraphernalia were found nearby. Myrick's family filed a lawsuit against the police and settled out of court for $400,000 a day before the trial was to begin. Myrick was suffering from leukaemia at the time of his death.

N

Jack Nance

(RICHARD JACKSON NANCE)
Born April 22, 1935
Died April 7, 2000
A music industry veteran, Jack Nance was a childhood friend of Conway Twitty. A native of Newport, Arkansas, Nance attended college before settling in Nashville to pursue a career in music. Drawn to Sun Records, Nance played the drums on the Sonny Burgess-led group The Pacers, appearing on the tracks 'Red Headed Woman' and 'Restless'. Leaving Sun Records, Nance joined Conway Twitty's band for a tour of Canada. After a performance at a lounge in Hamilton, Ontario, Nance called Twitty over and the pair completed a song that Nance had started – Twitty's breakthrough hit, 'It's Only Make Believe', which became an international smash. Leaving Twitty in 1960, Nance toured with Roy Orbison before taking a promotional position with Dick Clark's Caravan of Stars shows. Nance subsequently worked as an artist agent, promoter, and road manager for a bevy of acts including The Moody Blues, Sonny and Cher, Three Dog Night, The Rolling Stones, Elvis Presley, and for several Motown acts including The Temptations.
CAUSE: Lung cancer. He died in Nashville.

Joe Nanini

(OLIVER JOSEPH NANINI)
Born 1955
Died December 4, 2000
An inventive percussionist, Joe Nanini was a member of new-wave group Wall Of Voodoo. Born in Japan into a military family, Nanini received his first drum set at age seven. Settling in California, he played in a series of jazz and punk bands including The Bags. By 1979, Nanini joined new-wave act Wall Of Voodoo. A non-traditional musician, Nanini incorporated his wife's kitchen pots and pans into his drum kit. From their album *Call Of The West*, Wall Of Voodoo scored an early MTV hit with a quirky tune co-written by Nanini, 'Mexican Radio'. Disheartened by lead singer Stan Ridgway's departure from the group in 1983, Nanini soon followed. After working on a Ridgway solo project and briefly joining the alternative country group Lonesome Strangers, Nanini was employed as a session player at Dangerhouse Records.
CAUSE: Suffering a blood clot in his brain, he died at his home in Atlanta.

Syd Nathan

(SYDNEY NATHAN)
Born April 27, 1904
Died March 5, 1968
Crucial to the rise of R&B in the late Forties was the eccentric owner of the Cincinnati-based King-Federal Records. A one-man operation, the label was the brainchild of a registered blind, guitar-chomping asthmatic named Syd Nathan. After his Florida photo developing business went bankrupt, Nathan returned to his home city of Cincinnati in 1939, where he opened a record store, selling used jukebox records he'd purchased for two cents each. Overwhelmed by the demand, Nathan realised the potential profit in manufacturing his own discs and built his own record plant, with the aid of five investors who poured $25,000 into a former ice warehouse. An extremely frugal entrepreneur, Nathan refused to outsource any of the work involved in making a record, except for the inner LP sleeves. In 1946, King split into two divisions; while the King label continued its output of "hillbilly" records, the new Queen label was launched to issue jazz and "race" records, beginning with R&B shouter Bull Moose Jackson. By

1947, Nathan supplemented the King-Queen portfolio by purchasing master discs from competitors and expanding into the exploding gospel market with acts such as The Wings Over Jordan Choir. Merging the Queen subsidiary back into King Records, the label achieved R&B chart action with pioneering hits like Wynonie Harris' 'Good Rockin' Tonight'. Capitalising on the booming R&B market, Nathan bought out several competitors, including DeLuxe, Miracle, Bethlehem, Rockin' and Glory Records and, overwhelmed by the success of King's R&B roster, launched another subsidiary, Federal Records, headed by producer Ralph Bass. Bass' first success at Federal came with the bawdy, much-banned single, 'Sixty Minute Man' by The Dominoes, the best-selling R&B hit of 1951. Besides Bass, Nathan surrounded himself with a host of talented managers: Henry Stone, Seymour Stein, and a pioneering black record executive, Henry Glover. By the early Fifties, the King-Federal roster included The Dominoes, Hank Ballard & The Midnighters, Charles Brown, Freddy King, Earl Bostic, Little Willie John, Roy Brown and The "5" Royales. In 1956, King achieved crossover success with 'Please, Please, Please', the début release by newcomer James Brown. Operating a massive distribution network, Nathan managed to thrive at a time when other independent labels were selling out to the majors but, when accused in 1960 of making payola payments to deejays, Nathan and King Records never recovered. Except for James Brown who kept the label afloat, King had little success in the Sixties and, out of economic necessity, Nathan was forced in 1967 to merge King with Starday Records. After Nathan's death the following year, King was sold to Starday, which shut down the Cincinnati studio in 1970.

CAUSE: In poor health for several years, he succumbed to heart disease compounded by pneumonia. He died in Miami.

Bobby Neal

Born July 19, 1947
Died December 31, 1985

Missouri-reared member of Ricky Nelson's back-up group, The Stone Canyon Band, Bobby Neal toured with Nelson beginning in the late Seventies.

CAUSE: He died in an on-board fire in the DC-3 plane, near Dekalb, Texas, en route from Guttersville, Alabama, to Dallas for half-time festivities at the Cotton Bowl. Neal, Nelson, and all of the others in the cabin section of the craft died from smoke inhalation. Both pilots survived.

Joe Negronie

Born September 7, 1940
Died September 5, 1978

The baritone vocalist of the Fifties pop/doo-wop group, Frankie Lymon & The Teenagers, Puerto Rican-born Joe Negronie moved to New York City with his family at a young age. There Negronie and Puerto Rican friend Herman Santiago were joined by two black classmates from Edward W. Stitt Junior High, Sherman Garnes and Jimmy Merchant, in forming a vocal group, The Premiers. Soon after they added young Frankie Lymon, The Premiers/Ermines were discovered by former Valentines' lead singer turned producer Richard Barrett. Signed to George Goldner's Gee Records in late 1955, the group recorded their self-penned composition, 'Why Do Birds Sing So Gay?' But at Barrett's insistence, Frankie Lymon replaced Herman Santiago as lead singer, the group was renamed The Teenagers, and the song was retitled 'Why Do Fools Fall In Love?' A multi-million seller, the song catapulted the five teens to massive fame. Dropping out of school, Negronie and the rest of the group hit the road for a succession of tours. The Teenagers enjoyed a brief

hit run with 'I Want You To Be My Girl' (1956), 'I Promise To Remember' (1956), and from the Alan Freed film *Rock Rock Rock*, 'I'm Not A Juvenile Delinquent' (1956). Although promised a trust fund by their record company, each member would receive only $1,000 at age 21. With Lymon convinced to leave the group for a solo career, The Teenagers struggled along with a new lead singer, Bill Lobrano. Signing away all future rights to their music in exchange for the use of The Teenagers name, the group recorded its final single in 1960.
CAUSE: Brain aneurysm.

Fred Neil

Born March 16, 1936
Died July 7, 2001
A prolific singer-songwriter, folk-blues artist Fred Neil was an institution in the folk music houses of Greenwich Village during the Sixties. The son of a jukebox industry executive, Neil began playing guitar in his teens and left home to join a gospel group. After releasing several unsuccessful solo singles in the late Fifties, he was hired as a staff writer at Southern Music; among his compositions during this period were the often recorded 'Come Back Home Baby' and the 1961 Roy Orbison hit 'Candy Man'. Continuing to pursue a solo career, Neil became a regular at the folk clubs and coffee houses of Greenwich Village and was occasionally joined on stage by Bob Dylan. Signed by Elektra, Neil teamed with Miami-based folkie Vince Martin on the Paul Rothchild-produced album, *Tear Down The Walls*, which featured guest musicians Felix Pappalardi and John Sebastian and the popular Neil composition 'The Other Side Of This Life', later covered by Sebastian's group, The Lovin' Spoonful, and Jefferson Airplane. The song also appeared on Neil's first solo album, the moody and bluesy *Bleecker & MacDougal*, released by Elektra Records in 1965. Aided by his manager Herb Cohen, Neil then signed with Capitol Records and issued three albums for the label that continued to earn critical, but not commercial success. One of the tracks from his first Capitol album, 'Everybody's Talkin'', became a hit for Harry Nilsson in 1969 after its inclusion in the Dustin Hoffman film *Midnight Cowboy*, while 'The Dolphins' was covered by fellow cult folkie Tim Buckley. By the mid Seventies, Neil became a semi-recluse and rarely performed.
CAUSE: Natural causes. He died in Key West, Florida.

Alex Nelson

(ALEXANDER D. NELSON)
Born February 24, 1963
Died May 17, 2004
A guitarist for Los Angeles-based, theatrical heavy-metal band Lizzy Borden, Alex Nelson replaced Tony Matuzak in 1986. Formed in the early Eighties, the band was a popular concert draw, particularly on the West Coast, but managed to sell few records. Nelson first appeared on the album *The Murderess Metal Roadshow*. After a hiatus lasting for most of the Nineties, Lizzy Borden regrouped in 2000 and released *Deal With The Devil*.
CAUSE: He died in a daytime, head-on collision in Palm Springs, which involved a total of three cars. Driving his Ford Explorer left of centre into oncoming traffic, he sideswiped a pick-up truck before hitting another vehicle head on.

Doug Nelson

(DOUGLAS D. NELSON)
Born November 12, 1953
Died November 7, 2000
A member of blues prodigy Jonny Lang's backing band, bass player Doug Nelson was hired in 1997. Hailing from Nebraska, Nelson had previously toured with Olivia Newton-John and had engineered tracks on a Frank Sinatra album.

CAUSE: He was struck by a passing pick-up truck while walking home from a restaurant on Highway 65 near his home in McGregor, Minnesota.

George Nelson

Born c. 1926
Died 1959

Baritone vocalist of the early doo-wop group The Orioles, the shy and diminutive George Nelson began performing in the mid Forties. After a talent show in 1947, winner Sonny Til teamed with several of the evening's other contestants, including Nelson, to form a group called The Vibranairs. A jazz aficionado who was influenced by Louis Armstrong, Nelson would occasionally share the lead vocal duties. Fronted by Til, and soon managed by songwriter Deborah Chessler, the group auditioned on *Arthur Godrey's Talent Scout* radio programme in 1948. Impressing Godrey, the group landed a spot on Godrey's more popular daytime show; there they met record label owner Jerry Blain who renamed the group The Orioles. Beginning with the Chessler composition 'It's Too Soon To Know' (1948), The Orioles enjoyed a string of pioneering doo-wop hits including '(It's Gonna Be A) Lonely Christmas' (1948), and 'Tell Me So' (1949). Tragedy struck the group in 1950 when bandmate Tommy Gaither was killed in a serious auto accident just outside Baltimore and Nelson himself was seriously injured. Developing a drinking problem, Nelson soon lost interest in performing and began missing rehearsals; he was occasionally replaced on stage by their new guitarist Ralph Williams. After recording the touching gospel number 'Crying In The Chapel' in 1953, Nelson left the group; he was replaced by Gregory Carrol, formerly of The Four Buddies. With The Orioles disbanding in 1954, Sonny Til would occasionally form new versions of the group.
CAUSE: He died from an asthma attack.

Mercury Nelson

(CHARLES RICHARD NELSON)
Born December 19, 1964
Died March 9, 1995

The lead singer of the doo-wop styled rap quartet The Force MDs, Mercury Nelson rooted his sound in old-style vocal harmony. Launched on the street corners of Staten Island, New York in 1982 as an a cappella group called The LDs, the group added Nelson two years later. Soon adding a turntable-artist and adopting a harder street-savvy sound, the group was renamed Dr. Rock & The MCs. Discovered by New York City DJ Mr. Magic, the renamed Force MDs signed with Tommy Boy Records. After charting with the Mr. Magic co-produced single 'Let Me Love You', and then reaching the R&B Top 10 with 'Tears', The Force MDs landed their first crossover pop entry with the Jimmy Jam/Terry Lewis production 'Tender Love'; the group had performed the latter song in the film *Krush Groove*. Remaining an R&B favourite, The Force MDs returned to the charts with 'Love Is A House' and 'Touch And Go', and in 1987 toured with Madonna. The group released its third album in 1990, *Step To Me*.
CAUSE: He died of a heart attack in Staten Island, New York.

Nate Nelson

(NATHANIEL NELSON)
Born April 10, 1932
Died June 2, 1984

The tenor vocalist in two legendary R&B vocal groups, The Flamingos and The Platters, Nate Nelson was trained on the gospel music of his Baptist church. After completing a navy stint in the early Fifties, Nelson formed a Chicago-based vocal group The Velvetones (not the more famous outfit). But after meeting the struggling, three-year-old Flamingos at Martin's Corner nightclub in 1953, Nelson joined the group on a part-time basis as the replacement for Sollie

McElroy who was eased out of the line-up. Recording in 1955 at the Chicago-based Parrot label, Nelson shared lead vocal duties with Johnny Carter on the minor hit 'I'm Yours'. Now at the Chess subsidiary Checker Records, Nelson assumed the lead vocal duties as the blues and harmony-based ballad group enjoyed a string of hits with 'When' (1955), 'Please Come Back Home' (1955), and a Nelson composition which was covered by Pat Boone 'I'll Be Home' (1956). The Flamingos disbanded after recording the beautiful ballad 'The Vow' (1956). After briefly recording as a solo act at Chess, Nelson relocated to Pittsburgh in 1957; there he formed a new Flamingos line-up and released several substandard releases at Decca Records. Relocating to New York City and signing with George Goldner's End Records, Nelson and The Flamingos enjoyed renewed fame with 'Lovers Never Say Goodnight', the timeless ballad 'I Only Have Eyes For You' (1959), and an uncharacteristic uptempo track, the Sam Cooke-penned 'Nobody Loves Me Like You' (1960). Leaving The Flamingos in 1962, Nelson emerged in the Herb Reed-led Platters; signed to Musicor Records in 1966, The Platters scored a pair of hits with the pop-soul flavoured 'I Love You A Thousand Times' and 'With This Ring' (1967); an intermittent member of the group, Reed quit for good in 1982.
CAUSE: Heart disease. Unable to locate a donor heart, he died at Brigham and Women's Hospital in Boston.

Phyllis Nelson

Born 1951
Died 1998
A one-hit wonder, Philadelphia-based R&B singer Phyllis Nelson topped the UK charts in 1985 with 'Move Closer'. The song returned to the charts in 1994 after its inclusion in a television commercial. Working in the music industry since the early Seventies, Nelson was a member of various acts and had been a member of Major Harris' backing vocal group Brown Sugar. Nelson's son Marc Nelson was an early member of Boys II Men but quit to pursue a solo career.
CAUSE: Breast cancer.

Rick Nelson

(ERIC HILLIARD NELSON)
Born May 8, 1940
Died December 31, 1985
Television actor turned teenage heart-throb, "Ricky" Nelson was reared in a showbiz family. The son of bandleader Ozzie Nelson and singer Harriet Hilliard, Ricky Nelson joined his parents' radio sitcom *The Adventures Of Ozzie & Harriet* in 1949. Following the success of a feature-film *Here Comes The Nelsons*, the Nelson clan transferred their show to television in October 1952 (the radio version of the show continued for a few years). In an attempt to impress his girlfriend, in 1957 the boyish Ricky Nelson sang Fats Domino's 'I'm Walking' on the programme. With fans creating a demand for a single, Nelson landed a surprise million-selling, US Top 10 hit. A talented multi-instrumentalist, Nelson surrounded himself with a top quality band that included 16-year-old guitar virtuoso James Burton. Aided by weekly television exposure, Nelson scored three dozen hits including 'Stood Up' (1957), the Sharon Sheeley-penned 'Poor Little Fool' (1958), 'Nobody Else But You' (1959), 'It's Late' (1959), and the double-sided entry 'Travelin' Man'/'Hello Mary Lou' (1961), the latter penned by Gene Pitney. Shortening his name to the more mature sounding Rick Nelson in 1961, he let his crew-cut grow out and two years later signed with Decca Records in a lucrative deal that was negotiated by his lawyer father. His singing career was stalled by the British Invasion, however, and Nelson managed few hits at the label. Turning to the big screen,

Nelson starred in several films, including the western *Rio Bravo, The Wackiest Ship In The Army*, and *Love And Kisses*. Now married, Nelson was joined on the cast of *Ozzie & Harriet* in the mid Sixties by his real-life wife Kristin Harmon (sister of actor Mark Harmon), but after a remarkable 14-year run, the show was cancelled in September 1966. In an attempt to rekindle his music career, Nelson turned to country and folk music. His 1968 album, *Another Side Of Rick* was highlighted by three Tim Hardin compositions. Forming The Stone Canyon Band, Nelson returned to the charts with the Bob Dylan song 'She Belongs To Me'. Now sporting long hair, Nelson was heckled at a rock revival show at New York's Madison Square Garden in the autumn of 1971 when he tried to perform new material for a crowd that was expecting to hear his old hits. Nelson chronicled the event in his final pop hit 'Garden Party' (1972). After parting with The Stone Canyon Band and undergoing a painful divorce, Nelson briefly flirted with jazz in the late Seventies. Nelson later returned to acting, appearing in several TV series and starring in the 1983 television film, *High School U.S.A.*, in which his mother portrayed a secretary. Having formed a new line-up of The Stone Canyon Band, Nelson enjoyed renewed popularity on the oldies circuit. Rick Nelson's daughter, Tracy, became a television actress (*Father Dowling Mysteries*), and his twin sons Matthew and Gunner formed a hard rock duo called Nelson.
CAUSE: He died from smoke inhalation as the result of an on-board aeroplane fire near DeKalb, Texas. Six others died including his fiancee Helen Blair (27), soundman Clark Russell, and the members of his back-up group The Stone Canyon Band, Andy Chapin (20), Rick Intveld (22), Bobby Neal (38), and Patrick Woodward (35). Both pilots survived. It was rumoured that the fire was caused by the freebasing of cocaine gone awry but investigators found no drugs or drug paraphernalia on board, and blamed the fire on a faulty gasoline heater. Nelson had purchased the DC-3 in May 1985 from Jerry Lee Lewis, and the craft had been forced to make two emergency landings in the previous six months. After almost hitting a farm house and then shearing off the top of a wooden utility pole, the burning plane landed in a field. Nelson and his band were en route from Guttersville, Alabama, to Dallas for the half-time festivities at the Cotton Bowl.
FURTHER READING: Basche, Philip. (1992). *Teenage Idol, Travelin' Man: The Complete Biography Of Rick Nelson*. New York: Hyperion.

Walter "Papoose" Nelson

Born c. 1930
Died February 28, 1962
Guitarist on many of Fats Domino's hits, Walter "Papoose" Nelson joined the group in 1955 beginning with 'Ain't That A Shame', and continuing with 'Blueberry Hill' and 'Blue Monday'. Nelson also worked with Clarence "Frogman" Henry and Professor Longhair.
CAUSE: He died of a drug overdose in a New York City hotel room.

Nervous Norvus

(JAMES DRAKE)
Born March 24, 1912
Died May 1968
Novelty-styled Fifties pop-rock singer whose biggest hit came with 'Transfusion' (1956), Nervous Norvus had previously recorded under his real name. A much banned hit, 'Transfusion' had been recorded originally by The Four Jokers. A former truck driver, he followed up with another novelty hit 'Ape Call'. After his brief career subsided, he returned to driving a truck and occasional radio work.
CAUSE: Unknown.

Mickey Newbury

(Milton S. Newbury, Jr.)
Born May 19, 1940
Died September 29, 2002
A singer-songwriter, Mickey Newbury was successful with several of his compositions in the Sixties. Breaking into music at age 15 as a member of an R&B group, Joe D'Ambra & The Embers, Newbury recorded a single at Mercury Records in 1960. After serving in the Air Force, Newbury moved to Nashville in 1963 and signed as a songwriter to Acuff-Rose in 1964 and, over the years achieved hits in various genres including: 'Just Dropped In (To See What Condition My Condition Was In)' (Kenny Rogers & The First Edition), 'Here Comes The Rain, Baby' (Eddie Arnold), 'Time Is A Thief' (Solomon Burke) and 'Sweet Memories' (Andy Williams). Recording as a solo act beginning in 1968, he scored his only pop hit in 1971 with 'An American Trilogy', a song which would become a staple at Elvis Presley concerts.
Cause: Emphysema. He died at his home in Vida, Oregon.

Anthony Newley

(George Anthony Newley)
Born September 24, 1931
Died April 14, 1999
A consummate entertainer, Anthony Newley had great success as an actor, playwright, lyricist, and crooner. Born in East London, he dropped out of school at 14. Drawn to acting while working as an office boy, he gained fame with his masterful role as the cockney-accented Artful Dodger in Dean Lean's 1948 film version of *Oliver Twist*. Portraying an Elvis Presley-like rock star who is drafted in the film *Idle On Parade* (1959), Newley landed a surprise hit with 'I've Waited So Long' (1959). Signed to Decca Records, Newley scored several Top 10 British hits including, 'Why' (1960), 'Do You Mind' (1960), and 'Strawberry Fair' (1960). Teaming with composer Leslie Bricusse, Newley co-wrote and starred in the stage musical *Stop The World – I Want To Get Off*, which earned a Grammy for 'What Kind Of Fool Am I'; the pair subsequently composed the James Bond theme 'Goldfinger', a hit for Shirley Bassey. But Newley's most endearing role came in the 1967 film musical, *Doctor Dolittle*; he also composed the score and appeared in the film *Willy Wonka And The Chocolate Factory* (1971) which spawned the Sammy Davis, Jr. hit 'Candy Man'. Relocating to the US in the Seventies, he was a leading cabaret entertainer in Las Vegas where he was allegedly presented with a Jaguar by the local Mafiosi who were delighted by the number of punters he drew in. Thrice married, Newley joined former wife Joan Collins in 1991 on the BBC television series, *Tonight At Eight-Thirty*. David Bowie has gone on record as saying that Newley's singing style was a strong influence on his early recordings.
Cause: Diagnosed with renal cancer in 1985, he had a kidney removed. After several years of remission, he succumbed to the disease at his home in Jensen Beach, Florida.

Richard Nickens

Born 1936
Died August 3, 1991
Bass singer of the Fifties Chicago-based, doo-wop group The El Dorados, Richard Nickens appeared on the group's hit 'At My Front Door' (1955). Nickens left the group in 1955 to join the army.
Cause: Cancer. He was diagnosed with the disease in 1988.

Nico

(Kristina Pavloski)
Born October 16, 1938
Died July 18, 1988
A model, actress and briefly the singer with the pioneering art-rockers The Velvet Underground, Nico was raised

in the turmoil of post-World War II West Germany. Embracing the arts, Nico landed a bit part in the 1961 Fellini film *La Dolce Vita*, and at 14 worked as a fashion model in London and Paris before settling in New York. When avant-garde artist Andy Warhol became the manager/producer of The Velvet Underground, he placed Nico at the front of the group as the co-lead vocalist. Though not fully accepted by the other members of the band, the mysterious Nico was visually stunning with her Marlene Dietrich-like features and German-accent, and she quickly earned a reputation as a *femme fatale*. After playing at various Greenwich Village clubs and galleries and appearing in a series of Warhol-staged performance art events, VU signed with Verve Records in 1966. The group sold few copies of their début effort *The Velvet Underground And Nico* (1967), a controversial record that was ignored by radio, not least because of its drug related tracks 'Heroin' and 'Waiting For The Man', both sung by Lou Reed, and suggestive social comment like 'Femme Fatale' and 'All Tomorrow's Parties', both sung by Nico. With Warhol sidelined by self-appointed VU leader Reed, Nico was dismissed from the group in 1968. Playing an Indian harmonium, and embracing dark, metaphysical poetry, Nico subsequently released a series of commercially unsuccessful solo records, beginning with an album of cover songs *Chelsea Girls*, which included compositions by Reed, Bob Dylan, Tim Hardin and a young Jackson Browne. A subsequent album, *Marble Index* (1969), was produced by her longtime collaborator, former VU member John Cale. Remaining in the rock media limelight during this period, Nico was romantically linked with Iggy Pop, Jim Morrison, Leonard Cohen and Jackson Browne. Returning to France in 1972, Nico made her first appearance in a Philippe Garrel-directed film *The Inner Scar*. After briefly reuniting with VU for a 1974 Paris concert, she teamed with Cale on the album *The End*, the project featuring guest players Phil Manzanera and Brian Eno, then of Roxy Music. Relocating to Manchester, England, in 1979, Nico became addicted to heroin and for many years lived in reduced circumstances in the Prestwich area of the city where she was often seen riding around on a bicycle. Her regular companion during this time was the poet John Cooper Clarke. Again teaming with Cale, Nico fronted a group called The Faction for the 1985 album, *Camera Obscura*. She toured in support of the project, and subsequently released two live albums. Nico had finally beaten her longtime chemical addiction shortly before her death.

CAUSE: Thrown from her bicycle, she suffered a cerebral haemorrhage. She was bicycling on the Mediterranean island of Ibiza.

FURTHER READING: Young, James. (1994). *Nico: The Last Bohemian: Songs They Never Play On The Radio*. London: Arrow.

Robert Nighthawk

(ROBERT LEE MCCOLLUM)
Born November 30, 1909
Died November 5, 1967

A Delta-influenced, slide-blues guitarist, Robert Nighthawk released his finest work beginning in the late Forties on Aristocrat/Chess and United Records. Self taught on the harmonica as a child, he was taught to play the guitar by his cousin Houston Stackhouse. After joining Stackhouse on the gin-joint circuit, Nighthawk relocated to St. Louis in the mid Thirties. Quick to pull up sticks, Nighthawk preferred life on the road. First recording in 1937 under the name Robert McCoy, Nighthawk gained a following via a series of Southern radio shows. Aided by Muddy Waters in signing with Aristocrat Records in 1948, Nighthawk enjoyed success with

the Tampa Red compositions, 'Anna Lee Blues' and 'Sweet Black Angel'; at United, Nighthawk recorded the masterful 'Kansas City Blues' and 'Crying Won't Help You'. By the mid Sixties, Nighthawk's talented studio band featured Buddy Guy and Walter "Shakey" Horton.
CAUSE: Natural causes. Suffering from ill health, he retired from music and moved back to his hometown of Helena, Mississippi.

Harry Nilsson

(HARRY EDWARD NELSON, III)
Born June 15, 1941
Died January 15, 1994
A talented singer and songwriter, Harry Nilsson was best known for his hit recording of 'Without You', a song he didn't write, and for his exploits with his friend John Lennon. Born in Brooklyn, New York, Harry "Nelson" moved to Los Angeles at age 10 with his divorced mother, a part-time songwriter. After returning to New York City, the very shy Nilsson dropped out of high school at 15. Hitch-hiking back to California a few months later, he worked at a movie theatre and then at First National Bank. During this period, he began writing commercial jingles, and recorded under a series of monikers including Bo Pete, Foto-Fi-Four and, with Ron Story, The Ric-A-Shays; he also sold three compositions to Phil Spector, two of which were recorded by The Ronettes. Reluctantly leaving his lucrative banking position in 1967, he signed with RCA Records. He adopted the Swedish spelling of his surname, and for most of his career was known only as Nilsson. With his impassioned, sad voice, and quirky, folk-like compositions, Nilsson created a fan base with his début release, the Rick Jarrard-produced *Pandemonium Shadow Show*. Breaking through with his follow-up album *Aerial Ballet* (1968), Nilsson recorded a lilting cover of Fred Neil's 'Everybody's Talkin'' which, although not a hit when first released, was featured in the Academy Award-winning film *Midnight Cowboy*, after which it hit the charts and earned Nilsson a Grammy. Another track, the Nilsson-penned 'One' would later be covered by Three Dog Night. After composing the music for the 1968 film *Skidoo*, Nilsson released Harry (1969), which included 'Puppy Song', later a hit for David Cassidy. The next album, *Nilsson Sings Newman* (1970) was a fulsome tribute to songwriter Randy Newman. It was followed by the soundtrack of the film, *The Point* (1970). A perfectionist who rarely performed live, Nilsson released his best selling album in 1972 with *Nilsson Schmilsson*, the project highlighted by the chart-topping, Grammy-winning hit 'Without You' (written by Pete Ham and Tommy Evans of Badfinger), 'Jump Into The Fire' and the novelty tune 'Coconut'. A second 1972 release, *Son Of Schmilsson*, also fared well, spawning the pop hit 'Spaceman', and the following year he recorded an album of standard ballads, *A Little Touch Of Schmilsson In The Night*, which was produced by former Beatles publicist Derek Taylor and on which he was backed by a full orchestra. By this time Nilsson had become something of a party animal and friend of the rock elite whose rowdy behaviour was chronicled in the press. He made no secret of his admiration for The Beatles, having earlier recorded a montage of Beatles songs, and he palled around with Ringo Starr, working on the film score of *Son Of Dracula* (1974). He also befriended John Lennon during his separation from wife Yoko Ono, and was involved in various well-publicised drunken episodes with the former Beatle. After providing backing vocals on Lennon's 1974 album *Walls And Bridges*, Nilsson persuaded Lennon to produce his album *Pussycats*. His popularity fading, Nilsson last hit the charts in 1978 with the compilation, *Greatest Hits*.

Switching to Mercury Records in 1980, he released his first album as "Harry" Nilsson, *Flash Harry*. Then, after composing the score for the film Popeye (1981), Nilsson wrote the music for the children's television programme, *Ziggy's Gift*. Appalled by the death of Lennon at the hands of a gun-toting lunatic, Nilsson spoke out in favour of gun control, always a lost cause in American politics. Despite his reputation, Nilsson's early experience in banking had turned him into a shrewd businessman. He managed himself, negotiated his own very lucrative record contracts and invested his money wisely, buying property in London, New York and Los Angeles, and becoming involved in a successful film distribution company. Spending the Eighties out of the limelight and away from the music industry, Nilsson returned to the studio shortly before his death, finishing an album's worth of material. Nilsson enjoyed renewed popularity in 1998 when four of his compositions were included on the soundtrack album of *You've Got Mail.*
CAUSE: Heart disease. A prodigious drinker who often carried a bottle around with him, he suffered a massive heart attack in February, 1993, and never fully recovered. He died at his home in Agoura Hills, California.

Walter D. Nims

Born September 11, 1943
Died March 31, 2000
A songwriter and guitarist, Walter Nims broke into music as a member of Tom King & The Starfires, the house band for the Cleveland-based, syndicated pop music programme, *Big Five Show* (later renamed *Upbeat*). Nims subsequently joined a latter version of The Outsiders, which by 1968 had spawned another group, Climax; Nims penned the group's romantic ballad, 'Precious And Few' (1972). Another Climax track, 'Rock And Roll Heaven', was later reworked for a hit by The Righteous Brothers. Stricken from poor health, Nims left the Midwest for The West Coast, and continued to write music.
CAUSE: Suffering complications from a stroke, he died at his home in Agoura, California.

Mana "China" Nishiura

Born October 11, 1971
Died November 4, 2005
The drummer of Japanese rock band Shonen Knife, Mana "China" Nishiura was a touring member from 2001 to 2004 and was also a member of the Japanese psychedelic-rock act DMBQ.
CAUSE: While travelling with a tour manager and fellow members of DMBQ on the New Jersey turnpike en route to a gig in Brooklyn, the group's van was struck by a car driven by 22-year-old Sara Jacobi. As the van rolled over several times, Nishiura was ejected and died instantly. While the other passengers in the van suffered moderate to serious injuries, Jacobi was unhurt.

Jack Nitzsche

(BERNARD ALFRED NITZSCHE)
Born April 22, 1937
Died August 25, 2000
A prolific producer and songwriter, Jack Nitzsche had a long and varied career. Born in Chicago but raised in Michigan, Nitzsche taught himself music through a mail correspondence course, and played saxophone in a local band during his teens. Moving to Los Angeles in 1955, he continued his formal musical training and was eventually hired by Sonny Bono, then an A&R executive at Specialty Records. After paying his dues as a studio musician, Nitzsche was hired by producer Phil Spector in 1962, and formulated the complex "Wall Of Sound" arrangements for many of Spector's classics including 'He's A Rebel', 'Be My Baby', 'Baby, I Love You', and later, 'River Deep, Mountain High'. Occasionally working with The Rolling Stones, Nitzsche

played piano on such hits as '(I Can't Get No) Satisfaction', 'Paint It, Black' and 'Let's Spend The Night Together' and harpsichord/percussion on the 1965 B-side 'Play With Fire'. Nitzsche managed some success as a solo artist in 1963 with a minor hit, the classic instrumental 'The Lonely Surfer', lifted from his solo album for Reprise Records. As a songwriter, Nitzsche joined Sonny Bono in composing the pop standard 'Needles And Pins' for Nitzsche's then-girlfriend Jackie DeShannon but which became a universal hit for The Searchers in 1964. Beginning in the mid-Sixties, Nitzsche produced a wide variety of pop, rock and folk artists, including Tim Buckley, Lesley Gore, Bobby Darin, Buffalo Springfield and, frequently, Neil Young. Nitzsche's later production credits include John Hiatt, Rick Nelson, The Neville Brothers, Michelle Phillips and alternative/punk artists The Germs, Mink DeVille and Graham Parker. Focusing on scoring film music for the last two decades of his career, Nitzsche worked on dozens of projects including *The Exorcist*, *One Flew Over The Cuckoo's Nest*, and *Mermaids*. He also earned two Academy Award nominations for *An Officer And A Gentleman*. Nitzsche was supposedly a descendant of German philosopher Friedrich Nietzsche.
CAUSE: He suffered a heart attack brought on by a recurring bronchial infection. He died at Queen of Angels Hospital in Hollywood, California.

Lynne Nixon

Born 1939
Died January 2001
A member of Fifties doo-wop quartet The Aquatones, soprano Lynne Nixon provided the lovely vocals on the Long Island-based group's only hit 'You'. Initially hired as a backing vocalist in 1957, she was quickly promoted to the lead spot. Retiring from music in 1962, she joined her husband in operating a restaurant in New York City. Nixon did not join a revived version of the group in 1998.
CAUSE: Cancer.

Jerry Nolan

Born May 7, 1945
Died January 14, 1992
The drummer of the proto-glam, pre-punk band The New York Dolls, Brooklyn-born Jerry Nolan enjoyed much fame but little commercial success. Raised in a military family, Nolan was frequently uprooted during his childhood; while his father was stationed in Hawaii, 10-year-old Nolan was taught to play drums by a young black serviceman. First joining a rock band while living in Oklahoma, Nolan later settled in New York City, alternating his time between membership in a gang and drumming. While backing cross-dressing musical artist Wayne County, Nolan occasionally shared the bill with another gender-bending act, The New York Dolls, and when original Dolls drummer Billy Murcia died in 1972, Nolan was brought into the David Johansen-fronted band. Becoming a fixture at venues like The Mercer Arts Center and Max's Kansas City, the Dolls were signed by Mercury Records, though the company was hardly sympathetic to their ambitions or style. Recording two critically acclaimed proto-punk albums the Todd Rundgren-produced *New York Dolls* (1973) and the George "Shadow" Morton-produced *Too Much Too Soon* (1974) the group landed only sporadic airplay with influential singles such as 'Personality Crisis', 'Trash', 'Looking For A Kiss' and their only real hit, a cover of The Cadets' novelty number, 'Stranded In The Jungle'. Their relationship with Mercury deteriorated, not least because of their reckless behaviour and habitual drunkenness. Much loved by rock critics who sensed in them a refreshingly liberating attitude

that challenged the increasingly well mannered AOR rock favoured by radio stations and record companies, the Dolls earned a justified reputation as profligate delinquents. In truth, they were about two years ahead of their time, as the inexorable rise of the anarchic punk movement would soon demonstrate. Dropped by Mercury and subsequently managed by clothes shop owner Malcolm McLaren, The Dolls traded their lipstick and glam clothing for a shocking, Red Chinese motif. But with McLaren unable to salvage the group's career, Nolan and Johnny Thunders left and teamed with bass player Richard Hell to form The Heartbreakers (not Tom Petty's group). Popular in Britain, The Heartbreakers often shared bills with The Clash and the McLaren-managed Sex Pistols. (The Dolls were an immense influence on McLaren's stewardship of the Pistols.) Recorded for Track Records, The Heartbreakers' 1977 album *L.A.M.F.* was highlighted by 'Born To Loose' and the drug-themed 'Chinese Rocks'. In late 1978, Nolan formed his own group with ex-Doll Arthur Kane, the poorly received Idols, who sometimes backed Sid Vicious after the break-up of The Sex Pistols. Nolan briefly headed a Swedish-based group in 1982, The Tenerrifa Cowboys. Frequent collaborators, Nolan and Thunders were planning to work together again in early 1991. Like his friend Johnny Thunders who would also die young, Nolan was a heroin addict for much of his adult life.
CAUSE: Nolan died after long-term treatment for bacterial meningitis and pneumonia. Suffering a stroke, he passed away while in a coma, thus becoming the third member of The New York Dolls, after Billy Murcia and Thunders, to die prematurely.
FURTHER READING: Antonia, Nina. (1998). *The New York Dolls: Too Much Too Soon*. London: Omnibus.

Larry "Big Twist" Nolan

Born 1938
Died March 14, 1990
Leader of the modern R&B group, Big Twist & The Mellow Fellows, the portly Larry "Big Twist" Nolan earned his nickname from his habit of dancing the twist on stage. A native of Terre Haute, Indiana, Nolan sang in his church choir before becoming a rock drummer. Nolan had joined the first line-up of The Mellow Fellows in the mid Fifties as a drummer and vocalist; a successful midwest bar band, the outfit was formed by two brothers. Teaming with two students at Southern Illinois University in 1970, Nolan formed a new version of The Mellow Fellows. Although managing little airplay, the constantly touring group recorded for Flying Fish and Alligator Records, and were popular on national blues circuits with danceable material such as '300 Pounds Of Heavenly Joy', 'Too Much Barbeque', 'Steamroller Blues' and 'The Sweet Sound Of Rhythm & Blues'. Not a blues purist group, the Chicago-styled Mellow Fellows combined blues with soul. Nolan's group also backed James Brown, Big Joe Turner and others. With Nolan's health failing due to kidney problems, Martin Albritton would share some of the vocal duties.
CAUSE: Heart failure. Suffering with severe kidney problems, Nolan had been on dialysis since 1988. He died at his home in Broadview, Illinois.

Jimmy Nolen

Born April 3, 1934
Died December 18, 1983
A noteworthy Oklahoma-born guitarist, Jimmy Nolen initially recorded as a solo act in 1954, before joining Johnny Otis' band in 1957. As a member of The Johnny Otis Show, Nolen appeared on the hit, 'Willie And The Hand Jive'. Leaving Otis in 1961, Nolen briefly backed harmonica player George Smith. As a member of James Brown's Fabulous Flames from 1965 until his

death in 1983, Nolen's groundbreaking riffs would define funk guitar.
CAUSE: Suffering a heart attack on December 16, 1983, while on tour with James Brown in Atlanta, he died two days later.

Klaus Nomi

(KLAUS SPERBER)
Born January 24, 1944
Died August 6, 1983
An androgynous German-born, opera-trained, new wave artist, Klaus Nomi performed idiosyncratic, falsetto versions of mostly rock oldies. Drawn to opera in his youth, he was a frequent stage extra, and then an usher at the Deutsche Opera in Berlin. Amusing his co-workers with his Maria Callas impersonation, Nomi was frustrated by his inability to be taken seriously as an opera singer. Landing in New York City in 1972, he took a day job as a pastry chef at the World Trade Center and, by night, he began developing his musical act in the East Village clubs. Discovered by David Bowie, Nomi was invited to sing back-up for a *Saturday Night Live* appearance in 1979. Thanks to Bowie's influence he was signed to RCA Records. Nomi (an anagram of the magazine *Omni*) incorporated elements of science-fiction, classical opera, and Japanese kabuki into his stage act, which for a time featured two male dancers. Donning his signature white-face make-up, black lipstick and Bauhaus-style costumes, Nomi had limited commercial appeal. The compilation album *Eclipsed* was issued by Razor & Tie Records in 1999.
CAUSE: AIDS. He was diagnosed with the disease only a few months before his death.

Daniel "Sonny" Norton

Born c. 1933
Died 1972
The vocalist of the early Fifties doo-wop group The Crows, Daniel "Sonny" Norton provided the lead on their early pop-crossover, million-selling hit, 'Gee'. Formed on the sidewalks of Harlem, The Crows found fame at George Goldner's Rama Records. Enjoying only a brief spell of popularity, the group disbanded in 1955. "Gee" is sometimes considered the first rock'n'roll song.
CAUSE: Unknown.

Notorious B.I.G.

(CHRISTOPHER WALLACE)
Born May 21, 1972
Died March 9, 1997
A rising East Coast "gangster rap" star, Notorious B.I.G. (also known as Biggie Smalls) was an imposing figure at 6 foot 3 inches, 320 pounds. Raised in the Bedford-Stuy section of Brooklyn, he sold crack cocaine in his teens. After recording some demos with neighbourhood rap group OGB, he was discovered by Big Daddy Kane's deejay, Mister Cee. Soon hyped by *The Source* magazine, Notorious B.I.G. was signed by Puffy Combs to Uptown Records. Switching to Combs' new Bad Boy Entertainment label, Notorious B.I.G. chronicled his violent past on his début, million-selling album *Ready To Die*. Frequently in trouble on charges of drug possession and assault, he was voted top rapper of the year in 1995 at the *Billboard* Awards; he also claimed best rap single for 'One More Chance'/'Stay With Me'. On the cover of *The Source* at the time of his death, he was promoting his upcoming release *Life After Death*; posthumously released, the album topped the charts and was highlighted by the hit single and MTV video, 'Mo' Money Mo' Problems'. Notorious B.I.G. also co-penned Junior M.A.F.I.A.'s 1995 hit 'Player's Anthem', and provided the rap backing on Mary J. Blige's hits 'Real Love' and 'What's The 411'.
CAUSE: After attending the 11th annual *Soul Train* Music Awards, he was shot to death while leaving the post-award party at the Petersen Automotive Museum in Los Angeles. Sitting in the

passenger seat of his GMC Suburban, he was struck by a shower of bullets fired from a passing vehicle. The attack was attributed to the rivalry between the "East Coast" and the "West Coast" gangster rap camps, as retribution for the death of Tupac Shakur who was shot dead and robbed of $40,000 in jewelry. Shakur had blamed a previous 1994 shooting and beating on Notorious B.I.G., and subsequently attacked him on the track 'Hit 'Em Up'. After an 18-month investigation, in 2005 the FBI rejected a conspiracy theory that a rogue Los Angeles police officer was involved in the murder. In response, the family of Notorious B.I.G. sued the police department and were awarded $1.1 million by a federal court. In 1999, a jailed former police officer became a suspect in the rapper's murder.

John Novarese

(Angelo John Novarese)

Born November 13, 1923

Died June 23, 1996

The longtime proprietor of Hi Records since shortly after its inception in the mid Fifties, John Novarese operated the Memphis-based label along with partner Joe Cuoghi. Novarese and Cuoghi had combined the label with their 10-year-old record wholesale business, Poplar Tunes. The business was located across the street from Novarese's home and family grocery store. A successful organization, Hi Records was home to hit acts such as The Bill Black Combo and Ace Cannon. Hiring Willie Mitchell as the label's music director, Hi Records had success with soul acts Al Green and Syl Johnson. Purchased by Creem Records in 1977, Hi Records was closed two years later. The son of Italian immigrants, Novarese earned a degree from Memphis State University and had fought in the Army Air Corps during World War II.

Cause: Cancer. He died at his home in Memphis.

Bradley Nowell

Born February 22, 1968

Died May 25, 1996

The lead singer and guitarist of the ska-influenced punk-rock group Sublime, Bradley Nowell was raised in Long Beach, California. A surfer who formed his first rock band at age 13, he was diagnosed with Attention Deficit Disorder and placed on Ritalin, a drug he would later blame for his progression to heroin. With Sublime garnering a strong fan base throughout California, Nowell dropped out of college in 1990, a semester shy of earning a finance degree. After releasing two albums on its own Skunk Records (including *40 Oz. To Freedom* which spawned the underground hit 'Date Rape'), Sublime signed with the MCA-related Gasoline Alley Records in 1994. Remaining relatively unknown until Nowell's sudden death, the group landed several posthumous radio and MTV hits including 'What I Got', the reggae-influenced 'Santaria' and 'Wrong Way'. Sublime's unreleased sessions were assembled on the 1998 album *Second-Hand Smoke.*

Cause: He died from an accidental heroin overdose at his motel room in San Francisco. Near death when he was discovered by a bandmate, he died at the scene soon after. The coroner found heroin, valium and alcohol in his system. Nowell had married the mother of his child seven days earlier.

Bobby Nunn

Born September 20, 1925

Died November 5, 1986

The booming bass vocalist and original member of The Coasters, former boxer Bobby Nunn hit the stage on the advice of musician/nightclub owner Johnny Otis. A native of Birmingham, Alabama, Nunn joined The A-Sharp Trio in 1950 at Otis' Barrelhouse nightclub in Los Angeles. Renamed The Four Bluebirds by Otis, the group would soon evolve into The Robins. After backing a young Esther Phillips on 'Double Crossin' Blues', The Robins broke away from Otis and teamed in 1951 with a pair of young, white, R&B aficionados, Jerry Leiber and Mike Stoller. After producing several Robins releases, Leiber & Stoller recorded The Robins at their own Sparks label. Unhappy with Nunn's lead vocal on 'Riot In Cell Block #9' (1954), Leiber & Stoller brought in guest singer Richard Berry, but Nunn's bass returned to prominence as the group followed up with 'Framed' (1955). With Leiber & Stoller hired by Atlantic Records as independent producers, The Robins' final Spark hit, 'Smokey Joe's Cafe' (1955), was also released on Atlantic's Atco subsidiary. Bobby Nunn and lead tenor Carl Gardner followed Leiber & Stoller to Atlantic, becoming The Coasters. Joined by Leon Hughes, Billy "Bip" Guy and Adolph Jones, Nunn and Gardner scored several strong crossover hits beginning in 1956 with the moody and exotic 'Smokey Joe's Cafe'. Leiber & Stoller then took the group in a pop direction, The Coasters enjoyed a pop smash with the double-sided hit 'Searchin''/'Youngblood'. Tired of life on the road, the married Nunn wanted to spend more time with his family. Leaving the group, he was replaced by Will "Dub" Jones. In the Seventies Nunn toured the oldies circuit with his own Coasters group. CAUSE: He died from a heart attack at his home in Los Angeles.

Laura Nyro

(LAURA NIGRO)
Born October 18, 1947
Died April 8, 1997
The daughter of a professional jazz trumpeter, Bronx-born singer Laura Nyro had greater success as a songwriter than as a performer. Composing her first song at age eight, she nurtured her talent at the High School of Music and Art in Manhattan. Recording a much-ignored début album at 19, *More Than A New Discovery* (1966), the project instead spawned a trio of cover hits: 'Stoney End' (Barbra Streisand), 'And When I Die' (Blood, Sweat & Tears) and 'Wedding Bell Blues' (The Fifth Dimension). Having alienated the crowd with her odd costume, Nyro was mercilessly booed off-stage at the Monterey Pop Festival in 1967, and thereafter she rarely performed in public. Hiring the young David Geffen as her manager, Nyro switched to Columbia Records where she would release her breakthrough album *Eli And The Thirteenth Confession*, which was highlighted by 'Stoned Soul Picnic' (a hit for The Fifth Dimension), and 'Eli's Coming' (a Top 10 hit for Three Dog Night). Nyro followed this up with the genre-crossing album *New York Tendaberry*, which yielded a third cover-hit for The Fifth Dimension, 'Save The Country'. Nyro landed her sole chart hit with a cover of the Goffin-King standard, 'Up On The Roof', which appeared on the emotive and politically charged album *Christmas And The Beads Of Sweat*. She later recorded an album's worth of cover hits, and was backed by LaBelle on the Gamble & Huff-produced *Gonna Take A Miracle* (1971). After retiring from music for four years, Nyro divorced her husband and returned to the studio in 1976 to record *Smile*. A reclusive, cult figure who preferred to expend her energy in social activism in the latter part of her life, Nyro toured for the first time in over a decade in 1988, a performance captured on *Live At The Bottom Line*. Her final studio recordings, *Angel In The Dark*, were released in 2001. CAUSE: Ovarian cancer. She died at her home in Danbury, Connecticut.

O

Berry Oakley

(Raymond Berry Oakley)
Born April 4, 1948
Died November 11, 1972
The bass player of the legendary Southern rock group The Allman Brothers Band, Berry Oakley was reared on blues music in his native Chicago. Moving to Sarasota, Florida, in his teens, Oakley landed his first professional gig with The Romans, Tommy Roe's touring back-up band. Forming a politically orientated rock group, Second Coming, in the late Sixties, Oakley was joined by Dickey Betts, Gregg Allman, and lastly, Duane Allman. With Duane Allman signed to Capricorn Records, he built a new group with members of his former bands, Second Coming and Hourglass. Relocating to Macon, Georgia, The Allman Brothers Band began an arduous touring schedule. While guitarist Duane Allman was the soul of the group, Oakley was its conscience. Released in late 1969, The Allman Brothers' self-titled début album was a moderate success, highlighted by the Southern-flavoured, blues-rock gems 'Whipping Post' and 'Dreams'. At the forefront of the emerging Southern rock genre, The Allman Brothers enjoyed fame with the albums *Idlewild South* (1970), the live *At Fillmore East* (1971), and the final project with Duane Allman *Eat A Peach* (1972). Oakley was killed while working on the group's fifth album, *Brothers And Sisters*, which contained the hits, 'Ramblin' Man' and 'Jessica'. Oakley was replaced in the group by Lamar Williams.
Cause: He died in a motorcycle accident in Macon, Georgia – less than a mile from where bandmate Duane Allman met his demise a year earlier. After crashing into the side of a city bus, Oakley refused medical treatment and went home. He later died of a brain haemorrhage at the Macon Medical Center.
Further Reading: Freeman, Scott. (1995). *Midnight Riders: The Story Of The Allman Brothers Band.* New York: Little, Brown.

Bishop O'Brien

(Joel O'Brien)
Born July 27, 1943
Died September 9, 2004
A multi-instrumentalist who drummed in James Taylor's early group The Flying Machine, Bishop O'Brien also backed Taylor on his début 1968 album for The Beatles' Apple Records label. Moving to Los Angeles, O'Brien formed the rock soul band Jo Mama, and most of the group, including O'Brien, backed Carole King on her first three albums, including the million-selling *Tapestry*. By 1973, O'Brien had settled in Woodstock, New York, where he worked with Robbie Dupree and joined a series of jazz, R&B, and even country bands. O'Brien later worked in Europe before returning to the US.
Cause: Cancer. He died at his home in Mar Vista, California.

Phil Ochs

Born December 19, 1940
Died April 9, 1976
A politically motivated singer-songwriter in the folk tradition, Texas-born Phil Ochs was largely apolitical during his upbringing in suburban Columbus, Ohio. Enrolling at Ohio State University in 1958, he decided to major in journalism after a gruelling 15-day detention in a Florida prison. Publishing a radical, off-campus publication called *The Word*, Ochs dropped out of college as a protest when the official student newspaper refused to run his pro-Castro article. Taught to play the guitar by his college roommate Jim Glover, Ochs performed in Cincinnati

and Cleveland. Relocating to Greenwich Village and perfecting his craft, Ochs became a fixture in the Dylan-led folk community with his politically charged material. Embracing left-wing causes, Ochs first gained national acclaim in 1962 with the angry protest song, 'The Cuban Invasion'. Signing with Elektra Records in 1964, Ochs followed the Dylan style of protest singers with the albums *All The News That's Fit To Sing* and *I Ain't Marching Anymore*, the latter highlighted by its masterful anti-war title track and 'Draft Dodger Rag'. Although he was blacklisted on radio for his political views, Ochs landed airplay via Joan Baez's rendition of his composition 'There But For Fortune' which reached the UK Top Ten in late 1965. Ochs befriended Dylan but they fell out over political issues and it has been suggested that Dylan wrote his scathing put-down 'Positively Fourth Street' partly as a tirade against Ochs. Moving to A&M Records, Ochs took a slight commercial turn with *Pleasures Of The Harbor* (1967), the album highlighted by 'The Party' and 'Outside A Small Circle Of Friends'. True to his politics, Ochs was immersed in the violent turmoil of the 1968 Democratic convention in Chicago, and was among those dissidents who attempted to nominate a pig as a presidential candidate. Alienating his fans, Ochs recorded the rock-flavoured, ironically titled *Greatest Hits* in 1970; in a reference to an Elvis release, the back of the album cover read, "50 Phil Ochs Fans Can't Be Wrong." He further angered, or at least confused, his fans by appearing on stage at New York's Carnegie Hall in a gaudy, Elvis-like, gold lamé suit, and releasing a live album from the show. Depressed and disillusioned by both the music industry and the folk movement, Ochs settled in Los Angeles in the early Seventies and performed only sporadically thereafter. After producing an album for folk singer Sammy Walker, Ochs returned to journalism, writing for the British listings magazine *Time Out*. He also travelled extensively, to South America, Australia and Africa where he was the victim of a mugging which permanently damaged his vocal cords. At the time of his death he was living in New York and abusing alcohol, a sorry figure around the Greenwich Village clubs where he had once been a popular performer. Phil Ochs' brother Michael, the owner of one of the world's leading rock photo archives, compiled a posthumously released Phil Ochs album *Chords Of Fame* (1976).
CAUSE: He committed suicide by hanging at his sister's home in Far Rockaway, New York. Like his father and brother, Ochs suffered from chronic depression. Having been treated by a psychiatrist a week earlier, Ochs had refused to take the prescribed anti-depressants. Ochs had also been distraught over his inability to write new material.
FURTHER READING: Eliot, Marc. (1990). *Phil Ochs, Death Of A Rebel: A Biography*. London: Omnibus.

O.D.B.

(RUSSELL TYRONE JONES)
Born November 15, 1968
Died November 13, 2004
A founding member of influential Nineties rap act Wu-Tang Clan, O.D.B. (an abbreviation of Ol' Dirty Bastard) also pursued a thriving solo career. O.D.B – who occasionally used other nicknames including Dirt McGirt, Osiris, and Big Baby Jesus – earned notoriety for his brazen behaviour, both on and off stage, which culminated in a series of well-publicised arrests. Born in Brooklyn, he teamed with cousins Robert Diggs and Gary Grice to merge their common appreciation of kung fu movies and rap music into the stage act, Wu-Tang Clan. Devised as a musical collective to cultivate solo careers, Wu-Tang Clan created a stir with its 1993 début

album, *Enter The Wu-Tang (36 Chambers)*. That same year, O.D.B. was convicted of second-degree assault, and the following year he was shot in the stomach by a rival rapper. Following in the wake of Wu-Tang bandmate Method Man, O.D.B. went solo; signing with Elektra, he became an instant media star with his 1995 release *Return To The 36 Chambers: The Dirty Version*, which spawned the hits 'Brooklyn Zoo' and 'Shimmy Shimmy Ya'. O.D.B. also provided a cameo rap on the remix of Mariah Carey's hit 'Bad Boy'. By 1997, O.D.B. rejoined Wu-Tang Clan for their much anticipated follow-up album, *Wu-Tang Forever*; but months after its release, O.D.B. was arrested for failing to pay $35,000 in child support to the mother of three of his at least 13 children. The following year, he launched his own urban-style clothing line, My Dirty Wear. Then in a bizarre stunt at the 1998 Grammy Awards, he angrily rushed the stage after losing the "Song of the Year" prize and interrupted the winner's speech. By year's end, O.D.B. had been convicted of assault, shot in a robbery attempt, arrested for shoplifting in Virginia Beach and arrested again for making "terrorist threats". Faring no better in 1999, he was frequently arrested, and by August had entered a drug rehab programme. But despite his rocky personal life, he managed to reach the Top 10 with his second solo album, *Nigga Please*. Though ordered by the court to extend his stay in drug rehab, he escaped two months before the completion of the programme. Though a wanted man, O.D.B. made a public appearance at the Wu-Tang Clan release party for the group's album *The W*. Not surprisingly, the project featured O.D.B. on just one track, 'Conditioner'. In April 2001, O.D.B. finally went to prison, given the minimum sentence of two to four years for cocaine possession. While behind bars, a third O.D.B. album was issued from sessions recorded while he was on the run, the poorly received *The Trials And Tribulations Of Russell Jones*. Although O.D.B. attempted suicide before beginning his prison term, he pledged to clean up his act upon his discharge in 2003. At the time of his death, he was working on a comeback album for Roc-A-Fella Records and was slated to perform at a Wu-Tang reunion concert. A 1995 album was issued posthumously.
CAUSE: He collapsed in the lounge of Wu-Tang's Manhattan recording studio, 36 Records LLC, after complaining of chest pains earlier in the day. The coroner's report attributed O.D.B.'s death to the combined effects of cocaine and the prescription pain medication Tramadol.

Bertrand Odom

Born June 10, 1932
Died August 17, 2004
The bass player behind soul great James Brown from 1958 to 1968, Bertrand Odom appeared on dozens of hit recordings including 'Try Me', 'Papa's Got A Brand New Bag', 'Cold Sweat' and 'It's A Man's, Man's, Man's World'. Odom had originally joined the touring version of James Brown & The Famous Flames in 1958 after completing an army stint. Upon his retirement from The Fabulous Flames in 1968, Odom continued working for Brown in various capacities until 1998. In the early Seventies, Odom was a member of Maceo & All The Kings Men, an outfit consisting of former James Brown sidemen.
CAUSE: Kidney failure. He died at a hospital in his home town of Mobile, Alabama.

Brian O'Hara

Born March 12, 1942
Died June 27, 1999
Liverpudlian Brian O'Hara was the leader of The Fourmost, one of Brian Epstein's stable of pop acts. Forming a duo with childhood schoolmate Billy Hatton, they performed around

Liverpool as The Two Jays. Encouraged to expand into a group after nearly winning a talent show at the Pavilion Theatre, The Four Jays alternated between skiffle and rock as they performed in the clubs on the Isle of Wight in the mid Fifties. The senior member, guitarist and vocalist of the group, O'Hara worked as an accountant during the day. In the wake of The Beatles, the renamed Fourmost were signed by Epstein as another promising Mersybeat group, scoring UK hits with the Lennon & McCartney compositions 'Hello Little Girl', and 'I'm In Love'. Sharing bills with The Beatles and other NEMS acts and appearing in the rock film *Ferry Cross The Mersey* in 1964, The Fourmost lost their momentum with the illness and subsequent death of bandmate Mike Millward in 1966, together with Epstein concentrating his energies on The Beatles. During this period, the group endured a long residency in a variety show at the London Palladium with Cilla Black, Frankie Laine, and others. Falling from the public eye, the group faded after their final hit, 'Girls, Girls, Girls' (1966). Leaving rock music for the world of dinner clubs and cabaret, O'Hara often toured with Frankie Laine. Resisting his band's desire to return to contemporary music, O'Hara disbanded The Fourmost in 1978. O'Hara hired three new backing members, but sold them the rights to the group's name. The group's original surviving members reunited in 1990 at a John Lennon tribute concert at Liverpool's Philharmonic Hall. O'Hara later worked as a mobile disc jockey.
CAUSE: Suicide by hanging at his home in the Waverley district of Liverpool.

Frank O'Keefe

Born March 18, 1950
Died February 26, 1995
The founding bassist of the Seventies Southern-rock band The Outlaws, Florida-native Frank O'Keefe had joined several friends to form the group in 1972. Discovered at a small Georgia nightclub by Clive Davis who had just formed Arista Records, The Outlaws were signed in 1974. Featuring twin lead guitars, the group's début album *The Outlaws* (1975) was certified gold and contained the epic Southern rock anthem, 'Green Grass And High Tide'. O'Keefe appeared on two more Outlaws albums, *Lady In Waiting* (1976) and *Hurry Sundown* (1977), before being ousted from the band in 1977 due to his heavy drug and alcohol use. Unable to earn a living as a musician, he returned to Clearwater, Florida, and worked as a house painter.
CAUSE: Overdosing on prescription tranquillisers, cocaine, and methadone, he died at his apartment in St. Petersburg, Florida. The local medical examiner ruled the death a suicide.

Johnny O'Keefe

(JOHN MICHAEL O'KEEFE)
Born January 19, 1935
Died October 6, 1978
Australia's first rock star, Johnny O'Keefe is best known for his much covered, self-penned standard 'Real Wild Child' (1958). Initially recording mostly cover versions of American hits in the Fifties, the charismatic performer had limited success in the US, where he tried to promote himself as 'The Boomerang Boy'. With his backing band, The Dee Jays, the exuberant O'Keefe performed to packed houses of screaming adolescent girls in his native country. In all, O'Keefe recorded over 50 albums. In the Seventies, he formed an entertainment management company. O'Keefe was celebrated in the low budget, 1986 film biography, *Shout! The Story Of Johnny O'Keefe*. In 1986 Iggy Pop enjoyed a major hit with O'Keefe's 'Real Wild Child'.
CAUSE: Heart attack. He died at his suburban Sydney home.

Criss Oliva

(CHRISTOPHER OLIVA)
Born April 3, 1963
Died October 17, 1993
The guitarist for the heavy metal group Savatage, Criss Oliva backed his brother Jon on lead vocals. Formed in 1983 as a trio called Metropolis, the Florida-based group often employed symphonic backing on its albums, and managed a minor hit with the track 'Jesus Saves'. Chriss Oliva's final Savatage album was *Edge Of Thorns*.
CAUSE: He was killed in an automobile accident near his home in Clearwater, Florida, when his vehicle was struck head-on by a drunk driver. Seated next to him, Oliva's wife was severely injured.

Oliver

(WILLIAM OLIVER SWOFFORD)
Born February 22, 1945
Died February 11, 2000
A Sixties folk-pop singer, William "Oliver" Swofford had a pair of Top 10 singles in 1969. First hitting the stage in his teens, he joined two bands at the University of North Carolina, a bluegrass outfit called The Virginians and then a country-rock band called The Good Earth. With the aid of producer Bob Crewe, Oliver nearly topped the charts with 'Good Morning Starshine', a song from the musical *Hair*, and followed with 'Jean', from the film *The Prime Of Miss Jean Brodie*. Abandoning music in 1982, he worked in the construction and pharmaceutical fields.
CAUSE: Cancer. He died in Shreveport, Louisiana.

Joe Olivier

(JOSEPH N. OLIVIER)
Born October 12, 1937
Died December 25, 2001
A member of Bill Haley & The Comets during the late Fifties, guitarist Joe Olivier appeared on several releases including the album *Rockin' Around The World*. Born in the Netherlands, Olivier (often misspelled in reference sources as "Oliver") played second guitar behind Haley. A baritone vocalist, Olivier occasionally performed as Haley's opening act and issued a few solo singles during this period. He left the music business in the Sixties.
CAUSE: While recovering from diabetes-related surgery, he died at his home in Marcy, New York.

Mark Olson

(MARK DANIEL OLSON)
Born July 12, 1951
Died April 25, 1991
A member of Motown rock act Rare Earth, keyboardist Mark Olson joined in early 1971 as a replacement for Kenny James and appeared on the hits 'I Just Want To Celebrate' and 'Hey Big Brother'. A native of Fargo, North Dakota, Olson began playing piano at his church during early childhood. Relocating to the Detroit area, he joined future rock singer Meatloaf and others in a local production of the rock musical *Hair* before joining Rare Earth. Formed in 1969, Rare Earth experienced numerous personnel changes before disbanding in 1974. In later years, Olson rejoined Rare Earth for reunion tours and also headed his own group, The Mark Olson Band.
CAUSE: Liver disease.

Hugh O'Neill Jr.

Born 1958
Died January 20, 1999
The drummer of the Boston-based surf-punk band The Queers, Hugh O'Neill Jr. joined the second line-up of the group in 1986, beginning with the album *Grow Up*. Signing with Lookout Records (home of Green Day), The Queers merged the styles of The Ramones with The Beach Boys on their upbeat, politically incorrect material. Falling ill, O'Neill left the group in 1996.
CAUSE: Inoperable brain cancer. He

died at Oak Knoll Healthcare Center in his hometown of Ashland, Massachusetts.

Roy Orbison

(ROY KELTON ORBISON)
Born April 23, 1936
Died December 6, 1988
A legendary rock crooner who broke out of the country and rockabilly traditions, Roy Orbison enjoyed massive fame in the early Sixties with his dramatic songs of doomed romance. A native of Vernon, Texas, Orbison received informal guitar lessons from a neighbour. After appearing on a series of local radio programmes during his childhood, he formed a popular, regional teenage country group, The Wink Westerners. While studying geology in college, he was urged by classmate Pat Boone to take a rockabilly turn. Renaming his group The Teen Kings, Orbison recorded the rockabilly-flavoured single 'Ooby Dooby' at Norman Petty's small studio in Clovis, New Mexico; with the track leased to Jewel Records, Orbison landed a regional hit. Aided by Johnny Cash, Orbison then signed with Sun Records where he recorded an updated version of 'Ooby Dooby'; a minor national hit, it would be Orbison's sole chart entry at the label. Unhappy with the rockabilly and novelty-styled material he was obliged to record with Sun chief Sam Phillips, Orbison left the label and settled in Nashville. After The Everly Brothers recorded the Orbison composition 'Claudette', he was signed as a songwriter by the Acuff-Rose publishing firm. Now managed by Wesley Rose (the Rose in Acuff-Rose) and signed to Monument Records, Orbison released a series of failed singles until he found his niche as a moody, pop-rock crooner. With his soaring three-octave vocal range, Orbison drew legions of fans with plaintive, slightly eerie, songs such as 'Only The Lonely' (1960), 'Running Scared' (1961), 'Crying' (1961), 'Dream Baby' (1961), 'In Dreams' (1961)' and 'It's Over' (1964). His biggest hit came with the uncharacteristically uptempo 'Pretty Woman' (1964). Orbison first introduced his trademark, Ray Ban Wayfarer model, black sunglasses at an Alabama concert, and popularised his new look during a 1963 British tour with the then-upstart Beatles. Switching to MGM Records in 1965, Orbison also starred in the film *The Fastest Guitar Alive*. Tragedy struck Orbison when he lost two of his three sons in a house fire and lost his wife Claudette in a 1966 motorcycle accident. Thereafter the melancholy nature of his songs struck a sympathetic chord in audiences everywhere, especially Great Britain. Fading from the US charts, Orbison married German-born Barbara Wellhonen in 1969, and relocated to Germany. Although remaining a star in Britain, his return to the US in 1977 went unnoticed. Orbison experienced an uphill comeback in the Eighties, opening on an Eagles tour in 1980, and teaming up with Emmylou Harris for the Grammy-winning hit, 'That Loving You Feeling Again'. He also enjoyed Top 10 hit covers of his compositions, 'Crying' (Don McLean) and 'Pretty Woman' (Van Halen). When his moody classic 'In Dreams' was featured prominently in the David Lynch film *Blue Velvet*, Orbison was poised for a comeback. He was then invited to join the studio supergroup The Traveling Wilburys (alongside Bob Dylan, George Harrison, Tom Petty and Jeff Lynne) under the moniker of Lefty Wilbury (after Lefty Frizzell), who enjoyed a surprise hit with the rollicking album *The Traveling Wilburys Volume 1*, highlighted by the single 'Handle With Care'. At the time of his death, Orbison was nearly as popular as he had been during his early Sixties heyday. In fact, with movies, record deals and other projects in the works, he was again approaching major

league status. Completed shortly before his death, Orbison's solo album *Mystery Girl*, spawned a Top 10 posthumous hit with 'You Got It' (1989). Orbison's 'Pretty Woman' enjoyed a second chart run after its exposure as the title track of Julia Roberts' 1990 film of the same name. An Orbison monument was erected in his hometown of Wink, Texas in 1991.
CAUSE: He died after suffering a massive heart attack while visiting his mother at her home in Henderson, Tennessee. Orbison had undergone triple-bypass heart surgery a decade earlier.
FURTHER READING: Clayson, Alan. (1989). *Only The Lonely: Roy Orbison's Life And Legacy*. New York: St. Martin's. Amburn, Ellis. (1990). *Dark Star: The Roy Orbison Story*. New York: Carol.

Orion

(JIMMY HODGES ELLIS)
Born February 26, 1945
Died December 12, 1998
A notorious Elvis impersonator, Orion released a series of Presley-styled recordings beginning in 1978. Initially performing under his real name of Jimmy Ellis, he first recorded in 1964. With Sun Records sold in 1969, new owner Shelby Singleton issued Orion's versions of Presley's early Sun releases of 'That's All Right (Mama)' and 'Blue Moon Of Kentucky' without any artist credit, thereby suggesting the singles were alternative Presley takes. Then, after Presley's death in 1977, Singleton overdubbed Orion's vocals on to some Jerry Lee Lewis tracks which were issued as "Jerry Lee Lewis and friend", with the implication that they were lost Presley tracks. Wearing a mask on stage and on his album covers, Orion even sang with Presley's former backing group, The Jordanaires. After landing a minor chart hit in 1981 with 'Rockabilly Rebel', Orion's career nose-dived in 1983 when he tried performing without his trademark mask. He later operated a pawn shop and worked as a bail bondsman.
CAUSE: He was shot and killed in a robbery at a convenience store that he operated near Selma, Alabama. Also killed was his ex-wife, Elaine Thompson; another woman, Helen King, was seriously injured. Three young suspects were later apprehended and charged with murder.

Benjamin Orr

(BENJAMIN ORZECHOWSKI)
Born September 8, 1947
Died August 3, 2000
The bassist of Boston-based rock act The Cars, Benjamin Orr also provided an occasional lead vocal. The son of Russian immigrants, Orr was raised in suburban Cleveland. Enamoured of The Beatles, Orr joined a local rock group, The Grasshoppers, aged 15, on lead vocals and guitar. After having a pair of local hits, The Grasshoppers were hired as the house band on the locally produced, syndicated, *American Bandstand*-inspired music show *Upbeat*, but with several of the band members drafted to fight in the Vietman War, the group was forced to disband. After passing through two more bands, Orr teamed up with Ric Ocasek to form a series of bands in Cleveland, Columbus and New York City, before making Boston their home. There in 1972, the pair added keyboardist Greg Hawkes to form a folk group, Milkwood, who recorded an album for Paramount Records. Adding guitarist Elliott Easton, they formed a rock band called Cap'n Swing who, inspired by the punk movement and adding drummer David Robinson, morphed into the new-wave quintet, The Cars. Playing bass by this time, Orr also provided the backing vocals on the band's début hit, the power-pop anthem 'Just What I Needed'. Initially a regional hit, the track wound up on their 1978 Elektra Records self-titled début album. Remaining a radio favourite over the next decade, The

Cars issued a number of anthemic hits including 'My Best Friend's Girl', 'Let's Go', 'Shake It Up', 'You Might Think' and 'Tonight She Comes'. Orr provided an occasional lead vocal, including on the hit ballad 'Drive'. After The Cars disbanded in 1986, Orr released a solo album *The Lace*, which spawned the hit 'Stay The Night', and after taking a respite from the music industry on his Vermont farm, he formed The Orr Band in 1994. Though diagnosed with cancer in May 1999, Orr refused to cancel a scheduled tour with his new group, Big People.
CAUSE: Diagnosed with pancreatic cancer in May 1999, he was told he had six months to live. He died at his home in Atlanta.

Jinny Osborn

(VIRGINIA COLE)
Born April 25, 1927
Died May 19, 2003
As a member of the all-girl, barbershop-style vocal group The Chordettes, Jinny Osborn had several pop hits in the Fifties. A native of Seattle, Washington, Osborn was the daughter of O.H. "King" Cole, the president of the Barbershop Harmony Society. Aided by Cole's musical and financial guidance, the Sheboygan, Wisconsin-based a cappella act was an immediate sensation and after touring heavily throughout the Midwest, The Chordettes garnered national exposure as regulars on Arthur Godfrey's popular radio and television programmes. In 1950, Godfrey aided the group in landing a recording contract with Columbia but he fired them in 1953, and replaced them with The McGuire Sisters. Also that year, a pregnant Osborn left The Chordettes and was temporarily replaced by Margie Needham. Moving to Cadence Records in 1954, The Chordettes veered away from their barbershop roots and adopted a more mainstream pop sound. Returning to the group following their chart success with 'Mr. Sandman', Osborn appeared on The Chordettes subsequent hits such as 'Born To Be With You', 'Just Between You And Me' and 'Lollipop'. In 1957, the group performed on the début episode of the national version of Dick Clark's *American Bandstand.* After Osborn quit the group in 1961, The Chordettes were unable to find a suitable replacement and eventually they disbanded. Jinny retired from music and settled in southern California.
CAUSE: Cancer. She died in Palm Springs, California.

Danny Overbea

Born February 3, 1926
Died May 11, 1994
A Philadelphia-born guitarist and balladeer, Danny Overbea broke into music in the early Fifties in a Cleveland-based trio called The Three Earls. A consummate performer, Overbea was soon a frequent solo act on Alan Freed's early rock concerts in the Cleveland/Akron area. Relocating to Chicago, Overbea scored a pair of rock'n'roll styled hits – 'Train, Train, Train' (1953) and the often-recorded '40 Cups Of Coffee' (1953) – on the Chess Records subsidiary Checker. Also a fine balladeer, Overbea had regional successes with 'You're Mine' and 'A Toast To Lovers'. Retiring from music in 1976, he later worked as an elementary school music teacher.
CAUSE: Stricken with cancer and suffering heart problems, he died at a Chicago hospital.

Malcolm Owen

Born c. 1955
Died July 14, 1980
Lead singer of late Seventies British punk rock group The Ruts, Malcolm Owen incorporated reggae rhythms in his group's politically orientated material. Signing with Virgin Records, The Ruts released two albums

beginning with 1979's *The Crack*, which was highlighted by 'Babylon's Burning'. After Owen's death, the remaining members of the group emerged as The Ruts D.C.
CAUSE: Drug overdose.

A.L. Owens

(ARTHUR LEE OWENS)
Born November 28, 1930
Died October 4, 1999
A singer-songwriter, A.L. "Doodle" Owens penned material for Brenda Lee ('Johnny One Time'), George Jones ('Wine Colored Roses'), and Charlie Pride ('Afraid Of Losing You' and 'All I Have To Offer You'). A native of Waco, he moved to Nashville in 1965. Also a recording artist, his best known release came with 'Honky Tonk Toys'.
CAUSE: Heart attack.

Donnie Owens

Born February 8, 1932
Died October 27, 1994
A one-hit wonder, Donnie Owens was aided by guest guitarist Duane Eddy on the rockabilly-flavoured 'I Need You' (1958). Discovered by country singer Jimmy Wakely, Owens also worked with Lee Hazelwood, Waylon Jennings and Skip & Flip.
CAUSE: He was accidentally shot to death at a Phoenix motel by his girlfriend, Chato D'Rea. D'Rea, who was the manager of the motel, inadvertently shot Owens in the stomach while trying to ward off a man who was threatening him.

P

Gene Page

(EUGENE EDGAR PAGE, JR.)
Born October 13, 1938
Died August 24, 1998
Producer and arranger for Diana Ross, Lionel Richie and Whitney Houston, Gene Page first gained fame in the Sixties for his work with The Righteous Brothers on their 1964 hit 'You've Lost That Lovin' Feelin''. After a stint at Motown Records, he took a turn toward Philly soul with The Love Unlimited Orchestra's disco instrumental, 'Love's Theme'. Frequently employing a string section on his mostly ballad productions, Page's work includes 'Stoney End' (Barbra Streisand), 'The Greatest Love Of All' (Whitney Houston), 'Her Town, Too' (James Taylor & J.D. Souther), and 'Endless Love' (Lionel Richie and Diana Ross). Attempting a solo career, Page recorded for Atlantic and Arista Records, landing a minor R&B hit in 1978 with an instrumental version of the theme from *Close Encounters Of The Third Kind.*
CAUSE: He died from an undisclosed long-term illness in Los Angeles.

Bruce Palmer

Born September 9, 1946
Died October 1, 2004
The original bass player for the influential but short-lived classic West Coast rock band Buffalo Springfield, the mysterious Bruce Palmer failed to achieve the same level of success as his bandmates. Hailing from Canada, he broke into music as a member of a British Invasion covers band, Jack London & The Sparrows. By 1966, Palmer traded places with the bassist of The Mynah Birds – a group which included Rick James and, for a short time, Neil Young. Recording an album's worth of material for Motown Records, none of the tracks were released once the label discovered James' AWOL military status. After the group disbanded, Palmer and Young travelled to Los Angeles, where they teamed with Dewey Martin, Richie Furay and Stephen Stills to form the electric folk-rock act Buffalo Springfield. After completing sessions for the group's début album, Palmer was busted for drug possession and deported back to Canada. As a recurring member of Buffalo Springfield, Palmer played on all three of the group's albums but, due to his precarious immigration status and frequent drug use, Palmer was eventually fired and replaced by Jim Messina before the group finally split in 1968. Pursuing a solo career in the Seventies, Palmer released the poorly received jazz-rock album, *The Cyrcle Is Complete*, which featured his early musical compatriot Rick James. In the early Eighties, Palmer toured with Neil Young and later joined former bandmate Dewey Martin in the revival group, Buffalo Springfield Revisited. In 1988 Buffalo Springfield re-formed in private for rehearsals and sessions at Young's ranch.
CAUSE: Heart attack. He died in Belleville, Ontario, Canada.

Robert Palmer

Born June 19, 1945
Died November 20, 1997
Music critic, author, producer and historian, Robert Palmer was from 1976–88 the first full-time rock critic on *The New York Times*, and was a frequent contributor to *Rolling Stone* magazine. An author, he penned several music books including *Rock And Roll: The Unruly History*, and the definitive tome on Delta blues, *Deep Blues*. As a music producer at Fat Possum Records, he oversaw the blues acts R.L. Burnside and Junior Kimbrough; he also co-founded the Memphis Blues Festival in 1966. As a

musician, the Arkansas-born Palmer recorded two major label albums in the late Sixties with a group called The Insect Trust.
CAUSE: Stricken with liver disease after a 1995 bout of hepatitis, he died while awaiting a liver transplant. He died at Westchester County Medical Center in Valhalia, New York.
FURTHER READING: Palmer, Robert. (1995). *Rock & Roll: An Unruly History*. New York: Harmony.

Robert Palmer

(ROBERT ALAN PALMER)
Born January 19, 1949
Died September 26, 2003
A charismatic entertainer and dapper dresser, singer Robert Palmer owed his success in the Eighties to a series of stylish music videos. Born in England but raised on the island of Malta, Palmer listened to American rock music on Armed Forces Radio during his youth. After joining his first band at age 15, he recorded three albums as a member of the soul group Dada (later known as Vinegar Joe). Gaining a solo record deal with Island Records, Palmer released his R&B-inflected début album *Sneakin' Sally Through The Alley* in 1975, backed by members of The Meters and Little Feat, and scored an AOR hit with the title track. Entering the Top 40 for the first time in 1978 with 'Every Kinda People', Palmer flirted with disco (he would return to the charts with an updated version of the song in 1992) and veered towards rock with the frenetic 'Bad Case Of Loving You (Doctor, Doctor)'. In 1985, Palmer joined what was intended as a studio-only, synth rock supergroup, The Power Station, which included members of Duran Duran. A much hyped outfit featuring Palmer on lead vocals, they had hits with 'Some Like It Hot' and a cover of T. Rex's 'Get It On (Bang A Gong)'. Teaming with producer Bernard Edwards of Chic for the album *Riptide*, Palmer scored his career-defining hit in 1986 with 'Addicted To Love', the accompanying MTV video featured Palmer backed by a horde of leggy, dark-haired women pretending to play guitars. His hit run continued over the next several years with 'I Didn't Mean To Turn You On', 'Simply Irresistible', 'Early In The Morning' and a medley of Marvin Gaye classics, 'Mercy Mercy Me'/'I Want You'. Palmer joined the original line-up of The Power Station in 1997. Palmer's final album, the bluesy *Drive*, was issued in 2003.
CAUSE: Suffering a massive heart attack, he died at Warwick Hospital in Paris.

Larry Palumbo

Born 1941
Died 1960
The baritone vocalist of the late Fifties doo-wop vocal group The Earls, Larry Palumbo left before they scored their biggest hit, 'Remember Then'. Palumbo first joined a predecessor of The Earls in 1957 called The High Hatters. He left the group in 1959 to join the service.
CAUSE: Suffering a blood clot during a military parachuting exercise, he passed away after a two-month coma.

John Panozzo

Born September 20, 1948
Died July 16, 1996
The drummer for Styx, the popular American AOR band of the Seventies, Chicago-born John Panozzo learned his craft from an uncle. Teaming with his twin brother, bassist Chuck Panozzo, John performed in a series of Chicago rock bands beginning in 1963. By the late Sixties, the Panozzo brothers had formed a group with future Styx guitarist Tommy Shaw and accordion player, Dennis DeYoung. Discovered in 1971 by record label chief Bill Traut, the group was signed to the Wooden Nickel label; Traut renamed the group Styx, after the mythological Greek river of the dead. Releasing their début album *Styx* in

1971, the group landed its breakthrough pop hit in 1975 with a three-year-old track, the Dennis DeYoung-penned ballad 'Lady'. One of the country's top pop-rock bands in the second half of the Seventies, Styx recorded a series of million-selling albums including *The Grand Illusion* (1977), *Pieces Of Eight* (1978), and *Paradise Theater* (1981). A concept project aided by MTV exposure, Styx's 1983 album *Kilroy Was Here* attacked censorship and spawned the hits 'Mr. Roboto' and the touching ballad, 'Don't Let it End'. During the middle of a tour in support of the *Kilroy* album, co-lead singer Tommy Shaw quit the band for a solo career. With replacement singer-guitarist Glen Burtnik, Styx reunited in 1990 for the album *Edge Of The Century*. Styx enjoyed a surprise hit in 1991 when their single 'Show Me The Way' was adopted as an unofficial anthem of the Persian Gulf War. In poor health and suffering an injured right arm, Panozzo was unable to join the group for its 77-date reunion tour in 1996 and was replaced by drummer Todd Sucherman.
CAUSE: A hard drinker, he died of bleeding ulcers and cirrhosis of the liver. He was found unconscious at his Chicago home.

Felix Pappalardi

(FELIX PAPPALARDI, JR.)
Born December 20, 1939
Died April 17, 1983
The bass player and co-leader of famed, early heavy-metal group Mountain, Bronx-born Felix Pappalardi was a fan of Baroque music in his youth. He was formally trained on the piano before moving to the viola. Studying music at the University of Michigan, he dropped out in 1962 to join the army reserves. Returning to New York City on his discharge, he sought a position in one of the city's orchestras. After discovering the Greenwich Village folk scene, he was soon performing with folkies such as Richie Havens, Tim Hardin and Ian & Sylvia. Initially entering the studio as an arranger, he worked with Tom Rush and Tom Paxton. Graduating to production work, he teamed with Tim Hardin, Joan Baez, The Lovin' Spoonful and The Youngbloods. But Pappalardi's greatest achievement came with the rock supergroup Cream; co-writing their hit 'Strange Brew' (1967) and occasionally providing backing piano, Pappalardi produced the masterful albums *Disraeli Gears* (1967), *Wheels Of Fire* (1968), and *Goodbye* (1969). After producing several singles for the Leslie West-headed group The Vagrants, Pappalardi produced the album *Leslie West – Mountain*. Impressed with West's guitar work, Pappalardi teamed with the heavyweight guitarist in 1969 to form Mountain. Their fourth public performance would come at the Woodstock festival, assaulting the attendees with a blend of hard blues and buzzing heavy metal. Signed to Windfall Records, Mountain enjoyed instant fame with the albums *Mountain* (1969) and *Mountain Climbing!* (1970), the latter featuring 'Never In My Life' and their crunching, guitar-rock anthem, 'Mississippi Queen'. Although the group split in 1972, Pappalardi would occasionally reform Mountain. Teaming with Jerry Shirley and Joey Molland in the short-lived group Natural Gas, Pappalardi recorded one album before they disbanded in 1976. Also that year, Pappalardi released the first of his two solo albums *Felix Pappalardi & Creation*. After years of studio and stage work, Pappalardi was declared legally deaf in the late Seventies. At the time of his death, Pappalardi was working on an album with French singer, Enrico Macais, and on a Broadway play with wife Gail Collins.
CAUSE: He was shot to death in the neck by his wife Gail Collins (who was also his songwriting partner) while he

was lying in the bed of their Manhattan apartment. Collins claimed that the gun had accidentally discharged. With Pappalardi and his former Mountain bandmates involved in a lawsuit, they were initially treated as suspects and questioned by police. Collins was acquitted of second degree murder but was convicted of criminal negligent homicide and was sentenced to 16 months to four years in prison. In October 1983, Pappalardi's father, Felix Pappalardi Sr., sued Collins in a Manhattan court for "wilfully and maliciously" shooting his son.

Priscilla Paris

Born November 21, 1944
Died March 5, 2004
A member of the girl group The Paris Sisters, Priscilla Paris had formed the San Francisco-based trio with her two older sisters, Albeth and Sherrell. Discovered by The Andrews Sisters, the trio first recorded for Decca Records in 1954. Emerging as the group's lead singer, Priscilla Paris provided the yearning vocals on the lush, Phil Spector-produced Top 10 single, 'I Love How You Love Me' (1961). The group returned to the Top 40 only once more with 'He Knows I Love Him Too Much' (1962). After parting with Spector, The Paris Sisters recorded for several labels in the Sixties – most notably Warner-Reprise – before Priscilla chose to focus on a solo career. In all, Priscilla Paris recorded three solo albums beginning with 1967's *Priscilla Sings Herself.*
CAUSE: She suffered severe injuries during a fall in Paris, France. She had moved to the city in the late Seventies.

(Little) Junior Parker

(HERMAN PARKER, JR.)
Born March 27, 1932
Died November 18, 1971
A prolific Memphis-based blues singer and harmonica player, (Little) Junior Parker is best known as the composer of 'Mystery Train'. Born in West Memphis, Arkansas, he practised his harmonica when he wasn't working in the cotton fields. A chance meeting with blues legend Sonny Boy Williamson inspired Parker to pursue his craft. Hitting the road in 1949 behind Howlin' Wolf, Parker shared the stage with another talented harmonica player, James Cotton. Parker formed his own group, The Blue Flames, in 1950 and moonlighted in a loose-knit Memphis-based group, The Beale Streeters, alongside Johnny Ace and B.B. King. Aided by talent scout Ike Turner, Parker recorded his first solo session for Modern Records in 1952. With his popularity growing via regular radio performances, Parker switched to Sam Phillips' Sun Records in 1953, recording four tracks, and scoring an R&B hit in 1953 with 'Feelin' Good'. The most famous of the four songs was a Parker original called 'Mystery Train' which was immortalised in 1955 by labelmate Elvis Presley. At Sun Records, Phillips helped to soften and refine Parker's earthy-blues sound. Drawn to Don Robey's Duke Records, Parker enjoyed a string of R&B hits at the label including 'Next Time You See Me' (1957), 'Sweet Home Chicago' (1958), 'Five Long Years' (1959), 'Driving Wheel' (1961), 'In The Dark' (1961), and 'Annie Get Your Yo-Yo' (1962). Leaving Duke Records in 1967, Parker had limited success with his more polished approach. Parker recorded the album *I Tell Stories Sad And True* (1971) shortly before his death.
CAUSE: Suffering from a brain tumour, he died during surgery in Blue Island, Illinois.

Colonel Tom Parker

(ANDREAS CORNELIUS VAN KUIJK)
Born June 26, 1909
Died January 21, 1997
The controversial figure who controlled every aspect of Elvis Presley's career, Colonel Tom Parker was crucial in the rise of the young

singer and in maintaining Presley's high profile. Research into Parker's ancestry has revealed that he was an illegal alien from Holland who was therefore unable to apply for a US passport, which partly explains why he refused to permit Presley to tour overseas. This never became public knowledge during Presley's lifetime, which suggests that Presley himself was uncertain about his manager's background. Parker crossed the Atlantic on a Dutch merchantman, jumped ship, and lied about his identity in order to join the US Army, serving in Hawaii. After leaving the army and working in a series of odd jobs in carnivals (and as a dog catcher) in the Florida area, he broke into show business in the early Forties as a promoter of country & western concerts and as a booking agent to country performers. He was given his "Colonel" nickname by Louisiana governor Jimmie Davis. Turning to artist management, Parker signed the emerging Eddy Arnold in 1948 but the relationship soured. He was also involved with country star Hank Snow. Mesmerised by the reaction to the raw Elvis Presley, Parker pressured the young performer into signing a management deal after having first convinced Presley's parents of his suitability. Thereafter he never took on another client. Parker quickly signed Elvis to RCA Records in a deal which netted the young singer $35,000, a huge sum at that time. From then on Parker controlled every detail of Presley's career, all the while maintaining an inscrutable image as a kind of benevolent father figure to Elvis who at the same time was as sharp as a razor when it came to business deals. His strategy with Elvis was to minimise exposure in order to maximise demand, thereby confining Presley to a life of pampered unreality which in the long term would prove disastrous for his mental health. Throughout the Sixties Parker signed his client to a series of immensely profitable film deals, even though the quality of these movies was almost always lamentably poor. Quality control was never high on Parker's list of priorities; instead he bombarded RCA, movie theatres and fan clubs with ream after ream of cheaply produced Elvis flyers, each one drawing attention to Elvis' latest product, be it a record or film. As tireless in his promotion as he was tasteless in its execution, Parker raked in almost half of Presley's earnings and netted himself further income through lucrative side-deals with RCA, the song publishers Hill & Range and various film companies. Although unhappy with the quality of the film scripts and the songs he was obliged to sing in them, Presley remained loyal to Parker, most likely because neither he nor his father could conceive an alternative way of doing business. Having shrewdly observed that takings from his films and sales of records were declining and that a new or at least different career direction was therefore necessary, Parker masterminded Presley's return to the stage at Las Vegas in 1969. In 1973, he controversially sold the rights to Presley's back catalogue to RCA for a lump sum in lieu of future royalties, a deal which netted Elvis a relatively paltry figure for what is amongst the most valuable catalogues in popular music. However, for all the allegations that Parker swindled Presley out of millions, he nevertheless succeeded brilliantly in maintaining Presley's profile and income during lean periods. How that income was ultimately spent was never Parker's concern, nor was the fact that Presley never received prudent investment advice. Indeed, Parker himself is alleged to have squandered most of his colossal earnings on the gaming tables in Las Vegas. Following Presley's death in 1977, Parker was involved in a lawsuit with the singer's estate, the court ordering him to sell his rights in Presley

for $2 million. In the Nineties, Parker worked as a consultant for the Hilton Hotel in Las Vegas where he lived in a complimentary suite. He also had a home in Palm Springs.
CAUSE: Stroke. He died at Valley Hospital in Las Vegas.
FURTHER READING: O'Neal, Sean. (1998). *My Boy Elvis: The Colonel Tom Parker Story*. New York: Barricade. Vellenga, Dirk, with Farren, Mick. (1988). *Elvis And The Colonel*. New York: Delacorte.

Ian Parkin

Born 1950
Died July 1995
The rhythm guitarist of glam-influenced, British progressive-rock act Be-Bop Deluxe, Ian Parkin appeared on the group's first album *Axe Victim* (1974). Formed in 1972 by guitarist Bill Nelson, the group was aided by deejay John Peel in securing a recording contract. Shortly after the release of *Axe Victim*, Nelson disbanded the group and formed a new outfit from the remnants of Cockney Rebel. Parkin later joined a series of pub bands.
CAUSE: Unknown.

Larry Parnes

(LAURENCE MAURICE PARNES)
Born 1930
Died August 4, 1989
During the second half of the Fifties, Larry Parnes was a dominant figure in the history of UK rock'n'roll and the first major pop manager/impresario of his era. After working in his family's clothing business, he became interested in the theatre and after a meeting with publicist John Kennedy discovered rock'n'roll. His first major signing was Tommy Hicks, renamed Tommy Steele, who went on to become the first significant post-Elvis UK rocker. Parnes rapidly discovered a veritable stable of home grown stars, who were blessed with such exotic names as Marty Wilde, Vince Eager, Dickie Pride, Duffy Power and Johnny Gentle. Arguably Parnes' most potent discovery was Billy Fury, whose career he managed until the end of the Sixties. Another important Parnes' signing was Joe Brown, a gifted guitarist who subsequently enjoyed a career in film and theatre. Parnes was noted for his patriarchal approach in overseeing the conduct of his young charges. His power in the industry was such that few dared rebel against his advice. At a time when the career of a teenage pop star was inevitably ephemeral, Parnes expertly executed that tricky transition to more traditional areas of showbusiness. It was no coincidence that Tommy Steele, Joe Brown and Marty Wilde all went on to enjoy success in stage musicals and films. As well as managing artists, Parnes was also one of the biggest pop promoters of the period. At one point, he employed The (Silver) Beatles to back his singer Johnny Gentle on a tour of Scotland. Parnes even had the chance to sign The Beatles as their sole promoter but declined the offer. By the mid Sixties, he had effectively retired from pop management and spent more time working on musicals. His influence on the British pop music industry remains incalculable and he was without doubt the blueprint for the legion of pop managers that followed in his wake.
CAUSE: He died suddenly after an illness possibly related to a 1981 bout of meningitis.
FURTHER READING: Rogan, Johnny. (1987). *Starmakers & Svengalis: The History Of British Pop Management*. London: Queen Anne Press.

Eddie Parry

Born 1946
Died 1995
As lead vocalist for the Merseybeat band, The Dennisons, Eddie Parry had a pair of minor British hits with a composition co-written by Parry, 'Be My Girl' (1963) and a cover of Rufus

Thomas' 'Walkin' The Dog' (1964). On several occasions, the group appeared on the same bill as The Beatles at Liverpool's Cavern Club. Parry left the group in 1965.
CAUSE: Heart attack.

Gram Parsons

(CECIL INGRAM CONNOR)
Born November 5, 1946
Died September 19, 1973
A talented singer, guitarist and songwriter, Gram Parsons was a key figure in the rise of country rock whose recorded legacy continues to inspire generations of 'new' country performers. Raised in Florida and Georgia, Parsons was the heir to a vast fortune derived from orange plantations. As a teenager he formed a series of R&B-influenced rock groups including The Legends, which included future solo pop star Jim Stafford. Drawn to folk hootenannies and then discovering the Greenwich Village music scene in 1962, Parsons changed musical allegiances and formed The Village Vanguard (named after a coffee house). After recording as a member of The Shilos, Parsons relocated to Cambridge, Massachusetts, in 1965 with the intention of attending Harvard University. Seldom attending classes, he instead formed the pioneering country-rock group, The International Submarine Band. Spawning scores of imitators, the group released a single unheralded album, *Safe At Home* (1967). In early 1968, Parsons was invited to join The Byrds, then performing as a trio. Along with bassist Chris Hillman, he pushed them towards a more country direction, and soon they were recording in Nashville and even appearing on the Grand Ole Opry. The highly influential *Sweetheart Of The Rodeo* (1968) emphasised Parsons' importance to the group and included one of his best songs, 'Hickory Wind'. Prior to its release, he left The Byrds in controversial circumstances on the eve of their tour of South Africa. Later that year, he reunited with Hillman to form The Flying Burrito Brothers and pursue what he eloquently described as "cosmic American music". The results were evident on the following year's *The Gilded Palace Of Sin*, one of the best country rock albums ever released. It was followed by the less impressive but still interesting *Burrito Deluxe*, which included a reading of Jagger/Richard's 'Wild Horses'. By 1970, Parsons had grown tired of The Flying Burrito Brothers and, backed by his trust fund, he was able to finance a solo career without the rigours of constant touring. Leaving the group in 1970 to pursue a solo career, Parsons was sidelined by a motorcycle accident. Parsons befriended Keith Richards of The Rolling Stones in 1971 and was present during the recording of their *Exile On Main Street* album in the South of France. That album's country influences can probably be attributed largely to Parsons. Returning to the US, he formed a talented backing group, The Fallen Angels, which included singer Emmylou Harris. Signing a solo record deal with Warner-Reprise, Parsons recorded a pair of well-received albums, *GP* (1973) and *Grievous Angel* (1974). Following Parsons' untimely death, Emmylou Harris hired his back-up band. The Parsons/Harris duet 'Love Hurts' was later nominated for a Grammy.
CAUSE: Drug overdose. He consumed a fatal quantity of alcohol and morphine. Found unconscious in his room at the Joshua Tree Motel in California, he died at the nearby High Valley Memorial Hospital. Parsons had spent his last day at a tiny bar, drinking and playing pool. In the fulfilment of a macabre pact, two members of his road crew, Phil Kaufman and Michael Martin, stole Parsons' casket as it was being placed onto a plane for a family funeral in Louisiana. Telling

authorities that funeral plans had changed, the pair signed a receipt, using the name Jeremy Nobody, and placed the coffin in a borrowed hearse. They first stopped at a bar to toast their departed friend, then purchased gasoline for the planned funeral pyre at the Joshua Tree Monument, near Los Angeles. The fire was quickly spotted and the fire department arrived on the scene before the cremation was complete. Kaufman was charged only with stealing a coffin and fined $750; the fine was paid through money raised at a subsequent wake. Two months later, ex-Byrd Clarence White was killed in a hit-and-run car crash. Parsons' life had been full of tragedy: his father committed suicide while Parsons was in grade school; his alcoholic mother killed herself when he was 18.

FURTHER READING: Fong-Torres, Ben. (1991). *Hickory Wind: The Life And Times Of Gram Parsons.* New York: Pocket. Rogan, Johnny. (1997). *The Byrds – Timeless Flight Revisited – The Sequel.* London: Rogan House.

Jim Pash

Born December 23, 1948
Died April 29, 2005

A founding member of Sixties surf-rock pioneers The Surfaris, guitarist/saxophonist Jim Pash did not appear on the group's timeless classic 'Wipe Out'. Pash was absent from the session because his father insisted he work at the family store that evening. Intended as the B-Side of 'Surfer Joe', 'Wipe Out' was recorded in only two takes and became a Top Five hit in the US and UK during the summer of 1963. The group rode out the surf craze and disbanded in 1967. In later years, Pash joined reunions of the group.

CAUSE: He succumbed to congestive heart failure at his home in Yucca Valley, California, while awaiting a liver transplant.

Jaco Pastorius

(JOHN FRANCIS PASTORIUS III)
Born December 1, 1951
Died September 12, 1987

A brilliant jazz-rock fusion bassist, Pennsylvania-born Jaco Pastorius was a revolutionary player who took the bass into the forefront with his intricate harmonics and nimble finger-work. Originally a drummer, he switched to bass guitar at 16 and joined a series of Tampa Bay rock bands. Gaining his first taste of success at age 19, he enlisted in Wayne Cochran's band in 1970, but was fired for overshadowing the group's leader. After performing with Blood, Sweat & Tears in 1975, and impressing the group's drummer Bobby Colomby, Pastorius signed a recording contract the following year. A watershed year for Pastorius, in 1976 he played on albums for Joni Mitchell, Ian Hunter, Pat Methany, and Al Di Meola; he also garnered fame and respect within the jazz community for his work on Weather Report's pivotal release, *Weather Report*, his first of six albums with the group; additionally that year, Pastorius recorded a stunning self-titled début album, which was highlighted by 'Portrait Of Tracy' and 'Donna Lee'. Forming Word Of Mouth in 1980, Pastorius toured for the next three years. A popular session player, Pastorius later recorded with Herbie Hancock and Sly Stone. Recording three solo albums in all, Pastorius earned three Grammy nominations. Abusing drugs and alcohol, and suffering from manic-depression, Pastorius was once confined to the psychiatric ward of New York's Bellevue Hospital.

CAUSE: Assaulted outside a Ft. Lauderdale, Florida, after-hours bar, the Midnight Bottle Club, he died in a nearby hospital. He had tried to kick in the door of the club after he was refused admittance. Suffering a fractured skull, he never came out of a coma. The bouncer, martial-arts expert Luc Haven, was convicted of

manslaughter for kicking Pastorius in the head, but he served only four months in prison.
FURTHER READING: Milkowski, Bill. (1996). *Jaco: The Extraordinary Life Of Jaco Pastorius*. San Francisco: Miller Freeman.

Nee-Daku Patato

(DARKU ADAMS)
Born 1932
Died January 1, 1995
As the conga player of the British-based group Osibisa, Nee-Daku Patato played on a pair of 1976 hits, 'Sunshine Day' and 'Dance The Body Music'. Comprising musicians from Ghana and Nigeria, Osibisa merged African percussion and a Latin horn section with a splash of reggae. Joining in the Seventies, Patato appeared on the albums, *Black Magic Night*, *African Flight*, *Unleashed (Live In India)*, *Live At The Marquee* and *Movement*. In the early Nineties, Patato joined world-music jazz ensemble, Trever Watts Moire Music Drum Orchestra.
CAUSE: Unknown. He died in Ghana.

Dave Patillo

Born July 4, 1914
Died September 1967
Tenor and occasional bass player in the Forties/Fifties doo-wop vocal group, The Red Caps, Dave Patillo had initially sung second tenor in the predecessor of the Los Angeles-based outfit, The Four Blackbirds. Formed at Jefferson High School, the group recorded in the late Thirties on Vocalion and Melotone Records. Signing with Beacon Records in the early Forties, the group landed on the pop charts with 'I've Learned A Lesson I'll Never Forget' (1943) and 'No One Else Will Do'. Moving to Mercury Records in 1946, the renamed Steve Gibson and The Red Caps secured a hit with 'Wedding Bells Are Breaking Up That Old Gang Of Mine' (1948). Moving to RCA, The Redcaps scored their final hit in a duet with songstress Damita Jo, 'I Went To Your Wedding' (1952). Patillo left the group in 1956.
CAUSE: Unknown. He died in Los Angeles.

Edward Patten

(EDWARD ROY PATTEN)
Born August 22, 1939
Died February 24, 2005
A member of perennial R&B/soul act Gladys Knight & The Pips, Edward Patten joined the group in the early Fifties. A family ensemble which began as a gospel act at Atlanta's Mount Moriah Baptist Church, the group performed popular music as The Pips and religious music as The Fountaineers but with two of the three female members leaving to get married, Edward Patten joined the group and his cousin, Gladys, emerged as the group's lead singer. After scoring their début hit in 1961 with 'Every Beat Of My Heart' (via two different versions, both of which charted), a pregnant Gladys Knight left the group. Struggling without Gladys, The Pips were forced to work as session singers, and upon Knight's return in 1964, the group scored a pair of minor hits on Van McCoy's Maxx label. Overruling Gladys Knight's objections, the group voted to sign with Motown in 1965 and, as beneficiaries of the label's hit factory, they enjoyed a string of hits with 'Everybody Needs Love', 'I Heard It Through The Grapevine', 'If I Were Your Woman', and their only self-composed Motown hit, 'I Don't Want To Do Wrong'. Disheartened by their treatment at the label, Gladys Knight & The Pips left Motown following the expiration of their contract in 1972. Lured to Buddah Records with a lucrative advance, the group continued their chart run, beginning with the Grammy-winning, 'Midnight Train To Georgia'. When Motown scored a surprise hit in 1973 with a leftover track, 'Neither One Of Us', the group sued their former label over unpaid royalties. The group's

Buddah hits continued with 'Best Thing That Ever Happened To Me', 'On And On' and the medley 'The Way We Were'/'Try To Remember'. During this period, the group landed its own NBC variety show and Knight starred in the film *Pipe Dreams* but after receiving a bad cheque for $100,000 from Buddah, the group filed suit against their label. With lawsuits abounding, Gladys Knight & The Pips were barred from recording together, and instead released separate albums. Reunited at CBS Records in 1980, Gladys Knight & The Pips recorded the poor-selling Ashford & Simpson-produced album *About Love*. Switching to MCA Records in 1987, the group scored a pair of R&B chart hits with 'Love Overboard' and 'Lovin' On Next To Nothin''. Soon after, Gladys Knight left The Pips for a solo career but, as separate acts, again both Knight and The Pips fared poorly. Patten later co-founded the Atlanta-based label Crew Records, where he sang backup for a number of artists.
CAUSE: Suffering a series of strokes, he died at St. Mary's Mercy Hospital in the Detroit suburb of Livonia, Michigan. He was in poor health and retired from performing after suffering his first stroke in 1995.

Lover Patterson

Born c. 1930
Died 1965
An R&B singer/songwriter and manager, Lover Patterson entered the music field as the valet for The Orioles. Leaving to join The (Five) Crowns, he quickly emerged as the group's manager. But when a member failed to show up for a performance, Patterson would join the group and pretend to sing along. Adding Ben E. King to the group, Patterson signed the talented vocalist to a personal contract. Meanwhile, when manager George Treadwell fired the entire line-up of The Drifters, he hired The Crowns as a replacement group. Remaining with the group as their road manager, Patterson quit after his many squabbles with Treadwell. Patterson co-penned The Drifters' hit 'There Goes My Baby', and in the mid Sixties recruited a short-lived, competing Drifters group.
CAUSE: Unknown.

Mike Patto

(MICHAEL PATRICK MCGRATH)
Born September 22, 1942
Died March 4, 1979
Scottish-born leader and vocalist of the early Seventies British rock band Patto, Mike Patto broke into music in 1966 as a member of the London-based group, The Bo Street Runners. After a brief stint with The Chicago Line, Patto released a solo single on Columbia Records before joining the Ollie Halsall-led psychedelic-pop group Timebox in 1967. Signing with Deram Records, the group managed a moderately successful British hit single with 'Beggin''. Taking a progressive rock turn by 1970, the renamed Patto released three influential, but poor selling albums in the early Seventies beginning with the Vertigo release *Patto*. Disbanding the group in 1974, and retaining guitarist Ollie Halsall, Mike Patto formed Boxer. After releasing three albums, Patto disbanded the group in 1977. Patto then joined a latter line-up of Spooky Tooth, providing the vocals on the album, *The Mirror*. At the time of his death he was working with a studio group called Hinckley's Heroes.
CAUSE: Throat cancer.

Charley Patton

Born 1887
Died April 28, 1934
A pioneering Delta blues guitarist, Charley Patton was instrumental in defining the genre. A native of Edwards, Mississippi, Patton was raised on the notorious Dockery

plantation. Preferring to play guitar instead of working the fields, Patton was often joined by guitarist Willie Brown. Performing for large audiences in gin joints and at weekend plantation shows, the small-framed, charismatic Patton earned a reputation as a quick-tempered, hard-drinking womaniser. A consummate entertainer, the gruff-voiced Patton employed a percussive, down-home guitar style. Recording prolifically for Paramount Records beginning in 1929, Patton infused social and religious commentary into classics such as 'Pony Blues' and 'Poor Me'; Patton was often joined in the studio by guitarists Willie Brown and Son House, and pianist Louise Johnson. His health failing, Patton recorded his final tracks in New York City in 1934. Patton's finest work was assembled on the Yazoo album, *King Of The Delta Blues*.
CAUSE: Heart disease.
FURTHER READING: Calt, Stephen. (1988). *King Of The Delta Blues: The Life And Times Of Charley Patton*. Newton, NJ: Rock Chapel.

Clarence Paul

(CLARENCE PAULING)
Born March 19, 1928
Died May 6, 1995
Best known as a Motown songwriter, vocalist Clarence Paul first gained fame as a member of the popular Fifties doo-wop group, The "5" Royales. Born in the Winston-Salem area of North Carolina, Paul initially joined several family members, including brother Lowman, in a family gospel group, The Royal Sons Quintet. With Apollo Records showing interest in the group, the renamed Royal Sons released two well-received singles in 1951. But with the label wanting a more rocking sound, the group emerged as a secular R&B band, The "5" Royales. Following the release of their début non-religious single 'Too Much Of A Little Bit', Clarence Pauling left the group. Paul then joined a pair of leading gospel groups, Wings Over Jordan and The Coleman Brothers. Then, after serving in the Korean War, Paul pursued a solo R&B career in the late Fifties, recording for Federal, Roulette, and Hanover Records, and though Paul was unsuccessful as a solo act, his material received airplay via popular cover versions by Roy Hamilton and Hank Ballard. Inspired by his successes, he moved to Detroit to work as a full-time songwriter, and shortened his last name from "Pauling" to "Paul". There, he frequently aided neighbour Steveland Morris (later known as Stevie Wonder) in his musical pursuits. Both Wonder and Paul signed to Motown Records where Paul assumed production and songwriting duties, overseeing Wonder's 'Fingertips' and 'Hey Love', and working with Marvin Gaye. Paul and Wonder also scored a duet hit in 1966 with a cover of Dylan's 'Blowin' In The Wind'; the pair later penned Aretha Franklin's hit 'Until You Come Back To Me'. Leaving Motown in the late Sixties, Paul later worked at MGM Records. Abusing drugs and experiencing tax problems, Paul was later hired by Motown executive Mickey Stevenson for his new Venture Records label.
CAUSE: In poor health for some time, he succumbed to complications from heart disease and diabetes. He died in Los Angeles.

Lowman Pauling

(LOMOND PAULING)
Born July 14, 1926
Died December 26, 1973
Guitarist, songwriter, and bass vocalist of the Fifties doo-wop group The "5" Royales, North Carolina-born Lowman Pauling was reared in a coal-mining community in West Virginia. Nicknamed "Pete", Pauling constructed a home-made guitar, before receiving a store-bought version from his musician father. In the early

Forties Lowman Pauling joined several family members, including brother Clarence, in the Winston-Salem based family gospel group, The Royal Sons Quintet. Though not achieving the stature of gospel stars like The Soul Stirrers, the group enjoyed a regional following. With Apollo Records showing interest in the group, the renamed Royal Sons released two well-received singles in 1951. But with the label wanting a more rocking sound, the group emerged as a secular R&B band, The "5" Royales. Their début single, 'Too Much Of A Little Bit', featured a rare lead by Lowman Pauling. Although a talented bluesy guitarist who always played his instrument on stage, Pauling was not permitted to play on the group's sessions until their fifth release. Completing their metamorphosis from gospel to R&B, the John Tanner-fronted "5" Royales recorded their first of many Pauling-penned, sexually tinged hits with 'Baby, Don't Do It' (1952). Backed by the Charlie Ferguson Orchestra, the group continued its hit run with 'Help Me Somebody'/'Crazy, Crazy, Crazy' (1953), 'Too Much Lovin'' (1953), and 'I Do' (1954). Switching to King Records, The "5" Royales managed two more hits, 'Tears Of Joy' (1957) and 'Think' (1957). One of their releases, the Pauling/Ralph Bass composition, 'Dedicated To The One I Love' (1954), was a bigger hit for both The Shirelles and The Mamas & The Papas. (Meanwhile, Pauling sued Apollo Records and his publishing company over unpaid royalties.) Although their chart run had waned, the group would remain a strong live draw into the early Sixties. Temporarily leaving The "5" Royales in 1960 to pursue a solo career, Pauling stayed with the group until its demise in 1965, releasing a final single as El Pauling and The "5" Royales. Remaining in the music industry, Pauling worked with several artists including Sam & Dave.
CAUSE: He died of a seizure in Manhattan.

Johnny Paycheck

(DONALD EUGENE LYTLE)
Born May 31, 1938
Died February 18, 2003
An outlaw-style country singer-guitarist who garnered occasional crossover airplay, Johnny Paycheck began playing in bar bands at a young age. While in the Navy, he spent two years confined in a military penitentiary for assaulting an officer. Relocating to Nashville, Paycheck was befriended by music executive Buddy Killen, signing a songwriting deal with Tree Publishing and a recording contract with Decca Records, initially recording under the name, Donny Young. Over the next several years, he joined the backing bands of the city's leading country stars, Ray Price, Porter Wagoner, Faron Young and, for a four year stint beginning in 1962, George Jones. Legally changing his name to Johnny Paycheck in 1965, he began his long string of country hits, including 'Little Darlin'', the Grammy-nominated 'She's All I Got', 'Mr. Lovemaker', and his enduring signature piece, 'Take This Job And Shove It', which spawned the 1981 film of the same name. Teaming with his former boss George Jones, Paycheck had several duet hits beginning with the 1978 cover of the Chuck Berry classic 'Mabellene'. In 1989, Paycheck began a two-year prison stint for shooting a man in a barroom fight and in 1997 he became a member of the Grand Ole Opry.
CAUSE: Suffering from emphysema for a number of years, he succumbed to respiratory failure. He died in Nashville.

Gordon Payne

Born c. 1935
Died 1975
Latter-day member of the Fifties

doo-wop vocal outfit The Four Fellows, Gordon Payne joined after they had scored their sole chart hit, 'Soldier Boy'.
CAUSE: Leukaemia. He died in California.

Brenda Payton

Born 1949
Died June 14, 1992
Lead singer for the Philadelphia R&B ballad group, Brenda & The Tabulations, Brenda Payton enjoyed hits with 'Dry Your Eyes' (1967) and 'Right On The Tip Of My Tongue' (1971). The group released three albums, *Dry Your Eyes* (1967), *Brenda & The Tabulations*, and *I Keep Coming Back For More* (1977).
CAUSE: Unknown.

Lawrence Payton

Born March 2, 1938
Died June 20, 1997
A member of the legendary, Sixties Motown group The Four Tops, Detroit native Lawrence Payton was the group's most musically skilled member. An athlete in high school, Payton had joined friends Obie Benson, Abdul Fakir and lead singer Levi Stubbs in 1954, originally as a doo-wop group called The Four Aims. Regulars on the Southern chitlin' circuit, the renamed Four Tops briefly recorded in the early Sixties at Columbia, and then Riverside Records, and for a time shared a bill with crooner Billy Eckstine. Though initially rejected by Motown chief Berry Gordy Jr. in 1959, the now polished and professional quartet was signed to Motown's short-lived jazz subsidiary, Workshop Jazz. With these sessions shelved, The Four Tops were reassigned to songwriters Holland-Dozier-Holland. Taking a pop-soul turn, The Four Tops enjoyed a defining string of H-D-H Motown hits beginning with 'Baby I Need Your Loving' (1964) and continuing with 'I Can't Help Myself' (1965), 'Reach Out I'll Be There' (1966), 'Standing In The Shadows Of Love' (1966), and 'Bernadette' (1967). With the departure of H-D-H from Motown, The Four Tops continued with cover hits such as Left Banke's 'Walk Away Renee' (1968), Tim Hardin's 'If I Were A Carpenter' (1968) and, in a duet with The Supremes, Ike and Tina Turner's 'River Deep Mountain High' (1970). Lured to ABC-Dunhill Records with promises of top-notch material, The Four Tops adopted a smoother soul sound. After enjoying hits with 'Keeper Of The Castle' (1972) and the million-selling 'Ain't No Woman (Like The One I've Got)' (1973), The Four Tops faded from the charts. Pursuing a solo project in 1974, Payton landed a minor R&B hit at ABC-Dunhill with 'One Woman Man'. Releasing two albums at Casablanca, The Four Tops scored a comeback hit in 1981 with 'When She Was My Girl'. The group returned to Motown Records in 1983 following their appearance on Motown's televised anniversary special.
CAUSE: Liver cancer. He died at his suburban Detroit home. Until his death The Four Tops held the record as the longest surviving intact group.
FURTHER READING: Taraborrelli, J. Randy. (1986). *Motown: Hot Wax, City Cool & Solid Gold.* New York: Dolphin/Doubleday. George, Nelson. (1985). *Where Did Our Love Go?: The Rise & Fall Of The Motown Sound.* Omnibus Press: London.

Gene Pearson

Born September 15, 1935
Died April 6, 2000
A member of a trio of notable doo-wop outfits, tenor vocalist Gene Pearson first made his mark in the early Fifties as a member of The Rivileers. One of hundreds of aspiring New York City-based, street corner vocal groups, The Rivileers had regional success beginning with 'A Thousand Stars' (1953). Subsequently joining The

Embers, Pearson co-wrote a number of their releases including 'How Do You Feel?'. Landing in the Rudy Lewis/Charlie Thomas-led version of The Drifters in early 1963 as a baritone vocalist, Pearson appeared on several of the group's hits including 'Under The Boardwalk' and 'Saturday Night At The Movies'. Pearson left the group in 1966 and, in the late Nineties, he was performing on the oldies circuit with The Rivileers.
CAUSE: Unknown. He died in Brooklyn, New York.

John Pechickjian

Born 1951
Died December 25, 2000
Johnny Tillotson's guitarist and musical director for 26 years, John Pechickjian oversaw the sessions for hits such as 'Poetry In Motion', 'Without You', 'It Keeps Right On A-Hurtin'' and 'Talk Back Trembling Lips'.
CAUSE: Natural causes. He died in Los Angeles.

Daryl Pediford

Born c. 1955
Died October 30, 2004
A guitarist and vocalist, Daryl Pediford was a member of the Trans-Siberian Orchestra. Combining hard rock with classical music, the 60-piece New York City-based orchestra employed various vocal choirs and soloists. Trained in soul and gospel, Pediford provided the lead vocals on the group's renditions of 'Three Kings' and 'Music Box Blues', and last appeared on the album *The Lost Christmas Eve*. Pediford was previously a guitarist for Kool & The Gang.
CAUSE: Unknown.

Paul Peek

(PAUL EDWARD PEEK, JR.)
Born June 23, 1937
Died April 3, 2001
A member of Gene Vincent's backing band The Blue Caps, Paul Peek replaced rhythm guitarist Willie Williams in 1956. Playing Spanish and steel guitar since his mid-teens, Peek was hired by the rebellious Vincent after a chance meeting in Washington DC. Within weeks of joining the group, Peek was in a Hollywood studio shooting a performance of the group's previous hit 'Be-Bop-A-Lula' for the Jane Mansfield film *The Girl Can't Help It*; to the astonishment of Vincent, Peek stole the scene with his exuberant antics. Developing "The Clapper Boys" stage routine with bandmate Tommy Facenda, Peek and Facenda flanked Vincent, providing backing vocal harmonies and synchronised hand claps, as seen in the group's performance of 'Baby Blue' from the 1958 film *Hot Rod Gang*. Peek played his Gretsch guitar on a number of Blue Caps' tracks including the hits 'Lotta Lovin'' and 'Dance To The Bop' before parting with Vincent to pursue a solo career, spending the next 40 years performing in nightclubs and occasionally as part of Blue Caps revival acts. Recording sporadically, Peek managed to place two singles on the lower reaches of the pop charts.
CAUSE: Stricken with liver disease and skin cancer, he underwent surgery in February 1999. He died at his home in the Atlanta suburb of Lithonia, Georgia.

John Peel

(JOHN ROBERT PARKER RAVENSCROFT)
Born August 30, 1939
Died October 26, 2004
The most well-liked British deejay of the rock era, John Peel's influence could make or break new acts but it was his undying support for maverick artists that earned him the admiration of fans. Born into a comfortable upbringing in the town of Heswall near Liverpool, Peel was drawn to rock music after hearing Elvis on the radio. After completing his two years of National Service in the British Army in 1959, Peel's father arranged

his passage to America where he worked in the textile business. He also worked as an insurance salesman, and was hired as a deejay on an R&B programme at WRR in Dallas. Then, during the rise of Beatlemania in 1964, thanks to his ties to Liverpool, Peel became the "official" Beatles correspondent with another Dallas station, KLIF. This led to minor local celebrity status because, as Peel later admitted, no one bothered to ask him whether he'd actually met the Fab Four! He then took a radio job in Oklahoma, before landing at a station in California in 1966, where he first heard and nurtured the cult psychedelic group, The Misunderstood, encouraging them to go to England, and another underground legend, Don van Vliet – a.k.a. Captain Beefheart – who he retained a lifelong affection for. Returning to Great Britain under stressful personal circumstances in the spring of 1967, his American radio credentials led to him being hired, untested, in pirate radio. In the years leading up to popular music receiving widespread airplay on the BBC, the genre was the domain of illegal, pirate radio stations who broadcasted from ships on the open sea. One of these stations was Radio London, where Peel was first heard in the UK on a programme which evolved into *The Perfumed Garden*. Reading poetry – some sent to him by a young Marc Bolan of Tyrannosaurus Rex whom Peel championed – and playing records brought back or imported from the US, he was an immediate sensation. With the demise of the pirates, in September 1967, Peel was hired by the BBC to co-host a Sunday afternoon record programme, *Top Gear*, with DJs Pete Drummond and later Tommy Vance on the corporation's newly established station, Radio One. Eventually he became sole presenter and controlled his own playlists which reflected his eclectic tastes. Remaining at the station for the rest of his career, Peel outlasted all of his contemporaries and spent nearly four decades promoting new acts on his night-time programme. Playing an eclectic mix of rock, blues and folk, Peel initially aided the careers of T. Rex, Pink Floyd, David Bowie, and The Faces. As well as radio, Peel was also seen as a host on the late Sixties BBC TV arts programme *How It Is* and also went out on the road, playing records at hippie concerts and festivals in the late Sixties and early Seventies. In 1969, Peel launched his own record company, Dandelion Records, with record executive Clive Selwood, that folded after three years. In the studio, Peel was just as willing to break the rules. His straightforward style, and occasional blunders, saw him voted *Melody Maker*'s top DJ 11 times in a row. By 1976, Peel veered away from classic and progressive rock artists and began championing the burgeoning punk and new-wave movement, giving airplay to such bands as The Sex Pistols, The Clash, Joy Division, and The Undertones, becoming the first DJ to play a record twice in a row with the latter's 'Teenage Kicks' – his favourite record of all time. This policy of giving a hearing to alternative or "challenging" music continued throughout the Eighties and Nineties with Peel's late-night, three times a week show aiding the careers of The Smiths, The Fall, Pulp, Nirvana and P.J. Harvey to name the more well known among hundreds who owe him a debt of gratitude. Often airing exclusive material, Peel recorded over 2,000 artists in what became known as "The Peel Sessions", of which a number were issued on a label launched by Peel and Selwood, Strange Fruit Records. Arguably, Peel's most fertile period occurred during his partnership with show producer, John Walters. The two were frequently at odds,

sometimes over the choice of material Peel favoured but this contributed to a healthy working and personal relationship that lasted until Walters' death. The pair also contributed a column to the now defunct rock publication *Zigzag*, and in the early Seventies Peel contributed a weekly column to *Sounds* magazine. During his latter years, Peel sometimes broadcast his programme from his country cottage near Suffolk where he lived in contented domesticity with his wife Sheila (universally known as "The Pig", Peel's nickname for her!) whom he married in 1974 and their four children. He also took on secondary jobs such as commercial voice-overs and, in direct opposition to his role of champion of the bizarre, the host of Radio 4's Saturday morning programme *Home Truths*. Among his many awards, Peel was honoured with an Order of the British Empire in 1998.
CAUSE: A diabetic, he suffered a heart attack while on holiday with his wife in Cuzco, Peru.

Leon Peels

Born 1936
Died April 10, 1999
The lead vocalist of The Blue Jays, Leon Peels formed the doo-wop vocal group in the Fifties with friends from a local basketball court. A native of Arkansas, Peels was raised in Venice, California. After three years of informal practice, The Blue Jays landed a recording contract in 1961 with Milestone Records, a label launched by former doo-wop/country singer Werly Fairborn. Penned by Leon Peels and bandmate Alex Manigo, the quintet's first of five singles, 'Lover's Island', entered the Top 40 in 1961. But shortly thereafter their label declared bankruptcy and The Blue Jays disbanded in 1962. Then with Fairborn joining partner Madelon Baker to form a new label, Peels was teamed with a backing band called The Hi Tensions for a regional hit, 'A Casual Kiss'. Returning to the stage in the Eighties, Peels and The Blue Jays recorded a single in 1989.
CAUSE: Cancer.

Paul Pena

Born January 26, 1950
Died October 1, 2005
A bluesman who wrote The Steve Miller Band's Top 10 hit 'Jet Airliner' (1977), Paul Pena is better known for his Tuvan-style throat singing and was the subject of the 1999 Academy Award-nominated film *Genghis Blues*. Nearly blind throughout his entire life due to congenital glaucoma, Pena was introduced to the Central Asian musical form in the Eighties while listening to a Moscow-based shortwave broadcast.
CAUSE: Suffering from complications of diabetes and pancreatitis, he died in San Francisco.

Brian Pendleton

Born April 13, 1944
Died May 16, 2001
The rhythm guitarist of British R&B/rock act The Pretty Things, Brian Pendleton appeared on the group's early records. The Pretty Things were formed by singer Phil May and guitarist Dick Taylor, who had just left an embryonic line-up of The Rolling Stones in 1962. A native of Wolverhampton, Pendleton joined the "Pretties" a year later. Among the first British groups to achieve mainstream success with blues/R&B material, the long-haired Pretty Things wore their hair longer than any other British group – even The Rolling Stones, a group they were constantly compared to. The group's UK chart entries between 1964/66 ran (in order): 'Rosalyn', 'Don't Bring Me Down' (banned in the US due to its lyrics), 'Honey, I Need', 'Cry To Me', 'Midnight To Six Man' and 'Come See Me', but the group were unable to make headway in the US, partly due to their wild sound and

image. Experiencing personal problems, Pendleton quit the band in 1966 and soon dropped out of the music scene altogether. He made a brief appearance with the group in 1995 at the legendary 100 Club in London, performing on the encore 'Rosalyn'. At the time of his death, he was looking forward to receiving long-overdue Pretty Things' royalties.
CAUSE: Stricken with cancer, he was found dead near the front door of his home in Maidstone, Kent.

Hugo Peretti

Born December 6, 1916
Died May 1, 1986
A successful producer and songwriter of Italian descent who teamed with cousin Luigi Creatore as Hugo & Luigi, Hugo Peretti was a former trumpeter who broke into music as a Broadway pit musician. After recording a number of children's songs at Mercury Records in the early Fifties, Hugo & Luigi produced The Gaylords' Top 10 hit 'The Little Shoemaker' in 1954; on the track, Peretti sang one of the verses in Italian and was billed on the label as Hugo Perelli. Also at Mercury, the pair oversaw the recordings of jazz chanteuse Sarah Vaughan and cover-record queen Georgia Gibbs. Within a couple of years, Hugo & Luigi were soon key players in New York's rising rock and R&B scene. After buying a share of Roulette Records, the pair wrote material under the pseudonym, Mark Markwell; there they had their best success with pop-rockabilly teen idol Jimmie Rodgers on 'Honeycomb', 'Kisses Sweeter Than Wine', and a pair of Hugo & Luigi compositions, 'Oh, Oh, Falling In Love Again' and 'Secretly'. As independent producers, Hugo & Luigi then signed a five-year pact with RCA, their hit run continuing with 'I Will Follow' (Little Peggy March), 'Shout' (The Isley Brothers), 'Tell Laura I Love Her' (Ray Peterson), and a pair of songs they co-wrote, 'The Lion Sleeps Tonight' (The Tokens) and 'Can't Help Falling In Love' (Elvis Presley). However, their biggest prize came when Sam Cooke left Keen Records for RCA. With the aid of Hugo & Luigi, Cooke's hit run intensified with polished soul gems such as 'Chain Gang', 'Cupid', and 'Another Saturday Night'. As recording artists themselves, Hugo & Luigi scored a pair of minor hits at RCA with 'La Plume De Ma Tante' (1959) and 'Just Come Home' (1960). After their contract with RCA expired in 1964, Hugo & Luigi teamed with George Weis to pen the Broadway musical *Maggie Flynn* – a poorly received Civil War-era play which was forced to close after ten weeks. Later launching Avco Records, Hugo & Luigi wrote and produced hits for The Stylistics, and their last major success came in 1975 with the production of the chart-topping disco smash, 'The Hustle' (Van McCoy). Hugo and partner Luigi retired in 1979.
CAUSE: He died in Englewood, New Jersey, following a lengthy undisclosed illness.

Carl Perkins

(CARL LEE PERKINGS)
Born April 9, 1932
Died January 19, 1998
A pioneering rockabilly singer, Carl Perkins was a contemporary of Elvis Presley at Sun Records. Born on a sharecropping farm in the Mississippi River town of Tiptonville, Tennessee, Perkins picked cotton from the age of four. Here Perkins was exposed to the gospel and blues strains of bellowing black field-labourers. Raised in a dirt-poor home without electricity, Perkins was taught to play the guitar by an elderly black neighbour. With his father bedridden with tuberculosis, Carl Perkins joined brothers Jay and Clayton at a mattress factory; the siblings also formed a country band, The Perkins Brothers. With the addition of drummer W.S. "Fluke" Holland, the group settled into a

country-R&B hybrid that featured Carl Perkins' prominent electric-guitar leads. Encouraged by the success of Elvis Presley's innovative rendition of Bill Monroe's 'Blue Moon Of Kentucky', the Perkins brothers auditioned at Sun Records in 1954. Initially bombing with a song he had written at age 13, 'Movie Magg' (which was released on the Sun subsidiary, Flip), Carl Perkins soon toured with labelmates Elvis Presley and Johnny Cash. Following the sale of Presley's contract, Sun Records chief Sam Phillips was determined to mould Perkins into the next Elvis; but with the lanky Perkins possessing none of Presley's raw sensuality or confidence, that did not happen. Perkins did manage a trailblazing multi-format smash with the rockabilly standard 'Blue Suede Shoes' (1956), the song penned by Perkins at his kitchen table at three in the morning. With his star in the ascent, Perkins suffered a serious setback. En route to New York City for appearances on the nationally televised programmes, *The Perry Como Show* and *The Ed Sullivan Show*, the group's car was involved in a head-on collision. Carl suffered a fractured skull and neck and Jay Perkins was seriously injured. While 'Blue Suede Shoes' dominated the airwaves and gave Sun Records its first million-seller, Perkins was in a hospital bed recuperating. Returning to the studio, Perkins moved to the country market, securing three Top 10 country hits in the late Fifties with 'Boppin' The Blues', 'Your True Love' and 'Dixie Fried'. Leaving Sun Records with his career in decline, Perkins began abusing alcohol. While touring through Britain, Perkins was approached by Ringo Starr who asked if The Beatles could record his songs. Perkins' stature was quickly revitalised by The Fab Four's recordings of 'Honey, Don't', 'Everybody's Trying To Be My Baby' and 'Matchbox'. In 1967, Perkins joined Johnny Cash as both a backing guitarist and as an opening act; Perkins also appeared on Cash's television programme and penned his chart-topping country hit 'Daddy Sang Bass' (1969). Leaving Cash in 1975 to form a band with sons, Stan, Greg, and Steve, Perkins began adding Christian songs into his rock'n'roll repertoire. Attempting a comeback with the album *Old Blue Suede's Back*, Perkins remained an active performer in the Eighties, working with former Sun labelmates Johnny Cash and Roy Orbison; in 1989, Perkins co-wrote and performed on The Judds' number 1 country hit, 'Let Me Tell You About Love'. Having lost several relatives to cancer, Perkins beat a bout of throat cancer in 1991. Recorded at the Sun studio, the 1996 tribute album, *Go Cat Go!* teamed Perkins with Paul Simon, Tom Petty, and others.
CAUSE: Suffering several strokes in the last few years of his life, he died from complications at Jackson-Madison County General Hospital in Jackson, Tennessee.
FURTHER READING: Perkins, Carl. (1996). *Go, Cat, Go!: The Life And Times Of Carl Perkins, The King Of Rockabilly*. New York: Hyperion.

Clayton Perkins

(LLOYD CLAYTON PERKINGS)
Born 1935
Died December 25, 1973
The brother of rockabilly star Carl Perkins, Clayton Perkins was the bassist in his brother's band. Working the sharecropping fields of Tennessee as a young child, Clayton Perkins submitted a fake birth certificate at age 14 to join the marines, but quit after a very short time. Playing an upright bass, Clayton teamed with brothers Jay and Carl as The Perkins Brothers. Signed by Sun Records, the group was involved in a serious car crash in 1956 as Carl Perkins' début hit, 'Blue Suede Shoes', was storming up the charts.

Fired by Carl Perkins in 1963, Clayton Perkins became depressed, never to work again. Abusing alcohol, he became estranged from his family.
CAUSE: Suicide. Lying alone in bed, he shot himself with a .22 pistol, a few weeks after undergoing stomach surgery.
FURTHER READING: Perkins, Carl. (1996). *Go, Cat, Go!: The Life And Times Of Carl Perkins, The King of Rockabilly*. New York: Hyperion.

Greg Perkins

(GREGORY JAY PERKINS)
Born January 15, 1959
Died November 18, 2005
The son of rockabilly pioneer Carl Perkins, bass guitarist Greg Perkins played in his father's band for 28 years. Also a songwriter, Greg Perkins co-wrote many of the band's songs, and his brother Stan was drummer.
CAUSE: In poor health for several years, he succumbed to cancer.

Jay Perkins

(JAMES BUCK PERKINGS)
Born 1930
Died October 21, 1958
The brother of rockabilly star Carl Perkins, Jay played acoustic guitar in his brother's band. Sickly for the remainder of his life following a bout of double pneumonia at the age of two, Perkins joined his parents and siblings in picking cotton as soon as he was able. Playing an acoustic guitar behind brother Carl's electric model, Jay teamed with brothers Clayton and Carl as The Perkins Brothers. Signed by Sun Records, the group was involved in a serious car crash in 1956 as Carl Perkins' début hit, 'Blue Suede Shoes', was storming up the charts. With Jay Perkins' health worsening in the summer of 1958, brother Carl quit touring to spend time with him.
CAUSE: Injured in a car accident en route to television appearances in New York City, Jay Perkins never fully recovered. While Jay and Carl Perkins' were riding in the back seat of the loaned luxury Chrysler, Clayton, W.S. Holland, and the driver, Stewart Pinkhams, sat in front. Carl Perkins writes in his first autobiography: "Our car hit an old pick-up truck five miles from Dover, Delaware. Clayton, W.S., and Stewart were thrown from the car but received only minor cuts. W.S. found me lying face down in a pool of water and thought I was dead. He dragged me to a grassy bank. Jay was still in the car." While Jay suffered a broken neck, the pick-up driver died. His injuries still evident, Jay Perkins eventually rejoined his brother's band. In January 1958, he fell ill on tour and died soon after from a brain tumour.
FURTHER READING: Perkins, Carl. (1996). *Go, Cat, Go!: The Life And Times Of Carl Perkins, The King Of Rockabilly*. New York: Hyperion.

Luther Perkins

Born January 8, 1928
Died August 5, 1968
Johnny Cash's guitarist in the Tennessee Three, Luther Perkins was a rudimentary musician who usually played just the bass strings of his instrument. A former car mechanic, Perkins first teamed with Cash in 1954, performing around Memphis as a country and religious act. Perkins switched from an acoustic to an electric guitar in 1955 just as Cash signed to Sun Records. Backing Cash, Perkins appeared on a string of records, beginning with 'Cry! Cry! Cry!' (1955). Perkins was replaced in Cash's band by Carl Perkins (no relation) in 1968.
CAUSE: Falling asleep while smoking, he died at his home from burns and smoke inhalation.

Freddie Perren

(FREDERICK J. PERREN)
Born May 15, 1943
Died December 16, 2004
A producer and songwriter, Freddie

Perren is best known for his work at Motown Records. While pursuing a degree in musicology at Howard University, Perren worked in a record store and also played in a local band who, one night, opened up for soul singer Jerry Butler. Perren filled in on piano for an absent band member, and ended up touring in Butler's band for the next 18 months. Perren then teamed with former college classmate Fonce Mizell, Motown writer Deke Richards and Motown chief Berry Gordy, Jr. in a songwriting/production ensemble called The Corporation. The quartet wrote a number of hit singles for The Jackson 5 including 'I Want You Back', 'The Love You Save', 'ABC' and the Michael Jackson solo release 'Ben', from the film of the same name. In partnership with Mizell, Perren penned the score for the film *Hell Up In Harlem* as well as material for Edwin Starr and the post-Smokey Robinson line-up of The Miracles. Focusing on production work, Perren had much success in the disco field: 'If I Can't Have You' by Yvonne Elliman, 'More Than A Woman' by Tavares and 'Boogie Fever' by The Sylvers. Forming his own production company, MVP, Perren's hit run continued with a pair of Peaches & Herb hits, 'Shake Your Groove Thing' and 'Reunited', as well as 'I Will Survive' by Gloria Gaynor. Perren continued his work as a songwriter and producer until suffering a debilitating stroke in 1993.
CAUSE: Heart failure. He died in Chatsworth, California.

Pete Perryer

Born c. 1947
Died September 6, 2005
As lead singer and drummer of the David Gilmour-assisted British country-rock band Unicorn, Pete Perryer issued several albums in the Seventies. Their music impressed the Pink Floyd guitarist so much that he immediately offered to produce them and get them management and recording contracts when he heard them perform in 1973. Gilmour produced and performed on the albums *Blue Pine Trees*, *Too Many Crooks* and *One More Tomorrow*.
CAUSE: Heart attack.

John Persh

Born November 23, 1942
Died January 1981
As a member of Detroit-based, blue-eyed soul-rock band Rare Earth, John Persh (a.k.a. John Parrish) had several crossover hits. Formed in 1961 as The Sunliners by Gil Bridges and Pete Rivera, Persh was added the following year. After recording for a series of labels over several years, the group was spotted by Motown session musician Dennis Coffey. Signing with the label in 1969, the renamed Rare Earth became the most successful white act in Motown's history, featuring Persh on bass guitar and trombone. Rare Earth had a brief hit run with a pair of Temptations' cover versions, 'Get Ready' and '(I Know) I'm Losing You' as well as 'Born To Wander', 'I Just Want To Celebrate' and 'Hey Big Brother'. Persh left the group in late 1971.
CAUSE: He contracted a staphylococcal infection following a bout of pneumonia.

Lennie Peters

(LEONARD SERGEANT)
Born 1933
Died October 10, 1992
Half of the Seventies British pop duo, Peters and Lee, Lennie Peters enjoyed several UK hits beginning with 'Welcome Home' (1973). A former lounge pianist, the London-born singer-songwriter was blind since age 16, the result of two separate accidents. Originally a solo act, Peters released three singles in the Sixties, making his radio début on the BBC in 1963. Joining The Migil Five on piano in 1964, he left before the group scored its

only hit with 'Mockingbird Hill'. Singing mostly romantic ballads, Peters and partner Diane Lee formed a duo in 1970, and were incorrectly assumed by the public to be husband and wife. After disbanding the duo in 1980, Peters reunited with Lee in 1986, touring until a year before his death. The duo had just completed the sessions for their sixteenth album *Through The Years*.
CAUSE: Bone cancer. He died in Enfield, England.

Ray Peterson

Born April 23, 1935
Died January 25, 2005
A pop-rock singer, Ray Peterson possessed a pleading and vulnerable voice, similar to that of his idol Roy Orbison. Peterson had initially considered a career in music during his teens while practising the guitar as he recuperated from polio at a Texas hospital. Settling in Los Angeles, Peterson signed with RCA Records and had several hits, beginning with 'The Wonder Of You' (1959), which was later a hit for Elvis Presley, and the teen tragedy classic, 'Tell Laura I Love Her' (1960). Forming his own label, Dunes Records, Peterson continued his hit run with a cover of the often-recorded standard, the Phil Spector-produced 'Corrina, Corrina' (1960) and the syrupy ballad 'Missing You' (1961). The only other act at Dunes – Curtis Lee – hit the charts with 'Pretty Little Angel Eyes'. Peterson later flirted with country music.
CAUSE: Cancer. He died in Smyrna, Georgia.

Robert Peterson

Born 1937
Died January 12, 1987
Songwriter for The Grateful Dead, Robert Peterson penned 'Pride Of Cucamonga', 'Unbroken Chain', and 'New Potato Caboose'.
CAUSE: He died of an undisclosed illness at his home near San Francisco.

Charles Pettigrew

Born May 12, 1963
Died April 6, 2001
A member of R&B duo Charles & Eddie, Philadelphia native Charles Pettigrew teamed with singer Eddie Chacon to score the pop hit 'Would I Lie To You?' (1992). While studying jazz vocal singing at the Berklee College of Music, Pettigrew was previously a member of the pop group Down Avenue. In 1998, Pettigrew joined Talking Heads spin-off group, Tom Tom Club.
CAUSE: Cancer. He died in Philadelphia.

Norman Petty

Born May 25, 1927
Died August 15, 1984
A pioneering record producer best known for his association with Buddy Holly, Norman Petty originally gained fame in the early Fifties as the leader of a pop-jazz outfit, The Norman Petty Trio. A mostly self-taught pianist, Petty performed regularly on a Clovis, New Mexico, radio station beginning at age 13. After a stint in his late teens as a disc jockey, he left for Dallas, finding a part-time position at Jim Beck's studio. After forming The Norman Petty Trio, which included his wife Vi on piano, Petty returned to Clovis in 1954 and built a small recording studio in his home. Releasing the single 'Mood Indigo' on his own NorVaJak label, Petty garnered local airplay; picked by an RCA subsidiary for national distribution, Petty and his trio landed their first of two pop hits. With his studio becoming popular with regional musicians, Petty attracted the likes of Roy Orbison, The Rhythm Orchids (Buddy Knox and Jimmy Bowen), and most importantly, Buddy Holly. With his band The Crickets, Holly was aided by Petty in defining his rockabilly style. Recording a new version of his Decca release 'That'll Be the Day', Holly landed a chart-topping, million-selling hit. Petty emerged as

the group's manager, and also demanded songwriting credits on a number of Holly compositions. Unhappy with the arrangement, Holly would part with Petty in 1958 and pursue an ill-fated solo career. Following Holly's tragic death in 1959, Petty issued a series of overdubbed Holly sessions but there always remained the suggestion that he had somehow swindled Holly out of the rights to his own work. Petty would continue to have chart success in the early Sixties with 'Wheels' by The String-a-Longs and 'Sugar Shack' by Jimmy Gilmer & The Fireballs. He also worked with Brian Poole & The Tremeloes, playing piano on their hits 'Someone, Someone' and 'The Three Bells'. Remaining in Clovis, Petty later operated a local radio station. Selling his Buddy Holly publishing rights to Paul McCartney in 1974, Petty refused to grant permission for his character to be included in the 1978 film *The Buddy Holly Story*.
CAUSE: Leukaemia. He died at Methodist Hospital in Lubbock, Texas.
FURTHER READING: Goldrosen, John; & Beecher, John. (1996). *Remembering Buddy: The Definitive Biography Of Buddy Holly*. London: Omnibus.

"Lonesome" Dave Peverett

Born April 16, 1943
Died February 7, 2000
The lead singer of Seventies hard rock group Foghat, Dave Peverett was born in Dulwich, south London, but raised in nearby Brixton. Peverett had performed on the London club circuit from 1963, and he was asked by guitarist Kim Simmonds to join the second line-up of Savoy Brown in 1967. Influenced by blues greats such as Buddy Guy and John Lee Hooker, Peverett brought his purist electric-blues guitar work to the popular progressive blues-rock outfit. As a pivotal member of Savoy Brown, Peverett recorded five albums and took over the lead vocal duties on the 1970 release, *Looking In*. Tiring of Simmonds' dictatorial control, Peverett and bandmates bassist Tony Stevens and drummer Roger Earl left to form their own group, Foghat. Discovered by US impresario Albert Grossman at a London nightclub in 1971, Foghat left England for the US and signed with Bearsville Records. From their self-titled, Dave Edmunds-produced, début album, Foghat scored a breakthrough hit with a cover of Willie Dixon's 'I Just Want To Make Love To You' (1972). With the band a greater success in the US than in their native England, Foghat settled in Long Island, New York. From their 1975 album *Fool For The City*, Foghat cemented their AOR fanbase with the title track and the masterful rock standard, 'Slow Ride'. Although not their finest outing, Foghat's seventh release *Foghat Live* (1977) became their best seller. After briefly disbanding in 1980, Foghat started touring three years later. Disbanding again in 1985, two competing line-ups hit the road in the early Nineties, before merging in 1993. Foghat enjoyed renewed interest in the Nineties with the inclusion of a track in the *Dazed And Confused* soundtrack. Recording their final album, *Road Cases*, in 1999, Foghat toured until shortly before Peverett's death.
CAUSE: While battling kidney cancer, he contracted double pneumonia and died at an Orlando hospital. He was diagnosed with cancer in 1998.

Tracy Pew

Born December 19, 1957
Died July 5, 1986
The outspoken, leather-clad, hard-drinking bassist of the Australian alternative rock band The Birthday Party, Tracy Pew joined several art school dropouts in Melbourne including Nick Cave in The Boys Next Door, a predecessor of the group in 1977. Relocating to London in 1980, The Birthday Party gained an

underground cult following with their two album releases, *Prayers On Fire* and *Junkyard*. Imprisoned for drunk-driving in late 1981, Pew was temporarily replaced in the band. Moving to Berlin, The Birthday Party released a pair of unnoticed EPs, before disbanding in 1983. Pew subsequently joined The Saints. Cave later pursued a solo career before forming The Bad Seeds.
CAUSE: Suffering an epileptic seizure while in a bathtub, he died from head injuries.
FURTHER READING: Brokenmouth, Robert. (1996). *Nick Cave: The Birthday Party & Other Epic Adventures*. London: Omnibus.

Kristen Pfaff

Born May 26, 1967
Died June 16, 1994
The bassist of the Courtney Love-led, Seattle-based grunge band Hole, New York-native Kristen Pfaff was classically trained on piano. Attending the University of Minnesota, she was instrumental in launching a campus radio station. After learning to play the bass guitar, she toured as a member of a local group called Janitor Joe, during which time she caught the attention of Hole's guitarist Eric Erlandson. Joining a reassembled version of Hole in 1993, Pfaff was hired by Courtney Love after she caught a performance of Janitor Joe. Moving to Seattle, Pfaff appeared on the second Hole album, the critically acclaimed angst-driven *Live Through This*, which was highlighted by 'Doll Parts' and 'Violet'. With Hole on hiatus after the death of Courtney Love's husband Kurt Cobain, Pfaff rejoined Janitor Joe for a European tour. Pfaff was later replaced in Hole by Melissa Auf Der Maur.
CAUSE: Heroin overdose. She was discovered in her bathtub, with drug paraphernalia at her side. Pfaff's family ordered Love not to attend the funeral. Pfaff's death came just two months after the suicide death of Love's husband, Kurt Cobain.
FURTHER READING: Rossi, Melissa. (1996). *Courtney Love: Queen Of Noise*. New York: Pocket.

Dewey Phillips

Born May 13, 1926
Died September 28, 1968
An influential DJ at WHBQ in Memphis during the Fifties, Dewey Phillips was the first person to play an Elvis Presley disc on the radio. On the evening of July 10, 1954, Sun Records owner Sam Phillips (no relation) asked Dewey Phillips to play an acetate of Presley's 'That's All Right' on his *Red, Hot & Blue* programme. When the phone lines began lighting up, the fast-talking DJ informed Sam Phillips that he had a huge hit on his hands. After playing the record over and over again, he invited the shy 19-year-old Presley into the studio for an on-air interview. Presley obliged, having been dragged out of a nearby cinema where he was watching a film, and Phillips was astonished to discover that he was white. With 7,000 copies of the record pressed for local sales, Presley was on his way to becoming a star. Nicknamed Daddy-O, Phillips joined WHBQ in 1952, initially being given a 15-minute programme. A talented personality whose radio jive targeted blacks and teens, Phillips was soon given a three-hour shift in the coveted evening slot. Fired in the Sixties, Phillips drifted from station to station, in his last years working in Little Rock, Arkansas. A hard-drinker who was hooked on pain killers after two debilitating car crashes, Dewey was eventually left homeless, and was dependent on friends for shelter.
CAUSE: Heart attack. He died at the home of a cousin.

Doug Phillips

Born 1945
Died May 5, 1995
The bass player and vocalist of the California-based rock group The Dartells, Doug Phillips enjoyed a sole

hit with 'Hot Pastrami' (1963). Phillips was still a senior in high school when the record hit the charts. He later fronted The New Concepts, and then a hard rock group, Cottonwood.
CAUSE: Unknown.

Earl Phillips

Born April 25, 1920
Died November 20, 1990
A Chess and Vee-Jay session drummer in the Fifties, Tennessee-born Earl Phillips played behind Jimmy Reed and others.
CAUSE: Unknown.

Ernesto Phillips

(ERNESTO MCKENZIE PHILLIPS)
Born July 13, 1953
Died March 25, 2004
As the leader of Eighties R&B/dance group Starpoint, Ernesto Phillips placed over two dozen singles on the R&B charts. A guitarist and trumpeter, Phillips formed the family group, originally called Licyndiana, in Maryland with his brothers but the group only gelled after adding new lead vocalist Renee Diggs. Signed in 1980 by Casablanca/Chocolate City Records, Starpoint scored club hits with 'I Just Wanna Dance With You' and 'Keep On It'. After passing through Boardwalk Records, the group then joined Elektra in 1984, reaching the Top 40 for the only time with the club classic, 'Object Of My Desire'. The group remained a staple of R&B radio for the rest of the decade with hits such as 'What You Been Missin'', 'Restless', 'He Wants My Body' and 'Say You Will'. The group disbanded in the early Nineties. As a songwriter and producer, Phillips worked with Toni Braxton, Kimberly Scott and Millie Vanilli.
CAUSE: Stroke. He died in Baltimore.

John Phillips

Born c. 1930
Died date unknown
A short-term member of Fifties R&B/doo-wop act The Clovers, singer-guitarist John Phillips was hired upon the departure of lead tenor John "Buddy" Bailey, who had been drafted into the army. Touring with The Clovers throughout the East Coast, Phillips never recorded with the group and was replaced after just six months in early 1953 by Charlie White.
CAUSE: Unknown.

John Phillips

(JOHN EDMUND ANDREW PHILLIPS)
Born August 30, 1935
Died March 18, 2001
The leader of talented folk-rock quartet The Mamas & The Papas, singer-guitarist John Phillips masterfully arranged the group's complicated vocal harmonies. Born in Parris Island, South Carolina, Phillips relocated to New York City where he formed the Greenwich Village folk trio The Journeymen, including Scott McKenzie, who issued three albums on Capitol Records. While on a West Coast tour, husband and father Phillips met 17-year-old Michelle Gilliam. Following the demise of The Journeymen in 1964, Phillips and his now second wife Michelle teamed with Denny Doherty as The New Journeymen. While on an extended holiday jaunt in the Virgin Islands, the trio bumped into a friend from New York City, singer Cass Elliot. Camping out on the beach, the group composed and sang songs which would later appear on their first album. With "Mama" Cass Elliot begrudgingly joining the group, the foursome was initially hired to provide the backing vocals for friend Barry McGuire's album *This Precious Time*, which was released on producer Lou Adler's new Dunhill label. After impressing Adler with their repertoire of original material, they were signed by Dunhill as The Mamas & The Papas. Produced by Adler, the group's début single 'California Dreamin'' – an amalgamation of folk and electric rock featuring their distinctive four-part

vocal harmonies – was a US number four hit in 1965 (though only a Top 30 hit in the UK), and The Mamas & The Papas became instant media darlings with their youthful exuberance and psychedelic costumes. Treated as rock royalty in the late Sixties, the group's brief two year tenure yielded the hits 'Monday, Monday' (a US number one and UK number three in 1966), 'I Saw Her Again' (a song Phillips' wrote about Michelle's infidelity with Doherty), 'Dedicated To The One I Love' (a cover of the version by vocal group The "5" Royales), and the autobiographical 'Creeque Alley'. John Phillips also composed Scott McKenzie's hippie anthem 'San Francisco (Wear Some Flowers In Your Hair)', a worldwide number one during that halcyon "Summer of Love" in 1967. Embracing the spirit of the era, John and Michelle Phillips teamed with Lou Adler and publicist Derek Taylor to coordinate the three-day Monterey Pop Festival – the first and arguably most successful of its kind. As a result of simmering internal strife and the sale of Dunhill to ABC Records, The Mamas & The Papas disbanded in 1968 and Phillips released his well-received solo album, *The Wolfking Of LA*, in 1970. Under the threat of a lawsuit, the group briefly reunited to record their final studio album, *People Like Us*. Following his divorce from Michelle, Phillips married actress Genevieve Waite and turned to stage and film production, financing the Robert Altman-produced comedy *Brewster McLoud* as well as staging a disastrous Broadway musical, *Man On The Moon*. Spending much of the Seventies in a drug haze, Phillips was arrested in 1981 for trafficking; convicted by year's end, he entered drug rehab as did his actress daughter Mackenzie Phillips who had co-starred in the Seventies sitcom *One Day At A Time*. In 1982, Phillips re-formed The Mamas & The Papas with Spanky McFarland (formerly of Spanky & Our Gang) as Mama Cass' replacement. By 1986, the group included Doherty, MacFarlane, John Phillips and his daughter Mackenzie. Also that year, Phillips published his best-selling autobiography *Papa John*. At the time of his death, Phillips was completing a solo album.

CAUSE: Heart failure. He died at the University of California, Los Angeles Medical Center. After years of drug abuse, Phillips had received a liver transplant in 1992.

Linn V. Phillips

(LINN V. PHILLIPS III)
Born August 1, 1947
Died March 23, 1993

Founding guitarist and vocalist of the oldies revival act, Flash Cadillac, Linn V. Phillips appeared with the group in several films including *American Graffiti*. A native of Pennsylvania, Phillips had formed the group in 1969 with several other students at the University of Denver. Releasing their début album in 1973, *Flash Cadillac And The Cadillac Kids*, the group landed two pop hits, 'Good Times Rock & Roll' (1975), and featuring the spoken snippets of deejay Wolfman Jack, 'Did You Boogie (With Your Baby)' (1976).

CAUSE: Heart attack. He died backstage after a sold-out concert with The Tulsa Philharmonic Orchestra.

"Little" Esther Phillips

(ESTHER MAE JONES)
Born December 23, 1935
Died August 7, 1984

A legendary R&B singer, Texas-born "Little" Esther veered toward jazz and soul in the latter part of her career. Moving to the Watts section of Los Angeles at age nine, she lived in the vicinity of a chicken farm owned by bandleader/nightclub owner Johnny Otis. Invited by Otis in 1950 to watch a recording session by The Robins, Esther sang on a session as a lark; belting out 'Double Crossing Blues', it would be her first of many hits. The

underage Phillips soon joined Otis' orchestra for a three year stint and was billed as Little Esther with The Johnny Otis Orchestra. A large figured girl who was exposed to drugs at an early age, Little Esther could belt out the blues with her streetwise delivery. Although she managed two more R&B hits at Savoy, 'Mistrustin' Blues' (1950) and 'Cupid's Boogie' (1950), she left the label over the underpayment of royalties. After moving to King-Federal Records, where Otis' orchestra continued to back her, she unsuccessfully sued her old label which had continued to release her material. Recording a series of duets at King-Federal with acts such The Dominoes, Big Al Downing, Little Willie Littlefield, and two noteworthy singles with Bobby Nunn, Phillips landed her final hit at the label in 1952 in a collaboration with Mel Walker, 'Ring-A-Ding-Doo'. Parting with Otis and leaving the label in 1953, Phillips switched to Decca in 1954. But with her output affected by her heavy drinking, Little Esther briefly retired from music. Returning to Houston for what would be a two-year respite, she was considered a has-been at age 19. Then after some poorly received sessions at Savoy, Phillips joined Lennox Records in 1962. With her voice maturing, she topped the charts with a cover of the standard, 'Release Me' (1962). Then joining Atlantic Records in 1964, she was paired with some of the label's greatest jazz and blues talents. There her hits continued with a cover of Dinah Washington's 'What A Diff'rence A Day Makes' (1963) and a retitling of The Beatles' 'And I Love Him' (1965). After entering rehab in 1969, the following year she recorded the King Curtis-produced live album, *Burnin'*. Switching to Creed Taylor's Kudel label in 1972, Phillips scored a hit album with *From A Whisper To A Scream*, and in 1973, landed a surprise pop hit with a Grammy-nominated disco version of 'What A Diff'rence A Day Makes'; she lost the Grammy to Aretha Franklin who then handed the trophy to Phillips. Phillips continued to record regularly into the Eighties. Her final album, *A Way To Say Goodbye*, was released shortly before her death.
CAUSE: Suffering from heart, liver, and kidney problems, she died at U.C.L.A Harbor Medical Center in Carson, California.

Sam Phillips

(SAMUEL CORNELIUS PHILLIPS)
Born January 5, 1923
Died July 30, 2003
The founder of the legendary Sun Records, Sam Phillips played an integral role in the genesis of rock'n'roll through his discoveries of Jerry Lee Lewis, Carl Perkins, Johnny Cash and a former truck driver named Elvis Presley. A native of Florence, Alabama, Phillips barely survived a childhood bout of pneumonia. Exposed to blues music on his father's cotton farm, Phillips was captivated by the impassioned wailings of the black migrant workers. Following his father's death, Phillips quit high school to support the family. Yearning to be a lawyer but unable to afford law school tuition, he instead took a short course in broadcasting at a local technical college. After working behind the microphone at a series of radio stations, Phillips spent four years as a radio announcer and sound engineer at WREC in Memphis. Frustrated by the departure of local blues talent for Chicago, Phillips constructed a recording studio in a converted radio repair shop. Launched in 1949, the Memphis Recording Service initially survived by offering amateurs the opportunity to cut their own vanity records at $1.99 per song. Attracting the region's finest blues talent to his tiny rudimentary studio, Phillips was the first to record Howlin' Wolf, B.B. King and Junior Parker. Initially operating as an independent producer,

Phillips sold master discs to large independent record companies such as Los Angeles' Modern/RPM and Chicago's Chess. Scoring his first R&B smash hit with 'Rocket 88' by Ike Turner & The Kings Of Rhythm (erroneously attributed on the label by Chess Records to lead singer Jackie Brenston), Phillips produced what is often considered the first rock'n'roll song. Angered by Chess' signing of Howlin' Wolf, Phillips launched his own record company in March 1952 with a loan from record label owner Jim Bulleit. Sun's early roster included Billy Lee Riley, Harmonica Frank, and Rufus Thomas, Jr., who in 1953 gave the label its first hit with 'Bear Cat', a note-for-note sequel to Big Mama Thornton's 'Hound Dog'. Instrumental in the success of Sun Records were Phillips' brother Jud, office manager Marion Keisker, and producers Bill Justis and Jack Clement. Actively searching for a white artist who could sing R&B, Phillips realised this goal in 1954 when a young guitarist named Elvis Presley came to Sun to record a song for his mother's birthday. Backed by guitarist Scotty Moore and bassist Bill Black, Presley would record five singles for the label, beginning with a countrified cover of Arthur Crudup's R&B release 'That's All Right (Mama)'. After a bidding war, Phillips sold Presley's contract to RCA Records in 1956 for $35,000, and was also offered an executive post at the label which he declined. As well as using the money to help budding rockers such as Jerry Lee Lewis and Carl Perkins, who were drawn to the label on the heels of Presley's meteoric success, Phillips earned millions by investing as an original shareholder of the Holiday Inn motel chain. Though moving his studio to a larger building in 1960, and opening a satellite studio in Nashville the following year, Phillips was soon too busy overseeing several radio stations to tend to his label. (Several Sun rockers like Charlie Rich, Johnny Cash and Conway Twitty emerged as country superstars after joining other labels. Another Sun act, Roy Orbison, also found success elsewhere.) Closing Sun Records in 1968, Phillips sold the label's catalogue to Shelby Singleton, Jr. the following year. In 1987, the Sun studio was sold to musician Gary Hardy, who restored the building as a tourist attraction and in 1988, U2 recorded three tracks for their *Rattle And Hum* film and album at the studio. In 1994, Phillips loaned the original Sun studio equipment to the Rock and Roll Hall of Fame.
CAUSE: Suffering from respiratory problems, he died at St. Francis Hospital in Memphis.

Piano Red

(WILLIAM LEE PERRYMAN)
Born October 19, 1911
Died July 25, 1985
An albino blues pianist whose recording career spanned the Twenties to the Eighties, Piano Red collaborated with the finest blues including Barbecue Bob and Blind Willie McTell. Self-taught, Piano Red left his sharecropping family during his teens to find work as a musician in Atlanta. Signing with RCA Records in 1950, his R&B hits included the million-selling rock'n'roll-styled 'Rockin' With Red', 'Red's Boogie', and 'The Wrong Yo Yo' (1951). As Dr. Feelgood & The Interns, he scored a crossover hit in 1962 with 'Doctor Feelgood'. He spent the last part of his career alternating between his base in Atlanta and touring Europe. His composition 'Mister Moonlight' was recorded by The Beatles on their album *Beatles For Sale*.
CAUSE: Diagnosed with cancer in 1984, he died the following year at his home in Atlanta.

Kenny Pickett

(KENNETH GEORGE PICKETT)
Born September 3, 1942
Died January 10, 1997

The lead singer of the idiosyncratic British art-rock band Creation, Kenny Pickett would use spray paint on stage, while guitarist Eddie Phillips played his instrument with a violin bow. Previously known as The Mark Four, the group had some minor success with the Pickett co-penned single release, 'Hurt Me If You Will'. The renamed Creation were guided by Tony Stratton-Smith and Planet Records owner/producer Shel Talmy for their début single 'Making Time'. Embracing psychedelia, Creation landed its biggest hit in 1966 with the feedback-filled 'Painter Man' (the song was later reprised by Boney M). But following the bankruptcy of Planet Records, the group disbanded in 1968. Pickett later became a tour manager for Led Zeppelin and Steppenwolf, and wrote Clive Dunn's chart-topping 1971 British hit 'Grandad'. In the Eighties, Pickett headed the Kennedy Express, before briefly reforming Creation. Creation's finest output is compiled on the 1998 album *Our Music Is Red With Purple Flashes*.
CAUSE: Unknown. He collapsed and died during an encore of 'Johnny B. Goode' at a gig at a pub in Mortlake, south west London. An autopsy failed to reveal the cause of death.

Wilson Pickett

Born March 18, 1941
Died January 19, 2006
A giant of soul, Wilson Pickett dominated the pop and R&B charts in the Sixties. Born into a family of 10 children, Pickett was reared on a sharecropping farm in Prattville, Alabama. With his parents divorcing, at 16 Pickett moved to Detroit to live with his father. Dropping out of high school, Pickett formed a gospel group called The Violinaires. Overheard singing on his front porch by Willie Schofield of The Falcons (of 'So Fine' fame), Pickett was brought into the group. With his gospel strains adding to the group's doo-wop sound, Pickett was criticised by his mother for embracing "the devil's music". Receiving financial backing from Atlantic Records co-owner Jerry Wexler, The Falcons recorded at Detroit's LuPine Records, gaining a Top 10 R&B hit with 'I Found A Love' (1962) featuring Pickett's frenetic, raspy lead vocals. But, unhappy with his paltry salary, Pickett quit the group. After failing an audition at Atlantic Records, Pickett recorded a self-penned track 'If You Need Me' for Double-L Records (co-owned by Lloyd Price), which competed on the charts with a version by Solomon Burke on Atlantic. Ironically, the two singers soon toured together and the label relented and signed Pickett as a solo act. Teamed with pop producer Bert Berns, Pickett's early Atlantic releases flopped but, undeterred, Jerry Wexler sent Pickett to Memphis to work with the Stax studio band. Aided by Stax session guitarist Steve Cropper, Pickett co-wrote 'In The Midnight Hour', a song which employed a strong, danceable 2/4 beat and set the pattern for "Wicked" Wilson Pickett's future hits. A soaring star, the energetic Pickett crisscrossed the country and toured the UK, continuing his hit run with 'Don't Fight It' (1965) featuring the backing vocals of Patti LaBelle & The Bluebelles, and '634-5789' (1966). However, with Stax demanding a greater share of the profits, Pickett relocated to Rick Hall's Muscle Shoals Fame Studio and recorded several cover songs: Chris Kenner's 'Land Of A 1000 Dances' (1966), Sir Mack Rice's 'Mustang Sally' (1966), a new version of his earlier Falcons hit 'I Found A Love' (1967), Solomon Burke's 'Everybody Needs Somebody To Love' (1967) and Dyke & The Blazers' 'Funky Broadway' (1968). Then in 1968, a then-unknown Muscle Shoals studio guitarist named Duane Allman convinced Pickett to record The

Beatles' 'Hey Jude', which became an unlikely soul ballad hit in early '69. Teaming with an upstart production company led by the Philadelphia-based Gamble & Huff, Pickett's appearances in the R&B charts continued with 'Engine Number Nine' (1970) and 'Don't Let The Green Grass Fool You' (1971). Backed by Muscle Shoals players, Pickett landed a million-selling hit with the impromptu composition 'Don't Knock My Love – Pt. 1' (1972). Quitting Atlantic over ever present monetary issues, Pickett signed with RCA records in 1973 and, moving in a more pop direction, he managed only a few more R&B hits such as 'Take A Closer Look At The Woman You're With' (1973) and 'Soft Soul Boogie Woogie' (1973). With his career nosediving, Pickett briefly recorded on his own label, Wicked Records, and then jumped from label to label. Having staunchly avoided the disco craze, Pickett relented and released a pair of poorly received dance albums in the late Seventies. Often in trouble with the law, Pickett was sentenced to a year in prison in 1993. After recording an album for Motown in 1987, Pickett experienced new-found notoriety with the inclusion of his music in a 1991 film about a white Irish soul band *The Commitments* but, continuing to experience problems with the law, Pickett was unable to reinvigorate his career and was sentenced to a year in prison in 1996 for using cocaine while on probation. Pickett released his final album in 1999, *It's Harder Now*.
CAUSE: He suffered a heart attack and died at a hospital near his home in Reston, Virginia.

Howard Pickup

(HOWARD BOAK)
Born 1951
Died July 1997
As lead guitarist and co-founder of early British punk band The Adverts, Howard Pickup was at the forefront of the punk movement. Signing to Stiff Records in 1976 on the advice of their friends The Damned, the London-based Adverts initially made waves with the self-deprecating single 'One-Chord Wonders' (1977). A rough, untrained aggregate, the group re-recorded the track for their first album, the youthful, angst-filled, *Crossing The Red Sea*. But The Adverts' greatest success came with the irreverent single, 'Gary Gilmore's Eyes', the song penned by the group's chief songwriter and vocalist, Tim "TV" Smith. The Adverts released one more studio album, *Cast Of Thousands*, before breaking up at the end of the punk rock era.
CAUSE: He was diagnosed with an inoperable brain tumour just weeks before his death.

Jeffrey Lee Pierce

Born June 27, 1958
Died March 31, 1996
Bluesy vocalist of the influential Los Angeles-based punk group The Gun Club, Texas-born Jeffrey Lee Pierce merged blues with rockabilly. Relocating to the West Coast, Pierce was a huge fan of Blondie when he formed The Creeping Rituals in 1979. By 1981, he joined a year-old quartet called The Gun Club (which included future Cramps guitarist Kid Congo). Previously a writer for underground newspapers, Pierce penned dark, despairing songs. Marked by Pierce's howling vocals, the group's début album *Fire Of Love* (1981) was issued on Slash/Ruby Records, the project featuring a Robert Johnson cover, 'Preachin' The Blues'. Relocating to England in the mid Eighties, Pierce released a solo effort in 1985, *Wildweed*. Occasionally reforming The Gun Club beginning in 1987, Pierce released material on several labels including Chris Stein and Debbie Harry's Animal Records, his finest project coming with *In Exile* (1992). A world traveller who developed a

fascination for the Far East, Pierce later became a Buddhist.
CAUSE: He suffered a stroke and died from a brain haemorrhage while visiting his father at a hospital in Salt Lake City. Pierce was very ill in his last months, his poor health exacerbated by drugs and alcohol.

Paula Pierce

Born June 23, 1960
Died August 10, 1991
Singer-guitarist of Los Angeles-based, psychedelic-tinged retro rock band The Pandoras, Paula Pierce co-founded the all-girl act with bassist Gwynne Kahn. Hailing from Orange County, Pierce remained with the group throughout its many personnel changes. After signing with Elektra Records in 1987, The Pandoras veered towards hard rock and later issued a pair of EPs on Enigma Records.
CAUSE: After an exercise session at her apartment, she suffered an aneurysm while taking a shower.

Craig Pike

Born January 25, 1963
Died May 23, 1993
A Los Angeles-born bassist who backed Iggy Pop from 1990–91, Craig Pike moved to London in 1992 and formed his own rock band, The Hypnotics. At the time of his death, he was preparing to record a major label début album.
CAUSE: He died in a car crash in London.

Rob Pilatus

Born June 8, 1965
Died April 3, 1998
A member of the disgraced pop-rap duo Milli Vanilli, Rob Pilatus joined partner Fabrice Morvan to front the sham musical group. The son of a black American soldier and a German dancer, Pilatus ran away from home and emigrated to the US where he found work as a breakdancer and model. Pilatus first teamed with Morvan in a Los Angeles-based duo in 1984. Finding little success, the svelte, dreadlocked duo found their way to Germany, coming under the tutelage of producer Frank Farian (who had earlier found success with Boney M). With their entire chart run lasting a little over a year, Milli Vanilli placed four singles in the Top 5 including 'Girl You Know It's True' and the ballad 'Girl I'm Gonna Miss You'. Their début album sold seven million copies, and they won a 1989 Grammy for Best New Artist. Although at first they denied it, they were later obliged to admit that they did not sing their songs, and the duo was stripped of its Grammy. In an attempt to repair their reputation, the duo provided their own vocals on a poorly received album, *Rob And Fab* (1993). A much-watched 1997 VH-1 documentary chronicled the duo's rise and fall.
CAUSE: Pilatus was found dead in a hotel near Frankfurt, Germany, having suffered heart failure as the result of a lethal combination of drugs and alcohol; traces of cocaine and anti-depressants were also found in his bloodstream. He had appeared at a studio the previous day in a very inebriated state. Pilatus had been in and out of detox several times and was planning to enter a drug clinic the following week in Bombay, India. Exhibiting a history of depression, he had attempted suicide in 1991.

Lonnie Pitchford

Born October 8, 1955
Died November 8, 1998
A Delta-style blues revivalist, Lonnie Pitchford is best known as a master of an African-styled, single-stringed instrument called the diddley bow. With his haunting voice and rural-styled acoustic guitar, he became an overnight sensation following his appearance at the National Folk Festival in 1974. Tutored by Robert Junior Lockwood, the stepson of blues great Robert Johnson, Pitchford was a

carpenter by trade who built his instruments (and even his own home). Pitchford released his only album in 1994, *All Around Man*, and earned a Grammy nomination for his work on *Roots Of Rhythm & Blues: A Tribute To The Robert Johnson Era*. At the time of his death, he was completing a second solo album.
CAUSE: Suffering from AIDS, he succumbed to complications from pneumonia. He died at his home in Lexington, Mississippi.

Barbara Pittman

Born April 25, 1938
Died October 28, 2005
The most successful female artist at Sun Records and labelmate Elvis Presley's one-time girlfriend, rockabilly singer Barbara Pittman recorded as both a solo artist and as a member of The Sunrays. Though never achieving a national hit, she remained a popular performer around Memphis and throughout Europe.
CAUSE: Heart failure. She died at her home in Memphis.

David Platz

Born January 13, 1929
Died May 20, 1994
A soft-spoken giant in the British music publishing world, David Platz headed the independent firm, Essex Music. Born in Hanover, Germany, 10-year-old Platz and his sister arrived in Britain in 1939 having fled the Nazi persecution of Jews. Though possessing no formal education in music, Platz was hired as a messenger at Southern Music in London's famed music industry corridor, Denmark Street. Rising through the ranks, in 1946 he was named manager of the organisation's Latin American Music subsidiary. Leaving Southern in 1955, he co-founded Essex Music with American partner Howard Richmond. Keenly aware of emerging musical tastes, Platz acquired the song publishing rights of Fifties pioneers Lonnie Donegan and Chris Barber. With the rise of British rock in the Sixties, Essex signed The Rolling Stones, Moody Blues, Procol Harum, The Who, David Bowie and The Move. Platz also funded Denny Cordell's Deram-affiliated production company, Straight Ahead Productions; and with Cordell reviving the EMI subsidiary, Regal Zonophone, Platz acquired the musical publishing of its acts Joe Cocker and Marc Bolan. Platz also operated a pair of record labels, Fly and Cube. Platz and Richmond parted bitterly in 1979, the process dragging out until 1993. Platz later concentrated his efforts on running Bucks Music enterprises, targeting television music and film scores.
CAUSE: Platz succumbed to motor neurone disease. He had been diagnosed 17-months earlier.

Derrick Plourde

Born October 17, 1971
Died March 30, 2005
A Southern California drummer who joined a number of West Coast punk bands, Derrick Plourde is best known for working with The Ataris. Initially a member of pop-punk act Lagwagon, Plourde appeared on a trio of albums with the group, beginning with *Duh* (1992). Leaving Lagwagon after the release of *Hoss*, Plourde joined guitarist Joey Cape to form Bad Astronauts. Plourde co-founded the Santa Barbara-based act The Ataris in 1997, leaving after the release of their début album *Anywhere But Here*, and later worked with the punk-ska act The Mad Caddies, performing on their album *Rock The Plank* (2001).
CAUSE: He shot himself in an apparent suicide.

Rudy Pompilli

(RUDOLPH POMPILLI)
Born April 16, 1924
Died February 5, 1976
The saxophonist and longtime

bandleader for Bill Haley's Comets, Rudy Pompilli was born in Chester, Pennsylvania, of Italian heritage. A self-taught musician, he joined Ralph Martieri's orchestra in the early Fifties, and in 1953 was voted Best New Saxophonist in a *Down Beat* magazine poll. While leading a jazz group called The Merry Men in 1953, Pompilli first met Haley who was then managing Chester radio station WPWA. Joining The Comets in September 1955, Pompilli arrived on the heels of their massive hit, 'Rock Around The Clock'. In spite of his conservative, scholarly appearance, Pompilli was an attention grabber, playing his instrument while lying on his back with his feet flailing in the air. Pompilli's first hit with Haley came with the double-sided entry, 'R-O-C-K'/'Rock-A-Beatin' Boogie', and continued with 'See You Later Alligator' (1956), 'Rip It Up' (1956), and 'Rudy's Rock', a sax heavy number written by Pompilli and Ralph Jones, and featured in the film *Rock Around The Clock*. Like many Fifties rock pioneers, Bill Haley and The Comets soon fell from popularity in the US while remaining in demand in Britain. With Haley moving to Mexico to escape his debts, The Comets were let go in 1962. Returning to Chester, Pennsylvania, Pompilli performed in local night spots. Rejoining Haley in 1964, Pompilli frequently organised new versions of The Comets. But with Haley becoming unreliable, Pompilli and the band were sometimes forced to take the stage without their lead singer. For a time, Pompilli assumed the name Rudy Pell and led his own band, The Happy Days.

CAUSE: He fell ill in 1974 during a European tour. Although he attributed his symptoms to the flu, he was diagnosed with lung cancer upon his return to the US.

FURTHER READING: von Hoelle, John; & Haley, John W. (1990). *Sound And Glory: The Incredible Story Of Bill Haley*. Wilmington, DE: Dyne-American.

Doc Pomus

(JEROME SOLON FELDER)
Born June 27, 1925
Died March 14, 1991

A former blues singer turned songwriter, Doc Pomus penned dozens of hits beginning in the Fifties. The son of a blue-collar lawyer, the Brooklyn-born Pomus got around on crutches following a childhood bout with polio. A loyal fan of Big Joe Turner, Pomus taught himself to play the saxophone. By the age of 18, he was studying political science at Brooklyn College during the day and belting out the blues at George's Tavern in Greenwich Village at night. Afraid of embarrassing his family, the former Jerome Felder assumed the stage name of Doc Pomus. Aided by his idol Big Joe Turner, Pomus composed several songs for the veteran blues shouter including 'Still In Love' (1950), 'Boogie Woogie Country Girl' (1956), and 'I Need A Girl' (1957). Entering the studio, Pomus was less successful as a recording artist; backed by top-notch session musicians such as King Curtis and Mickey Baker, Pomus quit recording after his record company sabotaged what was looking to be his first hit, 'Heartlessly'. Devastated by the experience, he gave up recording for a career as a songwriter. After landing his first Top 10 R&B hit in 1956 with Ray Charles' 'Lonely Avenue', Pomus followed with his début Top 10 pop entry, 'Youngblood' by The Drifters. Hiring the young Mort Shuman as his collaborator in 1956, Pomus and his new partner teamed with Big Joe Turner to compose Turner's 1957 R&B hit, 'Love Roller Coaster'. During this period, Pomus also wrote magazine fiction and briefly operated a tiny record label. Signing with the Hill & Range Publishing Company and moving into the legendary Brill Building, Pomus and Shuman landed their first pop hit with 'Plain Jane' by Bobby Darin, and followed with a trio of Fabian hits, 'I'm A Man', 'Hound Dog Man', and 'Turn

Me Loose', the latter initially offered to Elvis Presley. Other Pomus and Shuman hit compositions include 'Teenager In Love' (Dion & The Belmonts), 'This Magic Moment' (The Drifters; Jay & The Americans), 'Hushabye' (The Mystics), 'Suspicion' (Terry Stafford), 'Sweets For My Sweet' (The Drifters; The Searchers), and 'Save The Last Dance For Me' (The Drifters). Elvis Presley later appreciated Pomus' talent. Together with or apart from Shuman, Pomus composed 16 songs for The King in his post-army days including 'A Mess Of Blues', '(Marie's The Name) His Latest Flame', 'Viva Las Vegas', and 'Little Sister'. The duo soon settled into a songwriting pattern in which Pomus penned most of the lyrics, while Shuman composed the melodies. Suffering many calamities in 1965, Pomus divorced his wife, was abandoned by his writing partner, and suffered a devastating fall which damaged his legs. Quitting his musical craft and working as a professional gambler for the next decade, Pomus was drawn back into music by New Orleans pianist Dr. John in the mid Seventies. In the late Seventies, Pomus was instrumental in assembling The Blues Brothers band for John Belushi and Dan Aykroyd, and produced Big Joe Turner's Grammy-winning album, *Blues Train* (1983). Shortly before his death, Pomus provided music for the film *Dick Tracy* and worked on the album, *Johnny Adams Sings Doc Pomus*. Released in 1995, the tribute album, *Till The Night Is Gone* featured performances by Bob Dylan, Lou Reed, Dion and Los Lobos.
CAUSE: Lung cancer. He died at Tisch Hospital at Manhattan's University Medical Center. Shuman died a few months later.

"Groovey" Joe Poovey

(ARNOLD JOSEPH POOVEY)
Born May 10, 1941
Died October 6, 1998

A raspy-voiced, Texas-based rockabilly singer and songwriter, "Groovey" Joe Poovey began as a childhood country performer. A frequent guest of The Big D Jamboree beginning at age 12, he was backed by his band, The Hillbilly Boys. Inspired by Elvis Presley after opening for the explosive entertainer in 1955, Poovey took a turn toward rockabilly. Playing a twangy guitar, Poovey scored two regional hits with 'Ten Long Fingers' and 'Move Around'. Leaving the stage, Poovey later worked as a country deejay under the radio name of Johnny Dallas. But with Britain's Sussex Records reissuing Poovey's 'Ten Little Fingers' in 1980, he was soon touring that country as a rediscovered rockabilly star. Poovey's finest work was collected on the posthumously issued *Greatest Grooves* (1999). Poovey's compositions have been recorded by the likes of Johnny Paycheck and George Jones.
CAUSE: Never fully recovering from a heart attack, he died in his sleep at his home in Dallas.

Denniz Pop

(DAG VOLLE)
Born April 26, 1963
Died August 30, 1998

Swedish pop producer who worked with Dr. Alban, Ace Of Base, Papa Dee, The Backstreet Boys, and others, Denniz Pop usually collaborated with co-producer Max Martin. A former deejay and concert promoter, Pop co-founded a pair of labels, SweMix and Cheiron.
CAUSE: Cancer. He died at a hospital in Stockholm, Sweden.

Joseph Pope

(JOSEPH LEE POPE)
Born November 6, 1933
Died March 16, 1996

Lead singer of the Sixties, Atlanta-based R&B vocal group, The Tams, Joseph Pop enjoyed his biggest hit in 1963 with 'What Kind of Fool (Do You Think I Am)'. Formed in

Atlanta in 1952 as The Four Dots, the group also featured his brother Charles Pop. After scoring their final US hit in 1968 with 'Be Young, Be Foolish, Be Happy' The Tams landed a pair of British hits, the chart-topping reissue of their 1964 release, 'Hey Girl Don't Bother Me' (1971) and, inspired by the shag dance movement, 'There Ain't Nothing Like Shaggin'' (1987).
CAUSE: Heart failure. He died at a Veteran's Administration hospital in Atlanta.

Jeff Porcaro

(JEFFREY THOMAS PORCARO)
Born April 1, 1954
Died August 5, 1992
A prolific session drummer and founding member of Toto, Jeff Porcaro was raised in a musical family in southern California, his father being a jazz percussionist. Playing professionally while still attending Grant High School, Porcaro worked as a drummer on television's *The Sonny & Cher Show*. By 1974, Porcaro had replaced original Steely Dan drummer Jim Hodder, appearing on the album *Katy Lied*. After playing on the Tommy Bolin album *Teaser*, Porcaro emerged as one of the most in-demand session players in Los Angeles, working with Boz Scaggs, Aretha Franklin, Jackson Browne and others. Forming Toto in 1977, Porcaro teamed with five other session players, including his brother Steve on keyboards and Bobby Kimball on lead vocals. A polished power-pop band, Toto reached the US Top 10 with its début single, 'Hold The Line' (1978). A perennial favourite for the next decade with their straightforward melodies, skilled musicianship and flawless production-work, Toto enjoyed heavy airplay with 'I'll Supply The Love' (1979), '99' (1980), and from its opus, *Toto IV*, 'Rosanna' and 'Africa'. Experiencing numerous personnel changes, by 1986 the group was fronted by new lead singer Dennis Fredericksen. With Jeff Porcaro and other members involved in various side-projects, Toto disintegrated in the late Eighties. After a two-year hiatus, and with new lead singer Jean-Michel Byron, Toto released a compilation album *Past And Present 1977–1990* (1990). During his career, Jeff Porcaro performed on hundreds of albums and was immensely respected and liked by other musicians. One of rock's finest drummers, he also worked with Michael Jackson, Don Henley, Dire Straits, Rickie Lee Jones, Hall & Oates, Manhattan Transfer, Joe Cocker and Bonnie Raitt. Shortly before his death, Porcaro and Toto had finished a new album for European and Asian release entitled *Kingdom Of Desire*.
CAUSE: It was originally reported that Porcaro had died after a lethal allergic reaction to a lawn chemical, Dursban, while working in his yard in the Los Angeles suburb of Hidden Hills. However, a coroner ruled his death a heart attack resulting from long-term cocaine use. There were no traces of pesticide found in his body.

Janice Pough

Born 1945
Died 1980
The second vocalist of pioneering girl group The Bobbettes, Janice "Jannie" Pough sang on several hits beginning in the late Fifties. Formed in 1955 at a public school in Manhattan by eight girls, aged 11 to 15, the group was originally called The Harlem Queens. Pared down to a quintet in 1957, the renamed Bobbettes were discovered by music manager James A. Dailey at a performance on a local television talent programme. The group's début release 'Mr. Lee' – written about their fifth grade teacher – was a Top 10 smash but their career stalled as they were unable to perform in nightclubs because of their age, and they failed to return to the Top 40. In 1962, The Bobbettes provided the backing vocals on the Johnny Thunder hit, 'Loop De Loop'.

CAUSE: She was stabbed to death by a stranger as she walked down a street in Jersey City, New Jersey.

Jon-Jon Poulos

(JOHN POULOS)
Born March 31, 1948
Died March 26, 1980
The drummer for the Sixties pop-rock group The Buckinghams, Chicago-born Jon-Jon Poulos passed through several bands before joining a popular local outfit called The Pulsations. Teaming with members of a group called The Centuries, The Pulsations were renamed The Buckinghams in 1965. After appearing on a local variety television show, the group had limited success with its first locally released singles. Then, after scoring its first national hit with 'Kind Of A Drag' in 1967, The Buckinghams signed with CBS Records. Dominating the US charts in 1967, the group managed a quick run of hits with 'Don't You Care', a cover of Cannonball Adderley's 'Mercy, Mercy, Mercy', 'Hey Baby (They're Playing Our Song)', and their last Top 40 entry, 'Susan'. After riding a massive wave of popularity, the group would fail to place another single in the Top 40. With The Buckinghams disbanding in 1970, Poulos worked in artist management; one of his acts was a duo of former Buckinghams, Tufano & Giammerse.
CAUSE: Drug-related heart failure. He died in Chicago.

Cozy Powell

(COLIN POWELL)
Born December 29, 1947
Died April 5, 1998
Heavy metal drummer Cozy Powell performed with a who's who of hard-rock royalty. A native of Cirencester, England, Powell was adopted, never meeting his birth parents. A technical but bombastic drummer, Powell passed through several Sixties bands including The Sorcerers and Big Bertha. In 1971 he joined the second version of The Jeff Beck Group, appearing on the albums *Rough And Ready* (1971) and *Jeff Beck Group* (1972). When Beck disbanded the group, Powell formed his own outfit, Bedlam. Hired by producer Mickie Most as a session player at RAK Records, Powell performed on record behind acts such as Hot Chocolate and Donovan. Encouraged by Most, Powell scored a couple of solo British Top 10 hits, 'Dance With The Devil' (1973) and 'Na Na Na' (1974). When guitarist Ritchie Blackmore left Deep Purple to form his own group Rainbow, Powell was invited to join the perennial hard rock band. A consummate performer who earned a reputation for his extended concert drum solos, Powell remained with Rainbow for five albums, quitting in 1980. He then passed through The Michael Schenker Group and Whitesnake, before working as a replacement for Carl Palmer in the group they called Emerson, Lake and Powell. In 1989, he joined a latter-day version of Black Sabbath which he was forced to leave after a 1991 riding accident. Additionally, Powell performed on Roger Daltrey's Keith Moon tribute, 'Under A Raging Moon', recreating the frenetic energy of the late Who drummer. He also appeared on Robert Plant's 1982 solo album *Pictures At 11*. At the time of his death, Powell had just completed a solo album, and had performed on album projects for Brian May and Judas Priest's Glenn Tipton.
CAUSE: A lover of fast cars and motorcycles, he died in an auto accident near his home in Bristol, England. Distracted while talking on his cellular phone, he lost control of his vehicle and crashed his Saab 9000 into the crash barrier on the M4 motorway. He had broken several ribs earlier in the year in a motorcycle mishap.

William Powell

(William Powell, Jr.)
Born January 20, 1942
Died May 26, 1977

The lead tenor/baritone vocalist of the popular soul group The O'Jays, William Powell joined a predecessor of the group in his native Canton, Ohio, in 1957. Formed at McKinley High School as The Triumphs, the group consisted of Powell, Walter Williams, Eddie Levert and two others. Dropping out of school after 11th grade, Powell appeared with the group at local YMCA dances and at talent shows, frequently crossing paths with another up and coming group, Ruby and The Romantics. Renamed The Mascots by King Records chief Syd Nathan, the group issued two obscure singles. Soon aided by popular Cleveland deejay Eddie O'Jay, the group began building a following throughout the Midwest. Taking their mentor's name in 1961, the renamed O'Jays struggled along in the Sixties, recording for several labels. Teaming with producer and songwriter H.B. Barnum in 1963, The O'Jays scored several R&B chart entries at Imperial Records, hitting the Top 20 with 'Stand In For Love' (1966). After scoring a Top 10 R&B hit at Bell Records with 'I'll Be Sweeter Tomorrow' (1967), the group temporarily disbanded following the departure of original member Bill Isles. Finally hitting the big time under the care of the production team of Kenny Gamble and Leon Huff, The O'Jays pared down to a trio of Powell, Levert, and Williams by 1971. Thereafter The O'Jays enjoyed a long string of hits beginning with the million-sellers, 'Back Stabbers' (1972) and 'Love Train' (1973). One of the decade's most popular soul acts, The O'Jays continued their chart dominance with 'Put Your Hands Together' (1974), 'For The Love Of Money' (1974), 'I Love Music' (1975), and 'Livin' For The Weekend' (1976). Severely ill, Powell left the group before the start of a scheduled US tour in 1975; the group had just finished recording the album *Family Reunion*. He was replaced by Sammy Strain, formerly of Little Anthony & The Imperials.

Cause: Powell was diagnosed with cancer a year before his death while hospitalised for injuries received in an auto accident. With the disease progressing into its final stages, he was forced to retire from the group in February 1976. He died at Aultman Hospital in Canton, Ohio.

Perez Prado

(Damaso Perez Prado)
Born December 11, 1916
Died November 14, 1989

Nicknamed "The King of the Mambo", Cuban-born Perez Prado was at the forefront of the mambo craze of the mid Fifties. A member of a series of casino orchestras in pre-Castro Havana, Prado relocated to Mexico in 1948 and formed his own orchestra. The originator of the emerging mambo movement, Prado combined Afro-Cuban rhythms and big band swing. Employing a strong brass section, and punctuating his songs with vocal grunts, Prado became a sensation during his long residency at the Mexico City nightclub, Club 1-2-3. As a result of Sonny Burke scoring a US hit with a reworked version of Prado's 'Que Rico Mambo' as 'Mambo Jambo' in 1951, Prado performed for packed houses throughout the US. Challenging Bill Haley's success in 1955, Prado remained atop the charts for 10 weeks with the instrumental smash, 'Cherry Pink And Apple Blossom White'. After a lull, Prado returned to the charts in 1958 with his final hit, 'Patricia', later featured in the film *La Dolce Vita*, which was reprised in 1962 as the reworked 'Patricia Twist'. Dropped by RCA Records in 1963, Prado returned to Mexico and spent the next decade touring throughout Latin America, before retiring in the mid Seventies. Prado's music had a remarkable revival

in the late Nineties when 'Guaglione', used in a British commercial for Guinness ale, was reissued and reached the British Top 5. When Prado's 'Mambo No. 5' was employed in another Guinness commercial, the track was updated for an international smash by Lou Bega, and was subsequently chosen as the theme music for televised cricket on UK television's Channel 4. Another Prado classic, 'Sway', was reworked by Shaft as 'Mucho Mambo', a British Top 10 hit.
CAUSE: Stroke. He died in Mexico City.

Dave Prater

(DAVID PRATER, SR.)
Born May 9, 1937
Died April 9, 1988
A member of the gritty Sixties duo Sam & Dave, Dave Prater helped define soul music. A native of Ocilla, Georgia, he learned to sing in his church's gospel choir. The son of a labourer, he moved to Miami after high school to pursue a singing career. Working at a diner as a cook, one of his regular customers was another struggling singer named Sam Moore. Prater and Moore would soon cross paths at a talent show, at which the club owner insisted the two singers combine their talents as a duo. Signed by Morris Levy of Roulette Records, Sam & Dave released several unsuccessful singles beginning with 'I Need Love' (1962). Switching to Atlantic Records in 1965, Sam & Dave were recorded at Stax studios in Memphis and were teamed with songwriters Isaac Hayes and Dave Porter. Backed by Booker T. & The MGs and The Memphis Horns, Sam & Dave pumped out a sinewy string of gospel-inspired, gritty soul hits beginning with 'You Don't Know Like I Know' (1966). Nicknamed "Double Dynamite", the pair found crossover success with 'Hold On, I'm Coming' (1966), their Grammy-winning signature piece, 'Soul Man' (1967), 'I Thank You' (1968) and 'Wrap It Up' (1968). With Stax's arrangement with Atlantic Records expiring in 1968, Sam & Dave's fortunes waned as they recorded with a new group of musicians and songwriters. Except for the million-selling single, 'Soul Sister, Brown Sugar' (1968), the duo would never return to the Top 40. Also that year, Prater escaped prosecution after shooting his wife. Frequently feuding with his partner, Prater left Moore in 1970. Then, after recording as a solo act for Alston Records, Prater would occasionally reteam with Moore throughout the Seventies, landing a minor hit with a cover of The Beatles' 'We Can Work It Out'. When The Blues Brothers reprised 'Soul Man' in 1979, Sam & Dave enjoyed a comeback on the oldies circuit. The pair appeared in the Paul Simon film *One Trick Pony* and were invited to open for British punk rockers, The Clash. Remaining hostile toward each other, the battling duo disbanded for good in 1982. For a time Prater teamed with Sam Daniels as the new Sam & Dave, until his former partner launched a legal action.
CAUSE: He was killed in a car crash near Sycamore, Georgia, on his way to his mother's house in Ocilla, Georgia. Prater was ejected from the vehicle and died at the scene, while his passenger remained in the car and was seriously injured.
FURTHER READING: Moore, Sam. (1998). *Sam And Dave: An Oral History*. New York: Avon.

Mike Pratt

Born June 7, 1931
Died July 10, 1976
A member of Tommy Steele's backup band The Cavemen, Mike Pratt had far greater success as an actor. A former advertising copywriter, London-born Pratt was drawn to the entertainment field after a stint as a stage assistant. A talented jazz-trained pianist and guitarist, Pratt teamed with

Lionel Bart to perform around London in 1956. Together with an unknown singer named Tommy Hicks, Pratt and Bart formed a trio, The Cavemen, who gained a manager, Larry Parnes, and a contract with Decca Records. With Hicks transformed into rocker Tommy Steele, beginning with the 1956 début release 'Rock With The Caveman' (as Tommy Steele & The Steelmen), the group became an instant sensation among British youth. After topping the charts with a rockabilly-tinged cover of Guy Mitchell's 'Singing The Blues', Steele subsequently recorded compositions usually written by Pratt and Bart. The 1957 biopic *The Tommy Steele Story*, for which Steele, Pratt and Bart composed 12 songs in a week, spawned the hit singles 'Butterfingers' and 'Water, Water'/'A Handful Of Songs'. The soundtrack album to a follow-up Steele film, 1958's *The Duke Wore Jeans*, featuring additional Pratt/Bart compositions, topped the charts. With Steele spending more of his time as a stage and film actor and Bart moving into stage writing, Pratt formed a side group, The Cotton Pickers. Following Steele's lead, Pratt took a series of roles in television and film, often as the villain. His best-known role was as Jeff Randall in the British detective comedy *Randall & Hopkirk (Deceased)*.
CAUSE: Lung cancer.

George Prayer

Born c. 1943
Died 1992
The original baritone vocalist of The Moroccos, a Chicago-based doo-wop outfit, George Prayer formed the group with several friends in 1952. Signing with United Records in 1954, the group found fame after the addition of former Flamingos tenor, Sollie McElroy, and scored several regional hits beginning with a cover of 'Somewhere Over the Rainbow' (1955). The Moroccos disbanded in 1957.
CAUSE: Unknown.

Elvis Presley

(ELVIS AARON PRESLEY)
Born January 8, 1935
Died August 16, 1977
The undisputed king of rock'n'roll, Elvis Presley irrevocably altered the direction of 20th Century popular music. Elvis was not the originator of rock'n'roll, nor the first to release a rock'n'roll record, but he was its first real star and his image as the wild, hillbilly cat, his pelvis gyrating while his quiff flapped up and down over his forehead, is forever etched on the genre. No other single entertainer, musical or otherwise, exerted as much influence on the social upheavals that occurred in the USA in the Fifties, and though his undignified decline in the Seventies foreshadowed an early, drug-related, death, Presley remains a hero to millions. His record sales are incalculable, his popularity and influence is exceeded only by The Beatles, and his legacy is a vast catalogue of recordings, the earliest of which form the bedrock of rock'n'roll.
A surviving twin and an only child, Elvis Aaron Presley was born at 4:35 a.m. on January 8, 1935 in East Tupelo, Mississippi. Reared in a poor, religious home by an overprotective mother and a Depression-scarred father, Presley sang at the Tupelo Pentecostal First Assembly of God Church at age two, and was later exposed to the emotional black gospel stylings of interracial tent revivals. Given a guitar by his mother at age 12, the young Presley was grounded in country & western music but he was also listening to Memphis radio station WDIA, which played "sinful" R&B and blues. In an attempt to escape poverty, the unemployed Vernon Presley moved his family 90 miles north to Memphis in September 1948. Attending L.C. Humes High School, Elvis made few friends and was instead drawn to black hangouts in the city's Beale Street. After graduating from high school, Presley was hired as a

truck driver by Crown Electric but already he was showing signs of an unusual individuality, dressing in flashy clothes and combing his long hair into a quiff. Too poor to live on his own, Elvis continued to share his parents' home in the Lauderdale public housing complex and despite his exuberant nature was a respectful son. Walking into the Sam Phillips-owned Sun Studio in 1953, Presley paid $3.98 to make a two-song, birthday record for his mother, singing 'My Happiness' and 'That's When Your Heartaches Begin', and impressing office manager Marion Keisker. When Presley returned the following year to cut another disc, Keisker took down Elvis' name and address. During this period, Presley was hired as an intermission act for a local country group, Doug Poindexter and The Starlite Wranglers. At Keisker's suggestion, Sam Phillips called Presley into the Sun studios for a try-out in April 1954. Returning in July, Phillips backed him with a pair of session players from The Starlite Wranglers, guitarist Scotty Moore and stand-up bass player Bill Black. Impressing Phillips with an impromptu, countrified version of Arthur Crudup's blues number 'That's All Right (Mama)', Presley returned the following day and recorded a rockabilly rendition of Bill Monroe's bluegrass waltz 'Blue Moon Over Kentucky'. When Memphis disc jockey Dewey Phillips (no relation to Sam Phillips) began playing an acetate of 'That's All Right (Mama)' a few days later on his *Red, Hot, And Blue* R&B radio show, the song was rush-released as the first of Presley's five Sun singles. Initially embraced by country audiences, Presley and his backing duo of "Scotty & Bill" opened up for crooner Slim Whitman and appeared on *The Louisiana Hayride*. Then, after scoring a second regional hit with a rockabilly-flavoured cover of Roy Brown's R&B song 'Good Rockin' Tonight', Presley was invited to perform at The Grand Ole Opry in Nashville where, billed as "The Hillbilly Cat", he received only a polite reception. Landing his first national hits in mid-1955, Presley appeared on the country charts with a hot cover of Arthur Gunter's recent R&B entry, 'Baby Let's Play House', and followed this with a double-sided hit, a cover of labelmate Junior Parker's 'Mystery Train' and 'I Forgot To Remember To Forget'. In 1956 Presley signed a management contract with former carnival huckster Colonel Tom Parker, who engineered his move to RCA who paid a then amazing $35,000 to Phillips for his Sun contract. Retaining Scotty & Bill, and adding drummer D.J. Fontana, Presley topped the US charts with his dramatic label début, 'Heartbreak Hotel'. Parker was quick to sign a three-film deal worth $450,000, and Presley's début feature *Love Me Tender* packed theatres. Dominating the charts in 1956, Presley notched a string of number 1 hits, 'I Want You, I Need You, I Love You', 'Love Me Tender' and, now backed by a white gospel group The Jordanaires, the double-sided smash, 'Don't Be Cruel'/'Hound Dog'. Presley set sales records and was an overnight sensation, oozing a raw sexuality which shocked middle America and brought stern criticism from conservative columnists. Teenage girls thought differently and his raw, hip-gyrating performances caused riots at concerts throughout the American south and, eventually, the entire country. As a result of the controversy he aroused, Presley was filmed from the waist up on his third and final *Ed Sullivan Show* appearance on January 6, 1957, a futile gesture that served only to emphasise the sensual nature of his performance. Presley's first two albums, *Elvis Presley* and *Elvis*, both shot to the top of the *Billboard* LP charts and contain many of the most exciting rock'n'roll songs of the era. With the money rolling in,

Presley purchased his Graceland mansion in Memphis in March 1957 for $102,500, and in its garage there appeared the first of several Cadillacs. There were three more movies, *Loving You*, *Jailhouse Rock* and *King Creole* – the latter usually cited as Presley's best – before Elvis was drafted into the army, and the hits continued with 'Too Much', 'All Shook Up', '(Let Me Be Your) Teddy Bear' and, from the film of the same name, 'Jailhouse Rock'. By this time Scotty and Bill had quit after a pay dispute but top quality musicians were drafted in as replacements, including guitarist Chet Atkins and pianist Floyd Cramer. Presley was sworn into the US Army on March 24, 1958, as US Private 53310761 but a few months later he was granted special leave to be by his dying mother's bedside. Grief-stricken, he never really recovered from his mother's death and was always able to dominate his weak-willed father. Subsequently stationed near Frankfurt in West Germany, Presley lived off base in a house with his father and grandmother; here Presley would first meet his future wife, the then 14-year-old Priscilla Ann Beaulieu. After being promoted to sergeant in January 1960, Presley was discharged soon after. In spite of his two-year absence, RCA continued to issue Presley material and his hits during his army spell included 'Hard Headed Woman' (1958), 'One Night' (1958) and 'A Fool Such As I' (1959). After his army service, Presley was actively promoted as an all-round entertainer. The image change was immediately evident on the mega-selling chart topper 'It's Now Or Never' (1960), based on the Italian operatic melody, 'O Sole Mio'. The melodramatic 'Are You Lonesome Tonight' (1960), originally recorded by Al Jolson in 1927, again emphasised Presley's move away from rock'n'roll, a point reinforced by two further 1961 hits, 'Wooden Heart' and 'Surrender'. However, he was still capable of bringing life to some upbeat pop items, such as the Doc Pomus-Mort Shuman coupling '(Marie's The Name) His Latest Flame'/ 'Little Sister'. Presley had released his first devotional album, *His Hand In Mine*, in 1960 and thereafter took a keen interest in alternative religious theories and spiritualism. Shortly after his discharge from the army, Presley ceased live and television appearances, concentrating instead on a movie career of doubtful integrity. At the insistence of Col. Parker, he appeared in light-hearted, mediocre feature films, all of them low budget exploitation movies which presented little in the way of a challenge to either their star or their audiences. Most of the films spawned corresponding hit albums and singles including 'Can't Help Falling In Love' from *Blue Hawaii* (1961), 'Follow That Dream' from the film of the same name (1962), 'Return To Sender' from *Girls! Girls! Girls!* (1962), 'Viva Las Vegas' from the film of the same name (1964), and 'Puppet On A String' from *Girl Happy* (1965). Significantly, Presley's biggest hit from the mid Sixties was 'Crying In The Chapel', a song that dated back to 1960. Although fans continued to enjoy songs like 'Frankie and Johnny', 'Love Letters' and 'If Every Day Was Like Christmas', Presley's strike rate was no longer as strong as it had been. By this time Elvis had become neutered, and it was difficult to equate the sexually explicit Presley of the Fifties with his increasingly wholesome film characters. He had also become sidelined in the rock world by The Beatles and other groups, and was now seen as something of an anachronism, reclusive and ludicrously out of touch with current trends as the Sixties progressed. It was therefore no surprise that by 1966 his records were no longer selling as they once had and the movies were no longer guaranteed box-office successes. Presley married the former Priscilla Ann Beaulieu on May 1, 1967; exactly nine months later, the Presleys celebrated the birth of their only child, daughter Lisa Marie. These changes in his personal life seemed to inspire Elvis to change the direction of his career and he enjoyed a major comeback with the success of an NBC television special in December 1968. Dressed in a skin-tight black leather outfit and looking more handsome than ever before, Elvis re-emerged as a performer of remarkable vitality. An attendant hit, 'If I Can Dream', was particularly impressive. Shortly afterwards he opened a season at the Las Vegas Hilton, thus embarking on the final portion of his career as a cabaret entertainer and touring rock superstar. Thereafter Presley became a major Las Vegas tourist draw and blue-chip box-office sell-out in large arenas throughout the US. His voice matured, he abandoned the facile film songs and returned to the Top 10 with a series of strong recordings, including 'Suspicious Minds' (1969), 'In The Ghetto' (1969), 'Kentucky Rain' (1970), 'The Wonder of You' (1970) and, reminiscent of his early rockers, 'Burning Love' (1972). Elvis had started abusing prescription drugs while in the army, and continued to do so for the rest of his life. By 1970 he was swallowing huge quantities of pills to wake up and to fall asleep. Elvis legally separated from Priscilla in February 1972, divorcing her 20 months later. Thereafter he was accompanied by a series of beautiful women but by the mid Seventies he'd become a parody of himself, hulking and overweight but still packing concert halls in spite of his diminished performances. Presley's image in the Seventies has become something of a cliché: Elvis dressed in bejewelled white outfits with billowing sleeves and ludicrously flared trousers, karate-kicking his way across the stage and distributing silk scarves to female fans while going through the motions of singing his greatest hits. He was now a cultural icon with legions of rabid fans who excused his shortcomings, but as the Seventies progressed he was increasingly felled by ill-health. His once innovative and invigorating stage shows became a tired routine and he relied increasingly on live recordings to keep his name in the marketplace. He collapsed on stage twice during this period, a bloated and sad figure. This was the final image of Elvis Presley, but it says much for the iconographic power of his persona that he would be remembered almost as three separate people, each embodying a different age of rock. From the black-haired hillbilly cat of the Fifties through to the jewel-encrusted Vegas star of the Seventies, Elvis became all things to all men, rising above the one-dimensional image that is all too often foisted upon pop stars. His sudden death came as a great shock and yet it was not entirely unexpected given his recent decline. A month before his demise, the biography *Elvis: What Happened?*, written by former employees, detailed his personal problems in harrowing detail. In the days following his death, his record sales sold out all over the world and the single 'Way Down' provided a final UK number 1 hit. With Elvis' life and death continuing to fascinate fans and historians alike, an entire Elvis Presley cottage industry flourished. Merchandising of Elvis now goes far beyond records, books and movies, and the official Elvis Presley-related companies were worth over $100 million by 1992, considerably more than Elvis was ever worth when he was alive and considerably more than he left in his will. Visited by 700,000 pilgrims a year, Graceland has become a leading tourist destination, placed on the National Register of Historic Places in 1991. Presley was inducted into the Rock and Roll Hall of Fame in its premier year of 1986. Elvis scored a surprise hit in 2002 with a remixed version of a track from 1968, 'A Little Less Conversation', earning $34 million in royalties and other income. In 2004, Lisa Marie Presley sold most of her interests in Elvis Presley Enterprises to Robert F.X. Sillerman, founder of the music and sports promotion firm SFX Entertainment for $50 million and a 15 per cent holding in the new company. (Priscilla Presley walked away with $6.5 million and a 10-year consulting contract, worth $560,000 annually.)

CAUSE: His body was discovered by his 'fiancee' Ginger Alden on the floor of his personal bathroom at his Graceland mansion. Dressed in his pyjamas, he was rushed to Memphis Baptist Memorial Hospital where doctors worked in vain to resuscitate the fallen singer. On the day of his death, Presley was scheduled to begin a two-week East Coast tour, with the first stop at Portland, Maine (many of the 4,000 $15 tickets were returned for a refund). Traces of many prescription drugs were found in Presley's bloodstream. In the days following his death, thousands of fans gathered outside Graceland, some of whom were allowed to file past the casket containing the singer's body. During the eulogy, Rex Humbard claimed that Elvis had premonitions of his death. Originally buried in a public cemetery, Elvis was reintered in the rear garden of Graceland. Aside from a few small bequests and instructions to provide for his close blood relations, Elvis left his entire estate to his daughter Lisa Marie, in trust until she reached her 25th birthday. His ex-wife, Priscilla, was appointed co-executor and it is largely through her enterprise and clear-sighted business sense that the Elvis industry has prospered so successfully since his death.

FURTHER READING: Goldman, Albert. (1981). *Elvis: The Last 24 Hours.* New York: McGraw-Hill. Guralnick, Peter. (1994). *Last Train To Memphis: The Rise Of Elvis Presley.* New York: Little, Brown. Guralnick, Peter. (1999). *Careless Love: The Unmaking Of Elvis Presley.* New York: Little Brown.

Nigel Preston

Born c. 1959
Died May 7, 1992

The original drummer of the British punk-metal group The Cult, Nigel Preston was previously a member of Sex Gang Children. In 1983 Preston joined singer Ian Astbury in a group called Southern Death Cult. After shortening its name to The Cult in early 1984, the group landed a Top 30 album in Britain, *Dreamtime* (1984). Preston would leave The Cult in mid-1985 shortly after the release of its first big hit, 'She Sells Sanctuary', and was replaced by drummer Mark Brzezicki of Big Country. Preston then passed through a pair of bands, Theatre Of Hate and The Gun Club.

CAUSE: Unknown. He died in London.

Rod Price

(RODERICK MICHAEL PRICE)
Born November 22, 1947
Died March 22, 2005

As a member of hard rock group Foghat, Rod Price toured endlessly for much of the Seventies. Reared on American blues, Rod Price had passed through a series of British blues-rock bands in the late Sixties. In 1971, Price joined a trio of former Savoy Brown members to form Foghat. Discovered by Bob Dylan's ex-manager Albert Grossman at a London nightclub in 1971, Foghat left England for the US and signed with Grossman's Bearsville Records. Fronted by vocalist "Lonesome" Dave Peverett, Foghat managed a surprise hit single in 1972 with a reworked version of the Muddy Waters blues standard, 'I Just Want To Make Love To You'. Enjoying far greater success

in the US than in their native Britain, Foghat settled in Long Island, New York, and cemented their AOR fanbase with the tracks 'Fool For The City' and the driving rock standard 'Slow Ride', from their 1975 album *Fool For The City*. Although not their finest outing, Foghat's seventh release, *Foghat Live* (1977), would be their greatest seller. Tired of touring, Price quit in 1981, but with Foghat garnering new-found popularity after the inclusion of their music in the hit film *Dazed And Confused*, Price joined a re-formed version of the band in 1993. Foghat recorded their final album featuring original singer "Lonesome" Dave Peverett a year before his death in 2000. Returning to his blues roots, Price issued the solo albums *Open* (2000) and *West Four* (2003). During his long career, Price worked with such blues greats as Duster Bennett, Champion Jack Dupree, Honey Boy Edwards, John Lee Hooker and Muddy Waters.
CAUSE: He suffered head trauma during a fall precipitated by a heart attack in a stairway at his home in Wilton, New Hampshire.

Dave Prichard

(DAVID E. PRICHARD)
Born November 27, 1963
Died February 27, 1990
The lead guitarist of the Eighties heavy metal band Armored Saint, Dave Prichard formed the Los Angeles-based quintet in 1981. After one of their tracks was included on a metal compilation EP, *Metal Massacre II*, the group was signed by Chrysalis Records. Releasing a trio of studio albums beginning with thrash-metal outing *March Of The Saint* (1984), Armored Saint opened for rock heavyweights such as Metallica, Judas Priest and Aerosmith. Though poised for stardom, Armored Saint never developed a fan base and were dropped by their record label. Although the group had disbanded after Prichard's death, they belatedly completed *Symbol Of Salvation* (1991). Vocalist John Bush later joined Anthrax, before re-forming Armored Saint in 1998, with new guitarist Jeff Duncan.
CAUSE: Leukaemia.

Dickie Pride

(RICHARD CHARLES KNELLAR)
Born October 21, 1941
Died March 26, 1969
A member of Larry Parnes' stable of pop singers, the talented Dickie Pride never attained his potential. Trained at the Royal College of Church Music, he was drawn to skiffle in his early teens. Discovered in a tiny pub in Tooting at age 16 by pianist Russ Conway, Pride was signed by Parnes the following week, joining the likes of Tommy Steele and Billy Fury. Dubbed "The Sheik of Shake", Pride was a charismatic and energetic performer. Landing his only chart hit with 'Primrose Lane' (1959), Pride was unhappy with the quality of the material he was forced to sing. Parnes also vetoed Pride's intention to hire The (Silver) Beatles as his backing band for a tour. Exhibiting erratic behaviour and frequently clashing with Parnes, Pride split from his manager in late 1960 though Parnes continued to book him for occasional concerts. In 1963, Pride tried to resurrect his career by forming a trio, The Gov'nors, but after sharing a bill on British television with the far superior Beatles, Pride disbanded his group. While working a day job in a sewing machine factory, Pride attempted a series of comebacks, and landed an opening slot on a Stevie Wonder tour. With his drug use intensifying, Pride was institutionalised in 1967, and after exhibiting violent tendencies, underwent a radical frontal lobotomy. He later found employment as a truck driver. Chronicling Pride's career, the stage show, *Pride With Prejudice*, débuted in London in 1999.

CAUSE: Long-term LSD and heroin abuse. He was found dead at his mother's home.

Louis Prima

(LOUIS LEO PRIMA)
Born December 7, 1911
Died August 24, 1978
A bubbly, upbeat swing musician who survived into the rock era and had a resurgence of popularity in the late Nineties, Louis Prima was a consummate entertainer. With his strong Italian features, the New Orleans native was frequently mistaken for a black man. Though trained on the violin, Prima was inspired by the bustling local Dixieland jazz scene and switched to the cornet. After spending time in a theatre pit orchestra, Prima headed for New York City in 1934 with encouragement from Guy Lombardo. Taking New York by storm, Prima penned Benny Goodman's hit 'Sing, Sing, Sing' (1938), and formed his own rollicking band. By the mid Forties Prima had become one of the country's top live entertainers; discovering his key to success, Prima exploited his ethnicity with a series of comical, Italian-accented hits such as 'Angelina', 'Please No Squeeza Da Banana' and 'Josephina, Please No Lean On The Bell'. Reinventing himself during the rise of rock in the early Fifties, Prima enjoyed a new wave of popularity as he teamed on stage and record with Keely Smith (his fourth of five wives from whom he was divorced in 1961), and a talented bandleader and saxophonist Sam Butera (and The Witnesses). Prima's hits during this period included 'Just A Gigolo (I Ain't Got Nobody)', 'Jump, Jive And Wail', and 'That Old Black Magic' (1956) and he remained a fixture on the Las Vegas strip. His welcome worn out in Vegas by the early Seventies, Prima returned to New Orleans and subsequently provided the voice of King Louie The Orangutan in the animated film *The Jungle Book*, singing 'I Wanna Be Like You'. With the rise of the lounge and neo-swing movement of the late Nineties, Prima experienced posthumous interest. Although The Brian Setzer Orchestra had reprised 'Jump, Jive And Wail', Prima's original version was featured in a popular Gap commercial. Another of Prima's hits, 'Just A Gigolo (I Ain't Got Nobody)', had been revived a decade earlier by David Lee Roth. His music also appeared in films such as *Mad Dog And Glory* (1993). Keely Smith remained active in music, releasing a new album in 2000.
CAUSE: Undergoing surgery in 1975 to remove a brain tumour, he lapsed into a coma, remaining hospitalised for three years until his death in New Orleans.

Barry Pritchard

Born April 3, 1944
Died January 11, 1999
A member of British pop group The Fortunes, Barry Pritchard fronted the act along with Glen Dale (real name: Richard Garforth). Originally formed as an acoustic trio called The Cliftones (after Clifton Hall School where they met), the Birmingham-based act originally consisted of Pritchard, Rod Allen and Glen Dale. Expanding to an electric quintet and renaming themselves The Merry Men backing London singer Robbie Hood, they became The Fortunes Rhythm Group in 1963, shortened to The Fortunes when the group was signed by Decca. Their début single 'Summertime Summertime' failed to chart but the follow-up 'Caroline' was used as the theme song by pirate station Radio Caroline in 1964. The Fortunes reached the Top Five in 1965 with the Roger Greenaway/Roger Cook ballad, 'You've Got Your Troubles' (1965). Highlighted by the group's three-part vocal harmony, the song was followed by similar ballad hits such as 'Here It

Comes Again' (1965) and 'This Golden Ring' (1966), but after the murder of their manager Reg Calvert and the departure of key member Glen Dale, the group struggled over the next several years. Signing with Capitol Records and belatedly returning to the charts, The Fortunes scored a US hit with 'Here Comes That Rainy Day Feeling Again' (1971) and a pair of UK hits, 'Freedom Come, Freedom Go' (1971) and 'Storm In A Teacup' (1972). Leaving the group in 1995 due to declining health, Pritchard settled in Spain.
CAUSE: Heart attack.

Mel Pritchard

(MELVIN PAUL PRITCHARD)
Born January 20, 1948
Died January 27, 2004
An original member of British progressive-rock band Barclay James Harvest, drummer Mel Pritchard developed a unique, pared down style. Playing drums since his childhood, Pritchard and lifelong friend Les Holroyd were previously members of an Oldham blues-rock band called The Wickeds. After adding two members from a rival band, The Keepers, the group emerged as Barclay James Harvest. Initially signed to EMI, releasing a single in 1968 on Parlophone and recording five albums for Harvest, the group fared poorly, unfairly attacked by rock journalists as "the poor man's Moody Blues", despite standout tracks such as 'She Said' and 'Mockingbird'. The group nonetheless persevered, cultivating a fanbase in continental Europe, particularly in Germany. In 1973 BJH signed with Polydor Records and broke through the following year with the album *Barclay James Harvest – Live*, featuring their trademark Mellotron. Subsequent albums – including *The Honoured Ghosts*, *Octobertron*, *Gone To Earth*, *XII*, *A Concert For A People* and *Victims Of Circumstance* – found some success in the UK. After suffering serious injuries in a car accident, Pritchard refused to retire, though he eventually switched to a less strenuous electronic drum kit. Following the release of 1997's *River Of Dreams*, the group splintered. Pritchard joined the group's bassist Les Holroyd for the album *Revolution Days* and a subsequent tour which was billed as Barclay James Harvest featuring Les Holroyd.
CAUSE: He died in his sleep at his flat in Greenfield, England.

Professor Longhair

(HENRY ROELAND BYRD)
Born December 19, 1918
Died January 30, 1980
Nicknamed the grandfather of rock'n'roll, boogie-woogie pianist Professor Longhair predated Fifties rockers such as Little Richard and Jerry Lee Lewis. Born Henry Byrd in Bogalusa, Louisiana, he was taught to play guitar by his mother in a New Orleans tenement. Finding an abandoned piano at age 15, he learned his craft by watching experienced players. Sneaking into nightclubs with a charcoal moustache, he was taken under the wing by stride-style pianist Tuts Washington. Soon crossing paths with Jerry Roll Morton, Champion Jack Dupree and Sonny Boy Williamson, the impressionable young musician developed his own primitive, unorthodox style. Incorporating the structure and percussion of Mexican mariachi music having been exposed to the genre during a stint in the Civilian Conservation Corps in the late Thirties, Byrd had his career interrupted by World War II. After his discharge he returned to New Orleans in 1944, but left music to work as a cook. Returning to the stage in 1947, he joined The Mid-Drifs; shaving his head in 1948, he was nicknamed Professor Longhair by the owner of New Orleans' famed Caladonia Inn. Signed to Star Talent Records as Professor Longhair and The Shuffling

Hungarians, he recorded 'She Ain't Got No Hair' (1949) and an early version of his signature piece 'Mardi Gras In New Orleans' (1950), the tune emerging as the theme song of the pre-Lenten Mardi Gras Festival. Reworking 'She Ain't Got No Hair' as 'Bald Head' (1950) at Mercury Records under the moniker of Roy Byrd & His Blues Jumpers, he finally landed his first national hit. He subsequently recorded for Federal, Wasco, and Atlantic Records under a series of names. Then in 1954, he suffered a debilitating stroke and was hospitalised for a year. Later recording for a series of labels, he teamed with vocalist Earl King to score a minor hit in 1964 with 'Big Chief'. Ailing, and having earned little in royalties, Professor Longhair was living in a state of near-destitution by the late Sixties. Making a spectacular comeback after a stunning performance at the second annual New Orleans Jazz and Heritage Festival in 1971, the toothless performer began receiving a stream of job offers. He was hired to perform by Paul McCartney in 1976, the concert captured on the album *Live On The Queen Mary*. Enjoying an extended residency at Tipitina's, a nightclub named after one of his compositions, Professor Longhair remained a favourite at music festivals.
CAUSE: He died in his sleep of natural causes at his home in New Orleans.

Arthur Prysock

Born January 2, 1929
Died June 21, 1997
A popular, elegant, R&B baritone balladeer who was often compared to crooner Billy Eckstine, Arthur Prysock gained fame as a member of Buddy Johnson's band. Born in South Carolina, Prysock left home at age 13 to work as a car mechanic in Connecticut. Discovering a propensity for music, Prysock found local club work and was hired in 1945 by the touring Buddy Johnson when his orchestra's vocalist had fallen ill. As the featured vocalist in Johnson's band, Prysock appeared on several hits, including 'They Say I'm The Biggest Fool' (1945), 'Jet My Love' (1947), and 'Because' (1950). But when Johnson left Decca Records in 1950, Prysock remained at the label as a solo act, and continued his hit run with 'I Didn't Sleep A Wink Last Night' (1952). Switching to Old Town Records, Prysock enjoyed further success. His career halted by the rise of rock, Prysock signed with Verve Records in 1964; taking a jazz turn, he recorded an album with Count Basie in 1965. Beginning in 1971, Arthur Prysock frequently teamed with his brother, saxophonist Red Prysock. Working as a cabaret singer, he landed a surprise hit in 1976 with the disco-flavoured, 'When Love Is New', and later earned a pair of Grammy nominations.
CAUSE: Aneurysm. He died in a Bermuda hospital following a long-term illness.

Red Prysock

(WILBERT PRYSOCK)
Born February 2, 1926
Died July 19, 1993
A legendary R&B tenor saxophonist, South Carolina-native Red Prysock followed his brother to Hartford, Connecticut, in 1942. But while the underage Arthur Prysock was performing with The Buddy Johnson Orchestra in the mid Forties, Red Prysock joined the army and mastered several instruments while serving in World War II. Discharged in 1947, Prysock became a popular session player, working with Tiny Bradshaw and Tiny Grimes. A leading R&B "honker", Prysock joined many Alan Freed revues in the Fifties and performed alongside honker great Sam "The Man" Taylor. Releasing his own material, Prysock enjoyed some airplay with 'Wiggles', and with its great horn solo, 'Hand Clappin''. Beginning in 1971, Red Prysock frequently

performed with his brother, vocalist Arthur Prysock. Red Prysock's finest output is compiled on the AVI album *The Best Of Red Prysock* (1996).
CAUSE: After suffering a series of heart attacks, he died in Chicago.

Rainer Ptacek

Born June 7, 1951
Died November 12, 1997
Inventive Czech-American slide and dobro, blues-styled guitarist and songwriter who was based in Tucson, Arizona, Rainer Ptacek escaped with his family from Communist East Berlin in 1953. Trained on the violin but switching to guitar, he was chiefly employed as a guitar repairman. Forming a series of blues groups including Das Combo, Ptacek collaborated with the uncredited Billy Gibbons of ZZ Top on the 1993 album *The Texas Tapes*; Ptacek's final album, *Nocturnes*, was recorded in 1995. A tribute album, *Inner Flame*, was released shortly before his death.
CAUSE: Lymphoma and an inoperable brain tumour. He had been diagnosed two years earlier.

Richie Puente

(RICHARD ANTHONY PUENTE)
Born June 15, 1953
Died July 18, 2004
A member of Latin-rooted disco era group Foxy, percussionist Richie Puente was the son of jazz bandleader Tito Puente. Nicknamed "Kiki", Richie Puente formed Foxy in 1974 with guitarist-vocalist Ish "Angel" Ledesma. Hired as the session band for Miami-based T.K. Records, the group also scored its own hits with 'Get Off Your Aahh! And Dance' (1976), 'Get Off' (1978), 'Hot Number' and 'RRRRRRock' (1979). Puente also worked with Eddie Money, George and Gwen McRae, Abba and Peter Frampton.
CAUSE: He succumbed to the long-term effects of a chronic, debilitating disease, viral encephalopathy. Puente was employed as a percussionist for The Miami City Ballet when in 2001 he began to suffer seizures; doctors initially misattributed the symptoms to the belated effects of a violent assault eight years earlier.

Tito Puento

(ERNEST ANTHONY PUENTE, JR.)
Born April 20, 1923
Died May 31, 2000
A giant of Latin-based jazz who emerged during the mambo craze of the Fifties, percussionist and bandleader Tito Puento influenced a host of Latin-rockers. A master at tambales, the New Yorker of Puerto Rican descent passed through a series of outfits before launching his own orchestra in 1948. One of his compositions, 'Oye Come Va', was reworked by Santana for their album *Abraxas*. Puento garnered renewed interest thanks to the 1992 film, *The Mambo Kings*. In 1995, he appeared on an episode of *The Simpsons*.
CAUSE: Suffering from heart disease, he died in a New York City hospital.

Dave "Grape" Purple

(DAVID ALAN PURPLE)
Born February 27, 1945
Died June 16, 2001
As bassist of Chicago-based pop-rock band The Cryan' Shames, Dave "Grape" Purple enjoyed a minor hit with 'Sugar And Spice' (1966). Drafted into the military, he left the group in 1967 and later worked as a recording engineer for Chess and Stax/Volt Records, earning a Grammy for engineering Isaac Hayes' chart-topping single 'Theme From Shaft'.
CAUSE: Unknown. He died in the Nashville suburb of Antioch, Tennessee.

Q

Clarence E. Quick

Born February 2, 1937
Died May 5, 1983

Vocalist for the Fifties doo-wop group The Del Vikings, Clarence Quick was raised in Brooklyn. A bass vocalist, he was previously teamed with his cousin William Blakely to form a local vocal group, The Mellowlarks. Joining the US Air Force, Quick was stationed in Pittsburgh. There he formed an off-hours vocal group, The Del Vikings, in 1956 with several other servicemen. After winning a number of Armed Forces talent contests, the group caught the attention of Pittsburgh deejay Barry Kaye. Recording in Kaye's small basement studio, the group was also aided by local record distributor Joe Averbach. One of the first racially integrated rock groups, The Del Vikings enjoyed a genre-defining hit with the Quick-composition, 'Come Go With Me'; initially released by the small Fee Bee label, the record was picked up by the larger Dot label. Because the group members were still serving in the Airforce, not every member appeared on every record. After following up with another Quick-penned hit, 'Whispering Bells', The Del Vikings splintered into two different groups. While Fee Bee retained the group led by Kripp Johnson and Don Jackson, Mercury controlled the group led by Clarence Quick. Quick's group scored a US Top 40 hit with 'Cool Shake' (1957), and appeared in the film, *The Big Beat* (1957), but the Fee Bee group was less successful. However, fans, distributors, and record stores soon backed off from both groups. Quick's group was eventually joined by members of the competing line-up in the early Sixties. After recording for several labels including ABC-Paramount, the group disbanded in 1965. Johnson joined a revival version of The Del Vikings in 1980.
CAUSE: Heart attack.

Robert Quine

Born December 30, 1942
Died May 31, 2004

A founding member of punk group Richard Hell & The Voidoids, Robert Quine was an innovative guitarist whose unorthodox riffs influenced many punk axemen. Born in Akron, Ohio, Quine was reared on acoustic blues and bebop jazz and, while attending law school in the late Sixties, he became infatuated with the avant-garde rock of The Velvet Underground. After failing his bar exam, he relocated to New York City where he wrote books on tax law. Taking a position at a bookstore, he was befriended by fellow employee Richard Hell, who was then (1974) a member of the band, Television. In 1976 Quine was invited to join Hell in his band, The Voidoids, who were eventually signed by Sire Records. Appearing on the ground-breaking *Blank Generation* album (1977), Quine infused components of jazz and progressive rock. Although enjoying limited commercial success, The Voidoids spawned a host of imitators. After the release of the group's follow-up album *Destiny Street* (1982), Quine was hired by Lou Reed, performing on Reed's albums *The Blue Mask* (1982), *Legendary Hearts* (1983), and *Live In Italy* (1984). Quine also worked with Tom Waits, Matthew Sweet, Marianne Faithfull, Lydia Lunch, and Material. Quine's cousin, Dan Auerbach is part of the blues duo, The Black Keys.
CAUSE: Despondent and reclusive after the deaths of his mother in 2002 and his wife, Alice, in 2003, Quine overdosed at his Manhattan apartment. His body was discovered five days later on June 5th. Found at his side was a large quantity of heroin and a suicide note. In poor health for most of his adult life, he had previously attempted suicide a month before his death.

R

Eddie Rabbitt

(EDWARD THOMAS RABBITT)
Born November 27, 1944
Died May 7, 1998
A much respected singer-songwriter, Eddie Rabbitt was a star in both the country and pop fields. Born in Brooklyn but raised in East Orange, New Jersey, Rabbitt made his unheralded recording début at 20th Century Records in 1964. Yearning for success, Rabbitt moved to Nashville in 1968 and gained fame when Elvis Presley recorded his composition 'Kentucky Rain'. Placing a dozen hits on the country charts before making his pop début, Rabbitt first crossed over in 1979 with the title track of the film *Every Which Way But Loose*. His pop hits continued with 'Suspicions'; from the film *Roadie*, 'Drivin' My Life Away'; the number one single, 'I Love A Rainy Night'; and 'Step By Step'. Teaming with Crystal Gayle in 1982, Rabbitt recorded the enduring, tender ballad hit 'You And I'. Following the death of his infant son from liver disease in 1985, Rabbitt expended much of his energy on children's charities. Rabbitt later scored a series of country hits including a cover of Dion's 'The Wanderer' (1988) and 'On Second Thought' (1989).
CAUSE: A long-term smoker, he was diagnosed with lung cancer in March 1997.

Carl Radle

Born June 18, 1942
Died May 30, 1980
Best known for his long association with Eric Clapton, Carl Radle was self-taught on bass guitar, picking up the instrument at 15. Playing locally around his home of Tulsa, Oklahoma, Radle joined a band led by Leon Russell. With Russell relocating to the West Coast in the late Sixties, Radle soon followed. Quickly finding session work, Radle backed Gary Lewis & The Playboys before forming his own Los Angeles-based group, Colors. Aided by Russell in 1969, Radle then joined Delaney & Bonnie & Friends for an extended caravan-style tour and subsequent album, *The Original Delaney & Bonnie: Accept No Substitute*. With the group hired as Blind Faith's opening act, Radle was befriended by Eric Clapton. After leaving Blind Faith, Clapton recorded his first solo album in 1970, and asked Radle, Leon Russell and other members of Delaney & Bonnie to join him. A breakthrough album, *Eric Clapton* was highlighted by 'Let It Rain', J.J. Cale's 'After Midnight' and the Leon Russell composition, 'Blues Power'. By mid-1970, Clapton's session group would evolve, with only a few changes, into Derek & The Dominoes. After appearing on the seminal Clapton album, *Layla And Other Assorted Love Songs*, Radle quit the group over personality differences with Clapton. During this period Radle joined Joe Cocker's 20-musician ensemble for the *Mad Dogs And Englishmen* tour, backed George Harrison on *All Things Must Pass*, and appeared at the charity concert and subsequent album, *The Concert For Bangla Desh*. Returning to Tulsa, Radle briefly reunited with Russell. Rejoining Clapton's group in 1973, Radle appeared on four albums – *461 Ocean Boulevard, There's One in Every Crowd*, the live *E.C. Was Here*, and the classic *Slowhand* – performing on tracks such as 'I Shot The Sheriff' (1974), 'Lay Down Sally' (1977), 'Wonderful Tonight' (1978) and 'Promises' (1978). Clapton hired a new backing band in 1979 with new bass player Dave Markee.
CAUSE: Long-term alcohol and heroin abuse resulting in kidney shutdown.

FURTHER READING: Schumacher, Michael. (1998). *Crossroads: The Life And Music Of Eric Clapton*. New York: Warner.

Ma Rainey

(GERTRUDE MELISSA NIX PRIDGETT)
Born April 26, 1886
Died December 22, 1939
Dubbed "The Mother of the Blues", the former Gertrude Pridgett was born in Columbus, Georgia, to former Vaudeville actors. Leaving home at 14, she joined a touring song and dance revue, The Rabbit Foot Minstrels. Marrying the troupe manager William Rainey, she formed a new act with her husband, "Ma & Pa Rainey, Assassinators of the Blues". Creating a new genre of vaudeville blues, Rainey toured throughout the South. After leaving her husband in 1917, "Madame" or Ma Rainey formed The Georgia Jazz Band. A bawdy and boisterous entertainer who belted out double-entendre lyrics, the gold-toothed Rainey draped herself in oversized-feathers, glitzy golden necklaces, and flashy gowns. Cutting her first sessions at age 37 in 1923, Rainey was backed at Paramount Records by leading musicians of the day including Fletcher Henderson, Louis Armstrong, and Coleman Hawkins. Issuing a run of strong selling 78s such as 'Lawd, I'm Down Wid De Blues', 'Ma Rainey's Black Bottom', and the often-recorded 'See See Rider Blues', Rainey had limited success outside the black market. With blues declining in popularity, Rainey was dropped by Paramount in 1928. Abandoning blues after the death of a sister in 1935, Rainey joined a Baptist church and sang spirituals in her later years.
CAUSE: She suffered a heart attack in Columbus, Georgia.
FURTHER READING: Jones, Hettie. (1995). *Big Star Fallin' Mama*. New York: Viking.

Ben Raleigh

Born June 16, 1913
Died February 26, 1997
A lyricist who worked with Herb Alpert and Otis Blackwell, Ben Raleigh penned 'Wonderful Wonderful', 'She's A Fool', 'Tell Laura I Love Her', and the theme from the *Scooby Doo* show. He won a Grammy for the Lou Rawls hit, 'Love Is A Hurtin' Thing'.
CAUSE: He died from injuries suffered in a kitchen fire at his home in Hollywood, California.

Don Ralke

Born July 13, 1920
Died January 26, 2000
A prolific but relatively unknown composer and arranger, Michigan-born Don Ralke provided the music for a number of US television programmes including *77 Sunset Strip*, *Hawaiian Eye*, *Laverne & Shirley* and *Happy Days*. He also produced or arranged scores of hit records including 'The Mountain's High' (Dick & Dee Dee), 'There I've Said It Again' (Sam Cooke), 'Ringo' (Lorne Greene), 'The Birds And The Bees' (Jewel Akens), 'Kookoo, Lend Me Your Comb' (Edd "Kookie" Byrnes) and '16 Reasons' (Connie Stevens).
CAUSE: He died from natural causes at Kaiser Hospital in Santa Rosa, California.

Buck Ram

(SAMUEL RAM)
Born November 21, 1907
Died January 1, 1991
A composer, manager and producer of many Fifties R&B artists, Buck Ram was especially successful with The Platters. Born a child prodigy in Chicago to well-off parents, Samuel "Buck" Ram attended law school at age 15, passing the California bar exam at 21. During his late teens, he dropped out of school for a year to work as a saxophone player on a radio show. Drawn to music and deciding not to work in the legal field, he took a

position at the Mills Music publishing house in the Thirties, working as an arranger for Cab Calloway, Count Basie and Glenn Miller. A prolific songwriter who penned classics such as 'I'll Be Home For Christmas' and 'Have Mercy', Ram assumed various pseudonyms including Lynn Paul and Ande Rand. With the big band era finished at the close of World War II, Ram found himself living in Los Angeles and briefly pursued a solo career at Savoy Records. Entering the business side of music as a manager, Ram had his first major success with The Three Suns, the group scoring several hits including the Ram co-composition, 'Twilight Time'. Nurturing young, raw talent, Ram became heavily involved in the genesis of the West Coast doo-wop and R&B scene. Forming Personality Productions in Los Angeles, Ram managed a host of pioneering acts including The Penguins, Sugar & Spice, Shirley Gunter, Joe Houston, Young Jessie, The Flairs and The Colts. But Ram would have the greatest success with Tony Williams and The Platters; honed and heavily tutored by Ram, The Platters dominated the charts in the last half of the Fifties with a remarkable string of Top 10 crossovers including the Ram-penned 'Twilight Time' and '(You've Got) The Magic Touch', The Platters faded from the charts with the departure of Tony Williams in 1961. For a number of years, Ram promoted his own touring version of the group as Buck Ram's Platters. In a lingering lawsuit that was filed in 1974, Ram lost the exclusive use of The Platters' name to former member Paul Robi in 1989.
CAUSE: Natural causes. He died after a lengthy illness at Valley Hospital in Las Vegas, Nevada.

Glenn Rambo

(GLENN MARSHALL RAMBO)
Born December 4, 1970
Died circa October 1, 2005
A co-founder of New Orleans-based heavy metal group Soilent Green, vocalist Glenn Rambo was a member from 1987 to 1988. A veteran of the city's rock scene, he later passed through a series of bands, including his final group, Swarm.
CAUSE: In the aftermath of Hurricane Katrina, he was found dead along with his mother at her home in Violet, Louisiana. Both had drowned. Neither Rambo nor his mother owned a car so that they were unable to reach safety.

Bobby Ramirez

Born 1949
Died July 24, 1972
The drummer in Edgar Winter's short-lived backing group, White Trash from 1971–72, Bobby Ramirez appeared on Epic Records releases, *White Trash* and *Roadwork*. With the break-up of White Trash in mid-1972, Winter formed the more successful Edgar Winter Group.
CAUSE: He died in a Chicago bar fight.

Dee Dee Ramone

(DOUGLAS GLENN COLVIN)
Born September 18, 1952
Died June 5, 2002
A member of legendary punk band The Ramones, in concert bassist Dee Dee Ramone led off each song with a frenetic "one, two, three, four". Growing up in Germany with his army father, the former Douglas Colvin spent his latter teen years in Queens, New York. A self-described juvenile delinquent, he was involved in drugs and prostitution. Dee Dee formed The Ramones as a surf-rock band in 1974 with his "brothers" Joey, Tommy and Johnny. (The Ramones surname was chosen by Dee Dee in tribute to one of Paul McCartney's early pseudonyms, Paul Ramone.) Rejecting the popular music of the day, the group began infusing musical elements from unconventional proto-punk acts such as MC5, The Stooges and The New York Dolls with the classic '60s AM

pop of the Spector girl groups, surf music and The British Invasion. Signing with Sire Records, the group issued its classic self-titled début album in 1976 which became the touchstone for all the punk influenced music that followed, particularly for nascent UK bands like The Sex Pistols and The Clash. Continuing to define the punk genre on a series of albums – *Leave Home* (1977), *Rocket To Russia* (1977) and *Road To Ruin* (1978) – The Ramones masterminded such brilliant three minute gems as 'Sheena Is A Punk Rocker', 'I Wanna Be Sedated' and 'Do You Remember Rock'n'Roll Radio?' (from 1980's *End Of The Century*, produced by their idol Phil Spector) which, much to their chagrin, failed to gain airplay because of the dreaded punk credentials. As the group's chief songwriter, Dee Dee Ramone wrote or co-wrote 'Teenage Lobotomy', 'Psycho Therapy', 'Rockaway Beach', 'Too Tough To Die' and the punk anthem about heroin use, 'Chinese Rocks'. Constantly feuding with his bandmates, Dee Dee left the group in 1989 and pursued an unlikely solo career as a rapper under the moniker, Dee Dee King, recording the poor-selling hip hop album, *Standing In The Spotlight*. Returning to his punk roots, he released a trio of solo albums including an album of Ramones covers, *Greatest And Latest*. Rejoining The Ramones, Dee Dee composed 'Pet Sematary' for the Stephen King film of the same name, and appeared on the group's final studio album, 1995's *¡Adios Amigos!* Having played over 2,000 shows over 10 years, The Ramones disbanded the following year. Also the author of several books, Dee Dee penned the novel *Chelsea Horror Hotel* and an autobiography, *Lobotomy: Surviving The Ramones*. During the group's induction into the Rock and Roll Hall of Fame just 11 weeks before his death, Dee Dee proclaimed at the podium: "I'd like to congratulate myself, and thank myself, and give myself a big pat on the back."

CAUSE: He accidentally overdosed at his Hollywood home and was found dead on his couch by his wife Barbara who had returned from shopping. Investigators reported finding drug paraphernalia on a nearby counter including a syringe. Dee Dee had struggled with drug and alcohol addiction for most of his life. The coroner ruled the cause of death as "morphine intoxication by self injection".

Joey Ramone

(JEFFREY HYMAN)
Born May 19, 1951
Died April 15, 2001

The lanky and towering frontman of The Ramones, singer Joey Ramone became a role model for the meek outsider attracted to rock'n'roll, providing a role model for the likes of Kurt Cobain. Wearing dark glasses overshadowed by a long mane of hair, Joey emerged as an unofficial godfather of punk. From a New York Jewish background, raised in the urban environment of Queens, Joey was reared on Sixties pop and rock. Encouraged by his artistic mother to learn an instrument, at age 13 he began playing the drums, in emulation of his idols Ringo Starr and Keith Moon. Briefly studying jazz drumming, the former Jeffrey Hyman took the name Jeff Starship and joined a number of local bands. In 1974, he joined his drinking buddies in forming what was intended to be a surf-rock band. Although originally the group's drummer, Joey was moved forward as the lead singer while Tommy Ramone took on the drums role when no one suitable could be found. Rejected by Rick Derringer's Blue Sky label, The Ramones were instead signed by Seymour Stein at Sire Records (a label that embraced early punk and new wave music). Dressed like a Bowery street gang in sneakers, torn jeans and leather jackets, The

Ramones prized songwriting and melody over extravagant stage shows, extended soloing and rock star pretension. Honing their sound at CBGB's, The Ramones were forefathers of a new movement alongside Television, The Patti Smith Group, Blondie, and Talking Heads. During their first tour through the UK in July 1976, The Ramones' London performance provided an inspiration to both The Clash and The Sex Pistols while also in the audience were Chrissie Hynde, members of The Damned and other aspirant punks who went on to form bands. Released in 1976, the group's début album *The Ramones* was an anomaly during the AOR stadium rock of the period; the album featured crafty, short, Sixties-styled rock ditties such as 'Blitzkrieg Bop' and 'I Wanna Be Your Boyfriend'. Equally creative were the follow-ups, *Leave Here, Rocket To Russia* and *Road To Ruin*. Though severely introverted and suffering from obsessive compulsive disorder for much of his life, Joey sardonically sang about mental illness on songs like 'Teenage Lobotomy' and 'I Wanna Be Sedated', while his Jewish lineage didn't prevent him from singing tongue-in-cheek about Nazis ('Today Your Love, Tomorrow The World'). Although the group would never place a single on the US pop charts and mainstream American radio ignored them, The Ramones scored several UK hits including 'Sheena Is A Punk Rocker' (1977) and the Phil Spector-produced 'Baby, I Love You' (from the 1980 album *End Of The Century*). After Johnny stole Joey's girlfriend in the early Eighties, tensions within the band increased. Although both men remained in the group during its entire run, they hardly ever spoke to each other again. A year after releasing their final studio album, the appropriately titled *¡Adios Amigos!*, The Ramones disbanded in 1996. At the time of his death, Joey Ramone was working on his first solo album – the posthumously issued *Don't Worry About Me*. Over the years, The Ramones' influence spawned a host of musical progeny including Green Day and Blink-182.

CAUSE: Lymphoma. He had been ill for some time but continued to tour. He died at the Presbyterian Hospital in New York City while listening to U2's 'In A Little While'.

Johnny Ramone

(JOHN CUMMINGS)
Born October 8, 1948
Died September 15, 2004

As a key member of The Ramones, guitarist Johnny Ramone provided a barrage of buzz saw riffs. Born on Long Island, but raised in the Queens section of New York City, he attended college in the mid Sixties to avoid military call-up. Dropping out of school, he took a series of menial jobs and while working with Dee Dee Ramone (Douglas Colvin), as a construction worker, the former John Cummings purchased a guitar. Both into music and rock gigs, the pair decided to form a surf band that included John's childhood friend, drummer Tommy Ramone (Thomas Erdelyi), and lanky vocalist Joey Ramone (Jeffrey Hyman). The group immediately caused a stir (often for the wrong reasons!) upon their début at CBGB's in August 1974. Taken under the wing of their manager, music insider Danny Fields, the group was signed by Seymour Stein of Sire Records and released their self-titled debut album in 1976. As the architect of the band, Johnny Ramone was instrumental in shaping all aspects of their music and public persona. Playing a quick succession of three-minute songs – starting with a shouted "one, two, three, four" from Dee Dee – The Ramones toured incessantly. Spawning a host of imitators, the group irreverently wore leather jackets, torn T-shirts and cheap tennis shoes, topped by bowl-cut long, straight manes. On stage, Johnny Ramone would stand in an aggressive

pose, legs apart, with his hair flailing to the music, chopping at his Mosrite guitar in a blurred series of down strokes. Although the group never managed a chart hit in the US, among the group's enduring tracks were 'Sheena Is A Punk Rocker', 'I Wanna Be Sedated', the sing-along "Hey Ho! Let's Go!" anthem 'Blitzkrieg Bop' and the title track of their campy 1979 film *Rock 'n' Roll High School.* Teaming with eccentric producer Phil Spector in 1980, The Ramones barely survived multiple confrontations with Spector who at one point pulled a gun on the group. The resulting album, *End Of The Century,* would turn out to be the group's biggest seller, although at least half the band members disowned it. As the group's outspoken conservative, Johnny tried to block drug and political references from the group's lyrics and played begrudgingly on songs like the anti-Reagan 'Bonzo Goes To Bitburg' (1985). When Joey's girlfriend left him for Johnny in the early Eighties, a permanent rift ensued; though Johnny and Joey both remained dedicated to the band, the two hardly spoke to each other again. With little to show financially for 10 years of hard work, The Ramones remained on the road until disbanding in 1996, travelling the entire time not in a luxurious tour bus but in decrepit vans. Following the break-up, Johnny Ramone retired from music and sold off his guitars, moving to the West Coast to follow his beloved baseball. The 2004 Ramones documentary, *End Of The Century,* painted Johnny Ramone in an unfavourable light as an overcontrolling tyrant.
CAUSE: He died at his home in Los Angeles after battling prostate cancer for five years.

Mike Ramsden

(MICHAEL JOHN RAMSDEN)
Born June 21, 1943
Died January 17, 2004
A member of the British group The Silkie, Mike Ramsden formed the quartet in 1963 with his future wife Sylvia and two other students at Hull University. Managed by Brian Epstein, The Silkie reached the Top 10 with their folk-tinged cover of The Beatles' 'You've Got To Hide Your Love Away', which featured performing and production involvement from Lennon, McCartney and Harrison. After touring across the UK and continental Europe in the Sixties, the group disbanded. In 1971, Ramsden teamed with architect Jim Goodwin to launch the annual Totnes Raft Race, eventually raising over £600,000 for charity.
CAUSE: He underwent a kidney transplant, but died ten years later after the organ failed. He died at the Royal Devon and Exeter Hospital in Wonford.

Teddy Randazzo

(ALESSANDRO RANDAZZO)
Born May 13, 1935
Died November 21, 2003
A songwriter and performer, Brooklyn born Teddy Randazzo became the lead singer and accordion player of The Three Chuckles at age 15. After scoring a Top 20 hit in 1954 with 'Runaround', the group made a series of appearances on *The Ed Sullivan Show,* and appeared in the rock films *Hey, Let's Twist*; *The Girl Can't Help It*; and a pair of Alan Freed productions, *Mister Rock And Roll* and *Rock, Rock, Rock.* As a songwriter, Randazzo co-composed 'Goin' Out Of My Head', 'Hurts So Bad', 'It's Gonna Take A Miracle', 'I'm On The Outside (Looking In)', 'Pretty Blue Eyes' and 'Christmas Love'. Purchasing a holiday home in Hawaii, Randazzo later worked with a number of traditional Hawaiian musical acts.
CAUSE: He died in his sleep at his home in Orlando, Florida. Although the cause of death was not disclosed, he had suffered a heart attack in the early Eighties.

Bill Randle

(William McKinley Randle, Jr.)
Born March 14, 1923
Died July 9, 2004
An influential deejay with star-making power, Bill Randle was best known for bringing an unknown singer named Elvis Presley to Cleveland for his first-ever concert north of the Mason-Dixon line. After the performance, Randle turned down Presley's offer to become his manager. Randle was influential in aiding the careers of entertainers such as Johnnie Ray, The Crew-Cuts, Bobby Darin and Tony Bennett. A nationally known figure throughout the Fifties, Randle introduced Presley on one of his *Ed Sullivan Show* performances, and was named the top deejay in America by *Time* magazine. At one time, Randle's radio programme garnered over 50 per cent of the audience in Cleveland. Randle was also a professor, attorney, and had earned three Masters degrees.
Cause: Cancer. He died at the Hospice of the Western Reserve in Cleveland.

Bill Randolph

Born March 19, 1951
Died June 19, 2001
The bass player of Southern-flavoured rock group Point Blank, "Wild" Bill Randolph began his career in the nightclubs of Dallas in the late Sixties, before touring with John Lee Hooker for a year. Joining the Texas-based rock group Rock Point in the late Seventies, he appeared on their third album *Airplay* (1979). The group scored its only Top 40 hit in 1981 with 'Nicole' and disbanded shortly after the release of their final album, *On A Roll.* Randolph left music for a career in printing.
Cause: He suffered a heart attack at his home near Lake Texoma, Texas.

Danny Rapp

Born May 10, 1941
Died April 5, 1983
The namesake and lead singer of early rock'n'roll band Danny & The Juniors, Danny Rapp formed a predecessor of the group, The Juvenairs, while attending John Bartram High School in Philadelphia. After performing in front of the home of former singer Johnny Medora, the group was introduced to local music promoter and record label owner Artie Singer. With Singer hired as their manager, the group recorded a self-penned composition 'Do The Bop', named after a then-popular dance craze. Asked by Singer for a recommendation, Dick Clark suggested a title change to 'At The Hop'. Released on Singer's small label, Singular Records, the single was only a local hit until the group was invited to perform on Dick Clark's *American Bandstand* as a last-minute replacement. With ABC-Paramount Records acquiring the master disc, 'At The Hop' (1958) was a number one hit. Later in the year, Danny & The Juniors followed up with 'Rock And Roll Is Here To Stay' and 'Dottie'. Heading the relatively clean-cut rock group, the pompadoured Rapp was a great dancer who tutored his bandmates. Switching to Swan Records in 1960, the group would score its final Top 40 hit with 'Twistin' U.S.A'. After signing to Guyden Records in early 1963, the group broke up. Occasionally reforming, Danny & The Juniors would sporadically record. After reforming in the early Seventies for Dick Clark's oldies shows, Danny & The Juniors split amicably into two camps in 1978, with Rapp's group the more popular. Rapp later took a managerial position in a toy factory.
Cause: Suicide by gunshot at the Yacht Club motel in Quartzsite, Arizona, during a four-week engagement at the Pointe Tapatio Resort in Phoenix. Reportedly a heavy drinker, Rapp had been despondent and unruly while performing earlier in the day.

Lou Rawls

(LOUIS ALLEN RAWLS)
Born December 1, 1935
Died January 6, 2006
A versatile, velvety voiced soul singer who earned respect for his social activism, Lou Rawls was rooted in the gospel tradition. Born in Chicago, Rawls was exposed to gospel music at a young age by his grandmother. Singing in a series of local gospel harmony acts, Rawls teamed with Sam Cooke in The Teenage Kings Of Harmony, subsequently joining The Holy Wonders before replacing Cooke in The Highway QCs. By 1954, Rawls made his recording début at Specialty Records as a member of The Chosen Gospel Singers. Relocating to Los Angeles in the mid Fifties, Rawls joined the popular Pilgrim Travelers, his stint interrupted by two years in the army. With The Pilgrim Travelers disbanding in 1959, Rawls switched to secular music, and was discovered at a Hollywood nightclub in 1962 by Capitol Records producer Nik Venet. That same year, Rawls rejoined Sam Cooke to provide the call-and-response vocals on the bluesy 'Bring It On Home To Me', as well as a strong backing vocal on the flip side, the rock standard 'Having A Party'. Anchored in jazz and blues, Rawls released *Stormy Monday*, the first of many albums at Capitol, backed on the sessions by The Les McCann Trio. Turning towards soul, Rawls topped the R&B charts in 1966 with the title track of his Grammy-nominated album, *Love Is A Hurtin' Thing*. Signing with Philadelphia International Records in 1975, Rawls reached his commercial peak with such orchestrated and polished hits as 'Lady Love', 'See You When I Git There' and his signature piece, 'You'll Never Find Another Love Like Mine'. Also an actor, Rawls made numerous television appearances beginning with a bit part in *77 Sunset Strip* and as a cowboy in *The Big Valley*, and starred in his own summer replacement series in 1969, *Lou Rawls & The Golddiggers*. Rawls' many film roles include *Blues Brothers 2000* and *Leaving Las Vegas*. In 1976, Rawls became the corporate spokesman for Anheuser-Busch and provided the voice-overs for many of their commercials. Continuing in voice-over work, he appeared in a number of *Garfield* television specials. As an activist, Rawls launched *The Lou Rawls Parade Of Stars*, which raised $200 million over three decades to benefit the United Negro College Fund. In his latter years, Rawls frequently performed in Las Vegas.
CAUSE: He was diagnosed with lung cancer in December 2004, and in May 2005, brain cancer. He died after a month-long hospitalisation at Cedars-Sinai Medical Center in Los Angeles.

Harry Ray

(HARRY MILTON RAY)
Born December 15, 1946
Died December 1, 1992
A member of two R&B ballad groups – The Moments and Ray, Goodman & Brown – bass-baritone vocalist Harry Ray was born in New Jersey. Singing on street corners, Ray first joined an amateur group called The Voltaires. By 1970, he joined a latter line-up of the Washington DC-based R&B vocal group, The Moments, shortly after the release of their biggest seller, 'Love On A Two Way Street'. When bandmate Harry Brown came down with throat problems, Ray was asked to sing lead on their next release, an R&B hit remake of The Ink Spots' standard, 'If I Didn't Care'; as a result of the record's success, Ray and Brown would later alternate lead vocal duties. Single-handedly keeping their record label afloat, The Moments enjoyed a string of R&B entries including Ray co-compositions, 'Sexy Mama' (1974) and 'Look At Me (I'm In Love)' (1975). With All Platinum Records owning the rights to The Moments'

name, the trio left the label and in 1979 emerged at Polydor Records as Ray, Goodman & Brown. From their label début, *Ray, Goodman & Brown*, the trio scored a million-selling smash hit with elegant ballad, 'Special Lady'. After the release of *Ray, Goodman & Brown II* in 1982, Ray left to pursue a solo career, and was replaced by Kevin Owens. He released an ignored solo album, *It's Good To Be Home* (with its minor hit 'Sweet Baby'), and subsequently reunited with his former group.
CAUSE: Suffering from long-term hypertension, he died of a massive stroke in Boundbrook, New Jersey.

Johnnie Ray

(JOHN ALVIN RAY)
Born January 10, 1927
Died February 24, 1990
An innovative, Fifties pop crooner who bridged white ballads with R&B, Johnnie Ray's emotional, gut-wrenching delivery pre-dated rock but at the same time anticipated its manner. Part-Blackfoot Indian, Ray was rendered deaf at age 11 after falling on his head while playing with friends. Shunned and friendless due to his handicap, Ray regained partial hearing at 15, and wore a hearing aid for life. Playing the piano since his childhood, the talented Ray landed on a local radio show with Jane Powell. Attracted by the lure of Hollywood, he left home in 1948. Playing in a series of piano lounges, first in Los Angeles, and then in the midwest, Ray was taught to sing R&B during a residency in Akron, Ohio. Often alienating audiences with his overly dramatic stage antics, the contorted and weeping Ray would fervently yank at his hair, and scream out lyrics. An emotional powder keg, he soon acquired several nicknames including "The Prince Of Wails" and "The Nabob Of Sob". During an extended engagement at the Flame Club in Detroit, Ray was discovered by DJ Robin Seymore. Signing with Columbia Records and working with producer Mitch Miller, Ray's début single, 'Whiskey Gin', sold poorly outside the midwest. The follow-up, a double-sided hit 'Cry'/'The Little White Cloud That Cried', featured Ray's exaggerated falsetto vocals; a two-million-selling smash, 'Cry' dominated the pop airwaves and even crossed over onto the R&B charts with many listeners believing he was black. With Ray emerging as a pre-rock teen-idol, 'Cry' paved the way for white singers to sing R&B. Unfortunately, Ray's own singing career did not survive into the rock era. With his ensuing releases tamed by producer Mitch Miller, Ray continued his run with 'Please, Mr. Sun'/'Here I Am – Broken Hearted' (1952), 'Walking My Baby Back Home' (1952), 'Somebody Stole My Gal' (1953), 'Such A Night' (1954), and 'Hey There'/'Hernando's Hideaway' (1954). Moving into film, Ray appeared in several features including *There's No Business Like Show Business* (1954). Abusing alcohol and arrested several times on morals charges, Ray left the stage in 1965. Returning to touring in the mid Seventies, Ray was disheartened with his relegation to the oldies circuit. Remaining a huge draw in Britain, the ageing crooner assumed the role of an Elvis-like, Las Vegas entertainer in his last years.
CAUSE: Liver failure. A heavy drinker, Ray had suffered from cirrhosis. Entering a ten-day coma, he died at Cedars-Sinai Medical Center in Los Angeles.
FURTHER READING: Whiteside, Jonny. (1994). *Cry: The Johnny Ray Story*. New York: Barricade.

Raybeez

(RAYMOND BARBIERI)
Born November 27, 1961
Died September 11, 1997
Lead singer of the politically charged, New York-based hardcore group Warzone since its inception in 1984,

Raybeez had previously been the drummer in a similar outfit, Agnostic Front. At the time of his death, Raybeez had completed work on the Warzone album, *Fight For Justice*. CAUSE: Bacterial pneumonia. He died in New York City.

Razzle

(NICHOLAS DINGLEY)
Born December 2, 1963
Died December 8, 1984
The drummer and only British member of Hanoi Rocks, Razzle joined the two-year-old Scandinavian hard rock group in 1982. Born on the Isle of Wight but raised in Coventry, England, Razzle was inspired in his teens by The Sex Pistols. Passing through a series of metal and punk bands, he recorded a single with The Dark. Razzle joined Hanoi Rocks as a replacement for original drummer Gyp Casino after catching a gig at the Zig Zag club in London. Headed by vocalist Mike Monroe and featuring a two guitar assault, the hard rocking Hanoi Rocks adopted a glam persona in a cross between The Rolling Stones and The New York Dolls. Relocating from Stockholm to London in early 1982, Hanoi Rocks signed with Lick Records. After releasing their breakthrough album *Back To Mystery City Beat*, which featured the track 'Malibu Beach Nightmare', Hanoi Rocks signed a three record deal with CBS Records in 1983. Ironically, Hanoi Rocks co-headlined a tour in late 1984 with former New York Dolls members, Johnny Thunders and Jerry Nolan. Released shortly before Razzle's death, *Two Steps On The Move* was highlighted by 'Underwater World' and a cover of Creedence Clearwater Revival's 'Up Around The Bend'. Although Hanoi Rocks were relatively unknown in the US, the group was also quite popular in Japan. After temporarily replacing Razzle with former Clash drummer Terry Chimes, Hanoi Rocks disbanded in December 1984.

CAUSE: He died in an automobile accident in Redondo Beach, California. Razzle was the passenger in a sports car driven by Motley Crue's Neil Vincent when the 1972 Ford Pantera collided with two other cars, striking the second vehicle head on. Razzle and Vincent were returning to Vincent's home from a beer run. Vincent suffered facial cuts and cracked ribs and was charged with vehicular manslaughter and driving under the influence. His blood alcohol level was .17 per cent. Razzle was pronounced dead on arrival at Redondo's South Bay Hospital. The 20-year-old driver and 18-year-old passenger of the second car, a Volkswagon, both suffered head injuries and required physical rehabilitation. The driver of the other vehicle was uninjured. Neil Vincent pleaded guilty to drunken driving and manslaughter charges; he was sentenced to five years probation, 30 days in jail, 200 hours of community service, and ordered by a court to pay $2.6 million to his victims; of that figure, Razzle's estate received $200,000. (Neil Vincent left Motley Crue in 1992 and became a full-time racing-car driver.)

Eugene Record

(EUGENE BOOKER RECORD)
Born December 23, 1940
Died July 22, 2005
A former taxi driver and original member of soul group The Chi-Lites, lead singer and guitarist Eugene Record also emerged as their producer and chief songwriter. Formed in Chicago in 1960 as a doo-wop outfit called Marshall & The Hi-Lites, the renamed group signed with Brunswick Records in 1968. Beginning with the 1969 single 'Give It Away', The Chi-Lites enjoyed a long and fruitful run on the R&B charts. Record co-penned and sang falsetto on their breakthrough crossover ballad hit 'Have You Seen Her?' with wife, singer (and Brunswick labelmate) Barbara Acklin. The enduring song was later

covered by and became a hit for MC Hammer in 1990. The Chi-Lites followed up with another Record-composed ballad, the chart-topping 'Oh Girl' (which was later revived by Paul Young in 1990). Record left the group for a solo career in 1976, but managed just one hit with 'Laying Beside You' (1977). In 1980, the original four members of The Chi-Lites regrouped, recording for a series of labels and scoring with several singles on the R&B charts, most notably 'Bottom's Up' (1983). After leaving The Chi-Lites in 1990 (to be replaced by Anthony Watson) Record turned to gospel music, issuing the religious album *Let Him In* (1998). In 2003 Record shared a Grammy Award for the Beyoncé Knowles' hit 'Crazy In Love', which prominently sampled the horn riff from The Chi-lites' 1970 R&B hit 'Are You My Woman? (Tell Me So)'. CAUSE: Cancer. He died at his daughter's home in suburban Chicago.

Sharon Redd

Born October 19, 1945
Died May 1, 1992
A former backing singer for Bette Midler, Sharon Redd later pursued a solo career. Signed to Prelude Records, the classically trained Redd recorded three albums for the label and had a pair of disco/club hits in the early Eighties with 'Can You Handle It?' and 'Beat The Street'. She also had a leading role in an Australian production of the rock musical *Hair*. CAUSE: Pneumonia.

Noel Redding

(NOEL DAVID REDDING)
Born December 25, 1945
Died May 11, 2003
The bassist in The Jimi Hendrix Experience from 1966 to 1969, Noel Redding provided a platform for Hendrix's complex and mesmerising guitar. Born in the coastal town of Folkestone, Kent, Redding mastered the mandolin and violin during his childhood, before switching to guitar. During the rise of the British beat boom, Redding played rhythm guitar in several covers bands and, by age 17, was working in a pair of rock groups in the rough clubs of Hamburg, Germany. As a member of The Loving Kind, who were managed by Gordon Mills, he released three singles for the Pye label subsidiary Piccadilly in 1966. Meanwhile, at a New York City nightclub, a young guitarist and leader of an R&B group called Jimmy James & The Blue Flames was performing to an audience that included former Animals' bassist Chas Chandler. As Hendrix's new manager, Chandler brought the talented guitarist to London and started auditions for a touring band. Originally trying out for the vacant guitarist's role in Eric Burdon's New Animals in September 1966, Redding was hired in part because Hendrix admired his afro hairstyle. Switching from rhythm guitar to bass, Redding quickly taught himself how to play on Chandler's borrowed bass guitar. A week later, former child actor-turned-drummer Mitch Mitchell was added to complete the trio. Though intended as a temporary backing outfit, The Jimi Hendrix Experience quickly gelled and the arrangement became permanent. While Hendrix would be paid fifty per cent of the group's profits, the rest was to be split between Redding and Mitchell. Released in Britain in late 1966, Hendrix's first British hit, 'Hey Joe', was based on the Billy Roberts arrangement of the folk standard also recorded by The Byrds, Love, The Leaves and folkie Tim Rose. Following-up with the British hits 'Purple Haze' and 'The Wind Cries Mary', Hendrix remained relatively unknown in his native country. Then, at Paul McCartney's insistence, Hendrix was added to the bill for the Monterey Pop Festival in June 1967, which resulted in his first significant American exposure. Dominating the

show, Hendrix shocked the audience when he set his guitar on fire with lighter fluid. Releasing two classic and innovative albums in 1967 – *Are You Experienced* and *Axis: Bold As Love* – The Jimi Hendrix Experience set a new standard for guitar oriented rock, with classic tracks such as 'Are You Experienced?', 'Fire' and 'Foxy Lady'. While the group's fortunes as a live act continued to escalate in America in 1968, tensions simmered between Hendrix and Redding, particularly in the studio where Redding walked out of sessions for the group's dynamic version of Bob Dylan's 'All Along The Watchtower' (Hendrix ended up playing bass). The number of parasites hanging around Jimi only contributed to the tension, causing Chas Chandler to quit as manager during elongated sessions for the Experience's third album (and the last to feature Redding), the double *Electric Ladyland*. Despite their differences Hendrix encouraged Redding's songwriting efforts, and the Experience recorded several Redding compositions, of which 'She's So Fine' and 'Little Miss Strange' were released on *Axis: Bold As Love* and *Electric Ladyland* respectively. The Experience situation was not democratic enough for Redding who during his final stages with the group formed his own outfit, Fat Mattress, with former Loving Kind member Neil Landon on vocals, Jim Leverton on bass, Eric Dillon (drums) and Redding (guitar). The group supported The Jimi Hendrix Experience at a prestigious Royal Albert Hall concert in London in February 1969 – Redding's last English shows with the guitar genius – and also on an American and Canadian tour, during which Hendrix was arrested for heroin possession in Toronto in May 1969. Redding officially left The Jimi Hendrix Experience after a disastrous gig at the Denver Pop Festival on June 29, 1969, and the Experience as they were known was disbanded. Having recorded and released a self-titled début album for Polydor, Redding was fired from his own group who went on to record a follow-up, *Fat Mattress II*, with replacement Steve Hammond before splitting. With his Hendrix money frozen because of business complexities at the time of Hendrix's death in September 1970, Redding consequently joined a Los Angeles-based heavy metal band, Road, who recorded an album for Kama Sutra Records. Settling in Cork, Ireland, Redding teamed with Eric Bell of Thin Lizzy and two others to form The Noel Redding Band, recording a pair of albums in the mid Seventies for RCA. In later years, Redding sporadically recorded and toured as part of various all-star aggregations, including Shut Up Frank, featuring Dave Clark (guitar), ex-Animals' keyboardist Dave Rowberry and ex-Kinks' drummer Mick Avory. In 1991, Redding published his autobiography *Are You Experienced?*, written with the help of longtime girlfriend Carol Appleby who was tragically killed just prior to the book's publication. In the book, Redding revealed that in 1974, he and Mitch Mitchell were forced out of financial desperation into legally signing away any rights to future royalties from their Hendrix-era recordings. In 1992 Redding was inducted into the Rock and Roll Hall of Fame as a member of The Jimi Hendrix Experience and following the 1997 introduction of the Fender manufactured Noel Redding Jazz Bass, Redding became a promotional spokesman for the company. Redding released his final album in 2002, a live project, *From Bunkr-Prague*, which included some Hendrix songs. At the time of his death an ongoing lawsuit to reclaim his Hendrix monies was unresolved.

CAUSE: He died suddenly in the bathroom of his home in Clonakilty, Ireland. Authorities later attributed the death to natural causes.

Otis Redding

(OTIS REDDING, JR.)
Born September 9, 1941
Died December 10, 1967

A soul music giant, the gritty-voiced Otis Redding was born into poverty at a housing project in the musically rich community of Macon, Georgia. After forming his own gospel choir at his preacher father's small Mount Ivy Baptist Church, Redding mastered the drums, piano and guitar by playing along with his records. Inspired by the success of fellow Macon resident Little Richard, Redding formed an R&B band against the wishes of his deeply religious father. Dropping out of school to support his family after his father fell ill, Redding spent his weekends entering talent contests with his Little Richard-like delivery. Beginning in 1958, Redding occasionally joined guitarist Johnny Jenkins' group The Pinetoppers; after hiring an unlikely 18-year-old, white, R&B fan Phil Walden as their manager, The Pinetoppers secured bookings throughout the South. Recording two solo singles, Redding landed scattered airplay with the upbeat 'Shout Bamalama'. After accompanying Johnny Jenkins and The Pinetoppers to the Stax-Volt studio in Memphis in 1952, Redding recorded two unscheduled solo tracks at the end of a Pinetoppers session. Backed by the house band, Booker T & The MGs, Redding recorded two songs for what would become his first single, 'Hey, Hey Baby' and the gospel-tinged, slow-climbing, B-side hit, 'These Arms Of Mine'. Recording at the Stax-Volt studios but signed by Atlantic-Atco, Redding developed a fruitful writing relationship with MGs' guitarist Steve Cropper. Recorded in 24 hours, the album *Otis Blue* (1965) spawned the hits 'I've Been Loving You Too Long' and a Redding composition that Aretha Franklin redefined two years later, 'Respect'. Although he was a soul superstar, the gruff-voiced Redding initially found limited pop crossover acceptance as he continued his hit run with a remake of the 1933 Ted Lewis release 'Try A Little Tenderness' (1966). During this period Redding joined Phil Walden in forming Jotis Records, their greatest success coming with Arthur Conley's Top 10 hit 'Sweet Soul Music' (1967). Pairing with R&B songstress Carla Thomas in 1967 as "The King & Queen", Redding scored hits with 'Tramp', 'Knock On Wood' and 'Lovey Dovey'. Desperately yearning for crossover acceptance, Redding performed at rock venues like the Fillmore and Whisky A-Go-Go and, more importantly, at the Monterey Pop Festival in June 1967 when he won over a predominantly white crowd and was poised for superstardom. Veering away from his hard-soul style, Redding was targeting the pop market with '(Sittin' On) The Dock Of The Bay'. Rush-released after Redding's death, the song earned Redding a posthumous US number one single and two Grammy Awards and was followed by nearly a dozen posthumous hits. Redding's music was a central theme of the film, *The Commitments* (1991).

CAUSE: Aeroplane crash. Redding was in Cleveland to appear on the syndicated television programme *Upbeat* (on the same bill as Mitch Ryder) and to perform three concerts at Leo's Casino nightclub (8 p.m., 10:30, and 1 a.m.). Arriving an hour late for the taping of his *Upbeat* segment, Redding attributed the delay to electrical problems with his plane. On the road for a series of one-night stands, Redding was booked the following day for a performance at the Factory nightclub near the University of Wisconsin; ironically, Redding's scheduled opening act was a band called The Grim Reaper. Despite adverse weather conditions, the conscientious Redding was determined to fulfil his contractual obligations and flew out of foggy

Cleveland. While attempting a daytime, instrument landing three miles south of Madison Municipal Airport, Redding's new $20,000 Beechcraft plane lost power, went into a spin, and dropped into the icy waters of lake Monoma at 3:28 p.m., half a mile offshore. Besides Redding, four of the five members of his back-up touring band, The Bar-Kays, also perished – only Ben Cauley survived to hear the voices of fellow bandmates whom he was unable to save. Dead by drowning were Ron Caldwell (19), Carl Cunningham (18), Phalin Jones (18) and Jimmy King (18). Also dead were the pilot, Richard Fraser (26), and Redding's valet, Matthew Kelley (17). Redding was seated in the front, next to the pilot. Andrew Love and Wayne Jackson of The Memphis Horns had earlier declined to join the tour.
FURTHER READING: Schiesel, Jane. (1973). *The Otis Redding Story*. Garden City, NJ: Doubleday.

Bill Reed

Born January 11, 1936
Died October 22, 2004
A member of popular Fifties doo-wop group The Diamonds, Bill Reed provided the prominent bass vocal on most of their hits. Raised in Toronto, Reed was taught to sing and harmonise by his father. Formed at the University of Toronto as a barbershop-style vocal group, The Diamonds were inspired by the success of fellow Canadian vocal group, The Crew-Cuts, who had scored a hit covering The Chords' 'Sh-Boom'. Taking a similar route, The Diamonds recorded a series of cover hits beginning with Frankie Lymon & The Teenagers' 'Why Do Fools Fall In Love?'. Recording a cover version of The Gladiolas' R&B hit 'Little Darlin'', The Diamonds revamped the sombre romantic ballad into an upbeat, satirical piece complete with castanets, novelty-style falsetto vocals and Reed's mocking, spoken-word soliloquy. One of the best-selling singles of the rock era, The Diamonds' rendition prevented the original from reaching the Top 40 pop chart. Follow-up hits included Buddy Holly's 'Words Of Love' (1957), 'Zip Zip' (1957), 'Silhouettes' (1957) and, capitalising on the Stroll dance craze, an original composition, 'The Stroll' (1957). In early 1958, Reed left the group and was replaced by Evan Fischer. Reed later worked in record promotion, and on occasion would rejoin The Diamonds for a performance.
CAUSE: Cancer. He died at the Hospice of Martin and St. Lucie in Port St. Lucie, Florida.

Dean Reed

Born September 22, 1938
Died June 17, 1986
Virtually unknown in his native land, Denver-born Dean Reed was a pop music superstar in the Soviet Union and in his adopted home of East Germany. After scoring a minor US hit in 1959 with 'The Search', the left-wing activist left for the other side of the Iron Curtain. Also an actor, he appeared in 18 films including the Italian western *Adios Sabata* (1985). Having retained his US citizenship, Reed occasionally visited his homeland. Actor Tom Hanks announced plans for a Reed biopic in 2005.
CAUSE: He died under mysterious circumstances. Reed was found fully clothed in the driver's seat of his car on the bottom of a lake near Berlin. Suffering marital problems, he left a suicide note addressed to German ruler Erich Honecker, written on the back of a screenplay. Fearing a public relations disaster, Honecker personally ordered the note to be hidden away in a government safe. Instead, Reed's death was ruled a swimming accident. But years after the fall of Communism, the note surfaced and was published by the German tabloid *Bild*.

Jimmy Reed

Born September 6, 1925
Died August 29, 1976

A country blues guitarist, Jimmy Reed was reared in a Mississippi sharecropping family. After passing through a gospel vocal group, Reed was taught to play guitar by childhood friend and future blues star, Eddie Taylor. Settling in the Chicago area in 1947, Reed worked in the steel mills. Accompanying himself on the guitar and harmonica, he also landed an occasional stage gig. Buying a table-top record-making machine, Reed peddled his amateur recordings to Vee-Jay Records in 1953. Reunited in the studio with Eddie Taylor, Reed scored a local hit with 'Found My Baby' (1953). But with several follow-up singles garnering little attention, Reed took a job as a butcher for Armour meats. With the release of a nearly two-year-old track 'You Don't Have To Go', Reed scored his first national hit and was able to quit his day job. Grounded in a backwoods Delta style, Reed's hit run continued with 'Ain't That Lovin' You Baby' (1956), 'Can't Stand To See You Go' (1956), 'You've Got Me Dizzy' (1956), and a crossover pop hit, 'Honest I Do' (1957). With the popularity of blues waning in the early Sixties, Reed's last major hit came in 1961 with his self-penned and often recorded standard, 'Bright Lights Big City'. Abusing alcohol since navy days, Reed began missing concerts as his health failed. Following Vee-Jay's bankruptcy in 1965, Reed recorded for a series of labels beginning with Exodus. Suffering a severe epileptic seizure in 1969, Reed spent the next three years convalescing. Finally quitting the bottle in 1975, Reed died a year later.

CAUSE: He died in San Francisco after performing at the Savoy Club in nearby Oakland. A myth later circulated that Reed was buried in a whiskey-shaped coffin.

Johnny Reed

(JOHN T. REED)
Born August 16, 1923
Died June 18, 2005

A member of pioneering R&B vocal group The Orioles, Johnny Reed sang bass and occasionally played stand-up acoustic bass. Hailing from Baltimore, Reed played in a number of local jump-blues and jazz acts and while performing with the house band at The Avenue Cafe, Reed first met singer Sonny Til who had just won an amateur competition. Joining Til in The Vibranaires, Reed wasn't a full-time member until the group appeared on *The Arthur Godfrey Show*. Managed by a young songwriter named Deborah Chessler, the renamed Orioles scored a crossover hit with the Chessler composition 'It's Too Soon To Know'. Helping to define modern, black vocal harmony singing, The Orioles had a series of doo-wop hits on the R&B charts, including '(It's Going To Be A) Lonely Christmas', 'Tell Me So', 'A Kiss And A Rose', 'Forgive And Forget' and a cover of Margaret Whiting's 'What Are You Doing New Year's Eve?'. However, tragedy struck the group in 1950 when one of the group's vehicles was involved in a serious accident, killing member Tommy Gaither and injuring Reed and others. Forced to curtail their touring and recording schedule, The Orioles disappeared from the charts for two years until 1952, when the group scored a comeback hit with 'Baby Please Don't Go', and then crossed over to the pop charts with the gospel standard 'Crying In The Chapel' (1953), later a hit for Elvis Presley in 1965. The Orioles scored their final hit the following year with the similar 'In The Mission Of St. Augustine'. Unhappy with the group's financial situation, Reed quit the band in early 1955, to be replaced by Maurice "Tank" Hicks, and later joined Deek Watson's version of The Ink Spots.

During the induction of The Orioles into the Rock and Roll Hall of Fame in 1995, Reed was presented the award by the group's original manager Deborah Chessler. Also that year, Reed joined Bobby Thomas' Orioles, and retired several years later.
CAUSE: Natural causes. He died at Kimball Medical Center in Lakewood, New Jersey.

James Reese

Born December 7, 1941
Died October 26, 1991
The rhythm guitarist of the Sixties garage rock band, The Bobby Fuller Four, James Reese had previously played the keyboards in a local group in his native El Paso, Texas, called Bob Taylor & The Counts. After backing Fuller in 1961 on several self-released singles, Reese joined The Bobby Fuller Four, a group that featured the alternating lead guitars of Reese and Fuller. Relocating to Los Angeles and recording for Bob Keene's Del-Fi/Mustang Records, the group scored a garage classic with a cover of The Crickets' 1961 release, 'I Fought The Law'. Following Fuller's mysterious death in 1966, the group disbanded and returned to Texas.
CAUSE: Heart attack.

Bert Reid

(BERTRAM CHARLES REID, JR.)
Born October 25, 1956
Died December 12, 2004
As the bass vocalist and occasional saxophonist of American disco/funk group The Crown Heights Affair, Bert Reid played on the hits 'Galaxy Of Love' (1978) and 'You Gave Me Love' (1980). Reid joined the New York City-based act in 1975 just in time to appear on their second album. In 1986, Bert Reid, his brother Raymond and Ray Anderson left the group. Reid and Anderson formed a production team, working with Unlimited Touch and after parting with Anderson, Reid oversaw Raw Silk and Denroy Morgan. Reid joined a revival version of The Crown Heights Affair in 1999.
CAUSE: Pneumonia-related lung cancer. He died at St. Vincent's Hospital in New York City.

David Reilly

Born May 5, 1971
Died October 16, 2005
The lead singer and co-founder of American synth/industrial rock group God Lives Underwater. Formed in 1993 with Jeff Turzo, the group was initially signed to Rick Rubin's American Recordings label before moving to Interscope Records, where the album *Life In The So-Called Space Age* included the radio hit, 'From Your Mouth'. Moving to the 1500/Riffage label, the group was in the middle of recording a follow-up album in 2000 when their record company went bankrupt and Reilly's fiancée perished in a train accident. Some of the tracks from these sessions later appeared in 2004 on the group's semi-autobiographical release *Up Off The Floor*. After issuing a solo EP, *Inside*, that same year, Reilly signed with Sony/Ruff Nation and was working on his first full-length solo project.
CAUSE: He succumbed to complications from an untreated oral infection.

Keith Relf

Born March 24, 1943
Died March 14, 1976
The original lead singer and harmonica player of the influential British blues rock group The Yardbirds, Keith Relf was a serious blues record collector. Born in Richmond, in south west London, Relf almost died at age three from asthma, a condition which haunted him throughout his life. After dropping out of Kingston Art College, Relf drifted from job to job while assembling The Metropolitan Blues Quartet in 1963 with rhythm guitarist Chris Dreja, lead guitarist Anthony Topham, drummer Jim McCarty and

bassist Paul Samwell-Smith. Renamed The Yardbirds by Relf, the group found their voice in late 1963 when guitarist Eric Clapton replaced Topham. When the London-based Yardbirds backed visiting bluesman Sonny Boy Williamson during a winter British tour, the association was captured on the album *With Sonny Boy Williamson* (1964). Signing with British EMI's Columbia label, The Yardbirds scored a minor chart hit with an R&B cover, 'Good Morning Little Schoolgirl'. Although Relf emerged as the chief songwriter, the group recorded a host of Chicago blues standards. His asthma aggravated by performing in smoke-filled venues, Relf would temporarily leave the group after suffering a collapsed lung. The Yardbirds reached number one in the UK with 'For Your Love', a guitar-driven, title track, a song written by future 10cc member Graham Gouldman. Unhappy that the group was veering away from its blues core, Clapton quit and was replaced by guitarist Jeff Beck. The Yardbirds' hit run then continued with another Gouldman composition, 'Heart Full Of Soul', followed by 'Evil Hearted You', 'Shapes Of Things' and Tiny Bradshaw's rock standard, 'Train Kept A-Rollin'' which was a track recorded at Sun Studios in Memphis during their first US tour. Releasing two solo singles at Columbia Records in 1966, Relf scored a minor British hit with pop-textured 'Mr. Zero'. When Samwell-Smith departed to become a record producer in 1966, session guitarist Jimmy Page was added, initially on bass guitar, but Dreja soon switched to bass, enabling The Yardbirds to boast a particularly effective – albeit short-lived – twin lead guitar line-up. Releasing their second studio album *Over, Under, Sideways, Down*, The Yardbirds veered further away from their blues roots as they charted with the psychedelic title track. Beck quit the group towards the end of 1966 after the release of the single, 'Happenings Ten Years Time Ago'. Hiring new manager Peter Grant and joined by new producer Mickie Most, The Yardbirds continued with 'Little Games' (1967) and a cover of Manfred Mann's 'Ha! Ha! Said The Clown' (1967). Unhappy with the excessive tinkerings of the pop-trained Mickey Most, The Yardbirds disbanded in July 1968. Needing to fulfil contractual obligations, Page took control and formed a replacement group as The New Yardbirds, which evolved into Led Zeppelin. Relf and McCarty then launched the progressive rock group, Renaissance, joined by Relf's sister Jane and two others. Relf left the group after they released two poor-selling albums, *Renaissance* and *Illusion*. Relf then produced the experimental British rock group Steamhammer. After that group disbanded, Relf retained guitarist Martin Pugh and bassist Louis Cennamo (who had also been in Renaissance) to form Armageddon. Signed by A&M, the group recorded an ignored, self-titled album before disbanding. After passing through Medicine Head, Relf teamed with his sister and McCarty in a group called Illusion.

CAUSE: He was electrocuted by a faulty amplifier while playing his guitar at his home. An alternative explanation suggests that Relf was electrocuted while standing over a hidden power socket near the fireplace in his home.

FURTHER READING: Platt, John. (1983). *Yardbirds*. London: Sidgwick & Jackson.

Leon Rene

Born February 6, 1902
Died May 30, 1982

A songwriter/musician turned record company owner, Leon Rene was a classically trained pianist. While the leader of a jazz group called The Southern Syncopators, Rene honed his songwriting skills, penning the standard 'When the Swallows Come

Back to Capistrano' in 1940. Teaming with brother Otis, Leon Rene also composed 'I Sold My Heart To The Junkman' and 'I Lost My Sugar In Salt Lake City', the latter a hit for both The Ink Spots and Glenn Miller. Natives of New Orleans, the Rene brothers then opened their first of two West Coast-based labels, Exclusive Records; aided by musical director Buddy Baker, the Rene brothers recorded groundbreaking proto-R&B hits by Ivory Joe Hunter, Johnny Moore's Three Blazers, and Joe Liggins. Launching Class Records in 1951, the brothers recorded early rock and R&B acts such as Richard Berry and Bobby Day. Class Records was closed in 1962.
CAUSE: Heart disease. He died in Los Angeles.

Nadine Renee

(NADINE SHAMIR)
Born 1972
Died December 2, 2004
As a member of R&B/dance group Planet Soul, Nadine Renee scored a million-selling hit in 1995 with 'Set U Free'. Born in New York City but raised in Miami, she recorded two independently released albums during her late teens and, after working as a receptionist at MCA, formed Planet Soul with Miami disc jockey George Acosta. She left the group in 1996, being replaced by Brenda Dee, to pursue a solo career.
CAUSE: She died from childbirth complications at North Shore Hospital in Miami, Florida.

Jeannie Reynolds

Born c. 1955
Died July 1980
A disco artist who recorded for Casablanca Records, Jeannie Reynolds scored hits with 'The Phones Been Jumping All Day' (1975) and 'The Fruit Song' (1976). Her brother is Dramatics' vocalist L.J. Reynolds.
CAUSE: A murder-suicide, she first killed her two children.

Herbert "Toubo" Rhoad

Born October 1, 1944
Died December 8, 1988
The backing baritone singer of the Brooklyn-based a cappella soul group The Persuasions, Herbert "Toubo" Rhoad had previously sung in a series of doo-wop groups in his native South Carolina. Moving to New York City in his mid-teens, he was nicknamed "Toubo" by his Hispanic friends. Formed in 1962, The Persuasions recorded for Frank Zappa's Bizarre Records; releasing several a cappella albums in the Sixties, the group frequently opened for Zappa's Mothers of Invention. Fronted by Jerry Lawson, the group fared poorly after adding instrumental backing in the late Seventies. As session singers, The Persuasions have backed Don McLean, Paul Simon and Stevie Wonder. The Persuasions had reunited shortly before Rhoad's death in early 1988.
CAUSE: Suffering an aneurysm shortly before a scheduled performance in Sacramento, he died the following day. His ashes were scattered off the San Francisco coast.

Randy Rhoads

(RANDALL WILLIAM RHOADS)
Born December 6, 1956
Died March 19, 1982
An inventive guitarist who achieved cult status after his death, Randy Rhoads gained much exposure as a member of Ozzy Osbourne's backing band. Born in Burbank, California, Rhoads first picked up the guitar at age six, switching to an electric model at age eight; by his early teens, he was studying classical guitar. His mother a music teacher and music store owner, Rhoads began teaching guitar at age 18. In 1975, Rhoads joined friend Kevin DuBrow in forming a heavy metal group, Quiet Riot. Unable to interest any US labels, the group

signed with Japan's Sony/CBS Records. With Rhoads the visual focus of the group's stage shows, Quiet Riot released two poorly produced Japanese-only albums, *Quiet Riot* (1977) and *Quiet Riot II* (1978), the latter highlighted by 'Slick Black Cadillac'. Returning to Los Angeles and still unable to land a US record deal, the despondent Rhoads left the group after being offered a position in Black Sabbath founder Ozzy Osbourne's backing band. A surprise Top 10 smash, Osbourne's début album *Blizzard Of Oz* (1981) was highlighted by 'Mr. Crowley' and the fiery 'Crazy Train', the latter featuring Rhoads' searing triple-tracked guitarwork. A guitar hero who won the best new talent award in a *Guitar Player* readers' poll, the nimble-fingered Rhoads was a great asset to Osbourne. With his début album still in the charts, Osbourne released the certified platinum, *Diary Of A Madman*; but during a tour in support of the album Rhoads was killed in a bizarre accident. At a 1992 Ozzy Osbourne-headlined, benefit concert to mark the 10th anniversary of Rhoads' death, fans went on a rampage and caused $100,000 in property damage. A Randy Rhoads scholarship in classical guitar is awarded annually at UCLA. At the time of his death, Rhoads was planning to record an album of classical material.

CAUSE: Rhoads was killed during a brief stopover en route to Orlando for a performance at the Rock Superbowl XIV festival on a bill with UFO and Foreigner. Needing parts for their tour bus, driver Andrew Aycock stopped for the night at his home in Leesburg, Florida. Spotting several aeroplanes on a small, nearby airfield, Aycock (who was a licensed pilot) decided to "borrow" a plane the following morning. Jumping into the 1955 Beechcraft Bonanza with Aycock were Randy Rhoads and the group's costume designer, 58-year-old Rachel Youngblood. With Osbourne and the rest of the band sleeping on the bus, Aycock repeatedly circled the vehicle, buzzing within a few yards. On the fourth pass, the plane bumped the bus and collapsed the roof. In the process the plane clipped a wing, ricocheted off a tree and the ground, and then crashed into a nearby house, setting the building ablaze. All aboard the plane were killed instantly. While no one in the vicinity offered aid, the uninjured Osbourne heroically ran into the burning house to rescue a deaf man. A coroner's report found cocaine in Aycock's system. Aycock had previously crashed another aeroplane, killing a passenger. One theory suggests that the 36-year-old pilot tried to fly the plane into his ex-wife who was on the ground.

FURTHER READING: Wall, Mick. (1985). Ozzy Osbourne: Diary Of A Madman. London: Zomba.

"Lightning Bug" Rhodes

(WALTER RHOADES)
Born September 4, 1939
Died July 4, 1990

A guitarist who played with B.B. King, Otis Redding, and for much of his career, Wilson Pickett, "Lightning Bug" Rhodes also recorded a solo blues classic, 'Pickin' Daddy'. Based in Chapel Hill, North Carolina, during the Eighties, he led The Lightning Bug Blues Band.

CAUSE: He suffered a heart attack at a motel swimming pool in Rockingham, North Carolina.

Todd Rhodes

(TODD WASHINGTON RHODES)
Born August 31, 1900
Died June 4, 1965

A Kentucky-born pianist, Todd Rhodes launched his career in the late Twenties as a founding member of the RCA-Victor group, McKinley's Cotton Pickers. With the group disbanding in 1934, Rhodes moved to Detroit and led his own jazz combo. After a brief

retirement in the mid Forties, he recorded in 1947 for the King-distributed labels, Vitacoustic and Sensation Records. Landing at King Records in 1948, Rhodes scored two instrumental hits with 'Pot Likker' and a low-down blues number used by DJ Alan Freed as his theme song, 'Blues For The Red Boy'. In addition, Rhodes and his group were frequently employed as the house band at King Records. In the early Fifties, Rhodes and his band toured Europe with vocalist LaVern Baker. Disbanding his group in the late Fifties, he toured as a solo act into the Sixties.
CAUSE: Unknown. He died in Flint, Michigan.

Charlie Rich

Born December 14, 1932
Died July 25, 1995
Nicknamed "The Silver Fox", Charlie Rich was born into a family of cotton farmers in Colt, Arkansas. Joining his first band at age 14, he spent a year studying musical theory at the University of Arkansas. While serving an Air Force stint in Oklahoma, Rich mastered the saxophone and piano, and formed a country/pop group, The Velvetones. After his discharge he returned to his father's cotton farm in West Memphis. Rich also found work as a lounge musician and a session player at Sun Records, where he backed rockabilly artists Jerry Lee Lewis, Ray Smith and Billy Lee Riley. Recording under his own name in 1958 for the Sun Records subsidiary, Phillips International, Rich landed two minor rockabilly-styled hits with 'Whirlwind' and the bluesy 'Lonely Weekends'. With the decline of the label, Rich left Sun Records in 1963. After an uneventful stay at RCA/Groove Records, Rich scored a hit in 1965 with 'Mohair Sam' at Smash Records. Then, after a brief stint at the Memphis-based Hi Records, during which he recorded the Hank Williams' tribute album *Charles Rich Sings Country And Western*, he emerged as a country music star at Epic Records. Reunited with producer Billy Sherrill (of Tammy Wynette fame), Charlie Rich enjoyed a country hit with 'I Take It On Home' and scored two career-defining pop and country hits in 1973 with the million-sellers, 'Behind Closed Doors' and 'The Most Beautiful Girl'. Rich faded from the music charts in the early Eighties, but remained a strong concert draw.
CAUSE: Suffering a blood clot in his lung, he was found dead in a Hammond, Louisiana, motel. For much of his life he had been a heavy drinker.

Norman P. Rich

Born February 26, 1930
Died January 17, 1970
A member of Billy Stewart's band, Norman P. Rich appeared on several Sixties R&B hits including, 'I Do Love You' and the frenetic cover of George Gershwin's 'Summertime'.
CAUSE: Car crash. Experiencing brake problems, the new car in which Stewart and the group were riding struck a bridge abutment and plunged into a river.

Johnnie Richardson

(JOHNNIE LOUISE SANDERS)
Born June 25, 1940
Died October 25, 1988
The female half of R&B, vocal duo Johnnie & Joe, Johnnie Richardson teamed with the older Joe Rivers. The daughter of the owner of J&S records, Zell Sanders, Alabama-born Richardson was raised in a musical household in Harlem. Recording at J&S Records, Johnnie & Joe scored a string of R&B hits including 'I'll Be Spinning' (1957), 'It Was There' (1957), 'I Was So Lonely' (1957), and their biggest, the Top 10 'Over The Mountain, Across The Sea' (1957). Though not romantically involved, the public assumed the pair were married;

in fact, the duo was chaperoned on its tours by Richardson's mother. Aided by her mother, the teenage Richardson also formed her own shortlived label in 1958; heading Dice Records, Richardson oversaw several artists including The Avalons and a girl group, The Clickettes ('Because Of My Best Friend'). Richardson also sang back-up for J&S act The Jaynetts; while not appearing on their Top 10 R&B hit 'Sally, Go 'Round The Roses' (1964), she did sing on most of the tracks on their album, *Sally Go 'Round The Roses* (1964). Leaving J&S, Johnnie & Joe fared poorly at a succession of labels. Later appearing on the oldies circuit, Johnnie & Joe last reunited in 1983 for the album, *Kingdom Of Love*; that same year, Richardson released a solo album, *Double Dealing*.
CAUSE: Alternately attributed to tuberculosis or stroke, she died in the hallway outside her manager's office.

Randy Rickman

(RANDY LEON RICKMAN)
Born November 14, 1953
Died October 17, 2004
A guitarist and vocalist who worked with many notable acts, Randy Rickman is best known for his stint with late Seventies AOR act Exile (of 'Kiss You All Over' fame). Rickman also worked with Rich Mullens, Charlie Daniels, Steppenwolf, Three Dog Night, Charlie Rich and, in the early Nineties, was a member of the perennial rock act Head East. Turning to Christian music, Rickman launched his own studio and promotion company.
CAUSE: Unknown. He died at his home in Beaumont, California.

Jimmy Ricks

Born August 6, 1924
Died July 2, 1974
The leader and bass singer for The Ravens, Jimmy "Ricky" Ricks aided in the transition of the pop-vocal sound of The Ink Spots to modern Fifties doo-wop. Born in Florida but raised in New York City, he formed The Ravens in 1946 while employed as a nightclub waiter. Adding tenor singer Maithe Marshall in 1947, the group achieved its classic sound with Ricks' booming bass lead playing off Marshall's falsetto vocals. Signing with Herb Abramson's National Records, The Ravens dominated the R&B chart with hits such as 'Write Me A Letter' and 'Send For Me If You Need Me'. Simultaneously attempting a solo career, Ricks released 'Oh Babe' (1950), with musical backing from Benny Goodman's group. Moving to Mercury, The Ravens continued their hit run with 'Rock Me All Night Long'; by this time, the group's sound was dominated by Ricks' lead vocals. But experiencing frequent personnel changes, The Ravens lost much of their fan base. Leaving the group in 1956 to pursue a solo career, Rick fared poorly with his releases at Josie Records. Landing at Atlantic Records in 1960, Ricks teamed with LaVern Baker for a minor hit with the Leiber & Stoller composition, 'You're The Boss'. Ricks remained active in the music industry until shortly before his death.
CAUSE: Heart attack. He died in New York City.

Tommy Ridgley

(THOMAS HERMAN RIDGLEY)
Born October 30, 1925
Died August 11, 1999
A New Orleans R&B singer, gospel trained Tommy Ridgley learned to play blues piano while stationed in the Pacific region during World War II. Returning to New Orleans, he was hired as a vocalist by producer Dave Bartholomew. Forming his own band, Ridgley recorded for a series of labels including Decca and Atlantic, billed as "The New King Of The Stroll". On the brink of national success, he landed a series of regional hits including

'Shrewesbury Blues', 'Jam Up' and 'When I Meet My Girl'. One of his releases, 'Tra-La-La', was covered by Pat Boone. A fixture on The New Orleans Jazz & Heritage Festival since 1972, Ridgley released a comeback album in 1995, *Since The Blues Began*.
CAUSE: Lung cancer. He died at East Jefferson Hospital in New Orleans.

Greg Ridley

Born October 23, 1947
Died November 19, 2003
Bass player of British rock acts Spooky Tooth and Humble Pie, Greg Ridley spent most of his youth playing in blues and rock bands. One of these was an R&B outfit called The VIPs who briefly included keyboardist Keith Emerson. Signed to Island Records and renamed Art, the group released an obscure album, *Supernatural Fairy Tales* (1967), which included their version of Buffalo Springfield's 'For What It's Worth'. After the addition of keyboardist-vocalist Gary Wright, the group took a turn towards harder rock and evolved into Spooky Tooth, with Ridley appearing on the group's first two critically acclaimed albums – *It's All About* (1968) and their commercial breakthrough *Spooky Two*. In early 1969, Ridley was invited by Steve Marriott of The Small Faces to join a new group with Peter Frampton and Jerry Shirley. Formed at the time of the "supergroup", Humble Pie were signed to Andrew Oldham's Immediate label, recording two albums and gaining a Top Five hit with their first single, 'Natural Born Bugie'. Following the label's bankruptcy the group switched to A&M and scored US radio hits with 'I Don't Need No Doctor' and, after Frampton was replaced by Clem Clempson in 1971, 'Thirty Days In The Hole'. Their albums from this period such as *Rockin' The Fillmore*, *Smokin'* and *Eat It* were also more successful in America than the UK and Humble Pie became one of the main touring rock acts of the era. Following the band's break-up in 1975, Ridley worked with Steve Marriott and then joined Clempson and drummer Cozy Powell in the trio Strange Brew which lasted just two months after Clempson broke his wrist. Ridley retired from music in 1977 but after a Humble Pie reunion in 2001 to mark the 10th anniversary since Steve Marriott's death, Ridley hit the road as Greg Ridley's Humble Pie.
CAUSE: While battling throat cancer, he suffered a stroke and went into a coma. He died at Alicante Hospital in Javea, Spain.

Clarence Rigsby

Born c. 1942
Died 1978
The lead tenor of Texas-based doo-wop group The Velvets, Clarence Rigsby joined three classmates in 1960 in a group formed by their 25-year-old English teacher Virgil Johnson. Befriended by Roy Orbison, The Velvets signed with Monument Records where they experienced a brief chart run in the early Sixties with 'Tonight (Could Be The Night)' and the Orbison-penned, 'Laugh'.
CAUSE: Car crash.

Miguel Rios

Born 1943
Died March 28, 1977
A one-hit wonder, Miguel Rios turned the closing portion of Beethoven's Ninth symphony, 'Ode To Joy', into a pop hit in 1970 as 'A Song Of Joy (Himno A La Alegria)'. Born in Grenada, Spain, he left school to form a rock band in the late Sixties. A pop star in his native country, Rios had recorded several versions of the Beethoven piece.
CAUSE: Unknown.

Minnie Riperton

Born November 8, 1948
Died July 12, 1979
A versatile vocalist who mastered a

variety of musical styles, Minnie Riperton was active in fine arts from an early age. Reared in a rough Chicago neighbourhood, she sang gospel in her church before taking ballet and dance lessons at Lincoln Center at age 10. Riperton studied classical music and opera singing for several years. Discovered by executives of Chess Records at a high school performance, Riperton was initially hired as a receptionist at the label and was also placed in a pop group called The Gems. With her nimble five-octave soprano voice, she also provided back-up vocals for artists such as Johnny Nash, Billy Stewart and Etta James. Recording under the pseudonym Andrea Davis, Riperton scored a local hit with 'Lonely Girl'. Marrying in 1967, Riperton then joined Rotary Connection as the only female member. A rock outfit assembled by Marshall Chess, it was intended as a one-shot studio group. A strangely pseudo-psychedelic band which sang mostly rock covers, the group was an underground favourite. With Riperton often providing the co-lead, Rotary Connection released six albums, and landed an album-rock hit from their début set, 'Turn Me On'. After recording a much-ignored solo album at Janus Records in 1970, *Come To My Garden*, and briefly reteaming with her former group as The New Rotary Connection, Riperton retreated to Florida with her husband for the next two years. Returning to music in 1973, Riperton joined Stevie Wonder's backing vocal group, Wonder Love. Subsequently singing with Epic Records, Wonder produced her début album *Perfect Angel*, which included the chart-topping ballad, 'Lovin' You' (1975). Her hit run continued with 'Inside My Love' (1975), the disco-flavoured 'Stick Together' (1977), and 'Memory Lane' (1979). Released shortly before her death, the Grammy-nominated *Minnie* spawned a trio of R&B hits, 'Memory Lane' (1979), 'Lover And Friend' (1979) and 'Here We Go' (1980). Riperton's husband assembled her final sessions on the Grammy-nominated set, *Love Lives Forever* (1980). Riperton's daughter, Maya Randolph, became a cast member of the television series, *Saturday Night Live*.
CAUSE: Breast cancer. She disclosed her condition on national television, shocking *Tonight Show* guest host Flip Wilson. Diagnosed in 1976, she became a spokeswoman for the American Cancer Society in the last few years of her life. She kept the severity of her condition hidden from both the public and most of her family.

Robert Ritter

Born c. 1958
Died June 28, 1990
A guitarist/bassist, Rob Ritter (a.k.a. Rob Graves) joined a series of Los Angeles punk bands. A native of Detroit, he joined The Bags, a ground-breaking punk band founded in 1977 by sisters Alice and Pat Bag. Releasing their first single in 1979, 'Survive', the group also appeared in the punk documentary *The Decline Of Western Civilization*. After the group disbanded in 1981, Rob Ritter joined The Gun Club, a group led by Jeffrey Lee Pierce; after appearing on the album *Fire Of Love*, Ritter left the group and changed his name to Rob Graves. Graves subsequently co-founded the goth-metal band 45 Grave, recording a number of innovative records including the album *Sleep In Safety*, before they disbanded in 1985. Graves then teamed with bandmate Don Bolles and two others to form Silver Chalice. Graves later re-formed 45 Grave for occasional performances. At the time of his death, Graves was travelling with members of the group Celebrity Skin.
CAUSE: He overdosed on heroin while in the back of a van in New York City.

Marty Robbins

(MARTIN DAVID ROBINSON)
Born September 26, 1925
Died December 8, 1982
A popular country and pop singer who flirted with rockabilly in the late Fifties, Marty Robbins was a native of Glendale, Arizona, who landed his own radio show in the late Forties with The K-Bar Cowboys. After being given his own local television programme in Phoenix, *Western Caravan*, Robbins was aided by Little Jimmy Dickens in signing with Columbia Records. Starting out in the western tradition with his first country chart hit, 'I'll Go On Alone' in 1952, Robbins enjoyed a long string of hits that would span three decades. In 1954 he recorded a country cover of 'That's All Right', the Arthur Crudup number later made famous by Elvis Presley. A versatile performer, Robbins took a pop turn with the rise of rock'n'roll, landing pop airplay with rockabilly influenced numbers such as 'Singing The Blues' (1957), 'A White Sports Coat' (1957), 'The Story Of My Life' (1957) and 'She Was Only Seventeen' (1958). Introduced to Hawaiian music during a World War II navy stint, he released an album's worth of Hawaiian material, *Songs Of The Islands*, in 1957. In 1959, Robbins reached number one in the US and enjoyed an international hit with 'El Paso', which was included on his massive selling and highly influential *Gunfighter Ballads And Trail Songs*. Other notable successes included 'Big Iron', 'Running Gun' and 'The Fastest Gun Around'. A member of The Grand Ole Opry since 1953, Robbins became the first country performer to play Las Vegas in 1963. He reached number five in the UK charts with 'Devil Woman' in 1962. As well as racking up a startling number of country successes during the Sixties, Robbins starred in another television series, *The Drifter*, featured in eight western movies and even penned a cowboy novel, *The Small Man*. He also received countless country music awards and accolades. Robbins scored his final country hit in 1983 with the posthumously released Top 10 entry 'Honkytonk Man'. His finest work was compiled in the 1993 box set *The Essential Marty Robbins: 1951–1982*.
CAUSE: Heart attack. He died in Nashville.
FURTHER READING: Pruett, Barbara J. (1991). *Marty Robbins: Fast Cars And Country Music*. Metuchen, NJ: Scarecrow.

Doug Roberts

Born June 15, 1941
Died November 18, 1981
Latter drummer for the Sixties group, Jimmy Gilmer & The Fireballs, Doug Roberts appeared on several hits including the million-selling 'Sugar Shack' (1963) and 'Bottle Of Wine' (1968). Roberts had replaced Eric Budd, who was drafted in 1962, and stayed with the group until its break-up in 1969.
CAUSE: Unknown.

Ed Roberts

(EDWARD L. ROBERTS)
Born April 24, 1936
Died August 15, 1993
The first tenor of the pop-soul group Ruby & The Romantics, Ed Roberts teamed with several friends in Akron, Ohio, originally as an all-male outfit called The Supremes. After failing to find success in New York City, the group returned to Akron and added novice female vocalist Ruby Nash. Signing with Kapp Records, which insisted that Nash assume lead vocal duties, the redubbed Ruby & The Romantics enjoyed several hits including 'Our Day Will Come' and 'Hey There Lonely Boy'. But after leaving Kapp for ABC Records, Roberts and the other male members of the group soon quit the group. Settling in New York, Roberts later worked at a bank.
CAUSE: Cancer. He died at his home in New Rochelle, New York.

Jim Roberts

(JAMES TALMADGE ROBERTS)
Born September 29, 1944
Died October 29, 2002
A member of avant-garde rock band Seatrain, Jim Roberts was initially hired as a lyricist, but almost immediately, he became a full-time member, playing guitar and mandolin as well as providing an occasional lead vocal. Formed from the remnants of The Blues Project, Seatrain infused elements of rock, folk and bluegrass on their 1969 album *Sea Train*. Working with producer George Martin on the albums *Seatrain* and *The Marblehead Messenger*, the group experienced numerous personnel changes. Roberts quit in 1972.
CAUSE: Cancer. He died in York, Pennsylvania.

Malcolm Roberts

(MALCOLM JAMES ROBERTS)
Born March 31, 1944
Died February 7, 2003
A ballad singer, previously an actor, from Manchester, Malcolm Roberts had a pair of schmaltzy UK hits with 'May I Have The Next Dream With You?' (1968) and 'Love Is All' (1969). With no further hits, Roberts remained a popular entertainer into the Eighties and, as a songwriter, he penned 'Contact', recorded by Edwin Starr in 1979, and Britain's 1992 Eurovision entry 'One Love'.
CAUSE: He suffered a heart attack and died near his home in Chertsey, Surrey.

Don Robey

(DONALD DEARIC ROBY)
Born November 1, 1903
Died June 16, 1975
One of the first black Americans to launch a successful record company, Don Robey was notorious for his aggressive business practices. A native of Houston, Robey had quit high school a year before graduation for a career as a professional gambler. After lending money to a local music promoter to stage a concert, Robey became intrigued with show business. After staging a number of ballroom dances in Houston, he launched a venue called the Bronze Peacock Dinner Club (which for a time permitted gambling in a back room). When opening a record store and an artist management company, Robey was unhappy with the treatment by Alladin Records of one of his acts, Clarence "Gatemouth" Brown, and decided to enter the record business himself. Although Peacock Records was launched as a vehicle to record Brown, Robey also introduced a gospel division, enjoying strong sales with The Five Blind Boys, The Dixie Hummingbirds, and Spirit Of Memphis Quartet. Robey also built a significant R&B and blues roster, notably Marie Adams and Big Mama Thornton. After forcibly buying out Memphis-based Duke Records from deejay James Mattis in 1952, Robey inherited a strong stable of acts that included Johnny Ace and, later, Junior Parker. Teamed with the talent of arranger/trumpeter Joe Scott, Robey had his greatest success with Bobby "Blue" Bland. Launching a pop and soul subsidiary in 1957, Back Beat Records, Robey had chart success with The Casuals, Joe Hinton, Roy Head, and O.V. Wright. Selling Duke/Peacock in 1973 to ABC-Dunhill, Robey was retained as a consultant.
CAUSE: He suffered a heart attack at his home in Houston.
FURTHER READING: Gart, Galen. (1990). *Duke/Peacock Records: An Illustrated History With Discography*. Milford, NH: Big Nickel.

Paul Robi

Born August 20, 1931
Died February 1, 1989
The baritone vocalist of the popular R&B group The Platters, Paul Robi was reared on gospel music, working as a choir leader by the late Forties.

Switching to secular music in the early Fifties, he sang R&B in his native New Orleans. Moving to Los Angeles in 1953, Robi joined The Platters in July 1954 as the replacement for Alex Hodge who had got into trouble for selling marijuana to a police officer. Led by Tony Williams, The Platters had formed a year earlier at a Los Angeles high school. Managed by Buck Ram, The Platters enjoyed a string of R&B-inflected pop ballad hits including 'Only You' (1955), 'The Great Pretender' (1955), '(You've Got) The Magic Touch' (1956), and 'My Prayer' (1956). Robi provided a rare lead vocal on the album track, 'Glory Of Love'. The group's career was scarred when on August 10, 1959, Robi and other male members of The Platters were arrested in a Cincinnati motel for having sex with underage women; they were later acquitted of the charges. The Platters' final Top 10 hit came in 1960 with a remake of the standard, 'Harbour Light'. With Williams leaving the group, The Platters left Mercury Records on a sour note in 1962. Despondent over the group's misfortunes, Robi began abusing alcohol and left The Platters in 1964. In the early Seventies, Robi joined a revival version of The Platters, performing until a year before his death. In a lawsuit filed in 1974 against Buck Ram over the ownership of The Platters' name, Robi emerged victorious shortly before his death in 1989; following an appeal, Robi's widow was awarded a $3.5 million settlement and Ram's trademark registration of the group's name was cancelled.
CAUSE: Pancreatic cancer.

Alvin "Shine" Robinson

Born December 22, 1937
Died January 25, 1989
A New Orleans R&B guitarist and singer, Alvin "Shine" Robinson is best known for the minor hits 'Down Home Girl', which was covered by The Rolling Stones on their second UK album, and 'Something You Got' (1964). As a session player, Robinson backed Joe Jones on 'You Talk Too Much'. Moving to the West Coast, he later joined Dr. John's backing band.
CAUSE: He died after a long-term, undisclosed illness, possibly a heart ailment.

Darren Robinson

Born June 10, 1967
Died December 10, 1995
Before the emergence of the gangster rap genre in the late Eighties, rap music was dominated by upbeat acts such as Run D.M.C. and The Fat Boys. A visual focal point of The Fat Boys, the 400lb Darren Robinson was dubbed The Human Beat Box for his ability to generate percussive grunts and other comical vocal sounds. Teaming with fellow New York City natives Mark "Prince Markie Dee" Moreles and Damon "Kool Rock-ski" Wimbley, Robinson formed a heavy-set group in 1983 called Disco 3. Signed to a record deal, the trio amassed such hefty room service bills during a European tour that their angry promoter dubbed them "the fat boys", and the name stuck. Produced by pioneering rapper Kurtis Blow, The Fat Boys were initially billed as a novelty act as they enjoyed R&B chart hits with 'Jail House Rap' (1984) and 'Sex Machine' (1986). Leaving Sutra for Tin Pan Alley/Polydor Records, The Fat Boys landed two pop-crossover, hit duets, 'Wipe Out' (1986) with The Beach Boys, and 'The Twist (Yo Twist)' (1988) with Chubby Checker. Also appearing on the big screen, The Fat Boys were portrayed in farcical roles in the films, *Krush Groove and Disorderlies*. Leaving behind their lighthearted personas, in 1989 the trio attempted an ill-received "gangster rap" album, *On And On*. The group was further harmed when Robinson was prosecuted on complicity charges in sexual liaison with a minor. After Moreles left the

group in 1991 to pursue a solo career, Robinson and Wimbley performed as a duo, produced other rap acts, and occasionally hosted the cable programme *Yo MTV Raps*. The Fat Boys reunited ten days before Robinson's death to record a new album.
CAUSE: He suffered a heart attack after falling off a chair during a performance for friends at his home in New York City. He had recently been diagnosed with lymphoedema.

Fenton Robinson

Born September 23, 1935
Died November 26, 1997
A Mississippi-born electric bluesman, the velvety-voiced Fenton Robinson incorporated jazz stylings into his refined sound. Relocating to Memphis at age 16, Robinson backed Rosco Gordon on his 1956 hit 'Keep On Doggin''. Forming the Dukes in 1957, Robinson recorded his first solo material for the new Meteor label. Discovered the following year by Bobby "Blue" Bland, Robinson was signed by Duke Records; here he recorded 'Mississippi Steamboat' and, featuring James Booker on piano, 'As The Years Go Passing By'. Moving to Chicago in 1962, Robinson was a fixture in the city's blues clubs, often collaborating with Otis Rush and Junior Wells. Recording his elegant signature piece 'Somebody Loan Me A Dime' in 1967, Robinson later sued Boz Scaggs who claimed authorship. Signing with Alligator Records in 1974, Robinson re-recorded 'Somebody Loan Me A Dime' as the title track of his début album. He continued to tour and record into the Nineties.
CAUSE: Complications from brain cancer. He died in Rockford, Illinois.

Joe Robinson

(JOSEPH R. ROBINSON, JR.)
Born July 25, 1932
Died November 5, 2000
The co-founder of Sugarhill Records, Joe Robinson teamed with his wife, former R&B hit singer Sylvia Vanderpool, to form the Englewood, New Jersey-based label in 1979. Streetwise and gruff, Robinson was a lifelong entrepreneur who had previously operated several bars in New York City. It was Robinson who years earlier had encouraged his wife to form her successful singing duo, Mickey & Sylvia. In 1968, the Robinsons launched a soul label, All-Platinum Records, that had its greatest success with the single 'Pillow Talk' by Sylvia (none other than Sylvia Robinson). With All-Platinum filing for bankruptcy in the late Seventies, the Robinsons chose to launch another label, Sugarhill Records, financed by music mogul Morris Levy. Best known for its pioneering "old skool" rap releases, in 1979 the label issued the genre-defining track 'Rapper's Delight' by a trio of unknown rappers assembled by Sylvia Robinson which she dubbed The Sugarhill Gang. The first rap single to reach the US pop charts, 'Rapper's Delight' was originally considered a novelty song; the single sold extremely well both in its edited form and as a 12-inch single which featured the original 15-minute version. Capitalising on the success of The Sugarhill Gang, the label signed a host of budding rappers including Spoonie Gee, Kool Moe Dee, The Crash Crew, Positive Force and the first all-female rap act The Sequence; another rap act at the label, Grandmaster Flash & Furious Five with Melle Mel, issued the ground-breaking, socially conscious single 'The Message'. After signing an unfavourable distribution deal with MCA in 1983, Joe and Sylvia Robinson bought out Levy's share of the label but, struggling to adapt to changing musical trends and falling into debt to MCA, the Robinsons

were forced to sell their Chess Records catalogue to MCA. After battling MCA in court, the Robinsons emerged with the sole ownership of the Sugarhill catalogue, which they sold to Rhino Records for a hefty price in 1995. The Sugarhill studio burned down in 2002.
CAUSE: Cancer.

Vickie Sue Robinson

Born May 31, 1954
Died April 27, 2000
A disco star in the Seventies, Vickie Sue Robinson scored a major hit with the career-making release 'Turn The Beat Around'. The biracial Philadelphian daughter of showbiz parents, she first performed with her mother, radical folk singer Marian Robinson, at the Philadelphia Folk Festival in 1960. Moving to New York City at age 10, she appeared on the original Broadway cast of the rock opera *Hair* in her teens and, later, in the original stage production of *Jesus Christ Superstar*. Originally blending jazz and folk, she performed on the bohemian folk coffee-house circuit and after earning some recording experience behind Todd Rundgren and as a member of a Japanese rock band, Robinson was signed to RCA Records in 1975. At the forefront of the disco movement, Robinson recorded one of the genre's defining hits, the Grammy-nominated title track of her second album, *Turn The Beat Around*; but her follow-up singles, 'Daylight' and 'Hold Tight', barely dented the charts. While battling drug addiction, Robinson issued a series of albums in the Eighties and worked as a backing vocalist for Cher and Michael Bolton. When Gloria Estefan released a faithful rendition of 'Turn The Beat Around' in 1995, Robinson's career was re-ignited, having a British dance hit with 'House Of Joy'. Though diagnosed with cancer in 1997, Robinson collaborated with her husband Bill Good to produce an autobiographical off-Broadway revue in 1999, *Behind The Beat*.
CAUSE: Cervical cancer. She died at her home in Wilton, Connecticut.

Barbara "Sandi" Robison

(BARBARA JEANNE MOYER)
Born October 14, 1945
Died April 22, 1988
A member of The Crosswinds and The Peanut Butter Conspiracy, Barbara "Sandi" Robison broke into music in a West Coast duo with her husband, comedy folk singer Robbie Robison. Discovered while performing in a trio with her husband, Sandi was hired as the lead singer of a pioneering folk-rock group which evolved into The Crosswinds. Eventually joined by future Jefferson Airplane member Spencer Dryden, the group was renamed The Ashes. When Robison became pregnant, the group disbanded in 1966. Restarting her musical career, she joined a pair of former bandmates to form the psychedelic band The Peanut Butter Conspiracy. Signing with Columbia Records, the group recorded a pair of excellent but ignored albums, while the Gary Usher-produced track 'It's A Happening Thing', from their début album, was a West Coast hit. The group disbanded in 1969 after recording a final album for Warner/Challenge. Robison then joined the Los Angeles production of the rock musical, *Hair*, for an 18 month stint.
CAUSE: Toxic shock poisoning. She fell ill while performing in Butte, Montana, and died 16 days later at a hospital in Billings.

Rockin' Dopsie

(ALTON JAY RUBIN, SR.)
Born February 10, 1932
Died August 26, 1993
A popular Louisiana-born Cajun accordionist, Rockin' Dopsie was nicknamed "The Crown Prince of Zydeco Music" following the death of

pioneer Clifton Chenier in 1987. Combining strains of jazz and R&B, Rockin' Dopsie headed the spirited accordion-driven zydeco band, The Zydeco Twisters, which included his two sons. Also a session player, he backed Paul Simon, Bob Dylan, and Cyndi Lauper.
CAUSE: He suffered heart failure while at the steering wheel of his vehicle, en route from Lafayette to Opolousas, Louisiana.

Rockin' Sidney

(SIDNEY SIMIEN)
Born April 9, 1938
Died February 25, 1998
The first zydeco artist to score pop airplay, Rockin' Sidney earned a Grammy for the self-composed, novelty-styled single '(Don't Mess With My) Toot Toot' (1986). Infusing R&B into his brand of danceable zydeco, Rockin' Sidney began his recording career in the mid Fifties as a blues guitarist and singer. Switching to the squeeze-box accordion in the early Eighties, he embraced the regional zydeco music.
CAUSE: Lung cancer. He died in Lake Charles, Louisiana.

Joe Rock

(JOSEPH VINCENT ROCK)
Born May 16, 1936
Died April 4, 2000
A producer, manager, and lyricist, Joe Rock was responsible for the success of both The Jaggerz and The Skyliners. After entering the music industry as a session vocalist and member of The Marquees in his native Pittsburgh, Rock switched to promotion and artist management in the late Fifties, grooming a local white doo-wop outfit, The Crescents, whom he renamed The Skyliners after they were signed by Calico Records. Teaming with lead singer Jimmy Beaumont, Rock co-wrote the group's biggest hit, the elegant doo-wop standard, 'Since I Don't Have You'. Rock had penned the song's lyrics after his girlfriend had left town for a new life in Oklahoma. Rock and Beaumont continued to collaborate on future releases such as 'This I Swear' and Rock also worked with Johnny Day (of Stax Records), The Jaggerz of 'The Rapper' fame (featuring future solo star Donnie Iris), and co-wrote 'Dreams To Remember' with Otis Redding. Rock settled in Nashville in 1993.
CAUSE: He died in a Nashville hospital after undergoing open-heart surgery.

David Rockola

(DAVID C. ROCKOLA)
Born January 23, 1897
Died January, 26 1993
The founder of the company that manufactured Rockola jukeboxes, Canadian-born David Rockola launched the Chicago-based company in 1926 as the Rockola Scale Co. Adapting to new technologies, the business added the production of pinball machines in 1933, and jukeboxes two years later. Manufacturing tens of thousands of machines, Rockola enjoyed a boom with the rise of the 45rpm record in the Fifties. With his machines omnipresent, in some countries jukeboxes were simply called "rockolas". Working at the plant well past his 90th birthday, Rockola sold the company in 1992.
CAUSE: He died of natural causes in Chicago.

Jose L. Rodriguez

Born March 25, 1944
Died April 20, 1996
Recording engineer who worked with dance and R&B artists such as Culture Club, Take That, Gloria Gaynor, Jodeci, and Mary J. Blige, Puerto Rican-born Jose L. Rodriguez also played a significant role in the development of the 12-inch single format.
CAUSE: AIDS. He died in New York City.

Jimmy Rogers

(James A. Lane)
Born June 3, 1924
Died December 19, 1997
A Mississippi-born Chicago-based, electric blues guitarist, pianist, and harmonica player, the self-taught Jimmy Rogers is best known for his membership in Muddy Waters' first band. After struggling in the St. Louis blues scene in the Thirties, Rogers arrived in Chicago in 1939. Working street corners for tips in his early years, he was given a break in 1946 by Sunnyland Slim, which led to gigs with Big Bill Broonzy and Sonny Boy Williamson. Teaming with Waters soon after his arrival in Chicago in 1947, the trio was completed with the addition of guitarist Blue Smitty. When Blue Smitty left and harp virtuoso Little Walter joined, Rogers switched from the harmonica to second guitar. A monumental outfit that was informally known as The Headhunters, Rogers, Waters, and Little Walter reshaped and came to define modern Chicago blues. After some scattered recordings, the trio recorded for Aristocrat/Chess Records. As a member of Muddy Waters' band (which now included Otis Spann) until 1955, Rogers appeared on hits such as 'Louisiana Blues' and 'Honey Bee'. Rogers also pursued a solo career in the Fifties beginning with 'That's All Right', and continuing with 'Walking By Myself' (a reworking of T-Bone Walker's 'Why Not'), 'Chicago Bound' and 'Luedella'. Retiring from music for much of the Sixties, Rogers operated a clothing store which was torched following the murder of Martin Luther King. After returning to the studio in 1971 to record his first album *Gold-Tailed Bird*, Rogers toured internationally. Recorded shortly before Rogers' death, *Blues Blues Blues* featured a host of guest players, including Eric Clapton, Mick Jagger and Taj Mahal. Rogers' early output is compiled on the album *The Complete Chess Recordings*.
Cause: He died in a Chicago hospital following surgery for an intestinal infection caused by colon cancer.

John Rogers

Born c. 1940
Died 1963
The leader of Adam Faith's backing band The Roulettes, bassist John Rogers backed Faith on one album and a handful of singles. Pursuing a simultaneous recording career apart from Faith, The Roulettes failed to reach the charts. Following his death, Rogers was replaced in The Roulettes by John "Mod" Rogan.
Cause: Car crash.

Robert Rolontz

Born December 14, 1920
Died June 14, 2000
A music industry veteran, Robert Rolontz began as an R&B reporter for *Billboard* magazine in the early Fifties. Hired as a musical director for labels such as RCA/Groove and Vic Records, he produced Mickey & Sylvia's ground-breaking multi-tracked hit, 'Love Is Strange'. Returning to *Billboard* in 1958, he was eventually promoted to music editor, during which time he penned the instructional tome, *How To Get Your Song Recorded*. Hired by Atlantic Records in 1965 as the vice-president of advertising and publicity, he worked on campaigns for a host of acts including Aretha Franklin, Cream, Led Zeppelin, and The Rolling Stones. Rolontz would later move to Atlantic's sister company, Warner Communications. In 1989, Rolontz was the force behind the creation of the Ralph J. Gleason Music Book Awards.
Cause: Unknown.

Tony Romeo

Born 1939
Died June 23, 1995
A producer and songwriter, Tony Romeo is best known for his work with Lou Christie, The Cowsills, and The Partridge Family. His compositions included 'Indian Lake' (The Cowsills),

'I Think I Love You' (The Partridge Family), 'Blessed Is The Rain' (Brooklyn Bridge) and 'I'm Gonna Make You Mine' (Lou Christie). Also a recording artist, Romeo scored solo hits with 'Go Johnny Go' and 'Carnival Girl'.
CAUSE: Heart attack. He died at his home in Pleasant Valley, New York.

Mick Ronson

Born May 26, 1949
Died April 29, 1993
A much respected guitarist, Mick Ronson is best known for having been David Bowie's foil in his Spiders From Mars band in the early Seventies. Reared on classical music in his native Hull, England, Ronson mastered the violin and piano during his childhood. Discovering rock music and acquiring an electric guitar during his mid-teens, Ronson passed through several bands including The Hullabaloos and The Rats. After moving to London in 1969, Ronson appeared on an album behind British folk singer Michael Chapman. In 1970, Ronson joined David Bowie's backing band. Rising to fame as an androgynous, glam-rocker behind Bowie, the blond-haired Ronson appeared on five Bowie albums beginning with *The Man Who Sold The World*, and continuing with *Hunky Dory*, and *The Rise And Fall Of Ziggy Stardust & The Spiders From Mars*. Ronson also performed on the Lou Reed, Bowie-produced *Transformer* (1972), the project highlighted by 'Walk On The Wild Side'. Ronson's stage persona was also an important factor in Bowie's breakthrough with the Spiders: invariably dressed in a gilded satin jumpsuit open to his navel, Ronson cut quite a dash and at one stage in the show Bowie would kneel and lick Ronson's guitar strings in a pseudo-sexual gesture that greatly appealed to Bowie's increasingly large gay following. After the 1973 release of Bowie's *Pin-Ups* album, Ronson began work on his first album, *Slaughter On 10th Avenue* (the project featuring all the musicians that appeared on *Pin-Ups*). He also provided string arrangements on Pure Prairie League's second album *Bustin' Out*. With Bowie dismissing Ronson and the other members of his Spiders backing band in 1973, Ronson joined the soon to disband, Ian Hunter-led group, Mott The Hoople. Ronson subsequently teamed with Hunter as The Hunter-Ronson Band, with both simultaneously involved in solo projects. While Ronson released *Play, Don't Worry* (1975), Ian Hunter issued a self-titled album which spawned the hit, 'Once Bitten, Twice Shy', which featured Ronson's guitar work. He also supplied the blazing guitar on the Hunter hit, 'Cleveland Rocks' (1979). Ronson produced Roger McGuinn's 1976 solo album *Cardiff Rose*, and in 1975, when he was living in New York, was a surprise addition to Bob Dylan's Rolling Thunder Revue, appearing on the live album *Hard Rain*. Ronson reunited with Hunter for an album in 1989, *YUI Orta*. In 1992, Ronson produced the Morrissey album *Your Arsenal*. His final stage appearance was at the Freddie Mercury tribute in London on April 20, 1992, when he performed 'All The Young Dudes' and 'Heroes' with Bowie and Hunter.
CAUSE: Diagnosed with liver cancer in 1991, he succumbed to the disease two years later. He died in London.

Root Boy Slim

(FOSTER MACKENZIE III)
Born July 9, 1945
Died June 8, 1993
A pioneering Washington DC-based R&B-based alternative artist, Root Boy Slim launched his career in a punk rock group called The Sex Change Band. Notorious for his outrageous stage act, Slim released six politically charged albums with tracks such as 'Dare To Be Fat' and 'You Can't Quit

My Club'. Banned on many college campuses, Slim would vomit on stage at the close of his signature finale, 'Boogie 'Til You Puke'.
CAUSE: Heart failure. He died at his home in Orlando.

Tim Rose

(TIMOTHY ALAN PATRICK ROSE)
Born September 23, 1940
Died September 24, 2002
A talented singer-songwriter who is best known for popularising the folk standard 'Hey Joe', the gruff-voiced Tim Rose never achieved the fame or success he was due. Born in Washington DC, he studied to become a priest, but was forced to leave the seminary for improper conduct. After returning from stints in the merchant marines and Air Force, he pursued a career in music. Drawn to the booming Greenwich Village folk scene, Rose joined The Smoothies (a.k.a. The Journeymen), which included future folk-rock stars Scott McKenzie and John Phillips. In 1963, Rose teamed with (Mama) Cass Elliot and James Hendricks to form a folk trio, The Big 3 and, as well as a successful residency at the Bitter End folk club in Greenwich Village, the group recorded a pair of albums – *The Big 3* (1963) and *The Big 3: Live At The Recording Studio* (1964) – and garnered attention with their many television performances. The group disbanded after Rose clashed with Elliot over the group's direction: while she preferred to remain strictly acoustic, Rose wanted to add electric guitars. Signing as a solo act with CBS Records, Rose issued a critically acclaimed self-titled album in 1967 which was highlighted by the tracks 'Morning Dew', 'Come Away Melinda' and 'Hey Joe'. After recording a series of poor-selling albums over the next decade, Rose eventually settled in London. Returning to New York City in the late Seventies, he quit music for a time. After finding work as a session singer, he returned to college and worked as a stockbroker until the Wall Street crash of 1987. Sporadically performing over the next 15 years, Rose was aided in his comeback by Nick Cave, who had covered Rose's version of 'Hey Joe' for the *Kicking Against The Pricks* album. Rose issued his final album in 2002, *American Son*.
CAUSE: He died shortly after colon cancer surgery at Middlesex Hospital in London. His weak heart was stressed by the operation.

Peter Rosen

Born c. 1944
Died 1969
The original bassist of the funk-rock group War, Peter Rosen was responsible for their association with former Animals' frontman Eric Burdon at MGM Records. In early 1970, Rosen convinced producer Jerry Goldstein to bring Burdon to one of the group's concerts. Rosen had joined a predecessor of War in 1968 when the band was known as The Creators, and then, Nightshift. Rosen had passed away before War entered a recording studio.
CAUSE: Drug overdose.

John Rostill

Born June 16, 1942
Died November 26, 1973
The bassist in Cliff Richard's backing group The Shadows, John Rostill joined in late 1963 as a replacement for Brian Locking. Previously a member of The Interns, Rostill appeared on a number of Cliff Richard hits including 'The Minute You're Gone', 'Visions' and 'Congratulations'. Aside from their long-standing role as Cliff Richard's backing band, The Shadows had their own strong hit run and although this was slowing down by the time Rostill joined the group, they enjoyed two Top Ten hits, 'The Rise And Fall Of Flingel Bunt' and 'Don't Make My Baby Blue', during his tenure. Although The Shadows disbanded in

1969, they made a major comeback in the late Seventies. Also a successful songwriter, Rostill penned the Olivia Newton-John hits, 'Let Me Be There', 'Please Mr. Please', and 'If You Love Me (Let Me Know)'.
CAUSE: He was electrocuted by his guitar while writing songs in his recording studio in Radlett, Hertfordshire.
FURTHER READING: Turner, Steve. (1994). *Cliff Richard: The Biography*. Oxford, England: Lion.

Paul A. Rothchild

Born April 18, 1935
Died March 30, 1995
Prolific producer best known for his work with The Doors at Elektra Records, Paul A. Rothchild joined the label in 1963 after leaving Prestige Records, and had overseen a series of pioneering folk acts including Fred Neil, Tom Paxton, and Phil Ochs, and white blues pioneer, Paul Butterfield. With the signing of The Doors to Elektra in late 1966, Rothchild collaborated with engineer Bruce Botnick in solidifying their blues-based rock sound beginning with the album *The Doors*, which featured the breakthrough hit, 'Light My Fire'. Rothchild subsequently produced dozens of rock albums including *Pearl*, Joplin's widely acclaimed posthumous album. He later produced the soundtracks for the films, *The Rose* and *The Doors*.
CAUSE: Diagnosed with lung cancer in 1990, he succumbed to the disease five years later. He died at his home in West Hollywood, California.

Dave Rowberry

(DAVID ERIC ROWBERRY)
Born July 4, 1940
Died circa June 6, 2003
A member of British Invasion R&B band The Animals, keyboardist Dave Rowberry was added during the height of the group's popularity. A jazz-trained musician, Rowberry had joined The Mike Cotton Jazzmen in 1962 but, with the arrival of the British beat boom, the group quickly veered towards popular music. Renamed The Mike Cotton Sound, the group released a self-titled album for Columbia and often backed visiting American singers such as Gene Pitney and Solomon Burke. With the departure of Alan Price from The Animals in May 1965, Rowberry was hired as his replacement, and within weeks found himself touring America. After parting with their producer Mickie Most, the group enjoyed more freedom in the studio, and Rowberry appeared on two of the group's albums – *Animalisms* (confusingly released as two different albums under that title in the UK and US) – and the hits, 'Inside – Looking Out', 'Don't Bring Me Down' and 'See See Rider'. After The Animals split in mid 1966 Rowberry turned to session work, playing with a variety of artists over the ensuing decades. He also performed with ex-Jimi Hendrix Experience bassist Noel Redding and ex-Kinks' drummer Mick Avory in a pub rock outfit, Shut Up Frank. In 1994, Rowberry was excluded from The Animals' induction into the Rock and Roll Hall of Fame but joined two former bandmates, Hilton Valentine and John Steele, in The Animals II, and, in 2000, as The Animals & Friends.
CAUSE: Suffering from heart problems, he was found dead in his apartment in Hackney, London, on June 6. It was undetermined how long he had been dead.

Dave Rowbotham

Born 1958
Died January 1992
Guitarist for The Durutti Column, Dave Rowbotham joined the Manchester, England-based group in 1978. One of the first bands signed to Factory Records, Durutti Column was assembled by label founder Tony

Wilson around the idiosyncratic vocalist Vini Reilly. Vacillating between folk and techno music, the group's first tracks were issued on *A Factory Sampler EP*. Subsequent releases were essentially solo Reilly projects. Rowbotham and a few of his bandmates subsequently formed The Moth Men. Rowbotham was the subject of The Happy Monday's song, 'Cowboy Dave'.
CAUSE: He was killed in a knife attack in Manchester. The murder was never solved.

Dick Rowe

Born 1922
Died June 6, 1986
For many years the head of the (British) Decca Records A&R department, Dick Rowe will be forever and unfairly known as the man who turned down The Beatles. Initially a producer at Decca, Rowe had success in the Fifties with pop acts such as The Stargazers ('Broken Wings'), Dickie Valentine ('Finger Of Suspicion') and Jimmy Young ('Unchained Melody'). Briefly leaving Decca, he worked at Top Rank where he had success with the Joe Meek-produced John Leyton. Back at Decca, Rowe worked with Billy Fury, overseeing the young rocker's move towards high quality ballads and chart hits. Rowe and his assistant Mike Smith rejected The Beatles after an audition in January 1962, supposedly telling the group's manager Brian Epstein that "guitar groups are on their way out", an accusation Rowe emphatically denied. In fact, The Beatles had already been rejected by every other major label, none of which, unlike Rowe, had even bothered to offer them an audition. Decca would instead sign Brian Poole and The Tremeloes, the chief reason being that they were based in Dagenham in East London, while The Beatles were from Liverpool which would make it more difficult for them to attend recording sessions. Realising his error, Rowe subsequently signed several other Merseybeat acts including Beryl Marsden, The Big Three and Pete Best, the ousted Beatle. In some respects Rowe made up for his mistake by signing The Rolling Stones, largely on the advice of Beatle George Harrison. Rowe's other successful signing included Dave Berry, John Mayall's Bluesbreakers, Them, The Moody Blues, The Zombies, The Small Faces, The Animals and Unit Four Plus Two. Rowe enjoyed a thriving relationship with most of the big-name managers of the period and was well liked. After signing the immensely successful pop crooners Tom Jones and Engelbert Humperdinck, Rowe left the music industry in the late Sixties.
CAUSE: Complications from diabetes.

Hadie Rowe

(HADIE C. ROWE, JR.)
Born September 19, 1928
Died September 19, 1998
The baritone vocalist of early doo-wop act The Larks, Hadie Rowe left just as the group was achieving fame. From North Carolina, Rowe joined several friends in the late Forties to form a spiritual group, The Southern Harmonaires. The group evolved into The Jubilators, and recorded under both names in 1950, as well as recording as The Selah Singers and The 5 Barons. Veering from religious to secular music in 1951 as The (Five) Larks, the doo-wop group were signed to Apollo Records but just as The Larks were about to record the first of two R&B hits, Rowe was drafted into the army.
CAUSE: Unknown.

Sean Rowley

Born 1969
Died November 12, 1992
The keyboard player and lead vocalist of Cause And Effect, Sean Rowley formed the nucleus of the

Sacramento-based techno-pop group in 1988 with lyricist and guitarist Rob Rowe. From their début album *Another Minute* (1991), the group enjoyed two dance/alternative hits with 'You Think You Know Her' and 'What Do You See'.
CAUSE: Died of a heart attack brought on by an asthma attack during a pre-concert soundcheck at the Glam Slam nightclub in Minneapolis. The group was on tour with Information Society.

Lillian Roxon

Born February 1, 1932
Died August 9, 1973
An Italian-born, Australian-raised, and New York-based music critic, Lillian Roxon wrote the first ever rock reference book of its kind, *Rock Encyclopedia*, in 1969. Arriving in New York City in 1962, she initially worked as a freelance journalist, before landing her own column in *Mademoiselle* magazine.
CAUSE: Severe asthma attack.

Dallas "Digger" Royal

Born c. 1950
Died 1991
The drummer of Australian blues-influenced, heavy-metal band Rose Tattoo, Dallas "Digger" Royal joined the group in 1977, just in time for the sessions of their début single. Royal was previously a member of a latter line-up of the Melbourne-based boogie rock band Buster Brown. Although Rose Tattoo became an institution in their native land, the group's greatest international success came with the albums *Rock 'N' Roll Outlaw* (1980) and *Assault And Battery* (1981). During the early Eighties, the group toured the US as the opening act for Aerosmith and ZZ Top, but was billed as a punk outfit by the rock press for its UK performances. Royal and two other members left the group in early 1983.
CAUSE: Cancer.

Michael Rudetski

Born 1959
Died August 6, 1986
A keyboard player from New York City, who had previously worked with a number of East Coast bands, Michael Rudetski performed on the 1986 Culture Club album, *From Luxury To Heartache.*
CAUSE: He overdosed on heroin at the London home of singer Boy George. A week earlier, Boy George had been fined for heroin possession. Rudetski's parents were unsuccessful in their wrongful death lawsuit against Boy George.

David Ruffin

(DAVIS ELI RUFFIN)
Born January 18, 1941
Died June 1, 1991
The co-leader of the Motown group The Temptations during the Sixties, David Ruffin provided the vocals on a string of soul chestnuts. Born near Meridian, Mississippi, Ruffin was raised by his grandmother following the death of his mother. Displaying musical talent at an early age, Ruffin joined a number of local gospel groups. After moving to Detroit with his family in the late Forties, he spent two years in another gospel group, The Dixie Nightingales. Switching to secular music in the mid Fifties, Ruffin joined The Voice Masters; recording three singles in 1959 for Anna Records (a predecessor of Motown), the group also included future songwriting talent Lamont Dozier. After failing an audition with Harvey Fuqua for his new version of The Moonglows, Ruffin spent two years as a nightclub singer in Cleveland. Returning to Detroit in 1961, Ruffin found work as a studio drummer. Still pursuing a solo career, Ruffin landed a local hit with 'Mr. Bus Driver Hurry'. Then, with the departure in 1963 of original member Eldridge Bryant from the Motown, male vocal group The Temptations, Ruffin was brought in as his

replacement. Beginning their collaboration with songwriter and producer Smokey Robinson, The Temptations scored their first crossover hit with the Robinson-penned 'The Way You Do The Things You Do' (1964). With Ruffin then assuming most of the lead vocal duties, The Temptations enjoyed a remarkably successful series of crossover hits beginning with the Motown-defining standard 'My Girl' (1965), and continuing with 'Ain't Too Proud To Beg' (1966), 'Beauty Is Only Skin Deep' (1966), '(I Know) I'm Losing You' (1966), and 'I Wish It Would Rain' (1968). After years of trying to bully his bandmates, the headstrong Ruffin was ousted from the group; his final release with the group came with 'Please Return Your Love To Me'. Contractually prevented from leaving Motown, Ruffin subsequently pursued a solo career; but to his chagrin, he was only marginally successful. Recording two solo albums in 1969, he scored his début hit with the ballad 'My Whole World Ended'. Billed as The Ruffin Brothers, David Ruffin also recorded a much-ignored album with his brother Jimmy, *I Am My Brother's Keeper*. Ruffin left Motown in 1975 after scoring a final solo hit with 'Walk Away From Love'. Switching to Warner Brothers Records, Ruffin recorded two moderately selling albums. Ruffin and bandmate Eddie Kendrick briefly returned to The Temptations in 1982 for the *Reunion* album and tour. He would later team up with Kendrick for a collaborative hit single with Daryl Hall & John Oates, 'A Nite At The Apollo Live! The Way You Do The Things You Do/My Girl'. A subsequent album, *Ruffin And Kendrick* (1987) spawned a couple of minor R&B hits, 'I Couldn't Believe' and 'One More For The Road'. Away from music, Ruffin attempted to raise horses on a Michigan farm. A long-time drug user, Ruffin was arrested in Detroit for crack cocaine possession and was sentenced to drug treatment. Ruffin toured with The Temptations until three weeks before his death.

CAUSE: Drug overdose. Ruffin collapsed at a crack house after reportedly sharing ten vials of crack cocaine in a 30-minute period. The unconscious Ruffin was hurriedly dropped off by a limo at the University of Pennsylvania Hospital in Philadelphia. After giving hospital workers the identity of the fallen star, the limo driver sped away. Lacking any formal identification, the deceased Ruffin had to be identified by FBI fingerprinting. The coroner ruled Ruffin's death an accidental overdose. He was carrying $40,000 in cash and travellers cheques which disappeared; a subsequent police probe was unable to locate the missing valuables. With Ruffin financially destitute, Michael Jackson offered to pay the funeral expenses.

FURTHER READING: Turner, Tony. (1992). *Deliver Us From Temptation: The Tragic And Shocking Story Of The Temptations And Motown*. New York: Thundermouth.

Joel Rundell

Born c. 1967
Died August 8, 1990

The original guitarist of alternative rock act Better Than Ezra, Joel Rundell perished before the group achieved fame. Formed in 1988 in New Orleans by students at Louisiana State University, the group earned accolades with its cassette-only release *Surprise*, in 1990. Disbanding after Rundell's death, the group re-emerged several months later as a trio.

CAUSE: Suicide by gunshot.

Jimmy Rushing

(JAMES ANDREW RUSHING)
Born August 26, 1903
Died June 8, 1972

A blues and jazz shouter, Oklahoma-born Jimmy Rushing launched his professional career in the

mid Twenties. Honing his craft as the featured vocalist in The Count Basie Orchestra, Rushing provided the vocals on Basie's hits 'Boogie Woogie' and 'Evening'. With Basie disbanding his outfit in 1950, Rushing formed his own group. A remarkably versatile high tenor vocalist, he easily switched between smooth jazz and rough, uptempo blues. Nicknamed "Five-By-Five", because of his large frame, Rushing toured heavily until shortly before his death. He appeared in the 1969 film, *The Learning Tree.*
CAUSE: Cancer. He died in New York City.

Bobby Russell

Born April 19, 1940
Died November 19, 1992
A pop-rock songwriter, Bobby Russell penned the hits 'Little Green Apples' (O.C. Smith), 'Honey' (Bobby Goldsboro), and 'The Night The Lights Went Out In Georgia' (Vicki Lawrence). A native of Nashville, Russell also passed through a series of rock and country groups, and sang backing vocals on Ronnie And The Daytonas' hit 'G.T.O.'.
CAUSE: Heart disease. He died in Nicholasville, Kentucky.

Patty Russell

Born 1942
Died September 5, 1998
The lead singer of soul group Patty & The Emblems, Patty Russell scored a minor hit in 1964 with the Leon Huff composition 'Mixed-Up, Shook-Up Girl'. Formed in Camden, New Jersey, the group recorded for several labels in the Sixties.
CAUSE: Leukaemia.

Thermon Ruth

Born March 6, 1914
Died September 13, 2002
A member of early doo-wop act The Larks, Thermon Ruth had previously spent decades performing African-American religious music. At age 13 in 1927, Ruth began singing traditional spirituals in the Brooklyn-based ensemble The Selah Jubilee Singers. Relocating to North Carolina in the Forties, the group evolved into a modern, vocal harmony-styled gospel group but, unhappy with their new direction, Ruth and bandmate Allen Bunn quit in 1949 and formed The Jubilators. The following year, the group recorded a number of singles under their own name as well as under the monikers The Southern Harmonaires and The Selah Singers (including 'Down Here I've Done My Best' which featured Ruth on lead vocals). Veering from religious to secular music in 1951, renamed as The (Five) Larks and fronted by Gene Mumford, the group were signed by Apollo Records, scoring a pair of doo-wop hits with 'Hopefully Yours' and the elegant ballad 'My Reverie'. Thermon Ruth returned to North Carolina and later worked as a gospel deejay under the moniker "T. Ruth".
CAUSE: Unknown.

Chico Ryan

(DAVID-ALLEN RYAN)
Born April 9, 1948
Died July 26, 1998
A member of Sixties pop-rock group The Happenings, Chico Ryan is better remembered for his long-term stint with the revival oldies band Sha Na Na. Born in Arlington, Massachusetts, Ryan toured during his college years as the bass player for Massachusetts-based rock act The Rockin' Ramrods. Discovered by Freddie Cannon, the group eventually released one major label album for MGM under the moniker Puff. After passing through a local group called The Minutemen, Ryan joined the touring version of New Jersey-based vocal group The Happenings, best known for their hits 'See You In September', 'Go Away Little Girl' and 'I Got Rhythm'. After forming a

group called Rainface, Ryan joined Sha Na Na in 1973 as a replacement for founding member Bruce Clarke. Appearing on their syndicated US television programme during its full run from 1977 to 1981, Ryan sang lead vocal on their rendition of 'Teenager In Love'. Ryan and the group also appeared in the 1978 film musical *Grease* as Johnny Casino & The Gamblers. Ryan later toured with a revived version of Bill Haley's Comets.
CAUSE: He died in a suburban Boston convalescence facility after suffering an undisclosed accident.

Marion Ryan

(MARION SAPHERSON)
Born February 4, 1933
Died January 15, 1999
Marion Ryan was a prominent British pop singer in the Fifties, and mother of the Ryan Twins, Paul and Barry, who were also successful pop singers. Born in Leeds, in Northern England, Ryan made BBC broadcasts with the Ray Ellington Orchestra during the mid Fifties and toured the country in variety shows, often alongside her friend and rival Alma Cogan. Promoted as a glamour girl and even as "Britain's answer to Marilyn Monroe", Ryan recorded for the Pye label and reached the Top 10 with 'Love Me Forever' in 1958. She starred on several programmes including *The Marion Ryan Show* and the ITV quiz-show *Spot The Tune*. Also a film actress, she appeared alongside singing star Tommy Steele in *It's All Happening*. Like many others of her era she was eclipsed by the advent of The Beatles, and she retired in the Sixties having married Harold Davison, a leading London impresario. Her twin sons Paul (who predeceased her) and Barry Ryan were the products of an earlier marriage.
CAUSE: Heart attack. She died at Boca Raton Community Hospital in Florida, where she was admitted after contracting pneumonia.

Paul Ryan

Born October 24, 1948
Died November 29, 1992
Half of the Sixties British pop-rock twin duo which was formed with his brother Barry, Paul Ryan was the son of British entertainer Marion Ryan. With their mother becoming a star, the twins were sent to live with their grandmother. Following their mother into the British charts, Paul and Barry Ryan scored several hits including 'Don't Bring Me Your Heartaches' (1965) and 'I Love Her' (1966). With the duo disbanding in 1968, Paul Ryan became a full-time songwriter, penning brother Barry's million-selling début single 'Eloise' (1968), a song reprised in 1976 by The Damned. Ryan also wrote 'I Will Drink The Wine' for his godfather Frank Sinatra. After living in the US during the Seventies, Paul Ryan returned to London in 1985 and operated a chain of hair salons.
CAUSE: Cancer. He died at Cromwell Hospital in London.

John Ryanes

Born November 16, 1940
Died May 30, 1972
The bass vocalist for the one-hit wonder group The Monotones, the gospel trained John Ryanes joined his brother Warren and several friends from a housing project in Newark, New Jersey, to launch the doo-wop outfit in 1955. Signed with Hull/Mascot Records in 1957, The Monotones scored a hit with the self-penned 'Book Of Love' (1958), the song inspired by a toothpaste commercial. The group would never reappear in the charts.
CAUSE: Unknown.

Warren Ryanes

Born December 14, 1937
Died June 1982
The baritone vocalist for the one-hit wonder group The Monotones, the gospel-trained Warren Ryanes joined

his brother John and several friends from a housing project in Newark, New Jersey, to launch the doo-wop outfit in 1955. After appearing on *Ted Mack's Amateur Hour*, The Monotones signed with Hull/Mascot Records. After landing in the Top 5 with 'Book Of Love', the group would never reappear in the charts.
CAUSE: Unknown.

S

Alex Sadkin

Born April 9, 1949
Died July 25, 1987
A British-born pop-rock producer, Alex Sadkin worked with Bob Marley, Talking Heads, Foreigner, Duran Duran, Grace Jones, Robbie Nevil, and others. At the time of his death, he was scheduled to produce an album for Ziggy Marley & The Melody Makers.
CAUSE: He died in an auto accident near Kingston, Jamaica.

Ssgt. Barry Sadler

Born October 15, 1939
Died October 31, 1989
An American soldier turned unlikely pop star, Staff Sergeant Barry Sadler topped the US charts in 1966 with 'The Ballad Of The Green Berets'. The son of professional gamblers, he dropped out of high school during the ninth grade, and was soon playing the drums in a local Colorado band. After a four-year Air Force stint, he returned briefly to civilian life in 1962 and spent his nights playing guitar in a rock band. Joining the US Army in 1963 and assigned to Vietnam, he worked as a medic in the Special Forces (also known as the Green Berets). After suffering a severe leg injury, he was honorably discharged in 1965. Returning home to his wife, he worked as a military recruiter. Intended as a promotional tool, Sadler recorded the patriotic ditty, 'The Ballad Of The Green Berets'. Re-recording the song for RCA Records in 1966, Sadler secured an unlikely worldwide smash. After landing some acting roles, Sadler moved to Nashville in 1972 and opened a bar. Also a successful author, he penned the instructional guide, *Everything You Wanted To Know About The Music Industry*, and wrote two dozen military action novels beginning with *The Moi*. Making the news from time to time, the self-described soldier of fortune was arrested on two separate shooting incidents, one in 1978, the other in 1981. Settling in Guatemala City in 1984, he frequently provided locals with medical care and established a trust fund for Vietnamese orphans.
CAUSE: He succumbed to brain damage sustained in shooting incident in 1988 during one of his mercenary jobs in central America. Three versions of the incident exist: he was being robbed; he was the target of an assassination; or he accidentally shot himself in the head while showing off his gun. What is known for certain is that he was shot in the frontal lobe with a .380 Pietro Beretta in a taxicab on a main Guatemalan highway. Flown to the US for treatment, he shuffled through a number of Veterans' Administration hospitals. An ugly battle over Sadler's guardianship pitted his mother against his wife and son. A judge eventually placed Sadler under the supervision of an independent guardian, a Nashville attorney. Sadler died at a V.A. hospital in Murfreesboro, Tennessee.

Doug Sahm

(DOUGLAS WAYNE SAHM)
Born November 6, 1941
Died November 19, 1999
A much respected Tex-Mex musician, Doug Sahm was the lead vocalist of The Sir Douglas Quintet and The Texas Tornados. From San Antonio, Sahm began singing and performing on the radio at age five as "Little" Doug. By eight, he was a regular on *The Louisiana Hayride* and, at 11, sang at Hank Williams' penultimate concert. At 14, he made his recording début as Little Doug & The Bandits and after having a series of local hits, Sahm jumped on the British Invasion bandwagon in 1964 and adopted an English sounding moniker, The Sir

Douglas Quintet. To maintain the ruse, the group refused to tour until their electric organ-heavy début single, 'She's About A Mover', was firmly in the Top 40. Featuring Sahm on lead vocals and guitar, the group followed up with 'The Rains Came' (1966). The group was widely admired by fellow musicians, particularly Bob Dylan, but after a marijuana bust in Corpus Christi in 1967, Sahm relocated to San Francisco and formed a new band. Sahm became a regular at the Avalon Ballroom and landed a hit with 'Mendocino' (1968) but, tiring of San Francisco's hippie scene, Sahm disbanded his group and returned to Texas in 1971. Sahm released his powerful solo album *The Return Of Doug Saldana* and also flirted with acting, portraying a drug dealer in the Kris Kristofferson film, *Cisco Pike*. Signed to Atlantic Records by Jerry Wexler, he recorded the masterful *Doug Sahm And Band*, with guest musicians Bob Dylan, Dr. John, and accordionist Flaco Jiminez. Re-forming The Sir Douglas Quintet in 1977, Sahm continued his heavy touring schedule, which included an opening slot with The Pretenders. While visiting Vancouver in 1986, Sahm formed an unlikely Cajun/country group called The Formerly Brothers who enjoyed Canadian success and won a Juno Award. Teaming with then-slumping country singer Freddie Fender and two others in 1989, Sahm reinvigorated his career with The Texas Tornados. Beginning with the Grammy-winning, self-titled début, the group released seven albums and scored a regional hit with '(Hey Baby) Que Paso'. Sahm also continued to record with The Sir Douglas Quintet, a final album coming with *S.D.Q. '98*. Sahm had completed a solo country record shortly before his death, the posthumously released *The Return Of Wayne Douglas*. Sahm's youngest son, Shandon, is a drummer in The Meat Puppets.

CAUSE: He was found dead in a Taos, New Mexico, hotel room after suffering a heart attack.

Oliver Sain

Born March 1, 1932
Died October 28, 2003

A talented blues-trained saxophonist, producer and bandleader, Oliver Sain scored an unlikely disco hit in 1976 with 'Party Hearty'. Born in Mississippi, but raised in the Memphis area, Sain performed in groups with Howlin' Wolf, Fontella Bass, Ike Turner, Bobby McClure and Little Milton. Settling in St. Louis, Sain operated the Archway recording studio and continued to perform right up to his death.

CAUSE: Bladder cancer. He died at his home in St. Louis.

Alex St. Clair

(ALEXIS CLAIR SNOUFFER)
Born September 14, 1941
Died circa January 6, 2006

The founder of Captain Beefheart & The Magic Band, Alex St. Clair was reared on the blues. While playing trumpet in his high school band, St. Clair became friends with classmate Frank Zappa and both teenagers eventually bought guitars and practised playing along to R&B and blues records. In 1958, St. Clair formed an R&B group called The Omens, which included former members of Zappa's band The Blackouts. When Zappa opened his legendary recording studio in Cucamonga, California, various like-minded musicians – including all the original members of The Magic Band – spent hours jamming together, with some of the material captured on tape. Following the break-up of The Omens in 1962, St. Clair played in a series of short-lived bands before landing at a Lake Tahoe resort where he maintained slot machines while playing in a Top 40 covers band. Returning to California in 1964, he

assembled Captain Beefheart & The Magic Band with Paul Blakely, Doug Moon, Jerry Handley and lead singer Don Van Vliet. Although St. Clair was the group's original leader, Vliet subtly took over the reins and assumed the persona of Captain Beefheart. The group soon experienced internal conflicts, with Vliet wanting to go in an experimental direction while St. Clair preferred a more commercially accessible sound. Building a fanbase in Los Angeles, the group issued a few singles on the A&M label and then recorded their début album *Safe As Milk* for Buddah (1967), which included the slide guitar work of new member Ry Cooder. Tired of battling Vliet over control of the group, St. Clair quit in 1968 after the release of the album *Strictly Personal*. Passing through a number of covers bands over the next few years, St. Clair also produced and performed on Denny King's 1972 album *The Evil Wind Is Blowing*. Invited by Vliet in late 1972 to rejoin Captain Beefheart & The Magic Band on guitar, St. Clair toured extensively the following year and appeared on the poorly received album *Unconditionally Guaranteed*. After constantly battling Vliet over money, St. Clair quit before a scheduled tour in 1974. Remaining on friendly terms with Vliet, St. Clair contributed the track 'Owed T'Alex' to Beefheart's 1979 album *Shiny Beast* and after returning to the bar circuit for the remainder of the decade, St. Clair left music altogether. A heavy drinker, he later entered rehab twice.
CAUSE: Unknown. His body was discovered in his apartment in Lancaster, California.

Dick St. John

(RICHARD GOSTING)
Born 1940
Died December 27, 2003
The male half of Sixties pop duo Dick & Deedee, Dick St. John began singing with classmate Mary "Deedee" Sperling while attending junior high school in Santa Monica, California. Recording three singles on Lama Records – a label owned by their manager – the duo garnered some local airplay but it wasn't until 'Mountain's High' was picked up for national distribution by Liberty Records, that they reached the Top 10. Signing with Warner Brothers, the duo followed up with another hit, the John D. Loudermilk composition 'Thou Shalt Not Steal' in 1964. Leaving Warner Brothers in 1967, the duo recorded for Dot Records where St. John issued a pair of solo singles, including a cover of the John Denver composition 'Leaving On A Jet Plane' (1969). After the duo disbanded in the early Seventies, St. John retired from music. In the Nineties, St. John was joined by his wife Sandy in a new version of Dick & Deedee.
CAUSE: He struck his head during a fall from a ladder at his home near Pacific Palisades, California. He died soon after at UCLA Medical Center.

Kyu Sakamoto

Born November 10, 1941
Died August 12, 1985
A native of Kawasaki, Japan, Kyu Sakamoto landed a surprise international hit in 1963 with a Japanese-language record, 'Sukiyaki'. A former jazz club singer, he signed with Toshiba Records in 1959 and scored a string of hits in his native country. One of his releases 'Ue O Muite Aruto' (which translated means 'Let's Walk With Our Faces Up'), was issued in Britain under the title of 'Sukiyaki' (1963); subsequently released in the US, the song was a Top 10 smash in both countries. A follow-up single 'China Nights', fell just short of the Top 40. With new English lyrics, 'Sukiyaki' returned to the pop charts via a pair of cover versions, in 1981 by A Taste Of Honey, and in 1995 by 4 P.M. Sakamoto was also an actor and radio star.

CAUSE: Aeroplane crash. En route from Tokyo to Osaka on JAL Flight 123, the 747 lost portions of its tail section. The craft eerily spiralled down for 30 minutes, giving passengers time to write farewell notes to their loved ones. The craft crashed into a heavily wooded mountainside, killing 520 people.

Ian Samwell

(IAN RALPH SAMWELL)
Born January 19, 1937
Died March 13, 2003
A songwriter, producer and guitarist, Ian "Sammy" Samwell is best remembered for his affiliation with Cliff Richard. Born in Lambeth, south London, Samwell joined Richard's backing group The Drifters after one of their performances at London coffeehouse, the 2I's. A former skiffle guitarist, Samwell wrote Richard's ground-breaking B-side hit 'Move It' (1958), one of Britain's first bona fide rock'n'roll songs, as well as Richard's 'Dynamite', 'Mean Streak', 'Never Mind', 'High Class Baby', 'Steady With You', 'Fall In Love With You', 'My Feet Hit The Ground', 'I Cannot Find A True Love' and 'Gee Whiz It's You'. An average calibre guitarist, Samwell switched to bass when Hank Marvin and Bruce Welch were added to the group but when bassist Jet Harris joined the line-up, Samwell stepped aside and, after briefly acting as the group's manager, left the group. After a stint in the early Sixties as a popular deejay at the Lyceum Ballroom, Samwell turned to production work and oversaw early sessions by John Mayall, The Small Faces (for whom he co-wrote their first single 'Whatcha Gonna Do About It') and The Aynsley Dunbar Retaliation, as well as Georgie Fame's first album, the live recording *Rhythm And Blues At The Flamingo*. By the late Sixties, Samwell was hired as a staff producer at Warner Brothers' London studio, and discovered acts such as Linda Lewis and Al Jarreau. Samwell also produced Claudia Lennear, Isaac Guillory, as well as the début self-titled album by America (who were then being managed by his close friend and fellow deejay, Jeff Dexter) which spawned the hits 'A Horse With No Name' and 'I Need You'. Samwell subsequently produced the original cast album for Robert Stigwood's London production of *John, Paul, George, Ringo . . . & Bert*. In the late Seventies, Samwell managed and produced three albums for Hummingbird, who consisted of members from Jeff Beck's former backing band. Relocating to Sacramento, California, in 1980, Samwell worked with an emerging band, Bourgeois Tagg, and continued his involvement in the music industry before being diagnosed with an enlarged heart. Cliff Richard's 1995 re-recording of 'Move It' included an additional verse penned by Samwell.
CAUSE: Heart failure. He had received a heart transplant in 1991 after friends helped defray the $100,000 cost. He died at Mercy San Juan Hospital in Sacramento, California.

Gar Samuelson

(GARY SAMUELSON)
Born February 18, 1958
Died July 14, 1999
The original drummer of Megadeth, Gar Samuelson joined the thrash metal band in 1983. Hailing from Dunkirk, New York, Samuelson started out as a jazz drummer. When guitarist Dave Mustaine left Metallica to form Megadeth, Samuelson was among the recruits. Releasing the low-budget indie album *Killing Is My Business . . . And Business Is Good*, Megadeth attracted the attention of Capitol Records. Solidifying their fan base with the brash and confident *Peace Sells . . . But Who's Buying?* (1986), Megadeth took a political turn. However, after repeatedly sparring with Mustaine,

Samuelson was fired from the band. Settling in Orange City, Florida, he operated his own recording studio and also teamed with his two brothers in the progressive metal band, Fatal Opera.
CAUSE: Liver disease.

Bob Sanderson

(DAVID ROBERT SANDERSON)
Born November 18, 1935
Died June 25, 1994
The guitarist of the one-hit wonder rock group The Royaltones, Bob Sanderson appeared on the instrumental hit 'Poor Boy' (1958).
CAUSE: Heart attack. He died in Dearborn Heights, Michigan.

Mark Sandman

Born September 24, 1952
Died July 3, 1999
The lead singer, bassist and songwriter of Boston-based alternative-rock trio Morphine, Mark Sandman employed a lo-fi sound that depended on inexpensive instruments. A guitar-less trio consisting of a drummer, bassist and baritone saxophonist, Morphine's sound was further punctuated by Sandman's deep eerie vocals. A former fisherman and taxi driver, Sandman earned a degree in political science from the University of Boston. As a member of the blues-rock band Treat Her Right, Sandman appeared on three albums in the Eighties. Forming Morphine in 1990, Sandman signed with a series of labels, before landing his biggest hit with the surreal 'Cure For Pain' (1993). During this period, Sandman pursued several side projects including The Pale Brothers and, with Chris Ballew, Supergroup. Sandman had completed a new album, *Night*, a week before his death. The surviving members of the group later launched a nine-piece ensemble called Orchestra Morphine.
CAUSE: He suffered a heart attack while performing near Rome, on the second day of a three-day music festival. After collapsing two songs into the group's set, he died en route to a local hospital.

Mongo Santamaria

(RAMOON SANTAMARIA)
Born April 7, 1917
Died February 1, 2003
A Cuban-born bandleader, Mongo Santamaria scored a Top 10 instrumental hit in 1963 with 'Watermelon Man'. Formerly a member of big bands led by Tito Puente, Perez Prado and Cai Tjader, Santamaria formed his own Afro-Latin group in 1961. Santamaria's only other Top 40 hit came with an instrumental version of The Temptations' hit 'Cloud Nine'.
CAUSE: Natural causes. He died at the Baptist Hospital in Miami, Florida.

Joe Santollo

Born July 23, 1943
Died June 3, 1981
The backing tenor for the doo-wop styled, New Jersey vocal outfit The Duprees, Joe Santollo had initially joined a precursor of the Joey Vann-fronted group in 1959 called The Parisiennes. Grounded in harmony-based ballads, the well-practised quintet signed with Coed Records in 1962 with the aid of new manager George Paxton. The Duprees scored their début hit with a dramatic reading of Jo Stafford's 1952 ballad, 'You Belong To Me' (1962); a follow-up hit, 'My Own True Love' (also known as 'Tara's Theme'), was a vocal version of the *Gone With The Wind* theme. The Duprees completed their Top 40 run with a pair of Joni James' covers, 'Why Don't You Believe Me' (1963) and 'Have You Heard' (1963). Signed to Columbia Records in 1965 and sporting new lead vocalist Mike Kelly, The Duprees fared poorly with their updated sound.
CAUSE: Heart attack. He died in Jersey City, New Jersey.

Pattie Santos

(Patricia D. Santos)
Born November 16, 1944
Died December 14, 1989
Vocalist and percussionist of the San Francisco-based progressive-rock pioneers It's A Beautiful Day, Pattie Santos co-founded the group in 1968 with classically trained electric violinist and vocalist David LaFlamme. Hired as an opening act for Cream in 1968, the group caught the attention of Columbia Records. From their self-titled début album, the group enjoyed an underground hit with the exotic single 'White Bird' (1968). Santos appeared on five albums, leaving the group in 1973. After forming Pharoes Whistle in 1975, Santos later teamed with former Pablo Cruise member Bud Cockrell, and released an album *Cockrell And Santos* (1978).
Cause: She died in a car accident near Healdsburg, California. According to the State Highway Patrol, she had been drinking and travelling at high speed when she missed a curve in the road and crashed into two trees.

Scatman John

(John Larkin)
Born March 13, 1942
Died December 3, 1999
A jazz-trained singer who had a pair of unlikely scat-styled club hits in the Nineties, California-native Scatman John found success on pop charts very late in life. A lifelong stutterer, he joined a series of jazz acts as a pianist in the Los Angeles area. Making his unplanned singing début during a performance on a cruise ship in 1984, he improvised a series of bebop-like nonsense syllables. Soon drawing enthusiastic crowds in both Sweden and Germany, he came to the attention of producer Manfred Zahringer. Signed by BMG-Germany, Scatman John scored a pair of international hits in 1995 with 'Scatman (Ski-Ba-Bop-Ba Do Bop)' and 'Scatman's World'.
Cause: Cancer. He died at his home in Los Angeles.

Stefanie Sargent

(Stefanie Ann Sargent)
Born June 1, 1968
Died June 27, 1992
The original guitarist of the Seattle all-girl grunge quartet, 7 Year Bitch, Stefanie Sargent formed the group with other employees of a health food store. A native of Seattle, Sargent left high school two years early at age 16. Performing in a series of West Coast bands, she returned to Seattle in the late Eighties and joined 7 Year Bitch in 1990. Fronted by guitarist and vocalist Selene Vigil, 7YB garnered favourable rock press with their début single, 'Lorna'. After an opening slot for The Red Hot Chili Peppers, 7YB signed with the tiny C/Z Records. Tracks from their early singles and EPs were compiled on the group's début album, *Sick 'Em*, which was released shortly after Sargent's death.
Cause: She died from an alcohol and heroin overdose. A syringe was found near her body.

Clarence G. Satchell

Born April 15, 1940
Died December 30, 1995
A horn player for the percussion-heavy funk band The Ohio Players, Clarence "Satch" Satchell was stricken with polio as a child in his native suburban Cleveland. Formed in Dayton, Ohio, in the early Sixties as The Untouchables, the Robert Ward-headed trio was quickly expanded with trumpeter Ralph "Pee Wee" Middlebrook and Clarence Satchell, who played saxophone and occasionally flute. Finding little luck with their early releases, the group also backed The Falcons on their 1962 R&B hit, 'I Found A Love'. Ward left in 1964, and was replaced by Leroy Bonner. Merging with another group in 1967 and now featuring Joe Harris (later of Undisputed Truth) on lead

vocals, the renamed The Ohio Players worked as session players at a hometown label, Compass Records. There, the group scored a minor hit with 'Trespassin''. Signing with the Detroit-based Westbound Records in 1971, The Ohio Players scored their first major hit with the synthesizer-heavy, novelty-styled 'Funky Worm' (1973). At Satchell's insistence, the group's album covers regularly featured photos of scantily clad women. Moving to Mercury Records, the group landed a string of funk-based crossover hits with 'Skin Tight' (1974); from a controversial album of the same name, 'Fire' (1974); 'Love Rollercoaster' (1975); and 'Who'd She Coo?' (1976). After much internal squabbling, Satchell left the group in the late Seventies.
CAUSE: Brain aneurysm. He died in Dayton.

Louis Satterfield

Born April 3, 1937
Died September 27, 2004
A bass guitarist and trombone player, Louis Satterfield is best known for a stint with Earth, Wind & Fire. Originally a nightclub musician in Chicago, the Mississippi-born Satterfield had previously teamed with drummer Maurice White in a group headed by trumpeter Charles Handy called The Jazzmen. Satterfield and White were hired by producer Billy Davis in the mid Sixties as the nucleus of the house band at Chess Records, and appeared on countless recordings, most notably Fontella Bass' 1965 hit 'Rescue Me', for which Satterfield provided the prominent bass line. With Chess in decline during the early Seventies, Satterfield left to join a jazz/funk outfit, The Pharoahs, and appeared on their album *Awakening*. The Pharoahs evolved into The Phenix Horns and were hired by Maurice White as the horn section in his new soul/funk group Earth, Wind & Fire. Satterfield moonlighted over the next few years, performing as a member of Earth, Wind & Fire and teaming with White to produce a number of R&B acts including Denise Williams and The Emotions. Parting with White in 1981, Satterfield worked primarily as a session player, backing artists such as Phil Collins (whom he would later battle over royalties), providing the horns on the Genesis hit 'Abacab'. At the time of his death, Satterfield was touring with Cash McCall.
CAUSE: Unknown. He died in Chicago.

John Baker Saunders

Born September 23, 1954
Died January 15, 1999
The bassist of the short-lived Seattle supergroup Mad Season, John Baker Saunders conceived the group with Mike McCready while both men were confined to a drug rehab facility in Minnesota. Formed in 1995, Mad Season included Saunders, McCready (Pearl Jam), Layne Staley (Alice In Chains), and Barrett Martin (Screaming Trees). Releasing the album *Above*, the group scored a pair of AOR/alternative-rock hits with 'River And Deceit' and 'I Don't Know Anything'. A native of Montgomery, Alabama, Saunders had previously been aligned with blues artists in Chicago and Minneapolis, including Little Pat Rushing and Hubert Sumlin. Later a member of The Walkabouts, Saunders toured Europe and appeared on the album *Nighttown*.
CAUSE: He died of a drug overdose in Seattle.

Red Saunders

Born March 12, 1912
Died March 4, 1981
A popular bandleader who led the house band at Chicago's famed jazz/R&B nightspot The Club DeLisa, Red Saunders scored a novelty R&B hit in 1952 with 'Hambone' which featured the juba-style percussion

backing of The Hambone Kids (a group that included future soul star Dee Clark). A classically trained drummer, Saunders recorded for several labels beginning with Savoy Records in 1945. At OKeh Records in the early Fifties, Saunders was usually fronted by his group's featured vocalist, Jumpin' Joe Williams.
CAUSE: Unknown.

Bill "Little Bo" Savich

Born August 2, 1939
Died January 4, 2002
As drummer of the Ohio-based rock instrumental group Johnny & The Hurricanes, Bill "Little Bo" Savich played on several hits. Previously a member of The Royaltones (of 'Poor Boy' fame), Savich joined a similar group led by saxophonist Johnny Paris, The Hurricanes. Replacing original drummer Tony Kaye in 1959, Savich joined just as the group was enjoying success with their million-selling single, 'Red River Rock'. Savich subsequently provided the backbeat on their hits, 'Reveille Rock', 'Beatnik Rock' and 'Down Yonder'. Savich left the group in 1963 and later worked as a taxidermist.
CAUSE: Cancer. He died in Detroit, Michigan.

Johnny Sayles

Born February 9, 1937
Died August 17, 1993
A Texas-born, Chicago-based hard-soul singer, Johnny Sayles grew up listening to blues and honky tonk music. While attending Prairie View University, he formed his own campus-based band. Dropping out of college to pursue a career in music, he moved to St. Louis where he initially took a series of day jobs to support his family. After passing through a number of local groups in the city's plentiful nightclubs, Sayles joined the city's top drawing band, Ike Turner's Kings of Rhythm. After briefly returning to college, Sayles joined The Five Du-Tones revue in the early Sixties as a replacement for Johnny Taylor. Soon making Chicago his home, Sayles recorded for several of the city's labels his finest output coming at Mar-V-Lus and Minit – Sayles pounded out virile, hard-edged soul chestnuts such as 'Don't Turn Your Back On Me' and 'Anything For You'. Recording for Dakar Records, Sayles released his only album, *Man On The Inside* (1970). Leaving music in the late Seventies, Sayles worked as a guard at the state prison in Joliet, Illinois. Returning to a full-time music career in the early Eighties, Sayles was joined by the Tommy Jamison's Soul Invader's band as he became a fixture at blues festivals and in Chicago nightclubs.
CAUSE: He died from a heart attack at the suburban Chicago home of Tommy Jamison.

Skip Scarborough

(CLARENCE ALEXANDER SCARBOROUGH)
Born November 26, 1944
Died July 3, 2003
An R&B songwriter, keyboardist and producer, Skip Scarborough worked with scores of acts during his prolific career. His compositions include: 'Love Ballad' (LTD), 'Can't Hide Love' (Earth, Wind & Fire), 'Lovely Day' (Bill Withers), 'Don't Ask My Neighbors' (The Emotions) and 'Love Me Or Let Me Be Lonely' (The Friends Of Distinction). The co-writer of Anita Baker's 'Giving You The Best That I've Got', Scarborough earned a Grammy Award in 1988, and as a keyboard player and producer he worked with Creative Source, Blue Magic, Phyllis Hyman, Nancy Wilson, Bobbi Humphrey and Con Funk Shun. In the Nineties, Scarborough turned his attention to gospel music.
CAUSE: Cancer. He died in Los Angeles.

Joe Schermie

(JOSEPH EDWARD SCHERMETZLER, JR.)
Born February 12, 1948
Died March 25, 2002

A member of Los Angeles pop-rock group Three Dog Night from 1968 to 1973, bass player Joe Schermie brought Latin influences to the group's sound. Born into a showbiz family in Madison, Wisconsin, Schermie often visited his parents' nightclub. Initially playing the drums before moving to bass guitar, he moved with his family to Phoenix and while playing in a number of rock bands – often with Mexican musicians – Schermie was drawn to the blues. Meanwhile, Three Dog Night had formed in 1967 by a trio of vocalists – Cory Wells, Danny Hutton and Chuck Negron – and expanded into a seven-man outfit the following year. Schermie had previously worked with Wells in the short-lived Cory Wells Blues Band and was flown in from Phoenix when Three Dog Night's original bass player was dismissed after kicking Negron's dog! In turn, Schermie brought in two additional members, Floyd Sneed and Michael Allsup. Signed by ABC-Dunhill, the group graduated from playing Los Angeles nightclubs to headlining stadium shows in a very short time. Dominating the US pop charts for several years, the group forged a career by reinterpreting the compositions of talented – often unknown – songwriters: 'One' (Harry Nilsson), 'Eli's Coming' (Laura Nyro), 'Mama Told Me Not To Come' (Randy Newman), 'Joy To The World' (Hoyt Axton) and 'Liar' (Russ Ballard). Despite being one of the more successful rock acts of the period, Three Dog Night failed to generate much respect in the serious rock community. Wanting to write and produce his own material, Schermie left Three Dog Night in 1973 after the release of their ninth album, a live project from shows at Tokyo and Frankfurt, *Around The World With Three Dog Night*. He was replaced by Jack Ryland, formerly with Helen Reddy. Pursuing a solo career, Schermie worked with Kim Fowley, Stephen Stills, Yvonne Elliman and Gayle McCormick of the group Smith. Although Schermie did not join in on any Three Dog Night reunions, he occasionally performed with Chuck Negron and worked on an album with Floyd Sneed under the moniker K.A.T.T.
CAUSE: Heart attack. He died in Los Angeles.

Bob Scholl

Born July 14, 1938
Died August 27, 1975
Along with brother Jerry and three others, Bob Scholl formed one of the first interracial rock groups, The Mello-Kings. Assembled in 1956 at a high school in Mount Vernon, New York, originally as the Mellotones, the group scored its sole hit in 1957 with the elegant doo-wop standard 'Tonight Tonight'.
CAUSE: Boating accident.

William Schwann

Born May 13, 1913
Died June 7, 1998
The founder of the *Schwann* record catalogue, William Schwann launched the monthly publication in 1949 to keep track of records for his retail store in Cambridge, Massachusetts. Soon closing the store to devote his energies to publishing the catalogue, Schwann hired a staff of employees to document all available releases.
CAUSE: He died of natural causes in Burlington, Massachusetts.

Gene Schwartz

(EUGENE SCHWARTZ)
Born December 16, 1920
Died May 4, 1999
A co-founder of Laurie Records, Gene Schwartz formed the label in 1958 with his brother Bob and two others. The Schwartz brothers had previously worked at the tiny Mohawk label, where Dion (DiMucci) had made his first recordings. Beginning with the Bob Schwartz-produced Dion & The

Belmonts' hit 'I Wonder Why', Laurie was behind the early Sixties chart successes of Randy & The Rainbows, The Jarmels, The Five Discs, The Del Satins, The Chiffons, and The Passions. Laurie survived The Beatles by issuing British Invasion singles by acts such as Gerry & The Pacemakers, and by purchasing master discs from other labels (such was the case with 'He's So Fine' by The Chiffons). Continuing in the pop-rock vein during the late Sixties, Laurie had further hits with 'Little Bit O'Soul' (The Music Explosion), 'Abraham, Martin And John' (Dion) and 'Snoopy vs. The Red Baron' (The Royal Guardsmen). By the mid Seventies, Laurie had evolved into a reissue label. Later renamed 3C (Continental Communications), the label was absorbed by EMI-Capitol in 1992.
CAUSE: Having already been diagnosed with Parkinson's disease, he suffered a stroke. He died in Newport Beach, California.

Ingo Schwichtenberg

Born May 18, 1965
Died March 8, 1995
A founding member of German heavy metal band Helloween, the always smiling Ingo Schwichtenberg was a resourceful drummer. Signed by Noise Records, the group contributed a pair of tracks for the compilation album *Death Metal*, before recording an EP *Helloween*. Schwichtenberg recorded five albums with the band – *Walls Of Jericho*, *Keeper Of The Seven Keys Part I*, *Keeper Of The Seven Keys Part II*, *Pink Bubbles Go Ape* and *Chameleon* – and got airplay in the UK with tracks such as 'Dr. Stein', 'I Want Out' and 'Kids Of The Century'. Schwichtenberg was forced from the band because of alcohol and drug problems in 1993.
CAUSE: Battling a host of personal demons, he committed suicide. Suffering from manic depression, he jumped in front of a train near Hamburg, Germany.

Bobby Scott

Born January 29, 1937
Died November 5, 1990
A one-hit wonder, jazz pianist Bobby Scott scored a pop hit in 1956 with 'Chain Gang'. Also a producer, Scott worked with Marvin Gaye, Bobby Darin, Harry Belafonte, and Aretha Franklin. Scott also co-wrote several hits including 'A Taste Of Honey' (Herb Alpert; The Beatles) and 'He Ain't Heavy, He's My Brother' (The Hollies). Scott released a final album shortly before his death, *For Sentimental Reasons*.
CAUSE: Lung cancer. He died in New York City.

Bon Scott

(RONALD BELFORD)
Born July 9, 1946
Died February 19, 1980
The lead singer of the popular heavy-metal band AC/DC, the raspy-voiced Bon Scott spawned a host of imitators. Born in Kirriemuir, Scotland, Scott joined his father's band as a bagpipe player at age 11, staying with the group for five years. Switching to drums, Scott joined his first rock band in 1965, The Spectors. Later teaming with Vince Lovegrove to form a pop-rock outfit The Valentines, Scott shared the lead vocal duties with Lovegrove. Recording on Australia's Clarion, and then Philips Records, The Valentines scored their biggest hit in 1969 with 'My Old Man's A Groovy Old Man'. After the group disbanded in 1970, Scott joined another Australian band, Fraternity; edging toward hard-rock, Scott recorded two albums with the group, *Livestock* (1971) and *Flaming Galah* (1973). After leaving Fraternity in 1973 and joining The Mount Lofty Rangers, Scott suffered a motorcycle accident and was unable to record with the group. Meanwhile, Angus Young and his brother Malcolm had emigrated to Sydney, Australia, in 1973. Settling in Melbourne, the brothers disbanded one group and

started another, asking their roadie, fellow-Scotsman Bon Scott, to join as the lead vocalist. Joined by bassist Mark Evans and drummer Phillip Rudd, AC/DC earned a strong Australian following. With his unpredictable demeanour, Scott was a perfect choice as the leader of a heavy-metal rock group. Produced by former members of the Sixties pop group The Easybeats, George Vanda and the Youngs' older brother George, AC/DC recorded a pair of strong albums in 1975, *High Voltage* and *TNT*. Signing with Atlantic Records in early 1976 and moving to Britain, AC/DC placed an album in the British Top 20, *Let There Be Rock* (1977). Lacing his performances with bawdy humour, the smoky-voiced Scott was complimented by the crunching guitar riffs of Angus Young who wore a British schoolboy outfit. Returning to Australia to record *Powerage* (1978), AC/DC also released a live project from a Scottish performance, *If You Want Blood, You've Got It*. Meanwhile, AC/DC would belatedly break into the US market in 1979 with the platinum-certified release *Highway To Hell*, which featured a scorching title track. At the peak of their success at the time of Scott's death, AC/DC continued with singer Brian Johnson. Reissued in 1981, the five-year-old Scott-fronted AC/DC album *Dirty Deeds Done Dirt Cheap* became an instant classic with hit tracks such as 'Dirty Deeds', 'Problem Child', and 'Big Balls'. With the album's success, AC/DC became the only artists of the Eighties to place three Top 10 albums in the US charts in one calendar year.
CAUSE: Although acute alcohol poisoning was originally reported as the cause of death, the coroner's report revealed that Scott had suffocated on his own vomit in the back seat of a car after a heavy night of drinking and substance abuse. Scott and friend Alistair Kinnear had spent much of the evening at a London nightclub, The Music Machine, in Camden Town. Instead of dropping off Scott at his central London flat, Kinnear drove to his home in Dulwich, south-east London. Unable to rouse the sleeping Scott, Kinnear returned with a blanket and left a note with directions to his third-floor residence but with Scott failing to arrive, Kinnear returned to the vehicle the following morning to discover Scott unconscious. Rushed to King's College Hospital, Scott was pronounced dead on arrival.
FURTHER READING: Putterford, Marc. (1992). *AC/DC: Shock To The System*. London: Omnibus. Huxley, Martin. (1996). *AC/DC: The World's Heaviest Rock*. London: Boxtree. Walker, Clinton. (1994). *Highway To Hell: The Life And Times Of AC/DC Legend Bon Scott*. Australia: Verse Chorus.

Clifford Scott

Born June 21, 1928
Died April 19, 1993
San Antonio-based tenor saxophone and flute player, Clifford Scott was a member of Bill Doggett's group from the mid Fifties to the early Sixties; during this period, he co-wrote and provided the distinctive solo on the driving R&B instrumental 'Honky Tonk'. Scott also performed with Charles Brown, The Lionel Hampton Orchestra, Roy Milton, and Freddie King. Also a solo act, Scott released several albums.
CAUSE: Unknown.

George Scott

(GEORGE SCOTT III)
Born c. 1953
Died August 5, 1980
An experimental bass player, George Scott launched his professional career behind progressive rocker John Cale, performing on the album, *Sabotage/Live*. Scott then joined the James Chance-led African-rock group The Contortions, and in 1979, The Raybeats. Later in 1979, he joined an avant-garde, New York City-based rock group led by new-wave singer

Lydia Lunch, 8 Eyed Spy. Scott passed away before the group recorded its first studio album.
CAUSE: Unknown. He died suddenly in New York City.

George "King" Scott

Born 1930
Died February 1968
The leader of the Cleveland-based soul group The Hesitations, George "King" Scott provided the vocals on their biggest pop hit, a cover of the film theme 'Born Free'.
CAUSE: He was accidentally shot and killed by the group's tenor, Fred Deal.

Joe Scott

Born c. 1912
Died 1979
A talented Texas-born R&B songwriter, arranger, trumpeter, and bandleader at Duke/Peacock Records, Joe Scott is best known for his work with Bobby "Blue" Bland. Harnessing Bland's vocal style during an 18-year association, Scott led a tight session band on soul chestnuts such as 'Farther Up The Road', 'Cry Cry Cry', and 'I Pity The Fool'. Scott also worked with the bluesmen Clarence "Gatemouth" Brown and Little Junior Parker, soul diva Aretha Franklin, rocker Roy Head, and gospel acts The Staple Singers and The Dixie Hummingbirds.
CAUSE: Unknown.

Ronnie Scott

(RONALD SCHATT)
Born January 28, 1927
Died December 23, 1996
A leading British jazz musician, Ronnie Scott was better known as the proprietor of London's leading jazz nightclub, called Ronnie Scott's, in Soho's Frith Street. A talented tenor saxophonist, the London-born Scott founded the club in 1959 with partner Peter King, booking only British acts during its first two years. With his deadpan voice and droll sense of humour, Scott introduced shows at the venue which at times presented jazz influenced rock performers and cross-over acts like The Charlie Watts Big Band. Jimi Hendrix's last public performance, albeit jamming along with Eric Burdon & War, was at Ronnie Scott's club. Also, The Who showcased *Tommy* for the press in 1969. Scott broke into music with Ted Heath's band in the Forties. He later performed on the Queen Mary transatlantic cruise ship and had co-led The Jazz Couriers along with Tubby Hayes. Scott's banter was captured on the 1997 album, *Whenever I Want Your Opinion I'll Give It To You.* A second Ronnie Scott's Club was eventually opened in Birmingham.
CAUSE: He overdosed on prescription barbiturates and whiskey at his London apartment; he had taken cocaine the previous day. Scott had been distraught over his approaching 70th birthday, a failed five-year relationship, and serious dental problems which prevented him from playing the saxophone. A coroner brushed aside a verdict of suicide and ruled death from "misadventure". However, according to Scott's son, it was his third suicide attempt in the last years of his life. Shortly before his death, Scott had mailed a suicide note to his former fiancée who had spurned his marriage proposal. Scott's father had also taken his own life after a cancer diagnosis. The funeral procession wound its way through Soho, past the club, on its way to the church service.
FURTHER READING: Fordham, John. (1986). *Let's Join Hands And Contact The Living: Ronnie Scott & His Club.* London: Elm Tree.

Walter Scott

(WALTER NOTHEIS, JR.)
Born February 7, 1943
Died December 27, 1993
The lead singer of the pop-rock outfit Bob Kuban & The In Men, Walter Scott had joined the St. Louis-based group in 1963. Scott provided urgent

vocals on the group's biggest hit, a horn and electric organ drenched lament about marital infidelity, 'The Cheater'. Leaving the group in 1966, Scott was joined by two members of The In Men in a regional group called The Guise. Following a nervous breakdown, Scott reconciled with Kuban in 1968 for a short-lived version of The In Men. Scott spent the Seventies at the helm of a nationally touring oldies group, The Cheaters. Scott reunited with Kuban in 1983 for a television appearance and resulting tour.
CAUSE: Disappearing under mysterious circumstances, Scott was last seen on December 27, 1983 on his way to purchase a car battery. The following day, his abandoned car was found at a local airport. Scott's remains were located four years later in his neighbour concrete cistern. Neighbour Jim Williams was romantically entangled with Scott's wife, JoAnn Notheis, and killed both Scott and his own wife. Williams was convicted of double murder.
FURTHER READING: Priesmeyer, Scottie. (1996). *The Cheaters: The Walter Scott Murder*. St. Louis: Tula.

Ray Scragg

(RAYMOND ARTHUR SCRAGG)
Born August 4, 1946
Died February 7, 2001
As the rhythm guitarist for Merseybeat band The Dennisons, Ray Scragg scored a pair of minor UK hits with '(Come On) Be My Girl' (1963) and a cover of the R&B standard 'Walkin' The Dog' (1964). The group appeared on the same bill as The Beatles at Liverpool's Cavern Club on a number of occasions. The Dennisons disbanded in 1965.
CAUSE: Throat cancer.

Son Seals

(FRANK SEALS)
Born August 14, 1942
Died December 20, 2004
A three-time W.C. Handy Award winner, bluesman Son Seals made his recording début in 1973 with the Alligator Records release *The Son Seals Blues Band*. Originally a drummer, he switched to guitar at age 18, playing the club scene of south Chicago in 1971, sharing stages with such blues greats as Junior Wells, Buddy Guy, James Cotton, Albert King and Hound Dog Taylor.
CAUSE: Complications from diabetes. He died in Chicago.

"Big Al" Sears

(ALBERT OMEGA SEARS)
Born February 22, 1910
Died March 23, 1990
A popular jazz and R&B tenor saxophonist, "Big Al" Sears was one of the most influential "honkers" of the Fifties. A veteran player who got his break in Chick Webb's band in 1928, Sears briefly headed his own small combo in 1941. Sears subsequently joined Andy Kirk, Lionel Hampton, and as a replacement for Ben Webster in Duke Ellington's Orchestra from 1944 to 1949. While a member of Johnny Hodges' group in 1949, Sears penned the Hodges' hit, 'Castle Rock'. Embracing R&B in the Fifties, Sears was a central figure in Alan Freed's house band and was frequently teamed on stage with other honker greats such as Sam "The Man" Taylor and Red Prysock. Hired in the Sixties as an executive at ABC-Paramount Records, Sears also recorded a series of jazz albums. After retiring from the label in 1980, Sears remained a popular figure on the R&B and blues circuit until shortly before his death.
CAUSE: He died of lung cancer at his home in Long Island, New York.
FURTHER READING: Shaw, Arnold. (1978). *Honkers And Shouters*. New York: Macmillan.

Zenas Sears

Born July 14, 1913
Died October 4, 1988
A pioneering white DJ, Zenas Sears

introduced R&B and blues acts on his programme at a state-owned radio station, WGST in Atlanta. Hired in 1944, the Ohio-born Sears initially began playing black musical styles two years later under the radio name "Daddy" Sears. Alienating pro-segregationists, he received frequent death threats. Also a talent scout, Sears discovered Billy Wright, Tommy Brown, Chuck Willis, and was instrumental in the launching of Little Richard, all of whom performed at Sears' live broadcasts from the 81 Theater in Atlanta. Fired from WGST in 1954 by the governor, Sears landed at WOAK. Sears was active in the turbulent Civil Rights struggle during the Sixties.
CAUSE: Suffering a debilitating stroke in the mid Eighties, he was confined to a nursing home during his last years.
FURTHER READING: Smith, Wes. (1989). *The Pied Pipers Of Rock'n'Roll.* Marietta, GA: Longstreet.

Tony Secunda

(ANTHONY MICHAEL SECUNDA)
Born August 24, 1940
Died February 10, 1995
A noted British music entrepreneur, Tony Secunda was involved in a myriad of entertainment industry pursuits, including concert promotion, artist management, and the operation of a clandestine pirate station, the Monte Carlo-based Radio Geronimo. Secunda was known as one of the great sensationalist managers of the Sixties in the tradition of Andrew Oldham and Kit Lambert. Quitting school in his teens, Secunda worked in the art department of Fleetway Press, served coffee at the famous 2Is, then joined the Merchant Navy as an 18-year-old deck boy. He jumped ship at Long Beach, California, then returned to the UK. Motivated to stage rock music concerts in Britain, Secunda teamed with former singer Rory Blackwill to book rising youthful proto-rockers such as Georgie Fame, Johnnie Angel, and Johnny Kidd. Secunda subsequently joined a circus, then took up wrestling promotion. Venturing to South Africa, Secunda teamed with friend and former singer-turned-music promoter Mickie Most to stage a series of rock'n'roll shows. Returning to London, Secunda's success was interrupted in 1961 by a one-year sentence for marijuana possession. Released just as Britain was enjoying a Beatles explosion, Secunda jumped on The Fab Four bandwagon and profited from Beatles merchandising. Parlaying his earnings to launch an artist management company with Alex Murray, Secunda initially managed Leslie Duncan before discovering The Moody Blues. He enjoyed far greater success with another Birmingham act, The Move, with whom he employed various sensationalist publicity stunts involving strippers and on-stage violence. He famously cost The Move all their royalties from the hit 'Flowers In The Rain' after libelling the British Prime Minister Harold Wilson on a saucy postcard. He subsequently managed Procol Harum, who had already achieved success with 'A Whiter Shade Of Pale', and T. Rex, whose singer Marc Bolan later nicknamed Secunda "Telegram Sam". By the early Seventies, Secunda teamed with producer Denny Cordell at the reactivated Regal Zonophone label. Semi-retired, Secunda moved to the US, working with The Dwight Twilly Band. Returning to England for a time, Secunda worked with Gary Shearston, Steeleye Span, Motorhead and The Pretenders. He later settled in California where he worked in record promotion and as a literary agent.
CAUSE: Heart attack. He died at his home in San Anselmo, California.
FURTHER READING: Rogan, Johnny. (1987). *Starmakers & Svengalis: The History Of British Pop Management.* London: Queen Anne Press.

Selena

(SELENA QUINTANILLA-PEREZ)
Born April 16, 1971
Died March 31, 1995
A Tejano pop music star who was dubbed "The Mexican Madonna", Selena was on the verge of mainstream US stardom at the time of her death. Her father a former bandleader, Texas-native Selena impressed her parents when she began singing at the age of three. By the time she was nine, Selena was placed at the helm of a newly assembled musical group, Selena Y Los Dinos (Selena & The Guys) performing at her family's new restaurant. With their business headed toward bankruptcy, the family loaded their musical gear and settled in nearby Corpus Christi. Managed by her doting and earnest father, Abraham Quintanilla, Jr., Selena dropped out of school in eighth grade to further her musical ambitions. Having released three independent albums and drawing thousands to her concerts, Selena was signed by Capital/EMI Latin in 1989. Her star in the ascent, Selena won a Grammy for *Live* (1993) and topped the Latin charts with her album *Amor Prohibido*. Also in 1994, Selena opened the first of her two boutiques, hiring her fan club president, Yolanda Saldivar, as manager. Infusing her Mexican heritage into her music, Selena sang exclusively in Spanish on the first five of her major label albums. Poised for crossover appeal at the time of her death, Selena had begun recording English-language songs for her next album; posthumously released, *Dreaming Of You* was a surprise million-selling mainstream smash. Selena was portrayed by Jennifer Lopez in the title role of the 1997 biopic *Selena*.
CAUSE: She was murdered by the president of her fan club, 32-year-old registered nurse, Yolanda Saldivar. Confronting Saldivar at her motel room in Corpus Christi, Texas, over $30,000 in missing funds, Selena was shot in the shoulder. After struggling to reach the motel lobby, she was rushed to a local hospital where, with a major artery shattered, she soon bled to death. After the shooting, the armed Saldivar held police at bay for ten hours. Saldivar was convicted and sentenced to life in prison. During court testimony, Saldivar claimed she had also planned to kill herself but the gun misfired. The gun was shredded in 2002 after a lengthy legal fight.
FURTHER READING: Potoski, Joe Nick. (1996). *Selena*. New York: Boulevard.

Ronnie Self

Born July 5, 1938
Died August 28, 1981
A songwriter and obscure rockabilly artist, Ronnie Self scored a minor hit on Sun Records with 'Bop-A-Lena'. Nicknamed "Mr. Frantic", Self recorded the original version of the garage classic 'I Fought The Law' in 1961. Also a songwriter, he penned the Brenda Lee hits, 'Sweet Nothings', 'Everybody Loves Me But You', 'Anybody But Me', 'I'm Sorry', and with fellow Springfield, Illinois-native Wayne Carson Thompson, The Box Top hits, 'The Letter', 'Soul Deep', and 'Neon Rainbow'.
CAUSE: Long-term effects of alcoholism.

Joe Seneca

(JOSEPH MCGEE)
Born January 14, 1919
Died August 15, 1996
A singer and songwriter, Joe Seneca also worked as a film actor in later life. After graduating from a Cleveland high school in the mid Thirties, Seneca formed a song and dance trio called The Jungle Boys, which on their arrival in New York City was dubbed The Three Riffs. A popular stage act that lasted into the Fifties, The Three Riffs recorded for Decca, Apollo, and Atlantic. Belatedly discovering a talent for writing songs, Seneca penned the hits 'Break It To Me Gently' (Brenda

Lee), 'It's Gonna Work Out Fine' (Ike & Tina Turner) and 'Talk To Me, Talk To Me' (Little Willie John). In his best-known film role, Seneca portrayed an ageing blues singer in *Crossroads*; co-starring Ralph Macchio, the film was centred on a lost Robert Johnson song.
CAUSE: He died from a heart attack brought on by an asthma attack at his home in Roosevelt Island, New York.

David Seville

(ROSS S. BAGDASARIAN, SR.)
Born January 27, 1919
Died January 16, 1972
Best known as the creator of musical cartoon singing group, The Chipmunks (Alvin, Simon and Theodore), David Seville entered show business as a struggling actor. The son of an Armenian-born, California grape farmer, Seville was born in Fresno. Leaving for New York City at age 19 to appear in his cousin, William Saroyan's play, *The Time Of Your Life*, Seville was hired as a stage manager for another show. After serving a four-year stint in the US Air Force in the mid Forties, Seville married and settled in Los Angeles. Turning to songwriting, Seville had several early successes. With the aid of friend Mitch Miller, Seville's novelty composition 'Come On-A My House' (1951) was a million-selling, smash hit for Rosemary Clooney (the song had originally been recorded the previous year by Kay Armen). Seville followed up with 'Hey Brother, Pour The Wine' (1954), a hit for Dean Martin, and the often recorded instrumental, 'Armen's Theme' (1956). Initially recording in 1954 under his real name, Ross Bagdasarian, Seville would later employ a host of pseudonyms. After buying an expensive tape recorder in late 1957 and experimenting with the speed control, Seville discovered that he could produce what sounded like multiple voices. Manipulating the tape speed, he sang 'Witch Doctor' as a duet between his normal and accelerated voice. Reluctantly released in 1958 by the almost bankrupt Liberty Records under the moniker David Seville, the novelty record was a multi-million seller. Employing the same method, Seville soon invented a trio called The Chipmunks. Taking The Chipmunks' names – Simon, Theodore, and Alvin – from those of Liberty Records' chiefs, Seville scored another million-selling smash with 'The Chipmunk Song'. The Chipmunks hits continued with 'Alvin's Harmonica' (1959), 'Ragtime Cowboy Joe' (1959), 'Alvin's Orchestra' (1960), 'Rudolph The Red Nosed Reindeer' (1960), and 'The Alvin Twist' (1962). Then in 1961 The Chipmunks hit the small screen as a cartoon show; beginning its first year in prime-time evenings, *The Alvin Show* then moved to Saturday mornings. Jumping on the British Invasion bandwagon, Alvin and the boys recorded an album of Beatles songs in 1964, *The Chipmunks Sing The Beatles Hits*. After releasing his final Chipmunks album in 1967, Seville teamed the fictional trio with blues-rock group Canned Heat in 1968 for an updated recording of the 'Chipmunk Song'. In all, Seville won three Grammy Awards in his lifetime. Also an actor, Seville appeared in such films as *Viva Zapata!* (1952), *Stalag 17* (1953), *Rear Window* (1954), and *The Proud And The Profane* (1956). Shortly before his death, Seville retired his Chipmunks and moved towards mainstream rock music. Seville's son, Ross Bagdasarian, Jr., a Stanford law graduate, resurrected The Chipmunks in 1977. With the help of his wife, actress Janice Karmen, Bagdasarian marketed a string of Chipmunks projects including a new NBC cartoon television series in 1983. 'Witch Doctor' reached the British Top 10 in 1999 via a version by the group, Cartoons.
CAUSE: Heart attack. He died in Beverly Hills.

FURTHER READING: Bagdasarian, Ross. (1998). *Alvin And The Chipmunks: Forty Years In A Nutshell.* Los Angeles: General Publishing.

Phil Seymour

Born May 15, 1952
Died August 17, 1993
A talented guitarist, Phil Seymour was also the lead singer of The Dwight Twilley Band. Born in Tulsa, Oklahoma, Seymour met his future recording partner, fellow British Invasion fanatic Dwight Twilley, at a mid Sixties screening of The Beatles' film *A Hard Day's Night.* Quitting high school in 1969 to join Twilley in a duo called Oister, Seymour relocated to Memphis in search of a recording contract. Returning to Tulsa, Seymour joined a local group, El Roacho, but quit after the group signed with Columbia Records in 1972. Rejoining Twilley, Seymour worked as a session player at Denny Cordell's Tulsa-based Shelter Records. Recorded over several gruelling sessions over a period of a year, *Sincerely* was a retro-rocking album of all Twilley compositions. Although Seymour was the lead vocalist and Twilley remained in the background, usually playing drums, bass guitar, or providing vocal harmony, the group was billed as The Dwight Twilley Band. But from the project, the group scored a power-pop styled hit with the upbeat 'I'm On Fire' (1975). True to their influences, the British-looking band enjoyed a strong fan base in the emerging Los Angeles punk/new-wave scene. With their follow-up album delayed by their label's financial problems, *Twilley Don't Mind* (1977) stalled on the charts. Shelter Records labelmate Tom Petty supplied guitar on two tracks, and Twilley and Seymour reciprocated, singing on Petty's début album. Leaving Twilley for a solo career, Seymour recorded two albums for Boardwalk Records. Recorded while Seymour was hampered with a broken finger, his début disc, *Phil Seymour* (1980), featured his only solo hit, 'Precious To Me'. Abusing drugs and refusing to tour to promote his second album, Seymour was dropped by his label. Also a session player, Seymour backed Moon Martin, Peter Noone and Del Shannon on the oldies circuit. Seymour also sang lead vocals on a few tracks of The Textones début album, *Mission Midnight* (1984).
CAUSE: Diagnosed with lymphoma in 1985, he died of the disease at the Tarzana Medical Center near Los Angeles.

Bob Shad

Born February 12, 1920
Died March 13, 1985
A veteran jazz and rock producer, Robert Shad learned his craft working with blues acts at Gold Star Records in Houston during the late Forties. Launching his own label in 1948, Sittin' In With Records, Shad landed hits by Peppermint Harris and others. With Mercury acquiring the label in 1951, Shad was retained as an A&R director. At Mercury, Shad worked with The Platters, Sarah Vaughan, Cannonball Adderley, Quincy Jones, Big Bill Broonzy, and Patti Page. Launching Time/Shad and Mainstream Records in the mid Sixties, Shad produced the early sessions of both Ted Nugent and Janis Joplin; by the Seventies, Shad was concentrating his efforts on jazz acts.
CAUSE: Heart attack. He died in Beverly Hills, California.

Tupac Shakur

(TUPAC AMARU SHAKUR)
Born June 16, 1971
Died September 13, 1996
Gangster rapper and actor, Tupac Shakur celebrated the self-described "thug life". Shakur was reared in a politically charged environment, his mother arrested as a member of the radical Black Panthers when she attempted to bomb several buildings in

New York City. Born in the Bronx but moving to Baltimore, Shakur studied acting at a public high school for the performing arts, and began composing rap songs after the death of a friend in a shooting accident. Moving to suburban San Francisco with his family, "2 Pac" was drawn to the urban street life of nearby Oakland. Joining forces in the early Nineties with rap group Digital Underground, Shakur was initially employed as a roadie, and on occasion, a rapper. Signed by Interscope Records in 1992 as a solo act, Shakur released his début album *2Pacalypse Now*, highlighted by street-wise tracks such as 'Trapped' and 'Brenda's Got A Baby'. Although his lyrics were rife with violent and misogynist messages, Shakur was nominated for a NAACP Image Award. After appearing in the film *Juice*, Shakur followed up with another hit album, *Strictly 4 My N.I.G.G.A.S.*, and hit the charts with the singles 'I Get Around' and 'Keep Ya Head Up'. Frequently in the news for a series of arrests, Shakur garnered further fame as the co-star of the film, *Poetic Justice*. Shakur narrowly escaped death in 1994 when he was shot by intruders in the lobby of a New York City recording studio, and robbed of $40,000 worth of jewellery. At the forefront of gangster rap, Shakur enjoyed superstar status in the black community with the album, *Me Against The World* (1995), and after signing with Death Row Records, *All Eyez On Me* (1996). Frequently in trouble with the law, Shakur was placed on probation for assault and battery, and he served eight months in prison on assault charges. Free on $1.4 million bail at the time of his death, he was scheduled to be sentenced on a weapons conviction later the same week. A posthumously released album *The Don Killuminati* furthered Shakur's urban legend. The 2004 film documentary *Tupac: Resurrection* and accompanying soundtrack were solid hits. Poems composed by Shakur as a teenager were posthumously compiled in the book, *The Rose That Grew From Concrete*.

CAUSE: Shakur was the victim of a drive-by shooting on the Las Vegas strip while en route from the Mike Tyson–Bruce Seldon heavyweight title fight to a party. Shakur and Death Row Records chairman Marion "Suge" Knight were shot while stopped at a red light. With Knight at the steering wheel of his black BMW 750, a Cadillac with four people inside pulled up and started shooting. Shakur and his entourage had got into a brawl earlier in the evening outside a Las Vegas hotel. A similar tussle had erupted at the MTV awards in New York City. Shot four times in the chest, Shakur was listed in critical condition following three operations at University Medical Center. Initially expected to survive, Shakur had his right lung removed the next day, and died six days later. Suffering only a minor head wound, 31-year-old Marion Knight was treated and released. With the shooting attributed in the media to a gang-related feud between East Coast and West Coast rappers, police received little cooperation from witnesses; even Knight eluded police investigators. A member of Shakur's backing band who witnessed the shooting was later shot to death. Shakur became an instant cultural icon in the urban community, and many of his fans believe he faked his death. In 2002, *The Los Angeles Times* reported that Notorious B.I.G. paid to have Shakur killed shortly after Shakur's entourage assaulted Orlando Anderson at the MGM Grand. But B.I.G.'s family claimed to have an audiotape to prove that he was in a New York City studio the night of the shooting.

FURTHER READING: White, Armond. (1997). *Rebel For The Hell Of It: The Life Of Tupac Shakur*. London: Quartet.

Haroon Shamsher

Born November 14, 1965
Died July 8, 1999
Half of the London-based duo Joi, Haroon Shamsher teamed with his brother Farook to fuse Indian and Pakistani rhythms with modern dance grooves. Born in London, the pair grew up watching Indian musicians record in a makeshift studio in the rear of their father's retail store. After 10 years as popular club deejays, the pair began recording their own material in their father's studio. First making waves when *NME* named 'Desert Storm' single of the week, Joi became club favourites in Britain. Signed to Peter Gabriel's Real World Records, Joi released their début album in 1998, *One And One Is One*.
CAUSE: He succumbed to heart failure after a week-long illness. He suffered a heart attack during a hospital examination. Though ill, he had performed the night before.

Del Shannon

(CHARLES WEEDON WESTOVER)
Born December 30, 1939
Died February 8, 1990
A classic pop-rock singer who often sang about broken hearts, the brooding Del Shannon broke on the musical scene in the early Sixties with the irresistible 'Runaway'. A native of Coopersville, Michigan, Shannon picked up the ukulele before switching to the guitar at age thirteen. A reluctant member of his high school football team, Shannon yearned to be a musician, teaching himself to play by watching country & western players in a rough Grand Rapids club. Drafted, Shannon spent four months of his military stint working in the Special Services as a radio entertainer in West Germany. Returning to Michigan in 1960, Shannon and keyboard player Max Crook occasionally performed with the house band at The Hi-Lo Club in Battle Creek. Approached after a performance by popular Michigan DJ/producer Ollie McLaughlin, Shannon and Crook landed a recording contract with Embee Records. At their second session, the duo recorded 'Runaway', a hook-laden pop masterpiece that featured Shannon's eerie R&B influenced falsetto vocal and Crook's space age-like Musitron keyboard riffs. With his yearning, impassioned voice, Shannon followed up with 'Hats Off To Larry' (1961), 'So Long Baby' (1961), and 'Little Town Flirt' (1963). While touring Britain in 1963 on the same bill as the meteoric Beatles, Shannon offered to help the group by covering one of their compositions. He thus became the first artist to chart in the US with a Lennon-McCartney song, scoring a minor hit in 1963 with 'From Me To You'. (Lennon later denied giving Shannon permission to record the song.) With his career marred by contractual problems in late 1963, Shannon attempted to release material on his own Berlee label. Switching to Amy Records, Shannon weathered the British Invasion and returned to the charts with a cover of Jimmy Jones' 'Handy Man' (1964), 'Keep Searchin'' (1964), and 'Stranger In Town' (1965). Shannon's composition 'I Go To Pieces' was a Top 10 hit in 1965 for Peter & Gordon. Switching to Liberty Records in 1966, Shannon lost much of his artistic freedom and was forced to record material against his wishes. Liberty also refused to release Shannon's experimental album with Rolling Stones' manager Andrew Loog Oldham, *Home And Away* (1966). Inspired by The Beatles' *Sgt. Pepper* project, Shannon subsequently released a much-ignored, psychedelic-styled concept album under his real name, *The Further Adventures Of Charles Westover*. With his success as a recording artist stymied in the late Sixties, Shannon turned to record production. Discovering a female-led rock group called Smith, Shannon re-worked their cover hit, 'Baby It's You' (1969),

produced Brian Hyland's 'Gypsy Woman' (1970), and collaborated with Dave Edmunds and Jeff Lynne. Recording little in the Seventies, Shannon toured heavily throughout Europe and made a fortune through a series of real estate investments. Breaking free of his longtime drinking problem, Shannon began working on a new album in the late Seventies. What started as a country music project took a rock turn on the advice and production help of longtime fan, Tom Petty. Three years in the making, *Drop Down And Get Me* (1981) spawned a Top 40 hit cover of Phil Phillips' 'Sea Of Love'. A star on the oldies circuit at the time of his death, Shannon was completing a Tom Petty/Jeff Lynne-aided album, the posthumously released *Rock On* (1991).
CAUSE: A likely suicide, Shannon died from a gunshot wound with a .22 rifle in the den of his recently purchased Santa Clarita, California home. His wife, LeAnne Westover, claimed that the anti-depressant drug, Prozac, that Shannon was taking was responsible for Shannon's actions and took the matter to court, suing pharmaceutical makers, Eli Lilly & Co. for "wrongful death, negligence, and fraud".

Alexander Sharp

Born December 1919
Died January 1970
The backing tenor vocalist of the pioneering doo-wop group The Orioles, Alexander Sharp was an original member of the Sonny Til-fronted outfit. Formed in Baltimore in 1947 as The Vibranaires, the group was signed after a performance on Arthur Godfrey's *Talent Scout Show*. A harmony-based doo-wop group, The Orioles enjoyed a strong hit run with 'It's Too Soon To Know' (1948); a song that their manager had intended to give to Savannah Churchill and then Dinah Washington, 'Tell Me So' (1949); and a pop crossover smash, 'Crying In The Chapel' (1953). A heavy-set, burly man, Sharp possessed a very high tenor which contrasted with Sonny Til's more fluid lead. With the traffic death of the group's original guitarist Tommy Gaither while returning from a performance, The Orioles severely curtailed their touring schedule. This lack of exposure hindered the group's success. Sharp left after the release of 'If You Believe' in 1954. In the Sixties, Sharp joined a revival version of The Ink Spots.
CAUSE: Heart attack.

Sonny Sharrock

(WARREN HARDING SHARROCK)
Born August 27, 1940
Died May 26, 1994
Best known as a jazz and rock guitarist, Sonny Sharrock emerged from a late Fifties family doo-wop group The Echoes. After briefly attending the Berklee College of Music, Sharrock moved to New York City and apprenticed under several experimental jazzmen including Sun Ra and Pharoah Sanders. Playing a crashing style of guitar, Sharrock was admired by fans of rock and jazz alike. Sharrock subsequently teamed with flautist Herbie Mann in 1967 on both the stage and on sessions. During this period, Sharrock also recorded his first solo album, *Black Woman* (1970). Re-emerging in the Eighties, Sharrock frequently worked with bassist/producer Bill Laswell and appeared on several albums with The Last Exit. Shortly before his death, Sharrock had signed with RCA to record a rock oriented album. Sharrock also provided the theme for the cable cartoon programme, *Space Ghost: Coast To Coast*.
CAUSE: Heart attack. He died at his home in Ossining, New York.

Will Shatter

(RUSSELL WILKINSON)
Born June 10, 1956
Died December 15, 1987
The co-leader of the punk quartet

Flipper, Will Shatter teamed with Bruce Lose to provide a double-barrel bass and vocal attack. Formed in 1979 during the San Francisco punk exposure, Flipper emerged from the ashes of another punk group, Negative Trend. Signing with a new indie label, Subterranean Records, Flipper made waves with their début album *Generic Flipper*, which was highlighted by 'Life' and a new version of their previously released single, the bombastic 'Sex Bomb'. Preferring extended, repetitive mid-tempo songs, Flipper stood apart from their contemporaries such as The Dead Kennedys. Disbanding after Shatter's death, the remaining members of Flipper reunited in 1992 for the album *American Grafishy*.
CAUSE: He died from an accidental heroin overdose while enrolled in a detox programme. Also dying of heroin overdoses were Shatter's brief replacement, John Dougherty, and a bassist in an early version of the group, Ricky Williams.

Arnold Shaw

Born June 28, 1909
Died September 26, 1989
A pianist turned rock and R&B researcher, Arnold Shaw penned several pioneering historical works including *The Rockin' '50s*, *The World of Soul*, and *The Jazz Age: Popular Music In The Twenties*. But his most significant work was the groundbreaking tome, *Honkers And Shouters*, a study of the emergence of rock'n'roll. Shaw later founded the Popular Music Research Center at the University of Nevada where he taught pop music courses for ten years. Educated at Columbia University, Shaw began his professional career as a pianist and composer, before learning the music industry ropes in the Forties as the director of publicity and advertising at the Leed Music Corporation (now MCA).
CAUSE: Cancer. He died at his home in Las Vegas.
FURTHER READING: Shaw, Arnold. (1978). *Honkers And Shouters*. New York: Macmillan.

Greg Shaw

(GREGORY ALAN SHAW)
Born January 31, 1949
Died October 19, 2004
A renegade rock'n'roll entrepreneur, Greg Shaw was actively involved in various musical pursuits throughout his 40 year career. A native of San Francisco, Shaw became absorbed by San Francisco's Haight-Ashbury cultural revolution and, in 1966, launched the pioneering rock magazine *Mojo-Navigator Rock & Roll News*. Shaw befriended Jann Wenner who started his own publication, *Rolling Stone*, in November 1967. Ceasing publication of *Mojo-Navigator* due to time constraints, Shaw relocated to Los Angeles and started publishing an oldies fanzine *(Who Put The) Bomp* and began a long-term, A-to-Z project *The Encyclopedia Of British Rock*. Also working at United Artists Records, Shaw assumed a number of behind-the-scene duties as the Assistant Head of Creative Services, and was also appointed the editor of a music publication financed by UA, *Phonograph Record Magazine*. Leaving United Artists in 1974, Shaw became the manager of the rock'n'roll group The Flamin' Groovies. After releasing a single, 'You Tore Me Down', on his newly formed label Bomp Records, Shaw persuaded Seymour Stein to sign the group to Sire Records. Accompanying the band during their European tours in 1976, Shaw immersed himself in the burgeoning punk scene and became friends with numerous acts including The Sex Pistols. During this period, Shaw was hired by Sire to edit a number of rock books and he also wrote one of his own, an Elton John biography. After parting with The Flamin' Groovies at the end of 1976, Shaw spent the rest of the decade involved with punk rock but

failed in his attempt to convince Sire to sign The Sex Pistols. Eventually disillusioned by the commercialisation of punk, he closed *Bomp* magazine and focused on Sixties garage rock. From his massive record collection, Shaw began issuing the *Pebbles* compilation series of lost gems (he picked the name *Pebbles* as a nod to the earlier *Nuggets* series produced by Lenny Kaye). In the Eighties, Shaw operated the Cavern Club in Hollywood and produced material by a number of emerging garage-rock bands on his new Voxx label, including The Miracle Workers, The Pandoras, The Crawdaddys and The Fuzztones. Leaving Los Angeles for England, Shaw launched Ubik Records, which was torpedoed after the label distributing his releases went bankrupt. Returning to California, he revived Bomp Records and spent most of the Nineties reissuing the Bomp catalogue on compact disc.
CAUSE: Heart failure. In poor health for many years, in 1999 he underwent kidney transplant and pancreas surgery.

Bobby Sheehan

Born June 12, 1968
Died August 20, 1999
The bassist of the John Popper-led, blues-rock group Blues Traveler, Bobby Sheehan grew up a self-described "Deadhead", reared on the folksy blues-rock of The Grateful Dead. Blues Traveler was formed by four former high school friends in 1988 in Princeton, New Jersey, originally as The Blues Band. The last member to join the group, Sheehan was educated at the Berklee School of Music in Boston. Regulars on the New York City blues circuit, the quartet frequently shared bills with up-and-coming bands such as Phish and The Spin Doctors. Aided by fan and rock promoter Bill Graham, Blues Traveler landed key gigs and drew the attention of A&M Records. Becoming an overnight sensation after the release of their self-titled début album in 1990, Blues Traveler resorted to using fictional names in order to keep playing smaller venues in New York City. Ironically, the group was unable to get onto a national tour, and instead organised the H.O.R.D.E. (Horizons Of Rock Developing Everywhere) Festival in 1992. Evolving into a popular annual event, the multi-act H.O.R.D.E. Festival was embraced as an alternative to the more youth-oriented Lollapalooza. Remaining popular with fans, Blues Traveler won a Grammy in 1995 for the track 'Runaround', from their five-million-selling album *Four.* Moving to New Orleans in 1996 and building a home studio, Sheehan began working on a solo album.
CAUSE: Accidental drug overdose. He was found dead at his home in New Orleans, after ingesting a combination of heroin, Valium, and cocaine. His body was discovered by his friends, who initially attributed the death to sleep apnoea. Sheehan had pleaded guilty to drug possession in 1998, after being apprehended at Winnipeg airport with less than a gram of cocaine, and was sentenced to two years of unsupervised probation.

Sharon Sheeley

Born April 4, 1940
Died May 18, 2002
A talented songwriter, Sharon Sheeley will always be remembered as the fiancée of the late Eddie Cochran. Born in Los Angeles, Sheeley had her first success when Ricky Nelson scored a hit with her composition, 'Poor Little Fool' in 1958. Sheeley had been introduced to Eddie Cochran by her ex-boyfriend Don Everly and after writing 'Love Again', the B-side of Eddie Cochran's hit 'Summertime Blues', she began dating the rockabilly singer. Cochran also recorded the Sheeley composition, 'Cherished Memories', and a song she co-wrote with Cochran's older brother, Bob, the 1959 hit 'Somethin' Else'. Then in early 1960, Cochran and

another rockabilly singer, Gene Vincent, headed to the UK for a successful ten-week tour. A second ten-week leg was quickly scheduled but, homesick and invited by his record company to finish recording an album, Cochran wanted to return to the US for a two-week respite. Sheeley had flown to London a day or two earlier to celebrate her 20th birthday with Cochran. Shortly after midnight on April 17, 1960, en route from the Royal Hotel in Bristol to Heathrow Airport in London for a flight the next afternoon, tour manager Patrick Thompkins informed the driver, George Martin (*not* the future Beatles producer), that he was going in the wrong direction. While attempting to stop and turn around just outside Chippenham, Wiltshire, Martin lost control of the Ford Consul Saloon, blew a tyre and struck a solid lamp-post. While Sheeley suffered a broken pelvis, and Vincent multiple non-life threatening injuries, Cochran had taken the brunt of the crash as he attempted to shield Sheeley, and was thrown from the vehicle, striking his head on the ground; he passed away less than a day later. After returning to the US, Sheeley teamed with Jackie DeShannon for a series of songwriting collaborations: 'Dum Dum' (Brenda Lee), 'Heart In Hand' (Brenda Lee), '(He's) The Great Impostor' (The Fleetwoods), 'Trouble' (The Kalin Twins) and 'Breakaway' (Irma Thomas; Tracey Ullman). Sheeley later wed Jimmy O'Neill, host of the Sixties music programme *Shindig!*
CAUSE: She suffered a cerebral haemorrhage and died five days later at Sherman Oaks Hospital Medical Center. She was buried next to Eddie Cochran.

Bobby Sheen

(ROBERT JOSEPH SHEEN)
Born May 17, 1941
Died November 23, 2000
As the lead singer of early Sixties pop-rock group Bob B. Soxx & The Blue Jeans, Bobby Sheen was teamed by producer Phil Spector with former Blossoms alumni Darlene Love and Fanita James. The trio reached the Top 10 with an updated version of the Disney classic 'Zip-A-Dee Doo-Dah' in 1963 and followed up with 'Why Do Lovers Break Each Other's Heart?' Born in St. Louis but raised in Los Angeles, Sheen was discovered by Philles label co-owner Lester Sill. Sheen joined a revival version of The Coasters in the late Seventies.
CAUSE: Pneumonia. He died in Los Angeles.

Roscoe Shelton

Born August 22, 1931
Died July 27, 2002
A Southern soul singer, Tennessee-born Roscoe Shelton scored a pair of R&B chart hits with 'Strain On My Heart' (1965) and 'Easy Going Fellow' (1966). He was previously a member of several Nashville area gospel groups, including The Fireside Gospel Singers and The Fairfield Four.
CAUSE: Unknown. He died in Nashville.

Gerry Shephard

Born December 28, 1951
Died May 6, 2003
As a member of glam rocker Gary Glitter's stage group The Glitter Band, guitarist Gerry Shephard stood out playing his trademark star-shaped instrument. Formed in the wake of Glitter's breakthrough 1972 smash hit 'Rock And Roll Part 1', The Glitter Band appeared with their leader on tours and television appearances but never in the studio. In late 1973, Glitter and his musical partner Mike Leander decided to record separately The Glitter Band. Headed by baritone sax player John Rossall, The Glitter Band reached the UK Top 10 with their début single, a Rossall-Shephard composition 'Angel Face' (1974), and followed through with two more Top 10 entries that year, 'Just For You' and 'Let's Get Together Again'. Changing

gears, the group traded stompers for ballads in 'Goodbye My Love', 'The Tears I Cried', 'Love In The Sun' and 'People Like You, And People Like Me'. Although Glitter announced his retirement in 1976, The Glitter Band persevered and scored a club/dance hit that year with 'Makes You Blind'. Following the departure of Rossall, the group signed with CBS Records and changed its name to The G Band but after dropping the glam sound for hard rock, sales of the album *Paris Match* were disappointing. In 1978, Shephard and bandmate Pete Phipps teamed with former Sparks keyboardist Peter Oxendale under the moniker Shephard/Oxendal to record a poor-selling album. When Glitter decided to resurrect his career in 1980, The Glitter Band also re-formed; but eventually, the group split into two camps, with one line-up unsuccessfully suing its counterpart over control of the group name. Following Gary Glitter's much publicised sexual misdeeds, both versions of The Glitter Band found themselves shunned by British concert promoters. Falling ill, Shephard retired from music in 2002.
CAUSE: Cancer.

James "Shep" Sheppard

(JAMES SHANE SHEPPARD)
Born September 24, 1935
Died January 24, 1970
The leader of a pair of Fifties doo-wop vocal groups, The Heartbeats and Shep & The Limelites, James "Shep" Sheppard grew up in Queens, New York, where he attended The Food & Maritime Trades Vocational High School. Leaving a mediocre vocal group in late 1954 for a more polished outfit called The Hearts, Sheppard emerged as the group's lead tenor and chief songwriter. Renamed The Heartbeats, the heavily rehearsed quintet signed with Network, and then, Hull Records, releasing a number of poor selling but exquisite singles including 'Darling How Long', and 'Your Way'. Embracing elements of rock in their tight, ballad-rooted vocal harmony, The Heartbeats managed a sole hit with a B-side entry, the melancholy 'A Thousand Miles Away'. Written by Sheppard about the loss of a girlfriend, the rising single was sold by Hull to the larger Gee/Rama label. With the exception of another ballad, 'Everybody's Somebody's Fool' (1957), The Heartbeats would arouse little interest. Alienating his bandmates with his oversized ego, Sheppard was eventually abandoned by The Heartbeats in 1959. After briefly attempting a solo career as a nightclub singer, Sheppard formed an R&B trio called Shep & The Limelites with Clarence Bassett and Charles Baskerville. Returning to Hull Records, Sheppard and the group released an answer song to The Heartbeats' 'A Thousand Miles Away' called 'Daddy's Home' (1961). After scoring a final hit in 1962 with 'Our Anniversary', the group disbanded in 1966, only to reform three years later to work the oldies circuit. Returning to the charts on three occasions, 'Daddy's Home' was reprised by Jermaine Jackson, Cliff Richard, and Color Me Badd.
CAUSE: Sheppard was found stabbed and beaten to death in his car on the Long Island Expressway in New York City. Penniless and in debt at the time of his death, he was probably murdered by loan sharks.

Sherrick

(LAMOTTE SMITH)
Born July 6, 1957
Died January 22, 1999
An R&B multi-instrumentalist, Sherrick scored his only hit with 'Just Call' (1987). Based in Los Angeles and previously a member of the Motown act Kagny, Sherrick was given his stage name by Raynoma Gordy, the former wife of Berry Gordy, Jr.
CAUSE: Unknown. He died in Los Angeles.

Johnny Shines

(JOHN NED SHINES)
Born April 26, 1915
Died April 20, 1992
Legendary Tennessee-born blues guitarist who frequently teamed with Robert Johnson in the mid Thirties, Johnny Shines helped define modern blues. Settling in Chicago in 1941, Shines worked with the city's leading bluesmen including Muddy Waters and Big Bill Broonzy. After leaving music in the late Fifties, Shines was rediscovered during the blues boom of the late Sixties. Later settling in Tuscaloosa, Alabama, he became a fixture in the city's blues scene. Shines was nominated for a Grammy in 1980 for the album *Hangin' On*, which he recorded with Robert Jr. Lockwood.
CAUSE: Suffering a stroke in 1980, his health had deteriorated.

Charlie Shivers

(WESLEY CLARENCE SHIVERS)
Born 1934
Died April 7, 1961
A legendary figure in rockabilly who turned down numerous recording contracts, Charlie Shivers preferred to record at his home studio in Kentucky. The son of a US diplomat, Shivers forsook a professional music career for a position in his family's engineering firm in Panama. At his home studio, Shivers recorded tracks with Elvis Presley, Hank Williams, and Johnny Burnette.
CAUSE: He died in a methane gas explosion at his home near Scottsville, Kentucky. A subsequent fire also destroyed his many unreleased master tapes.

Dave Shogren

(DAVID P. SHOGREN)
Born October 10, 1950
Died December 14, 1999
A founding member of The Doobie Brothers, San Francisco-native Dave Shogren played the bass and keyboards, and provided backing vocals on the group's first album. Formed as a biker band called Pud in 1970 by Shogren, Tom Johnston and John Hartman, The Doobie Brothers recorded a number of demos under the guidance of Moby Grape member Skip Spence. Signed to Warner Brothers by producer/A&R man Ted Templeman, the Doobies fared poorly with their predominantly acoustic, self-titled début album. Leaving the group in 1971, Shogren operated a recording studio for many years. In the mid Nineties, he teamed with Brad Feager to form Parrot Audio Books, publishing 12 cassette books in all, including biographies of John Denver and Burt Reynolds. In 1996, Shogren teamed with two other short-term Doobie Brother members, Chet McCracken and Cornelius Bumpus, to record a dubious album of new versions of the group's hits. When the trio began touring as The Original Doobie Brothers, they were met with a lawsuit. The group was forced by the court to change their name to SMB Former Doobie Brothers Performing the Hits of The Doobie Brothers.
CAUSE: Contracting pneumonia, he died in his sleep at his home in San Diego, California.

Mort Shuman

Born January 12, 1938
Died November 3, 1991
A prolific songwriter, who along with Doc Pomus wrote scores of early rock hits, Mort Shuman was a native of Brighton Beach, New York, where as a teen he mastered both the piano and guitar. He developed an interest in writing music while attending college. Offered an apprenticeship position under songwriter Doc Pomus in 1956, Shuman initially contributed little to Pomus' compositions. Moving into the famous Brill Building in New York City in 1959, the pair were hired by the Hill and Range Publishing Company. Falling into a pattern, Shuman wrote most of the music while Pomus penned the lyrics. Shuman would often add Mexican and Caribbean metres and

rhythms to make Pomus' R&B-flavoured compositions more commercial. Enjoying several successes in 1959, Pomus and Shuman wrote Dion & The Belmonts' 'Teenager In Love' and provided teen idol Fabian with three hits, 'I'm A Man', 'Hound Dog Man' and 'Turn Me Loose' (a song written with Elvis Presley in mind). Other Pomus and Shuman hit compositions included 'This Magic Moment' (The Drifters; Jay & The Americans), 'Hushabye' (The Mystics), 'Suspicion' (Terry Stafford), 'Sweets For My Sweet' (The Drifters; The Searchers), and 'Save The Last Dance For Me' (The Drifters). They wrote a number of songs for Elvis Presley after his discharge from the service, including 'A Mess O' Blues', '(Marie's The Name) His Latest Flame', 'Kiss Me Quick', 'Surrender', 'Viva Las Vegas' and 'Little Sister'. Strangely, Shuman would never meet Presley. Apart from Pomus, Shuman wrote or co-wrote 'Little Children' (Billy J. Kramer & The Dakotas), 'Love's Just A Broken Heart' (Cilla Black); and 'Sha La La La Lee' (The Small Faces). After writing hundreds of songs together, in 1965 Shuman left Pomus and moved to Paris, angry over US policies toward Vietnam. While living in France, Shuman wrote a number of French hit compositions, released several successful solo albums, and produced the musical, *Jacques Brel Is Alive And Well And Living In Paris*. Settling in London in 1986, he produced another musical, *Save The Last Dance For Me*. In the Eighties, Shuman recorded his own version of 'Save The Last Dance For Me'.
CAUSE: Suffering a liver ailment, he had undergone a transplant several months before his death. He died in London.

Lester Sill

Born January 13, 1918
Died October 31, 1994
A music industry legend, Lester Sill began as a nightclub owner in 1945. After taking a job as a record salesman for the Los Angeles-based R&B label Modern Records in the late Forties, he moved to the recording side of the label, producing Charles Brown and Hadda Brooks. Teaming with songwriters Jerry Leiber and Mike Stoller to launch Spark Records in 1953, Sill enjoyed a number of pioneering West Coast R&B hits with The Robins. Turning to artist management in the late Fifties, Sill oversaw the career of guitarist Duane Eddy. Then in 1961, Sill co-founded Philles Records with Phil Spector, making stars out of The Crystals, The Ronettes and other girl groups. Spector eventually bought out Sill's share in the company. Sill spent the next two decades working at Screen Gems Music.
CAUSE: He died from an undisclosed, long-term illness at Cedars-Sinai Medical Center in Los Angeles.

Jimmy Silva

Born May 31, 1952
Died December 23, 1994
A recording artist and songwriter whose compositions were recorded by The Smithereens and The Young Fresh Fellows, Jimmy Silva had previously been a member of the late Sixties group, The Empty Set, which released two albums for Poplama Records. He later formed Jimmy Silva and The Goats.
CAUSE: Complications from chicken pox.

Al Silver

Born January 9, 1914
Died March 4, 1992
The founder of the pioneering New York City-based rock and R&B record companies, Herald and Ember, Al Silver signed acts such as The Mellow Kings, The Turbans, The Silhouettes, Faye Adams, The Five Willows, and The Five Satins. Silver later worked with music mogul Morris Levy at

Roulette Records. Retiring in 1975, Silver moved to Florida and opened a record store.
CAUSE: Unknown. He died in Ft. Lauderdale, Florida.

"Waxie Maxie" Silverman

(MAXWELL SILVERMAN)
Born May 25, 1910
Died August 29, 1989
The founder of a legendary Washington DC record store chain, "Waxie Maxie" Silverman worked as a talent scout at Atlantic Records in its early days, and promoted the careers of acts such as LaVern Baker, The Clovers, and The Orioles. A native of New York City, he founded his first store in Washington DC in 1937, and it became a mecca for jazz and blues enthusiasts. The 33-store chain was sold shortly after Silverman's death for $11.75 million.
CAUSE: Heart failure. He died at the Washington Hospital Center.

Shel Silverstein

(SHELDON SILVERSTEIN)
Born September 25, 1930
Died May 10, 1999
A prolific songwriter and award-winning children's author, Chicago-native Shel Silverstein broke into the entertainment industry as a cartoonist and writer for *Playboy* magazine upon its inception in 1953. After a stint in the Korean War, Silverstein returned to Chicago where, frequenting the Gates of Horn folk/blues club, he was commissioned as a lyricist by singer-songwriter Bob Gibson. Quickly turning to popular music, Silverstein penned hundreds of songs including, 'The Unicorn' (The Irish Rovers), and a pair of Dr. Hook & The Medicine Show hits, 'Sylvia's Mother' and 'The Cover Of The "Rolling Stone"'. As a country lyricist, he composed 'A Boy Named Sue' (Johnny Cash) and 'One's On The Way' (Loretta Lynn). Attempting a solo career, Silverstein recorded over a dozen, mostly comedy, albums beginning with *Hairy Jazz* (1959) and also wrote several film scores including *Ned Kelly* and *Postcards From The Edge*, the latter earning an Academy Award nomination for the track, 'I'm Checkin' Out'.
CAUSE: Suffering from long-term coronary disease, his dead body was found by a maid in the bedroom of his home in Key West, Florida.

John Simmons

Born 1949
Died March 16, 1990
A member of the Seventies soul group The Reflections, the New York City-born John Simmons provided the lead vocals on several R&B hits beginning with 'Three Steps From True Love' (1975). In the mid Eighties, he worked as a pianist and arranger for Stephanie Mills and Whitney Houston.
CAUSE: Respiratory illness. He died in East Orange, New Jersey.

Nina Simone

(EUNICE KATHLEEN WAYMON)
Born February 21, 1933
Died April 21, 2003
Nicknamed the High Priestess of Soul, Nina Simone is best known for her politically charged material of the Sixties. The daughter of weekend preachers, Simone learned to play the piano at age three. A gifted child, she excelled both academically and musically, playing the organ in her parents' church. Briefly attending the prestigious Juilliard School of Music, she abandoned her goal of becoming a classical musician after she was unable to pay her tuition fees. After landing a nightclub gig in 1954, she changed her name to Nina Simone, so as not to shame her religious parents. Discovered by label owner Sid Nathan, Simone scored her breakthrough single in 1959 with a George Gershwin composition from *Porgy And Bess*, 'I Loves You, Porgy'. With a wide repertoire that

included jazz, soul, blues and gospel, Simone became popular on both sides of the Atlantic with hits including the standard 'Nobody Knows You When You're Down And Out' (1960), 'Trouble In Mind' (1961), 'Don't Let Me Be Misunderstood' (1964 – a bigger pop hit when rearranged by UK group The Animals much to Ms. Simone's ire!), a cover of Screamin' Jay Hawkins' 'I Put A Spell On You' (1965), a double-sided UK chart entry 'Ain't Got No One – I Got No Life'/'Do What You Gotta Do' (1968) and a cover of The Bee Gees' 'To Love Somebody' (1969). Simone became active in the civil rights movement, recording influential anthems such as 'Four Women' and the often recorded song which she co-wrote with Weldon Irvine, Jr., 'To Be Young, Gifted And Black'. With her personal life and career in tatters, Simone left the US in 1971. Upon her return in 1978, she was charged with tax evasion. Continuing to record on a series of labels over the next two decades, she settled in France in 1993. Simone's music received a new lease of life when 'My Baby Just Cares For Me' and 'Feeling Good' were used in television commercials in the UK – the former becoming a surprise Top Five UK hit in 1987. Though seriously ill, she continued to perform until several months before her death. In 2006, Mary J. Blige portrayed Nina Simone in an MTV-produced biopic.
CAUSE: She passed away from undisclosed causes at her home in Carry Le Rouet, near Marseille, France.

Will Sin

(WILLIAM SINNOTT)
Born December 23, 1960
Died May 23, 1991
A member of the Scottish techno-pop, rave favourites The Shamen, Will Sin joined the group in 1988. Formed in Scotland in 1986 by Colin Angus, The Shamen were transformed into a synthesizer band with the addition of the technologically proficient Sin. Sin and Angus had previously worked together as psychiatric nurses. Leaving Scotland for London in late 1988, Sin and Angus embraced the emerging rave scene. Launching their own multi-media, caravan rave tour which was dubbed Synergy, The Shamen were joined by a host of like-minded groups and DJs for a two-year trek across Britain. An underground favourite, the group's third album, *Entact*, sold 100,000 copies in Britain. At the time of Sin's death, the group was targeting the pop charts with 'Move Any Mountain – Progen 91' (1991), the song a reworked version of their two-year-old release, 'Progren'.
CAUSE: He accidentally drowned off the Canary Islands during a video shoot for the group's forthcoming single, 'Move Any Mountain – Progen 91'. He was pulled under by a strong current while swimming off the coast of the isle of Gomera.

Frank Sinatra

(FRANCIS ALBERT SINATRA)
Born December 12, 1915
Died May 14, 1998
One of the century's most dynamic and resilient entertainers, Frank Sinatra emerged out of the crooner tradition to become a legendary figure in the US entertainment worlds. A charismatic and golden-voiced singer, Sinatra laid the groundwork for the rock star of the Fifties with his teen-idol status among legions of World War II-era bobbysoxers. Inspired to pursue a career in music after attending a Bing Crosby concert in 1936, Sinatra initially formed a vocal group called The Hoboken Four. While working as a singing waiter in Teaneck, New Jersey, Sinatra was discovered by Harry James, and hired as a featured soloist in his big band. He then landed a prized spot as a vocalist in The Tommy Dorsey Orchestra, and soon emerged as a national star. After overshadowing

the visibly annoyed Dorsey at a residency at New York's Paramount Theater in 1942, Sinatra left his orchestra to pursue a solo career. Inspiring mob scenes in front of theatres, Sinatra performed to an onslaught of screaming young women. Signing with Columbia Records, Sinatra dominated the charts well into the rise of the rock era. Among his hits during this period were 'Dream', 'Nancy (With The Laughing Face)', 'The Coffee Song', 'The Things We Did Last Summer', 'Full Moon' and 'Empty Arms'. In 1953, Sinatra signed to Capitol Records and worked with arranger Nelson Riddle on standards such as 'Young At Heart' and 'Come Fly With Me', both notable for his command of phrasing. He also recorded several successful 10-inch albums, including 1954's *Songs For Young Lovers*. His swaggering confidence and seemingly effortless ability to phrase lyrics were evident on standards such as 'Young At Heart' and 'Come Fly With Me'. Also a *bona fide* film actor, Sinatra solidified his fame in *From Here To Eternity*, for which he would earn an Oscar nomination. Known for his cavalier lifestyle, Sinatra was a member of a closeknit group of hard drinking intimates known as the Hollywood Rat Pack. Their members also included comedian Joey Bishop, actor and Kennedy associate Peter Lawford, and singers Sammy Davis Jr, and Dean Martin. Nicknamed "Old Blue Eyes" and "The Chairman Of The Board", Sinatra was an enduring figure in the music world whose alleged friendship with Mafia figures was well known. In 1956, Sinatra recorded his classic *Songs For Swinging Lovers*, which included a sumptuous reading of Cole Porter's 'I've Got You Under My Skin'. The album would later feature in all-time great album polls, more than 40 years after its original release. During 1957, Sinatra won an Oscar for his reading of the ballad, 'All The Way'. His career temporarily stalled by the rise of rock in the late Fifties, Sinatra viciously attacked the new music and was particularly scathing about Elvis Presley. The hatchet was buried shortly after Presley left the US Army in 1960 and appeared alongside Sinatra in a TV special, the senior man evidently recognising that it was in his interests to embrace rather than reject the emerging culture changes. With Dave Cavanaugh installed as producer, Sinatra completed *Only The Lonely* (1958) and the best-selling *Come Dance With Me, Come Fly With Me* (1959), the latter highlighted by 'April In Paris'. Dropped by Capitol Records, he launched Reprise Records in 1962 and entered a renewed period of popularity. By 1963, Sinatra had sold a majority shareholding in Reprise to Warner Brothers and the label continued to enjoy success thereafter. Meanwhile, Sinatra's recordings betrayed a stronger jazz feel, reinforced by the presence of arrangers Count Basie and Quincy Jones. During this period, Sinatra also worked with Ella Fitzgerald, Duke Ellington and Antonio Carlos Jobim. After enjoying success recording standards like 'It Was A Very Good Year', Sinatra unexpectedly hit the top of the charts in 1966 with 'Strangers In The Night', which even managed to hold off The Beatles' 'Paperback Writer' from entering the charts at number one. A follow-up, 'That's Life', was another standard that featured frequently in his repertoire. By this point, Sinatra's daughter Nancy was enjoying solo success in her own right, so the two united for the duet 'Something Stupid', which topped the charts on both sides of the Atlantic. By the end of the Sixties, Sinatra was still a formidable figure in the music marketplace and released the definitive version of 'My Way' (whose English lyrics were provided by Paul Anka). The song became Sinatra's signature tune and broke chart records in the UK by

remaining in the listings for a staggering 124 weeks, a feat that has yet to be matched. Briefly retiring in 1971, he re-emerged two years later as a Las Vegas favourite. Returning to the charts in 1982, Sinatra scored a hit with the bombastic, 'Theme From New York, New York'. Its sequel, 'L.A. Is My Lady', did not fare as well (an MTV video for the single featured members of Van Halen). Sinatra made many comebacks in his declining years, touring with Liza Minelli and Sammy Davis Jr. An American institution, Sinatra continued to record until shortly before his death, his final album coming with *Duets II*, on which he sang with several rock stars.
CAUSE: After years of poor health, he died in the emergency room of Cedars-Sinai Medical Center in Los Angeles.
FURTHER READING: Freedland, Michael. (1998). *All The Way: A Biography Of Frank Sinatra*. London: Orion. Kelley, Kitty. (1986). *His Way: The Unauthorised Biography Of Frank Sinatra*. New York: Bantam.

Kenny Sinclair

(KENNETH FRANCIS SINCLAIR, JR.)
Born August 4, 1939
Died March 16, 2003
A member of Los Angeles-based doo-wop group The Six Teens, tenor Kenny Sinclair sang behind lead vocalist Trudy Williams on the 1956 hit 'A Casual Look'. Sinclair left the group in 1957 and was replaced by Richard Owens. Still at high school, Sinclair joined a series of similar groups. By 1959, Sinclair and former Six Teens bandmate Darryl Lewis co-founded The Elements and recorded a single on the Titan label. Evolving into The Elgins (not the Detroit group of the same name) the group recorded several singles before emerging as The Bagdads in the late Sixties. For a time, Sinclair was a member of a revival version of The Olympics.
CAUSE: Prostate cancer. He died in Rialto, California.

The Singing Nun (Sister Luc-Gabrielle)

(JEANINE DECKERS)
Born October 17, 1933
Died April 1, 1985
Nicknamed The Singing Nun, Sister Luc-Gabrielle scored an unlikely hit in 1963 with 'Dominique'. Approaching the Belgium offices of Philips Records, she wanted to record an album as a gift for friends and students at the Fichermont Monastery. Impressed by the sessions, Philips initially pressed an additional 1,000 copies of the album for general sale. A strong seller across Europe, the album was subsequently released in the US as by The Singing Nun. The album was ignored until music publisher Paul Kapp released one of the tracks as a single. A surprise smash, 'Dominique' topped the charts for over two months and landed Sister Luc-Gabrielle on *The Ed Sullivan Show*. All of the profits from her recordings were spent on missionary projects. Leaving the Dominican order in 1966 and taking her given name, Jeanine Deckers, she continued her charity work with the Catholic Church.
CAUSE: She died in a suicide pact with a female companion, Annie Pescher, in Wavre, Belgium. Despondent that their funding had dried up, the two women overdosed on barbiturates and alcohol.

Freddie Slack

(FREDERIC CHARLES SLACK)
Born August 7, 1910
Died August 10, 1965
A popular bandleader in the Forties, the classically trained Freddie Slack mixed boogie-woogie and jazz styles and was an integral cog in the development of jump-blues and R&B. A lively pianist, Slack had previously worked in the big bands of Ben Pollack and Jimmy Dorsey. Joining Bill Bradley's band in 1939, he took the

outfit in a boogie-woogie direction. Leaving to front his own West Coast group in 1941, Slack scored his first major hit with the early crossover entry, 'Cow Cow Boogie', with the vocal by his combo's attractive singer, Ella Mae Morse. One of the first acts signed to the fledgling Capitol Records, Slack hired the then-unknown Texas blues guitarist T-Bone Walker, recording proto-R&B styled hits with 'Mr. Five By Five' (1942) and featuring a revolutionary single-string guitar solo, 'Riffette' (1942). Slack's other hits included 'Strange Cargo' and in a reunion with Morse, the boogie-woogie styled 'House Of Blue Lights' (1946). Abandoning his orchestra for a combo in the early Fifties, Slack was relegated to smaller venues.
CAUSE: He died under mysterious circumstances in his Hollywood, California, apartment.

Chuck Slater

Born c. 1950
Died c. 1985
As the drummer of Toronto-based pop act Ocean, Chuck Slater had a hit with the gospel-tinged 'Put Your Hand In The Hand' (1971). After scoring a Canadian-only hit with 'I've Got A Dream', Ocean disbanded in 1975.
CAUSE: Suicide.

Hillel Slovak

Born April 13, 1962
Died June 27, 1988
The original guitarist with the funk rock band The Red Hot Chili Peppers, Isreali-born Hillel Slovak relocated to the Los Angeles area with his family when he was five. A huge Kiss fan, Slovak teamed with future RHCP drummer Jack Irons to form a band while in junior high school. While attending Fairfax High School, Irons and Slovak joined Michael Balzary (a.k.a. Flea) and vocalist Anthony Kiedis to form Anthem School, a hard rock outfit that played Kiss and Led Zeppelin covers. After graduating, Slovak teamed with Irons to form a new wave group called What Is This, and for a time joined Balzary in a latter line-up of the James Chance-led punk rock group, The Contortions. Meanwhile, Anthony Kiedis had dropped out of college in 1983 to join Michael Balzary in forming a new band; adding their old friends, Slovak and Irons, the group jelled into The Red Hot Chili Peppers. Often performing naked, with white tube socks covering their genitalia, the group quickly built a local following. Following an impromptu gig at a Los Angeles dance club, the group signed with EMI Records. Produced by Gang Of Four's Andy Gill, The RHCP's début album, *The Red Hot Chili Peppers* (1984), was poorly received, largely because the group were unable to recreate its powerful live performances in the studio. Busy moonlighting with Irons in another group, What Is This?, Slovak wrote tracks for a Chili Peppers' psychedelic-styled dance project but did not perform on the sessions. Taking a light-hearted turn with the George Clinton-produced follow-up, *Freaky Styley* (1985), the group enjoyed some airplay with 'Jungle Man'. With the release of their third album, *Uplift Mojo Party Plan* in 1987, The Chili Peppers finally succeeded in capturing the energy of their live performances on record. With drug use intensifying within the band, drummer Jack Irons left and later joined Pearl Jam.
CAUSE: Abusing heroin for several years, Slovak overdosed while enrolled in a detox programme. His body was found two days later in his apartment in Hollywood. A coroner's report was inconclusive. As a result of Slovak's death, bandmate Anthony Kiedis kicked his heroin habit.
FURTHER READING: Thompson, Dave. (1993). *Red Hot Chili Peppers*. New York: St. Martin's.

Al Smith

(ALBERT B. SMITH)
Born November 23, 1923
Died February 7, 1974
A Chicago-based blues and R&B producer, bandleader and bassist at Vee-Jay Records, Al Smith worked with Buddy Guy, John Lee Hooker, and others.
CAUSE: He suffered a heart attack, his heart weakened by years of diabetes.

Bessie Smith

Born April 15, 1894
Died September 26, 1937
A classic blues singer, Bessie Smith was nicknamed "The Empress Of The Blues". Trained in the vaudeville tradition, Smith delivered a more refined style of blues than her contemporaries. Orphaned in the slums of Chattanooga, Tennessee, Smith survived by performing on street corners. Hitting the stage in 1912, initially as a dancer, she joined The Rabbit Foot Minstrels touring revue, apprenticing under Ma Rainey. After honing her act at a residency at Charles Bailey's 81 Theater in Atlanta, Smith was leading her own troupe by 1920. Signing with Columbia Records in 1923 to the label's new black division, Smith was backed by pianist Clarence Williams on her début release, a hit cover of Alberta Hunter's 'Down Hearted Blues'. Following with the self-penned million-seller, 'Tain't Nobody's Bizzness If I Do', Smith recorded a string of strong sellers including 'Careless Love Blues' and 'A Good Man Is Hard To Find', and bawdy numbers with *double entendre* lyrics such as 'Empty Bed Blues' and 'Need A Little Sugar In My Bowl'. Appearing on stage in a full regalia of long gowns, drapes of beads, and feather hats, the confident and commanding singer did not actively pursue a crossover audience, and preferred to perform in black-oriented venues and Southern tent shows. Smith made her only film appearance as she sang the title track in the low-budget film, *St. Louis Blues* (1929). With old-style country blues falling out of popularity, Smith's 1929 recording of 'Nobody Knows You When You're Down And Out' predicted her own downfall. Relegated to smaller gin-joints, she was lured back into a recording studio by jazz producer John Hammond. Smith was buried in an unmarked grave, but Janis Joplin paid half the costs to erect a marker in 1970.
CAUSE: She suffered mortal injuries when her wooden-framed Packard automobile struck a truck near Clarksdale, Mississippi. A passing white doctor arrived at the scene two minutes after the crash but was unable to save Smith. *Downbeat* magazine later propagated a myth that Smith died after being refused treatment by a white-only hospital.
FURTHER READING: Oliver, Paul. (1959). *Bessie Smith*. London: Cassell.

Clarence "Pine Top" Smith

Born June 11, 1904
Died March 15, 1929
A groundbreaking performer, Clarence "Pine Top" Smith launched the boogie-woogie piano craze of the Thirties with his 1928 recording of 'Pine Top's Boogie Woogie'. He died before reaping fame.
CAUSE: He was shot and killed in a Chicago nightclub by a stray bullet shot by a food vendor who was trying to break up a fight. Smith was dancing with a woman at the time, and was not playing piano as is commonly reported. Shot in the chest, Smith was taken to Henrotin Hospital where he died the following day.

Elliott Smith

(STEVEN PAUL SMITH)
Born August 6, 1969
Died October 21, 2003
An introspective and moody singer-songwriter, Elliott Smith was on

the verge of a commercial breakthrough at the time of his death. Born in Omaha, Nebraska, Smith was raised in Dallas before relocating to Portland, Oregon, at age 14. After earning a college degree in philosophy and legal theory, he returned to Portland and launched a punk band, Heatmiser. As a side project, Smith released a series of moody, low-key albums, and garnered national attention when Portland-based film director Gus Van Sant used several of Smith's songs, including the Oscar-nominated 'Miss Misery', for the soundtrack of the 1997 film, *Good Will Hunting*. After signing with Dreamworks Records, Smith failed to find mainstream success with *XO* and *Figure 8*. At the time of his death Smith had nearly completed the tracks for another album, *From A Basement*, which was posthumously released in 2004.
CAUSE: Although police called the death a suicide, a coroner's report concluded that Smith died from two stab wounds to the chest, which could have been inflicted by his own hand or by somebody else. He died in Los Angeles.

Frank Smith

(JOHN F. SMITH)
Born May 17, 1939
Died November 26, 2000
As one of two bass singers in The Monotones, Frank Smith scored a doo-wop hit in 1958 with 'Book Of Love'. Formed in a Newark, New Jersey housing project in 1955, the group attracted attention after appearing on *Ted Mack's Amateur Hour* the following year. Smith toured with a revived version of the group, beginning in the Seventies.
CAUSE: Lung cancer. He died in Newark, New Jersey.

Frank Esler-Smith

Born June 5, 1948
Died March 1, 1991
The London-born keyboard player and songwriter for the soft-rock group Air Supply, Frank Esler-Smith previously worked in the mid Seventies as the music director for the Australian stage production of *Jesus Christ Superstar*. Future Air Supply bandmate Russell Hitchcock starred in the production. By 1976, the pair decided to form a singing duo. With that outfit disbanding, Russell formed Air Supply later in the year. After signing with Arista Records in 1979, the Melbourne-based Air Supply was expanded by the addition of several members including the thin and bearded Esler-Smith. Headed by Russell Hitchcock and Graham Russell on lead vocals, Air Supply enjoyed a strong run of mostly ballad hits, beginning with 'Lost In Love' (1979) and continuing with 'All Out Of Love' (1980), 'Every Woman In The World' (1980), 'The One That You Love' (1981), 'Here I Am' (1981), 'Sweet Dreams' (1982), 'Even The Nights Are Better' (1982), and the uncharacteristically dramatic 'Making Love Out Of Nothing At All' (1983). A minor Air Supply hit 'Power Of Love' (1985) was later a bigger success for both Jennifer Rush and Laura Branigan. With the group's success waning, Air Supply disbanded in 1988.
CAUSE: Pneumonia. He died in Melbourne, Australia.

Fred "Sonic" Smith

Born September 13, 1949
Died December 4, 1994
The co-lead guitarist of the free form radical rock band MC5, Fred "Sonic" Smith shared guitar duties with Wayne Kramer. A native of West Virginia, Smith was raised in the Detroit area. Expelled from school at 15, the rebellious Smith teamed with Kramer to form The Bounty Hunters. Evolving into MC5 (short for Motor City 5), the group added bassist-turned-lead vocalist Rob Tyner. Earning a strong following in the Detroit and Ann Arbor areas, the rowdy, hard drinking group was

banned from many larger clubs. One of two early singles, 'Looking At You', was a minor local hit. Managed by noted underground entrepreneur John Sinclair, MC5 became the house band for the radical White Panther Party, and increasingly infused anti-government themes into their lyrics and performances, which often included destroying a US flag. The group subsequently garnered much press for their appearance at the 1968 Democratic national convention in Chicago. Catching the attention of Elektra Records, MC5 released their landmark début, *Kick Out The Jams*, which is often cited as the first punk rock album. The group were obliged to re-write the lyrics to the album's title track in order to placate record stores and radio stations. Splitting from Sinclair shortly before he was imprisoned for marijuana possession, MC5 had tired of defending his White Panther political dogma. Dropped by Elektra and signed to Atlantic, MC5 released the Jon Landau-produced album, *Back In The USA* (1970). Hailed by critics but ignored by consumers, the album was uncharacteristically apolitical with youth-celebrating tracks such as 'High School' and 'Teenage Lust'. Atlantic quietly released a third album, *High Time*, (half the tracks penned by Smith), and MC5 disbanded in 1972 shortly after completing a European tour. Smith and a pair of MC5 members subsequently formed Ascension, the group lasting six months. Smith later joined The Scott Morgan Group, which also featured MC5 bassist Michael Davis and included former members of The Stooges and other Detroit punk bands. The group evolved into The Sonic Rendezvous Band in 1979–80. After marrying punk singer/poet Patti Smith in 1980, Smith left music to start a family. In 1988, Smith produced, played on, and co-wrote many of the tracks of his wife's comeback album, *Dream Of Life*. After the death of MC5 member Rob Tyner in 1991, Smith joined his former MC5 bandmates in 1991 for a reunion concert. At the time of his death, Smith was producing his wife's next album and was assembling a Sonics Rendezvous compilation album.
CAUSE: Heart failure. He died at St. John's Hospital in Detroit.

George "Smitty" Smith

Born November 16, 1943
Died December 1970
The original lead singer of The Manhattans, George "Smitty" Smith passed away before the group crossed over into the pop market in the Seventies. Formed in New York City from the ashes of a group called The Statesmen (not the popular R&B group), the group was initially known as The Dulcets. After releasing an obscure single in 1961, the group evolved into The Manhattans the following year. Briefly recording for the Bobby Robinson-owned Enjoy Records as Ronnie & The Manhattans, the group spent several years at Carnival Records, signed after a losing performance at an Apollo Nightclub amateur competition. At Carnival Records, The Manhattans recorded several R&B hits with Smith at the helm including, 'I Wanna Be (Your Everything)' (1965), 'Follow Your Heart' (1965), and 'I Call It Love' (1967). Signing with the King subsidiary, Deluxe Records, the group continued its run of moderate R&B hits.
CAUSE: Spinal meningitis.

Jerome Smith

Born June 18, 1953
Died July 28, 2000
A rhythm guitarist for the Seventies ensemble KC & The Sunshine Band, Jerome Smith played on a series of upbeat disco hits. Co-founding the group in 1973 along with lead singer Harry Casey and several others, Smith was previously a session player best known for providing the riff on the

George McRae hit 'Rock Your Baby'. The Sunshine Band was assembled at the Miami-area T.K. Studios originally as The Sunshine Junkanoo Band and their début single, 'Blow Your Whistle', appeared on the R&B charts. After scoring a pair of UK pop hits in 1974 with 'Queen Of Clubs' and 'Sound Your Funky Horn', the group began its chart domination on both sides of the Atlantic with hook-filled hits such as 'Get Down Tonight', 'That's The Way (I Like It)', '(Shake, Shake, Shake) Your Booty' and 'Keep It Comin' Love'. Battling drug addiction, Smith left the group in 1979. Smith also worked with controversial R&B singer Blowfly and joined a touring version of Australian band The Divinyls.
CAUSE: While working at a construction site in West Palm Beach, Florida, he fell from the bulldozer he was operating and was crushed by the machine.

Mamie Smith

Born May 26, 1883
Died August 16, 1946
A little-known vaudeville singer, Mamie Smith made history in 1920 when she recorded the first blues record, 'Crazy Blues'. Released by the OKeh Record Company, the 78 r.p.m. single sold several hundred thousand copies and established blues as a viable commercial format, with records purchased by blacks and whites alike. Backed by The Jazz Hounds, Smith continued to record until 1931, releasing 31 discs in all. Born in Cincinnati, she had left home at age 10 to become a dancer in a white touring revue.
CAUSE: Unknown. She died at Harlem Hospital in New York City.

Marshall Smith

(MARSHALL O'NEAL SMITH)
Born June 27, 1949
Died October 14, 2005
A member of Southern boogie-rock band Wet Willie in the late Seventies, Marshall O'Neal Smith appeared on two albums. After a stint in college, Smith was drafted into the army and worked in a military band while based in South Korea. Returning to his native Alabama, he spent several years in a touring soul group called Piranha. In 1977, Smith joined a revised line-up of Wet Willie, first appearing on the album *Manorisms*, which featured the Smith co-penned hit 'Street Corner Serenade'. The follow-up, *Which One's Willie?*, spawned the disco-flavoured hit 'Weekend'. After the group disbanded in 1980, Smith moved to Atlanta but later returned to work with a series of groups in Mobile, Alabama.
CAUSE: Unknown.

Mike "Smitty" Smith

Born March 27, 1941
Died March 6, 2001
A member of Paul Revere & The Raiders during its peak period, drummer Mike "Smitty" Smith appeared on most of their Sixties hits. Costumed in colourful 18th century American Independence military garb, the high-energy American group adopted a British Invasion-styled sound. Originally a guitarist, Smith had previously joined a pair of friends during the late Fifties in operating a teen music club, The Headless Horseman. As a member of the club's house band, Smith had the opportunity to hone his musical skills. Meanwhile, fellow Portland musicians Mark Lindsay and Paul Revere scored a national hit in 1961 with 'Like Long Hair', and after completing their military obligations in 1962, Lindsay and Revere re-formed Paul Revere & The Raiders, hiring Smith who was forced to switch from the guitar to drums. As the house band for Dick Clark's daily music television programme *Where The Action Is* starting in 1965, Paul Revere & The Raiders emerged as stars in their own right. Beginning with their regional

cover hit 'Louie Louie', the group scored an impressive string of pop-rock hits between '65 and '67 including 'Just Like Me', 'Kicks', 'Hungry', 'Good Thing' and 'Him Or Me – What's It Gonna Be?' Leaving the group in 1967, Smith joined fellow Raiders, Phil "Fang" Volk and Drake Levin, to form the rock group Brotherhood, who released three unsuccessful albums on RCA Records. Smith returned to The Raiders in late 1971, appearing on the group's number-one single 'Indian Reservation', before leaving the band again in late 1972. Smith would occasionally return for reunion shows.
CAUSE: Natural causes. He died at his home in Kailua Kona, Hawaii.

O.C. Smith

(OCIE LEE SMITH, JR.)
Born June 21, 1932
Died November 23, 2001
A soul singer-turned-preacher, O.C. Smith was trained in jazz music. Born in Mansfield, Louisiana, but raised in Little Rock, Arkansas, and then Los Angeles, Smith was taught to sing by his mother, a music teacher. After earning a degree in psychology at Southern University, he was drafted into the military in 1953 where he served as an entertainer in the Special Forces unit. After his discharge in 1956, Smith relocated to New York City where he spent several years performing in jazz acts, including Sy Oliver's group before joining Count Basie in 1961 as the replacement for vocalist Joe Williams. After parting with Basie in 1963, Smith returned to Los Angeles and signed with Columbia Records, where he managed his first success with the controversial, Dallas Frazier composition 'The Son Of Hickory Holler's Tramp', which barely grazed the US Top 40 but was a number two hit in Britain in 1968. His follow-up, the touching 'Little Green Apples', became his signature piece and earned a Grammy Award for Song of the Year. Smith's other hits included 'Friend, Lover, Woman, Life' (1969), 'Daddy's Little Man' (1969), 'La La Peace Song' (1974) and 'Together' (1976). Entering the ministry in 1980, Smith later cultivated a large congregation in Los Angeles.
CAUSE: Heart attack. He died in Ladera Heights, California.

Ray Smith

(RAYMOND EUGENE SMITH)
Born October 30, 1934
Died November 29, 1979
An early rockabilly singer, Ray Smith was reared on country music in the backwoods of Melber, Kentucky. The son of an itinerant labourer, Smith dropped out of school in the eighth grade to support his sister's family. Married at 18, Smith quit his job at a shoe factory to join the Air Force. Ordered to enter a talent show by his sergeant at Sampson Air Force Base, Smith won first place. Subsequently forming a country trio while stationed at George Air Force Base in Victorville, California, Smith was a local hit. On his discharge from the Air Force in June 1956, Smith returned to Kentucky and formed a country/rockabilly band called The Rock'n'Roll Boys. Appearing on local radio and landing a television show on WPSD in Paducah, Kentucky, Smith was discovered by former country singer turned manager, Charlie Terrell. Smith agreed to a management deal on the condition Terrell land him a recording contract. Quickly signed to Sun Records in 1958, Smith was backed by Charlie Rich on piano for his first single, 'So Young'. Switching to Judd Records (operated by Sam Phillips' brother, Judd), Smith scored his best known hit with the rockabilly standard, 'Rockin' Little Angel'. After failing with a series of uncharacteristic ballads, Smith briefly returned to Sun Records. Later settling in Canada, he toured until shortly before his death.

Smith penned Conway Twitty's 1970 hit, '15 Years Ago'.
CAUSE: Suicide by gunshot at his home in Burlington, Ontario, Canada.

Scott Smith

(DONALD SCOTT SMITH)
Born February 13, 1955
Died November 30, 2000
As bass guitarist for the Canadian rock band Loverboy, Scott Smith performed on a string of AOR hits in the Eighties. A native of Vancouver, British Columbia, Smith had previously been a member of Hurricane Hannah and singer Lisa Dal Bello's backing band. At the same time, Loverboy was formed in Calgary in 1979 by guitarist Paul Dean and vocalist Mike Reno as a studio-only duo, but expanded the following year into a five-man band with Smith replacing short term original bassist Jim Clench. Owing much of their success to their exposure on MTV, Loverboy received heavy airplay on both pop and AOR radio with their début single, the hard rocking 'Turn Me Loose', followed by a series of radio-friendly hits over the next several years, including 'The Kid Is Hot Tonite', 'Working For The Weekend', 'When It's Over', 'Lovin' Every Minute Of It' and 'This Could Be The Night'. After releasing the poor-selling *Wildside* album in 1987, the group briefly disbanded the following year. Despite several attempts over the years, Loverboy was never able to break into the UK market. Smith was replaced in the band by Ken "Spider" Sinnaeve, formerly of Streetheart.
CAUSE: Smith was sailing with his fiancée Yvonne Mayotte and friend Bill Ellis from Vancouver en route to a marina near Los Angeles. He was on deck during rough weather, steering the boat when a massive wave struck. Smith, not wearing a life jacket, fell overboard just south of San Francisco's Golden Gate Bridge. The other two passengers were below deck when the incident occurred and after an unsuccessful two-day Coastguard search for his body, Smith was officially declared "lost at sea". Smith's family later mounted their own unsuccessful search. An experienced yachtsman, he had owned the 37-foot sailboat for 18 months.

Tab Smith

(TALMADGE SMITH)
Born January 11, 1909
Died August 17, 1971
A jazz trained alto saxophonist who switched to R&B in the late Forties, Tab Smith had honed his talent in the bands of Teddy Wilson, Count Basie, and Luck Millinder. As a solo act, Smith landed on the R&B charts with a pair of entries, 'I'll Live True To You' (1945) which featured the vocals of Trevor Bacon, and the chart-topping instrumental, 'Because Of You' (1951). Smith retired from music in the late Fifties.
CAUSE: Unknown.

Warren Smith

Born February 7, 1932
Died January 30, 1980
An early Sun Records rockabilly artist, Warren Smith scored a minor hit in 1957 with the Roy Orbison composition, 'So Long, I'm Gone'. Discovering Smith, Orbison had convinced Sam Phillips to sign the singer to Sun. Leaving Sun Records in 1959 and moving to California, Smith switched to country music. Signing with Mercury Records, Smith landed several charts hits in the early Sixties, and frequently opened up for Johnny Cash. Suffering severe injuries in a car crash in 1965, he was forced from music for nearly a decade.
CAUSE: He suffered a heart attack in Longview, Texas.

William Smith

Born 1944
Died December 1, 1997
The lead vocalist and keyboardist of

Canadian one-hit wonders, Motherlode, William "Smitty" Smith co-wrote their single 'When I Die' (1969) with the group's sax player Steve Kennedy. Formed in London, Ontario, the group disbanded within months of them scoring their only chart hit. Smith formed a new version of Motherlode in 1973 who recorded the poor-selling *Tuffed Out* album.
CAUSE: Heart attack.

Snakefinger

(PHILIP CHARLES LITHMAN)
Born June 17, 1949
Died July 1, 1987
A London-born multi-instrumentalist, Philip Lithman – better known as Snakefinger – earned notoriety for his membership of the avant-garde rock group The Residents. Emerging from the British blues scene, he originally worked in groups such as Junior's Blues Band and Smiley. Travelling to San Francisco in 1971, Lithman spent six months performing on local stages with The Residents and, returning to England the following year, he teamed with ex-Mighty Baby guitarist Martin Stone to form the popular touring pub-rock band Chilli Willi & The Red Hot Peppers. Following the group's disbandment in 1975, manager Jake Riviera went on to co-found Stiff Records, while Snakefinger went to Canada where he toured with Long John Baldry. Returning to California, Snakefinger rejoined The Residents for studio and stage work, and appeared on several electronic albums including *Fingerprince* and *Satisfaction*. Rejecting offers from major labels, Snakefinger issued solo material on The Residents' own label, Ralph Records.
CAUSE: He suffered a heart attack while performing in Linz, Austria, with his band The Vestal Virgins. He had been hospitalised for several months in 1980 after suffering a previous heart attack.

Richard Sohl

Born 1953
Died June 3, 1990
The keyboard player and songwriter for the art-rock act The Patti Smith Group, Richard Sohl was hired by the group in 1973 after answering an advertisement placed by Smith and guitarist Lenny Kaye. A proto-punk New York City outfit led by radical poet Patti Smith, the group regularly performed at CBGB's. Financially backed by the art photographer Robert Mapplethorpe, the group released its first single, 'Hey Joe'/'Piss Factory', on the MER label in 1974. Signed with Arista Records in 1974, the group recorded two rock-based, socially biting albums, *Horses* (1975) and *Radio Ethiopia* (1976). After missing a number of performances, Sohl left the group in the summer of 1977 and was replaced by Bruce Brody (formerly with John Cale). The Patti Smith Group would score its biggest hit the following year with the Smith/Bruce Springsteen composition, 'Because The Night'. Sohl reunited with Smith in 1988 for her comeback album, *Dream Of Life*.
CAUSE: Heart attack. He died in Long Island, New York.
FURTHER READING: Johnstone, Nick. (1997). *Patti Smith: A Biography*. London: Omnibus.

Clifford Solomon

Born January 17, 1931
Died June 21, 2004
A tenor saxophonist, Clifford Solomon worked with many R&B and blues greats such as Charles Brown, Ray Charles, Big Joe Turner, Lionel Hampton, Ike & Tina Turner, Johnny Otis and John Mayall. From Los Angeles, Solomon broke into music at age 16 in a touring USO band. By 1951, he had joined Charles Brown's backing band and later spent extended stints in Ike & Tina Turner's band and with Ray Charles.
CAUSE: Unknown. He died in Los Angeles.

Bert Sommer

Born February 7, 1949
Died July 23, 1990
Briefly a member of Sixties pop-rock group The Left Banke, Bert Sommer was hired in 1967 during a dispute with lead singer Michael Brown. Sommer later earned notoriety by joining the Broadway production of the rock musical *Hair* and performing as a solo act at the original Woodstock Festival where he received a standing ovation for his performance of Simon & Garfunkel's 'America'. Recording for a number of labels including Capitol, Sommer issued his final self-titled solo album in 1977.
CAUSE: Liver failure.

Alex Soria

Born 1965
Died December 13, 2004
The founder of Canadian punk band The Nils, singer-songwriter Alex Soria never achieved the level of success he deserved. Forming the group at the age of 12 in 1977, Alex Soria was joined by his older brother Carlos and two others. By 1979, the group began performing around Montreal and earned praise for Soria's inventive compositions and adept guitarwork. Releasing one album on a subsidiary of Profile Records, the critically acclaimed group failed to break through into the international market. At the height of The Nils' career, their record company went bankrupt and the group was legally prevented from signing with another label. Soria later formed another punk group, Chino.
CAUSE: Struggling with drug addiction, he panicked upon seeing the police and stepped in front of an oncoming train in St. Henri, Quebec.

Jimmy Soul

(JAMES MCCLEESE)
Born August 24, 1942
Died June 25, 1988
Best known for the hilarious romp, 'If You Want To Be Happy', New York City-born Jimmy Soul was trained in gospel music, where as a member of The (Sensational) Nightingales he was known as "The Wonder Boy". Switching to secular doo-wop, 19-year-old Soul signed with SPQR Records in 1962, and recorded a pair of soul/calypso-styled dance hits beginning with 'Twistin' Matilda' (1962). Initially offered to Gary US Bonds, Soul's follow-up, 'If You Want To Be Happy' (1963), was a near-novelty soul hit about marrying an unattractive woman. Drafted into the Vietnam War in 1967, Soul developed a life-long problem with drugs and alcohol.
CAUSE: He died of a heart attack at the Otisville Corrections Facility in Otisville, New York, where he was serving a drug conviction. It was his third long-term jail sentence.

Soulja Slim

(JAMES TAPP)
Born September 9, 1977
Died November 26, 2003
A gangster rapper who had frequent brushes with the law, Soulja Slim released his début album, *Give It 2 'Em Raw*, on rapper Master P's label, No Limit Records. After completing a three-year prison term for armed robbery, Slim followed up in 2001 with *The Streets Made Me*. Launching his own imprint, Cut Throat Committy, Soulja Slim released *Years Later* and, on Koch Records, *Years Later . . . A Few Months After*. Often compared lyrically to Tupac Shakur for his characterisation of ghetto society, Soulja Slim provided a guest rap on the Juvenile hit 'Slow Motion' and also worked with Snoop Doggy Dog, C-Murder and The ReBirth Brass Band.
CAUSE: He was shot several times, execution style, after getting out of a car in front of the home he had purchased for his mother in New Orleans. Although an arrest was later made, the murder remained unsolved.

Ironically, authorities posthumously implicated Soulja Slim in the murder of a 30-year-old man.

Epic Soundtracks

(KEVIN PAUL GODFREY)
Born March 23, 1959
Found Dead December 1, 1997
The founding drummer of the pioneering, British proto-punk, avant-garde rock band, Swell Maps, Epic Soundtracks formed the group in the early Seventies in his native Birmingham, with vocalist brother Nikki Sudden. Experimenting with percussion and electronics on indie hit singles such as 'Read About Seymour' and 'Dresden Style', Swell Maps found scant interest until the punk explosion of 1977. Also an artist, Soundtracks designed the covers to the group's albums, *A Trip To Marineville* and *Jane From Occupied Europe*. With Swell Maps disbanding in 1980, Soundtracks teamed with his brother in The Jacobites, and later played drums and keyboards for other underground rock groups. After a three-year stint with Crime & The City Solution, he formed These Immortal Souls, releasing two albums during the group's five-year run, as well as holding down a day job at a vintage record shop. Recording the first of five solo albums in 1992, Soundtracks was joined by guests Dinosaur Jr. and Sonic Youth on *Rise Above*.
CAUSE: He overdosed on drugs in his apartment. His body was discovered two weeks later.

Angel South

(LUCIEN J. GONDRON)
Born February 1, 1943
Died June 4, 1998
A Texas-based blues-rock guitarist, Angel South played behind B.J. Thomas in the late Sixties before joining Grammy-winning, jazz-rock band Chase in the early Seventies. Following the deaths in a plane crash of the group's leader Bill Chase and five other members, South pursued a solo career. A native of Beaumont, South spent his early years working with Janis Joplin and brothers Johnny and Edgar Winter.
CAUSE: Prostate cancer.

Otis Spann

Born March 21, 1930
Died April 25, 1970
A much respected Chicago-based blues pianist and singer, Otis Spann is celebrated as a member of Muddy Waters' virtuoso band at Chess Records. Born in Jackson, Mississippi, Spann learned to play the organ in his stepfather's church. Drawn to the regional blues scene, the teenage Spann began performing in gin joints. After stints in the boxing ring and the army, Spann relocated to Chicago in 1951 where he worked in bands behind Memphis Slim and Roosevelt Sykes. Forming his own group, Spann landed a residency at the Tick Tock nightclub. Working first as a session player behind Muddy Waters in 1952, he joined his band the following year. Appearing on most of Waters' recordings until 1969, Spann can be first heard on 'Blow Wind Blow'. Also touring with Waters, Spann proved his worth as a solo act with his strong vocal performance at Newport in 1960, the tracks captured on the album, *Muddy Waters At Newport*. With Chess choosing to limit Spann's solo activities, Spann landed at Nat Hentoff's jazz label, Candid Records; he backed Robert Jr. Lockwood and recorded his first solo album in 1960, *Otis Spann Is The Blues*. Spann was usually backed by Muddy Waters or members of his band. Recording at Blue Horizon, Spann teamed with members of Fleetwood Mac (including Peter Green) on the album, *Biggest Thing Since Colossus*; the project spawned his only hit single, 'Hungry Country Girl'.
CAUSE: Cancer. He died at Cook County Hospital in Chicago.

John Spence

Born February 2, 1969
Died December 21, 1987
The original vocalist of Orange County, California-based ska-alternative group No Doubt, John Spence shared the duties with the precocious Gwen Stefani. The group was conceived by John Spence and Eric Stefani while they were employees at a Dairy Queen restaurant in 1986. Named after Spence's favourite expression, "No Doubt", the group garnered local success with their quirky material. A charismatic performer who did back-flips on stage, Spence was not an especially talented singer. Following his sudden death, Spence was replaced by Alan Meade, who quit and defaulted the duties to Eric Stefani's younger sister, Gwen Stefani. Releasing their début, self-titled album in 1992, No Doubt enjoyed international success.
CAUSE: Suicide. He shot himself in the head at an Anaheim, California, park.
FURTHER READING: Rogers, Kalen. (1997). *The Story Of No Doubt*. New York: Omnibus.

Skip Spence

(ALEXANDER LEE SPENCE, JR.)
Born April 18, 1946
Died April 16, 1999
A member of two pioneering psychedelic era, San Francisco groups – The Jefferson Airplane and Moby Grape – Skip Spence suffered a debilitating, drug-induced fate similar to that of Pink Floyd's Syd Barrett. A native of Windsor, Ontario, Canada, Spence was reared in a musical household, his father a professional jazz musician who relocated the family several times. After completing a navy stint in 1965, Spence settled in the San Francisco Bay Area where he was drawn to the bohemian folk music community in Sausalito. While practising with the newly formed, pioneering acid-rock band Quicksilver Messenger Service, Spence was asked by Marty Balin to join Jefferson Airplane as the replacement for the short-lived original member Jerry Peloquin. Although primarily a guitarist, Spence was hired as the group's drummer. Eventually fronted by a former model Grace Slick, The Jefferson Airplane released their much ignored début album in 1966, *Jefferson Airplane Takes Off*, which included four Spence compositions. Quitting Jefferson Airplane over artistic differences, Spence reverted to the guitar. Spence subsequently formed Moby Grape, a leaderless, blues-psychedelic quintet which included guitarist Peter Lewis (son of actress Loretta Young). Musically more sophisticated than their San Francisco contemporaries, Moby Grape was courted by a dozen labels. Signing with Columbia Records, the group issued the heralded album *Moby Grape*, which was highlighted by '8:05' and the Spence-composed hit single, 'Omaha'. Although poised for stardom, Moby Grape was torpedoed by poor management, heavy drug use, frequent arrests, and poor marketing by their record label which among other blunders simultaneously released five singles from the album on the same day. After a solid year on the road, Moby Grape began recording their second album, *Wow*; but with Spence's mind destroyed by a recent LSD binge, he tried to attack a bandmate with an axe during the sessions; subsequently institutionalised, Spence was diagnosed with paranoid schizophrenia. Upon his release, Spence briefly pursued a solo career. Playing all the instruments and writing all the songs, he released a dark, introspective solo album, *Oar*, which has since become a cult favourite. Spence subsequently aided a San Jose bar band, Pud, which later evolved into The Doobie Brothers. Institutionalised for many of his latter years, Spence subsisted on welfare

and panhandling, and often lived on the streets. Recorded shortly before his death, the tribute album, *More Oar*, featuring Beck, Robert Plant, and others, was released. Spence was not a part of any of the latter incarnations of The Jefferson Airplane/Starship.
CAUSE: Admitted to the Dominican Hospital in Santa Cruz, California, for a bout of pneumonia, his conditioned worsened. The official cause of death was listed as lung cancer.
FURTHER READING: Gleason, Ralph J. (1969). *The Jefferson Airplane And The San Francisco Sound.* New York: Ballantine.

C.P. Spencer

(CRATHMAN PLATO SPENCER)
Born January 13, 1938
Died October 20, 2004
A member of soul group The Originals, C.P. Spencer was also a session vocalist at Motown. Originally a doo-wop singer, in 1953 Spencer joined The 5 Jets, which included future hit songwriter Roquel "Billy" Davis. After Davis moved to the role of manager, the group was renamed The Five Stars, and with the additions of Lamont Dozier, Ty Hunter and David Ruffin, the group evolved into The Voice Masters. After recording for the Gwen Gordy-owned label Anna Records, the group disbanded and a number of members, including Spencer, were subsequently hired as session vocalists by Gordy's brother, Berry, who was launching his own label, Motown. At Motown, Spencer also joined The Originals, a group led by Joe Stubbs, the brother of Four Tops' singer Levi Stubbs, sharing the tenor role with Henry Dixon. After Joe Stubbs left to join The Contours, The Originals scored a pair of crossover hits with the Marvin Gaye produced and composed 'Baby, I'm For Real' (1969) and 'The Bells' (1970). Spencer left the group in 1971 and was replaced by his former bandmate, Ty Hunter. In 1978 Spencer rejoined The Originals as the group was entering its disco phase.
CAUSE: Heart attack. He died in Oak Park, Michigan.

Alan Spenner

Born c. 1950
Died August 1991
The bassist and leader of the blue-eyed British soul group Kokomo, Alan Spenner was a member of all three incarnations of the group. Formed in 1973, the critically acclaimed outfit recorded three albums at Columbia Records, managing its only chart success with the single 'A Little Bit Further Away'. In the late Seventies, Spenner joined Bryan Ferry on several Roxy Music projects and a host of solo efforts. Also a popular session player, Spenner backed dozens of acts.
CAUSE: Asthma. He died in London.

Jakson "Thunderfoot" Spires

(JACK W. SPIRES)
Born April 12, 1951
Died March 16, 2005
A core member of popular touring ensemble The Southern Rock All-Stars, veteran drummer Jakson "Thunderfoot" Spires had formed the band with Dave Hlubek of Molly Hatchet, Jay Johnson of The Rossington-Collins Band and Charles Hart of Radio Tokyo. They performed material by their respective bands and cover versions by other acts of the genre, including Lynyrd Skynyrd and The Allman Brothers as The Southern Rock All-Stars were unable to garner airplay with their original material. A founding member and chief songwriter of the Southern rock band Blackfoot, Spires co-wrote their hits 'Highway Song' and 'Fly Away', until the group disbanded in 1986. Also a session player, Jakson worked with Benny Mardones, Phil Lynott, Willie Dixon and Albert King.
CAUSE: He suffered a brain aneurysm and died after three days on life

support at a hospital in Fort Pierce, Florida.

Victoria Spivey

(VICTORIA REGINA SPIVEY)
Born October 15, 1906
Died October 3, 1976
A jazz and blues songstress, Victoria Spivey enjoyed a long fruitful career, outlasting her classic-blues contemporaries. Beginning her career as a piano player in the red-light district of her native Houston, she was mentored by Blind Lemon Jefferson and Ida Cox. Recording for a series of labels beginning with OKeh Records, Spivey moaned and wailed on her self-penned chestnuts such as 'TB Blues' and 'Dope Head Blues'. Spivey also worked as a staff songwriter for the St. Louis Music Company. Joining a series of musical stage revues in the Thirties and Forties, she also appeared in the all-black film musical, *Hallelujah!*. After abandoning blues for gospel during the Fifties, she returned to her blues roots in 1962 with the launching of her own label, Spivey Records. Embraced during the blues boom of the late Sixties, Spivey remained a regular on the blues festival circuit until her death.
CAUSE: Unknown. She died in New York City.

Mark Spoon

(MARKUS LOFFEL)
Born November 27, 1966
Died on or shortly before January 9, 2006
A member of German dance duo Jam & Spoon, Mark Spoon formed the Frankfurt-based act with Jam El Mar (born Rolf Ellmer). A former record company executive and nightclub owner, Spoon hired American singer Plavka Lonich for the group's UK chart hits, 'Right In The Night' (1994), 'Find Me' (1994) and 'Angel' (1995). Also recording as Tokyo Ghetto Pussy, the duo had club hits with 'Stella' (1992) and 'Everybody On The Floor (Pump It)' (1995). Later recording under the moniker Storm, the pair had a 1998 UK hit with 'Positiva'. As deejays, Jam and Spoon remixed songs by artists such as Technotronic, The Pet Shop Boys and Moby.
CAUSE: He died at his apartment in Frankfurt, Germany, as the result of a heart attack.

Dusty Springfield

(MARY ISABEL CATHERINE BERNADETTE O'BRIEN)
Born April 16, 1939
Died March 2, 1999
Dubbed Britain's soul diva, the much-revered Dusty Springfield scored a string of melodramatic soul-flavoured pop hits in the Sixties. Educated in a convent, she first sang in public in 1957, occasionally joining her brother for folk club performances. In 1958, she joined an all-girl trio, The Lana Sisters, and performed middle-of-the-road fare in cabarets. Then in 1960, she formed a pop-folk trio with her brother Dion, and friend Tim Field. Seeking a folksy stage name, the former Mary O'Brien became Dusty Springfield, while Dion became Tom. Enjoying several hits including 'Island Of Dreams' (1962) and their only US Top 40 entry, 'Silver Threads And Golden Needles' (1962), the trio was voted the top vocal group for two years in a *New Musical Express* poll. But during the trio's first tour of the US in 1963, Springfield was captivated by Motown soul and abandoned folk music. Pursuing a solo career, she scored one of the first British Invasion hits with her début release, 'I Only Want To Be With You' (1964). Dropping her rather frumpy folk uniform, Springfield was soon sporting a beehive hairdo, thick eye-eyeliner, and glamorous outfits. Borrowing Phil Spector's "Wall Of Sound" recording technique, Springfield owed much of her success to the strong material provided by Burt Bacharach. With her hit run stronger in her native Britain than in the US, Springfield charted with

'Wishin' And Hopin'' (1964), 'In The Middle Of Nowhere' (1965), 'You Don't Have To Say You Love Me' (1966), 'All I See Is You' (1966), 'The Look Of Love' (1967) and 'I Close My Eyes And Count To Ten' (1968). Venturing to Memphis and working with veteran Atlantic producers Jerry Wexler, Tom Dowd, and Arif Mardin, she recorded her musical opus, the critically acclaimed album *Dusty In Memphis* (1969) which spawned the hits 'Son Of A Preacher Man' and 'Windmills Of Your Mind'. Notoriously insecure, the husky voiced Springfield rarely performed in concert. Her career displaced by the hippie movement, Springfield relocated to New York, and then in 1972, Los Angeles where she met with mixed fortunes. With her career floundering in the late Seventies, Springfield worked as a session singer. She subsequently acknowledged drink and drug problems. In 1987 in a duet with longtime fans Neil Tenant and Chris Lowe – The Pet Shop Boys – Springfield returned to the Top 10 with 'What Have I Done To Deserve This?' Signing with the duo's label, Parlophone Records, she was the recipient of several Pet Shop Boys compositions including 'Nothing Has Been Proved'. Springfield enjoyed further interest when Quentin Tarantino creatively employed 'Son Of A Preacher Man' in the film *Pulp Fiction*. Springfield was diagnosed with cancer in 1994 shortly before completing her final album *A Very Fine Love*. In 1998, she sold the rights to her 275 songs to Prudential Insurance for $15 million. In early 1999 she was awarded an OBE in the British Honours List but was too ill to attend Buckingham Palace to receive the award from the Queen. She died 11 days before she was to be formally inducted into The Rock 'n' Roll Hall of Fame.

CAUSE: She died from breast cancer at her home in Henley alongside the Thames River west of London. A large crowd of fans gathered as her coffin was carried in a horse-drawn glass hearse through the streets of Henley on the day of her funeral.

FURTHER READING: O'Brien, Lucy. (1999). *Dusty*. London: Sidgwick & Jackson. Leeson, Edward. (1999). *Dusty Springfield*. London: Omnibus.

Jimmy Springs

Born September 5, 1911
Died October 4, 1987

The drummer and high-tenor vocalist of the pioneering, Forties/Fifties Los-Angeles-based doo-wop vocal outfit The Red Caps, Illinois-born Jimmy Springs worked as a musician since the Thirties. Joining a Mills Brothers copy-outfit called The Dixie Cups, Springs imitated a trumpet; after touring with a Vaudeville revue, the group landed a spot on Gene Autry's nationally broadcast barn dance. Relocating to California, the group experienced several name changes including The Jones Boys and The Four Toppers before emerging as The Red Caps. Signing with Beacon Records, the group landed on the pop charts with 'I've Learned A Lesson I'll Never Forget' (1943) and 'No One Else Will Do'. Moving to Mercury Records in 1946, the renamed Steve Gibson & The Red Caps landed a hit with 'Wedding Bells Are Breaking Up That Old Gang Of Mine' (1948). Moving to RCA, the group scored their final hit in a duet with Damita Jo, 'I Went To Your Wedding' (1952). The group also appeared in several musical films including *Mystery In Swing*. Springs left the group in 1955, before joining a new Steve Gibson-led line-up in 1959.

CAUSE: Unknown. He died in Philadelphia.

"Wild" Jimmy Spruill

Born June 1, 1934
Died February 3, 1996

A New York City-based blues session guitarist, "Wild" Jimmy Spruill worked

with John Hammond Jr., The Shirelles, Tarheel Slim, Little Anthony & The Imperials, Elmore James, and others. Into the mid Sixties, he was utilised as session guitarist for Bobby Robinson's Fire/Fury Records, playing on Wilbert Harrison's 'Kansas City', Buster Brown's 'Fanny Mae' and Dave "Baby" Cortez's 'Happy Organ'. Tiring of session work, he formed an East Coast nightclub trio with singer Tommy Knight and drummer Popsy Dixon.
CAUSE: He died from a heart attack while travelling home on a bus to the Bronx, New York. He had been visiting friends in Florida.

Dorothy Squires

(EDNA MAY SQUIRES)
Born March 25, 1915
Died April 14, 1998
A Welsh-born pop singer who was popular in Britain in the Forties and Fifties, Dorothy Squires led a particularly tumultuous life. Though she trained as a nurse, Squires moved to London to pursue a singing career. After a stint with American pianist Charlie Kunz, she was hired in 1938 by bandleader Billy Reid. Though Reid was married, he caused a scandal by cohabiting with Squires, who was 22 years his junior. The pair formed a successful duo, The Composer & His Voice, and landed major hits with Reid compositions such as 'Gypsy' and 'I'm Walking Behind You'. Squires' relationship with Reid ended in 1950 after a vicious fist fight at The Llanelli, the theatre Reid owned. Squires then began an affair with her future husband, the then-unknown actor Roger Moore (12 years her junior). While Moore's career took off in the Sixties, Squires fell from popularity, her first hit in eight years coming with 'Say It With Flowers' (1961). With her marriage to Moore on the rocks, Squires began to abuse alcohol and was belatedly divorced from Moore in 1969, after which she attempted a series of comebacks. Returning to the charts with 'For Once In My Life' (1969), 'Till' (1969) and 'My Way' (1970), Squires silenced her detractors when she sold out the London Palladium. As her behaviour became ever more erratic, Squires often found herself on the scandal pages and was arrested on numerous occasions for public drunkenness and assault, but when she was charged with offering a bribe to a BBC producer, she alienated her otherwise loyal fanbase. Becoming what lawyers refer to as a "vexatious litigant", she filed more than 20 legal actions in 10 years, claiming among other things, assault, libel, and piracy of her autobiography. In the late Nineties, she was involved in a dispute over the ownership of several of her songs. Although she had earned a fortune, she lost a mansion to fire, and was forced to file for bankruptcy twice. Evicted from her home in 1988, she accepted the gift of a house from a longtime fan.
CAUSE: Suffering from lung and bladder cancer, she died after a two-month stay at Llwynypia Hospital in Mid Glamorgan, South Wales. Almost destitute, her medical bills were paid by her former husband, Roger Moore.

Terry Stafford

Born November 22, 1941
Died March 17, 1996
An Elvis sound-alike, Terry Stafford was a one-hit wonder who landed on the charts in 1964 with, 'Suspicion' (1964). The song first appeared on Presley's 1962 album *Pot Luck*. Also a songwriter, the Oklahoma-born Stafford penned 'Amarillo By Morning' (George Strait), 'Say, Has Anybody Seen My Sweet Gypsy Rose' (Tony Orlando & Dawn), and 'Big In Texas' which Buck Owens reworked as 'Big in Vegas'.
CAUSE: Unknown. He died in Amarillo, Texas.

Layne Staley

(LAYNE THOMAS STALEY)
Born August 22, 1967
Died circa April 5, 2002
As lead singer of Alice In Chains, Layne Staley was at the forefront of the first wave of the Seattle grunge movement. Hailing from Kirkland, Washington, Staley began playing the drums and guitar as a young child. Joining a series of glam-metal bands, Staley was usually the drummer and vocalist; one of these groups was a cross-dressing act called Alice N' Chains. In 1987 Staley formed another glam band, Diamond Life, with Jerry Cantrell, Sean Kinney and Mike Starr but, with the decline of hair-metal, the group veered towards hard-rock as Alice In Chains. In the wake of fellow grunge act Nirvana's massive breakthrough, Alice In Chains reached the US charts in 1991 with *Facelift*, featuring the Grammy-nominated track 'Man In The Box'. More metal-oriented than their grunge contemporaries, the group achieved full superstardom with 1992's *Dirt*; half of the album's dark and brooding tracks such as 'Rooster', 'Would' and 'Them Bones' chronicling Staley's heroin addiction. Kurt Cobain's sudden death in April 1994 briefly convinced Staley to quit drugs but as the *Jar Of Flies* EP entered the album charts in 1994 in the number one position, Layne regressed back into his heroin addiction and the group was forced to cancel a tour with Metallica. As a side project, Staley formed the Seattle supergroup Mad Season, which included Pearl Jam's Mike McCready and The Screaming Trees' Barrett Martin. Their album, *Above* (1995), featured the radio hits, 'River Of Deceit' and 'I Don't Know Anything'. Meanwhile as Layne's personal troubles intensified, Alice In Chains released their final studio album in 1995. The group subsequently issued a pair of compilations and two live albums, including an *MTV Unplugged* project. Becoming reclusive after the drug-related bacterial infection death of his girlfriend in October 1996, Layne retreated from music altogether. Spending nearly all his time in his penthouse condominium, he never recorded or performed again.
CAUSE: He was discovered dead in his apartment on April 19. He had been dead for about two weeks. A heroin cooking device and syringe were found near his body. His death was ruled an accidental "acute intoxication due to the combined effects of opiate [heroin] and cocaine".

"Baby" Lloyd Stallworth

(LLOYD EUGENE STALLWORTH)
Born April 15, 1941
Died October 27, 2002
A member of James Brown's revue The Famous Flames, "Baby" Lloyd Stallworth initially joined Brown as his valet. Becoming a dancer, and then a backing singer, Stallworth co-wrote Brown's 1961 hit, 'Lost Someone' and also recorded occasional solo material, including a single produced by Brown, 'There's Something On Your Mind'. After spending seven years in Brown's revue, Stallworth took a position as a member of Brown's clerical staff.
CAUSE: Natural causes. He died in Tampa, Florida.

Darron Stankey

Born July 5, 1942
Died May 11, 2005
A founding member of pop vocal group The Innocents, Darron Stankey sang on a pair of Top 40 hits. Originally formed in Los Angeles in 1958 as The Emeralds, the group replaced a number of its members in 1959 before becoming The Echoes; initially being hired by Herb Albert to provide backing vocals at Andex Records. Signing with Indigo Records, the renamed Innocents scored their first hit with 'Honest I Do' followed by, after appearing on *American Bandstand*, 'Gee Whiz'. Meanwhile,

14-year-old vocalist Kathy Young had scheduled a session at the same studio used by The Innocents. When the producer was unimpressed with her remake of The Rivileers' 'A Thousand Stars', he asked The Innocents to provide backing vocals. The resulting session produced a million-selling single, which was followed by the stylistically similar 'Happy Birthday Blues', but their hits dried up after The Innocents moved to Warner-Reprise Records. In the spring of 1966, Stankey and two former members of The Innocents launched their own label, Sugar Beats Records.
CAUSE: Cancer.

Vivian Stanshall

Born March 21, 1943
Died March 5, 1995
The leader of the British art-rock band, The Bonzo Dog (Doo-Dah) Band, Vivian Stanshall merged theatrics, comedy and rock'n'roll. Born in the Essex resort town of Southend, the rebellious Stanshall was kicked out of private school in his teens. During a stint in the Merchant Navy, he picked up his lifelong drinking habit. After enrolling in a London art school, he immersed himself in the Teddy Boy movement and on graduating, he decided to pursue music on a full-time basis. Formed in London in 1965 as a Twenties-style revivalist outfit by fellow art students, Rodney Slater and Roger Ruskin Spear, The Bonzo Dog Doo-Dah Band was soon expanded with trumpeter/vocalist Stanshall and guitarist/keyboard player Neal Innes. Infusing rock music into their act, the costumed band performed musical sketches, combining old style theatrics and slapstick comedy. After appearing in The Beatles' television film *Magical Mystery Tour*, The Bonzo Dog Doo-Dah Band scored their first hit with the novelty-styled 'I'm The Urban Spaceman' (1968), produced by Paul McCartney (under the pseudonym Apollo C. Vermouth). Shortening their moniker in late 1968 to The Bonzo Dog Band, the group landed on the British album charts with *The Doughnut in Granny's Greenhouse* (highlighted by the track 'Do Blue Men Sing The Whites?'), *Tadpoles* and *Keynsham*. The group found little success in the US, as American audiences were unable to relate to the band's zany and particularly British sense of humour. With The Bonzo Dog Band disbanding in early 1970, Stanshall shaved his head and formed a group called Big Grunt. He suffered a nervous breakdown in late 1970, and was institutionalised for seven weeks. A reformed Bonzo Dog Band released one further album, the aptly titled, *Let's Make Up And Be Friendly* (1971). Remaining active in the Seventies, Stanshall worked as a comic and disc-jockey, and his distinguished accent was also in demand for voice-overs. Stanshall and his friend Keith Moon became known as rock's practical jokers and on one famous occasion they dressed as Nazi soldiers to visit several London bars. Stanshall was featured on Mike Oldfield's *Tubular Bells* and wrote the lyrics to the song 'Arc Of A Diver' for Steve Winwood. He subsequently launched a pair of music/comedy troupes, Gerry Atric & The Aging Orchestra and Viv & His Gargantuan Chorus. He also wrote and starred in the cult movie *Sir Henry At Rawlinson's End*. After beating a tranquillizer addiction in the early Nineties, Stanshall worked as an actor in television commercials and stage musicals. He was working on a new album for his own label at the time of his death.
CAUSE: He died in a fire at his London apartment near Alexandra Palace.

Pops Staples

(ROEBUCK STAPLES)
Born December 28, 1914
Died December 19, 2000
The patriarch of the veteran soul/gospel act The Staple Singers, Pops Staples enjoyed a long and fruitful career. A

singer-songwriter and guitarist, Staples was reared on black spiritual singing as well as the Delta blues of Howlin' Wolf and Charley Patton. While a member of The Gospel Trumpets in the early Thirties, he mastered the guitar and after moving his family to Chicago in 1936 (where his brother became the pastor at the Mount Zion Church), Staples launched a family musical group in 1948. First recording in 1953, The Staple Singers initially sold few records outside of the Chicago area. Featuring Pops Staples' distinctive guitar-heavy sound, the group hit its stride after signing with Vee-Jay Records in 1959. Although Pops Staples provided the vocals on many of the group's early releases, including '(This May Be) The Last Time' – the chorus later "borrowed" by The Rolling Stones for their 1965 hit – Pops daughter Mavis soon assumed lead vocal duties. After signing with Stax Records, the group enjoyed a strong hit run on the R&B charts in the Seventies with: 'Heavy Makes You Happy', 'This World', 'City In The Sky', as well as a number of crossover hits including, 'Respect Yourself', 'I'll Take You There', 'If You're Ready' and 'Let's Do It Again'. As The Staples, the group's hit run slowed at Warner Brothers in the late Seventies and early Eighties. Pops Staples appeared in the films *Wattstax* (1973), *The Last Waltz* (1978), David Byrne's *True Stories* (1986) and *Wag The Dog* (1997). He also earned a Grammy nomination for the solo album *Peace To The Neighborhood* and won a Grammy for the solo track 'Father, Father'. In 1998, he was awarded a National Heritage Fellowship from the National Endowment For The Arts.
CAUSE: Stricken with Bell's palsy, he suffered concussion from a fall near his home. He later died in his sleep.

Edwin Starr

(CHARLES EDWIN HATCHER)
Born January 21, 1942
Died April 2, 2003

A soul singer, Edwin Starr is best remembered for his Vietnam-era protest song 'War'. Born in Nashville but raised in Cleveland, he often performed on local television talent shows before forming a teenage doo-wop group The Future Tones. After completing a military stint in 1962, he replaced Howard Tate as the organist in Bill Doggett's touring band. Starr was occasionally allowed to sing one or two songs per show in what had previously been an exclusively instrumental combo. After Doggett refused to record his song inspired by a James Bond movie, Starr quit to pursue a solo career at Ric-Tic Records scoring a Top 10 R&B hit with 'Agent Double-O-Soul' (1965), followed by 'Back Street', 'Stop Her On Sight (S.O.S.)' and, as a songwriter, 'Oh How Happy' by The Shades Of Blue. When Motown Records purchased Ric-Tic, Starr was teamed with master producers Johnny Bristol and Harvey Fuqua for his first Top 10 pop hit, '25 Miles' (1968). When a Temptations' album track, 'War', started receiving airplay, Motown was apprehensive about releasing it as a single. Instead, they had Starr cover the controversial anti-war song, who turned it into a number one smash, followed by a similarly themed Top 40 hit, 'Stop The War Now'. Leaving Motown in 1974 following a dispute over royalties, Starr released some disco material in the late Seventies, including 'Contact'. Moving to England in 1983, Starr formed a small orchestra and frequently toured across Europe. In 1986, Bruce Springsteen reached the charts with a live version of 'War'.
CAUSE: Heart attack. He died in Chigwell, England.

Ruby Starr

(CONSTANCE MIERZWIAK)
Born November 30, 1949
Died January 14, 1995

As a guest vocalist for the Southern rock band Black Oak Arkansas, Ruby

Starr provided the co-vocals on the group's only Top 40 hit, a cover of the R&B standard 'Jim Dandy' (1974). She would also appear on the group's concert album, *Live! Mutha*. Reared on country music, the Toledo, Ohio-native was discovered by members of Black Oak Arkansas while she was performing in a Chicago nightclub with The Ruby Jones Band. After leading her own band in Milwaukee, Wisconsin, she joined a country music review in Las Vegas.
CAUSE: Cancer of the brain and lungs. She died in Toledo.

John "Scooter" Steele

(JOHN THOMAS STEELE)
Born c. 1936
Died April 28, 1997
The bass singer of Fifties doo-wop group The (Five) Willows, John "Scooter" Steele was inspired by the music of The Dominoes. Formed in 1950 as a quintet called The Dovers, the Harlem-based group originally included future record label owner Bobby Robinson and, later, future Drifters member Doc Green. After recording a self-financed début single in 1953, The (Five) Willows continued to record for a series of labels until gaining a crossover hit in 1956 with the upbeat 'Church Bells May Ring', a track that featured a young Neil Sedaka playing chimes. Unfortunately for Steele, he was unable to attend the session and was replaced on the record by Richard Simon. Quitting in 1956, Steele was replaced in the group by Freddy Donovan. Steele joined a touring revival version of the group in the Eighties.
CAUSE: Unknown.

John Steele

(JOHN THOMAS STEELE)
Born March 9, 1934
Died April 28, 1997
The bass singer of the Fifties, Harlem-based doo-wop group The (Five) Willows from 1951–55, John Steele had initially joined a precursor of the teenage outfit called The Dovers. Appearing on the doo-wop standard 'The White Cliffs Of Dover', Steel left the group before the release of their biggest hit, 'Church Bells May Ring'. With The Willows hitting the oldies circuit in 1983, Steele rejoined the original line-up.
CAUSE: He died of an undisclosed illness at his apartment in Harlem.

Doug Stegmeyer

(DOUGLAS ALAN STEGMEYER)
Born 1952
Died August 24, 1995
The bassist and leader of Billy Joel's band, Doug Stegmeyer joined "The Piano Man" in 1972. Stegmeyer and Joel had been friends since their mid-teens in their hometown of Hicksville, New York. Playing both an electric and upright bass, Stegmeyer performed on dozens of hits including 'The Piano Man', 'Just The Way You Are', and 'It's Still Rock And Roll To Me'. Stegmeyer was fired in 1988 after the release of *The Bridge* album, dismissed along with guitarist Russell Javors and saxophonist Mark Rivera.
CAUSE: Suicide. He was found dead of a gunshot wound at his apartment in Smithtown, New York.
FURTHER READING: Geller, Debbie. (1985). *Billy Joel: An Illustrated Biography*. New York: McGraw-Hill.

Ray Stephens

Born 1955
Died October 4, 1990
The lead singer of Village People from 1984–85, Ray Stephens joined the group during its post-disco era heyday. Also an actor, Stephens appeared in the Broadway shows, *Your Arm's Too Short To Box With God* and *On The Twentieth Century*. He also sang the theme song to the Stephen King film, *Cat's Eye*.
CAUSE: He died from an undisclosed illness in New York City.

Van Stephenson

(Van Wesley Stephenson)
Born November 4, 1953
Died April 8, 2001
A Nashville based singer-songwriter, Van Stephenson was also a member of the trio, BlackHawk. Born in Hamilton, Ohio, but raised in Nashville, Stephenson became a minister before switching careers to become a staff writer for House Of Gold, where he landed his first major success with the Crystal Gayle country hit 'Your Kisses Will'. Also pursuing a solo career, Stephenson had a solo pop-rock hit with 'Modern Day Delilah' (1984). Teaming with songwriter Dave Robbins in the early Eighties, Stephenson penned a number of hits for Restless Heart, Dan Seals and others. In 1992, Stephenson and Robbins teamed with former Outlaws member Henry Paul to form the country trio, BlackHawk, one of the most successful country acts in the Nineties, with over a dozen chart hits including 'Every Once In A While', 'I'm Not Strong Enough To Say No' and 'There You Have It'. Diagnosed with cancer in 1999, Stephenson quit the group the following year.
Cause: Skin cancer. He died in Memphis.

Charles Stepney

Born March 26, 1931
Died May 17, 1976
A producer and songwriter, Charles Stepney is best known for his work with the Seventies soul/funk group Earth, Wind & Fire. Honing his craft in the mid Sixties as the staff arranger at the Chess Records' subsidiary Cadet, Stepney churned out a series of soul classics by artists such as Marlena Shaw and Ramsey Lewis. Teamed with producer/songwriter Bobby Miller, Stepney had his greatest success with The Dells on hits such as 'Oh What A Night' and 'Stay In My Corner'. At the label, Stepney was also hired as the arranger and co-producer for a newly assembled rock/R&B outfit, Rotary Connection; although the group would enjoy moderate success on underground rock radio, lead vocalist Minnie Riperton would later emerge as a hit solo act. When former Ramsey Lewis member Maurice White launched Earth, Wind & Fire in 1969, he turned to Stepney for his expertise. With their smooth horn section and elegant harmonies, EW&F brought a sophistication to R&B with hits such as 'Mighty Mighty', 'Shining Star', and 'Sing A Song'. Stepney and White teamed in 1976 to form Kalimba Productions, named after one of the group's hits. The pair produced albums for Deniece Williams and The Emotions. Stepney passed away during the sessions for the EW&F album *Spirit*, which contained the group's first British hit, 'Saturday Night'.
Cause: Heart attack. He died in Chicago.

Guy Stevens

Born April 13, 1943
Died August 29, 1981
A former British deejay turned rock producer, Guy Stevens was a well respected arbiter of taste for the British mod scene of the mid Sixties. Having developed an early interest in American rock'n'roll, soul and R&B, Stevens ran the UK division of the Sue record label for Chris Blackwell, and used it to put out obscure singles not only from the US Sue group of labels, but from any number of tiny independent record companies, and some of the bigger ones. Stevens was also president of the Chuck Berry Appreciation Society, and had a say in the UK releases that the Pye record label put out by Chuck Berry, Bo Diddley and others on the Chess and Checker labels. Stevens even flew to America to help secure Chuck Berry's release from prison, not that Berry thanked him for his efforts, and brought him to the UK for his first tour. As a deejay at the Scene Club in Soho, London, Stevens' impeccable

taste for rock'n'roll, R&B, ska, jazz and soul meant that his weekly record sessions became a Mecca for the burgeoning Mod movement. His stunning record collection was made available to the likes of such acts as The High Numbers (later The Who) from which to build their stage repertoire. He also put together several compilations of the Sue and Chess catalogue for Island. Moving into music he appeared as part of the 1967 artist collective Hapshash & The Coloured Coat, and produced such Island acts as The VIPs (who evolved into Art and then Spooky Tooth), Free and Mott The Hoople. An amiable eccentric, Stevens was highly respected in the industry though he spent time in jail for drug offences and, during one session with Mott The Hoople, destroyed a studio clock when someone pointed out that the session was running into overtime. Having lain low for several years with various alcohol-related problems, in 1979 he was invited to produce The Clash's third and arguably most defining album, *London Calling*. His production techniques at Wessex Studios were eccentric to say the least, with chairs being thrown about to coax better performances from the musicians while he filled a piano with beer to try to make it sound better.
CAUSE: Heart attack. He died in London.

B.W. Stevenson

(LOUIS CHARLES STEVENSON)
Born October 5, 1949
Died April 28, 1988
An early country-rocker, B.W. Stevenson sported a beer gut, a big hat, and a full beard. Born and raised in Dallas, he attended North Texas State University on a voice scholarship. While serving in the army in the late Sixties, he was nicknamed "B.W." (short for Buckwheat). Returning to Texas and performing in Austin nightclubs, he was signed by RCA Records. Releasing his self-titled début album in 1970, Stevenson merged his raw bluesy vocals with Southern, country-flavoured guitar riffs. Stevenson initially charted with the self-penned composition, 'Shambala' (1973), a few months before Three Dog Night's more popular cover version. From Stevenson's third album, he scored his breakthrough hit with the pleading title track, 'My Maria' (1973). The following year, Stevenson was the featured act on the first episode of the perennial PBS music programme, *Austin City Limits*. Later releasing two albums at Warner Brother Records, Stevenson scored a minor pop hit in 1977 with, 'Down To The Station'. Moving to Nashville in 1987, Stevenson worked as a full-time songwriter.
CAUSE: He died after heart surgery at a Veterans' Administration hospital in Nashville.

Andy Stewart

Born 1934
Died October 11, 1993
A popular Scottish radio star, Andy Stewart scored a major international hit in 1961 with 'The Scottish Soldier'. Stewart, invariably dressed in a kilt, was a regular on the BBC TV programme, *The White Heather Club* and a familiar face at New Year's Eve shows in the Sixties and Seventies.
CAUSE: Heart attack. He died in Arbroath, Scotland.

Billy "Fat Boy" Stewart

(WILLIAM LARRY STEWART)
Born March 24, 1937
Died January 17, 1970
An R&B singer and piano player who scored a string of hits in the mid Sixties, Washington DC-native Billy Stewart received his musical training as a member of his family's gospel group, The Stewart Gospel Singers. Encouraged to learn the piano by his mother, Stewart soon left gospel for pop music. After passing through a

local group called The Graham Crackers, Stewart joined his uncle's group, "Houn' Dog" Ruffin, as a vocalist. Winning a talent show as a soloist at The Howard Theater in Washington DC, Stewart sang his own R&B arrangement of the *Porgy & Bess* standard, 'Summertime'. Asked in 1956 to join Bo Diddley's band, the young Stewart honed his keyboard skills during the next few years. Occasionally recording as a solo act at Diddley's label, Chess/Argo Records, Stewart's début single, 'Billy's Blues', was plagiarised by Mickey & Sylvia for their 1957 hit, 'Love Is Strange'. Stewart sued to receive writer's credit but lost. Stewart did not again record until 1962 when under new manager Allen Meyerhoff, he scored a minor R&B hit with 'Reap What You Sow'/'Fat Boy'. A large man who was nicknamed "Fat Boy" and "Motor Mouth", Stewart possessed an idiosyncratic, fast-fire, stuttering-like delivery in which words were doubled up. Stewart enjoyed a strong hit run in the mid Sixties with 'Strange Feeling' (1963); 'Count Me Out' (1964); and a pair of self-penned releases, 'I Do Love You' (1965) and 'Sitting In The Park' (1965). But his biggest pop hit came with his frenetic cover of the standard, 'Summertime' (1966). In the late Sixties, Stewart's life was marred by vehicle mishaps. In 1968, one of the automobiles carrying Stewart's entourage crashed and burned killing all but one occupant, trumpeter Cuba Sanchez. Then a year later, Stewart was injured in a motorcycle accident. A final road tragedy ended Stewart's life in 1970.

CAUSE: Stewart died instantly along with three members of his band, The Soul Kings, when their automobile struck a bridge support on Interstate-95, and tumbled down an abutment into the Neuse River, one mile south of Smithfield, North Carolina, while en route to an engagement in Columbia, South Carolina. The wheels of Stewart's brand new, week-old Ford Thunderbird had locked up. Stewart's manager was following in a second car and had noticed the wobbling wheels; Stewart had planned on servicing the vehicle after reaching the next stop. Also killed were Norman P. Rich, William Cathey, and Rico Hightower. Suing the Ford Motor Company, Stewart's family reached an out-of-court settlement.

Ernest "Snuffy" Stewart

Born April 10, 1950
Died April 26, 1997

Best known as the keyboard player for the disco group KC & The Sunshine Band, Miami-born Ernest "Snuffy" Stewart was added in 1980 in order to give the group's leader more opportunity to concentrate on his singing. Stewart had previously worked as a session player for the pop/soul group The Cornelius Brothers and Sister Rose.

CAUSE: Asthma attack. He was found dead at his home in Opa Locka near Fort Lauderdale, Florida.

Ian Stewart

Born July 18, 1938
Died December 12, 1985

A founding member of The Rolling Stones who was demoted to sideman and road manager, Ian Stewart stayed out of the limelight during the next two decades but remained an essential member of the band. Born during his family's visit to relatives in the Scottish fishing village of Pittenween, Stewart was raised in Surrey. Taught to play the piano as a child, Stewart answered an ad placed by blues fanatic Brian Jones in *Jazz News* in the hopes of forming an R&B blues band, and was the first hired. Eventually, Mick Jagger, Keith Richards, and Dick Taylor would also join, as well as a succession of drummers. Taking their name, The Rolling Stones, from a Muddy Waters' song, by early 1963 Dick Taylor had

left and Bill Wyman and Charlie Watts were in place. The group was discovered during their weekly Sunday residency at the Crawdaddy Club, in Richmond, Surrey by future manager Andrew Oldham in April 1963. However, Oldham decided that Stewart's somewhat portly appearance and lantern jaw were inappropriate for the image he had in mind for the group. Stewart thus became an "unofficial" Rolling Stone, heard but not seen for the next two decades, though often referred to as the "Sixth Stone" by those who understood his role with the band. In addition to being road manager, he played keyboards, appeared on most of the group's studio albums, and occasionally he joined them onstage. Eventually, he was given the title of company secretary. As well as running the Stones' rehearsal space in Bermondsey, south London (where The Faces with Rod Stewart first played together), "Stu", as he was known to all, administered The Rolling Stones Mobile Studio, used by the likes of The Who and Led Zeppelin. The Zeppelin track, 'Boogie With Stu' (1975), featured Stewart tinkling the ivories. In 1979, Stewart formed Rocket 88, his own part-time boogie band, which included Jack Bruce, Alexis Korner and Charlie Watts, and also sat in with various musicians he admired, including Ronnie Lane's Slim Chance. Though the Stones have never been known for their sentimentality, tucked away on their 1986 album, *Dirty Work*, is Stewart's inimitable boogie-woogie piano, isolated to provide an uncredited eleventh track as a touching memorial from the band who loved him. He was, according to Keith Richards, "the glue that held the bits together".
CAUSE: Heart attack. He died in his doctor's office at the Harley Street Clinic in London. Never again would the Stones hear his immortal, "Come on my little showers of shit, you're on," as he herded them towards the stage of some gigantic auditorium.
FURTHER READING: Hotchner, A.E. (1990). *Blown Away: The Rolling Stones And The Death Of The Sixties*. New York: Simon & Schuster. Norman, Philip. (1984). *The Stones*. London: Elm Tree.

Jermaine Stewart

(WILLIAM JERMAINE STEWART)
Born September 7, 1957
Died March 17, 1997
An eighties pop-soul performer, Jermaine Stewart was also a one-time member of Shalamar. Trained on piano and reared on Motown soul, Stewart was a *Soul Train* dancer in the Seventies when the programme was filmed in Chicago. Joining Shalamar as a backing dancer/vocalist in 1980, Stewart remained in the shadows of the Howard Hewitt-led group. With Shalamar about to disband, Stewart left the group in 1983 and was encouraged to pursue a solo career by bandmate Jodie Watley. After providing the backing vocals on Culture Club's hit 'Miss Me Blind', Stewart was aided by the group's bassist Mike Craig, who financed a solo demo recording. After scoring a minor R&B hit with the title track of his début solo album *Word Is Out* (1984), Stewart enjoyed a dance-club smash with 'We Don't Have To Take Our Clothes Off' (1986), the song penned by his producer Narada Michael Walden and Preston Glass. Stewart's final successes came with 'Jody' (1986), 'Say It Again' (1988), and the Top 10 British chart entry, 'Get Lucky' (1988). Embracing house music in the Nineties, Jackson fared poorly with the 1992 album, *Set Me Free*.
CAUSE: Liver cancer. He died at Oak Forest Hospital in Oak Forest, Illinois.

Michael Stewart

(MICHAEL GASSEN STEWART)
Born April 19, 1945
Died November 13, 2002

The rhythm guitarist and drummer of the Sixties group We Five, Michael Stewart was the younger brother of one-time Kingston Trio member John Stewart. Hailing from Southern California, Michael Stewart joined Jerry Burgan to launch a folk group in 1963, The Ridge Runners. Expanded to a quintet and moving to San Francisco, the renamed We Five was signed by A&M Records in 1965. Employing complex harmonies, the group took a turn towards folk-rock, reaching the Top 10 that year with the Grammy-nominated single 'You Were On My Mind'. We Five managed just one more hit with the peace anthem written by Dino Valenti, 'Let's Get Together' (also covered by Jefferson Airplane and later a Top 10 hit for The Youngbloods under the title 'Get Together') before disbanding in 1968. In the early Seventies, Michael Stewart occasionally performed with his brother, John. Turning to production work, Michael Stewart collaborated with Tom Jones, Kenny Rankin, Ahmad Jamal, and was nominated for a Grammy for the Billy Joel album *Piano Man*.
CAUSE: He died after a long, undisclosed illness in Sacramento, California.

Rob Stinson

Born December 17, 1959
Died February 15, 1995
The lead guitarist of the influential Eighties pop-punk band The Replacements, Rob Stinson was the group's visual focus, appearing on stage in a dress or only in his underwear. A native of Waconia, Minnesota, Stinson had received a guitar for a Christmas present at age 11. Joined by his 12-year-old brother Tommy on bass and drummer Chris Mars, Stinson fronted a trio in 1978 called Dogbreath. Adding Paul Westerberg on vocals and guitar, the renamed Replacements got their break as a last-minute replacement at a local venue. Signing with the indie label TwinTone Records, the group released four albums including the irreverent and sloppy *Sorry Ma, Forgot To Take Out The Garbage* (1981) and the masterful *Let It Be* (1984). Signed by Sire Records' chief Seymour Stein, The Replacements made their major label début with the much acclaimed album, *Tim* (1985), which was highlighted by 'World Class Fad'. But with Stinson's increasing substance abuse interfering with his guitar work, he was fired from the band in 1986. Stinson formed a series of bands, including his last, The Bleeding Hearts. His brother Tommy Stinson later formed the group, Bash And Pop.
CAUSE: A victim of an accidental drug overdose, his body was discovered in his Minneapolis apartment on Saturday, February 18. Diagnosed as a manic-depressive in 1994, Stinson had been placed on medication.

Jesse Stone

Born November 16, 1901
Died April 1, 1999
Best known for his work behind the scenes at Atlantic Records, Jesse Stone worked with R&B stars such as The Drifters, Ray Charles, Ruth Brown, The Clovers, and Big Joe Turner. A prolific songwriter who often used the pseudonym Charles Calhoun, he penned a number of R&B standards. Born in Atchinson, Kansas, he first hit the stage at age five in his parents' minstrel act. Beginning his musical career as a jazz musician, he was a fixture in the nightclubs of Kansas City, cutting his first record in 1927, 'Starvation Blues'. Then after leading his own regional band (which included Coleman Hawkins and Budd Johnson), he passed through the Duke Ellington and Jimmie Lunceford orchestras. As a songwriter in the Forties, he had success with 'Sorgham Switch' (Jimmy Dorsey) and 'Idaho' (Guy Lombardo; Benny Goodman). Attracted by the novelty jump-blues of Louis Jordan,

Stone recorded a series of comical records for RCA and MGM Records. But with Ahmet Ertegun and his brother Nesuhi launching Atlantic Records in 1947, Jesse Stone was hired as a songwriter and arranger, and frequently joined his bosses on back-road talent hunts across the country. One of Stone's discoveries was session saxophonist King Curtis. Stone's hit compositions at Atlantic included 'Money Honey' (The Drifters), 'Cole Slaw' (Frank Culley), 'Shake, Rattle, And Roll' (Big Joe Turner), 'Flip Flop And Fly' (Big Joe Turner), 'Down In The Alley' (The Clovers), and 'Your Cash Ain't Nothing But Trash' (Clovers). Many of his songs were covered by others, notably Elvis Presley. Quitting Atlantic in 1956 after being refused part ownership of the label, he launched his own Brill Building publishing company, Roosevelt Music. Stone also worked for several other labels including Capitol, Reprise, CBS, and Aladdin, and penned further hits including 'Don't Let Go' (Roy Hamilton) and 'Smack Dab In The Middle' (Ray Charles). After leaving music in the late Sixties, he married and returned to New York. He retired to Florida in 1983.
CAUSE: Suffering from long-term kidney and heart problems, he died at a hospital near his home of Altamonte Springs, Florida.

Rory Storm

(ALAN CALDWELL)
Born c. 1940
Died September 28, 1972
The leader of the Merseybeat group Rory Storm & The Hurricanes, Rory Storm was a contemporary of The Beatles. Also an athlete, Storm simultaneously competed in sporting events. Storm formed a skiffle group in 1957 with friend Johnny Byrnes. Regulars at Liverpool's Cavern club, in mid-1959 the group switched to rock music as Al Storm & The Hurricanes. But by year's end Alan Caldwell became Rory Storm, and the group was expanded to a quartet and later a quintet that included drummer Ringo Starr. Emerging as one of Liverpool's most popular groups, The Hurricanes were among the first from the city to perform in Hamburg, Germany, where The Beatles would hone their skills. Briefly under the management of Brian Epstein, Rory & The Hurricanes were unable to create their own material and like so many other Merseyside bands they were left behind in the wake of The Beatles. The group disintegrated after the onstage death of guitarist Ty Brian in 1967. Rory Storm's sister Iris was married to singer Alvin Stardust.
CAUSE: Stricken with heart problems and devastated by two events – the death of his father and the break-up with his fiancée – he took a large quantity of sleeping pills and was found with his head in an oven. Storm's mother, Violet, killed herself the same day; in her suicide note, it was obvious that she had told Rory about her decision to end her life, which compounded his desperate state of mind.

Todd Storz

(ROBERT TODD STORZ)
Born May 8, 1924
Died April 13, 1964
The father of Top 40 radio, Todd Storz introduced the format in the mid Fifties in Omaha, New Orleans, and Kansas City. The first such format was introduced at KOWH in Omaha, a station given to Storz by his father. The idea of limiting a playlist to forty selections was born out of Storz's and station's programmer Bill Stewart's observation that teenagers tended to repeatedly play the same few songs on a local jukebox. After applying the formula, KOWH went from last to first place in the ratings.
CAUSE: Probably a cerebral haemorrhage.
FURTHER READING: Fong-Torres, Ben.

(1998). *The Hits Keep On Coming: The History of Top 40 Radio*. San Francisco: Miller Freeman.

Lynn Strait

(JAMES LYNN STRAIT)
Born August 7, 1968
Died December 11, 1998
A member of the Nineties heavy metal band Snot, Lynn Strait provided the lead vocals on the group's Geffen Records release, *Get Some* (1997). A controversial act, Snot was often targeted by authorities.
CAUSE: He died in a three-car crash near Santa Barbara, California. Also killed was Strait's dog Dobbs, which was pictured on the cover of the group's first album.

Gary Strater

Born 1951
Died September 19, 2004
A member of Illinois-based, melodic progressive-rock band Starcastle, bassist Gary Strater backed lead vocalist Terry Luttrell. The group was launched in 1969, originally as St. James, by students at the University of Illinois in Champaign. Often compared to the group Yes, Starcastle placed three albums on the US charts beginning with a symphonic, self-titled début release in 1976. After the group disbanded, Strater worked as a session player and joined a covers band, ESP. Strater later re-formed Starcastle for the 2001 album *Chronos*, which was issued on his own label Sunsinger Records. Strater also recorded a solo album around the same time.
CAUSE: Cancer of the liver and pancreas. He died at his home.

Tony Stratton-Smith

Born 1933
Died March 19, 1987
A sports writer turned record industry mogul, the avuncular Tony Stratton-Smith founded independent British label Charisma Records in 1969. Nicknamed "Strat", he was initially drawn to the music industry by his friends Kit Lambert and Brian Epstein. Stratton-Smith had previously written about soccer for several British newspapers including *The Daily Express* and after writing several football biographies he continued to edit a soccer yearbook into the Seventies, using the profits to help fund Charisma. He also wrote the book *The Rebel Nun* about South American martyr Mother Maria Skobtzova who was stabbed during a pursuit of Nazi war criminal Martin Boorman who was alleged to have survived World War II and gone into hiding in South America. After first dabbling in music publishing, Stratton-Smith switched to artist management, overseeing the trio Paddy, Klaus & Gibson who were taken over by his friend Brian Epstein. Stratton-Smith also managed Creation, The Koobas and Beryl Marsden. Undeterred by their limited success, Stratton-Smith launched his own label, Charisma Records, and henceforth became known as a generous patron of talented rock musicians whose work was not necessarily in line with commercial trends. If "Strat" believed in an artist there were few lengths to which he would not go to secure their ultimate success, an attitude that endeared him to many in the industry. Signing a host of groups, the label's first success came in 1970 with The Nice, led by keyboard player Keith Emerson. They were followed by Newcastle-based folk rockers Lindisfarne, and public school progressive rockers Genesis, both of whom were initially managed by "Strat". Charisma thrived with a small stable of acts that also included Van Der Graaf Generator, Rare Bird, Bell 'N Arc and Audience. Charisma also released records by the Monty Python's Flying Circus comedy team, the poet Sir John Betjeman and sports broadcasters Peter O'Sullivan and John Arlott. The signing of O'Sullivan, doyen of horse racing commentators,

reflected Stratton-Smith's keen interest in the turf. At one time he owned a string of racehorses and sponsored a Charisma Handicap Stakes race at Kempton Park, west of London. Charisma also launched a literary division, publishing poetry and music related books, and had a stake in the music magazine *Zig Zag*. By the Eighties, the label had added Hawkwind, Julian Lennon and Malcolm McLaren to their roster but "Strat" was tiring of the music industry and devoting more and more of his time to racing. A year before his death Stratton-Smith sold Charisma Records to Virgin Records founder Richard Branson for £4,000,000, largely on the strength of the Genesis catalogue and his contracts with Peter Gabriel and Phil Collins. Retiring to the Canary Islands as a tax exile, he opened a nightclub called The Final Crease.
CAUSE: Stomach cancer. He died while visiting the English Channel island of Jersey. His ashes were scattered over Newbury Racecourse in Southern England, and that afternoon one of Strat's horses, Sergeant Smoke, romped home at odds of 20–1.
FURTHER READING: Rogan, Johnny. (1987). *Starmakers & Svengalis: The History Of British Pop Management.* London: Queen Anne Press.

Henry Strong

Born c. 1920
Died July 1954
A blues harmonica player in Muddy Waters' blues band in the Fifties after the departures of Little Walter and Walter Horton in 1953, Henry Strong performed on standards such as 'I Just Want To Make Love To You'.
CAUSE: He was stabbed by his girlfriend and then bled to death in the back seat of Muddy Waters' car.

Jimmy Strong

Born c. 1936
Died January 29, 1970
The younger brother of Nolan Strong, Jimmy Strong had joined his brother's Detroit-based doo-wop group, The Diablos, in 1955 as the replacement for tenor Juan Guitieriez. But following Nolan Strong's departure for the army, Jimmy Strong assumed the lead vocal duties in the group from 1956–58, appearing on only one single, 'Oh Harriet'.
CAUSE: Unknown.

Nolan Strong

Born January 22, 1934
Died February 21, 1977
The leader of the Fifties Detroit-based R&B group, The Diablos, the Alabama-born Nolan Strong was reared on gospel music. Formed in 1950 at Detroit's Central High School, The Diablos were signed by Fortune Records in 1953. After finding local success the following year with 'Adios My Love', the group followed with their first national hit, the often recorded romantic ballad, 'The Wind' (1954). With a new line-up, Strong and The Diablos landed their highest chart entry with the uptempo, bluesy 'The Way You Dog Me Around' (1956). With Nolan Strong beginning a two-year army stint in 1956, his brother Jimmy Strong took over lead vocal duties. But by the time Nolan Strong returned in 1958, the group was in its waning days. Strong later scored a minor solo hit with 'Mind Over Matter' (1962).
CAUSE: Unknown. He died at his home in Detroit.

Joe Strummer

(JOHN GRAHAM MELLOR)
Born August 21, 1952
Died December 22, 2002
As a member of politically-charged punk group The Clash, guitarist Joe Strummer helped to alter the face of British rock. Born in Ankara, Turkey, the son of a low-level British diplomat, Strummer was educated at a boarding school before dropping out in his mid-teens. Having played in a

duo called The Vultures, in the mid Seventies he formed an R&B-rooted, pub-rock act, The 101ers. Although playing mostly covers, Strummer wrote their best known original, 'Keys To Your Heart'. After catching an early performance of The Sex Pistols when they supported The 101ers, Strummer quit and, through Malcolm McLaren's assistant Bernard Rhodes, he joined guitarist Mick Jones, Paul Simonon (bass), Terry Chimes (drums) and additional guitarist Keith Levene, to form The Clash in June 1976. Managed by Rhodes, The Clash began playing gigs supporting The Sex Pistols before Levene dropped out. (He later appeared in John Lydon's post-Pistols outfit, P.I.L.) In December 1976, The Clash joined the Pistols' infamous *Anarchy In The U.K.* tour, which after an avalanche of bad press was reduced to just three stops. Signed by CBS Records in 1977, seen as a sell-out by some of their more fervent following, the band released their first UK single 'White Riot'. The Clash sound infused elements of punk, rock and reggae as evidenced by their quickly-recorded self-titled album, featuring tracks mostly penned by Strummer and Jones. Emerging as the group's chief lyricist, Strummer explored topics such as racial inequality, police brutality and the entrenched establishment. The album remained unreleased for nearly three years in the US where it sold strongly as an import. When it was released there by Epic Records, several crucial UK single-only releases such as 'Complete Control', 'Clash City Rockers' and 'White Man In Hammersmith Palais' were added. A second, less well-received album, *Give 'Em Enough Rope*, appeared in 1978, followed by *The Cost Of Living* EP and their breakthrough album, *London Calling* (both 1979) featuring the memorable title track and a last-minute uncredited addition, 'Train In Vain (Stand By Me)' which became a minor US hit. Recording the self-produced, three-disc set *Sandinista!* (1980), The Clash purposely took a non-commercial route which received a critical battering and further divided their original audience. On the eve of a tour to promote the Glyn Johns-produced follow-up *Combat Rock* (1982), Strummer unexpectedly went AWOL but was eventually tracked down in Paris. His actions hinted at the tensions within the band. Drummer Nicky "Topper" Headon's drug problems had become a liability and he was sacked to be temporarily replaced by his predecessor Terry Chimes. Thanks to *Combat Rock* including the group's most commercial tracks, Jones' 'Should I Stay Or Should I Go' (later successfully used in the early Nineties for a Levi's TV ad) and the MTV staple 'Rock The Casbah', The Clash were making inroads into America. A 1982 US tour included opening stadium shows for The Who and a headlining slot on the 1983 US Festival – all of which served to make a mockery of the band's original punk credo. In '83, Strummer and Simonon fired Jones and, after releasing the critically savaged album *Cut The Crap*, The Clash was disbanded by Strummer in 1986. Jones went on to head Big Audio Dynamite and their second album featured Strummer's active involvement. Forming his own short-lived group Latino Rockabilly War, Strummer starred in the film *Straight To Hell*, had a minor solo UK hit with 'Love Kills', written for the film *Sid & Nancy*, and provided the score for the film *Walker*. With a new backing band – which included Jack Irons of Red Hot Chili Peppers – Strummer recorded the album *Earthquake Weather* (1989). Strummer quashed rumours of a Clash reunion by joining the touring version of The Pogues, producing their album *Hell's*

Ditch, as well as briefly substituting for lead singer Shane MacGowan on a subsequent tour. Forming The Mescaleros in the late Nineties, Strummer was working on sessions for the group's third album at the time of his death.
CAUSE: He suffered a heart attack at his home in Somerset.

Jud Strunk

(JUSTIN STRUNK, JR.)
Born June 11, 1936
Died October 15, 1981
A pop-country banjo player and vocalist, Jud Strunk landed his sole pop hit in 1973 with 'Daisy A Day'. A native of Jamestown, New York, he had been a regular on television's *Laugh In* and had appeared in the Broadway musical, *Beautiful Dreamer*. Later buying a wood cabin in Maine, he was unsuccessful in his bid for a state senate seat.
CAUSE: He crashed his recently purchased, open-cockpit, World War II vintage aeroplane into the mountainous forests of western Maine, while attempting to land at the Carabassett Valley Airport. Also killed was his passenger Richard Ayotte.

Joe Stubbs

(JOSEPH STUBBLES)
Born 1942
Died January 19, 1998
A member of the soul/R&B group The Falcons from 1957–60, Joe Stubbs replaced Eddie Floyd as lead singer. A native of Detroit, Stubbs provided the lead vocals on their hits, 'You're So Fine' (1959), 'Just For Your Love' (1959) and 'The Teacher' (1960). (The group landed its next hit in 1962 with new lead singer Wilson Pickett.) With his brother, Levi, a member of The Four Tops, Joe Stubbs occasionally joined that group for their stage shows. Hired by Motown, Stubbs briefly worked with The Contours and The Originals. Then in 1969, Stubbs formed an R&B group, 101 Proof Aged in Soul, landing a crossover, Top 10 hit with 'Somebody's Been Sleeping' (1970). Stubbs later joined a revival version of The Falcons.
CAUSE: Long-term heart condition.

Sugar Shaft

(ANTHONY HARDIN)
Born 1970
Died September 1, 1995
A member of the militant, Brooklyn-based rap outfit X Clan, deejay Sugar Shaft co-founded the group in 1984. Recording for Atlantic and 4th & Broadway Records, X Clan recited Afrocentric messages over sampled loops, and frequently criticised white rappers. The group's first album, *To The East Blackwards*, featured the hit single, 'Raise The Flag'. Sugar Shaft also worked with former X Clan member, Professor X.
CAUSE: AIDS.

Danny Sugerman

(DANIEL S. SUGERMAN)
Born October 11, 1954
Died January 5, 2005
Co-author of the best-selling Jim Morrison biography *No One Here Gets Out Alive*, Danny Sugerman was a Doors insider who personally witnessed some of the most outlandish behaviour in the annals of rock history. Befriended by Morrison in 1967, Sugerman finagled his way onto The Doors' payroll, initially by performing clerical tasks such as answering the group's fan mail. Following Morrison's death in Paris in 1971, Sugerman managed the careers of the group's surviving members as well as Iggy Pop, another rocker who could match Morrison for hedonism. Turning to journalism, Sugerman launched the magazine *Heavy Metal Digest*. In 1980, *No One Here Gets Out Alive*, co-written with *Rolling Stone* writer Jerry Hopkins, was published, becoming one of the most acclaimed books in rock'n'roll history. Sugerman

followed with an autobiographical sequel, *Wonderland Avenue: Tales Of Glamour And Success* that charted his narcotic downfall and rehabilitation, and a Guns N' Roses biography, *Appetite For Destruction*. Sugerman continued to oversee various Doors projects and was a consultant for the 1991 Oliver Stone biopic *The Doors* starring Val Kilmer as Morrison.
FURTHER READING: Sugerman, Danny. (1989). *Wonderland Avenue: Tales Of Glamour And Excess*. New York: Morrow.
CAUSE: A heavy smoker, he succumbed to lung cancer. He died at his home in Los Angeles.

Niki Sullivan

(NIKI MONROE SULLIVAN)
Born June 23, 1937
Died April 6, 2004
A member of Buddy Holly's backing band The Crickets, guitarist Niki Sullivan provided some of the best known riffs of the early rock era. Born in South Gate, California, but raised in Lubbock, Texas, Sullivan went to high school with Holly, and after an informal, after school, jam session, was asked to join Holly's group. Fronted by Holly on guitar and vocals, The Crickets eventually included Sullivan, drummer Jerry Allison and Joe B. Maudlin on bass. Travelling just across the state line to Clovis, New Mexico, in early 1957 the group began a fruitful relationship with independent producer Norman Petty. When the demo version of 'That'll Be The Day' was released on Decca subsidiary Brunswick Records, it far surpassed an overly produced version that was released on Decca by Buddy Holly & The Three Tunes. Topping the pop charts, the million-selling single propelled Holly & The Crickets into the national spotlight. With Norman Petty as their manager, the group set out on an East Coast tour, booked unseen, at the Apollo Theater in Harlem (the club believed it had hired the black doo-wop group led by Dean Barlow also called The Crickets). Initially heckled by the black audience, the Crickets were warmly received after performing a medley of Bo Diddley songs. In an effort to increase the group's exposure, a number of Crickets records were marketed as Holly solo releases on another Decca subsidiary, Coral. The "solo" Holly hit 'Peggy Sue' (originally titled 'Cindy Lou') landed the group an *Ed Sullivan Show* appearance. A follow-up single, 'Oh, Boy', featured 'Not Fade Away' on the flip side but, tiring of the hardships of the road, Sullivan left The Crickets at the end of 1957. He later recorded a few obscure singles as a solo act and as a member of a group he formed, Soul Incorporated. Sullivan did not rejoin his former bandmates in The Crickets until a Buddy Holly tribute in 1979.
CAUSE: Suffering a heart attack, he died in his sleep at his home in Sugar Creek, Missouri.
FURTHER READING: Sugerman, Danny. (1989). *Wonderland Avenue: Tales Of Glamour And Excess*. New York: Morrow.

Bert Summer

Born 1948
Died July 23, 1990
An actor and singer, Bert Summer starred in the Broadway production of *Hair*. He also scored a Top 40 hit in 1970 with 'We're All Playing In The Same Band'.
CAUSE: Liver failure.

J.D. Sumner

(JOHN DANIEL SUMNER)
Born November 19, 1914
Died November 16, 1998
A prolific gospel singer-songwriter, deep-bass vocalist J.D. Sumner was crucial to the establishment of the Gospel Music Association. Born in Lakeland, Florida, Sumner was drawn to music during childhood camp meetings and revivals. A member of The Blackwood Brother gospel group

1954–65, he joined a Southern-gospel group called The Stamps Quartet in 1965. The Stamps backed Elvis Presley on stage and in the studio from 1972 and until his death in 1977.
CAUSE: Heart attack. He was found dead in his hotel room in Myrtle Beach, South Carolina.

Sunnyland Slim

(ALBERT LUANDREW)
Born September 5, 1907
Died March 17, 1995
Mississippi-born Delta-styled, Chicago pianist bluesman extraordinaire, Sunnyland Slim was noted for bringing Muddy Waters into the studio. He earned his nickname in 1928 from his self-composed hit, 'Sunnyland Train', the song chronicling a train that had twice crashed. A self-taught player, Sunnyland Slim began his career as an itinerant musician in Memphis when in 1923 he hit the stage alongside Little Brother Montgomery. Later teaming with Tampa Red, and then Roosevelt Sykes, he also joined a revue led by Ma Rainey. Moving to Chicago in 1942, he initially joined Jump Jackson's band before collaborating with the likes of Big Bill Broonzy, Sonny Boy Williamson II, and an undiscovered Muddy Waters. Recording heavily for a series of labels including Chess, Vee-Jay, and Cobra, in 1947 he invited friend Muddy Waters to a session at Aristocrat Records. After backing Sunnyland Slim on 'Johnson Machine Gun', Waters sang lead on a pair of tracks including 'Little Anna Mae'. Aristocrat soon became Chess, and Waters emerged as the label's workhorse. Possessing a powerful voice that was legendary for shattering microphones, Sunnyland Slim enjoyed hits with 'Going Back To Memphis', 'Devil Is A Busy Man', and 'When I Was Young'. Still performing in the Eighties, he led The Big Four Band and operated his own label, Airway Records.
CAUSE: His health deteriorating in the last years of his life, he died from kidney inflammation at the Thorek Hospital in Chicago.

Sun Ra

(HERMAN BLOUNT)
Born May 22, 1914
Died May 30, 1993
An avant-garde keyboardist and bandleader who claimed to have been born on Saturn, the former Herman "Sonny" Blount was reared in jazz and blues. A native of Birmingham, Alabama, he moved to Nashville and played piano behind R&B shouter Wynonie Harris. Drawn to the Chicago blues scene in the mid Forties, he worked as an arranger for Fletcher Henderson and landed a position in the house band at the famed Club DeLisa. Forming his own free-form bebop group in the Fifties, he led a small ensemble which was alternately called The Arkestar, The Cosmo Jet, or The Solar-Myth Arkestra. Changing his name to Sun Ra, he infused new age culture, African symbolism, and astronomical imagery on progressive jazz albums such as *Cosmic Tones For Mental Therapy* (1961). In the forefront for employing musical electronics, he played an electric piano in 1956 and a Moog synthesizer in 1969. Gaining some acceptance in the Seventies, he was frequently derided for his idiosyncratic philosophies.
CAUSE: Stroke. He died at the Baptist Medical Center-Princeton in Birmingham, Alabama.
FURTHER READING: Szwed, John F. (1998). *Space Is The Place: The Lives And Times Of Sun Ra*. New York: Da Capo.

George Suranovich

(GEORGE PAUL SURANOVICH)
Born June 15, 1944
Died February 15, 1990
A latter member of the Los Angeles-based, Arthur Lee-led rock group Love, George Suranovich replaced drummer Michael Stuart in

1968 (Stuart had replaced original member Alburn Pfisterer). With Lee taking the group in a hard-rock direction, Suranovich appeared on the albums, *Four Sail* (1969) and *Out Here* (1969). Having been temporarily replaced in early 1970 by Drachen Theaker, Suranovich returned for a final Love album, *False Start* (1970). After playing behind Eric Burdon in the early to mid Seventies, Suranovich reappeared in another version of Love in 1977; a live album was subsequently issued by Rhino Records. A fixture on the Pittsburgh music scene for the remainder of his career, Suranovich also joined the touring oldies revues of Chuck Berry, Bo Diddley, The Platters, and The Drifters.
CAUSE: Congestive heart failure. He died in Pittsburgh.

Screaming Lord Sutch

(DAVID EDWARD SUTCH)
Born November 10, 1940
Died June 16, 1999
Though better known in the UK for his political aspirations as the "leader" of the Monster Raving Loony Party, Screaming Lord Sutch first came to prominence as the singer with The Savages, a theatrical rock act from pre-Beatles era England. Born in West Hampstead, north-west London, Sutch began his working life as a plumber's mate, joining the existing Savages in 1960. At this time he boasted the longest hair in rock, all 18 inches of it, and was regarded as a "wild man of pop" long before the emergence of The Rolling Stones. Based in Wembley, the Sutch-led Savages recorded but never reached the charts, perhaps because for all his showmanship Sutch's vocal talents were somewhat limited. However, they toured extensively with a variety of line-ups which at times included Carlo Little on drums, Ritchie Blackmore on guitar and Nicky Hopkins on piano among others less well known. Nicknamed "Lord" Sutch for the top hat he invariably wore, Sutch was the consummate stage performer: for Bobby Darin's 'Bull Moose', he put on a helmet with two foot long horns; for 'Blue Suede Shoes', he pranced around in boots painted lurid blue; during the group's self-penned single 'Till The Following Night', he emerged from a coffin; and on 'Great Balls Of Fire' he jumped around the stage holding a biscuit tin which he'd set alight. Too outrageous – and loud – for public consumption, there is no question that Sutch and his group influenced many future rock stars and in the Seventies he persuaded some of them, including Jimmy Page, Jeff Beck, and Noel Redding, to join him on an album entitled *Lord Sutch And Heavy Friends*. Latterly he became a well-known fringe candidate at UK parliamentary elections and by-elections, campaigning at times as the leader of the Teenage Party or the Monster Raving Loony Party, the latter inspired by a sketch from the *Monty Python's Flying Circus* troupe. His career as a candidate began in 1964 when he was persuaded by then manager Reg Calvert to stand for the National Teenage Party at Stratford-on-Avon, a seat vacated by John Profumo, who had been forced to resign for his role in the Christine Keeler sex scandal that effectively ousted the Conservative Government. Shortly after this Sutch and Calvert launched Radio Sutch, the second British pirate radio station (after Radio Caroline) from an abandoned fort off the Essex coast. In September 1964 Sutch sold the station to Calvert for the then astronomical sum of £5,000. Sutch was a much-loved figure in Britain, a true eccentric whose sense of humour often pricked the pomposity of British politics.
CAUSE: Despondent after the deaths of his mother and pet dog and financially insolvent, Sutch hung himself at his mother's home.

Stuart Sutcliffe

(STUART FERGUSSON VICTOR SUTCLIFFE)
Born June 23, 1940
Died April 10, 1962
A member of the early Beatles, Stuart Sutcliffe was a close friend of the teenage John Lennon and is generally credited with having influenced the group in their choice of hairstyle. Born in Edinburgh, Scotland, Sutcliffe moved with his family to Liverpool as a young child. While attending The Liverpool College of Art, he met Lennon, who was a year behind him. After selling his first painting in 1959 for the then impressive sum of £65, Sutcliffe was persuaded by Lennon to buy a bass guitar and join his fledgling group. With a line-up of Lennon, Paul McCartney, George Harrison, drummer Pete Best and the musically inept Sutcliffe, the group assumed various names including The (Silver) Beatles. Auditioning in 1960 for British promoter Larry Parnes for a chance to back the rising Billy Fury, The Beatles were instead assigned to another Parnes act, Johnny Gentle, with whom they toured Scotland. Visiting Hamburg, Germany in August of 1960, The Beatles honed their musical skills with gruelling, nightly shifts lasting several hours. With his sunglasses and leather jacket, Sutcliffe was a shy performer who would often play with his back to the audience to hide his inability on bass. Except for the occasional Eddie Cochran cover and Elvis Presley's 'Wooden Heart', Sutcliffe rarely sang lead vocals. While the other members of the group spent their days sleeping, Sutcliffe worked on his paintings. Although the audiences at the Star Club were mainly seamen in search of drink and prostitutes, The Beatles somehow came to the attention of young artists Astrid Kirschherr and her then-boyfriend, Klaus Voormann. Sutcliffe and Kirschherr began a relationship and in June 1961, Sutcliffe abandoned the group to study art under Eduardo Paolozzi at Hamburg University. Remaining in Hamburg while the other Beatles returned to Liverpool, Sutcliffe subsequently moved in with Kirschherr, a photographer whose pictures of the early Beatles in and around Hamburg would eventually become world famous. Sutcliffe died just as The Beatles arrived in Hamburg for a third visit. Sutcliffe was later pictured on the cover of The Beatles' album, *Sgt. Pepper's Lonely Hearts Club Band.* Several of Sutcliffe's paintings have been displayed in British art galleries; a number of his works were auctioned by Sotheby's in 1991.
CAUSE: Cerebral haemorrhage. Complaining of severe headaches, he went to doctors who were unable to see anything wrong in X-rays. In bed for two weeks, he was discovered unconscious by Kirschherr at their apartment and died in an ambulance en route to a Hamburg hospital. The haemorrhage was likely the result of either a fall down steps or a kick to the head during a fight after one of The Beatles' early performances.
FURTHER READING: Williams, Kay. (1996). *Stuart: The Life And Art Of Stuart Sutcliffe*. Guildford, England: Genesis.

Stacy Sutherland

Born May 28, 1946
Died August 24, 1978
An original member of The 13th Floor Elevators, guitarist Stacy Sutherland provided the psychedelic riffs for the Texas-based garage band. Conceived by Tommy Hall in 1965, the group was fronted by vocalist/guitarist Roky Erikson who had just scored a regional hit with 'You're Gonna Miss Me' as a member of The Spades. Composed by Erikson, 'You're Gonna Miss Me' was re-recorded for the group's moderate-selling début album, *Psychedelic Sounds Of The 13th Floor Elevators*. Taking large quantities of LSD for musical inspiration, the group

was the frequent target of police harassment and arrests. Following Erikson's imprisonment on a drug possession charge, the group disbanded in early 1968. Sutherland joined a 13th Floor Elevators reunion tour in 1977 which did not include Roky Erikson.
CAUSE: He was shot dead by his wife following a domestic argument.

Darrell Sweet

Born May 16, 1947
Died April 30, 1999
Darrell Sweet was the drummer in the hard-working Scottish rock band Nazareth who broke through with their Razamanaz (1973) album which was produced by Deep Purple bassist Roger Glover. Born in Bournemouth, on the south coast of England, Sweet's family moved to Glasgow, Scotland, where he studied accountancy while playing in a semi-pro covers band called The Shadettes who changed their name to Nazareth after hearing the lyrics to 'The Weight' by The Band. Nazareth turned professional and moved to London in 1970, securing a record deal a year later. Their manager, Scottish bingo entrepreneur Bill Fehilly, financed their début album. Although the band's style was rooted in blues rock, with the slide guitar work of Manuel 'Manny' Charlton to the fore, Nazareth scored hit singles with heavily re-arranged cover versions, including Joni Mitchell's 'This Flight Tonight', which reached UK number 11 in 1973, and Tomorrow's 'My White Bicycle', UK number 14 in 1975. Limited US success came a year later with their version of Boudleaux Bryant's 'Love Hurts' which reached number eight in the US *Billboard* charts, but the band found greater acceptance in Canada. Nazareth relied on constant gigging to maintain their fan-base but suffered a serious loss when their manager Fehilly died, and was replaced by a man who allegedly swindled the band out of thousands of pounds. Various personnel shifts saw Nazareth at a low ebb in the Eighties, especially in the UK where fans were thin on the ground, but they regrouped in 1992 and continued to perform before loyal fans in Continental Europe (especially Scandinavia and Germany), Russia, Japan, Brazil and Canada.
CAUSE: Heart attack. Sweet died in New Albany, Indiana, while on tour in the US.

Peter Sweval

(PIET SWEVAL)
Born April 13, 1948
Died January 23, 1990
A member of the rock groups Looking Glass and Starz, bassist Sweval veered from mainstream pop to hard metal within a few years. Formed by Sweval and two other students at Rutgers University in New Jersey during the late Sixties, Looking Glass played frat houses and college bars. Disbanding after graduation, the group was revived a year or two later and signed by Epic Records. Looking Glass topped the pop charts with a B-side hit, 'Brandy (You're A Fine Girl)' (1972) and, after a few misses, the group returned to the Top 40 with 'Jimmy Loves Mary-Ann'. Out of the ashes of Looking Glass, Sweval and bandmate Lawrence Gonsky formed a New York City group called Fallen Angels, releasing two singles and recording an album which went unissued for over two decades. After their contract with Arista Records unravelled, the group evolved into the heavy metal band Starz, fronted by singer Michael Lee Smith (brother of singer-actor Rex Smith) and signed to Capitol Records by Kiss' manager Bill Aucoin. Starz's self-titled 1976 début album was a blues-inspired, mainstream heavy metal venture and was followed by the similar *Violation* (1977), which spawned the band's only Top 40 hit 'Cherry Baby'. After the release of *Attention Shoppers!*, Sweval was fired for not wanting to take a turn towards

harder rock and was replaced by Orville Davis. Sweval then joined disco group The Skatt Brothers, recording one album for Casablanca Records in 1979.
CAUSE: Cancer.

Roosevelt Sykes

Born January 31, 1906
Died July 17, 1983
A legendary blues pianist and singer, Roosevelt Sykes influenced an entire generation of blues players with his inventive boogie-woogie based delivery. Born in Arkansas but raised in St. Louis, Sykes was a self-taught player, leaving home at 15 to work as an itinerant musician. First recording at OKeh Records in 1929 under the name of Dobby Bagg (one of his three pseudonyms), he scored a hit with 'Forty-Four Blues'. After spending most of the next decade in a series of St. Louis groups, Sykes moved to Chicago in 1941. Forming his own combo, The Honeydrippers, Sykes scored several hits including covers of Cecil Gant's 'I Wonder' and Joe Liggins' 'The Honeydripper'. A dapper dresser who possessed a genial disposition, Sykes was a true crowd pleaser. A prolific songwriter who advanced the blues idiom, Sykes penned a number of classics including 'Night Train', 'Nighttime Is The Right Time', and 'Forty-Seventh Street Jive'. With the ascent of electric blues in Chicago in the mid Fifties, Sykes disbanded The Honeydrippers and relocated to New Orleans, becoming a mainstay in the city's music scene. He frequently toured Europe in the Sixties and Seventies, and later became a deacon in a Baptist church.
CAUSE: Heart attack. He died at Charity Hospital in New Orleans.

Edmund Sylvers

(EDMUND THEODORE SYLVERS)
Born January 25, 1957
Died March 11, 2004
A member of the family soul/disco act The Sylvers, tenor vocalist Edmund Sylvers formed the group with several of his siblings. After winning a talent contest at a Los Angeles high school, the act was signed in 1972 by Mike Curb at MGM Records. With Edmund on lead vocals, the group had two R&B chart hits with their first two singles, 'Fool's Paradise' and 'Wish That I Could Talk To You'. Switching to Capitol Records where they teamed with former Motown producer Freddie Perren, The Sylvers topped the pop charts with the disco style ditty 'Boogie Fever' (1975), followed by two more crossover entries, 'Hot Line' (1976) and 'High School Dance' (1977). Moving to the Casablanca label, The Sylvers scored their final hit with 'Don't Stop, Get Off' (1978). Casablanca's attempt to promote Edmund Sylvers as a solo act failed as he managed just one minor R&B hit with 'That Burning Love' (1980). As a session percussionist, he worked with The Whispers, Janet Jackson and Carrie Lucas.
CAUSE: Lung cancer. He died in Richmond, Virginia.

Sylvester

(SYLVESTER JAMES)
Born September 6, 1947
Died December 16, 1988
An outlandish, androgynous, glitter-wearing Seventies disco star, "Sylvester" James was born and raised in south Los Angeles. Growing up in a Pentecostal church, he toured professionally as a child on the gospel circuit under the guidance of his grandmother, a blues singer in the Thirties. Moving to San Francisco in 1967, he joined a musical troupe called The Cockettes, an all-male drag revue that sang show tunes. Quitting in 1972 to attempt a solo career, Sylvester appeared in the Los Angeles production of *Hair*. Initially assuming the stage name of Ruby Blue, he performed in the style of a torch singer like Billie Holiday (whom

he claimed as a cousin); during this period, he began hormonal therapy to alter his gender. Signed to Blue Thumb Records in 1973, Sylvester and his backing group, The Hot Band (which featured future Journey guitarist Neil Schon), recorded two unsuccessful albums; tackling rock material with his funky gospel-trained falsetto, Sylvester was unable to find an audience. Rediscovered in 1977 by Fantasy Records A&R man Harvey Fuqua (formerly of The Moonglows), Sylvester embraced the disco craze. From his second Fuqua-produced album, *Step II* (1978), the cross-dressing, overweight, and openly homosexual performer was thrust into the national limelight with two high-energy disco standards, 'Dance (Disco Heat)' and 'Mighty Real'. But with the death of disco in the summer of 1979, Sylvester tried in vain to reignite his career. Releasing a number of albums in the Eighties including, *Mutual Attraction* (1986), Sylvester scored club hits with 'Do You Wanna Funk?' (1982) and 'Someone Like You' (1987). Sylvester appeared in the 1980 Bette Midler film, *The Rose*. Sylvester's back-up group, Two Tons Of Fun, included Martha Wash and later evolved into the soul group, The Weather Girls.
CAUSE: Although it is generally reported that Sylvester succumbed to AIDS, he was never diagnosed. He died in Oakland, California.

Margo J. Sylvia

(MARGO J. LOPEZ)
Born April 4, 1936
Died October 25, 1991
A member of R&B vocal group The Tune Weavers, Margo J. Sylvia provided the pleading lead vocals on the group's signature piece, 'Happy, Happy Birthday Baby'. Formed in Boston in the mid Fifties with her older brother Gilbert Lopez as The Tone Weavers, the group was expanded by Sylvia's husband, Johnny Sylvia, and a cousin, Charlotte Davis. With a DJ mispronouncing their name at a dance as The Tune Weavers, the group adopted the new moniker. Rooted in the light jazz/torch standards tradition, the group was discovered by Frank Paul who became their manager. Pregnant with her first child during the recording session for 'Happy, Happy Birthday Baby', Sylvia had penned the song with Lopez. Released on Frank Paul's small Casa Grande label, the song was soon picked up by the larger Chess/Checker label in 1957. A smash hit, the single propelled the group onto a series of caravan revues. But never scoring another hit and receiving few royalties, The Tune Weavers disbanded in 1962. Although Sylvia attempted a nightclub career in Boston, she soon abandoned music to raise six children. Moving to the West Coast in the Eighties, she launched a music publishing firm with her son and brother. In the Eighties, Sylvia released new material at Classic Artist Records and returned to the oldies circuit.
CAUSE: Suffering a heart attack and stroke, she died at a San Diego hospital.

Stan Szelest

(STANLEY MARTIN SZELEST)
Born February 11, 1942
Died January 20, 1991
A session keyboard player and original member of Ronnie Hawkins & The Hawks, the classically trained Stan Szelest had gravitated toward a boogie-woogie style piano in his mid-teens. A native of Buffalo, he ventured across the border to Hamilton, Ontario, to join a local bar band called The Tremblers. After crossing paths with a nationally touring band led by rockabilly artist Ronnie Hawkins, Szelest and bandmate Rebel Payne joined his backing band, The Hawks, shortly after the release of Hawkins' hit

single, 'Mary Lou'. (The Hawks would later evolve into The Band.) After leaving The Hawks and returning to college to study engineering, Szelest briefly joined The Bill Black Combo in 1960. But tiring of one night stands, Szelest returned to Buffalo in late 1960 and formed the perennial local rock band, Stan & The Ravens; after recording two bluesy singles, The Ravens disbanded in 1964. Szelest would frequently rejoin Hawkins' band in the next decade, appearing on several of his albums. A popular session player in the Seventies, Szelest toured with Neil Young, Jackson Browne, and Maria Muldaur, and also joined Lonnie Mack's band in 1977, appearing on the album, *Lonnie Mack And Pismo*. Relocating to Woodstock in the Eighties and reforming The Ravens, Szelest would occasionally perform in a loose knit group with former Hawks/Band members Garth Hudson and Levon Helm. At the time of his death, Szelest was working on an album with the remnants of The Band; the group had just signed a four-album deal with Columbia.
CAUSE: Heart attack. He died in Woodstock, New York.
FURTHER READING: Hoskyns, Barney. (1993). *Across The Great Divide: The Band And America*. New York: Hyperion.

T

Ron Tabak

Born c. 1953
Died December 16, 1984
The original vocalist of the Canadian rock group Prism, Ron Tabak had been a veteran of Vancouver bar bands. Formed in 1976 out of the ashes of a legendary group called Sunshyne, Prism experienced frequent personnel changes including the move of Bruce Fairborn from the line-up to producer. From their début album *Prism*, the group scored a major Canadian hit with 'Spaceship Superstar'. Although Jim Valance would leave the group, he would continue to contribute material, often in collaboration with the then-unknown Bryan Adams. Though remaining a force in Canada, Prism would have limited success elsewhere. With the moody Tabak in frequent trouble with the law, and following the failure of the group's fourth album, *Young And Restless*, Tabak was fired in 1981, and replaced by former Burton Cummings back-up singer, Henry Small. Tabak joined a series of local bands, but was in discussions to rejoin Prism at the time of his death.
CAUSE: While bicycling across Vancouver en route to the home of bandmate Al Harlow, Tabak was sideswiped by a passing car, striking his head. Tabak was taken by ambulance to Burnaby Hospital. Having injured his head the previous week in a mugging, Tabak became agitated when informed he hadn't suffered further injuries. Arrested by police, he was found unconscious while in his cell. Most sources mistakenly attribute his death to a car crash.

Tampa Red

(HUDSON WHITTAKER)
Born December 25, 1900
Died March 19, 1981
A legendary pioneering pre-war, bottleneck-style blues guitarist, Tampa Red was Chicago's first guitar star. A native of Atlanta, Tampa Red scored several bawdy hits in the Twenties, including a duet with frequent partner Georgia Tom, 'It's Tight Like That'. Considered a novelty number in the new "hokum" genre, the song sold very well and gave the renamed Hokum Boys a series of risqué blues hits. But with Georgia Tom (Thomas A. Dorsey) abandoning blues in 1931, Tampa Red moved to Chicago in the Thirties to pursue a solo career. A blues giant who usually recorded for Bluebird Records, Tampa Red teamed on recordings with bluesmen such as Leroy Carr, Big Maceo Merriweather, and Big Bill Broonzy. With his music out of fashion by the late Forties, Tampa Red was also hindered by a crippling drinking problem. After retiring from music in 1960, he re-emerged during the blues revival of the late Sixties. A prolific songwriter, Tampa Red's compositions include 'Sweet Black Angel' and 'Let Me Play With Your Poodle'.
CAUSE: Abusing alcohol much of his life, he died of natural causes.

Gene Tanner

(EUGENE TANNER)
Born February 1, 1936
Died December 29, 1994
The tenor vocalist of Fifties doo-wop group The "5" Royales, North Carolina-born Tanner joined the act during its peak period at the invitation of his older brother, lead singer Johnny Tanner. Joining in December 1953 as the replacement for Otto Jeffries, Gene Tanner first appeared on the Top 10 R&B entry 'I Do' (1954). Leaving Apollo for King Records, The "5" Royales would remain a popular concert draw but did not appear on the charts again until 1957 when Gene Tanner provided lead vocals on the Top 10 R&B hits 'Joy' and 'Think'. A follow-up single

(with Gene Tanner on lead vocals), 'Dedicated To The One I Love', wasn't a chart hit for the group but was later revived by both The Shirelles and The Mamas & The Papas. Becoming involved in litigation with labelmate James Brown, The "5" Royales were forced to leave King Records in 1961. After several more recording sessions over the next three years, the group disbanded in 1964.
CAUSE: Unknown. He died in Winston-Salem, North Carolina.

Johnny Tanner

(JOHN L. TANNER, SR.)
Born November 28, 1926
Died November 8, 2005
The tenor vocalist of Fifties doo-wop group The "5" Royales, North Carolina-born John Tanner had previously been a member of the Winston-Salem based gospel group The Royal Sons Quintet. Formed in 1942 by brothers Lowman, Clarence and Curtis Pauling, the gospel act emerged as a regional favourite and, after a two-year military stint, Johnny Tanner returned to the fold in 1950. In 1952, the group recorded two well-received gospel singles for Apollo Records but with the label wanting a more rock sound, the group emerged as a secular R&B band. One of the most successful acts of the era, the group débuted on the R&B charts in 1952 with the chart-topping 'Baby Don't Do It' which featured Tanner's impassioned lead vocals. The group returned to the top of the charts with 'Help Me Somebody'/'Crazy, Crazy, Crazy' and continued their hit run with 'Too Much Lovin' (Much Too Soon)' and 'I Do'. Leaving Apollo for King Records, the group remained a popular concert draw but it would be three years before they returned to the charts in 1957 with a pair of Top 10 R&B hits, 'Joy' and 'Think'. Involved in litigation with labelmate James Brown, The "5" Royales were forced to leave King Records in 1961. John Tanner left the group in 1963 and retired from music. He later worked at a Methodist church in Winston-Salem.
CAUSE: Bone cancer. He died at Wake Forest University Baptist Medical Center in Winston-Salem, North Carolina.

Nat Tarnopol

Born January 26, 1931
Died December 15, 1987
A record industry heavyweight who joined Brunswick Records as A&R chief in 1957, Nat Tarnopol broke into the music industry as a concert promoter. When his boss Al Green (not the soul singer) passed away in 1957, Tarnopol assumed the reins of a pair of publishing companies and the managerial duties over several acts including Jackie Wilson. Employing heavy-handed tactics and paying his artists little, Tarnopol was notorious within the music industry. After assuming half-ownership of the Brunswick subsidiary from Decca Records in the late Fifties, Tarnopol's prosperity was due in part to the talented Jackie Wilson. Building Brunswick into a top soul and R&B label, Tarnopol also had successes with Gene Chandler, The Chi-Lites, The Artistics, Percy Mayfield, Big Maybelle, and Young-Holt Unlimited. After demanding a financial audit of his parent label in 1970, Tarnopol emerged as the sole owner of Brunswick Records. A frequent target of federal prosecutors, in 1976 Tarnopol was convicted of conspiracy. Although sentenced to three years in jail, the conviction was overturned three years later on a technicality. Suffering a massive heart attack in 1982, Tarnopol effectively retired from the music industry. Brunswick Records was reactivated as a reissue label in 1995 by Tarnopol's children, Paul and Maria.
CAUSE: Heart failure. He died in Las Vegas.

Bob Tate

(ROBERT TATE, JR.)
Born 1932
Died August 3, 1993
A member of Sam Cooke's band, Oklahoma-born Bob Tate had moved to Los Angeles in 1956 after a navy stint. A classically trained saxophonist, he was initially hired as an arranger by bandleader Johnny Otis. Working with Cooke from 1958 until his mysterious death in 1964, Tate provided the sax on hits such as 'Bring It On Home To Me' and 'Twistin' The Night Away'. Tate also worked with T-Bone Walker, The Coasters, and Lou Rawls. Returning to his home in Phoenix, he performed on the local circuit during the next decade.
CAUSE: He succumbed to diabetes-related kidney failure. After suffering a heart attack, he was too weak to undergo dialysis treatment. He died at his home in Arizona.

Bruce Tate

Born 1935
Died 1973
A member of the pioneering Los Angeles doo-wop group The Penguins, Bruce Tate enjoyed brief fame in the mid Fifties. When tenor Cleveland "Cleve" Duncan met bass vocalist and songwriter Curtis Williams in 1954, they decided to form a vocal R&B group. Hiring a member from their respective schools, Williams brought on second tenor Dexter Tisby, and Duncan enlisted his friend, baritone vocalist, Bruce Tate. Not a particularly good student, an opportunity to sing in a group greatly appealed to Tate. Signed to Doo-Tone records, The Penguins recorded 'Earth Angel' in a garage studio as the B-side of 'Hey Senorita'. With lead vocals by Duncan, the romantic ballad had evolved from Williams' association with singer-songwriter Jesse Belvin. A rare crossover hit, 'Earth Angel' sold two-million copies and became a doo-wop standard. The group's newly hired manager, Buck Ram, subsequently placed the group with the larger Mercury Records, where their career fizzled. Killing a pedestrian and charged with manslaughter in November 1955, Tate dropped out of the group. He was replaced by Randy Jones.
CAUSE: Unknown.

Alex Taylor

Born 1947
Died March 12, 1993
The eldest sibling of the Taylor musical clan – Livingston, Kate, and the more famous James – Alex Taylor and his siblings were immortalised in the early Seventies on the cover of *Rolling Stone* as "the first family of rock". The first of the Taylor siblings to form his own group, Alex Taylor formed The Fabulous Corsairs, an early Sixties R&B group in Chapel Hill, North Carolina. For a time, the group would be expanded with James Taylor before he left for London on the first stage of a very successful solo career. (Alex Taylor's son, James, was the inspiration for the title track of James Taylor's 1970 album, *Sweet Baby James*.) More blues and R&B-orientated than his folk-based siblings, Alex Taylor recorded two solo albums at Capricorn Records in the early Seventies. Managing only limited success, Taylor recorded intermittently during the next decade for Dunhill and Bang Records. Also a jingle artist, he appeared in ads for Levi's and Kentucky Fried Chicken. In 1986, Taylor joined blues harpist James Montgomery to form the R&B group, The East Coast Funkbusters. At the time of his death, Taylor was working on his third solo album.
CAUSE: He suffered an alcohol-related heart attack on March 7 while working on his third album at King Snake Records studio. Falling into a coma, he died five days later in Sanford, Florida. Taylor had been in and out of detox programmes for various addictions much of his life.

Dallas Taylor

Born May 22, 1936
Died November 14, 1986
The leader of the Fifties, Chicago doo-wop group The Danderliers, Dallas Taylor provided the tenor vocals on their only national hit, the Top 10 R&B entry, 'Chop Chop Boom' (1955). After the group disbanded in the late Fifties, Taylor briefly joined The Dells and appeared on the single, 'Swingin' Teens' (1961).
CAUSE: Heart attack.

Derek Taylor

(DEREK WYN TAYLOR)
Born May 7, 1932
Died September 7, 1997
As the publicist and general aide to The Beatles, the urbane Derek Taylor maintained a high profile throughout much of the Sixties and his experience and company were eagerly sought after throughout his life. Trained as a journalist, Taylor worked for *The Daily Express* in Manchester, England, where he reviewed a Beatles concert on May 30, 1963, and by his own admission "fell in love" with the group. He met them backstage, befriended Beatles' manager Brian Epstein and was subsequently hired as his personal assistant. One of Taylor's earliest assignments was to ghost-write a George Harrison column for a national newspaper, and as a result he and Harrison formed a lasting friendship. Taylor also ghost-wrote Epstein's autobiography, *A Cellarful Of Noise*, and thus became one of the group's few close and trusted retainers. Leaving The Beatles' employ after an argument with Epstein (apparently because Taylor borrowed Epstein's limousine without permission), Taylor moved to California, and worked as a publicity agent for The Byrds, The Beach Boys, Buffalo Springfield and Paul Revere & The Raiders. He also helped in the staging of The Monterey International Pop Festival in 1967. With the death of Epstein and the launch of The Beatles' business venture Apple Corps in 1968, Taylor was invited back to England to work for the group. As the head of press at Apple, Taylor again worked closely with The Beatles until their demise in 1970. A lavish spender, he orchestrated a string of publicity stunts and maintained an open-door policy at his Apple office. As interviewees The Beatles were in constant demand and it was Taylor's unenviable task to decline far more interview requests than were granted. To his eternal credit, Taylor nevertheless became one of the most popular professionals in the industry, one of very few men to perfect the art of saying "no" graciously. His all-round courtesy and gift for dealing with potentially tricky situations was such that many of his friends believed he would have been better employed as a diplomat working for the government. When Apple folded, Taylor was hired as a publicity executive at WEA Records, initially in London and later as a vice-president of Warner Brothers Records in California. Although not a record producer in the formal sense, he oversaw the production of his friend Harry Nilsson's *A Little Touch Of Schmillson In The Night*. Leaving Warner Brothers in the late Seventies to pursue a career as an author, he penned the memoir *As Time Goes By*. It was followed by *Fifty Years Adrift*, a largely autobiographical limited edition, and *It Was Twenty Years Ago Today*, a memoir about the year 1967, the year that *Sgt Pepper's Lonely Hearts Club Band* was released. He also helped George Harrison with his autobiography, *I Me Mine*. Retained as a consultant by Apple Corps in the Nineties, he oversaw various later Beatles projects including the *Live At The BBC* albums and the *Anthology* series. At the time of his death he was working on The Beatles' official coffee-table biography, *The Beatles Anthology*, the text of which included

his own interviews with Paul, George and Ringo, as well as retrospective material on John Lennon.
CAUSE: Throat cancer. He died at his home near Sudbury, England.
FURTHER READING: Taylor, Derek. (1984). *Fifty Years Adrift*. Genesis: Guildford, England.

Eddie Taylor

Born January 29, 1923
Died December 25, 1985
A popular Chicago guitarist, Eddie Taylor was a key member in a series of leading blues bands in the Fifties. Arriving in Chicago in 1949, Taylor spent several years in a band led by Jimmy Reed, whom he had tutored on guitar as a child back in Mississippi. Backing Reed on a number of fruitful sessions at Vee-Jay Records, Taylor also scored his own hit at the label with 'Bad Boy'. A talented sideman, Taylor also joined the bands of Elmore James and John Lee Hooker. Merging modern funk with electric blues in the Seventies, Taylor's finest output was captured on the 1972 album, *I Feel Bad*.
CAUSE: Unknown. He died in Chicago.

Hound Dog Taylor

(THEODORE ROOSEVELT TAYLOR)
Born April 12, 1915
Died December 17, 1975
A Mississippi-born slide-blues guitarist who aided in the success of the fledgling Alligator Records, Hound Dog Taylor was little known outside Chicago until the release of his début album in 1971, *Hound Dog Taylor & The Houserockers*. With his rocking, rip-roaring guitar work and raw vocals, he created an immediate sensation on stripped down blues numbers such as 'She's Gone' and 'Give Me Back My Wig'. He released two more studio albums, *Natural Boogie* and the posthumously released live set, *Beware Of The Dog*.
CAUSE: Lung cancer. He died in Chicago.

Johnny Taylor

(JOHN HARRISON TAYLOR)
Born May 5, 1938
Died May 31, 2000
A gritty soul singer, Johnny Taylor thrived on the charts for over four decades. Born near West Memphis, Taylor was a neighbour of bluesman Junior Parker. Landing in Chicago around 1950, Taylor vacillated between the sacred and the profane, initially joining The Highway QCs gospel group in 1953 as the replacement for Sam Cooke who was joining the legendary Soul Stirrers. After a couple of years, Taylor quit the group to join the Vee-Jay Records doo-wop outfit, The Five Echoes. When Cooke departed The Soul Stirrers in 1957 to pursue a career in secular pop music, Taylor was again brought in to replace Cooke as the lead tenor. Quitting in 1959, Taylor briefly took to the pulpit as a preacher. Returning to music in 1961, Taylor signed with the Cooke co-owned SAR label. Emerging as a soul singer, Taylor scored a minor hit the following year with the Cooke-penned 'Rome Wasn't Built In A Day'. After Cooke's mysterious death in 1964 and the subsequent closure of SAR Records, Taylor signed with Stax. Nicknamed "The Philosopher of Soul", Taylor enjoyed a long string of gritty, Don Davis-produced hits including the two-million selling 'Who's Making Love?' (1968), 'Jody's Got You Girl And Gone' (1971), and the million-selling 'I Believe In You (You Believe In Me)' (1973). But with the demise of Stax in 1975, Taylor moved to Columbia Records. Flirting with disco, Taylor scored the biggest pop hit of his career with 'Disco Lady' (1976), the first single to earn Platinum certification in the US. Taking a turn toward bluesy soul, Taylor issued a series of brilliant albums for Malaco Records beginning in 1984.
CAUSE: After suffering a heart attack at his suburban Dallas home, he died at

nearby Charleton Methodist Medical Center.

Little Johnny Taylor

(JOHNNY LAMONT MERRETT)
Born February 11, 1943
Died July 17, 2002
A soul-blues singer and harmonica player, Little Johnny Taylor is often confused with R&B singer Johnnie Taylor who passed away in 2000. Born near Memphis but raised in Los Angeles, Little Johnny Taylor learned his passionate vocal phrasings while singing gospel music in his church. After passing through a number of gospel acts, including The Mighty Clouds Of Joy, he switched to secular music and, while working with R&B bandleader Johnny Otis, Taylor impressed audiences with his falsetto bursts. Pursuing a solo career, Taylor first recorded in 1960 for Hunter Hancock/Roger Davenport's Swingin' Records. Moving to Galaxy Records, Taylor first hit the R&B chart in 1963 with 'You'll Need Another Favor' and the soul-blues classic 'Part Time Love', his signature piece and only Top 40 crossover hit. Leaving Galaxy for Ronn Records in 1968, Taylor continued his hits with 'Everybody Knows About My Good Thing Pt. 1' (1971) and 'Open House At My House (Part 1)' (1972). After briefly taking a turn towards funk in the late Seventies, Taylor returned to his soul-blues roots and continued performing until a few years before his death.
CAUSE: Suffering complications of diabetes, he died at the Conway Regional Medical Center in Conway, Arkansas.

Lynne Taylor

Born 1928
Died 1982
A member of the folk-pop trio The Rooftop Singers, the jazz-trained, Lynn Taylor was previously a vocalist in orchestras led by Buddy Rich and Benny Goodman. Formed in 1962 by Bill Svanoe and former Weavers/Tarriers member Erik Darling, The Rooftop Singers scored a pair of hits, 'Tom Cat', and the chart-topping remake of Gus Cannon and The Jugstompers' 1930 release 'Walk Right In' (1963). Both tracks were culled from their début Vanguard Records release, *The Rooftop Singers.*
CAUSE: Unknown.

Mel Taylor

Born September 24, 1933
Died August 11, 1996
The drummer for legendary surf group The Ventures, Mel Taylor was inspired in his youth by jazz drummer Gene Krupa. Born in Brooklyn but moving to Tennessee in his early teens, Taylor initially played the guitar. Forming Mel Taylor and The Twilight Ramblers in the mid Fifties, he landed his own local radio show. Moving to Los Angeles in the late Fifties, he performed at the Palomino Club, and appeared as a session player on Bobby "Boris" Pickett's 'Monster Mash'. First guesting on a Ventures session in 1961, Taylor joined the group two years later as a replacement for Howie Johnson who had been seriously injured in a car crash. Playing on all of their Sixties hits except 'Walk, Don't Run', Taylor briefly left the group in 1967 to pursue a solo career. Continuing his session work, Taylor provided drums on a number of Herb Alpert & The Tijuana Brass hits, including 'The Lonely Bull'. Taylor again left The Ventures in 1973 to form Mel Taylor and The Dynamics but returned to the group in 1978. Mel's brother, Lawrence Taylor, was the bassist for the blues group, Canned Heat.
CAUSE: Cancer. Suffering from flu-like symptoms at the start of a Japanese tour with The Ventures, his condition worsened. Contracting pneumonia, he was hospitalised. Doctors in Japan subsequently diagnosed Taylor with lung cancer. Returning home, he died shortly thereafter.

Richard Taylor

(Richard Alanzo Taylor)
Born 1940
Died December 7, 1987
The baritone vocalist of the veteran soul group The Manhattans, Richard Taylor had previously formed a vocal group called The Statesmen while serving in the Air Force. On his discharge, Taylor and some of The Statesmen settled in New York City and formed The Dulcets with lead singer George Smith. After releasing an obscure single in 1961, The Dulcets evolved into The Manhattans the following year. Briefly recording for the Bobby Robinson-operated Enjoy Records as Ronnie & The Manhattans, the group spent several years at Carnival Records, signed after a losing performance at an Apollo Nightclub amateur competition. At Carnival Records, the group scored several R&B hits with Smith including, 'I Wanna Be (Your Everything)' (1965), 'Follow Your Heart' (1965), and 'I Call It Love' (1967). Signing with the King subsidiary, Deluxe Records, the group continued its run of moderate R&B hits. Following the death of original lead vocalist George "Smitty" Smith, the group hired Gerald Alston and supplanted their soul-based sound with a mature, ballad format. Signed to Columbia Records in 1973, The Manhattans found new success with a string of Bobby Martin produced and arranged R&B and pop hits including, 'One Life To Live' (1972), 'There's No Me Without You' (1973), and 'Don't Take Your Love' (1974). But The Manhattans' biggest hit would come in 1976 with a million-selling composition penned by the group's bass vocalist, Wilfred "Blue" Lovett, 'Kiss And Say Goodbye'. But following a lengthy illness, Taylor was forced to leave The Manhattans in 1976, his last hit with the group coming with 'I Kinda Miss You' (1976). After attempting a solo career, Taylor converted to Islam, taking the name Abdul Rashid Talhah.
Cause: The cause was never disclosed. He died in Kansas City, Kansas.

Ted Taylor

(Austin Taylor)
Born February 16, 1934
Died October 23, 1988
A popular soul singer, Ted Taylor emerged from the gospel and doo-wop traditions. Reared on gospel music in rural Okmulgee, Oklahoma, near Tulsa, Taylor was captivated as a child by the emotional strains of gospel singers like R.H. Harris and Sam Cooke. After passing through The Mighty Clouds Of Joy, Taylor joined The Santa Monica Soul Seekers, a gospel group that included Lou Rawls; but after the group signed with Modern Records in 1954, the label owners convinced both Rawls and Taylor to switch to R&B. Crossing the threshold into secular music, Taylor provided the first tenor in The Cadets/Jacks (the group recorded simultaneously under both names). As The Jacks, Taylor and the group enjoyed a hit with 'Why Don't You Write Me' (1955), and as The Cadets, 'Don't Be Angry' (1955). (Taylor was not on The Cadets' hit remake of The Jayhawks' raucous 'Stranded In The Jungle'.) Leaving for a solo career in 1956, Taylor took a stylistic turn toward R&B and blues. With his searing, high-pitched voice often leaping into a falsetto, Taylor enjoyed a series of moderate R&B hits with 'Days Are Dark' (1958), a remake of Chuck Willis' 'Be Ever Wonderful' (1959), 'Stay Away From My Baby' (1965), 'Something Strange Is Goin' On In My House' (1970) and 'How's Your Love Life Baby' (1971). Frequently jumping labels, Taylor achieved neither mass stardom nor wealth due to his business naiveté. After flirting with disco in the late Seventies, Taylor released his final album on his own SPG label in 1987.
Cause: Automobile accident. Taylor was killed during a tour through

Louisiana when his car struck the rear of a truck.

Vince Taylor

(BRIAN MAURICE HOLDEN)
Born July 14, 1939
Died August 31, 1991
A pioneering, London-born, leather-clad rock singer, Vince Taylor was forced to go to France to become a star. Though born in Britain, he was raised in the US and returned to London in 1958. Originally a member of The Playboys, a group that also included Tony Sheridan and Brian Bennett, Taylor and the group were frequent guests on the BBC television show, *Oh Boy!*, and scored an influential rock hit with the Taylor-penned, 'Brand New Cadillac'. Shocking audiences, the grunting and growling Taylor would make his stage entrance shackled up inside an iron cage. With the group disbanding in 1959, Taylor assembled a new line-up of The Playboys, and backed Screaming Lord Sutch in 1960. After filling in for an ailing Gene Vincent on a tour through France, Taylor moved to that country in the early Sixties. Embraced as a genuine rock star, for a time Taylor's popularity rivalled that of the "French Elvis", Johnny Halliday (who ironically was backed by former members of The Playboys). Touring and recording prolifically for the next three decades, Taylor remained relatively unknown in Britain. A rough character, Taylor was frequently confined to prison cells and psychiatric wards in later life. His troubled career and messianic pronouncements provided the inspiration for David Bowie's character Ziggy Stardust.
CAUSE: Cancer. He died in Lausanne, France.

Vinnie Taylor

(CHRIS DONALD)
Born 1948
Died April 19, 1974
A member of Sha Na Na, Vinnie Taylor provided the guitar in the revivalist group. Born in San Salvador where his father worked for the US State Department, Taylor discovered rock'n'roll after moving back to the US in 1960 at age 12. First studying the piano and violin, he switched to classical guitar. Drawn to surf music, Taylor passed through a series of groups before joining Sha Na Na (named from the lyrics of The Silhouettes' 1958 hit 'Get A Job'). Greasing his back hair and sporting dark sunglasses and long sideburns, Taylor was quick to learn the group's complex, stage choreography. A theatrical group, Sha Na Na was vital to the rock revivalist movement of The Seventies. Taylor died before Sha Na Na premiered its syndicated television programme in 1977.
CAUSE: Drug, probably heroin, overdose. He died in his room at a Holiday Inn in Charlottesville, Virginia, after a performance at the University of Virginia.

Tommy Tedesco

Born July 3, 1930
Died November 10, 1997
A prolific session guitarist, Tommy Tedesco performed on sessions behind acts such as The Beach Boys, The Monkees, and Frank Sinatra. A native of Niagara Falls, New York, Tedesco quit music for three years at age 13 when an instructor called him his worst student ever. After completing an army stint in the early Fifties, Tedesco joined Ralph Marterie's Orchestra, appearing with the group on Hoagy Carmichael's West Coast-based television programme in 1953. Leaving Marterie and remaining in Los Angeles, Tedesco was hired as a session musician for *The Adventures Of Ozzie And Harriet*, a gig that would lead to countless TV and film assignments, including *The Godfather, Green Acres, Batman, M*A*S*H, Charlie's Angels, Happy Days*, and *Butch Cassidy And The Sundance Kid.*

Much respected by his fellow musicians, Tedesco played guitar on dozens of hits, including 'Strangers In The Night' (Frank Sinatra), 'Viva Las Vegas' (Elvis Presley), 'Little Old Lady From Pasadena' (Jan & Dean), several Beach Boys classics including 'Good Vibrations', and countless Phil Spector "wall of sound" sessions at Philles Records behind girl groups such as The Crystals and The Ronettes. Also a member of various studio groups, Tedesco recorded with The Routers and The Marketts. Pursuing a solo career in 1978, he recorded several instrumental albums, and began to perform regularly in public. Tedesco also wrote a column for *Guitar Player* magazine, and wrote several guitar instruction books.
CAUSE: Lung cancer and a brain tumour. He died at his home in Northridge, California.

Richard Tee

(RICHARD TEN RYK)
Born November 24, 1943
Died August 19, 1993
A popular, classically trained session pianist, Brooklyn-born Richard Tee attended the Manhattan School of Music. Initially hired as a session player for Motown Records, he backed Marvin Gaye on early recordings such as 'Hitch Hike'. Returning to his native New York, Tee played on sessions behind Aretha Franklin, Billy Joel, Carly Simon, Joe Cocker, and Herbie Mann. Then in 1976, Tee joined the R&B/jazz group Stuff; featuring guitarist Eric Gale, they released two albums in the late Seventies and appeared in the Paul Simon film *One Trick Pony*. Tee subsequently joined Simon's band for a world tour in 1991. Writing *Mama, I Want to Sing*, Tee based the off-Broadway musical on the life of gospel/pop singer Doris Troy. Tee later led his own jazz ensemble, The Richard Tee Committee.
CAUSE: Prostate cancer. He died at Calvary Hospital in New York City.

Richard Tepp

(HOWARD RICHARD TEPP)
Born March 14, 1947
Died June 17, 2004
As the vocalist of Sixties garage-rock act Richard & The Young Lions, Richard Tepp enjoyed brief fame. Forming as The Emeralds in Newark, New Jersey, in 1965, Tepp initially sang cover versions of British Invasion hits. Renamed The Original Kounts and then Richard & The Young Lions, the group found its greatest fanbase in Detroit where they performed for huge crowds. However when the group's producers insisted that Tepp record with session musicians, the band soon split but not before landing a hit with the fuzz-guitar classic 'Open Up Your Door'. Tepp later hired replacement band members. At the time of Tepp's death, the group's original line-up had re-formed for a just-completed film biography and album produced by Steven Van Zandt.
CAUSE: Leukaemia. He died at Kingston Hospital in Kingston, New Jersey.

Tammi Terrell

(THOMASINA MONTGOMERY)
Born April 29, 1945
Died March 16, 1970
Best known for her collaborations with Marvin Gaye, soul singer Tammi Terrell began entering talent shows at age 11 in her native Philadelphia. As Tammy Montgomery, she toured with the James Brown Revue and released several singles in the early Sixties, landing scattered airplay with the Brown-produced, 'I Cried' (1963). Relocating to New York City in the mid Sixties, she attended the University of Pennsylvania and married professional boxer Ernie Terrell. Discovered by a Motown talent scout while performing in a Detroit nightclub, Terrell wowed the audience with her sensual, uplifting persona. Teamed with producers Harvey Fuqua and Johnny Bristol, Terrell placed a

trio of moderately selling singles on to the R&B charts in 1966. Duetting with Marvin Gaye in 1967, Terrell was the third of Gaye's four female singing partners at Motown. Becoming soulmates, they first landed on the charts with the Nick Ashford/Valerie Simpson composition, 'Ain't No Mountain High Enough' (1967), and continued their hit run with sincere, emotionally charged numbers such as 'Your Precious Love' (1967), 'If I Could Build My World Around You' (1967), 'Ain't Nothing Like the Real Thing' (1968), 'You're All I Need To Get By' (1968), 'Keep On Lovin' Me Honey' (1968) and 'You Ain't Livin' Till You're Lovin'' (1969). After collapsing on a Virginia stage into Gaye's arms in 1967, Terrell was diagnosed with a brain tumour. Although Terrell and Gaye collaborated on three albums, it was later rumoured that Valerie Simpson substituted for the ailing Terrell on some tracks on the third album, including the hits, 'What You Gave Me' and 'The Onion Song'.
CAUSE: Diagnosed with brain cancer, she underwent six operations in two years. She died at Graduate Hospital in Philadelphia.

Dewey Terry

(DEWEY STEVEN TERRY, JR.)
Born July 17, 1937
Died May 11, 2003
Half of the duo Don & Dewey, singer and keyboardist Dewey Terry formed the doo-wop outfit with Don "Sugarcane" Harris. Terry was raised in Los Angeles listening to his parents' boogie-woogie and jazz records and began his musical career as a falsetto singer in The Squires, a doo-wop vocal group formed at John Muir High School in Pasadena, California. From the group, Terry teamed with childhood friend Don Harris to form Don & Dewey. Although the pair had only limited success as recording artists, their self-composed releases were bigger cover hits for other acts: 'Justine' (The Righteous Brothers), 'Big Boy Pete' (The Olympics), 'I'm Leaving It All Up To You' (Dale & Grace; Donnie & Marie Osmond), 'Ko-Ko Joe' (Jerry Reed) and 'Farmer John' (The Premiers; The Searchers; Neil Young). By 1964, Don & Dewey were briefly members of Little Richard's backing band. Reuniting with Harris beginning in 1975, Terry would occasionally hit the oldies circuit. Later emerging as a guitar-slinging R&B solo act in the mould of Guitar Slim, Terry spent the next two decades touring across the US and Europe. Following Harris' death in 1999, Terry occasionally performed as Don & Dewey with replacement member Ron Shy.
CAUSE: Suffering from throat cancer for two years, he died at Cedars-Sinai Medical Center in Los Angeles.

Sonny Terry

(SAUNDERS TERRILL)
Born October 24, 1911
Died March 12, 1986
A folk-blues harmonica player who frequently collaborated with Brownie McGhee, Sonny Terry bridged 19th century folk balladry with acoustic Delta blues. Blind in both eyes from two separate incidents (at ages five and eighteen), Terry first attracted attention as backing player for blues guitarist Blind Boy Fuller, appearing on a number of Vocalion recordings beginning in 1937. Invited to New York City by producer/promoter John Hammond, Terry appeared at the celebrated Spirituals to Swing concert in 1938. First meeting acoustic guitarist Brownie McGhee in 1939, Terry teamed with his long time collaborator in 1941 after the death of Fuller. Relocating to New York City, Terry and McGhee were befriended by like-minded folk-blues singer Leadbelly, and landed gigs in the city's politically charged folk clubs. McGhee toured and recorded prolifically at a

variety of record labels, usually with Terry at his side; for a time, the pair even hit the Broadway stage as actors in Tennessee Williams' *Cat On A Hot Tin Roof*. Travelling to Britain in the Fifties, the duo influenced an entire generation of budding blues musicians. Parting with McGhee in the mid Seventies in a bittersweet break-up, Terry continued to record and tour, and made an appearance in the film *The Color Purple*.
CAUSE: Natural causes. He died in Mineola, New York.

Joe Tex

(JOSEPH ARRINGTON, JR.)
Born September 8, 1933
Died August 13, 1982
A popular soul singer who scored a string of hits beginning in the mid Sixties, the sandpaper-voiced Joe Tex frequently talked his way through his autobiographical songs. Born into poverty in Navasota, Texas, and raised in suburban Houston, Tex was discovered by Arthur Prysock after winning an amateur show performance at Harlem's Apollo Theater. Signed by King Records in the mid Fifties, Tex recorded several poor-selling singles. After a stint at Ace Records, he switched to Anna Records and garnered scattered airplay with his first "talking" song, a cover of Etta James' 'All I Could Do Was Cry'. Tex's fortunes soon improved at Dial Records, a label formed by country music publisher and producer Buddy Killen. Failing to chart during his first four years at Dial, Tex was initially successful as a songwriter, penning the James Brown hit, 'Baby You're Right' (1961). With Killen nearly giving up on Tex, a final session was scheduled at Fame Studios in Muscle Shoals, Alabama. Released against Tex's wishes, 'Hold What You've Got' became his first national hit. Enjoying a remarkable string of soul hits at Dial Records, Tex dominated the R&B charts with 'I Want To Do (Everything For You)', 'A Sweet Woman Like You' (1965), 'S.Y.S.L.J.F.M' (1966), 'Show Me' (1967), and 'Skinny Legs And All' (1967). An R&B superstar during the Sixties, Tex was a rousing, energetic performer whose stage antics rivalled James Brown. Also a funk pioneer, Tex scored the biggest US hit of his career with gritty 'I Gotcha' (1972); but while the single was sitting atop the pop charts, Tex adopted the name Joseph Hazziez and left music to spread the teachings of Black Muslem sect leader, Elija Muhammad. Following Muhammad's death in 1975, Tex returned to a career in music, and landed his last hit in 1977 with the disco-flavoured, 'Ain't Gonna Bump No More (With No Big Fat Woman)'.
CAUSE: He suffered a heart attack at his home in Navasota, Texas. At the time of his death, he had been touring in an oldies soul revue with Wilson Pickett and Solomon Burke.

Gary Thain

Born May 15, 1948
Died December 15, 1975
The bass player of the British heavy-metal group Uriah Heep, Gary Thain preferred to allow flashier members of the band to take the spotlight. Born in New Zealand and moving to England in the mid Sixties, Thain joined Keef Hartley's blues-rock group in 1969 for a three-year stint, beginning with the album *Halfbreed*. Leaving in 1972 to join Uriah Heep, Thain replaced the ailing Paul Newton. Thain joined just as the group was celebrating its first million-seller, *Demons And Wizards* (1972), the album containing the group's only Top 40 hit, 'Easy Livin''. Leaving Mercury Records for Warner Brothers in 1973, the group scored airplay with 'Stealin'', the track culled from their label début, *Sweet Freedom*. A popular if critically unfashionable touring band, Uriah Heep sustained a long career without the help of rock critics or much radio airplay. After recording his fifth album

with the group, *Wonderworld* (1974), Thain quit, angry over receiving an electric shock while on stage in Dallas. Following a five-month recuperation, Thain was left with a slight limp. Also a session player, Thain backed a number of artists including Champion Jack Dupree, Ken Hensley, Miller Anderson and Martha Valez.
CAUSE: Accidentally overdosing, he had been abusing drugs for years.

Sister Rosetta Tharpe

(ROSETTA NUBIN)
Born March 20, 1921
Died October 9, 1973
A gospel singer and guitarist who influenced many R&B singers, Arkansas-born Sister Rosetta Tharpe belted out gospel, blues, and jazz during her long career. After recording for Decca Records in 1938, Tharpe joined the bands of Cab Calloway and Lucky Millinder in the early Forties. By the mid Forties, she scored several influential hits including, 'Strange Things Are Happening Everyday' (1945), 'Up Above My Head, I Hear Music In The Air' (1948), and a moving rendition of 'Silent Night' (1949). Although Tharpe continued to sing gospel music in the church, she belted out jazz in nightclubs. Tharpe later toured England with traditional jazz bandleader, Chris Barber.
CAUSE: Suffering a stroke in 1970, her health had deteriorated. She died in Philadelphia.

Drachen Theaker

Born c. 1946
Died 1992
A drummer best known for his stint in The Crazy World Of Arthur Brown, Drachen Theaker was an original member of the outrageous theatrical act. A jazz trained musician, Theaker had previously worked with both Jimmy Cliff and The Measles, an R&B group which had created a stir with their first (1965) single 'Casting My Spell'. After nearly joining Jimi Hendrix's Experience in 1966, Theaker teamed with ex-Reading University student, Arthur Brown. Though a promising début, 'Devil's Grip', failed to chart in 1967, the atmospheric 'Fire', produced by Who manager/producer Kit Lambert, reached number one in the UK in the summer of 1968. Angry over how Lambert had mixed down most of his drum parts on the group's self-titled début album, Theaker left the band just as 'Fire' was climbing the charts and was replaced by Carl Palmer. Spending several months with the Los Angeles-based psychedelic band Love, Theaker worked on the 1969 albums *Four Sail* and *Out Here*; Theaker also aided Warren Zevon on his début album *Wanted – Dead Or Alive*. Maintaining his ties with Arthur Brown, Theaker formed Rustic Hinge; some tracks from these sessions – which did not feature Brown – were released in 1988. Theaker subsequently worked with Deep Fix and a latter version of the progressive-rock act High Tide.
CAUSE: Brain tumour.

Bob Thiele

Born July 27, 1922
Died January 30, 1996
Longtime producer and record company executive at Decca Records, Bob Thiele was instrumental in the early career of Buddy Holly. A former jazz radio DJ and big-band leader who at 18 launched his own label, Signature Records, Thiele recorded jazz acts such as Erroll Garner and Coleman Hawkins. Hired by the Decca subsidiary, Coral Records in 1949, he transferred his Signature catalogue to the label. With the departure of Milt Gabler for Decca, Thiele became the head of Coral's A&R department and had great chart success with The McGuire Sisters, Teresa Brewer, and Lawrence Welk. His greatest achievement came when he bought Buddy Holly's master for 'That'll Be

The Day', a record issued on another Decca subsidiary, Brunswick. Thiele then signed Jackie Wilson who was also placed on Brunswick. Leaving Decca for Dot Records, Thiele produced pop singer Pat Boone. Forming Impulse Records in 1961, Thiele recorded the finest in jazz including Archie Shepp and John Coltrane. A Thiele co-composition, 'What A Wonderful World', was a hit for Louis Armstrong.
CAUSE: He died of kidney failure at Roosevelt Hospital in New York.
FURTHER READING: Thiele, Bob. (1995). *What A Wonderful World: A Lifetime Of Recordings*. New York: Oxford University.

Jon Thomas

Born 1918
Died October 28, 1995
An R&B/blues keyboardist, Jon Thomas scored his biggest hit with 'Heartbreak (It's Hurtin' Me)' (1960). A native of Cincinnati, Thomas had worked as a session player at King Records in the late Fifties.
CAUSE: Prostate cancer.

Leon Thomas

Born October 4, 1937
Died May 8, 1999
A one-time member of Santana, Leon Thomas is better known for his African-tinged experimental jazz. After studying music at Memphis State University, Thomas settled in New York City in the Fifties. After a decade on the jazz and blues circuit, he teamed with experimental jazz saxophonist Pharaoh Saunders, a fruitful partnership which spawned several highly regarded albums and the classic, 'The Creator Has A Master Plan'. Pursuing a solo career in 1969, Thomas released a number of albums on Bob Thiele's Flying Dutchman label and performed on Louis Armstrong's final recording session. Invited to join the Latin-tinged rock band Santana as a multi-instrumentalist and singer, Thomas appeared on the live album *Lotus* (1973). For the album *Welcome* (1973), Thomas provided the lead vocals on the tracks 'When I Look Into Your Eyes' and 'Light Of Life'. Struggling with a drug problem, Thomas left Santana in 1973. Recording sporadically during the next two decades, Thomas reunited with Saunders in the Nineties.
CAUSE: Suffering from leukaemia, he suffered a massive heart attack and died at Lincoln Hospital in the Bronx, New York.

Rufus Thomas

Born March 26, 1917
Died December 15, 2001
A celebrated Memphis-based R&B artist, Rufus Thomas was an outrageous dresser who often hit the stage in capes, feathers and white boots. Born in rural Mississippi but raised in Memphis, Thomas broke into show business in 1936 as a comedian, singer and dancer in the legendary travelling black troupe, The Rabbit-Foot Minstrels. By 1940, Thomas had gained notoriety as the emcee of a local talent show at the Palace Theater on Beale Street; the venue would launch the careers of numerous recording stars including Bobby "Blue" Bland and B.B. King. Joining the staff at WDIA in 1948, Thomas began a decades-long career in broadcasting. Also pursuing a singing career, Thomas scored his first national hit in 1953 with the Sam Phillips-produced 'Bear Cat', which was an answer record to Big Mama Thornton's 'Hound Dog'. Joined by his teenage daughter Carla at the new Satellite label, Thomas scored a regional hit with the self-penned duet ''Cause I Love You'. With Satellite renamed Stax, Thomas became one of the label's first hit acts with 'Walking The Dog' (1963) and 'Can Your Monkey Do The Dog?' (1964). After a recording respite, Thomas enjoyed new-found popularity in the early

Seventies as he returned to the charts with 'Do The Funky Chicken' (1970), '(Do The) Push And Pull Part I' (1970) and 'The Breakdown (Part I)' (1971). Nicknamed "the Ambassador Of Beale Street", Thomas last performed at the Memphis In May Beale Street Music Festival in 2000.
CAUSE: Heart failure. He had undergone open-heart surgery in 1998. He died in Memphis.

Tasha Thomas

Born 1950
Died October 15, 1984
Best known as a cabaret performer and disco singer, Alaska-born Tasha Thomas enjoyed several club hits in the late Seventies including 'Shoot Me (With Your Love)' and 'Midnight Rendezvous', and starred in the Broadway production of *The Wiz*. Also a session vocalist, she backed Kiss, Diana Ross, Stevie Wonder, Carly Simon and Al Kooper.
CAUSE: Cancer. She died in New York City.

Sonny Thompson

(ALFONSO THOMPSON)
Born August 22, 1916
Died August 11, 1989
A popular Chicago-based R&B pianist and bandleader, Mississippi-born Sonny Thompson scored several instrumental hits at Miracle Records in the late Sixties including 'Long Gone, Pts. 1 & 2' (1948), 'Late Freight' (1948), and 'Blue Dreams' (1949). While employed as a session player by King-Federal, Thompson continued his hit run with another instrumental, 'Mellow Blues, I & II' (1950) and featuring the vocals of Lula Reed, 'I'll Drown In My Tears' and 'Let's Call It A Day' (1952). Promoted to the label's A&R department in 1959, Thompson signed blues guitarist Freddy King the following year. Leaving King-Federal in 1964, Thompson joined King's band, and later Otis Rush's group.
CAUSE: Diabetes. He died in Chicago.

Tony Thompson

(ANTHONY T. THOMPSON)
Born November 15, 1954
Died November 12, 2003
A member of both Chic and Power Station, drummer Tony Thompson provided the backbeat on numerous dance-oriented hits. From New York City, Thompson took drum lessons from Narada Michael Walden and broke into music as a backing session player for Patti LaBelle. After meeting Nile Rodgers at an audition, Thompson was hired in the jazz-rock group The Big Apple Band who floundered until adding female vocalists, veering towards disco and changing their name to Chic. Eventually signed by Atlantic Records, Chic scored several influential disco hits including 'Dance, Dance, Dance (Yowsah, Yowsah, Yowsah)', 'Le Freak', 'I Want Your Love' and the frequently sampled 'Good Times'. Following Chic's demise in 1982, Thompson and his Chic-cohorts worked as session musicians, appearing on Diana Ross' *Diana*, Madonna's *Like A Virgin*, David Bowie's *Let's Dance* and Mick Jagger's *She's The Boss*. In 1985, Thompson joined what was intended as a studio-only, synth-rock band, Power Station, including members of Duran Duran and featuring Robert Palmer on lead vocals, who landed hits with 'Some Like It Hot' and a cover of T. Rex's 'Get It On (Bang A Gong)'. When the band hit the road, Palmer was replaced by Michael des Barres. The original line-up briefly reunited in 1997. Thompson did not join any of the Chic reunions in the Nineties.
CAUSE: Renal cell cancer. He died in Encino, California.

Big Mama Thornton

(WILLIE MAE THORNTON)
Born December 11, 1926
Died July 25, 1984
Earning the nickname "Big Mama"

for her 350 pound weight, blues singer Willie Mae Thornton growled and moaned through her records. Born a minister's daughter in Montgomery, Alabama, Thornton was a member of Sammy Green's nationally touring, Atlanta-based Hot Harlem Revue from 1941–48; a featured vocalist, she also played drums and harmonica. Settling in Houston in 1948, Thornton recorded for E&W Records before catching the attention of Peacock Records owner Don Robey. With her initial releases fizzling, Thornton was teamed with Johnny Otis and his powerful R&B orchestra. Recording the Jerry Leiber and Mike Stoller composition 'Hound Dog', Big Mama Thornton landed her sole chart hit with this lowdown, million-selling single. Elvis Presley would record a different, rock-flavoured version of the song several years later. A captivating stage performer whose best work was never captured on record, Thornton sold few discs after leaving Peacock. Falling out of popularity in the late Fifties, Thornton settled in the San Francisco Bay Area, where she performed with local blues groups. Rediscovered after a commanding performance in 1964 at the Monterey Jazz Festival, Thornton toured heavily throughout Europe. Joined by an all-star cast which included Muddy Waters, Otis Spann and James Cotton, Thornton recorded the Arhoolie album, *Big Mama With The Chicago Blues Band*. Taking a soul turn on *Stronger Than Dirt* (1969), she attempted material such as 'Funky Broadway'. One of Thornton's hit compositions, 'Ball And Chain', was redefined by white blues-rock singer Janis Joplin. In declining health in later years, Thornton settled in Los Angeles.

CAUSE: Abusing alcohol for decades, she succumbed to heart and liver problems. At the time of her death, she had withered to less than 100 pounds. She died in Los Angeles.

Melanie Thornton

Born May 13, 1967
Died November 24, 2001

The lead singer of R&B/dance duo La Bouche, Melanie Thornton was reared on Motown classics. Born in Charleston, South Carolina, Thornton left the US for Germany in 1992 in an attempt to further her musical career. Befriended by Milli Vanilli svengali Frank Farian, Thornton was paired with rapper Lane McCray in 1995 to form La Bouche and had a pair of international club hits with 'Be My Lover' (1995) and 'Sweet Dreams' (1996). Thornton left the group in February 2000 for a solo career.

CAUSE: She died in an aeroplane crash while on a publicity tour to promote her solo album *Ready To Fly*. The Crossair Avro RJ100 Jumbolino crashed in a wooded area two miles short of Zurich airport. Of the 33 persons aboard the Swiss flight from Berlin to Zurich, only nine survived. In addition to Thornton, two of the three members of German/Dutch pop trio Passion Fruit also perished in the crash.

Johnny Thunders

(JOHN ANTHONY GENZALE, JR.)
Born July 15, 1952
Died April 23, 1991

The outlandish guitarist of the legendary glam rock group, The New York Dolls, Johnny Thunders was a legend in the punk-rock community. Born in Queens, New York, Thunders planned on pursuing a career in baseball until he quit high school as the result of an argument with the baseball coach over the length of his hair. Soon heading a rock group called Johnny and The Jaywalkers, Thunders had already adopted a glam persona and wore women's blouses, cowboy scarves and make-up. Using the stage name of Johnny Volume, Thunders joined drummer Billy Murcia and guitarist Sylvain Sylvain in 1971 to form Actress. Evolving into The Dolls in late 1971, and then The New York Dolls, the androgynously attired group added vocalist David Johansen (then known as David Jo Hansen). After a series of shows at the Mercer Arts Center in Greenwich Village, the Dolls became the house band at Max's Kansas City until banned when two members were caught smoking cocaine in the bathroom. Signed to Mercury Records in an alliance that harboured distrust on both sides, The Dolls recorded two critically acclaimed proto-punk albums – the Todd Rundgren-produced *New York Dolls* (1973) and the George "Shadow" Morton-produced *Too Much Too Soon* (1974). The New York Dolls landed only spotty airplay with influential singles such as 'Personality Crisis', 'Trash' and their only real hit, a cover of The Cadets' novelty number, 'Stranded In The Jungle'. Dropped by Mercury, not least because of their reckless ways, and latterly managed by former shop owner Malcolm McLaren, The Dolls traded their lipstick and glam clothing for Red Chinese outfits. With McLaren unable to salvage the group's career, Nolan and Johnny Thunders quit and teamed with bass player Richard Hell to form The Heartbreakers (not Tom Petty's group). Popular in Britain, The Heartbreakers often shared bills with The Clash and The Sex Pistols who were then managed by McLaren. Recorded for Track Records, The Heartbreakers' 1977 album *L.A.M.F.* was highlighted by 'Born To Loose' and the drug-themed 'Chinese Rocks'; with Thunders often in detox programmes, the song mirrored his life. After the break-up of The Heartbreakers, Thunders stayed on in England and signed with Real Records. Releasing his first solo album *So Alone* (1978), Thunders enjoyed an underground hit with 'You Can't Put Your Arms Around A Memory' (1978); helping on the sessions were Steve Jones, Paul Cook, Chrissie Hynde, Phil Lynott, and Steve Marriott. After a problem with his visa, Thunders left England and returned to New York and temporarily regrouped The Heartbreakers. In 1979, Thunders joined former MC5 member Wayne Kramer in the Detroit-based group, Gangwar. His heroin addiction intensifying, Thunders made light of his problem on the aptly titled solo album, *Too Much Junkie Business*. Spending much of the Eighties in England, Thunders released *Que Sera Sera* in the early Eighties and his final album, *Copy Cats*, in 1988. He then formed a band called The Oddballs but was unable to secure a record deal for them. Leaving The Oddballs on hold, Thunders had arranged to meet up with former Dolls drummer Jerry Nolan and Oddballs guitarist Stevie Klasson in New Orleans when he died.

CAUSE: Thunders died while staying in a New Orleans' boarding house, the St. Peter House. Although alcohol, cocaine and methadone were found in his system, a post mortem examination revealed that he was suffering lymphatic leukaemia. The room had been ransacked by the time police had arrived. According to former bandmate Sylvain Sylvain, Thunders was introduced to heroin by Iggy Pop. Rumours of Thunders' death had circulated from time to time in the Seventies and Eighties.

FURTHER READING: Antonia, Nina. (1987). *Johnny Thunders: In Cold Blood*. London: Jungle Books. Antonia, Nina. (1998). *The New York Dolls: Too Much Too Soon*. London: Omnibus.

Andrew Tibbs

(MELVIN ANDREW GRAYSON)
Born February 2, 1929
Died May 5, 1991

A Chicago-based blues singer, Andrew Tibbs gained fame for giving Phil and Leonard Chess their first pre-Chess

Records hit at Aristocrat Records with 'I Feel Like Cryin'' (1949). Tibbs later teamed with brother Kenneth as The Tibbs Brothers, recording at Atco Records in 1956. Disillusioned by the life of a musician, he quit the music industry.
CAUSE: He died in Chicago.

Sonny Til

(EARLINGTON CARL TILGHMAN)
Born August 8, 1925
Died December 9, 1981
The lead vocalist of the early R&B group The Orioles, the charismatic Sonny Til influenced a generation of doo-wop singers with his stellar delivery. A native of Baltimore, Til sang in his high school choir. Drafted during World War II, he sang in the USO. Upon his return to Baltimore, Til was convinced by his girlfriend to enter a talent contest as a solo vocalist. Tall, thin, confident and possessing a strong high tenor voice, he won first prize. There he met and then teamed up with three other contestants to form a Ravens-like four-part harmony group called The Vibranairs. Fronted by Til, and soon managed by fledgling songwriter Deborah Chessler, the group auditioned for *Arthur Godfrey's Talent Scout* radio programme in 1948. Losing to George Shearing but impressing Godfrey, the group landed a spot on Godfrey's more popular daytime show. There they met record label owner Jerry Blain who renamed the group The Orioles, after Maryland's official state bird. Beginning with the Chessler composition and crossover hit 'It's Too Soon To Know' (1948), The Orioles enjoyed a string of pioneering doo-wop hits which included '(It's Gonna Be A) Lonely Christmas' (1948), 'Tell Me So' (1949), and the double-sided entry, 'What Are You Doing New Year's Eve'/'Lonely Christmas' (1949). Tragedy struck the group in 1950 just outside Baltimore when one of the band's vehicles was involved in a serious auto accident, killing Tommy Gaither and injuring two others. Severely curtailing their touring schedule, The Orioles saw their career decline. After a two-year absence from the charts, The Orioles returned with 'Baby, Please Don't Go' (1952). During this period, Til also released a number of solo singles and duets with Edna McGriff. Featuring Til's emotionally charged lead vocal, The Orioles scored their second crossover hit with a cover of the gospel-rooted, Darrell Glenn-penned standard, 'Crying In The Chapel'. Hoping to repeat their success, The Orioles managed one final hit with another gospel-styled number, 'In The Mission Of St. Augustine' (1953) but disintegrated after the release of the single, 'If You Believe'. Attempting to salvage the group, Til hired The Regals as the new Orioles. Signing with Vee-Jay, they managed a minor R&B hit with 'Happy Till The Letter' (1956). After disbanding The Orioles in 1958, Til pursued an ill-fated solo career at Jubilee, and then Roulette Records. Forming several incarnations of The Orioles beginning in the early Sixties, Til performed until shortly before his death in 1981.
CAUSE: Heart failure complicated by diabetes. He died at Veteran's Memorial Hospital in Baltimore.

Sandra Tilley

Born May 6, 1946
Died September 9, 1983
A latter member of Martha Reeves & The Vandellas, Sandra Tilley joined the group in 1970. Orphaned in her native Cleveland at age two, Tilley was encouraged by her grandmother to join a series of gospel groups. After passing through a latter version of The Orlons, Tilley joined the Motown act, The Velvelettes, scoring a minor R&B hit in 1966 with an updated version of 'These Things Will Keep Me Loving You', but with Motown spending few resources on the group, The

Velvelettes floundered. After working as a Motown session vocalist in the late Sixties, Tilley replaced the fired Rosalyn Ashford in The Vandellas. A popular touring band, Martha Reeves & The Vandellas placed several singles on the R&B charts during this period, including, '(We've Got) Honey Love' (1970), 'Bless You' (1971), and 'In And Out Of My Life' (1972). With the emotionally troubled Reeves disbanding The Vandellas in late 1971, Tilley married and settled down in Houston.
CAUSE: She suffered a brain haemorrhage while vacationing in Las Vegas.

Clyde Tillis

Born January 29, 1925
Died December 1980
An occasional member of the Los Angeles-based, Bobby Day-led doo-wop group The Hollywood Flames, second tenor Clyde Tillis originally joined in 1951 as the replacement for Willie Ray Rockwell. Tillis appeared on various recordings including the upbeat crossover hit 'Buzz-Buzz-Buzz' (1958). He also worked with The Harmony Kings.
CAUSE: Unknown. He died in Los Angeles.

Georgeanna Tillman

(GEORGEANNA MARIE TILLMAN)
Born February 5, 1944
Died January 6, 1980
A founding member of The Marvelettes, Georgeanna Tillman formed the girl-group in 1960 with classmates at Inkster High School in Inkster, Michigan, initially as The Marvels. After winning a Motown-sponsored talent contest, the group later landed a recording contract with the label, becoming Motown's first hit girl-group. Featuring Marvin Gaye as a session drummer, The Marvelettes' début single 'Please Mister Postman' gave Motown its first million-seller. The first Motown act to choreograph their stage shows, the bouffanted Marvelettes were embraced by pop and R&B audiences alike. The Marvelettes' hit run continued with 'Playboy' (1962), 'Beechwood 4-5789' (1962), and 'Strange I Know' (1962). In 1964, Tillman married the lead singer of The Contours, Billy Gordon. Leaving the group the following year due to declining health, Tillman took a position as a Motown secretary. Tillman's estate and another member of The Marvelettes sued Motown Records in 1986 over past royalties. A minor rock classic, 'Please Mr. Postman' was recorded by The Beatles and The Carpenters.
CAUSE: Stricken with sickle cell anaemia and lupus, she died in suburban Detroit.

Abe Tilmon

(ABRIM TILMON)
Born January 12, 1945
Died July 1982
A member of the funk/soul vocal group Detroit Emeralds, Abe Tilmon join his brothers Ivory, Cleophus and Raymond in their hometown of Little Rock, Arkansas. Signed with Ric-Tic Records in 1967, the group managed a minor R&B hit with 'Show Time' (1968). A major force in the group, Abe Tilmon was the arranger, guitarist and chief songwriter. Signing with Detroit's Westbound label in 1970, the group was reduced to a trio of Abe and Ivory Tilmon and new lead vocalist James Mitchell. Backed by a number of former Motown session players, Detroit Emeralds landed on the charts with 'Do Me Right' (1971), 'You Want It, You Got It' (1972), 'Baby Let Me Take You (In My Arms)' (1972), and 'You're Gettin' A Little Too Smart' (1973). The group's final hit came in 1977 with a 12-inch disco remix of a five-year-old track, 'Feel The Need In Me'. That same year, two members of the group would leave to form The Floaters. Leaving the group soon after, Abe Tilmon would launch a competing

version of Detroit Emeralds.
CAUSE: He suffered a heart attack and died at his home in the suburban Detroit community of Southfield, Michigan.

Tiny Tim

(HERBERT KHAURY)
Born April 4, 1930
Died November 30, 1996
With his stringy long hair, pasty-white make-up, oversized nose, falsetto voice and mismatched ukulele, Tiny Tim emerged as an unlikely pop star in the late Sixties. Born Herbert Khaury in New York City, he began performing in 1954. Initially taking the stage name of "Larry Love The Singing Canary", he joined a New York City freak show. Adopting the Tiny Tim persona in 1958, he garnered an underground fan base with his updated renditions of pop hits from the Twenties and Thirties. His fame nurtured by a series of television appearances, Tiny Tim was a regular on *Rowan & Martin's Laugh-In* and *The Johnny Carson Show*. Then in 1968, Tiny Tim landed a massive hit with the novelty-styled 'Tip-Toe Thru' The Tulips With Me' (1968), a remake of Nick Lucas' pop hit. He also released three albums at Reprise Records, beginning with the Top 10 entry, *God Bless Tiny Tim*. Marrying 17-year-old Miss Vicki (Budinger) in a televised ceremony witnessed by 40 million viewers, Tiny Tim fathered one daughter, Tulip Victoria. Remaining an odd curiosity on the concert trail, Tiny Tim returned sporadically to the recording studio. Although exhibiting outlandish behaviour towards the end of his life, Tiny Tim was in the midst of a comeback.
CAUSE: Falling ill during a charity function at the Women's Club of Minneapolis, he collapsed after walking off the stage during the middle of a rendition of 'Tip-Toe Thru' The Tulips With Me'. Stricken with heart problems, he died at a nearby hospital; he had suffered a previous heart attack two months earlier at a Massachusetts ukulele festival.

Sean Tolby

(DAVID JACKSON TOLBY)
Born July 27, 1943
Died November 1990
The guitarist and backing vocalist of Sixties psychedelic rock act The Chocolate Watch Band, Sean Tolby joined the San Jose-based group in 1965 after leaving California surf band, The Topsiders. Although The Chocolate Watch Band experienced numerous personnel changes, Tolby performed on all three of the group's Tower (a subsidiary of Capitol) albums beginning with *No Way Out* (1967), produced by Ed Cobb. The group disbanded in 1969 and briefly re-formed the following year. Tolby left music and later worked as a carpenter. The Chocolate Watch Band occasionally re-form to play various garage rock festivals.
CAUSE: Unknown.

Steve Peregrine Took

(STEPHEN ROSS PORTER)
Born July 28, 1949
Died October 27, 1980
The founding member of Tyrannosaurus Rex alongside Marc Bolan, percussionist Steve Peregrine Took joined former child actor Bolan in the late Sixties to form the psychedelic-tinged folk-rock duo. Taking his name from a Hobbit character in the fantasy world of J.R.R. Tolkien's *The Lord Of The Rings*, the former Steve Porter joined Bolan's group after answering a newspaper advertisement. Hired as a drummer, but soon switching to the bongos, Peregrine Took also shared vocal duties with Bolan. Tyrannosaurus Rex quickly found a following within the British underground. With the group's music textured by exotic imagery, Bolan and Peregrine Took were attired in a combination of troubadour garb and wizard-like costumes. While Bolan

espoused liberal political beliefs, Peregrine Took was a genuine radical. Aided by pirate radio DJ John Peel, the pair recorded with producer Tony Visconti at Regal Zonophone Records. Their début album, *My People Were Fair And Had Sky In Their Hair, But Now They're Content To Wear Stars On Their Brows* (1968) spawned the British hit 'Debora'. Taking a turn toward progressive rock on their third album *Unicorn*, Tyrannosaurus Rex would land minor hits with 'One Inch Rock' and 'King Of The Rumbling Spires'. Heavily involved in LSD, Peregrine Took left the group at the completion of a tour in late 1969 and eloped with an American fan. Recruiting Mickey Finn in Took's place, Bolan abandoned his former underground following and re-emerged as the leader of the slightly abbreviated T. Rex, which quickly captured a teenybop following with a slew of catchy pop singles based around boogie rhythms. Peregrine Took subsequently joined a pair of progressive-rock acts, The Pink Fairies and Shagrat. After pursuing an ill-fated solo career under the management of Tony Secunda, he dropped out of the music scene. Secunda would later help Peregrine Took in retrieving unpaid royalties.
CAUSE: After a night of ingesting morphine, he snacked on cherries and choked on a pip.
FURTHER READING: Paytress, Mark. (1992). *Twentieth Century Boy: The Marc Bolan Story*. London: Sidgwick & Jackson.

Rudy Toombs

(RUDOLPH TOOMBS)
Born 1914
Died 1962
A proficient, under-appreciated, early R&B songwriter at Atlantic Records, Rudy Toombs penned many hits including '5-10-15 Hours' (Ruth Brown), and 'Teardrops From My Eyes' (Ruth Brown, Louis Jordan). In his youth, Toombs had appeared on the Apollo Theater stage as a tap dancer.
CAUSE: Mugged and viciously beaten by three men on a Harlem street, he suffered brain damage and died soon after.

David Torbert

Born June 7, 1948
Died December, 1982
A founding member of The Grateful Dead offshoot group The New Riders Of The Purple Sage, bassist David Torbert formed the outfit in 1969 with Grateful Dead leader Jerry Garcia. Torbert had first crossed paths with Garcia on the San Francisco coffee house circuit in the early Sixties. Previously a member of The New Delhi, Torbert was joined by guitarist Davis Nelson and vocalist/guitar player John Dawson in launching The New Riders Of The Purple Sage as an alter ego for Jerry Garcia and other members of The Grateful Dead. Reciprocating, Torbert appeared on The Grateful Dead album, *American Beauty*. With The New Riders becoming The Grateful Dead's regular opening act, Garcia could not keep up with membership of two groups and was replaced by Canadian folk guitarist Buddy Cage. A quirky country-rock flavoured group, The New Riders Of The Purple Sage were readily accepted by The Dead's legions of fans. Assuming greater influence within the group, Torbert insisted on the inclusion of early rock standards such as 'Willie And The Hand Jive' on their second album, *Powerglide* (1972). Then after scoring an album-rock hit with 'Don't Need No', the group decided to tour apart from The Dead in 1972. The group had moderate successes with the albums, *Gypsy Cowboy* (1972) and their biggest seller, *The Adventures Of Panama Red* (1973), which contained their pro-marijuana, near-novelty hit, 'Panama Red'. While crowds were initially strong, the group's popularity apart from The

Dead would wither in just a couple of years. Shortly before the release of their 1974 live album, *Home, Home On The Road*, Torbert left the group and was replaced by former Byrds member Skip Battin. Torbert subsequently joined Kingfish which, after the addition of Bob Weir in 1976, was considered another Grateful Dead offshoot. The group released four albums including, *Heaven Help The Fool* (1978).
CAUSE: Heart attack.

Peter Tosh

(WINSTON HUBERT MACINTOSH)
Born October 19, 1944
Died September 11, 1987
The outspoken guitarist and pianist of the reggae supergroup The Wailers, Peter Tosh was frequently the target of Jamaican authorities. Nicknamed the Bush Doctor, Tosh was raised in the Trenchtown ghetto of Kingston, Jamaica, where as a child he sang in church. Building a home-made guitar, in the early Sixties Tosh jumped on the "ska" bandwagon, embracing the hybrid of American R&B and Caribbean percussion. After attempting a solo career under various names including Peter Touch, Tosh formed a proto-reggae group in 1963 with friends Bob Marley and Bunny Livingston. Recording dozens of strong-selling locally released singles on the Leslie Kong-owned Kong label, the group would earn little. A talented guitarist, Tosh tutored Marley on the intricacies of writing music, and was an uncredited songwriter on many of the group's later works. When Marley left for Wilmington, Delaware in 1966 to live with his mother, The Wailers disbanded until Marley returned to Jamaica to avoid the US draft. Reforming in late 1968, The Wailers launched their own Tuff Gong label, and teamed with producer Lee "Scratch" Perry. The group was augmented by brothers Aston and Carlton Barrett. During this period, all the group members would convert to Rastafarianism, a sect that amongst other tenets considered marijuana consumption to be a sacrament. Although continuing to release local singles on their own Tuff Gong label, The Wailers signed a recording deal with Chris Blackwell at Island Records. Sparking interest when released in 1972, the albums *Catch A Fire* and *Burnin'* contained politically charged tracks such as 'I Shot The Sheriff' and 'Get Up, Stand Up'. The group's fame spread enormously when Eric Clapton took 'I Shot The Sheriff' to the top of the US charts in 1974. Angered by Marley's increasing control of the group, both Tosh and Livingston quit in late 1973. A controversial and militant figure, Tosh was politically active in Jamaican politics and the proposed legalisation of marijuana. Financed by Eric Clapton's bassist Carl Radle, Tosh released *Legalize It*, the album's title track referring to marijuana and, like much of Tosh's output, promptly banned from the airwaves by the Jamaican government. Teaming with bassist Robbie Shakespeare and drummer Sly Dunbar, Tosh recorded *Equal Rights* (1977), the project containing the hit 'Stepping Razor' and a version of 'Get Up, Stand Up'. After a spectacular performance at the One Love Peace Concert, Tosh was invited to open for The Rolling Stones, and after recording a duet hit with Mick Jagger, a cover of The Temptations' '(You've Got To Walk And) Don't Look Back' (1978), Tosh signed with Rolling Stone Records. The over-produced *Bush Doctor* featured a photograph of Tosh's body scarred from a brutal police beating suffered earlier in the year. Later signing with EMI Records and now backed by Word, Sound & Power, Tosh released his best selling US album, *Mama Africa* (1983), and scored a rare pop hit with a cover of the Chuck Berry standard, 'Johnny B. Goode'. A subsequent album, *Captured Live* (1984), earned a Grammy nomination. Following Marley's death, Tosh was involved in a

series of tenuous lawsuits against his record companies, ex-wives, and former bandmates. Tosh released the autobiographical album, *No Nuclear War* (EMI), shortly before his death and was scheduled to begin a world tour.
CAUSE: Tosh was shot to death at his Kingston home by burglars. Riding souped-up motorcycles, three gunmen rode up to Tosh's house; dressed in a business suit, one of the men was an acquaintance of Tosh and talked his way into the residence. When Tosh laughed at the intruders as they demanded money, he was violently beaten. Not satisfied with the quantity of loot, the robbers lashed out at their victims, killing Tosh and two others and wounding four more; each victim was shot in the back of the head. Besides Tosh, the other victims were Wilton "Doctor" Brown (a herbalist and Tosh's vegetarian cook) and radio disc jockey Jess "Free I" Dixon. The injured included Tosh's common-law wife, Marlene Brown. The men then ransacked the house and took additional valuables. Tosh's previous home had been burned down by arsonists the previous year. A *Rolling Stone* magazine investigator later contended that the robbery was actually an attempt to mask a feud. Tosh's killer, Dennis "Leppo" Lobban, an ex-convict, was found guilty and sentenced to death by hanging. The other two men were killed under unusual circumstances on the streets of Jamaica. While Tosh suspected that his life was in danger, he expected to be murdered by the local police. Tosh's murder was documented in the 1992 film *Steeping Razor: Red X*.
FURTHER READING: White, Timothy. (1998). *Catch A Fire: The Life Of Bob Marley*. New York: Henry Holt.

Frank Tovey

Born September 8, 1956
Died April 3, 2002
Originally known as Fad Gadget, the outrageous Frank Tovey was at the forefront of the UK electronica movement. A former performance artist, Tovey signed to Mute Records in 1979 under the moniker Fad Gadget. Reverting to his given name in 1984, Tovey toned down his stage antics after seriously injuring both legs. A leading underground artist during the Eighties, he spawned a host of imitators and Tovey toured through Europe as the opening act for Depeche Mode to coincide with the 2001 release of *The Best Of Fad Gadget*.
CAUSE: Suffering from heart problems since childhood, he succumbed to a heart attack at his home in London.

David Townsend

Born 1955
Died October 29, 2005
A member of the Eighties smooth R&B trio Surface, guitarist and keyboardist David Townsend spent a decade as a producer before stepping in front of the microphone. Townsend first broke into music as a touring guitarist for The Isley Brothers. In 1973, he joined the R&B group Port Authority and formed a songwriting partnership with bandmate David "Pic" Conley. With additional songwriter, Bernard Jackson, the trio were hired by EMI Music and by the early Eighties, they decided to form their own group, Surface. After an unproductive stint at Salsoul Records, Surface scored nearly a dozen Top 10 R&B hits, mostly ballads, beginning in 1987 with 'Happy' and 'Lately', continuing with 'I Missed', 'Closer Than Friends', a million-selling crossover hit 'Shower Me With Your Love', 'You Are My Everything', 'Can We Spend Some Time?', another million-seller 'The First Time' and 'All I Want Is You', featuring Regina Belle on backing vocals. Apart from Surface, Townsend worked with a variety of pop and R&B artists including Rebbie Jackson, Jermaine Jackson, Sister Sledge, The Isley Brothers, Aretha

Franklin and New Edition. Re-forming Surface months before his death, Townsend was working on a new album. David Townsend's father was singer Ed Townsend.
CAUSE: Unknown. He died at his home in Northridge, California.

Ed Townsend

(EDWARD BENJAMIN TOWNSEND)
Born April 16, 1929
Died August 13, 2003
A singer and songwriter, Ed Townsend is best known for writing Marvin Gaye's 'Let's Get It On'. Born in Fayetteville, Tennessee, Townsend sang gospel music in his father's church choir. After earning a law degree from Arkansas State College, Townsend spent two years in the military, stationed in South Korea. Relocating to Los Angeles in 1954, he hosted a local television programme and also recorded several unsuccessful singles. During this period, he also composed songs for Bull Moose Jackson, Etta James and others but when he tried to peddle one of his compositions to Capitol Records, the label suggested he record the song himself. The ballad 'For Your Love' (1959) became Townsend's only hit, reaching the Top 10. Despite having a powerful and emotive voice, Townsend had far greater success as a producer and songwriter for Ben E. King, Big Maybelle, Chuck Jackson, The Shirelles, The Main Ingredient, The Impressions and others. Inspired by his personal fight against drug and alcohol addiction, Townsend wrote and co-produced 'Let's Get It On', a 1973 smash hit for Marvin Gaye. As a producer, Townsend worked at Vee Jay, Capitol, Mercury, and Scepter Records. Ed Townsend's son was singer David Townsend of the R&B group Surface.
CAUSE: He suffered a heart attack and died at a hospital in San Bernardino, California.

Ron Townson

Born January 20, 1947
Died August 2, 2001
As a member of soul-rock act The Fifth Dimension, Ron Townson had a string of Sixties and Seventies hits. Born in St. Louis, he was reared on gospel music, and spent eight years as a member of the popular gospel act Wings Over Jordan. Attending Lincoln University, he studied opera and directed school choirs. After a stint in the military, Townson moved to Los Angeles where he toured with Nat "King" Cole and Dorothy Dandridge. Then in 1966, Townson formed The Versatiles, which included the future husband-and-wife team of Marilyn McCoo and Billy Davis, Jr. Discovered by singer Johnny Rivers, the group was signed to his Soul City label. After scoring a regional hit with 'I'll Be Loving You For Ever', the group retooled its image and was renamed The 5th Dimension. Sporting psychedelic outfits and targeting crossover audiences, the group reached the Top 40 in 1967 with a cover of The Mamas & The Papas' 'Go Where You Want To Go'. Recording a number of Jimmy Webb songs, The 5th Dimension followed up with the Grammy-winning 'Up, Up And Away' and also recorded several Laura Nyro compositions, including a pair of platinum-sellers, 'Stoned Soul Picnic' and 'Wedding Bell Blues'. Considered the group's signature piece, the medley from the rock musical *Hair* – 'Aquarius'/'Let The Sun Shine In' – was a masterful amalgam of soul and psychedelia. Focusing on ballads by the early Seventies, The 5th Dimension continued their hit run with 'One Less Bell To Answer', '(Last Night) I Didn't Get To Sleep At All' and 'It Could Reach You'. After The 5th Dimension splintered in the late Seventies, Townsend formed his own group, Ron Townson & Wild Honey. He later re-formed The 5th Dimension with two original members

but was forced to retire from performing in 1997 due to declining health.
CAUSE: He died at his home in Las Vegas after a four-year battle with kidney disease.

Nick Traina

(NICHOLAS JOHN STEEL)
Born May 1, 1978
Died September 20, 1997
The eldest son of best-selling author Danielle Steel, Nick Traina joined the punk rock band, Link 80, in 1995 as a singer and songwriter. Forming another punk group, Knowledge, a month before his death, Traina recorded a number of tracks, posthumously released on the album, *A Gift Before I Go*.
CAUSE: A manic-depressive, he was found dead from a self-inflicted overdose of morphine in his bedroom at his mother's home in San Francisco.
FURTHER READING: Steel, Danielle. (1998). *The Story Of Nick Traina: His Bright Light.* New York: Delacorte.

Buddy Trenier

(CONSTANTINE MAXWELL TRENIER)
Born December 11, 1913
Died March 15, 1999
A member of the proto-R&B band The Treniers, baritone vocalist Buddy Trenier joined an act started by his twin brothers Claude and Cliff following a military stint. A very popular touring act in the R&B field, the group scored hits with 'Go Go Go' (1951) and 'Get Out Of The Car' (1955) on Okeh Records. Having developed a choreographed singing and comedy routine, The Treniers were one of the first black acts to perform regularly in Las Vegas and often appeared on national television programmes such as *The Ed Sullivan Show* and *The Merv Griffin Show*. The Treniers also appeared in a number of early rock'n'roll films including *The Girl Can't Help It* and *Don't Knock The Rock*. After retiring from the group in 1985, Buddy Trenier made occasional appearances, his last being just two months before his death.
CAUSE: In poor health for some time, he suffered a stroke in 1991 as well as battling lung cancer. He died at Nathan Adelson Hospice in Las Vegas.

Claude Trenier

Born July 14, 1919
Died November 17, 2003
A member of the proto-R&B group The Treniers, vocalist Claude Trenier had formed the act as a duo with his twin brother Cliff. The brothers had previously formed an act while attending college, but with World War II underway, the group disbanded as members were drafted. In 1944, Claude Trenier joined The Jimmie Lunceford Orchestra with Cliff joining a year later. Fired by Lunceford, both brothers were eventually hired by Big Jim Wynn & His Bobolibans. By 1947, Claude and Cliff began recording on Mercury Records as The Trenier Twins. Joined by brother Buddy, the renamed Treniers signed with Okeh Records for their hits 'Go Go Go' (1951) and 'Get Out Of The Car' (1955). A very popular touring act in the R&B field, The Treniers performed in Las Vegas nightclubs for over five decades.
CAUSE: Cancer. He died in Las Vegas.

Cliff Trenier

Born July 14, 1919
Died March 2, 1983
Best known as a member of Fifties R&B group The Treniers, Cliff Trenier was a music veteran by that time. Along with twin brother Claude, Cliff Trenier formed the Alabama State Collegians in the late Thirties. With Claude leaving the group in 1943 to join The Jimmie Lunceford Orchestra, Cliff joined the following year. Emerging as a duo in 1947, The Trenier Twins recorded for several labels beginning with Mercury. Adding brothers Buddy and Milt, the renamed

Treniers joined OKeh Records, landing R&B hits with 'Go Go Go' (1951) and 'Get Out Of The Car' (1955). Known for their comedic routines, The Treniers appeared in several rock films including *Don't Knock The Rock* and *The Girl Can't Help It.*
CAUSE: Cancer. He died in Las Vegas.

Domenic Troiano

Born January 17, 1946
Died June 3, 2005
A jazz-influenced singer-songwriter and guitarist who gained prominence in the Canadian rock band The Guess Who, Domenic Troiano also worked with a number of other noteworthy acts. A native of Italy, he emigrated as a child with his family to Toronto, Canada, breaking into music as the replacement for Robbie Robertson in Ronnie Hawkins' backing band. Leaving after a year, Troiano joined a series of acts before landing in The Five Rogues, a Toronto-based blue-eyed soul band which soon changed its name to Mandala. After creating a buzz in Toronto, the group had several local hits and toured America. Though Atlantic Records bought the group's recording contract, Mandala was unable to break into the US market and after disbanding in 1969, Troiano and two of his bandmates formed Bush who recorded an album for ABC-Dunhill before breaking up in 1971. While working on sessions for his first solo album, Troiano joined The James Gang as replacement for Joe Walsh while simultaneously working on his own solo material. Troiano appeared on two James Gang albums, *Straight Shooter* and *Passin' Thru,* before joining The Guess Who in late 1974 as a replacement for lead guitarist Kurt Winter, appearing on two albums, *Flavours* and *Power In The Music.* With The Guess Who disbanding in late 1975, Troiano resumed his solo career, recording *Burning At The Stake,* for Capitol Records, followed by two more projects in the late Seventies. Attempting one last shot at fame, Troiano formed Black Market but, unhappy with the poor chart performance of the album *Changing Of The Guard,* he quit. Troiano later provided music for television programmes and worked as a session player.
CAUSE: Prostate cancer.

Roland Trone

Born July 2, 1936
Died May 1982
The "Don" in the R&B duo Don & Juan (the moniker inspired by the Errol Flynn portrayal of Don Juan), Alabama-born Roland Trone was previously a member of a touring version of The Ink Spots. Abandoned by the rest of the group following an engagement in 1960, Trone settled in Long Beach, New York. While painting the exterior of an apartment building, he met the building's superintendent, former Genies member Claude "Juan" Johnson. Joining forces as both house painters and a musical duo, Don & Juan were overheard by a customer who aided them in landing a recording contract with Big Top Records. Issued as a B-side in 1962, the ballad 'What's Your Name' became their signature piece. But with their managers shuffling them through several record labels, Don & Juan disappeared from the charts after a second hit, 'Magic Wand'. Disbanding in 1967, Don & Juan reunited in 1981. Johnson later formed a new version of Don & Juan with Genies bandmate Alexander Faison.
CAUSE: Unknown. He died in Long Beach, New York.

Larry Troutman

Born August 12, 1944
Died April 25, 1999
The congo player/percussionist and former manager of the Dayton, Ohio-based funk/R&B group Zapp,

Larry Troutman had teamed to form the group with brothers Lester, Terry, and Roger. The brainchild of Roger Troutman, the group had been launched in the mid Seventies as Roger and The Human Body. Releasing a self-financed album in 1975, *Introducing Roger*, the group garnered regional attention and were the opening act on a George Clinton/ Parliament-Funkadelic show. Clinton subsequently introduced them to Warners, where they recorded their 1980 début album under the new name Zapp. Bootsy Collins co-produced *Zapp*, which was followed by a Top Five R&B hit, 'More Bounce to the Ounce' (1980). Their hits included 'Dance Floor' (1982), 'Do Wah Ditty (Blow That Thing)' (1982) and 'I Can Make You Dance' (1983). With Roger Troutman enjoying success as a solo act apart from Zapp, Larry Troutman stopped performing with the group in the mid Eighties. Returning to Dayton, Larry Troutman took a position in Troutman Enterprises, his family's recording, bus company, and real estate business.

CAUSE: In a murder-suicide, Larry Troutman shot his brother Roger Troutman several times in an alley behind the family's music studio in Dayton. Climbing into his car, Larry Troutman then shot himself in the head and crashed into a tree. A disagreement over the direction of the family's financially struggling business was the most likely cause of the shootings.

Roger Troutman

Born November 29, 1951
Died April 25, 1999

A funk/R&B star in the Eighties, Roger Troutman usually used only his first name. A multi-instrumentalist who had mastered the bass guitar, keyboard, and harmonica, Troutman formed his first of many musical groups in his native Dayton, Ohio, in 1962. Forming a musical group with his brothers called Roger and The Human Body, Troutman released a self-financed album in 1975, *Introducing Roger*. With the project garnering regional attention, the group earned an opening slot on a George Clinton/Parliament-Funkadelic show. Aided by Clinton in landing a recording contract with Warner Records, the renamed Zapp released their major label début in 1980. With Bootsy Collins co-producing and guesting on the album *Zapp*, the group secured a Top Five R&B hit with 'More Bounce To The Ounce' (1980). Employing a vocoder voice-synthesizer, Roger Troutman provided the idiosyncratic robotic-like vocals on the group's hits, 'Dance Floor' (1982), 'Do Wah Ditty (Blow That Thing)' (1982) and 'I Can Make You Dance' (1983). Simultaneously pursuing a solo career, Troutman hit the R&B charts with a cover of the Motown standard 'I Heard It Through The Grapevine' (1981) and 'Do The Roger' (1981), the singles culled from the album *The Many Faces Of Roger*. With Zapp on hiatus in the Eighties, Roger Troutman landed his only solo crossover hit in 1987 with the Top 10 entry, 'I Want To Be Your Man'. As a producer, Troutman worked with Zapp backing vocalist Shirley Murdock, Dayton, Sugarfoot, and Bobby Glover. Pared down to a quartet of Troutman brothers in the Nineties, the group was renamed Roger and Zapp. Flirting with rap, Troutman collaborated with Tupac Shakur and Dr. Dre on the Grammy-nominated single 'California Love'. At the time of his death, Troutman was working on an album project that he had titled, *Roger And Friends*.

CAUSE: In a murder-suicide, Roger Troutman was shot several times by his brother Larry Troutman in an alley behind the family's music studio in Dayton. Climbing into his car, Larry Troutman then shot himself in the head and crashed into a tree. Roger Troutman died following surgery at Good Samaritan Hospital. A disagreement over the direction of the family's financially struggling business was the likely cause of the shootings.

Roger Troutman II

Born January 31, 1970
Died January 22, 2003
The son of the late Roger Troutman, R&B vocalist Roger Troutman II often recorded with his father. Beginning in 1985, the younger Troutman played keyboards or bass guitar and provided backing vocals on tracks for R&B acts such as Shirley Murdock, The Human Body, Jesse Rae and Sugarfoot. Aided by many family members including his father, the younger Troutman released the 1989 album *A Pinch Of Lynch* under the name Robert T. Lynch. Later recording as Roger Troutman II, he released the album *The Second Coming* a year after his father's death; the album featured a guest vocal by Gap Band lead singer Charlie Wilson.
CAUSE: Suffering a head injury as the result of a fall in Minneapolis, he died several months later from complications.

Doris Troy

(DORIS HIGGINSON)
Born January 6, 1937
Died February 16, 2004
A respected soul singer, Doris Troy later worked as a session vocalist for a number of leading rock acts. Born and raised in New York City, Troy performed gospel in her church but was inspired to sing secular music after working as an usher at the Apollo Theater. Breaking into music in the Fifties, Troy joined two friends to form The Halos and recorded as a member of the duo Jay & Dee, as well as being a backing vocalist for such R&B greats as The Drifters, Solomon Burke and Chuck Jackson. However, Troy had greater success as a songwriter, using her grandmother's nom de plume of Payne, with Dee Clark scoring an R&B hit in 1960 with 'How About That?', on Vee Jay. Teaming with Gregory Carroll to co-write her best-known song, 'Just One Look', Troy took a demo cut at Sue Records to Atlantic. The label decided to issue the demo featuring Troy on lead vocals, which reached the US Top 10 and, when covered by The Hollies in 1964, a UK number two. Enjoying a second UK Top 40 hit with 'What'cha Gonna Do About It' (1964), Troy moved to England in 1969. Continuing her career as a session singer, she backed Billy Preston, who convinced George Harrison to sign her to Apple Records; recording a self-titled album with contributions from Harrison, Ringo Starr, Eric Clapton and Stephen Stills. Moving to Polydor Records, she recorded a live, upbeat gospel album, *The Rainbow Testament* (1972). Working with Pink Floyd, she provided the prominent gospel-like wails on the group's masterpiece *Dark Side Of The Moon* and also worked with Atomic Rooster, Nick Drake, Peter Frampton and The Rolling Stones. Beginning in 1983, Troy starred in the autobiographical musical *Mama, I Want To Sing*; written by Troy's sister, the touring production continued with Doris Troy in the lead role until 1998.
CAUSE: Suffering from emphysema, she died in a Las Vegas hospital.

Roger "Jellyroll" Troy

(ROGER MCGAHA)
Born c. 1945
Died March 15, 1991
The bass player of the Chicago-based blues-rock band Electric Flag, Roger "Jellyroll" Troy had initially led his own group, releasing an album at Kapp Records in 1971, *Jellyroll*. Replacing original Electric Flag bassist Harvey Brooks in 1974, Troy joined a supergroup of Buddy Miles, Nick Gravenites, Barry Goldberg, and Michael Bloomfield on the Atlantic Records album *The Band Kept Playing*;

but the project was a commercial failure and the group disbanded after one public performance. After releasing a solo album, *Roger Troy* (1976), Troy joined Michael Bloomfield for five albums beginning with *If You Love Those Blues* (1977). Troy later played the bass on Nick Gravenites' album, *Blue Star*, and worked as a session player for James Brown, Jerry Garcia, Lonnie Mack and Huey Lewis.
CAUSE: Complications from open-heart surgery.

Alonzo Tucker

Born 1915
Died 1977
A guitarist, arranger and songwriter for the Detroit-based doo-wop harmony group The Royals/Midnighters, Alonzo Tucker was far older than his bandmates. When Hank Ballard joined in 1953, Tucker befriended the former auto-assembly line worker when the others in the group considered firing him. Leaving The Midnighters in the early Sixties, Tucker worked with soul star Jackie Wilson, co-composing his hits, 'Years From Now'/'You Don't Know What It Means' (1961), 'Baby Work Out' (1963), and 'Baby Don't Get It' (1963). Tucker spent his last years behind the scenes at Brunswick Records.
CAUSE: Unknown.

Luther Tucker

Born January 20, 1936
Died June 18, 1993
A popular Memphis-born, Chicago-based string-bending blues guitarist, Luther Tucker first gained fame when in 1955 he joined Little Walter's band, The Jukes. A prolific player, Tucker backed Muddy Waters, Howlin' Wolf, Jimmy Rogers, Elvin Bishop and, for extended periods in the Sixties, James Cotton and Otis Rush. Settling in San Francisco, Tucker spent three years in John Lee Hooker's band, before heading his own group and recording several albums. After spending much of the Eighties living in Europe, he returned to San Francisco. Tucker appeared on James Cotton's 1988, Grammy-nominated album, *Live At Antones*.
CAUSE: He died of a heart attack in suburban San Francisco.

Mick Tucker

(MICHAEL THOMAS TUCKER)
Born July 17, 1949
Died February 14, 2002
The drummer with Seventies British glam rock group The Sweet, Mick Tucker had first performed with future Sweet vocalist Brian Connolly in a Middlesex pub band called Wainwright's Gentlemen. After Connolly was fired, Tucker joined him in a new group, The Sweet Shop. Signed by Fontana Records in 1968, and renamed The Sweet, the group released one flop single on Fontana, 'Slow Motion', followed by three equally unsuccessful singles on Parlophone, featuring original guitarist Frank Torpey. Replacing Torpey with Andy Scott and signing to RCA while reducing the name further to Sweet, their first single for the label, 'Funny Funny', released in 1971, was written by Nicky Chinn and Mike Chapman – the songwriting partnership behind the group's hits up to 1974. Despite the band's reluctance, session players were used on such early novelty hits as 'Co-Co', 'Poppa Joe', and 'Little Willy' but, gradually evolving into a make-up wearing, glam-rock group, they were eventually permitted to perform on such hits as 'Blockbuster', 'Hell Raiser', 'Ballroom Blitz', 'Teenage Rampage' and 'The Six Teens'. Sweet had surprise success in the US charts with the self-penned hit 'Fox On The Run' but, wanting to pursue more serious rock, they parted company with Chinn and Chapman in 1974. From the album *Level Headed*, the group scored its final Top 10 hit in 1978 with 'Love Is Like Oxygen'. Following the departure of Connolly in 1978, Sweet

was pared down to a trio which allowed Tucker the opportunity to provide lead vocals on two tracks for the album *Cut Above The Rest* (1979). After disbanding in 1982, Sweet returned on occasion in various incarnations, with members sometimes battling over ownership of the group's name.
CAUSE: He died in Welwyn Garden City, Hertfordshire, after battling leukaemia for five years

Tommy Tucker

(ROBERT HIGGENBOTHAM)
Born March 5, 1933
Died January 22, 1982
A R&B vocalist, Springfield, Ohio-native Tommy Tucker is best known for his hit 'Hi-Heel Sneakers'. A formally trained clarinet player, Tucker taught himself to play the piano by listening to old jazz and blues 78s. Receiving his "Tommy Tucker" nickname while a star football player in high school, he later entered the boxing ring. Joining an uncle's band, The Bob Wood Orchestra, in the late Forties, Tucker alternated between the piano and clarinet. After the orchestra disbanded in 1955, Tucker formed a rock vocal group called The Dusters, releasing an obscure single the following year. Subsequent singles as both The Cavaliers and The Belvaderes also failed to garner interest. Moving to Dayton and joining a bar band, Tucker was aided by his savvy manager, Johnny Smith, in signing with Hi Records in 1959. Then moving to New Jersey, he also fared poorly with his Atlantic Records releases. But aided by former Atlantic co-owner Herb Abramson, a demo of Tucker's self-penned, guitar-heavy, novelty-styled single, 'Hi-Heel Sneakers' was leased to Checker Records in 1963. The song was inspired by an oddly dressed woman at one of his nightclub shows. Issued as a single in its demo form, the song was a surprise R&B and pop hit. Releasing several more singles at the label, Tucker's only other success came with 'Long Tall Shorty' (1964). Leaving music in the late Sixties, Tucker settled in East Orange, New Jersey, where he took a position as a real estate agent. Returning to the studio in 1979, Tucker was joined by Bo Diddley on a pair of albums, *Mother Trucker* and *The Rocks Is My Pillow*.
CAUSE: Poisoning. He died after inhaling carbon tetrachloride while refinishing the wood floors of his home. (Alternatively, Tucker's death has been attributed to food poisoning, contracted after consuming a hamburger.) He died at College Hospital in Newark, New Jersey.

William Tucker

(EDWIN WILLIAM TUCKER)
Born 1961
Died May 14, 1999
A talented guitarist, producer and songwriter, New Jersey-born William Tucker formed his first significant band in the late Eighties with future Rollins Band members Andrew Weiss and Sim Cain. Moving to Chicago in 1989, he worked with a series of gothic and industrial bands including Thrill Kill Kult, Ministry, Pigface, KMFDM, and Foetus. Tucker also taught guitar to Dean Ween of the alternative rock band Ween.
CAUSE: He committed suicide at his apartment in Chicago. After ingesting a number of pills, he slashed his throat. He had reportedly suffered from an undisclosed illness.

Charlie Tumahai

Born 1949
Died December 21, 1995
A latter member of the Seventies progressive-rock group Be-Bop Deluxe, Auckland, New Zealand-born bassist Charlie Tumahai joined the third incarnation of the Bill Nelson-fronted outfit. Inspired by local showbands, Tumahai left his homeland at age 17 to work as a professional musician,

performing throughout Australia, Vietnam, and a host of other exotic locales. Returning to Australia in the mid Seventies, he joined a group which evolved into The Little River Band; frustrated with the group's early failures, he quit. Leaving for England in 1974, he soon recorded his first of five albums with Be-Bop Deluxe, including *Sunburst Finish* which featured the hit 'Ships In The Night' (1976). Nicknamed "The Mad Maori" by his bandmates, Tumahai provided the bass behind Nelson's exquisite guitar lead. Nelson dissolved the group in 1978. Returning to New Zealand in 1985, Tumahai joined a regional touring group called The Herbs, on bass and lead vocals.
CAUSE: Heart attack. He died in Auckland.

"Big" Joe Turner

(JOSEPH VERNON TURNER)
Born May 18, 1911
Died November 24, 1985
A blues baritone boogie-woogie shouter who shifted into rock and R&B in the Fifties, Kansas City native Joe Turner was reared on his mother's blues 78s. Breaking both legs at age 12 while escaping a building, Turner was told by doctors he would never walk again. But after a year of crawling on floors, Turner regained his mobility. Taught the rudiments of blues by three uncles, Turner also collected tips for a series of blind, street corner blues guitarists; eventually accompanying these bluesmen on vocals, Turner later formed a sidewalk jug band. Sneaking into a Kansas City nightclub by donning a painted moustache, he pestered boogie pianist Pete Johnson into letting him sing. Alternating between mixing drinks behind the bar and belting the blues on stage, Turner was not yet 20. Cementing an association that would last 13 years, Turner and Johnson gained national acclaim with their performance at the legendary From Spirituals To Swing revue at Carnegie Hall. After landing a residency at the Cafe Society, the pair released the boogie-woogie scorcher, 'Roll 'Em Pete' (1938), which was followed by 'Cherry Red' (1939) and 'Wee Baby Blues' (1941). Apart from Johnson, Turner performed with jazz greats such as Art Tatum, Count Basie, Duke Ellington, and recorded with William "The Lion" Smith and Freddie Slack. After riding the boogie-woogie explosion in New York, Turner and Johnson left for the West Coast and recorded for a number of labels. Parting with Johnson and returning to New York City in the early Fifties, the reinvented Turner made a spectacular comeback. After scoring a hit at Freedom Records with 'Still In The Dark' (1950), Turner signed with Atlantic in 1951. Embraced by R&B fans, the towering Turner enjoyed a strong string of rock-flavoured hits with 'Chains Of Love' (1951), 'Honey Hush' (1953), 'Shake, Rattle, And Roll' (1954), 'Flip, Flop And Fly' (1955), and a cover of the Twenties blues standard, 'Corrine Corrina' (1956). (Bill Haley & The Comets would record a partially sanitised version of 'Shake, Rattle, And Roll'.) After appearing in the low-budget rock flick, *Shake, Rattle And Rock* (1956), Turner reunited with the ailing Johnson and recorded new versions of their early hits on the album, *Joe Turner Sings Kansas City Jazz: The Boss Of The Blues*. Dropped by Atlantic Records in 1959, Turner toured internationally for the next two decades. In frail health in the Eighties, Turner performed while sitting in a chair.
CAUSE: Suffering stroke and kidney failure, he died at his Inglewood, California home.

Titus Turner

Born May 1, 1933
Died September 13, 1984
An Atlanta-born R&B artist and songwriter, Titus Turner scored his

own hit in 1959 with 'Return Of Stagolee', and penned the hits, 'Hey, Baby Doll' (The Clovers) and 'Tell Me Why' (The Crew Cuts; Elvis Presley). Turner recorded regularly through the Sixties.
CAUSE: Unknown. He died in Atlanta.

Conway Twitty

(HAROLD LLOYD JENKINS)
Born September 1, 1933
Died June 5, 1993
A country music superstar who began in the rockabilly vein, Conway Twitty was raised on a houseboat just north of the blues centre of Clarksdale, Mississippi. Given a ukulele and then guitar, he formed his first of many bands at age 10. Drafted shortly after high school graduation, he was unable to accept a contract with The Philadelphia Phillies. While stationed in Japan, he joined a country group; but upon his return, rock music was beginning to make inroads. Attracted to the sounds of Elvis Presley and Carl Perkins, he added R&B to his country and gospel repertoire, and formed The Rockhousers. A seasoned musician, he began to perform in small clubs and impromptu outdoor concerts throughout Mississippi and nearby states. Signed to Sun Records by Sam Phillips as a solo act and songwriter, the former Harold Jenkins was forced to change his name. As Conway Twitty, he scored a minor hit with his début release, 'I Need Your Lovin''. After switching to MGM Records, Twitty scored a career-defining hit with a tear-jerker he co-wrote with Jack Nance which had been rejected by Elvis Presley, the chart-topping 'It's Only Make Believe' (1958). Twitty also registered a UK Top Five hit in 1959 with 'Mona Lisa'. Initially considered a rock act, his only other major rock-styled hit came with 'Lonely Blue Boy' (1960). Unhappy with the direction of rock music in the early Sixties, Twitty abandoned the genre. Having secretly written country songs which he gave to other artists, Twitty was initially ignored by rock and country fans alike. Singing in a traditional country style, Twitty soon churned out a river of number one country singles beginning with 'Next In Line' in 1968, and continuing with 'Hello Darlin'' (1970), 'Baby's Gone' (1973), and 'Julia' (1987). Twitty also recorded a number of successful duets with country queen Loretta Lynn, including their first number one hit, 'After The Fire Is Gone'. The character of Conrad Birdie in the Broadway production, *Bye Bye, Birdie* was patterned on Twitty.
CAUSE: Complaining of stomach problems the week before his death, Twitty was found unconscious on the floor of his tour bus by band members who had gone out to buy food. After extensive surgery to repair a ruptured blood vessel in his stomach, Twitty died of a heart attack the next day at the Cox Medical Center in Springfield, Missouri.
FURTHER READING: Cross, Wilbur. (1986). *The Conway Twitty Story*. Garden City, NJ: Doubleday.

Alvin "Red" Tyler

Born December 5, 1925
Died April 3, 1998
A baritone saxophonist who performed on dozens of hits via his work at the Dave Bartholomew-produced sessions at the J&M studio in New Orleans, Alvin "Red" Tyler backed leading rock and R&B artists such as Fats Domino, Lloyd Price, Jimmy Clanton, and Little Richard. After learning to play the saxophone while serving in the navy, Tyler enrolled in music school on a G.I. scholarship in 1947. Surrounded by the Crescent City's top session players including Lee Allen and Earl Palmer, Tyler joined Bartholomew's house band in 1949, first performing on Fats Domino's début hit, 'They Call Me The Fat Man'. Parting with Bartholomew in the early Sixties, Tyler

co-founded AMO Records with producer Harold Battiste, and had success with Lee Dorsey and Barbara George. Leaving music in 1967, Tyler took a job in liquor sales. Returning to his first love, jazz music, Tyler formed his own group which recorded on Rounder Records. In the mid Eighties, Tyler joined a band led by Dr. John. CAUSE: Natural causes. He died in New Orleans.

Rob Tyner

(ROBERT DERMINER)
Born December 12, 1944
Died September 17, 1991
The lead vocalist of the proto-punk, free-form rock band MC5, Rob Tyner had reluctantly joined the group in 1965. The Detroit-born Tyner had originally intended to manage the group, then called The Bounty Hunters, but was instead hired as a bassist. Quitting in 1964 but returning the following year, Tyner switched to the lead vocal position. A guitar-orientated garage rock group that featured the talents of Fred "Sonic" Smith and Wayne Kramer, MC5 (short for Motor City Five) earned a strong following in the Detroit and Ann Arbor areas. Releasing a couple of local singles, 'Looking At You' was a minor local hit. Managed by the noted radical John Sinclair and becoming the house band for his White Panther Party, MC5 increasingly infused anti-government themes into their lyrics and performances, which often included destroying a US flag. The group subsequently garnered much press for their appearance at the 1968 Democratic national convention in Chicago. Catching the attention of Elektra Records, MC5 released their landmark début, *Kick Out The Jams*, which is often cited as the first punk-rock album. The album's title track had to be rewritten before the record received airplay or was stocked in some record stores. Splitting from Sinclair shortly before he was imprisoned for marijuana possession, MC5 had tired of defending his White Panther political dogma. With Tyner uttering profanities in concert, MC5 had their own brushes with the law and were frequently the targets of obscenity charges. Dropped by Elektra and signed to Atlantic, MC5 released the Jon Landau-produced album, *Back In The USA* (1970); hailed by critics but ignored by consumers, the album was uncharacteristically apolitical with youth-celebrating tracks such as 'High School' and 'Teenage Lust'. After Atlantic quietly released a third album, *High Time*, MC5 disbanded in 1972 after completing a European tour. In the Seventies, Tyner turned to freelance song writing and photography. Angering his former band mates in 1977, Tyner formed his own short-lived version of MC5 with an all-new line-up. That same year he also recorded a one-off single with Eddie & the Hot Rods, 'Till The Night Is Gone (Let's Rock)'. In the late Eighties he managed an all-girl, Detroit-based group, The Vertical Pillows. Returning to the studio, Tyner released a solo album in 1990, *Blood Brothers*, on the small R&A label. Tyner was working on the liner notes for an MC5 compilation CD at the time of his death.
CAUSE: He suffered a heart attack. His body was discovered behind the wheel of his parked car in the driveway of his Berkley, Michigan home. He died 45 minutes later at nearby Beaumont Hospital.

U

Gary Usher

(Gary Lee Usher)
Born December 14, 1938
Died May 25, 1990
A behind-the-scenes architect of the surf genre, Gary Usher worked with The Beach Boys, The Hondells, The Surfaris, Dick Dale, and others. Breaking into music as a performer, Usher scored a minor hit in 1960 with 'Driving Insane'. Drawn to the surf/hot rod genre, Usher provided the musical scores for several beach films in the Sixties, and collaborated with Brian Wilson on co-writing six tracks on the first Beach Boys' album *Surfin' Safari*, including '409', 'Lonely Sea' and the introspective 'In My Room'. Hired as a staff producer by CBS Records in the mid Sixties, Usher produced three classic Byrds albums: *Younger Than Yesterday*, *The Notorious Byrd Brothers* and *Sweetheart Of The Rodeo*. He also produced Chad & Jeremy's concept album, *Of Cabbages And Kings*, a high-budget work whose extravagance caused concern to the fiscally minded Columbia Records. In late 1967 he formed a studio group called Sagittarius with Bruce Johnston and Curt Boettcher, and utilised an early 16-track board for a session which spawned the underground, psychedelic-styled 'My World Fell Down'. In 1969 Usher launched his own short-lived label, Together Records, and subsequently worked at RCA Records. After a brief retirement in the mid Seventies, Usher produced albums for Chicago, The Commodores, Roger Daltrey, Laura Branigan, and Gino Vannelli. After reteaming with Brian Wilson in the mid Eighties on the solo album *Brian Wilson*, Usher returned to his surf roots on the 1987, Frankie and Annette beach movie spoof, *Back To The Beach*. Usher's final chart success came with The Fat Boys/Beach Boys novelty rendition of 'Wipe Out'.
Cause: Cancer. He died in Los Angeles.
Further Reading: McParland, Stephen J. (1993). *The California Sound: An Insider's Story: The Authorised Biography Of Gary Lee Usher*. Ann Arbor: MI: Popular Culture Ink.

V

Ritchie Valens

(RICHARD STEVEN VALENZUELA)
Born May 13, 1942
Died February 3, 1959

With three hits in the US pop charts at the time of his death, Ritchie Valens was poised to become America's first real Chicano rock star. Born in suburban Los Angeles to Mexican-Native American parents, Valens built his first guitar in a junior-high wood shop class. Joining a local interracial rock group The Silhouettes (not the famous Philadelphia group) in 1957 on guitar, he would emerge as the lead singer. Discovered in 1958 by Bob Keene of Del-Fi Records, Valens was tutored on guitar by labelmate Dick Dale. Valens' début release, the rockabilly-inflected 'Come On, Let's Go' (1958), was a slow chart-climber. Quickly following up with the Top 5 'Donna', Valens had written the ballad for girlfriend Donna Ludwig; also a hit, the record's B-side, 'La Bamba', was a Spanish folk standard that dated to the late 17th century. By year's end, Valens would guest twice on Dick Clark's *American Bandstand* and perform 'Ooh My Head' in the Alan Freed, cheapie rock film *Go Johnny Go*; chubby, Valens would appear much older than his actual age of 17. After some final studio sessions in January 1959, Valens hit the road as the headliner of the ill-fated Winter Dance Party Tour on a bill with Buddy Holly, The Big Bopper, and others. The 1987 Valens biopic *La Bamba* featured Lou Diamond Phillips in the title role; a hit soundtrack spawned a pair of cover hits by Los Lobos, 'La Bamba' and 'Come On, Let's Go'.

CAUSE: A much chronicled event, Ritchie Valens, Buddy Holly, The Big Bopper, and a pilot died in an aeroplane crash. Frustrated with the broken heater in their dilapidated tour bus, Valens and the others wanted to avoid the region's below-zero temperature and had instead chartered a small plane. Holly's guitarist, Tommy Allsup, lost the last seat in a coin-toss with Valens, with the excited Valens exclaiming that he had never before won anything. Departing from nearby Mason City, Iowa, in a blinding snowstorm en route to their next show in Fargo, North Dakota, the craft took off at 1:50 in the morning, and went down just minutes later at the edge of a cornfield in Clear Lake, Iowa. Pilot error was cited as the cause of the crash; suffering vertigo, newlywed Roger Peterson flew directly into the ground. With the wreckage undiscovered until the following morning, there was no chance of survivors due to the inclement elements. Aeroplane crash or not, the Winter Dance Party Tour continued with a revised line-up, including Frankie Avalon, Jimmy Clanton, and at one stop, 15-year-old Robert Velline (a.k.a. Bobby Vee) and his band The Shadows. The tour began on January 23, 1959 at George Devine's Ballroom in Milwaukee, Wisconsin, and ended on schedule at the Illinois State Armory in Springfield on February 15. Ironically, Valens had developed a fear of planes when in 1957 the debris from an overhead collision of two aircrafts killed several of his classmates who were on the school playground. Attending his grandfather's funeral that day, Valens was not in school.

FURTHER READING: Mendheim, Beverly. (1987). *Ritchie Valens: The First Latino Rocker.* Tempe, AZ: Bilingual Press.

Dino Valenti

(CHESTER POWERS)
Born November 7, 1943
Died November 16, 1994

A crucial figure in the formation of the

pioneering acid rock band Quicksilver Messenger Service, Dino Valenti also had success as a songwriter. A native of Danbury, Connecticut, Valenti embraced the emerging Greenwich Village folk movement in the Sixties. Relocating to the West Coast, he immersed himself in the San Francisco folk/beatnik scene, living in a commune in Venice in a volatile household that included David Crosby, Paul Kantner and David Freiberg. Valenti recorded several folk-rock styled demos at World Pacific and was signed to Elektra in 1964 as a soloist, releasing the label's twelfth single 'Don't Let It Down'. Its B-side 'Birdses', partly inspired several of his contemporaries to call themselves The Byrds. Switching musical gears in 1964 after meeting John Cipollina, Valenti formed Quicksilver Messenger Service. Blending psychedelia with folk-rock, QMS followed in the wake of a similar local group, The Charlatans. Shortly after booking gigs for the group, Valenti was jailed on a drug conviction for which he served nine months of a one-to-ten year sentence, and was forced to sell the rights of his composition 'Get Together' to fund his defence. The song subsequently became a national hit for The Youngbloods and a much-used anthem for various advertisers and organisations. Its loss caused Valenti millions. After his release in 1970, Valenti recorded a folk rock album, *Dino Valenti,* and when Cipollina left QMS the same year during the recording sessions for their fourth album, *Just For Love,* Valenti returned to the group on guitar and lead vocals. From this project, QMS would land their biggest hit with the psychedelic-styled 'Fresh Air'. Under Valenti's leadership, QMS lost its fanbase. A 1975 QMS reunion and album *Solid Silver* fared poorly. Valenti has been frequently miscredited with writing 'Hey Joe', the folk standard popularised by The Leaves, The Byrds and Jimi Hendrix. Later pressings credit the song to Chester Powers.
CAUSE: Although the cause was never disclosed, Valenti's death was probably related to brain surgery. He died in Santa Rosa, California.

Dickie Valentine

(RICHARD BRICE)
Born November 4, 1929
Died May 6, 1971
A British pop singer who enjoyed considerable fame in the Fifties, Dickie Valentine broke into show business at age three in the film comedy, *Jack's The Boy.* While working as a stagehand during his teens, Valentine was befriended by entertainer Bill O'Conner who paid for his singing lessons. Joining Ted Heath's band as a vocalist, Valentine entertained audiences with his impersonations of a multitude of crooners including Mario Lanza and Johnnie Ray. Becoming a pre-rock teen idol, Valentine was frequently voted top British singer in *NME* polls. Signing with Decca, he enjoyed a strong hit run including 'Broken Wings' (1953), 'Finger Of Suspicion' (1954) and 'Christmas Alphabet' (1955). Though he had fallen from the pop charts by 1960, Valentine remained a popular concert draw right up to his death.
CAUSE: He was involved in an car accident when returning from a concert in Wales.

Earl Van Dyke

Born July 8, 1930
Died September 19, 1992
A classically trained Motown arranger and session keyboard player, Earl Van Dyke joined the label in 1961, co-heading the studio band, nicknamed The Funk Brothers, by 1964. Largely unknown to the public, or the millions of fans who bought Tamla records during the Sixties, The Funk Brothers performed on dozens of hits for virtually all the singers and groups who recorded for Motown,

among them The Temptations, The Four Tops, The Supremes, and Marvin Gaye. Leaving Motown in 1971, he continued to work as a session musician for hire, and for a time he led Freda Payne's backing band. He later taught music in a Detroit high school, retiring in 1991.
CAUSE: Prostate cancer. He died in Detroit.
FURTHER READING: George, Nelson. (1985). *Where Did Our Love Go?: The Rise & Fall Of The Motown Sound.* Omnibus Press: London.

Frederick Van Pallandt

(BARON FREDERICK JAN GUSTAV FLORIS VAN PALLANDT)
Born May 14, 1934
Died May 15, 1994
Half of the popular blue-blood, Danish husband and wife pop duo, Nina and Frederick, Frederick Van Pallandt scored several British ballad hits including 'Little Donkey' (1960) and 'Sucu Sucu' (1961). The jet-setting couple divorced in 1976. After residing for several years on the island of Ibiza, Van Pallandt later settled on the island of Mindoro in the Philippines.
CAUSE: He was murdered at his mansion on Mindoro, apparently by a professional 'hitman'. Also killed was his girlfriend Susannah. The motive for the killing was never established.

Dave Van Ronk

(DAVID R. VAN RONK)
Born June 30, 1936
Died February 10, 2002
Nicknamed "The Mayor of Greenwich Village", Dave Van Ronk was a folk-blues guitarist who befriended a young Bob Dylan upon his arrival in Greenwich Village. Van Ronk recorded nearly two dozen albums during his long career, with his final album issued in 2001. He also collaborated with The Hudson Dusters.
CAUSE: Colon cancer. He died at New York University Medical Center.

Townes Van Zandt

Born March 7, 1944
Died January 1, 1997
Although Texas-based singer songwriter Townes Van Zandt never managed to score a hit, his compositions were recorded by a host of star acts and his reputation remains high. Dropping out of the University of Colorado to become a folk singer, he settled into the Houston club scene. Unable to support himself as a musician, he attempted to enlist for the Vietnam War but was rejected due to psychological problems. Relocating to Memphis in 1968, Van Zandt recorded his first of 15 albums, *For The Sake Of The Song.* A country-rock performer who was rooted in the blues, he wrote a host of tragic folk ballads with clever melodies and introspective, evocative and poetic lyrics. His benchmark album *High, Low, And In Between* (1972), was highlighted by 'If I Needed You' and 'Pancho And Lefty', the latter track a number one country single for Willie Nelson. Van Zandt's material would also be recorded by Lyle Lovett, Emmylou Harris, The Cowboy Junkies, Joe Ely and Nanci Griffith. Abusing alcohol and in poor health, Van Zandt did not record from 1978 to 1987. Returning to the music scene, he recorded his final album in Ireland with local musicians, the Celtic-flavoured, *No Deeper Blue* (1995). Shortly before he died Van Zandt gave his wife a number of tapes containing unreleased tracks, and told her that once he passed away she would be a "very busy girl". The tracks were overdubbed and compiled on the 1999 album *A Far Cry From Dead.*
CAUSE: Heart attack. He died at his home in Smyrna, Texas.

Ronnie Van Zant

Born January 15, 1949
Died October 20, 1977
The leader and vocalist of Southern rock giants Lynyrd Skynyrd, Ronnie Van Zant abandoned a budding

baseball career for rock music on hearing The Rolling Stones. While attending a Jacksonville high school, Van Zant teamed in 1965 with childhood friends, guitarists Allen Collins and Gary Rossington, to form My Backyard, a cover band that played Cream and Hendrix material and a few originals. Composing most of the group's material with Collins, Van Zant usually provided the lyrics. Evolving into Lynyrd Skynyrd, the group was named after an unpopular gym teacher, Leonard Skinner. After extensive club work and a few local record releases, Lynyrd Skynyrd signed with MCA Records in 1973. Produced by Al Kooper, their début album *Pronounced Leh-Nerd Skin-Nerd* (1973) was highlighted by the rock standard, 'Free Bird', a dedication to the late Duane Allman of The Allman Brothers. Featuring Van Zant's deep, raunchy voice, the guitar orientated group became leaders of the new Southern rock genre. Hiring a third guitar player in time for their second album *Second Helping* (1974), Lynyrd Skynyrd scored their first Top 10 pop hit with 'Sweet Home Alabama', a blistering answer to Neil Young's anti-Southern laments, 'Southern Man' and 'Alabama'. Around this time they befriended The Who, with whom they toured as a support act in 1973, and were managed by Englishman Peter Rudge, then also managing The Who's American affairs and all tours by The Rolling Stones. Under Rudge's guidance Skynyrd toured relentlessly both at home and in Europe – they supported the Stones at Knebworth in 1976 – and the hard work resulted in platinum sales for their live album *One More From The Road* (1976). Hard drinkers and abusers of drugs, Skynyrd gained a fearsome reputation as hell-raisers both for fighting amongst themselves and with others. Van Zant – a noted brawler – was frequently arrested for violent outbursts in the mid Seventies. Adding the brother and sister team of Steve and Cassie Gaines, Lynyrd Skynyrd launched a 50-city US tour in 1977 to promote their new album *Street Survivors*; which spawned the hits 'What's Your Name' and 'That Smell', the album cover featuring a shot of the group members engulfed in flames. Shortly before his death, Van Zant was planning to record a country album with Steve Gaines. Van Zant sang barefoot on stage – "I like to feel the stage burn," he was quoted as saying – and without his leadership Lynyrd Skynyrd had little option but to disband after his death. The group reunited in the Eighties and, as a tribute to their former singer and guiding light, played 'Free Bird' as an instrumental while a single spotlight picked out Ronnie Van Zant's characteristic wide-brimmed hat atop a microphone stand placed centre stage.

CAUSE: The group was en route from Greenville, South Carolina, to Baton Rouge, Louisiana, when the group's plane ran out of gas after the pilots had accidentally jettisoned fuel. The pilots radioed the tower in Houston asking for the coordinates to a small airfield in McComb, Mississippi; but forced to land in a swamp near Gillsburg, the plane struck the base of a tree head-on. All the passengers, except Van Zant, who was asleep on the floor of the plane, were buckled in their seat belts. The crash killed Van Zant, bandmates Steve and Cassie Gaines, road manager Dean Kilpatrick, and both pilots. Van Zant was hurled into a tree and died from head injuries. Of the 20 others injured, eight were hospitalised. One of the injured, Allen Collins, walked several miles to get help. With rescuers unable to fly into the marshy, wooded site, local farmers carried the victims to safety. In a gruesome, shameful display, souvenir hunters descended on the site, pilfering items from the craft as well as from the injured and dead. In 1982, Van Zant's 300-pound marble grave slab was stolen. One surviving roadie later committed suicide; another roadie was murdered by a girlfriend.

Tommy Vance

(RICHARD ANTHONY CRISPIAN FRANCIS PRUE HOPE-WEST)
Born July 11, 1941
Died March 6, 2005
A longtime deejay at BBC Radio 1 as presenter of the popular *Friday Rock Show*, gravel-voiced Tommy Vance began his career in the US using the on-air name Rick West. Born in Oxford, and having served in the navy, Vance got his first break in America on Los Angeles station KHJ where he appropriated the name Tommy Vance which had been left unused by another presenter. After returning to the UK, his first broadcasting stint was at pirate stations Radio Caroline and London, followed by a period in 1967 co-hosting *Top Gear* with John Peel on the newly inaugurated Radio 1. Vance hosted his own slot on Capital Radio in the Seventies and during his 15 years with Radio 1 (commencing in 1978) his *Friday Rock Show* became something of an institution. In later years, as well as innumerable voice-overs, Vance hosted a TV version of the *Friday Rock Show* on the VH1 network in the UK, as well as his own radio show on digital station Virgin Classic Rock.
CAUSE: He suffered a stroke and died three days later at Darent Valley Hospital near Dartford, Kent.

Luther Vandross

(LUTHER RONZONI VANDROSS)
Born April 20, 1951
Died July 1, 2005
An R&B crooner renowned for his heart-rending ballads, Luther Vandross dominated the charts beginning in the Eighties. Born into a musical family in Manhattan, Vandross taught himself to play the piano beginning at age three. Drawn to soul divas during his youth, he was influenced by Aretha Franklin, The Shirelles and, especially, Dionne Warwick and, with his older sister Pat, a member of the doo-wop group The Crests, Vandross began singing with neighbourhood friends. Joining a 16-member ensemble called Listen My Brother, Vandross sang on the premiere episode of the PBS educational programme *Sesame Street* in November 1969, and enjoyed his first taste of success when one of his compositions, 'Everybody Rejoice', was included in the 1972 Broadway production of the musical *The Wiz*. After a chance meeting with David Bowie in 1974, who hired him to sing backing on the *Young Americans* album, Vandross became a much in-demand session vocalist. Over the next decade, Vandross worked with a who's who of music royalty including Quincy Jones, Bette Midler, Lou Rawls, Roberta Flack, Chic, Carly Simon, Ringo Starr, Todd Rundgren and The Average White Band. During this period, Vandross could also be heard in commercial jingles for Pepsi Cola, Burger King, Miller Beer, KFC and General Electric. In 1976, Vandross formed a group called Luther, who recorded a pair of albums for Cotillion Records and had a pair of minor R&B hits before disbanding. Soon Vandross became the unidentified voice in a number of studio-only ensembles by the names of The New York City Band, Bionic Boogie and even a disco-styled Beach Boys group called The Good Vibrations. Vandross was also hired by a pair of Italian producers as the lead vocalist of what had been intended as another studio-only creation, Change. After quitting Change, Vandross demanded that the producers pay him a cut of the royalties instead of a flat fee. He then produced and financed his own solo album *Never Too Much*, which was released by Epic Records, and reached the top position on the R&B charts with the self-composed single 'Never Too Much' followed by a

hit run of smooth love ballads which included: 'It's Over Now', 'Give Me The Reason', 'Stop To Love', 'Any Love', 'Here And Now', the medley 'Power Of Love'/'Love Power', 'Don't Want To Be A Fool' and 'Your Secret Love'. His collaborative hits included: 'If This World Were Mine' with Cheryl Lynn, 'How Many Times Can We Say Goodbye' with Dionne Warwick, 'There's Nothing Better Than Love' with Gregory Hines, 'Endless Love' with Mariah Carey, and 'The Best Things In Life Are Free' with Janet Jackson, BBD and Ralph Tresvant. Vandross also wrote and co-produced several Aretha Franklin hits including 'Jump To It'. Although Vandross' releases occasionally crossed over to the pop charts, he achieved far wider airplay on urban radio and his greatest success came with the touching Richard Marx co-penned ballad 'Dance With My Father', which earned four Grammys. In the last years of his life, Vandross suffered from various physical maladies.
CAUSE: Battling a chronic weight problem, he suffered a stroke in April 2003. Never fully recovering, he collapsed during a physical therapy session at John F. Kennedy Medical Center in Edison, New Jersey and died. Vandross also suffered from diabetes, which ran in the family and had taken the lives of two siblings as well as his father when Luther was just eight.

Joey Vann

(JOSEPH CANZANO)
Born April 3, 1943
Died February 28, 1984
The lead vocalist of the New Jersey-based, white R&B vocal group The Duprees, Joey Vann enjoyed several hits in the early Sixties. Forming several doo-wop outfits in the mid Fifties, Vann teamed with vocalist Tom Bialoglow in 1959 to form The Parisiennes. Practising heavily, the group was signed to Coed Records in 1962 with the aid of new manager George Paxton. Débuting with a cover of Jo Stafford's 1952 hit 'You Belong To Me', The Duprees employed a Fifties-style group harmony sound. The Duprees' hits continued with 'My Own True Love' (also known as 'Tara's Theme'), and two Joni James' covers, 'Why Don't You Believe Me' (1963) and 'Have You Heard' (1963). Leaving the group in 1964 for a solo career, Vann was replaced by Mike Kelly. Attempting a comeback in 1974, Vann would sporadically return to the stage.
CAUSE: Heart attack.

Randy Vanwarmer

(RANDALL EDWIN VANWARMER)
Born March 30, 1955
Died January 12, 2004
A one-hit wonder, singer-songwriter Randy Vanwarmer is best known for his hit 'Just When I Needed You Most'. Born in Indian Hills, Colorado, he moved to England with his family, aged 15, after the death of his father. As a songwriter, Vanwarmer was befriended by Ian Kimmet of Island Music, and when Kimmet found a position at Bearsville Records, he helped Vanwarmer sign with the label. Returning to the US, Vanwarmer scored his sole Top 40 hit with a ballad he had written when aged 18, 'Just When I Needed You Most' (1979), a yearning song about unrequited love. Recording a total of four albums at Brownsville, he was unable to score another hit. Vanwarmer also wrote a number of country hits: 'I Guess It Never Hurts To Hurt Sometimes' (The Oak Ridge Boys), 'I'm In A Hurry (And Don't Know Why)' (Alabama) and 'I Will Whisper Your Name' (Michael Johnson).
CAUSE: He had undergone a bone marrow transplant for treatment of leukaemia at the Fred Hutchinson Cancer Research Center in Seattle, but died after suffering complications.

Kin Vassy

Born August 16, 1943
Died June 15, 1994
A member of Kenny Rogers & The First Edition and a touring member of Frank Zappa & The Mothers of Invention, Kin Vassy also had success as a songwriter, penning material for Ray Charles, Anne Murray, and Bonnie Raitt.
CAUSE: Cancer. He died in Los Angeles.

Frankie Vaughan

(FRANCIS ABELSON)
Born February 3, 1928
Died September 17, 1999
In a throwback to the music hall tradition, British pop crooner Frankie Vaughan would take the stage in an elegant top hat and cane. Born in Liverpool, Vaughan was reared in a poor environment. While studying commercial art at the Leeds College of Art, Vaughan won a singing competition and after touring for three years as a dance band crooner, he achieved fame only after he started recording. Considered to be Britain's Frank Sinatra, Vaughan was a major British star with hits such as 'Istanbul' (1954), 'Garden Of Eden' (1957), 'Kisses Sweeter Than Wine' (his only US hit, 1957), 'Judy' (1958), 'Tower Of Strength' (1961), and a song that became his signature tune, 'Give Me The Moonlight'. He donated the profits from his hit 'Green Door' to the British Boy Clubs, where he was helped during his youth. An outspoken social critic, he railed against juvenile delinquency and criticised the behaviour of rock entertainers such as Elvis Presley and The Beatles. As an actor, he appeared in a number of teen-oriented films, playing a pop singer in two of them, *The Heart Of A Man* and *The Lady Is A Square*. Drawn to Hollywood, he appeared opposite Marilyn Monroe in *Let's Make Love*. Remaining popular in Britain, in the Seventies he hosted his own television series and set a record with his three-month run at London's Talk Of The Town nightclub. He also starred in a London theatrical production of *42nd Street* in the Eighties.
CAUSE: Afflicted with heart disease for a number of years, he suffered a heart attack at his home in High Wycombe. He had undergone emergency heart surgery four months before his death.

Stevie Ray Vaughan

(STEPHEN RAY VAUGHAN)
Born October 3, 1954
Died August 27, 1990
A legendary blues rock guitarist with few equals, Stevie Ray Vaughan had reached the zenith of his "guitar god" status at the time of his death. Born in the Dallas, Texas, suburb of Oak Cliff, Vaughan was taught a series of rudimentary chords at the age of eight by his older brother, Jimmie; Stevie would idolise and attempt to emulate his older brother throughout his career. Discovering blues music in his mid-teens, Vaughan spent more time in nightclubs than in school. Passing through a series of local groups including The Chantones, Vaughan briefly played bass guitar in his brother's blues rock group, Texas Storm. With only a limited blues scene in Dallas, Vaughan ventured to Austin in early 1972. Buying a '59 Stratocaster, he joined Marc Benno & The Nightcrawlers, a group that seemed poised for stardom, but after touring as an opening act for a number of established rock acts, The Nightcrawlers were dropped by A&M Records, who shelved their completed album. Devastated, Vaughan returned to the Austin blues bar scene and in 1975 joined an R&B group, The Cobras. (Meanwhile, brother Jimmie had just formed The Fabulous Thunderbirds.) Opening up for the visiting Albert King, Vaughan amazed the seasoned bluesman who took Vaughan under his wing. Vaughan left The Cobras in late 1977 to form Triple

Threat, an R&B outfit that featured his girlfriend, Lou Ann Barton, on vocals. Following Barton's departure in 1979, the none-too-confident Vaughan took the group in an instrumental direction before disbanding them in 1981 and forming his more famous outfit, Double Trouble, with bassist Tommy Shannon and drummer Chris Layton. Vaughan's skill was evident at his stunning performance at the Montreux Jazz Festival in Switzerland on July 17, 1982. Standing out from the predominantly jazz performers with his blazing guitar solos, the unknown Vaughan stole the show. He also impressed David Bowie, who was in the audience, who invited him to play guitar on his album, *Let's Dance* (1983). Offered a paltry salary to tour behind Bowie, Vaughan refused and the incident made headline news in the music press, not least because Vaughan's guitar work was regarded by critics as a highlight of *Let's Dance.* Courted by producer/talent scout John Hammond, Vaughan signed with Epic Records in 1982. From his début album, *Texas Flood,* Vaughan scored a pair of driving album-rock hits with 'Love Struck Baby' and 'Pride And Joy'. Next he won a *Guitar Player* readers' poll, and almost single-handedly reinvigorated the blues genre. Sporting a floppy black hat and goatee, Vaughan wowed audiences with fast and furious guitar solos of extraordinary fluency. Vaughan's success continued with two platinum certified albums, *Couldn't Stand The Weather* (1984) and *Soul To Soul* (1985). Playing duelling guitars with Sixties surf-guitar legend Dick Dale, in 1987 Vaughan recorded a rocked-out version of The Chantays' instrumental classic 'Pipeline' for the surf film, *Back To The Beach* (1987), the single earning a Grammy nomination. During his long years on the road Vaughan had developed a serious drug and alcohol problem and in 1986 he checked into a rehab clinic to dry out, putting his career on hold for three years. Vaughan's comeback album *In Step* (1989) enjoyed a very long chart run and was highlighted by the tracks 'Tightrope', 'The House Is Rockin'' and 'Crossfire'. Shortly before his death, Vaughan had finished recording a long-overdue collaborative album with his brother Jimmie, the posthumously released, Grammy-winning *Family Style* (1990). In all, Stevie Ray Vaughan earned nine Grammy nominations during his lifetime. Epic Records continued to release material by Vaughan throughout the Nineties. Vaughan's sidemen, Tommy Shannon and Chris Layton, went on to form a series of bands together including Storyville, before releasing an album as Double Trouble in 2001, *Been A Long Time.*

CAUSE: After performing 'Sweet Home Chicago' as the final encore with his brother Jimmie, Robert Cray, and headliner Eric Clapton, at the Alpine Valley outdoor amphitheater in East Troy, Wisconsin, Stevie Ray convinced Jimmie to give up the last seat on a departing helicopter. Flying in dense fog, the chopper crashed into a man-made ski slope a mile from the venue. All aboard, including three members of Clapton's entourage, died immediately on impact. The search for the craft did not begin for four hours. The pilot had been involved in two previous crashes.

FURTHER READING: Patoski, Joe Nick. (1993). *Stevie Ray Vaughan: Caught In The Crossfire.* Boston: Little, Brown.

R.J. Vealey

(ROBERT JASON VEALEY)
Born September 29, 1962
Died November 13, 1999

The drummer of the Atlanta Rhythm Section, R.J. Vealy joined the band in 1995. A native of West Virginia, Vealy was reared on classic rock but drawn to jazz during his college years. After joining a techno-pop band in the Eighties called Fashion Reaction, he was hired by The Atlanta Rhythm

Section, recording two albums with the group.
CAUSE: He suffered a heart attack shortly after a concert at the University of Central Florida in Orlando. Complaining of indigestion, he collapsed backstage and died at the scene. Tests later determined that his heart had been weakened by cocaine abuse. A coroner's report attributed his death to heart disease and chronic cocaine abuse.

Carlos Vega

Born December 7, 1957
Died April 6, 1998
The Cuban-born drummer for James Taylor since 1985, Carlos Vega appeared on four albums, *Never Die Young*, *New Moon Shine*, *Hourglass*, and *Live*. A popular session drummer who was discovered by jazzman Lee Ritenour, Vega also backed George Benson, Laura Branigan, Sheena Easton, Don Felder, Olivia Newton-John, and The Weather Girls.
CAUSE: He committed suicide by gunshot on a deserted road overlooking Los Angeles. He had been scheduled to appear with James Taylor on *The Oprah Winfrey Show* the following day.

Nik Venet

(NIKOLAS KOSTANTINOS VENETOULIS)
Born December 3, 1936
Died January 2, 1998
A veteran staff producer at Capitol Records, Nik Venet oversaw 300 albums including projects by The Beach Boys, King Curtis, John Stewart, and Glen Campbell. A native of Baltimore, Venet mastered the banjo and guitar as a child. Moving to New York City, he worked in a variety of music industry positions including as a Brill Building songwriter. After failing as a solo act at RCA Records, Venet flirted briefly with film and television acting. Hired as an A&R man and producer by Capitol Records, Venet landed his first success with The Beach Boys. With an eye for talent, Venet also signed Lou Rawls, John Stewart, and Linda Ronstadt & The Stone Poneys. Leaving Capitol for United Artist Records in 1971 and launching his own production company, Venet worked with Frank Zappa and Don McLean. In 1995 Venet launched his own label, Evening Star Records.
CAUSE: He died from a rare form of lymphoma at the County-USC Medical Center in Los Angeles. He had been hospitalised for four months.

Vik Venus

(JACK SPECTOR)
Born September 15, 1928
Died March 8, 1994
An American DJ, Vik Venus scored a novelty hit in 1969 with 'Moonflight'. A veteran of the New York City airwaves, he worked at a series of radio stations including WMCA, WHN, and WCBS. Nicknamed "Jake", Venus was the subject of The Del Lords' song, 'Saint Jake'.
CAUSE: He died while on the air at Long Island, New York, radio station WHLI. After several minutes of silence from the DJ booth, a station employee burst into the studio and found Venus unconscious.

Harrison Verrett

Born February 27, 1907
Died October 1965
Years before he joined his young brother-in-law's R&B band, Harrison Verrett had taught the teenage Fats Domino the basics of the piano. When the former Antoine Domino emerged as a hit act at Imperial Records in the Fifties, he hired his former teacher Verrett as a backing pianist. A popular local musician in his native New Orleans, Verrett married Domino's sister in the mid Forties.
CAUSE: Unknown.

Henry Vestine

Born December 25, 1944
Died October 21, 1997
The lead guitarist of the Sixties

blues-rock group Canned Heat, Henry Vestine was rooted in pre-war blues. Having been told at age five that his hands were too small for the guitar, the Washington DC-native initially learned to play the accordion. He took up guitar at the age of 11. An unorthodox player, Vestine received only limited musical training in his teens. Reared on a mixture of country, rock and especially blues, Vestine amassed an impressive collection of blues records and became friends with fellow blues enthusiast Bob "The Bear" Hite. A member of the first line-up of Frank Zappa's band, The Mothers (of Invention), Vestine quit in 1966 after Zappa signed with Verve Records and demanded a long-term commitment from the group's members. When Bob Hite and Al "Blind Owl" Wilson formed Canned Heat in 1966 from the remnants of an acoustic California jug band, Vestine asked to join. Electrifying their sound, the unsigned group delivered a solid set at the Monterey Pop Festival in June 1967, and as a result of this exposure, the group was signed by Liberty Records. Their début album *Canned Heat* (1967) was a critical success and a moderate seller, containing blues standards such as Elmore James' 'Dust My Broom'. Their follow-up release, *Boogie With Canned Heat* (1968), was more successful and the group enjoyed their first pop hit with a reworking of an old blues song 'On The Road Again', which became a hippie anthem. Combining psychedelic textures over a solid blues foundation, the group became a favourite of the Sixties flower power crowd. Nicknamed "he Sunflower", Vestine provided an LSD-inspired brand of fuzztone and feedback-filled guitar work. The group's third album *Living The Blues* (1969) was highlighted by 'Going Up The Country', which borrowed the melody of a Henry Thomas blues standard. Vestine left Canned Heat after a performance at the Fillmore in August 1969 just weeks before the group's landmark performance at Woodstock. After passing through various incarnations of Canned Heat in the Seventies, Vestine relocated to Eugene, Oregon, in the Eighties. Performing with a series of local groups, he later released his first solo album.
CAUSE: Respiratory failure. After finishing a tour of France, he was found dead in a Paris hotel room.

Sid Vicious

(JOHN SIMON RITCHIE)
Born May 10, 1957
Died February 2, 1979
The iconic bass player of pioneering punk rock group The Sex Pistols, the surly Sid Vicious became a punk hero, his tragic life and squalid death an abject lesson in how lethal sudden fame can be. Born in London, the former John Ritchie grew up in a turbulent, broken home. A loner who frequently changed schools before finally dropping out at age 15, his first job was in a garment factory. Enrolling in a college photography course, he met and befriended future bandmate John Lydon and thereafter followed the fortunes of the fledgling Sex Pistols as they performed around London. He was allegedly responsible for throwing a glass that ricocheted off a pillar and blinded a girl in one eye during a Sex Pistols show at London's 100 Club, where he also attacked noted *New Musical Express* critic Nick Kent with a bicycle chain. Such behaviour evidently endeared Ritchie to The Sex Pistols and, having adopted the name Sid Vicious, he was invited by Rotten to join the group in March 1977 as the replacement for original bassist Glen Matlock, sacked by all accounts because he liked The Beatles. This occurred shortly after the group had been dropped by EMI Records following their controversial TV appearance on the *Today* show, during which host Bill Grundy was referred to

on air as 'a dirty fucker'. Musically inept, Vicious had previously been a member of a loose aggregation of would-be punks who called themselves Flowers Of Romance. Under the guidance of svengali-like manager Malcolm McLaren, The Sex Pistols now included Vicious, vocalist Johnny Rotten (Lydon), drummer Paul Cook and guitarist Steve Jones. A neurotic, heavy-drug user given to self-mutilation, the unpredictable Vicious was often the visual focus in the group. Unable to dance, Vicious instead invented a solitary dance called "the pogo", the precursor of slam dancing and moshing. Signed and quickly dropped by A&M Records, The Sex Pistols finally landed at Virgin Records in May 1977. Their single 'God Save The Queen', released to coincide with the Queen's Silver Jubilee, signalled the explosion of punk rock. Then, in a publicity stunt gone awry, The Sex Pistols rented a boat named The Queen Elizabeth and threw a party on the River Thames; the craft was boarded by police who arrested members of the group, their management and other guests. With much of Britain appalled at the antics of these scruffy outlaws, The Sex Pistols were forced to tour under a series of pseudonyms. Finally permitted airplay on the BBC, the group enjoyed hits with socially biting numbers such as 'Pretty Vacant' (1977) and 'Holidays In The Sun' (1977). The group would release only one studio album, *Never Mind The Bollocks, Here's The Sex Pistols*. During this period, Vicious began dating Nancy Spungen, a middle-class girl from suburban Philadelphia with a history of emotional problems. Launching their ill-fated tour of the US in January 1978, The Sex Pistols were often met with hostile audiences. Ten days into the tour at the Winterland Auditorium in San Francisco on January 18, a disgusted Johnny Rotten stopped the show and, after uttering the words "Ever get the feeling you've been cheated?" disbanded the group. Within a few days, Vicious overdosed on heroin and was hospitalised. A month later, Vicious and Spungen were arrested on drug possession charges. Returning to London, Vicious performed with Johnny Thunders in the group, The Living Dead. Entering the studio, Vicious recorded an album's worth of material, highlighted by a tongue-in-cheek cover of the pop standard 'My Way'. After vacationing in Paris, Vicious returned to the US. Backed by members of The New York Dolls, he made his New York City solo début at Max's Kansas City and was unmercifully heckled. Sharing a run-down Chelsea Hotel apartment with girlfriend Nancy Spungen, Vicious spent most of his time strung out on heroin, and after one of their many drug-induced violent exchanges, on October 12, 1978, Vicious woke up and found Spungen dead. He was charged with her murder. Sex Pistols manager Malcolm McLaren hired high profile attorney F. Lee Bailey to investigate Spungen's death. Two weeks later, Vicious unsuccessfully tried to kill himself by slashing his wrists. He was sent to the psychiatric ward of New York's Rikers Island Prison. Released on bail, Vicious was dead before he could be prosecuted. Vicious and Spungen's relationship was chronicled in the 1986 Alex Cole film *Sid & Nancy*, with Gary Oldman portraying Vicious and Chloe Webb as Nancy. A slow seller in the US, *Never Mind The Bollocks* was finally certified gold in 1987 a decade after its release. In a 2002 *Q* magazine interview, John Lydon said of *Sid & Nancy*, "It's a work of fabrication, plain and simple."

CAUSE: A day after his release on $50,000 bail, Vicious was found dead from a heroin overdose in a Greenwich Village apartment. Vicious reportedly preferred death over a long prison sentence and begged his mother for an injection of heroin. Spungen's mother

Ann McDonald would not permit Vicious to be buried next to her daughter. According to *The Village Voice*, Vicious' remains were secretly scattered over Spungen's grave. (An alternative story has Vicious' mother unceremoniously disposing of his ashes in a trash receptacle at a New York City airport.) Vicious' controversial and outspoken mother, Ann Beverly, unexpectedly wealthy after receiving a percentage of the Pistols' royalties, committed suicide by drug overdose on September 6, 1996, at the age of 44.

FURTHER READING: Bateson, Keith, and Parker, Allen. (1991). *The Life & Death Of Sid Vicious: The Official Biography*. London: Omnibus. Savage, Jon. (1991). *England's Dreaming*. London: Faber & Faber.

Jack Vigliatura

(JOHN VIGLIATURA IV)
Born December 20, 1973
Died September 8, 1995

The lead singer and lyricist of the Nineties alternative rock outfit For Squirrels, Jack Vigliatura formed the group in Gainesville, Florida. For Squirrels scored a posthumous MTV and radio hit with 'The Mighty K.C.', the song about the deceased Kurt Cobain. The track was culled from their début album, *Example*.

CAUSE: With Vigliatura driving the group's tour van, the rear right tyre exploded and the vehicle flipped over several times. Killed were Vigliatura and two passengers. The group was returning home from a CMJ convention performance at CBGBs in New York City.

Gene Vincent

(EUGENE VINCENT CRADDOCK)
Born February 11, 1935
Died October 12, 1971

A much-revered rockabilly pioneer, Gene Vincent was tormented for much of his life through a leg injury sustained during military service. A native of Norfolk, Virginia, he entered the Navy in 1952 after lying about his age. He almost lost his leg in a traffic accident while making a courier delivery, his military motorcycle colliding with a car. Honorably discharged, Vincent honed his guitar skills during his convalescence, and while in hospital, he paid fellow patient Donald Graves $25 for the rights to the composition 'Be-Bop-A-Lula' (1956). Out of the hospital and still wearing a leg cast, Vincent performed sporadically in local clubs where he was spotted by local DJ Bill "Sheriff Tex" Davis, who helped him record a demo. Envious of RCA's success with Elvis Presley, Capitol Records were on the lookout for a rocker and Vincent, still on crutches, was selected from hundreds of auditions. Although the A-side of his début single 'Woman Love' fared poorly and was even banned by the BBC, the B-side, 'Be-Bop-A-Lula', was an instant smash. With his backing band The Blue Caps, Vincent would never attain the same level of success as Presley but his peculiar breathless style and leather clad image won him many fans, especially in the UK. Appearing in his first of two films, *The Girl Can't Help It* (1956), Vincent had his cast painted to match his other pant leg. With Vincent constantly on the road during the next two years, his leg would never properly heal, and his cast was later replaced by a permanent brace. After scoring hits with 'Race With The Devil' (1956), 'Lotta Lovin'' (1957) and 'Dance To The Bop' (1958), Vincent was forced to leave the US for a time due to a conflict with the Musicians' Union. Relocating to England, Vincent was guided by television producer Jack Good who encouraged the black leather image and exaggerated limp which gave the star his iconic edge. Further UK hits followed with 'Pistol Packing Mama' and 'She She Little Sheila'. Vincent was promoted by Don Arden who also managed him for a period. After a sold-out tour through Japan, Vincent appeared on the same bill as fellow early rocker Eddie Cochran in 1960, and was a passenger in the car in which Cochran was killed in the UK on April 17, 1960. He remained in England until the ascendancy of The Beatles, riding out the rockabilly craze and continuing to perform in clubs. Returning to the US in 1965, he was advised by doctors to have his leg amputated. Refusing, he continued to fight the pain with large doses of aspirin and liquor. In 1969 he returned to the UK, but his alcoholism had transformed him into a bloated figure and a parody of the once great showman of the Fifties. A comeback album *I'm Back And I'm Proud* fared less well than hoped and Vincent continued touring with pick-up bands, often appearing in France. In 1971 he completed two albums for Kama Sutra, *If Only You Could See Me Today* and *The Day The World Turned Blue*, but neither could arrest his continued physical decline. For all that, he remained a legend to his coterie of fans and one of the most important and tragic underachievers from the late Fifties school of rock'n'roll.

CAUSE: Vincent died at Intervalley Community Hospital in Newhall, California, from complications of ulcers and long-term alcohol and aspirin abuse. His health in decline, Vincent had last performed eight days earlier in Liverpool, England. According to a 1993 *Goldmine* magazine report, Vincent's worried parents had gone to his home. Walking through the front door, "Vincent tripped and fell, bursting his chronic ulcers, and began vomiting blood." His mother later commented: "After he died, he had the sweetest smile on his face. He wanted to die. He was glad to think he was getting out of the mess he was in."

FURTHER READING: Hagarty, Britt. (1983). *The Day The Earth Turned Blue: A Biography Of Gene Vincent*. Poole, England: Blandford.

Johnny Vincent

(JOHN VINCENT IMBRAGULIO)

Born October 3, 1927

Died February 4, 2000

The owner of New Orleans' biggest independent label, Ace Records, John Vincent released dozens of national hits. After serving a military stint during World War II, Vincent returned to his home in Jackson, Mississippi and, after operating a tiny jukebox company, he took a position at a regional record distributor. Subsequently opening a record store and tiny blues label, Champion Records, Vincent attracted the attention of record mogul Art Rupe. Hired by Rupe as a talent scout and record salesman for Specialty Records, Vincent produced a hit for Guitar Slim but was fired by Rupe for demanding promised royalties from the record. Vincent then launched Ace Records in 1955, initially discovering success with local R&B acts such as Huey "Piano" Smith ('Rocking Pneumonia And The Boogie Woogie Flu'), but faring even better with teen idol pop acts such as Frankie Ford ('Sea Cruise') and Jimmy Clanton ('Just A Dream', 'Venus In Blue Jeans'). After entering an ill-fated distribution agreement in 1963 with financially troubled Vee-Jay Records, Ace was forced to close within three years. Remaining an entrepreneur, Vincent launched a restaurant, nightclub, and a recording studio. After several failed attempts, he revived Ace Records in the Nineties and had success with Willie Clayton. Vincent sold the Ace catalogue to British company Westside and formed a new label, Avanti Records.

CAUSE: Suffering pneumonia and heart failure, he died in Jackson, Mississippi.

Eddie "Cleanhead" Vinson

Born December 19, 1917

Died July 2, 1988

An early Houston-born alto saxophone player and singer, Eddie "Cleanhead" Vinson emerged from the jazz tradition

as a member of travelling bands led by Chester Boone and Milton Larkin. Dubbed "Cleanhead" after shaving his head, he began touring with blues guitar legend Big Bill Broonzy in 1940. Moving to New York City in 1942, Vinson joined The Cootie Williams Orchestra, providing the spirited vocal on 'Cherry Red'. Leaving Williams in 1945, Vinson formed his own 16-piece jump-blues styled orchestra, scoring a national hit with 'Kidney Stew Blues'. Retiring from music in 1954, he returned to Houston and recorded only sporadically. Rediscovered in 1967 by bandleader Johnny Otis, Vinson returned to the blues circuit. He later toured and recorded with Count Basie's Orchestra and Cannonball Adderley. His latter solo albums included *Cleanhead's Black* and *You Can't Make Love Alone.*
CAUSE: Stricken with throat cancer, he suffered a heart attack during a chemotherapy treatment. He died at a Los Angeles hospital.

Frank Virtue

(FRANCIS F. VIRTUOSO)
Born January 21, 1921
Died June 11, 1994
A Philadelphia-born producer and bandleader, Frank Virtue had a Top 10 instrumental hit in 1959 with 'Guitar Boogie Shuffle' with his group The Virtues. Opening his own recording studio in 1962, Virtue worked with Barbara Mason ('Yes, I'm Ready'), Eddie Holman ('Hey There Lonely Girl') and many others.
CAUSE: Unknown. He died at Nazareth Hospital in Philadelphia.

Janet Vogel

Born June 10, 1942
Died February 21, 1980
The soprano for the Fifties, Pittsburgh-based, all-white doo-wop outfit The Skyliners, Janet Vogel initially joined a precursor of the group called The Crescents. Managed by former Marquees singer Joe Rock, the Jimmy Beaumont-fronted Skyliners signed with Calico Records in late 1958. The Skyliners landed in the Top 10 with their début release, the elegant ballad 'Since I Don't Have You' which featured orchestral backing and closed with Vogel's high-pitched warbles. Often surprising audiences which assumed the group was black, The Skyliners continued their hit run with 'This I Swear' (1959), the slow chart-climber 'It Happened Today' (1959), and borrowing The Clovers' arrangement, the standard 'Pennies From Heaven' (1960). Tiring of life on the road, Vogel left the group in 1961. Regrouping in the Seventies, four of the five original members of The Skyliners hit the oldies circuit and scored a regional hit with the Doc Pomus composition, 'Where Have They Gone'. The Skyliners classic 'Since I Don't Have You' has been recorded by a number of artists including Chuck Jackson (1964), Eddie Holman (1970), Art Garfunkel (1979), Don McLean (1981) and even Guns N'Roses (1994).
CAUSE: She committed suicide by carbon-monoxide poisoning in the garage of her Pittsburgh home.

Jim Voight

Born September 24, 1946
Died November 7, 2000
A member of Sixties psychedelic rock band The Peanut Butter Conspiracy, drummer Jim Voight provided the backbeat for the West Coast act. The son of journalists, Voight won a Hollywood Bowl battle of the bands contest during his high school years as a member of The Elementary School Band. While attending college, he joined a group called The Interns, followed by folk-rock act The Ashes. As replacement for original drummer Spencer Dryden, who quit to join Jefferson Airplane, Voight recorded one album with the group. After adding vocalist Barbara "Sandi" Robison in late 1966, The Ashes

temporarily disbanded upon Robison's pregnancy but re-emerged as The Peanut Butter Conspiracy. Signing with Columbia Records, the group recorded a pair of excellent but ignored albums; from their début Gary Usher-produced album *The Peanut Butter Conspiracy Is Spreading*, the group scored a West Coast hit with 'It's A Happening Thing'. The group disbanded in 1969 after recording a final album for Warner/Challenge. Voight toured in various bands over the next several years before retiring from music.
CAUSE: Heart attack. He died in South Pasadena, California.

Roger Voudouris

(JOHN ROGER VOUDOURIS)
Born December 29, 1954
Died August 3, 2003
A one-hit wonder, singer-songwriter Roger Voudouris had a pop-rock chart hit with 'Get Used To It' in 1979. Hailing from Sacramento, California, he was previously a member of Voudouris/Kahne, a duo formed with David Kahne. Pursuing a solo career in 1978, Voudouris was signed by Warner Brothers and was popular in Japan and Australia during the Eighties.
CAUSE: Liver disease. He died at his home in the Sacramento suburb of Land Park, California.

W

Doreen Waddell

Born 1967
Died March 1, 2001

A member of dance/soul group Soul II Soul and techno-pop act The KLF, vocalist Doreen Waddell often performed under the stage name of Do'reen. From London, she was raised in a series of foster homes. Discovered by producer Beresford Romeo (a.k.a. Jazzie B.), Waddell was added to Soul II Soul, an act which featured several lead vocalists, and her lead vocals on three tracks including the hit 'Feel Free' appeared on the 1989 album *Club Classics Vol. One*. Waddell then joined The KLF in the early Nineties but, after dropping out of the music scene, she fell upon hard times.
CAUSE: After security guards at a Tesco supermarket in Shoreham-on-Sea, Sussex, accused her of shoplifting, she fled the building through a rear fire exit. Dashing over an embankment and into traffic on the nearby A27 highway, she was fatally struck by three vehicles. She was pronounced dead on arrival at a nearby hospital and was not identified for several days.

Chuck Wagon

(ROBERT DAVIS)
Born c. 1957
Died June 1981

The keyboard player of the pioneering California-based punk-rock outfit The Dickies, Chuck Wagon was a core member of the group along with vocalist Leonard Phillips and guitarist Stan Lee. Initially launched as an experimental jazz-rock combo called Jerry Kids, the group took a punk turn in 1977 after Wagon and his bandmates caught a performance by The Damned. One of the first US punk bands signed to a major label, The Dickies made their A&M Records début with *The Incredible Shrinking Dickies* (1979). Celebrating absurdity in costume and song, The Dickies churned out a series of quirky two-minute romps. Often recording cover songs, The Dickies tore through irreverent renditions of rock standards such as 'Nights In White Satin' and 'Paranoid'. Although immensely popular in Los Angeles, the group managed only limited success in the rest of the country. In Britain, the group placed several singles on the charts including the Top 10 entry, the theme from 'Banana Splits' (1979). Wagon released a solo EP in 1980.
CAUSE: Suicide by gunshot.

Steve Wahrer

Born November 22, 1941
Died January 21, 1989

The drummer of the Sixties surf-flavoured garage-rock group Trashmen, Steve Wahrer co-founded the Minneapolis-St. Paul quartet in 1962. After recording unsuccessfully for Soma Records, the Dal Winslow-fronted group landed at Garrett Records in 1963. Taking a stylistic turn toward surf music, The Trashmen landed a career-defining hit in 1963 with the uproarious 'Surfin' Bird', the song based on The Rivington's novelty hit 'Papa-Oom-Mow-Mow'. The group managed a second hit the following year with the similar-sounding 'Bird Dance Beat'. With The Trashmen disbanding in 1967, Wahrer found work as a local session player. Beginning in 1975, Wahrer rejoined The Trashmen for occasional oldies shows.
CAUSE: Throat and spinal cancer. He died at North Memorial Hospital in suburban Minneapolis.

Bruce Waibel

Born July 9, 1958
Died September 2, 2003

An innovative bassist whose style was rooted in Southern rock, Bruce Waibel was a member of Gregg Allman's backing band and hair metal act, Firehouse. Hailing from Dover, New Jersey, Waibel began playing guitar aged nine. Joining Gregg Allman's band as guitarist in 1982, Waibel switched to bass in 1985 and appeared on two studio albums, *I'm No Angel* (1987) and *Just Before The Bullets Fly* (1988). Parting with Allman in 1992, Waibel performed with a number of local groups in Sarasota, Florida before replacing Perry Richardson in Firehouse, in 2000, appearing on their seventh album, *02*. While with Firehouse, he also played in guitarist Bill Leverty's side project Wanderlust. Wanting to spend more time with his family, Waibel quit both groups. Waibel also worked with Dickey Betts and Rick Derringer.
CAUSE: Unknown. He was found dead at his home in Sarasota, Florida.

Patrick Waite

Born June 16, 1958
Died February 18, 1993
The bass player of the British pop-reggae sensation Musical Youth, Patrick Waite was born in Jamaica, but raised in Birmingham, England, by his father who was a former reggae performer. Under their father's guidance, Patrick and his brother Junior Waite were joined by another pair of brothers in 1981 to form a musical group. Although initially featuring their father on lead vocals, the group was completed with the addition of 14-year-old lead singer, Dennis Seaton. Signed by MCA after attracting the attention of influential British DJ John Peel, Musical Youth landed a pop-reggae hit with the Pete Waterman-produced 'Pass The Dutchie' (1983). Immensely popular in Britain during the next two years, the group disbanded after the release of their poor-selling second album. Turning to drugs and crime, Patrick Waite spent time behind bars. Waite and the group had been planning a comeback shortly before his death.
CAUSE: Suffering from an undiagnosed viral infection and a resulting enlarged heart and lung congestion, he collapsed while visiting a friend's home in Birmingham. Hitting the floor, he struck his head and died instantly. No drugs were found in his system.
FURTHER READING: Thompson, Caro. (1983). *Musical Youth: The Official Biography*. London: Virgin.

Freddie Waits

Born 1940
Died November 18, 1989
A prolific drummer, Freddie Waits performed with a series of R&B balladeers including Ivory Joe Hunter, Percy Mayfield and Little Willie John. Rooted in jazz, Waits was trained on flute before switching to drums, and for a time worked with Ella Fitzgerald and Milt Jackson. After a stint as a Motown session player in the Sixties, Waits relocated to New York and formed The New York Jazz Sextet. He later joined The Billy Taylor Trio.
CAUSE: Kidney failure. He died in New York City.

Junior Walker

(OSCAR G. MIXON)
Born June 14, 1931
Died November 23, 1995
The leader of Jr. Walker & The All Stars, saxophone player Junior Walker merged jazz and soul to create an instantly identifiable sound. Born in Arkansas but raised in South Bend, Indiana, Walker was reared on jazz music. Forming his first group The Jumping Jacks with future All Stars-member Willie Woods, Walker performed on a local music television programme. Relocating to St. Louis for a time, Walker honed his sax skills in Albert King's backing band. Returning to South Bend and forming a new group, Walker frequented the Battle Creek/Detroit club circuit in

the Sixties. Discovered by former Moonglows singer Harvey Fuqua, Jr. Walker & The All Stars first recorded as an instrumental outfit on the Fuqua-owned Harvey Records in 1962, releasing the obscure single, 'Twist Lackawanna'. With Harvey Records purchased by Motown, Walker's group recorded on the Motown subsidiary, Soul Records. Then with the scheduled singer absent during the session for the group's first hit, the Walker-penned 'Shotgun', the apprehensive Walker was forced into singing the lead vocals. The group continued its strong hit run into the Seventies, churning out a series of smooth soul-funk entries, including two Holland-Dozier-Holland compositions, '(I'm A) Road Runner' (1966) and 'How Sweet It Is (To Be Loved By You)', as well as 'What Does It Take (To Win Your Love)' (1969), 'These Eyes' (1969), and 'Gotta Hold On To This Feeling' (1970). With his group falling from the charts, Walker returned to his jazz roots in the Seventies. Except for providing the sax solo on Foreigner's 1981 Top 10 hit 'Urgent', Walker remained out of the limelight in the Eighties.
CAUSE: Diagnosed with cancer in 1993, he died at his home in Battle Creek, Michigan.

Randy "Stretch" Walker

Born 1968
Died November 30, 1995
A rapper, session drummer, synthesiser player, and producer, Randy "Stretch" Walker worked with Tevin Cambell, Vanessa Williams, and Mariah Carey. His best known work came as a producer and back-up vocalist for Tupac Shakur. Walker was a member of the Los Angeles-based, Tommy Boy Music gangster rap group Live Squad who scored a hit in 1992 with 'Heartless/Murderer'.
CAUSE: He was shot dead by three gunmen while he was driving his minivan in Queens, New York. Walker's vehicle then struck a tree and a parked car before overturning. Walker was one of several people whom Tupac Shakur had accused of his own shooting in 1994. Ironically, Walker was murdered on the first anniversary of Shakur's shooting.

T-Bone Walker

(AARON THIBEAUX WALKER)
Born March 28, 1910
Died March 16, 1975
A bluesman extraordinaire, T-Bone Walker has been called the century's first guitar hero. Reared in Dallas by his mother, Walker launched his musical career at age eight by collecting tips for blues guitarist Blind Lemon Jefferson. Taught the ukulele, and then guitar by his mother, Walker was also influenced by the gospel music of his Holiness church. After frequently joining his stepfather's amateur blues group as a singer and dancer, Walker joined a travelling medicine show at 14, and then a musical revue led by blues songstress Ida Cox at 17. Returning to Dallas, Walker was hired as a banjo player in Lawson Brooks' 16-piece band. Winning a talent contest in 1929, Walker earned a week-long stint with Cab Calloway and a recording session with Columbia Records. Backed by pianist Douglas Fernell, Walker made his recording début with the obscure single, 'Trinity River Blues', under the moniker Oak Cliff T-Bone. Settling in Oklahoma in 1933, Walker took guitar lessons, and teamed with fellow pupil and future jazz legend Charlie Christian in the same year; both men were still playing acoustic instruments. Relocating to California in 1936 at his wife's urging, Walker was hired by bandleader Big Jim Wynn, initially as a dancer. Buying an early Gibson electric guitar so as to be heard over boisterous crowds, Walker popularised the instrument within the blues world. Although Walker was not the first

bluesman to play an electric guitar, he was the most important as he incorporated jazz horn-like riffs into the blues idiom. Hired by popular bandleader Les Hite in 1939, Walker scored his first hit the following year with 'T-Bone Blues'. Leaving Hite in 1941 to start his own band, Walker began recording for a new label, Capitol Records. Teamed with pianist Freddie Slack, Walker landed a double-sided hit, 'I Got A Break Baby'/ 'Mean Old World' (1942). More significantly, Walker introduced his much-copied single-string guitar riff on the 1943 instrumental pop hit 'Riffette' (1943). After recording a series of poor-selling discs for the Chicago-based Rhumboogie label (named after a nightclub), Walker returned to Los Angeles and signed with Black & White Records. After initially targeting the emerging teenage market with the hit single 'Bobby Sox Blues' (1947), Walker made his groundbreaking recordings. Featuring his trademark single-string guitar work on the striking 'Call It Stormy Monday', Walker emerged as the country's leading blues guitarist. It became his signature tune, and features one of the most copied guitar riffs in R&B and rock history. Returning to Capitol Records in 1950, Walker churned out a string of influential releases. Criss-crossing Europe during the next two decades, Walker returned to the US for the blues revival of the Sixties. Walker won his first Grammy in 1970 for the album *Good Feelin'*. The following year, Walker enjoyed renewed interest when The Allman Brothers covered 'Call It Stormy Monday'.
CAUSE: Suffering a debilitating stroke in 1974, he succumbed to pneumonia the following year. He died in a Los Angeles nursing home.
FURTHER READING: Dance, Helen Oakley. (1990). *Stormy Monday: The T-Bone Walker Story*. New York: Da Capo.

Sippie Wallace

(BEAULAH THOMAS)
Born November 1, 1898
Died November 1, 1986
A classic blues singer and pianist, Sippie Wallace launched her career in the Twenties alongside contemporaries such as Bessie Smith and Victoria Spivey. The daughter of a Baptist deacon, Wallace abandoned spirituals for the jazz and blues of a Dallas-based tent show. Moving to Chicago in 1923, she took the nickname of "The Texas Nightingale". Signed to OKeh Records, she recorded dozens of 78s beginning with 'Up The Country Blues' (1923), one of many songs penned by her brothers. A leading blues star in The Twenties, Wallace enjoyed a string of bawdy hits including 'I'm A Mighty Tight Woman' and 'Bedroom Blues'. But following the death of her husband and a brother, Wallace abandoned blues music in the Thirties and returned to gospel. Only occasionally performing the blues in the next three decades, Wallace was lured back to the stage by Victoria Spivey during the blues boom of the Sixties. After recording the collaborative album *Sippie Wallace And Victoria Spivey*, Wallace suffered a debilitating stroke in 1970. Wallace entered another phase of her career in 1982 when she was befriended by singer Bonnie Raitt, with whom she recorded the duet 'Women Be Wise'. Wallace's 1983 album, the Raitt-produced *Sippie*, was nominated for a Grammy.
CAUSE: Suffering a heart attack during a tour through Germany, she returned to the US. She died later in the year in a Detroit hospital.

Steve Waller

(STEVEN CHARLES WALLER)
Born June 6, 1951
Died February 6, 2000
A member of Manfred Mann's Earth Band, Steve Waller replaced Dave Flett in early 1979. From London, Waller

was a self-taught musician inspired by the refined blues of B.B. King. Formerly a member of UK funk group Gonzalez, Waller appeared on their disco hit, 'Haven't Stopped Dancing Yet'. First appearing on the Earth Band album *Angel Station*, Waller also performed on *Chance*, *Somewhere In Africa* and the live project *Budapest*. Having been fired from the group in 1983, Waller worked with Kevin Coyne, Roger Ruskin Spear of The Bonzo Dog Band and reportedly turned down an offer to join Whitesnake.
CAUSE: His health was wrecked by years of alcohol abuse.

Steve Walsh

Born 1959
Died July 4, 1988
A veteran soul deejay who got his broadcasting start at UK pirate station Radio Invicta, Steve Walsh scored a cover hit with Fatback's 'I Found Lovin''; upon its release in 1987, the original version also re-charted. Walsh just missed the UK Top 40 with a cover of 'Ain't No Stoppin' Us Now'. Also a club deejay, he hosted *Soul Night Out* for Radio London.
CAUSE: Suffering injuries in a car accident in the resort of Ibiza, he returned to London for surgery. While recuperating, he suffered a massive heart attack.

Billy Ward

(ROBERT WILLIAMS)
Born September 15, 1921
Died February 16, 2002
The founder and manager of Fifties R&B group The Dominoes, Billy Ward was a shrewd businessman. A native of Los Angeles, the former child prodigy studied at the Art Institute of Chicago and at Juilliard in New York City. After working for the head of Rose Ann Marks, a Broadway advertising company in the late Forties, Ward decided to break into popular music. Assembling an R&B group, Ward hoped to capitalise on the doo-wop craze and after catching a performance in 1950 by former gospel singer Clyde McPhatter at an Apollo Theater amateur night, Ward knew he had found his lead vocalist. In addition to McPhatter the group – originally named The Ques – included Joe Lamont, Charlie White and Bill Brown. Ward was joined by Rose Ann Marks in managing the group and in writing most of their material. He played piano, occasionally sang backing vocals – but more importantly – hired and fired members at will. After winning an Arthur Godfrey *Talent Scouts* competition, the renamed Dominoes were signed by producer Ralph Bass to Federal Records, a new division of King Records. The group's début single 'Do Something For Me' (1951), featuring McPhatter's high tenor vocals, was an R&B hit and quickly propelled The Dominoes into the limelight. Initially, confused record buyers presumed that Ward was either lead singer or McPhatter's brother. A follow-up, the bawdy 'Sixty Minute Man', became the biggest R&B hit of the Fifties. Despite many stations banning the record, it received crossover airplay and spawned numerous answer records. Although McPhatter provided the group with a number of hits including 'Have Mercy Baby' and 'The Bells', he parted with Ward in 1953 after demanding an increase in his paltry $100 weekly salary. Ward subsequently replaced McPhatter with former boxer Jackie Wilson, who himself was fired in 1956 after getting into a fistfight with Ward. Taking a turn toward Mills Brothers-style harmony pop with new lead singer Gene Mumford, the renamed Billy Ward & The Dominoes employed lush orchestral backing on pop standards such as 'Star Dust' and 'Deep Purple'. Ward continued to form new versions of The Dominoes until 1965.

CAUSE: Natural causes. He died at the Centinela Park Convalescent Hospital in Los Angeles.

Jeff Ward

Born November 28, 1962
Died March 19, 1993
Jeff Ward briefly passed through leading industrial rock bands Ministry and Nine Inch Nails. At the time of his death, Ward was the drummer for Low Pop Suicide which had just released the album, *On The Cross Of Commerce.* Ward's brother, Jason, is the bass player of the group, Flotsam And Jetsam.
CAUSE: He committed suicide by carbon-monoxide poisoning at his home in Chicago. He was struggling to break a drug habit.

Si Waronker

(SIMON WARONKER)
Born March 5, 1915
Died June 6, 2005
The founder of Liberty Records, Simon "Si" Waronker enjoyed a number of pop and rock hits in the Fifties and Sixties. A musical prodigy as a child, Waronker studied the violin in France and Germany, and barely escaped from the Nazis at the start of the Second World War. Returning to Los Angeles, Waronker began a two decade long stint in 1936 with the 20th Century Fox studio orchestra. In 1955, he was asked by his cousin, Herb Newman, to start a record company but with Waronker taking too long to decide, Newman went ahead and launched his own label, Era. Soon after, Waronker moonlighted from his position at Fox to start Liberty Records. Initially focusing on the same sort of Hollywood music that he was performing at Fox, Waronker scored his first pop hit for Liberty with the jazz-flavoured 'Cry Me A River' recorded by actress Julie London and continued in 1956 with Patience & Prudence's 'Tonight You Belong To Me'. Keeping the label financially afloat during this period, the former Ross Bagdasarian scored hits as both David Seville and The Chipmunks, a trio of cartoon character-style voices – Alvin, Simon and Theodore named after Liberty vice president Alvin Bennett, Si Waronker and recording engineer Theodore "Ted" Keep – created by manipulating the speed of a tape recorder. Expanding into the emerging rock market, the label signed rockabilly singer Eddie Cochran, and later, Bobby Vee, The Rivingtons, Johnny Burnette, Jan & Dean, Johnny Rivers, The Ventures, and a latter version of Billy Ward & The Dominoes. Other Liberty artists included Henry Mancini, Timi Yuro, The Fleetwoods, Gene McDaniels, Rod McKuen, Gary Lewis & The Playboys, exotica founder Martin Denny, and a number of country acts including Floyd Tillman, June Carter, Bob Wills and a young singer-songwriter, Willie Nelson. After suffering the second of two strokes over a two-year period in 1963, Waronker sold the label to Avnet for $12 million. Waronker's son Lenny would later run Warner Brothers Records, producing artists such as Randy Newman, James Taylor and Captain Beefheart.
CAUSE: He died of natural causes at his home in Beverly Hills, California.

Delores Warren

Born 1953
Died February 22, 1985
A member of Eighties R&B vocal group Krystol, Delores Warren had hits with 'Passion From A Woman' (1986) and 'Precious, Precious' (1986). Warren and fellow Krystol member Robyrda Stiger were previously members of all-female R&B trio Alton McClain & Destiny, who scored a crossover hit in 1979 with 'It Must Be Love'. Warren was married to record producer Skip Scarborough.
CAUSE: Car crash.

Earle Warren

(EARL RONALD WARREN)
Born July 1, 1914
Died July 1, 1994
A saxophonist who performed with Count Basie from 1937–1945, Earle Warren later led Johnny Otis' R&B group in the Fifties. Warren also toured with The Coasters, The Platters, and The Drifters. Turning to jazz in the Seventies, Warren joined a series of combos before leading his outfit, The Countsmen.
CAUSE: Natural causes. He died in Ohio.

Clint Warwick

(ALBERT CLINTON ECCLES)
Born June 25, 1940
Died May 15, 2004
The original bass player in the first line-up of The Moody Blues, Clint Warwick co-founded the act in 1964 with Denny Laine, Mike Pinder, Ray Thomas and Graeme Edge. Born in Birmingham, Warwick was lured into music by the skiffle boom. During the rise of rock'n'roll, he was influenced by The Shadows and formed a series of early Sixties pub and club bands around Birmingham, including Gerry Day & The Dukes. With The Dukes evolving into The MB5, and then The Moody Blues, the group was discovered by producer Tony Secunda. Signed by Decca Records, the group topped the UK charts in late 1964 with a cover of Bessie Banks' 'Go Now!'. Warwick appeared on two more minor UK hits from 1965, 'I Don't Want To Go On Without You' and 'From The Bottom Of My Heart', as well as the group's début album *The Magnificent Moodies.* Leaving the band in mid-1966 to spend more time with his wife and new baby, Warwick was replaced by Rod Clarke. But just months later the group disbanded and was re-formed (without Laine) in early 1967 as a progressive-rock act featuring new members Justin Hayward and John Lodge. Retiring from music altogether, Warwick returned to his position as a carpenter. A few years before his death, he was attempting a musical comeback.
CAUSE: Suffering from liver disease, he died at Good Hope Hospital near Birmingham.

Dinah Washington

(RUTH LEE JONES)
Born August 29, 1924
Died December 14, 1963
The first queen of R&B, Dinah Washington was a versatile singer who was rooted in the jazz and gospel traditions. The daughter of a maid and professional gambler, the former Ruth Lee Jones was born in Tuscaloosa, Alabama, but raised on Chicago's south side. Learning to play the piano at a young age by accompanying her pianist mother at St. Luke's Baptist Church, Washington also joined the church choir at age eight. After touring Chicago's gospel circuit in an act with her mother, in 1940 Washington joined the pioneering all-girl revue, The Sallie Martin Colored Ladies Quartet. Flirting with secular music without her mother's knowledge, Jones won an amateur contest at Chicago's Regal Theater with a rendition of 'I Can't Face The Music', a song she would later record. Auditioning for Joe Glazer, Washington was recommended to Lionel Hampton whose jazz orchestra she joined in 1943 for a three-year stint as the featured vocalist, a decision that devastated her mother. With Hampton contractually barred by Decca Records from recording with Washington, she signed with music critic Leonard Feather's small Keynote label. Accompanied by a sextet from Hampton's orchestra, Washington landed two blues hits in 1944 with the Leonard-penned, 'Salty Papa Blues' and 'Evil Gal Blues'. After parting with Hampton, Washington signed with Apollo, and then Mercury Records, beginning her amazing solo hit run in 1948 with 'Ain't Misbehavin'' and 'West Side Baby'. Possessing a sharp tongue, quick wit and a violent

temper, the gun-toting, blonde-wigged Washington struck fear in the hearts of promoters, club owners, musicians and her many paramours and husbands one of whom she physically assaulted on stage. Often recording cover versions of pop hits, Washington landed on the R&B charts with 'Wheel Of Fortune' (1952) and 'I Don't Hurt Anymore' (1953). Although Mercury refused to market her records to pop audiences, Washington crossed over in 1959 with the Clyde Otis-produced ballad, 'What A Diff'rence A Day Makes' (1959) and a reissue of her earlier R&B hit, 'Unforgettable' (1959). Teamed against her wishes with crooner Brook Benton for a host of tension-filled sessions, Washington continued her pop run with 'Baby (You've Got What It Takes)' (1960) and 'A Rockin' Good Way' (1960). A heavy spender, Washington was lured to Roulette Records in 1961 with a large advance. Although absent from the charts in the last part of her career, Washington remained a strong concert draw. Pursuing other business ventures, she also operated a talent agency and Detroit restaurant, and was a mentor to Aretha Franklin. Washington's life was celebrated in the stage musical *Dinah Was*. Singer Patti Austin is Washington's goddaughter.
CAUSE: After years of abusing alcohol and diet pills, Washington died in Detroit from an accidental overdose of brandy and diet pills while watching television, apparently determining to lose weight before a major concert in Chicago. Her weight-loss regimen also included mercury injections. She was found unconscious by football player Dick "Night Train" Lane, the last of her many husbands and live-in boyfriends.

Grover Washington, Jr.

Born December 12, 1943
Died December 17, 1999
A versatile jazz-pop saxophonist, Grover Washington, Jr. epitomised the smooth jazz style. From Buffalo, he played the saxophone from the age of ten, leaving home at 16 for a four-year stint with an Ohio-based group, The Four Clefs and, after serving in the army, he settled in Philadelphia in 1967. A session player at Prestige Records, Washington had his first success when he backed organist Johnny "Hammond" Smith. Signed to Kudu Records by producer Creed Taylor, Washington recorded tracks for what would be his album, *Inner City Blues* (1972), after Hank Crawford had missed the scheduled session. Making waves in 1975 with a pair of Top 10 instrumental albums, *Feels So Good* and the Bob James-arranged, *Mister Magic*, Washington combined jazz with funky soul as he dominated the jazz charts for the next decade. Washington teamed with soul crooner Bill Withers for the crossover pop hit 'Just The Two Of Us', in 1981. The track was culled from the million-selling album *Winelight*, which yielded two Grammys. Washington's saxophone can be heard on the themes for the television programmes, *Moonlighting* and *The Cosby Show*.
CAUSE: He suffered a heart attack and collapsed in his dressing room after taping four songs for the CBS programme, *The Early Show*. Rushed to St. Luke's-Roosevelt Hospital in New York City, he died an hour later. Taped on Friday evening, Washington's performance aired the following morning. Washington had been suffering from prostate cancer at the time of his death.

Tuts Washington

(ISIDORE WASHINGTON)
Born January 24, 1907
Died August 5, 1984
A legendary New Orleans-based stride and boogie-woogie pianist, Tuts Washington was a fixture of New Orleans jazz nightclubs. First hitting the stage in the Twenties, he frequented the French Quarter into the Forties with his amalgamation of blues,

jazz and ragtime influences. During this period, Washington tutored another piano great, Professor Longhair, and for a time was a backing member of Smiley Lewis' band. Washington's only solo album, the traditional-styled *New Orleans Piano Professor*, was released a year before his death. The documentary *Piano Players Rarely Play Together*, featured the trio of Washington, Professor Longhair and their disciple, Allen Toussaint.
CAUSE: He died while performing in the Louisiana Folk Life Center at the World's Fair in New Orleans.

Johnny "Guitar" Watson

Born February 3, 1935
Died May 17, 1996
A flamboyant Texas-style R&B guitarist, Johnny "Guitar" Watson moved to Los Angeles from his native Houston at age 15 and was hired as a pianist in Chuck Higgins' backing band The Mellowtones. Forming his own band, Watson signed with the King subsidiary Federal Records and initially recorded as Young John Watson. An upbeat, humorous but brash performer, Watson abandoned the piano for guitar in 1954 and adopted a new moniker; as Johnny "Guitar" Watson, he recorded the stunning instrumental 'Space Guitar'. Landing at RPM Records the following year, Watson scored a hit cover of Earl King's 'Those Lonely, Lonely Nights'. Passing through several labels, Watson continued his hit run with 'Gangster Of Love' (1957) and 'Cuttin' In' (1962). After experimenting with jazz piano in the Sixties, Watson collaborated with R&B singer Larry Williams. Adopting a funk-based sound in the Seventies, Watson enjoyed newfound popularity with gritty hits such as 'I Don't Want To Be A Lone Ranger' (1975), 'Superman Lover' (1976), and 'A Real Mother For Ya' (1977). Returning to the studio for the first time since 1980, Watson scored his final hit in 1994 with 'Bow Wow', from the Grammy-nominated album of the same name. He later appeared on Bo Diddley's 1996 album, *A Man Amongst Men*.
CAUSE: He collapsed after taking the stage at the Yokohama Blues Cafe in Yokohama, Japan, stricken by a heart attack.

Johnny Watt

Born 1938
Died 1983
The leader of Los Angeles-based R&B group, Rochell and The Candles, Johnny Watt enjoyed a hit in 1961 with the doo-wop styled, 'Once Upon A Time'.
CAUSE: Unknown.

Noble "Thin Man" Watts

Born February 17, 1926
Died August 24, 2004
A legendary saxophonist, Noble "Thin Man" Watts was one of the leading players during the rise of rock'n'roll. Classically trained on the violin as a child, he was drawn to the sax and trumpet during his teens. Enrolled in A&M University, he joined the marching band, which at the time included future jazz greats, brothers Nat and Cannonball Adderley. Immediately after graduation, Watts was hired as a member of The Griffin Brothers' touring band. Watts then joined Paul "Hucklebuck" Williams' band, and would earn his nickname from one of Williams' recordings, 'Thin Man'. After a brief association with Lionel Hampton, Watts joined the touring troupes of a number of early rock'n'roll packages in the Fifties, including many promoted by Alan Freed. Watts' only solo success came in 1957 with the single, 'Hard Times (The Slop)'. Returning to music in the late Eighties, Watts worked with The Blues Creepers, recording their fine album *Return Of The Thin Man* (1987). In 2003, an annual music festival named after Watts was launched in his home town of DeLand, Florida.

CAUSE: Suffering from emphysema and pneumonia, he died at a retirement facility in DeLand, Florida.

Bernie Wayne

Born March 6, 1919
Died April 18, 1993
A pop songwriter, Bernie Wayne composed 'Blue Velvet' (Tony Bennett, The Clovers, Bobby Vinton), 'You Walk By' (Guy Lombardo), 'Laughing On The Outside' (Sammy Kaye, Dinah Shore and others) and 'Vanessa' (Hugo Winterhalter). Wayne gained attention for penning the perennial jingle for Chock Full O'Nuts coffee and a song popularised by Bert Parks on the annual Miss America pageant, 'There She Is'. As the A&R director at 20th Century Fox in the Sixties, Wayne produced several soundtracks including *Zorba The Greek*.
CAUSE: Heart failure. He died in Marina del Ray, California.

Carl Wayne

(COLIN TOOLEY)
Born August 18, 1943
Died August 31, 2004
As the lead singer of UK pop-rock act The Move, Carl Wayne was notorious for on-stage antics which often included the demolition of effigies, televisions – and at a New Year's Eve 1966 performance at London's Roundhouse – a car. From Birmingham, Wayne broke into music in a local group, The Vikings, in 1963. Renamed Carl Wayne & The Vikings, including ex-Denny Laine and The Diplomats drummer Bev Bevan, the group endured gruelling stints in German red-light district nightclubs. In January 1966, Wayne, Bevan and Vikings' bassist Chris "Ace" Kefford united with fellow Birmingham musicians Roy Wood from Mike Sheridan & The Nightriders and Trevor Burton from Danny King and The Mayfair Set to form The Move. Signing with Deram Records, the Tony Secunda-managed group began a UK hit streak in 1966 with 'Night Of Fear', and followed up over the next two years with 'I Can Hear The Grass Grow', 'Flowers In The Rain' (the first-ever song to be played on the BBC's new commercial station, Radio 1), 'Fire Brigade' and the chart-topping 'Blackberry Way'. After a dispiriting American tour in 1969, Wayne left The Move the following year. Turning towards mainstream pop music, Wayne launched an unsuccessful solo career. As an actor, he occasionally took television roles on programmes such as *Crossroads* and spent six years in the London musical, *Blood Brothers*. Wayne was hired in 2000 as the replacement for Allan Clarke in The Hollies.
CAUSE: Suffering from cancer of the esophagus, he died in his sleep at his home in Pryfor, England.

David Wayne

(DAVID WAYNE CARNELL)
Born January 1, 1958
Died May 10, 2005
The powerful vocalist of Seattle-based thrash-metal band Metal Church, David Wayne appeared on the group's first two Elektra albums, *Metal Church* and *The Dark*. Founded by guitarist Kurt Vanderhoof in 1982, Metal Church was repeatedly compared to Metallica, with whom they often shared the same bill. Leaving Metal Church in 1988, Wayne was replaced by Mike Howe of the group Heretic. In an odd twist, Wayne later hired two former members of Heretic for his band, Reverend; the group recorded two albums and a pair of EPs. Wanting a more stable life, Wayne returned from Los Angeles to Seattle in 1993 and spent a year in a local covers band. Rejoining Metal Church in 1999 for the reunion album *Masterpeace*, Wayne confused record buyers by releasing a "solo" album under the moniker, Metal Church, in 2001.
CAUSE: He never recovered from

injuries sustained in a head-on car collision.

Mick Wayne

Born c. 1945
Died June 26, 1994
The guitarist of The Pink Fairies, Mick Wayne joined the British rock group in late 1972 as a replacement for Paul Rudolph. Breaking into music as a member of The Hullabaloos in 1967, Wayne subsequently co-founded the pop-rock group Junior's Eyes in 1968. Under the production of Tony Visconti, Junior's Eyes released the critically acclaimed album *Battersea Power Station* and backed David Bowie on *Space Oddity*. Spending the next two decades as a session player, Wayne travelled to the US shortly before his death to record a solo album.
CAUSE: He was killed in a fire at a friend's home in Michigan.

Thomas Wayne

(THOMAS WAYNE PERKINS)
Born July 22, 1940
Died August 15, 1971
A one-hit wonder, Mississippi-born Thomas Wayne attended the same Memphis high school as Elvis Presley. Forming a female backing group called The De-Lons while in high school, Wayne recorded at the Scotty Moore co-owned label, Fernwood Records. While The De-Lons recorded some unnoticed singles, Thomas Wayne reached the Top 10 with his Moore-produced cover of an obscure single, 'Tragedy'. A similar sounding follow-up, 'Eternally', received only scattered airplay. Meanwhile, after Presley was discharged from the army, he recorded a Wayne composition, 'The Girl Next Door Went A'Walking'. After briefly operating his own label Chalet Records, Wayne later worked as a producer and recording engineer.
CAUSE: He died in a head-on car crash near Memphis. Wayne's brother Luther Perkins, a guitarist with Johnny Cash, also met an untimely demise.

William Henry Weatherspoon

Born February 11, 1936
Died July 17, 2005
A producer and songwriter, William Henry Weatherspoon frequently collaborated at the Motown label with James Dean (not the actor). Weatherspoon broke into music in 1956 as a member of a Detroit-based doo-wop group, The Tornados, formed by Charles Sutton of The Midnighters. After the group disbanded in 1960, Weatherspoon subsequently worked as a songwriter and producer for the small Correct-Tone label. Hired by Motown in the mid Sixties, Weatherspoon and Dean were often teamed with a third songwriter at Motown as they composed hits such as 'What Becomes Of The Brokenhearted' (Jimmy Ruffin), 'I've Passed This Way Before' (Jimmy Ruffin), 'I Am The Man For You Baby' (Edwin Starr) and 'It's So Hard Being A Loser' (The Contours). When Motown's legendary songwriting trio Holland-Dozier-Holland left the label and started Invictus Records, Weatherspoon and Dean followed them in 1968. At the new firm, Weatherspoon often teamed with Angelo Bond, co-writing The Embers' hit 'I'm Not My Brother's Keeper' and a trio of hits – 'Women's Love Rights', 'Love And Liberty' and 'Rip Off' – for Laura Lee. Following the closure of Invictus, Weatherspoon returned to Motown in 1980; still teamed with Bond, Weatherspoon wrote for The Temptations and a number of newer artists. In later years, Weatherspoon launched his own gospel music production company.
CAUSE: He suffered a probable heart attack and was found dead in his home in the Detroit suburb of Lathrup Village, Michigan.

Fred Webb

Born c. 1946
Died 1990
The keyboardist of San Francisco-based folk/psychedelic rock act It's A Beautiful Day, Fred Webb joined in 1970 as replacement for Linda LaFlamme. Bringing a more mainstream rock sound to the band, Webb appeared on four albums before the group disbanded in 1974.
CAUSE: Unknown.

Melvin Webb

Born c. 1945
Died 1973
The drummer for perennial pop/soul band Bloodstone, Melvin Webb co-founded the group in 1962 as The Sinceres. Originally an a cappella, doo-wop styled outfit, the group left its Kansas City base for Los Angeles in the late Sixties. Though unsigned, Bloodstone toured England with singer Al Green in 1972 and after earning accolades for their soulful performances, they were signed by Decca Records. Webb appeared on the group's first three albums including their best seller, *Natural High* (1973), providing the drum work on several hits, including the million-selling 'Natural High' (1973), 'Never Let You Go' (1973) and 'Outside Woman' (1974). Webb also worked with Jeffrey Osborne.
CAUSE: Diabetes.

Charlie Webber

(CHARLES D. WEBBER)
Born November 15, 1944
Died January 17, 2003
A founding member of The Swingin' Medallions, trumpet player Webber formed the group in 1962 with several friends in Greenwood, South Carolina. A one-hit wonder, the group scored a Top 10 entry with the raucous, frat-rock standard, 'Double Shot (Of My Baby's Love)'. Webber left the group in the late Sixties and went to work in law enforcement.
CAUSE: Cancer. He died at his home in Greenwood, South Carolina.

Katie Webster

(KATHRYN JEWEL THORNE)
Born September 9, 1939
Died September 5, 1999
Nicknamed "The Swamp Boogie Queen", Katie Webster was a powerful two-fisted piano player who spanned the genres of gritty R&B, blues, and boogie-woogie. Reared on gospel music in her minister father's church, she was not permitted to play secular music at home but as a child prodigy in Louisiana she quickly became a much in-demand session player, performing on hundreds of records. Also a recording artist, she released a string of swamp-blues singles beginning in the late Fifties for the Excello and Goldband labels. As the opening act and pianist in Otis Redding's band beginning in 1964, Webster bowed out for several months due to a pregnancy and was not on the aeroplane that killed Redding and several members of his backing band in December 1967. Devastated by the tragedy, Webster retired from music, and became a carer for her ailing parents. Returning to the stage in 1982, she recorded for Arhoolie and Alligator Records, and became a huge star in Europe. Although suffering a moderate stroke in 1993, she returned to the stage as often as she was able.
CAUSE: Heart failure. She died at her home in suburban Houston.

Julius Wechter

Born May 10, 1935
Died February 1, 1999
A member of Herb Alpert's band The Tijuana Brass, Julius Wechter also led his own spin-off group, The Baja Marimba Band. Raised in Los Angeles, Wechter had previous success in the Fifties as a songwriter and as a vibes player in the Hawaii-based The Martin Denny Group. Returning to Los Angeles, he found session work as a

percussionist behind The Beach Boys, The Righteous Brothers and Sonny & Cher. Frequently teaming with Herb Alpert beginning with the 1962 album, *The Lonely Bull*, Wechter also composed Alpert's hit 'The Lonely Bull' (better known as *The Dating Game* theme). Formed by Wechter on a lark, The Baja Marimba Band featured no Mexican musicians but were a sensation in the Sixties, recording 18 albums in a five-year span and regularly appearing in Las Vegas. Wechter later composed music for television, and in 1990 formed The Baja Marimbas.
CAUSE: Lung cancer. He died at his home in Calabasas, California.

Wes Wehmiller

(JOHN WESLEY WEHMILLER)
Born September 12, 1971
Died January 30, 2005
The bassist of Duran Duran from 1997 to 2001, Wes Wehmiller joined the group for a number of world tours, but stepped aside when the original line-up re-formed. Born in New York City but raised near Philadelphia, Wehmiller studied at Berklee College of Music. Moving to the West Coast in 1993, he collaborated with a number of jazz and rock acts, including Warren Cuccurullo, Mike Keneally and Missing Persons. At the time of his death, Wehmiller was preparing for a tour in a band with Dweezil Zappa.
CAUSE: Thyroid cancer. He died in his sleep at his home in California.

Pete Welding

Born November 15, 1935
Died November 17, 1995
A rock journalist, record producer and record label owner, Pete Welding was reared on modern jazz. After discovering blues music in the Fifties, the Philadelphia-native became a scholar whose writing appeared on the liner notes of dozens of albums. Also a music journalist, he became the editor of *Downbeat* magazine. Launching Testament Records in 1963 with the inaugural release by Bill Jackson, Welding concentrated on blues and gospel acts such Dr. Ross, Johnny Shines, and Fred McDowell. Relocating to the West Coast in 1966, Welding enrolled in the folk music department at the University of California, where he would nurture a friendship with future folklorist David Evans. After taking a position at Epic Records in 1969, he landed at Playboy Records in 1972, and later, in the special products division at Capitol Records where in 1995 he began releasing a series of archival blues albums. Welding's essays were compiled in 1991 for the book, *Bluesland*.
CAUSE: Heart attack. He died at Rancho Cucamonga, California.

Brandi Wells

(MARGUERITE J. PINDER BANNISTER)
Born May 13, 1955
Died March 25, 2003
A former member of Major Harris' backing vocal group Brown Sugar, Philadelphia-born Brandi Wells later joined a series of R&B acts. After parting with Harris, she formed a vocal session group called Breeze which backed artists such as Billy Paul and "Fat" Larry James. With Breeze evolving into the disco group Slick, Wells had a pair of UK hits in 1979 with 'Space Bass' and 'Sexy Cream'. Emerging as a solo act in 1981, Wells was backed by topnotch session players including Thom Bell and Dexter Wansel. Recording for the WMOT label, Wells scored a pair of minor US R&B hits with 'When It's Love' (1981) and 'Watch Out' (1982). She released a second album in 1985, *21st Century Fox*.
CAUSE: Unknown. She died in Chester, Pennsylvania.

Ed Wells

Born July 20, 1937
Died February 18, 2001
A songwriter and founding member of

Los Angeles-based doo-wop group The Six Teens, backing tenor Ed Wells sang behind lead vocalist Trudy Williams on the 1956 hit 'A Casual Look'. With all the members still attending school, they were only able to perform at weekends. Wells remained with the group until 1968, at which time he relocated to New York City, and was later employed as a social worker.
CAUSE: Cancer. He died in Rialto, California.

Junior Wells

(AMOS WELLS BLAKEMORE, JR.)
Born December 9, 1934
Died January 15, 1998
A blues harmonica virtuoso, Junior Wells was tutored in his childhood by Little Junior Parker. Leaving West Memphis for Chicago in 1946, Wells formed a blues group called The Little Boys. Popular in the clubs of Chicago, the group underwent several name changes including The Dueces and The Aces. When Little Walter left Muddy Waters for a solo career in 1952, Wells was briefly hired as his replacement. (Meanwhile, Wells' backing group The Aces would back Little Walter in the studio.) Pursuing a solo career, Wells was backed by The Aces at his early sessions at States Records. Landing at Chief/Profile Records in 1957 and produced by label head Mel London, Wells recorded vocal-heavy blues gems such as 'Little By Little' (1959) and 'Messin' With The Kid' (1960). In the mid Sixties, Wells joined forces with blues guitarist Buddy Guy, their best work captured on their first of several collaborative albums, *Hoodoo Man Blues* (1965). Touring together until the Nineties, the pair once opened for The Rolling Stones. Shortly before his death, Wells shot a scene for the film *Blues Brothers 2000*.
CAUSE: Suffering a heart attack on September 4, 1998, he was left in a coma. At the time he was receiving chemotherapy treatment for leukaemia and lymphoma. He died at Michael Reese Hospital in Chicago.

Mary Wells

(MARY ESTHER WELLS)
Born May 13, 1943
Died July 26, 1992
A popular soul singer in the Sixties, Detroit-native Mary Wells was one of Motown's first hit acts. A sickly child, stricken with both meningitis and tuberculosis, Wells began singing publicly at age three in her church. Performing in her high school choirs, Wells was a classmate of two future members of The Temptations. Yearning to become a songwriter but unable to transcribe her compositions on paper, she instead sang for Motown chief Berry Gordy, Jr.; impressing Berry with her vocal prowess, she was instead signed as a solo act. Intending the song for Jackie Wilson, Wells scored her first hit with the self-composed 'Bye Bye Baby'. Aided by singer-songwriter Smokey Robinson, Wells continued her hit run with a trio of Top 10 entries in 1962, 'The One Who Really Loves You', 'You Beat Me To The Punch', and 'Two Lovers'. But Wells biggest hit came with the Robinson-penned 'My Guy' (1964), giving Motown its first million-seller. Wells' last major hit came later in the year in a duet with labelmate Marvin Gaye, the double-sided entry 'What's The Matter With You'/'Once Upon A Time'. Unhappy with Motown's tight control and lack of individual attention, Wells left the label in 1964 and signed a multi-year contract with 20th Century Fox. Drawn to the company because of its film division, she had hoped to pursue a career in acting but her new label was unable to promote an established star in the R&B field, and Wells fared poorly with the albums *Mary Wells* and *Love Songs To The Beatles*. Subsequently recording for Atco, and then, Jubilee, Wells managed

a sole hit with 'Dear Lover' (1966). Finally hitting the big screen, Wells made her film début in the 1967 box-office bomb, *Catalina Caper,* for which she sang the title track. Retiring from music in the Seventies to raise a family, Wells returned to occasional club work in 1978. Recording for Reprise, and then, Epic Records, Wells scored her final hit in 1982 with the disco-styled, 'Gigolo', from the album *In And Out Of Love*. In declining health, uninsured and unable to pay her rent, Wells subsequently lost her home and went into debt. Naive about the trappings of the music industry, Wells had earned little during her Motown days. The Rhythm and Blues Foundation raised $50,000 to pay for her medical care, with Diana Ross donating an additional $15,000. The impoverished death of another major Sixties singing star served as a catalyst for the music industry to fund an economic safety net for its veteran acts.
CAUSE: A heavy smoker, she succumbed to cancer of the larynx. She had suffered with throat problems for several years and was diagnosed with cancer in 1990. She died at UCLA's Kenneth Norris Jr. Cancer Center in Los Angeles.

Dottie West

(DOROTHY MARIE MARSH)
Born October 11, 1932
Died September 4, 1991
A country singer-songwriter, Dottie West achieved some crossover pop success in duets with Kenny Rogers, including 'What Are We Doin' In Love?' and 'All I Ever Need Is You'. A native of Tennessee, she had earned a degree in cello at Tennessee Tech. Moving to Cleveland, she hosted a local, country music television programme. After landing a recording contract with Starday in 1959, her first success came as a songwriter, penning the Jim Reeves hit, 'Is This Me?' Signing with RCA Records in 1963, West joined The Grand Ole Opry the following year. In addition to Kenny Rogers, West would also record duets with Jim Reeves, Don Gibson and Jimmy Dean.
CAUSE: With her car breaking down near Opryland, she accepted a ride from a friend, 81-year-old George Thackston. His car crashed in the Opry car park and West ruptured her liver. She underwent three operations and died four days later at Vanderbilt Medical Center.
FURTHER READING: Berryhill, Judy. (1995). *Country Sunshine: The Dottie West Story*. Nashville: Eggman.

Ricky West

(RICHARD ALLEN WESTFIELD)
Born May 7, 1943
Died 1985
An early member of funk/R&B ensemble Kool & The Gang, keyboardist Ricky West appeared on the hits 'Funky Stuff' (1973), 'Jungle Boogie' (1973) and 'Hollywood Swinging' (1974), one of nearly two dozen songs he wrote for the group. West joined brothers Ronald and Robert Bell in the New Jersey-based group The Jazziacs in 1964. Veering toward soul, the group, renamed Kool & The Gang, recorded their début album in 1971. Leaving the group in 1977, West formed the group North, East, South, West, named after a track he wrote for Kool & The Gang's 1973 album *Good Times*.
CAUSE: He died from an undisclosed illness.

Rudy West

Born July 25, 1932
Died May 14, 1998
As the lead singer of the pioneering doo-wop group The Five Keys, Rudy West was instrumental in transforming the genre from the pop flavour of The Ink Spots and The Mills Brothers to its modern, street-corner form. A product of two pairs of brothers, Rudy and Bernie West and Ripley and Raphael Ingram, The Five Keys were launched

in 1949 as a gospel quartet called The Sentimental Four. Switching to secular music, the group parlayed an Apollo Theater talent contest win into a recording contract with Aladdin Records. Replacing the drafted Raphael Ingram with Maryland Pierce and Dickie Smith, the renamed Five Keys reworked Benny Goodman's 1936 hit 'Glory Of Love' for their second single; a million-selling, chart-topping R&B hit, the elegant ballad propelled the group to stardom. Drafted along with bandmate Dickie Smith, Rudy West left the group in 1953 and was replaced by Ulysses K. Hicks. Returning to The Five Keys in 1955, West sang co-lead on the group's ballad hit, a cover of Chuck Willis' 'Close Your Eyes'. Tiring of the road and earning little, West retired from the group in 1958. After pursuing a brief and unfruitful solo career the following year at King Records, West would record only sporadically. Taking a job with the US Postal Service, he retired in 1981. West occasionally led revival versions of The Five Keys until just days before his death.
CAUSE: His body weakened by cancer treatments, he suffered a heart attack. He died at his home in Chesapeake, Virginia.

Jimmy Weston

Born 1940
Died June 10, 1993
A member of the Fifties Brooklyn-based doo-wop group The Danleers, Jimmy Weston provided the lead vocals on their romantic ballad hit, 'One Summer Night' (1958). The group's Mercury Records output is compiled on the album, *The Best Of The Danleers: The Mercury Years*.
CAUSE: Unknown.

Peetie Wheatstraw

(WILLIAM BUNCH)
Born December 21, 1902
Died December 21, 1941
Nicknamed "The Devil's Son-In-Law" and "The High Sheriff From Hell", bluesman Peetie Wheatstraw attributed his musical prowess to a dalliance with Satan. A pioneering Delta-styled pianist and singer who settled in St. Louis, Wheatstraw worked with Kokomo Arnold, Charlie McCoy and Lonnie Johnson. Releasing nearly 80 singles in his brief career, Wheatstraw was very popular in the Thirties with bawdy releases such as 'Big Leg Woman' and 'I Want Some Seafood'. Many of Wheatstraw's recording sessions were punctuated with the cries of, "ooh, well well".
CAUSE: His car was struck by a train at a crossing. He died 26 days after his last recording session.
FURTHER READING: Garon, Paul. (1971). *The Devil's Son-in-Law.* London: Studio Vista.

Nancy Whiskey

(ANNE ALEXANDRA YOUNG WILSON)
Born March 4, 1935
Died February 1, 2003
A member of The Chas McDevitt Skiffle Group, Scottish-born Nancy Whiskey provided the lead vocals on the group's two biggest late Fifties hits – an upbeat rendition of 'Freight Train' and 'Greenback Dollar'. Under the stage name of Nancy Wilson, she had previously played guitar and sung in the folk clubs of Glasgow. After leaving McDevitt, she formed her own group, Nancy Whiskey & Her Skifflers, who included Bob Kelly, her future husband, on piano. After the birth of a daughter in 1958, Whiskey put aside her musical career. In 1999, Whiskey performed with skiffle pioneer Lonnie Donegan at the Royal Albert Hall.
CAUSE: Heart attack.

Barry White

(BARRY EUGENE CARTER)
Born September 12, 1944
Died July 4, 2003
A sultry, deep-voiced R&B crooner, Barry White had a long and varied career as a singer, songwriter and

producer. Born in Galveston, Texas, but raised in Los Angeles, White began his musical schooling in a Baptist church choir, where he was quickly promoted to the role of director. Aged 11, he played piano on the Jesse Belvin classic 'Goodnight My Love', and from the age of 14, White suddenly possessed his trademark deep and booming voice. After quitting school a year later, White joined a soul band, The Upfronts, as the bass singer, recording one single and, when caught stealing expensive tyres he was briefly jailed. White found employment in a production capacity for a succession of Los Angeles labels, and provided the arrangement for the 1963 Bob & Earl hit 'Harlem Shuffle'. By 1965, he had recorded his first solo single, 'Man Ain't Nothin'' under the name Lee Barry. Turning to production work, White collaborated with Danny Wagner, Viola Wills and Felice Taylor, and was hired as an A&R man by Mustang/Bronco Records. By the early Seventies White had organised an all-girl, R&B group, Love Unlimited, producing and composing the group's début single 'Walkin' In The Rain With The One You Love' (1972), on which White also provided the spoken dialogue. After Love Unlimited's backing group, the 40-piece Love Unlimited Orchestra, scored a surprise hit with the instrumental 'Love's Theme', he began recording the act as a separate entity. White simultaneously concentrated on a solo career and became a staple on R&B radio with lushly orchestrated hits beginning with 'I'm Gonna Love You Just A Little More Baby', continuing with 'Never, Never Gonna Give Ya Up', 'Can't Get Enough Of Your Love, Babe', 'You're The First, The Last, My Everything' and the sensual 'It's Ecstacy When You Lay Down Next To Me'. After an impressive decade, White launched his own Unlimited Gold label but, entering into a rocky distribution deal with CBS, White fared poorly. Signing with A&M Records in 1987, White began a new phase of his career characterised by a string of R&B hits. In 2000 White earned two Grammys for the track 'Staying Power'. Ironically he had shunned the ceremony for several years after losing the Grammy for Best New Artist in 1974. At the time of his death, White was completing a duets album.

CAUSE: Kidney failure. His kidneys were damaged by chronic high blood pressure. He had been hospitalised for nearly 10 months after suffering a stroke in September 2002. He died at Cedars-Sinai Medical Center in Los Angeles.

Bill White

Born 1973

Died September 8, 1995

The bassist of the Nineties alternative-rock outfit For Squirrels, Bill White joined lead singer Jack Vigliatura and others to form the group in Gainesville, Florida. For Squirrels would score a posthumous MTV and radio hit with 'The Mighty K.C.', the song about the deceased Kurt Cobain. The track was culled from their début album, *Example*.

CAUSE: With the group's lead singer Jack Vigliatura at the wheel of the group's tour van, the rear right tyre exploded and the vehicle flipped over several times, killing Vigliatura, White, and manager Tim Benson.

Bukka White

(BOOKER T. WASHINGTON WHITE)

Born November 12, 1906

Died February 26, 1977

A pioneering country blues slide guitarist, Bukka White was taught to play guitar by his railroad worker father. Inspired by Delta guitar legend Charley Patton, White pursued a career in music. Initially recording under the moniker of Washington White, he alternated between blues and gospel material for his first sessions for Victor Records in 1930. Leaving music

for a time, he boxed and played baseball in the Negro leagues. Imprisoned for assault in 1937, he escaped from prison and landed in Chicago. After recording 'Shake 'Em On Down' and 13 other masterful tracks for Vocalion, he was recaptured by the authorities. Released from prison in 1940, he enjoyed a few more years of recording success with his percussive, improvisational style. Relocating to Memphis, he hit the stage only sporadically, sometimes with his cousin B.B. King. Tracked down by two blues researchers in 1963, White was rediscovered during the blues revival of the Sixties. White's output is compiled on the 1994 Legacy Records release, *The Complete Bukka White*.
CAUSE: Cancer. He died in Memphis.

Carl White

Born June 21, 1932
Died January 7, 1980
The lead singer and songwriter of the comical R&B musical group The Rivingtons, Carl White launched his musical career in The Limelighters, joining the three-year-old Los Angeles-based doo-wop group in 1955. With the group occasionally recording as The Tenderfoots, White provided the lead vocals on their releases on Federal Records in 1955. Rejoined by their former lead singer Thurston Harris, the group reverted to The Limelighters. Evolving into The Sharps in 1956, the group recorded for a variety of labels. Then with Harris emerging as a solo act, The Sharps provided the backing on his 1957 hit 'Little Bitty Pretty One'. Aided by music publisher Lester Sill, the group subsequently sang back-up for a number of performers including The Heartbreakers, Paul Anka, and Duane Eddy. In the early Sixties, The Sharps evolved into The Crenshaws, and finally, The Rivingtons. Signing with Liberty Records in 1962, the group scored a pair of novelty-styled, Carl White/Rocky Wilson-composed hits, 'Papa-Oom-Mow-Mow' (1962) and 'The Bird Is The Word' (1963). The garage-rock band The Trashmen would revive 'The Bird Is The Word' in 1964. White later joined revival versions of The Rivingtons.
CAUSE: Acute tonsillitis. He died at his Los Angeles home.

Charlie White

Born 1930
Died c. 1995
A member of the pioneering R&B/doo-wop groups The Dominoes and The Clovers, tenor Charlie White sang on a string of R&B hits. In 1950, White teamed with Bill Brown, Willie Lamont and former gospel singer Clyde McPhatter to form The Ques, a group assembled and managed by songwriter-pianist Billy Ward. Renamed as The Dominoes and signed to the new King Records subsidiary Federal, the group worked under the guidance of producer Ralph Bass. With McPhatter on high lead tenor and White on backing tenor harmony, The Dominoes' hits included 'Do Something For Me' (1951), the bawdy crossover smash 'Sixty Minute Man' and 'I Am With You'. Though the group was successful, White quit and was replaced by James Van Loan. Initially intending to join The Clovers, White instead formed The Checkers, who unsuccessfully recorded for King Records. White eventually joined The Clovers in late 1952 as replacement for John "Buddy" Bailey who had been drafted into the army. After providing the powerful lead vocals on the R&B hits 'Good Lovin'' and the double-sided chart entry 'Little Mama'/'Lovey Dovey', White left The Clovers in 1954 to join The Playboys and was replaced by Billy Mitchell.
CAUSE: Unknown.

Clarence White

Born June 6, 1944
Died July 14, 1973
A country-rock pioneer and latter

member of The Byrds, Clarence White was born into a musical family in Lewiston, Maine. With his family settling in Burbank, California, White teamed with his two brothers, Roland and Eric, in 1954 to form The Country Boys. The group released a couple of singles and appeared on television's *The Andy Griffith Show*. By 1962, with White playing bluegrass in the tradition of Doc Watson, the group evolved into the more successful Kentucky Colonels, arguably the most accomplished urban bluegrass ensemble of the era. The Kentucky Colonels issued two albums for World Pacific, *The New Sound Of Bluegrass America* and *Appalachian Swing*. White later moved into session work, backing acts as varied as Pat Boone, Ricky Nelson, Randy Newman and The Monkees. During this period he also teamed up with Gene Parsons to form the country rock group Nashville West. After a session for The Byrds, White was asked by Roger McGuinn to join a new line-up of the group in 1968. Employing a device called the stringbender which made a Fender Telecaster sound like a steel-string guitar, White infused an element of country music into the group's next album, *Dr. Byrds & Mr. Hyde* (1969). White would appear on a series of consistent, moderately selling Byrds albums including *Ballad Of Easy Rider* (1970), the two-disc, *(Untitled)* (1970), *Byrdmaniax* (1971), and *Farther Along* (1971); unfortunately, few hits would emerge from these projects. After frequent line-up changes, McGuinn finally disbanded The Byrds in 1973. Continuing his session work in the Seventies, White backed Jackson Browne, Gene Clark, and toured behind Emmylou Harris, Gene Parsons, and Gram Parsons. After rejoining The Kentucky Colonels in 1973, White also recorded several tracks for a planned solo album at Warner Brothers.
CAUSE: He was run down and killed by a drunk driver while loading instruments into his vehicle after a performance in Palmdale, California. White died two months before another ex-Byrd, Gram Parsons.
FURTHER READING: Rogan, Johnny. (1997). *The Byrds: Timeless Flight Revisited The Sequel*. London: Rogan House.

Cliff White

(CLIFTON M. WHITE)
Born October 6, 1921
Died April 2, 1998
Initially a session player at Specialty Records, Cliff White emerged as the guitarist and bandleader for Sam Cooke. Born in Dallas, but raised in Monterey, California, White was aided in the mid Forties by Louis Armstrong in landing a position in The Mills Brothers' backing band. An integral part of Cooke's success, White appeared on all of his hits including 'You Send Me' and 'Cupid'. After Cooke's death in 1964, White worked as a session player and formed a series of small bands. He later co-authored the Sam Cooke biography, *You Send Me: The Life And Times Of Sam Cooke*, a winner of the seventh annual Ralph J. Gleason Award.
CAUSE: Diabetes. He died at Midway Hospital Medical Center in Los Angeles.

Josh White

(JOSHUA WHITE)
Born February 11, 1914
Died September 6, 1969
A folk-blues singer, South Carolina-native Josh White frequently performed alongside contemporaries such as Woody Guthrie and Sonny Terry. Acting as a guide for several blind blues singers during his childhood, White toured throughout the South. Recording heavily beginning in the Thirties, White released blues material under the name Pinewood Tom and gospel as Joshua White, The Singing Christian. Relocating to New

York City in the mid Thirties, White was embraced by the city's left-wing intelligentsia for his politically charged lyrics. White also had success as an actor, appearing in the films *Crimson Canary* and *The Walking Hills*, and the plays *John Henry* and *The Man Who Went To War*. With his large repertoire of folk, blues, and protest songs, White found much success in Britain during the Fifties.

CAUSE: He died during an operation to replace a defective heart valve. He died in Manhasset, New York.

FURTHER READING: Siegel, Dorothy Schainman. (1982). *The Glory Road: The Story Of Josh White*. San Diego: Harcourt Brace Jovanovich.

Robert White

Born November 19, 1936
Died October 27, 1994

A session guitarist at Motown Records from 1959 to 1972, Robert White was an integral member of the label's house band, The Funk Brothers. Previously a guitarist at the Harvey Fuqua-owned Harvey Records, White had toured behind Fuqua's new Moonglows line-up, which at the time included a young Marvin Gaye. With Gordy hiring the finest in local jazz-trained musicians for his new Motown label, White was joined by bassist James Jamerson, keyboardist Earl Van Dyke, drummer Benny Benjamin, and others to back the label's stable of hits acts including The Four Tops, Marvin Gaye, and The Temptations. When Gordy moved the bulk of Motown's activities to Los Angeles in 1972, White remained in Detroit. Seldom employed by Motown during this period, White left the label in 1975. After relocating to Los Angeles in the Seventies, White joined a Temptations reunion in 1982. Although appearing on scores of hit records, White remained virtually unknown to the public.

CAUSE: He died following heart surgery.

Ronnie White

Born April 5, 1939
Died August 26, 1995

A founding member of The Miracles, Ronnie White was once Smokey Robinson's paperboy and had a crush on one of his sisters. A fan of jazz and doo-wop music in his youth, White had first formed an informal vocal group with Smokey Robinson and Pete Moore at age 11. While attending Detroit's Northern High School, White joined Robinson and three others to form The Five Chimes. Renamed The Matadors, the group auditioned for Jackie Wilson's manager, Nat Tarnapol, and a budding songwriter named Berry Gordy Jr. Impressed with Robinson's original compositions, Gordy became manager of the renamed Miracles. With The Miracles landing local airplay with 'Got A Job' (an answer song to The Silhouettes hit 'Get A Job') and hitting the national charts with 'Bad Girl', Gordy ended his practice of leasing records to other labels. The Miracles soon gave Gordy's Motown Records its first Top Five smash with the Robinson-penned 'Shop Around' (the song was initially intended for Barrett Strong). After a disastrous performance at The Apollo Theater, The Miracles were one of the first recipients of Motown's artists development department. As Motown's first superstar act, The Miracles unleashed a string of usually romantic hits with 'You've Really Got A Hold On Me' (1963), 'Mickey's Monkey' (1963), a song impromptly written on stage, 'Ooh Baby Baby' (1965), and 'Going To A Go-Go' (1966). Also a songwriter, White usually collaborated with Robinson on the hits, 'My Girl' (The Temptations), 'Don't Look Back' (The Temptations, Peter Tosh), 'One More Heartache' (Marvin Gaye), and 'You Beat Me To The Punch' (Mary Wells). Renamed Smokey Robinson & The Miracles in 1966, the group continued its run with 'More Love' (1967) and 'I Second

That Emotion' (1967). Tiring of his squabbles with White, Robinson briefly disbanded the group in 1968. Later announcing his retirement from The Miracles, Robinson repeatedly postponed his departure for four years, during which time the group landed on the charts with 'Tears Of A Clown' (1970) and 'I Don't Blame You At All' (1971). Replacing Robinson in 1972 with Billy Griffin (and later, his brother Donald Griffin), The Miracles managed only two more Top 40 hits including the chart-topping 'Love Machine (Part 1)'. Leaving Motown for CBS, The Miracles released two poor-selling albums before disbanding in 1978.
CAUSE: Leukaemia. He died in Detroit.
FURTHER READING: Robinson, Smokey; & Ritz, David. (1989). *Inside My Life*. New York: McGraw-Hill.

Timothy White

Born January 25, 1952
Died June 27, 2002
The influential editor of the music industry weekly *Billboard*, Timothy White enjoyed a distinguished career in music journalism. Born in Paterson, New Jersey, White had previously worked at Associated Press (1972–75), *Crawdaddy* (1976–78) and as senior editor at *Rolling Stone* (1978–82). Landing at the helm of *Billboard* in 1991, White penned a weekly column, "Music To My Ears", profiling both new and established artists, and these columns were later published in book form. His other books included *Catch A Fire: The Life Of Bob Marley*; *James Taylor: Long Ago And Far Away*; *The Nearest Faraway Place: Brian Wilson, The Beach Boys, The Southern California Experience*; *The Entertainers* and the award-winning *Rock Lives: Profiles And Interviews*. White also hosted the ABC Radio Network interview programme, *Timothy White's Rock Stars/The Timothy White Sessions*.
CAUSE: He suffered a heart attack while riding in a lift at *Billboard*'s New York offices. He was rushed to a nearby hospital, where he passed away.

John Whitehead

(JOHN CAVADUS WHITEHEAD II)
Born July 10, 1948
Died May 11, 2004
One half of Philadelphia-based R&B duo McFadden & Whitehead, John Whitehead scored a disco-era hit in 1979 with 'Ain't No Stoppin' Us Now'. Friends since high school, McFadden and Whitehead had broken into music in a doo-wop act, The Epsilons. After spending a year opening for Otis Redding, the group later sang back-up for Arthur Conley and sang on his 1967 hit 'Sweet Soul Music'. Following Redding's death that same year, the group was renamed Talk Of The Town, and recorded a few obscure singles for producers Kenny Gamble and Leon Huff on their North Bay label. Continuing to work with Gamble and Huff at their new Philadelphia International label, McFadden & Whitehead earned notoriety for their songwriting successes beginning with 'Back Stabbers' (The O'Jays), continuing with 'I'll Always Love My Mama' (The Intruders) and a number of hits for Harold Melvin & The Blue Notes including 'Bad Luck', 'Wake Up Everybody' and 'Where Are All My Friends?' McFadden & Whitehead also worked with Archie Bell and The Drells, Melba Moore, Gloria Gaynor and Freddie Jackson. Whitehead spent time in jail in the mid Eighties for tax evasion and, upon his release, recorded the suitably titled album *I Need Money Bad*. McFadden's eldest sons, Kenny and Johnny, placed several singles on the R&B charts in the Nineties as Whitehead Bros. Gene McFadden died in 2006.
CAUSE: While working on a car behind his home in Philadelphia, Whitehead and his friend Oemidd Johnson, 20, were shot multiple times by two young

men. Although Whitehead was killed, Johnson survived.

Chris Whitley

Born August 31, 1960
Died November 20, 2005
A brooding Texas-based singer-songwriter, Chris Whitley merged modern country with alternative rock. Born in Texas, Whitley spent most of the Eighties in Belgium heading a funk-rock group called A Noh Rodeo. Returning to the US, he signed with Columbia Records as a solo act in 1991 and after débuting with the critically acclaimed album *With The Law*, Whitley toured as opening act for Tom Petty. Though not commercially successful, Whitley released a series of critically praised, introspective, genre-blending albums – *Din Of Ecstasy* (1995), *Terra Incognita* (1996) and *Dirt Floor* (1998) – that put him at the forefront of the emerging alt-country movement. Flirting with jazz, Whitley teamed with Billy Martin and Chris Wood of the trio Medeski, Martin & Wood for *Perfect Day* (2000), an album of cover songs by artists such as Bob Dylan, Lou Reed and Robert Johnson. Whitley followed with a pair of disparate albums: the electronica-influenced *Rocket House* (2001) and an acoustic set of all original tracks *Hotel Vast Horizon* (2004). Recording prolifically, Whitley's final works included the solo acoustic project *Weed*, the internet-only release *War Crime Blues* and the moody *Soft Dangerous Shores*. His health worsening, Whitley cancelled a series of tour dates just a matter of weeks before his death.
CAUSE: Suffering from lung cancer, he was diagnosed with the condition just five weeks before his death. He died at a friend's home in suburban Houston.

Danny Whitten

Born May 8, 1943
Died November 18, 1972
A member of Neil Young's sometimes backing group Crazy Horse, Danny Whitten provided the backing vocals and guitar on a number of Young's early albums. In the mid Sixties, Whitten had formed an a cappella group called Danny and The Memories. Evolving into a pop-rock outfit called The Rockets, the group was renamed Crazy Horse just weeks after the release of their album *The Rockets* (1968), which contained four Whitten compositions. The group teamed up with Young after he was invited to sit in with them during a performance at The Whisky A-Go-Go in Los Angeles. (Whitten had first met Young during the sessions for the first Buffalo Springfield album.) With Buffalo Springfield disbanding, Young split his time between a stint in Crosby, Stills, Nash & Young and a solo career. Crazy Horse first collaborated with Young on the album *Everybody Knows This Is Nowhere* (1969), which featured 'Down By The River' and 'Cinnamon Girl'. Abusing heroin during the sessions of what would become *After The Goldrush* (1970), Whitten was fired by Young. Recorded without Young, Crazy Horse issued an album in 1971. Featuring guitarist Nils Lofgren and keyboardist Jack Nitzche, *Crazy Horse* (1971) contained several Whitten-penned gems, including 'I Don't Want To Talk About It', which was later a hit for both Rod Stewart and Everything But The Girl. Backed in the studio by The Stray Gators, Young asked Whitten to join in the sessions. Having forsaken heroin but now taking other drugs, Whitten was again fired by an anguished Young.
CAUSE: After he was fired by Neil Young, Whitten was paid in cash and given a plane ticket back to Los Angeles. Spending his wages on near-pure heroin, he overdosed. Young lamented the incident in the song, 'The Needle And The Damage Done'. Neil Young roadie Bruce Berry later died of a drug overdose.
FURTHER READING: Rogan, Johnny.

(1983). *Neil Young: Here We Are In The Years*. London: Proteus. Williams, Paul. (1997). *Love To Burn: Thirty Years Of Speaking Out*. London: Omnibus.

Jessie Whitten

Born c. 1950
Died 1976
The second guitarist of the Seventies disco group Heatwave, Jessie Whitten was the last member hired. He died shortly after the release of the album *Too Hot To Handle*, which was highlighted by the international hit, 'Boogie Nights' and the ballad, 'Always And Forever'. Whitten was replaced in Heatwave by former Foundations member Ray Carter.
CAUSE: He was stabbed to death while visiting Chicago.

Wally Whyton

Born September 23, 1929
Died January 22, 1997
The leader of the shortlived British outfit The Vipers (Skiffle Group), Wally Whyton enjoyed a brief hit run in the Fifties. Formed in 1956, the group gained fame at the 2Is coffee bar in London's Soho, the city's first ever rock'n'roll venue. Co-penned by Whyton, The Vipers' début hit 'Don't You Rock Me Daddy-O' (1957) was also a bigger hit for skiffle star Lonnie Donegan. Placing two more singles on the British charts in 1957, The Vipers followed up with 'Cumberland Gap' (1957) and 'Streamline Train' (1957); another single, 'Maggie May', was banned by the BBC. Originally an acoustic outfit, The Vipers went electric with the addition of Jet Harris and guitar-master Hank Marvin. (The group would evolve into an instrumental band called The Drifters, the forerunners of Cliff Richard's Shadows.) With the demise of the skiffle craze, Whyton emerged as a popular folk singer. Subsequently working in television, he appeared on the popular Sixties British puppet shows, *Small Time* and *Five O'Clock Club*. Turning his attention to radio in 1967, he hosted *Country Meets Folk*. His most enduring success came with the BBC country music programme *Country Club*. Nicknamed "The Voice Of Country Music", he remained its host from 1974–1995.
CAUSE: Cancer. He died in London.

Wildchild

(ROGER MCKENZIE)
Born 1971
Died November 25, 1995
A one-hit British dance/pop artist, Wildchild enjoyed a hit shortly before his death in 1995 with the Fatboy Slim-remix of the synthesizer-laden, club anthem 'Renegade Master'. Living in the US at the time of the song's chart ascent, he returned to England for a performance on *Top Of The Pops* and died soon after. Wildchild also operated his own record label, Dark & Black.
CAUSE: He died from an undiagnosed heart condition.

Alexander Wilde

Born 1938
Died November 13, 1998
As a member of Sixties soul group Patty & The Emblems, Alexander Wilde scored an R&B hit in 1964 with 'Mixed-Up, Shook-Up Girl'. Formed in Camden, New Jersey, the group had no further chart success.
CAUSE: Unknown.

Leon Wilkeson

(LEON RUSSELL WILKESON)
Born April 2, 1952
Died July 27, 2001
The original bassist of tragedy-prone Southern rock band Lynyrd Skynyrd, Leon Wilkeson survived the infamous 1977 aeroplane crash which claimed the lives of several band members. Born in Texas to a Navy pilot but raised in Jacksonville, Florida, Wilkinson was previously a member of a group headed by Donnie Van Zant

called The Collegiate, which later evolved into .38 Special. By 1972, Wilkeson had joined another Jacksonville band, Lynyrd Skynyrd founded by Donnie Van Zant's brother Ronnie. Hired in 1972 as the replacement for original bassist Larry Jungstrom, an apprehensive Wilkeson temporarily quit the band during the recording of their début album, *Pronounced Le-Nerd Skin-Nerd* (1973); solidifying the Southern rock genre, the album spawned the hits 'Gimme Three Steps', 'Simple Man' and the anthemic 'Free Bird'. Lynyrd Skynyrd followed up with equally strong albums including *Second Helping* (1974), *Nuthin' Fancy* (1975), *Gimme Back My Bullets* (1976) and *One More From The Road* (1976). A week after the release of their 1977 album *Street Survivors*, the sleeve for which ironically showed the group engulfed in flames, disaster struck. En route from Greenville, South Carolina, to Baton Rouge, Louisiana, the band's chartered plane ran out of fuel after the pilots accidentally jettisoned it, and crashed into a wooded swamp near Gillsburg, Mississippi. Ronnie Van Zant, band members Steve and Cassie Gaines, road manager Dean Kilpatrick and both pilots were killed. Instead of helping the injured, hundreds of scavengers converged on the site and shamelessly looted any souvenirs they could find. A number of the remaining passengers were seriously injured, including Wilkeson who was initially pronounced dead on arrival at a local hospital. Eventually revived, he later claimed to have seen images of Ronnie Van Zant and the late Duane Allman telling him to go back. In 1979, Wilkeson and Lynyrd Skynyrd member Billy Powell joined several other Jacksonville musicians to form Alias, but after releasing one poor-selling album, *Contraband*, the group disbanded. Invited by Charlie Daniels to perform at the 1979 edition of the annual charity event Volunteer Jam, Wilkeson and the other surviving Lynyrd Skynyrd members were heartened by the reunion and decided to regroup. Out of respect for their deceased bandmates, the group took the name The Rossington-Collins Band, recording a pair of well-received albums, *Anytime, Anyplace, Anywhere* (1980) and *This Is The Way* (1981), as well as an AOR hit, 'Don't Misunderstand Me'. After the group disbanded, Wilkeson joined most of the members to form The Allen-Collins Band who issued just one album, *Here, There & Back* (1983). On the tenth anniversary of the tragic crash, the surviving members of Lynyrd Skynyrd reunited for what was intended as a one-off but soon turned into a sold-out, emotionally charged tour. Ronnie Van Zant's younger brother, Johnny, was enlisted as the new lead singer. Over the following years, Wilkeson continued to record and tour with various incarnations of the group.
CAUSE: In poor health for years, he suffered from chronic liver and lung disease. He was found dead in his hotel room on Ponte Vedra Beach in Jacksonville, Florida.

Elbert Wilkins

Born May 1, 1947
Died December 13, 1992
The baritone vocalist of perennial Detroit-based soul group The Dramatics, Elbert Wilkins replaced original member Robert Ellington. Headed by founder Ron Banks, after an inauspicious start the group signed with Stax-Volt Records in 1968 and had hits with 'Whatcha See Is Whatcha Get' (1971), 'In The Rain' (1972), 'Toast To The Fool' (1972), and 'Hey You! Get Off My Mountain' (1973). In 1973, Wilkins and William "Wee Gee" Howard left The Dramatics to form a competing version of the same group. Signed by Mainstream Records, the Howard/Wilkins line-up managed

just one R&B hit 'No Rebate On Love' (1975) during its four-year run.
CAUSE: Heart attack.

Kevin Wilkinson

(KEVIN MICHAEL WILKINSON)
Born June 11, 1958
Died July 17, 1999
A prolific drummer, Kevin Wilkinson worked for a series of new wave acts including Squeeze, Holly & The Italians, and The Waterboys. Having started on the drums at the age of seven Wilkinson began playing professionally in his mid-teens. In the late Seventies he joined the arty punk band Stadium Dogs and his first exposure to large audiences came as the drummer for Swedish alternative rocker, Magnus Uggla. By 1981, Wilkinson had joined the transplanted, American retro-styled band, Holly & The Italians. Hired in 1983 by The Waterboys (a band that included Karl Wallinger), Wilkinson appeared on their album, *A Pagan Place* (1984). Joining China Crisis about the same time, Wilkinson appeared on four albums. It was the most successful period of his career, and Wilkinson appeared on nearly a dozen British hits including 'Black Man Ray', 'King In A Catholic Style' and 'Best Kept Secret'. With China Crisis disbanding in 1989, Wilkinson joined Fish, a band led by Marillion's former vocalist, and in the Nineties he was constantly on the road as a member of a series of new wave revival outfits. In 1994, he performed with The Proclaimers and Andy Stewart. The following year he joined Squeeze, appearing on the album *Ridiculous*. Beginning in 1998, Wilkinson had been scheduled to start a US tour backing Howard Jones. Several weeks before his death, Wilkinson had organised a relief concert for refugees from Kosovo.
CAUSE: He committed suicide by hanging at his home near Swindon. He had been suffering from depression, brought on by a personal and financial crisis.

Big Joe Williams

(JOSEPH LEE WILLIAMS)
Born October 16, 1899
Died December 17, 1982
A Mississippi-born, Delta-styled bluesman who recorded prolifically for over half a century, Big Joe Williams was a powerful stage performer. Reared on a cotton farm, Williams joined The Rabbit Foot Minstrels in the Twenties. An itinerant bluesman who initially assumed the moniker Po' Joe Williams, he recorded for Bluebird Records in the Thirties. Employing his trademark nine-string guitar, his early hits included 'Please Don't Go', 'Highway 49', and 'Crawlin' King Snake'. After a stint as a labourer in the Depression-era WPA programme, he returned to the road where he collaborated with blues greats such as Robert Nighthawk, Peetie Wheatstraw and Sonny Boy Williamson (#1). Embraced by newfound audiences in the Sixties, Williams recorded prolifically for a series of labels including Delmark and Arhoolie.
CAUSE: Cardiac arrhythmia. Hospitalised for a week, his chronic heart condition had been exacerbated by both lung disease and diabetes.

Bobby Williams

Born 1936
Died 1961
The second tenor and pianist of the Fifties, Harlem-based teenage doo-wop group The Mello-Moods, Bobby Williams frequently shared lead vocal duties with Ray "Buddy" Wooten. Recording for Robin Records, the group landed its sole R&B chart entry with a cover of the 1936 standard, 'Where Are You (Now That I Need You)' (1952). Williams later teamed with two of his bandmates to form The Solitaires. Williams and The Solitaires recorded a series of enduring doo-wop chestnuts at Old Town Records including 'The Wedding' (1955). Williams left in 1956 and did not

appear on the group's biggest hit 'Walkin' Along' (1957).
CAUSE: Unknown.

Curtis Williams

Born December 11, 1934
Died c. 1980
A songwriter and member of several leading Los Angeles doo-wop groups in the Fifties including The Penguins, Curtis Williams alternated between bass and baritone vocals. Williams initially formed The Flamingos (not the famous Chicago group) in 1951 with a who's who of doo-wop vocalists, Richard Berry, Cornelius Gunter and Alex Hodge. Williams then recorded several tracks as a member of The (Hollywood) Flames, a prolific group which was headed by Robert Byrd (aka Bobby Day). Then when Williams met tenor Cleveland "Cleve" Duncan at a talent show in 1954, the pair decided to form a vocal R&B group; adding a member from their respective schools, Williams hired Dexter Tisby, and Duncan enlisted Bruce Tate. Named after the cartoon character on the back of a Kool cigarette pack, The Penguins were signed by Doo-Tone Records. A straightforward, expressive singer, Williams was also the group's pianist and chief songwriter. Recording 'Earth Angel' in a garage studio, the track was intended as the B-side of 'Hey Senorita'. With lead vocals by Duncan, the romantic ballad had evolved from Williams' association with singer-songwriter Jesse Belvin (a complex lawsuit later gave Belvin part-songwriting credit). An early rare crossover hit, 'Earth Angel' sold two million copies and became a doo-wop standard. The group's newly hired manager, Buck Ram, subsequently placed the group with the larger Mercury Records. Unhappy with his lack of royalty payments, Williams sued his former record company for $100,000, claiming that his contract was invalid because he signed it while a minor. Bombing at Mercury, The Penguins moved to Atlantic where they scored a minor R&B hit with 'Pledge Of Love'. With his former wife suing over unpaid alimony, Williams quit the group and skipped town. Rejoining The Hollywood Flames (now called The Satellites) as a baritone vocalist, Williams sang back-up on the Thurston Harris hit 'Little Bitty Pretty One'. Featuring Bobby Day on lead vocals, The Hollywood Flames landed their own hit in 1957 with 'Buzz-Buzz-Buzz'; the group would also back Day on several of his solo releases including 'Rockin' Robin'. With Donald Height providing the lead vocal, The Hollywood Flames scored their final hit in 1961 with 'Gee'.
CAUSE: Unknown.

Danny Williams

Born January 7, 1942
Died December 6, 2005
A ballad singer, Danny Williams had several British hits in the early Sixties. Born in South Africa, Williams was discovered by producer Norman Newell in 1957 while touring through Britain in an African review, The Golden City Dixies, and in 1960 he relocated to the UK. Often compared to Johnny Mathis, Williams had success with a chart-topping version of Henry Mancini's 'Moon River', along with 'Jeannie', 'The Wonderful World Of The Young' and 'Tears', while his only US hit came in 1964 with 'White On White'. Suffering from a nervous breakdown in 1968, Williams declared bankruptcy in 1970. Later becoming a fixture on the cabaret circuit, Williams made an unexpected return to the UK charts in 1977 with 'Dancin' Easy', based on a television commercial for a martini mix.
CAUSE: Cancer.

David Williams

Born February 29, 1972
Died August 14, 2002
The energetic lead singer of heavy metal outfit Drowning Pool, David

Williams passed away just as the group was achieving stardom. Previously an instrumental trio, Drowning Pool was formed in 1998 by a pair of New Orleans musicians, guitarist C.J. Pierce and drummer Mike Luce. A veteran of the Dallas music scene, Williams was last to join the band. After creating a buzz as the opening act on tours with Sevendust and Kittie, Drowning Pool was signed by Windup Records and their début album *Sinner*, issued in 2001, was certified platinum; the video for 'Bodies' becoming an MTV staple. In 2002, the group was invited to appear on the second Ozzfest tour.
CAUSE: He was found dead on the band's tour bus after it reached its destination of Manassas, Virginia. The group had performed at an Ozzfest stop the night before in Indianapolis. An autopsy attributed the death to cardiomyopathy, a heart condition.

Dootsie Williams

(WALTER WILLIAMS)
Born 1911
Died 1991
A record company owner best remembered for his success with the doo-wop standard 'Earth Angel', former MGM Records employee Dootsie Williams operated the tiny Dootone label in Los Angeles. The leader of jazz combo The Harlem Dukes during the Thirties, Williams had also written a number of songs for artists such as Amos Milburn and Count Basie. Launching the label Blue Records from the front of his home in 1949, Williams renamed the firm Dootone in 1951. Issuing a wide variety of genres including jazz, R&B and spoken comedy, Williams also released early singles by Johnny Creach, later known as violinist "Papa" John Creach when performing with Jefferson Airplane in the Seventies. The most notable comedian to record at Dootone was John Elroy Sanford, who as Redd Foxx issued a series of bawdy, best-selling albums for the label until his contract was bought out in 1967 by Frank Sinatra. Dootone's greatest chart success came in the Fifties when a group of students from Fremont High School calling themselves The Penguins recorded the timeless ballad 'Earth Angel'. Despite a cover version by The Crew-Cuts, the original rendition featuring the lead vocals of Cleveland Duncan crossed over into the pop Top 10. When The Penguins' manager wanted to move the group to a larger label, Williams wound up with part ownership of the composition and all of the publishing rights. Other rock and R&B acts at the label included The Medallions, Don Julian & The Meadowlarks, The Calvanes, Roy Milton and Chuck Higgins. In 1956, Williams was forced to rename his label Dooto when the Duo-Tone Needle Company threatened litigation over the similar sounding names. Dooto remained financially afloat into the Seventies by reissuing the material of Redd Foxx, who by 1972 was starring in the hit sitcom *Sanford & Son*.
CAUSE: Natural causes.

Eddie Williams

Born June 12, 1912
Died February 18, 1995
The bassist of the pioneering Los Angeles-based proto-R&B group Johnny Moore and The Three Blazers, Texas-native Eddie Williams had much success in the mid Forties. Formed by guitarist Johnny Moore in 1942, The Three Blazers initially included Williams and pianist Garland Finney. With the departure of Finney the following year, the group would settle into its classic line-up with the addition of singer and pianist Charles Brown. After recording several singles at the tiny Atlas label, The Three Blazers found fame at Eddie Messner's Philo Records. Composed by Brown, 'Drifting Blues' was an influential hit during the rise of R&B. Refusing to be tied down to a single label, the group

enjoyed hit releases at several record companies. Featuring Brown's jazz-blues, elegant, ballady voice, and Moore's jazzy guitar, the group dominated jukeboxes with 'Sunny Road', 'So Long', 'New Orleans Blues' and the perennial favourite, 'Merry Christmas, Baby'. With the addition in 1948 of Johnny Moore's younger brother, jazz guitarist Oscar Moore, both Williams and Brown would soon leave the group. Williams later joined a series of groups including The Four Tunes and Jewel Akens.
CAUSE: Suffering a debilitating stroke, he never recovered.

Fleming Williams

Born December 26, 1943
Died February 15, 1998
A member of California-based disco/soul trio The Hues Corporation, Fleming Williams provided the lead vocals on the chart-topping 1974 single, 'Rock The Boat'. Highlighted by a fast shuffle beat, the record initially bombed until several months later when club deejays in New York City discovered the track. A native of Michigan, Williams quit the group in late 1974 and was replaced by Tommy Brown.
CAUSE: Drug related.

George Williams

(GEORGE REGINALD WILLIAMS, JR.)
Born December 6, 1935
Died July 28, 2004
A member of Philadelphia-based soul-pop group The Tymes, vocalist George Williams enjoyed a long career in music. After an army stint, he returned to Philadelphia and took a series of jobs including a position at Einstein Medical Center, where he met singer Norman Burnett of a local vocal harmony group called The Latineers. With Williams joining the group as lead singer in 1961, The Latineers were discovered at a local talent contest by A&R director Billy Jackson of Parkway Records. Signing with Parkway, the renamed Tymes enjoyed three Top 40 hits in 1963, the Williams' co-composition 'So Much In Love', a cover of Johnny Mathis' 'Wonderful! Wonderful!' and 'Somewhere'. Adding a pair of female singers in the early Seventies, the group returned to the Top 40 in 1974 with 'You Little Trustmaker' and UK number one, 'Ms. Grace'. After the group left RCA Records in 1977, Williams moved to England, performing as a solo act and recording with the funk group The Chosen Three. In 2000, Williams reunited with The Tymes for a doo-wop programme on PBS, and resettled in the US in 2002.
CAUSE: Cancer. He died at his home in Maple Shade, New Jersey.

Hank Williams

(HIRAM KING WILLIAMS)
Born September 17, 1923
Died January 1, 1953
A country music legend who set the stage for the rock'n'roll rebel of the Fifties, Hank Williams led a tortured existence, not least because he suffered from a debilitating back ailment throughout his adult life. With his father committed to the psychiatric ward of a veterans' hospital, Hiram "Hank" Williams began drinking at age 11. Reared during the Depression by his imposing church organist mother, Williams was drawn to the music and moral base of his Baptist church. Spurning a formal education, Williams acquired an acoustic guitar and was informally tutored by a black street musician named Rufe "Tee-Tot" Payne. Forming an early version of The Drifting Cowboys at age 14, Williams was soon performing in honky-tonk bars throughout the South. After garnering a touch of fame with a radio show at WSFA in Montgomery, Williams was convinced in 1946 by his strong-willed wife, the former Audrey Sheppard, to settle in Nashville. Initially hired as a songwriter by the Acuff-Rose publishing company, Williams was signed to the new MGM

label the following year. Although barely literate, Williams was a talented songwriter who was capable of expressing core human emotions. After scoring his first hits with the upbeat 'Move It On Over' (1947) and a countrified version of an early Tin Pan Alley song, 'Lovesick Blues' (1949), Williams earned a spot in the *Louisiana Hayride* radio programme. Lured to the Grand Ole Opry and subsequently given his own programme on WSM, the gawky Williams became a superstar in the country field. Never veering far from his Christian principles, Williams also issued a string of religious numbers under the pseudonym Luke The Drifter. Dominating the country charts during his brief career, Williams enjoyed hits with 'I'm So Lonesome I Could Cry' (1950), 'Cold, Cold Heart' (1951), 'Hey, Good Lookin'' (1951), 'Jambalaya' (1952), and the double-sided entry, 'Kaw-Liga'/'Your Cheatin' Heart'. The appeal of Williams was underlined by the concomitant success of his country hits by mainstream pop artists. Tony Bennett transformed 'Cold Cold Heart' into a million-seller, while Frankie Laine enjoyed success with 'Hey Good Lookin'' and Jo Stafford charted with 'Jambalaya'. Williams' own success on record was undermined by his continual problems with alcohol, a condition made worse by his reliance on pain-killers. His unpredictability and tardiness eventually cost him his marriage and his residency on the Grand Ole Opry. In a vulgar display of ostentation and financial need, he organised his second marriage in New Orleans with a gig, open to the public for the price of a ticket. Returning to the smaller *Louisiana Hayride*, Williams quit two months later due to declining health. His son, Hank Williams, Jr., later emerged as a country star in his own right. The popularity of Hank Williams increased substantially after his death in 1953. The double A-side 'Your Cheatin' Heart'/'Kaw-Liga' topped the pop and country charts. Thereafter his back catalogue was plundered by countless new country and pop acts, with many of the songs emerging as standards that are likely to be included among the most memorable melodies of the century.

CAUSE: His health wrecked by years of drug and alcohol abuse, Williams died in the back seat of a baby-blue Cadillac convertible en route to Ohio where he was scheduled to play two New Year's Day shows at the Canton Memorial Auditorium. In the driver's seat was Charles Carr, a 17-year-old college freshman on his Christmas break. A coroner's report ruled the death a heart attack. Williams attributed his drug use to painful, chronic injuries suffered during a pair of horse riding accidents.

FURTHER READING: Caress, Jay. (1979). *Hank Williams: Country Music's Tragic King*. New York: Stein and Day.

Joe Williams

(JOSEPH GOREED)

Born December 12, 1918

Died March 29, 1999

A smooth baritone vocalist who skilfully shifted between blues and big-band jazz, the affable Joe Williams enjoyed decades of fame. A native of Cordele, Georgia, he moved with his family to Chicago at age four. After forming a gospel quartet called The Jubilee Boys at 15, he barely survived a bout of tuberculosis. Influenced by blues shouter Big Joe Turner, Williams switched to secular music at 16, and was simultaneously a member of bands led by Joe Long and Jimmy Noone. After a stint with Coleman Hawkins (1941–42) and then Lionel Hampton, Williams landed in Andy Kirk's ensemble (1946–47). Suffering personal problems, the dejected Williams left music in 1947, but after taking a series of non-musical jobs, Williams returned to the stage.

Backed by King Kolax's R&B band, Williams made his solo recording début in 1951 with 'Every Day I Have The Blues'. Then after a stint with Red Saunders, Williams joined The Lionel Hampton Orchestra in 1954 as a replacement for Jimmy Rushing. With the careers of both Basie and Williams reinvigorated, their album *Count Basie Swings, Joe Williams Sings* (1955) was highlighted by 'In The Evening', 'Teach Me Tonight', and the definitive version of 'Every Day I Have The Blues'. Leaving Basie in 1961 to form his own group, Williams was backed on sessions by leading jazzmen such as George Shearing and Cannonball Adderly. In the Eighties, Williams portrayed the recurring role of Grandpa Al on the top-rated television programme, *The Cosby Show*.

CAUSE: Suffering respiratory problems and acute obstructive pulmonary disease, he was admitted to Sunrise Hospital in Las Vegas. After a week, he walked out of the hospital. With no money, he walked several miles on foot and was only a few blocks from his home when he collapsed and died on a city sidewalk.

Johnny Williams

(JOHN LEE WILLIAMS)
Born October 27, 1940
Died December 19, 2004

A member of perennial vocal R&B act The Drifters, Johnny Williams joined the Ben E. King version of the group in 1959, but left after a year. A tenor vocalist, Williams provided the lead vocal on the 1959 B-side hit, 'True Love, True Love', backed King on the A-side hit, 'Dance With Me', and sang on 'This Magic Moment', 'Lonely Winds', 'Save The Last Dance For Me' and 'I Count The Tears'. Williams was also hired to fill in for King in the touring version of The Drifters. Both Williams and King left the group in late 1960. Williams later recorded a number of solo singles and was a member of The Embraceables.

CAUSE: Unknown. He died in a Mobile, Alabama, hospital.

Lamar Williams

Born January 14, 1949
Died January 25, 1983

The bass player in the tragedy-ridden Southern rock group The Allman Brothers Band, Lamar Williams replaced founding member Berry Oakley in January 1973. A native of Gulfport, Mississippi, Williams was hired on the recommendation of band member Jai Johanny Johanson, who had known Williams from Gulfport. Trained in R&B, Williams was a very different player than the blues-based Oakley. Williams first appeared on the group's album *Brothers And Sisters*, which spawned the country-rock styled hits, 'Rambling Man' and 'Jessica'. The group experienced much internal strife in the mid Seventies when leader Gregg Allman testified in a drug trial against the group's former road manager. Recorded amid much acrimony, *Win, Lose Or Draw* (1975) spawned the album rock hits 'Nevertheless' and 'Louisiana Lou And The Three Card Monty John'. With The Allman Brothers Band disbanding in 1976, Williams joined bandmates Chuck Leavell and Jai Johanny Johanson in a group called We Three, before forming the more stable, Sea Level. Departing from the blues rock of The Allmans, Sea Level vacillated between soft, electric-jazz and funky R&B. Although only moderately successful, Sea Level experienced no desertions when The Allman Brothers Band reformed in 1978. Signed to the same label as The Allmans, Capricorn Records, Sea Level released the first of five albums in 1977. The group would disband a year after releasing its final album, *Ballroom* (1980).

CAUSE: Cancer. A Vietnam veteran, Williams attributed his condition to exposure to herbicide Agent Orange. He died in Los Angeles.

Larry Williams

Born May 10, 1935
Found dead January 2, 1980
An underrated Fifties R&B singer who struggled with his own insecurities, Larry Williams was born in a Creole community near New Orleans. After entering a number of local talent shows in the Forties, Williams briefly settled in Oakland where he employed a trained monkey in his stage act. Relocating to San Francisco at age 16, Williams joined The Lemon Drops, and was tutored by the group's leader on piano and bass guitar. Returning to New Orleans in the Fifties, Williams joined a band led by R&B singer Lloyd Price. Soon perfecting his pounding style of piano playing, Williams emerged as an explosive singer and performer. But with Price entering the service, Williams was not popular enough to maintain the group. After a stint with Fats Domino as a roadie and sometimes musician, Williams signed a solo contract with Specialty Records (labelmate Little Richard would befriend Williams and offer him part-time employment). Landing his first hit in 1957, Williams recorded a cover version of Price's 'Just Because'; but while both singles reached the R&B charts, Price's original rendition barely eclipsed the remake. Williams followed with a series of hook-laden, rock'n'roll classics such as 'Short Fat Fanny' (1957), 'Bony Moronie' (1957), and 'Dizzy Miss Lizzy' (1958). Leaving Specialty in 1959, Williams was convicted of narcotics possession the following year. His career sidetracked by negative publicity, Williams managed to record some material for Chess Records before entering prison. Williams would soon regain a level of fame when The Beatles recorded 'Dizzy Miss Lizzy' (on their *Help!* album), and two other Williams songs, 'Slow Down' (on their *Twist And Shout* EP) and 'Bad Boy'. On his release, Williams was hired as a talent scout for the CBS subsidiary OKeh Records. Teaming with Johnny Watson in the mid Sixties, Williams scored minor hits with 'Mercy, Mercy, Mercy' (1967) and 'Nobody' (1968). During this period Williams would also produce a pair of Little Richard albums. According to Etta James in her autobiography, Williams was a very successful burglar during this period; then, after a stint as the head of Angel Town Records, Williams lived very comfortably as a pimp.
CAUSE: He committed suicide by gunshot at his Los Angeles home. His body was discovered several days later. Friends insisted that Williams was murdered by members of an organised crime syndicate.

L.C. Williams

Born March 12, 1930
Died October 18, 1960
A Houston-based blues singer, L.C. Williams scored his sole R&B hit with 'Ethel Mae' (1949). Frequently touring with Lightnin' Hopkins, Williams earned the nickname Lightnin' Jr.
CAUSE: Suffering with tuberculosis, he died from a collapsed lung.

Louis Williams

Born February 24, 1941
Died October 13, 2002
The lead vocalist and chief songwriter of Memphis-based Southern soul group The Ovations, Louis Williams was often compared to Sam Cooke. Signed by Goldwax Records, the group scored a pair of R&B hits with 'It's Wonderful To Be In Love' (1965) and 'Me And My Imagination' (1967). After the group disbanded, Williams formed a new line-up of The Ovations in 1972 with former members of Ollie & The Nightingales. The new group placed two more singles on the R&B charts, 'Touching Me' (1972) and the Sam Cooke-based medley 'Having A Party'.
CAUSE: Unknown. He died at the Methodist Healthcare University Hospital in Memphis.

Marion Williams

Born August 29, 1927
Died July 2, 1994
A pioneering gospel singer who influenced scores of R&B and rock acts, including Little Richard and Aretha Franklin, Miami-born Marion Williams first performed in church at age three alongside her soloist mother. During a visit to Philadelphia at age 17, Williams sang at a church concert and was subsequently invited to join The Clara Ward Singers. With her pentecostal fire, Williams became the group's lead singer in 1947, appearing on the gospel classics 'I'm Climbing Higher And Higher', 'Packin' Up', and 'Surely God Is Able'. Possessing a soaring, melodic voice, Williams infused elements of both blues and R&B into her delivery. Leaving Ward in 1959, Williams formed her own group, The Stars Of Faith, before pursuing a solo career in 1965. After decades of turning aside offers to perform in nightclubs and sing non-religious material, Williams appeared in 1980 at the Cookery in Greenwich Village.
CAUSE: A diabetic, she developed severe kidney problems and succumbed to vascular disease. She died in Philadelphia.

Nat D. Williams

Born October 19, 1907
Died October 27, 1983
A pioneering R&B DJ at WDIA in Memphis, Nat D. Williams was a moonlighting school teacher when in 1948 he brought his own records to the station. Heard on the AM dial in dozens of states, Williams spawned a host of imitators. Also a journalist, he penned a column for *The Tri State Defender*. His health eroding in the Seventies, Williams retired from radio.
CAUSE: He died from the effects of a stroke, suffered several years before his death.

Paul Williams

Born July 2, 1939
Died August 17, 1973
The second tenor and guitarist for the Motown soul giants The Temptations (1960–71), Paul Williams went to high school in Birmingham, Alabama, with future Temptations member Eddie Kendricks. Alternating his time between football and music, Williams was a skilled guitarist and bassist in several local doo-wop groups. Relocating to Detroit, Williams reunited with Kendricks. Discovered by manager Milton Jenkins, Williams and Kendricks were placed in a new group called The Cavaliers. Soon renamed The Primes, the vocal group was signed by Motown Records in 1960. With Jenkins also managing a group led by Otis Williams (no relation) called The Distants, the two groups were merged in 1961 to form The Elgins. Soon renamed The Temptations, the group landed its first hit in 1962 with 'Dream Come True'. Quiet and moody, Williams was the group's original lead singer but was pushed to the background with the arrival of David Ruffin in 1963. (Ruffin had replaced Elbridge Bryant who was fired for attacking Williams.) Beginning their fruitful collaboration with songwriter and producer Smokey Robinson, The Temptations scored their first crossover hit with the Robinson-penned 'The Way You Do The Things You Do' (1964). With Ruffin then assuming most of the lead vocal duties, The Temptations enjoyed a remarkably successful series of crossover hits, beginning with the Motown-defining standard 'My Girl' (1965) and continuing with 'Ain't Too Proud To Beg' (1966), 'Beauty Is Only Skin Deep' (1966), '(I Know) I'm Losing You' (1966) and 'I Wish It Would Rain' (1968). Williams would provide a rare lead on the group's R&B hit 'Don't Look Back' (1965). Following David Ruffin's departure in 1968, the group adopted a harder,

rock-orientated sound on hits such as 'Cloud Nine' (1968), 'I Can't Get Next To You' (1969), 'Psychedelic Shack' (1970), and 'Ball of Confusion' (1970). Abusing alcohol, Williams left the group in 1971. From an album recorded a year earlier, Williams' last hit with The Temptations came with 'It's Summer' (1971). Williams was replaced in the group by Richard Street, who had been hired earlier to cover for the ailing Williams in the studio and on stage.
CAUSE: He committed suicide by gunshot, pushed to the brink by marital woes, $100,000 in debt, and an alcohol addiction. Wearing only swimming trunks, he was found dead in the front seat of his car near Motown's Hitsville studio in Detroit.
FURTHER READING: Romanowski, Patricia; & Williams, Otis. (1989). *Temptations*. New York: Simon & Schuster.

Paul "Hucklebuck" Williams

Born July 13, 1915
Died September 14, 2002
A popular R&B bandleader, Paul "Hucklebuck" Williams scored a number of R&B hits in the late Forties. Previously a member of a band led by jazzman King Porter, Williams was discovered by Savoy Records producer Teddy Reig. He earned his nickname after the chart smash 'The Hucklebuck' which spent 14 weeks atop *Billboard's* R&B chart. Featuring a driving tenor sax, the song's melody borrowed from both Charlie Parker's 'Now's The Time' and Lucky Millinder's 'D Natural Blues', and was later recorded by countless acts including Kate Smith, Frank Sinatra and Louis Armstrong. Williams' other hits included 'Thirty-Five Thirty' (1948), 'Waxey Maxie' (1948), 'Walkin' Around' (1949) and 'Pop-Corn' (1949), and all were instrumentals excepting 'He Knows How To Hucklebuck' (1949), which featured a vocal by Joan Shaw. Williams gained historical notoriety when on March 21, 1952 at the Cleveland Arena, he was the only act who performed at Alan Freed's Moondog Coronation Ball, an oversold concert which prematurely ended in a riot. Williams retired from the stage in 1964.
CAUSE: He died in Harlem after suffering a heart attack.

Rozz Williams

(ROGER ALAN PAINTER)
Born November 6, 1963
Died April 1, 1998
The lead singer and lyricist of Los Angeles-based gothic rock band Christian Death, Rozz Williams predated Marilyn Manson with his outrageous stage antics, Nazi imagery and attacks on organised religion. Formed in Los Angeles in 1979, the group released their morbid début, *Only Theater Of Pain*, in 1982, the album featuring tracks such as 'Burnt Offerings' and 'Spiritual Cramp'. After relocating to Europe, the group briefly disbanded. Forming a new version of Christian Death in 1984 with members of Pompeii 99, Williams would leave the group two years later. Returning to San Francisco, Williams subsequently pursued a solo career before forming Shadow Project in 1987 with his wife, Eva O. Forming a competing version of Christian Death in 1989, Williams released material on Cleopatra Records. Relocating Shadow Project to Los Angeles, Williams recorded four albums with the group. Returning to solo work in 1995, Williams recorded two albums including the spoken-work project, *The Whorses' Mouth*.
CAUSE: Williams committed suicide by hanging at his home in West Hollywood, California. Stricken with manic-depression, he was also battling heroin addiction.

Scott Williams

(James Scott Williams II)
Born 1966
Died April 26, 2004
A member of New Orleans-based heavy metal group Soilent Green, bassist Scott Williams joined in 1992. The group had formed in 1988, taking its name from the 1973 Charlton Heston sci-fi film *Soylent Green*. Merging metal, blues-rock and hardcore punk, the group ground out a fanbase through the Nineties with albums such as *A String Of Lies*, the critically acclaimed *Sewn Mouth Secrets* and *A Deleted Symphony*. Williams and another bandmate suffered broken bones in December 2001 when the group's tour van flipped over in Washington state. After Williams was involved in a second accident several months later, he left the group.
Cause: He was murdered by his roommate Tracey Scott, who then turned the gun on himself. Both men died at the scene. After arguing at a restaurant, the men returned to their home in the suburban New Orleans community of Gretna, where the murder/suicide occurred.

Tony Williams

Born April 5, 1928
Died August 14, 1992
As the masterful lead vocalist of The Platters, Tony Williams merged R&B with traditional balladry on a string of elegant crossover hits in the last half of the Fifties. Trained on the gospel music of his Baptist church in Elizabeth, New Jersey, Williams later received classical voice lessons. Part American-Indian, Williams entered a series of New Jersey talent shows before winning first place at The Apollo Theater amateur night. After a stint in the US Airforce in the Forties, Williams struggled to find work as a singer. Taking the advice of his sister Linda Hayes (who had scored an R&B hit with 'Yet I Know'), Williams relocated to Los Angeles. Arriving in 1952, Williams replaced Cornell Gunter in a struggling R&B group called The Platters. Recording at the King Records subsidiary Federal, the group fared poorly with its rough, R&B-flavoured material. Hiring manager Buck Ram, The Platters left Federal. Heavily tutored by Ram, The Platters adopted a smoother, doo-wop harmony sound. Also managing The Penguins (who had just scored a major hit with 'Earth Angel'), Ram convinced Mercury Records to sign both groups. Recording a new, polished version of their earlier Federal release 'Only You (And You Alone)' (1955), The Platters landed in the Top 10 and appeared in the Alan Freed film, *Rock Around The Clock*. Initially unhappy with Ward's choice of ballad material, Williams and his bandmates wanted to record upbeat material; hating 'The Great Pretender' (1955), Williams and The Platters were pleasantly surprised when the single became their first pop chart-topper. The most successful R&B group of the decade, The Platters continued their strong run of enchanting ballad hits with '(You've Got) The Magic Touch', 'My Prayer', 'Twilight Time', and a definitive 'Smoke Gets In Your Eyes'. Uncredited by Buck Ram, Williams often aided in the composition of much of the group's material. The Platters' career was irrevocably harmed when on August 10, 1959, the four male members were arrested in a Cincinnati motel for having sex with women who were under 21. Although Lynch and the others were acquitted of the charges, the group never truly recovered from the scandal. The Platters scored their final Top 10 hit in 1960 with a cover of the standard, 'Harbor Lights'. While still a member of The Platters, Williams recorded his first solo record, 'A Girl Is A Girl Is A Girl Is A Girl' (1959); surprisingly, it bombed. Beginning with the single 'Red Sails In The Sunset', Williams received additional prominence in the

group which was renamed The Platters Featuring Tony Williams. Leaving The Platters in June 1960 after multiple personality clashes with back-up singer Herb Reed, Williams was replaced in the group by Johnny Barnes, and then, Sonny Turner. With Williams' sudden departure, Ram and The Platters were sued by Mercury Records. Pursuing a solo career, Williams fared poorly with his Reprise and Philips releases. Abusing alcohol and near financial ruin, Williams rebounded after his new wife/manager regained his past royalties. Forming a competing version of The Platters, Williams spent years on the road and was especially popular in Japan. But after years of litigation, in July 1982 the New York Supreme Court ruled against Williams and barred him from using "The Platters" name. Williams eventually joined an authorised Platters group. In 1990, an appeals court cancelled Buck Ram's trademark registration of The Platters name. Though severely ill, Williams was forced out of financial necessity to tour until several months before his death.
CAUSE: A heavy smoker who also suffered from diabetes and emphysema, he died in his sleep at his Manhattan apartment.

Wendy O. Williams

(WENDY ORLEANS WILLIAMS)
Born May 28, 1949
Died April 6, 1998
As the leader of The Plasmatics, shock-rock pioneer Wendy O. Williams combined heavy metal with punk. Born in Rochester, New York, but raised in nearby Webster, Williams launched her show business career at the age of six as a dancer on *The Howdy Doody Show*. Taking clarinet lessons at the Eastman School of Music, she later joined her junior high band. Committing a variety of rebellious acts in her mid-teens, she was arrested at 15 for sunbathing in the nude. Quitting high school and hitting the road in her late teens, Williams hitchhiked to Colorado and then Florida, taking odd jobs including a stint as a lifeguard. After drifting through Europe, she returned to the US in 1976 and became a go-go dancer at a New York City theatre operated by the Yale-educated Rod Swenson. Conceived by Swenson, The Plasmatics débuted at CBGBs in 1978. After releasing a pair of indie EPs, the group signed with Stiff Records in 1980, recording the brash punk/metal album *New Hope For The Wretched.* Sporting a blue mohawk and covering her breasts with shaving cream and strategically placed band-aids, Williams was arrested in Milwaukee and Cleveland on lewdness charges. Williams and the group garnered substantial press coverage for their outrageous stage act which included the chain-sawing of guitars and televisions. After releasing three albums at Stiff, The Plasmatics' major label début came in 1982 with the Capitol Records set, *Coup d'Etat*, the album cover picturing Williams straddling a tank. With The Plasmatics disbanding in the mid Eighties, Williams released several solo albums including the Gene Simmons aided, Grammy-nominated *W.O.W.* Also flirting with acting, Williams appeared in the films *Reform School Girls* and *Pucker Up And Bark Like A Dog.* A reformed Plasmatics last toured in 1988. Outside of music, Williams devoted her time to animal welfare.
CAUSE: Suicide by gunshot. Her body was found in the woods near her home in Storrs, Connecticut, by her former manager Rod Swenson. Williams had been despondent for some time and had planned her suicide well in advance.

Willie Williams

Born March 13, 1922
Died December 8, 1988
A drummer in Howlin' Wolf's Chicago-based band, Willie Williams

had previously formed a blues band in St. Louis. He scored his best known hit with 'Wine Headed Woman'.
CAUSE: Unknown. He died in Chicago.

Billy Williamson

Born February 9, 1925
Died March 22, 1996
An original member of Bill Haley & The Comets, steel guitarist Billy Williamson also backed Haley in his earlier groups. Williamson and pianist Johnny Grande first teamed with Haley, then a Western swing singer, in 1950 to form Bill Haley & His Saddlemen. Recording for several labels, the group slowly mixed elements of R&B into their sound. Discarding the cowboy attire and moving further away from their country roots, the renamed Bill Haley & The Comets signed with Essex Records where they ascended the pop charts with 'Crazy, Man, Crazy', 'Fractured' and 'Live It Up'. Aided by songwriter/publisher Jim Meyers, the group then signed with Decca Records, recording the Meyers-penned '(We're Gonna) Rock Around The Clock', which, initially, was only a moderate hit in 1954. However, with the inclusion of the song in the opening credits of the film *The Blackboard Jungle*, the single was re-released, topped the pop charts and went on to launch the rock'n'roll era. Williamson and the rest of the group then appeared in their own film, the musical *Rock Around The Clock* (1956), where they performed six songs. Bill Haley & The Comets followed up with a string of infectious rockabilly-inflected hits in the last half of the Fifties including 'Razzle-Dazzle', 'Burn That Candle', a cover of Bobby Charles' 'See You Later Alligator', 'R-O-C-K', a cover of Little Richard's 'Rip It Up', 'Rudy's Rock' and 'Skinny Minny'. During his time with Haley, Williamson provided an occasional lead vocal on tracks such as 'Jamaica D.J.' and 'Hide And Seek'. In trouble with the IRS, Haley moved the group to Mexico in 1960, and occasionally slipped back into the US for a performance. After a 13-year run, both Grande and Williamson parted with Haley in 1963; Williamson was replaced by Nick Nastos. In subsequent years, Williamson rebuffed invitations to rejoin the group.
CAUSE: Cancer.

Sonny Boy Williamson

(JOHN LEE WILLIAMSON)
Born March 30, 1914
Died June 1, 1948
An innovative, Delta-styled blues harmonica player and singer, Arkansas-born Sonny Boy Williamson (#1) was a self-taught musician. Mastering the instrument at a young age, Williamson toured throughout the South with the likes of Robert Nighthawk and Sleepy John Estes. Landing in Chicago in 1934, Williamson was signed by Lester Melrose to RCA-Bluebird Records in 1937. Beginning with the frequently covered 'Good Morning Schoolgirl' (1937), Williamson recorded heavily during the next decade. A crucial figure in the rise of blues, Williamson furthered the role of the harmonica in the blues genre. As the Forties progressed, Williamson's sound became more urban and his singing more raucous on hits such as 'Shake The Boogie' (1947) and the posthumously released 'Better Cut That Out' (1948). Williamson's name was later appropriated by Aleck Ford "Rice" Miller, who for a time pretended to be the dead bluesman.
CAUSE: He was murdered in Chicago, repeatedly struck in the head during a street robbery.

Sonny Boy Williamson

(ALECK FORD "RICE" MILLER)
Born December 5, 1899
Died May 25, 1965
A popular blues harmonica player and guitarist who had appropriated the name of Sonny Boy "John Lee"

Williamson, the former Aleck Ford "Rice" Miller surpassed the success of his namesake. An itinerant musician in the Twenties, the Mississippi-native travelled throughout the Delta region as Little Boy Blue. After teaming with blues legends such as Robert Johnson and Elmore James, Williamson adopted the moniker, The One Man Band. Hosting the legendary radio blues programme, *The King Biscuit Time* at KFFA in Helena, Arkansas, beginning in 1941, he was forced by the show's sponsor to adopt the name of popular bluesman Sonny Boy Williamson. But when the real Williamson arrived in Helena to end the charade, he was chased out of town. Emerging as a more skilled musician than Williamson #1, Sonny Boy Williamson #2 became a radio star and was crucial in the dissemination of blues music throughout the region. Moving to Detroit for a time, Williamson teamed with pianist Boogie Woogie Red. Then after recording in 1951 at the small Mississippi-based Trumpet Records, Williamson relocated to Chicago in 1955 when Chess/Checker Records bought his contract. Aided by Muddy Waters and Jimmy Rodgers, Williamson landed his first national hit with 'Don't Start Me Talkin'' (1955); he followed up with 'Keep It To Yourself' (1956) and 'Help Me' (1963). Another of his compositions, 'One Way Out', was later a hit for The Allman Brothers. Arriving in Europe in 1963, Williamson was greeted by throngs of blues fans. While in England, he toured and recorded with The Yardbirds and The Animals, and influenced an entire generation of budding blues musicians. Returning to Arkansas in 1964, Williamson reprised his *King Biscuit* programme.
CAUSE: Heart attack. He died in bed at a boarding house in Helena, Arkansas. He had been ill for some time and had returned home to die.

Chuck Willis

Born January 31, 1928
Died April 10, 1958
A R&B singer and songwriter who died at the height of his career, Atlanta-native Chuck Willis was discovered in the Forties by legendary DJ Zenas "Daddy" Sears. A house painter during the day, Willis was a huge draw around Atlanta. After passing through a Southern musical revue, the Broadway Follies, in 1951 Willis was signed as a solo act to Columbia/OKeh Records by OKeh label head Danny Kessler. With his laid-back delivery, Willis landed on the R&B charts with 'My Story' (1952), 'Goin' To The River' (1953), 'Don't Deceive Me' (1953), and 'I Feel So Bad' (1954). Switching to Atlantic Records in 1956, Willis turned toward rock'n'roll. Sporting a flashy turban, his hits continued with 'It's Too Late' (1956), and the double-sided entry 'Juanita'/'Watcha' Gonna Do When Your Baby Leaves You' (1956). Willis was also a prolific songwriter whose compositions were recorded by a who's who of early rock: The Five Keys, The Cadillacs, and The Clovers. Written for Ruth Brown, 'Oh, What A Dream' topped the R&B charts. Willis crossed over into the pop chart with a cover of the blues standard, 'C.C. Rider' (1957), for which he was nicknamed "The King Of Stroll" by Dick Clark. Willis followed up with 'Betty And Dupree' and the posthumously released, million-selling double-sided single, the aptly titled 'What Am I Living For'/'Hang Up My Rock And Roll Shoes'. His son Chick Willis is a blues singer and guitarist.
CAUSE: Suffering from a bleeding stomach ulcer, he died on the operating table in Atlanta, Georgia.

Alan "Blind Owl" Wilson

Born July 4, 1943
Died September 3, 1970
The vocalist, rhythm guitarist and harmonica player of the blues rock

group Canned Heat, Boston native Alan "Blind Owl" Wilson was an outstanding talent and, like the rest of Canned Heat, a serious blues record collector. Wilson co-founded Canned Heat in 1966 with fellow blues aficionado Bob "The Bear" Hite from the remnants of an acoustic California jug band. Electrifying its sound, the unsigned group delivered a solid set at the Monterey Pop Festival in June 1967. As a result of this exposure, the group was signed by Liberty Records. Their début album *Canned Heat* (1967) was a critical success and a moderate seller, containing blues standards such as Elmore James' 'Dust My Broom'. But breaking through with their follow-up release, *Boogie With Canned Heat* (1968), Canned Heat enjoyed their first pop hit with a reworking of an old blues song 'On The Road Again', which featured Wilson's falsetto vocals and became a hippie anthem. Combining psychedelic textures over a folk and blues foundation, the group became a favourite of the Sixties flower power crowd. The group's follow-up album *Living The Blues* (1969) was highlighted by 'Going Up The Country', the song borrowing the melody of a Henry Thomas blues standard. Turning in a spectacular performance at the Woodstock Festival in August 1969, Canned Heat were embraced by fans and critics alike. Despite Wilson's sudden death in 1970, the remaining members of Canned Heat began a planned European tour several days later. Issued just after Wilson's death, the album *Future Blues* (1970) spawned the Top 40 hit 'Let's Work Together'.

CAUSE: Chronically despondent and once admitted to a psychiatric clinic, Wilson overdosed on barbiturates. Friends claimed that he tried to kill himself on three previous occasions. He was found dead in a sleeping bag behind bandmate Bob Hite's house in Topanga Canyon, California, with an empty bottle of pills at his side.

B.J. Wilson

(BARRIE JAMES WILSON)
Born March 18, 1947
Died October 8, 1990

The highly rated drummer of the symphonic rock band Procol Harum, B.J. Wilson employed a powerful, bombastic, thick drum sound. A native of Southend, England, Wilson had replaced drummer Mick Brownlee in 1962 in the British R&B group The Paramounts. Signing with Parlophone Records, The Paramounts scored their sole chart hit with a cover of The Coasters' 'Poison Ivy' (1964). After The Paramounts disbanded in 1966, Wilson worked as a session player for Cat Stevens and Lulu. Meanwhile, former Paramounts lead singer Gary Brooker teamed with songwriter Keith Reid to form Procol Harum. Following the release in 1967 of their début smash 'A Whiter Shade Of Pale', B.J. Wilson answered an advertisement in a British music magazine and was hired as the replacement for drummer Bobby Harrison. Another ex-Paramount, Robin Trower, also joined at this time. A revolutionary art/progressive group, Procol Harum followed up with 'Homburg' (1967) and strong albums such as *Shine On Brightly* (1968), *A Salty Dog* (1969), *Home* (1970) and Trower's last with the group, *Broken Barricades* (1971). In 1968 Wilson was invited by Jimmy Page to become the drummer of Led Zeppelin, but he declined and Page recruited John Bonham instead. True to their classical sound, Procol Harum was backed by The Edmonton Symphony Orchestra for their 1972 album, *Live In Concert*, and they landed a Top 10 hit with a new, orchestral version of their 1967 track 'Conquistador' (1972). Although the group's later albums *Grand Hotel* (1973), *Exotic Birds And Fruit* (1974), and *Procol's Ninth* (1975) were strong sellers, Procol Harum managed only one more hit with the Top 20 British

entry, 'Pandora's Box'. After a two-year hiatus, Procol Harum was reformed by Wilson and Brooker for a final album, the Leiber & Stoller-produced *Something Magic* (1977). Later employed as a session player, Wilson worked with John Hiatt, Frankie Miller, Lou Reed, and for an extended period, Joe Cocker. In very poor health, Wilson was unable to join the reunion of Procol Harum in the Eighties and was replaced by Mark Brzezicki of Big Country.
CAUSE: He was stricken with pneumonia while in a drug-induced coma. A prodigious drinker throughout his adult life, Wilson consumed a massive quantity of drugs in 1987, and remained in a near-vegetative state for the next three years.

Carl Wilson

(CARL DEAN WILSON)
Born December 21, 1946
Died February 6, 1998
A founding member of The Beach Boys, Carl Wilson was the youngest of the three Wilson brothers and the most mentally stable, and he was largely responsible for holding the group together during the many times that crises rocked the band. He was the group's principal guitar player and he also possessed a fine falsetto voice which was often underused, mainly because of elder brother Brian and lead singer Mike Love's equally prodigious talents in this area. Formed in 1961 as The Pendletones by the trio of Wilson brothers – Brian, Dennis, and Carl – the group was completed with cousin Mike Love and, eventually, Brian's college friend, Al Jardine. Under the control of the domineering family patriarch Murry Wilson, the group was tutored in vocal harmony. A self-taught guitarist, Carl Wilson was very serious about his playing and in later years would become the owner of an expansive guitar collection, including one of the very first Fender Stratocasters ever built. After a session at the tiny X label, the renamed Beach Boys switched to the Candix label and scored a regional hit with Brian's composition 'Surfin''. With the label closing, The Beach Boys signed with Capitol Records and scored their first Top 40 hit with 'Surfin' Safari' (1962). Often assisting brother Brian on production, Carl Wilson also provided essential backing harmonies on hits such as 'Surfin' USA' (1963), 'Fun, Fun, Fun' (1964), 'I Get Around' (1964), 'Dance, Dance, Dance' (1964), a remake of Bobby Freeman's 'Do You Wanna Dance' (1965), 'Help Me Rhonda' (1965), 'California Girls' (1965), and a cover of The Regents' 'Barbara Ann' (1966), the latter featuring session vocalist Dean Torrance of Jan & Dean. As the Sixties progressed Brian Wilson became a victim of psychedelic drugs and chronic insecurity, and his fear of flying and stage fright led to his quitting the road in favour of a studio role. With Bruce Johnston taking over on bass, Carl was obliged to assume a greater role as a singer on stage. With Brian still in command, The Beach Boys tackled mature material on their masterpiece *Pet Sounds*, an album widely hailed by critics but, at the time, a commercial failure. Among its many delights was a rare and quite transcendental lead vocal by Carl Wilson on the hit single 'God Only Knows'. Thereafter Carl always sang this song in concert to fervent applause from Beach Boys fans. The relative failure of *Pet Sounds* plunged Brian Wilson further into depression, leaving Carl to pick up the reins and hold the band together. The group's career was under threat again in early 1967 when Carl received his draft notice, but he escaped service as a conscientious objector. He was subsequently arrested by the FBI for refusing to take the Oath of Allegiance and assigned civilian duties as a bedpan changer, a job he successfully avoided. Nevertheless, the legal ramifications

resulting from his draft status dragged on interminably. In 1969 he produced and provided lead vocals on 'I Can Hear Music' and, for a time, took over vocal duties during the group's concerts. Landing at Warner-Reprise Records in 1970, The Beach Boys maintained their credibility with *Surf's Up* (1971) and *Holland* (1973). Between these two releases, they issued *Carl And The Passions/So Tough*, its title borrowed from one of the names that the group used prior to the formation of The Beach Boys, as well as underlining Carl's increasing importance in guiding their career. By 1974 they were transformed into an oldies band by the extraordinary success of the double compilation *Endless Summer* which gathered together all their Sixties hits and reached number one in the US charts. Subsequently signing for $8 million with CBS-Caribou Records in 1979, the group continued to release albums of new material which were largely ignored, even though Brain Wilson was persuaded out of retirement to contribute on some later albums. At the same time The Beach Boys remained an enormous concert draw, among the biggest in the world, although at times they were on the verge of collapse due to internal squabbling, financial irregularities and mismanagement. Leaving the group in 1981, Carl Wilson recorded a pair of commercially ignored albums, *Carl Wilson* (1981) and *Youngblood* (1983), and toured with his own band. Later rejoining The Beach Boys, Carl provided the lead vocals on their major comeback hit 'Kokomo' from the Tom Cruise film, *Cocktail*. Wilson toured with the group until several months before his death. The Beach Boys' saga was featured, and occasionally ridiculed, in the 1988 television film, *Summer Dreams: The Story Of The Beach Boys*. Despite the deaths of Carl and Dennis Wilson, and Brian Wilson apparently estranged from singer Mike Love, a Wilson-less Beach Boys somehow continue as a touring band under Love's leadership.

CAUSE: Diagnosed with lung cancer, he suffered a common complication when the disease spread to his brain. Diagnosed a year earlier, he died in Los Angeles.

FURTHER READING: Gaines, Steven. (1986). *Heroes And Villains: The True Story Of The Beach Boys*. New York: New American Library. Leaf, David. (1978). *The Beach Boys And The California Myth*. New York: Grossett & Dunlap. White, Timothy. (1997). *The Nearest Faraway Place: Brian Wilson, The Beach Boys And The Southern California Experience*. New York: Henry Holt.

Dennis Wilson

(DENNIS CARL WILSON)
Born December 4, 1944
Died December 28, 1983

The drummer and middle Wilson brother in the pioneering surf rock group The Beach Boys, Dennis Wilson was the only member who could actually surf, picking up the sport in the Fifties. His enthusiasm for surfing unquestionably influenced elder brother Brian to begin writing songs about the craze. Formed in 1961 as The Pendletones by the trio of Wilson brothers – Brian, Dennis, and Carl – the group was completed with cousin Mike Love and, eventually, by Brian's college friend, Al Jardine. Under the management of the domineering family patriarch Murry Wilson, the group was taught vocal harmony though by all accounts they needed little encouragement. A self-taught drummer, Dennis Wilson was content to remain in the shadows of elder brother Brian and younger brother Carl. The renamed Beach Boys scored a regional hit with 'Surfin'' on Candix. The Beach Boys then signed with Capitol Records and scored their first Top 40 with 'Surfin' Safari' (1962). The group's hits continued with 'Surfin'

U.S.A.' (1963), 'Fun, Fun, Fun' (1964), 'I Get Around' (1964), 'Dance, Dance Dance' (1964), a remake of Bobby Freeman's 'Do You Wanna Dance' (1965), 'Help Me Rhonda' (1965); 'California Girls' (1965), and a cover of The Regents' 'Barbara Ann' (1966). With Brian abandoning the road for the studio, the group tackled more mature material on *Pet Sounds*, by the Beach Boys standards a largely experimental album that predated The Beatles' *Sgt. Pepper* project, and featured tracks such as 'Sloop John B.', 'Wouldn't It Be Nice' and 'God Only Knows'. As the uncontrollable free spirit of the group, Dennis Wilson befriended Charles Manson at a hippie commune and invited Manson to live at his home. It soon became overrun with freeloaders, most of them teenage girls under Manson's spell. Wilson recorded a Manson composition, 'Cease To Exist', which was retitled 'Never Learn Not To Love' and released as the B-side of The Beach Boys' 1968 single, 'Bluebirds Over The Mountain'. Landing at Warner-Reprise Records in 1970, The Beach Boys maintained their credibility with *Surf's Up* (1971) and *Holland* (1973) but were transformed into an oldies band by the extraordinary success of the double compilation *Endless Summer* (1974) which gathered together all their Sixties hits and reached number one in the US charts. In 1970, Dennis Wilson pursued a side project as Dennis Wilson and Rumbo (aka Daryl Dragon), releasing the single 'Sound Of Free'. The duo was disbanded when Wilson severely injured his hand after punching a window. The injury also temporarily removed him from The Beach Boys, and he was replaced on tour by Ricky Fataar. Also flirting with acting, Wilson studied under Lee Strasberg and co-starred with James Taylor in the film, *Two Lane Blacktop* (1971). Dennis, along with Carl, also guested as vocalist on Chicago's US Top 20 hit 'Wishing You Were Here'. Providing fodder for the socialite pages, Wilson dated a series of celebrities during this period, including Christine McVie and Ronald Reagan's daughter, Patti Davis. With Brian Wilson returning to the band, The Beach Boys landed their only Top 10 hit of the decade in 1976 with a cover of Chuck Berry's 'Rock And Roll Music'. Becoming the first Beach Boy to release a solo album, Dennis Wilson played most of the instruments on the critically acclaimed and self-produced *Pacific Ocean Blue* (1977). Signing for $8 million with CBS-Caribou Records in 1979, The Beach Boys remained bogged down due to internal squabbling, although Dennis returned to the line-up in 1981. Their career was reignited in 1983 when Secretary of the Interior James Watt tried to cancel an Independence Day concert by the group, charging that they attracted the "wrong element"; while Watt would soon lose his job, The Beach Boys were embraced by a new generation of fans. Often absent from the group in the Eighties due to personal and drug problems, Dennis Wilson rejoined the Beach Boys on tour a month before his death. He enjoyed a particularly tempestuous personal life, having been married five times, twice to the same woman and once to an illegitimate daughter of singer Mike Love with whom he was frequently estranged.

CAUSE: A drunken and disillusioned Dennis Wilson died in a freak diving accident. Spending the day on a friend's boat near Marina del Ray, California, Wilson repeatedly dived into 10–12 feet of chilly December water. Swimming to the ocean floor, he made a game out of retrieving items which he himself had thrown overboard when a yacht he had once owned was moored above. During one of his dives he struck his head on the bottom of the boat while surfacing. With his blood-alcohol level at 0.26 per cent, the severely inebriated Wilson lost consciousness and drowned. A week before his death, Wilson had been admitted to a drug and alcohol treatment centre at nearby St. John's Hospital. At the time of his death he was reported to be virtually destitute, his fortune squandered on drugs and alcohol, and living rough when friends were unwilling to accommodate him. Although he had never served in the Coast Guard or US Navy, he was given an official Coast Guard funeral and buried at sea.

FURTHER READING: Gaines, Steven. (1986). *Heroes And Villains: The True Story Of The Beach Boys*. New York: New American Library. Leaf, David. (1978). *The Beach Boys And The California Myth*. New York: Grossett & Dunlap. White, Timothy. (1997). *The Nearest Faraway Place: Brian Wilson, The Beach Boys And The Southern California Experience*. New York: Henry Holt. Wincentsen, Ed. (1990). *Denny Remembered: Dennis Wilson In Words and Pictures*. El Paso, TX: Vergin.

Jackie Wilson

(JACK LEROY WILSON)
Born June 9, 1934
Died January 20, 1984

A vibrant, energetic performer who was dubbed "Mr. Excitement", Jackie Wilson masterfully glided between pop standards and upbeat soul. Reared in a Detroit ghetto, the church-trained Wilson joined The Ever Ready Gospel Singers while in his mid-teens. Lying about his age to enter the boxing ring, 16-year-old Wilson quickly abandoned the sport to appease his mother. As Sonny Wilson, he also pursued a singing career. Winning a number of local talent shows, he released a pair of obscure singles in 1951 at Dee Gee Records, including his future show-stopper, 'Danny Boy'. After passing through The Thrillers (the forerunner of The Royals/Midnighters), Wilson was discovered by King-Federal talent scout Johnny Otis, but while label chief Syd Nathan signed The Royals, he rejected the solo Wilson. Subsequently auditioning for bandleader Billy Ward of The Dominoes, Wilson initially apprenticed under Clyde McPhatter. With McPhatter abruptly leaving the group in 1953, Wilson assumed the lead tenor position. A member of The Dominoes for four years, Wilson provided the lead on the pop/soul flavoured hits 'You Can't Keep A Good Man Down' (1953), 'Rags To Riches' (1954), and the crossover entry, 'St. Therese Of The Roses' (1956). Leaving The Dominoes after a physical altercation with Ward, Wilson was signed to the Decca subsidiary, Brunswick Records with the aid of new manager Al Green (not the soul singer). With the label's musical director Dick Jacobs targeting the crossover market, Wilson was backed by a small orchestra and white backing singers. Wilson scored his first pop hit with 'Reet Petite', a song penned by cousin Billy Davis and boxing friend Berry Gordy, Jr. Composing several tracks with Gordy, Wilson emerged as a pop and R&B star with the hits 'To Be Loved' (1958), 'Lonely Teardrops' (1958), 'That's Why (I Love You So)' (1959), and 'I'll Be Satisfied' (1959). Aided by influential DJ Alan Freed, Wilson appeared in the rock film, *Go Johnny Go* (1959), from which he landed an R&B hit with 'You Better Know It'. Under the subsequent management of Nat Tarnopol, Wilson recorded uncharacteristically substandard material, and would earn little during the next decade. He continued his hit run with 'Night' (1960), 'Alone At Last' (1960), 'My Empty Arms' (1961), and 'Baby Workout', and teamed on record with LaVern Baker, Linda Hopkins, and Count Basie. Relocating to Chicago in 1966, Wilson was produced by Carl Davis. Wilson's career went into decline after '(Your Love Keeps Lifting Me) Higher And Higher' (1967) and 'I Get The Sweetest Feeling' (1968). Struck with a series of personal tragedies in the Sixties, Wilson entered

drug rehabilitation in 1968. Davis later attempted to revive Wilson's career, producing the poor selling album *Beautiful Day* (1973). Joining Dick Clark for a pair of oldies revues, Wilson enjoyed newfound fame in 1974, but on September 25, 1975, Wilson collapsed from a heart attack while performing at the Latin Casino nightclub in Camden, New Jersey. Falling from the stage and striking his head on the concrete floor, he stopped breathing and suffered permanent brain damage. Emerging from a coma after three months, Wilson was thereafter largely unresponsive. Institutionalised in the Medford Leas Retirement Community in 1977, Wilson died a forgotten man seven years later. Although The Spinners donated $60,000 for his medical care, much of the money was spent on litigation as family members fought over control of his estate. Wilson's early hit 'Reet Petite' reached number one on the British pop charts two years after his death. Wilson's goddaughter is singer Jody Watley.
CAUSE: Admitted to Burlington County Hospital on January 8, 1984, he died two weeks later. The exact cause of death was not revealed. Due to continued litigation among his family members, Wilson was buried in an unmarked grave. Wilson's strange death was one of many tragedies to befall his family: son Jackie, Jr. was killed in 1970 during a burglary; daughter Sandra Wilson Abrams died from a heart attack in 1977; and daughter Jacqueline Wilson was an innocent bystander when she was shot and killed during a drug related drive-by shooting.
FURTHER READING: Douglas, Tony. (1997). *Lonely Teardrops: The Jackie Wilson Story*. London: Sanctuary.

J. Frank Wilson

(JOHN FRANK WILSON)
Born December 11, 1941
Died October 4, 1991
A one-hit wonder, Texas-native J. Frank Wilson was reared on Cajun and Tex-Mex music. Discharged from the airforce in 1962, Wilson was hired as the lead vocalist of an instrumental trio called The Cavaliers. Discovered by independent record producer Sonley Roush, Wilson and The Cavaliers were convinced to sing a cover of Wayne Cochran's tragic, necra-rock themed, 'Last Kiss'. With the single hitting the US Top 10, the emotionally troubled Wilson, unable to handle fame, was quickly abandoned by The Cavaliers. His career quickly fading, Wilson managed only minor hits with a cover of Dorsey Burnette's 'Hey Little One' (1964) and a remake of 'Last Kiss' (1973).
CAUSE: Kidney failure. He died in Lufkin, Texas.

Johnny "Peanuts" Wilson

(JOHNNY ANCIL WILSON)
Born November 28, 1935
Died September 1980
An early member of Roy Orbison's country/rockabilly backing group The Teen Kings, Johnny "Peanuts" Wilson joined on rhythm guitar in 1955. Recording and touring with Orbison in the late Fifties, Wilson appeared on the first two versions of Orbison's rockabilly ditty 'Ooby Dooby', including the chart hit for Sun Records. During this period, Wilson also co-wrote several songs with Orbison. Over the next few years, Wilson also issued several solo singles.
CAUSE: Unknown.

Meri Wilson

(MARY EDNA EDGEMON)
Born June 15, 1949
Died December 28, 2002
A one-hit wonder, Meri Wilson scored a Top 20 novelty hit in 1977 with 'Telephone Man'. Born in Nagoya, Japan, while her father served in the US Air Force, Wilson was raised in Marietta, Georgia. After earning a pair of music degrees, she became a model and jingle singer in Dallas. Discovered

by former Bloodrock vocalist Jim Rutledge, she teamed with music producer Owen "Boomer" Castleman and recorded the self-composed 'Telephone Man'. In 1999, Wilson recorded an updated version of her earlier hit, now retitled 'Internet Man'.
CAUSE: She was involved in a single car accident near her home in Americus, Georgia.

Paul Wilson

Born January 6, 1935
Died May 15, 1988
A founding member of the celebrated Fifties doo-wop group The Flamingos, Paul Wilson was the group's baritone singer. The Flamingos were formed in 1950 by four cousins from the choir at the Jewish-affiliated, Chicago's Church of God and Saints of Christ. Signing with Chance Records in 1952, the group recorded several stunning, regional hit singles including the lovely 'Golden Teardrops'. After passing through the Chicago-based Parrot label, The Flamingos landed at the Chess subsidiary Checker Records. Featuring Nate Nelson on lead, the harmony-based ballad group enjoyed a string of hits with 'When' (1955), 'Please Come Back Home' (1955), and a song covered by Pat Boone, 'I'll Be Home' (1956). With two members of the group drafted in 1956, The Flamingos disbanded soon after the session for 'The Vow' (1956). Regrouping the following year and signing with Decca Records, the group fared poorly at the label. Moving to New York City and landing at End Records, The Flamingos struck gold with the elegant Paul Wilson co-penned ballad 'Lovers Never Say Goodbye'. Soon after, the group would score the biggest hit of its career with the exquisite doo-wop standard, 'I Only Have Eyes For You' (1959). The group's hit run continued with the Sam Cooke-penned, uncharacteristically uptempo 'Nobody Loves Me Like You Do' (1960) and 'Mio Amore' (1960). Wilson left the group in the Sixties.
CAUSE: Unknown.

Ricky Wilson

Born March 19, 1953
Died October 12, 1985
A founding member of Athens, Georgia-based, idiosyncratic new-wave group The B-52's, Ricky Wilson joined future bandmate Keith Strickland in a high school band called Black Narcissus. After graduating, Wilson and Strickland drifted through Europe. Returning to Athens, the pair formed a band with Wilson's sister Cindy, Fred Schneider, and Kate Pierson. Named for the bouffant hairdos of the two female members, the bizarrely attired B-52's popularised thrift-store clothing. Formed in 1976, the group made their public début soon after at a private Valentine's Day party. An immediate sensation in the Southern college town of Athens, the group initially performed with the taped accompaniment of a rhythm guitar, congas and tambourines. As the group's arranger and lead guitarist, Ricky Wilson teamed with electric keyboard player Kate Pierson to provide the group's trademark electronic-pop sound. Making their nightclub début in front of a sparse crowd at Max's Kansas City in New York City, The B-52's soon emerged as new-wave favourites. Attracting industry attention after pressing 2,000 copies of 'Rock Lobster' (a record cited by John Lennon as indicative of Yoko Ono's influence on new wave pop), The B-52's were signed in 1978 by Chris Blackwell of Island Records in the UK and Warner Brothers in the US. Featuring the quirky lead vocals of Fred Schneider, the group's début album, *The B-52's* (1979), became an instant classic with upbeat, lyrically amusing dance rock numbers such as 'Rock Lobster', 'Planet Claire', 'Strobe Light', and 'Quiche Lorraine'. Following up with Top 20 album *Wild*

Planet (1980), The B-52's enjoyed club and underground airplay with 'Private Idaho'. Further releases *The Party Mix Album* (1981), the David Byrne-produced *Mesopotamia* (1982), and *Whammy* (1983) were steady sellers. Showing signs of a serious illness in 1983, Ricky Wilson was forced to retire after completing the sessions for the album *Bouncing Off The Satellites* (1986). In disarray after Wilson's death, The B-52's would not record for the next several years. Keith Strickland would later assume the guitar duties, and Wilson's sister Cindy left the group in 1991 to spend more time with her family.
CAUSE: AIDS-related cancer. He died in a New York City hospital.
FURTHER READING: Brown, Rodger Lyle. (1991). *Party Out Of Bounds: The B-52's, R.E.M. & The Kids Who Rocked Athens*, Georgia. New York: New American Library.

Ron Wilson

Born March 9, 1945
Died May 19, 1989
A founding member of Sixties surf-rock group The Surfaris, Ron Wilson provided the timeless drum solo on the group's instrumental classic 'Wipe Out'. Intended as the B-side to 'Surfer Joe', 'Wipe Out' was recorded in only two takes. Featuring its memorable witch's laugh opening, 'Wipe Out' landed in the Top 10 in 1963. With most of the group members still attending high school, The Surfaris limited their touring to the Los Angeles area. After experiencing a number of problems at Dot Records, the group signed with Decca later in 1963, where they managed only limited record sales. After riding out their fame, The Surfaris disbanded in the late Sixties, occasionally re-forming for oldies revues. Leaving the music industry, Wilson became financially destitute late in life. Two years older than the Surfaris three guitarists, Ron Wilson was the cousin of Beach Boys members Brian, Carl, and Dennis Wilson.
CAUSE: Brain aneurysm. He died in Dutch Flats, California.

Tom Wilson

Born March 25, 1931
Died September, 1978
A talented producer at CBS Records, Tom Wilson was best known for his work with Bob Dylan and Simon & Garfunkel. Producing Dylan's 1965 album, *Highway 61 Revisited*, Wilson allowed an unknown pianist named Al Kooper to play the swirling, atmospheric Hammond organ on 'Like A Rolling Stone'. Signing Simon & Garfunkel to CBS, Wilson gained accolades for dubbing drums, electric guitar, and bass on to the duo's previously ignored, acoustic track, 'Sound Of Silence' which became a US Number 1 hit as a result. Later moving to Verve Records, Wilson produced The Velvet Underground, Nico and, after catching a performance of Frank Zappa at the Whisky-A-Go-Go nightclub, the début album by The Mothers of Invention, *Freak Out!* Wilson also produced albums for Country Joe & The Fish, Eric Burdon & The Animals, Cecil Taylor, John Coltrane, and Fraternity of Man.
CAUSE: Heart attack.

Victor Ray Wilson

Born February 20, 1959
Died April 30, 1996
Nicknamed "Beatmaster V", Victor Ray Wilson was the original drummer of the rap/heavy metal outfit Body Count, the backing group of controversial gangster rapper Ice-T. Formed in south-central Los Angeles in 1989, Body Count included several friends from Crenshaw High School. First teaming with Ice-T in 1991 for the Lollapalooza tour, the group released its début album in 1992. A strong seller, *Body Count* created a storm of controversy with

inflammatory tracks such as 'KKK Bitch' and 'Cop Killer', the latter glorifying the murder of police officers in the wake of the Rodney King beating. With the album criticised by actor Charlton Heston and others, police groups organised a boycott of the group's label, Time-Warner. With their label buckling, Ice-T and Body Count were signed by Virgin Records. The group's follow-up album, *Born Dead* (1994), was less incendiary.
CAUSE: Leukaemia. He died at his home in Los Angeles.

Ronald Winans

Born June 30, 1956
Died June 17, 2005
A member of the celebrated, R&B-styled family gospel act The Winans, Ronald Winans was the second eldest in a large family of ten siblings. Teaming in the late Seventies with his three younger brothers – Marvin, Carvin and Michael – Ronald first formed the contemporary-style gospel act. Beginning with their début album *Introducing The Winans* (1981), they merged modern soul and R&B with traditional gospel themes and drew praise for tracks like 'The Question Is'. Signing with the Quincy Jones-owned Qwest label in 1985, the group simultaneously built audiences in the gospel and secular communities, appearing on the R&B charts with 'Let My People Go', continuing with the Anita Baker duet 'Ain't No Need To Worry' featuring a guest rap by Teddy Riley, 'It's Time', 'A Friend', 'When You Cry', and 'Payday'. Establishing a series of gospel workshops in 1987, Ronald formed an offshoot group, Ron Winans Family & Friends, which spawned the careers of Darrell Hines, Kayla Parker and Donnie McClurkin as well as other members of the Winans family including the youngest two siblings, BeBe and CeCe, who formed a successful gospel duo. The entire Winans family assembled for a tour across the US in 2002. In January 2005, Ronald released his final album, *Ron Winans Family & Friends V: A Celebration*, exactly eight years after nearly losing his life from a heart attack. In addition to his musical career, Ronald Winans was a minister and operated a number of restaurants in partnership with singer Gladys Knight.
CAUSE: Contracting pneumonia following a bout of congestive heart failure, he died at Harper Hospital in Detroit. He had previously suffered a heart attack in 1997 and was declared "clinically dead" at the time but, after his family prayed over him, he miraculously returned to life.

Kai Winding

(KAI CHRESTEN WINDING)
Born May 18, 1922
Died May 6, 1983
Born in Denmark, but a resident of the US from 1934, jazz trombonist Kai Winding landed a Top 10 hit in 1963 with 'More', the instrumental theme from the film *Mondo Cane*. Winding had performed with Benny Goodman and Stan Kenton in the Forties, and in a combo with J.J. John in the mid Fifties. Winding was later hired by Hugh Hefner as the musical director for his chain of Playboy clubs, and in the Seventies he joined Merv Griffin's television band.
CAUSE: Complications from a brain tumour. He died in Yonkers, New York.

Billy Windsor

(JAMES WINDSOR)
Born 1944
Died January 5, 1994
A vocalist, songwriter, and rhythm guitarist, Billy Windsor backed rock artist Danny Gatton off and on for 20 years. Windsor's last collaborative effort with Gatton came with the 1993 Elektra Records release, *Cruisin' Dueces*. Windsor also operated a nightclub.
CAUSE: He suffered a heart attack at

his home in Hughesville, Virginia. Gatton died later in the year.

Kurt Winter

Born April 2, 1946
Died December 14, 1997
A member of Canadian rock band The Guess Who, Winnipeg-native Kurt Winter appeared on a number of hook-laden hits in the Seventies. Winter was previously a member of the group Brother, which was signed to the same label as The Guess Who. With founder Randy Bachman leaving the group in 1970, Kurt Winter and Greg Leskiw were added as his replacements. Joining just after the success of 'American Woman', the pair first appeared on the album *Share The Land*, which featured two Winter-composed hits, 'Bus Rider' and 'Hand Me Down World'. Nicknamed "The Walrus", Winter also co-wrote The Guess Who hits, 'Clap For The Wolfman' and 'Raindance'. Winter and bandmate Don McDonell were fired in 1974 by Burton Cummings. The Guess Who would disband the following year.
CAUSE: Suffering from a long-term bleeding ulcer, he succumbed to liver failure. He died in a Winnipeg, Manitoba, hospital.

Jimmy Witherspoon

Born August 8, 1923
Died September 18, 1997
A blues shouter, Jimmy Witherspoon enjoyed a strong hit run in the Forties. A native of Arkansas, Witherspoon left the world of gospel music and moved to Los Angeles at age 16. After a stint in the merchant marines, Witherspoon returned to California in 1944. Auditioning for bandleader Jay McShann during a stop in Vallejo, California, the deep-voiced Witherspoon replaced vocalist Walter Brown in 1944. Remaining in the shadows of McShann's band, Witherspoon was little known until the release of the chart-topping R&B smash 'Ain't Nobody's Business', the track featuring the bluesy piano of Jay McShann. Amicably parting with McShann in 1947, Witherspoon landed a major hit with a cover of the blues standard 'Ain't Nobody's Business' (1949) and followed up with 'In The Evening When The Sun Goes Down' (1949), 'No Rollin' Blues' (1949), and 'Wind Is Blowing'. His career hampered by the rise of doo-wop groups, Witherspoon declared bankruptcy in 1953. Rediscovered after an appearance at the 1959 Monterey Jazz Festival, Witherspoon took a stylistic turn toward jazz. During the next decade, he would record with leading jazzmen such as Gerry Mulligan, Jack McDuff, and Richard "Grooves" Holmes. Also an actor, Witherspoon appeared in several feature films including *To Sleep With Anger*, and in the Seventies gave up touring for DJ work at KMET in Los Angeles. Lured back to the stage by Eric Burdon, Witherspoon landed a surprise R&B chart hit in 1975 with 'Love Is A Five Letter Word'. Although diagnosed with throat cancer in the 1984, and told by doctors he would never again sing, Witherspoon was back on the road within a year. Performing until shortly before his death, he earned a Grammy nomination for the album *Live At The Mint* (1995).
CAUSE: Succumbing to throat cancer, he died in his sleep at his home in Los Angeles.

Norma-Jean Wofford

Born October 20, 1938
Died April 30, 2005
Nicknamed "The Duchess", Norma-Jean Wofford tantalised audiences with her skin-tight stage outfits as a member of Bo Diddley's band. A native of Pittsburgh, she was trained to play guitar by Diddley and joined his touring group in 1962 as a replacement for Peggy Jones. In order to protect her from the dangers of the

road, Diddley would claim she was his sister. First recording with Diddley on the album *Bo Diddley & Company*, she was prominently featured on his album covers, and also backed Diddley in the 1965 concert performance film *The Big TNT Show*. Leaving Bo's group in 1966 to marry, she settled in Florida. CAUSE: Unknown.

Wolfman Jack

(ROBERT WESTON SMITH)
Born January 21, 1938
Died July 1, 1997
A legendary rock DJ and impresario, Wolfman Jack first garnered fame in the Sixties on a Mexican radio station just south of the Texas border. A native of Brooklyn, he was initially drawn to rock music as a fan of DJ and promoter Alan Freed. Pestering Freed at his legendary Paramount Theater concerts in the Fifties, the young teenager gradually gained Freed's trust and was permitted backstage. Subsequently hanging out with a radio engineer at WNJR in New Jersey in his late teens, he learned the business of radio. Booted from his home by his father's new wife, the teenager moved in with a married sister and attended broadcasting school. Landing a DJ position at a black Virginia radio station WYOU, he initially assumed the moniker of Daddy Jules. Fooling audiences with his black-styled dialect, he would adopt several radio names before settling on "Wolfman Jack". Gaining control of Mexican border station XERF, which illegally boomed a massive 250,000 watts, Wolfman Jack could be heard in two-thirds of the US. In addition to playing music, he made millions by hawking a variety of mail-order products. Returning to the US and taping his Mexican radio show, he took a second DJ post at KCIJ in Shreveport, Louisiana. Remaining a shadowy figure until making his first public appearances in 1963, Wolfman Jack emerged as a rock celebrity. Moving to Minneapolis, he was placed in charge of KUXL, where he DJd under his real name, Bob Smith. Simultaneously assuming control of Tijuana-based XERB from 1966–71, he programmed the Mexican R&B station from a Los Angeles studio. Finally going legit in 1971, Wolfman Jack landed at prominent stations KDAY in Los Angeles, and then, WNBC in New York. Meanwhile, he syndicated his XERB programmes for airing on US Armed Forces Radio. Landing a Top 40 hit in 1974, Wolfman Jack provided the talking co-vocals on The Guess Who's single 'Clap For The Wolfman'. Also appearing on television, he co-hosted the NBC night music programme, *Midnight Special*, from 1972–81. As an actor, he portrayed himself in the 1974 film *American Graffiti*, and subsequently turned down a role in TV's *Happy Days*. Comfortably wealthy, Wolfman Jack remained out of the media spotlight in the Eighties.
CAUSE: Although trimming 40 pounds shortly before his death, he remained severely overweight. Suffering a heart attack in the driveway of his home in Belvidere, North Carolina, he hugged his wife and then collapsed. He had just completed a 20-day promotional tour for his just published autobiography.
FURTHER READING: Wolfman Jack. (1995). *Have Mercy: Confessions Of The Original Rock'n'Roll Animal*. New York: Warner.

Richard Wolfson

(RICHARD JONATHAN WOLFSON)
Born April 25, 1955
Died February 1, 2005
A member of indie new-wave rock act Fischer-Z, multi-instrumentalist Richard Wolfson played on a pair of minor UK Eighties hits, 'The Worker' and 'So Long'. He later joined Andy Saunders to head the multi-media act Towering Inferno. A self-taught

guitarist, Wolfson studied theatre and music at the University of York.
CAUSE: He suffered a ruptured aorta.

John Wolters

(JOHN CHRISTIAN WOLTERS)
Born April 28, 1945
Died June 16, 1997
The drummer and backing vocalist of Dr. Hook, John Wolters initially joined a predecessor of the group in 1968 called The Chocolate Papers. Leaving the following year, Wolters rejoined the Ray Sawyer-fronted country-rock group in 1974 after they had established themselves with the international hit 'Sylvia's Mother'. With Dr. Hook jumping to Capitol Records, Wolters initially appeared on the group's label début, *Bankrupt* (1975), which was highlighted by a cover of Sam Cooke's 'Only Sixteen'. The follow-up album, *A Little Bit More*, featured 'A Little Bit More' and the British hit, 'If Not You'. Taking a pop turn, Dr. Hook continued their hit run with "Sharing The Night Together' (1978), 'When You're In Love With A Beautiful Woman' (1979), 'Better Love Next Time' (1979), and 'Sexy Eyes' (1980). With the group disbanding in 1982, Wolters later worked at Hearts of Space Records.
CAUSE: Liver cancer. He died in San Francisco.

Harry Womack

(HARRIS WOMACK)
Born June 25, 1945
Died March, 1974
A member of the Sixties family soul group The Valentinos, Harry Womack enjoyed a brief hit run in the Sixties. Discovered during a 1952 stop in Cleveland by Sam Cooke who was then the lead singer of the gospel greats The Soul Stirrers, Harry Womack was a member of a child gospel act with his brothers Cecil, Curtis, Friendly and Bobby. Signed to the Sam Cooke-owned SAR label in 1962 initially as a gospel group called The Womack Brothers, Bobby Womack and the others switched to secular music as The Valentinos. Under the personal direction of Cooke, The Valentinos scored a Top 10 R&B hit with 'Lookin' For A Love' (1962). A later release, 'It's All Over Now' (1964), was a much bigger hit for The Rolling Stones. With the closure of SAR Records following Cooke's death in 1965, The Valentinos signed with Chess Records.
CAUSE: He was stabbed to death by his wife.

Andrew Wood

Born January 8, 1966
Died March 19, 1990
A pioneering grunge-rocker, Andrew Wood achieved little in the way of fame during his brief career but his attitude and style were an inspiration to several groups that came out of his native Seattle in the early Nineties, most notably Nirvana and Pearl Jam. Wood began writing music as a young child and, adopting the stage name of Landrew The Love Child in 1980, became the lead singer of a punk-rock band called Malfunkshun. With the group taking a glam-rock turn, Wood donned glittery costumes and platform boots, sticking out like a sore thumb in the middle of Seattle's hard rock scene. The group floundered after contributing tracks for a few local compilation albums, and disbanded in 1988. Wood subsequently teamed with the remnants of another local group, Green River, and formed The Lords Of The Wasteland. With Wood playing bass and providing lead vocals in the renamed Mother Love Bone, the group found an immediate local following with its punk-grunge hybrid sound. After recording a critically acclaimed EP for Starday/Polydor in 1989, the band was poised for stardom. With Wood quitting drugs for the sake of the band (he had previously been admitted to a rehab programme in 1985), Mother Love Bone recorded their first full album in 1990, *Apple*; the project

was posthumously released after Wood's death. Wood had also been in discussions to record a solo album. Members of Mother Love Bone later surfaced in the groups Temple Of The Dog, Soundgarden and Pearl Jam.
CAUSE: After completing the sessions for the group's only album, Wood returned to his drug habit and overdosed on heroin. Found unconscious by his girlfriend, he died three days later after life-support was disconnected.

Chris Wood

Born June 24, 1944
Died July 12, 1983
A member of the legendary British rock group Traffic, Birmingham-born Chris Wood juggled his time in the mid-Sixties between art school and musical pursuits. Playing a variety of instruments including saxophone, flute, and keyboard, Wood passed through several local bands such as Sounds Of Blue, Locomotive and, in their embryonic stage, Chicken Shack. In 1966, Wood joined Jim Capaldi, Dave Mason and former Spencer Davis Group vocalist Steve Winwood in forming Traffic. Wood and Winwood had often crossed paths in the clubs of Birmingham. Setting up camp in a house deep in the Berkshire countryside, the group worked together on the songs for its first album and established a much copied modus operandi for "getting it together in the country". Signed by Island Records in 1967, Traffic announced themselves with three charming hit singles 'Paper Sun', 'Hole In My Shoe' and 'Here We Go Round The Mulberry Bush', and thereafter concentrated on the albums market. Their début album, *Mr. Fantasy*, was a pioneering foray into psychedelic rock; the title track rumoured to be a tribute to Jimi Hendrix. A year later the group's eponymous second album included the much-covered track 'Feelin' Alright'; another cut, '40,000 Headmen', was highlighted by Wood's exquisite flute playing. A versatile musician, Wood introduced a host of non-traditional instruments into Traffic's music, and often played the electric organ or piano on stage while Winwood played guitar. With Traffic disbanding in late 1968, Wood joined bandmates Dave Mason and Jim Capaldi in the short-lived group, Mason, Capaldi, Wood & Frog. During this time, Wood was also involved with Dr. John and Ginger Baker's Airforce. In 1970, Wood and Capaldi were invited by Winwood to help him record a solo album. In the event, this turned out as another Traffic album, *John Barleycorn Must Die*, from which the group would land a hit with 'Empty Pages'. Following the release of *The Low Spark Of High Heeled Boys* (1971), which was highlighted by 'Rock'n'Roll Stew', the group was sidelined when Winwood was stricken with peritonitis. After experiencing a series of personnel changes, Traffic released *Shoot Out At The Fantasy Factory* (1973), which contained the Wood composition, 'Tragic Magic'. Traffic disbanded the following year after the release of *When The Eagle Flies*. As a session player, Wood also worked with Jimi Hendrix, Jim Capaldi, John Martyn, Shawn Phillips, and Third World. Wood was working on a solo album at the time of his death.
CAUSE: A known abuser of drugs and alcohol, Wood's death is alternately attributed to cancer or liver failure. Either way, Wood had been ill for some time and died at Queen Elizabeth Hospital in Birmingham. Traffic's sometime percussionist, Reebob Kwaku Baah, had died of a brain haemorrhage earlier in the year.

Kent Wood

(KENT RICARDO WOOD)
Born 1967
Died December 31, 2005
A member of R&B/rap act E.U., Kent Wood replaced original keyboardist

Jerry Parker. Emerging from Washington DC's "go-go" music scene, E.U. (short for Experience Unlimited) scored several club hits beginning in 1988 with 'Da' Butt' from the film *School Daze*. E.U. followed with the Wood co-composition 'Buck Wild', 'Taste Of Your Love' and 'I Confess', and backed Salt-N-Pepa on the hit 'Shake Your Thing'. A self-taught musician, Wood also worked with Eva Cassidy, Chuck Brown, and with Britney Spears on her hit album *Oops! . . . . I Did It Again*.
CAUSE: He died in a single car accident on Route 3 in Orange County, Virginia. He had just left his preacher father's church.

Peter Woods

Born 1950
Died December 1993
A talented session player who worked with a series of leading pop and rock acts, keyboardist Peter Woods (a.k.a. Peter Wood) joined Sutherland Brothers & Quiver – an amalgamation of two separate acts – in 1972. After recording three albums and achieving two UK hits in 1976 with 'Arms Of Mary' and 'Secrets', Woods left to form Natural Gas (with Joey Molland, Mark Clarke and Jerry Shirley) releasing a self-titled album. During the mid to late Seventies, Woods also appeared on a number of Al Stewart albums – including *Past, Present And Future*, *Modern Times*, *Year Of The Cat* and *Time Passages* – and occasionally joined Stewart on the road. Woods also played with Pink Floyd on *The Wall* tour, and later backed Roger Waters for *The Wall* performance in Berlin in July 1990. A prolific session player, Woods also worked with Lou Reed (*New Sensations*), Curved Air (*Midnight Wire*), Tom Paxton (*Something In My Life*), Joan Armatrading (*Joan Armatrading*), Wishbone Ash (*Locked In*), Freddie Salem (*Cat Dance*), Cyndi Lauper (*True Colors*; *She's So Unusual*), Graham Parker (*The Up Escalator*), Carly Simon (*Hello Big Man*), Martin Briley (*Dangerous Moments*), Scandal (*Warrior*) and Julian Lennon (*Valotte*).
CAUSE: Suicide. He died in New York City.

Sonny Woods

Born c. 1930
Died September 1982
The bass vocalist of the popular Fifties R&B group The Royals/Midnighters, Sonny Woods was born in Winston-Salem, North Carolina, but raised in Detroit. After a stint as a chauffeur/ roadie for The Orioles, Woods quit in December 1951 after a traffic accident which killed member Tommy Gaither. Returning to Detroit, Woods formed a vocal group called The Thrillers, which soon evolved into The Royals. Hearing fellow Ford assembly-line worker Hank Ballard singing on the job, Woods invited him to join the group. Signing with King Records with the aid of Johnny Otis, The Royals landed a string of hits beginning with 'With Every Beat Of My Heart' (1952). With Lawson Smith drafted into the army, Ballard emerged as the group's new lead singer. When audiences began confusing The Royals with their much more successful labelmates, the similarly named "5" Royales, Woods' group reaped unexpected interest. Dropping romantic ballads for a raunchy brand of R&B, The Royals landed in the R&B charts with the bawdy 'Get It'. Forced by their label to change their moniker, the renamed Midnighters scored one of the most influential R&B hits of the decade with 'Work With Me Annie' (1954). Banned by radio for its sexually charged lyrics, the song spawned a massive Annie craze. While The Midnighters would follow with 'Annie Had A Baby', 'Annie's Aunt Fanny', and 'Henry's Got Flat Feet', a host of R&B acts would release their own Annie answer songs, most notably Etta James' similarly patterned 'The Wallflower Song (Roll With Me

Henry)'. Other Midnighters hits included 'Sexy Ways' (1954) and 'It's Love Baby (24 Hours A Day)' (1955). Although landing few hits in the next several years, The Midnighters remained a popular concert attraction. Leaving The Midnighters in 1958, Woods was replaced by Norman Thrasher. Woods later worked in record distribution.
CAUSE: He suffered a heart attack in Atlanta.

Willie Woods

Born September 5, 1936
Died May 27, 1997
A songwriter and guitarist with Jr. Walker & The All Stars, Willie Woods was a member of the R&B group during its entire hit run. Woods and Walker had previously been bandmates in a mid Fifties, South Bend, Indiana-based R&B group called The Jumping Jacks. Discovered by former Moonglows singer Harvey Fuqua, the group first recorded on the Fuqua-owned Harvey Records in 1962. When Harvey Records was purchased by Motown, the group recorded for the Motown subsidiary Soul Records, landing a Top 10 entry with 'Shotgun'. The group's hit run continued into the Seventies with '(I'm A) Road Runner' (1966), 'How Sweet It Is (To Be Loved By You)', and 'What Does It Take (To Win Your Love)' (1969).
CAUSE: Lung cancer. He died in Kalamazoo, Michigan.

Patrick Woodward

Born August 29, 1948
Died December 31, 1985
The bassist of Ricky Nelson's back-up group The Stone Canyon Band, Patrick Woodward was hired by Nelson in 1983. Nelson had caught a performance of a Long Beach, California-based group called The Rockin' Shadows and hired both Woodward and bandmate Rick Intveld.
CAUSE: He died as the result of an on-board fire in a DC-3 aeroplane, near Dekalb, Texas, en route from Guttersville, Alabama, to Dallas for half-time festivities at the Cotton Bowl. Killed were Ricky Nelson and six others. The pilots survived. A wrongful death lawsuit was later filed by Woodward's widow Jodie against four aviation firms.

Allen Woody

(DOUGLAS ALLEN WOODY)
Born October 2, 1956
Died circa August 26, 2000
The bassist and mandolin player of Georgia-based jam band Gov't Mule, Nashville native Allen Woody was reared on blues and Southern rock. After joining a band headed by former Lynyrd Skynyrd drummer Artimus Pyle, Woody was introduced to The Allman Brothers' drummer Butch Trucks. When The Allman Brothers re-formed after a seven-year hiatus in 1989, Woody was hired as bassist; the fourth person to hold the bass player's position in the group. Woody also co-wrote a number of songs for the group and, as a side project, he teamed with bandmates Warren Hayes and Matt Abts to form the trio Gov't Mule. Though Woody and Abts left the Allmans in 1997 to devote their energies to their new band, they remained on friendly terms. Gov't Mule released several albums including *Live . . . With A Little Help From Our Friends* (1999), which featured musicians from Sea Level, The Allman Brothers and Parliament-Funkadelic.
CAUSE: He was discovered dead in his room at the Marriott Court Hotel in Queens, New York. Although an autopsy was unable to determine the cause of his death, he probably died from a heart attack.

Sheb Wooley

(SHELBY F. WOOLEY)
Born April 10, 1921
Died September 17, 2003

Primarily a country singer, Sheb Wooley scored a crossover hit with one of his many novelty songs, the chart-topping 'The Purple People Eater' (1958). Also an actor, he appeared in numerous films and on television shows such as *Rawhide*, *The Lone Ranger* and *Death Valley Days*. He sometimes recorded under the name Ben Colder.
CAUSE: Leukaemia. He died at Skyline Medical Center in Nashville.

Hal Worthington

(HAROLD WORTHINGTON)
Born 1947
Died February 20, 1990
The leader of The Unifics, Hal Worthington formed the soul outfit in 1967 while attending Howard University in his hometown of Washington DC. Featuring lead singer Al Johnson, The Unifics delivered tight, soulful harmonies. Impressed by the dance moves of Motown groups such as The Temptations and Four Tops, Worthington choreographed The Unific's stage show. Signed by Kapp Records in 1968, the group was teamed with producer Guy Draper for the hits 'Court Of Love' (1968), 'The Beginning Of My End' (1968), and 'It's A Groovy World' (1969). After the group was dropped by Kapp in 1969, Worthington and bandmate Michael Ward quit the following year. The Unifics disbanded in 1972.
CAUSE: He was killed in a Washington DC suburb, shot to death by two gunmen at Player's Billiard Parlor and Restaurant. He was an innocent bystander during a gang related shooting. The gunmen were later captured.

Doug Wray

(DOUGLAS LEON WRAY)
Born July 4, 1933
Died April 1984
A member of Link Wray's backing band The Ray Men, drummer Doug Wray had performed with his brother for a decade before achieving success in the late Fifties. Joined by a third brother, Vernon, Doug and Link Wray originally formed The Lazy Pine Wranglers, renamed The Palomino Ranch Hands and then Link Wray & His Ray Men, who had two instrumental hits on the pop charts, 'Rumble' and 'Raw-Hide'. Before forming The Ray Men, Doug had been a member of Jimmy Dean's group and, in later years, operated a barber shop, occasionally rejoining brother Link in the studio and on stage.
CAUSE: Heart attack.

Link Wray

(FREDERICK LINCOLN WRAY, JR.)
Born May 2, 1929
Died November 5, 2005
Best remembered for his raw fuzz guitar and power chord style, rockabilly pioneer Link Wray achieved his sound by putting holes in his speakers. From Dunn, North Carolina, Link claimed to have learned to play guitar at age eight from a travelling circus performer named Hambone. After serving in the Army and contracting tuberculosis, which led to the loss of a lung, Link initially assembled a group with his brothers Vernon and Doug and cousin Shorty Horton called The Lazy Pine Wranglers; later renamed Lucky Wray & The Palomino Ranch Hands and finally Link Ray & His Ray Men. In the late Fifties the group had two instrumental hits, the influential 'Rumble' (in 1958), which was widely banned by radio stations across America, despite the fact that it had no lyrics, and a cover of 'Raw-Hide'. Link Wray continued to make instrumental records before temporarily retiring from music in the late Sixties. Attempting a comeback during the late Seventies, Wray collaborated with rockabilly revivalist Robert Gordon and drew further interest when his music was cited by a new wave of garage acts like The Cramps, whose sound owed him a considerable debt. Settling in Copenhagen, Denmark,

Wray continued to tour on the back of this interest and received more exposure as a result of 'Rumble' being included in Quentin Tarantino's quirky film *Pulp Fiction*. A number of guitarists have cited Wray as an influence including Pete Townshend (who wrote the liner notes to Wray's 1974 album *The Link Wray Rumble*), Dave Davies and Jerry Garcia.
CAUSE: Probably heart failure. He died in Copenhagen, Denmark.

Billy Wright

Born May 23, 1918
Died October 28, 1991
A flamboyant R&B singer who influenced many rock and blues singers including Little Richard, Atlanta-native Billy Wright began singing as a child at The Mount Vernon Baptist Church. Switching to secular music in his teens, Wright emerged as a top-notch nightclub entertainer. Aided by Paul Williams (of 'The Hucklebuck' fame), Wright was signed by Savoy Records. With his wailing gospel/blues delivery, Wright scored several R&B hits including the double-sided entry, 'Blues For My Baby'/'You Satisfy' (1949), 'Stacked Deck' (1951), and 'Hey Little Girl' (1951). Renowned for his pompadour and flashy, outrageous costumes, he was nicknamed "The Prince Of Blues". Wright remained active in Atlanta into the Seventies as a performer and nightclub emcee.
CAUSE: Pulmonary embolism. He died in Atlanta.

Harold "Sonny" Wright

Born c. 1935
Died April 7, 1996
The lead singer of the Fifties Harlem-based doo-wop outfit The Diamonds (not the white, Toronto group), Harold "Sonny" Wright formed the group in 1951 originally as The Three Aces. Featuring Wright's smooth tenor, the group's hits at Atlantic Records included 'A Beggar For Your Kisses', 'I'll Live Again', and 'Romance In The Dark'. After disbanding The Diamonds, Wright joined a succession of groups beginning with The Metronomes. After beating a drug addiction in the Sixties, Wright launched The ARC Choir, a gospel ensemble initially formed to raise money for The Addicts Rehabilitation Center in Harlem.
CAUSE: Heart failure. He died at his apartment in Harlem.

O.V. Wright

(OVERTON VERTIS WRIGHT)
Born October 10, 1939
Died November 16, 1980
A gospel-trained soul artist who scored a long string of minor Southern-style, R&B hits, Tennessee-native O.V. Wright emerged out of the gospel tradition. A deeply soulful singer in the tradition of Otis Redding, Wright joined a series of leading gospel groups, Spirit Of Memphis, The Highway QCs, and the legendary Soul Stirrers. Switching to secular material, Wright débuted on Goldwax Records in 1964 with the sizzling 'That's How Strong My Love Is'. Landing at the Duke subsidiary Back Beat Records, Wright hit his stride with producer Willie Mitchell on soulful gems such as 'You're Gonna Make Me Cry' (1965), 'Eight Men, Four Women' (1967), and 'Ace Of Spades' (1970). Jailed on a drug conviction, Wright's career was interrupted in the Seventies. Wright subsequently signed with Hi Records in 1975 and was befriended by labelmate Otis Clay.
CAUSE: Heart failure. Stricken while on stage at Joe Moore's Lakeside Lounge in Grand Bay, Alabama, he was rushed to Providence Hospital in nearby Mobile the following morning where he died shortly thereafter. He had a history of heart problems.

Syreeta Wright

Born August 3, 1946
Died July 6, 2004
A recording artist at Motown, Syreeta

Wright was initially hired as a secretary for producer William "Mickey" Stevenson. Originally from Pittsburgh, at age 11 she had moved to Detroit with her mother. Wright occasionally joined Stevenson on Motown sessions, providing backing vocals or handclaps. Finally permitted to issue her own material, in 1968 she recorded the Nick Ashford and Valerie Simpson-produced single 'I Can't Give Back The Love I Feel For You' under the name Rita Wright. According to Mary Wilson in her autobiography *Dream Girls: My Life As A Supreme*, Wright angered Motown chief Berry Gordy by refusing to replace the departing Diana Ross in The Supremes in 1969. As a songwriter, Wright joined her future husband Stevie Wonder in composing 'Signed, Sealed, Delivered, I'm Yours' (1970) and The Spinners' hit 'It's A Shame' (1970). Wonder produced Wright's début album, *Syreeta*, the first of nine albums during her career and, although the couple divorced in 1974, Wright continued to provide backing vocals on Wonder's releases, wrote many of his lyrics and was a member of his touring group, Wonderlove. In 1980, she teamed with Billy Preston for the ballad 'With You I'm Born Again' and in the wake of the single's success, Motown issued an album of Wright/Preston duets. As a session vocalist, Wright also worked with Michael Bolton, Quincy Jones, Kirk Whalum and Nelson Rangell. In 1994, Wright joined a touring production of *Jesus Christ Superstar* in the role of Mary Magdalene.
CAUSE: She died in Los Angeles after suffering from bone cancer for two years.

Johnny Wyatt

Born October 6, 1938
Died December 1983
As a member of Los Angeles-based R&B group Rochell & The Candles, Johnny Wyatt scored a crossover hit in 1961 with 'Once Upon A Time'. The record was released on the Swingin' label, co-owned by legendary Los Angeles deejay Hunter Hancock. Wyatt also released a series of solo singles and headed his own group, The Hightones.
CAUSE: Unknown.

Howard Wyeth

(HOWARD PYLE WYETH)
Born April 22, 1944
Died March 29, 1996
The drummer for Bob Dylan during his Rolling Thunder Revue in the mid Seventies, Howard Wyeth also appeared on two Dylan albums, *Desire* and *Hard Rain*. Wyeth also backed Roger McGuinn and Don McLean, and appeared on four albums with Robert Gordon. In the Nineties, he was leading The Howie Wyeth Ragtime Band in the clubs of New York City.
CAUSE: Heart attack. He died at St. Vincent's Hospital in New York City.

Tammy Wynette

(VIRGINIA WYNETTE PUGH)
Born May 5, 1942
Died April 6, 1998
A country music superstar, singer Tammy Wynette was dubbed "The First Lady Of Country Music". Her father dying when she was not yet one, Wynette was raised by her mother and grandmother in Birmingham, Alabama. After teaching herself to play the guitar and piano, Wynette took formal singing lessons. Divorced at a young age, Wynette was forced to supplement her beautician earnings with nightclub work to pay the medical bills when the youngest of her three children was stricken with spinal meningitis. After appearing in 1965 on a local television programme *The Country Boy Eddie*, and then the nationally syndicated *Porter Wagoner Show*, she relocated to Nashville in 1966. Aided by her longtime manager Billy Sherrill, Wynette landed the first

of dozens of country hits with a Johnny Paycheck co-composition 'Apartment No. 9' (1966). The following year, she would score the first of 20 country chart toppers with 'Take Me To Your World'. Wynette scored the biggest hit of her career with the first of two crossover hits, the anti-feminist paean 'Stand By Your Man' (1968), a song featured in the film *Five Easy Pieces*. Marrying country star George Jones in 1969, it was no secret that Wynette suffered abuse from her hard-drinking husband. Billed as Mr. and Mrs. Country Music, the couple collaborated on a number of recordings before divorcing in 1975. (Wynette reunited with George Jones in the studio for several projects in the Nineties including the 1995 album *One* and a subsequent 35-city tour.) In 1978 Wynette married her former producer George Richey, the last of her four husbands. Dogged by poor health in the Eighties, Wynette had limited chart success but remained a revered figure in country circles. In 1992, she landed a surprise hit, 'Justified & Ancient', with the British electronic duo KLF. Teaming with Dolly Parton and Loretta Lynn in 1993, Wynette recorded the album *Honky Tonk Angels*. In all, Wynette would record over 50 albums.
CAUSE: Suffering from poor health for much of her life, she had undergone approximately 20 operations for various ailments. Her personal physician, Dr. Wallis March, attributed Wynette's death to a blood clot in the lung, which occurred while napping on a couch in her Nashville home. Unconvinced by the official ruling, Wynette's daughters contacted the Nashville medical examiner, and demanded the body be exhumed for an autopsy. They subsequently sued her mother's doctor and manager-husband for $50 million, charging that Wynette's health was not well monitored. After Wynette's widower, George Richey, ordered the exhumation, he was dropped from the lawsuit. The coroner's report confirmed the doctor's findings of death. In 2002, a secret out-of-court settlement was reached between Dr. March and Wynette's daughters.
FURTHER READING: Wynette, Tammy. (1980). *Stand By Your Man: An Autobiography*. New York: Pocket.

Phillipe Wynne

(PHILIP WALKER)
Born April 3, 1938
Died July 14, 1984
The tenor vocalist in The Spinners, Cincinnati-born Phillipe Wynne was reared on gospel music in his church choir. In 1968, Wynne toured Europe with The Afro-Kings but he refused to live on the African continent and quit the group. Returning to Cincinnati and attending Xavier University, he auditioned for The Spinners in 1971, replacing G.C. Cameron on lead vocals when the group left Motown for Atlantic Records. The Spinners also included baritone Henry Fambrough, bass vocalist Pervis Jackson, and two more tenors, Billy Henderson and Bobbie Smith. With Wynne composing most of the group's hits, The Spinners were at the forefront of "Philly Soul" with hits such as 'I'll Be Around' (1972), 'Could It Be I'm Falling In Love?' (1972) and 'One Of A Kind (Love Affair)' (1973). Leaving the group in 1977, Wynne scored his final Spinners hit with 'Rubberband Man'. Wynne was replaced by John Edwards, who had previously filled in during Wynne's hospitalisation in 1975 for tonsillitis. Shortening his last name to Wynn, as a soloist, he managed only one hit, 'Hats Off To Mama', a single culled from his Atlantic album, *Starting All Over*. In the Eighties, Wynne joined George Clinton's P-Funk family during the 'Uncle Jam' tour and appeared on Funkadelic's R&B hit, '(Not Just) Knee Deep – Part 1' (1979). After fulfilling his legal obligations to

Clinton, in 1983, Wynne released a self-titled album, aided by Sugar Hill label owner Sylvia Robinson.
CAUSE: Heart attack. He collapsed during a solo performance after jumping into the audience at the Jack London Square nightclub in Oakland, California.

Y

Yana

(Pamela Guard)
Born February 16, 1932
Died November 21, 1988
A British pop singer and actress, the elegant Yana had several hits in the Fifties. A former fashion model, she began her career when dared by friends to take the stage. Impressing the club owner, she was hired on the spot. In the Fifties, Yana starred in her own BBC television series, and later appeared in numerous stage musicals. Retiring from music for a time in the early Eighties, she worked in a pharmacy.
Cause: Suffering from throat cancer, she died at Middlesex Hospital in London.

Rev. Marvin J. Yancy

Born May 31, 1950
Died March 22, 1985
An R&B songwriter and record producer, Reverend Marvin J. Yancy was also pastor of a Chicago church. Teaming in 1971 with Chuck Jackson (the younger brother of Jesse Jackson, and not the more famous soul singer of the same name), Yancy had intended to form a writing and production team but after a year of collaborative work, Yancy and Jackson formed the popular soul group, The Independents. Preferring a behind the scenes role, Yancy quit the group. With Yancy and Jackson teaming on production and songwriting, The Independents enjoyed a hit run in the early Seventies with: 'Just As Long As You Need Me, Part 1' (1972), the million-selling 'Leaving Me' (1973), 'It's All Over' (1973), and 'Let This Be A Lesson To You' (1974). Beginning in 1975, Yancy and Jackson began collaborating with Yancy's future wife, Natalie Cole, producing all of her material until 1982. Yancy won Grammys for producing Cole's hits, 'This Will Be', 'Inseparable', and 'Sophisticated Lady'. (Yancy and Cole divorced in 1979.) Yancy also worked with gospel acts and was nominated for a Grammy for an album by his church's choir. Trained at the Moody Bible Institute and the Chicago Bible Institute, Yancy succeeded his father in 1977 as the pastor of the Fountain of Life Baptist Church.
Cause: He suffered a heart attack at his home in Chicago.

Zal Yanovsky

(Zallman Yanovsky)
Born December 19, 1944
Died December 13, 2002
A member of The Lovin' Spoonful, bohemian Zallman "Zal" Yanovsky provided the lively guitar on most of the group's hits. Hailing from Toronto, Yanovsky dropped out of Downsview Collegiate Institute at 16. Drawn to folk music, he worked the Toronto coffee-shop circuit. He moved to Israel to live in a kibbutz, but was kicked out after driving a tractor through a building. Returning to Toronto in 1961, he joined a group headed by Denny Doherty called The Halifax Three. While in New York City, Yanovsky met Cass Elliot at a party she hosted in February 1964 to watch the Beatles' first performance on *The Ed Sullivan Show*. Within months, Yanovsky, Elliot, Doherty and James Hendricks had formed the short-lived folk act The Mugwumps. In early 1965, Yanovsky joined vocalist John Sebastian, drummer/vocalist Joe Butler and bassist Steve Boone to form The Lovin' Spoonful. After an extended stint at the Night Owl club in Greenwich Village, the group signed with Kama Sutra Records. An instant sensation, The Lovin' Spoonful scored a series of upbeat, hook-filled pop hits such as 'Do You Believe In Magic', 'You Didn't Have To Be So Nice',

'Daydream', 'Did You Ever Have To Make Up Your Mind?' and 'Summer In The City'. After a marijuana bust in Berkeley, Yanovsky reportedly eluded prosecution and deportation back to Canada by aiding police in the arrest of his drug dealer. With *Rolling Stone* and others calling for a boycott, Yanovsky was forced to quit in 1967 and was replaced by Jerry Yester, from The Association. After recording a poorly received solo album, *Alive And Well In Argentina*, in 1968, Yanovsky briefly worked with Tim Buckley and Kris Kristofferson. Yanovsky subsequently moved into television production, including the Canadian series *Magistrate's Court*. In 1980 the original line-up of The Lovin' Spoonful reunited for an appearance in the Paul Simon film *One Trick Pony*. Leaving music altogether, Yanovsky settled in Kingston, Ontario, where he operated a restaurant named Chez Piggy. At the time of his death, Yanovsky was preparing to join John Sebastian for a short UK tour.
CAUSE: He suffered a heart attack and died suddenly at his home outside Kingston, Ontario.

Max Yasgur

Born December 15, 1919
Died February 3, 1973
The owner of a dairy farm where the famed 1969 Woodstock festival was staged, Max Yasgur was paid $50,000 in advance for the use of a 40-acre section of his large farm. When the officials at nearby Woodstock, New York, refused to permit the event, organisers moved the site 50 miles south-east to Yasgur's farm in Bethel. The three-day festival, which starred Jimi Hendrix, The Who and Janis Joplin, drew 400,000 spectators from August 15 to 17. With organisers unprepared for the huge crowd, Yasgur and many local residents provided a large quantity of free food and other provisions. But with concertgoers having wreaked havoc to the area, Yasgur's neighbours were angry about the property damage and sued him in 1970 for $35,000. A year later Yasgur sold his farm and retired to Florida. Yasgur's 600-acre farm was later subdivided with part of it sold for housing development. Musical tributes to Yasgur include 'For Yasgur's Farm' by Mountain and Joni Mitchell's 'Woodstock' which was also recorded by Crosby, Stills, Nash & Young and Matthews Southern Comfort.
CAUSE: Heart attack. He died at Fisherman's Hospital in Marathon, Florida.
FURTHER READING: Spitz, Bob. (1979). *Barefoot In Babylon: The Creation Of The Woodstock Festival*. New York: Viking.

Evelyn Young

Born 1928
Died October 2, 1990
A flamboyant Memphis-based saxophone player who played on many early B.B. King sessions in the Fifties including 'Three O'Clock Blues', Evelyn Young was nicknamed "The Whip". Accompanied by a chaperone, Young was a child prodigy who performed in the blues clubs of Beale Street beginning at age 14. Later becoming a fixture in the nightclubs of New Orleans, she would also record with Rufus Thomas, Little Richard, and Bobby "Blue" Bland.
CAUSE: Heart failure. She died at Methodist Hospital South in Memphis.

Karen Young

Born March 23, 1952
Died January 26, 1991
A disco singer who scored a club hit in 1977 with 'Hot Shot', Karen Young had previously worked as a commercial jingle singer. 'Hot Shot' returned to the British charts in 1997, remixed by Mo' Bizz Records as 'Hot Shot "97"'.
CAUSE: Bleeding ulcer. She died in Philadelphia.

Paul Young

Born June 17, 1947
Died July 15, 2000

Not to be confused with his fellow British solo pop/soul singer from the Eighties, Paul Young enjoyed several hits as lead singer of pop-rock outfit Mike & The Mechanics, formed in 1985 by Genesis guitarist Mike Rutherford and former Ace frontman Paul Carrack. A music veteran when he joined the group, Paul Young had been apprenticed on the West German club circuit in the early Sixties, passing through a series of bands – Johnny Dark & The Midnights, The Toggery Five, Young & Renshaw – before gaining prominence in the late Seventies in Sad Café whose second album *Misplaced Ideals* yielded a pair of hits, 'Everyday Hurts' and the Young co-penned 'Run Home Girl'. Rutherford assembled Mike & The Mechanics in the wake of Genesis bandmate Phil Collins' massive solo success. With Young and Carrack sharing lead vocal duties, the group had hits with 'Silent Running' (1986), 'All I Need Is A Miracle' (1986), and a song inspired by the death of Rutherford's father, 'The Living Years' (1989). Although the group was commercially ignored in the US during the Nineties, Mike & The Mechanics continued their hit run in Britain with 'Word Of Mouth' (1991) and 'Over My Shoulder' (1995). They were working on their fifth album at the time of Young's death.

CAUSE: He suffered a heart attack at his home in Altrincham, Cheshire and was pronounced dead on arrival at Wythenshawe Hospital.

Timi Yuro

(ROSEMARIE TIMOTEA AURRO)
Born August 4, 1940
Died May 30, 2004

With her soulful and haunting alto voice, Timi Yuro was often compared to Dinah Washington and Nancy Wilson. Originally from Chicago, she moved to Los Angeles with her family in 1952. Signing with Liberty Records in 1959, Yuro scored her first hit with a cover of Roy Hamilton's 'Hurt' (1961), a song which became her signature piece. Drawn to country music after hearing Ray Charles' *Modern Sounds In Country And Western Music*, Yuro recorded a similar album, including tracks by a then-unknown songwriter, Willie Nelson. Switching labels in 1974, Yuro recorded at Mercury with little success and, after briefly returning to Liberty Records, she retired from music in 1969. She returned to the stage in the mid Seventies, but was stricken with throat cancer several years later. In 1982, Willie Nelson graciously invited Yuro to his studio to record the album, *Timi Yuro – Today*.

CAUSE: Brain cancer. She died at her home in Las Vegas.

Z

Mia Zapata

Born August 25, 1965
Died July 7, 1993
The lead singer of the Seattle punk-rock band The Gits, Mia Zapata was murdered on the eve of the group's national breakthrough. Raised in Louisville, Kentucky, she attended Antioch College in Ohio where in 1989 she formed The Gits with bassist Matt Dresdner. As the group's songwriter, the hard-drinking and apolitical Zapata distanced herself from the burgeoning riot-girl movement. Shortly before Zapata's death, The Gits had completed tracks for their second indie album, *Enter: The Conquering Chicken*. Joan Jett teamed with The Gits in 1996 for the album *Evil Stag*.
CAUSE: She was raped and then murdered by strangulation. After spending the evening drinking with friends at the Comet Tavern in Seattle, she left at 2 a.m. and was headed for a friend's apartment a block away. Her body was found at 3:21 a.m. on the sidewalk next to a Catholic community services building, and not in an alley as is commonly reported. She had been murdered at an unknown location, with her body dumped from a vehicle. In 2003, Jesus Mezqueia was charged with her death. A convicted felon, he was living in the Florida Keys and was connected to the murder through evidence collected from a nationwide DNA database of violent offenders. Her death spawned the 1996 indie Seattle, 2-CD set, *Home Alive: The Art Of Self-Defense*. Zapata's murder was re-enacted in 1995 on television's *America's Most Wanted.*

Frank Zappa

(FRANK VINCENT ZAPPA, JR.)
Born December 21, 1940
Died December 4, 1993
A pioneering rock virtuoso, experimentalist and often serious musician, Frank Zappa managed only limited radio airplay during his prolific career but probably released more albums than any other artist in the rock field. Of Sicilian/Greek heritage, Zappa was born in Baltimore, but was frequently uprooted by his father who worked in the defence industry. Idolising the obscure avant-garde classical musician Edgar Varese, Zappa composed classical pieces in his youth. Drawn towards rock and doo-wop while attending high school, Zappa was hired as the drummer for a local group called The Ramblers. Switching to guitar in 1956, Zappa formed an eight-piece R&B group with Don Van Vliet (later known as Captain Beefheart) called The Black-Outs. After two stabs at college, Zappa decided on self-education and spent countless hours in the library studying music theory. While working as a lounge musician, Zappa wrote and produced a classical music score for a low budget art-film, *The World's Greatest Sinner* (1960). Teaming with former doo-wop singer Ray Collins, Zappa penned The Penguins elegant single 'Memories Of El Monte'. Taking the profits from scoring another low-budget film, *Run Home Slow*, Zappa purchased a recording studio for $2,300. Collaborating with Collins, Zappa released a stream of obscure singles under various monikers including The Masters. When an undercover officer paid $100 for a "bawdy" party tape of faked moaning, Zappa was arrested on indecency charges. Indignant at being entrapped in this way, Zappa emerged as a First Amendment champion who would fight all forms of censorship for the rest of his life. Settling in Los Angeles, Zappa then joined The Soul Giants, an R&B group led by his former collaborator, Ray Collins. Emerging as the leader of the renamed

Muthers (later The Mothers), Zappa took the group in an avant-garde direction, lacing their lyrics with satire and sexual puns. Discovered by producer Tom Wilson, Zappa was signed to MGM's new Verve subsidiary and forced to change the name of his group to The Mothers Of Invention. Releasing rock music's first double album, *Freak Out!* (1966), Zappa embarked on a career in which he would constantly reinvent himself. A concert favourite who landed scant radio airplay, not least because his lyrics were looked on as either subversive or licentious (or both), Zappa surrounded himself with a rotating line-up of dozens of talented musicians. Temporarily disbanding The Mothers Of Invention, Zappa left Verve in 1969 for Warner/Reprise Records, and with manager Herb Cohen formed two production companies, Bizarre and Straight (later evolving into DiscReet). During this period, Zappa also oversaw efforts by Lenny Bruce, Captain Beefheart, Tim Buckley, and Alice Cooper. Initially a bigger sensation in Britain, Zappa scored Top 20 albums in 1970 with the critically acclaimed *Hot Rats* and a final project with the original Mothers of Invention, *Burnt Weenie Sandwich*. Various line-ups of The Mothers (now minus the "Of Invention" suffix) included George Duke, Jack Bruce, Dale Bozzio, Lowell George, Steve Vai, and former Turtles members Mark Volman and Howard Kaylan (aka Flo and Eddie). Zappa was known as a stern bandleader, insisting on rigorous rehearsal schedules and banning drugs and alcohol from dressing rooms. Conversely, his long unkempt hair, moustache, beard and sexually charged lyrics encouraged the widely held but incorrect view that Zappa was a hedonistic freak, a belief given further credence when he was photographed on a toilet seat, his trousers around his ankles. The photograph became a widely circulated poster, prompting Zappa to comment often and with no little irony that this was the sole image most people had of him. In 1971 Zappa's career was sidetracked by a series of misfortunes. His band's equipment was destroyed by fire at a performance in Switzerland; then, in London, the jealous boyfriend of a female fan pushed Zappa into the orchestra pit at the Rainbow Theatre, breaking his leg and damaging his back and larynx. Zappa was confined to a wheelchair for nine months and his singing voice dropped by a third-octave. Later enjoying a brief period of commercial success, Zappa landed radio airplay with 'Dinah-Moe Humm' (1973) from the album *Over-Nite Sensation*, and 'Don't Eat The Yellow Snow' (1974) from the album *Apostrophe*. This was not to last and Zappa was soon in dispute with his record labels. Eventually he was awarded the masters tapes of his five Verve albums and, after sparring with Warner Brothers over the lyrical content of his 1978 album, *Zappa in New York*, he won the rights to his entire Warner catalogue in 1983. After launching Zappa Records, Zappa earned his first Grammy-nomination for the anti-disco album, *Sheik Yerbouti* (1979), which spawned his highest-charting solo single, 'Dancin' Fool'. Also that year, Zappa released the first volume of a rock opera, *Joe's Garage, Act I*. Forming Barking Pumpkins Records and hiring guitarist Steve Vai in 1981, Zappa attacked conservatives on the album *You Are What You Is*. The following year, Zappa released the first of another three-volume set, the career retrospective *Shut Up 'n Play Yer Guitar*. Also in 1982, Zappa scored his sole entry in the US Top 40 with a parody of dimwitted teenagers in 'Valley Girl', a duet with his daughter, Moon Unit, from the album *Ship Arriving Too Late To Save A Drowning Witch*. Indulging his love of classical music, Zappa organised a Varese tribute concert in 1981, and released the albums, *The London Symphony Orchestra: Zappa Vol. 1* (1983) and *Boulez Conducts Zappa: The Perfect Stranger* (1984). An outspoken critic of the Tipper Gore-led Parents Music Resource Center (PMRC), Zappa publicly attacked music censorship and addressed several congressional committees, chronicling the issue on the track 'Porn Wars' from his album, *Frank Zappa Meets The Mothers Of Prevention* (1985). Having won the rights to most of his early work, Zappa angered his fans by reissuing the albums with newly added drum and bass tracks. He also challenged bootleggers by issuing illicit product on a pair of box sets, *Beat The Boots*. On visits to Europe Zappa befriended Vaclac Havel, the post-Communist President of Czechoslovakia, who appointed him in 1991 the country's Cultural Liaison Officer with the West, a role which Zappa hoped might allow him access to various Government departments. Around the same time he announced his intention of standing as an independent candidate in the forthcoming US Presidential election. Regrettably, his cancer diagnosis prevented him from following through with his candidature. In the middle of a prolific string of releases that included the six-volume live series, *You Can't Do That On Stage Anymore*, Zappa penned an autobiography in 1991, *The Real Frank Zappa Book*. At the time of his death, Zappa was working on several projects including the posthumously released, *Civilization Phaze III* (1995). Since his death Rykodisc has reissued over 50 Frank Zappa albums, all of them remastered and repackaged with great attention to detail.

CAUSE: Zappa's children, Moon Unit and Dweezil, disclosed their father's diagnosis of prostate cancer in 1991 amid rumours that he was too ill to attend the tribute, Zappa's Universe. He died at his Los Angeles home.

FURTHER READING: Slavin, Neil. (1997). *Electric Don Quixote: The Story Of Frank Zappa*. London: Omnibus.

Lena Zavaroni

Born November 4, 1963
Died October 1, 1999

A child singer, Lena Zavaroni led a tragic life. After winning a talent competition over five weeks on the ITV television show, *Opportunity Knocks*, the Scottish-born nine-year-old drew comparisons to a young Judy Garland. Embraced by British audiences, in 1974 she scored a pair of hits, 'Personality' and a cover of the Johnny Otis Show's 'Ma He's Making Eyes At Me'. Managed by Dorothy Solomon (partner of Phil Solomon), at age 13 Zavaroni became the youngest performer ever to headline the London Palladium. She also starred in two television programmes but, unable to deal with the stresses of youthful stardom, she suffered from depression and the eating disorder, anorexia nervosa. After retiring in 1989, she was financially destitute by the mid Nineties.

CAUSE: In an attempt to cure her chronic depression and anorexia, she underwent a brain surgery procedure called a leucotomy. After the operation, she developed a blood infection which led to heart failure.

Gary Zekley

Born 1943
Died 1995

A singer-songwriter and producer, Gary Zekley worked with several pop-rock artists in the Sixties. Based in Los Angeles, in 1966 Zekley was asked by Dean Torrence (of Jan & Dean) for some original compositions for a solo project. After Torrence recorded 'Like A Summer Rain' and 'Yellow Balloon', Zekley was unhappy with the results. Zekley went to Canterbury Records where the label head insisted that

Zekley issue the song himself. Recorded with studio musicians, Zekley's version, credited to The Yellow Balloon, became a Top 40 hit, and prevented Torrence's rendition from charting. Teaming with Tommy James, Zekley co-produced the self-titled 1969 album by The Clique, and co-wrote several of the tracks including 'Superman', which was later covered by R.E.M in 1986. Other Zekley co-compositions included: 'Hallelujah' (Sweathog), 'I Can't Break Away' (Chuck Jackson; Big Pig), and a pair of Grass Roots hits, 'I'd Wait A Million Years' and 'Sooner Or Later'.
CAUSE: Heart attack.

Warren Zevon

(WARREN WILLIAM ZEVON)
Born January 24, 1947
Died September 7, 2003
An edgy singer-songwriter whose lyrics sometimes bordered on the macabre, Warren Zevon was an AOR staple during the last half of the Seventies. Born in Chicago to Russian immigrant parents but raised in Los Angeles, Zevon studied classical piano during his childhood. Dropping out of high school at age 17, he moved to New York City where he failed as a folk singer. Returning to California, Zevon found work writing and performing advertising jingles and, in 1965 he formed a folk duo with Violet Santangelo called Lyme & Cybelle, who recorded a trio of obscure singles for White Whale Records the following year. Pursuing a solo career, Zevon recorded his début album in 1969, *Wanted – Dead Or Alive*; one of the tracks, 'She Quit Me', was included in the Academy Award-winning film *Midnight Cowboy*. By the early Seventies, Zevon was working as a pianist and musical director for The Everly Brothers and, aided by rock luminaries such as Phil Everly, Glenn Frey and Carl Wilson, he recorded his second solo album in 1976, the Jackson Browne-produced *Warren Zevon*, which featured 'Hasten Down The Wind'. Garnering attention on FM radio, Zevon issued his seminal *Excitable Boy* album in 1978, which featured the title track, 'Lawyers, Guns And Money', as well as his enduring chart hit, 'Werewolves Of London'. That same year, Linda Ronstadt scored a hit with a Zevon composition, 'Poor Poor Pitiful Me', which originally appeared on his second album. Following an interruption to his career due to substance abuse, Zevon teamed with R.E.M. in 1984 to record an album as The Hindu Love Gods. In the months leading up to his death, Zevon met his impending demise head on. Continuing to work on his final album project *The Wind*, he filled his days with media interviews.
CAUSE: A former smoker who had quit in 1996, he was diagnosed with lung cancer in August 2002. He died at his home in Los Angeles.

Armand Zone

Born c. 1954
Died 1996
The keyboard player and original vocalist of Seventies art-rock group The Fast, Armand Zone had limited success outside of New York City. The Fast were formed in 1972 by brothers Miki and Armand "Mandy" Zone as a roots-rock glam band and were often later compared to The New York Dolls and The Ramones. Though Armand was the group's original lead singer, he moved to keyboards in 1975 when younger brother, Paul, took over the role. Unhappy with his role as a sideman, Armand Zone left The Fast in 1978 and after issuing a single featuring Blondie guitarist Gary Valentine, Zone formed his own group, Ozone, issuing a series of singles and EPs between 1979 and 1984. Armand Zone's brothers Miki and Paul would emerge in a popular techno/dance act, Man 2 Man. Following the death of his brother Miki, Armand reunited with

Paul in the late Eighties to work on the album *After The Zone Brothers*. Armand Zone's solo output was chronicled in the 2003 release, *Alone Fantasy Fone: The Armand Zone Collection*.
CAUSE: AIDS.

Miki Zone

(MICHAEL ZONE)
Born c. 1953
Died December 31, 1986
As guitarist for the New York City-based, Seventies art-rock group The Fast, Miki Zone was constantly on the verge of stardom. The Fast were formed in 1972 by brothers Miki and Armand "Mandy" Zone, later joined by their brother Paul. Often compared to The New York Dolls and The Ramones, The Fast failed to reach mass audiences. While many of The Fast's contemporaries were signed by major labels during the late Seventies, the group was tied down to a small independent company which had issued two of their tracks on the 1976 *Max's Kansas City* compilation. For a time in the late Seventies, the group toured as The Miki Zone Zoo. At a 1979 performance in Boston, the group was noticed by Ric Ocasek of The Cars, who produced their début album, *For Sale*, which included the group's earlier material as well as six tracks produced by Ocasek. With their second (and final) album, *Leather Boys From The Asphalt Jungle*, The Fast were central in the creation of the Goth movement, with the group members draped in black. Following the break-up of The Fast in 1984, Miki and Paul Zone teamed with electronica wizard Man Parrish to form the trio Man 2 Man. Released in 1986, the group's club-classic 'Male Stripper' reached the UK Top 10 two months after the death of Miki Zone.
CAUSE: AIDS related. After returning from England, he died in a New York City hospital.

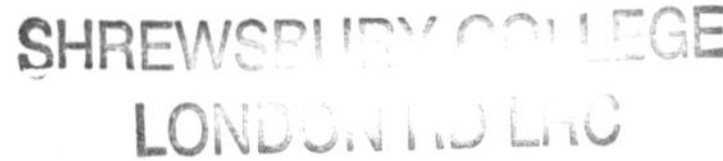